W9-BLI-622

PRENTICE HALL

LITERATURE

THE AMERICAN EXPERIENCE • VOLUME ONE

COMMON CORE EDITION

Upper Saddle River, New Jersey

Boston, Massachusetts

Chandler, Arizona

Glenview, Illinois

PRENTICE HALL

LITERATURE

THE AMERICAN EXPERIENCE • VOLUME ONE

COMMON CORE EDITION

Upper Saddle River, New Jersey

Boston, Massachusetts

Chandler, Arizona

Glenview, Illinois

ALWAYS LEARNING

PEARSON

Acknowledgments

Grateful acknowledgment is made to the following for copyrighted material:

Advancement Project "10 Things Every Florida Poll Worker Should Know" from *http://www.advancementproject.org*. Used by permission.

Archaeology Magazine "A Community's Roots" by Samir S. Patel from *http://www.archaeology.org*. Copyright © 2006 by The Archaeological Institute of America. Used by permission.

Arte Publico Press "The Latin Deli: An Ars Poetica" by Judith Ortiz Cofer from *The Latin Deli*. Used with permission from the publisher of "The Americas Review" (Copyright © 1992 Arte Publico Press-University of Houston).

The James Baldwin Estate "The Rockpile" is collected in *Going to Meet the Man*, © 1965 by James Baldwin. Copyright renewed. Published by Vintage Books. Used by arrangement with the James Baldwin Estate.

Susan Bergholz Literary Services "Antojos" by Julia Alvarez from *Antojos*. Copyright © 1991 by Julia Alvarez. Later published in slightly different form in *How the Garcia Girls Lost Their Accents*, Copyright © 1991 by Julia Alvarez. Published by Plume, an imprint of Dutton Signet, a division of Penguin USA, Inc., and originally in hardcover by Algonquin Books of Chapel Hill. "Straw into Gold: The Metamorphosis of the Everyday" by Sandra Cisneros from *The Texas Observer*. Copyright © 1987 by Sandra Cisneros. First published in *The Texas Observer*, September 1987. Used by permission of Susan Bergholz Literary Services, New York, NY and Lamy, NM. All rights reserved.

BOA Editions Limited "The Gift" by Li-Young Lee from Rose. Copyright © 1986 by Li-Young Lee. All rights reserved. "Study the Masters" by Lucille Clifton from *Blessing the Boats: New and Selected Poems 1988–2000*. Copyright © 2000 by Lucille Clifton. Used with the permission of BOA Editions, Ltd. www.boaeditions.org.

Brooks Permissions "The Explorer" by Gwendolyn Brooks from *Blacks*. Used by permission of Brooks Permissions. Copyright © 1991 by Gwendolyn Brooks, published by Third World Press, Chicago.

The California Council for the Humanities "California Council for the Humanities/Our Mission/Our History" from *http://www.calhum.org*. Courtesy of the California Council for the Humanities and its California Stories Initiative. Copyright © 2007 by The California Council for the Humanities. Used by permission.

California Department of Water Resources "California Water Plan Highlights" from *Department of Water Resources Bulletin 160-05*. Copyright © 2005 California Department of Water Resources.

California Secretary of State "Poll Worker Advertisement" from *www.sos.ca.gov/elections/outreach/posters/pollworker.pdf*. Used by permission.

Sandra Dijkstra Literary Agency "Mother Tongue" by Amy Tan from The Joy Luck Club. Copyright © 1989 by Amy Tan. Used by permission of the author and the Sandra Dijkstra Literary Agency. Copyright © 1989 by Amy -Tan. First appeared in *Threepenny Review*.

Doubleday "Cuttings (later)" by Theodore Roethke from Collected Poems of Theodore Roethke. "Cuttings" by Theodore Roethke from *The Collected Poems of Theodore Roethke. The Collected Poems of Theodore Roethke by Theodore Roethke*, copyright © 1946 by Editorial Publications, Inc. Used by permission of Doubleday, a division of Bantam Doubleday Dell Publishing Group.

Richard Erdoes "When Grizzlies Walked Upright" by Modoc Indians from *American History Customized Reader*. Used by permission.

Faber and Faber Limited "Mirror" by Sylvia Plath from *Crossing the Water*. Copyright © 1963 by Ted Hughes. Used by permission.

Farrar, Straus & Giroux, LLC "Losses" by Randall Jarrell from *The Complete Poems by Randall Jarrell*. Copyright © 1969, renewed 1997 by Mary von S. Jarrell. "The Death of the Ball Turret Gunner" by Randall Jarrell from *The Complete Poems of Randall Jarrell*. Copyright © 1969, renewed 1997 by Mary von S. Jarrell. "The First Seven Years" by Bernard Malamud from *The Magic Barrel*. Copyright © 1950, 1958 and copyright renewed 1977, 1986 by Bernard Malamud. "Coyote v. Acme" by Ian Frazier from *Coyote v. Acme*. Copyright © 1996 by Ian Frazier. "One Art" by Elizabeth Bishop from *Geography III*. Copyright © 1979, 1983 by Alice Helen Methfessel. "Filling Station" by Elizabeth Bishop from *The Complete Poems 1927–1979* by Elizabeth Bishop. Copyright © 1979, 1983 by Alice Helen Methfessel. Used by permission of Farrar, Straus and Giroux, LLC.

Florida Master Site File from *http://www.flheritage.com*. Used by permission.

Fulcrum Publishing "The Earth on Turtle's Back" by Joseph Bruchac and Michael J. Caduto from *Keepers of the Earth: Native American Stories and Environmental Activities for Children*, © 1998. Used by permission of Fulcrum Publishing, Inc.

Georgia State University "Georgia State University's Web Accessibility Policy," copyright © 2006 is used with permission from the University System of Georgia by and on behalf of Georgia State University.

Graywolf Press "Traveling Through the Dark" by William Stafford from *Stories That Could be True: New and Collected Poems*. Copyright 1962, 1998 by the Estate of William Stafford. Used from *The Way It Is: New and Selected Poems* with the permission of Graywolf Press, Saint Paul, Minnesota.

Harcourt, Inc. "Chicago" by Carl Sandburg from *Chicago Poems*, copyright © 1916 by Holt, Rinehart and Winston and renewed 1944 by Carl Sandburg. "Grass" by Carl Sandburg from *Chicago Poems*. Copyright © 1916 BY Holt, Rinehart and Winston and renewed 1944 by Carl Sandburg. "Everyday Use" by Alice Walker from *In Love & Trouble: Stories of Black Women*, copyright © 1973 by Alice Walker. "The Jilting of Granny Weatherall" by Katherine Anne Porter from *Flowering Judas and Other Stories*, copyright © 1930 and renewed 1958 by Katherine Anne Porter. "The Life You Save May Be Your Own" by Flannery O'Connor from *A Good Man is Hard to Find and Other Stories*, copyright © 1953 by Flannery O'Connor and renewed 1981 by Regina O'Connor. "A Worn Path" by Eudora Welty from *A Curtain of Green and Other Stories*, copyright 1941 and renewed in 1969 by Eudora Welty. Used by permission of Harcourt, Inc. This material may not be reproduced in any form or by any means without the prior written permission of the publisher.

HarperCollins Publishers, Inc. From "Dust Tracks on a Road" by Zora N. Hurston. Copyright © 1942 by Zora Neale Hurston; renewed © 1970 by John C. Hurston. "Mirror" by Sylvia Plath from *Crossing the Water*. Copyright © 1963 by Ted Hughes. Originally appeared in The New Yorker. "Where Is Here?" by Joyce Carol Oates. Copyright © 1992 by The Ontario Review, Inc. Used by permission of HarperCollins Publishers. Excerpt from *Black Boy* by Richard Wright. Copyright © 1944, 1945 by Richard Wright.

Harvard University Press "Because I could not stop for Death (#712)", "I heard a Fly buzz—when I died (#465)", "My life closed twice before its close— (#1732)", "The Soul selects her own Society (#303)", "There's a certain Slant of light (#258)", "There is a solitude of space (#1695)", by Emily Dickinson from *The Poems of Emily Dickinson*. Used by permission of the publishers and the Trustees of Amherst College from *The Poems of Emily Dickinson*, Thomas H. Johnson, ed., Cambridge, Mass.: The Belknap Press of Harvard University Press, Copyright (c) 1951, 1955, 1979 by the Presidents and Fellows of Harvard College.

Acknowledgments continue on page R80, which constitutes an extension of this copyright page.

Cover: (Bkgd) ©Ted Mead/Getty Images, (L) ©James Forte/Getty Images, (B) ©Tom Merton/OJO Images/Getty Images, (TL, BC) ©Blaine Harrington III/CORBIS, (CR) ©Uli Wiesmeier/zefa/CORBIS

PEARSON

ISBN-13: 978-0-13-320869-6
ISBN-10: 0-13-320869-9
6 7 8 9 10 VO57 15 14 13

Master Teacher Board

Heather Barnes
Language Arts Instructor
Central Crossing High School
Grove City, Ohio

Lee Bromberger
English Department Chairperson
Mukwonago High School
Mukwonago, Wisconsin

Cathy Cassy
Communication Arts Curriculum Supervisor 6-12
St. Louis Public Schools
St. Louis, Missouri

Judy Castrogiavanni
English Teacher
Abington Heights School
Clarks Summit, Pennsylvania

Ann Catrillo
Sr. English & AP Teacher; Department Chairperson
East Stroudsburg High School South
East Stroudsburg, Pennsylvania

Susan Cisna
Instructor Middle School Education
Eastern Illinois University
Charleston, Illinois

Linda Fund
Reading Specialist
Ezra L. Nolan Middle School #40
Jersey City, New Jersey

Gail Hacker
Adjunct Professor
Springfield College School of Human Services
North Charleston, South Carolina

Patricia Matysik
English Department Chairperson
Belleville West Middle School
Belleville, Illinois

Gail Phelps
Literacy Intervention Coach
Oak Grove High School
Little Rock, Arkansas

Julie Rucker
Literacy Coach/English Teacher
Tift County High School
Tifton, Georgia

Kathy Ryan
Curriculum Coordinator
Rockwood Schools
St. Louis, Missouri

Matthew Scanlon
Vice Principal
Kinnelon High School
Kinnelon, New Jersey

Renee Trotier
Freshman Principal
Lafayette High School
Wildwood, Missouri

Carolyn Waters
Language Arts Supervisor
Cobb County Schools
Marietta, Georgia

Martha Wildman
Social Studies Teacher
Las Cruces Public Schools
Las Cruces, New Mexico

Melissa Williams
District Supervisor
Delsea Regional Schools
Franklinville, New Jersey

Charles Youngs
English Language Arts Facilitator
Bethel Park High School
Bethel Park, Pennsylvania

Contributing Authors

The contributing authors guided the direction and philosophy of Pearson Prentice Hall Literature. Working with the development team, they helped to build the pedagogical integrity of the program and to ensure its relevance for today's teachers and students.

Grant Wiggins, Ed.D., is the President of Authentic Education in Hopewell, New Jersey. He earned his Ed.D. from Harvard University and his B.A. from St. John's College in Annapolis. Grant consults with schools, districts, and state education departments on a variety of reform matters; organizes conferences and workshops; and develops print materials and Web resources on curricular change. He is the coauthor, with Jay McTighe, of Understanding by Design and The Understanding by Design Handbook, the award-winning and highly successful materials on curriculum published by ASCD. His work has been supported by the Pew Charitable Trusts, the Geraldine R. Dodge Foundation, and the National Science Foundation. *The Association for Supervision of Curriculum Development (ASCD), publisher of the "Understanding by Design Handbook" co-authored by Grant Wiggins and registered owner of the trademark "Understanding by Design", has not authorized, approved, or sponsored this work and is in no way affiliated with Pearson or its products.*

Jeff Anderson has worked with struggling writers and readers for almost 20 years. Anderson's specialty is the integration of grammar and editing instruction into the processes of reading and writing. He has published two books, *Mechanically Inclined: Building Grammar, Usage, and Style into Writer's Workshop,* and *Everyday Editing: Inviting Students to Develop Skill and Craft in Writer's Workshop,* as well as a DVD, *The Craft of Grammar.* Anderson's work has appeared in *English Journal.* Anderson won the NCTE Paul and Kate Farmer Award for his *English Journal* article on teaching grammar in context.

Arnetha F. Ball, Ph.D., is a Professor at Stanford University. Her areas of expertise include language and literacy studies of diverse student populations, research on writing instruction, and teacher preparation for working with diverse populations. She is the author of *African American Literacies Unleashed* with Dr. Ted Lardner, and *Multicultural Strategies for Education and Social Change.*

Sheridan Blau is Professor of Education and English at the University of California, Santa Barbara, where he directs the South Coast Writing Project and the Literature Institute for Teachers. He has served in senior advisory roles for such groups as the National Board for Professional Teaching Standards, the College Board, and the American Board for Teacher Education. Blau served for twenty years on the National Writing Project Advisory Board and Task Force, and is a former president of NCTE. Blau is the author of *The Literature Workshop: Teaching Texts and Their Readers,* which was named by the Conference on English Education as the 2004 Richard Meade Award winner for outstanding research in English education.

William G. Brozo, Ph.D., is a Professor of Literacy at George Mason University in Fairfax, Virginia. He has taught reading and language arts in junior and senior high school and is the author of numerous texts on literacy development. Dr. Brozo'z work focuses on building capacity among teacher leaders, enriching the literate culture of schools, enhancing the literate lives of boys, and making teaching more responsive to the needs of all students. His recent publications include *Bright Beginnings for Boys: Engaging Young Boys in Active Literacy* and the *Adolescent Literacy Inventory.*

Doug Buehl is a teacher, author, and national literacy consultant. He is the author of *Classroom Strategies for Interactive Learning* and coauthor of *Reading and the High School Student: Strategies to Enhance Literacy;* and *Strategies to Enhance Literacy and Learning in Middle School Content Area Classrooms.*

Jim Cummins, Ph.D, is a professor in the Modern Language Centre at the University of Toronto. He is the author of numerous publications, including *Negotiating Identities: Education for Empowerment in a Diverse Society.* Cummins coined the acronyms BICS and CAPT to help differentiate the type of language ability students need for success.

Harvey Daniels, Ph.D., has been a classroom teacher, writing project director, author, and university professor. "Smokey" serves as an international consultant to schools, districts, and educational agencies. He is known for his work on student-led book clubs, as recounted in *Literature Circles: Voice and Choice in Book Clubs & Reading Groups* and *Mini Lessons for Literature Circles.* Recent works include *Subjects Matter: Every Teacher's Guide to Content-Area Reading* and *Content Area Writing: Every Teacher's Guide.*

Jane Feber taught language arts in Jacksonville, Florida, for 36 years. Her innovative approach to instruction has earned her several awards, including the NMSA Distinguished Educator Award, the NCTE Edwin A. Hoey Award, the Gladys Prior Award for Teaching Excellence, and the Florida Council of Teachers of English Teacher of the Year Award. She is a National Board Certified Teacher, past president of the Florida Council of Teachers of English, and is the author of *Creative Book Reports* and *Active Word Play.*

Danling Fu, Ph.D., is Professor of Language and Culture in the College of Education at the University of Florida. She researches and provides inservice to public schools nationally, focusing on literacy instruction for new immigrant students. Fu's books include *My Trouble is My English* and *An Island of English* addressing English language learners in the secondary schools. She has authored chapters in the *Handbook of Adolescent Literacy Research* and in *Adolescent Literacy: Turning Promise to Practice.*

Kelly Gallagher is a full-time English teacher at Magnolia High School in Anaheim, California. He is the former co-director of the South Basin Writing Project at California State University, Long Beach. Gallagher wrote *Reading Reasons: Motivational Mini-Lessons for the Middle and High School, Deeper Reading: Comprehending Challenging Texts 4-12,* and *Teaching Adolescent Writers.* Gallagher won the Secondary Award of Classroom Excellence from the California Association of Teachers of English—the state's top English teacher honor.

Sharroky Hollie, Ph.D., is an assistant professor at California State University, Dominguez Hills, and an urban literacy visiting professor at Webster University, St. Louis. Hollie's work focuses on professional development, African American education, and second language methodology. He is a contributing author in two texts on culturally and linguistically responsive teaching. He is the Executive Director of the Center for Culturally Responsive Teaching and Learning and the co-founding director of the Culture and Language Academy of Success, an independent charter school in Los Angeles.

Dr. Donald J. Leu, Ph.D., teaches at the University of Connecticut and holds a joint appointment in Curriculum and Instruction and in Educational Psychology. He directs the New Literacies Research Lab and is a member of the Board of Directors of the International Reading Association. Leu studies the skills required to read, write, and learn with Internet technologies. His research has been funded by groups including the U.S. Department of Education, the National Science Foundation, and the Bill & Melinda Gates Foundation.

Jon Scieszka founded GUYS READ, a nonprofit literacy initiative for boys, to call attention to the problem of getting boys connected with reading. In 2008, he was named the first U.S. National Ambassador for Young People's Literature by the Library of Congress. Scieszka taught from first grade to eighth grade for ten years in New York City, drawing inspiration from his students to write *The True Story of the 3 Little Pigs!, The Stinky Cheese Man,* the *Time Warp Trio* series of chapter books, and the *Trucktown* series of books for beginning readers.

Sharon Vaughn, Ph.D., teaches at the University of Texas at Austin. She is the previous Editor-in-Chief of the *Journal of Learning Disabilities* and the co-editor of *Learning Disabilities Research and Practice.* She is the recipient of the American Education Research Association SIG Award for Outstanding Researcher. Vaughn's work focuses on effective practices for enhancing reading outcomes for students with reading difficulties. She is the author of more than 100 articles, and numerous books designed to improve research-based practices in the classroom.

Karen K. Wixson is Dean of the School of Education at the University of North Carolina, Greensboro. She has published widely in the areas of literacy curriculum, instruction, and assessment. Wixson has been an advisor to the National Research Council and helped develop the National Assessment of Educational Progress (NAEP) reading tests. She is a past member of the IRA Board of Directors and co-chair of the IRA Commission on RTI. Recently, Wixson served on the English Language Arts Work Team that was part of the Common Core State Standards Initiative.

COMMON CORE
Contents in Brief

The selections in this book are presented through the lens of three Essential Questions:

What makes American literature American?

What is the relationship between literature and place?

How does literature shape or reflect society?

Introductory Unit: Common Core Student Workshops xlvi

Building Academic Vocabulary
Writing an Objective Summary
Comprehending Complex Texts
Analyzing Arguments

Unit 1: A Gathering of Voices 1

Literature of Early America (beginnings to 1750)

Extended Studies Speeches; Benjamin Franklin

Writing Workshop: Autobiographical Narrative
Communications Workshop: Evaluate Persuasive Speech
Vocabulary Workshop: Using a Dictionary and Thesaurus

Unit 2: A Growing Nation 208

Literature of the American Renaissance (1800 to 1870)

Extended Studies Edgar Allan Poe; Transcendentalism; Poetry

Writing Workshop: Reflective Essay
Communications Workshop: Write and Deliver a Persuasive Speech
Vocabulary Workshop: Etymology: Political Science/History Terms

Unit 3: Division, Reconciliation, and Expansion 460

Literature of the Civil War and the Frontier (1850 to 1914)

Extended Studies Narrative Nonfiction; Mark Twain

Writing Workshop: Historical Investigation Report
Communications Workshop: Oral Interpretation of a Literary Work
Vocabulary Workshop: Words from Mythology and Religious Traditions

Unit 4: Disillusion, Defiance, and Discontent 688

Literature of the Modern Age (1914 to 1945)

Extended Studies Short Stories; Langston Hughes

Writing Workshop: Multimedia Presentation
Communications Workshop: Analyze a Nonprint Political Advertisement
Vocabulary Workshop: Etymology: Scientific, Medical, and Mathematical Terms

Unit 5: Prosperity and Protest 964

Literature of the Postwar Era (1945 to 1970)

Extended Study	Drama
Writing Workshop:	Persuasive Essay
Communications Workshop:	Analyze and Evaluate Entertainment Media
Vocabulary Workshop:	Idioms and Idiomatic Expressions

Unit 6: New Voices, New Frontiers 1276

Literature of the Contemporary Period (1970 to Present)

Extended Study	The Essay
Writing Workshop:	Short Story
Communications Workshop:	Compare Print News Coverage
Vocabulary Workshop:	Cognates

Resources

Reading and Vocabulary Handbook R1
Literary Handbook R18
Writing Handbook R34
21st Century Skills R47
Communications Handbook R53
Grammar, Usage, and Mechanics Handbook R56
Indexes R64
Acknowledgments (continued) R80
Credits R81

COMMON CORE
Unit 1 ▪ Table of Contents

A Gathering of Voices

Literature of Early America (Beginnings to 1800)

Multiple Perspectives on the Era

Snapshot of the Period		INSTRUCTIONAL ESSAY AND GRAPHICS	2
Historical Background		INSTRUCTIONAL ESSAY	4
Essential Questions Across Time: Early America		INSTRUCTIONAL ESSAY	6
RECENT SCHOLARSHIP			
William L. Andrews	**America Begins with a Promise and a Paradox**	ESSAY	14
Integrate and Evaluate Information			16

PART ONE: **MEETING OF CULTURES**

Comparing Literary Works: Mythic Archetypes

Onondaga	**The Earth on Turtle's Back**	MYTH	20
Modoc	**When Grizzlies Walked Upright**	MYTH	24
Navajo	***from* The Navajo Origin Legend**	MYTH	27
THEMES ACROSS CENTURIES: Author's Insights			
Susan Power	***Introduces* Museum Indians**	ESSAY	32
Susan Power	**Museum Indians**	ESSAY	34
Dekanawidah	***from* The Iroquois Constitution**	POLITICAL DOCUMENT	42

Comparing Literary Works: Problems and Solutions

Alvar Núñez Cabeza de Vaca	***from* A Journey Through Texas**	EXPLORATION NARRATIVE	48
García López de Cárdenas	**Boulders Taller Than the Great Tower of Seville**	EXPLORATION NARRATIVE	52
William Bradford	***from* Of Plymouth Plantation**	NARRATIVE ACCOUNT	58
	The Mayflower	HISTORY CONNECTION	60

Contemporary Connection: Exploration Past and Present

Steve Squyres	***from* Mars Rover Mission Update**	BLOG	69

PART TWO: **THE PURITAN INFLUENCE**

Anne Bradstreet	**To My Dear and Loving Husband**	POEM	76
	The Tenth Muse	WORLD LITERATURE CONNECTION	78
Edward Taylor	**Huswifery**	POEM	82
Jonathan Edwards	***from* Sinners in the Hands of an Angry God**	SERMON	86
	Biblical Imagery	LITERATURE CONNECTION	88

* INFORMATIONAL TEXT HIGHLIGHTED

PART THREE: **A NATION IS BORN**

Extended Study: Speeches

Elements of Speeches 96

Frederick Douglass	***from* What to the Slave Is the Fourth of July** EXEMPLAR	SPEECH	97
Patrick Henry	**Speech in the Virginia Convention**	SPEECH	100
Benjamin Franklin	**Speech in the Convention**	SPEECH	105

Comparing Literary Works: Appeals to Audience

Thomas Jefferson	**The Declaration of Independence** EXEMPLAR	POLITICAL DOCUMENT	112
	John Locke and the Social Contract	PHILOSOPHY CONNECTION	114
Thomas Paine	***from* The American Crisis** EXEMPLAR	POLITICAL ESSAY	117
Phillis Wheatley	**To His Excellency, General Washington**	POEM	124

Reading for Information: Analyzing Functional and Argumentative Texts

	How to Watch a Debate	FUNCTIONAL TEXT	129
	Help North Texas Vote	ARGUMENTATIVE TEXT	132

Extended Study: Benjamin Franklin

Literary History: Franklin's World		INSTRUCTIONAL ESSAY	134
Meet the Author: Benjamin Franklin		BIOGRAPHY	136
Benjamin Franklin	***from* The Autobiography**	AUTOBIOGRAPHY	140
	Socrates	WORLD LITERATURE CONNECTION	142
	Benjamin Franklin in Our World	CULTURAL CONNECTION	146
William L. Andrews	**Benjamin Franklin: America's Everyman**	ESSAY	147
Benjamin Franklin	***from* Poor Richard's Almanack**	PROVERBS	148
	Proverbs: The Wisdom of Many	WORLD LITERATURE CONNECTION	151

Comparing Autobiography Past and Present

	A Gallery of Autobiography	ILLUSTRATED HISTORY	156
Sandra Cisneros	**Straw Into Gold: The Metamorphosis of the Everyday**	AUTOBIOGRAPHY	158

THEMES ACROSS CENTURIES: Author's Insights

William L. Andrews	**Introduces Olaudah Equiano**	ESSAY	166
Olaudah Equiano	***from* The Interesting Narrative of the Life of Olaudah Equiano**	AUTOBIOGRAPHY	170
	The Slave Trade	ECONOMIC CONNECTION	174

Research Project: Primary Sources

John Adams	**Letter from the President's House**	LETTER	181
Abigail Adams	**Letter to Her Daughter From the New White House**	LETTER	182
Benjamin Henry Latrobe	**Floor Plan of the President's House**	BLUEPRINT	184

Writing Workshop: Autobiographical Narrative 188

WRITE GUY *Jeff Anderson, M.Ed.*	**What Do You Notice?**	188
Susan Power	**On Choosing the Right Word**	191

Communications Workshop: Evaluate Persuasive Speech 196

Vocabulary Workshop: Using a Dictionary and Thesaurus 198

Common Core Assessment Workshop: Test-Taking Practice SAT PREP ACT 200

Common Core Assessment Workshop: Performance Tasks 204

Independent Reading 206

Pearson Prentice Hall	Native American Literature	ANTHOLOGY
Phillis Wheatley	The Complete Writings EXEMPLAR	POETRY
Alvar Núñez Cabeza de Vaca	Chronicle of the Narváez Expedition	NARRATIVE ACCOUNT
J. Hector St. John de Crevecoeur	Letters from an American Farmer	EPISTOLARY LETTERS
Olaudah Equiano	The Interesting Narrative of the Life of Olaudah Equiano	AUTOBIOGRAPHY
Alexis de Tocqueville	Democracy in America EXEMPLAR	POLITICAL SCIENCE
Alan Taylor	American Colonies: The Settling of North America	HISTORY
David McCullough	1776 EXEMPLAR	HISTORY

A Growing Nation

Literature of the American Renaissance (1800 to 1870)

Multiple Perspectives on the Era

Snapshot of the Period		INSTRUCTIONAL ESSAY AND GRAPHICS	210
Historical Background		INSTRUCTIONAL ESSAY	212
Essential Questions Across Time: The American Renaissance		INSTRUCTIONAL ESSAY	214
RECENT SCHOLARSHIP			
Gretel Ehrlich	**Inspired by Nature**	ESSAY	222
Integrate and Evaluate Information			224

PART ONE: **FIRESIDE AND CAMPFIRE**

Washington Irving	**The Devil and Tom Walker**	SHORT STORY	228
	The Faust Legend	WORLD LITERATURE CONNECTION	235

Research Project: Primary Sources

Thomas Jefferson	**Commission of Meriwether Lewis**	COMMISSION	245
Meriwether Lewis	**Crossing the Great Divide**	FIELD REPORT	250

Comparing Literary Works: Meter and Mood

Henry Wadsworth Longfellow	***from* The Song of Hiawatha**	POEM	258
	The Fireside Poets	LITERATURE CONNECTION	259
	The Tide Rises, The Tide Falls	POEM	260
William Cullen Bryant	**Thanatopsis**	POEM	262
Oliver Wendell Holmes	**Old Ironsides**	POEM	266

PART TWO: **SHADOWS OF THE IMAGINATION**

Nathaniel Hawthorne	**The Minister's Black Veil**	SHORT STORY	272
	Jonathan Edwards, Puritans, and Sermons of Fear	HISTORY CONNECTION	276

Extended Study: Edgar Allan Poe

Meet the Author: Edgar Allan Poe		BIOGRAPHY	288
	Poe and Pop Culture	CULTURAL CONNECTION	290
Edgar Allan Poe	**The Fall of the House of Usher**	SHORT STORY	292
	On Writing "The Raven"	LITERARY CRITICISM	311
	The Raven	POEM	312

Comparing Gothic Literature Past and Present

The Gothic Family Tree		ILLUSTRATED LITERARY HISTORY	322
Joyce Carol Oates	**Where Is Here?**	SHORT STORY	325
Herman Melville	***from* Moby Dick**	NOVEL EXCERPT	336
	The Golden Age of Yankee Whaling	HISTORY CONNECTION	344
	The Whale as Archetype	HUMANITIES CONNECTION	346

PART THREE: THE HUMAN SPIRIT AND THE NATURAL WORLD

Extended Study: Transcendentalism

Literary History: The Transcendentalists

Transcendentalism: The Seekers		INSTRUCTIONAL ESSAY	360
THEMES ACROSS CENTURIES: Scholar's Insights			
Charles Johnson	**On Ralph Waldo Emerson**	ESSAY	362
Ralph Waldo Emerson	***from* Nature**	ESSAY	366
	***from* Self-Reliance**	ESSAY	369
	Concord Hymn	POEM	371
THEMES ACROSS CENTURIES: Scholar's Insights			
Gretel Ehrlich	**Introduces Henry David Thoreau**	ESSAY	374
Henry David Thoreau	***from* Walden** EXEMPLAR	ESSAY	378
	Mount Olympus	WORLD LITERATURE CONNECTION	382
	***from* Civil Disobedience**	ESSAY	388

Reading for Information: Analyzing Functional and Expository Texts

	Water on Tap	FUNCTIONAL TEXT	*393*
	South Florida Environmental Report	EXPOSITORY TEXT	395

Contemporary Connection: Embracing Wilderness Past and Present

Bridget Besaw	**Thoreau-Wabanaki Trail**	PHOTOGRAPHS	398

PART FOUR: AMERICAN MASTERS

Extended Study: Poetry

Elements of Poetry			402
Billy Collins	**Man Listening to Disc** EXEMPLAR	POEM	403
Emily Dickinson	**Because I could not stop for Death** EXEMPLAR	POEM	408
	I heard a Fly buzz—when I died	POEM	410
	There's a certain Slant of light	POEM	412
	My life closed twice before its close	POEM	413
	Capturing the Moment	WORLD LITERATURE CONNECTION	413
	The Soul selects her own Society	POEM	414
	The Brain—is wider than the Sky	POEM	415
	There is a solitude of space	POEM	416
	Water, is taught by thirst	POEM	417
Galway Kinnell	**Reckless Genius**	LITERARY CRITICISM	418
Walt Whitman	***from* Preface to the 1855 Edition of Leaves of Grass**	ESSAY	426
	***from* Song of Myself** EXEMPLAR	POEM	428
	When I Heard the Learn'd Astronomer	POEM	432
	By the Bivouac's Fitful Flame	POEM	433
	I Hear America Singing	POEM	434
	A Noiseless Patient Spider	POEM	436
James E. Miller, Jr.	**America's Epic**	LITERARY CRITICISM	437

Writing Workshop: Reflective Essay 440

WRITE GUY

Jeff Anderson, M.Ed.	**What Do You Notice?**	440
Gretel Ehrlich	**On Using Layers of Meaning**	443

Communications Workshop: Write and Deliver a Persuasive Speech 448

Vocabulary Workshop: Etymology: Political Science/History Terms 450

Common Core Assessment Workshop: Test-Taking Practice SAT PREP ACT 452

Common Core Assessment Workshop: Performance Tasks 456

Independent Reading 458

Nathaniel Hawthorne	The Scarlet Letter EXEMPLAR	NOVEL
Walt Whitman	Leaves of Grass EXEMPLAR	POETRY
Edgar Allan Poe	Complete Stories and Poems EXEMPLAR	STORIES AND POETRY
Emily Dickinson	Complete Poems of Emily Dickinson EXEMPLAR	POETRY
Ralph Waldo Emerson	Selected Writings of Ralph Waldo Emerson	ESSAYS AND POEMS
Henry David Thoreau	Walden *and* Civil Disobedience	ESSAYS
David Colbert, Editor	Eyewitness to America: 500 Years of American History in the Words of Those Who Saw It Happen EXEMPLAR	HISTORY
Daniel Boorstin, Editor	An American Primer EXEMPLAR	HISTORY

Division, Reconciliation, and Expansion

Literature of the Civil War and the Frontier (1850 to 1914)

Multiple Perspectives on the Era

Snapshot of the Period INSTRUCTIONAL ESSAY AND GRAPHICS 462
Historical Background INSTRUCTIONAL ESSAY 464
Essential Questions Across Time: The Civil War and the Frontier INSTRUCTIONAL ESSAY 466
RECENT SCHOLARSHIP
Nell Irvin Painter **Defining an Era** ESSAY 474
Integrate and Evaluate Information 476

PART ONE: **A NATION DIVIDED**

Ambrose Bierce **An Occurrence at Owl Creek Bridge** SHORT STORY 480
The Battle of Shiloh HISTORY CONNECTION 485

Research Project: Primary Sources
Mary Chesnut ***from* Mary Chesnut's Civil War** DIARY 495
Warren Lee Goss **Recollections of a Private** JOURNAL 500
Randolph McKim **A Confederate Account of the Battle of Gettysburg** DIARY 502

Stephen Crane **An Episode of War** SHORT STORY 508
Photographer Mathew Brady HUMANITIES CONNECTION 509

Extended Study: Narrative Nonfiction
Defining Narrative Nonfiction 516
Richard Wright ***from* Black Boy** EXEMPLAR AUTOBIOGRAPHY 517
Frederick Douglass ***from* My Bondage and My Freedom** AUTOBIOGRAPHY 520
Slave Narratives HISTORY CONNECTION 526

Comparing Literary Works: Refrains
Traditional **Go Down, Moses** SPIRITUAL 532
Traditional **Swing Low, Sweet Chariot** SPIRITUAL 534

Comparing Literary Works: Writer's View of Civil War
Abraham Lincoln **The Gettysburg Address** SPEECH 538
Robert E. Lee **Letter to His Son** LETTER 541

Contemporary Connection: Civil War Writings Past and Present
Anthony Minghella ***from* Cold Mountain** SCREENPLAY EXCERPT 546

THEMES ACROSS CENTURIES: Scholar's Insights
Nell Irvin Painter ***Introduces* Sojourner Truth** ESSAY 550
Sojourner Truth **An Account of an Experience With Discrimination** FIRST-PERSON ACCOUNT 554

Reading for Information: Analyzing Functional and Expository Texts
A Community's Roots EXPOSITORY TEXT 559
Virginia Department of Historic Resources Form FUNCTIONAL TEXT 561

PART TWO: FORGING NEW FRONTIERS

Extended Study: Mark Twain
Literary History: Twain's World INSTRUCTIONAL ESSAY 564
Meet the Author: Mark Twain BIOGRAPHY 566
Mark Twain ***from* Life on the Mississippi** AUTOBIOGRAPHY 570
***from* How to Tell a Story** LITERARY CRITICISM 575
The Notorious Jumping Frog of Calaveras County SHORT STORY 576

Comparing Humor Past and Present
"School" of American Humor ILLUSTRATED LITERARY HISTORY 586
Bill Bryson ***from* The Life and Times of the Thunderbolt Kid** MEMOIR 589

Jack London **To Build a Fire** SHORT STORY 596
Dogs and the Yukon HISTORY CONNECTION 602

Research Project: Primary Sources
Miriam Davis Colt **Heading West** PERSONAL HISTORY 617
Chief Joseph **I Will Fight No More Forever** SPEECH 622

PART THREE: LIVING IN A CHANGING WORLD

Kate Chopin **The Story of an Hour** SHORT STORY 628
Challenging Women's Roles WORLD LITERATURE CONNECTION 631
Paul Laurence Dunbar **Douglass** POEM 636
We Wear the Mask POEM 638
Edwin Arlington Robinson **Luke Havergal** POEM 642
Richard Cory POEM 644

Interactive resources provide personalized instruction and activities online.

	Dramatic Monologue	WORLD LITERATURE CONNECTION	646
Edgar Lee Masters	**Lucinda Matlock**	POEM	646
	Richard Bone	POEM	647
Willa Cather	**A Wagner Matinée**	SHORT STORY	652
	Wagnerian Opera	MUSIC CONNECTION	656

Writing Workshop: Historical Investigation Report 664

WRITE GUY

Jeff Anderson, M.Ed.	**What Do You Notice?**	664
Nell Irvin Painter	**On Using Research**	669

Communications Workshop: Oral Interpretation of a Literary Work 676

Vocabulary Workshop: Words from Mythology and Religious Traditions 678

Common Core Assessment Workshop: Test-Taking Practice SAT PREP ACT 680

Common Core Assessment Workshop: Performance Tasks 684

Independent Reading 686

Mark Twain	The Adventures of Huckleberry Finn	NOVEL
Willa Cather	My Ántonia	NOVEL
Edgar Lee Masters	Spoon River Anthology	POETRY
Henry L. Gates, Jr., Editor	The Classic Slave Narratives	AUTOBIOGRAPHY
Frederick Douglass	Narrative of the Life of Frederick Douglass EXEMPLAR	AUTOBIOGRAPHY
Diane Ravitch, Editor	The American Reader: Words That Moved a Nation EXEMPLAR	NONFICTION
David Haward Bain	Empire Express: Building the First Transcontinental Railroad	HISTORY
James McPherson	What They Fought For 1861–1865 EXEMPLAR	HISTORY

Disillusion, Defiance, and Discontent

Literature of the Modern Age (1914 to 1945)

Multiple Perspectives on the Era

Snapshot of the Period		INSTRUCTIONAL ESSAY AND GRAPHICS	690
Historical Background		INSTRUCTIONAL ESSAY	692
Essential Questions Across Time: The Modern Age		INSTRUCTIONAL ESSAY	694
RECENT SCHOLARSHIP			
Tim O'Brien	**Literature as a Magic Carpet**	ESSAY	702
Integrate and Evaluate Information			704

PART ONE: FACING TROUBLED TIMES

T. S. Eliot	**The Love Song of J. Alfred Prufrock** EXEMPLAR	POEM	708
	Modernism	HUMANITIES CONNECTION	713

Comparing Literary Works: Imagism

Ezra Pound	**A Few Don'ts**	LITERARY MANIFESTO	719
	In a Station of the Metro	POEM	722
William Carlos Williams	**The Red Wheelbarrow**	POEM	723
	This Is Just to Say	POEM	723
	The Great Figure	POEM	724
H. D.	**Pear Tree**	POEM	725

F. Scott Fitzgerald	**Winter Dreams**	SHORT STORY	730
	Fitzgerald's Elusive Women	CULTURAL CONNECTION	742
	The Jazz Age	CULTURAL CONNECTION	746
John Steinbeck	**The Turtle *from* The Grapes of Wrath**	NOVEL EXCERPT	758

Research Project: Primary Sources

Dorothea Lange	**Migrant Mother**	PHOTOGRAPHS	767
Woody Guthrie	**Dust Bowl Blues**	BALLAD	768

W. H. Auden	**The Unknown Citizen**	POEM	774
E. E. Cummings	**old age sticks**	POEM	780
	anyone lived in a pretty how town	POEM	781

Comparing Literary Works: Theme

Wallace Stevens	**Of Modern Poetry**	POEM	786
Archibald MacLeish	**Ars Poetica**	POEM	789
Marianne Moore	**Poetry**	POEM	791

COMMON CORE
Unit 4 ▪ Table of Contents

PART TWO: FROM EVERY CORNER OF THE LAND

Extended Study: Short Stories

Elements of Short Stories			796
Sarah Orne Jewett	***from* A White Heron** EXEMPLAR	SHORT STORY	797
Ernest Hemingway	**In Another Country**	SHORT STORY	800
THEMES ACROSS CENTURIES: Author's Insights			
Tim O'Brien	***Introduces* Ambush**	ESSAY	808
Tim O'Brien	**Ambush**	SHORT STORY	810
William Faulkner	**A Rose for Emily**	SHORT STORY	816
	Two Influential Writers	LITERATURE CONNECTION	820
	Nobel Prize Acceptance Speech	SPEECH	828
Katherine Anne Porter	**The Jilting of Granny Weatherall**	SHORT STORY	834
	House Calls	HISTORY CONNECTION	836
Eudora Welty	**A Worn Path**	SHORT STORY	848
	The Hero's Quest	WORLD LITERATURE CONNECTION	851
James Thurber	**The Night the Ghost Got In**	HUMOROUS ESSAY	860

Comparing Literary Works: Personification

Carl Sandburg	**Chicago**	POEM	868
	Grass	POEM	870
Robert Frost	**Birches**	POEM	874
	Stopping by Woods on a Snowy Evening	POEM	877
	Mending Wall EXEMPLAR	POEM	878
	"Out, Out—"	POEM	880
	Acquainted With the Night	POEM	882
	Terza Rima	WORLD LITERATURE CONNECTION	883
	The Gift Outright	POEM	884

Contemporary Connection: Cartooning as Literature

Jules Feiffer	**Trapped in a Comic Book**	GRAPHIC STORY	889

Interactive resources provide personalized instruction and activities online.

PART THREE: THE HARLEM RENAISSANCE

Extended Study: Langston Hughes

Literary History: Langston Hughes and Harlem		INSTRUCTIONAL ESSAY	896
Langston Hughes		BIOGRAPHY	898
Langston Hughes	**The Negro Speaks of Rivers**	POEM	902
	I, Too	POEM	904
	Dream Variations	POEM	906
	Refugee in America	POEM	907

Comparing Poetry of Cultural Identity

Poetry of Identity		ILLUSTRATED LITERARY HISTORY	912
Lucille Clifton	**Study the Masters**	POEM	915
Colleen McElroy	**For My Children**	POEM	916

Comparing Literary Works: Imagery

Claude McKay	**The Tropics in New York**	POEM	923
Arna Bontemps	**A Black Man Talks of Reaping**	POEM	924
Countee Cullen	**From the Dark Tower**	POEM	926

Zora Neale Hurston	***from* Dust Tracks on a Road**	AUTOBIOGRAPHY	930
	Zora Neale Hurston Rediscovered	LITERATURE CONNECTION	935

Reading for Information: Analyzing Functional and Expository Texts

	Son of Citation Machine	FUNCTIONAL TEXT	939
	Wikipedia Article, Atlanta Braves	EXPOSITORY TEXT	941

Writing Workshop: Multimedia Presentation 944

Tim O'Brien **On Revision** 947

Communications Workshop: Analyze a Nonprint Political Advertisement 952

Vocabulary Workshop: Etymology: Scientific, Medical, and Mathematical Terms 954

Common Core Assessment Workshop: Test-Taking Practice SAT PREP ACT 956

Common Core Assessment Workshop: Performance Tasks 960

Independent Reading 962

William Faulkner	As I Lay Dying EXEMPLAR	NOVEL
F. Scott Fitzgerald	The Great Gatsby EXEMPLAR	NOVEL
Ernest Hemingway	A Farewell to Arms EXEMPLAR	NOVEL
Robert Frost	The Complete Poems EXEMPLAR	POETRY
Zora Neale Hurston	Dust Tracks on a Road	AUTOBIOGRAPHY
John Keegan	The First World War	HISTORY
Studs Terkel	Hard Times: An Oral History of the Great Depression	HISTORY
Eric Foner and John A. Garraty, Editors	The Reader's Companion to American History EXEMPLAR	HISTORY

Prosperity and Protest

Literature of the Post-War Era (1945 to 1970)

Multiple Perspectives on the Era

Snapshot of the Period		INSTRUCTIONAL ESSAY AND GRAPHICS	966
Historical Background		INSTRUCTIONAL ESSAY	968
Essential Questions Across Time: The Post-War Era		INSTRUCTIONAL ESSAY	970
RECENT SCHOLARSHIP			
Arthur Miller	**The Purpose of Theater**	ESSAY	978
Integrate and Evaluate Information			980

PART ONE: WAR SHOCK

Comparing Literary Works: Author's Perspective

John Hersey	***from* Hiroshima**	NONFICTION	984
	B-29 Bombers	HISTORY CONNECTION	986
	World War II	HISTORY CONNECTION	992
Randall Jarrell	**The Death of the Ball Turret Gunner**	POEM	997

Research Project: Primary Sources

	Junk Rally	POSTER	1003
Dr. Seuss	**The Battle of the Easy Chair**	EDITORIAL CARTOON	1004
Editors of The New York Times	**Backing the Attack**	EDITORIAL	1005

PART TWO: TRADITION AND REBELLION

Flannery O'Connor	**The Life You Save May Be Your Own**	SHORT STORY	1012
Bernard Malamud	**The First Seven Years**	SHORT STORY	1028
Lawrence Ferlinghetti	**Constantly Risking Absurdity**	POEM	1042

Contemporary Connection: Artistic Upstarts Past and Present

Improv Everywhere	**Subway Birthday**	ELECTRONIC NONFICTION NARRATIVE	1047

Sylvia Plath	**Mirror**	POEM	1052
Anne Sexton	**Courage**	POEM	1053
Theodore Roethke	**Cuttings**	POEM	1058
	Cuttings (later)	POEM	1060

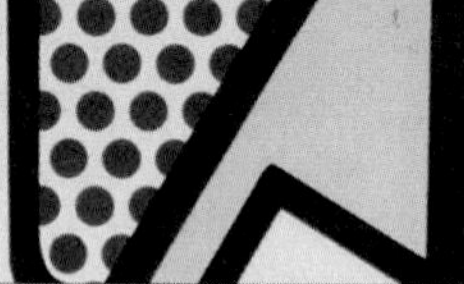

Comparing Literary Works: Repetition and Parallelism

Gwendolyn Brooks	**The Explorer**	POEM	1064
Robert Hayden	**Frederick Douglass**	POEM	1066
Elizabeth Bishop	**One Art**	POEM	1072
	The Villanelle	LITERATURE CONNECTION	1073
	Filling Station	POEM	1074

PART THREE: **LITERATURE OF PROTEST**

James Baldwin	**The Rockpile**	SHORT STORY	1082
	James Baldwin and the Church	CULTURAL CONNECTION	1088
Toni Morrison	**Life in His Language**	EULOGY	1096

Comparing Literary Works: Rhetorical Devices

John F. Kennedy	**Inaugural Address**	SPEECH	1104
Martin Luther King, Jr.	***from* Letter from Birmingham City Jail**	LETTER	1109

Extended Study: Drama

Defining Drama		INSTRUCTIONAL ESSAY	1116
Lorraine Hansberry	***from* A Raisin in the Sun** EXEMPLAR	DRAMA	1117
Author in Depth: Arthur Miller		BIOGRAPHY	1118
THEMES ACROSS TIME: Author's Insights			
Arthur Miller	**Miller on *The Crucible***	ESSAY	1120
	The Crucible, Act 1	DRAMA	1126
	History Repeats Itself	HISTORY CONNECTION	1132
	Maxim Gorky	WORLD LITERATURE CONNECTION	1137
	The Inquisition	HISTORY CONNECTION	1145
	The Crucible, Act 2	DRAMA	1161
	Arthur Miller and the Blacklist	HISTORY CONNECTION	1166
	Bertolt Brecht	WORLD LITERATURE CONNECTION	1171
	Twentieth-Century Drama	LITERARY HISTORY	1184
	The Crucible, Act 3	DRAMA	1187
	Federico García Lorca	WORLD LITERATURE CONNECTION	1199
	Puritans and Nathaniel Hawthorne	HISTORY CONNECTION	1208
	The Crucible, Act 4	DRAMA	1217
	Wole Soyinka	WORLD LITERATURE CONNECTION	1223
	Being Abigail Williams	MEDIA CONNECTION	1226

Comparing Political Drama Past and Present

Political Drama Around the World ILLUSTRATED LITERARY HISTORY 1238

George Clooney and Grant Heslov ***from* Good Night, and Good Luck** SCREENPLAY 1241

Reading for Information: Analyzing Argumentative and Expository Texts

Brooks Atkinson **The Crucible** ARGUMENTATIVE TEXT 1251

Kenneth Turan **Hysteria Resides at the Heart of the Frantic "Crucible"** ARGUMENTATIVE TEXT 1252

Mel Gussow **A Rock of the Modern Age, Arthur Miller Is Everywhere** EXPOSITORY TEXT 1253

Writing Workshop: Persuasive Essay 1256

WRITE GUY
Jeff Anderson, M.Ed. **What Do You Notice?** 1256

Arthur Miller **On Using Historical Facts** 1259

Communications Workshop: Analyze and Evaluate Entertainment Media 1264

Vocabulary Workshop: Idioms and Idiomatic Expressions 1266

Common Core Assessment Workshop: Test-Taking Practice SAT PREP ACT 1268

Common Core Assessment Workshop: Performance Tasks 1272

Independent Reading 1274

James Baldwin	Baldwin: Early Stories and Novels	FICTION
Cary Nelson, Editor	Anthology of Modern American Poetry EXEMPLAR	POETRY
Saul Bellow	The Adventures of Augie March EXEMPLAR	NOVEL
Arthur Miller	Death of a Salesman EXEMPLAR	DRAMA
Lorraine Hansberry	A Raisin in the Sun EXEMPLAR	DRAMA
Martin Luther King, Jr.	A Call to Conscience: The Landmark Speeches of Dr. Martin Luther King	SPEECHES
Christian G. Appy	Patriots: The Vietnam War Remembered from All Sides	PRIMARY SOURCE
Andrew Chaikin	A Man on the Moon: The Voyages of the Apollo Astronauts	HISTORY

Interactive resources provide personalized instruction and activities online.

New Voices, New Frontiers

Literature of the Contemporary Period (1970 to Present)

Multiple Perspectives on the Era

Snapshot of the Period — INSTRUCTIONAL ESSAY AND GRAPHICS 1278
Historical Background — INSTRUCTIONAL ESSAY 1280
Essential Questions Across Time: The Contemporary Period — INSTRUCTIONAL ESSAY 1282

RECENT SCHOLARSHIP
Julia Alvarez — **All-American Writer** — ESSAY 1290
Integrate and Evaluate Information 1292

PART ONE: **CONTEMPORARY FICTION**

THEMES ACROSS CULTURES: Author's Insights
Julia Alvarez — ***Introduces* Antojos** — ESSAY 1294
Antojos — SHORT STORY 1298
The Dominican Republic — GEOGRAPHY CONNECTION 1301
Alice Walker — **Everyday Use** — SHORT STORY 1312
Raymond Carver — **Everything Stuck to Him** — SHORT STORY 1326

PART TWO: **CONTEMPORARY POETRY**

William Stafford — **Traveling Through the Dark** — POEM 1336
Denise Levertov — **The Secret** — POEM 1339
Li-Young Lee — **The Gift** — POEM 1342

Comparing Literary Works: Social Commentary
Martín Espada — **Who Burns for the Perfection of Paper** — POEM 1348
Yusef Komunyakaa — **Camouflaging the Chimera** — POEM 1350
Naomi Shihab Nye — **Streets** — POEM 1353

Stanley Kunitz — **Halley's Comet** — POEM 1358
The Poets Laureate — LITERARY HISTORY 1362
Judith Ortiz Cofer — **The Latin Deli: An Ars Poetica** EXEMPLAR — POEM 1366
Ars Poetica — WORLD LITERATURE CONNECTION 1368

Contemporary Connection: Poetry and Numbers
The Fibonacci Sequence — POEMS 1371

PART THREE: CONTEMPORARY NONFICTION

Extended Study: The Essay

Defining the Essay 1374

H. L. Mencken **"American Slang" *from* The American Language** EXEMPLAR — ESSAY 1375

William Safire **Onomatopoeia** — ESSAY 1378

Ian Frazier **Coyote v. Acme** — ESSAY 1384

Anna Quindlen **One Day, Now Broken in Two** — ESSAY 1394

Research Project: Primary Sources

Sean Ramsay **Urban Renewal** — ORAL HISTORY TRANSCRIPT 1401

William Harvey **Playing for the Fighting Sixty-Ninth** — E-MAIL 1403

Comparing Literary Works: Identity

Amy Tan **Mother Tongue** EXEMPLAR — ESSAY 1410

Rita Dove **For the Love of Books** — ESSAY 1418

Comparing Literary Works: Point of View

Maxine Hong Kingston ***from* The Woman Warrior** — MEMOIR 1426

N. Scott Momaday ***from* The Names** — MEMOIR 1434

The Centaur — MYTHOLOGY CONNECTION 1437

Reading for Information: Analyzing Functional and Expository Text

Demographic Aspects of Surnames — EXPOSITORY TEXT 1443

The Statue of Liberty/Ellis Island Foundation — EXPOSITORY TEXT 1446

Writing Workshop: Short Story 1448

WRITE GUY

Jeff Anderson, M.Ed. **What Do You Notice?** 1448

Julia Alvarez **On Flashback and Exposition** 1451

Communications Workshop: Compare Print News Coverage 1456

Vocabulary Workshop: Cognates 1458

Common Core Assessment Workshop: Test-Taking Practice SAT PREP ACT 1460

Common Core Assessment Workshop: Performance Tasks 1464

Independent Reading 1466

Billy Collins Sailing Alone Around the Room EXEMPLAR — POETRY

Toni Morrison The Bluest Eye EXEMPLAR — NOVEL

Cristina Garcia Dreaming in Cuban EXEMPLAR — NOVEL

Jhumpa Lahiri The Namesake EXEMPLAR — NOVEL

Wole Soyinka Death and the King's Horseman EXEMPLAR — DRAMA

Rita Dove Mother Love: Poems EXEMPLAR — POETRY

Pearson Prentice Hall Nonfiction Readings Across the Curriculum — NONFICTION

Lee Gutkind, Editor On Nature: Great Writers on the Great Outdoors — NONFICTION

Malcolm Gladwell The Tipping Point: How Little Things Can Make a Big Difference EXEMPLAR — NONFICTION

Literature

▶ Stories

Adventure Stories

***from* Moby-Dick**
Herman Melville 336

An Occurrence at Owl Creek Bridge
Ambrose Bierce 480

To Build a Fire
Jack London 596

Allegories

The Turtle
John Steinbeck 758

Graphic Novels

Trapped in a Comic Book
Jules Feiffer 889

Humor/Satire

The Notorious Jumping Frog of Calaveras Country
Mark Twain 576

Myths

The Earth on Turtle's Back
Onondaga 20

When Grizzlies Walked Upright
Modoc 24

***from* The Navajo Origin Legend**
Navajo 27

Realistic Fiction

An Episode of War
Stephen Crane 508

The Story of an Hour
Kate Chopin 628

A Wagner Matinée
Willa Cather 652

Winter Dreams
F. Scott Fitzgerald 730

***from* The White Heron** EXEMPLAR
Sarah Orne Jewett 797

In Another Country
Ernest Hemingway 800

Ambush
Tim O'Brien 810

The Jilting of Granny Weatherall
Katherine Anne Porter 834

A Worn Path
Eudora Welty 848

The Life You Save May Be Your Own
Flannery O'Connor 1012

The First Seven Years
Bernard Malamud 1028

The Rockpile
James Baldwin 1082

Antojos
Julia Alvarez 1298

Everyday Use
Alice Walker 1312

Everything Stuck to Him
Raymond Carver 1326

Science Fiction/Fantasy/Gothic

The Devil and Tom Walker
Washington Irving 228

The Minister's Black Veil
Nathaniel Hawthorne 272

The Fall of the House of Usher
Edgar Allan Poe 292

Where Is Here?
Joyce Carol Oates 325

A Rose for Emily
William Faulkner 816

▶ Drama

Multi-Act Plays

***from* A Raisin in the Sun** EXEMPLAR
Lorraine Hansberry 1117

The Crucible
Arthur Miller 1124

Screenplays

***from* Cold Mountain**
Anthony Minghella 546

***from* Good Night, and Good Luck**
George Clooney, Grant Heslov 1241

▶ Poetry

Ballads

Dust Bowl Refugee
Woody Guthrie 768

Dramatic Monologue

Lucinda Matlock
Edgar Lee Masters 646

Richard Bone
Edgar Lee Masters 647

The Love Song of J. Alfred Prufrock EXEMPLAR
T. S. Eliot 708

The Death of the Ball Turret Gunner
Randall Jarrell 997

Epics

***from* The Song of Hiawatha**
Henry Wadsworth Longfellow 258

Formal Verse

To My Dear and Loving Husband
Anne Bradstreet 76

Huswifery
Edward Taylor 82

To His Excellency, General Washington
Phillis Wheatley 124

The Tide Rises, The Tide Falls
Henry Wadsworth Longfellow 260

Old Ironsides
Oliver Wendell Holmes 266

Douglass
Paul Laurence Dunbar 636

We Wear the Mask
Paul Laurence Dunbar 638

Acquainted With the Night
Robert Frost 882

The Tropics in NY
Claude McKay 923

A Black Man Talks of Reaping
Arna Bontemps 924

From the Dark Tower
Countee Cullen 926

Frederick Douglass
Robert Hayden 1067

One Art
Elizabeth Bishop 1072

Poetry and Numbers: The Fibonacci Sequence
Gregory Pincus, Patricia Lee Lewis,
Athena Kildegaard, Patricia Vogel 1371

Free Verse

***from* Song of Myself** EXEMPLAR
Walt Whitman 428

When I Heard the Learn'd Astronomer
Walt Whitman 432

By the Bivouac's Fitful Flame
Walt Whitman 433

I Hear America Singing
Walt Whitman 434

A Noiseless Patient Spider
Walt Whitman 436

Constantly Risking Absurdity
Lawrence Ferlinghetti 1042

Lyrical Poems

Thanatopsis
William Cullen Bryant 262

Man Listening to Disc EXEMPLAR
Billy Collins 403

Because I could not stop for Death EXEMPLAR
Emily Dickinson 408

I heard a Fly buzz—when I died
Emily Dickinson 410

There's a certain Slant of light
Emily Dickinson 412

My life closed twice before its close
Emily Dickinson 413

The Soul selects her own Society
Emily Dickinson 414

The Brain—is wider than the Sky
Emily Dickinson 415

There is a solitude of space
Emily Dickinson 416

Water, is taught by thirst
Emily Dickinson 417

In a Station of the Metro
Ezra Pound 722

The Red Wheelbarrow
William Carlos Williams 723

This Is Just to Say
William Carlos Williams 723

The Great Figure
William Carlos Williams 724

Pear Tree
H. D. 725

old age sticks
E. E. Cummings 780

Of Modern Poetry
Wallace Stevens 786

Ars Poetica
Archibald MacLeish 789

Poetry
Marianne Moore 791

Chicago
Carl Sandburg 868

Grass
Carl Sandburg 870

Birches
Robert Frost 874

Stopping by Woods on a Snowy Evening
Robert Frost 877

Mending Wall EXEMPLAR
Robert Frost 878

The Negro Speaks of Rivers
Langston Hughes 902

I, Too
Langston Hughes 904

Dream Variations
Langston Hughes 906

Study the Masters
Lucille Clifton 915

For My Children
Colleen McElroy 916

Mirror
Sylvia Plath 1052

Courage
Anne Sexton 1053

Cuttings
Theodore Roethke 1058

Cuttings (later)
Theodore Roethke 1060

The Explorer
Gwendolyn Brooks 1064

The Filling Station
Elizabeth Bishop 1075

The Secret
Denise Levertov 1339

Camouflaging the Chimera
Yusef Komunyakaa 1350

Streets
Naomi Shihab Nye 1353

The Latin Deli: An Ars Poetica EXEMPLAR
Judith Ortiz Cofer 1366

Narrative Poems

The Raven
Edgar Allan Poe 312

Luke Havergal
Edward Arlington Robinson 642

Richard Cory
Edward Arlington Robinson 644

The Unknown Citizen
W. H. Auden 774

anyone lived in a pretty how town
E. E. Cummings 781

"Out, Out—"
Robert Frost 880

Traveling Through the Dark
William Stafford 1336

The Gift
Li-Young Lee 1342

Who Burns for the Perfection of Paper
Martin Espada 1348

Halley's Comet
Stanley Kunitz 1358

Songs/Spirituals

Go Down, Moses
Traditional 532

Swing Low, Sweet Chariot
Traditional 534

Informational Text—Literary Nonfiction

▶ Argument

Opinion Pieces

Backing the Attack
Editors of The New York Times 1005
from **Letter from Birmingham City Jail**
Martin Luther King, Jr. 1109
Review of *The Crucible*
Brooks Atkinson 1251
Hysteria Resides at Heart of the Frantic "Crucible"
Kenneth Turan 1252

Speeches/Sermons

from **Sinners in the Hands of an Angry God**
Jonathan Edwards 86
from **What to the Slave Is the Fourth of July?** EXEMPLAR
Frederick Douglass 97
Speech in the Virginia Convention
Patrick Henry 100
Speech in the Convention
Benjamin Franklin 105
The Gettysburg Address
Abraham Lincoln 538
I Will Fight No More Forever
Chief Joseph 622
Nobel Prize Acceptance Speech
William Faulkner 828
Inaugural Address
John F. Kennedy 1104

▶ Exposition

Essays About Art, Literature, and Language

Promise and Paradox: American Autobiography
William L. Andrews 14
Susan Power Introduces "Museum Indians"
Susan Power 32
William L. Andrews Introduces Olaudah Equiano
William L. Andrews 166
Inspired by Nature
Gretel Ehrlich 222
On Writing "The Raven"
Edgar Allan Poe 311
Charles Johnson Introduces Ralph Waldo Emerson
Charles Johnson 362
Gretel Ehrlich Introduces Henry David Thoreau
Gretel Ehrlich 374
Reckless Genius: Emily Dickinson
Galway Kinnell 418
from **Preface to the 1855 Edition of *Leaves of Grass***
Walt Whitman 426
America's Epic
James E. Miller, Jr. 437
Defining an Era
Nell Irvin Painter 474
Nell Irvin Painter Introduces Sojourner Truth
Nell Irvin Painter 550
from **How to Tell a Story**
Mark Twain 575
Literature as a Magic Carpet
Tim O'Brien 703
A Few Don'ts
Ezra Pound 719
Migrant Mother
Dorothea Lange 767
Tim O'Brien Introduces "Ambush"
Tim O'Brien 808
The Purpose of Theater
Arthur Miller 978
Life in His Language: James Baldwin
Toni Morrison 1096
Arthur Miller Introduces *The Crucible*
Arthur Miller 1120
On "Antojos"
Julia Alvarez 1294
American Slang *from* The American Language EXEMPLAR
H. L. Mencken 1375
Onomatopoeia
William Safire 1379

Essays About Ideas

from **Nature**
Ralph Waldo Emerson 366
from **Self-Reliance**
Ralph Waldo Emerson 369
from **Walden** EXEMPLAR
Henry David Thoreau 378
from **Civil Disobedience**
Henry David Thoreau 388

Historical Accounts

from **A Journey Through Texas**
Alvar Núñez Cabeza de Vaca 48
Boulders Taller Than the Great Tower of Seville
García López de Cárdenas 52
from **Of Plymouth Plantation**
William Bradford 58
Crossing the Great Divide
Meriwether Lewis 250
from **Mary Chesnut's Civil War**
Mary Chesnut 495
Recollections of a Private
Warren Lee Goss 500

Range of Reading: Complete Contents by Genre

A Confederate Account of the Battle of Gettysburg
Randolph McKim ... 502

***from* Heading West**
Miriam Davis Colt ... 617

Urban Renewal
Sean Ramsey ... 1401

Playing for the Fighting Sixty-Ninth
William Harvey ... 1403

Humorous Essays

The Night the Ghost Got In
James Thurber ... 860

Coyote v. Acme
Ian Frazier ... 1384

Journalism

A Community's Roots (abstract)
Samir S. Patel ... 559

***from* Hiroshima**
John Hersey ... 984

A Rock of the Modern Age, Arthur Miller Is Everywhere
Mel Gussow ... 1253

Letters

Letter from the President's House
John Adams ... 181

Letter to Her Daughter From the New White House
Abigail Adams ... 182

Letter to His Son
Robert E. Lee ... 541

Memoirs/Autobiography

***from* The Autobiography**
Benjamin Franklin ... 140

Straw Into Gold: The Metamorphosis of the Everyday
Sandra Cisneros ... 158

***from* The Interesting Narrative of the Life of Olaudah Equiano**
Olaudah Equiano ... 170

***from* Black Boy** EXEMPLAR
Richard Wright ... 517

***from* My Bondage and My Freedom**
Frederick Douglass ... 520

An Account of an Experience With Discrimination
Sojourner Truth ... 554

***from* Life on the Mississippi**
Mark Twain ... 570

***from* The Life and Times of the Thunderbolt Kid**
Bill Bryson ... 589

***from* Dust Tracks on a Road**
Zora Neale Hurston ... 930

***from* The Woman Warrior**
Maxine Hong Kingston ... 1426

***from* The Names**
N. Scott Momaday ... 1434

Personal Essays

Museum Indians
Susan Power ... 34

All-American Writer
Julia Alvarez ... 1291

One Day, Now Broken in Two
Anna Quindlen ... 1394

Mother Tongue EXEMPLAR
Amy Tan ... 1410

For the Love of Books
Rita Dove ... 1418

Political Documents

***from* The Iroquois Constitution**
Dekanawidah ... 42

The Declaration of Independence EXEMPLAR
Thomas Jefferson ... 112

***from* The American Crisis** EXEMPLAR
Thomas Paine ... 117

Commission of Meriwether Lewis
Thomas Jefferson ... 245

Scientific Accounts

***from* Mars Rover Mission Update**
Steve Squyres ... 69

Water on Tap
United States EPA ... 393

Kissimmee River Restoration
and Upper Basin Initiatives ... 395

Technical Accounts

Demographic Aspects of Surnames from Census 2000
David L. Word, Charles D. Coleman ... 1443

▶ Functional Text

How to Watch a Debate ... 129

Help North Texas Vote ... 132

Floor Plan of President's House
Benjamin Latrobe ... 184

Government Form
Virginia Department of Historic Resources ... 561

Online Citation Organizer ... 939

Wikipedia Entry ... 941

Mission Statement
The Statue of Liberty–Ellis Island Foundation ... 1446

Informational Text—Literary Nonfiction

▶ Historical and Literary Background

Unit 1: A Gathering of Voices

Literature of Early America (Beginnings to 1800)
Snapshot of the Period 2

***Richard Lederer* Developing American English**
Our Native American Heritage 9

William L. Andrews
America Begins with a Promise and a Paradox 14

Unit 2: A Growing Nation

Literature of the American Renaissance (1800 to 1870)
Snapshot of the Period 210

***Richard Lederer* Developing American English**
The Truth About O.K. 221

Gretel Ehrlich
Inspired by Nature 222

Unit 3: Division, Reconciliation, and Expansion

Literature of the Civil War and the Frontier (1850 to 1914)
Snapshot of the Period 462

***Richard Lederer* Developing American English**
Mark Twain and the American Language 471

Nell Irvin Painter
Defining an Era 474

Unit 4: Disillusion, Defiance, and Discontent

Literature of the Modern Age (1914 to 1945)
Snapshot of the Period 690

***Richard Lederer* Developing American English**
Slang as It Is Slung 701

Tim O'Brien
Literature as a Magic Carpet 702

Unit 5: Prosperity and Protest

Literature of the Post-War Era (1945 to 1970)
Snapshot of the Period 966

Arthur Miller
The Purpose of Theater 978

Unit 6: New Voices, New Frontiers

Literature of the Contemporary Period (1970 to Present)
Snapshot of the Period 1278

***Richard Lederer* Developing American English**
Brave New Words 1287

Julia Alvarez
All-American Writer 1290

▶ The American Experience—Reading in the Humanities

Anne Bradstreet and John Berryman 7
African Americans and Women in the Revolution 11
Thomas Paine: Essayist, Hero of the Revolution, Father of the Internet? 12
The Mayflower 60
Biblical Imagery 88
John Locke and the Social Contract 114
Benjamin Franklin in Our World 146
The Slave Trade 174
Sacajawea, Guide for Lewis and Clark 215
Walden Pond and Tinker Creek 217
Emily Dickinson: Poet, Recluse . . . Gamer? 218
Jonathan Edwards, Puritans, and Sermons of Fear 276
The Golden Age of Yankee Whaling 344
Realism in Painting: The Ashcan School 467
Mark Twain, The Original Time Traveler 468
Photographer Mathew Brady 509
Slave Narratives 526
Women Get the Vote 695
William Faulkner: Hollywood Screen Doctor 698
Modernism 713
The Jazz Age 746
Two Influential Writers 820
Zora Neale Hurston Rediscovered 935
The Landscapes of Richard Diebenkorn 971
Jack Kerouac: King of the Roadtrip 972
Rachel Carson and Environmental Writing 977
World War II 992
Southern Regionalism 1021
Arthur Miller and the Blacklist 1166
A. R. Ammons, Emersonian Postmodernist 1277
Stephanie Strickland: Hypertext Poetry Pioneer 1288

▶ Literature in Context—Reading in the Content Areas

The Fireside Poets
Literature 259

Poe and Pop Culture
Culture 290
The Whale as Archetype
Humanities 346
The Battle of Shiloh
History 485
Dogs and the Yukon
History 602
Wagnerian Opera
Music 656
Fitzgerald's Elusive Women
Culture 742
House Calls
History 836
B-29 Bombers
History 986
The Villanelle
Literature 1073
James Baldwin and the Church
Culture 1080
History Repeats Itself
Social Studies 1132
The Inquisition
History 1145
Puritans and Nathaniel Hawthorne
History 1208
Being Abigail Williams
Media 1226
The Dominican Republic
Geography 1301
The Centaur
Mythology 1437

▶ World Literature Connections

The Tenth Muse 78
Proverbs 151
The Faust Legend 235
Mount Olympus 382
Capturing the Moment 413
Challenging Women's Roles 631
Dramatic Monologue: Robert Browning 646
The Hero's Quest 851
Terza Rima: Dante 883
Political Drama: Maxim Gorky 1137
Political Drama: Bertolt Brecht 1171
Political Drama: Federico García Lorca 1199
Political Drama: Wole Soyinka 1223
Ars Poetica 1368

▶ Literary History

All the News That's Fit to Print 134
A Gallery of Autobiography 156
The Gothic Family Tree 322
Transcendentalism: The Seekers 360
Mark Twain: The American Bard 564
"School" of American Humor 586
The Harlem Renaissance 896
Poetry of Identity 912
The Beats 1044
Political Drama Around the World 1238
The Poets Laureate 1362

Writing Workshops

Narrative Text: Autobiographical Narrative 188
Explanatory Text: Reflective Essay 440
Informative Text: Historical Investigation Report 664
Informative/Explanatory Text: Multimedia Presentation 944
Argumentative Text: Persuasive Essay 1256
Narrative Text: Short Story 1448

Vocabulary Workshops

Using a Dictionary and Thesaurus 198
Etymology: Political Science and History Terms 450
Words from Mythology and Religious Traditions 678
Etymology: Scientific, Medical, and Mathematical Terms 954
Idioms and Idiomatic Expressions 1266
Cognates 1458

Test-Taking Practice

Social Science Passage, Editing in Context 200
Paired Passages, Editing in Context 452
Humanities Passage, Editing in Context 680
Long Reading Passage, Improving Sentences 956
Prose Fiction, Editing in Context 1268
Short Reading Passage, Improving Paragraphs 1460

Communications Workshops

Evaluate Persuasive Speech 196
Write and Deliver a Persuasive Speech 448
Oral Interpretation of a Literary Work 676
Analyze a Nonprint Political Advertisement 952
Analyze and Evaluate Entertainment Media 1264
Compare Print News Coverage 1456

Common Core State Standards Overview

The Common Core State Standards will prepare you to succeed in college and your future career. They are separated into four sections—Reading (Literature and Informational Text), Writing, Speaking and Listening, and Language. Beginning each section, the College and Career Readiness Anchor Standards define what you need to achieve by the end of high school. The grade-specific standards that follow define what you need to know by the end of your current grade level.

Common Core Reading Standards

College and Career Readiness Anchor Standards

Key Ideas and Details

1. Read closely to determine what the text says explicitly and to make logical inferences from it; cite specific textual evidence when writing or speaking to support conclusions drawn from the text.
2. Determine central ideas or themes of a text and analyze their development; summarize the key supporting details and ideas.
3. Analyze how and why individuals, events, and ideas develop and interact over the course of a text.

Craft and Structure

4. Interpret words and phrases as they are used in a text, including determining technical, connotative, and figurative meanings, and analyze how specific word choices shape meaning or tone.
5. Analyze the structure of texts, including how specific sentences, paragraphs, and larger portions of the text (e.g., a section, chapter, scene, or stanza) relate to each other and the whole.
6. Assess how point of view or purpose shapes the content and style of a text.

Integration of Knowledge and Ideas

7. Integrate and evaluate content presented in diverse formats and media, including visually and quantitatively, as well as in words.
8. Delineate and evaluate the argument and specific claims in a text, including the validity of the reasoning as well as the relevance and sufficiency of the evidence.
9. Analyze how two or more texts address similar themes or topics in order to build knowledge or to compare the approaches the authors take.

Range of Reading and Level of Text Complexity

10. Read and comprehend complex literary and informational texts independently and proficiently.

Grade 11 Reading Standards for Literature

Key Ideas and Details

1. Cite strong and thorough textual evidence to support analysis of what the text says explicitly as well as inferences drawn from the text, including determining where the text leaves matters uncertain.

2. Determine two or more themes or central ideas of a text and analyze their development over the course of the text, including how they interact and build on one another to produce a complex account; provide an objective summary of the text.

3. Analyze the impact of the author's choices regarding how to develop and relate elements of a story or drama (e.g., where a story is set, how the action is ordered, how the characters are introduced and developed).

Craft and Structure

4. Determine the meaning of words and phrases as they are used in the text, including figurative and connotative meanings; analyze the impact of specific word choices on meaning and tone, including words with multiple meanings or language that is particularly fresh, engaging, or beautiful. (Include Shakespeare as well as other authors.)

5. Analyze how an author's choices concerning how to structure specific parts of a text (e.g., the choice of where to begin or end a story, the choice to provide a comedic or tragic resolution) contribute to its overall structure and meaning as well as its aesthetic impact.

6. Analyze a case in which grasping point of view requires distinguishing what is directly stated in a text from what is really meant (e.g., satire, sarcasm, irony, or understatement).

Integration of Knowledge and Ideas

7. Analyze multiple interpretations of a story, drama, or poem (e.g., recorded or live production of a play or recorded novel or poetry), evaluating how each version interprets the source text. (Include at least one play by Shakespeare and one play by an American dramatist.)

8. (Not applicable to literature)

9. Demonstrate knowledge of eighteenth-, nineteenth-, and early-twentieth-century foundational works of American literature, including how two or more texts from the same period treat similar themes or topics.

Range of Reading and Level of Text Complexity

10. By the end of grade 11, read and comprehend literature, including stories, dramas, and poems, in the grades 11–CCR text complexity band proficiently, with scaffolding as needed at the high end of the range.

Grade 11 Reading Standards for Informational Text

Key Ideas and Details

1. Cite strong and thorough textual evidence to support analysis of what the text says explicitly as well as inferences drawn from the text, including determining where the text leaves matters uncertain.

2. Determine two or more central ideas of a text and analyze their development over the course of the text, including how they interact and build on one another to provide a complex analysis; provide an objective summary of the text.

3. Analyze a complex set of ideas or sequence of events and explain how specific individuals, ideas, or events interact and develop over the course of the text.

Craft and Structure

4. Determine the meaning of words and phrases as they are used in a text, including figurative, connotative, and technical meanings; analyze how an author uses and refines the meaning of a key term or terms over the course of a text (e.g., how Madison defines *faction* in *Federalist* No. 10).

5. Analyze and evaluate the effectiveness of the structure an author uses in his or her exposition or argument, including whether the structure makes points clear, convincing, and engaging.

6. Determine an author's point of view or purpose in a text in which the rhetoric is particularly effective, analyzing how style and content contribute to the power, persuasiveness, or beauty of the text.

Integration of Knowledge and Ideas

7. Integrate and evaluate multiple sources of information presented in different media or formats (e.g., visually, quantitatively) as well as in words in order to address a question or solve a problem.

8. Delineate and evaluate the reasoning in seminal U.S. texts, including the application of constitutional principles and use of legal reasoning (e.g., in U.S. Supreme Court majority opinions and dissents) and the premises, purposes, and arguments in works of public advocacy (e.g., *The Federalist,* presidential addresses).

9. Analyze seventeenth-, eighteenth-, and nineteenth-century foundational U.S. documents of historical and literary significance (including The Declaration of Independence, the Preamble to the Constitution, the Bill of Rights, and Lincoln's Second Inaugural Address) for their themes, purposes, and rhetorical features.

Range of Reading and Level of Text Complexity

10. By the end of grade 11, read and comprehend literary nonfiction in the grades 11–CCR text complexity band proficiently, with scaffolding as needed at the high end of the range.

Common Core Writing Standards

College and Career Readiness Anchor Standards

Text Types and Purposes

1. Write arguments to support claims in an analysis of substantive topics or texts, using valid reasoning and relevant and sufficient evidence.
2. Write informative/explanatory texts to examine and convey complex ideas and information clearly and accurately through the effective selection, organization, and analysis of content.
3. Write narratives to develop real or imagined experiences or events using effective technique, well-chosen details, and well-structured event sequences.

Production and Distribution of Writing

4. Produce clear and coherent writing in which the development, organization, and style are appropriate to task, purpose, and audience.
5. Develop and strengthen writing as needed by planning, revising, editing, rewriting, or trying a new approach.
6. Use technology, including the Internet, to produce and publish writing and to interact and collaborate with others.

Research to Build and Present Knowledge

7. Conduct short as well as more sustained research projects based on focused questions, demonstrating understanding of the subject under investigation.
8. Gather relevant information from multiple print and digital sources, assess the credibility and accuracy of each source, and integrate the information while avoiding plagiarism.
9. Draw evidence from literary or informational texts to support analysis, reflection, and research.

Range of Writing

10. Write routinely over extended time frames (time for research, reflection, and revision) and shorter time frames (a single sitting or a day or two) for a range of tasks, purposes, and audiences.

Grade 11 Writing Standards

Text Types and Purposes

1. Write arguments to support claims in an analysis of substantive topics or texts, using valid reasoning and relevant and sufficient evidence.

a. Introduce precise, knowledgeable claim(s), establish the significance of the claim(s), distinguish the claim(s) from alternate or opposing claims, and create an organization that logically sequences claim(s), counterclaims, reasons, and evidence.
b. Develop claim(s) and counterclaims fairly and thoroughly, supplying the most relevant evidence for each while pointing out the strengths and limitations of both in a manner that anticipates the audience's knowledge level, concerns, values, and possible biases.
c. Use words, phrases, and clauses as well as varied syntax to link the major sections of the text, create cohesion, and clarify the relationships between claim(s) and reasons, between reasons and evidence, and between claim(s) and counterclaims.
d. Establish and maintain a formal style and objective tone while attending to the norms and conventions of the discipline in which they are writing.
e. Provide a concluding statement or section that follows from and supports the argument presented.

2. Write informative/explanatory texts to examine and convey complex ideas, concepts, and information clearly and accurately through the effective selection, organization, and analysis of content.

a. Introduce a topic; organize complex ideas, concepts, and information so that each new element builds on that which precedes it to create a unified whole; include formatting (e.g., headings), graphics (e.g., figures, tables), and multimedia when useful to aiding comprehension.
b. Develop the topic thoroughly by selecting the most significant and relevant facts, extended definitions, concrete details, quotations, or other information and examples appropriate to the audience's knowledge of the topic.
c. Use appropriate and varied transitions and syntax to link the major sections of the text, create cohesion, and clarify the relationships among complex ideas and concepts.
d. Use precise language, domain-specific vocabulary, and techniques such as metaphor, simile, and analogy to manage the complexity of the topic.
e. Establish and maintain a formal style and objective tone while attending to the norms and conventions of the discipline in which they are writing.
f. Provide a concluding statement or section that follows from and supports the information or explanation presented (e.g., articulating implications or the significance of the topic).

3. Write narratives to develop real or imagined experiences or events using effective technique, well-chosen details, and well-structured event sequences.

a. Engage and orient the reader by setting out a problem, situation, or observation and its significance, establishing one or multiple point(s) of view, and introducing a narrator and/or characters; create a smooth progression of experiences or events.

b. Use narrative techniques, such as dialogue, pacing, description, reflection, and multiple plot lines, to develop experiences, events, and/or characters.
c. Use a variety of techniques to sequence events so that they build on one another to create a coherent whole and build toward a particular tone and outcome (e.g., a sense of mystery, suspense, growth, or resolution).
d. Use precise words and phrases, telling details, and sensory language to convey a vivid picture of the experiences, events, setting, and/or characters.
e. Provide a conclusion that follows from and reflects on what is experienced, observed, or resolved over the course of the narrative.

Production and Distribution of Writing

4. Produce clear and coherent writing in which the development, organization, and style are appropriate to task, purpose, and audience.

5. Develop and strengthen writing as needed by planning, revising, editing, rewriting, or trying a new approach, focusing on addressing what is most significant for a specific purpose and audience.

6. Use technology, including the Internet, to produce, publish, and update individual or shared writing products in response to ongoing feedback, including new arguments or information.

Research to Build and Present Knowledge

7. Conduct short as well as more sustained research projects to answer a question (including a self-generated question) or solve a problem; narrow or broaden the inquiry when appropriate; synthesize multiple sources on the subject, demonstrating understanding of the subject under investigation.

8. Gather relevant information from multiple authoritative print and digital sources, using advanced searches effectively; assess the strengths and limitations of each source in terms of the task, purpose, and audience; integrate information into the text selectively to maintain the flow of ideas, avoiding plagiarism and overreliance on any one source and following a standard format for citation.

9. Draw evidence from literary or informational texts to support analysis, reflection, and research.

a. Apply *grades 11–12 Reading standards* to literature (e.g., "Demonstrate knowledge of eighteenth-, nineteenth-, and early-twentieth-century foundational works of American literature, including how two or more texts from the same period treat similar themes or topics").
b. Apply *grades 11–12 Reading standards* to literary nonfiction (e.g., "Delineate and evaluate the reasoning in seminal U.S. texts, including the application of constitutional principles and use of legal reasoning [e.g., in U.S. Supreme Court Case majority opinions and dissents] and the premises, purposes, and arguments in works of public advocacy [e.g., *The Federalist*, presidential addresses]").

Range of Writing

10. Write routinely over extended time frames (time for research, reflection, and revision) and shorter time frames (a single sitting or a day or two) for a range of tasks, purposes, and audiences.

Common Core Speaking and Listening Standards

College and Career Readiness Anchor Standards

Comprehension and Collaboration

1. Prepare for and participate effectively in a range of conversations and collaborations with diverse partners, building on others' ideas and expressing their own clearly and persuasively.

2. Integrate and evaluate information presented in diverse media and formats, including visually, quantitatively, and orally.

3. Evaluate a speaker's point of view, reasoning, and use of evidence and rhetoric.

Presentation of Knowledge and Ideas

4. Present information, findings, and supporting evidence such that listeners can follow the line of reasoning and the organization, development, and style are appropriate to task, purpose, and audience.

5. Make strategic use of digital media and visual displays of data to express information and enhance understanding of presentations.

6. Adapt speech to a variety of contexts and communicative tasks, demonstrating command of formal English when indicated or appropriate.

Grade 11 Speaking and Listening Standards

Comprehension and Collaboration

1. Initiate and participate effectively in a range of collaborative discussions (one-on-one, in groups, and teacher-led) with diverse partners on *grades 11–12 topics, texts, and issues,* building on others' ideas and expressing their own clearly and persuasively.

a. Come to discussions prepared, having read and researched material under study; explicitly draw on that preparation by referring to evidence from texts and other research on the topic or issue to stimulate a thoughtful, well-reasoned exchange of ideas.

b. Work with peers to promote civil, democratic discussions and decision-making, set clear goals and deadlines, and establish individual roles as needed.

c. Propel conversations by posing and responding to questions that probe reasoning and evidence; ensure a hearing for a full range of positions on a topic or issue; clarify, verify, or challenge ideas and conclusions; and promote divergent and creative perspectives.

d. Respond thoughtfully to diverse perspectives; synthesize comments, claims, and evidence made on all sides of an issue; resolve contradictions when possible; and determine what additional information or research is required to deepen the investigation or complete the task.

2. Integrate multiple sources of information presented in diverse formats and media (e.g., visually, quantitatively, orally) in order to make informed decisions and solve problems, evaluating the credibility and accuracy of each source and noting any discrepancies among the data.

3. Evaluate a speaker's point of view, reasoning, and use of evidence and rhetoric, assessing the stance, premises, links among ideas, word choice, points of emphasis, and tone used.

Presentation of Knowledge and Ideas

4. Present information, findings, and supporting evidence, conveying a clear and distinct perspective, such that listeners can follow the line of reasoning, alternative or opposing perspectives are addressed, and the organization, development, substance, and style are appropriate to purpose, audience, and a range of formal and informal tasks.

5. Make strategic use of digital media (e.g., textual, graphical, audio, visual, and interactive elements) in presentations to enhance understanding of findings, reasoning, and evidence, and to add interest.

6. Adapt speech to a variety of contexts and tasks, demonstrating a command of formal English when indicated or appropriate. (See grades 11–12 Language standards 1 and 3 for specific expectations.)

Common Core Language Standards

College and Career Readiness Anchor Standards

Conventions of Standard English

1. Demonstrate command of the conventions of standard English grammar and usage when writing or speaking.

2. Demonstrate command of the conventions of standard English capitalization, punctuation, and spelling when writing.

Knowledge of Language

3. Apply knowledge of language to understand how language functions in different contexts, to make effective choices for meaning or style, and to comprehend more fully when reading or listening.

Vocabulary Acquisition and Use

4. Determine or clarify the meaning of unknown and multiple-meaning words and phrases by using context clues, analyzing meaningful word parts, and consulting general and specialized reference materials, as appropriate.

5. Demonstrate understanding of figurative language, word relationships, and nuances in word meanings.

6. Acquire and use accurately a range of general academic and domain-specific words and phrases sufficient for reading, writing, speaking, and listening at the college and career readiness level; demonstrate independence in gathering vocabulary knowledge when considering a word or phrase important to comprehension or expression.

Grade 11 Language Standards

Conventions of Standard English

1. Demonstrate command of the conventions of standard English grammar and usage when writing or speaking.

- a. Apply the understanding that usage is a matter of convention, can change over time, and is sometimes contested.
- b. Resolve issues of complex or contested usage, consulting references (e.g., *Merriam-Webster's Dictionary of English Usage, Garner's Modern American Usage*) as needed.

2. Demonstrate command of the conventions of standard English capitalization, punctuation, and spelling when writing.

- a. Observe hyphenation conventions.
- b. Spell correctly.

Knowledge of Language

3. Apply knowledge of language to understand how language functions in different contexts, to make effective choices for meaning or style, and to comprehend more fully when reading or listening.

a. Vary syntax for effect, consulting references (e.g., Tufte's *Artful Sentences*) for guidance as needed; apply an understanding of syntax to the study of complex texts when reading.

Vocabulary Acquisition and Use

4. Determine or clarify the meaning of unknown and multiple-meaning words and phrases based on *grades 11–12 reading and content*, choosing flexibly from a range of strategies.

a. Use context (e.g., the overall meaning of a sentence, paragraph, or text; a word's position or function in a sentence) as a clue to the meaning of a word or phrase.

b. Identify and correctly use patterns of word changes that indicate different meanings or parts of speech (e.g., *conceive, conception, conceivable*).

c. Consult general and specialized reference materials (e.g., dictionaries, glossaries, thesauruses), both print and digital, to find the pronunciation of a word or determine or clarify its precise meaning, its part of speech, its etymology, or its standard usage.

d. Verify the preliminary determination of the meaning of a word or phrase (e.g., by checking the inferred meaning in context or in a dictionary).

5. Demonstrate understanding of figurative language, word relationships, and nuances in word meanings.

a. Interpret figures of speech (e.g., hyperbole, paradox) in context and analyze their role in the text.

b. Analyze nuances in the meaning of words with similar denotations.

6. Acquire and use accurately general academic and domain-specific words and phrases, sufficient for reading, writing, speaking, and listening at the college and career readiness level; demonstrate independence in gathering vocabulary knowledge when considering a word or phrase important to comprehension or expression.

Introductory Unit

COMMON CORE Workshops

Building Academic Vocabulary

Writing an Objective Summary

Comprehending Complex Texts

Analyzing Arguments

Common Core State Standards

Reading Literature 2, 10
Reading Informational Text 2, 4, 5, 6, 8
Writing 1.a, 1.b, 1.e, 9, 9.b
Language 6

Building Academic Vocabulary

Academic vocabulary is the language used in school, on standardized tests, and—often—in the business world. Academic terms are more formal and specific than the informal vocabulary most people use among friends and family members. Success in school and later in work requires a clear understanding of different types of academic language. The Common Core State Standards require that you acquire and use grade-appropriate academic words and phrases.

Language 6. Acquire and use accurately general academic and domain-specific words and phrases, sufficient for reading, writing, speaking, and listening at the college and career readiness level; demostrate independence in gathering vocabulary knowledge when considering a word or phrase important to comprehension or expression.

Technical Domain-Specific Academic Vocabulary The literary concepts you will learn throughout this book are one type of academic language. These words are specific to the content area—the subject or discipline—of literature. Other disciplines, such as social studies, the sciences, mathematics, and the arts, have their own academic vocabularies. Some content-area words cross disciplines, or have different meanings when applied to different areas of study.

Technical words are an even more specialized type of domain-specific academic vocabulary. These are words and phrases, such as the following, that identify a precise element in the content area and usually do not appear in other disciplines:

Science: pipette; genome
Music: clef; libretto

Critical Reading and Thinking Terms Many academic terms define modes of thinking, discussing, or writing about ideas. In this book, these words appear in the Critical Reading questions at the ends of the selections. Such academic terms also appear in instructions and writing prompts.

A Note on Etymology

Etymology is the branch of linguistics that deals with word origins and the development of languages. Etymologists trace the history of a word in its own language, and then to even earlier sources in other, more ancient languages. Knowledge of a word's etymology will contribute to your understanding of its meaning and help you determine the meaning of other words that share its history. Etymological information for content-area words appears in the charts on the following pages.

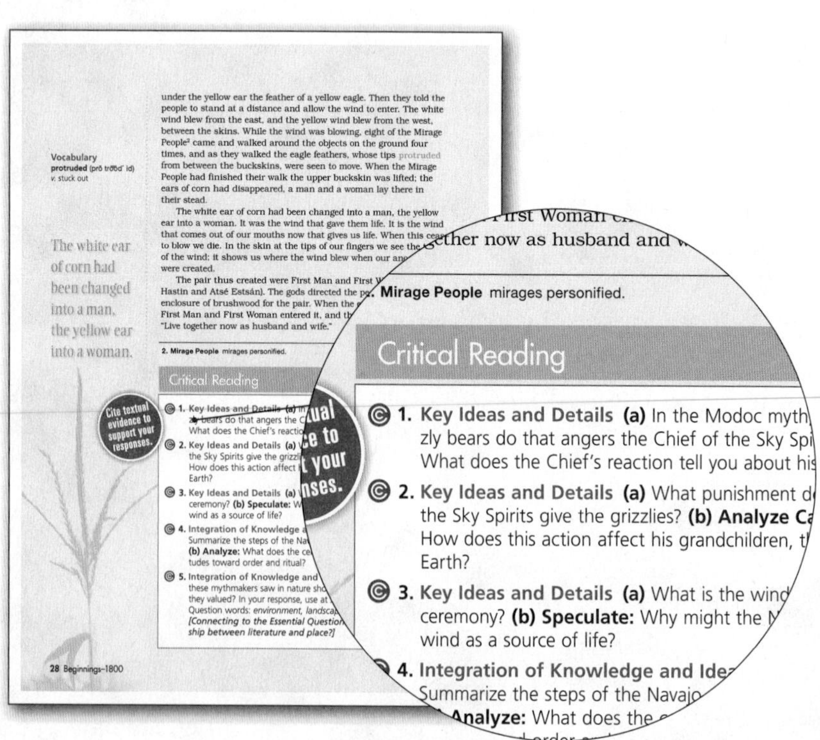

Technical Domain-Specific Academic Vocabulary

Knowledge of technical content-area academic words, and the roots and affixes that compose them, will help you in all of your school courses. As you review the charts below, recognize words that apply to content areas other than those specified here.

Technical Domain-Specific Academic Vocabulary: Science

Term	Meaning	Root/Affix
Accelerate	*v.* increase speed	Latin root *-celer-* = swift Words with the same root: accelerator *n.*; celerity *n.*
Catalyst	*n.* something that acts to bring about a result	Latin root *-cata-* = down; away Words with the same root: cataclysm *n.*; catapult *n.*
Chlorophyll	*n.* green pigment found in plant cells	Greek root *-chloro-* = green Words with the same root: chlorine *n.*; chlorosis *n.*
Chromosome	*n.* strand of proteins that carries the genes of a living creature	Greek prefix *chromo-* = color; pigment Words with the same prefix: chromatic *adj.*; chromate *n.*
Cytoplasm	*n.* colorless substance of a cell; outside the nucleus	Greek suffix *-plasm* = molded; formed Words with the same suffix: bioplasm *n.*; protoplasm *n.*
Entropy	*n.* lack of order that increases over time in a system	Greek root *-tropos-* = turning; deviation Words with the same root: tropical *adj.*; trophy *n.*; heliotrope *n.*
Enzyme	*n.* chemical substance produced by living cells that causes changes in other chemicals	Greek suffix *-zyme* = leavening (an agent that causes fermentation) Words with the same suffix: vitazyme *n.*; microzyme *n.*
Mitosis	*n.* method of cell division	Greek suffix *-osis* = action; process Words with the same suffix: prognosis *n.*; psychosis *n.*
Thermometer	*n.* instrument for measuring temperature	Greek root *-therme-* = hot Words with the same root: thermonuclear *adj.*; thermostat *n.*
Viscous	*adj.* having a thick and sticky fluid consistency	Latin prefix *visco-* = sticky Words with the same prefix: viscometer *n.*; viscosity *n.*

Ordinary Language: Ice cubes placed in water will begin to **break down.**

Academic Language: Ice cubes placed in water will begin the process of **entropy.**

Exploring Academic Vocabulary: Science

The word *thermometer* combines the Greek roots *-therme-*, which means "heat," and *-metr-*, which means "measure." Using this knowledge, determine the meaning of the following words derived from the same roots:

dynameter **odometer** **hypothermia** **thermography**

Then, use a dictionary to confirm the definitions you proposed. If a general dictionary is not sufficient, consult a specialized science dictionary to find the information you need. Explain how the meaning of each word relates to those of its Greek origins.

Technical Domain-Specific Academic Vocabulary: Mathematics

Term	Meaning	Root/Affix
Correlate	*v.* show mutual relationship between items	Latin prefix *cor-* = together; with Words with the same prefix: correspond *v.*; corrosion *n.*
Exponent	*n.* symbol placed above and to the right of a number or letter to show how many times that quantity is to be multiplied by itself	Latin suffix *-ponent* = to put; place; set Words with the same suffix: component *n.*; proponent *n.*
Inflection	*n.* change of a curve or arc from convex to concave or the reverse	Latin root *-flectere-* = to bend Words with the same root: reflection *n.*; deflect *v.*
Logarithm	*n.* power to which a base must be raised to produce a given number	Greek prefix *logos-* = word; speech; reason Words with the same prefix: logic *n.*; logotype *n.*
Statistics	*n.* numerical facts or data	Latin root *-stat-* = condition; position; state Words with the same root: statistical *adj.*; static *adj.*
Permutation	*n.* one of the ways in which a set of things can be arranged or ordered	Latin root *-mutare-* = change Words with the same root: mutable *adj.;* mutation *n.*
Estimate	*v.* calculate approximately	Middle French root *-estimer-* = value; appraise Words with the same root: estimation *n.*; esteem *v.*
Graphic	*adj.* relating to the use of diagrams, graphs, curves	Greek root *-graph-* = writing; drawing Words with the same root: telegraph *n.*; biography *n.*; autograph *n.*
Configure	*v.* construct; arrange	Latin root *-figura-* = shape; form; figure Words with the same root: disfigure *v.*; effigy *n.*

Ordinary Language: We arranged the **numerical information** in different charts.

Academic Language: We incorporated **statistical data** into charts.

Exploring Academic Vocabulary: Mathematics

The word *correlate* is built on the Latin prefix *cor-* (also *com-* or *con-*), which means "with" or "together." Using this knowledge, determine the meaning of the following words derived from the same prefix:

correspond **concert** **compress** **congruent**

Then, use an online or print dictionary to confirm the definitions you proposed. Explain how the meaning of each word relates to that of its Latin ancestor.

Technical Domain-Specific Academic Vocabulary: Social Studies

Term	Meaning	Root/Affix
Corporation	*n.* organization of many people authorized to act as a single person	Latin root *-corpus-* = body Words with the same root: corporeal *adj.*; incorporate *v.*
Demography	*n.* study of human populations	Greek prefix *demos-* = people Words with the same prefix: demographic *n.*; democracy *n.*
Economy	*n.* system by which a country's money and goods are used and produced	Greek suffix *-nomy* = law; received knowledge Words with the same suffix: economy *n.*; taxonomy *n.*
Invest	*v.* give money to a company in order to receive a profit	Latin root *-vestire-* = dress; clothe Words with the same root: vestment *n.*; investigation *n.*
Admiral	*n.* high-ranking Naval officer	Arabic root *-amir-* = leader Words with the same root: emirate *n.*; admiralship *n.*
Curfew	*n.* law requiring a population to stay indoors at a stated hour	Old French root *-covrir-* = to cover Words with the same root: covert *adj.*; coverlet *n.*
Lieutenant	*n.* someone who substitutes for another person of greater authority	Old French root *-lieu-* = place Word with the same root: milieu *n.*
Absolutism	*n.* system of government in which a ruler has unlimited power	Latin prefix *ab-* = away; from Words with the same prefix: absolve *v.*
Civic	*adj.* of a city, citizens, or citizenship	Latin root *-civ-* = citizen Words with the same root: civilian *n.*; civilization *n.*

Ordinary Language: The government urges citizens to **put money into** local businesses.

Academic Language: The government urges citizens to **invest in** local businesses.

Exploring Academic Vocabulary: Social Studies

The word *economy* is built on the Greek suffix *–nomy*, which means "law; body of received knowledge." Using this knowledge, determine the meaning of the following words derived from the same suffix:

taxonomy **autonomy** **astronomy** **gastronomy**

Then, use an online or print dictionary to confirm the definitions you proposed. Explain how the meaning of each word relates to that of its Greek ancestor.

Technical Domain-Specific Academic Vocabulary: Technology

Term	Meaning	Root/Affix
Gigabyte	*n.* unit of storage capacity in a computer system, equal to 1,073,741,824 bytes	Greek prefix *giga-* = giant Words with the same prefix: gigahertz *n.*; gigantic *adj.*
Macro	*n.* single computer instruction that represents a sequence of operations	Greek prefix *macro-* = long, tall, deep, large Words with the same prefix: macrobiotic *adj.*; macrocosm *n.*
Pixel	*n.* smallest unit of an image on a television or computer screen	Old French suffix *-el* = small one Words with the same suffix: satchel *n.*; model *n.*
Processor	*n.* central part of a computer that does the calculations needed to deal with the information it is given	from Latin root *-cedere-* = to go Words with the same root: proceed *v.*; recede *v.*
Simulation	*n.* situation that produces conditions that are not real but appear real	Latin root *-sim-* = like derived through Indo-European base *sem-/som-* = same; as one Words with the same root: ensemble *v.*; simultaneous *adj.*
Streaming	*n.* method of transmitting data so that it can be delivered and received in a steady stream	German root *-strom-* = current; river Words with the same root: mainstream *n.*; streamline *v.*
Transmitter	*n.* equipment that sends out radio or television signals	Latin prefix *trans-* = across Words with the same prefix: transportation *n.*; transcontinental *adj.*
Debug	*v.* find and correct defects	Latin prefix *de-* = down; from Words with the same prefix: defuse *v.*; defrost *v.*
Export	*v.* in computers, to save data in a format usable by another program	Latin root *-portare-* = to carry Words with the same root: import *v.*; airport *n.*
Binary	*adj.* made up of two parts or things; twofold	Latin root *-bin-* = together; double Words with the same root: binocular *n.*; binomial *n.*

Ordinary Language:
I asked the technician to **remove the defects from** my computer.

Academic Language:
I asked the technician to **debug** my operating system.

Exploring Academic Vocabulary: Technology

The word *simulation* comes from the Latin root *-sim-*, which means "like." This Latin root derives from the Indo-European base *sem-/som-*, which means "same; as one." Using your knowledge of these origins, determine the meaning of the following words derived from the same roots:

resemble **facsimile** **verisimilitude** **semblance**

Then, use a dictionary to confirm the definitions you proposed. Explain how the meaning of each word relates to that of its Indo-European base.

Technical Domain-Specific Academic Vocabulary: The Arts

Term	Meaning	Root/Affix
Allegro	*adv.* faster than allegretto but not so fast as presto	Latin root *-alacer-/-alacris-* = lively; brisk Words with the same root: allegretto *adj.*; *adv.*; alacrity *n.*
Alignment	*n.* arrangement in a straight line	Old French root *-lignier-* = to line Words with the same root: align *v.*; realign *v.*
Craftmanship	*n.* skill used in making handmade objects	Middle English suffix *-schipe*; derived through Anglian suffix *-scip* = state; condition; quality Words with the same suffix: friendship *n.*; dictatorship *n.*
Decrescendo	*n.* gradual decrease in volume	Old French *creissant*; derived through Latin root *-crescere-* = come forth; spring up; grow; thrive Words with the same root: crescent *n.*; increase *v.*
Baritone	*n.* male singing voice lower than a tenor and higher than a bass	Latin root *-tonus-* = sound; tone Words with the same root: monotone *n.*; intonation *n.*
Medium	*n.* material or technique used in art	Latin root *-medius-* = middle Words with the same root: media *n.*; mediate *v.*; median *adj.*
Musicality	*n.* sensitivity to, knowledge of, or talent for music	Latin suffix *-ity* = quality; state; degree Words with the same suffix: normality *n.*; publicity *n.*
Technique	*n.* method or procedure in rendering an artistic work	Indo-European prefix *tek-* = shape; make Words with the same prefix: technical *adj.*; technician *n.*
Tempo	*n.* speed at which a composition is performed	Latin root *-tempus-* = time Words with the same root: temporal *adj.*; temporary *adj.*

Ordinary Language: The dancers moved in a perfectly **straight line.**

Academic Language: The dancers moved in perfect **alignment** on stage.

Exploring Academic Vocabulary: The Arts

The word *craftsmanship* is built on the Anglian suffix *-scip*, which means "state, condition, quality." Using this knowledge, determine the meaning of the following words derived from the same suffix:

musicianship **readership** **friendship** **partnership**

Then, use an online or print dictionary to confirm the definitions you proposed. Explain how the meaning of each word relates to that of its Anglian ancestor.

Vocabulary Across Content Areas

You might recognize words that apply to content areas other than those specified in the charts on the previous pages. For example, notice how the word *accelerator* relates to two different content areas:

Science: accelerator *n.* nerve or muscle that speeds up a body function

Automotive Technology: accelerator *n.* device, such as the foot throttle of an automobile, for increasing the speed of a machine.

While the objects referred to in each definition are different, both of their functions relate to the Latin root *-celer-,* meaning "swift." As you read texts for school, recognize similarities in roots or affixes among words in different content areas. This will help you better understand specific terms and make meaningful connections among topics.

Academic Vocabulary: Critical Thinking Terms

Throughout this book, you will encounter academic vocabulary related to the process of critical thinking. Unlike content-area vocabulary, these words apply equally in all school studies. Being familiar with these academic vocabulary words will be useful as you approach high-stakes standardized tests such as the SAT and ACT. Academic vocabulary will also aid you as you encounter business materials in the workplace.

Term (verb form)	Meaning	Root/Affix
Advocate	Speak or write in support of	Latin root *-voc-* = speak; call Related words: advocate *n.*; advocacy *n.*
Anticipate	Prepare for or signal something	Latin prefix *ante-* = before Related words: anticipatory *adj.*; anticipation *n.*
Arrange	Put into order or sequence	Old French root *-rang-* = rank Related words: arrangement *n.*
Assess	Determine importance, size, or value	Latin root *-sed-/-sess-* = sit Related words: assessment *n.*
Categorize	Place in related groups	Greek prefix *kata-/cata-* = down; against Related words: category *n.*; categorical *adj.*
Compare	Examine in order to discover similarities	Latin root *-par-* = equal Related words: comparison *n.*; comparable *adj.*
Conclude	Determine through logical reasoning	Latin root *-clud-* = shut Related words: conclusion *n.*; conclusive *adj.*
Contrast	Examine in order to discover differences	Latin prefix *con-/com-* = with; together Related words: contrastable *adj.*
Debate	Discuss opposing reasons; argue	French root *-batre-* = to beat Related words: debatable *adj.*
Deduce	Infer from a general principle	Latin root *-duc-* = to lead Related words: deduction *n.*; deductive *adj.*
Defend	Maintain or support in the face of argument	Latin root *-fend-* = to strike; push Related words: defense *n.*; defendant *n.*

Term (verb form)	Meaning	Root/Affix
Describe	Represent in words	Latin root *-scrib-* = to write Related words: description *n.*; descriptive *adj.*
Design	Create; fashion or construct according to plan	Latin root *-sign-* = to mark Related words: design *n.*; designer *n.*
Devise	Form in the mind by new combinations of ideas; invent	Latin root *-vid-* = to separate Related words: devisable *adj.*
Differentiate	Recognize a difference	Latin suffix *-ate* = act Related words: different *adj.*; differentiation *n.*
Evaluate	Determine significance, worth, or condition through careful study	Old French root *-val-* = worth; value Related words: evaluation *n.*; evaluative *adj.*
Format	Arrange according to a design or plan	Latin root *-form-* = form, shape Related words: format *n.*; formation *n.*
Generalize	Draw a larger principle from details	Latin root *-genus-* = stock; kind Related words: generalization *n.*
Hypothesize	Develop a theory about	Greek prefix *hypo-* = under, beneath Related words: hypothesis *n.*; hypothetically *adv.*
Illustrate	Give examples that support an idea	Latin root *-lus-* = brighten; illuminate Related words: illustration *n.*; illustrative *adj.*
Interpret	Explain the meaning of	Latin root *-inter-* = between Related words: interpretation *n.*; interpreter *n.*
Investigate	Make a systematic examination	French root *-vestige-* = mark; trace; sign Related words: investigation *n.*; investigative *adj.*
Paraphrase	Express in one's own words what another person has said or written	Greek prefix *para-* = beside Related words: paraphraser *n.*
Predict	Foretell on the basis of observation, experience, or reason	Latin root *-dic-* = speak, tell, say Related words: prediction *n.*; predictable *adj.*
Refute	Prove an argument or statement false or wrong	Latin root *-fut-* = beat Related words: refutable *adj.*; refutably *adv.*
Sort	Put in place according to kind, class, or nature	Old French root *-sortir-* = allot; assort Related words: sorter *n.*
Speculate	Use evidence to guess what might happen	Latin root *-spec-* = look at; view Related words: speculation *n.*; speculative *adj.*
Structure	Create a general plot or outline	Latin root *-struct-* = to build; assemble Related words: structure *n.*; structural *adj.*
Validate	Prove to be factual or effective	Latin root *-val-* = be strong Related words: valid *adj.*; validity *n.*

Ordinary Language: She **explained the meaning of** the story's symbols.

Academic Language: She **interpreted** the meaning of the story's symbols.

Writing an Objective Summary

The ability to write objective summaries is important in college course work and in many careers, such as journalism, business, law, and research work. Writing an effective objective summary involves recording the key ideas of a text as well as demonstrating your understanding.

Common Core State Standards

Reading Informational Text
2. Determine two or more central ideas of a text and analyze their development over the course of the text, including how they interact and build on one another to provide a complex analysis; provide an objective summary of the text.

Reading Literature
2. Determine two or more themes or central ideas of a text and analyze their development over the course of the text, including how they interact and build on one another to produce a complex account; provide an objective summary of the text.

Characteristics of an Objective Summary

An effective objective summary is a concise overview of a text. Following are important elements of an objective summary:

- It is **focused,** relaying the main theme or central idea of a text. It includes specific, relevant details that support that theme or central idea, and it leaves out unnecessary supporting details.
- It is **brief,** although the writer must be careful to balance brevity and thoroughness and not misrepresent the text by eliminating important parts.
- It is **accurate** and captures the essence of the longer text it is describing.
- It is **objective.** The writer should refrain from inserting his or her own opinions, reactions, or personal reflections into the summary.

Remember that an objective summary is *not* a collection of sentences or paragraphs copied from the original source. It is *not* a long retelling of every event, detail, or point in the original text. Finally, a good summary does *not* include evaluative comments, such as the reader's overall opinion of or reaction to the selection.

Checklist for Writing an Objective Summary

Before writing an objective summary, be sure you are well acquainted with the text.

- **Understand the entire passage.** You must clearly understand the text's meaning, including any advanced or technical terminology. In your summary, refer to details from the beginning, middle, and end of the text.
- **Prioritize ideas and details.** Determine the main or central ideas of a text and identify the key supporting details. Make sure you recognize which details are less important so that you do not include them in your objective summary.
- **Identify the author's audience and purpose.** Knowing what the author intended to accomplish in the text as well as what audience it was designed to reach will help you summarize accurately.

INFORMATIONAL TEXT

Model Objective Summary

Note the key elements of an effective objective summary, called out in the sidenotes. Then, write an objective summary of a text you have recently read. Review your summary, and delete any unnecessary details, opinions, or evaluations.

Summary of "The Open Window"

"The Open Window," by Saki, ~~the pen name of H.H. Munro~~, is a short story about a nervous man by the name of Framton Nuttel. Set in rural England during the Victorian-Edwardian period, the story tells of a visit that Mr. Nuttel makes to a neighboring estate.

Mr. Framton Nuttel, who has been ordered by his physicians to rest and avoid excitement, has gone to the country for a "nerve cure." His sister has given him letters of introduction to various acquaintances of hers. Framton reluctantly takes his sister's suggestion and calls on the Sappletons.

When Framton arrives at the Sappleton estate, he is met by Mrs. Sappleton's fifteen-year-old niece, Vera. ~~She is quite a character.~~ Vera points to an open window and relates a tragic tale. She tells Framton that exactly three years ago, Mr. Sappleton, Mrs. Sappleton's two younger brothers, and their spaniel went out to hunt, leaving through that very window, and met their death in the bog. Their bodies have never been recovered. The niece explains that her aunt keeps the window open because she expects her husband and brothers to return some day.

Soon thereafter, Mrs. Sappleton enters the room and begins to speak of the hunters. Alarmed, Framton tries to change the topic. He rambles on about his health, noticing that Mrs. Sappleton keeps glancing out of the open window. Suddenly, Mrs. Sappleton exclaims, "Here they are at last!" Framton sees a look of horror in Vera's eyes. Then he turns and sees the figures of three men and a dog approaching. He frantically gathers his belongings and runs away.

As Mr. Sappleton enters through the window, he greets his wife and inquires about the man he spotted running away. Mrs. Sappleton responds that Framton Nuttel was a strange man who dashed off as if he had seen a ghost.

Then Vera mentions that Mr. Nuttel was most likely frightened by the dog. She says that he confided in her that he was once terrified by a pack of wild dogs.

The story ends with this sentence: "Romance at short notice was her specialty."

Eliminate unnecessary details.

A one-sentence synopsis highlighting the theme or central idea of the story can be an effective start to a summary.

This sentence states the writer's opinion and should not be included in an objective summary.

Relating the development of the text in chronological order makes a summary easy to follow.

The writer quotes the final sentence of the story because it is the key to understanding the plot.

Comprehending Complex Texts

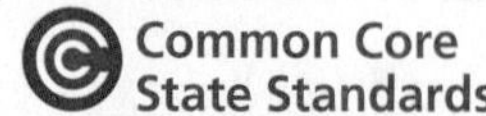
Common Core State Standards

Reading Literature 10. By the end of grade 11, read and comprehend literature, including stories, dramas, and poems, in the grades 11-CCR text complexity band proficiently, with scaffolding as needed at the high end of the range.

During the final years of high school, you will be required to read increasingly complex texts in preparation for college and the workplace. A complex text features one or more of the following qualities:

- challenging vocabulary
- long, complex sentences
- figurative language
- multiple levels of meaning
- unfamiliar settings and situations

The selections in this textbook provide you with a range of readings in many genres. Some of these texts will fall within your comfort zone, but others will be, and should be, more challenging. In order to comprehend and interpret complex texts, practice the reading strategies described here.

Strategy 1: Multi-draft Reading

Good readers develop the habit of rereading texts in order to comprehend them completely. To fully understand a text, try this multi-draft reading strategy:

1st Reading

The first time you read a text, read to gain its basic meaning. If you are reading a narrative text, look for the basics of the plot: what is happening, and to whom. If the text is nonfiction, look for central ideas and key supporting details. If you are reading poetry, read first to get a sense of who the speaker is. Also take note of the setting and situation.

2nd Reading

During your second reading of a text, focus on the artistry or effectiveness of the writing. Also take note of text structures and organizational patterns. Think about why the author made those choices and the effects they created. Then, examine the author's creative uses of language and the effects of that language. For example, has the author used rhyme, figurative language, or words with negative connotations? If so, to what effect?

3rd Reading

After your third reading, compare and contrast the text with others of its kind you have read. For example, you might compare poems from a certain time period or compare poems written by a single author. Evaluate the text's overall effectiveness and its central idea or theme.

Independent Practice

As you read this sonnet by William Shakespeare, practice the multi-draft reading strategy by completing a chart like the one below.

Sonnet 27

Weary with toil, I haste me to my bed,
The dear repose for limbs with travel tired;
But then begins a journey in my head
To work my mind, when body's work's expired:
For then my thoughts—from far where I abide—
Intend a zealous pilgrimage to thee,
And keep my drooping eyelids open wide,
Looking on darkness which the blind do see:
Save that my soul's imaginary sight
Presents thy shadow to my sightless view,
Which, like a jewel hung in ghastly night,
Makes black night beauteous, and her old face new.
　Lo! thus, by day my limbs, by night my mind,
　For thee, and for myself, no quiet find.

Multi-Draft Reading Chart

	My Understanding
1st Reading Look for key ideas and details that unlock basic meaning.	
2nd Reading Read for deeper meanings. Look for ways in which the author used text structures and language to create effects.	
3rd Reading Read to integrate your knowledge and ideas. Connect the text to others of its kind and to your own experience.	

Strategy 2: Close Read the Text

Complex texts require close reading, a careful analysis of word choices, phrases, and sentences. An awareness of literary techniques and elements, such as allusion, symbolism, analogy, and text structure, contributes to a deep understanding of a complex text. However, a starting point for close reading is comprehension, which is the foundation for interpretation and analysis. Use the following tips to comprehend the text:

Tips for Close Reading
1. Break down long sentences into parts. Look for the subject of the sentence and its verb. Then identify which parts of the sentence modify, or give more information about, its subject.
2. Reread passages. When reading complex texts, be sure to reread passages to confirm that you understand their meaning.
3. Look for context clues. There are several types of context clues, such as the following: **a.** Restatement of an idea. For example, in the example sentence, "to help . . . understand" restates the verb *clarify.* The sportscaster tried to **clarify** the offsides violation to help the spectators understand the referee's call. **b.** Definition of sophisticated words. In this sentence, the words *goes beyond* define the verb *transcends.* The watercolor painting **transcends,** or goes beyond, the expectations of the viewers. **c.** Examples of concepts and topics. The menu listed green beans, corn, and okra as side dishes. **d.** Contrasts of ideas and topics. In the following sentence, the examples help you understand the meaning of *claustrophobia.* Adam is **claustrophobic;** he is terrified of elevators and cannot tolerate being cooped up in small spaces.
4. Identify pronoun antecedents. If long sentences contain pronouns, reread the text to make sure you know to what the pronouns refer. The pronoun *its* in the following sentence refers to Yosemite National Park, not to the U.S. government. Yosemite National Park was set aside by the U.S. government for people to enjoy for **its** natural beauty.
5. Look for conjunctions, such as *and, or, yet,* and *however,* to understand relationships between ideas.
6. Paraphrase, or restate in your own words, passages of difficult text in order to check your understanding. Remember that a paraphrase is essentially a word-for-word restatement of an original text; it is not a summary.

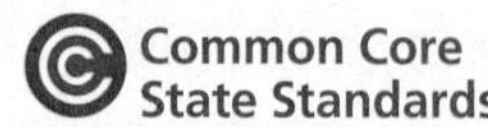

Reading Informational Text
4. Determine the meaning of words and phrases as they are used in a text, including figurative, connotative, and technical meanings; analyze how an author uses and refines the meaning of a key term or terms over the course of a text (e.g., how Madison defines *faction* in *Federalist* No. 10).

INFORMATIONAL TEXT

Close-Read Model

As you read this document, take note of the sidenotes that model ways to unlock meaning in the text.

from "The Perils of Indifference" by Elie Weisel

What is indifference? Etymologically, the word means "no difference." A strange and unnatural state in which the lines blur between light and darkness, dusk and dawn, crime and punishment, cruelty and compassion, good and evil.

What are its courses and inescapable consequences? Is it a philosophy? Is there a philosophy of indifference conceivable? Can one possibly view indifference as a virtue? Is it necessary at times to practice it simply to keep one's sanity, live normally, enjoy a fine meal and a glass of wine, as the world around us experiences harrowing upheavals?

Of course, indifference can be tempting—more than that, seductive. It is so much easier to look away from victims. It is so much easier to avoid such rude interruptions to our work, our dreams, our hopes. It is, after all, awkward, troublesome, to be involved in another person's pain and despair. Yet, for the person who is indifferent, his or her neighbors are of no consequence. And, therefore, their lives are meaningless. Their hidden or even visible anguish is of no interest. Indifference reduces the other to an abstraction. . . .

In a way, to be indifferent to that suffering is what makes the human being inhuman. Indifference, after all, is more dangerous than anger and hatred. Anger can at times be creative. One writes a great poem, a great symphony, one does something special for the sake of humanity because one is angry at the injustice that one witnesses. But indifference is never creative. Even hatred at times may elicit a response. You fight it. You denounce it. You disarm it. Indifference elicits no response. Indifference is not a response.

Indifference is not a beginning, it is an end. And, therefore, indifference is always the friend of the enemy, for it benefits the aggressor—never his victim, whose pain is magnified when he or she feels forgotten. The political prisoner in his cell, the hungry children, the homeless refugees—not to respond to their plight, not to relieve their solitude by offering them a spark of hope is to exile them from human memory. And in denying their humanity we betray our own.

Indifference, then, is not only a sin, it is a punishment. And this is one of the most important lessons of this outgoing century's wide-ranging experiments in good and evil. . . .

This list of contrasts helps you to know that "compassion" is the opposite of "cruelty."

Look for antecedents. The abstract noun *indifference* is referred to by the pronouns *its* and *it*.

Search for context clues. The words in blue are context clues that help you infer the meaning of the word that appears in yellow.

Break down this long sentence into parts. The text highlighted in yellow conveys the basic meaning of the sentence. The text highlighted in blue provides additional information.

The examples highlighted in pink help you understand that the word *plight* means "bad situation."

Strategy 3: Ask Questions

Be an attentive reader by asking questions as you read. Throughout this text, we have provided questions for you following each selection. Those questions are sorted into three basic categories that build in sophistication and lead you to a deeper understanding of the texts you read. Here is an example from this text:

Some questions are about **Key Ideas and Details** in the text. To answer these questions, you will need to locate and cite explicit information in the text or draw inferences from what you have read.

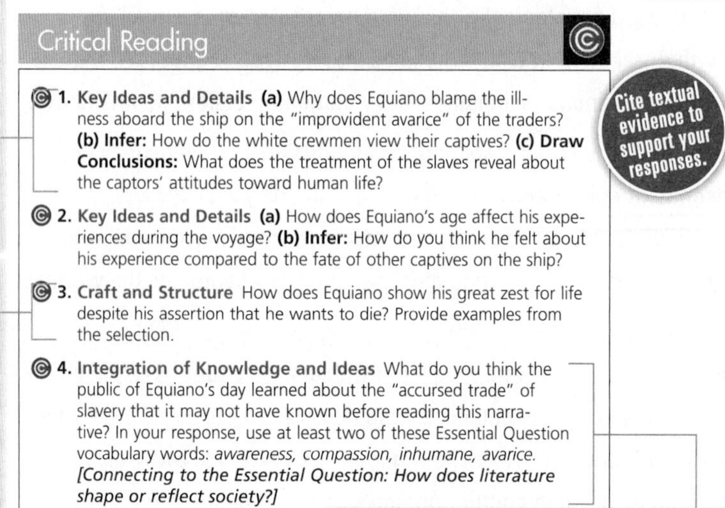

Critical Reading

Cite textual evidence to support your responses.

1. **Key Ideas and Details (a)** Why does Equiano blame the illness aboard the ship on the "improvident avarice" of the traders? **(b) Infer:** How do the white crewmen view their captives? **(c) Draw Conclusions:** What does the treatment of the slaves reveal about the captors' attitudes toward human life?
2. **Key Ideas and Details (a)** How does Equiano's age affect his experiences during the voyage? **(b) Infer:** How do you think he felt about his experience compared to the fate of other captives on the ship?
3. **Craft and Structure** How does Equiano show his great zest for life despite his assertion that he wants to die? Provide examples from the selection.
4. **Integration of Knowledge and Ideas** What do you think the public of Equiano's day learned about the "accursed trade" of slavery that it may not have known before reading this narrative? In your response, use at least two of these Essential Question vocabulary words: *awareness, compassion, inhumane, avarice. [Connecting to the Essential Question: How does literature shape or reflect society?]*

Some questions are about **Craft and Structure** in the text. To answer these questions, you will need to analyze how the author developed and structured the text. You will also look for ways in which the author artfully used language and how those word choices impacted the meaning and tone of the work.

Some questions are about the **Integration of Knowledge and Ideas** in the text. These questions ask you to evaluate a text in many different ways, such as comparing texts, analyzing arguments in the text, and using many other methods of thinking critically about a text's ideas.

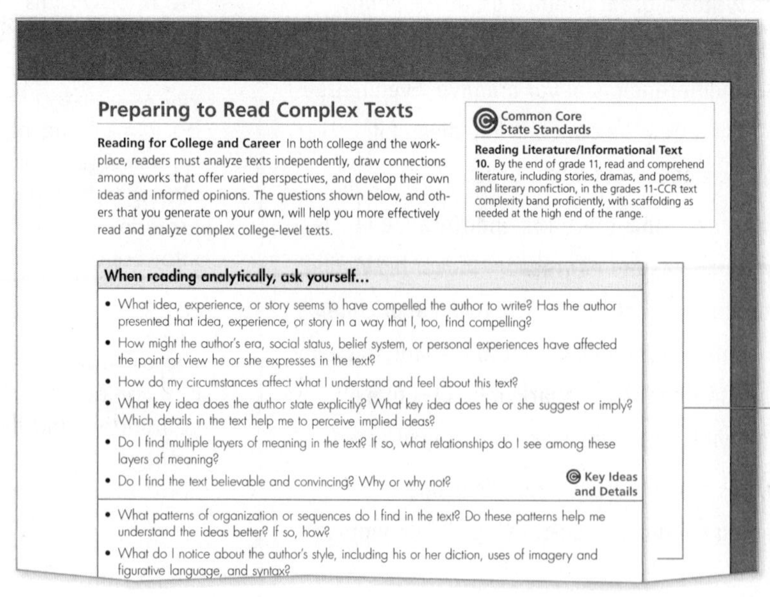

Preparing to Read Complex Texts

Reading for College and Career In both college and the workplace, readers must analyze texts independently, draw connections among works that offer varied perspectives, and develop their own ideas and informed opinions. The questions shown below, and others that you generate on your own, will help you more effectively read and analyze complex college-level texts.

Common Core State Standards

Reading Literature/Informational Text
10. By the end of grade 11, read and comprehend literature, including stories, dramas, and poems, and literary nonfiction, in the grades 11-CCR text complexity band proficiently, with scaffolding as needed at the high end of the range.

When reading analytically, ask yourself...

- What idea, experience, or story seems to have compelled the author to write? Has the author presented that idea, experience, or story in a way that I, too, find compelling?
- How might the author's era, social status, belief system, or personal experiences have affected the point of view he or she expresses in the text?
- How do my circumstances affect what I understand and feel about this text?
- What key idea does the author state explicitly? What key idea does he or she suggest or imply? Which details in the text help me to perceive implied ideas?
- Do I find multiple layers of meaning in the text? If so, what relationships do I see among these layers of meaning?
- Do I find the text believable and convincing? Why or why not?

Key Ideas and Details

- What patterns of organization or sequences do I find in the text? Do these patterns help me understand the ideas better? If so, how?
- What do I notice about the author's style, including his or her diction, uses of imagery and figurative language, and syntax?

As you read independently, ask similar types of questions to ensure that you fully enjoy and comprehend texts you read for school and for pleasure. Look for and use the sets of questions provided for Independent Reading at the end of each unit.

Model

Following is an example of a complex text. The call-out boxes show sample questions that an attentive reader might ask while reading.

from *1776* by David McCullough

On January 14, two weeks into the new year, George Washington wrote one of the most forlorn, despairing letters of his life. He had been suffering sleepless nights in the big house by the Charles. "The reflection upon my situation and that of this army produces many an uneasy hour when all around me are wrapped in sleep," he told the absent Joseph Reed. "Few people know the predicament we are in."

Filling page after page, he enumerated the same troubles and woes he had been reporting persistently to Congress for so long, and that he would report still again to John Hancock that same day. There was too little powder, still no money. . . . So many of the troops had given up and gone home had, against orders, carried off muskets that were not their own that the supply of arms was depleted to the point where there were not enough for the new recruits.

Sample questions:

Key Ideas and Details What central idea is revealed in this passage?

Craft and Structure Why does David McCullough use a direct quotation? What image does Washington create with the words "wrapped in sleep"?

Integration of Knowledge and Ideas What insight does this passage give you about Washington as a general? What insight do you gain about the Revolutionary War?

INFORMATIONAL TEXT

Independent Practice

Write three to five questions you might ask yourself as you read this passage from a speech delivered by James Bryant Conant, president of Harvard University, in 1940.

from "What Are We Arming to Defend?" by James Bryant Conant

. . . The history of this republic has been unique. And the uniqueness of our way of life rests not so much on constitutional democracy as on our social system—a system which is the embodiment of the golden mean of which I speak. I believe that fundamentally it is this unique form of society that we are really arming to defend. I believe that the ambition of every thoughtful citizen of this republic is to assist in keeping inviolate the free way of life which has developed on this continent in the last two hundred years.

. . . Let me examine for a moment the phrase "social mobility," for this is the heart of my argument. If large numbers of young people can develop their own capacities irrespective of the economic status of their parents, then social mobility is high. . . . Such is the American ideal.

Analyzing Arguments

The ability to evaluate an argument, as well as to make one, is a critical skill for success in college and in the workplace.

What Is an Argument?

An *argument* is a presentation of a controversial or debatable issue. In a formal, written argument, the writer logically supports a particular belief, conclusion, or point of view. A good argument is supported with sufficient and valid reasoning and evidence.

Purposes of Argument

There are three main purposes for writing a formal argument:

- to change the reader's mind about an issue
- to convince the reader to accept what is written
- to motivate the reader to take action, based on what is written

Elements of Argument

Claim (assertion)—what the writer is trying to prove
Example: Students should wear uniforms to public high schools.

Grounds (evidence)—the support used to convince the reader
Example: Students will focus less on what they and others are wearing and more on learning.

Justification—the link between the grounds and the claim; why the grounds are credible
Example: The purpose of school is to learn.

Evaluating Claims

When reading or listening to an argument, critically assess the claims that are made. Analyze the argument to identify claims that are based on fact or that can be proved true. Also evaluate evidence that supports the claims. If there is little or no reasoning or evidence provided to support the claims, the argument may not be sound or valid.

Analyzing and Evaluating Structures

As you read an argument, look for ways in which the writer uses structures. For example, the organizational structure, or order in which the writer presents claims and evidence, focuses and shapes the argument. Stylistic structural choices such as repetition and parallel structure can lend emotional power to an argument. Evaluate whether those structures strengthen or detract from the argument's effectiveness.

Common Core State Standards

Language 6. Acquire and use accurately general academic and domain-specific words and phrases, sufficient for reading, writing, speaking, and listening at the college and career readiness level; demonstrate independence in gathering vocabulary knowledge when considering a word or phrase important to comprehension or expression.

Reading Informational Text

5. Analyze and evaluate the effectiveness of the structure an author uses in his or her exposition or argument, including whether the structure makes points clear, convincing, and engaging.

6. Determine an author's point of view or purpose in a text in which the rhetoric is particularly effective, analyzing how style and content contribute to the power, persuasiveness, or beauty of the text.

Model Argument

from *The American Forests* by John Muir

The forests of America, however slighted by man, must have been a great delight to God; for they were the best he ever planted. The whole continent was a garden, and from the beginning it seemed to be favored above all the other wild parks and gardens of the globe . . .

. . . In the settlement and civilization of the country, bread more than timber or beauty was wanted; and in the blindness of hunger, the early settlers . . . regarded God's trees as only a larger kind of pernicious weeds, extremely hard to get rid of. Accordingly, with no eye to the future, these pious destroyers waged interminable forest wars; chips flew thick and fast; trees in their beauty fell crashing by millions, smashed to confusion, and the smoke of their burning has been rising to heaven more than two hundred years. . . . Thence still westward the invading horde of destroyers called settlers made its fiery way over the broad Rocky Mountains, felling and burning more fiercely than ever, until at last it has reached the wild side of the continent, and entered the last of the great aboriginal forests on the shores of the Pacific . . . Clearing has surely now gone far enough; soon timber will be scarce, and not a grove will be left to rest in or pray in. . . .

Every other civilized nation in the world has been compelled to care for its forests, and so must we if waste and destruction are not to go on to the bitter end . . . [T]he forest plays an important part in human progress, and that the advance in civilization only makes it more indispensable . . . But the state woodlands are not allowed to lie idle. On the contrary, they are made to produce as much timber as is possible without spoiling them. In the administration of its forests, the state righteously considers itself bound to treat them as a trust for the nation as a whole, and to keep in view the common good of the people for all time . . .

Notwithstanding all the waste and use which have been going on unchecked like a storm for more than two centuries, it is not yet too late, though it is high time, for the government to begin a rational administration of its forests. . . .

In their natural condition, or under wise management, keeping out destructive sheep, preventing fires, selecting the trees that should be cut for lumber, and preserving the young ones and the shrubs and sod of herbaceous vegetation, these forests would be a never failing fountain of wealth and beauty . . .

The outcries we hear against forest reservations come mostly from thieves who are wealthy and steal timber by wholesale. They have so long been allowed to steal and destroy in peace that any impediment to forest robbery is denounced as a cruel and irreligious interference with "vested rights" . . .

The introduction shows Muir's fondness for the forests of America.

As evidence, Muir describes the millions of trees that have been destroyed over the past 200 years.

Muir draws the logical conclusion for the audience that the trees will be gone if they continue to be cut down at the current rate.

Muir cites other civilized nations' actions as evidence that we must do the same.

Justification: Sustainable and productive forests are a national resource kept for the common good of the people.

Claim: It is time for the governments to begin a rational administration of the forests.

The opposition is addressed and refuted.

The Art of Argument: Rhetorical Devices and Persuasive Techniques

Rhetorical Devices

Rhetoric is the art of using language in order to make a point or to persuade listeners. Rhetorical devices such as the ones listed below are accepted elements of argument. Their use does not invalidate or weaken an argument. Rather, the use of rhetorical devices is regarded as a key part of an effective argument.

Examples of Rhetorical Devices	
Repetition The repeated use of certain words, phrases, or sentences	We are compelled to fight the **injustice** of low wages, the **injustice** of long hours, and the **injustice** of child labor.
Parallelism The repeated use of similar grammatical structures	Children should spend their time **playing active games, reading good books,** and **writing imaginative stories.**
Rhetorical Question Calling attention to the issue by implying an obvious answer	Aren't all people created equal?
Sound Devices The use of alliteration, assonance, rhyme, or rhythm	The savage settlers sowed only the seeds of greed to replace the trees they destroyed.
Simile and Metaphor Comparing two seemingly unlike things or asserting that one thing *is* another	Is **America** a **melting pot** or a **tossed salad**?

Persuasive Techniques

Persuasive techniques are often found in advertisements and in other forms of informal persuasion. Although techniques like the ones below are sometimes found in formal arguments, they should not be regarded as valid evidence.

Persuasive Techniques	
Bandwagon Approach/Anti-Bandwagon Approach Appeals to a person's desire to belong; Encourages or celebrates individuality	Our clothes are as unique as you are.
Emotional Appeal Evokes people's fear, anger, or desire	Soon, all you will see will be strip malls and parking lots.
Endorsement/Testimony Employs a well-known person to promote a product or idea	"I support this just cause. You should too!"
Loaded Language The use of words that are charged with emotion	The child laborers are slaves; their childhoods are owned by the factories.
"Plain Folks" Appeal Shows a connection to everyday, ordinary people	"My parents immigrated to this great land and started a new life."
Hyperbole Exaggerates to make a point	All the money in the world wouldn't solve the problem.

INFORMATIONAL TEXT

Model Speech

The excerpted speech below includes examples of rhetorical devices and persuasive techniques.

from *Strike Against War* by Helen Keller

. . . I think the workers are the most unselfish of the children of men; they toil and live and die for other people's country, other people's sentiments, other people's liberties and other people's happiness! The workers have no liberties of their own; they are not free when they are compelled to work twelve or ten or eight hours a day. They are not free when they are ill paid for their exhausting toil. They are not free when their children must labor in mines, mills and factories or starve, and when their women may be driven by poverty to lives of shame. They are not free when they are clubbed and imprisoned because they go on strike for a raise of wages and for the elemental justice that is their right as human beings . . .

As civilization has grown more complex the workers have become more and more enslaved, until today they are little more than parts of the machines they operate. Daily they face the dangers of railroad, bridge, skyscraper, freight train, stokehold, stockyard, lumber raft and mine. Panting and training at the docks, on the railroads and underground and on the seas, they move the traffic and pass from land to land the precious commodities that make it possible for us to live. And what is their reward? A scanty wage, often poverty, rents, taxes, tributes and war indemnities . . .

It is your duty to insist upon still more radical measure. It is your business to see that no child is employed in an industrial establishment or mine or store, and that no worker is needlessly exposed to accident or disease. It is your business to make them give you clean cities, free from smoke, dirt and congestion. It is your business to make them pay you a living wage. It is your business to see that this kind of preparedness is carried into every department on the nation, until everyone has a chance to be well born, well nourished, rightly educated, intelligent and serviceable to the country at all times.

Strike against all ordinances and laws and institutions that continue the slaughter of peace and the butcheries of war. Strike against war, for without you no battles can be fought. Strike against manufacturing shrapnel and gas bombs and all other tools of murder. Strike against preparedness that means death and misery to millions of human being. Be not dumb, obedient slaves in an army of destruction. Be heroes in an army of construction.

Helen Keller uses parallelism to emphasize her point.

The continued use of repetition gives the speech rhythm and emphasizes her points.

The metaphor compares the workers to the machine parts.

The alliteration gives variety to the speech.

Helen Keller answers the rhetorical question to drive home the irony of the word *reward*.

The continued parallelism and repetition shows the increasing passion of her argument.

The repetition in the conclusion calls the audience to action; Keller is now using commands.

The emotional appeal and loaded words add intensity to the argument.

Analyzing Legal Meanings and Reasoning

Reading historical and legal texts requires careful analysis of both the vocabulary and the logical flow of ideas that support a conclusion.

Common Core State Standards

Reading Informational Text

4. Determine the meaning of words and phrases as they are used in a text, including figurative, connotative, and technical meanings; analyze how an author uses and refines the meaning of a key term or terms over the course of a text.

8. Delineate and evaluate the reasoning in seminal U.S. texts, including the application of constitutional principles and use of legal reasoning and the premises, purposes, and arguments in works of public advocacy.

Writing

9. Draw evidence from literary or informational texts to support analysis, reflection, and research.

9.b. Apply grades 11–12 Reading standards to literary nonfiction.

Understanding Legal Meanings

The language of historical and legal documents is formal, precise, and technical. Many words in these texts have specific meanings that you need to understand in order to follow the flow of ideas. For example, the first amendment to the U.S. Constitution states that "Congress shall make no law respecting an establishment of religion, or prohibiting the free exercise thereof; or abridging the freedom of speech, or of the press…." To understand this amendment, it is important to know that in this context *exercise* means "practice," *abridging* means "limiting," and *press* means "media." To understand legal meanings:

- Use your knowledge of word roots to help you understand unfamiliar words. Many legal terms use familiar Greek or Latin roots, prefixes, or suffixes.
- Don't assume that you know a word's legal meaning: use a dictionary to check the meanings of key words to ensure that you are applying the correct meaning.
- Replace difficult words with synonyms to help you follow the logic of the argument.

Delineating Legal Reasoning

Works of public advocacy, such as court decisions, political proclamations, proposed laws, and constitutional amendments, use careful reasoning to support conclusions. These strategies can help outline the basic meanings of these texts:

- State the **purpose** of the document in your own words to help you focus on the writer's primary goal.
- Look for the line of reasoning that supports the **arguments** presented. To be valid and persuasive, key arguments should be backed up by clearly stated logical analysis. Be aware of persuasive techniques, such as citing facts and statistics, referring to expert testimonials, and using emotional language with strong connotations.
- Identify the **premises,** or evidence, upon which a decision rests. In legal texts, premises often include **precedents,** which are earlier examples that must be followed or else specifically overturned. Legal reasoning is usually based on the decisions of earlier trials. Be sure you understand precedents in order to identify how the court arrived at the current decision.

Writing about Legal Meanings

After reading the selection on the next page, write a detailed analysis of the meanings of the words *waive* and *waiver* in the *Miranda v. Arizona* decision. Explain the definitions of the terms as they are used in this context and provide an example that illustrates a situation in which a suspect "waives effectuation" of the rights outlined by this Supreme Court decision.

INFORMATIONAL TEXT

Model Court Decision

Note the strategies used to evaluate legal meanings and reasoning in this Supreme Court decision from 1966 regarding the rights of criminal suspects. The court addressed the admissibility of information obtained by police.

from *Miranda v. Arizona,* Opinion of the Supreme Court

We dealt with certain phases of this problem recently in *Escobedo v. Illinois.* There . . . law enforcement officials took the defendant into custody and interrogated him in a police station for the purpose of obtaining a confession. The police did not effectively advise him of his right to remain silent or of his right to consult with his attorney. Rather, they confronted him with an alleged accomplice who accused him of having perpetrated a murder. When the defendant denied the accusation . . . they handcuffed him and took him to an interrogation room. There, while handcuffed and standing, he was questioned for four hours until he confessed. During this interrogation, the police denied his request to speak to his attorney, and they prevented his retained attorney, who had come to the police station, from consulting with him. At his trial, the State, over his objection, introduced the confession against him. We held that the statements thus made were constitutionally inadmissible. . . .

. . . Our holding will be spelled out with some specificity in the pages which follow, but, briefly stated, it is this: the prosecution may not use statements, whether exculpatory or inculpatory, stemming from custodial interrogation of the defendant unless it demonstrates the use of procedural safeguards effective to secure the privilege against self-incrimination. By custodial interrogation, we mean questioning initiated by law enforcement officers after a person has been taken into custody or otherwise deprived of his freedom of action in any significant way. As for the procedural safeguards to be employed, unless other fully effective means are devised to inform accused persons of their right of silence and to assure a continuous opportunity to exercise it, the following measures are required. Prior to any questioning, the person must be warned that he has a right to remain silent, that any statement he does make may be used as evidence against him, and that he has a right to the presence of an attorney, either retained or appointed. The defendant may waive effectuation of these rights, provided the waiver is made voluntarily, knowingly and intelligently. If, however, he indicates in any manner and at any stage of the process that he wishes to consult with an attorney before speaking, there can be no questioning. Likewise, if the individual is alone and indicates in any manner that he does not wish to be interrogated, the police may not question him. The mere fact that he may have answered some questions or volunteered some statements on his own does not deprive him of the right to refrain from answering any further inquiries until he has consulted with an attorney and thereafter consents to be questioned.

The court cites and describes a **precedent**—an earlier court decision in which a suspect's confession was found inadmissible.

The word root *culp-* means "guilt," as in *culpable.* Context and prefixes combine to show that *exculpatory* means "proving innocence" and *inculpatory* means "proving guilt."

The **purpose** of the decision is stated: to guarantee that a suspect's statements are made in accordance with the rights granted by the U.S. Constitution. This **argument** is detailed and supported in the court decision. The context of the argument is the case summarized in the first paragraph.

Composing an Argument

Choosing a Topic

As you prepare to write an argument, choose a topic that interests you. The topic should be debatable or controversial to some degree.

Then, check to be sure you can make an arguable claim. Ask yourself:

1. What am I trying to prove? What ideas do I need to get across?
2. Are there people who would disagree with my claim? What counterclaims would they make?
3. Do I have evidence to support my claim? Is my evidence sufficient and relevant?

If you are able to put into words what you want to prove and answered "yes" to questions 2 and 3, you have an arguable claim.

Common Core State Standards

Writing

1.a. Introduce precise, knowledgeable claim(s), establish the significance of the claim(s), distinguish the claim(s) from alternate or opposing claims, and create an organization that logically sequences claim(s), counterclaims, reasons, and evidence.

1.b. Develop claim(s) and counterclaims fairly and thoroughly, supplying the most relevant evidence for each while pointing out the strengths and limitations of both in a manner that anticipates the audience's knowledge level, concerns, values, and possible biases.

1.e. Provide a concluding statement or section that follows from and supports the argument presented.

Introducing the Claim and Establishing Its Significance

Before you begin writing, determine how much your audience already knows about your chosen topic. Then, provide only as much background information as necessary. If there are issues surrounding your topic, you will need to clarify them for your audience and narrow the focus to your specific claim. Remember that you are not writing a summary of the issue—you are crafting an argument. Once you have provided context for your argument, you should clearly state your claim, or thesis.

Developing Your Claim with Reasoning and Evidence

Now that you have made your claim, support it with evidence, or grounds, and reasons for your claim. A valid argument should have multiple pieces of evidence to support the claim. Evidence can range from personal experience to researched data or expert opinion. Knowing your audience's knowledge level, concerns, values, and possible biases can help you decide what kind of evidence will have the strongest impact. Make sure your evidence is up to date and comes from a credible source. Be sure to credit your sources.

You should also address the opposing counterclaim within the body of your argument. Consider points you have made or evidence you have provided that a person might challenge. Decide how best to refute these counterclaims. One technique for defusing an opponent's claims is to agree with selected parts of them.

Writing a Concluding Statement or Section

Restate your claim in the conclusion of your argument, and summarize your main points. The goal of a concluding section is to provide a sense of closure and completeness to an argument. Make your concluding statement strong enough to be memorable and to leave the reader thinking.

Practice

Exploring both sides of an issue can be a good way to start planning an argument. Complete a chart like the one below to help you plan your own argument.

Topic: **Issue:** ____________________ ____________________	
Claim:	**Counterclaim:**
Grounds (Evidence): **1.** ____________ **2.** ____________ **3.** ____________	**Grounds (Evidence):** **1.** ____________ **2.** ____________ **3.** ____________
Justification: **1.** ____________ **2.** ____________ **3.** ____________	**Justification:** **1.** ____________ **2.** ____________ **3.** ____________

When you have completed the chart and developed your own precise claim, consider the following questions:

1. Who is your audience? What type of evidence can you use to best convince those who do not agree with your claim?
2. Is your evidence strong and difficult to dispute? If not, how can you strengthen it or find better evidence?
3. How will you refute the counterclaim? Are there any parts of the counterclaim you agree with?

Media Literacy Handbook

INTRODUCTION: Today, messages are transmitted across a variety of media modes, such as film, television, radio, and the Internet. As you interact with these messages each day—in images, advertisements, movies, and an array of different contexts—it is important to consider the potential influence of the medium.

- What is the intention of the message?
- How is it communicated?
- How do specific elements of the medium—such as color, image, or font—help convey the message?
- Why might the creator of the message have selected this medium?

These are the key issues of media literacy, the study of messages in the media and their impact.

Camera Shots and Angles

Filmmakers create camera shots and sequences to help them tell stories. Some shots capture an entire scene; others zoom in on specific characters.

FILM

Special Effects

Filmmakers use special effects to create on-screen illusions that bring the imagination to life.

Questions About Film Techniques

- What effect is created by the choice of camera angle shown in the image at left? Choose another camera angle and explain how that shot might convey a different message than the one shown here.
- Study the images above. In what way does the use of special effects make the film better for viewers?

Media Literacy Handbook

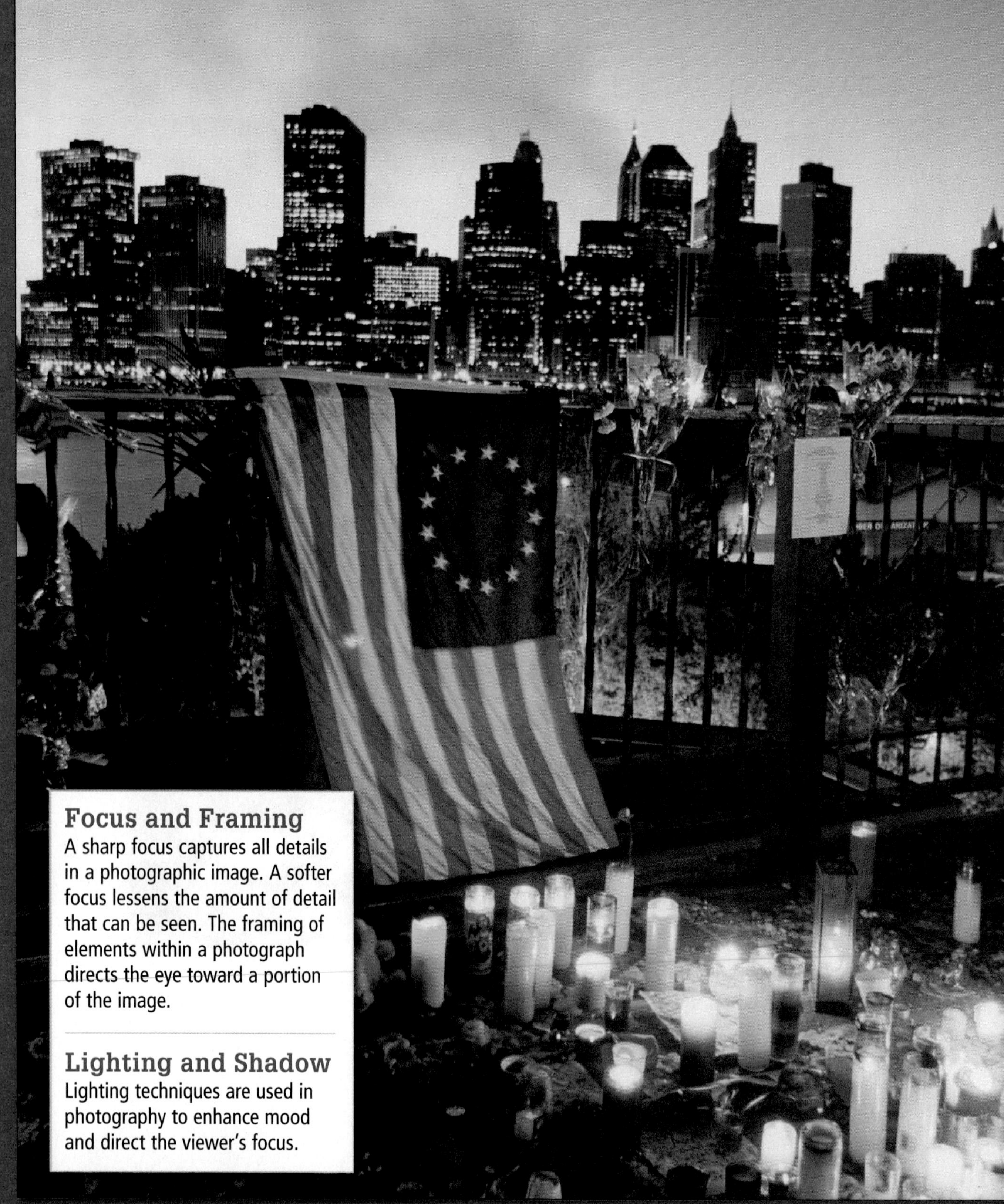

Focus and Framing

A sharp focus captures all details in a photographic image. A softer focus lessens the amount of detail that can be seen. The framing of elements within a photograph directs the eye toward a portion of the image.

Lighting and Shadow

Lighting techniques are used in photography to enhance mood and direct the viewer's focus.

Special Techniques

Most images you see today have been manipulated or changed in some way. Even a small change—such as an added graphic element or a difference in shading—can alter the mood of an image.

LUKE HAVERGAL

EDWIN ARLINGTON ROBINSON

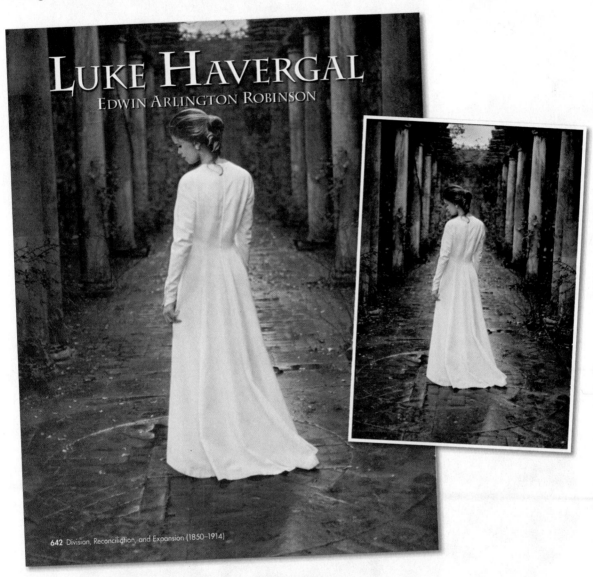

642 Division, Reconciliation, and Expansion (1850–1914)

Questions About Graphics and Photos

- What would be the effect if the image at left used a sharp focus instead of a combination of a sharp and soft focus?
- In what way does the use of color and light create mood in the photo at left?
- What special techniques were applied to the original photograph shown above right? What effect does the use of special techniques create?

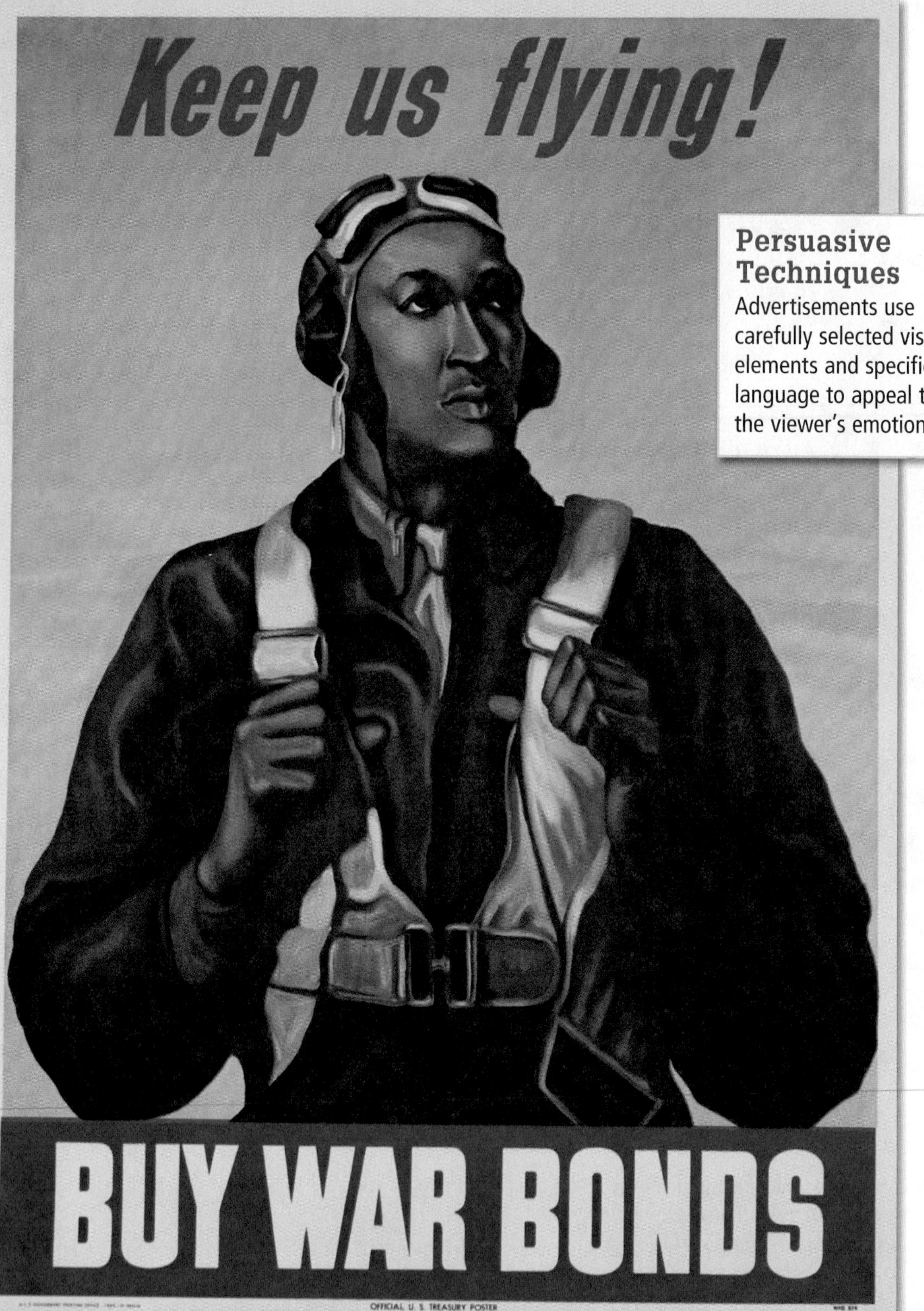

Persuasive Techniques
Advertisements use carefully selected visual elements and specific language to appeal to the viewer's emotions.

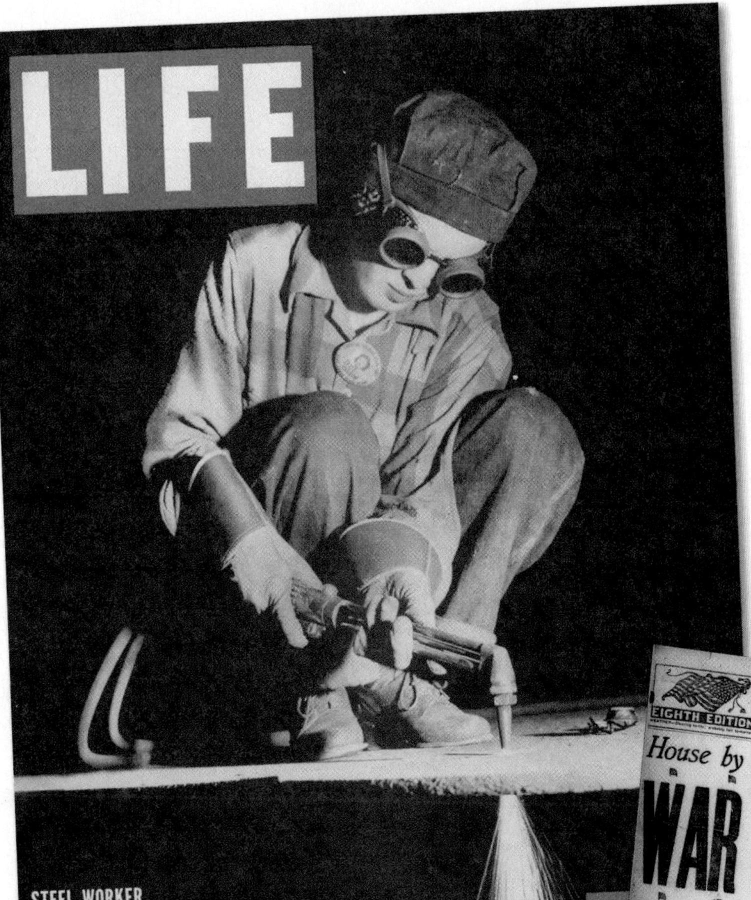

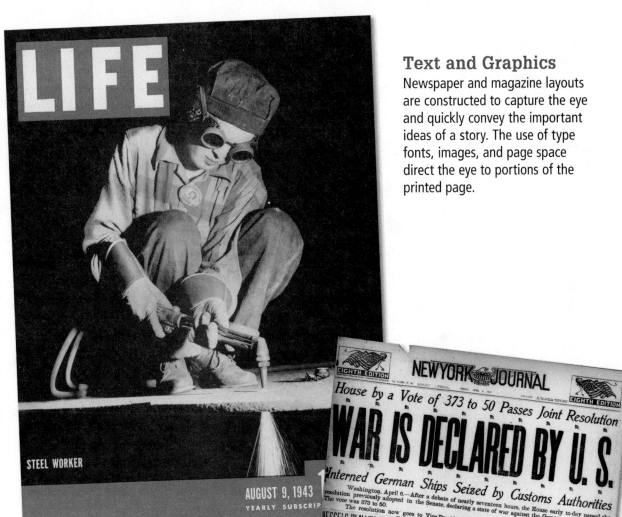

Text and Graphics

Newspaper and magazine layouts are constructed to capture the eye and quickly convey the important ideas of a story. The use of type fonts, images, and page space direct the eye to portions of the printed page.

EIGHTH EDITION NEW YORK JOURNAL EIGHTH EDITION

House by a Vote of 373 to 50 Passes Joint Resolution

WAR IS DECLARED BY U. S.

Interned German Ships Seized by Customs Authorities

Washington, April 6.—After a debate of nearly seventeen hours, the House early to-day passed the resolution previously adopted in the Senate, declaring a state of war against the Government of Germany. The vote was 373 to 50.

The resolution now goes to Vice-President Marshall, who must sign it in formal session of the Senate. It will then be taken before the President for his signature.

Amendments to prevent the use of United States military forces in Europe, Asia or Africa unless directed by Congress were voted down. The resolution adopted by the Senate on Wednesday was approved by the House without the crossing of a "t" or the dotting of an "i."

VESSELS IN PORT HERE TAKEN

ALLIES REST BEFORE BIG DRIVE

"LOVE U. S. BUT CAN'T VOTE FOR WAR"---MISS RANKIN

CARRANZISTAS

President's Historic Address Free to

Questions About Print Media

- What image or graphic dominates the advertisement at left? In what way does the use of language in the ad enhance its message?
- Which of the above grabs your attention: the image or the graphic on the magazine cover? Explain.
- What do you notice first on the newspaper's front page? What overall effect does the use of type size and fonts create?

How is this book organized?

- **There are six chronological units, starting with Native American beginnings and extending to the present.**
- **Each unit has an introduction that offers multiple perspectives on the history, culture, and literature of the time period.**

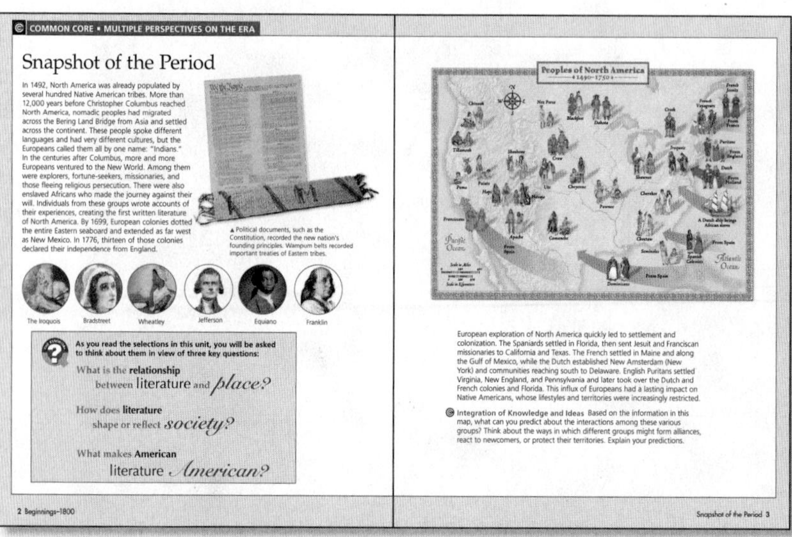

COMMON CORE • MULTIPLE PERSPECTIVES ON THE ERA

Snapshot of the Period

In 1492, North America was already populated by several hundred Native American tribes. More than 12,000 years before Christopher Columbus reached North America, nomadic peoples had migrated across the Bering Land Bridge from Asia and settled across the continent. These people spoke different languages and had very different cultures, but the Europeans called them all by one name: "Indians." In the centuries after Columbus, more and more Europeans ventured to the New World. Among them were explorers, fortune-seekers, missionaries, and those fleeing religious persecution. There were also enslaved Africans who made the journey against their will. Individuals from these groups wrote accounts of their experiences, creating the first written literature of North America. By 1699, European colonies dotted the entire Eastern seaboard and extended as far west as New Mexico. In 1776, thirteen of those colonies declared their independence from England.

▲ Political documents, such as the Constitution, recorded the new nation's founding principles. Wampum belts recorded important treaties of Eastern tribes.

The Iroquois | Bradstreet | Wheatley | Jefferson | Equiano | Franklin

As you read the selections in this unit, you will be asked to think about them in view of three key questions:

What is the relationship between literature and place?

How does literature shape or reflect society?

What makes American literature American?

2 Beginnings–1800

European exploration of North America quickly led to settlement and colonization. The Spaniards settled in Florida, then sent Jesuit and Franciscan missionaries to California and Texas. The French settled in Maine and along the Gulf of Mexico, while the Dutch established New Amsterdam (New York) and communities reaching south to Delaware. English Puritans settled Virginia, New England, and Pennsylvania and later took over the Dutch and French colonies and Florida. This influx of Europeans had a lasting impact on Native Americans, whose lifestyles and territories were increasingly restricted.

Integration of Knowledge and Ideas Based on the information in this map, what can you predict about the interactions among these various groups? Think about the ways in which different groups might form alliances, react to newcomers, or protect their territories. Explain your predictions.

Snapshot of the Period 3

A **"Snapshot"** shows you key people, places, and innovations. ▶

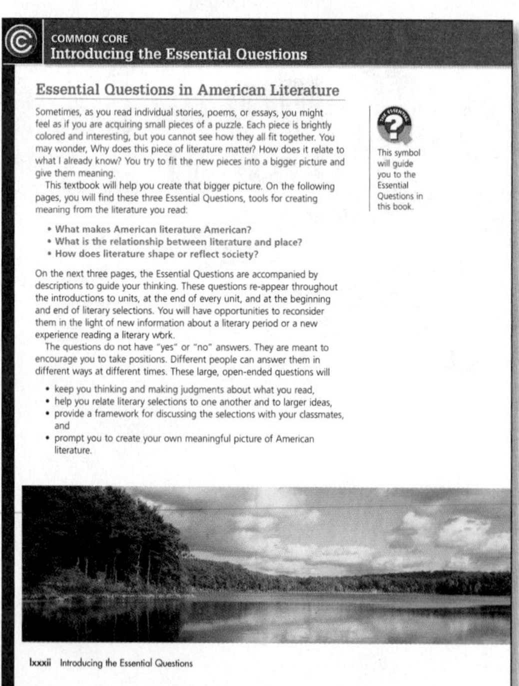

COMMON CORE
Introducing the Essential Questions

Essential Questions in American Literature

Sometimes, as you read individual stories, poems, or essays, you might feel as if you are acquiring small pieces of a puzzle. Each piece is brightly colored and interesting, but you cannot see how they all fit together. You may wonder, Why does this piece of literature matter? How does it relate to what I already know? You try to fit the new pieces into a bigger picture and give them meaning.

This textbook will help you create that bigger picture. On the following pages, you will find these three Essential Questions, tools for creating meaning from the literature you read:

- **What makes American literature American?**
- **What is the relationship between literature and place?**
- **How does literature shape or reflect society?**

On the next three pages, the Essential Questions are accompanied by descriptions to guide your thinking. These questions re-appear throughout the introductions to units, at the end of every unit, and at the beginning and end of literary selections. You will have opportunities to reconsider them in the light of new information about a literary period or a new experience reading a literary work.

The questions do not have "yes" or "no" answers. They are meant to encourage you to take positions. Different people can answer them in different ways at different times. These large, open-ended questions will

- keep you thinking and making judgments about what you read,
- help you relate literary selections to one another and to larger ideas,
- provide a framework for discussing the selections with your classmates, and
- prompt you to create your own meaningful picture of American literature.

This symbol will guide you to the Essential Questions in this book.

lxxxii Introducing the Essential Questions

▲ **Essential Questions** help you think about universal themes.

Historical Background summarizes key events of the era. ▼

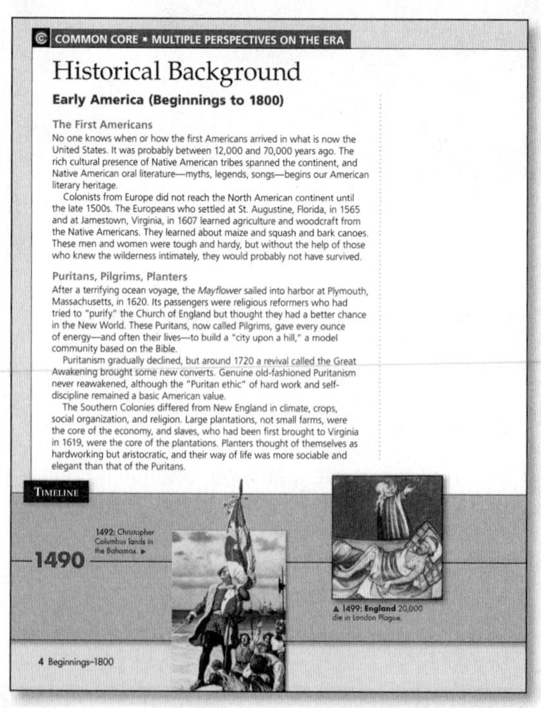

COMMON CORE • MULTIPLE PERSPECTIVES ON THE ERA

Historical Background

Early America (Beginnings to 1800)

The First Americans

No one knows when or how the first Americans arrived in what is now the United States. It was probably between 12,000 and 70,000 years ago. The rich cultural presence of Native American tribes spanned the continent, and Native American oral literature—myths, legends, songs—begins our American literary heritage.

Colonists from Europe did not reach the North American continent until the late 1500s. The Europeans who settled at St. Augustine, Florida, in 1565 and at Jamestown, Virginia, in 1607 learned agriculture and woodcraft from the Native Americans. They learned about maize and squash and bark canoes. These men and women were tough and hardy, but without the help of those who knew the wilderness intimately, they would probably not have survived.

Puritans, Pilgrims, Planters

After a terrifying ocean voyage, the *Mayflower* sailed into harbor at Plymouth, Massachusetts, in 1620. Its passengers were religious reformers who had tried to "purify" the Church of England but thought they had a better chance in the New World. These Puritans, now called Pilgrims, gave every ounce of energy—and often their lives—to build a "city upon a hill," a model community based on the Bible.

Puritanism gradually declined, but around 1720 a revival called the Great Awakening brought some new converts. Genuine old-fashioned Puritanism never reawakened, although the "Puritan ethic" of hard work and self-discipline remained a basic American value.

The Southern Colonies differed from New England in climate, crops, social organization, and religion. Large plantations, not small farms, were the core of the economy, and slaves, who had been first brought to Virginia in 1619, were the core of the plantations. Planters thought of themselves as hardworking but aristocratic, and their way of life was more sociable and elegant than that of the Puritans.

TIMELINE

1490

1492: Christopher Columbus lands in the Bahamas. ▶

▲ 1499: England 20,000 die in London Plague.

4 Beginnings–1800

How are the literary selections organized?

- **Each unit contains literary selections from the time period.**
- **Each selection has features to help you better understand the literature.**

Before You Read teaches you important skills and vocabulary. ▶

Vocabulary

prevalent (prev′ ə lənt) *adj.* widely existing or occurring (p. 229)

discord (dis′ kôrd′) *n.* lack of harmony; conflict (p. 230)

treacherous (trech′ ər əs) *adj.* dangerous (p. 230)

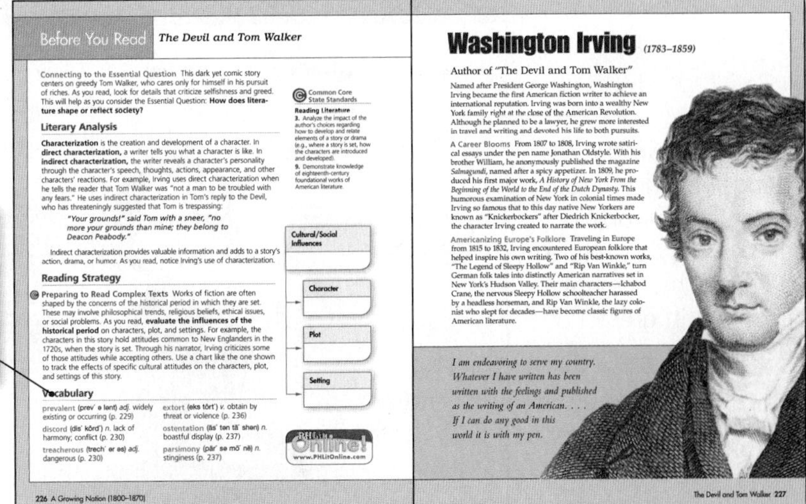

Before You Read | *The Devil and Tom Walker*

Connecting to the Essential Question This dark yet comic story centers on greedy Tom Walker, who cares only for himself in his pursuit of riches. As you read, look for details that criticize selfishness and greed. This will help as you consider the Essential Question: **How does literature shape or reflect society?**

Common Core State Standards

Reading Literature
3. Analyze the impact of the author's choices regarding how to develop and relate elements of a story or drama (e.g., where a story is set, how the characters are introduced and developed).
9. Demonstrate knowledge of eighteenth-century foundational works of American literature.

Literary Analysis

Characterization is the creation and development of a character. In **direct characterization,** a writer tells you what a character is like. In **indirect characterization,** the writer reveals a character's personality through the character's speech, thoughts, actions, appearance, and other characters' reactions. For example, Irving uses direct characterization when he tells the reader that Tom Walker was "not a man to be troubled with any fears." He uses indirect characterization in Tom's reply to the Devil, who has threateningly suggested that Tom is trespassing:

> *"Your grounds!" said Tom with a sneer, "no more your grounds than mine; they belong to Deacon Peabody."*

Indirect characterization provides valuable information and adds to a story's action, drama, or humor. As you read, notice Irving's use of characterization.

Reading Strategy

Preparing to Read Complex Texts Works of fiction are often shaped by the concerns of the historical period in which they are set. These may involve philosophical trends, religious beliefs, ethical issues, or social problems. As you read, **evaluate the influences of the historical period** on characters, plot, and settings. For example, the characters in this story hold attitudes common to New Englanders in the 1720s, when the story is set. Through his narrator, Irving criticizes some of those attitudes while accepting others. Use a chart like the one shown to track the effects of specific cultural attitudes on the characters, plot, and settings of this story.

Cultural/Social Influences
Character
Plot
Setting

Vocabulary

prevalent (prev′ ə lənt) *adj.* widely existing or occurring (p. 229)
discord (dis′ kôrd′) *n.* lack of harmony; conflict (p. 230)
treacherous (trech′ ər əs) *adj.* dangerous (p. 230)
extort (eks tôrt′) *v.* obtain by threat or violence (p. 236)
ostentation (äs′ tən tā′ shən) *n.* boastful display (p. 237)
parsimony (pär′ sə mō′ nē) *n.* stinginess (p. 237)

PHLit Online!
www.PHLitOnline.com

226 A Growing Nation (1800–1870)

Washington Irving (1783–1859)

Author of "The Devil and Tom Walker"

Named after President George Washington, Washington Irving became the first American fiction writer to achieve an international reputation. Irving was born into a wealthy New York family right at the close of the American Revolution. Although he planned to be a lawyer, he grew more interested in travel and writing and devoted his life to both pursuits.

A Career Blooms From 1807 to 1808, Irving wrote satirical essays under the pen name Jonathan Oldstyle. With his brother William, he anonymously published the magazine *Salmagundi*, named after a spicy appetizer. In 1809, he produced his first major work, *A History of New York From the Beginning of the World to the End of the Dutch Dynasty.* This humorous examination of New York in colonial times made Irving so famous that to this day native New Yorkers are known as "Knickerbockers" after Diedrich Knickerbocker, the character Irving created to narrate the work.

Americanizing Europe's Folklore Traveling in Europe from 1815 to 1832, Irving encountered European folklore that helped inspire his own writing. Two of his best-known works, "The Legend of Sleepy Hollow" and "Rip Van Winkle," turn German folk tales into distinctly American narratives set in New York's Hudson Valley. Their main characters—Ichabod Crane, the nervous Sleepy Hollow schoolteacher harassed by a headless horseman, and Rip Van Winkle, the lazy colonist who slept for decades—have become classic figures of American literature.

I am endeavoring to serve my country. Whatever I have written has been written with the feelings and published as the writing of an American. . . . If I can do any good in this world it is with my pen.

The Devil and Tom Walker 227

▲ **Author Biography** tells you about the author's life.

About the year 1727, just at the time that earthquakes were prevalent in New England, and shook many tall sinners down upon their knees, there lived near this place a meager, miserly fellow, of the name of Tom Walker. He had a wife as miserly as himself: they were so miserly that they even conspired to cheat each other. Whatever the woman could lay hands on, she hid away; a hen could not cackle but she was on the alert to secure the new-laid egg. Her husband was continually prying about to detect her secret hoards, and many and fierce were the conflicts that took place about what ought to have been common property. They lived in a forlorn-looking house that stood alone, and had an air of starvation. A few straggling savin trees, emblems of sterility, grew near it;

Literary Analysis
Characterization
What do you learn about Tom and his wife through this description?

◀ **While You Read questions** help you apply the skills as you read.

After You Read helps you practice the skills you have learned. ▶

Skills Practice

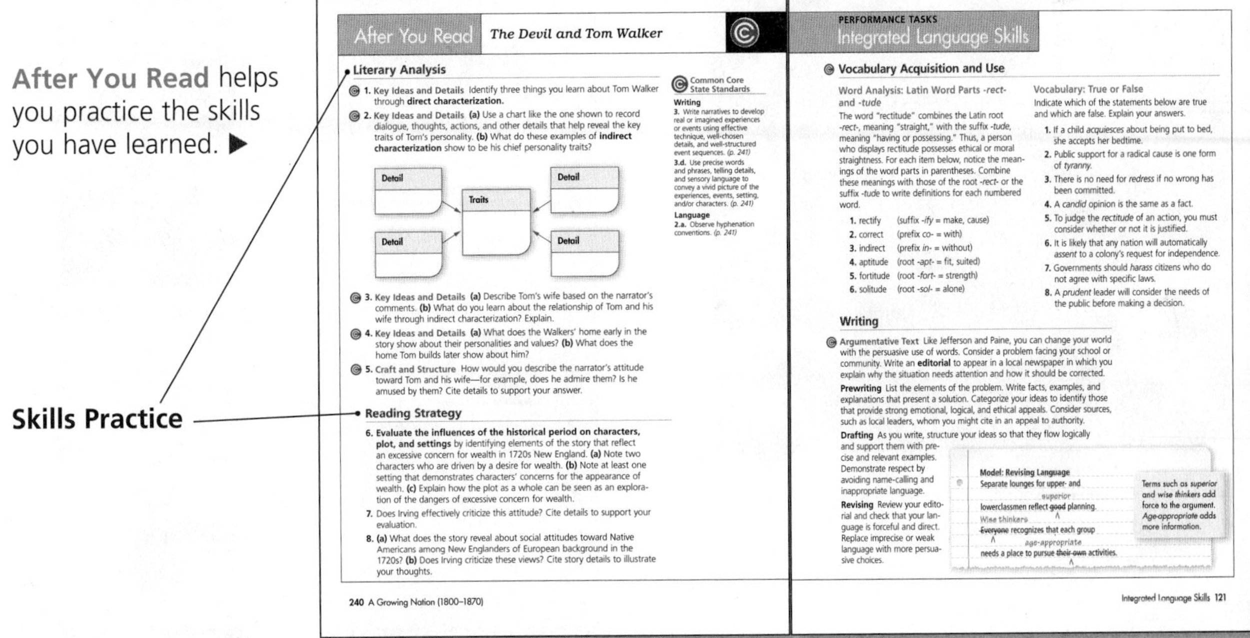

After You Read | *The Devil and Tom Walker*

Literary Analysis

1. **Key Ideas and Details** Identify three things you learn about Tom Walker through **direct characterization.**
2. **Key Ideas and Details** **(a)** Use a chart like the one shown to record dialogue, thoughts, actions, and other details that help reveal the key traits of Tom's personality. **(b)** What do these examples of **indirect characterization** show to be his chief personality traits?

Detail
Detail
Traits
Detail
Detail

3. **Key Ideas and Details** **(a)** Describe Tom's wife based on the narrator's comments. **(b)** What do you learn about the relationship of Tom and his wife through indirect characterization? Explain.
4. **Key Ideas and Details** **(a)** What does the Walkers' home early in the story show about their personalities and values? **(b)** What does the home Tom builds later show about him?
5. **Craft and Structure** How would you describe the narrator's attitude toward Tom and his wife—for example, does he admire them? Is he amused by them? Cite details to support your answer.

Reading Strategy

6. **Evaluate the influences of the historical period on characters, plot, and settings** by identifying elements of the story that reflect an excessive concern for wealth in 1720s New England. **(a)** Note two characters who are driven by a desire for wealth. **(b)** Note at least one setting that demonstrates characters' concerns for the appearance of wealth. **(c)** Explain how the plot as a whole can be seen as an exploration of the dangers of excessive concern for wealth.
7. Does Irving effectively criticize this attitude? Cite details to support your evaluation.
8. **(a)** What does the story reveal about social attitudes toward Native Americans among New Englanders of European background in the 1720s? **(b)** Does Irving criticize these views? Cite story details to illustrate your thoughts.

Common Core State Standards

Writing
3. Write narratives to develop real or imagined experiences or events using effective technique, well-chosen details, and well-structured event sequences. *(p. 241)*
3.d. Use precise words and phrases, telling details, and sensory language to convey a vivid picture of the experiences, events, setting, and/or characters. *(p. 241)*
Language
2.a. Observe hyphenation conventions. *(p. 241)*

240 A Growing Nation (1800–1870)

PERFORMANCE TASKS
Integrated Language Skills

Vocabulary Acquisition and Use

Word Analysis: Latin Word Parts *-rect-* and *-tude*

The word "rectitude" combines the Latin root *-rect-*, meaning "straight," with the suffix *-tude*, meaning "having or possessing." Thus, a person who displays rectitude possesses ethical or moral straightness. For each item below, notice the meanings of the word parts in parentheses. Combine these meanings with those of the root *-rect-* or the suffix *-tude* to write definitions for each numbered word.

1. rectify (suffix *-ify* = make, cause)
2. correct (prefix co- = with)
3. indirect (prefix *in-* = without)
4. aptitude (root *-apt-* = fit, suited)
5. fortitude (root *-fort-* = strength)
6. solitude (root *-sol-* = alone)

Vocabulary: True or False

Indicate which of the statements below are true and which are false. Explain your answers.

1. If a child *acquiesces* about being put to bed, she accepts her bedtime.
2. Public support for a radical cause is one form of *tyranny.*
3. There is no need for *redress* if no wrong has been committed.
4. A *candid* opinion is the same as a fact.
5. To judge the *rectitude* of an action, you must consider whether or not it is justified.
6. It is likely that any nation will automatically *assent* to a colony's request for independence.
7. Governments should *harass* citizens who do not agree with specific laws.
8. A *prudent* leader will consider the needs of the public before making a decision.

Writing

Argumentative Text Like Jefferson and Paine, you can change your world with the persuasive use of words. Consider a problem facing your school or community. Write an **editorial** to appear in a local newspaper in which you explain why the situation needs attention and how it should be corrected.

Prewriting List the elements of the problem. Write facts, examples, and explanations that present a solution. Categorize your ideas to identify those that provide strong emotional, logical, and ethical appeals. Consider sources, such as local leaders, whom you might cite in an appeal to authority.

Drafting As you write, structure your ideas so that they flow logically and support them with precise and relevant examples. Demonstrate respect by avoiding name-calling and inappropriate language.

Revising Review your editorial and check that your language is forceful and direct. Replace imprecise or weak language with more persuasive choices.

Model: Revising Language
Separate lounges for upper- and
superior
lowerclassmen reflect good planning.
Wise thinkers
Everyone recognizes that each group
age-appropriate
needs a place to pursue their own activities.
Terms such as superior and wise thinkers add force to the argument. Age-appropriate adds more information.

Integrated Language Skills 121

Special Features Bring American Literature to Life and Show Why It Matters Today

Extended Study brings you closer to an author's world or allows you to explore a literary movement or genre in great depth. ▶

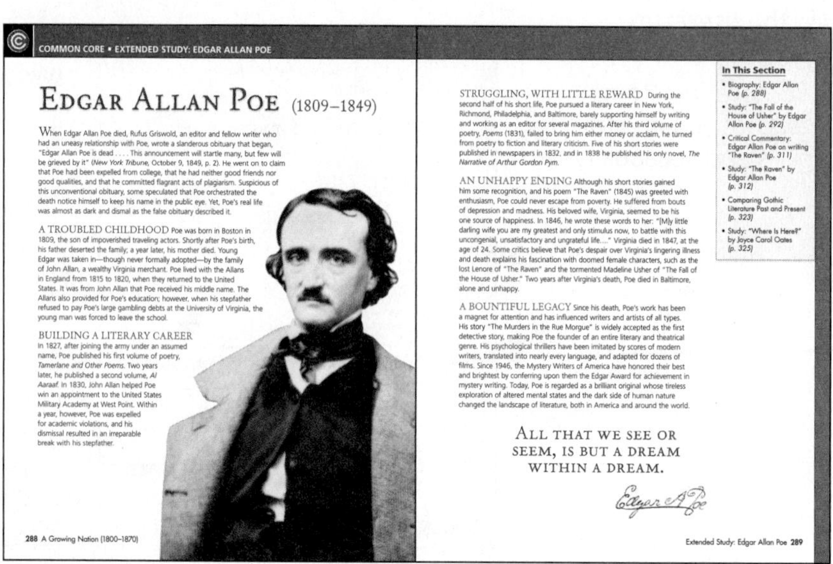

COMMON CORE • EXTENDED STUDY: EDGAR ALLAN POE

EDGAR ALLAN POE (1809–1849)

When Edgar Allan Poe died, Rufus Griswold, an editor and fellow writer who had an uneasy relationship with Poe, wrote a slanderous obituary that began, "Edgar Allan Poe is dead . . . . This announcement will startle many, but few will be grieved by it" (*New York Tribune*, October 9, 1849, p. 2). He went on to claim that Poe had been expelled from college, that he had neither good friends nor good qualities, and that he committed flagrant acts of plagiarism. Suspicious of this unconventional obituary, some speculated that Poe orchestrated the death notice himself to keep his name in the public eye. Yet, Poe's real life was almost as dark and dismal as the false obituary described it.

A TROUBLED CHILDHOOD Poe was born in Boston in 1809, the son of impoverished traveling actors. Shortly after Poe's birth, his father deserted the family; a year later, his mother died. Young Edgar was taken in—though never formally adopted—by the family of John Allan, a wealthy Virginia merchant. Poe lived with the Allans in England from 1815 to 1820, when they returned to the United States. It was from John Allan that Poe received his middle name. The Allans also provided for Poe's education; however, when his stepfather refused to pay Poe's large gambling debts at the University of Virginia, the young man was forced to leave the school.

BUILDING A LITERARY CAREER In 1827, after joining the army under an assumed name, Poe published his first volume of poetry, *Tamerlane and Other Poems*. Two years later, he published a second volume, *Al Aaraaf*. In 1830, John Allan helped Poe win an appointment to the United States Military Academy at West Point. Within a year, however, Poe was expelled for academic violations, and his dismissal resulted in an irreparable break with his stepfather.

STRUGGLING, WITH LITTLE REWARD During the second half of his short life, Poe pursued a literary career in New York, Richmond, Philadelphia, and Baltimore, barely supporting himself by writing and working as an editor for several magazines. After his third volume of poetry, *Poems* (1831), failed to bring him either money or acclaim, he turned from poetry to fiction and literary criticism. Five of his short stories were published in newspapers in 1832, and in 1838 he published his only novel, *The Narrative of Arthur Gordon Pym*.

AN UNHAPPY ENDING Although his short stories gained him some recognition, and his poem "The Raven" (1845) was greeted with enthusiasm, Poe could never escape from poverty. He suffered from bouts of depression and madness. His beloved wife, Virginia, seemed to be his one source of happiness. In 1846, he wrote these words to her: "[M]y little darling wife you are my greatest and only stimulus now, to battle with this uncongenial, unsatisfactory and ungrateful life...." Virginia died in 1847, at the age of 24. Some critics believe that Poe's despair over Virginia's lingering illness and death explains his fascination with doomed female characters, such as the lost Lenore of "The Raven" and the tormented Madeline Usher of "The Fall of the House of Usher." Two years after Virginia's death, Poe died in Baltimore, alone and unhappy.

A BOUNTIFUL LEGACY Since his death, Poe's work has been a magnet for attention and has influenced writers and artists of all types. His story "The Murders in the Rue Morgue" is widely accepted as the first detective story, making Poe the founder of an entire literary and theatrical genre. His psychological thrillers have been imitated by scores of modern writers, translated into nearly every language, and adapted for dozens of films. Since 1946, the Mystery Writers of America have honored their best and brightest by conferring upon them the Edgar Award for achievement in mystery writing. Today, Poe is regarded as a brilliant original whose tireless exploration of altered mental states and the dark side of human nature changed the landscape of literature, both in America and around the world.

ALL THAT WE SEE OR SEEM, IS BUT A DREAM WITHIN A DREAM.

In This Section

- Biography: Edgar Allan Poe *(p. 288)*
- Study: "The Fall of the House of Usher" by Edgar Allan Poe *(p. 292)*
- Critical Commentary: Edgar Allan Poe on writing "The Raven" *(p. 311)*
- Study: "The Raven" by Edgar Allan Poe *(p. 312)*
- Comparing Gothic Literature Past and Present *(p. 323)*
- Study: "Where Is Here?" by Joyce Carol Oates *(p. 325)*

288 A Growing Nation (1800–1870)

Extended Study: Edgar Allan Poe 289

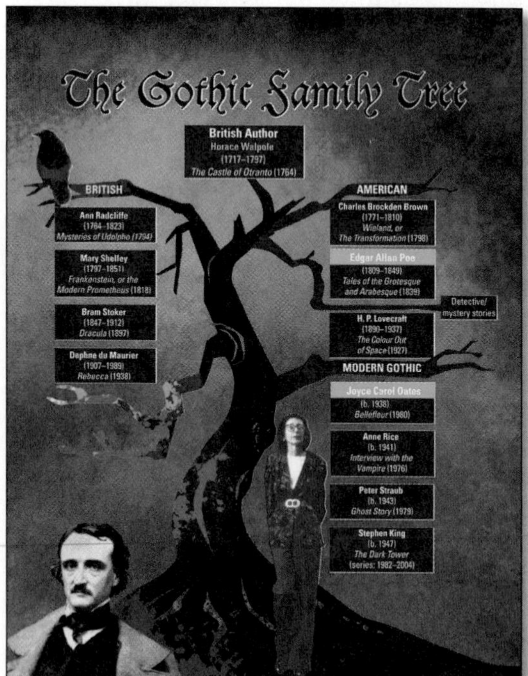

▲ **Illustrations** help you visualize literary history.

Themes Across Centuries, Genres, or Cultures features essays by today's writers on the topic of the classics. ▼

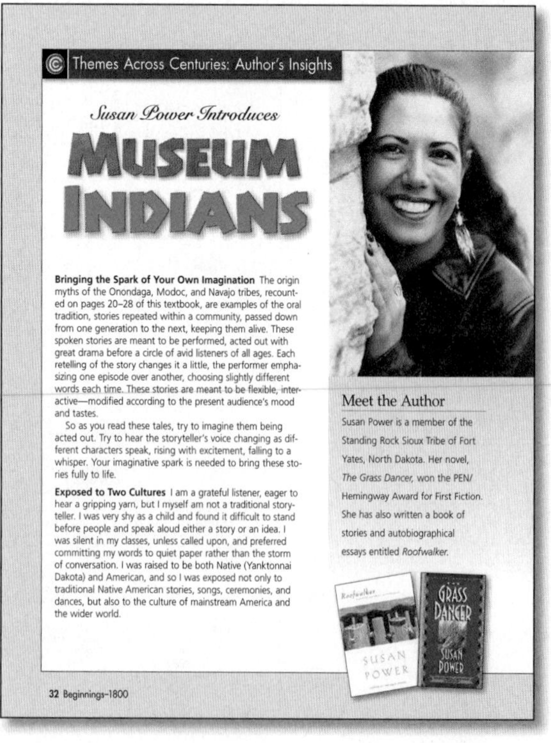

Themes Across Centuries: Author's Insights

Susan Power Introduces

MUSEUM INDIANS

Bringing the Spark of Your Own Imagination The origin myths of the Onondaga, Modoc, and Navajo tribes, recounted on pages 20–28 of this textbook, are examples of the oral tradition, stories repeated within a community, passed down from one generation to the next, keeping them alive. These spoken stories are meant to be performed, acted out with great drama before a circle of avid listeners of all ages. Each retelling of the story changes it a little, the performer emphasizing one episode over another, choosing slightly different words each time. These stories are meant to be flexible, interactive—modified according to the present audience's mood and tastes.

So as you read these tales, try to imagine them being acted out. Try to hear the storyteller's voice changing as different characters speak, rising with excitement, falling to a whisper. Your imaginative spark is needed to bring these stories fully to life.

Exposed to Two Cultures I am a grateful listener, eager to hear a gripping yarn, but I myself am not a traditional storyteller. I was very shy as a child and found it difficult to stand before people and speak aloud either a story or an idea. I was silent in my classes, unless called upon, and preferred committing my words to quiet paper rather than the storm of conversation. I was raised to be both Native (Yanktonnai Dakota) and American, and so I was exposed not only to traditional Native American stories, songs, ceremonies, and dances, but also to the culture of mainstream America and the wider world.

Meet the Author

Susan Power is a member of the Standing Rock Sioux Tribe of Fort Yates, North Dakota. Her novel, *The Grass Dancer*, won the PEN/Hemingway Award for First Fiction. She has also written a book of stories and autobiographical essays entitled *Roofwalker*.

32 Beginnings–1800

Contemporary Connections links the classics to today. ▶

The American EXPERIENCE

CONTEMPORARY CONNECTION

Thomas Paine: Essayist, Hero of the Revolution…Father of the Internet?

Thomas Paine believed that knowledge is power and that it belongs to all people, not just the wealthy or privileged. He believed that through knowledge, ordinary people could guarantee their own freedoms. Even at a time when the printed word was slow to publish and distribute, Paine's fiery words brought change, fueling both the American and the French revolutions.

While this pamphleteer and passionate advocate of communication is often seen as a pioneer of investigative journalism, perhaps his true legacy is the Internet. Writing in *Wired News* (issue 3.05–May 1995), journalist Jon Katz observed that regarding the Internet, Paine's "ideas about communications, media ethics, the universal connections between people, and the free flow of honest opinion are all relevant again, visible every time one modem shakes hands with another."

Paine once said, "Such is the irresistible nature of truth that all it asks, and all it wants, is the liberty of appearing." When the Internet is used in its best and highest forms, truth becomes available to anyone with a computer. Thomas Paine, advocate of "all mankind," might recognize the Internet as the true product of his own ideals.

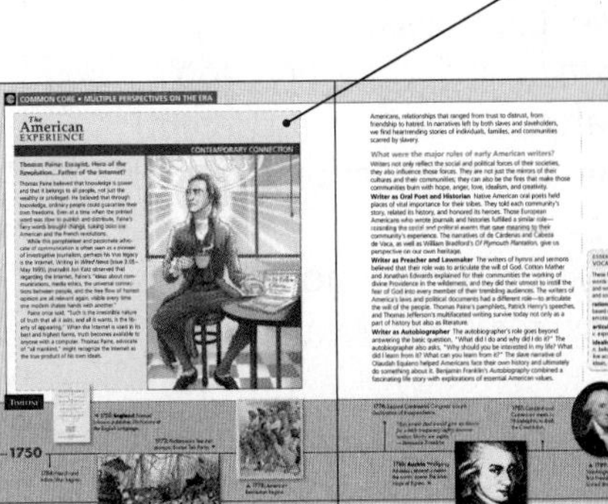

COMMON CORE • RESEARCH PROJECT

THE STORY BEHIND THE DOCUMENTS

President John Adams

Abigail Adams

Benjamin Henry Latrobe

In 1790—two years after the ratification of the Constitution and one year after George Washington was elected the nation's first president—the U.S. Congress passed the Residence Act. This act established a permanent national capital in a 10-square-mile tract of land along the Potomac River. Washington himself selected the site for the President's House, later known as the White House, in a wooded area on the banks of the river. In 1792, a competition was held to choose an architect for the presidential residence. It was hoped that the design would reflect the nation's noble ideals. Irishman James Hoban (1762–1831) won the competition.

Hoban's design for the President's House was a basic rectangular structure. The classic simplicity of this design would allow later presidents to make alterations according to the needs of the day. Thomas Jefferson, for one, would ask architect **Benjamin Henry Latrobe (1764–1820)** to complete and extend Hoban's design. Latrobe transformed Hoban's boxy original into the grand house with columns and covered entrances that today is widely recognized as the home of the President of the United States.

Construction of the original President's House began on October 13, 1792. The house would not near completion until some eight years later, when the second President of the United States, **President John Adams (1735–1826)** and his wife **Abigail Smith Adams (1744–1818)** took up residence there in November, 1800. Although their stay in the house would be brief, the Adamses graciously made do with less-than-perfect living conditions. Many of the walls were still unplastered. A giant hole marked the place where the grand staircase would someday be, and the six out of thirty-six rooms that were habitable were poorly lit and drafty. To keep the house even mildly warm, President Adams paid for firewood out of his own pocket. Unwilling to have the president's laundry hung about the yard, Abigail had lines strung in the large, unfinished East Room.

These were trying times for the Adamses. John was on the brink of losing his reelection to Thomas Jefferson, and Abigail had been ill. The couple was no doubt bolstered by their close companionship, a relationship documented in their letters. Throughout their courtship and marriage, John and Abigail wrote more than one thousand letters to one another. Although their letters are often affectionate and even playful, they also reflect the couple's underlying awareness that they were key players in the unfolding of history.

180 Beginnings–1800

Letter from the

PRESIDENT'S HOUSE

John Adams

BACKGROUND As John Adams wrote this letter, the outcome of the election of 1801, in which Thomas Jefferson was his opponent, was still uncertain. Anxious for the company and consolation of his wife, Adams seems to sense that defeat is likely.

President's house,
Washington City,
Nov. 2, 1800

My Dearest Friend,

We arrived here last night, or rather yesterday, at one o Clock and here we dined and Slept. The Building is in a State to be habitable. And now we wish for your Company. The Account you give of the melancholly State of our dear Brother Mr. Cranch[1] and his family is really distressing and must severely afflict you. I most cordially Sympathize with you and them. I have seen only Mr. Marshall and Mr. Stoddert, General Wilkinson and the two Commissioners Mr. Scott and Mr. Thornton.[2] I shall say nothing of public affairs. I am very glad you consented to come on, for you would have been more anxious at Quincy[3] than here, and I, to all my other Solicitudines Mordaces as Horace[4] calls them i.e. "biting Cares" should have added a great deal on your Account. Besides it is fit and proper that you and I should retire together and not one before the other. Before I end my Letter I pray Heaven to bestow the best of Blessings on this House and all that shall hereafter inhabit it. May none but honest and wise Men ever rule under this roof. I shall not attempt a description of it. You will form the best Idea of it from Inspection. Mr. Brisler[5] is very anxious for the arrival of the Man and Women and I am much more so for that of the Ladies. I am with unabated Confidence and affection your

John Adams

Vocabulary

account (ə kount') *n.* report or description

commissioners (kə mish' ə nərz) *n.* government officials

inspection (in spek' shən) *n.* examination

unabated (un ə bāt' təd) *adj.* not lessened or reduced

▲ sample of John Adams's handwriting

1. **Richard Cranch** President Adams's brother-in-law.
2. **Mr. Marshall. . . Mr. Thornton** Various officials and cabinet members.
3. **Quincy** the Adamses' hometown in Massachusetts.
4. **Horace** classical Roman poet.
5. **John Brisler** President Adams's servant.

Letter from the President's House

◀ **Primary Sources** features real documents that made history and supports in-depth research projects.

COMMON CORE • EXTENDED STUDY: BENJAMIN FRANKLIN

Comparing Literary Works

from ***The Autobiography*** by Benjamin Franklin • ***"Straw Into Gold: The Metamorphosis of the Everyday"*** by Sandra Cisneros

Comparing Autobiography Past and Present

Autobiographical Writing The first autobiography was the *Confessions* of St. Augustine, which was written in Latin sometime around A.D. 400. The form did not appear in English, though, until the late 1700s. It was during this "Golden Age" of nonfiction that Benjamin Franklin wrote his *Autobiography*. In doing so, he created a model for the American success story.

Over the next two centuries, major American autobiographies such as the *Narrative of the Life of Frederick Douglass* (1845) and Zora Neale Hurston's *Dust Tracks on a Road* (1942) paved the way for other related forms of nonfiction. These include *memoirs*, which are smaller in scope and less formal in tone, and *autobiographical essays*, which focus on a small slice of the writer's life in order to explore larger ideas. "Straw Into Gold," by Sandra Cisneros, is an example of an autobiographical essay.

These selections highlight some of the ways that American autobiography has evolved. They reflect vastly different historical periods and cultures as well as changing attitudes toward social status and gender. Despite these differences, both address a powerful American *theme*—success. As you read "Straw Into Gold," use a chart like the one shown to compare and contrast Franklin's and Cisneros's ideas about success.

	Franklin	Cisneros
What is success?		
What are its costs?		
What are its rewards?		

Common Core State Standards

Reading Informational Text
3. Analyze a complex set of ideas or sequence of events and explain how specific individuals, ideas, or events interact and develop over the course of the text.

Language
6. Demonstrate independence in gathering vocabulary knowledge when considering a word or phrase important to comprehension or expression.

Gather Vocabulary Knowledge

Sandra Cisneros uses related forms of the words *venture, nomad,* and *vagabond.* Use a **dictionary** to find each word's part of speech and definition. Then, employ other references to further explore these words:

- **History of Language:** Use a history of English to research each word's origins. Write a paragraph about the word's emergence in English.
- **Book of Quotations:** Use an online or print collection of quotations to find a statement or passage containing one of the words. In a paragraph, explain nuances in meaning that are evident from the context of the quotation.

Comparing References Compare and contrast what you learn about the words from each specialized reference.

PHLit Online! www.PHLitOnline.com

from The Autobiography • Straw Into Gold: The Metamorphosis of the Everyday 157

◀ **Reading for Information** features nonfiction texts you will encounter in daily life.

Consumer Guide

EPA United States Environmental Protection Agency

WATER ON TAP
what you need to know

Where Does My Drinking Water Come From And How Is It Treated?

The headings anticipate questions readers may have.

Your drinking water comes from **surface water** or **ground water.** The water that systems pump and treat from sources open to the atmosphere, such as rivers, lakes, and reservoirs is known as surface water. Water pumped from wells drilled into underground aquifers, geologic formations containing water, is called ground water. The quantity of water produced by a well depends on the nature of the rock, sand, or soil in the aquifer from which the water is drawn. Drinking water wells may be shallow (50 feet or less) or deep (more than 1,000 feet). More water systems have ground water than surface water as a source (approx. 147,000 v. 14,500), but more people drink from a surface water system (195 million v. 101,400). Large-scale water supply systems tend to rely on surface water resources, while smaller water systems tend to use ground water. Your water utility or public works department can tell you the source of your public water supply.

How Does Water Get To My Faucet?
An underground network of pipes typically delivers drinking water to the homes and businesses served by the water system. Small systems serving just a handful of households may be relatively simple, while large metropolitan systems can be extremely complex—sometimes consisting of thousands of miles of pipes serving millions of people. Drinking water must meet required health standards when it leaves the treatment plant. After treated water leaves the plant, it is monitored within the distribution system to identify and remedy any problems such as water main breaks, pressure variations, or growth of microorganisms.

How Is My Water Treated To Make It Safe?
Water utilities treat nearly 34 billion gallons of water every day.[1] The amount and type of treatment applied varies with the source and quality of the water. Generally, surface water systems require more treatment than ground water systems because they are directly exposed to the atmosphere and runoff from rain and melting snow. Water suppliers use a variety of treatment processes to remove contaminants from drinking water. These individual processes can be arranged in a "treatment train" (a series of processes applied in a sequence). The most commonly used processes include coagulation (flocculation and sedimentation), filtration, and disinfection. Some water systems also use ion exchange and adsorption. Water utilities select the treatment combination most appropriate to treat the contaminants found in the source water of that particular system.

Coagulation (Flocculation & Sedimentation): *Flocculation:* This step removes dirt and other particles suspended in the water. Alum and iron salts or synthetic organic polymers are added to the water to form tiny sticky particles called "floc," which attract the dirt particles.

Informational Text: Consumer Guide 393

Comparing Literature Past and Present shows the continuity of ideas, themes, and styles. ▶

Essential Questions in American Literature

Sometimes, as you read individual stories, poems, or essays, you might feel as if you are acquiring small pieces of a puzzle. Each piece is brightly colored and interesting, but you cannot see how they all fit together. You may wonder, Why does this piece of literature matter? How does it relate to what I already know? You try to fit the new pieces into a bigger picture and give them meaning.

This textbook will help you create that bigger picture. On the following pages, you will find these three Essential Questions, tools for creating meaning from the literature you read:

- **What makes American literature American?**
- **What is the relationship between literature and place?**
- **How does literature shape or reflect society?**

This symbol will guide you to the Essential Questions in this book.

On the next three pages, the Essential Questions are accompanied by descriptions to guide your thinking. These questions re-appear throughout the introductions to units, at the end of every unit, and at the beginning and end of literary selections. You will have opportunities to reconsider them in the light of new information about a literary period or a new experience reading a literary work.

The questions do not have "yes" or "no" answers. They are meant to encourage you to take positions. Different people can answer them in different ways at different times. These large, open-ended questions will

- keep you thinking and making judgments about what you read,
- help you relate literary selections to one another and to larger ideas,
- provide a framework for discussing the selections with your classmates, and
- prompt you to create your own meaningful picture of American literature.

What makes American literature *American?*

In one sense, anything written in America is American. But in a deeper way, literature is "American" because it says something fundamental about our identity as Americans. In fact, literature may be the most powerful creative expression of our national and cultural identity.

The selections in this book will spread before you styles, images, expressions, characters, themes, and stories that are uniquely American. By addressing this Essential Question in different ways throughout the book, you will find yourself getting to the heart of American literature.

As you read, keep in mind what it means to be "American." After all, it is American literature that enables us to tell ourselves who we are.

Thematic Vocabulary

To help as you explore this Essential Question, use words like these:

beliefs	**heritage**	**liberty**
diversity	**immigration**	**self-reliance**
freedom	**individualism**	

"What then is the American, this new man?"

—Michel-Guillaume Jean de Crèvecoeur

What is the relationship between literature and place?

Europeans imagined America before they knew it. Columbus envisioned a fabled land of gold and spices. Ponce de León dreamt that Florida was the home of a Fountain of Youth. Puritans escaping persecution planned to build a City on a Hill where freedom would reign. Meanwhile, Native Americans told stories inspired by the natural world in which they dwelled.

To dwell in a place is to live in it fully, to merge its real life with the imaginative life you live there. As Emily Dickinson wrote, "I dwell in Possibility." How do Americans shape and reflect all the possibilities of their dwelling place on the earth? How does geography help make literature? Do Americans respond to nature in a unique way?

As you read the selections in this book, consider what it means to live—and to create literature—in a particular place at a particular time.

Thematic Vocabulary

To help as you explore this Essential Question, use words like these:

environment	**natural**	**resources**	**urban**
frontier	**range**	**rural**	**wilderness**
landscape	**region**		

"...offer thanks to the earth where men dwell..."

—The Iroquois Constitution

How does literature shape or reflect *society?*

Literature is a product of the society from which it springs, reflecting the values, concerns, and spirit of a people. However, literature can be more than a passive mirror. It can act as a force that changes or shapes a society. Novels, stories, plays, poems, and literary nonfiction made by writers can entertain, inform, persuade, challenge, and move readers, both singly and in great numbers. Writers are the entertainers who amuse, the critics who confront, the teachers who share wisdom, and—sometimes—the visionaries who lead the way to the future. Every day, writers celebrate America, define it, defy it, and tell its story. As you read this textbook and keep asking this Essential Question, you will become aware of the defining interactions between American society and its literature.

Thematic Vocabulary

To help as you explore this Essential Question, use words like these:

humorist	**regionalism**	**storytelling**
myth	**satire**	**vernacular**
persona	**social critic**	**visionary**

"In bombers named for girls, we burned The cities we had learned about in school—"

—Randall Jarrell

LITERARY MAP OF THE UNITED STATES

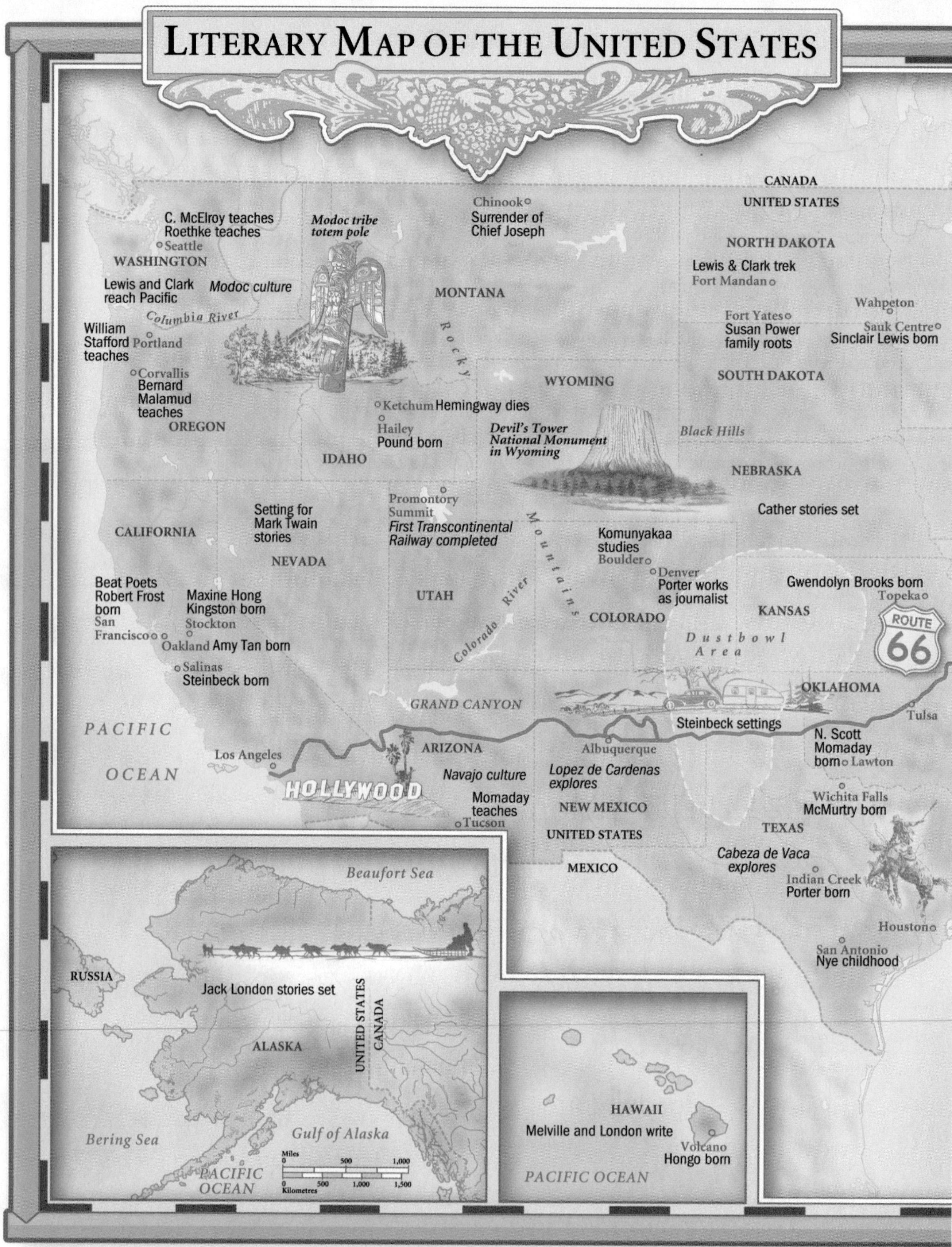

CANADA
UNITED STATES
C. McElroy teaches
Roethke teaches
Seattle
WASHINGTON
Modoc tribe totem pole
Chinook
Surrender of Chief Joseph
NORTH DAKOTA
Lewis & Clark trek
Fort Mandan
Lewis and Clark reach Pacific
Modoc culture
MONTANA
Columbia River
William Stafford teaches
Portland
Corvallis
Bernard Malamud teaches
OREGON
Rocky Mountains
Wahpeton
Fort Yates
Susan Power family roots
Sauk Centre
Sinclair Lewis born
SOUTH DAKOTA
WYOMING
Ketchum
Hemingway dies
Hailey
Pound born
IDAHO
Devil's Tower National Monument in Wyoming
Black Hills
NEBRASKA
Promontory Summit
First Transcontinental Railway completed
Cather stories set
CALIFORNIA
Setting for Mark Twain stories
NEVADA
Komunyakaa studies
Boulder
Denver
Porter works as journalist
Beat Poets
Robert Frost born
San Francisco
Maxine Hong Kingston born
Stockton
Oakland
Amy Tan born
Salinas
Steinbeck born
UTAH
Colorado River
COLORADO
Gwendolyn Brooks born
Topeka
KANSAS
ROUTE 66
Dustbowl Area
GRAND CANYON
OKLAHOMA
Tulsa
Steinbeck settings
PACIFIC OCEAN
Los Angeles
HOLLYWOOD
ARIZONA
Navajo culture
Albuquerque
Lopez de Cardenas explores
N. Scott Momaday born
Lawton
Momaday teaches
Tucson
NEW MEXICO
UNITED STATES
MEXICO
Wichita Falls
McMurtry born
TEXAS
Cabeza de Vaca explores
Indian Creek
Porter born
Houston
San Antonio
Nye childhood
Beaufort Sea
RUSSIA
Jack London stories set
UNITED STATES
CANADA
ALASKA
Bering Sea
Gulf of Alaska
PACIFIC OCEAN
Miles
0
500
1,000
Kilometres
0
500
1,000
1,500
HAWAII
Melville and London write
Volcano
Hongo born
PACIFIC OCEAN

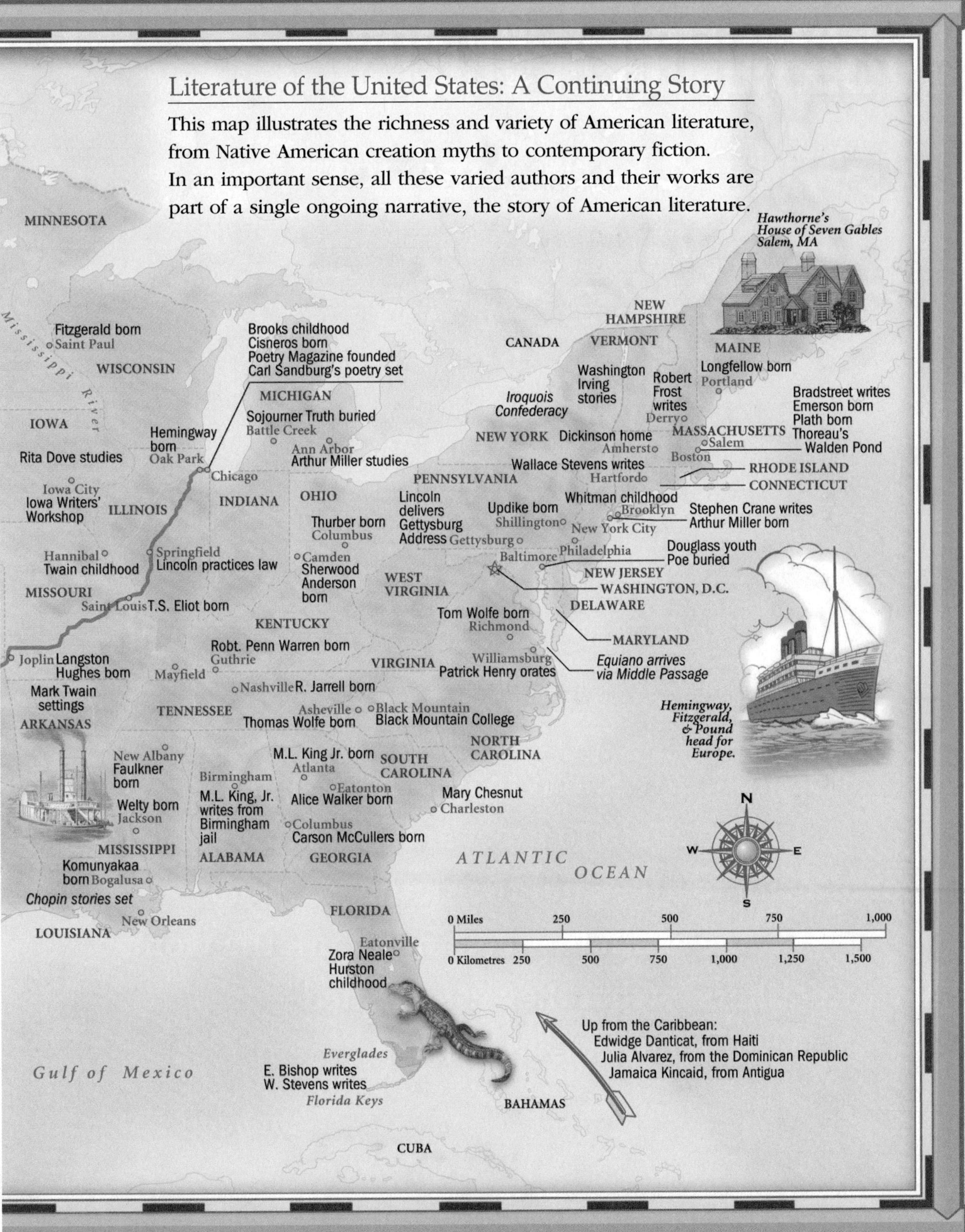

Literature of the United States: A Continuing Story
This map illustrates the richness and variety of American literature, from Native American creation myths to contemporary fiction. In an important sense, all these varied authors and their works are part of a single ongoing narrative, the story of American literature.
Hawthorne's House of Seven Gables Salem, MA
MINNESOTA
Mississippi River
Fitzgerald born
Saint Paul
WISCONSIN
Brooks childhood
Cisneros born
Poetry Magazine founded
Carl Sandburg's poetry set
MICHIGAN
Sojourner Truth buried
Battle Creek
Ann Arbor
Arthur Miller studies
IOWA
Hemingway born
Oak Park
Chicago
Rita Dove studies
Iowa City
Iowa Writers' Workshop
ILLINOIS
INDIANA
OHIO
Thurber born
Columbus
Hannibal
Twain childhood
Springfield
Lincoln practices law
Camden
Sherwood Anderson born
MISSOURI
Saint Louis
T.S. Eliot born
KENTUCKY
Joplin
Langston Hughes born
Robt. Penn Warren born
Guthrie
Mayfield
Nashville
R. Jarrell born
Mark Twain settings
ARKANSAS
TENNESSEE
Asheville
Black Mountain
Thomas Wolfe born
Black Mountain College
New Albany
Faulkner born
Birmingham
M.L. King Jr. born
Atlanta
Eatonton
Alice Walker born
Welty born
Jackson
M.L. King, Jr. writes from Birmingham jail
Columbus
Carson McCullers born
MISSISSIPPI
ALABAMA
GEORGIA
Komunyakaa born
Bogalusa
Chopin stories set
New Orleans
LOUISIANA
FLORIDA
Eatonville
Zora Neale Hurston childhood
Everglades
E. Bishop writes
W. Stevens writes
Florida Keys
Gulf of Mexico
CUBA
BAHAMAS
CANADA
NEW HAMPSHIRE
VERMONT
MAINE
Longfellow born
Portland
Washington Irving stories
Robert Frost writes
Derry
Iroquois Confederacy
NEW YORK
Dickinson home
Amherst
MASSACHUSETTS
Salem
Boston
Bradstreet writes
Emerson born
Plath born
Thoreau's Walden Pond
Wallace Stevens writes
Hartford
RHODE ISLAND
CONNECTICUT
PENNSYLVANIA
Lincoln delivers Gettysburg Address
Gettysburg
Updike born
Shillington
Whitman childhood
Brooklyn
New York City
Stephen Crane writes
Arthur Miller born
Philadelphia
Baltimore
Douglass youth
Poe buried
NEW JERSEY
WASHINGTON, D.C.
WEST VIRGINIA
DELAWARE
Tom Wolfe born
Richmond
MARYLAND
VIRGINIA
Williamsburg
Patrick Henry orates
Equiano arrives via Middle Passage
NORTH CAROLINA
SOUTH CAROLINA
Mary Chesnut
Charleston
Hemingway, Fitzgerald, & Pound head for Europe.
ATLANTIC OCEAN
N
W
E
S
0 Miles 250 500 750 1,000
0 Kilometres 250 500 750 1,000 1,250 1,500
Up from the Caribbean:
Edwidge Danticat, from Haiti
Julia Alvarez, from the Dominican Republic
Jamaica Kincaid, from Antigua

A Gathering of Voices

Literature of Early America

I come again to greet and thank the League;
    I come again to greet and thank the kindred;
I come again to greet and thank the warriors;
    I come again to greet and thank the women.
My forefathers—what they established—
    My forefathers—hearken to them!

- Iroquois Hymn

Unit 1

Beginnings to 1800

PHLit Online!
www.PHLitOnline.com

Hear It!
- Selection summary audio
- Selection audio

See It!
- Author videos
- Essential Question video
- Get Connected videos
- Background videos
- More about the authors
- Illustrated vocabulary words
- Vocabulary flashcards

Do It!
- Interactive journals
- Interactive graphic organizers
- Grammar tutorials
- Interactive vocabulary games
- Test practice

Snapshot of the Period

In 1492, North America was already populated by several hundred Native American tribes. More than 12,000 years before Christopher Columbus reached North America, nomadic peoples had migrated across the Bering Land Bridge from Asia and settled across the continent. These people spoke different languages and had very different cultures, but the Europeans called them all by one name: "Indians." In the centuries after Columbus, more and more Europeans ventured to the New World. Among them were explorers, fortune-seekers, missionaries, and those fleeing religious persecution. There were also enslaved Africans who made the journey against their will. Individuals from these groups wrote accounts of their experiences, creating the first written literature of North America. By 1699, European colonies dotted the entire Eastern seaboard and extended as far west as New Mexico. In 1776, thirteen of those colonies declared their independence from England.

▲ Political documents, such as the Constitution, recorded the new nation's founding principles. Wampum belts recorded important treaties of Eastern tribes.

The Iroquois

Bradstreet

Wheatley

Jefferson

Equiano

Franklin

As you read the selections in this unit, you will be asked to think about them in view of three key questions:

What is the **relationship** between literature and *place?*

How does **literature** shape or reflect *society?*

What makes **American** literature *American?*

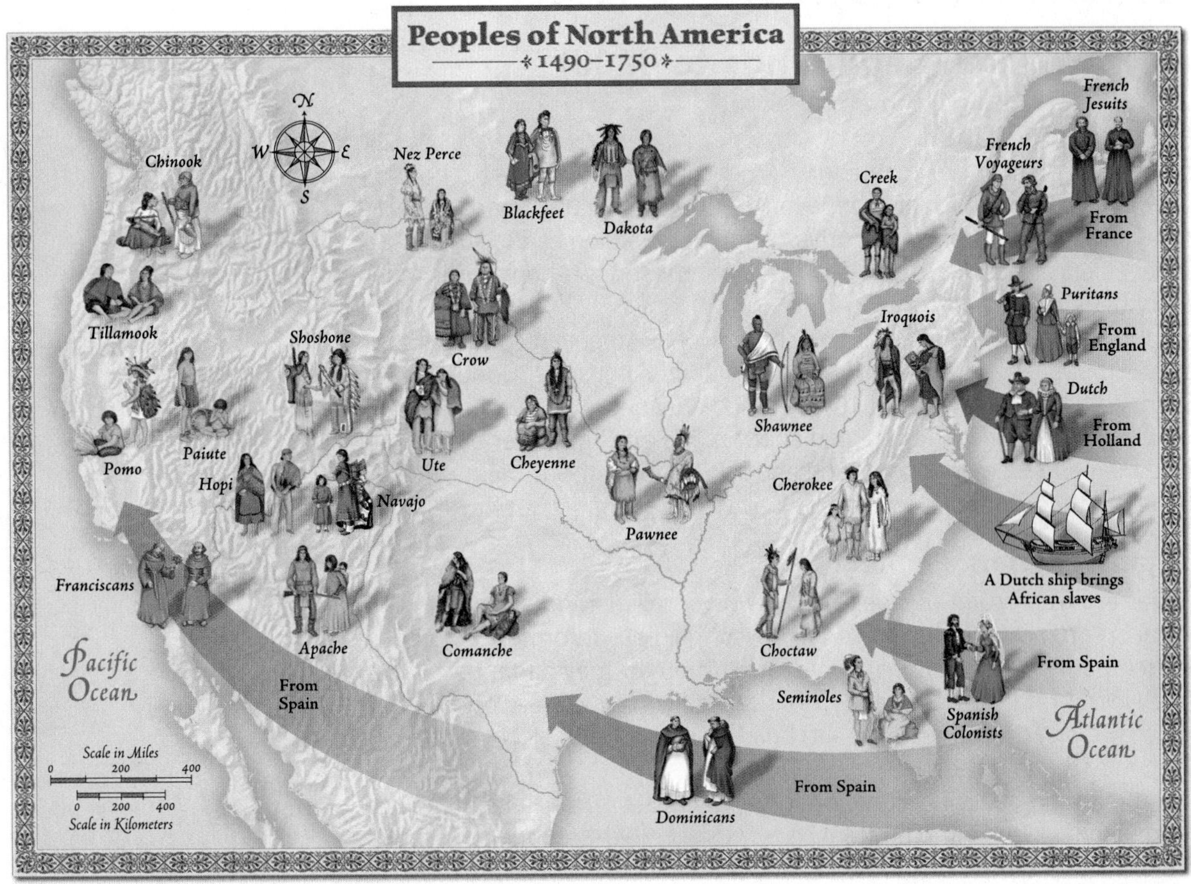

European exploration of North America quickly led to settlement and colonization. The Spaniards settled in Florida, then sent Jesuit and Franciscan missionaries to California and Texas. The French settled in Maine and along the Gulf of Mexico, while the Dutch established New Amsterdam (New York) and communities reaching south to Delaware. English Puritans settled Virginia, New England, and Pennsylvania and later took over the Dutch and French colonies and Florida. This influx of Europeans had a lasting impact on Native Americans, whose lifestyles and territories were increasingly restricted.

Integration of Knowledge and Ideas Based on the information in this map, what can you predict about the interactions among these various groups? Think about the ways in which different groups might form alliances, react to newcomers, or protect their territories. Explain your predictions.

Historical Background

Early America (Beginnings to 1800)

The First Americans

No one knows when or how the first Americans arrived in what is now the United States. It was probably between 12,000 and 70,000 years ago. The rich cultural presence of Native American tribes spanned the continent, and Native American oral literature—myths, legends, songs—begins our American literary heritage.

Colonists from Europe did not reach the North American continent until the late 1500s. The Europeans who settled at St. Augustine, Florida, in 1565 and at Jamestown, Virginia, in 1607 learned agriculture and woodcraft from the Native Americans. They learned about maize and squash and bark canoes. These men and women were tough and hardy, but without the help of those who knew the wilderness intimately, they would probably not have survived.

Puritans, Pilgrims, Planters

After a terrifying ocean voyage, the *Mayflower* sailed into harbor at Plymouth, Massachusetts, in 1620. Its passengers were religious reformers who had tried to "purify" the Church of England but thought they had a better chance in the New World. These Puritans, now called Pilgrims, gave every ounce of energy—and often their lives—to build a "city upon a hill," a model community based on the Bible.

Puritanism gradually declined, but around 1720 a revival called the Great Awakening brought some new converts. Genuine old-fashioned Puritanism never reawakened, although the "Puritan ethic" of hard work and self-discipline remained a basic American value.

The Southern Colonies differed from New England in climate, crops, social organization, and religion. Large plantations, not small farms, were the core of the economy, and slaves, who had been first brought to Virginia in 1619, were the core of the plantations. Planters thought of themselves as hardworking but aristocratic, and their way of life was more sociable and elegant than that of the Puritans.

TIMELINE

1490

1492: Christopher Columbus lands in the Bahamas. ▶

▲ **1499: England** 20,000 die in London Plague.

The Age of Reason

The Enlightenment shocked Puritan beliefs. Inspired by brilliant scientists such as Galileo and Newton, and philosophers such as Voltaire and Rousseau, the thinkers of this time valued science, logic, and reason over faith. They believed that people are good by nature and capable of building a better society. They spoke of a "social contract" that forms the basis of government, an idea that laid the groundwork for the American Revolution.

The Birth of the Nation

Taxes, taxes, and more taxes imposed by Britain kept beating down American colonists. The Stamp Act, the Townshend Acts, the Tea Act, the Coercive Acts—by 1774 the colonists had had enough. They met in Philadelphia for the First Continental Congress, and in 1775, minutemen at Lexington and Concord fired "the shot heard 'round the world."

Six long years of bloodshed followed. At Bunker Hill, Saratoga, and many other sites, colonists fought alongside French and African American soldiers, until the British finally surrendered at Yorktown in 1781. Even then, the "united" states disagreed fiercely among themselves until the Constitution and Bill of Rights were ratified.

Heroes of the Revolution—Washington and Adams—became the first two presidents. Thomas Jefferson, a hero of the Enlightenment, became the third. By 1800, the United States of America had firmly established its political identity. It would soon establish its cultural identity as well.

Key Historical Theme: Creating a Nation

- Europeans came to America to create a "city upon a hill," an ideal community founded on moral and religious values.
- Colonists, with the help of Native Americans, learned to make the wilderness productive, on both small farms and large plantations.
- The United States arose from Enlightenment ideas—that people are basically good and can use reason to create a better society.

1508: **Italy** Michelangelo begins painting ceiling of Sistine Chapel. ▼

1513: Juan Ponce de León lands on the Florida peninsula.

1513: Vasco Nuñez de Balboa reaches the Pacific Ocean.

▲ 1519: Magellan begins voyage around the world.

1519: **Spain** Chocolate introduced to Europe.

1521: **Mexico** Cortés conquers the Aztecs.

1555

Essential Questions Across Time

Early America (Beginnings to 1800)

THE ESSENTIAL
What is the relationship between literature and place?

What was the New World's natural environment?

About one century before the colonists arrived in North America, many people thought that crossing the Atlantic Ocean meant sailing off the edge of the earth. Instead, the first European colonists found a continent more magnificent, strange, and dangerous than any of them had ever imagined.

Place of Wonder The colonists discovered long shores and sandy beaches backed by vast forests. They found ranges of mountains and fertile valleys and an astounding variety of plants, fish, birds, and animals. Nature in America was built on an immense scale. The wilderness looked endless. Nevertheless, for all its intimidating size and wild variety, this new place had one overwhelmingly satisfying quality: It was not Europe.

At One with the Place From the beginning, then, America was a place apart—but it was not so in the eyes of the Native Americans. In fact, for most Native American cultures, the people belonged to the land. The deep forests and wide plains were simply to be used and cared for by the human beings who lived in them temporarily. The lands and waters were life-giving environments, and the animals were part of the community. The facts of nature could be harsh, but they were also to be celebrated in myths, rituals, and songs. Nature was not to be feared as an enemy or overcome as an obstacle, but honored as the source of life.

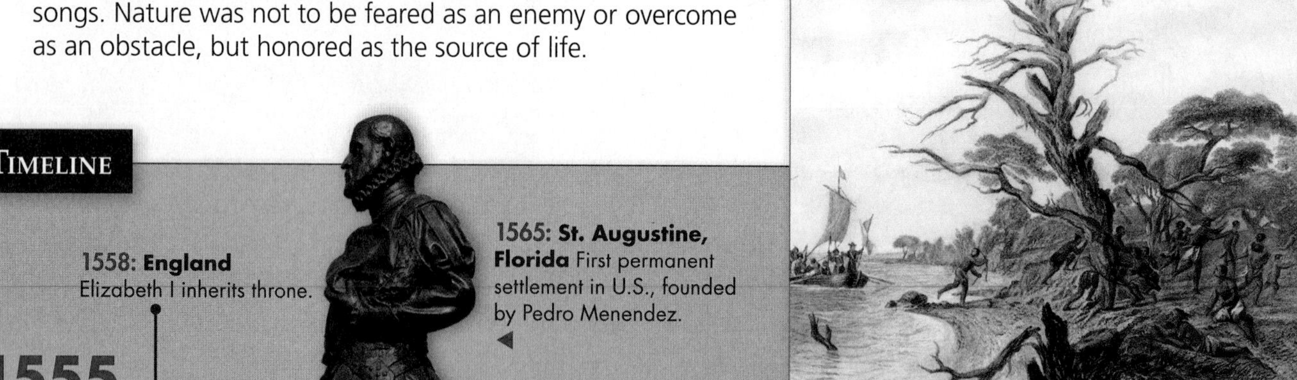

TIMELINE

1555

1558: **England** Elizabeth I inherits throne.

1565: **St. Augustine, Florida** First permanent settlement in U.S., founded by Pedro Menendez. ◀

1570: Iroquois Confederacy established to stop warfare among the Five Nations.

▲ 1587: English colony at Roanoke Island disappears; known as the Lost Colony.

What were the colonists' attitudes toward the New World environment?

For the colonists, the people did not belong to the land. Quite the opposite: Land belonged to people, and this land was to be claimed by Britain, France, and Spain. It was measured, divided, bought, sold, and governed as the property of European kings and trading companies. The Puritans, filled with religious zeal, may have wanted to build a "city upon a hill," but the hill would still belong to the King of England.

Dream vs. Reality During the seventeenth century, the colonists' attitude toward the American environment was a blend of dream and reality. The dream was to create a theocracy, an earthly community governed by religious principles. The reality was to avoid starving to death or falling prey to cold, disease, or animals. The colonists saw the continent's raw beauty, rich resources, and awe-inspiring possibilities. They also felt every day the hard facts of staying alive.

Independent Place and People By the eighteenth century, Europeans had gained a more secure foothold in America. Tree by tree, they had tamed a portion of the wilderness and built towns, roads, schools, and churches. They began to worry less about survival and more about self-government. They began to ask, "We live in an independent place, so why aren't we an independent people?" The effects of the Enlightenment began to set in, and people realized that they could belong to themselves rather than to a monarch. The spirit of self-reliance that had faced down the wilderness was the same spirit that would face down European kings. The place itself had taught Americans how to be Americans.

The American EXPERIENCE

A LIVING TRADITION

Anne Bradstreet and John Berryman

In the 1950s, American poet John Berryman responded powerfully to the life and work of Puritan poet Anne Bradstreet, who had lived 300 years earlier. In his long poem of praise called "Homage to Mistress Bradstreet," he reveals his understanding of her struggle to survive and to be a writer in seventeenth-century America. He imagines her winter ordeals and asserts that he is more sympathetic to her poetry than was her busy husband, Simon.

from "Homage to Mistress Bradstreet"

Outside the New World winters in grand dark
white air lashing high thro' the virgin stands

foxes down foxholes sigh,
surely the English heart quails, stunned.
I doubt if Simon than this blast, that sea,
spares from his rigor for your poetry
more. We are on each other's hands
who care. Both of our worlds unhanded us.
Lie stark,

thy eyes look to me mild. Out of maize & air
your body's made, and moves. I summon, see,
from the centuries it. . .

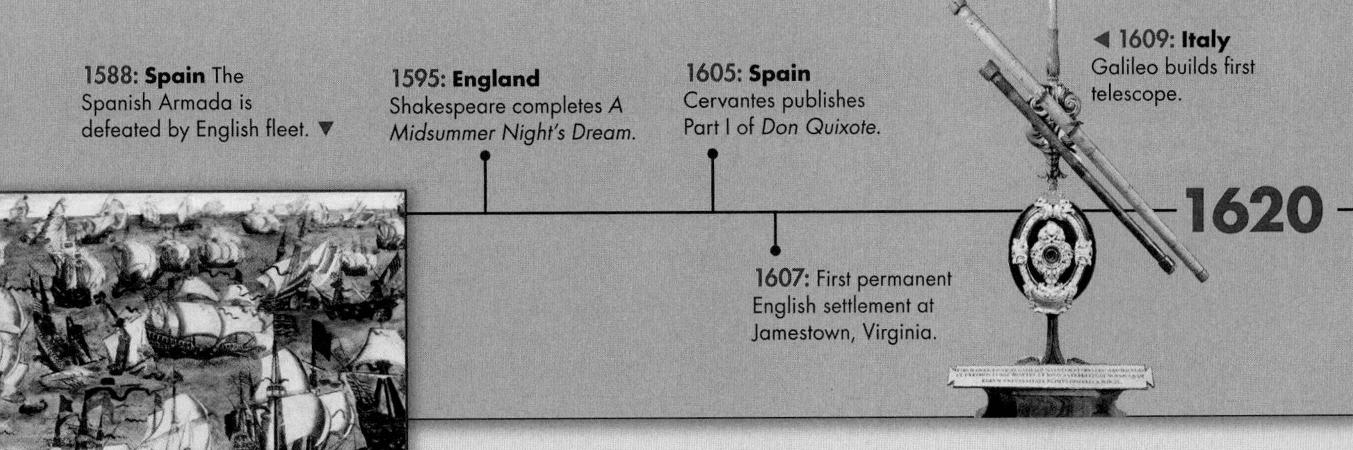

1588: Spain The Spanish Armada is defeated by English fleet. ▼

1595: England Shakespeare completes *A Midsummer Night's Dream.*

1605: Spain Cervantes publishes Part I of *Don Quixote.*

1607: First permanent English settlement at Jamestown, Virginia.

◀ **1609: Italy** Galileo builds first telescope.

How did attitudes toward nature show up in literature?

The close relationship between Native Americans and nature showed up in myths and legends. In these stories, people communicate with mountains and rivers. People and animals talk with each other and sometimes even change into each other. Human beings and nature live in harmony.

When the earliest explorers searched the continent, their responses to the land appeared in their journals and in the reports and letters they sent back home. Cabeza de Vaca recorded the natural wonders of the New World. William Bradford's *Of Plymouth Plantation*, the finest written work of the first European Americans, is filled with detailed descriptions of creating a colony in a place so delightful and so dangerous.

"Errand into the Wilderness" America's first literary family—Richard, Increase, and Cotton Mather—saw the environment from a religious point of view. Their writings describe a mission to combat evil in an "uncivilized" place. In time, this idea of the wilderness as a dark place of evil profoundly affected other writers. Forests and wild places play a large role, physically and symbolically, in the writings of American writers who would come later, including Washington Irving, James Fenimore Cooper, Nathaniel Hawthorne, and Mark Twain.

Place and Nation As the colonies developed, the power of reason began to make the continent a more hospitable place. Technology improved and agriculture flourished. In *Letters from an American Farmer*, Jean de Crèvecoeur even used the imagery of growing plants to emphasize the important idea that living in this particular place turned Europeans into Americans: "In Europe they were as so many useless plants ... they withered and were mowed down by want, hunger, and war; but now by the power of transplantation, like all other plants they have taken root and flourished!" The very name of the new nation reveals the influence of place: The "United States of America" is made of separate distinct places (states) united into one—a federal republic.

ESSENTIAL QUESTION VOCABULARY

These Essential Question words will help you think and write about literature and place:

magnificent (mag nif′ə sənt) *adj.* grandly beautiful; impressive

obstacle (äb′stə kəl) *n.* something that impedes progress

resources (rē′ sôrs əs) *n.* natural sources of wealth, such as land or minerals

TIMELINE

1620

1620: Pilgrims land at Plymouth, Massachusetts. ▼

1632: **India** Mughal Emperor Shah Jahan begins building the Taj Mahal as tomb for his wife Mumtaz. ▶

"For we must consider that we shall be a city upon a hill. The eyes of all people are upon us."
—John Winthrop, Governor of the Massachusetts Bay Colony from 1629–1649

1639: First printing press in English-speaking North America arrives in Massachusetts.

1640: *Bay Psalm Book* published; first book printed in the colonies.

What makes American literature *American?*

American literature, naturally, shares the basic characteristics of all literature—characters, plots, settings, images, and themes. However, American literature is much more than literary works written by Americans. It also embodies certain ideas, evokes certain places, and tells stories of certain kinds of characters. There are qualities that distinguish American literature and make it a unique cultural expression.

What is a theme, and how does it find expression in literature?

A theme is the central idea, message, or insight that a literary work reveals. A theme is not the subject of a work, but rather the insight that the work reveals about the subject. A work reveals its themes through characters' words and actions, through details of setting and plot, through imagery, and even through language and style.

What were early American themes?

Three themes dominate early American writing:

Wilderness Writers revealed insights into the nature and meaning of the wilderness by the details they used to describe it and by the stories they told of their physical, political, and spiritual struggles with it.

The American EXPERIENCE

DEVELOPING AMERICAN ENGLISH

Our Native American Heritage by Richard Lederer

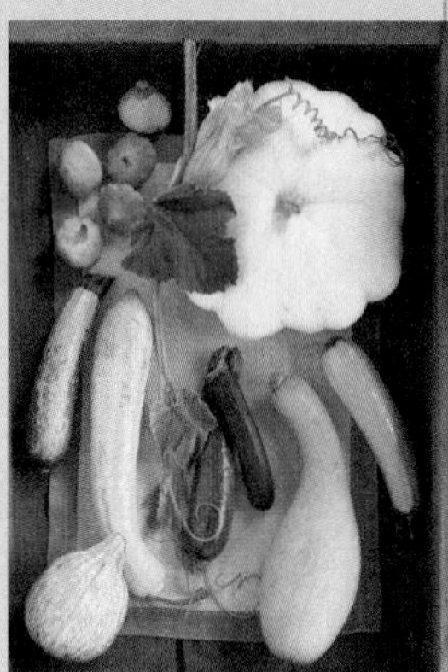

If you had been a settler in North America, you would have found many things in your new environment unknown to you. The handiest way of filling voids in your vocabulary would have been to ask local Native Americans what words they used. Colonists began borrowing words from Native Americans almost from the moment of their first contact, and many of those shared words have remained in our everyday language. They are part of what makes American literature American.

Anglicizing Pronouncing many of the Native American words was difficult for the colonists, so they often shortened or simplified the words. For example, *askútasquash* became "squash," *otchock* became "woodchuck," *rahaugcum* turned into "raccoon," and the smelly *segankw* transformed into "skunk." The North American menagerie brought more new words into the English language, including *caribou* (Micmac), *chipmunk* (Ojibwa), *moose* (Algonquian), and *muskrat* (Abenaki).

The Poetry of Place Names Some of our loveliest place names—*Susquehanna, Shenandoah, Rappahannock*—began life as Native American words. Such names are the stuff of poetry. Colonists freely used words of Indian origin to name states (half of all of them), cities, towns, mountains, lakes, rivers, and ponds.

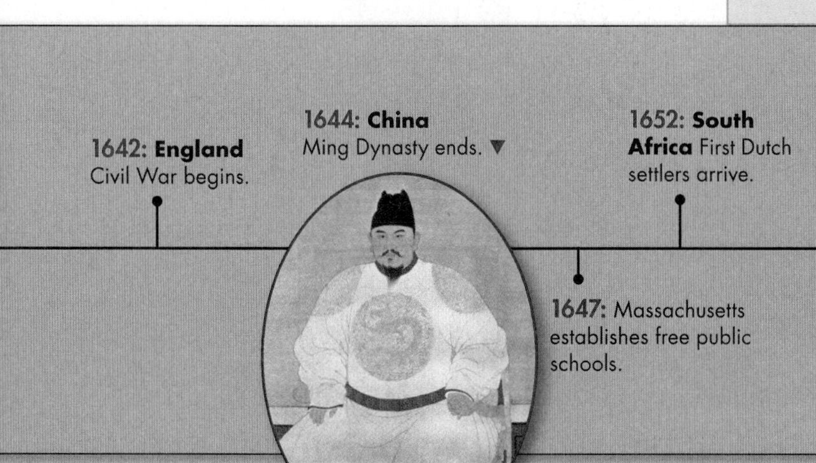

1642: **England** Civil War begins.

1644: **China** Ming Dynasty ends. ▼

1647: Massachusetts establishes free public schools.

1652: **South Africa** First Dutch settlers arrive.

◄ 1667: **England** Milton publishes *Paradise Lost.*

1685

Community In public writing such as pamphlets and newspapers, colonists and patriots conveyed the central message that America was a unique combination of community and independence.

Individualism In history and memoir, and in everything from laws to lyric poems, writers made clear that self-reliance and individualism are fundamental American values.

What is uniquely American about those themes?

The Place Americans recognized that they were in a unique place, a New World, only a small part of which they had even seen. Nothing in their European experience had prepared them for the splendors and the terrors of the American wilderness. Sometimes, America seemed to be the Garden of Eden, a newly created place of natural wealth. Sometimes, it seemed to be an enemy, a punishment, or a source of fear and death. These themes entered into the American literary imagination.

The Past When Americans wrote, they were aware of the many traditional European subjects and themes that were now of no importance to them. After all, there had been no Middle Ages or Renaissance in America. Europeans had medieval romances that told tales of knights and chivalry; Americans did not. Europeans had Shakespeare's tragedies of kings and princes; Americans did not. Europeans had a heritage of elegant and witty writing; Americans had a plain, straightforward way of writing. Americans did have histories and journals, prayers and sermons, speeches and essays. They even had some poems, but all of these imitated European styles. With the turn of the nineteenth century, American writers would begin to forge unique ways of expressing their unique experience.

The Vision The themes of independence and self-reliance are at the heart of Americans' vision of themselves as a new and unique people. They knew they were creating not only a new nation but a new kind of nation. That sense of newness marked Americans as a people of youth, innocence, optimism, risk-taking, and boundless originality.

ESSENTIAL QUESTION VOCABULARY

These Essential Question words will help you think and write about American literature:

independence (in′dē pen′ dəns) *n.* freedom from the control of others

straightforward (strāt for′ wərd) *adj.* direct; clear-cut

optimism (äp′ tə miz′ əm) *n.* hopefulness; a tendency to anticipate the best

TIMELINE

1685

1690: **India** Calcutta founded by the British.

1692: Salem witchcraft trials result in the execution of twenty people. ▼

▲ 1721: **Germany** Bach composes *The Brandenburg Concertos.*

1726: **England** Jonathan Swift publishes *Gulliver's Travels.* ▼

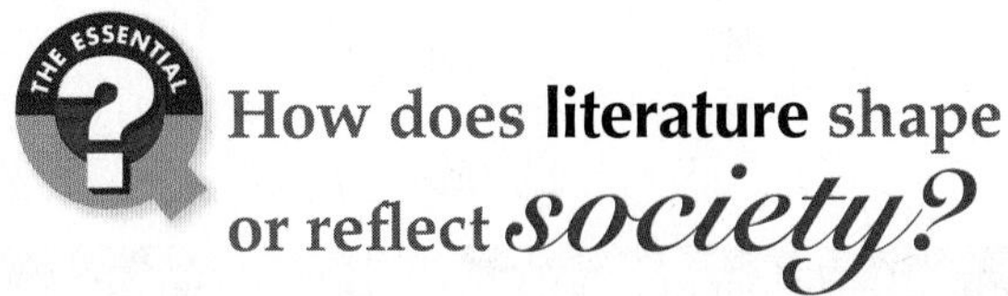

How does **literature** shape or reflect *society?*

What social and political forces affected early American literature?

Puritanism From the first, Puritanism influenced just about every aspect of colonial life. The impulse to escape to a New World and build a reformed and uncorrupted society shaped Puritan lawmaking, social relations, and daily life. Belief in predestination—John Calvin's doctrine that God has already decided who will be saved—made Puritans search every thought, action, and word for signs of grace. In hymns, sermons, histories, journals, and autobiographies, they aimed only for self-examination and spiritual insight.

The Enlightenment By the eighteenth century, the power of reason asserted itself in America. In speeches, pamphlets, essays, and newspaper articles, the spirit of the times called for debate, clear thinking, and reorganization of the political situation. The Declaration of Independence, for example, is not an outcry or an anarchic demand. It is a reasoned document, a controlled statement of the rational argument for independence.

Native Americans and African Americans Relations with Native Americans and the continued enslavement of African Americans left deep marks in American literature. In histories and captivity narratives, we have some record of relationships between colonists and Native

The American EXPERIENCE

CLOSE-UP ON HISTORY

African Americans and Women in the Revolution

In 1776, more than half a million African Americans lived in the colonies. At first, the Continental Congress did not permit enslaved or free African Americans to join the American army. However, when the British offered to free any male slave who fought for the king, George Washington changed American policy and allowed free African Americans to enlist. About 5,000 African Americans fought against the British. As this eyewitness account demonstrates, they fought with great courage:

Three times in succession, [African American soldiers] were attacked . . . by well-disciplined and veteran British troops, and three times did they successfully repel the assault, and thus preserve our army from capture.

Women also helped in the struggle for independence from Great Britain. When men went off to war, the women took on added work. They planted and harvested crops, and they made shoes and blankets and uniforms. Many followed their husbands and brothers to the front, where they washed, cooked, and cared for the wounded. Some even took part in battle, including a brave woman named Mary Hays, who carried water on the battle lines and became known as Molly Pitcher.

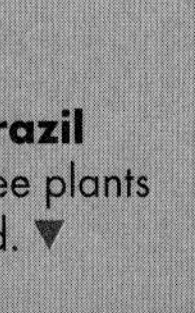

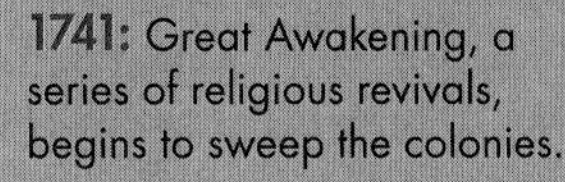

1727: Brazil First coffee plants cultivated. ▼

1735: John Peter Zenger acquitted of libel, furthering freedom of the press.

1741: Great Awakening, a series of religious revivals, begins to sweep the colonies.

▲ **1741:** Jonathan Edwards first delivers his sermon "Sinners in the Hands of an Angry God."

1748: France Montesquieu publishes *The Spirit of the Laws*, which later influences the U.S. Constitution.

1750

The American EXPERIENCE

CONTEMPORARY CONNECTION

Thomas Paine: Essayist, Hero of the Revolution...Father of the Internet?

Thomas Paine believed that knowledge is power and that it belongs to all people, not just the wealthy or privileged. He believed that through knowledge, ordinary people could guarantee their own freedoms. Even at a time when the printed word was slow to publish and distribute, Paine's fiery words brought change, fueling both the American and the French revolutions.

While this pamphleteer and passionate advocate of communication is often seen as a pioneer of investigative journalism, perhaps his true legacy is the Internet. Writing in *Wired News* (issue 3.05–May 1995), journalist Jon Katz observed that regarding the Internet, Paine's "ideas about communications, media ethics, the universal connections between people, and the free flow of honest opinion are all relevant again, visible every time one modem shakes hands with another."

Paine once said, "Such is the irresistible nature of truth that all it asks, and all it wants, is the liberty of appearing." When the Internet is used in its best and highest forms, truth becomes available to anyone with a computer. Thomas Paine, advocate of "all mankind," might recognize the Internet as the true product of his own ideals.

TIMELINE

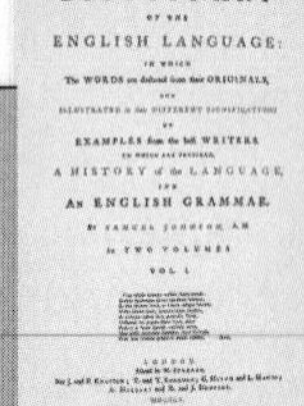

◀ 1755: **England** Samuel Johnson publishes *Dictionary of the English Language.*

1750

1754: French and Indian War begins.

1773: Parliament's Tea Act prompts Boston Tea Party. ▼

▲ 1775: American Revolution begins.

Americans, relationships that ranged from trust to distrust, from friendship to hatred. In narratives left by both slaves and slaveholders, we find heartrending stories of individuals, families, and communities scarred by slavery.

What were the major roles of early American writers?

Writers not only reflect the social and political forces of their societies, they also influence those forces. They are not just the mirrors of their cultures and their communities; they can also be the fires that make those communities burn with hope, anger, love, idealism, and creativity.

Writer as Oral Poet and Historian Native American oral poets held places of vital importance for their tribes. They told each community's story, related its history, and honored its heroes. Those European Americans who wrote journals and histories fulfilled a similar role—recording the social and political events that gave meaning to their community's experience. The narratives of de Cárdenas and Cabeza de Vaca, as well as William Bradford's *Of Plymouth Plantation,* give us perspective on our own heritage.

Writer as Preacher and Lawmaker The writers of hymns and sermons believed that their role was to articulate the will of God. Cotton Mather and Jonathan Edwards explained for their communities the working of divine Providence in the wilderness, and they did their utmost to instill the fear of God into every member of their trembling audiences. The writers of America's laws and political documents had a different role—to articulate the will of the people. Thomas Paine's pamphlets, Patrick Henry's speeches, and Thomas Jefferson's multifaceted writing survive today not only as a part of history but also as literature.

Writer as Autobiographer The autobiographer's role goes beyond answering the basic question, "What did I do and why did I do it?" The autobiographer also asks, "Why should you be interested in my life? What did I learn from it? What can you learn from it?" The slave narrative of Olaudah Equiano helped Americans face their own history and ultimately do something about it. Benjamin Franklin's *Autobiography* combined a fascinating life story with explorations of essential American values.

ESSENTIAL QUESTION VOCABULARY

These Essential Question words will help you think and write about literature and society:

rational (rash′ən əl) *adj.* based on reason, not emotion

articulate (är tik′ yo͞o lāt) *v.* express in words

idealism (ī dē′ əl iz′ əm) *n.* belief that one should live according to one's ideals, or high principles

1776: Second Continental Congress adopts Declaration of Independence.

"Any people that would give up liberty for a little temporary safety deserves neither liberty nor safety."
—Benjamin Franklin

1786: **Austria** Wolfgang Amadeus Mozart creates the comic opera *The Marriage of Figaro.* ▶

1787: Constitutional Convention meets in Philadelphia to draft the Constitution.

▲ 1789: George Washington elected first President of the United States.

1800

Recent Scholarship

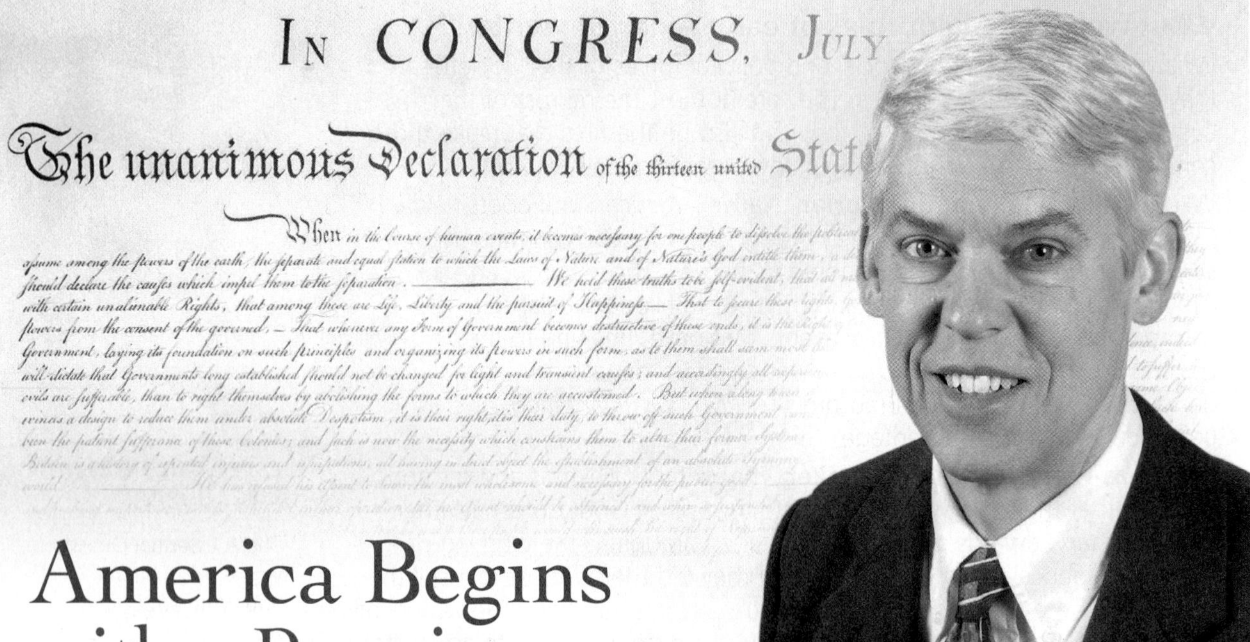

America Begins with a Promise and a Paradox

William L. Andrews

It's not just a coincidence that America's earliest literature is highly autobiographical. Nor is it by accident that autobiography emerged as a literary form about the same time that the United States became a new nation. Autobiography and America were made for each other.

The Promise: A New Person and a New Country

The revolution in the United States created a new person, as well as a new country. At least that's what the great spokesmen and propagandists of the Revolution, especially Thomas Jefferson, Patrick Henry, and Benjamin Franklin, claimed. Franklin, who wore a coonskin cap to the royal courts of Europe, became famous for inventing everything from streetlights to eyeglasses. But we read him today because his greatest invention was himself. Franklin gave the new nation (which he also helped to invent) its first literary classic. *The Autobiography of Benjamin Franklin* is the first great American success story: a tale of a poor boy who made good.

About the Author

William L. Andrews is an award-winning scholar and teacher whose work focuses on the historical links between white and black writers in the formation of American literature. In addition to his many scholarly publications, he has co-edited three major literature anthologies: *The Norton Anthology of African American Literature, The Oxford Companion to African American Literature,* and *The Literature of the American South: A Norton Anthology.* Andrews is currently the E. Maynard Adams Professor of English at the University of North Carolina, Chapel Hill.

The Paradox: Freedom and Slavery

In 1789 Franklin, head of Pennsylvania's largest antislavery society, signed a petition to Congress advocating an end to slavery. In the same year, a pioneering African American autobiography, *The Interesting Narrative of the Life of Olaudah Equiano,* adapted the success story to antislavery purposes. Before the American Revolution got under way, Phillis Wheatley, an African-born slave in Boston, published a book of poetry, written in the learned and ornate style of the day to show that the enslaved were just as intelligent and capable as their so-called masters. Yet when the revolutionary orator Patrick Henry demanded in 1775, "Give me liberty or give me death!" no one asked whether the slaves he held on his Virginia plantation deserved the same freedom he so passionately proclaimed.

When I was in the sixth grade in a public school not far from Patrick Henry's plantation, I studied Virginia history, a mandatory subject at the time. I remember learning then that my home state was "the mother of presidents." My teacher didn't mention that all of Virginia's great heroes, including Washington and Jefferson, were slaveholders as well. No one, not even the framers of the U.S. Constitution in 1787, had found a way to justify the presence of slavery in a land supposedly dedicated to freedom. Eventually the only solution to America's political paradox was civil war.

▲ **Critical Viewing** What image of the founding fathers—Franklin, Adams, and Jefferson—does this painting create? Which details support your response? **[Analyze]**

America's Destiny and a Persistent Question

Ever since the founding of the United States, Americans have trumpeted the new country's special destiny: to create a new form of government, democracy, that would reform humankind itself. The transplanted Frenchman Jean de Crèvecoeur believed that democracy would inspire in all who had immigrated to America an "original genius" that would bind them together in a shared national identity. America's dedication to human rights, particularly "life, liberty, and the pursuit of happiness," would give the new people of America a grand ideal and mission. The most important writers of the early Republic extolled the nation's founding ideals but often questioned the national commitment to them. Then as now we ask of ourselves: Has America become what Jefferson and Crèvecoeur imagined?

© Speaking and Listening: Collaboration

William L. Andrews raises an important question at the end of his essay: Has the United States become the country early citizens imagined? Conduct a **full-class discussion** about this issue. Work together to achieve the following goals:

- Determine the ideals held by Jefferson and his contemporaries.
- Come to a consensus about whether modern America has fulfilled these ideals.

As you conduct your discussion, work to engage everyone equally. Respond thoughtfully to different opinions and perspectives and resolve any contradictions. Cite specific examples from multiple relevant sources to support your opinions.

Integrate and Evaluate Information

1. Use a chart like the one shown to determine the key ideas expressed in the Essential Question essays on pages 6–13. Fill in two ideas related to each Essential Question, and note the groups most closely associated with each concept. One example has been done for you.

Essential Question	Key Concept	Group
Literature and Place		
American Literature	Self-determination	Revolutionaries like Thomas Jefferson
Literature and Society		

2. How do the visual sources in this section—illustrations, photographs, and maps—add to your understanding of the ideas expressed in words? Cite specific examples.
3. The Enlightenment belief in human goodness fueled the politics and literature of the American Revolution. How do other Revolutionary themes reflect a similar view of human nature? What conflicts with this optimism do you find in Puritan attitudes or other aspects of early colonial life? In your answer, cite evidence from the multiple sources presented on pages 4–15.
4. **Address a Question** William L. Andrews states that the American Revolution created "a new person, as well as a new country." What do you think "a new person" means? Does this idea still inform American identity? Integrate information from this textbook and other sources to support your ideas.

Reading Informational Text
7. Integrate and evaluate multiple sources of information presented in different media or formats as well as in words in order to address a question or solve a problem.

Speaking and Listening
1.b. Work with peers to promote civil, democratic discussions and decision-making, set clear goals and deadlines, and establish individual roles as needed. *(p. 15)*

Speaking and Listening: Oral Presentation

The spoken word had great power in early America. With a small group, research one of the early American spoken forms listed below. Then, develop an **oral presentation** in which you perform an example of the form.

- Native American oral histories
- Puritan sermons or hymns
- Early American speeches
- Revolutionary War songs

Solve a Research Problem: This assignment requires you to locate texts from the oral tradition, many of which predate recording devices. Formulate a plan to meet this research challenge. Identify print and media sources that provide reliable information about the content and style of forms in the oral tradition. Consider primary sources, such as journals, newspapers, and illustrations from the colonial era. Also consider secondary sources, such as writings by historians, interviews with scholars, and modern recordings, plays, or other dramatic interpretations. As part of your presentation, explain the process you used to identify information and solve the research problem.

ESSENTIAL QUESTION VOCABULARY

Use these words in your responses:

Place and Literature
wilderness
splendor
terrors

American Literature
independence
optimism
community

Literature and Society
govern
doctrine
heritage

For definitions and pronunciations, see the Glossary, pp. R1–R7.

PART 1

Meeting of Cultures

Before You Read

The Earth on Turtle's Back • *When Grizzlies Walked Upright* • from *The Navajo Origin Legend*

Connecting to the Essential Question These myths reveal the deep connections Native Americans saw between human society and the natural world. As you read, notice the qualities attributed to natural elements. Doing so will help as you consider the Essential Question: **What is the relationship between literature and place?**

Common Core State Standards

Reading Literature
2. Determine two or more themes or central ideas of a text and analyze their development over the course of the text, including how they interact and build on one another to produce a complex account.

Literary Analysis

An **origin myth** is a traditional story that explains how life began. Often, origin myths also explain how a feature of the world was formed or how a specific social custom began. As part of the *oral tradition*, myths were shared by generations of storytellers before being written down.

Like other stories, myths express **themes,** insights about life or the human condition. Because they have many layers of meaning, myths may even convey multiple themes. Often, myths from different places and times express similar themes. Such universal messages may be conveyed in **archetypes**—symbols, patterns, or character types that repeat across cultures. For example, these myths place archetypal significance on the cardinal directions:

> *Then they told the people to stand at a distance and allow the wind to enter. The white wind blew from the east, and the yellow wind blew from the west.*

Comparing Literary Works As you read these myths, look for patterns of events, images, or character types that might be *archetypes.* Compare and contrast the themes these archetypes carry in each myth.

Reading Strategy

Preparing to Read Complex Texts When you **establish a purpose for reading,** you determine the main reason for which you are reading a particular work—to learn, to be entertained, and so on. One purpose for reading these myths would be to learn about the *cultural characteristics* of Native American peoples. As you read, look for details that show how the people of each culture live, think, or worship. Use a chart like the one shown to record your observations.

Details	Cultural Characteristics
Chief says wife's dream has power.	Onondaga believe dreams convey messages.

Vocabulary

unconscious (un kän′ shəs) *adj.* having temporarily lost awareness; in a faint (p. 23)

depths (depths) *n.* the deepest areas (p. 23)

ancestors (an′ ses′ tərz) *n.* people from whom other people descend (p. 26)

protruded (prō tro͞o′ did) *v.* stuck out (p. 28)

ONONDAGA Tellers of "The Earth on Turtle's Back"

The Onondaga were key members of the Five Nations, or Iroquois Confederacy, in what is now upstate New York. Like other Iroquois, they lived in villages of wood-and-bark long houses occupied by related families. After siding with the British during the American Revolution, some Onondaga left for Canada after the British defeat. However, the majority returned to their ancestral valley in central New York state, near the lake that bears their name.

MODOC Tellers of "When Grizzlies Walked Upright"

The Modoc traditionally lived in what is now southern Oregon and northern California. There they farmed, fished, hunted, and became famous for their weaving. In the mid-nineteenth century, when the government tried to force the Modoc onto a reservation, they fought the resettlement under a leader known as Captain Jack. After several years of hostilities with United States troops, Captain Jack and his followers were forced to relocate to Oklahoma, although some were later able to return to Oregon.

NAVAJO Tellers of "The Navajo Origin Legend"

The largest Native American nation in the United States, the Navajo settled in the Southwest about a thousand years ago. Fierce warriors and hunters, they learned weaving and farming from the nearby Pueblo peoples, with whom they intermarried. Today, many Navajo live on a reservation that covers 24,000 square miles in Arizona, Utah, and New Mexico. Many Navajo still carry on their ancient customs, living in cone-shaped structures called hogans and practicing their tribal religion.

THE EARTH ON TURTLE'S BACK

ONONDAGA-NORTHEAST WOODLANDS
RETOLD BY MICHAEL CADUTO
& JOSEPH BRUCHAC

BACKGROUND Native Americans have great respect for the natural world. They believe that each living thing possesses a unique power that sustains it and affects others. This power is part of a greater power, which many Native American cultures recognize as a Great Spirit—the source of all life. These beliefs are reflected in Native American myths, such as the stories that follow.

Before this Earth existed, there was only water. It stretched as far as one could see, and in that water there were birds and animals swimming around. Far above, in the clouds, there was a Skyland. In that Skyland there was a great and beautiful tree.

Critical Viewing
What story could you tell to explain the markings on the turtle shell in this picture? **[Apply]**

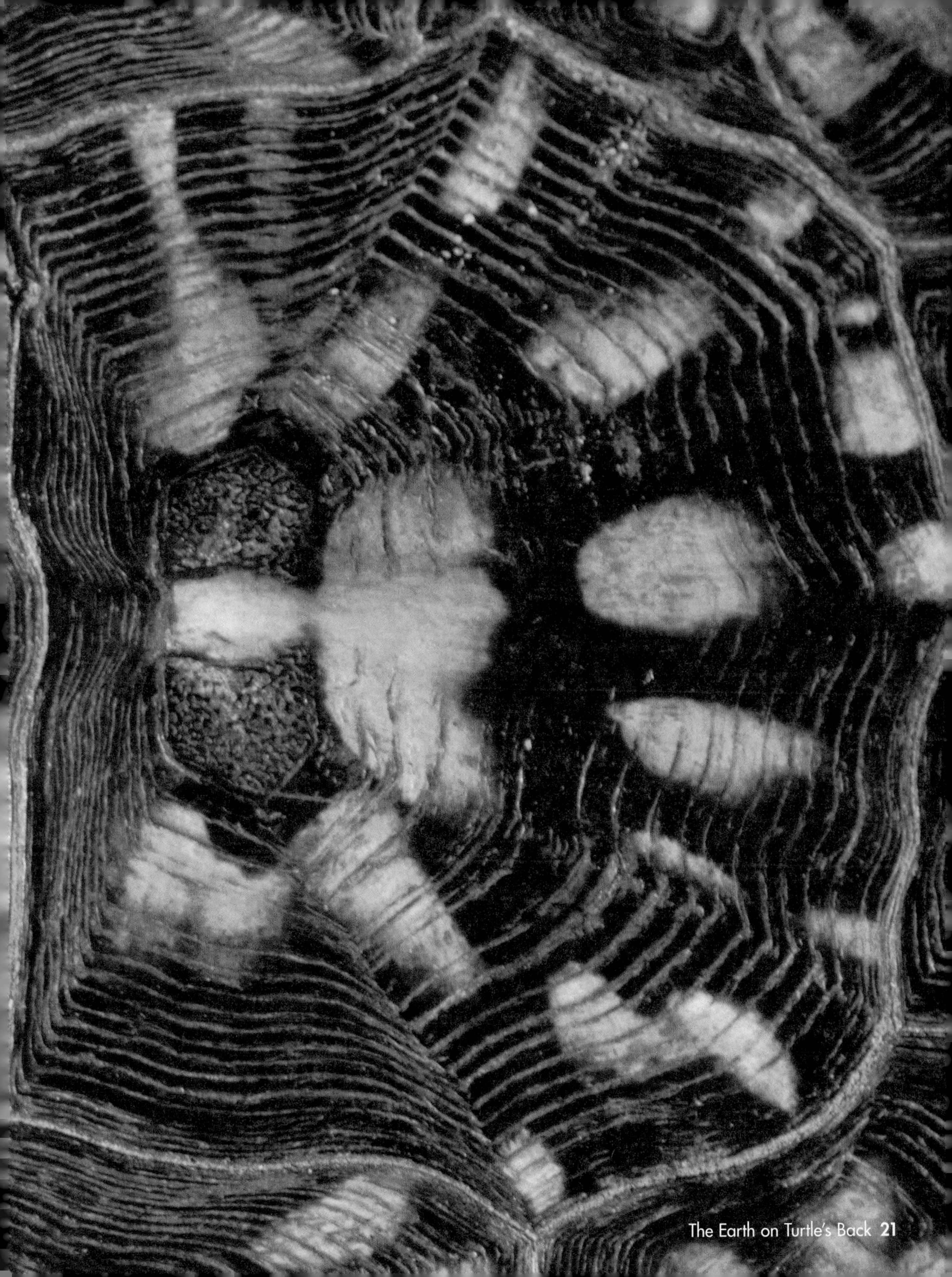

Literary Analysis
Origin Myths
How do the opening words of this story identify it as an origin myth?

Reading Strategy
Purpose for Reading: Cultural Characteristics
What does the chief's reaction to his wife's dream tell you about Onondaga beliefs?

Literary Analysis
Origin Myths
Why might characters in creation myths have generic names like "the Duck" or "the Beaver"?

It had four white roots which stretched to each of the sacred directions,[1] and from its branches all kinds of fruits and flowers grew.

There was an ancient chief in the Skyland. His young wife was expecting a child, and one night she dreamed that she saw the Great Tree uprooted. The next day she told her husband the story.

He nodded as she finished telling her dream. "My wife," he said, "I am sad that you had this dream. It is clearly a dream of great power and, as is our way, when one has such a powerful dream we must do all we can to make it true. The Great Tree must be uprooted."

Then the Ancient Chief called the young men together and told them that they must pull up the tree. But the roots of the tree were so deep, so strong, that they could not budge it. At last the Ancient Chief himself came to the tree. He wrapped his arms around it, bent his knees and strained. At last, with one great effort, he uprooted the tree and placed it on its side. Where the tree's roots had gone deep into the Skyland there was now a big hole. The wife of the chief came close and leaned over to look down, grasping the tip of one of the Great Tree's branches to steady her. It seemed as if she saw something down there, far below, glittering like water. She leaned out further to look and, as she leaned, she lost her balance and fell into the hole. Her grasp slipped off the tip of the branch, leaving her with only a handful of seeds as she fell, down, down, down, down.

Far below, in the waters, some of the birds and animals looked up.

"Someone is falling toward us from the sky," said one of the birds.

"We must do something to help her," said another. Then two Swans flew up. They caught the Woman From The Sky between their wide wings. Slowly, they began to bring her down toward the water, where the birds and animals were watching.

"She is not like us," said one of the animals. "Look, she doesn't have webbed feet. I don't think she can live in the water."

"What shall we do, then?" said another of the water animals.

"I know," said one of the water birds. "I have heard that there is Earth far below the waters. If we dive down and bring up Earth, then she will have a place to stand."

So the birds and animals decided that someone would have to bring up Earth. One by one they tried.

The Duck dove first, some say. He swam down and down, far beneath the surface, but could not reach the bottom and floated back up. Then the Beaver tried. He went even deeper, so deep that it all was dark, but he could not reach the bottom, either. The Loon tried, swimming with his strong wings. He was gone a long long time, but he, too, failed to bring up Earth. Soon it seemed that all had tried and all had failed. Then a small voice spoke.

"I will bring up Earth or die trying."

1. **the sacred directions** North, South, East, and West.

They looked to see who it was. It was the tiny Muskrat. She dove down and swam and swam. She was not as strong or as swift as the others, but she was determined. She went so deep that it was all dark, and still she swam deeper. She swam so deep that her lungs felt ready to burst, but she swam deeper still. At last, just as she was becoming unconscious, she reached out one small paw and grasped at the bottom, barely touching it before she floated up, almost dead.

When the other animals saw her break the surface they thought she had failed. Then they saw her right paw was held tightly shut.

"She has the Earth," they said. "Now where can we put it?"

"Place it on my back," said a deep voice. It was the Great Turtle, who had come up from the depths.

They brought the Muskrat over to the Great Turtle and placed her paw against his back. To this day there are marks at the back of the Turtle's shell which were made by the Muskrat's paw. The tiny bit of Earth fell on the back of the Turtle. Almost immediately, it began to grow larger and larger and larger until it became the whole world.

Then the two Swans brought the Sky Woman down. She stepped onto the new Earth and opened her hand, letting the seeds fall onto the bare soil. From those seeds the trees and the grass sprang up. Life on Earth had begun.

Vocabulary

unconscious (un kän′ shəs) *adj.* temporarily lost awareness; in a faint

depths (depths) *n.* the deepest areas

...THE TREES AND THE GRASS SPRANG UP. LIFE ON EARTH HAD BEGUN.

Critical Reading

Cite textual evidence to support your responses.

1. **Key Ideas and Details (a)** What happens to the young wife after the chief uproots the Great Tree? **(b) Interpret:** Why does this event generate concern among the animals?
2. **Key Ideas and Details (a)** What actions do the animals take when they realize the wife of the chief cannot live in water? **(b) Generalize:** How do these actions exhibit the best aspects of human nature?
3. **Craft and Structure (a)** What does the description of the Muskrat stress about her physical qualities? **(b) Interpret:** What message about human achievement is conveyed by the success of the Muskrat after the other creatures could not accomplish the same task?
4. **Integration of Knowledge and Ideas (a)** How would you characterize the Muskrat's swim and her decision to make it? **(b) Apply:** How does society benefit from actions like those of the Muskrat?

When Grizzlies Walked Upright

Modoc

Retold by
Richard Erdoes
and Alfonso Ortiz

Before there were people on earth, the Chief of the Sky Spirits grew tired of his home in the Above World, because the air was always brittle with an icy cold. So he carved a hole in the sky with a stone and pushed all the snow and ice down below until he made a great mound that reached from the earth almost to the sky. Today it is known as Mount Shasta.

Then the Sky Spirit took his walking stick, stepped from a cloud to the peak, and walked down the mountain. When he was about halfway to the valley below, he began to put his finger to the ground here and there, here and there. Wherever his finger touched, a tree grew. The snow melted in his footsteps, and the water ran down in rivers.

The Sky Spirit broke off the small end of his giant stick and threw the pieces into the rivers. The longer pieces turned into beaver and otter; the smaller pieces became fish. When the leaves dropped from the trees, he picked them up, blew upon them, and so made the birds. Then he took the big end of his giant stick and made all the animals that walked on the earth, the biggest of which were the grizzly bears.

Now when they were first made, the bears were covered with hair and had sharp claws, just as they do today, but they walked on two feet and could talk like people. They looked so fierce that the Sky Spirit sent them away from him to live in the forest at the base of the mountain.

Pleased with what he'd done, the Chief of the Sky Spirits decided to bring his family down and live on earth himself. The mountains of snow and ice became their lodge. He made a big fire in the center of the mountain and a hole in the top so that the smoke and sparks could fly out. When he put a big log on the fire, sparks would fly up and the earth would tremble.

Late one spring while the Sky Spirit and his family were sitting round the fire, the Wind Spirit sent a great storm that shook the top of the mountain. It blew and blew and roared and roared. Smoke blown back into the lodge hurt their eyes, and finally the Sky Spirit said to his youngest daughter, "Climb up to the smoke hole and ask the Wind Spirit to blow more gently. Tell him I'm afraid he will blow the mountain over."

As his daughter started up, her father said, "But be careful not to stick your head out at the top. If you do, the wind may catch you by the hair and blow you away."

The girl hurried to the top of the mountain and stayed well inside the smoke hole as she spoke to the Wind Spirit. As she was about to climb back down, she remembered that her father had once said you could see the ocean from the top of their lodge. His daughter wondered what the ocean looked like, and her curiosity got the better of her. She poked her head out of the hole and turned toward the west, but before she could see anything, the Wind Spirit caught her long hair, pulled her out of the mountain, and blew her down over the snow and ice. She landed among the scrubby fir trees at the edge of the timber and snow line, her long red hair trailing over the snow.

There a grizzly bear found the little girl when he was out hunting food for his family. He carried her home with him, and his wife brought her up with their family of cubs. The little red-haired girl and the cubs ate together, played together, and grew up together.

When she became a young woman, she and the eldest son of the grizzly bears were married. In the years that followed they had many children, who were not as hairy as the grizzlies, yet did not look exactly like their spirit mother, either.

All the grizzly bears throughout the forests were so proud of these new creatures that they made a lodge for the red-haired mother and her children. They placed the lodge near Mount Shasta—it is called Little Mount Shasta today.

After many years had passed, the mother grizzly bear knew that she would soon die. Fearing that she should ask of the Chief of the Sky Spirits to forgive her for keeping his daughter, she gathered all the grizzlies at the lodge they had built. Then she sent her eldest grandson in a cloud to the top of Mount Shasta, to tell the Spirit Chief where he could find his long-lost daughter.

Literary Analysis
Origin Myths
What natural feature of the world does the Sky Spirit create in this passage?

"But be careful not to stick your head out at the top. If you do, the wind may catch you by the hair and blow you away."

Who finds the red-haired daughter of the Sky Spirit?

Reading Strategy
Purpose for Reading: Cultural Characteristics
What does the Sky Spirit's reaction to his daughter and grandchildren suggest about Modoc attitudes toward obedience?

Vocabulary
ancestors (an´ ses´ tərz) *n.* people from whom other people descend

When the father got this news he was so glad that he came down the mountainside in giant strides, melting the snow and tearing up the land under his feet. Even today his tracks can be seen in the rocky path on the south side of Mount Shasta.

As he neared the lodge, he called out, "Is this where my little daughter lives?"

He expected his child to look exactly as she had when he saw her last. When he found a grown woman instead, and learned that the strange creatures she was taking care of were his grandchildren, he became very angry. A new race had been created that was not of his making! He frowned on the old grandmother so sternly that she promptly fell dead. Then he cursed all the grizzlies:

"Get down on your hands and knees. You have wronged me, and from this moment all of you will walk on four feet and never talk again."

He drove his grandchildren out of the lodge, put his daughter over his shoulder, and climbed back up the mountain. Never again did he come to the forest. Some say that he put out the fire in the center of his lodge and took his daughter back up to the sky to live.

Those strange creatures, his grandchildren, scattered and wandered over the earth. They were the first Indians, the **ancestors** of all the Indian tribes.

That's why the Indians living around Mount Shasta would never kill a grizzly bear. Whenever a grizzly killed an Indian, his body was burned on the spot. And for many years all who passed that way cast a stone there until a great pile of stones marked the place of his death.

"Get down on your hands and knees. You have wronged me, and from this moment all of you will walk on four feet and never talk again."

from The Navajo Origin Legend

Retold by Washington Matthews

On the morning of the twelfth day the people washed themselves well. The women dried themselves with yellow cornmeal; the men with white cornmeal. Soon after the ablutions were completed they heard the distant call of the approaching gods.[1] It was shouted, as before, four times—nearer and louder at each repetition—and, after the fourth call, the gods appeared. Blue Body and Black Body each carried a sacred buckskin. White Body carried two ears of corn, one yellow, one white, each covered at the end completely with grains.

The gods laid one buckskin on the ground with the head to the west; on this they placed the two ears of corn, with their tips to the east, and over the corn they spread the other buckskin with its head to the east; under the white ear they put the feather of a white eagle,

1. **the approaching gods** the four Navajo gods: White Body, Blue Body, Yellow Body, and Black Body.

under the yellow ear the feather of a yellow eagle. Then they told the people to stand at a distance and allow the wind to enter. The white wind blew from the east, and the yellow wind blew from the west, between the skins. While the wind was blowing, eight of the Mirage People[2] came and walked around the objects on the ground four times, and as they walked the eagle feathers, whose tips protruded from between the buckskins, were seen to move. When the Mirage People had finished their walk the upper buckskin was lifted; the ears of corn had disappeared, a man and a woman lay there in their stead.

Vocabulary
protruded (prō tro͞od′ id) *v.* stuck out

The white ear of corn had been changed into a man, the yellow ear into a woman. It was the wind that gave them life. It is the wind that comes out of our mouths now that gives us life. When this ceases to blow we die. In the skin at the tips of our fingers we see the trail of the wind; it shows us where the wind blew when our ancestors were created.

> The white ear of corn had been changed into a man, the yellow ear into a woman.

The pair thus created were First Man and First Woman (Atsé Hastin and Atsé Estsán). The gods directed the people to build an enclosure of brushwood for the pair. When the enclosure was finished, First Man and First Woman entered it, and the gods said to them: "Live together now as husband and wife."

2. **Mirage People** mirages personified.

Critical Reading

Cite textual evidence to support your responses.

1. **Key Ideas and Details (a)** In the Modoc myth, what do the grizzly bears do that angers the Chief of the Sky Spirits? **(b) Analyze:** What does the Chief's reaction tell you about his character?
2. **Key Ideas and Details (a)** What punishment does the Chief of the Sky Spirits give the grizzlies? **(b) Analyze Cause and Effect:** How does this action affect his grandchildren, the people of the Earth?
3. **Key Ideas and Details (a)** What is the wind's role in the Navajo ceremony? **(b) Speculate:** Why might the Navajo have viewed the wind as a source of life?
4. **Integration of Knowledge and Ideas (a) Summarize:** Summarize the steps of the Navajo creation ceremony. **(b) Analyze:** What does the ceremony show about Navajo attitudes toward order and ritual?
5. **Integration of Knowledge and Ideas** What do the qualities these mythmakers saw in nature show about the human traits they valued? In your response, use at least two of these Essential Question words: *environment, landscape, profound, cultivate.* ***[Connecting to the Essential Question: What is the relationship between literature and place?]***

After You Read

The Earth on Turtle's Back • *When Grizzlies Walked Upright* • from *The Navajo Origin Legend*

Literary Analysis

1. **Key Ideas and Details** **(a)** In which **origin myth** is the creation of the Earth unintentional, or almost an accident? **(b)** In which myth is the world's creation the result of a deliberate series of actions? Explain your answers.
2. **Key Ideas and Details** **(a)** In addition to the origins of life on Earth, what features of the land does the Modoc myth explain? **(b)** What social customs does the myth explain? **(c)** What does this suggest about the ways members of the Modoc tribe may have felt about the place in which they lived?
3. **Key Ideas and Details** **(a)** Which of the myths portrays the spirits or gods as generous and kind? **(b)** Which sees them as vengeful? Support your answers with details from the text.
4. **Key Ideas and Details** **(a)** In which myth is the world's creation the result of cooperation? **(b)** In which myth is it the result of aggression? **(c)** Do you think these differences suggest different views of life? Explain.
5. **Comparing Literary Works** **(a)** Using a chart like the one shown, note patterns, symbols, or character types that are similar in all three myths. **(b)** What common **themes** do these **archetypes** help express? Explain your thinking.

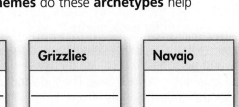

Details	Turtle's Back	Grizzlies	Navajo
Patterns			
Symbols			
Characters			

Reading Strategy

6. Assume that your **purpose for reading** these myths was to learn about the Native American cultures that produced them. **(a)** Identify at least two *cultural characteristics* that you learned from each myth. **(b)** What does each characteristic reveal about the general attitudes of the culture that produced it?
7. What similarities and differences do you see in the cultural attitudes expressed in these three myths? Explain your answers, citing details from the selections.
8. What are two other purposes you might have for reading these myths? Explain your answers.
9. Do the stories we tell today through film, TV, or books say something about who we are as a people? Explain your answer.

Common Core State Standards

Writing
3. Write narratives to develop real or imagined experiences or events using effective technique, well-chosen details, and well-structured event sequences. *(p. 30)*

Language
3.a. Vary syntax for effect. *(p. 31)*
4.a. Use context as a clue to the meaning of a word or phrase. *(p. 30)*

PERFORMANCE TASKS

Integrated Language Skills

Vocabulary Acquisition and Use

Word Analysis: Latin Root *-trud-* / *-trus-*

The Latin root *-trud-*, also spelled *-trus-*, means "push" or "thrust." Something that *protruded* was pushed out from where it was supposed to be. Use the context clues and your knowledge of the root *-trud-* / *-trus-* to explain the meaning of each italicized word below. Then, explain how the word's meaning reflects the meaning of the root.

1. Last night an *intruder* broke into the warehouse and robbed it.
2. The pastry bag *extruded* icing when the baker squeezed it.
3. In the quiet library, a noisy child is *obtrusive*.
4. Some uninvited guests are welcome, but others are simply *intrusive*.

Vocabulary: Context Clues

Answer each question. Then, explain how the context clues, or surrounding words and phrases, helped you determine your answer.

1. If Lola were *unconscious,* would you give her smelling salts or ask her to smile?
2. Which lives in the *depths* of the sea, an insect on the surface or a fish far below it?
3. Do people's *ancestors* usually inherit their money?
4. If a person's toes *protruded* from a sandal, could you see them, or would they be hidden?

Writing

Narrative Text Choose one of the three myths and turn it into a **play** that a group of classmates can perform for an audience.

Prewriting Reread the myth, listing each character and noting details about his or her appearance and personality. Also, list the various settings and jot down the actions that take place in each one. Then, decide if you will include a narrator who provides the audience with background information and transitions between scenes, or if you will rely solely on dialogue to tell the story.

Drafting List the characters. Then, organize the action into separate scenes that take place in each setting. Turn character's remarks or thoughts into dialogue. Use capital letters for the character names. Set stage directions that describe characters' behavior, tone, or actions in parentheses or brackets. Use italics to distinguish stage directions from dialogue.

Model: Setting Dialogue and Stage Directions

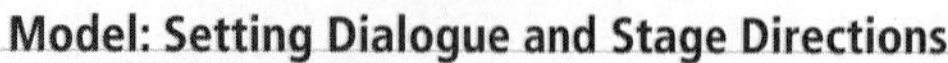

SPIRIT CHIEF [*angrily, stamping his feet*]: You have wronged me! You will now walk on all fours for eternity! [*The "bears" sink to their hands and knees and walk around the stage growling.*]

The use of italics and brackets clearly separates stage directions from dialogue.

Revising Read your draft aloud. If you find that some of the dialogue is hard to say, rewrite those sections so they sound more natural.

Conventions and Style: Coordinating Conjunctions

Include compound sentences in your writing by using **coordinating conjunctions** to combine short, choppy sentences. Coordinating conjunctions are words like *and, but, for, so,* and *yet* that connect words, phrases, or clauses of equal rank. Each coordinating conjunction shows a different relationship. For example, *and* shows addition or similarity, *but* and *yet* indicate contrast, and *or* and *nor* indicate a choice. *For* and *so* show a result.

Combining Sentences with Coordinating Conjunctions

Choppy: There was a great tree in Skyland. There was an ancient chief there, too.
Combined: There was a great tree *and* an ancient chief in Skyland.

Choppy: Several animals tried to swim the water's depths. The Muskrat succeeded.
Combined: Several animals tried to swim the water's depths, *but* the Muskrat succeeded.

Choppy: The Chief of the Sky Spirits must be strong. This being is in a position of power.
Combined: The Chief of the Sky Spirits must be strong, *for* he is in a position of power.

Punctuation Tip: If you use a coordinating conjunction to join two independent clauses, *place a comma before the coordinating conjunction.*

Practice In items 1–5, identify each coordinating conjunction and the words it connects. In items 6–10, combine the two sentences using a coordinating conjunction.

1. The Iroquois were five different tribes, yet they united to form one Indian nation.
2. The Sky Woman carries the seeds and allows them to fall.
3. The grizzlies were not supposed to act independently or challenge the chief.
4. Settlers conquered the Indians, but some tribes have survived.
5. Did the Modoc live in New York state or in Oregon?
6. The Chief of the Sky Spirits pledges to make the dream true. The Chief of the Sky Spirits is saddened by this pledge.
7. The chief has great power. He also has great responsibilities.
8. In one myth, an uprooted tree forms a hole in the sky. In another, a stone forms a hole.
9. They wanted potential allies to see the fire. They kept it burning constantly.
10. The woman gives her thanks to the swans. The woman gives her thanks to the turtle.

Writing and Speaking Conventions

A. Writing For each word pair listed below, write a sentence in which you link the two words or word groups using a coordinating conjunction. Then, tell what relationship is indicated by the conjunction.

1. swans—muskrat
2. under the sky—below the waters
3. the roots spread in all directions—they support the world

Example: swans—muskrat
Sentence: The swans and the muskrat display strength in different ways.
Relationship: similarity

B. Speaking Write and present a list of rules for your class. Use three different coordinating conjunctions. If you combine two independent clauses, remember to use a comma before the coordinating conjunction.

Further instruction and practice are available in *Prentice Hall Writing Coach.*

Susan Power Introduces

MUSEUM INDIANS

Bringing the Spark of Your Own Imagination The origin myths of the Onondaga, Modoc, and Navajo tribes, recounted on pages 20–28 of this textbook, are examples of the oral tradition, stories repeated within a community, passed down from one generation to the next, keeping them alive. These spoken stories are meant to be performed, acted out with great drama before a circle of avid listeners of all ages. Each retelling of the story changes it a little, the performer emphasizing one episode over another, choosing slightly different words each time. These stories are meant to be flexible, interactive—modified according to the present audience's mood and tastes.

So as you read these tales, try to imagine them being acted out. Try to hear the storyteller's voice changing as different characters speak, rising with excitement, falling to a whisper. Your imaginative spark is needed to bring these stories fully to life.

Exposed to Two Cultures I am a grateful listener, eager to hear a gripping yarn, but I myself am not a traditional storyteller. I was very shy as a child and found it difficult to stand before people and speak aloud either a story or an idea. I was silent in my classes, unless called upon, and preferred committing my words to quiet paper rather than the storm of conversation. I was raised to be both Native (Yanktonnai Dakota) and American, and so I was exposed not only to traditional Native American stories, songs, ceremonies, and dances, but also to the culture of mainstream America and the wider world.

Meet the Author

Susan Power is a member of the Standing Rock Sioux Tribe of Fort Yates, North Dakota. Her novel, *The Grass Dancer,* won the PEN/Hemingway Award for First Fiction. She has also written a book of stories and autobiographical essays entitled *Roofwalker.*

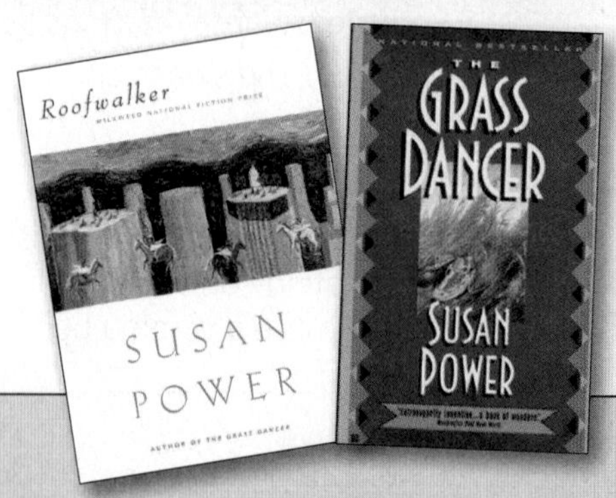

I loved reading and graduated from pop-up books and comics to the Nancy Drew mystery series and the *Chronicles of Narnia*. When I was about twelve, I began listening to recordings made of the plays of William Shakespeare and would memorize long passages that I delighted in performing privately, with no one but my mother and our cats to overhear. I didn't understand much of what was being spoken in the famous plays, but I was fascinated with the rhythmic poetry of the words, the dramatic plot lines, and thought to myself that Shakespeare would have felt at home in the Native world, dramatic as our oral literature can be.

Looking for My Own Experience I began writing my own poems, stories, essays, and political songs when I was very young—five or six years old. Perhaps I needed to write because, although I heard traditional stories of the people who came before me and inhabited this continent prior to European contact, and although I read dozens of books that taught me what it was like to live everywhere else in the world, I never found myself, my own experience, in either of these literatures: the oral tradition or the novels of the world. Where were the stories of little girls who attended church as well as a Native ceremony in the deep Wisconsin woods? Where were the books that told of a child who could perform a variety of traditional dances at an intertribal powwow and also excel in her ballet classes? I could not find myself on the literary map, and so I had to develop my own literature, plot my own place in this world.

But is my writing more Native than American? In my fiction and essays, Native American themes are emphasized—my characters believe, as I do, that everything is potentially alive, a creature of spirit, whether it be a person, an animal, a family car, a stone. But the language I use is English, the paintbrush of words I wield to draw you a picture of what I see with my eyes.

Oral Literature and Print The essay that follows, "Museum Indians," is a brief examination of my childhood in cultural terms—specifically, what it was like to be Native American in the city of Chicago. Notice that even though I have *written* several scenes describing adventures I shared with my mother, employing narrative strategies familiar to any reader of books, my mother is constantly *telling* me stories within the piece—instances of our own family oral tradition still in practice today. So I have captured the oral literature with my printed words.

Critical Reading

1. **Key Ideas and Details (a)** What reason does Power give to explain why she is not a traditional storyteller? **(b) Connect:** What life experiences do you think contributed to Power's decision to become a writer?
2. **Key Ideas and Details (a)** How does Power solve the problem of not finding her own experience in the literature she read as a child? **(b) Interpret:** According to Power, how do the dual influences of her childhood show up in her writing?

As You Read "Museum Indians" . . .

3. **Integration of Knowledge and Ideas** Look for details in the essay that show the contrast between the "Native" and the "American" that Power describes here.
4. **Integration of Knowledge and Ideas** Consider the ways in which Power is like her mother and the ways in which she is different.

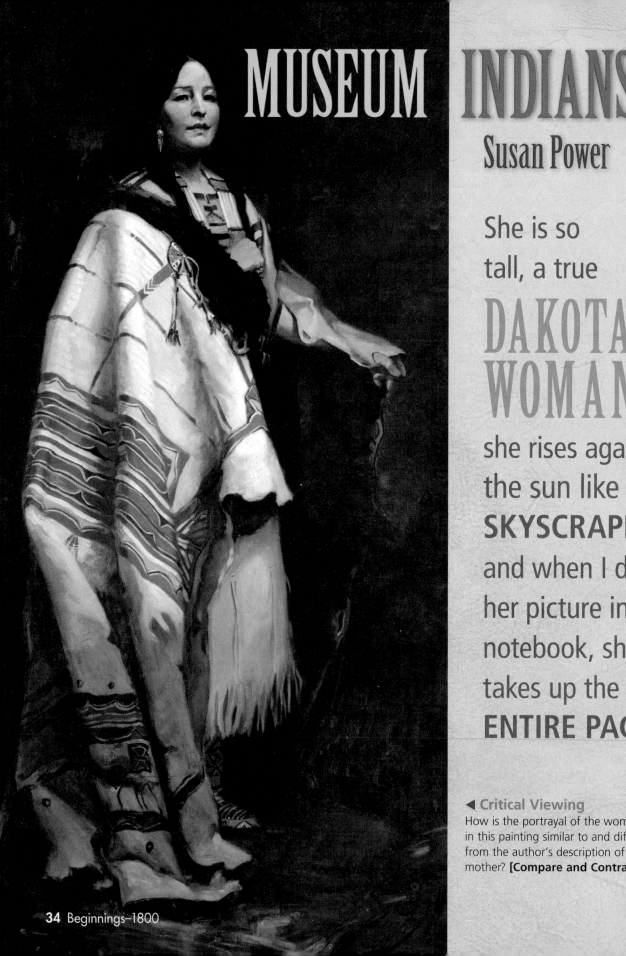

MUSEUM INDIANS

Susan Power

She is so tall, a true DAKOTA WOMAN; she rises against the sun like a **SKYSCRAPER,** and when I draw her picture in my notebook, she takes up the **ENTIRE PAGE.**

◀ **Critical Viewing**
How is the portrayal of the woman in this painting similar to and different from the author's description of her mother? **[Compare and Contrast]**

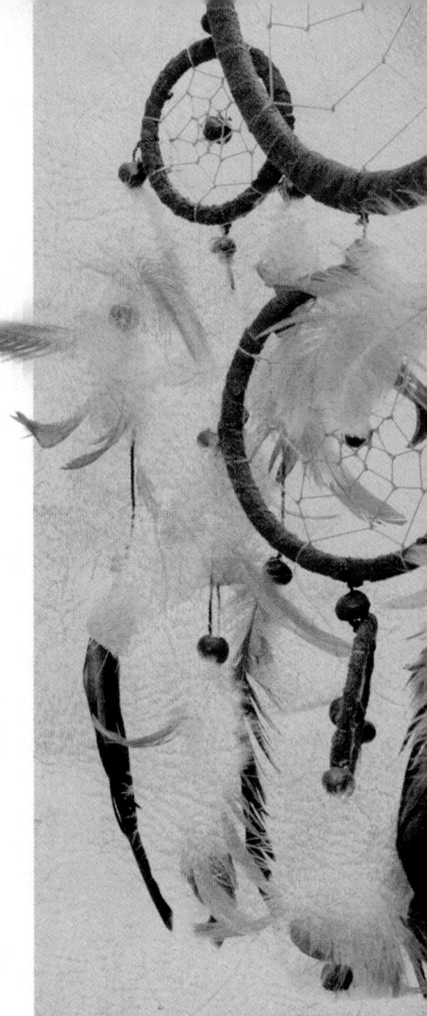

A snake coils in my mother's dresser drawer; it is thick and black, glossy as sequins. My mother cut her hair several years ago, before I was born, but she kept one heavy braid. It is the three-foot snake I lift from its nest and handle as if it were alive.

"Mom, why did you cut your hair?" I ask. I am a little girl lifting a sleek black river into the light that streams through the kitchen window. Mom turns to me.

"It gave me headaches. Now put that away and wash your hands for lunch."

"You won't cut my hair, will you?" I'm sure this is a whine.

"No, just a little trim now and then to even the ends."

I return the dark snake to its nest among my mother's slips, arranging it so that its thin tail hides beneath the wide mouth sheared by scissors. My mother keeps her promise and lets my hair grow long, but I am only half of her; my thin brown braids will reach the middle of my back, and in maturity will look like tiny garden snakes.

My mother tells me stories every day: while she cleans, while she cooks, on our way to the library, standing in the checkout line at the supermarket. I like to share her stories with other people, and chatter like a monkey when I am able to command adult attention.

Susan Power
Author's Insight
I compare my mother's braid to my own—hers is a "sleek black river," mine are "tiny garden snakes"—to underscore my childhood impression that I was so much smaller and weaker, a diluted version.

What does the author's mother do every day?

Susan Power

Author's Insight

I describe my mother as a "skyscraper" so the reader will have a visual image of my child's-eye view of her as a towering force.

Vocabulary

integral (in´ tə grəl) *adj.* essential

petrified (pe´ trə fīd´) *adj.* paralyzed as with fear

shrouded (shroud´ əd) *v.* wrapped

intrigues (in´ trēgz´) *n.* secrets

"She left the reservation when she was sixteen years old," I tell my audience. Sixteen sounds very old to me, but I always state the number because it seems integral to my recitation. "She had never been on a train before, or used a telephone. She left Standing Rock to take a job in Chicago so she could help out the family during the war. She was petrified of all the strange people and new surroundings; she stayed in her seat all the way from McLaughlin, South Dakota, to Chicago, Illinois, and didn't move once."

I usually laugh after saying this, because I cannot imagine my mother being afraid of anything. She is so tall, a true Dakota woman; she rises against the sun like a skyscraper, and when I draw her picture in my notebook, she takes up the entire page. She talks politics and attends sit-ins, wrestles with the Chicago police and says what's on her mind.

I am her small shadow and witness. I am the timid daughter who can rage only on paper.

We don't have much money, but Mom takes me from one end of the city to the other on foot, on buses. I will grow up believing that Chicago belongs to me, because it was given to me by my mother. Nearly every week we tour the Historical Society, and Mom makes a point of complaining about the statue that depicts an Indian man about to kill a white woman and her children: "This is the only monument to the history of Indians in this area that you have on exhibit. It's a shame because it is completely one-sided. Children who see this will think this is what Indians are all about."

My mother lectures the guides and their bosses, until eventually that statue disappears.

Some days we haunt the Art Institute, and my mother pauses before a Picasso.

"He did this during his blue period," she tells me.

I squint at the blue man holding a blue guitar. "Was he very sad?" I ask.

"Yes, I think he was." My mother takes my hand and looks away from the painting. I can see a story developing behind her eyes, and I tug on her arm to release the words. She will tell me why Picasso was blue, what his thoughts were as he painted this canvas. She relates anecdotes I will never find in books, never see footnoted in a biography of the master artist. I don't even bother to check these references because I like my mother's version best.

When Mom is down, we go to see the mummies at the Field Museum of Natural History. The Egyptian dead sleep in the basement, most of them still shrouded in their wrappings.

"These were people like us," my mother whispers. She pulls me into her waist. "They had dreams and intrigues and problems with their teeth. They thought their one particular life was of the utmost significance. And now, just look at them." My mother never fails to brighten. "So what's the use of worrying too hard or too long? Might as well be cheerful."

The Old Guitarist, ***Pablo Picasso***, 1903 (reproduction), The Art Institute of Chicago, ©2004 Estate of Pablo Picasso/Artists Rights Society (ARS), New York

◀ Critical Viewing
Compare and contrast the effect of the color blue in this painting and in the dress on page 38. **[Compare and Contrast]**

Before we leave this place, we always visit my great-grandmother's buckskin dress. We mount the stairs and walk through the museum's main hall—past the dinosaur bones all strung together, and the stuffed elephants lifting their trunks in a mute trumpet.

The clothed figures are disconcerting because they have no heads. I think of them as dead Indians. We reach the traditional outfits of the Sioux in the Plains Indian section, and there is the dress, as magnificent as I remembered. The yoke is completely beaded—I know the garment must be heavy to wear. My great-grandmother used blue

Vocabulary
disconcerting (dis′ kən surt′ iŋ) *adj.* upsetting

What do the author and her mother always do before leaving the museum?

beads as a background for the geometrical design, and I point to the azure[1] expanse.

"Was this her blue period?" I ask my mother. She hushes me unexpectedly, she will not play the game. I come to understand that this is a solemn call, and we stand before the glass case as we would before a grave.

"I don't know how this got out of the family," Mom murmurs. I feel helpless beside her, wishing I could reach through the glass to disrobe the headless mannequin. My mother belongs in a grand buckskin dress such as this, even though her hair is now too short to braid and has been trained to curl at the edges in a saucy flip.

We leave our fingerprints on the glass, two sets of hands at different heights pressing against the barrier. Mom is sad to leave.

"I hope she knows we visit her dress," my mother says.

There is a little buffalo across the hall, stuffed and staring. Mom

Susan Power
Author's Insight
"Was this her blue period?" my character asks, to draw a connection between Picasso's art (one phase of Picasso's painting is called his "blue period") and the exquisite beadwork of Native American women.

---

1. **azure** (azh′ ər) *adj.* sky blue.

doesn't always have the heart to greet him. Some days we slip out of the museum without finding his stall.

"You don't belong here," Mom tells him on those rare occasions when she feels she must pay her respects. "We honor you," she continues, "because you are a creature of great endurance and great generosity. You provided us with so many things that helped us to survive. It makes me angry to see you like this."

Few things can make my mother cry; the buffalo is one of them.

"I am just like you," she whispers. "I don't belong here either. We should be in the Dakotas, somewhere a little bit east of the Missouri River. This crazy city is not a fit home for buffalo or Dakotas."

I take my mother's hand to hold her in place. I am a city child, nervous around livestock and lonely on the plains.

I am afraid of a sky without light pollution—I never knew there could be so many stars. I lead my mother from the museum so she will forget the sense of loss. From the marble steps we can see Lake Shore Drive spill ahead of us, and I sweep my arm to the side as if I were responsible for this view. I introduce my mother to the city she gave me. I call her home.

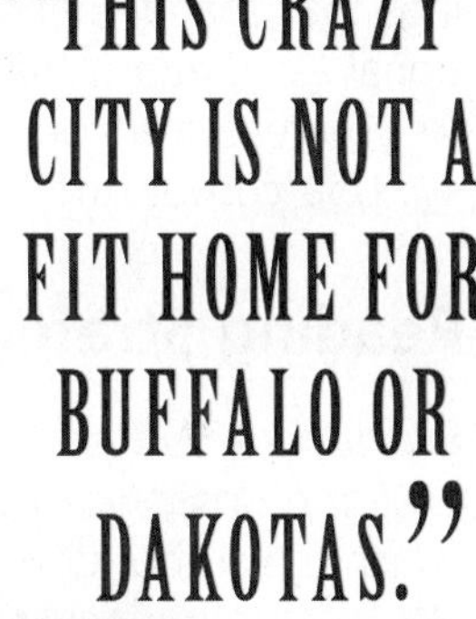
"THIS CRAZY CITY IS NOT A FIT HOME FOR BUFFALO OR DAKOTAS."

Critical Reading

1. **Key Ideas and Details (a)** What is the snake in Power's mother's dresser drawer? **(b) Interpret:** Why does she keep it there?
2. **Key Ideas and Details (a)** What complaint does Power's mother make about the statue at the Historical Society? **(b) Analyze:** What is the effect of her complaints? **(c) Contrast:** How does the statue contrast with the exhibit at the Art Institute?
3. **Craft and Structure (a)** What is unique about Power's relationship to the buckskin dress at the Art Institute? **(b) Interpret:** What is her mother's attitude toward seeing the dress there?
4. **Integration of Knowledge and Ideas (a)** In what ways does her mother identify with the buffalo? **(b) Contrast:** How is Power different from her mother? **(c) Generalize:** What does the final paragraph tell you about the relationship between the writer and her mother and their relationship with the city? Explain.
5. **Integration of Knowledge and Ideas** How do you think Power's mother influenced her as a writer? Base your answer on this essay.

Cite textual evidence to support your responses.

Before You Read

from the *Iroquois Constitution*

Connecting to the Essential Question The makers of this document use natural imagery to describe society and government. As you read, find details related to the forces of nature and consider whether nature provides a sound model for human society. This will help as you consider the Essential Question: **What is the relationship between literature and place?**

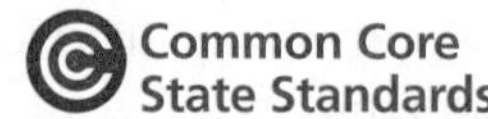

Reading Informational Text

1. Cite strong and thorough textual evidence to support analysis of what the text says explicitly as well as inferences drawn from the text.

6. Determine an author's point of view or purpose in a text in which the rhetoric is particularly effective, analyzing how style and content contribute to the power, persuasiveness or beauty of the text.

Literary Analysis

The Iroquois Constitution is a **political document** that defines the structure and practices of a political organization—the Iroquois Confederacy. One of the document's prominent features is its use of symbols. A **symbol** is a person, place, animal, or object that represents something else, often an abstraction. For example, in the Iroquois Constitution, a tree symbolizes the peace established among the uniting tribes:

> *I am Dekanawidah and with the Five Nations' confederate lords I plant the Tree of the Great Peace.*

Some symbols have a fixed meaning, representing the same thing in every context. A national flag is such a symbol. Other symbols have meanings that change depending on their context. Often, symbols have emotional associations that affect people more than the abstract ideas alone. As you read the Iroquois Constitution, think about the abstract ideas the symbols convey and how they intensify the emotional impact of the text.

Reading Strategy

Preparing to Read Complex Texts Political documents may express *explicit philosophical assumptions and beliefs*. These are statements in which the author directly states his or her point of view. A document may also express the writer's *implicit philosophical assumptions and beliefs,* or points of view that are suggested but not stated. To **analyze philosophical assumptions and beliefs,** follow the steps in the chart shown here.

Step One
Look for words that are negative or positive, such as *just*, *goodness*, or *evil*.
Step Two
Find statements that show specific ideas of right and wrong.
Step Three
Look for ideas that someone could argue against.

Vocabulary

disposition (dis´ pə zish´ ən) *n.* inclination; tendency (p. 43)

constitute (kän´ stə to͞ot) *v.* serve as the parts or basis of; form; comprise (p. 43)

tempered (tem´ pərd) *v.* treated to achieve just the right strength or balance (p. 44)

deliberation (di lib´ ər ā´ shən) *n.* careful consideration (p. 44)

oblivion (ə bliv´ ē ən) *n.* the condition of being completely forgotten (p. 44)

The Iroquois

Authors of the **Iroquois Constitution**

The Iroquois are a group of Native American tribes with closely related languages and cultural traditions. They often call themselves the People of the Long House, a reference to the long communal homes in which they traditionally lived. The Iroquois united in the sixteenth century or perhaps earlier, when—according to legend—a mystic and prophet named Dekanawidah traveled from village to village in what is now upstate New York, urging the tribes to stop fighting and band together. The result was a confederacy, or united group, often called the Five Nations. The confederacy initially included the Seneca, Cayuga, Onondaga, Oneida, and Mohawk tribes. In 1722 a sixth tribe, the Tuscarora, joined the group, which became known as the Six Nations.

A Colonial Power Even though their numbers were relatively small, unification made the Iroquois a powerful force in the colonial era. They gained control over many other Native American tribes and kept the Dutch and British from spreading much beyond New York's Hudson River. They often fought the French, who had allied with their enemies, the Algonquins and Hurons. The Iroquois, in turn, allied with the British, helping them win the French and Indian War (1754–1763). The American Revolution divided the Iroquois. While most tribes remained loyal to the British, the Oneida and some Tuscarora supported the colonists. After the war, some Iroquois resettled in Canada, and many Oneida moved to Wisconsin.

The Great Binding Law The agreement that united the Iroquois established a framework of laws and practices that helped make them the most highly organized Native American political body in colonial North America. Known as the Great Binding Law or Great Law of Peace, it was passed down orally for generations and recorded in shell beads called wampum that served as a memory device for oral recitation. The current version, now often called the Iroquois Constitution, was written down in the nineteenth century.

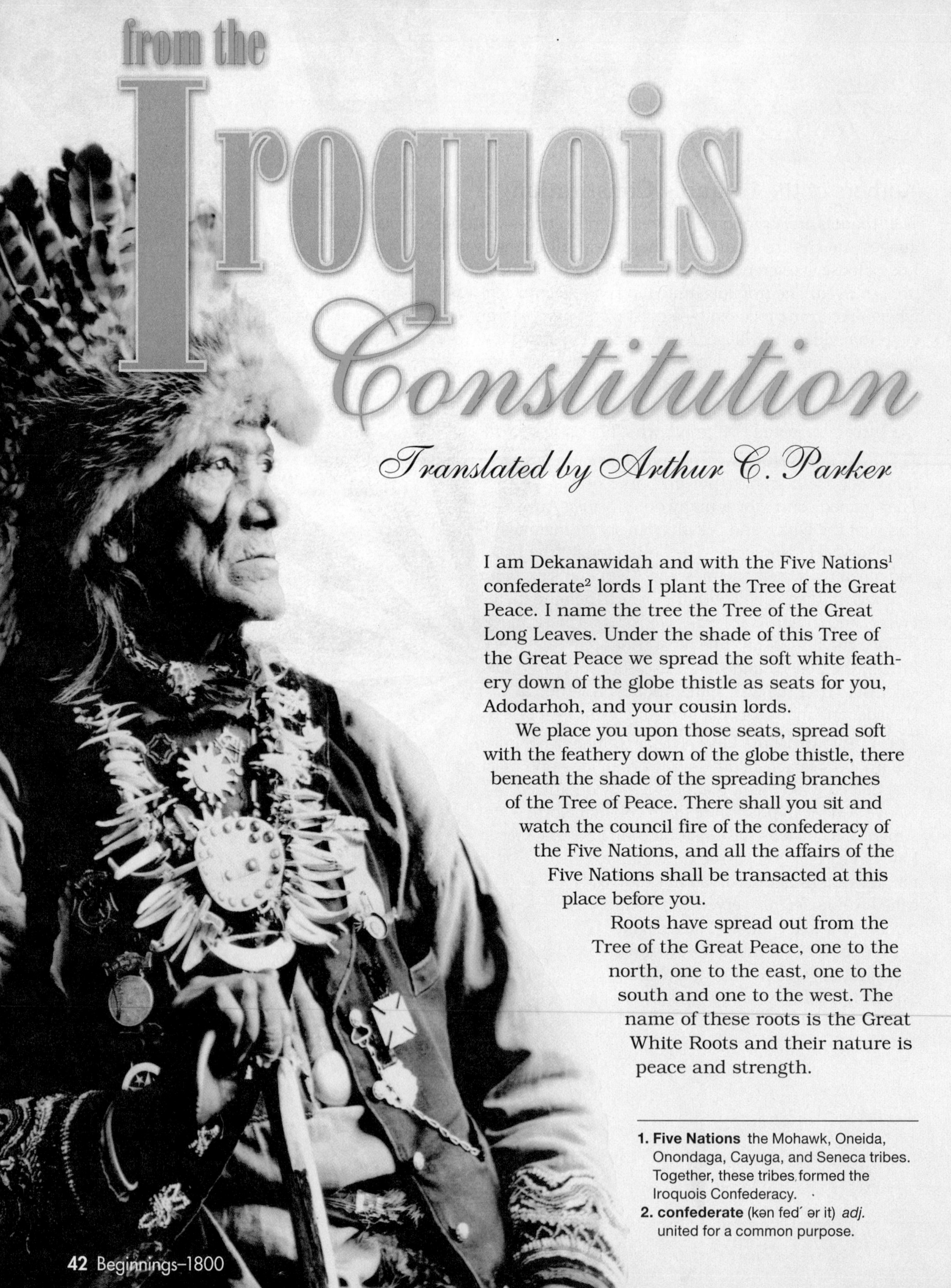

from the Iroquois Constitution

Translated by Arthur C. Parker

I am Dekanawidah and with the Five Nations[1] confederate[2] lords I plant the Tree of the Great Peace. I name the tree the Tree of the Great Long Leaves. Under the shade of this Tree of the Great Peace we spread the soft white feathery down of the globe thistle as seats for you, Adodarhoh, and your cousin lords.

We place you upon those seats, spread soft with the feathery down of the globe thistle, there beneath the shade of the spreading branches of the Tree of Peace. There shall you sit and watch the council fire of the confederacy of the Five Nations, and all the affairs of the Five Nations shall be transacted at this place before you.

Roots have spread out from the Tree of the Great Peace, one to the north, one to the east, one to the south and one to the west. The name of these roots is the Great White Roots and their nature is peace and strength.

1. **Five Nations** the Mohawk, Oneida, Onondaga, Cayuga, and Seneca tribes. Together, these tribes formed the Iroquois Confederacy.
2. **confederate** (kən fed′ ər it) *adj.* united for a common purpose.

If any man or any nation outside the Five Nations shall obey the laws of the Great Peace and make known their disposition to the lords of the confederacy, they may trace the roots to the tree and if their minds are clean and they are obedient and promise to obey the wishes of the confederate council, they shall be welcomed to take shelter beneath the Tree of the Long Leaves.

We place at the top of the Tree of the Long Leaves an eagle who is able to see afar. If he sees in the distance any evil approaching or any danger threatening he will at once warn the people of the confederacy.

The smoke of the confederate council fire shall ever ascend and pierce the sky so that other nations who may be allies may see the council fire of the Great Peace . . .

Whenever the confederate lords shall assemble for the purpose of holding a council, the Onondaga lords shall open it by expressing their gratitude to their cousin lords and greeting them, and they shall make an address and offer thanks to the earth where men dwell, to the streams of water, the pools, the springs and the lakes, to the maize and the fruits, to the medicinal herbs and trees, to the forest trees for their usefulness, to the animals that serve as food and give their pelts for clothing, to the great winds and the lesser winds, to the thunderers, to the sun, the mighty warrior, to the moon, to the messengers of the Creator who reveal his wishes and to the Great Creator who dwells in the heavens above, who gives all the things useful to men, and who is the source and the ruler of health and life.

Then shall the Onondaga lords declare the council open . . .

All lords of the Five Nations' Confederacy must be honest in all things . . . It shall be a serious wrong for anyone to lead a lord into trivial affairs, for the people must ever hold their lords high in estimation out of respect to their honorable positions.

When a candidate lord is to be installed he shall furnish four strings of shells (or wampum)[3] one span in length bound together at one end. Such will constitute the evidence of his pledge to the confederate lords that he will live according to the constitution of the Great Peace and exercise justice in all affairs.

When the pledge is furnished the speaker of the council must hold the shell strings in his hand and address the opposite side of the council fire and he shall commence his address saying: "Now behold him. He has now become a confederate lord. See how splendid he looks." An address may then follow.

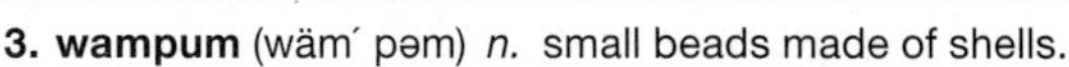

3. **wampum** (wäm′ pəm) *n.* small beads made of shells.

Vocabulary

disposition (dis′ pə zish′ ən) *n.* an inclination or tendency

constitute (kän′ stə to͞ot) *v.* serve as the parts or basis of; form; comprise

Reading Strategy

Analyzing Philosophical Assumptions and Beliefs What implicit beliefs are expressed in this paragraph?

What does the speaker say is the nature of the Great White Roots?

Literary Analysis
Political Document and Symbol
What agreement do the strings of shells, or wampum, symbolize?

Vocabulary
tempered (tem′ pərd) *v.* treated to achieve just the right strength or balance

deliberation (di lib′ ər ā′ shən) *n.* careful consideration

oblivion (ə bliv′ ē ən) *n.* the condition of being completely forgotten

At the end of it he shall send the bunch of shell strings to the opposite side and they shall be received as evidence of the pledge. Then shall the opposite side say:

"We now do crown you with the sacred emblem of the deer's antlers, the emblem of your lordship. You shall now become a mentor of the people of the Five Nations. The thickness of your skin shall be seven spans—which is to say that you shall be proof against anger, offensive actions and criticism. Your heart shall be filled with peace and good will and your mind filled with a yearning for the welfare of the people of the confederacy. With endless patience you shall carry out your duty and your firmness shall be tempered with tenderness for your people. Neither anger nor fury shall find lodgement in your mind and all your words and actions shall be marked with calm deliberation. In all of your deliberations in the confederate council, in your efforts at law making, in all your official acts, self-interest shall be cast into oblivion. Cast not over your shoulder behind you the warnings of the nephews and nieces should they chide you for any error or wrong you may do, but return to the way of the Great Law which is just and right. Look and listen for the welfare of the whole people and have always in view not only the present but also the coming generations, even those whose faces are yet beneath the surface of the ground—the unborn of the future nation."

Critical Reading

Cite textual evidence to support your responses.

1. **Key Ideas and Details (a)** What do the lords plant to commemorate their meeting? **(b) Analyze:** What do the roots of this plant symbolize?
2. **Integration of Knowledge and Ideas (a)** According to the Iroquois Constitution, what must confederate lords do to open a council meeting? **(b) Infer:** What does this decree suggest about the Iroquois?
3. **Integration of Knowledge and Ideas (a) Summarize:** Summarize the qualities and conduct required of council lords by the Iroquois Constitution. **(b) Synthesize:** How well do these qualities apply to leaders in the modern world?
4. **Integration of Knowledge and Ideas** Do you agree with and support the ideas presented in the Iroquois Constitution? Why or why not?
5. **Integration of Knowledge and Ideas** In what ways, both practical and spiritual, do the Iroquois rely on the natural world? Use these Essential Question words in your response: *cultivate, civilization, sacred.* ***[Connecting to the Essential Question: What is the relationship between literature and place?]***

After You Read from the *Iroquois Constitution*

Literary Analysis

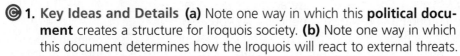

Language
4.a. Use context as a clue to the meaning of a word or phrase.

1. **Key Ideas and Details (a)** Note one way in which this **political document** creates a structure for Iroquois society. **(b)** Note one way in which this document determines how the Iroquois will react to external threats.
2. **Craft and Structure (a)** Use a chart like the one shown to list three **symbols** in the document and explain the abstract idea each one represents. **(b)** Which of these symbols has fixed meanings sometimes found outside of Iroquois culture? Cite examples to support your answer.

Symbol	Abstract Idea

Reading Strategy

3. **(a) Analyze explicit philosophical assumptions and beliefs** in this document by explaining how the Iroquois see the ideal relationship between a lord and his people. **(b) Analyze implicit philosophical assumptions and beliefs** by explaining the views of nature that underlie many of the statements.
4. Based on the details in the last paragraph, what philosophical beliefs did the Iroquois hold about the qualities that make one a good leader?

PERFORMANCE TASKS
Integrated Language Skills

Vocabulary Acquisition and Use

Sentence Completions Use the context clues, or surrounding words and phrases, to choose a word from the vocabulary list on page 40 that best completes each sentence. Explain your choices. Use each word only once.

1. Oil and vinegar ______ the main ingredients of that salad dressing.
2. To make a good decision, emotion must be ______ with reason.
3. I came to my conclusion after careful ______.
4. Someone with amnesia may live in a continuous state of ______.
5. Clio has a lazy ______, while her brother is inclined to work hard.

Writing

Found Poem A found poem is a poem created from writing or speech not intended to be poetry. Choose a passage from the Iroquois Constitution that you think is especially strong or beautiful. Turn it into a poem by rewriting it with line breaks like those of poetry. Organize the stanzas and place the line breaks where you feel they create the most impact. Read your poem aloud to verify your choices; revise them if necessary.

Before You Read

from *A Journey Through Texas* • *Boulders Taller Than the Great Tower of Seville*

Connecting to the Essential Question These accounts describe early meetings between Europeans and Native Americans. As you read, find details that show how the explorers and the native peoples react to each other. Doing so will help as you think about the Essential Question: **What is the relationship between literature and place?**

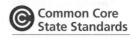

Common Core State Standards

Reading Informational Text
5. Analyze and evaluate the effectiveness of the structure an author uses in his or her exposition or argument, including whether the structure makes points clear, convincing, and engaging.

Literary Analysis

The Europeans who first came to the Americas related their experiences in **exploration narratives**—firsthand accounts of their travels. These accounts generally provide information in **chronological order,** describing events in the order in which they occurred. By creating a clear sequence of events, the explorers allowed readers back home in Europe to follow their journeys, step by step.

Comparing Literary Works Every journey presents conflicts and problems. As you read, use a chart like the one shown to *compare and contrast the problems* each explorer faced and the solutions he found.

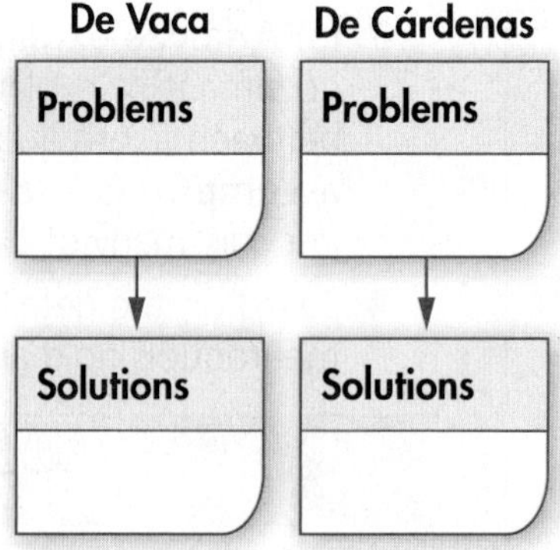

Reading Strategy

Preparing to Read Complex Texts When reading narrative accounts, analyze and evaluate the structure by making sure you are clear about the sequence in which events occur and the ways in which each event changes a situation. Pause and try to state events in order. To help, **recognize signal words** that clarify relationships of time and sequence, reason, or contrast.

Time: *After five days,* they had not *yet* returned.

Sequence: . . . and so we endured these seventeen days, *at the end of which* we crossed the river. . . .

Contrast: . . . *although* this was the warm season, no one could live in the canyon because of the cold.

Vocabulary

entreated (en trēt′ əd) *v.* begged; implored (p. 49)

feigned (fānd) *v.* pretended (p. 49)

subsisted (səb sist′ əd) *v.* remained alive; were sustained (p. 50)

successive (sək ses′ iv) *adj.* following one after another (p. 50)

advantageous (ad′ van tā ′ jəs) *adj.* favorable; beneficial (p. 51)

traversed (trə vurst′) *v.* moved over, across, or through (p. 51)

Alvar Núñez Cabeza de Vaca

(1490?–1557?)

Author of *A Journey Through Texas*

In 1528, Pánfilo de Narváez and 400 Spanish soldiers landed near Tampa Bay and set out to explore Florida's west coast. Alvar Núñez Cabeza de Vaca (äl′ bär n o͞on′ yes kä bā′ sä dā bä′ kä) was second in command. Beset by hostile natives, illness, and the prospect of starvation, Narváez and his men then set sail for Mexico in five flimsy boats, but he and most of the men drowned. Cabeza de Vaca and a party of about sixty survived and reached the Texas shore near present-day Galveston.

Shipwrecked without supplies, only fifteen of the group lived through the winter. In the end, Cabeza de Vaca and three others survived. They were captured by natives and spent the next several years in captivity. During that time, Cabeza de Vaca gained a reputation as a medicine man and trader. The four Spaniards finally escaped and wandered for eighteen months across the Texas plains. In 1536, the survivors finally reached Mexico City.

Invitation to Others Cabeza de Vaca's adventures and his reports on the richness of Texas sparked exploration of the region. In "A Journey Through Texas," he speaks of Estevanico, the first African to set foot in Texas.

In 1541, Cabeza de Vaca also led a 1,000-mile expedition through the south of present day Brazil to Asunción, the capital of Río de la Plata. He was appointed governor of the Río de la Plata region (now Paraguay), but he was ousted two years later as a result of revolt.

Through his journals, Cabeza de Vaca encouraged others, including Francisco Vásquez de Coronado, to explore America.

García López de Cárdenas

(c. 1540)

Author of *Boulders Taller Than the Great Tower of Seville*

García López de Cárdenas (gär sē′ ä lō′ pes dā kär′ dā näs) is best remembered as the first European to visit the Grand Canyon. As a leader of Francisco Vásquez de Coronado's expedition to New Mexico (1540–1542), Cárdenas was dispatched from Cibola (Zuni) in western New Mexico to see a river that the Moqui Native Americans of northeastern Arizona had described to one of Coronado's captains. The river was the Colorado. López de Cárdenas departed on August 25, 1540, reaching the Grand Canyon after a westward journey of about twenty days. He became the first European to view the canyon and its river, which from the vantage of the canyon's rim appeared to be a stream merely six feet wide! Unable to descend to the river, they took back to Europe descriptions that attempted to record the magnitude of the sight. López de Cárdenas reported that boulders in the Grand Canyon were taller than the 300-foot high Great Tower of Seville, one of the world's tallest cathedrals.

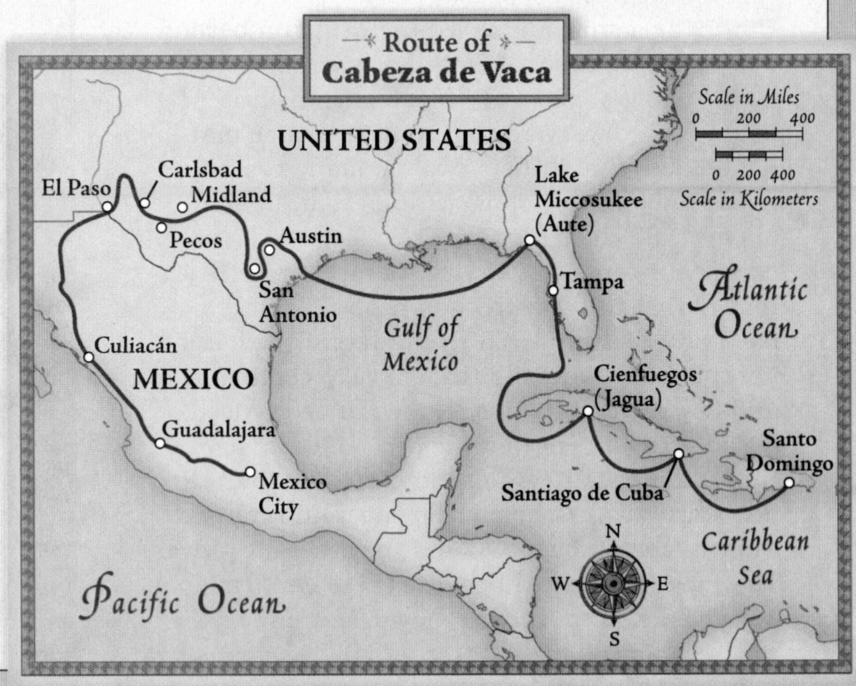

from

A JOURNEY THROUGH TEXAS

Alvar Núñez Cabeza de Vaca

BACKGROUND Alvar Núñez Cabeza de Vaca and three countrymen wandered for months through Texas as they journeyed toward the Spanish settlement in Mexico City. In the course of their travels, Cabeza de Vaca healed a Native American by performing the first recorded surgery in Texas. His resulting fame attracted so many followers that Cabeza de Vaca noted in his journal: "The number of our companions became so large that we could no longer control them." As the party continued traveling westward, they were well received by the native people they encountered.

The same Indians led us to a plain beyond the chain of mountains, where people came to meet us from a long distance. By those we were treated in the same manner as before, and they made so many presents to the Indians who came with us that, unable to carry all, they left half of it. . . . We told these people our route was towards sunset, and they replied that in that direction people lived very far away. So we ordered them to send there and inform the inhabitants that we were coming and how. From this they begged to be excused, because the others were their enemies, and they did not want us to go to them. Yet they did not venture to disobey in the end, and sent two women, one of their own and the other a captive. They selected women because these can trade everywhere, even if there be war.

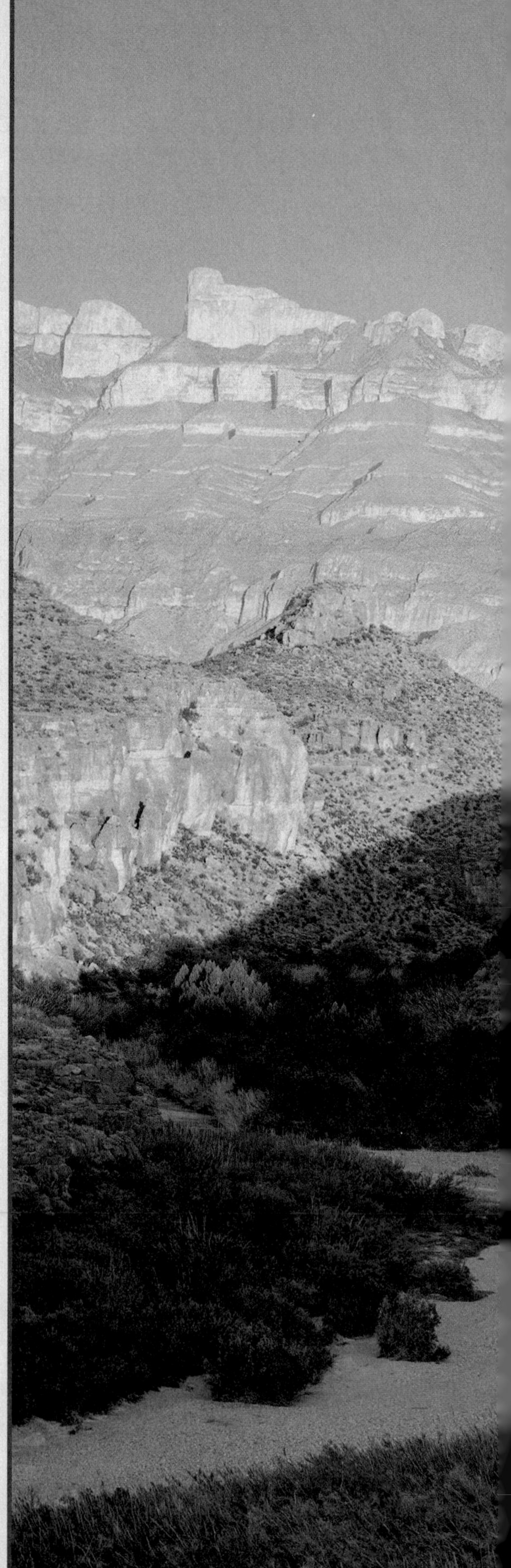

We followed the women to a place where it had been agreed we should wait for them. After five days they had not yet returned, and the Indians explained that it might be because they had not found anybody. So we told them to take us north, and they repeated that there were no people, except very far away, and neither food nor water. Nevertheless we insisted, saying that we wanted to go there, and they still excused themselves as best they could, until at last we became angry.

One night I went away to sleep out in the field apart from them; but they soon came to where I was, and remained awake all night in great alarm, talking to me, saying how frightened they were. They **entreated** us not to be angry any longer, because, even if it was their death, they would take us where we chose. We **feigned** to be angry still, so as to keep them in suspense, and then a singular[1] thing happened.

On that same day many fell sick, and on the next day eight of them died! All over the country, where it was known, they became so afraid that it seemed as if the mere sight of us would kill them. They besought[2] us not to be angry nor to procure the death of any more of their number, for they were convinced that we killed them by merely thinking of it. In truth, we were very much concerned about it, for, seeing the great mortality, we dreaded that all of them might die or forsake us in their terror, while those further on, upon learning of it, would get out of our way hereafter. We prayed to God our Lord to assist us, and the sick began to get well. Then we saw something that astonished us very much, and it was that, while the parents, brothers and wives of the dead had shown deep grief at their illness, from the moment they died the survivors made no demonstration whatsoever, and showed not the slightest feeling; nor did they dare to go near the bodies until we ordered their burial. . . .

The sick being on the way of recovery, when we had been there already three days, the women whom we had sent out returned, saying that they had met very few people, nearly all having gone after the cows, as it was the season. So we ordered those who had been sick to remain, and those who were well to accompany us, and that, two days' travel from there, the same women should go with us and get people to come to meet us on the trail for our reception.

The next morning all those who were strong enough came along, and at the end of three journeys we halted. Alonso del Castillo and Estevanico,[3] the negro, left with the women as guides, and the woman who was a captive took them to a river that flows between mountains, where there was a village, in which her father lived, and these were the first abodes we saw that were like unto real houses.

◀ Critical Viewing
In what ways might a landscape like the one in the photograph on the facing page pose difficulties for an expedition? **[Interpret]**

Vocabulary

entreated (en trēt′ əd) *v.* begged; pleaded

feigned (fānd) *v.* pretended

Reading Strategy
Recognizing Signal Words
Which words in this paragraph signal time and sequence relationships?

Why do the Indians fear going on ahead?

---

1. **singular** *adj.* strange.
2. **besought** (be sôt′) *v.* pleaded with.
3. **Estevanico** (es′ tā vä nē′ kō) Of Moorish extraction, Estevanico was the first African man to set foot in Texas.

Castillo and Estevanico went to these and, after holding parley[4] with the Indians, at the end of three days Castillo returned to where he had left us, bringing with him five or six of the Indians. He told how he had found permanent houses, inhabited, the people of which ate beans and squashes, and that he had also seen maize.

Of all things upon earth this caused us the greatest pleasure, and we gave endless thanks to our Lord for this news. Castillo also said that the negro was coming to meet us on the way, near by, with all the people of the houses. For that reason we started, and after going a league and a half met the negro and the people that came to receive us, who gave us beans and many squashes to eat, gourds to carry water in, robes of cowhide, and other things. As those people and the Indians of our company were enemies, and did not understand each other, we took leave of the latter, leaving them all that had been given to us, while we went on with the former and, six leagues beyond, when night was already approaching, reached their houses, where they received us with great ceremonies. Here we remained one day, and left on the next, taking them with us to other permanent houses, where they **subsisted** on the same food also, and thence on we found a new custom.

▲ **Critical Viewing**
What does this drawing suggest about the relationship between Cabeza de Vaca's party and the Native Americans? **[Interpret]**

Vocabulary
subsisted (səb sist′ əd) *v.* remained alive; were sustained

successive (sək ses′ iv) *adj.* one after another, in sequence

The people who heard of our approach did not, as before, come out to meet us on the way, but we found them at their homes, and they had other houses ready for us. . . . There was nothing they would not give us. They are the best formed people we have seen, the liveliest and most capable; who best understood us and answered our questions. We called them "of the cows," because most of the cows die near there, and because for more than fifty leagues up that stream they go to kill many of them. Those people go completely naked, after the manner of the first we met. The women are covered with deer-skins, also some men, especially the old ones, who are of no use any more in war.

Literary Analysis
Exploration Narratives
What information about the region and its people do you learn from this paragraph?

The country is well settled. We asked them why they did not raise maize, and they replied that they were afraid of losing the crops, since for two **successive** years it had not rained, and the seasons were so dry that the moles had eaten the corn, so that they did not dare to plant any more until it should have rained very hard. And they also begged us to ask Heaven for rain, which we promised to do. We also wanted to know from where they brought their maize, and they said it came from where the sun sets, and that it was found all over that country, and the shortest way to it was in that direction.

---

4. **holding parley** (pär′ lē) conferring.

We asked them to tell us how to go, as they did not want to go themselves, to tell us about the way.

They said we should travel up the river towards the north, on which trail for seventeen days we would not find a thing to eat, except a fruit called *chacan,* which they grind between stones; but even then it cannot be eaten, being so coarse and dry; and so it was, for they showed it to us and we could not eat it. But they also said that, going upstream, we could always travel among people who were their enemies, although speaking the same language, and who could give us no food, but would receive us very willingly, and give us many cotton blankets, hides and other things; but that it seemed to them that we ought not to take that road.

In doubt as to what should be done, and which was the best and most advantageous road to take, we remained with them for two days. They gave us beans, squashes, and calabashes.[5] Their way of cooking them is so new and strange that I felt like describing it here, in order to show how different and queer are the devices and industries of human beings. They have no pots. In order to cook their food they fill a middle-sized gourd with water, and place into a fire such stones as easily become heated, and when they are hot to scorch they take them out with wooden tongs, thrusting them into the water of the gourd, until it boils. As soon as it boils they put into it what they want to cook, always taking out the stones as they cool off and throwing in hot ones to keep the water steadily boiling. This is their way of cooking.

After two days were past we determined to go in search of maize, and not to follow the road to the cows, since the latter carried us to the north, which meant a very great circuit, as we held it always certain that by going towards sunset we should reach the goal of our wishes.

So we went on our way and traversed the whole country to the South Sea,[6] and our resolution was not shaken by the fear of great starvation, which the Indians said we should suffer (and indeed suffered) during the first seventeen days of travel. All along the river, and in the course of these seventeen days we received plenty of cowhides, and did not eat of their famous fruit (*chacan*), but our food consisted (for each day) of a handful of deer-tallow, which for that purpose we always sought to keep, and so endured these seventeen days, at the end of which we crossed the river and marched for seventeen days more. At sunset, on a plain between very high mountains, we met people who, for one-third of the year, eat but powdered straw, and as we went by just at that time, had to eat it also, until, at the end of that journey we found some permanent houses, with plenty of harvested maize, of which and of its meal they gave us great quantities, also squashes and beans, and blankets of cotton. . . .

5. calabashes (kal′ ə bash′ əz) *n.* dried, hollow shells of gourds used to hold food or beverages.
6. the South Sea the Gulf of Mexico.

Vocabulary

advantageous (ad′ van tā′ jəs) *adj.* favorable, profitable

traversed (trə vurst′) *v.* moved over, across, or through

Literary Analysis

Exploration Narratives What might readers back in Europe have thought about the group's determination to find maize?

With what information does Castilo return?

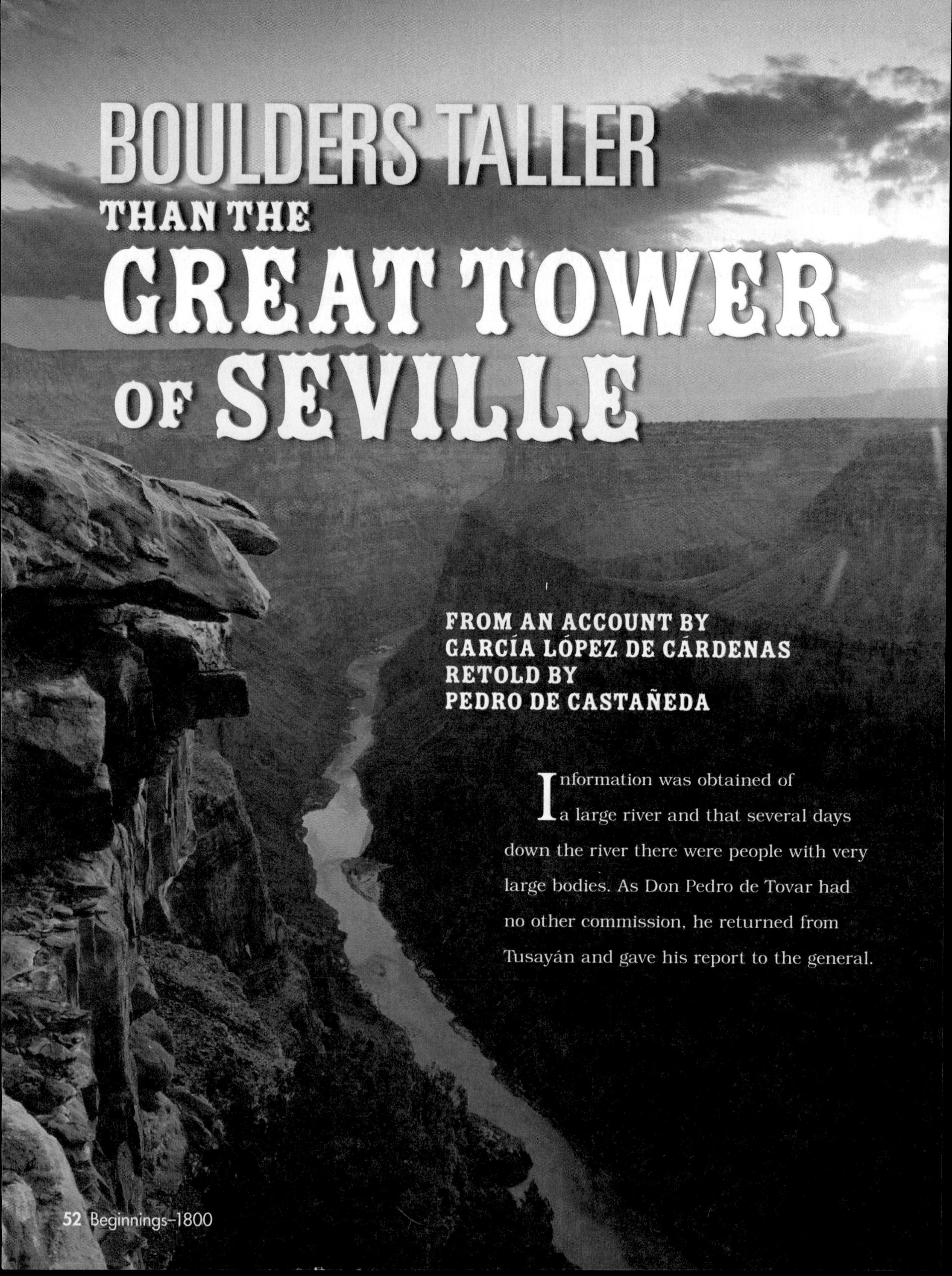

BOULDERS TALLER THAN THE GREAT TOWER OF SEVILLE

FROM AN ACCOUNT BY
GARCÍA LÓPEZ DE CÁRDENAS
RETOLD BY
PEDRO DE CASTAÑEDA

Information was obtained of a large river and that several days down the river there were people with very large bodies. As Don Pedro de Tovar had no other commission, he returned from Tusayán and gave his report to the general.

The latter at once dispatched Don García López de Cárdenas there with about twelve men to explore this river. When he reached Tusayán he was well received and lodged by the natives. They provided him with guides to proceed on his journey. They set out from there laden with provisions, because they had to travel over some uninhabited land before coming to settlements, which the Indians said were more than twenty days away. Accordingly when they had marched for twenty days they came to gorges of the river, from the edge of which it looked as if the opposite side must have been more than three or four leagues[1] away by air. This region was high and covered with low and twisted pine trees; it was extremely cold, being open to the north, so that, although this was the warm season, no one could live in this canyon because of the cold.

The men spent three days looking for a way down to the river; from the top it looked as if the water were a fathom[2] across. But, according to the information supplied by the Indians, it must have been half a league wide. The descent was almost impossible, but, after these three days, at a place which seemed less difficult, Captain Melgosa, a certain Juan Galeras, and another companion, being the most agile, began to go down. They continued descending within view of those on top until they lost sight of them, as they could not be seen from the top. They returned about four o'clock in the afternoon, as they could not reach the bottom because of the many obstacles they met, for what from the top seemed easy, was not so, on the contrary, it was rough and difficult. They said that they had gone down one-third of the distance and that, from the point they had reached, the river seemed very large, and that, from what they saw, the width given by the Indians was correct. From the top they could make out, apart from the canyon, some small boulders which seemed to be as high as a man. Those who went

FROM THE TOP THEY COULD MAKE OUT, APART FROM THE CANYON, SOME SMALL BOULDERS WHICH SEEMED TO BE AS HIGH AS A MAN.

Who is dispatched to explore the river?

1. **leagues** (lēgz) *n.* units of measurement of approximately three miles.
2. **fathom** (fa*th*′ əm) *n.* a unit of measurement equal to six feet.

▲ **Critical Viewing** Do the photographs on these two pages help you understand the explorers' confusion about the scale of the Grand Canyon? Explain. **[Connect]**

Reading Strategy
Recognizing Signal Words
What change do the words "up to that time" signal?

THOSE WHO WENT DOWN AND WHO REACHED THEM SWORE THAT THEY WERE TALLER THAN THE GREAT TOWER OF SEVILLE.

down and who reached them swore that they were taller than the great tower of Seville.[3]

The party did not continue farther up the canyon of the river because of the lack of water. Up to that time they had gone one or two leagues inland in search of water every afternoon. When they had traveled four additional days the guides said that it was impossible to go on because no water would be found for three or four days, that when they themselves traveled through that land they took along women who brought water in gourds, that in those trips they buried the gourds of water for the return trip, and that they traveled in one day a distance that took us two days.

This was the Tizón river, much closer to its source than where Melchior Díaz and his men had crossed it. These Indians were of the same type, as it appeared later. From there Cárdenas and his men turned back, as that trip brought no other results.

3. **great tower of Seville** The Giralda, the tower on the Cathedral of Seville in Spain, rises above the cathedral more than twice its height.

Critical Reading

Cite textual evidence to support your responses.

1. **Key Ideas and Details (a)** In the Cabeza de Vaca narrative, what conflict in the party occurs immediately before the Native Americans begin to fall ill? **(b) Draw Conclusions:** What do the Native Americans believe is the cause of their sickness? Explain.
2. **Key Ideas and Details (a)** Why do the native people in the settled areas no longer plant corn? **(b)** What do they ask the Spaniards to do to fix this problem? **(c) Interpret:** What does this request suggest about the Native Americans' view of the Spaniards?
3. **Key Ideas and Details (a)** In the Cárdenas narrative, what natural feature are Cárdenas and his men sent to explore? **(b) Infer:** Why do you think Coronado sends the group on this mission? Explain.
4. **Key Ideas and Details (a) Compare and Contrast:** How does the appearance of the river and the boulders from the top of the gorge differ from the reality close up? **(b) Identify Cause and Effect:** In what ways do these differences in perspective affect the explorers?
5. **Integration of Knowledge and Ideas** Judging from these accounts, what are some of the challenges Europeans faced in exploring—and understanding—the Americas? In your response, use at least two of these Essential Question words: *perspective, values, respect, alter.* ***[Connecting to the Essential Question: What is the relationship between literature and place?]***

After You Read

from ***A Journey Through Texas* • *Boulders Taller Than the Great Tower of Seville***

Literary Analysis

1. Key Ideas and Details Which details in these **exploration narratives** suggest how the Native Americans viewed the Europeans? Explain your choices.

2. Integration of Knowledge and Ideas **(a)** Why do you think the explorers in the Cárdenas party compare the boulders to the great tower of Seville? **(b)** What does this suggest about the ways in which people understand new experiences?

3. Craft and Structure **(a)** Use a chart like this one to list four events from each account in **chronological order.** **(b)** Why might each explorer have felt a responsibility to create a clear sequence of events for his readers?

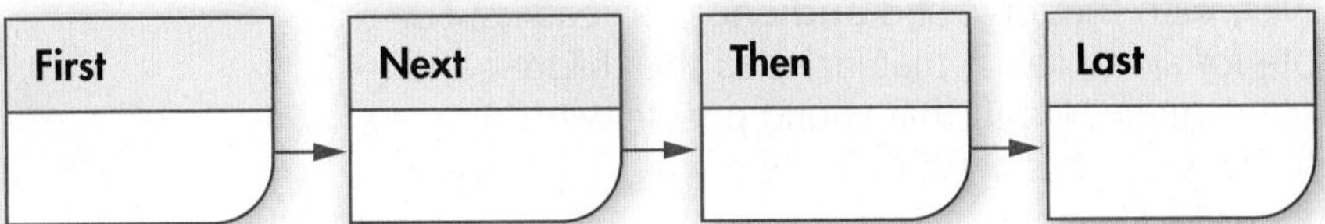

4. Comparing Literary Works **(a)** Note two problems each explorer faced and the solutions each found. **(b)** How were they similar and different?

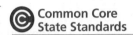

Common Core State Standards

Writing
2.d. Use precise language.

Language
5. Demonstrate understanding of figurative language, word relationships, and nuances in word meanings.

Reading Strategy

5. What type of relationship (time, sequence, reason, or contrast) is indicated by each of the italicized **signal words** in this passage? "*Nevertheless* we insisted, saying that we wanted to go there, and they *still* excused themselves as best they could, *until* at last we became angry."

PERFORMANCE TASKS
Integrated Language Skills

Vocabulary Acquisition and Use

Use New Words Use the following word pairs correctly in sentences:

1. entreated/danger
2. feigned/surprise
3. advantageous/win
4. traversed/journey
5. successive/days
6. subsisted/food

Writing

Explanatory Text Imagine that you are exploring a new territory. Write an **explorer's journal entry** that provides precise details about your discoveries. Choose a specific location and, if necessary, gather details through research so that your description is authentic. Share your draft with a partner. If your reader cannot "see" your description, replace weak words with vivid choices.

Weak word choice: The river *was* ten miles from end to end.
Strong word choice: The river *cut through* the mountains for ten miles.

Before You Read from *Of Plymouth Plantation*

Connecting to the Essential Question William Bradford's account reveals courage and perseverance in the face of harsh circumstances. As you read, find details that show how the settlers face and overcome challenges. Doing so will help as you consider the Essential Question: **What makes American literature American?**

Common Core State Standards

Reading Informational Text
6. Determine an author's point of view or purpose in a text in which the rhetoric is particularly effective, analyzing how style and content contribute to the power, persuasiveness, or beauty of the text.

Literary Analysis

An **author's purpose** is his or her reason for writing. General purposes for writing are *to inform, to entertain,* and *to persuade.* Authors also have specific purposes that vary with the topic and **audience,** or readers. For example, Bradford wrote for an audience that included the children and grandchildren of the first settlers. He felt that young people were straying from the Pilgrims' faith. He wrote this account for two specific purposes:

- **To inform:** Bradford sought to tell the new generation about the Pilgrims' history.
- **To persuade:** Bradford sought to inspire the new generation to uphold Puritan values.

As you read, thinking about Bradford's purposes will help you understand and interpret his ideas.

Reading Strategy

Preparing to Read Complex Texts Bradford wrote in *Puritan Plain Style*, which is relatively straightforward, but his writing can be challenging to modern readers. As you read, *monitor your understanding.* If you find you are not completely sure of the sequence of events or Bradford's insights, clarify the meaning by **breaking down long sentences.** To do so, separate a complex sentence into its essential parts—the subject (who or what) and the verb (action). This will help you isolate the main idea. As you read, use a chart like the one shown to analyze and interpret the meaning of complex sentences.

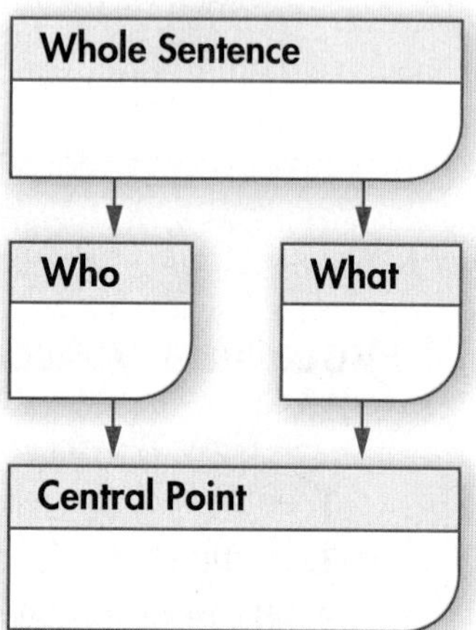

Vocabulary

peril (per´ əl) *n.* danger (p. 59)

habitation (hab´ i tā´ shen) *n.* place to live; group of homes or dwellings (p. 60)

subject to (sub´ jikt to͞o) *adj.* likely to be affected by something (p. 61)

adversity (ad vʉr´ sə tē) *n.* hardship; difficulty (p. 61)

calamity (kə lam´ ə tē) *n.* disaster; catastrophe (p. 62)

relent (ri lent´) *v.* become less harsh; be more merciful (p. 62)

William Bradford (1590–1657)

Author, *Of Plymouth Plantation*

Survival in North America was a matter of endurance, intelligence, and courage. William Bradford had all three qualities. Thirteen years after the first permanent English settlement was established in Jamestown, Virginia, Bradford helped lead the Pilgrims to what is now Massachusetts.

Seeking Freedom Bradford, who was born in Yorkshire, England, joined a group of Puritans who believed that the Church of England was corrupt. This group wished to separate from the church. In the face of stiff persecution, they eventually fled to Holland and from there sailed to North America. In *Of Plymouth Plantation,* Bradford provides an account of the experiences of these early settlers. Historians consider this account to be accurate.

A Long Leadership After the death of the colony's first leader, the Pilgrims elected Bradford governor. He was reelected thirty times. During his tenure, he organized the repayment of debts to financial backers, encouraged new immigration, and established good relations with the Native Americans, without whose help the colony never would have survived. He also instituted the town meeting within the colonies, a democratic process that continues to take place in state government today. Bradford was largely responsible for leading the infant colony through many hardships to success.

In 1630, Bradford began writing *Of Plymouth Plantation,* a firsthand account of the Pilgrims' struggle to endure, sustained only by courage and unbending faith. The work, written in the simple language known as Puritan Plain Style, was not published until 1856.

Our fathers were Englishmen which came over this great ocean, and were ready to perish in this wilderness.

from Of Plymouth Plantation

William Bradford

BACKGROUND In September of 1620, the tiny ship *Mayflower* set sail from Plymouth, England, bound for the Jamestown settlement in Virginia. The ship carried 102 Pilgrims, many of them members of a separatist religious congregation. During the stormy Atlantic crossing, the ship was blown off course, which forced it to miss its intended destination. The boat finally set anchor near Cape Cod, Massachusetts, in mid-November.

from Chapter 9

Of Their Voyage and How They Passed the Sea; and of Their Safe Arrival at Cape Cod

[1620] SEPTEMBER 6 . . . After they[1] had enjoyed fair winds and weather for a season, they were encountered many times with cross-winds, and met with many fierce storms, with which the ship was shrewdly[2] shaken, and her upper works made very leaky; and one of the main beams in the mid ships was bowed and cracked, which put them in some fear that the ship could not be able to perform the voyage. So some of the chief of the company, perceiving the mariners to fear the sufficiency of the ship, as appeared by their mutterings, they entered into serious consultation with the master and other officers of the ship, to consider in time of the danger; and rather to return than to cast themselves into a desperate and inevitable peril. And truly there was great distraction and difference of opinion amongst the mariners themselves; fain[3] would they do what could be done for their wages' sake (being now half the seas over), and on the other hand they were loath to hazard their lives too desperately. But in examining of all opinions, the master and others affirmed they knew the ship to be strong and firm under water; and for the buckling of the main beam, there was a great iron screw the passengers brought out of Holland, which would raise the beam into his place; the which being done, the carpenter and master affirmed that with a post under it, set firm in the lower deck, and other ways bound, he would make it sufficient. And as for the decks and upper works, they would caulk them as well as they could, and though with the working of the ship they would not long keep staunch,[4] yet there would otherwise be no great danger, if they did not over-press her with sails. So they committed themselves to the will of God, and resolved to proceed.

In sundry of these storms the winds were so fierce, and the seas so high, as they could not bear a knot of sail, but were forced to hull,[5] for diverse day together. And in one of them, as they thus lay at hull, in a mighty storm, a lusty[6] young man (called John Howland) coming upon some occasion above the gratings, was, with a seele[7] of the ship thrown into [the sea]; but it pleased God that he caught hold of the topsail halyards,[8] which hung overboard, and ran out at length; yet he held his hold (though he was sundry

◀ **Critical Viewing**
How does this photograph of a *Mayflower* replica help you better understand the Pilgrims' experience? **[Connect]**

Vocabulary
peril (per′ əl) *n.* danger

How is the ship damaged in the storm?

1. **they** Even though Bradford is one of the Pilgrims, he refers to them in the third person.
2. **shrewdly** (shro͞od′ lē) *adv.* severely.
3. **fain** (fān) *adv.* gladly.
4. **staunch** (stônch) *adj.* watertight.
5. **hull** *v.* drift with the wind.
6. **lusty** *adj.* strong; hearty.
7. **seele** *n.* rolling; pitching to one side.
8. **halyards** (hal′ yərdz) *n.* ropes for raising or lowering sails.

The American EXPERIENCE

HISTORY CONNECTION

The *Mayflower* was the British ship on which 102 Pilgrims sailed from Southampton, England, to North America during September, October, and November of 1620. In November, the Pilgrims disembarked at the tip of Cape Cod. Shortly before Christmas, they moved to the more protected site of Plymouth, Massachusetts. According to historians' estimates, the square-rigged *Mayflower* probably measured about 90 feet long and weighed 180 tons.

Connect to the Literature

What details in *Of Plymouth Plantation* suggest the kinds of challenges the travelers faced on the journey? What other challenges do you think travelers might face on a ship this size?

fathoms under water) till he was held up by the same rope to the brim of the water, and then with a boat hook and other means got into the ship again, and his life saved; and though he was something ill with it, yet he lived many years after, and became a profitable member both in church and commonwealth. In all this voyage there died but one of the passengers, which was William Butten, a youth, servant to Samuel Fuller, when they drew near the coast.

But to omit other things (that I may be brief), after long beating at sea they fell with that land which is called Cape Cod; the which being made and certainly known to be it, they were not a little joyful. After some deliberation had amongst themselves and with the master of the ship, they tacked about[9] and resolved to stand for the southward (the wind and weather being fair) to find some place about Hudson's River for their **habitation**. But after they had sailed that course about half the day, they fell amongst dangerous shoals[10] and roaring breakers, and they were so far entangled therewith as they conceived themselves in great danger; and the wind shrinking upon them withal,[11] they resolved to bear up again for the Cape, and thought themselves happy to get out of those dangers before night overtook them, as by God's providence they did. And the next day they got into the Cape harbor,[12] where they rid in safety. . . .

Being thus arrived in a good harbor and brought safe to land, they fell upon their knees and blessed the God of heaven, who had brought them over the vast and furious ocean, and delivered them from all the perils and miseries thereof, again to set their feet on the firm and stable earth, their proper element. . . .

But here I cannot but stay and make a pause, and stand half amazed at this poor people's present condition; and so I think will the reader too, when he well considers the same. Being thus passed the vast ocean, and a sea of troubles before in their preparation (as may be remembered by that which went before), they had now no friends to welcome them, nor inns to entertain or refresh their weather-beaten bodies, no houses or much less towns to repair to, to seek for succor.[13] It is recorded in Scripture[14] as a mercy to the apostle and his shipwrecked company, that the barbarians

Vocabulary
habitation (hab′ i tā′ shen) *n.* place to live; group of homes or dwellings

9. **tacked about** sailed back and forth so the wind would hit the sails at the best angles.
10. **shoals** (shōlz) *n.* sandbars or shallow areas that are dangerous to navigate.
11. **withal** (w*ith* ôl′) *adv.* also.
12. **Cape harbor** now called Provincetown Harbor.
13. **succor** (suk′ ər) *n.* help; relief.
14. **Scripture** In Acts 27–28, when the Apostle Paul and a group of other Christians are shipwrecked on the island of Malta, they are treated kindly by the "barbarians" who live there.

showed them no small kindness in refreshing them, but these savage barbarians, when they met with them (as after will appear) were readier to fill their sides full of arrows then otherwise. And for the season it was winter, and they that know the winters of that country know them to be sharp and violent, and subject to cruel and fierce storms, dangerous to travel to known places, much more to search an unknown coast. Besides, what could they see but a hideous and desolate wilderness, full of wild beasts and wild men? And what multitudes there might be of them they knew not. . . . What could now sustain them but the spirit of God and his grace? May not and ought not the children of these fathers rightly say: *Our fathers were Englishmen which came over this great ocean, and were ready to perish in this wilderness;*[15] *but they cried unto the Lord, and He heard their voice, and looked on their adversity, etc.*[16] *Let them therefore praise the Lord, because He is good, and His mercies endure forever. . . .*

from Book 2[17]

[1620] In these hard and difficult beginnings, they found some discontents and murmurings arise amongst some, and mutinous speeches and carriages in others; but they were soon quelled and overcome by the wisdom, patience, and just and equal carriage of things by the Governor[18] and better part, which cleaved faithfully together in the main. But that which was most sad and lamentable was that in two or three months' time, half of their company died, especially in January and February, being the depth of winter, and wanting houses and other comforts; being infected with the scurvy[19] and other diseases, which this long voyage and their inaccommodate[20] condition had brought upon them; so as there died sometimes two or three of a day, in the foresaid time; that of one hundred and odd persons, scarce fifty remained.

And of these in the time of most distress, there was but six or seven sound persons, who, to their great commendations be it spoken, spared no pains, night nor day, but with abundance of toil and hazard of their own health, fetched them wood, made them fires, dressed them meat, made their beds, washed their loathsome clothes, clothed and unclothed them; in a word, did all the homely[21] and necessary offices for them which dainty and queasy stomachs

Vocabulary

subject to (sub′ jikt to͞o) *adj.* likely to be affected by something

adversity (ad vʉr′ si tē) *n.* hardship; difficulty

What season was it when the Pilgrims arrived in Cape Cod?

---

15. **wilderness** Bradford is comparing the Pilgrims to the ancient Hebrews, who wandered in the desert after fleeing Egypt and before reaching the Promised Land.
16. **they cried . . . etc.** Bradford is paraphrasing a passage from the Hebrew Bible (Deuteronomy 26:7).
17. **Book 2** Here Bradford switches from chapter divisions to book divisions.
18. **Governor** John Carver (c. 1576–1621) was the first governor of Plymouth Colony but died during his first year of office. Bradford succeeded him as governor.
19. **scurvy** (skʉr′ vē) *n.* disease cause by a vitamin C deficiency.
20. **inaccommodate** (in′ ə käm′ ə dāt′) *adj.* unfit.
21. **homely** *adj.* domestic.

cannot endure to hear named; and all this willingly and cheerfully, without any grudging in the least, showing herein their true love unto their friends and brethren. A rare example and worthy to be remembered. Two of these seven were Mr. William Brewster,[22] their reverend Elder, and Myles Standish,[23] their Captain and military commander, unto whom myself, and many others were much beholden in our low and sick condition. And yet the Lord so upheld these persons, as in this general calamity they were not at all infected either with sickness, or lameness. And what I have said of these, I may say of many others who died in this general visitation,[24] and others yet living, that whilst they had health, yea, or any strength continuing, they were not wanting to any that had need of them. And I doubt not but their recompense is with the Lord.

Vocabulary
calamity (kə lam′ ə tē) *n.* disaster; catastrophe

But I may not here pass by another remarkable passage not to be forgotten. As this calamity fell among the passengers that were to be left here to plant, and were hasted ashore and made to drink water, that the seamen might have the more beer, and one[25] in his sickness desiring but a small can of beer, it was answered that if he were their own father he should have none; the disease began to fall amongst them also, so as almost half of their company died before they went away, and many of their officers and lustiest men, as the boatswain, gunner, three quartermasters, the cook, and others. At which the master was something stricken and sent to the sick ashore and told the Governor he should send for beer for them that had need of it, though he drunk water homeward bound.

Literary Analysis
Author's Purpose
Why do you think Bradford describes in such detail the different reactions of the crew and the Pilgrims to the illness?

But now amongst his company there was far another kind of carriage[26] in this misery then amongst the passengers; for they that had been boon[27] companions in drinking and jollity in the time of their health and welfare began now to desert one another in this calamity, saying they would not hazard their lives for them, they should be infected by coming to help them in their cabins, and so, after they came to die by it, would do little or nothing for them, but if they died let them die. But such of the passengers as were yet aboard showed them what mercy they could, which made some of their hearts relent, as the boatswain (and some others), who was a proud young man, and would often curse and scoff at the passengers; but when he grew weak, they had compassion on

Vocabulary
relent (ri lent′) *v.* become less harsh; be more merciful

---

22. **William Brewster** (1567–1644) one of the Pilgrim leaders.
23. **Myles Standish** (c. 1584–1656) professional soldier hired by the Pilgrims to be their military advisor. He was not originally a Puritan but later became a member of the congregation.
24. **visitation** *n.* affliction.
25. **one** Bradford is referring to himself.
26. **carriage** *n.* behavior.
27. **boon** *adj.* close.

him and helped him; then he confessed he did not deserve it at their hands, he had abused them in word and deed. O! saith he, you, I now see, show your love like Christians indeed one to another, but we let one another lie and die like dogs. . . .

All this while the Indians came skulking about them, and would sometimes show themselves aloof of, but when any approached near them, they would run away. And once they stole away their tools where they had been at work, and were gone to dinner. But about the 16th of March a certain Indian came boldly amongst them, and spoke to them in broken English, which they could well understand, but marveled at it. At length they understood by discourse with him that he was not of these parts, but belonged to the eastern parts, where some English ships came to fish, with whom he was acquainted, and could name sundry of them by their names, amongst whom he had got his language. He became profitable to them in acquainting them with many things concerning the state of the country in the east parts where he lived, which was afterwards profitable unto them; as also of the people here, of their names, number, and strength; of their situation and distance from this place, and who was chief amongst them. His name was Samoset;[28] he told them also of another Indian whose name was Squanto,[29] a native of this place, who had been

▲ Critical Viewing Do you think this picture is an accurate representation of the first Thanksgiving? Why or why not? **[Judge; Support]**

Who is Samoset, and how do the Pilgrims meet him?

---

28. **Samoset** (sam´ ə set´) (d. 1655) a Pemaquid tribal chief from Maine.
29. **Squanto** (skwän´ tō) (d. 1622) a member of the Pawtuxet tribe who in 1614 had been kidnapped by an English sea captain and taken to Spain to be sold as a slave. He escaped and eventually returned to Massachusetts in 1619, only to find that his home village had been destroyed by plague.

Reading Strategy
Breaking Down Long Sentences What is the essential action described in the sentence beginning "Being, after some time..."?

in England and could speak better English then himself. Being, after some time of entertainment and gifts, dismissed, a while after he came again, and 5 more with him, and they brought again all the tools that were stolen away before, and made way for the coming of their great sachem,[30] called Massasoit,[31] who, about four or five days after, came with the chief of his friends, and other attendance, with the aforesaid Squanto. With whom, after friendly entertainment, and some gifts given him, they made a peace with him (which hath now continued this 24 years)[32] in these terms:

1. That neither he nor any of his should injure or do hurt to any of their people.
2. That if any of his did any hurt to any of theirs, he should send the offender, that they might punish him.
3. That if anything were taken away from any of theirs, he should cause it to be restored; and they should do the like to his.
4. If any did unjustly war against him, they would aid him; if any did war against them, he should aid them.
5. He should send to his neighbors confederates, to certify them of this, that they might not wrong them, but might be likewise comprised in the conditions of peace.
6. That when their men came to them, they should leave their bows and arrows behind them.

Literary Analysis
Author's Purpose Why do you think Bradford refers to Squanto as a "special instrument"?

After these things he returned to his place called Sowams,[33] some 40 mile from this place, but Squanto continued with them and was their interpreter, and was a special instrument sent of God for their good beyond their expectation. He directed them how to set their corn, where to take fish and to procure other commodities, and was also their pilot to bring them to unknown places for their profit, and never left them till he died. He was a native of this place, and scarce any left alive besides himself. He was carried away with diverse others by one Hunt,[34] a master of a ship, who thought to sell them for slaves in Spain; but he got away for England and was entertained by a merchant in London and employed to Newfoundland and other parts, and lastly brought hither into these parts. . . .

---

30. sachem (sā′ chəm) chief.
31. Massasoit (mas′ ə soit′) (c. 1580–1661) the supreme sachem (chief) of the Wampanoag peoples.
32. now . . . 24 years The treaty actually lasted until King Philip's War began in 1675.
33. Sowams (sō′ ämz) present site of Warren, Rhode Island.
34. Hunt Thomas Hunt was captain of one of the ships in John Smith's expedition to Virginia.

[1621] . . . They began now to gather in the small harvest they had,[35] and to fit up their houses and dwellings against winter, being all well recovered in health and strength, and had all things in good plenty; for as some were thus employed in affairs abroad, others were exercised in fishing, about cod and bass and other fish, of which they took good store, of which every family had their portion. All the summer there was no want. And now began to come in store of fowl, as winter approached, of which this place did abound when they came first (but afterward decreased by degrees). And besides water fowl, there was great store of wild turkeys, of which they took many, besides venison, etc. Besides they had about a peck of meal a week to a person, or now since harvest, Indian corn to that proportion. Which made many afterwards write so largely of their plenty here to their friends in England, which were not feigned, but true reports.

35. They . . . had This section of Bradford's narrative is often titled "The First Thanksgiving."

Critical Reading

Cite textual evidence to support your responses.

1. **Key Ideas and Details (a)** What were some of the hardships the Pilgrims faced during their trip across the Atlantic and their first winter at Plymouth? **(b) Interpret:** What do their troubles tell you about the climate and landscape of Plymouth?
2. **Key Ideas and Details (a) Draw Conclusions:** What message do you think Bradford is trying to convey in this narrative? **(b) Apply:** How might the message have meaning for people today?
3. **Integration of Knowledge and Ideas Hypothesize:** In what ways might this account have been different if the Pilgrims had settled farther south?
4. **Integration of Knowledge and Ideas Evaluate:** Has this account changed your impression of the Pilgrims? Explain your answer.
5. **Integration of Knowledge and Ideas** How are the Pilgrims' values and beliefs evident in the ways they respond to problems? In your response, use at least two of these Essential Question words: *just, commitment, gratitude, conviction.* ***[Connecting to the Essential Question: What makes American literature American?]***

After You Read

from *Of Plymouth Plantation*

Literary Analysis

1. **Craft and Structure** Complete these sentences to describe Bradford's **purpose** for writing and the **audience** he wanted to reach:
   - Bradford wrote *Of Plymouth Plantation* in order to ______.
   - He wrote this historical account for an audience that included ______.
2. **Craft and Structure** Use a chart like the one shown to explore how specific details in Bradford's account help him achieve his purpose for writing. **(a)** Choose four details, descriptions, or incidents that you think are especially important to Bradford's narrative. **(b)** For each one, explain why you think Bradford chose to include it and how it helped him achieve his overall purpose for writing.

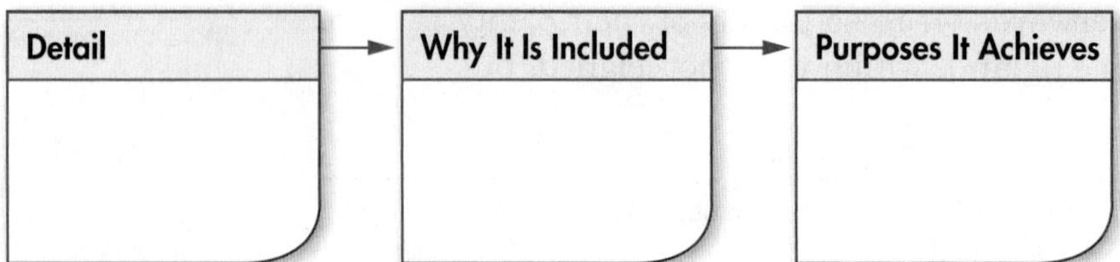

3. **Key Ideas and Details (a)** At what points does Bradford see religious or spiritual meaning in incidents that happen to the Pilgrims as a whole or to individuals? **(b)** In what ways does this both reflect his beliefs and support one of his purposes for writing?
4. **Integration of Knowledge and Ideas** Do you think Bradford succeeded in writing a document that fulfilled his original purpose? Explain why or why not.
5. **Integration of Knowledge and Ideas** In what ways are modern readers both similar to and different from Bradford's original audience?
6. **Integration of Knowledge and Ideas** Do you think that modern readers respond in the same way to Bradford's moral and religious goals as did his original readers? Explain.
7. **Integration of Knowledge and Ideas (a)** How might Bradford's first audience have responded to his depiction of Native Americans? **(b)** In what ways do today's readers bring a different perspective to this element of his narrative?

Reading Strategy

8. **(a)** Choose three sentences from the narrative that you find particularly challenging to understand. **(b) Break down the long sentences** into their essential parts—the subject and the verb. **(c)** Write the meaning of each sentence as you understand it.
9. **(a)** Choose a complex sentence and read it aloud at least twice, using punctuation to guide where to pause. **(b)** Then, restate the meaning of the sentence in simplified form.

Common Core State Standards

Writing

7. Conduct short as well as more sustained research projects to answer a question or solve a problem; narrow or broaden the inquiry when appropriate; synthesize multiple sources on the subject, demonstrating understanding of the subject under investigation. *(p. 67)*

Speaking and Listening

6. Adapt speech to a variety of contexts and tasks, demonstrating a command of formal English when indicated or appropriate. *(p. 67)*

Language

4.b. Identify and correctly use patterns of word changes that indicate different meanings or parts of speech. *(p. 67)*

PERFORMANCE TASKS

Integrated Language Skills

Vocabulary Acquisition and Use

Word Analysis: Related Forms of *peril*

The word *peril* comes from the Latin word *periculum*, which means "danger." Using your knowledge of the base word, fill in each blank with the word that best completes the sentence.

a. perilous **b.** perilously **c.** imperiled

1. Undertaking the risky voyage ______ the Pilgrims' lives.
2. The ship tossed ______ in the waves.
3. Building a new home in the wilderness was a ______ undertaking.

Vocabulary: Antonyms or Synonyms

Antonyms are words that have opposite meanings. Synonyms are words that have similar meanings. Decide whether the words in each of the following pairs are antonyms or synonyms. Then, explain your reasoning.

1. calamity, misfortune
2. relent, intensify
3. subject to, prone
4. adversity, ease
5. peril, safety
6. habitation, dwelling

Writing

Explanatory Text Imagine that time travel is possible and William Bradford is coming to speak at your school. Write the opening **speech** that will be used to introduce him to the assembly. Include information about his life and achievements, and explain why his perspective will be valuable to the audience.

Prewriting Reread the biography of Bradford on page 57 and the excerpt from his narrative. In a chart like the one shown, record questions you still have about Bradford. Then, use both print and electronic sources to find answers to these questions. Document answers and sources in your chart.

Using Clear Research Questions

Research Question	Answer	Source
1.		
2.		
3.		

Drafting As you draft, strike a tone that is informative and respectful, but friendly. Avoid using words that are either too complicated or too casual. Use appropriate formal English, but try to sound natural and fresh, rather than stiff or overly proper. To check your tone, pause to read your work aloud to yourself.

Revising Reread your introduction and make sure that all of the facts you have included are accurate. Double-check specific details and correct them as needed. Finally, read your work aloud as though you are delivering it for an audience. Replace words or sections that sound artificial or forced.

Exploration Past and Present

When producer Gene Roddenberry pitched a classic adventure drama to the NBC television network, his mission was to get the money he needed to explore new worlds on television. His series *Star Trek* debuted in 1966, and its opening phrase, "to boldly go where no man has gone before," became instantly memorable.

If space was a final frontier in twentieth-century science fiction, then Mars is "where no man has gone before" in twenty-first-century science fact. Just as the North American continent lured European explorers in the sixteenth century, the planet Mars lures scientists like Steve Squyres, the chief investigator for NASA's Mars Exploration Rover (MER) Project.

The rovers *Spirit* and *Opportunity* are twin robots that were launched toward Mars in 2003 to search for answers about the history of water on the Red Planet. From the moment they landed in early 2004, they began to send back amazing pictures, allowing people on Earth to see such Martian wonders as the floor of Victoria Crater: "We're still feeling a little awestruck," Squyres reports in his September 28, 2006, blog entry. López de Cárdenas probably felt the same when he first gazed upon the Grand Canyon.

Steve Squyres Scientist / Blogger

Steve Squyres became a geologist because he liked science and loved to climb mountains. However, he discovered his true passion when he was a graduate student at Cornell University. Looking for a subject for a term paper, he found a "room where they kept all the pictures from the *Viking* missions." Intending to look at these images of Mars explorations for a few minutes, Squyres says, "I was in that room for four hours." For the man who is now a professor at Cornell and also oversees the science operations of both Mars rovers and a team of 170 researchers at NASA's Jet Propulsion Laboratory, the Mars mission to seek "evidence concerning whether or not it once had liquid water and a habitable environment" was a success. However, Squyres is still not satisfied, saying he wants to "bring back samples." And that will require another mission, at least.

MISSION UPDATE

MARS BLOG BY STEVE SQUYRES

SEPTEMBER 28, 2006

Wow.

The last couple of days have been among the most exciting of the entire mission. The only other events I can compare this to are the two landings and the arrival of *Opportunity* at Endurance Crater. And in terms of sheer visual impact, this beats those.

Opportunity has arrived at Victoria Crater. As we expected, we came upon the view quite abruptly . . . it went from just the very tops of distant cliffs to a full-blown vista of the crater floor in just a handful of sols. And now we are perched just back from the lip of the crater at Duck Bay, with the whole thing laid out below us.

BLOG CONTINUES >>>

Our first order of business here, obviously, is going to be to take a very big Pancam panorama. We'll be starting on that very shortly, though of course it will take quite a while to get it all back to Earth. After that has been shot, we're heading for our next location . . . Cape Verde. We were considering both Cape Verde and Cabo Frio, and when we looked at all the factors together, Cape Verde won out. Wherever we stop next is where the rover will spend "superior conjunction"—the upcoming period when Mars will be out of sight behind the Sun, making communications impossible for a short while. Conjunction is coming soon, so we want to get to our conjunction spot quickly, and Cape Verde looked like an easier drive than Cabo Frio. Another factor is that we want to be parked on rock over conjunction, so that we can do some work on rock with the IDD. There seems to be good exposure of rock

BLOG CONTINUES >>>

- The distance between Earth and Mars varies from 33,900,000 to 249,000,000 miles because the two planets are orbiting the Sun at different speeds.
- Mars, named for the Roman war god, has two little moons: Phobos (fear) and Deimos (panic).
- Winds on Mars can blow up to 80 miles per hour, and dust storms sometimes blanket the planet for months.
- The gravity on Mars is only 38% as strong as the gravity on Earth.
- The temperature on Mars can be as warm as 80° Fahrenheit or as cold as -199° Fahrenheit.
- A Martian day is called a sol and lasts 24 hours, 39 minutes, and 35 seconds. A Martian year lasts 686.98 earth days.

MARS ROVER

Spirit took seven months to reach Mars from Earth.

Scientists communicate with the rovers twice per day, sending commands via the morning "uplink" and gathering data via the afternoon "downlink."

The rovers work on solar power that is absorbed during the day and stored in rechargeable batteries.

Data sent back by the rovers provides evidence that water once flowed across the surface of Mars.

There are two rovers—*Spirit* and *Opportunity*. Together, they have sent back more than 100,000 images of Mars.

Each rover carries specialized cameras, microscopic imagers, spectrometers, and rock abrasion tools.

at Cape Verde, but little or none of it at Cabo Frio. So Cape Verde it is. And how about that view?!? We're still feeling a little awestruck. The analytical part of my brain looks at that and is already doing science analysis and planning. The rest of me, though, just wants to sit back for a little while and take in the scenery.

This doesn't mean that we're going to traverse clockwise around the crater . . . we won't make that decision for quite a while yet. And it also doesn't mean we'll never go to Cabo Frio. And, to be honest, we can't even say for sure that we'll make it all the way to Cape Verde before conjunction . . . you have to be very careful when driving near cliffs this big! So we'll be driving slowly and cautiously. But Cape Verde is the next thing we're going to head off toward after we finish shooting the pan.

Critical Reading

1. **(a)** Note the names of two Martian locations or geographical features Squyres mentions. **(b) Describe:** What similarities do these names have to place names on Earth? **(c) Draw Conclusions:** Why might the scientists have chosen these names for each place?
2. Which details in the blog make it seem like Squyres is actually there on the planet instead of viewing it remotely? Explain your answer.
3. **(a) Analyze:** Which details in the text convey Squyres's excitement? Explain. **(b) Interpret:** What image of science and scientists does this blog convey? Explain.

Use these questions to hold a group discussion of "Mission Update":

4. **(a)** What are the risks of modern exploration—whether into space or into the deep sea? **(b)** Are the results worth the risks? Explain.
5. After reading this excerpt from Squyres's blog, how do you think our concepts of exploration and explorers have changed since Europeans first traveled in the Americas? In what way have those concepts remained the same as they once were?

PART 2

The Puritan Influence

Before You Read

To My Dear and Loving Husband

Connecting to the Essential Question The Puritans valued religious devotion, work, and duty over private emotions. Yet, Bradstreet's poems are filled with her feelings. As you read, notice details in this poem that refer to private feelings and those that refer to community or shared belief. Doing so will help as you consider the Essential Question: **What makes American literature American?**

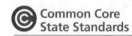

Reading Literature
5. Analyze how an author's choices concerning how to structure specific parts of a text contribute to its overall structure and meaning as well as its aesthetic impact.

Language
3.a. Apply an understanding of syntax to the study of complex texts when reading.

Literary Analysis

The Puritans' beliefs in modesty, hard work, and religious devotion were reflected in all aspects of their lives, from the simple, dark clothes they wore, to the spare furnishings they used, to the literature they wrote. The **Puritan Plain Style** is characterized by short words, direct statements, and references to everyday objects and experiences. Consider the simple, direct statements in these lines from Bradstreet's poem:

If ever two were one, then surely we,
If ever man were lov'd by wife, then thee.

Bradstreet's style may seem less plain to modern readers because of the outdated language, like the use of *thee* for *you*, and the **syntax,** or structure, of her sentences. She sometimes omits words, such as the verb *are* after *we* in the first line above, that we would include today. Her syntax also uses **inversion,** or the placing of sentence elements out of normal position. For example, instead of "let's so persevere in love," she says, "in love let's so persevere."

Reading Strategy

Preparing to Read Complex Texts To better understand a poem's *essential meaning*, **paraphrase** it, or restate it in your own words. Rewrite each sentence or clause in language and word order you understand. If necessary, consult the footnotes or a dictionary to clarify unfamiliar terms. Use a graphic organizer like the one shown to help clarify the lines of your paraphrase.

Poet's Version

My love is such that rivers cannot quench,
Nor ought but love from thee, give recompense.

Paraphrase

My love is so strong that rivers cannot relieve its thirst; only your love will satisfy me.

Vocabulary

quench (kwench) *v.* satisfy a thirst (p. 76)

recompense (rek´ əm pens´) *n.* something given or done in return for something else; repayment (p. 76)

manifold (man´ ə fōld´) *adv.* in many ways (p. 76)

persevere (pur´ sə vir´) *v.* continue despite hardship; persist (p. 76)

Anne Bradstreet *(1612–1672)*

Author of **"To My Dear and Loving Husband"**

Anne Bradstreet and her husband, Simon, arrived in the Massachusetts Bay Colony in 1630, when she was only eighteen. Armed with the convictions of her Puritan upbringing, she left behind her hometown of Northampton, England, to start afresh in America. It was not an easy life for Bradstreet, who raised eight children, suffered through multiple illnesses, and faced many hardships.

A Private Writer Made Public Despite the difficulties she endured, Bradstreet was able to devote her spare moments to the very "unladylike" occupation of writing. She wrote for herself, not for publication. Nevertheless, in 1650, John Woodbridge, her brother-in-law, arranged for the publication in England of a collection of her scholarly poems, *The Tenth Muse Lately Sprung Up in America, By a Gentlewoman of Those Parts.* Generally considered to be the first collection of original poetry written in colonial America, the book examined the rights of women to learn and express themselves. Bradstreet's later poems, such as "To My Dear and Loving Husband," are more personal, expressing her feelings about the joys and difficulties of everyday Puritan life. In one, she wrote about her thoughts before giving birth. In another, she wrote about the death of a grandchild.

Bradstreet's poetry reflects the Puritans' knowledge of the stories and language of the Bible, as well as their concern for the relationship between earthly and heavenly life. Her work also exhibits some of the characteristics of the French and English poetry of her day.

In 1956, the poet John Berryman wrote "Homage to Mistress Bradstreet," a long poem that pays tribute to this first American poet.

There is no object that we see; no action that we do; no good that we enjoy; no evil that we feel, or fear, but we may make some spiritual advantage of all: and he that makes such improvement is wise, as well as pious.

To My Dear and Loving Husband

Anne Bradstreet

Reading Strategy
Paraphrasing
How would you paraphrase these first two lines?

Vocabulary

quench (kwench) *v.* satisfy a thirst

recompense (rek′ əm pens′) *n.* repayment; something given or done in return for something else

manifold (man′ ə fōld′) *adv.* in many ways

persevere (pʉr′ sə vir′) *v.* persist; be steadfast in purpose

If ever two were one, then surely we.
If ever man were lov'd by wife, then thee;
If ever wife was happy in a man,
Compare with me ye women if you can.

I prize thy love more than whole mines of gold,
Or all the riches that the East doth hold.
My love is such that rivers cannot **quench**,
Nor ought[1] but love from thee, give **recompense**.
Thy love is such I can no way repay,

The heavens reward thee **manifold**, I pray.
Then while we live, in love let's so **persevere**,[2]
That when we live no more, we may live ever.

1. **ought** (ôt) *n.* anything whatever.
2. **persevere** pronounced (pʉr′ sə vir′) in the seventeenth century, and thus rhymed with the word *ever.*

Critical Reading 

1. **Key Ideas and Details** **(a)** What does the speaker value more than "whole mines of gold"? **(b) Distinguish:** What other images suggest the richness and abundance of the love the speaker and her husband share?
2. **Key Ideas and Details** **(a) Analyze:** What is the apparent contradiction in the last two lines? **(b) Draw Conclusions:** What does the last stanza reveal about Puritan beliefs in the afterlife?
3. **Craft and Structure** **(a)** Note where Bradstreet uses repetition in the first stanza. **(b) Analyze:** How does her use of repetition suggest a growing emotional intensity?
4. **Integration of Knowledge and Ideas** Which aspect of the speaker is more important in this poem—the private or the public self? Use at least two of these Essential Question words in your response: *community, personal, unique, social.* ***[Connecting to the Essential Question: What makes American literature American?]***

▲ Critical Viewing
How does this painting present Bradstreet as both poet and Puritan housewife? **[Analyze]**

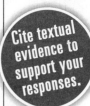

Cite textual evidence to support your responses.

WORLD LITERATURE IN CONTEXT

The Tenth Muse

Title page of *The Tenth Muse* by Anne Bradstreet, London, 1650 ▶

Anne Bradstreet's first book of poetry was published in England under the title *The Tenth Muse Lately Sprung Up in America.* In Greek Mythology, the original nine Muses were goddesses, daughters of Zeus, the ruler of the gods. The Muses were thought to be the source of inspiration for all artists, poets, musicians, dancers — and even philosophers. The Muses each had a specialty, as shown in the chart.

In Greek antiquity, the philosopher Plato referred to Sappho, the noted lyric poet, as The Tenth Muse because her poetry was so beautiful. The label lived through the centuries. Gifted, forward-thinking women writers are sometimes called "Tenth Muse." Anne Bradstreet was hailed as a Tenth Muse, as was her Mexican contemporary, Sor Juana Inés de La Cruz. Sor Juana was a noted poet and playwright, a fierce intellectual, and a woman of faith. She spent most of her adult life as a nun in the Convent of the Order of Saint Jerome. In 1689, an anthology of her poetry was published in Spain titled *The Overflowing of the Castalian Spring, by the Tenth Muse of Mexico.*

MUSE	SHE INSPIRED
CALLIOPE *"... beautiful of voice"*	*Eloquence and Epic Poetry*
ERATO *"... amorous"*	*Love Poetry, Lyrics, and Wedding Songs*
CLIO *"... glorious"*	*History*
EUTERPE *"... charming"*	*Music and Lyric Poetry*
MELPOMENE *"... the chanting one"*	*Tragedy*
POLYHYMNIA *"... the singer of many hymns"*	*Sacred Music*
TERPSICHORE *"... delighted with dance"*	*Choral Song and Dance*
THALIA *"... the blossoming one"*	*Comedy and Pastoral Poetry*
URANIA *"... the celestial one"*	*Astronomy*

CONNECT TO THE LITERATURE

Do you think that Tenth Muse is a fitting title for Anne Bradstreet? Why or why not?

◀ Sappho (c. 630 – c. 570 B.C.) Fresco painting Pompeii, Italy, 1st century A.D.

▼ Dance of Apollo with the Nine Muses (tempera on panel)

Sor Juana Inés de la Cruz, 18th century painting by Miguel Cabrera ▶

After You Read | *To My Dear and Loving Husband*

Literary Analysis

1. **Craft and Structure** Use a chart like the one shown to explore aspects of the poem that are typical of the **Puritan Plain Style.**

Style Element	Example
Short Words	
Direct Statements	
Familiar Objects/Experiences	

2. **Craft and Structure** Which aspects of the poem do not reflect the plainness of the Puritan ethic? Explain.
3. **Craft and Structure** **(a)** Which lines of the poem have customary **syntax? (b)** Which lines present examples of **inversion?** Explain your answers.

Reading Strategy

4. **Paraphrase** the last stanza as though you were explaining it to a friend.

Common Core State Standards

Writing

2. Write informative/explanatory texts to examine and convey complex ideas, concepts, and information clearly and accurately through the effective selection, organization, and analysis of content.

Language

5. Demonstrate understanding of figurative language, word relationships, and nuances in word meanings.

PERFORMANCE TASKS

Integrated Language Skills

Vocabulary Acquisition and Use

Word/Phrase Relationships Choose the letter of the situation that best reflects the meaning of the italicized word or phrase. Then, explain your answers.

1. *quench:* **(a)** filling up on snacks before dinner, **(b)** enjoying a glass of cool water after a long walk, **(c)** calming an unruly group of kids
2. *hard-earned recompense*: **(a)** getting a flat tire on the way to the dentist, **(b)** getting a day off after working late, **(c)** cleaning a messy room after a hard day
3. *increase manifold:* **(a)** receiving a small raise, **(b)** adding a drop to a full bucket, **(c)** getting a 300-percent return on an investment
4. *persevere:* **(a)** quitting when you get tired, **(b)** practicing until you improve, **(c)** arguing with a referee

Writing

Explanatory Text Write a brief **essay** in which you interpret the speaker's view of love and reward in this poem. First, review the poem for details relating to luxury and abundance. Then, explain how these images of wealth help the speaker express the depth of her love for her husband. Cite details from the text to support your ideas.

Before You Read *Huswifery*

Connecting to the Essential Question For most Americans, the values of working hard and being useful are important. Both can be traced back to the Puritans, who believed that all activity should have a practical purpose. As you read this poem, notice details that stress the usefulness of activity. This will help as you consider the Essential Question: **What makes American literature American?**

Common Core State Standards

Reading Literature
5. Analyze how an author's choices concerning how to structure specific parts of a text contribute to its overall structure and meaning as well as its aesthetic impact.

Literary Analysis

A **metaphor** is a figure of speech in which two very different subjects are shown to have a point of similarity. A metaphor may liken an abstract idea, such as love or friendship, to a concrete image:

Langston Hughes: "Life is a broken-winged bird."
Emily Dickinson: "Hope is the thing with feathers."

A **conceit,** also called an **extended metaphor,** is a metaphor taken to its logical limit. With a conceit, the metaphor does not end in a single line or image, but builds throughout the work. In this poem, Taylor uses the poetic structure itself to extend the metaphor of the spinning wheel into a conceit. Most poems are structured in individual **lines** organized into stanzas. A **stanza** is a group of consecutive lines that form a unit. Like a paragraph in prose, a stanza usually introduces and develops a new idea. Use a chart like the one shown to analyze how Taylor builds his conceit line by line and stanza by stanza.

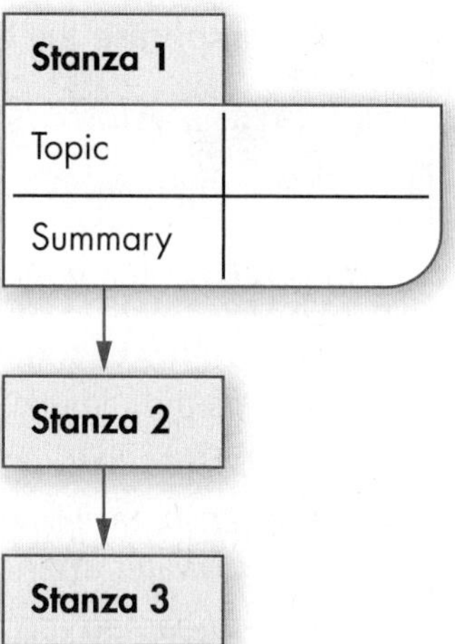

Reading Strategy

Preparing to Read Complex Texts The language of poetry is rich and dense, so you may find poetry more challenging than prose. As you read, monitor your comprehension to make sure you understand how Taylor builds his meaning. If you find the poem difficult, **adjust your reading rate** by slowing down. When you get to a complex image, you may slow down even more and take the time to form a clear, specific picture before you continue reading.

Vocabulary

affections (ə fek′ shənz) *n.* emotions (p. 82)

ordinances (ôrd′'n əns əz) *n.* sacraments or religious rites (p. 82)

judgment (juj′ mənt) *n.* power to form an opinion well; good sense (p. 82)

apparel (əp per′ əl) *n.* clothing (p. 82)

Edward Taylor (1642–1729)

Author of "Huswifery"

Puritanism was a religious reform movement that began in England in the sixteenth century. The Puritans sought to reform the Church of England and to reshape English society according to their beliefs. These efforts led to both civil strife and government persecution of the Puritans. In response, many Puritans, including Edward Taylor, fled to the American colonies.

Before his emigration to America, Edward Taylor worked as a teacher in England. Upon arriving in Boston in 1668, Taylor entered Harvard College as a sophomore, graduating in 1671. After graduation, he accepted the position of minister and physician in the small frontier farming community of Westfield, Massachusetts, and then walked more than one hundred miles, much of it through snow, to his new home.

Harsh Life in a New World Life in the village of Westfield was filled with hardships. Fierce battles between the Native Americans and the colonists left the community in constant fear. In addition, Taylor experienced many personal tragedies. Five of his eight children died in infancy; then, his wife died while she was still a young woman. He remarried and had five or six more children. (Biographers differ on the exact number.)

Edward Taylor is now generally regarded as the best of the North American colonial poets. Yet, because Taylor thought of his poetry as a form of personal worship, he allowed only two stanzas to be published during his lifetime. Some believe that he chose not to publish his poems because their joyousness and delight in sensory experience ran counter to Puritan attitudes that poetry be for moral instruction only. One of his nineteenth-century descendants donated Taylor's writings to Yale University. The stash of poems was discovered in the 1930s and, in 1939, *The Poetical Works of Edward Taylor* was published. Most of Taylor's poetry, including "Huswifery," uses extravagant comparisons, intellectual wit, and subtle argument to explore religious faith and affection.

Oh! that I ever felt what I profess.
'Twould make me then the
happi'st man alive.

Huswifery

Edward Taylor

Vocabulary

affections (ə fekʹ shənz) *n.* emotions

ordinances (ôrdʹʼn əns əz) *n.* sacraments or religious rites

judgment (jujʹ mənt) *n.* power to form an opinion well; good sense

apparel (əp perʹ əl) *n.* clothing

Make me, O Lord, Thy spinning wheel complete.
Thy holy word my distaff[1] make for me.
Make mine affections Thy swift flyers[2] neat
And make my soul Thy holy spoole to be.
My conversation make to be Thy reel
And reel the yarn thereon spun of Thy wheel.

Make me Thy loom then, knit therein this twine:
And make Thy holy spirit, Lord, wind quills:[3]
Then weave the web Thyself. The yarn is fine.
Thine ordinances make my fulling mills.[4]
Then dye the same in heavenly colors choice.
All pinked[5] with varnished flowers of paradise.

Then clothe therewith mine understanding, will,
Affections, judgment, conscience, memory
My words, and actions, that their shine may fill
My ways with glory and Thee glorify.
Then mine apparel shall display before Ye
That I am clothed in holy robes for glory.

1. **distaff** *n.* staff on which flax or wool is wound for use in spinning.
2. **flyers** *n.* part of a spinning wheel that twists fibers into yarn.
3. **quills** *n.* weaver's spindles or bobbins.
4. **fulling mills** *n.* machines that shrink and thicken cloth to the texture of felt.
5. **pinked** *v.* decorated with a perforated pattern.

Critical Reading

Cite textual evidence to support your responses.

1. **Key Ideas and Details (a)** What household activities are described in the first two stanzas? **(b) Analyze:** How do these images contribute to the idea of being "clothed in holy robes for glory," stated in the third stanza?
2. **Key Ideas and Details (a) Interpret:** What images in this poem may have contradicted the Puritan requirement that clothing be dark and plain? **(b) Deduce:** What do these images suggest about the speaker's feelings about God?
3. **Integration of Knowledge and Ideas** Do you think the Puritans would have considered this poem useful? In your answer, use at least two of these Essential Question words: *expression, practical, spiritual, labor.* ***[Connecting to the Essential Question: What makes American literature American?]***

After You Read Huswifery

Literary Analysis

1. **Craft and Structure (a)** In the first line, what request does the poet make? **(b)** Explain how this is a **metaphor**—what two dissimilar things are being compared? **(c)** What is the point of similarity between the two dissimilar things?
2. **Craft and Structure** Explain how the metaphors developed in each **stanza** build to a **conceit** for the poem as a whole.

Reading Strategy

3. Look back at how you **adjusted your reading rate** as you read the poem. Use a chart like the one shown to classify which lines you read at your usual speed and which you read more slowly. Use your chart to guide a second reading of the poem.

Average speed	More slowly

4. Explain how you integrated footnotes into your readings of the poem.

Common Core State Standards

Writing

2. Write informative/explanatory texts to examine and convey complex ideas, concepts, and information clearly and accurately through the effective selection, organization, and analysis of content.

2.d. Use precise language, domain-specific vocabulary, and techniques such as metaphor, simile, and analogy to manage the complexity of the topic.

PERFORMANCE TASKS

Integrated Language Skills

Vocabulary Acquisition and Use

True or False Decide whether each statement below is true or false. Explain each answer.

1. It is always possible to control your **affections,** regardless of the situation.
2. **Ordinances** should be fulfilled with respect and care.
3. Sleep deprivation can impair your **judgment.**
4. Wool, cotton, and polyester are examples of fine **apparel.**

Writing

Explanatory Text Taylor's poem describes the processes of turning raw materials into clothing. It works on two levels—as a description of an ordinary activity and as a metaphor for religious devotion. In a **reflective essay,** describe the procedure of a common household chore and explore how that task suggests a larger, or metaphoric, meaning. Include these elements:

- a complete, step-by-step description of the task from beginning to end
- vivid sensory details that appeal to the five senses
- a thoughtful insight about the meaning the task holds for you

Before You Read

from *Sinners in the Hands of an Angry God*

Connecting to the Essential Question This sermon had a powerful effect on its original audiences. As you read, note passages that you think most affected listeners. This will help as you consider the Essential Question: **How does literature shape or reflect society?**

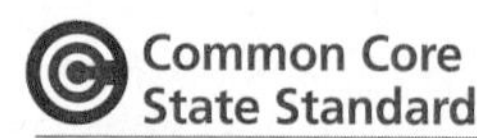

Reading Informational Text
6. Determine an author's point of view or purpose in a text in which the rhetoric is particularly effective, analyzing how style and content contribute to the power, persuasiveness, or beauty of the text.

Language
4. Determine or clarify the meaning of unknown and multiple-meaning words and phrases based on *grades 11–12 reading content.*
4.a. Use context as a clue to the meaning of a word or phrase

Literary Analysis

A **sermon** is broadly defined as a speech given from a pulpit in a house of worship. Like its written counterpart, the essay, a sermon conveys the speaker's message or point of view. As a form of **oratory,** or formal public speaking, sermons almost always display the following elements:

- They are *persuasive*, inspiring listeners to take action.
- They address the needs and concerns of the *audience,* or listeners.
- They *appeal to the emotions*.
- They include *expressive and rhythmic language*.

Often, orators also include images, patterns, characters, or stories from the Bible, myth, or classical literature. These **archetypes** add a deeper dimension for listeners who apply the ancient meanings to the new message. As you read, look for these elements of oratory in the sermon.

Reading Strategy

Preparing to Read Complex Texts As you read, monitor your comprehension of unfamiliar words and look for **context clues**—other words, phrases, and sentences—that can help you understand. For example, take the word *abominable* in this passage: "You are ten thousand times more abominable in his [God's] eyes, than the most hateful venomous serpent is in ours…." Edwards likens the way God views the sinner with the way we view a snake. From this clue, you can figure out that *abominable* must be close in meaning to *disgusting* or *horrible*. As you read, use a chart like the one shown to define other unfamiliar words by using context clues.

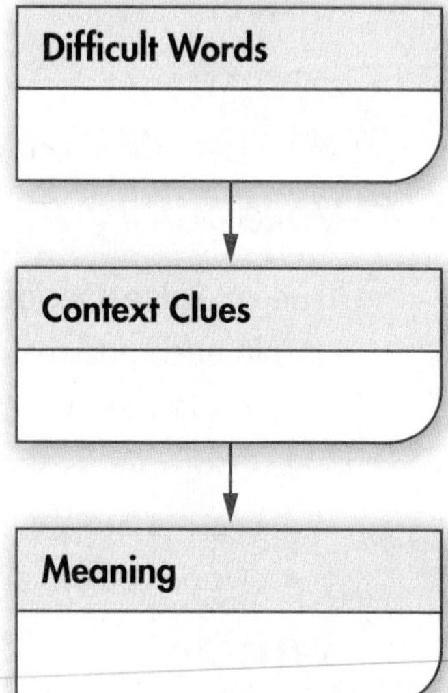

Vocabulary

constitution (kän′ stə to͞o′ shən) *n.* physical makeup of a person (p. 87)

prudence (pro͞o′ dəns) *n.* carefulness; caution (p. 88)

omnipotent (äm nip′ ə tənt) *adj.* all-powerful (p. 88)

mediator (mē′ dē ā tər) *n.* one who reconciles opposing groups (p. 89)

induce (in do͞os′) *v.* cause; bring about (p. 89)

Jonathan Edwards *(1703–1758)*

Author of "Sinners in the Hands of an Angry God"

The sermons of Jonathan Edwards were so filled with "fire and brimstone"—a phrase symbolizing the torments of hell endured by sinners—that his name alone was enough to make many eighteenth-century Puritans shake in their shoes. Yet, Edwards was not just a stone-faced religious zealot. He was also a man who believed in science and reason and who saw in the physical world the proof of God's presence and will.

A Born Preacher This great American theologian was born in East Windsor, Connecticut, where he grew up in an atmosphere of devout discipline. As a young boy, he is said to have demonstrated his religious devotion by preaching sermons to his playmates. He also displayed academic brilliance, learning to speak Latin, Greek, and Hebrew before he was twelve. Edwards entered the Collegiate School of Connecticut (now Yale University) at the age of thirteen and graduated four years later as valedictorian. He went on to earn his master's degree in theology.

The Great Awakening Edwards began his preaching career in 1727 as assistant to his grandfather, Solomon Stoddard. Stoddard was pastor of the church at Northampton, Massachusetts, one of the largest and wealthiest Puritan congregations. Edwards became the church pastor two years later when his grandfather died. Committed to a return to the orthodoxy and fervent faith of the Puritan past, Edwards became one of the leaders of the Great Awakening, a religious revival that swept the colonies in the 1730s and 1740s.

Fall from Favor As pastor of the church at Northampton, Edwards had instituted disciplinary proceedings against members of his congregation for reading what he considered improper books. In his sermons he denounced by name those he considered sinners. Such actions drew criticism and, in 1750, a council representing ten congregations dismissed Edwards as pastor.

After his dismissal, Edwards moved to Stockbridge, Massachusetts, where he preached to the Native Americans and wrote his most important theological works. He continued to preach and write until his death in 1758, shortly after becoming president of the College of New Jersey (now Princeton University). Although in most of his writings Edwards appeals to reason, his emotional sermon "Sinners in the Hands of an Angry God" is by far his most famous work. It demonstrates Edwards's tremendous powers of persuasion and captures the religious fervor of the Great Awakening.

▶ **Critical Viewing**
Edwards preached in churches similar to this. What values do you think are reflected in the style of this building? **[Analyze]**

from Sinners in the Hands of an Angry God

Jonathan Edwards

BACKGROUND Jonathan Edwards delivered this famous sermon to a congregation in Enfield, Connecticut, in 1741. Surprisingly, he spoke quietly and without emotion. According to one account, he read the six-hour work in a level voice, staring over the heads of his audience at the bell rope that hung against the back wall "as if he would stare it in two." Despite his calm manner, his listeners are said to have screamed in terror, and Edwards had to stop several times to ask for silence.

This is the case of every one of you that are out of Christ:[1] That world of misery, that lake of burning brimstone, is extended abroad under you. There is the dreadful pit of the glowing flames of the wrath of God; there is Hell's wide gaping mouth open; and you have nothing to stand upon, nor anything to take hold of; there is nothing between you and Hell but the air; it is only the power and mere pleasure of God that holds you up.

You probably are not sensible of this; you find you are kept out of Hell, but do not see the hand of God in it; but look at other things, as the good state of your bodily **constitution**, your care of your own life, and the means you use for your own preservation. But indeed these things are nothing; if God should withdraw his hand, they would avail no more to keep you from falling than the thin air to hold up a person that is suspended in it.

Vocabulary
constitution (kän′ stə to͞o′ shən) *n.* physical makeup of a person

Reading Check
Of what does Edwards believe his congregation is not "sensible"?

1. **out of Christ** not in God's grace.

The American EXPERIENCE

Biblical Imagery

Jonathan Edwards's frightening imagery of God's potential for wrath and destruction recalls stories of fires, floods, and divine retribution in the Old Testament of the King James Bible. While this imagery terrified Edwards's audience, they would have found it quite familiar. In fact, in 1741, when Edwards delivered this sermon, the King James Bible had been in wide circulation for 130 years. The first English version of the Bible to include both the Old and New Testaments, the King James Bible had been produced at the express request of the Puritans in England in 1611. This Bible, with its haunting language and powerful imagery, would have been common daily reading for most of Edwards's listeners.

Connect to the Literature

How do you think a contemporary audience of worshippers would react to this type of "fire and brimstone" biblical imagery?

Vocabulary

prudence (pro͞o′ dəns) *n.* carefulness; caution

omnipotent (äm nip′ ə tənt) *adj.* all-powerful

Your wickedness makes you as it were heavy as lead, and to tend downwards with great weight and pressure towards Hell; and if God should let you go, you would immediately sink and swiftly descend and plunge into the bottomless gulf, and your healthy constitution, and your own care and prudence, and best contrivance, and all your righteousness, would have no more influence to uphold you and keep you out of Hell, than a spider's web would have to stop a fallen rock. Were it not for the sovereign pleasure of God, the earth would not bear you one moment . . . The world would spew you out, were it not for the sovereign hand of Him who hath subjected it in hope. There are black clouds of God's wrath now hanging directly over your heads, full of the dreadful storm, and big with thunder; and were it not for the restraining hand of God, it would immediately burst forth upon you. The sovereign pleasure of God, for the present, stays[2] his rough wind; otherwise it would come with fury, and your destruction would come like a whirlwind, and you would be like the chaff of the summer threshing floor.

The wrath of God is like great waters that are dammed for the present; they increase more and more, and rise higher and higher, till an outlet is given; and the longer the stream is stopped, the more rapid and mighty is its course, when once it is let loose. It is true, that judgment against your evil works has not been executed hitherto; the Hoods of God's vengeance have been withheld; but your guilt in the meantime is constantly increasing, and you are every day treasuring up more wrath; the waters are constantly rising, and waxing more and more mighty; and there is nothing but the mere pleasure of God, that holds the waters back, that are unwilling to be stopped, and press hard to go forward. If God should only withdraw his hand from the floodgate, it would immediately fly open, and the fiery floods of the fierceness and wrath of God, would rush forth with inconceivable fury, and would come upon you with omnipotent power; and if your strength were ten thousand times greater than it is, yea, ten thousand times greater than the strength of the stoutest, sturdiest devil in Hell, it would be nothing to withstand or endure it.

The bow of God's wrath is bent, and the arrow made ready on the string, and justice bends the arrow at your heart, and strains the bow, and it is nothing but the mere pleasure of God, and that of an angry God, without any promise or obligation at all, that keeps the arrow one moment from being made drunk with your blood. Thus all you that never passed under a great change of heart, by the mighty power of the spirit of God upon your souls; all you that were never born again, and made new creatures, and raised from being dead in sin, to

2. **stays** (stāz) *v.* restrains.

a state of new, and before altogether unexperienced light and life, are in the hands of an angry God. However you may have reformed your life in many things, and may have had religious affections, and may keep up a form of religion in your families and closets,[3] and in the house of God, it is nothing but His mere pleasure that keeps you from being this moment swallowed up in everlasting destruction. However unconvinced you may now be of the truth of what you hear, by and by you will be fully convinced of it.

Those that are gone from being in the like circumstances with you, see that it was so with them; for destruction came suddenly upon most of them; when they expected nothing of it, and while they were saying, peace and safety: now they see, that those things on which they depended for peace and safety, were nothing but thin air and empty shadows.

The God that holds you over the pit of Hell, much as one holds a spider, or some loathsome insect over the fire, abhors you, and is dreadfully provoked: his wrath towards you burns like fire; he looks upon you as worthy of nothing else, but to be cast into the fire; he is of purer eyes than to bear to have you in his sight; you are ten thousand times more abominable in his eyes, than the most hateful venomous serpent is in ours. . . .

O sinner! Consider the fearful danger you are in: it is a great furnace of wrath, a wide and bottomless pit, full of the fire of wrath, that you are held over in the hand of that God, whose wrath is provoked and incensed as much against you, as against many of the damned in Hell. You hang by a slender thread, with the flames of divine wrath flashing about it, and ready every moment to singe it, and burn it asunder; and you have no interest in any **mediator**, and nothing to lay hold of to save yourself, nothing to keep off the flames of wrath, nothing of your own, nothing that you ever have done, nothing that you can do, to **induce** God to spare you one moment. . . .

When God beholds the ineffable[4] extremity of your case, and sees your torment to be so vastly disproportioned to your strength, and sees how your poor soul is crushed, and sinks down, as it were, into an infinite gloom; he will have no compassion upon you, he will not forbear the executions of his wrath, or in the least lighten his hand; there shall be no moderation or mercy, nor will God then at all stay his rough wind; he will have no regard to your welfare, nor be at all careful lest you should suffer too much in any other sense, than only that you shall *not suffer beyond what strict justice requires. . . .*

God stands ready to pity you; this is a day of mercy; you may cry now with some encouragement of obtaining mercy. But once the day of mercy is past, your most lamentable and dolorous[5] cries and shrieks

3. **closets** *n.* small, private rooms for meditation.
4. **ineffable** (in ef´ ə bəl) *n.* inexpressible.
5. **dolorous** (dō´ lər əs) *adj.* sad; mournful.

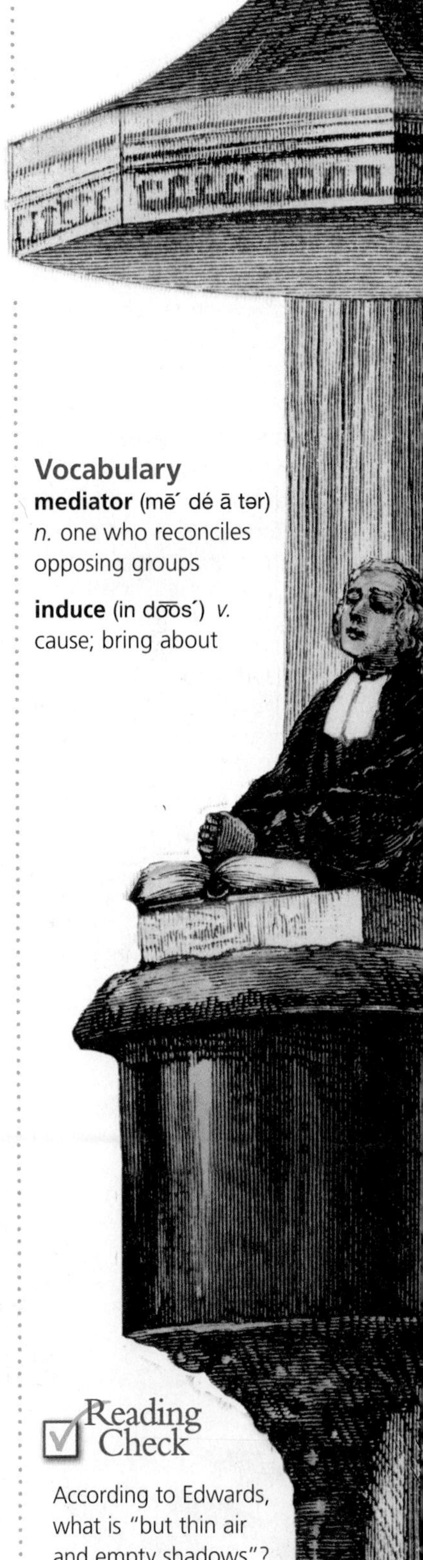

Vocabulary

mediator (mē´ dē ā tər) *n.* one who reconciles opposing groups

induce (in do͞os´) *v.* cause; bring about

Reading Check

According to Edwards, what is "but thin air and empty shadows"?

will be in vain; you will be wholly lost and thrown away of God, as to any regard to your welfare. God will have no other use to put you to, but to suffer misery; you shall be continued in being to no other end; for you will be a vessel of wrath fitted to destruction; and there will be no other use of this vessel, but to be filled full of wrath. . . .

Thus it will be with you that are in an unconverted state, if you continue in it; the infinite might, and majesty, and terribleness of the omnipotent God shall be magnified upon you, in the ineffable strength of your torments. You shall be tormented in the presence of the holy angels, and in the presence of the Lamb,[6] and when you shall be in this state of suffering, the glorious inhabitants of Heaven shall go forth and look on the awful spectacle, that they may see what the wrath and fierceness of the Almighty is; and when they have seen it, they will fall down and adore that great power and majesty. . . .

Reading Strategy
Using Context Clues
What clue does the reference to "forever" provide to the meaning of *boundless*?

It would be dreadful to suffer this fierceness and wrath of Almighty God one moment; but you must suffer it to all eternity. There will be no end to this exquisite horrible misery. When you look forward, you shall see a long forever, a boundless duration before you, which will swallow up your thoughts and amaze your soul; and you will absolutely despair of ever having any deliverance, any end, any mitigation, any rest at all. . . .

How dreadful is the state of those that are daily and hourly in the danger of this great wrath and infinite misery! But this is the dismal case of every soul in this congregation that has not been born again, however moral and strict, sober and religious, they may otherwise be. Oh that you would consider it, whether you be young or old! . . . Those of you that finally continue in a natural condition, that shall keep you out of Hell longest will be there in a little time! Your damnation does not slumber; it will come swiftly, and, in all probability, very suddenly upon many of you. You have reason to wonder that you are not already in Hell. It is doubtless the case of some whom you have seen and known, that never deserved Hell more than you, and that heretofore appeared as likely to have been now alive as you. Their case is past all hope; they are crying in extreme misery and perfect despair; but here you are in the land of the living and in the house of God, and have an opportunity to obtain salvation. What would not those poor damned hopeless souls give for one day's opportunity such as you now enjoy!

And now you have an extraordinary opportunity, a day wherein Christ has thrown the door of mercy wide open, and stands in calling and crying with a loud voice to poor sinners; a day wherein many are flocking to him, and pressing into the kingdom of God. Many are daily coming from the east, west, north and south; many that were very lately in the same miserable condition that you are in,

6. **the Lamb** Jesus.

are now in a happy state, with their hearts filled with love to him who has loved them, and washed them from their sins in his own blood, and rejoicing in hope of the glory of God. How awful is it to be left behind at such a day! To see so many others feasting, while you are pining and perishing! To see so many rejoicing and singing for joy of heart, while you have cause to mourn for sorrow of heart, and howl for vexation of spirit! . . .

Therefore, let everyone that is out of Christ now awake and fly from the wrath to come. The wrath of Almighty God is now undoubtedly hanging over a great part of this congregation: let everyone fly out of Sodom.[7] "Haste and escape for your lives, look not behind you, escape to the mountain, lest you be consumed."[8]

---

7. **Sodom** (säd′ əm) In the Bible, a city destroyed by fire because of the sinfulness of its people.
8. **"Haste . . . consumed"** from Genesis 19:17, the angels' warning to Lot, the only virtuous man in Sodom, to flee the city before they destroy it.

Critical Reading

Cite textual evidence to support your responses.

1. **Key Ideas and Details** **(a)** According to the opening paragraph, what keeps sinners from falling into hell? **(b) Interpret:** According to Edwards, what do his listeners mistakenly feel keeps them from falling into hell?
2. **Key Ideas and Details** **(a)** What words in the sermon's title suggest the emotional focus of Edwards's message? **(b) Analyze:** What additional traits does Edwards attribute to God as the sermon progresses?
3. **Key Ideas and Details** **(a)** Toward the end of the sermon, what does Edwards say sinners can obtain? **(b) Analyze Cause and Effect:** What must sinners do to obtain these things?
4. **Integration of Knowledge and Ideas** Given his purpose and the audience of worshipers to whom he spoke, do you think Edwards's sermon was effective? Why or why not?
5. **Integration of Knowledge and Ideas** This sermon played a significant role in reinvigorating Puritan faith during the 1740s. Why? State your opinion, using at least two of these Essential Question words: *powerful, beliefs, doctrine, faithful.* ***[Connecting to the Essential Question: How does literature shape or reflect society?]***

After You Read from *Sinners in the Hands of an Angry God*

Literary Analysis

1. **Key Ideas and Details (a)** What message is Edwards conveying in this **sermon? (b)** Note two places where he directly states his purpose and message.
2. **Key Ideas and Details** Explain how Edwards's purpose and message are *persuasive*. What does he want his listeners to do or think?
3. **Craft and Structure (a)** What is the main *emotional appeal* Edwards uses in his effort to move his congregation? **(b)** Considering Edwards's purpose, why is this an appropriate choice? Explain your answer.
4. **Craft and Structure (a)** What does Edwards seem to feel about those who maintain a "form of religion" or who seem "moral and strict"? **(b)** How does this part of his message show that Edwards understands his *audience* well?
5. **Craft and Structure (a)** Choose two passages that you find very powerful. **(b)** Analyze the reasons for your choice: are you responding to the message itself, to the *rhythmic and expressive language* in which it is framed, or to both?
6. **Craft and Structure** Why are images of the destructive power of nature appropriate to Edwards's message?
7. **Integration of Knowledge and Ideas** Do you think Edwards's **oratory** would have been equally effective if he had not had a reputation as a brilliant spiritual leader?
8. **Integration of Knowledge and Ideas** **(a)** Use a chart like the one shown to identify Biblical **archetypes**—images, patterns, characters, or stories—Edwards uses to describe God's wrath. **(b)** How does each archetype add to the power of Edwards's message?

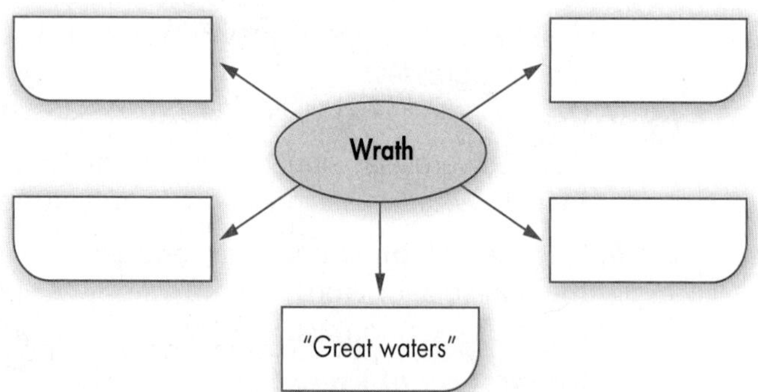

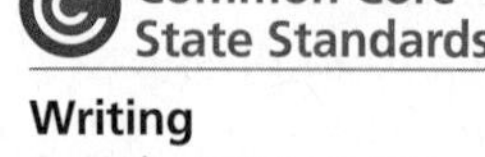

Writing

1. Write arguments to support claims in an analysis of substantive topics or texts, using valid reasoning and relevant and sufficient evidence. *(p. 93)*

Language

3.a. Vary syntax for effect. *(p. 94)*

5. Demonstrate understanding of figurative language, word relationships, and nuances in word meanings. *(p. 93)*

Reading Strategy

9. For each item below, **use context clues** to define the italicized words. Then, explain in your own words what each passage means.
   a. "you are every day treasuring up more wrath; the waters are constantly rising, and *waxing* more and more mighty…"
   b. "The God that holds you over the pit of Hell, much as one holds a spider, or some *loathsome* insect over the fire, *abhors* you, and is dreadfully provoked…"
   c. "…and you will absolutely despair of ever having any deliverance, any end, any *mitigation*, any rest at all…"

PERFORMANCE TASKS

Integrated Language Skills

Vocabulary Acquisition and Use

Word Analysis: Latin Prefix *omni-*

The Latin prefix *omni-* means "all" or "every." *Omnipotent,* then, means "all-powerful." Each of the adjectives below contains the prefix *omni-*. Use the information in parentheses to match each adjective with the situation to which it best applies.

1. omniscient (*sciens* = knowing)
2. omnivorous (*vor* = to eat)
3. omnipresent (*praesens* = present)

a. how a zoologist might describe an animal that eats both meat and plants

b. how a student might describe a brilliant teacher

c. how someone lost in the desert might describe the sun

Vocabulary: Analogies

Analogies show the relationship between pairs of words. Complete each analogy using a word from the vocabulary list on page 84. In each, your choice should create a word pair that matches the relationship between the first two words given. Then, explain your answers.

1. *Brilliant* is to *smart* as ______ is to *powerful.*
2. *Soul* is to *spiritual* as ______ is to *physical.*
3. *Translator* is to *languages* as ______ is to *enemies.*
4. *Argue* is to *reconcile* as ______ is to *prevent.*
5. *Loyalty* is to *faithless* as ______ is to *reckless.*

Writing

Argument A speaker's choice of persuasive techniques should depend on the audience and the occasion. Write an **evaluation** of the persuasive techniques that Edwards uses. Discuss the response he evokes in an audience and the ways he achieves it.

Prewriting To focus your writing, jot down examples of Edwards's uses of imagery, logical reasoning, and emotional appeals. Make sure all of your choices are relevant and provide sufficient support for your claims. Then, write one statement in which you evaluate their effectiveness in reaching an audience.

Drafting Use the statement you wrote as the basis for a strong, focused opening paragraph. Support your main point in the paragraphs that follow.

Model: Building Unity

Jonathan Edwards appealed to his audience's vulnerability by using powerful, elemental images of nature run amok. His images of air, water, and fire terrified his audience by summoning up mental pictures of unlimited natural destruction.

The paragraph contains a general statement followed by details of specific images used by Edwards.

Revising Read your evaluation as though you are seeing it for the first time. Eliminate any information that is unrelated to the main idea.

PERFORMANCE TASKS

Integrated Language Skills

Conventions and Style: Correlative Conjunctions

The use of *varied sentence structures* makes your writing more sophisticated and gives it a better flow. If you tend to use many short sentences, combine the ones that express related ideas into longer units. Correlative conjunctions can help you do this. A **correlative conjunction** is a word pair that is used to connect similar words or groups of words. Different correlative conjunctions show different relationships between ideas.

Using Correlative Conjunctions

Choppy Sentences: The sermon was frightening. The sermon was inspiring.
Combined: The sermon was *not only* frightening *but also* inspiring.

Choppy Sentences: The waters will be held back. If not, the flood gates will open.
Combined: *Either* the waters will be held back *or* the floodgates will open.

Common Correlative Conjunctions	
Both/and	Not only/but also
Either/or	Whether/or
Neither/nor	As/as

Tip: Use parallel grammatical structures after both parts of the correlative conjunction.

Practice In items 1–5, fill in the blanks with appropriate correlative conjunctions. In items 6–10, combine the two sentences using a correlative conjunction.

1. ______ the arrow will be released ______ it will not.
2. The sermon appeals ______ to people's fears ______ to their hopes.
3. Who decides ______ a person will go to heaven ______ burn in hell?
4. According to Edwards, ______ moral strictness ______ church attendance will reduce God's wrath.
5. The storm, ______ furious ______ dreadful, can be released at any time.
6. The sinner will not be spared. The serpent will not be spared.
7. He preached to Puritans. He also preached to Native Americans.
8. The storm imagery is eloquent. The storm imagery is powerful.
9. People could choose to be saved. They could choose to endure eternal suffering.
10. He can hold you out of the fire. He can withdraw His hand and let you fall.

Writing and Speaking Conventions

A. Writing For each word pair, write a sentence in which you link the two words or word groups using a correlative conjunction. Make sure to use the same grammatical structures after both parts of the correlative conjunction.

1. anger—mercy
2. miserable—eternal
3. to endure suffering—to rejoice in hope

Example: anger—mercy
Sentence: He can show either anger or mercy.

B. Speaking As a member of Edwards's congregation, write and present to the class a response to the sermon. Include two correlative conjunctions.

PH WRITING COACH
Further instruction and practice are available in *Prentice Hall Writing Coach*.

PART 3

A Nation is Born

SPEECH IS POWER: SPEECH IS TO PERSUADE, TO CONVERT, TO COMPEL.

— RALPH WALDO EMERSON

In This Section

- Defining Speeches *(p. 96)*
- Model: *from* "What to the Slave Is the Fourth of July?" by Frederick Douglass *(p. 97)*
- Study: "Speech in the Virginia Convention" by Patrick Henry *(p. 101)*
- Study: "Speech in the Convention" by Benjamin Franklin *(p. 105)*

For more practice analyzing speeches see pages 86, 538, 622, and 1104.

Defining Speeches

A **speech** is a nonfiction work that is delivered orally to an audience. Some speeches are fully composed before the speaker reads them aloud. Others are planned in notes or an outline to which the speaker refers as he or she talks.

Types of Speeches There are countless appropriate settings and purposes for speeches. Common types of speeches include the following:

- **Political Speech:** a speech focusing on an issue relating to government
- **Address:** a formal speech prepared for a special occasion, such as the dedication of a memorial or the inauguration of a new leader
- **Sermon:** a speech intended to provide religious instruction

Rhetorical Devices Regardless of the occasion, speeches typically include rhetorical devices—patterns of words and ideas that create emphasis, clarify meaning, and stir listeners' emotions. There are numerous rhetorical figures, including the following types.

- **Restatement:** expressing the same ideas using different words
  Abraham Lincoln: "...we can not dedicate—we can not consecrate—we can not hallow—this ground."
- **Anaphora:** repetition of the same word or group of words at the beginning of successive sentences, clauses, or phrases
  Winston Churchill: "We shall go on to the end, we shall fight in France, we shall fight on the seas and oceans..."
- **Rhetorical Questions:** questions asked for effect rather than answers
  Benjamin Franklin: "From such an assembly can a perfect production be expected?"

Close Read: Rhetorical Devices

These rhetorical devices appear in the Model text at right.

Repetition: restating an idea using the same words *Example: "The war is inevitable—and let it come! I repeat it, sir, let it come!" (Patrick Henry)*	**Antithesis:** juxtaposition of strongly contrasting words, images, or ideas *Example: "...ask not what your country can do for you—ask what you can do for your country." (John F. Kennedy)*
Parallelism: repeating a grammatical structure *Example: "With malice toward none; with charity for all..." (Abraham Lincoln)*	**Exclamation:** an emotional statement, often indicated in texts by an exclamation mark *Example: "...as for me, give me liberty or give me death!" (Patrick Henry)*

Model

About the Text Frederick Douglass (ca. 1818–1895) escaped from slavery and became a writer, orator, and abolitionist. On July 5, 1852, he delivered a speech at a celebration of the signing of the Declaration of Independence. In the speech he states, "This Fourth of July is *yours*, not *mine*. You may rejoice, I must mourn."

from "What to the Slave Is the Fourth of July?"
Frederick Douglass

Fellow Citizens, I am not wanting in respect for the fathers of this republic. The signers of the Declaration of Independence were brave men. They were great men too—great enough to give fame to a great age. It does not often happen to a nation to raise, at one time, such a number of truly great men. The point from which I am compelled to view them is not, certainly, the most favorable; and yet I cannot contemplate their great deeds with less than admiration. They were statesmen, patriots and heroes, and for the good they did, and the principles they contended for, I will unite with you to honor their memory.

They loved their country better than their own private interests; and, though this is not the highest form of human excellence, all will concede that it is a rare virtue, and that when it is exhibited, it ought to command respect. He who will, intelligently, lay down his life for his country, is a man whom it is not in human nature to despise. Your fathers staked their lives, their fortunes, and their sacred honor, on the cause of their country. In their admiration of liberty, they lost sight of all other interests.

They were peace men; but they preferred revolution to peaceful submission to bondage. They were quiet men; but they did not shrink from agitating against oppression. They showed forbearance; but that they knew its limits. They believed in order; but not in the order of tyranny. With them, nothing was "settled" that was not right. With them, justice, liberty and humanity were "final;" not slavery and oppression. You may well cherish the memory of such men. They were great in their day and generation. Their solid manhood stands out the more as we contrast it with these degenerate times.

How circumspect, exact and proportionate were all their movements! How unlike the politicians of an hour! Their statesmanship looked beyond the passing moment, and stretched away in strength into the distant future. They seized upon eternal principles, and set a glorious example in their defense. Mark them!

Fully appreciating the hardship to be encountered, firmly believing in the right of their cause, honorably inviting the scrutiny of an on-looking world, reverently appealing to heaven to attest their sincerity, soundly comprehending the solemn responsibility they were about to assume, wisely measuring the terrible odds against them, your fathers, the fathers of this republic, did, most deliberately, under the inspiration of a glorious patriotism, and with a sublime faith in the great principles of justice and freedom, lay deep the corner-stone of the national superstructure, which has risen and still rises in grandeur around you.

Repetition Repeated use of the word "great" supports the idea that Douglass honors the nation's founders. This allows listeners to more readily accept the argument he will later present that the founders' greatness does not excuse their support of slavery.

Antithesis Douglass's use of opposing ideas emphasizes the complexity of the founding fathers' beliefs and actions.

Exclamation Douglass uses exclamation to show the urgency of his feelings and to stir emotion in his audience.

Parallelism Douglass uses parallelism to add urgency to his accounting of the founding fathers' wisdom and courage.

Before You Read

Speech in the Virginia Convention • Speech in the Convention

Connecting to the Essential Question These speeches prompted great change. Henry's words spurred the American Revolution, and Franklin's helped to shaped our government. As you read, notice how each speaker stresses the need to deal in realities rather than illusions. Doing so will help as you think about the Essential Question: **How does literature shape or reflect society?**

Common Core State Standards

Reading Informational Text

6. Determine an author's point of view or purpose in a text in which the rhetoric is particularly effective, analyzing how style and content contribute to the power, persuasiveness, or beauty of the text.

9. Analyze seventeenth-, eighteenth-, and nineteenth-century foundational U.S. documents of historical and literary significance for their themes, purposes, and rhetorical features.

Literary Analysis

In these persuasive **speeches,** Henry and Franklin employ many of the **rhetorical devices** defined on page 96, including **restatement, repetition, parallelism,** and **rhetorical questions.** These devices serve to emphasize key points, make speeches memorable, and move listeners' emotions.

Persuasive orators like Henry and Franklin also use **allusions,** references to well-known people or events from history, literature, the Bible, and other sources. For example, in this passage, Patrick Henry alludes to the biblical figure of Judas, who betrayed Jesus "with a kiss":

> *Trust it not, sir; it will prove a snare to your feet. Suffer not yourselves to be betrayed with a kiss.*

As you read, notice examples of rhetorical devices and allusions and analyze how they contribute to the power and persuasiveness of each speech.

Comparing Literary Works To better appreciate these speeches about America's struggle for independence, **analyze the speakers' political assumptions**—the political ideas they take for granted. As you read, note the authors' beliefs about human nature and the role of government.

Reading Strategy

Preparing to Read Complex Texts While some listeners agree with a speaker, others may strongly disagree. A persuasive speech is effective when it both holds a friendly audience and convinces a hostile one. As you read these speeches, use a chart like the one shown to **critique their appeal to friendly and hostile audiences.**

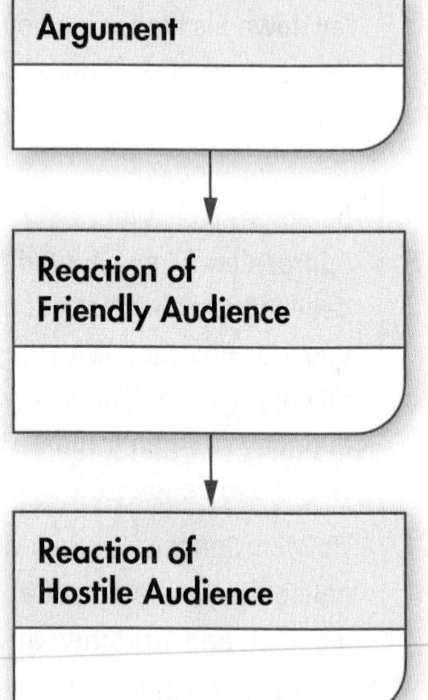

Vocabulary

insidious (in′ sid′ ē əs) *adj.* deceitful; treacherous (p. 101)

privileges (priv′ lij əz) *n.* special rights; advantages (p. 102)

vigilant (vij′ ə lənt) *adj.* alert to danger (p. 103)

despotism (des′ pət iz′ əm) *n.* absolute rule; tyranny (p. 105)

salutary (sal′ yoo ter′ ē) *adj.* beneficial; promoting a good purpose (p. 107)

unanimity (yoo′ nə nim′ ə tē) *n.* complete agreement (p. 107)

Patrick Henry (1736–1799)

Author of "Speech in the Virginia Convention"

It was said that Patrick Henry could move his listeners to anger, fear, or laughter more easily than the most talented actor. Remembered most for his fiery battle cry—"Give me liberty or give me death"—Henry is considered to be the most powerful orator of the American Revolution. He helped to inspire colonists to unite in an effort to win their independence from Great Britain.

Voice of Protest In 1765, Henry was elected to the Virginia House of Burgesses. Shortly after his election, he delivered one of his most powerful speeches, declaring his opposition to the Stamp Act. The Stamp Act, which was passed by the British Parliament, required American colonists to pay a tax on every piece of printed paper they used. Legal documents, newspapers, and even playing cards were all subject to the tax. Over the protests of some of its most influential members, the Virginia House adopted Henry's resolutions.

A Call to Arms In 1775, Henry delivered his most famous speech at the Virginia Provincial Convention. While most of the speakers that day argued that the colony should seek a compromise with the British, Henry boldly urged armed resistance to England. His speech had a powerful impact on the audience, feeding the revolutionary spirit that led to the signing of the Declaration of Independence.

In the years that followed, Henry continued to be an important political leader, serving as governor of Virginia and member of the Virginia General Assembly.

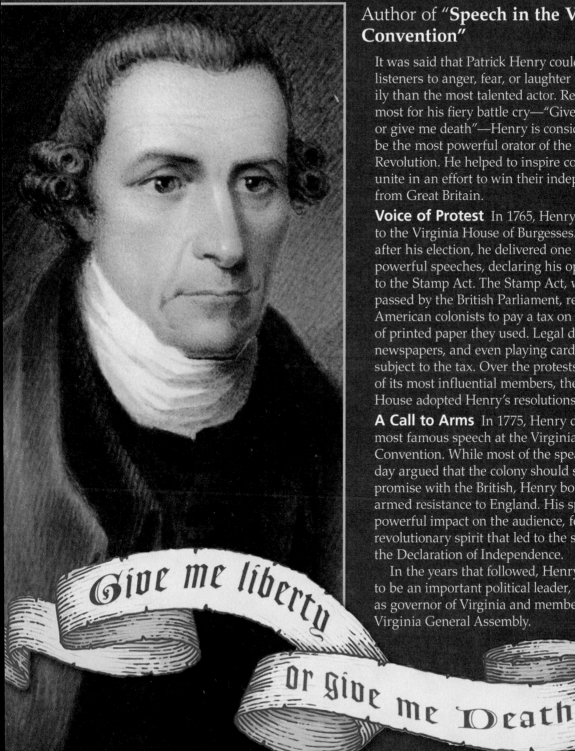

Give me liberty or give me Death!

Speech in the Virginia Convention

Patrick Henry

Patrick Henry Before the Virginia House of Burgesses, Peter F. Rothermel. Red Hill, The Patrick Henry National Memorial.

Background In this famous speech, Patrick Henry denounces the British king and urges the colonists to fight for independence. Making such a declaration took tremendous bravery. England was the world's most powerful country at the time, and the odds against the colonists were overwhelming. If the colonies had failed to win independence, Henry could have been executed for treason.

Mr. President: No man thinks more highly than I do of the patriotism, as well as abilities, of the very worthy gentlemen who have just addressed the house. But different men often see the same subject in different lights; and, therefore, I hope it will not be thought disrespectful to those gentlemen, if, entertaining, as I do, opinions of a character very opposite to theirs, I shall speak forth my sentiments freely and without reserve. This is no time for ceremony. The question before the house is one of awful moment[1] to this country. For my own part, I consider it as nothing less than a question of freedom or slavery. And in proportion to the magnitude of the subject ought to be the freedom of the debate. It is only in this way that we can hope to arrive at truth, and fulfill the great responsibility which we hold to God and our country. Should I keep back my opinions at such a time, through fear of giving offense, I should consider myself as guilty of treason toward my country, and of an act of disloyalty toward the Majesty of Heaven, which I revere above all earthly kings.

Mr. President, it is natural to man to indulge in the illusions of hope. We are apt to shut our eyes against a painful truth, and listen to the song of that siren till she transforms us into beasts.[2] Is this the part of wise men, engaged in a great and arduous struggle for liberty? Are we disposed to be of the number of those who having eyes see not, and having ears hear not,[3] the things which so nearly concern their temporal salvation? For my part, whatever anguish of spirit it may cost, I am willing to know the whole truth; to know the worst and to provide for it.

I have but one lamp by which my feet are guided, and that is the lamp of experience. I know of no way of judging of the future but by the past. And judging by the past, I wish to know what there has been in the conduct of the British ministry for the last ten years to justify those hopes with which gentlemen have been pleased to solace themselves and the house? Is it that **insidious** smile with which our petition has been lately received? Trust it not, sir; it will prove a snare to your feet. Suffer not yourselves to be betrayed with a kiss.[4]

1. **moment** importance.
2. **listen . . . beasts** In Homer's *Odyssey*, the enchantress Circe transforms men into swine after charming them with her singing.
3. **having eyes . . . hear not** In Ezekiel 12:2, those "who have eyes to see, but see not, who have ears to hear, but hear not" are addressed.
4. **betrayed with a kiss** In Luke 22:47–48, Jesus is betrayed with a kiss.

◀ **Critical Viewing**
Which details in this painting suggest the power of Patrick Henry's oratory? **[Analyze]**

Literary Analysis
Speeches and Allusions
Why do you think Henry makes allusions to Homer's *Odyssey* and the Bible?

Vocabulary
insidious (in sid′ ē əs) *adj.* deceitful; treacherous

Does Henry agree or disagree with those who spoke before him?

Spiral Review
Metaphor Cite details from throughout the speech that liken the growing tensions to an oncoming storm. How does this metaphor add to Henry's message?

Literary Analysis
Speeches and Rhetorical Questions What is the effect of the five rhetorical questions in this paragraph?

Vocabulary
privileges (priv´ lij əz) *n.* special rights; advantages

The battle, sir, is not to the STRONG alone; it is to the vigilant, the active, the brave.

Ask yourselves how this gracious reception of our petition comports with those warlike preparations which cover our waters and darken our land. Are fleets and armies necessary to a work of love and reconciliation? Have we shown ourselves so unwilling to be reconciled that force must be called in to win back our love? Let us not deceive ourselves, sir. These are the implements of war and subjugation—the last arguments to which kings resort.

I ask gentlemen, sir, what means this martial array, if its purpose be not to force us to submission? Can gentlemen assign any other possible motive for it? Has Great Britain any enemy in this quarter of the world, to call for all this accumulation of navies and armies? No, sir, she has none. They are meant for us: they can be meant for no other. They are sent over to bind and rivet upon us those chains which the British ministry have been so long forging.

And what have we to oppose to them? Shall we try argument? Sir, we have been trying that for the last ten years. Have we anything new to offer upon the subject? Nothing. We have held the subject up in every light of which it is capable; but it has been all in vain. Shall we resort to entreaty and humble supplication? What terms shall we find which have not been already exhausted? Let us not, I beseech you, sir, deceive ourselves longer. Sir, we have done everything that could be done to avert the storm which is now coming on. We have petitioned; we have remonstrated; we have supplicated; we have prostrated ourselves before the throne, and have implored its interposition[5] to arrest the tyrannical hands of the ministry and Parliament. Our petitions have been slighted; our remonstrances have produced additional violence and insult; our supplications have been disregarded; and we have been spurned with contempt from the foot of the throne! In vain, after these things, may we indulge the fond[6] hope of peace and reconciliation. There is no longer any room for hope. If we wish to be free, if we mean to preserve inviolate those inestimable **privileges** for which we have been so long contending, if we mean not basely to abandon the noble struggle in which we have been so long engaged, and which we have pledged ourselves never to abandon until the glorious object of our contest shall be obtained—we must fight! I repeat it, sir, we must fight! An appeal to arms and to the God of Hosts is all that is left us!

They tell us, sir, that we are weak—unable to cope with so formidable an adversary. But when shall we be stronger? Will it be the next week, or the next year? Will it be when we are totally disarmed, and when a British guard shall be stationed in every house? Shall we gather strength by irresolution and inaction? Shall we acquire the means of effectual resistance by lying supinely on our backs and hugging the delusive phantom of hope until our enemies shall have

---

5. interposition intervention.
6. fond foolish.

bound us hand and foot? Sir, we are not weak, if we make a proper use of those means which the God of nature hath placed in our power. Three millions of people, armed in the holy cause of liberty, and in such a country as that which we possess, are invincible by any force which our enemy can send against us. Besides, sir, we shall not fight our battles alone. There is a just God who presides over the destinies of nations and who will raise up friends to fight our battles for us. The battle, sir, is not to the strong alone;[7] it is to the vigilant, the active, the brave. Besides, sir, we have no election;[8] if we were base enough to desire it, it is now too late to retire from the contest. There is no retreat but in submission and slavery! Our chains are forged! Their clanging may be heard on the plains of Boston! The war is inevitable—and let it come! I repeat it, sir, let it come!

It is in vain, sir, to extenuate the matter. Gentlemen may cry, "Peace, peace"—but there is no peace. The war is actually begun! The next gale that sweeps from the north[9] will bring to our ears the clash of resounding arms! Our brethren are already in the field! Why stand we here idle? What is it that gentlemen wish? What would they have? Is life so dear, or peace so sweet, as to be purchased at the price of chains and slavery? Forbid it, Almighty God! I know not what course others may take; but as for me, give me liberty or give me death!

Vocabulary
vigilant (vij′ ə lənt) *adj.* alert to danger

---

7. **The battle . . . alone** "The race is not to the swift, nor the battle to the strong." (Ecclesiastes 9:11)
8. **election** choice.
9. **The next gale . . . north** In Massachusetts, some colonists had already shown open resistance to the British.

Critical Reading

Cite textual evidence to support your responses.

1. **Key Ideas and Details (a)** What measures does Henry say the colonists have already tried in their dealings with England? **(b) Analyze:** What examples does he provide to support his position that compromise with the British is not a workable solution?
2. **Key Ideas and Details (a)** What course of action does Henry want the colonists to take? **(b) Draw Conclusions:** What is Henry's answer to the objection that the colonists are not ready to fight the British?
3. **Integration of Knowledge and Ideas (a)** Do you think Henry was prepared to stand behind his words when he exclaimed, "Give me liberty or give me death"? Why, or why not? **(b) Deduce:** What does his willingness to make such an assertion reveal about his character? **(c) Extend:** If you had been in his place, would you have made such a statement? Why, or why not?
4. **Integration of Knowledge and Ideas Speculate:** What types of people living in the colonies at the time of Henry's speech might have reacted negatively to his words? Why?

BENJAMIN FRANKLIN

(1706–1790)

Author of **"Speech in the Convention"**

No other colonial American better embodied the promise of America than Benjamin Franklin. Through hard work, dedication, and ingenuity, Franklin was able to rise out of poverty to become a wealthy, famous, and influential person. Although he never received a formal education, Franklin made important contributions in the fields of literature, journalism, science, diplomacy, education, and philosophy.

A Persuasive Diplomat Franklin was a leader in the colonial movement for independence. In 1776, Congress sent him to France to enlist aid for the American Revolution. Franklin's persuasive powers proved effective, as he was able to achieve his goal. This turned out to be a pivotal breakthrough that may have been the deciding factor in the war.

Helping Forge a Nation In 1783, Franklin signed the peace treaty that ended the war and established the new nation. He returned home to serve as a delegate to the Constitutional Convention in Philadelphia. There, as politicians clashed over plans for the new government, Franklin worked to resolve conflicts and ensure ratification of the Constitution.

In spite of his contributions in so many other fields, Franklin is best remembered as a statesman and diplomat. He was the only American to sign all four documents that established the new nation: the Declaration of Independence, the treaty of alliance with France, the peace treaty with England, and the Constitution. (For more on Franklin, see pp. 136–137.)

"I confess, that I do not entirely approve of this Constitution at present…"

SPEECH *in the* CONVENTION

BENJAMIN FRANKLIN

BACKGROUND Following the American Revolution, each of the newly independent states created its own constitution. While Congress was able to pass limited laws, it had no power to tax the states or regulate issues, such as trade, that were affected by state boundaries. These problems led to the Constitutional Convention in 1787. Representatives from twelve states met to approve a national constitution. At the age of eighty-one, Benjamin Franklin represented Pennsylvania.

MR. PRESIDENT,

I confess, that I do not entirely approve of this Constitution at present; but, Sir, I am not sure I shall never approve it; for, having lived long, I have experienced many instances of being obliged, by better information or fuller consideration, to change my opinions even on important subjects, which I once thought right, but found to be otherwise. It is therefore that, the older I grow, the more apt I am to doubt my own judgment of others. Most men, indeed, as well as most sects in religion, think themselves in possession of all truth, and that wherever others differ from them, it is so far error. . . . Though many private Persons think almost as highly of their own infallibility as of that of their Sect, few express it so naturally as a certain French Lady, who, in a little dispute with her sister, said, "But I meet with nobody but myself that is *always* in the right." *"Je ne trouve que moi qui aie toujours raison."*

In these sentiments, Sir, I agree to this Constitution, with all its faults,—if they are such; because I think a general Government necessary for us, and there is no form of government but what may be a blessing to the people, if well administered; and I believe, farther, that this is likely to be well administered for a course of years, and can only end in **despotism**, as other forms have done before it, when the people shall become so corrupted as to need despotic government, being incapable of any other. I doubt, too, whether any other Convention we can obtain, may be able to make a better constitution; for, when you assemble a number of men, to have the advantage of their joint wisdom, you inevitably assemble with those men all their prejudices, their passions, their errors of opinion, their local interests, and their selfish views. From such an assembly can a *perfect* production be expected? It therefore astonishes me, Sir, to find this

Reading Strategy
Critiquing Appeal to Audiences In his reference to "faults," is Franklin appealing to those who are happy with the Constitution or those who are not? Explain.

Vocabulary
despotism (des′ pət iz′ əm) *n.* absolute rule; tyranny

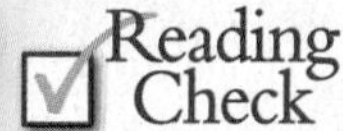

What does Franklin confess as he begins his speech?

WE THE PEOPLE

system approaching so near to perfection as it does; and I think it will astonish our enemies, who are waiting with confidence to hear, that our councils are confounded like those of the builders of Babel, and that our States are on the point of separation, only to meet hereafter for the purpose of cutting one another's throats. Thus I consent, Sir, to this Constitution, because I expect no better, and because I am not sure that it is not the best. The opinions I have had of its *errors* I sacrifice to the public good. I have never whispered a syllable of them abroad. Within these walls they were born, and here they shall die. If every one of us, in returning to our Constituents, were to report the objections he has had to it, and endeavour to gain Partisans in support of them, we might prevent its being generally received, and thereby lose all the salutary effects and great advantages resulting naturally in our favour among foreign nations, as well as among ourselves, from our real or apparent unanimity. Much of the strength and efficiency of any government, in procuring and securing happiness to the people, depends on *opinion*, on the general opinion of the goodness of that government, as well as of the wisdom and integrity of its governors. I hope, therefore, for our own sakes, as a part of the people, and for the sake of our posterity, that we shall act heartily and unanimously in recommending this Constitution, wherever our Influence may extend, and turn our future thoughts and endeavors to the means of having it *well administered.*

On the whole, Sir, I cannot help expressing a wish, that every member of the Convention who may still have objections to it, would with me on this occasion doubt a little of his own infallibility, and, to make manifest our *unanimity*, put his name to this Instrument.

◀ Critical Viewing
How is this painting of the ratifying of the Constitution similar to a literary allusion to classical mythology? **[Analyze]**

Vocabulary

salutary (sal′ yo͞o ter′ ē) *adj.* beneficial; promoting a good purpose

unanimity (yo͞o′ nə nim′ ə tē) *n.* complete agreement

Critical Reading

Cite textual evidence to support your responses.

1. **Key Ideas and Details (a)** Why does Franklin feel that unanimity among the delegates is essential to the success of the United States? **(b) Analyze:** What is his purpose in suppressing his "opinions" for the "public good"?
2. **Key Ideas and Details (a)** According to Franklin, why would any document created by committee be faulty? **(b) Generalize:** What is Franklin saying about human nature?
3. **Craft and Structure (a)** What three reasons does Franklin give for finally agreeing to accept the Constitution? **(b) Evaluate:** How effectively does he convey the thought process that brought him from doubt about the Constitution to a decision to accept it? Explain.
4. **Integration of Knowledge and Ideas** What connections do both Henry and Franklin make between the ability to face hard realities and ideas of loyalty to one's nation? In your response, use at least two of these Essential Question vocabulary words: *patriotism, responsibility, dispute, wisdom.* ***[Connecting to the Essential Question: How does literature shape or reflect society?]***

After You Read

Speech in the Virginia Convention • Speech in the Convention

Literary Analysis

Common Core State Standards

Writing

2. Write informative/ explanatory texts to examine and convey complex ideas, concepts, and information clearly and accurately through the effective selection, organization, and analysis of content. *(p. 109)*

2.a. Introduce a topic; organize complex ideas, concepts, and information so that each new element builds on that which precedes it to create a unified whole. *(p. 109)*

Language

5. Demonstrate understanding of figurative language, word relationships, and nuances in word meanings. *(p. 109)*

1. **Key Ideas and Details** Explain the persuasive message in each **speech:** What do Henry and Franklin want audiences to think and do?
2. **Craft and Structure** Use a chart like the one shown to note examples and describe the effects of each speaker's use of these **rhetorical devices: restatement, repetition, parallelism.**

	Example	Effect
Restatement		
Repetition		
Parallelism		

3. **Craft and Structure (a)** Identify at least two **rhetorical questions** from these speeches. **(b)** Explain how each question intensifies the emotion of the speech, clarifies an idea, or emphasizes a point.
4. **Craft and Structure** Explain the meanings each of the following classical and biblical **allusions** add to the speech:
   - Henry's allusion to sirens from Greek mythology
   - Henry's allusion to Judas's betrayal of Jesus in the Bible
   - Franklin's allusion to the builders of the Tower of Babel
5. **Integration of Knowledge and Ideas (a)** How is Franklin's experience as a diplomat reflected in his argument and the types of language he uses? **(b)** How is Henry's experience as a lawyer reflected in his?
6. **Comparing Literary Works (a)** What **political assumptions** does Henry make about the nature of government? **(b)** Does Franklin make similar assumptions? Defend and clarify your interpretation with elements from the texts.
7. **Analyzing Visual Information** Explain the humor in the cartoon shown on this page.

▼ *"Give me moderation or give me death!"*

VOTE
"Give me moderation or give me death!"

Reading Strategy

8. **Critique each speaker's appeal to friendly and hostile audiences.** Which speech do you think was more effective in holding a friendly audience and in reaching a hostile one? Explain your choice.
9. For each speech, note one argument that the speaker designed to appeal to a friendly audience and one intended to reach a hostile audience. Explain your choices.
10. In what ways does each speaker use "concession," or the acknowledgment of opposition arguments?

Integrated Language Skills

Vocabulary Acquisition and Use

Relate New Vocabulary to Familiar Words

The word *unanimity* comes from the Latin word *unanimus*, meaning "of one mind." Franklin did not feel the delegates to the Convention would ever be fully "of one mind." The word combines the prefix *uni-*, meaning "one," with the root *-anima-*, which means "being; soul; mind." Both word parts contribute to other words with which you are probably familiar. Write a definition for each word below. Then, explain how the meaning of the prefix or the root contributes to the meaning of each word.

1. animate
2. animation
3. universe
4. unify
5. unique

Vocabulary: Antonyms

For each vocabulary word, choose the letter of the antonym, or word that most closely expresses an opposite meaning. Then, explain your reasoning.

1. despotism **a.** tyranny; **b.** democracy; **c.** cruelty
2. privileges **a.** freedoms; **b.** fees; **c.** penalties
3. salutary **a.** damaging; **b.** beneficial; **c.** insensitive
4. insidious **a.** innocent; **b.** weary; **c.** sinister
5. unanimity **a.** harmony; **b.** discussion; **c.** discord
6. vigilant **a.** careless; **b.** watchful; **c.** forgetful

Writing

Explanatory Text Patrick Henry and Benjamin Franklin were master politicians who knew that success sometimes requires persistence and sometimes requires compromise. Write an **essay** in which you compare and contrast their views about when to compromise and when to stand firm.

Prewriting Review each speech, looking for details related to compromise and persistence. Use a chart like the one shown, or make one of your own design to organize your notes. Then, review your notes for patterns of similarity and difference. Write one sentence that states your *thesis*.

Model: Organizing Notes

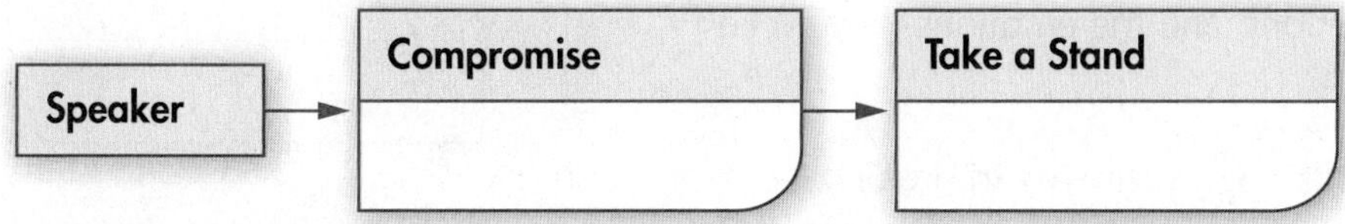

Drafting In your introduction, state the topic and summarize your main points. Then, draft one paragraph about Henry's political approach followed by one paragraph about Franklin's. Support your ideas with quotations.

Revising Reread your essay, making sure you have used sufficient evidence and that your ideas build to a logical conclusion. Check that you have separated longer direct quotations from paragraphs and set off shorter direct quotations with quotation marks.

Before You Read

The Declaration of Independence • from *The American Crisis, Number 1*

Connecting to the Essential Question Jefferson and Paine describe ideals that they were willing to fight to protect. As you read, notice the values that both Jefferson and Paine defend. Your observations will help as you reflect on the Essential Question: **What makes American literature American?**

Reading Informational Text

4. Determine the meaning of words and phrases as they are used in a text, including figurative, connotative, and technical meanings; analyze how an author uses and refines the meaning of a key term or terms over the course of a text.

8. Delineate and evaluate the reasoning in seminal U.S. texts and the premises, purposes, and arguments in works of public advocacy.

9. Analyze seventeenth-, eighteenth-, and nineteenth-century foundational U.S. documents of historical and literary significance for their themes, purposes, and rhetorical features.

Literary Analysis

Persuasion is writing that presents an *argument*, or message meant to get readers to think or act in a certain way. Effective persuasion uses the following techniques to build arguments:

- *Appeals to emotion* to influence readers' feelings
- *Appeals to logic* to show that an argument is well reasoned
- *Appeals to ethics* to show that an argument is just or fair
- *Appeals to authority* to show that a higher power supports the ideas

As you read, evaluate the reasoning and appeals each writer uses to construct his or her argument.

Comparing Literary Works Jefferson and Paine wrote for different **audiences,** or readers. Some of their readers were friendly and agreed with their ideas, whereas others were hostile and did not. Strong persuasive writers such as Jefferson and Paine attempt to address both types of audience. They anticipate reader concerns and build in counterclaims to address them. As you read, notice how these writers shape their messages to reach different audiences.

Reading Strategy

Preparing to Read Complex Texts When you **analyze word choice,** you study an author's words and observe how he or she uses and refines key terms over the course of a work. Persuasive writers may use words with strong *connotations* or associations to produce an intense emotional response. For example, the *denotation*, or basic meaning, of "evils" and "wrongs" is similar. However, the connotation of "evils" is stronger, making it a *charged or loaded word*. Use a chart like the one shown to note charged words, connotations, and the emotions they evoke.

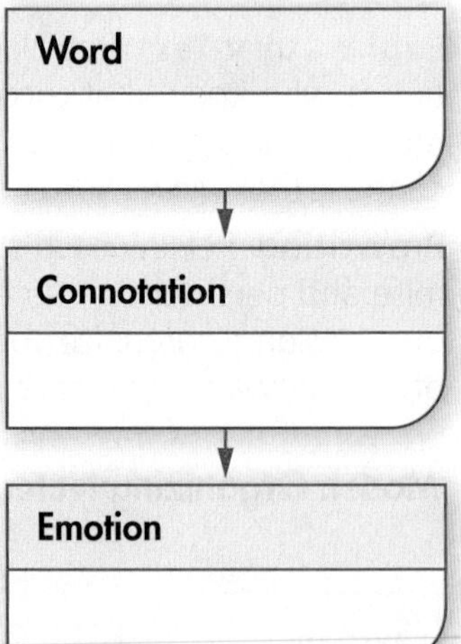

Vocabulary

candid (kan´ did) *adj.* honest; straightforward (p. 113)

assent (ə sent´) *n.* agreement (p. 113)

harass (hər´ əs) *v.* attack; bother (p. 114)

tyranny (tir´ ə nē) *n.* oppressive power (p. 114)

redress (ri dres´) *n.* compensation for a wrong done (p. 114)

acquiesce (ak´ wē es´) *v.* agree without protest (p. 115)

rectitude (rek´ ti to͞od) *n.* correctness; righteousness (p. 115)

prudent (pro͞o´ dənt) *adj.* sensible; careful (p. 118)

Thomas Jefferson (1743–1826)

Author of **The Declaration of Independence**

When you look at all of Thomas Jefferson's achievements, it seems almost nothing was beyond his reach. Not only did he help our nation win its independence and serve as its third president, but he also founded the University of Virginia, helped establish the public school system, designed his own home, invented a type of elevator for sending food from floor to floor, and created the decimal system for American money. He was a skilled violinist, an art enthusiast, and a brilliant writer.

Revolutionary Leader Born into a wealthy Virginia family, Jefferson attended the College of William and Mary and went on to earn a law degree. While serving in the Virginia House of Burgesses, he became an outspoken defender of American rights. When conflict between the colonists and the British erupted into revolution, Jefferson emerged as a leader in the effort to win independence.

Valued Statesman When the war ended, Jefferson served as the American minister to France for several years. He then served as the nation's first secretary of state and second vice president before becoming president in 1801. While in office, Jefferson nearly doubled the size of the nation by authorizing the purchase of the Louisiana Territory from France.

On the morning of July 4, 1826, the fiftieth anniversary of the Declaration of Independence, Jefferson died at the age of 83. John Adams, Jefferson's fellow contributor to the Declaration of Independence, died only several hours after his longtime friend. Adams's last words were "Thomas Jefferson still survives."

EXEMPLAR TEXT

The Declaration of Independence, John Trumbull, Yale University Art Gallery

The Declaration of Independence

Thomas Jefferson

BACKGROUND In 1776, Thomas Jefferson was chosen (with Franklin, Adams, and others) to write a declaration of the colonies' independence from England. The draft presented to the Second Continental Congress was largely Jefferson's work. To his disappointment, however, Congress made changes before approving the document. They dropped Jefferson's condemnation of the British for tolerating a corrupt Parliament, and they struck out a strong statement against slavery.

When in the course of human events, it becomes necessary for one people to dissolve the political bands which have connected them with another, and to assume among the powers of the earth, the separate and equal station to which the laws of nature and of nature's God entitle them, a decent respect to the opinions of mankind requires that they should declare the causes which impel them to the separation.

We hold these truths to be self-evident: that all men are created equal; that they are endowed by their Creator with certain unalienable rights; that among these are life, liberty and the pursuit of happiness; that to secure these rights, governments are instituted among men, deriving their just powers from the consent of the governed; that whenever any form of government becomes destructive of these ends, it is the right of the people to alter or to abolish it, and to institute new government, laying its foundation on such principles and organizing its powers in such form, as to them shall seem most likely to effect their safety and happiness. Prudence, indeed, will dictate that governments long established should not be changed for light and transient causes; and accordingly all experience hath shown, that mankind are more disposed to suffer while evils are sufferable than to right themselves by abolishing the forms to which they are accustomed. But when a long train of abuses and usurpations, pursuing invariably the same object, evinces a design to reduce them under absolute despotism,[1] it is their right, it is their duty, to throw off such government, and to provide new guards for their future security. Such has been the patient sufferance of these colonies; and such is now the necessity which constrains them to alter their former systems of government. The history of the present king of Great Britain is a history of repeated injuries and usurpations, all having in direct object the establishment of an absolute tyranny over these states. To prove this, let facts be submitted to a candid world.

He has refused his assent to laws the most wholesome and necessary for the public good.

He has forbidden his governors to pass laws of immediate and pressing importance, unless suspended in their operation till his assent should be obtained; and when so suspended, he has utterly neglected to attend to them.

He has refused to pass other laws for the accommodation of large districts of people, unless those people would relinquish the right of representation in the legislature, a right inestimable to them and formidable to tyrants only.

He has called together legislative bodies at places unusual, uncomfortable, and distant from the depository of their public records, for the sole purpose of fatiguing them into compliance with his measures.

He has dissolved representative houses repeatedly, for opposing with manly firmness his invasions on the rights of the people.

He has refused for a long time after such dissolutions to cause others to be elected, whereby the legislative powers, incapable of annihilation, have returned to the people at large for their exercise, the state remaining in the mean time exposed to all the dangers of invasion from without, and convulsions within.

He has endeavored to prevent the population of these states; for that purpose obstructing the laws for naturalization of foreigners, refusing to pass others to encourage their migration hither, and raising the conditions of new appropriations of lands.

He has obstructed the administration of justice, by refusing his assent to laws for establishing judiciary powers.

1. **despotism** (des′ pət iz′ əm) *n.* tyranny.

Literary Analysis

Persuasion

Why does Jefferson introduce the idea that one does not change a government for "light" causes?

Vocabulary

candid (kan′ did) *adj.* honest

assent (ə sent′) *n.* agreement

Why did Jefferson write this long list of facts?

The **American EXPERIENCE**

Philosophical Influence: John Locke and the Social Contract

In writing the Declaration of Independence, Jefferson drew on a theory of government devised by earlier European political thinkers, especially the Englishman John Locke (1632–1704). Locke argued that all people are born with certain *natural rights* that are not the property of governments. Locke's concept of the *social contract* also contributed to Jefferson's notion that governments derive their power from "the consent of the governed." According to Locke, when a ruler breaks the social contract by acting abusively, the people have the right to revolt against his rule. In 1776, that is what the American colonists did.

Connect to the Literature

Where in the Declaration does Jefferson echo Locke's idea that the people have the right to overthrow a government that breaks the social contract?

He has made judges dependent on his will alone, for the tenure of their offices, and the amount and payment of their salaries.

He has erected a multitude of new offices, and sent hither swarms of officers to harass our people and eat out their substance.

He has kept among us in times of peace standing armies without the consent of our legislatures.

He has affected to render the military independent of, and superior to, the civil power.

He has combined with others to subject us to a jurisdiction foreign to our constitution and unacknowledged by our laws, giving his assent to their acts of pretended legislation: for quartering large bodies of armed troops among us; for protecting them by a mock trial from punishment for any murders which they should commit on the inhabitants of these states; for cutting off our trade with all parts of the world; for imposing taxes on us without our consent; for depriving us, in many cases, of the benefits of trial by jury; for transporting us beyond seas to be tried for pretended offenses; for abolishing the free system of English laws in a neighboring province,[2] establishing therein an arbitrary government, and enlarging its boundaries, so as to render it at once an example and fit instrument for introducing the same absolute rule into these colonies; for taking away our charters, abolishing our most valuable laws, and altering fundamentally the forms of our governments; for suspending our own legislatures, and declaring themselves invested with power to legislate for us in all cases whatsoever.

He has abdicated government here, by declaring us out of his protection and waging war against us.

He has plundered our seas, ravaged our coasts, burned our towns, and destroyed the lives of our people.

He is at this time transporting large armies of foreign mercenaries to complete the works of death, desolation, and tyranny, already begun with circumstances of cruelty and perfidy scarcely paralleled in the most barbarous ages, and totally unworthy the head of a civilized nation.

He has constrained our fellow citizens taken captive on the high seas to bear arms against their country, to become the executioners of their friends and brethren, or to fall themselves by their hands.

He has excited domestic insurrections amongst us, and has endeavored to bring on the inhabitants of our frontiers, the merciless Indian savages, whose known rule of warfare is an undistinguished destruction of all ages, sexes, and conditions.

In every stage of these oppressions we have petitioned for redress in the most humble terms. Our repeated petitions have been answered only by repeated injury.

Vocabulary

harass (hər′ əs) *v.* attack; bother

tyranny (tir′ə nē) *n.* oppressive power

redress (ri dres′) *n.* compensation for a wrong done

Reading Strategy
Analyzing Word Choice
Why do you think Jefferson uses the words "ravaged" and "executioners"?

2. neighboring province Quebec.

A prince whose character is thus marked by every act which may define a tyrant is unfit to be the ruler of a free people.

Nor have we been wanting in attentions to our British brethren. We have warned them from time to time of attempts by their legislature to extend an unwarrantable jurisdiction over us. We have reminded them of the circumstances of our emigration and settlement here. We have appealed to their native justice and magnanimity and we have conjured[3] them by the ties of our common kindred to disavow these usurpations which would inevitably interrupt our connections and correspondence. They too have been deaf to the voice of justice and of consanguinity. We must therefore acquiesce in the necessity which denounces our separation and hold them, as we hold the rest of mankind, enemies in war, in peace friends.

We, therefore, the representatives of the United States of America in general congress assembled, appealing to the Supreme Judge of the world for the rectitude of our intentions, do in the name and by authority of the good people of these colonies, solemnly publish and declare that these united colonies are and of right ought to be free and independent states; that they are absolved from all allegiance to the British Crown, and that all political connection between them and the state of Great Britain is and ought to be totally dissolved; and that as free and independent states, they have full power to levy war, conclude peace, contract alliances, establish commerce, and to do all other acts and things which independent states may of right do.

And for the support of this declaration, with a firm reliance on the protection of divine providence, we mutually pledge to each other our lives, our fortunes and our sacred honor.

Vocabulary

acquiesce (ak′ wē es′) *v.* agree without protest

rectitude (rek ti to͞od) *n.* correctness; righteousness

---

3. **conjured** *v.* solemnly appealed to.

Critical Reading

Cite textual evidence to support your responses.

1. **Key Ideas and Details (a)** What points about human rights does Jefferson make at the beginning of the Declaration?
   (b) Analyze: Why does he begin with these observations before addressing the colonists' situation?
2. **Craft and Structure (a) Evaluate:** What is the most convincing evidence that Jefferson cites to support his points? Explain.
   (b) Evaluate: How would you rate the overall effectiveness of his argument? Why?
3. **Integration of Knowledge and Ideas Synthesize:** The period in which this document was written is often referred to as the Age of Reason because of the emphasis on logic and discipline at the time. What elements of Jefferson's Declaration reflect a faith in reason?

"I love the man that can **smile in trouble,** that can **gather strength** from distress, and **grow brave** by reflection."

Thomas Paine *(1737–1809)*

Author of **The American Crisis, Number 1**

Thomas Paine met Benjamin Franklin in London, and the introduction changed both his life and American history. Paine emigrated to the colonies from England in 1774. With a letter of introduction from Franklin, Paine began a career as a journalist. In January 1776, he published *Common Sense,* in which he argued that Americans must fight for independence. The pamphlet created a national mood for revolution.

Inspiring Essayist Paine enlisted in the American army toward the end of 1776. At that time, the army had just suffered a crushing defeat by the British in New Jersey and had retreated into Pennsylvania. The soldiers were suffering from freezing weather, a shortage of provisions, and low morale. Paine was writing the first of a series of essays entitled *The American Crisis.* Washington ordered Paine's essay read to his troops before they crossed the Delaware River to defeat the Hessians at the Battle of Trenton.

In 1787, several years after the end of the American Revolution, Paine traveled to Europe and became involved with the French Revolution. Though he wrote in support of the revolutionary cause in *The Rights of Man* (1791–1792), he was imprisoned for pleading against the execution of the overthrown French king. While in prison, he began writing *The Age of Reason* (1794), an attack on organized religion. The book turned American public opinion against him, and when he died in 1809, he was a broken man. Years later, however, Paine was once again recognized as a hero of the Revolution.

from

The American Crisis

Number 1

Thomas Paine

These are the times that try men's souls. The summer soldier and the sunshine patriot will, in this crisis, shrink from the service of his country; but he that stands it now, deserves the love and thanks of man and woman. Tyranny, like hell, is not easily conquered; yet we have this consolation with us, that the harder the conflict, the more glorious the triumph. What we obtain too cheap, we esteem too lightly:—'Tis dearness only that gives every thing its value. Heaven knows how to set a proper price upon its goods; and it would be strange indeed, if so celestial an article as Freedom should not be highly rated. Britain, with an army to enforce her tyranny, has declared, that she has a right (*not only to* TAX) but "*to* BIND *us in* ALL CASES WHATSOEVER," and if being *bound in that manner* is not slavery, then is there not such a thing as slavery

▲ Critical Viewing
In what ways does this cartoon mock Great Britain while celebrating the revolutionaries? **[Analyze]**

What does Paine say is not easily conquered?

Vocabulary
prudent (pro͞o′ dənt) *adj.* sensible; careful

upon earth. Even the expression is impious, for so unlimited a power can belong only to God.

Whether the Independence of the Continent was declared too soon, or delayed too long, I will not now enter into as an argument; my own simple opinion is, that had it been eight months earlier, it would have been much better. . . .

I once felt all that kind of anger, which a man ought to feel, against the mean[1] principles that are held by the Tories:[2] A noted one, who kept a tavern at Amboy, was standing at his door, with as pretty a child in his hand, about eight or nine years old, as most I ever saw, and after speaking his mind as freely as he thought was prudent, finished with this unfatherly expression, "*Well! give me peace in my day.*" Not a man lives on the Continent but fully believes that a separation must some time or other finally take place, and a generous parent would have said, "*If there must be trouble, let it be in my day, that my child may have peace;*" and this single reflection, well applied, is sufficient to awaken every man to duty. Not a place upon earth might be so happy as America. Her situation is remote from all the wrangling world, and she has nothing to do but to trade with them. A man may easily distinguish in himself between temper and principle, and I am as confident, as I am that God governs the world, that America will never be happy till she gets clear of foreign dominion. Wars, without ceasing, will break out till that period arrives, and the Continent must in the end be conqueror; for, though the flame of liberty may sometimes cease to shine, the coal never can expire.

America did not, nor does not, want force; but she wanted a proper application of that force. Wisdom is not the purchase of a day, and it is no wonder that we should err at first sitting off. From an excess of tenderness, we were unwilling to raise an army, and trusted our cause to the temporary defence of a well meaning militia. A summer's experience has now taught us better; yet with those troops, while they were collected, we were able to set bounds to the progress of the enemy, and, thank God! they are again assembling. . . .

. . . I turn with the warm ardour of a friend to those who have nobly stood, and are yet determined to stand the matter out: I call not upon a few, but upon all; not on THIS State or THAT State, but on every State; up and help us; lay your shoulders to the wheel; better have too much force than too little, when so great an object is at stake. Let it be told to the future world, that in the depth of winter, when nothing but hope and virtue could survive, that the city and the country, alarmed at one common danger, came forth to meet and to repulse it. Say not, that thousands are gone, turn out your tens of thousands; throw not the burden of the day upon Providence, but "*show your faith by your works,*" that God may bless you. It matters not where you live, or what rank of life you hold, the evil or the blessing will reach you all. The far and the near, the home counties and the back, the rich and the poor,

1. **mean** *adj.* small-minded.
2. **Tories** colonists who remained loyal to Great Britain.

shall suffer or rejoice alike. The heart that feels not now, is dead: The blood of his children shall curse his cowardice, who shrinks back at a time when a little might have saved the whole, and made *them* happy. I love the man that can smile in trouble, that can gather strength from distress, and grow brave by reflection. 'Tis the business of little minds to shrink; but he whose heart is firm, and whose conscience approves his conduct, will pursue his principles unto death. My own line of reasoning is to myself as straight and clear as a ray of light. Not all the treasures of the world, so far as I believe, could have induced me to support an offensive war, for I think it murder; but if a thief break into my house, burn and destroy my property, and kill or threaten to kill me, or those that are in it, and to "*bind me in all cases whatsoever,*" to his absolute will, am I to suffer it? What signifies it to me, whether he who does it, is a king or a common man; my countryman or not my countryman? whether it is done by an individual villain, or an army of them? If we reason to the root of things we shall find no difference; neither can any just cause be assigned why we should punish in the one case, and pardon in the other. . . .

These are the times that try men's souls.

There are cases which cannot be overdone by language, and this is one. There are persons too who see not the full extent of the evil that threatens them; they solace themselves with hopes that the enemy, if they succeed, will be merciful. It is the madness of folly to expect mercy from those who have refused to do justice; and even mercy, where conquest is the object, is only a trick of war: The cunning of the fox is as murderous as the violence of the wolf; and we ought to guard equally against both.

Critical Reading

Cite textual evidence to support your responses.

1. **Key Ideas and Details (a)** In the first paragraph, how does Paine say the "summer soldier" and the "sunshine patriot" will react to the American crisis? Why? **(b) Interpret:** In that same paragraph, with what ideas does Paine justify the struggle of revolution?
2. **Key Ideas and Details (a)** In the third paragraph, what anecdote, or story, does Paine tell? **(b) Draw Conclusions:** What point is Paine making by relating this anecdote?
3. **Integration of Knowledge and Ideas** Are the ideals Jefferson and Paine defend in these writings still important to Americans? Explain. In your response, use at least two of these Essential Question words: *patriotism, service, authority, equality. [Connecting to the Essential Question: What makes American literature American?]*

After You Read

The Declaration of Independence • from *The American Crisis, Number 1*

Literary Analysis

1. **Key Ideas and Details** Use a chart like the one shown to identify elements of **persuasion** in these selections. Classify the types of appeals Jefferson and Paine use to advance their arguments.

	Emotion	Logic	Ethics	Authority
Jefferson				
Paine				

2. **Key Ideas and Details (a)** What specific beliefs does each writer want his readers to hold? **(b)** What actions does each writer want his readers to take? Note details that support your answers.
3. **Craft and Structure (a)** Name two emotions to which Paine appeals in this excerpt. **(b)** Does he appeal more to emotion or to reason? Support your answer with examples from the text.
4. **Craft and Structure** What persuasive purpose does Paine's anecdote about the Tory serve?
5. **Comparing Literary Works (a)** Who are the intended **audiences** for each of these works? **(b)** What kinds of supporting evidence would you expect to see in writing meant for each audience? **(c)** Are your expectations borne out in these selections? Explain your reasoning.
6. **Craft and Structure** Jefferson presents a long list of grievances against King George. What counterclaim do you think the list attempts to answer? Explain.

Reading Strategy

7. **Analyze word choice** by examining *denotation* and *connotation:* **(a)** Write the denotative meaning of each numbered word below. **(b)** Write a suggested, or connotative, meaning for each word. **(c)** Explain the emotions each word evokes in you. **(d)** Which of these words is charged or loaded? Explain.

   1. liberty **2.** justice **3.** honor **4.** barbarous
8. Both Jefferson and Paine use the charged words "tyrant" and "tyranny" frequently. Do these words carry the same meanings for both writers? Explain.
9. In describing the colonists' British rulers, how does Paine's use of the word "thief" evoke a different response than would the word "supporters"?
10. Paine says, "There are cases which cannot be overdone with language." Do you think this statement is true? Explain your answer.

Common Core State Standards

Writing

1. Write arguments to support claims in an analysis of substantive topics or texts, using valid reasoning and relevant and sufficient evidence. *(p. 121)*

Language

4.b. Identify and correctly use patterns of word changes that indicate different meanings or parts of speech. *(p. 121)*

PERFORMANCE TASKS

Integrated Language Skills

Vocabulary Acquisition and Use

Word Analysis: Latin Word Parts *-rect-* and *-tude*

The word "rectitude" combines the Latin root *-rect-*, meaning "straight," with the suffix *-tude*, meaning "having or possessing." Thus, a person who displays rectitude possesses ethical or moral straightness. For each item below, notice the meanings of the word parts in parentheses. Combine these meanings with those of the root *-rect-* or the suffix *-tude* to write definitions for each numbered word.

1. rectify (suffix *-ify* = make, cause)
2. correct (prefix *co-* = with)
3. indirect (prefix *in-* = without)
4. aptitude (root *-apt-* = fit, suited)
5. fortitude (root *-fort-* = strength)
6. solitude (root *-sol-* = alone)

Vocabulary: True or False

Indicate which of the statements below are true and which are false. Explain your answers.

1. If a child *acquiesces* about being put to bed, she accepts her bedtime.
2. Public support for a radical cause is one form of *tyranny.*
3. There is no need for *redress* if no wrong has been committed.
4. A *candid* opinion is the same as a fact.
5. To judge the *rectitude* of an action, you must consider whether or not it is justified.
6. It is likely that any nation will automatically *assent* to a colony's request for independence.
7. Governments should *harass* citizens who do not agree with specific laws.
8. A *prudent* leader will consider the needs of the public before making a decision.

Writing

Argumentative Text Like Jefferson and Paine, you can change your world with the persuasive use of words. Consider a problem facing your school or community. Write an **editorial** to appear in a local newspaper in which you explain why the situation needs attention and how it should be corrected.

Prewriting List the elements of the problem. Write facts, examples, and explanations that present a solution. Categorize your ideas to identify those that provide strong emotional, logical, and ethical appeals. Consider sources, such as local leaders, whom you might cite in an appeal to authority.

Drafting As you write, structure your ideas so that they flow logically and support them with precise and relevant examples. Demonstrate respect by avoiding name-calling and inappropriate language.

Revising Review your editorial and check that your language is forceful and direct. Replace imprecise or weak language with more persuasive choices.

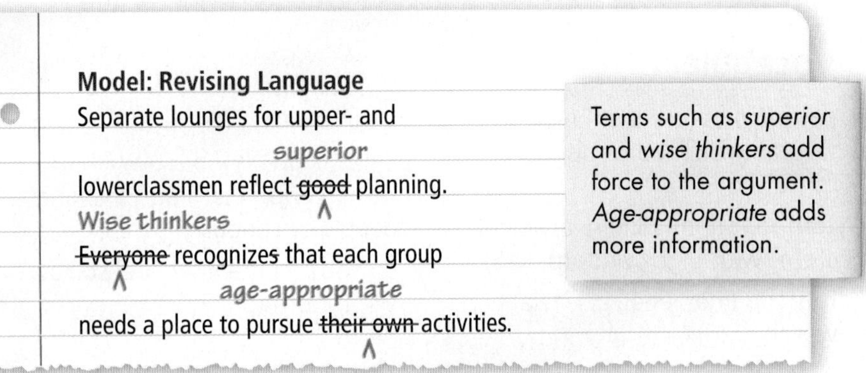

Model: Revising Language
Separate lounges for upper- and
superior
lowerclassmen reflect good planning.
Wise thinkers
Everyone recognizes that each group
age-appropriate
needs a place to pursue their own activities.
Terms such as *superior* and *wise thinkers* add force to the argument. *Age-appropriate* adds more information.

Before You Read

To His Excellency, General Washington

Connecting to the Essential Question In her poems, Phillis Wheatley often paid tribute to America, its leaders, and the ideals the new country represented to her. As you read, find details that show the qualities Wheatley most admires in George Washington. This will help as you consider the Essential Question: **What makes American literature American?**

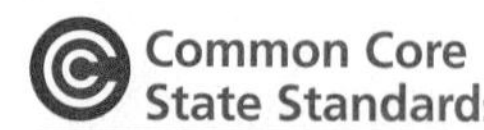

Reading Literature
5. Analyze how an author's choices concerning how to structure specific parts of a text contribute to its overall structure and meaning as well as its aesthetic impact.
9. Demonstrate knowledge of eighteenth-century foundational works of American literature.

Literary Analysis

Phillis Wheatley wrote in **heroic couplets,** a traditional *poetic form*, or structure. Heroic couplets were introduced into English literature by the poet Chaucer in the fourteenth century, but they earned their name from their use by sixteenth-century poets in dramatic works about heroes. Heroic couplets have the following elements:

- They are written in a sequence of rhyming *couplets*, or pairs of lines.
- Each couplet expresses a complete thought.
- They have *end rhyme*, or full rhyme at the end of each line.
- They are written in *iambic pentameter*, a meter in which five unstressed syllables are each followed by a stressed syllable.

The influence of traditional literature is also evident in Wheatley's many references to *archetypal figures* from **classical mythology.** In this poem, she even creates a new goddess, Columbia, to symbolize America. As you read, think about how these references add to Wheatley's presentation of Washington as a hero of mythic grandeur.

Reading Strategy

Preparing to Read Complex Texts As you read, monitor your comprehension. If you find you are unsure of the meaning of lines or sections, **reread** to clarify your understanding. You may need to reorder words or determine the nouns that confusing pronouns replace. As you reread, use a chart like the one shown to clarify the poem's meaning.

Original Sentence
How pour her armies through a thousand gates

Her refers to Columbia. Her armies is the subject of pour.

Clarified Meaning
How Columbia's armies pour through a thousand gates

Vocabulary

propitious (prō pish′ əs) *adj.* favorably inclined or disposed (p. 125)

tempest (tem′ pist) *n.* a violent storm with high winds (p. 125)

martial (mär′ shəl) *adj.* relating to war (p. 126)

implore (im plôr′) *v.* ask or beg earnestly; plead (p. 126)

pensive (pen′ siv) *adj.* thinking deeply or seriously (p. 126)

lament (lə ment′) *v.* feel sorrow for; mourn (p. 126)

Phillis Wheatley (1753?–1784)

Author of **"To His Excellency, General Washington"**

In an era when few women and even fewer slaves could read and write, Phillis Wheatley, a female slave, became one of the finest American poets of her day. A West African native, Wheatley was brought to America on a slave ship when she was about eight. She was lucky enough to be purchased by a Boston family who valued her intelligence and taught her to read and write. The Wheatleys converted their young slave to Christianity and gave her the Bible, Latin and Greek classics, and contemporary English poetry to read. Soon Wheatley was writing her own verse, publishing her first poem when she was just thirteen.

Fame Abroad at an Early Age In 1770, Wheatley won fame through a poem about the death of a celebrated English clergyman, George Whitehead. Three years later, two British aristocrats helped her publish a volume of poetry in London. Called *Poems on Various Subjects: Religious and Moral,* the book was probably the first published work by an African in the colonies. However, it was not published in America until 1786, two years after Wheatley's death.

A Falling and Rising Star Freed from slavery in 1773, Wheatley's final years were filled with hardship and sorrow. Three of her children died in infancy, and her husband was imprisoned for debt. Though she assembled a second collection of poetry, the manuscript was lost before publication, and Wheatley fell into obscurity as a poet. In the centuries since her death, however, her star has again risen. She is now seen as a noteworthy poet of early America and the first writer of African origin to gain a voice in American literature.

PHILLIS WHEATLEY, NEGRO SERVANT to Mr. JOHN WHEATLEY, of BOSTON.

The world is a severe schoolmaster, for its frowns are less dangerous than its smiles and flatteries, and it is a difficult task to keep in the path of wisdom.

FIRST in WAR,
FIRST in PEACE,
&
FIRST in the HEARTS
OF HIS
COUNTRYMEN.

Liberty and Washington, New York State Historical Association, Cooperstown

To His Excellency, General Washington

Phillis Wheatley

BACKGROUND In the early days of the American Revolution, Phillis Wheatley wrote a poem addressed to the commander of the American forces, George Washington. She sent him the poem in October of 1775, and he responded with sincere thanks and expressions of admiration. He also explained the reason he did not try to publish the poem was because it praised him so highly he was concerned he would appear vain.

Celestial choir! enthron'd in realms of light,
Columbia's scenes of glorious toils I write.
While freedom's cause her anxious breast alarms,
She flashes dreadful in refulgent arms.
See mother earth her offspring's fate bemoan,
And nations gaze at scenes before unknown!
See the bright beams of heaven's revolving light
Involved in sorrows and the veil of night!
The goddess comes, she moves divinely fair,
Olive and laurel binds her golden hair:
Wherever shines this native of the skies,
Unnumber'd charms and recent graces rise.
Muse![1] bow propitious while my pen relates
How pour her armies through a thousand gates,
As when Eolus[2] heaven's fair face deforms,
Enwrapp'd in tempest and a night of storms;
Astonish'd ocean feels the wild uproar,
The refluent surges beat the sounding shore;
Or thick as leaves in Autumn's golden reign,
Such, and so many, moves the warrior's train.
In bright array they seek the work of war,
Where high unfurl'd the ensign[3] waves in air.

1. **Muse** A Greek goddess, in this case Erato, who is thought to inspire poets. She is one of nine muses presiding over literature, the arts, and the sciences.
2. **Eolus** (ē´ ə ləs) the Greek god of the winds.
3. **ensign** (en´ sin) flag.

◀ Critical Viewing
Noting the symbols of the Revolutionary conflict, explain the action of the painting. **[Interpret]**

Vocabulary

propitious (prō pish´ əs) *adj.* favorably inclined or disposed

tempest (tem´ pist) *n.* A violent storm with high winds

What army is the poet celebrating?

Vocabulary

martial (mär′ shəl) *adj.* relating to war

implore (im plôr′) *v.* ask or beg earnestly; plead

pensive (pen′ siv) *adj.* thinking deeply or seriously

lament (lə ment′) *v.* feel sorrow for; mourn

Shall I to Washington their praise recite?
Enough thou know'st them in the fields of fight.
Thee, first in peace and honors,—we demand
The grace and glory of thy martial band.
Fam'd for thy valor, for thy virtues more,
Hear every tongue thy guardian aid implore!
One century scarce perform'd its destined round,
When Gallic[4] powers Columbia's fury found;
And so may you, whoever dares disgrace
The land of freedom's heaven-defended race!
Fix'd are the eyes of nations on the scales,
For in their hopes Columbia's arm prevails.
Anon Britannia[5] droops the pensive head,
While round increase the rising hills of dead.
Ah! cruel blindness to Columbia's state!
Lament thy thirst of boundless power too late.
Proceed, great Chief, with virtue on thy side,
Thy ev'ry action let the goddess guide.
A crown, a mansion, and a throne that shine,
With gold unfading, WASHINGTON! be thine.

---

4. **Gallic** (gal′ ik) French. The colonists, led by Washington, defeated the French in the French and Indian War (1754–1763).
5. **Britannia** England.

Critical Reading

Cite textual evidence to support your responses.

1. **Key Ideas and Details (a)** In lines 9–12, how is Columbia described? **(b) Deduce:** What does this image of Columbia suggest about the speaker's view of America?
2. **Key Ideas and Details (a)** In lines 13–20, to what natural phenomenon is the American army compared? **(b) Interpret:** What does this comparison suggest about the power of American military forces in battle?
3. **Key Ideas and Details (a)** Which details in the last two lines reflect the influence of the British political system? **(b) Deduce:** What position in a new government does the speaker assume Washington will occupy? **(c) Synthesize:** How do these details hint at the debate about the kind of government to be established after the war?
4. **Integration of Knowledge and Ideas** Do the qualities Wheatley attributes to Washington represent typically American values? In your response, use at least two of these Essential Question vocabulary words: *valor, boldness, principles, character. **[Connecting to the Essential Question: What makes American literature American?]***

After You Read | To His Excellency, General Washington

Literary Analysis

Common Core State Standards

Writing
1. Write arguments to support claims in an analysis of substantive topics or texts, using valid reasoning and relevant and sufficient evidence.

1. **Craft and Structure** To illustrate Wheatley's use of **heroic couplets,** select two lines from the poem. **(a)** Explain what the couplet means. **(b)** Identify the *rhyme*. **(c)** Indicate the patterns of stressed and unstressed syllables.
2. **Integration of Knowledge and Ideas** Use a chart like the one shown to list three **mythological references** in the poem. **(a)** Define each reference. **(b)** Explain what each reference adds to Wheatley's portrayal.

Mythological Reference	What It Contributes

Reading Strategy

3. **Reread** lines 35–38 to clarify their meaning. **(a)** To whom or what does the pronoun *thy* in line 38 refer? **(b)** Whose cruel blindness is the speaker talking about?
4. Reread the last four lines. **(a)** To whom does the pronoun *thy* refer? **(b)** Rewrite line 40 in a word order that is easier to understand.

PERFORMANCE TASKS
Integrated Language Skills

Vocabulary Acquisition and Use

Sentence Completions Complete each sentence with a word from the vocabulary list. Then, explain your choice.

1. We ______ the loss of these brave soldiers.
2. The good weather made it ______ to start the voyage.
3. The soldier knew a lot about ______ matters but little about daily life.
4. Her thoughtful expression reflected her ______ mood.
5. If captured, we must ______ our enemies to treat us with mercy.
6. The ship was tossed back and forth during the ______.

Writing

Argument A **memo** is a piece of *business writing* that usually begins with these headings: FROM: your name; TO: recipients' names; DATE: date of writing; SUBJECT: your topic. These headings are followed by text organized in paragraphs. Imagine that you are part of the team working on Washington's presidential campaign. Someone has proposed using Wheatley's poem in the campaign. Write a memo supporting or rejecting the idea. Defend your position using details from the poem.

Analyzing Functional and Expository Texts

Manual • Public Service Advertisement

Common Core State Standards

Reading Informational Text
5. Analyze and evaluate the effectiveness of the structure an author uses in his or her exposition or argument, including whether the structure makes points clear, convincing, and engaging.

About the Texts

A **manual** is an informational document that organizations publish to instruct readers in how to use a product or perform a task. Most manuals contain a statement of purpose; step-by-step instructions; and a list of requirements, tools, regulations, or suggestions.

A **public service advertisement** (PSA) presents information to the general public about issues that affect the common good. Unlike commercial advertisements, PSAs are broadcast or distributed for free. They may appear on posters, in newspapers, or on signs; be broadcast on TV, radio, or podcast; or appear on Web sites.

Reading Strategy

To be effective, functional and expository texts present information clearly so readers can understand and apply the information. To ensure a logical flow of ideas, writers may use specific patterns of organization, including the following structures:

- *Cause and effect* describes the results of an action.
- *Chronological order* identifies the sequence in which steps in a task should be performed.
- *Problem and solution* outlines a problem the text will help readers solve.

Text features—such as headings and subheads, boldface and italic type, bulleted lists, and images—help readers navigate the text. As you read these documents, **evaluate text features,** noting how they emphasize specific sections and help readers grasp the organizational structures. Use a chart like the one shown to identify text features and evaluate their purposes.

Content-Area Vocabulary

These words appear in the selections that follow. They may also appear in other content-area texts.

candidate (kan´ də dāt) *n.* person who seeks election to a political position

legislature (leg´ is lā´ chər) *n.* group of lawmakers who represent a state or nation

candid (kan´ did) *adj.* outspoken; open and sincere

officials (ə fish´ əlz) *n.* people who hold government offices or positions

Basic Elements		Purpose
Headings and subheads	Yes ❑ No ❑	
Boldfaced or italicized text	Yes ❑ No ❑	
Numbered or bulleted lists	Yes ❑ No ❑	
Photos or illustrations	Yes ❑ No ❑	

LEAGUE OF WOMEN VOTERS
Making Democracy Work

HOW TO WATCH A DEBATE

The title indicates the task being addressed.

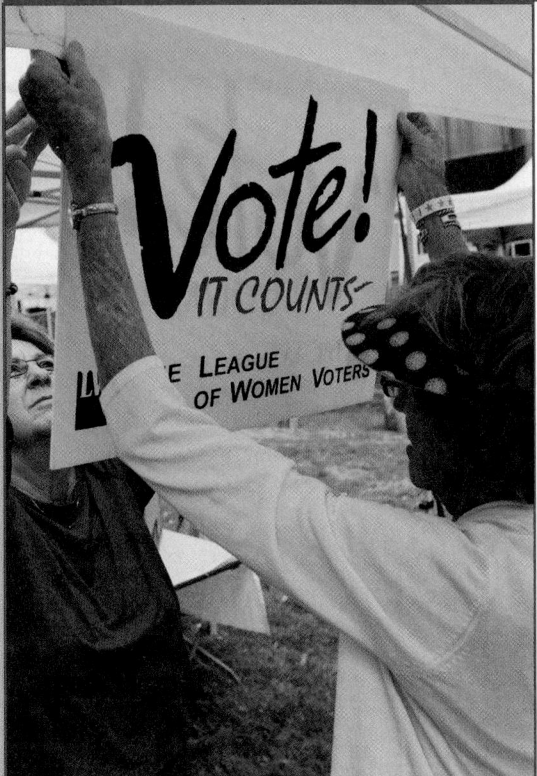

Stay Informed

Sign up for the League's e-newsletter and get all the latest information delivered to your inbox.

How to Watch a Debate

Headings guide readers through a step-by-step process.

Candidate debates have a long history in American politics. At every level of government—from city council to state **legislature**, from Congress to president of the United States—candidates participate in debates to help voters understand who they are and what they stand for.

Watching debates is an important way for voters to learn more about the candidates and the issues before the election, so that they can cast an informed vote. At the same time, voters need to view debates with a careful eye to get the most information. Candidates rehearse thoroughly for debates, making it hard to get **candid**, spontaneous answers. Debates can emphasize form over substance, such as the candidates' appearance instead of their stands on the issues. You may watch a debate and still not get answers to the questions you have about the candidates and issues.

Before the Debate

It will help if you take some time before the debate to

- follow the campaign to learn about the candidates and their backgrounds;
- find out what the important campaign issues are;
- decide what issues are most important to you;
- think about the questions you may have and the information you want to get from the debate to help you in your decision making;
- open your mind to new opinions/impressions of the candidate regardless of party affiliation.

You may want to make plans to get together with friends or family to watch the debate. Watching the debate in a group and discussing it afterward helps to clarify your thoughts about what was said in the debate and how the candidates performed.

A debate might not include all of the candidates for the office. Before the debate, note which candidates are included and which are not. If all candidates are not participating, try to find out why. Some debates include only candidates who have significant support, on the theory that the voters should be able to compare the candidates with a realistic chance of winning. Others invite all candidates who have qualified for the ballot. Sometimes candidates who are invited choose not to participate. Candidates with a strong lead might refuse to participate because they think there is no advantage to be gained by debating a lesser-known opponent.

During the Debate

When watching the debate, ask yourself questions like these to help you judge the fairness of the debate and the performance of the candidates:

The debate format and questions:

Italicized text emphasizes the importance of subheads.

- Does the format give each candidate an equal opportunity to speak and respond to questions?
- Are the questions clear, fair, and equally tough on all candidates?
- Do the questions cover the issues that are important to you?
- Is the moderator in control of the debate? Does the moderator need to say less and let the candidates say more?

The candidates:

- Do they answer questions directly, or do they evade them or fail to answer the specific question?

Bulleted lists provide a breakdown of important questions and steps.

- Do they give specifics about their stands on the issues, or do they speak in generalities? Do they support their positions and arguments with facts and figures?
- Do they talk about their own policies and positions, or do they mostly attack their opponents?
- Are their proposals realistic? Can they actually carry out the promises they are making?
- Do they appear sincere, confident, and relaxed?
- Do they show how their backgrounds and experience qualify them to hold the office?
- Are their answers consistent with their previous positions, and if not, do they explain why?
- What image are they trying to create?
- Do their responses appear overly rehearsed or "canned"?

Media coverage:

- If you are watching the debate on television, are reaction shots or other techniques used to create a sense of drama or conflict?
- Are you being influenced by comments made by reporters and commentators immediately before and after the debate?

Photographs add visual interest.

After the Debate

It will help clarify your thoughts about the candidates and the issues if you take some time after the debate to reflect on what you have just seen and heard. You can do this by

- comparing your impressions with those of others who watched the debate;
- asking yourself, based on the information you got from watching the debate, which candidate appears most qualified for the office;
- identifying the issues on which you agree with a candidate and those on which you disagree, and deciding whether that makes you more or less likely to vote for a particular candidate;
- asking yourself if you learned something new about the issues or the candidate;
- thinking about whether you have more questions about the issues or the candidates that you want to follow up;
- getting more information about the candidates' positions from news reports, candidate Web sites and nonpartisan voter information Web sites; and
- watching later debates for more information or to confirm your current impressions of the candidates.

Conclusion

A conclusion summarizes the information covered in the manual.

Candidate debates give voters a chance to hear the candidates speak and respond to their opponents. They give candidates a chance to present their message directly to a wide audience. As a voter, asking yourself the right questions before, during, and after the debate can help you make the most of this opportunity to learn about the candidates and the issues.

Public Service Announcement

HELP NORTH TEXAS VOTE
COLLEGE PROGRAM

The problem-and-solution organizational structure is established immediately.

Headings help readers follow the problem-and-solution organizational structure.

Did You Know?
Not having enough poll workers can force a polling site to close or lead to delays at the voting booth. According to election **officials**, the result could prevent people from exercising their right to vote.

Election Day Is Coming Soon
Sign up to become part of the *Help North Texas Vote College Program* and take on a larger role in the United States election process. The right to vote is the foundation of our democracy, and assuring access in all our communities is critical. Because of this, it is imperative that the election process run smoothly for everyone. A large part of this includes the people that actually work the polls on Election Day. By signing up on the HNTV Web site, you will provide your name to the county in which you are registered to vote, and if there is a need for poll workers in that county, it is very possible that you will be called upon to serve on Election Day.

The Need for Poll Workers
The number of poll workers serving on Election Day is consistently not adequate, according to the election officials in Dallas, Denton, and Tarrant counties. While an inadequate number of poll workers is a significant problem of its own, an added burden results from the lack of bilingual poll workers, including both Spanish and Vietnamese-speaking workers.

How to Become a Poll Worker
It's easy! Sign up on the *Help North Texas Vote* Web site and your information will be transferred to the county in which you are registered. Once the county officials receive your information, they will determine that county's need. Those needed will be called upon to attend poll-worker training. Training is typically held for a few hours over the course of one day. After you are trained, you are qualified to serve as a poll worker on Election Day.

Poll-Worker Requirements
Requirements for election poll workers are similar for Dallas, Denton, and Tarrant counties:

- Workers must be registered to vote in the county where they wish to work.
- Workers must not be an elected official or be an employee of an elected official.
- Workers must be able to arrive at their assigned polling site before the polls open and must remain until the polls are closed and results are either called in or transported.
- Workers should enjoy interaction with the public, be detail-oriented, be able to take direction well, and not be easily distracted.

What's in It for You?
Beyond the opportunity to fulfill a civic duty that aids fellow Texans, there are other advantages to working the polls on Election Day. If you are called and asked to become a poll worker, you will be compensated for your training and the days that you work. Additionally, we encourage students to work with faculty members to arrange criteria for extra credit where applicable.

The average age of a U.S. poll worker is 72, according to the U.S. Election Assistance Commission, and the numbers of active poll workers are dwindling. It has been reported that the current number of poll workers is well short of the 2 million needed for a national election.

After You Read

Manual • Public Service Announcement

Critical Reading

1. **Key Ideas and Details (a)** Which organizational structure is used in the manual—chronological order, cause-and-effect, or problem-and-solution? Explain. **(b)** Why is this structure appropriate—and common—in a "how-to" text such as this manual?
2. **Key Ideas and Details** Evaluate the text features used in the manual by considering whether they clarify or obscure the information. Explain your observations.
3. **Key Ideas and Details (a)** What organizational structure is used in the PSA? **(b)** In what ways do specific text features clarify that structure and emphasize distinct pieces of information?
4. **Content-Area Vocabulary (a)** Explain how the meaning of the Middle Dutch word *pol* ("head, top") contributes to the meaning of our English word *pollster.* **(b)** Determine the meaning of the following words derived from the same linguistic root: *outpoll, pollee.*

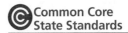

Common Core State Standards

Writing

1. Write arguments to support claims in an analysis of substantive topics or texts, using valid reasoning and relevant and sufficient evidence.

10. Write routinely over extended time frames and shorter time frames for a range of tasks, purposes, and audiences.

Timed Writing

Argument [40 minutes]

Format

An **argumentative essay** is not a piece of writing in which you start a fight. An argument is a well-reasoned position or opinion. In an essay, you must explain and support your argument.

These texts provide information intended to get readers more involved in the election process—a key requirement of good **citizenship**. Write an **argumentative essay** in which you take a position about the importance of **civic** involvement. Use evidence from these texts, as well as your own experience and knowledge, to defend your position.

Academic Vocabulary

The prompt asks you to address **citizenship** and **civic** involvement. Focus your response on ideas of community responsibility, rather than on personal benefits.

5-Minute Planner

Complete these steps before you begin to write.

1. Read the prompt carefully. List key words.
2. Draft a thesis that clearly responds to the prompt.
3. Skim the text for details you can use as evidence. **TIP** Organizational structures and text features can be used as evidence if they help support your thesis.
4. Reread the prompt, and draft your essay.

Literary History: Franklin's World

The American Revolution would not have happened when it did without the efforts of colonial newspapers, including those published by the Franklin brothers.

▲ **Critical Viewing** What does this scene of a coffee house and the facing samples of early newspapers indicate about the role of newspapers in colonial life? **[Analyze]**

All the News That's Fit to Print

"EXTRA! EXTRA! Read all about it! Newspapers banned! Journalists Jailed! Americans Fight for a Free Press!" Those might have been the headlines blaring from your local newspaper if you had lived in eighteenth-century America. Might have been, that is, if colonial newspapers had used headlines. America's earliest newspapers bore little resemblance to those we know today. They were crudely printed on wooden presses and contained only a clumsy illustration or two. Most were one or two pages, and their stories were often just a list of ship arrivals. Despite their primitive character, these early newspapers laid the groundwork for a uniquely American phenomenon: a free press that could criticize the government.

Trailblazers The first American newspaper, printed in Boston on September 25, 1690, was titled *Publick Occurrences, Both Foreign and Domestick*. The remarkable thing about *Publick Occurrences* was that it existed at all. England had no history of a free and independent press. If a newspaper criticized the crown, it could be shut down. Yet *Publick Occurrences* was published without British approval, and printed stories that the Massachusetts royal governor found offensive. As a result, it lasted exactly one issue.

Americans waited 14 years for another newspaper. In 1704, the Boston *News-Letter* appeared. Approved by the governor of Massachusetts, the *News-Letter* was little more than a British mouthpiece, careful not to offend colonial authorities.

The Franklin Brothers In contrast, other papers sought controversy. For example, the New England *Courant*, founded in 1721 by James Franklin, appeared without British approval. The paper jabbed mercilessly at the royal governor, and eventually landed Franklin in jail. He handed control of the paper to his 16-year-old brother, Benjamin—someone who would play his own significant role in our nation's history.

In 1729, Benjamin Franklin, now living in Philadelphia, founded the Pennsylvania *Gazette*. It was the first newspaper to carry weather reports, interviews, and cartoons, and it became the most successful paper in the colonies.

Freedom of the Press Is Born A landmark legal case helped establish freedom of the press in America. In 1733, John Peter Zenger, a German immigrant, began publishing the *New York Weekly Journal*. The paper immediately ran afoul of the royal governor by publishing articles critical of his policies. One year later, Zenger was thrown in jail for libel.

In his 1735 trial, Zenger's lawyer, Andrew Hamilton, argued that while Zenger had indeed printed material offensive to the governor, the material was true and, therefore, not libelous. Under British law, even true statements against the government could be legally silenced. Hamilton made an impassioned plea to the jury to defend the "cause of liberty . . . both of exposing and opposing arbitrary power . . . by speaking and writing truth."

The jury found Zenger innocent. As a result of the case, the British stopped prosecuting American journalists, even when their criticisms of the government grew intense in the years leading up to the American Revolution.

Revolutionary Journalists Most historians agree that the American Revolution would not have happened when it did without the efforts of colonial newspapers. Newspapers stoked the flames of revolution, coining phrases like "taxation without representation" and influencing public perception of England as an enemy. When the British Stamp Act of 1765 imposed a heavy tax on all printed materials, the press denounced the legislation and refused to pay the tax. Even though the Stamp Act was repealed in 1766, it united editors and publishers in support of independence. Indeed, in 1776, most newspapers printed the Declaration of Independence on their front page.

During the Revolution, newspapers brought accounts of military developments to an eager readership. By the end of the war, newspapers had gained enormous strength. American newspapers represented something the world had never before seen: a press committed to telling the truth, not pleasing the government.

In This Section

- Literary History *(p. 134)*
- Biography: Benjamin Franklin *(p. 136)*
- Study: from *The Autobiography* by Benjamin Franklin *(p. 141)*
- Critical Commentary: William L. Andrews on Ben Franklin *(p.147)*
- Study: from *Poor Richard's Almanack (p. 148)*
- World Literature Connection: African Proverbs *(p. 151)*
- Comparing Autobiographies *(p. 157)*
- Study: "Straw Into Gold: The Metamorphosis of the Everyday" by Sandra Cisneros *(p. 158)*

THE New-York Weekly JOURNAL

The Boston News-Letter.

Published by Authority.

Speaking and Listening: Media Review

Comprehension and Collaboration Today, electronic media, including TV, the Internet, and even cell phones, provide constant access to news. With a small group, read, watch, and listen to news presented in electronic formats. Divide the labor so that each person is responsible for a different media form. Prepare a set of guiding questions, such as those listed here, to focus your review:

- What is the quality of information provided by each media form?
- Are the same stories presented very differently in different formats?
- Is the coverage across media platforms equally objective and fair?

Organize your observations into a **report** to share with the class.

Benjamin Franklin (1706–1790)

From his teen years until his retirement at age forty-two, Benjamin Franklin worked as a printer. He got his start as an apprentice to his brother James Franklin, a Boston printer. By the time he was sixteen, Ben was not only printing, but writing parts of his brother's newspaper. Using the name "Silence Dogood," he wrote letters satirizing daily life and politics in Boston. When he was seventeen, Franklin moved to Philadelphia to open his own print shop. This move gave birth to one of his most enduring contributions to American culture, *Poor Richard's Almanack.* This annual publication, which was published from 1732 to 1757, contained information, observations, and advice and was a colonial bestseller.

The "Write Reputation" Just as he had signed "Silence Dogood" to the letters he wrote for his brother's paper, Franklin created a fictitious author/editor for the *Almanack.* The chatty Richard Saunders, or Poor Richard, first appeared as a dull and foolish astronomer. However, over the years his character developed, becoming more thoughtful, pious, and funny.

Secret to Success Like most almanacs, *Poor Richard's Almanack* contained practical information about the calendar, the sun and moon, and the weather. It also featured a wealth of homespun sayings and observations, or aphorisms, many of which are still quoted today. It was these aphorisms that made the *Almanack* a bestseller. Franklin included an aphorism at the top or bottom of most of the *Almanack*'s pages. The wit and brevity of these sayings allowed him to weave in many moral messages, while also entertaining his readers.

Man of Science When Franklin was forty-two, he retired from the printing business to devote himself to science. He proved to be as successful a scientist as he had been a printer. Over the course of his life, Franklin was responsible for inventing the lightning rod, bifocals, and a new type of stove. He confirmed the laws of electricity, charted the Gulf Stream, and contributed to the scientific understanding of earthquakes and ocean currents. In spite of all these achievements, Franklin is best remembered for his career in politics.

Statesman and Diplomat Franklin played an important role in drafting the Declaration of Independence, enlisting French support during the Revolutionary War, negotiating a peace treaty with Britain, and drafting the United States Constitution. In his later years, he was the United States ambassador to England and then to France. Even before George Washington earned the title, Franklin was considered to be "the father of his country."

The Autobiography Franklin wrote the first section of *The Autobiography* in 1771 when he was sixty-five years old. At the urging of friends, he wrote three more sections—the last shortly before his death—but succeeded in bringing the account of his life only to the year 1759. Though never completed, his *Autobiography*, filled with his opinions and advice, provides not only a record of his achievements but also an understanding of his extraordinary character.

"If you would
***NOT BE* Forgotten,**
As soon as you are
dead and rotten,
Either *write things*
worthy of reading,
Or ***DO things* worth**
the writing."

FRANKLIN'S FIRSTS

Benjamin Franklin was an inventions superstar. Practical yet inspired, Franklin never patented his inventions, writing that he was "glad of an opportunity to serve others by any invention of ours; and this we should do freely and generously."

Swim fin/fan: (Ben's childhood) Young Franklin thought he needed a bit more oomph during his swims. To increase his speed in the water, he concocted a fin, shaped like a lily pad, that he wore over his hands.

Fire Department: 1736 Franklin created the first fire department in Philadelphia. Sixteen years later, he set up the first fire insurance company.

Lightning Rod: 1752 Franklin's insight that lightning is a form of electricity led to his design of a pointed metal rod that attached to the top of a building with a wire running into the ground. Elegant and simple, this device reduced property damage and the numbers of lives lost to the fires caused by lightning strikes.

Glass Armonica: 1761 A more sophisticated version of filling up glasses with water and "playing" them by running your fingers around the edge of each, the armonica could produce chords and melodies. These instruments are still in use.

Glass Armonica ▼

Odometer: 1775 As postmaster of Philadelphia, Franklin wanted to boost efficiency by learning which routes were fastest. To measure distances, he attached an instrument to his carriage that counted the rotations of the axles, giving him the information he needed.

Bifocals: 1784 After getting frustrated with the need to keep switching between eyeglasses (one for seeing close up and one for seeing distances), Franklin had each pair cut in half horizontally and put one half of each lens into one frame. Many people use bifocals to this day.

Daylight Savings Time: 1784 Whether in jest or thrift, Franklin invented Daylight Savings Time, an idea that helps us spring forward and fall back each year as we make the most of natural light.

Before You Read

from *The Autobiography* • from *Poor Richard's Almanack*

Connecting to the Essential Question Scholar William L. Andrews has called Franklin's *Autobiography* "the first great American success story." As you read, notice the goals that Franklin set for himself, and think about how they reflect his values. This will help as you reflect on the Essential Question: **What makes American literature American?**

Common Core State Standards

Reading Informational Text

3. Analyze a complex set of ideas or sequence of events and explain how specific individuals, ideas, or events interact and develop over the course of the text.

9. Analyze eighteenth-century foundational U.S. documents of historical and literary significance for their themes, purposes, and rhetorical features.

Literary Analysis

The word **autobiography** is composed of three Greek roots: *-auto-*, which means "self," *-bio-*, which means "life," and *-graph-*, which means "write." Hence, an autobiography is a life history written by its subject. To later readers, an autobiography may provide a more intimate view of history than one might find in an official report or political document.

As an elder statesman, Franklin wrote his life story to serve as an example for young people and to offer advice. A similar motivation is at work in his writing of the **aphorisms**—short sayings with a message—for *Poor Richard's Almanack*. Like his life story, the aphorisms help to paint a portrait of Franklin's attitudes and the world he inhabited. As you read, use a chart like the one shown to record details that help you understand Franklin's values and the times in which he lived.

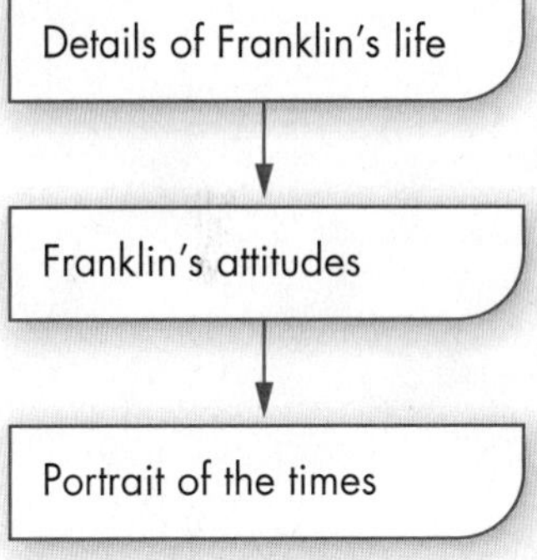

Reading Strategy

Preparing to Read Complex Texts In *The Autobiography*, you will read about Franklin's plan for self-improvement and the changes it made in his life. His plan can be seen as a *cause*, or the reason something happens, while each change may be seen as an *effect*, or the result. Some cause-and-effect relationships are simple.

Cause: Franklin wanted to organize his time

Effect: He prepared a notebook with a 24-hour schedule.

However, other cause-and-effect relationships are more complex. Many events have more than one cause or more than one effect. As you read, **analyze cause and effect** by pausing at important events and deciding, Why did this happen? What occurred as a result?

Vocabulary

arduous (är′ jo͞o əs) *adj.* difficult (p. 141)

avarice (av′ ə ris) *n.* greed (p. 142)

vigilance (vij′ ə ləns) *n.* watchfulness (p. 143)

incorrigible (in kôr′ ə jə bəl) *adj.* impossible to correct (p. 145)

posterity (päs ter′ ə tē) *n.* all future generations (p. 146)

squander (skwän′ dər) *v.* spend or use wastefully (p. 149)

from THE AUTOBIOGRAPHY

Benjamin Franklin

BACKGROUND Benjamin Franklin arrived in the city of Philadelphia in 1723 at the age of seventeen. He knew no one, and he had little money and fewer possessions. However, his accomplishments shaped the city in ways that are still visible today. He helped establish Philadelphia's public library and fire department, as well as its first college. In addition, through his efforts, Philadelphia became the first city in the colonies to have street lights. While Franklin was a brilliant man, some of his success can be attributed to sheer self-discipline, which is evident in this excerpt.

◀ **Critical Viewing**
This painting shows young Franklin arriving in Philadelphia, carrying all he owns. What point about Franklin might the artist be making? **[Draw Conclusions]**

It was about this time I conceived the bold and arduous project of arriving at moral perfection. I wished to live without committing any fault at any time; I would conquer all that either natural inclination, custom, or company might lead me into. As I knew, or thought I knew, what was right and wrong, I did not see why I might not always do the one and avoid the other. But I soon found I had undertaken a task of more difficulty than I had imagined. While my care was employed in guarding against one fault, I was often surprised by another; habit took the advantage of inattention; inclination was sometimes too strong for reason. I concluded, at length, that the mere speculative conviction that it was our interest to be completely virtuous was not sufficient to prevent our slipping; and that the contrary habits must be broken, and good ones acquired and established, before we can have any dependence on a steady, uniform rectitude of conduct. For this purpose I therefore contrived the following method.

In the various enumerations of the moral virtues I had met with in my reading, I found the catalog more or less numerous, as different writers included more or fewer ideas under the same name.

Vocabulary
arduous (är′ jo͞o əs) *adj.* difficult

Literary Analysis
Autobiography
What does Franklin's goal of moral "perfection" suggest about the values of the time period?

What project does Franklin undertake?

LITERATURE IN CONTEXT

World Literature

Socrates

A Greek philosopher and teacher who lived in the fifth century B.C., Socrates pioneered the kind of self-reflection that Benjamin Franklin undertakes with his moral improvement plan. Socrates believed that only through self-knowledge can people achieve virtue. Though he led many Athenians in searching for truth and defining rules for moral conduct, Socrates' criticism of the government resulted in his execution.

Connect to the Literature

Do you see any humor or irony in Franklin's plan for achieving humility—namely, by imitating Jesus and Socrates? Explain.

Temperance, for example, was by some confined to eating and drinking, while by others it was extended to mean the moderating every other pleasure, appetite, inclination, or passion, bodily or mental, even to our avarice and ambition. I proposed to myself, for the sake of clearness, to use rather more names, with fewer ideas annexed to each, than a few names with more ideas; and I included under thirteen names of virtues all that at that time occurred to me as necessary or desirable, and annexed to each a short precept, which fully expressed the extent I gave to its meaning.

These names of virtues, with their precepts, were:

1. Temperance Eat not to dullness; drink not to elevation.
2. Silence Speak not but what may benefit others or yourself; avoid trifling conversation.
3. Order Let all your things have their places; let each part of your business have its time.
4. Resolution Resolve to perform what you ought; perform without fail what you resolve.
5. Frugality Make no expense but to do good to others or yourself; i.e., waste nothing.
6. Industry Lose no time; be always employed in something useful; cut off all unnecessary actions.
7. Sincerity Use no hurtful deceit; think innocently and justly, and, if you speak, speak accordingly.
8. Justice Wrong none by doing injuries, or omitting the benefits that are your duty.
9. Moderation Avoid extremes; forebear resenting injuries so much as you think they deserve.
10. Cleanliness Tolerate no uncleanliness in body, clothes, or habitation.
11. Tranquillity Be not disturbed at trifles, or at accidents common or unavoidable.
12. Chastity Rarely use venery but for health or offspring, never to dullness, weakness, or the injury of your own or another's peace or reputation.
13. Humility Imitate Jesus and Socrates.

Vocabulary
avarice (av′ ə ris) *n.* greed

My intention being to acquire the *habitude* of all these virtues, I judged it would be well not to distract my attention by attempting the whole at once but to fix it on one of them at a time; and, when I should be master of that, then to proceed to another, and so on, till I should have gone through the thirteen; and, as the previous acquisition of some might facilitate the acquisition of certain others, I arranged them with that view, as they stand above. *Temperance* first, as it tends to procure that coolness and clearness of head, which is so necessary where constant vigilance was to be kept up, and guard maintained against the unremitting attraction of ancient habits and the force of perpetual temptations. This being acquired and established, *Silence* would be more easy; and my desire being to gain knowledge at the same time that I improved in virtue, and considering that in conversation it was obtained rather by the use of the ears than of the tongue, and therefore wishing to break a habit I was getting into of prattling, punning, and joking, which only made me acceptable to trifling company, I gave *Silence* the second place. This and the next, *Order,* I expected would allow me more time for attending to my project and my studies. *Resolution,* once become habitual, would keep me firm in my endeavors to obtain all the subsequent virtues; *Frugality* and *Industry* freeing me from my remaining debt and producing affluence and independence, would make more easy the practice of *Sincerity* and *Justice,* etc., etc. Conceiving then, that, agreeably to the advice of Pythagoras[1] in his *Golden Verses,* daily examination would be necessary, I contrived the following method for conducting that examination.

I made a little book, in which I allotted a page for each of the virtues. I ruled each page with red ink, so as to have seven columns, one for each day of the week, marking each column with a letter for the day. I crossed these columns with thirteen red lines, marking the beginning of each line with the first letter of one of the virtues, on which line and in its proper column I might mark, by a little black spot, every fault I found upon examination to have been committed respecting that virtue upon that day.

I determined to give a week's strict attention to each of the virtues successively. Thus, in the first week, my great guard was to avoid every[2] the least offense against *Temperance,* leaving the other virtues to their ordinary chance, only marking every evening the faults of the day. Thus, if in the first week I could keep my first line, marked *T.* clear of spots, I supposed the habit of that virtue so much strengthened, and its opposite weakened, that I might venture extending my attention to include the next, and for the following week keep both lines clear of spots. Proceeding thus to the last, I could go through a course complete in thirteen weeks, and four courses in a year. And like him who, having a garden to weed, does not attempt to eradicate all the bad herbs at once, which would exceed his reach and his strength, but works on one of the beds at a time, and, having accomplished the first, proceeds to a second, so I should have, I hoped, the encouraging pleasure of seeing on my pages the progress I made in virtue, by clearing successively my lines of their spots, till in the end, by a number of courses, I should be happy in viewing a clean book, after a thirteen weeks' daily examination. . . .

1. **Pythagoras** (pi thag´ ə rəs) Greek philosopher and mathematician who lived in the sixth century B.C.
2. **every** even.

Vocabulary
vigilance (vij´ ə ləns) *n.* watchfulness

Literary Analysis
Autobiography
What does the care with which Franklin makes his book tell you about his character?

What does Franklin hope to achieve in 13 weeks?

The precept of *Order* requiring that *every part of my business should have its allotted time,* one page in my little book contained the following scheme of employment for the twenty-four hours of a natural day.

The Morning Question. What good shall I do this day?	5	Rise, wash and address Powerful Goodness! Contrive day's business and take the resolution of the day; prosecute the present study, and breakfast.
	6	
	7	
	8	
	9	
	10	Work.
	11	
Noon	12	Read, or overlook my accounts, and dine.
	1	
	2	Work.
	3	
	4	
	5	Put things in their places. Supper. Music or diversion, or conversation. Conversation. Examination of the day.
	6	
Evening Question. What good have I done today?	7	
	8	
	9	
	10	Sleep.
	11	
	12	
Night	1	

I entered upon the execution of this plan for self-examination, and continued it with occasional intermissions for some time. I was surprised to find myself so much fuller of faults than I had imagined; but I had the satisfaction of seeing them diminish. To avoid the trouble of renewing now and then my little book, which, by scraping out the marks on the paper of old faults to make room for new ones in a new course, became full of holes, I transferred my tables and precepts to the ivory leaves of a memorandum book, on which the lines were drawn with red ink that made a durable stain, and on those lines I marked my faults with a black-lead pencil, which marks I could easily wipe out with a wet sponge. After a while I went through one course only in a year, and afterward only one in several years, till at length I omitted them entirely, being employed in voyages and business abroad, with a multiplicity of affairs that interfered; but I always carried my little book with me.

My scheme of *Order* gave me the most trouble; and I found that, though it might be practicable where a man's business was such as to leave him the disposition of his time, that of a journeyman printer, for instance, it was not possible to be exactly observed by a master, who must mix with the world and often receive people of business at their own hours. *Order,* too, with regard to places for things, papers, etc., I found extremely difficult to acquire. I had not been early accustomed to it, and, having an exceeding good memory, I was not so sensible of the inconvenience attending want of method. This article, therefore, cost me so much painful attention, and my faults in it vexed me so much, and I made so little progress in amendment, and had such frequent relapses, that I was almost ready to give up the attempt, and content myself with a faulty character in that respect, like the man who, in buying an ax of a smith, my neighbor, desired to have the whole of its surface as bright as the edge. The smith consented to grind it bright for him if he would turn the wheel; he turned, while the smith pressed the broad face of the ax hard and heavily on the stone, which made the turning of it very fatiguing. The man came every now and then from the wheel to see how the work went on, and at length would take his ax as it was, without farther grinding. "No," said the smith, "turn on, turn on; we shall have it bright by and by; as yet, it is only speckled." "Yes," says the man, "*but I think I like a speckled ax best.*" And I believe this may have been the case with many, who, having, for want of some such means as I employed, found the difficulty of obtaining good and breaking bad habits in other points of vice and virtue, have given up the struggle, and concluded that "*a speckled ax was best*"; for something, that pretended to be reason, was every now and then suggesting to me that such extreme nicety as I exacted of myself might be a kind of foppery in morals, which, if it were known, would make me ridiculous; that a perfect character might be attended with the inconvenience of being envied and hated; and that a benevolent man should allow a few faults in himself, to keep his friends in countenance.

In truth, I found myself **incorrigible** with respect to *Order*; and now I am grown old, and my memory bad, I feel very sensibly the want of it. But, on the whole, though I never arrived at the perfection I had been so ambitious of obtaining, but fell far short of it, yet I was, by the endeavor, a better and a happier man than I otherwise should have been if I had not attempted it; as those who aim at perfect writing by imitating the engraved copies, though they never reached the wished-for excellence of those copies, their hand is mended by the endeavor, and is tolerable while it continues fair and legible.

Literary Analysis
Autobiography
What does this anecdote about the man with the ax reveal about Franklin's sense of humor?

Vocabulary
incorrigible (in kôr´ ə jə bəl) *adj.* impossible to correct

Which virtue did Franklin hope to achieve by planning each day's activity?

Spiral Review
Audience For whom is Franklin writing? How do you think his sense of audience helped to shape this account of his life?

Vocabulary
posterity (päs ter ə tē) *n.* all future generations

It may be well my posterity should be informed that to this little artifice, with the blessing of God, their ancestor owed the constant felicity of his life, down to his seventy-ninth year in which this is written. What reverses may attend the remainder is in the hand of Providence; but, if they arrive, the reflection on past happiness enjoyed ought to help his bearing them with more resignation. To *Temperance* he ascribes his long-continued health, and what is still left to him of a good constitution; to *Industry* and *Frugality,* the early easiness of his circumstances and acquisition of his fortune, with all that knowledge that enabled him to be a useful citizen, and obtained for him some degree of reputation among the learned; to *Sincerity* and *Justice,* the confidence of his country, and the honorable employs it conferred upon him; and to the joint influence of the whole mass of the virtues, even in the imperfect state he was able to acquire them, all that evenness of temper, and that cheerfulness in conversation, which makes his company still sought for, and agreeable even to his younger acquaintance. I hope, therefore, that some of my descendants may follow the example and reap the benefit.

THE AMERICAN EXPERIENCE

BENJAMIN FRANKLIN *in Our World*

In *The Autobiography*, Benjamin Franklin describes his attempts to become a completely virtuous person. Though he thought he failed, Americans *do* view Franklin as a man of many virtues. He was civic-minded, intelligent, inquisitive, practical, and industrious. He embodies much that Americans value, which may be why his image is so visible in our world today. He is, in fact, an American icon.

CONNECT TO THE LITERATURE

What would you choose as Benjamin Franklin's most inspiring quality? Explain.

Benjamin Franklin National Memorial, The Franklin Institute, Philadelphia, PA ▶

Cartoon illustration of Ben Franklin from *Liberty's Kids* ▶

Ben Franklin Action Figure ▶

U.S. currency: $100 bill ▲

Critical Commentary

Ben Franklin, America's Everyman

William L. Andrews

William L. Andrews, an award-winning scholar and teacher, is the E. Maynard Adams Professor of English at the University of North Carolina, Chapel Hill.

It's not just a coincidence that America's earliest literature is highly autobiographical. Nor is it by accident that autobiography emerged as a literary form about the same time that the United States became a new nation. Autobiography and America were made for each other.

The revolution in the United States created a new person, as well as a new country. At least that's what the great spokesmen and propagandists of the Revolution, especially Thomas Jefferson, Patrick Henry, and Benjamin Franklin, claimed. Franklin, who wore a coonskin cap to the royal courts of Europe, became famous for inventing everything from street lights to eyeglasses. But we read him today because his greatest invention was himself. *The Autobiography* of Benjamin Franklin is the first great American success story: a tale of a poor boy who made good.

A New American Franklin's *Autobiography* has served for many generations as a blueprint for a new American man. This man was energetic, adaptable, shrewd, and, as the *Autobiography* makes very clear, success oriented. Industrious, frugal, temperate, orderly, and resolute, Franklin modeled for Americans a hero fulfilled by the work of this world, not longing for deliverance to the next. Yet in Franklin's autobiographical mirror his readers could see that success was not to be measured simply by acquiring the goods of this world but by "doing good" for the practical benefit of one's fellow Americans too.

An Achievable Good Franklin's "project of arriving at moral perfection," which he undertook when he was in his mid-twenties, epitomizes his audaciously American can-do spirit in at least two ways. First, it appears that the young Franklin really thought he could divest himself of all his faults simply by putting his mind and will to the task. Second, he seems to have been confident of success by approaching the task as a "project," not unlike some he'd already wrapped up, including the founding of the first lending library and the publication of *Poor Richard's Almanack*. Franklin doesn't hesitate to admit that he failed, but he insists that the effort he exerted was just as valuable to his character development as his unattained goal. Thus, as if following Poor Richard's counsel to "write injuries in dust, benefits in marble," Franklin's autobiographical account of his perfection project points finally to an achievable good, not an unreachable ideal.

Key Ideas and Details According to Andrews, why have generations of Franklin's readers treasured this episode of failure in a life of so many successes?

...his greatest INVENTION was himself.

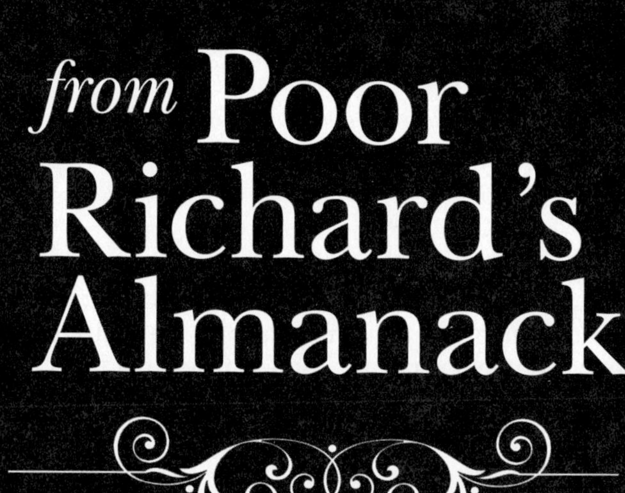

from Poor Richard's Almanack

Benjamin Franklin

- Fools make feasts, and wise men eat them.
- Be slow in choosing a friend, slower in changing.
- Keep thy shop, and thy shop will keep thee.
- Early to bed, early to rise, makes a man healthy, wealthy, and wise.
- Three may keep a secret if two of them are dead.
- God helps them that help themselves.
- The rotten apple spoils his companions.
- An open foe may prove a curse; but a pretended friend is worse.
- Have you somewhat to do tomorrow, do it today.
- A true friend is the best possession.
- A small leak will sink a great ship.
- No gains without pains.
- Tis easier to prevent bad habits than to break them.
- Well done is better than well said.
- Dost thou love life? Then do not squander time; for that's the stuff life is made of.
- Write injuries in dust, benefits in marble.
- A slip of the foot you may soon recover, but a slip of the tongue you may never get over.
- If your head is wax, don't walk in the sun.
- A good example is the best sermon.

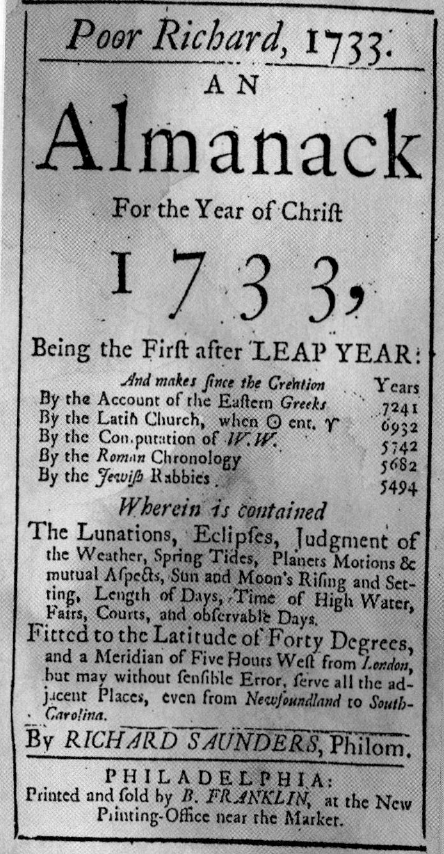

Poor Richard, 1733.

AN

Almanack

For the Year of Chrift

1733,

Being the Firft after LEAP YEAR:

And makes fince the Crehtion	Years
By the Account of the Eaftern *Greeks*	7241
By the Latin Church, when ☉ ent. ♈	6932
By the Computation of *W.W.*	5742
By the *Roman* Chronology	5682
By the *Jewifh* Rabbies	5494

Wherein is contained

The Lunations, Eclipfes, Judgment of the Weather, Spring Tides, Planets Motions & mutual Afpects, Sun and Moon's Rifing and Setting, Length of Days, Time of High Water, Fairs, Courts, and obfervable Days.

Fitted to the Latitude of Forty Degrees, and a Meridian of Five Hours Weft from *London*, but may without fenfible Error, ferve all the adjacent Places, even from *Newfoundland* to *South-Carolina*.

By *RICHARD SAUNDERS*, Philom.

PHILADELPHIA:
Printed and fold by *B. FRANKLIN*, at the New Printing-Office near the Market.

▲ Critical Viewing

The abbreviation "Philom." is short for *philomath*. The root *-philo-* means "love" and the suffix *-math-* means "learn." Can you infer what the word means? **[Infer Meaning]**

Vocabulary

squander (skwän′ dər) *v.* spend or use wastefully

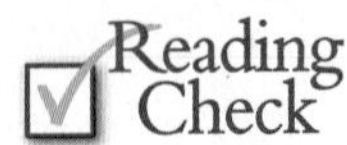

Which aphorisms offer advice about using time wisely?

❧ A good EXAMPLE is the best SERMON.

- ❧ Hunger is the best pickle.
- ❧ Genius without education is like silver in the mine.
- ❧ For want of a nail the shoe is lost; for want of a shoe the horse is lost; for want of a horse the rider is lost.
- ❧ Haste makes waste.
- ❧ The doors of wisdom are never shut.
- ❧ Love your neighbor; yet don't pull down your hedge.
- ❧ He that lives upon hope will die fasting.

Critical Reading

Cite textual evidence to support your responses.

1. **Key Ideas and Details** **(a)** What efforts does Franklin make to become more orderly? **(b) Infer:** Is he successful? Explain. **(c) Analyze:** What aspect of his attempt to become more orderly is illustrated by the anecdote of the man with the speckled ax?
2. **Key Ideas and Details** **(a)** When Franklin began his project, he was a young man. How do you think he felt at the time about his chances of attaining moral "perfection"? **(b) Compare and Contrast:** What insights does Franklin gain about the goal of achieving perfection as he gets older?
3. **Key Ideas and Details** **(a)** Note three aphorisms that deal directly with friendship. **(b) Analyze:** Is Franklin's message about friendship consistent? Explain.
4. **Key Ideas and Details** **(a)** According to the aphorism, what happens to a person who "lives upon hope"? **(b) Speculate:** What more reliable value would Franklin say a person can successfully "live upon"?
5. **Integration of Knowledge and Ideas** In what ways can analyzing one's own behavior contribute to personal growth?
6. **Integration of Knowledge and Ideas** With which of Franklin's aphorisms do you most strongly agree and disagree? Why?
7. **Integration of Knowledge and Ideas** In what ways do the goals Franklin sets for himself and the aphorisms he wrote express values that are still widely held in America? Explain. Use at least two of these Essential Question words: *individualism, thrifty, practical, humorous. [Connecting to the Essential Question: What makes American literature American?]*

WORLD LITERATURE CONNECTION

PROVERBS
THE WISDOM OF MANY

◀ Wooden helmet mask with beard (Congo)

The memorable aphorisms that Benjamin Franklin presents in *Poor Richard's Almanack* are grounded in the rich oral tradition of proverbs. A proverb is a traditional saying that offers a practical truth about life, work, love, death, and other universal experiences. Each proverb is a bit of cultural wisdom. A society's proverbs reflect the attitudes and worldviews of its people. Proverbs are handed down through generations and can be used to teach children, offer advice, settle arguments, or even help resolve legal disputes. The proverbs presented here are from various cultures on the African continent.

CONNECT TO THE LITERATURE

What similarities and differences do you notice between the African proverbs and Franklin's aphorisms?

AFRICAN PROVERBS

UGANDA: THE BAGANDA PEOPLE
Where there are no dogs, the wild cats move about freely.

LIBERIA: THE JABO PEOPLE
The butterfly that flies among the thorns will tear its wings.

~

Children are the wisdom of the nation.

SOUTH AFRICA: THE ZULU PEOPLE
There is no foot, which does not stumble.

GHANA: THE ASHANTI PEOPLE
Rain beats on a leopard's skin,
but it does not beat out the spots.

~

One falsehood spoils a thousand truths.

NIGERIA: THE YORUBA PEOPLE
He who is being carried does not
realize how far the town is.

TANZANIA AND KENYA: THE MASAI PEOPLE
The zebra cannot do away with his stripes.

~

Do not repair another man's fence
until you have seen to your own.

Mask with horns (Nigeria) ▶

After You Read

from ***The Autobiography*** •
from ***Poor Richard's Almanack***

Literary Analysis

1. **Key Ideas and Details** **(a)** Why do you think Franklin devoted such a large chunk of his **autobiography** to a discussion of his failures to achieve perfect virtue? **(b)** What message do both his efforts and his failures convey?
2. **Key Ideas and Details** **(a)** Do you think Franklin achieved the virtue of humility? Why or why not? **(b)** Do you find any evidence of pride—humility's opposite—in this account of his life?
3. **Craft and Structure** How do you think *The Autobiography* would be different if it were written about Franklin rather than by him?
4. **Integration of Knowledge and Ideas** **(a)** Note two details from this section of *The Autobiography* that reveal an aspect of ordinary, daily life in colonial America. **(b)** In what ways does this excerpt shed light on Franklin's era?
5. **Comparing Literary Works** **(a)** Are Franklin's struggles to improve himself related to the advice he offers in the **aphorisms**? **(b)** Do these aphorisms seem to be written by the same person who wrote *The Autobiography*? Why or why not?
6. **Integration of Knowledge and Ideas** Use a chart like this one to match three aphorisms with virtues from *The Autobiography*. Explain each choice.

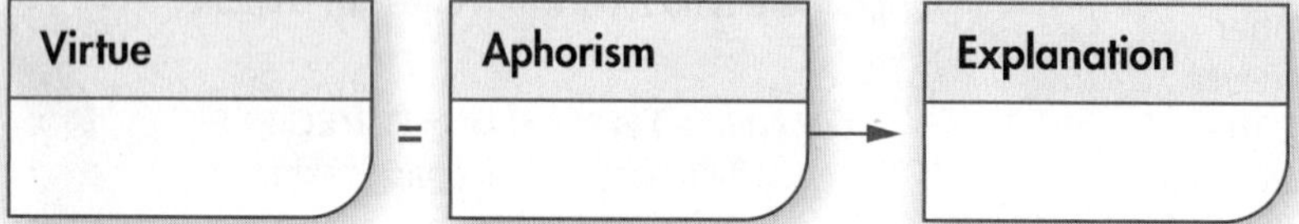

7. **Analyzing Visual Information** Based on what you know of the genre of autobiography, explain the humor in the cartoon shown on this page.

Reading Strategy

8. **Analyze cause and effect** in the anecdote about the man with the ax. **(a)** What goal propels the man to take an action? **(b)** What is the result of that action? **(c)** How does that result become the cause of another action or decision?
9. Choose one of Franklin's aphorisms and explain how it suggests a cause-and-effect relationship. For example, "No gains without pains" suggests that only through hard work (cause) can you achieve your goals (effect).

Common Core State Standards

Language

4.b. Identify and correctly use patterns of word changes that indicate different meanings or parts of speech.

5. Demonstrate understanding of word relationships and nuances in word meanings.

▼ *"I called for you creative people because I feel it's time to begin my autobiography."*

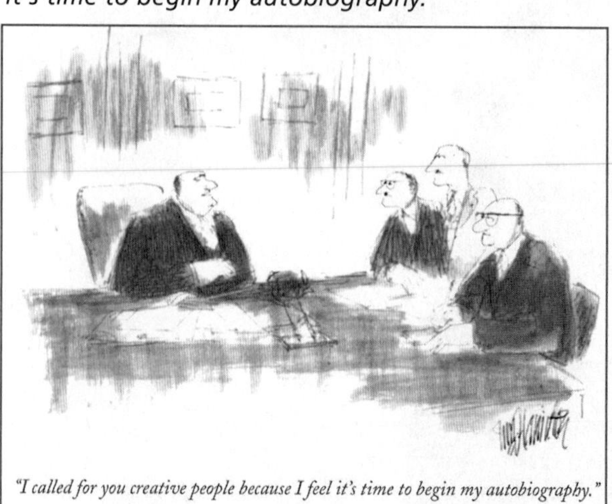

"I called for you creative people because I feel it's time to begin my autobiography."

PERFORMANCE TASKS

Integrated Language Skills

Vocabulary Acquisition and Use

Word Analysis: Patterns of Word Changes

The noun *vigilance*, meaning "watchfulness," contains the suffix *-ance*. Whenever you see a word with the *-ance* or *-ence* ending, you can be sure it is a noun. That suffix is a *pattern that indicates the word's function*. Words exhibit other patterns that indicate different meanings or functions. Write a definition for each italicized word below. Then, explain the word's function—noun, adjective, or adverb. Based on your answer, identify the letter pattern that indicates the word's function.

1. He was *vigilant* in his efforts to reform.
2. Through the night, the soldier stood watch *vigilantly*.
3. He showed great *avarice* in his drive for wealth.
4. Many great stories exist about *avaricious* characters.

Vocabulary: Analogies

Analogies show the relationships between pairs of words. Complete each analogy using a word from the vocabulary list on page 139. In each, your choice should create a word pair that matches the relationship between the first two words given. Then, explain your answers.

1. *Permission* is to *authorization* as ______ is to *greed*.
2. *Tragedy* is to *comedy* as ______ is to *negligence*.
3. *Contemporary* is to *now* as ______ is to *future*.
4. *Rare* is to *common* as ______ is to *easy*.
5. *Criticize* is to *praise* as ______ is to *save*.
6. *Fresh* is to *trite* as ______ is to *curable*.

Using Resources to Build Vocabulary

The Language of Failed Attempts

Although Franklin strives for moral perfection, he openly acknowledges his failure to meet his goals. Consider how these words help Franklin describe his failed attempt to be perfect:

debt	reverses
prattle	slipping
punning	temptations
relapses	vexed

Use a print or electronic dictionary to find a meaning for each word as it is used by Franklin. Then, write a short advice column in which you give readers suggestions that will help them avoid failure. Include each word at least once. You might use a question-and-answer format. Vocabulary words may appear in both the questions and answers.

PERFORMANCE TASKS

Integrated Language Skills

Writing

Informative Text In both life and literature, cause-and-effect relationships are far more complex than "A caused B." Often, one cause has multiple effects. Likewise, an effect can prompt other results, or new effects. In addition, while some effects can be anticipated, many are unforeseen and even surprising. Write an **analytical essay** in which you identify and explain the multiple effects of Benjamin Franklin's plan for self-improvement.

Prewriting Review *The Autobiography,* looking for events, changes, and insights that happened as a result of Franklin's plan. Use a chart like the one shown to identify multiple effects. After completing the chart, rank the effects from most important to least important.

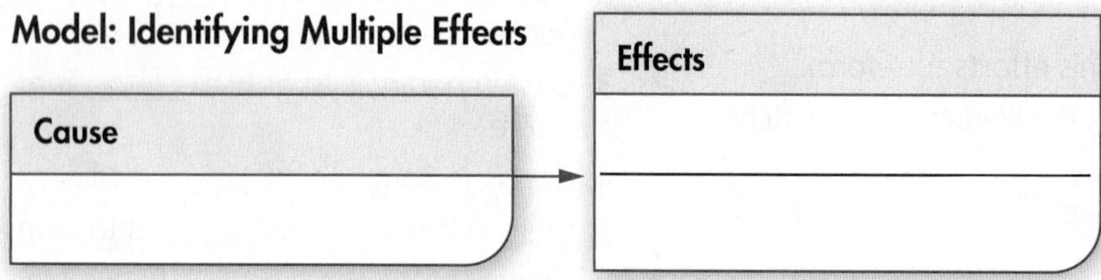

Drafting Start with a strong first sentence. You might use one of Franklin's aphorisms as a launching point. In the opening paragraph, state the topic of your essay and your *thesis*, or main idea. Then, follow these steps to structure the body of your essay:

- Describe the effects of Franklin's plan, devoting one paragraph to each effect. Make sure that each paragraph has a clear main idea.
- Follow *order-of-importance organization*, beginning with the least important effect and building toward the most important effect.
- In your conclusion, *summarize* the cause-and-effect relationships you have discussed.

Revising Reread your essay, making sure you have carefully explained the connections among your ideas. Consider reading your essay aloud so that you can hear sections that sound awkward or do not flow logically. Locate points in the text where the addition of *transitional words and phrases* will help clarify the flow of your ideas.

Transitional Words and Phrases	
as a result	outcome
because	since
for the reason that	therefore
in consequence	with the result that

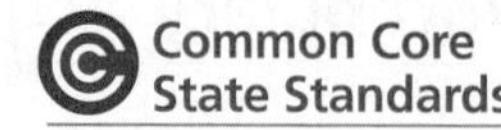

Common Core State Standards

Writing

2.a. Introduce a topic; organize complex ideas, concepts, and information so that each new element builds on that which precedes it to create a unified whole.

2.c. Use appropriate and varied transitions and syntax to link the major sections of the text, create cohesion, and clarify the relationships among complex ideas and concepts.

2.f. Provide a concluding statement or section that follows from and supports the information or explanation presented.

Language

3.a. Vary syntax for effect.

Conventions and Style: Subordinating Conjunctions

To increase the sentence variety in your writing, use subordinating conjunctions to combine short sentences. **Subordinating conjunctions** are words or phrases that join two complete ideas by making one idea subordinate to, or dependent on, the other. When you use **subordination,** you show which idea is more important.

Common Subordinating Conjunctions			
after	as though	if	unless
although	because	since	until
as if	before	so that	when
as long as	even though	than	where

Using Subordinating Conjunctions

Short Sentences: Ben Franklin moved to Philadelphia. He had very little money.
Combined: Benjamin Franklin had very little money *when* he moved to Philadelphia.

Short Sentences: Franklin used a pseudonym. Franklin became known as a good writer.
Combined: *Even though* he used a pseudonym, Franklin became known as a good writer.

Short Sentences: He would have to be more careful. He wanted to attain moral perfection.
Combined: He would have to be more careful *if* he wanted to attain moral perfection.

Punctuation Tip: When the dependent clause comes first in a sentence, use a comma between the clauses. When the independent clause comes first, do not separate the clauses with a comma.

Practice In items 1–5, add a subordinating conjunction to complete each sentence. In items 6–10, combine the two sentences using a subordinating conjunction.

1. Do not speak ______ you have something beneficial to say.
2. Practice temperance ______ you eat and drink.
3. Franklin worked on improving himself ______ it were his life's project.
4. ______ you speak, make sure your words are sincere.
5. ______ a line has no marks, he is improving in that particular category.
6. All things should have a place and time. Order is important.
7. Franklin listed the virtues in a certain order. This way, he could work through them methodically.
8. He tried. He did not achieve moral perfection.
9. People enjoyed the *Almanack.* The proverbs were entertaining.
10. You should use your time wisely. There is never enough of it.

Writing and Speaking Conventions

A. Writing For each item, write a sentence that joins the two ideas using an appropriate subordinating conjunction.

1. he wrote the book—his friends encouraged him
2. Franklin made a chart—he could track his progress
3. you follow these rules—you will be a better person

Example: He wrote the book *after* his friends encouraged him.

B. Speaking Make up two aphorisms that could each be a refrain for a song. Correctly use subordinating conjunctions in your refrains.

PH WRITING COACH
Further instruction and practice are available in *Prentice Hall Writing Coach.*

A GALLERY OF *Autobiography*

Self-Portraits in American Literature

Benjamin Franklin
(1706–1790)
The Autobiography

Henry David Thoreau
(1817–1862)
Walden

Frederick Douglass
(1817–1895)
My Bondage and My Freedom

Zora Neale Hurston
(1891–1960)
Dust Tracks on a Road

Richard Wright
(1908–1960)
Black Boy

Maya Angelou
(1928–)
I Know Why the Caged Bird Sings

Frank McCourt
(1930–2009)
Angela's Ashes

N. Scott Momaday
(1934–)
The Names: A Memoir

Maxine Hong Kingston
(1940–)
The Woman Warrior

Sandra Cisneros
(1954–)
Straw Into Gold: The Metamorphosis of the Everyday

Comparing Literary Works

from ***The Autobiography*** by Benjamin Franklin • ***"Straw Into Gold: The Metamorphosis of the Everyday"*** by Sandra Cisneros

Comparing Autobiographies Past and Present

Autobiographical Writing The first autobiography was the *Confessions* of St. Augustine, which was written in Latin sometime around A.D. 400. The form did not appear in English, though, until the late 1700s. It was during this "Golden Age" of nonfiction that Benjamin Franklin wrote his *Autobiography.* In doing so, he created a model for the American success story.

Over the next two centuries, major American autobiographies such as the *Narrative of the Life of Frederick Douglass* (1845) and Zora Neale Hurston's *Dust Tracks on a Road* (1942) paved the way for other related forms of nonfiction. These include *memoirs,* which are smaller in scope and less formal in tone, and *autobiographical essays,* which focus on a small slice of the writer's life in order to explore larger ideas. "Straw Into Gold," by Sandra Cisneros, is an example of an autobiographical essay.

These selections highlight some of the ways that American autobiography has evolved. They reflect vastly different historical periods and cultures as well as changing attitudes toward social status and gender. Despite these differences, both address a powerful American *theme*—success. As you read "Straw Into Gold," use a chart like the one shown to compare and contrast Franklin's and Cisneros's ideas about success.

	Franklin	Cisneros
What is success?		
What are its costs?		
What are its rewards?		

Common Core State Standards

Reading Informational Text
3. Analyze a complex set of ideas or sequence of events and explain how specific individuals, ideas, or events interact and develop over the course of the text.

Language
6. Demonstrate independence in gathering vocabulary knowledge when considering a word or phrase important to comprehension or expression.

Gather Vocabulary Knowledge

Sandra Cisneros uses related forms of the words *venture, nomad,* and *vagabond.* Use a **dictionary** to find each word's part of speech and definition. Then, employ other references to further explore these words:

- **History of Language:** Use a history of English to research each word's origins. Write a paragraph about the word's emergence in English.
- **Book of Quotations:** Use an online or print collection of quotations to find a statement or passage containing one of the words. In a paragraph, explain nuances in meaning that are evident from the context of the quotation.

Comparing References Compare and contrast what you learn about the words from each specialized reference.

Sandra Cisneros (b. 1954)

Author of "Straw Into Gold: The Metamorphosis of the Everyday"

Sandra Cisneros was born in Chicago into a large Mexican American family. Because her family was poor, Cisneros moved frequently and lived for the most part in small, cramped apartments. To cope with these conditions, she retreated into herself and spent much of her time reading fairy tales and classic literature.

Embracing Her Heritage Cisneros attended Loyola University in Chicago and, later, the prestigious Writer's Workshop at the University of Iowa. During her college years, Cisneros met writers from many other backgrounds. At first uncomfortable about her family's struggles, she soon realized that her heritage provided her with something unique. She began writing about her childhood in a book of connected short stories. *The House on Mango Street,* published in 1984, ushered Cisneros into the literary limelight.

Charting Her Success Cisneros's second book, *Woman Hollering Creek* (1991), confirmed her status as an important American writer. Since then, Cisneros has penned dozens of books, essays, poems, articles, and collections. Her most recent novel, *Caramelo* (2002), was selected for the Today Show Book Club and as notable book of the year by *The New York Times Book Review,* among others. Of her desire to write about her family and community, Cisneros has said, "I feel like a cartographer; I'm determined to fill a literary void."

All Autobiography? Translated into more than a dozen languages and taught in schools and universities around the world, Cisneros's works have not only filled a literary void, but charted new territory for writers who work in a semi-autobiographical vein. Frequently asked whether her fictional stories are "true" and whether she is their "main character," Cisneros responds: *"Yes, but no. . . . . I write what I see . . . or what happened to me that I can't forget, but also what happened to others I love, or what strangers have told me happened to them. . . . I take all of this and cut and paste it together to make a story, because in real life a story doesn't have shape, and it's the writer that gives it a beginning, a middle, and an end."*

STRAW INTO GOLD:
The Metamorphosis Of The Everyday

SANDRA CISNEROS

BACKGROUND The term "essay" from the French *essai,* meaning "try," historically described an exploratory piece of writing that lacked finish. Eventually, the essay lost its original "unfinished" sense and became a polished form of writing. Here, Sandra Cisneros recounts part of her own growth from "unfinished" to accomplished writer.

When I was living in an artists' colony in the south of France, some fellow Latin-Americans who taught at the university in Aix-en-Provence[1] invited me to share a home-cooked meal with them. I had been living abroad almost a year then on an NEA[2] grant, subsisting mainly on French bread and lentils while in France so that my money could last longer. So when the invitation to dinner arrived, I accepted without hesitation. Especially since they had promised Mexican food.

1. **Aix-en-Provence** (eks än prō väns′) city in southeastern France.
2. **NEA** National Endowment for the Arts.

Comparing Autobiographies
Are the challenges Cisneros describes similar in any way to those Franklin set for himself? Explain.

What I didn't realize when they made this invitation was that I was supposed to be involved in preparing this meal. I guess they assumed I knew how to cook Mexican food because I was Mexican. They wanted specifically tortillas, though I'd never made a tortilla in my life.

It's true I had witnessed my mother rolling the little armies of dough into perfect circles, but my mother's family is from Guanajuato,[3] *provinciales*,[4] country folk. They only know how to make flour tortillas. My father's family, on the other hand, is chilango,[5] from Mexico City. We ate corn tortillas but we didn't make them. Someone was sent to the corner tortilleria to buy some. I'd never seen anybody make corn tortillas. Ever.

Well, somehow my Latino hosts had gotten a hold of a packet of corn flour, and this is what they tossed my way with orders to produce tortillas. *Asi como sea.* Any ol' way, they said and went back to their cooking.

Why did I feel like the woman in the fairy tale who was locked in a room and ordered to spin straw into gold? I had the same sick feeling when I was required to write my critical essay for my MFA[6] exam—the only piece of noncreative writing necessary in order to get my graduate degree. How was I to start? There were rules involved here, unlike writing a poem or story, which I did intuitively. There was a step-by-step process needed and I had better know it. I felt as if making tortillas, or writing a critical paper for that matter, were tasks so impossible I wanted to break down into tears.

Vocabulary
intuitively (in to͞o′ i tiv lē) *adv.* without having to be taught; instinctively

capable (kā′ pə bəl) *adj.* having the skills needed to do something

Somehow though, I managed to make those tortillas—crooked and burnt, but edible nonetheless. My hosts were absolutely ignorant when it came to Mexican food; they thought my tortillas were delicious. (I'm glad my mama wasn't there.) Thinking back and looking at that photograph documenting the three of us consuming those lopsided circles I am amazed. Just as I am amazed I could finish my MFA exam (lopsided and crooked, but finished all the same). Didn't think I could do it. But I did.

I've managed to do a lot of things in my life I didn't think I was capable of and which many others didn't think me capable of either.

Especially because I am a woman, a Latina, an only daughter in a family of six men. My father would've liked to

3. **Guanajuato** (gwä′ nä hwä′ tō) state in central Mexico.
4. **provinciales** (prō bēn sē ä′ lās) "country folk" (Spanish).
5. **chilango** (chē län′ gō) "city folk" (Spanish).
6. **MFA** Master of Fine Arts.

La molendera (The grinder), Diego Rivera (1886–1957), 1926, oil on canvas, Museo Nacional de Arte Moderno, Instituto Nacional de Bellas Artes, Mexico City, D.F., Mexico, ©Banco de Mexico Diego Rivera & Frida Kahlo Museums Trust, Av. Cinco de Mayo No. 2, Col. Centro, Del. Cuauhtemoc 06059, Mexico, D.F., reproduction authorized by the Instituto Nacional de Bellas Artes y Literatura.

◀ Critical Viewing

Judging from this painting by Mexican artist Diego Rivera, explain the challenge tortilla making would present to someone who had never done it before. **[Connect]**

have seen me married long ago. In our culture, men and women don't leave their father's house except by way of marriage. I crossed my father's threshold with nothing carrying me but my own two feet. A woman whom no one came for and no one chased away.

To make matters worse, I had left before any of my six brothers had ventured away from home. I had broken a terrible taboo. Somehow, looking back at photos of myself as a child, I wonder if I was aware of having begun already my own quiet war.

I like to think that somehow my family, my Mexicanness, my poverty all had something to do with shaping me into a writer. I like to think my parents were preparing me all along for my life as an artist even though they didn't know it. From my father I inherited a love of wandering. He was born in Mexico City but as a young man he traveled into the U.S. vagabonding. He eventually was drafted and thus became a citizen. Some of the stories he has told about his first months in the U.S. with little or no English surface in my stories in *The House on Mango Street* as well as others I have in mind to write in the future. From him I inherited a sappy heart. (He still cries when he watches the Mexican soaps—especially if they deal with children who have forsaken their parents.)

Vocabulary

taboo (ta bo͞o′) *n.* something forbidden within a particular society or culture

What Mexican dish was Cisneros asked to prepare?

My mother was born like me—in Chicago but of Mexican descent. It would be her tough, streetwise voice that would haunt all my stories and poems. An amazing woman who loves to draw and read books and can sing an opera. A smart cookie.

When I was a little girl we traveled to Mexico City so much I thought my grandparents' house on La Fortuna, Number 12, was home. It was the only constant in our nomadic ramblings from one Chicago flat to another. The house on Destiny Street, Number 12, in the colonia Tepeyac,[7] would be perhaps the only home I knew, and that nostalgia for a home would be a theme that would obsess me.

Vocabulary
nostalgia (nä stal′ jə) *n.* a longing for something

My brothers also figured greatly in my art. Especially the oldest two; I grew up in their shadows. Henry, the second oldest and my favorite, appears often in poems I have written and in stories which at times only borrow his nickname, Kiki. He played a major role in my childhood. We were bunkbed mates. We were co-conspirators. We were pals. Until my oldest brother came back from studying in Mexico and left me odd-woman-out for always.

What would my teachers say if they knew I was a writer? Who would've guessed it? I wasn't a very bright student. I didn't much like school because we moved so much and I was always new and funny-looking. In my fifth-grade report card, I have nothing but an avalanche of C's and D's, but I don't remember being that stupid. I was good at art and I read plenty of library books and Kiki laughed at all my jokes. At home I was fine, but at school I never opened my mouth except when the teacher called on me, the first time I'd speak all day.

When I think how I see myself, it would have to be at age eleven. I know I'm thirty-two on the outside, but inside I'm eleven. I'm the girl in the picture with skinny arms and a crumpled shirt and crooked hair. I didn't like school because all they saw was the outside me. School was lots of rules and sitting with your hands folded and being very afraid all the time. I liked looking out the window and thinking. I liked staring at the girl across the way writing her name over and over again in red ink. I wondered why the boy with the dirty collar in front of me didn't have a mama who took better care of him.

Comparing Autobiographies
Why do you think Cisneros does not go into greater detail about the nature of her "hunger"?

I think my mama and papa did the best they could to keep us warm and clean and never hungry. We had birthday and graduation parties and things like that, but there was another hunger that had to be fed. There was a hunger I didn't even have a name for. Was this when I began writing?

---

7. colonia Tepeyac (cô lō′ nēä tā pā′ yäc) district of Mexico City.

In 1966 we moved into a house, a real one, our first real home. This meant we didn't have to change schools and be the new kids on the block every couple of years. We could make friends and not be afraid we'd have to say goodbye to them and start all over. My brothers and the flock of boys they brought home would become important characters eventually for my stories—Louie and his cousins, Meme Ortiz and his dog with two names, one in English and one in Spanish.

My mother flourished in her own home. She took books out of the library and taught herself to garden, producing flowers so envied we had to put a lock on the gate to keep out the midnight flower thieves. My mother is still gardening to this day.

This was the period in my life, that slippery age when you are both child and woman and neither, I was to record in *The House on Mango Street*. I was still shy. I was a girl who couldn't come out of her shell.

How was I to know I would be recording and documenting the women who sat their sadness on an elbow and stared out a window? It would be the city streets of Chicago I would later record, but from a child's eyes.

I've done all kinds of things I didn't think I could do since then. I've gone to a prestigious university, studied with famous writers, and taken away an MFA degree. I've taught poetry in the schools in Illinois and Texas. I've gotten an NEA grant and run away with it as far as my courage would take me. I've seen the bleached and bitter mountains of the Peloponnesus.[8] I've lived on a Greek island. I've been to Venice[9] twice. In Rapallo, I met Ilona once and forever and took her sad heart with me across the south of France and into Spain.

I've lived in Yugoslavia. I've been to the famous Nice[10] flower market behind the opera house. I've lived in a village in the pre-Alps[11] and witnessed the daily parade of promenaders.

I've moved since Europe to the strange and wonderful country of Texas, land of polaroid-blue skies and big bugs. I met a mayor with my last name. I met famous Chicana/o artists and writers and *politicos*.[12]

Texas is another chapter in my life. It brought with it the Dobie-Paisano Fellowship, a six-month residency on a 265-acre ranch. But most important Texas brought Mexico back to me.

Vocabulary

flourished (flur´ isht) *v.* grew strong, healthy, and happy; prospered

What happened to change Cisneros's life in 1966?

---

8. **Peloponnesus** (pel´ ə pə nē´ səs) peninsula forming the southeastern part of the Greek mainland.
9. **Venice** (ven´ is) seaport in northern Italy.
10. **Nice** (nēs) seaport and resort in southeastern France.
11. **pre-Alps** foothills of the Alps, a mountain range in south-central Europe.
12. **politicos** (pō lē´ tē cōs) "politicians" (Spanish).

Sitting at my favorite people-watching spot, the snaky Woolworth's counter across the street from the Alamo,[13] I can't think of anything else I'd rather be than a writer. I've traveled and lectured from Cape Cod to San Francisco, to Spain, Yugoslavia, Greece, Mexico, France, Italy, and finally today to Seguin, Texas. Along the way there is straw for the taking. With a little imagination, it can be spun into gold.

13. **the Alamo** (al′ ə mō′) mission in San Antonio, Texas, that was the scene of a famous battle between Texans and Mexican troops in 1836.

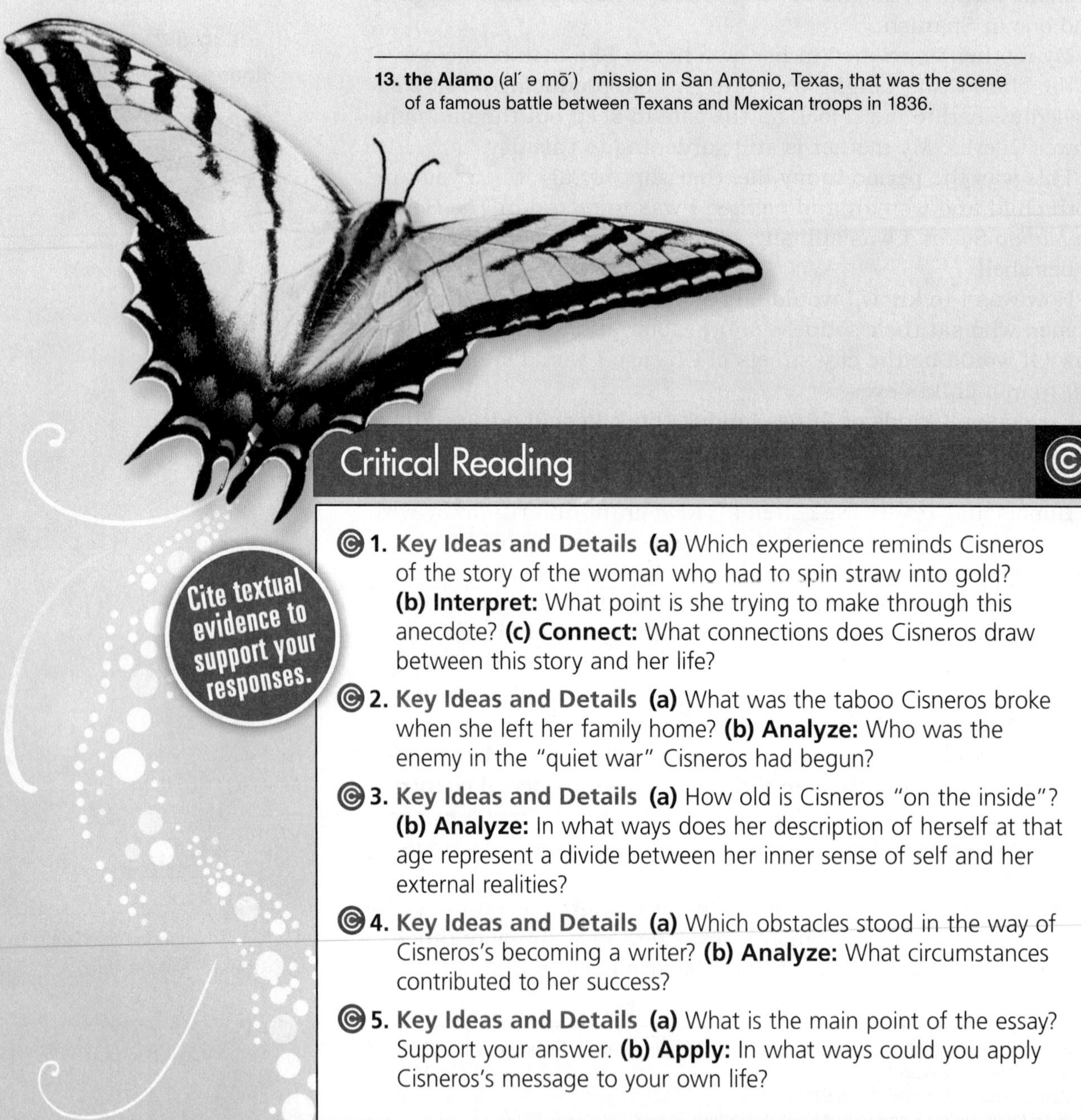

Critical Reading

Cite textual evidence to support your responses.

1. **Key Ideas and Details (a)** Which experience reminds Cisneros of the story of the woman who had to spin straw into gold? **(b) Interpret:** What point is she trying to make through this anecdote? **(c) Connect:** What connections does Cisneros draw between this story and her life?
2. **Key Ideas and Details (a)** What was the taboo Cisneros broke when she left her family home? **(b) Analyze:** Who was the enemy in the "quiet war" Cisneros had begun?
3. **Key Ideas and Details (a)** How old is Cisneros "on the inside"? **(b) Analyze:** In what ways does her description of herself at that age represent a divide between her inner sense of self and her external realities?
4. **Key Ideas and Details (a)** Which obstacles stood in the way of Cisneros's becoming a writer? **(b) Analyze:** What circumstances contributed to her success?
5. **Key Ideas and Details (a)** What is the main point of the essay? Support your answer. **(b) Apply:** In what ways could you apply Cisneros's message to your own life?

After You Read from *The Autobiography* • *Straw Into Gold*

Comparing Autobiography Past and Present

1. **Key Ideas and Details (a)** What facts about Franklin do you learn from reading his **autobiography** on pages 141–146? **(b)** What facts about Cisneros do you learn from reading her **autobiographical essay**?
2. **Key Ideas and Details** What information other than basic facts do you learn about each writer from these works? Cite details to support your answers.
3. **Key Ideas and Details (a)** What details does Cisneros include that you would find surprising in Franklin's writing? **(b)** Is this due to the time period, the writer's gender, the writer's cultural background, or another element? Explain.
4. **Integration of Knowledge and Ideas (a)** Judging from these two texts, how has American autobiography changed from the eighteenth to the twenty-first centuries? **(b)** In what ways is the genre the same? Support your answers with details from the texts.

Common Core State Standards

Writing

9. Draw evidence from literary or informational texts to support analysis, reflection, and research.

10. Write routinely over exended time frames and shorter time frames for a range of tasks, purposes, and audiences.

Timed Writing

Explanatory Text: Essay

Even though Franklin and Cisneros faced different obstacles, the *theme* of success—how to achieve it, what it is, and what it means—is a key element in both of their autobiographical works.

Assignment: Write an **essay** in which you *compare and contrast* each writer's ideas about success. Cite evidence from the texts to support your ideas. Use these questions to focus your analysis. **[40 minutes]**

- What challenges does each writer face? Are the challenges self-imposed, or do they come from without?
- What conclusions about success does each writer draw?
- Do these autobiographical works reveal connections between American identity and ideas of achievement or success?

Organize your ideas logically. You might focus on the features of one selection and then the features of the other. Alternatively, you might focus on points of similarity and difference, moving back and forth between the two selections.

USE ACADEMIC VOCABULARY

As you write, use academic language, including the following words or their related forms:

categorize
examine
insight
perception

For more on academic language, see the vocabulary charts in the introductory unit in this book.

5-Minute Planner

Complete these steps before you begin to write:

1. Read the assignment carefully. List key words and phrases.
2. Scan the autobiographies for evidence that relates to the ideas in your list. **TIP** As you scan the texts, jot down quotations or details that you might use in your essay.
3. Create a rough outline for your essay.
4. Reread the prompt, and draft your essay.

Themes Across Centuries: Scholar's Insights

William L. Andrews Introduces

The Interesting Narrative of THE LIFE OF OLAUDAH EQUIANO

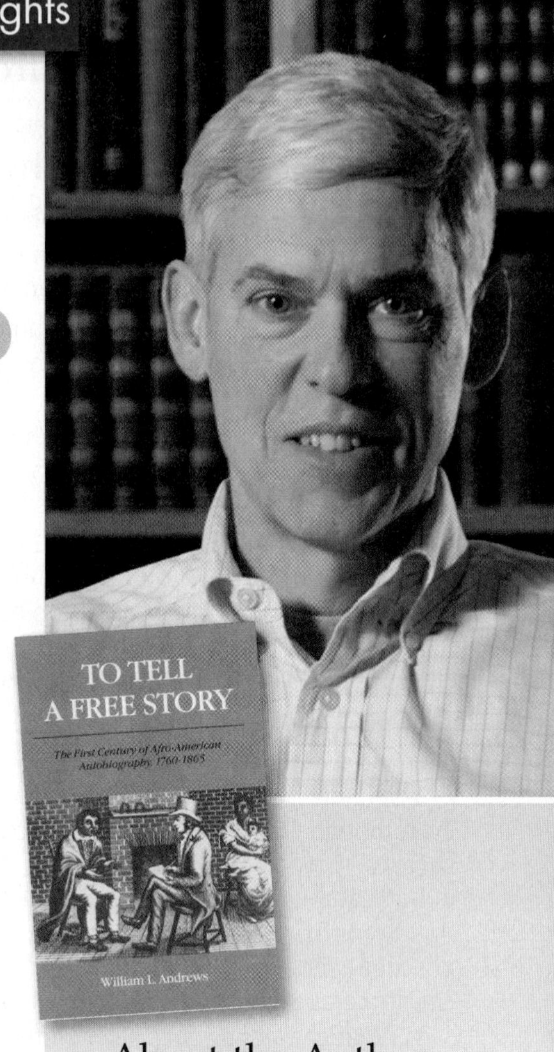

A Rare Firsthand Account of the Middle Passage One of the most astonishing facts about the Middle Passage—the Atlantic crossing of enslaved Africans to the Americas—is that, although millions of Africans endured it, and as many as one in eight died from it, history has preserved almost no firsthand accounts of it. *The Interesting Narrative of the Life of Olaudah Equiano* contains one of the rare detailed reports of the catastrophic journey that survives in English. Imagine how hard it would be for someone who had been through such a horrifying experience to write about it. Writing about past trauma almost certainly requires a person to relive it.

A Virtual Tour of the Slave Ship Equiano's account of the Middle Passage directly thrusts his reader, who Equiano expected would be either English or American, into a terrifying situation. Whatever Equiano's white readers thought about slavery, we can be pretty sure that they didn't want to think about how the Africans got to the Americas. By taking his reader on a virtual tour of the slave ship above and below decks, Equiano seems determined to confront his reader with the hideous—and generally hidden—truth about life aboard a slave ship.

The first stop is the ship's suffocating hold, where its human cargo was stored for most of the transatlantic voyage. Here we can see, hear, feel, and, especially, smell how "loathsome" a place it really was. Hell on earth would not be too strong a term to describe the hold of a slave ship.

Equiano doesn't confine us long in the miserable hold before taking us up into the fresh air, where we might hope for some relief from the horrors we've experienced. However, we soon find ourselves accompanied by dying Africans who've been brought up to the deck to perish of the illnesses they've contracted in the hold. Meanwhile, the European ship hands merely watch and wait, supremely indifferent to the suffering they witness.

About the Author

William L. Andrews is the series editor of North American Slave Narratives, Beginnings to 1920. His book *To Tell a Free Story* is a history of African American autobiography up to 1865.

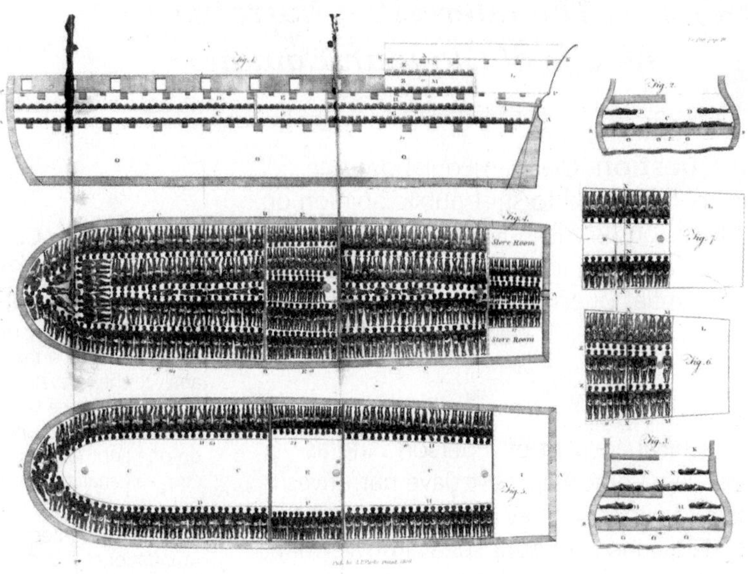

◀ **Critical Viewing** What do these design drawings of a slave ship tell you about slave traders' attitudes toward their captives? **[Analyze]**

Identifying With the Abused Africans The cruelty of the whites aboard the slave ship must have shocked Equiano's readers, particularly since, as whites themselves, they would likely have felt more in common with the Europeans on the ship than the Africans. But Equiano's storytelling gradually alienates his reader from the brutal whites while helping the reader to identify with the abused Africans.

Through the point of view of the ten-year-old African narrator, we inevitably feel the same shock and dread that the innocent African boy felt. Our sympathy with the narrator goes beyond pitying him as a victim, however. We follow as the curious African boy steps forward to take a peek through the ship's quadrant. As an unimagined world opens up to him, we realize that no matter how unjustly that new world may treat him in the future, Equiano the inquisitive, resilient traveler, will survive.

Thinking About the Commentary

1. **Key Ideas and Details (a)** What was the Middle Passage? **(b) Speculate:** Why do you think firsthand accounts of it are so rare?

2. **Key Ideas and Details (a)** What does Equiano show readers? **(b) Infer:** What do you think was his purpose in conducting this "virtual tour"?

As You Read ***The Interesting Narrative of the Life of Olaudah Equiano . . .***

3. **Key Ideas and Details** Identify details that justify Andrews's description of Equiano as "inquisitive" and "resilient."

Before You Read

from *The Interesting Narrative of the Life of Olaudah Equiano*

Connecting to the Essential Question Olaudah Equiano wrote about a personal ordeal. In doing so, he helped to shift public opinion on the issue of slavery. As you read, focus on details in Equiano's writing that you think would have been especially effective in changing public opinion. This will help as you consider the Essential Question: **How does literature shape or reflect society?**

Common Core
State Standards

Reading Informational Text

2. Determine two or more central ideas of a text and analyze their development over the course of the text, including how they interact and build on one another to provide a complex analysis; provide an objective summary of the text.

9. Analyze eighteenth-century foundational U.S. documents of historical and literary significance for their themes, purposes, and rhetorical features.

Literary Analysis

A **slave narrative** is an autobiographical account of a person's life as a slave. Written when slavery was a legal practice, most slave narratives have an implicit persuasive purpose: to expose the evils of slavery and, in so doing, turn the public against it. Equiano's account speaks powerfully against the slave trade. His style includes descriptive language that appeals to readers' emotions. Notice, for example, how descriptive words such as "shrieks" and "groans" evoke readers' sympathy and outrage in this description of the slave ship that brought Equiano from Africa:

> *The shrieks of the women, and the groans of the dying, rendered the whole a scene of horror almost inconceivable.*

As you read, recognize details that both convey Equiano's perceptions and experiences and register as strong emotional appeals against the institution of slavery. Consider how each detail contributes to the implicit case Equiano is building against the entire institution of slavery.

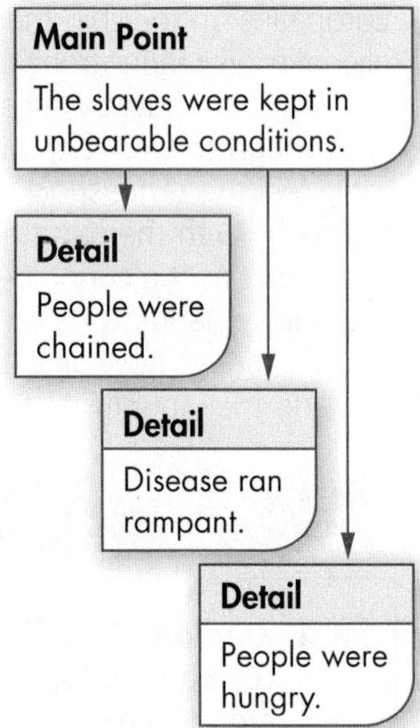
Main Point
The slaves were kept in unbearable conditions.
Detail
People were chained.
Detail
Disease ran rampant.
Detail
People were hungry.

Reading Strategy

Preparing to Read Complex Texts Some literature written long ago may be challenging to read. You can improve your comprehension by **summarizing to identify the main, or central, idea.** To do so, identify only the most important ideas and details in a passage. Include key information from the beginning, middle, and end. Then, gather that information into a brief statement. As you read, use a chart like the one shown to summarize.

Vocabulary

copious (kō´ pē əs) *adj.* plentiful; abundant (p. 172)

wretched (rech´ id) *adj.* deeply distressed; miserable (p. 172)

dejected (dē jek´ tid) *adj.* in low spirits; downcast; depressed (p. 173)

inseparable (in sep´ ə rə bəl) *adj.* not able to be divided; linked (p. 173)

heightened (hīt´ ənd) *v.* raised the level of (p. 174)

pacify (pas´ ə fī´) *v.* calm or soothe (p. 175)

PHLit Online!
www.PHLitOnline.com

Olaudah Equiano

(1745–1797)

Author of *The Interesting Narrative of the Life of Olaudah Equiano*

I believe there are few events in my life, which have not happened to many: it is true the incidents of it are numerous; and, did I consider myself an European, I might say my sufferings were great: but when I compare my lot with that of most of my countrymen, I regard myself as a particular favorite of Heaven, and acknowledge the mercies of Providence in every occurrence of my life.

When it was first published in 1789, the autobiography of Olaudah Equiano (ō lä o͞o′dā ek′wē ä′ nō) created a sensation. A best seller on both sides of the Atlantic, it made society face the cruelties of slavery and contributed to the banning of the slave trade in both the United States and England.

Childhood Interrupted The son of a West African tribal elder, Olaudah Equiano might have followed in his father's footsteps had he not been sold into slavery. Instead, when he was eleven years old, he and his sister were kidnapped from their home and sold to British slave traders. Separated from his sister, Equiano—like millions of other Africans—was shipped across the Atlantic Ocean under horrendous conditions. He was taken first to the West Indies and later brought to Virginia, where he was purchased by a British captain and employed at sea.

The Struggle for Liberty Renamed Gustavus Vassa, Equiano was enslaved for nearly ten years. After managing his master's finances and making his own money in the process, he amassed enough to buy his own freedom. In later years, he settled in England and devoted himself to the abolition of slavery. In addition to writing his two-volume autobiography to publicize the plight of slaves, he lectured and rallied public sympathies against the cruelties of slavery. He was also involved in the founding of Sierra Leone, the famous British colony established on the west coast of Africa for freed British slaves.

from The Interesting Narrative of THE LIFE OF OLAUDAH EQUIANO

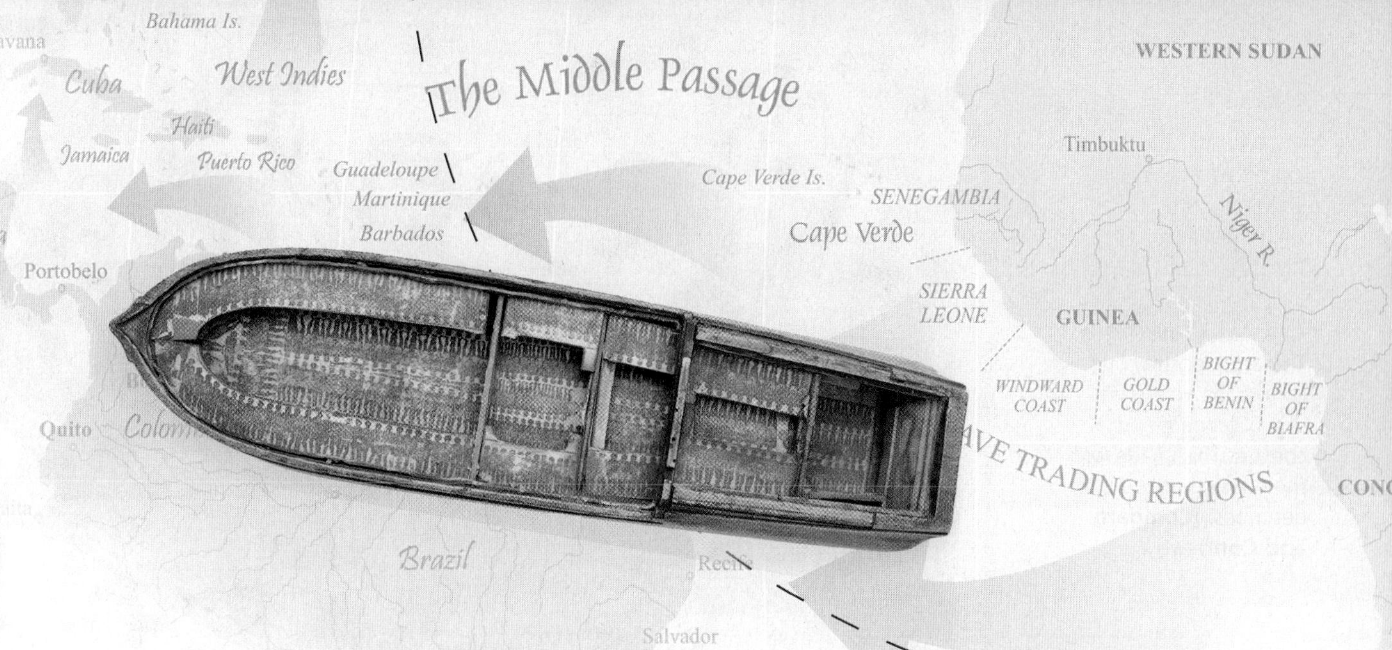

BACKGROUND In the first several chapters of his narrative, Olaudah Equiano describes how slave traders kidnapped him and his sister from their home in West Africa and transported them to the African coast. During this six- or seven-month journey, Equiano was separated from his sister and held at a series of way stations. After reaching the coast, Equiano was shipped with other slaves to North America. The following account describes this horrifying journey.

◀ ▲ **Critical Viewing**
In what ways do these images of slave ships help prove Equiano's point that the slavers were motivated by extreme greed? **[Verify]**

At last when the ship we were in, had got in all her cargo, they made ready with many fearful noises, and we were all put under deck, so that we could not see how they managed the vessel. But this disappointment was the least of my sorrow. The stench of the hold while we were on the coast was so intolerably loathsome, that it was dangerous to remain there for any time, and some of us had been permitted to stay on the deck for the fresh air; but now that the whole ship's cargo were confined together, it became absolutely pestilential. The closeness of the place, and the heat of the climate, added to the number in the ship, which was so crowded that each had scarcely room to turn himself, almost suffocated us.

According to Equiano, why does the hold become "pestilential"?

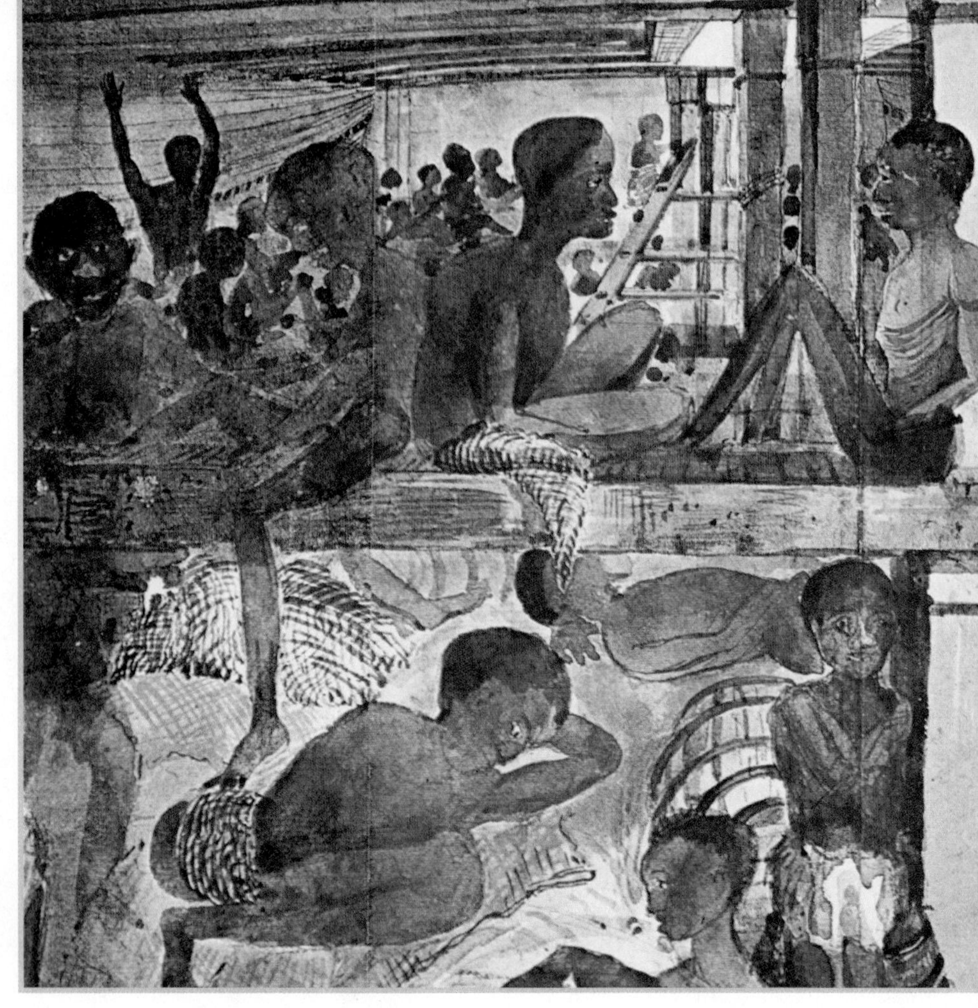

Slaves Below Deck (detail), Lt. Francis Meynell, National Maritime Museum, Greenwich

Critical Viewing ▶ The artist portrays conditions on a slave ship. Compare and contrast this image with the scene that Equiano describes. **[Compare and Contrast]**

Vocabulary

copious (kō´ pē əs) *adj.* plentiful; abundant

wretched (rech´ id) *adj.* deeply distressed; miserable

William L. Andrews
Scholar's Insight
The wasteful greed of European slave traders makes them so callous that they don't even care about the profits they lose when slaves die in transit aboard their ships. The words *improvident avarice* help Equiano portray slavery as both inhuman and unprofitable.

This produced copious perspirations, so that the air soon became unfit for respiration, from a variety of loathsome smells, and brought on a sickness among the slaves, of which many died—thus falling victims to the improvident avarice, as I may call it, of their purchasers. This wretched situation was again aggravated by the galling of the chains, now become insupportable, and the filth of the necessary tubs, into which the children often fell, and were almost suffocated. The shrieks of the women, and the groans of the dying, rendered the whole a scene of horror almost inconceivable. Happily perhaps, for myself, I was soon reduced so low here that it was thought necessary to keep me almost always on deck; and from my extreme youth I was not put in fetters.[1] In this situation I expected every hour to share the fate of my companions, some of whom were almost daily brought upon deck at the point of death, which I began to hope would soon put an end to my miseries. Often did I think many of the inhabitants of the deep much more happy than myself.

1. **fetters** (fet´ ərz) *n.* chains.

I envied them the freedom they enjoyed, and as often wished I could change my condition for theirs. Every circumstance I met with, served only to render my state more painful, and heightened my apprehensions, and my opinion of the cruelty of the whites.

One day they had taken a number of fishes; and when they had killed and satisfied themselves with as many as they thought fit, to our astonishment who were on deck, rather than give any of them to us to eat, as we expected, they tossed the remaining fish into the sea again, although we begged and prayed for some as well as we could, but in vain; and some of my countrymen, being pressed by hunger, took an opportunity, when they thought no one saw them, of trying to get a little privately; but they were discovered, and the attempt procured them some very severe floggings. One day, when we had a smooth sea and moderate wind, two of my wearied countrymen who were chained together (I was near them at the time), preferring death to such a life of misery, somehow made through the nettings and jumped into the sea; immediately, another quite **dejected** fellow, who, on account of his illness, was suffered to be out of irons, also followed their example; and I believe many more would very soon have done the same, if they had not been prevented by the ship's crew, who were instantly alarmed. Those of us that were the most active, were in a moment put down under the deck; and there was such a noise and confusion amongst the people of the ship as I never heard before, to stop her, and get the boat out to go after the slaves. However, two of the wretches were drowned, but they got the other, and afterwards flogged him unmercifully, for thus attempting to prefer death to slavery. In this manner we continued to undergo more hardships than I can now relate, hardships which are **inseparable** from this accursed trade. Many a time we were near suffocation from the want of fresh air, which we were often without for whole days together. This, and the stench of the necessary tubs, carried off many.

William L. Andrews
Scholar's Insight
The inexplicable cruelty of the Europeans, contrasted with the pleading and praying of the Africans, is designed to challenge the prejudices of Equiano's readers. These readers would have expected the supposedly heathen Africans, not the Christian Europeans, to be indifferent to human need.

Vocabulary

dejected (dē jek´ tid) *adj.* in low spirits; downcast; depressed

inseparable (in sep´ ə rə bəl) *adj.* not able to be divided; linked

What do some slaves do to escape the misery of the Middle Passage?

The
American EXPERIENCE

ECONOMICS

The Slave Trade

While some people came to the Western Hemisphere in search of a better life, others were brought against their will to be sold as slaves. The map shown here indicates the major slave trade routes.

The Atlantic crossing, known as the Middle Passage, was brutal. Africans were chained below decks in cramped, filthy spaces. Overcrowding, disease, and despair claimed many lives. Some Africans mutinied; others tried to starve themselves or jump overboard.

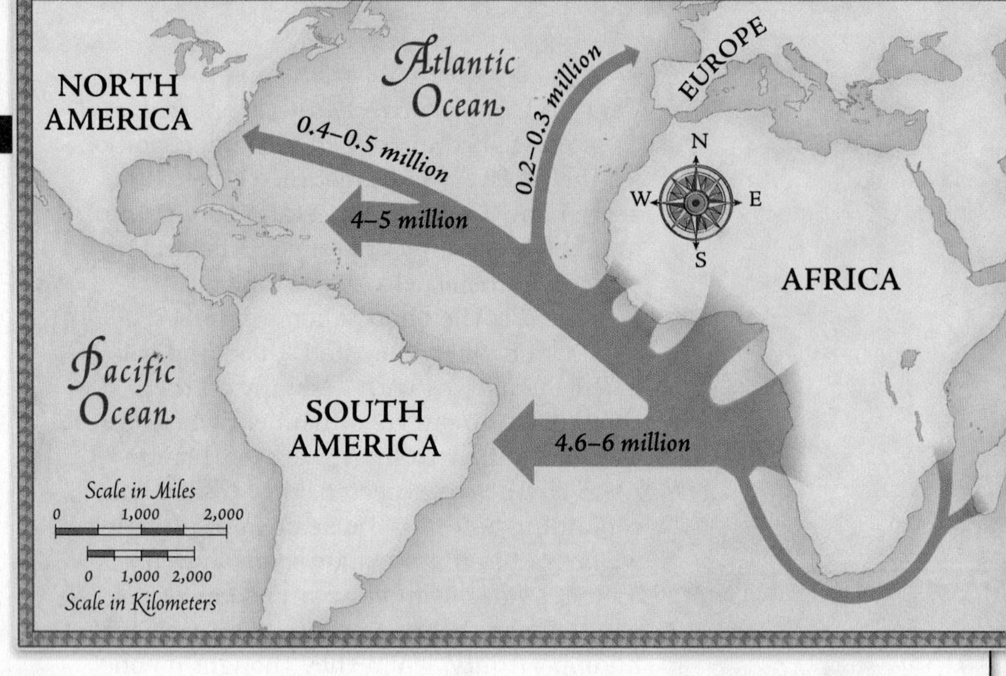

Atlantic Slave Trade Routes
1502–1870

Connect to the Literature

What seems to be Equiano's attitude toward the captives who preferred death to slavery?

During our passage, I first saw flying fishes, which surprised me very much; they used frequently to fly across the ship, and many of them fell on the deck. I also now first saw the use of the quadrant;[2] I had often with astonishment seen the mariners make observations with it, and I could not think what it meant. They at last took notice of my surprise; and one of them, willing to increase it, as well as to gratify my curiosity, made me one day look through it. The clouds appeared to me to be land, which disappeared as they passed along. This heightened my wonder; and I was now more persuaded than ever, that I was in another world, and that every thing about me was magic. At last, we came in sight of the island of Barbados, at which the whites on board gave a great shout, and made many signs of joy to us. We did not know what to think of this; but as the vessel drew nearer, we plainly saw the harbor, and other ships of different kinds and sizes, and we soon anchored amongst them, off Bridgetown.[3] Many merchants and planters now came on board, though it was in the evening. They put us in separate parcels,[4] and examined us attentively. They also made us jump, and pointed to the land, signifying we were to go there.

Vocabulary
heightened (hīt´ ənd) *v.* raised the level of

2. **quadrant** (kwä´ drənt) *n.* an instrument used by navigators to determine the position of a ship.
3. **Bridgetown** *n.* the capital of Barbados.
4. **parcels** (pär´ səlz) *n.* groups.

We thought by this, we should be eaten by these ugly men, as they appeared to us; and, when soon after we were all put down under the deck again, there was much dread and trembling among us, and nothing but bitter cries to be heard all the night from these apprehensions, insomuch, that at last the white people got some old slaves from the land to pacify us. They told us we were not to be eaten, but to work, and were soon to go on land, where we should see many of our country people. This report eased us much. And sure enough, soon after we were landed, there came to us Africans of all languages.

We were conducted immediately to the merchant's yard, where we were all pent up together, like so many sheep in a fold, without regard to sex or age. . . . We were not many days in the merchant's custody, before we were sold after their usual manner, which is this: On a signal given (as the beat of a drum), the buyers rush at once into the yard where the slaves are confined, and make choice of that parcel they like best. . . .

Vocabulary
pacify (pas′ ə fī′) *v.* to calm or soothe

William L. Andrews
Scholar's Insight
This reversal of the well-established European stereotype of the African as cannibal is one of Equiano's most effective ironies.

Critical Reading

Cite textual evidence to support your responses.

1. **Key Ideas and Details (a)** Why does Equiano blame the illness aboard the ship on the "improvident avarice" of the traders? **(b) Infer:** How do the white crewmen view their captives? **(c) Draw Conclusions:** What does the treatment of the slaves reveal about the captors' attitudes toward human life?

2. **Key Ideas and Details (a)** How does Equiano's age affect his experiences during the voyage? **(b) Infer:** How do you think he felt about his experience compared to the fate of other captives on the ship?

3. **Craft and Structure** How does Equiano show his great zest for life despite his assertion that he wants to die? Provide examples from the selection.

4. **Integration of Knowledge and Ideas** What do you think the public of Equiano's day learned about the "accursed trade" of slavery that it may not have known before reading this narrative? In your response, use at least two of these Essential Question vocabulary words: *awareness, compassion, inhumane, avarice. [Connecting to the Essential Question: How does literature shape or reflect society?]*

After You Read

from *The Interesting Narrative of the Life of Olaudah Equiano*

Literary Analysis

1. **Key Ideas and Details (a)** In his **slave narrative,** which physical hardships does Equiano say the captives suffered during the Middle Passage? **(b)** What emotional torments does he describe? **(c)** In what ways do these descriptions serve as appeals to readers' emotions? Explain.
2. **Key Ideas and Details (a)** Cite two examples of the slave traders' cruelty to the slaves. **(b)** What effect do you think this information would have had on readers in Equiano's day?
3. **Key Ideas and Details (a)** Cite two examples that show the slave traders' concern for the slaves. **(b)** What seems to motivate this concern? **(c)** Would you say this is genuine concern or something else? Explain.
4. **Craft and Structure (a)** Using a chart like the one shown, identify three examples of *descriptive language* in the narrative. **(b)** Explain how each example serves as a strong emotional appeal to the reader.

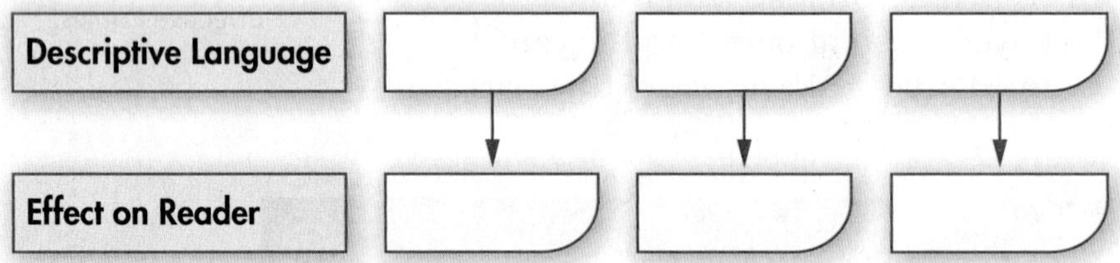

5. **Integration of Knowledge and ideas** Do you think it is better for people who are victims of injustice to record and even publicize their experiences or to maintain their privacy? Explain your answer.

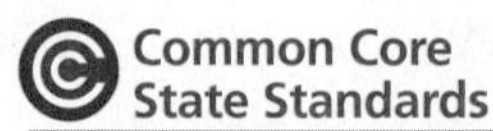

Common Core State Standards

Writing
7. Conduct short as well as more sustained research projects to answer a question or solve a problem; narrow or broaden the inquiry when appropriate; synthesize multiple sources on the subject, demonstrating understanding of the subject under investigation. *(p. 177)*

Language
4.d. Verify the preliminary definition of the meaning of a word or phrase. *(p. 177)*

Reading Strategy

6. **(a)** In **summarizing** the excerpt as a whole, what three central ideas would you include? **(b)** What is the single most essential message of Equiano's autobiographical account?
7. A summary of the first paragraph of the excerpt appears below. Revise this summary by deleting one piece of information that is not important enough to include, and adding one detail that is too important to omit.

   On the ship that took Equiano from Africa to the Americas, the slaves were kept in miserable conditions. It was hot and crowded. People were chained. Equiano wished he were a fish or another inhabitant of the deep.

8. **(a)** Summarize the events that occur after the ship reaches Bridgetown. **(b)** What is the central idea or essential message in that section of the narrative?

PERFORMANCE TASKS

Integrated Language Skills

Vocabulary Acquisition and Use

Word Analysis: Latin Root *-ject-*

The word *dejected* contains the Latin root *-ject-*, which means "throw." Someone who is *dejected* is thrown down, or downcast, by disappointment or sorrow. Use context clues and knowledge of the root *-ject-* to explain the meaning of each italicized word below. Also make clear how the word's meaning reflects the meaning of the root.

1. I was disappointed when the publisher *rejected* my manuscript.
2. The nurse gave me an *injection* in my arm.
3. Tanya *projected* her voice across the room.
4. We did not know the answer, but we offered our *conjectures* in a brainstorming session.
5. Pablo and Luisa were conversing when Celia *interjected* some remarks.
6. The guard *ejected* the misbehaving children.

Vocabulary: Categorize Key Vocabulary

Review the list of vocabulary words on page 168. Then, analyze the relationship between the italicized word and the words that follow it in each item below. For each grouping, determine a logical category, such as *synonyms, antonyms and synonyms*, or another category that you can defend. Explain your reasoning. Consult a dictionary if necessary.

1. *copious,* sparse, meager
2. *wretched,* desolate, pitiful
3. *dejected,* cheerful, lively
4. *inseparable,* divisible, isolated
5. *heightened,* sensitive, keen
6. *pacify,* agitate, incite

Writing

Informative Text Write the information for a large **museum placard** that visitors might read at the beginning of a museum exhibit about Olaudah Equiano and the slave trade during the eighteenth century. Use details from Equiano's narrative, as well as facts and data about the North American slave trade that you gather through research in other sources.

Prewriting Conduct research at the library or online to find public documents that *verify and clarify facts* and observations Equiano presents in his narrative. Organize your findings, perhaps drawing a map to trace the slave trade routes or marking dates and other key details on a timeline. Identify any *specialized vocabulary* you may need to define in order to make the material clear to a general reader.

Drafting As you draft, *consider your audience and purpose*. Begin with strong information, such as a startling anecdote or fact, that will draw the public into the exhibit. Remember that your audience probably has little prior knowledge about your topic. Use a chart like the one shown to anticipate readers' questions.

Revising Review your work, making sure you have clarified all unfamiliar facts or data. Add explanations as needed.

Model: Assessing Audience Knowledge

Detail	Prior Knowledge?	Action
Location of West Africa	Probably not	Explain
Average duration of Middle Passage	No	Provide data

Primary Sources

Letter
Letter from the President's House

Letter
Letter from the New White House

Floor Plan
President's House

Common Core State Standards

Reading Informational Text
9. Analyze seventeenth-, eighteenth-, and nineteenth-century foundational U.S. documents of historical and literary significance for their themes, purposes, and rhetorical features.

About the Text Forms

Today, you might send an IM or an e-mail to a distant friend, or simply make a phone call. In the past, though, people relied on **letters** to keep in touch. Private letters tend to be informal, spontaneous, and intended only for the reader to whom they are addressed. Most letters are not meant for publication. However, some letters, such as these by John and Abigail Adams, contain firsthand accounts of historical events and so are regarded as important primary source documents.

A **floor plan** is a diagram of one level of a building shown from an aerial point of view. It is usually drawn to scale and shows the relationships between rooms and other features. While this floor plan is an interesting primary source document in its own right, you may also use it to *verify and clarify* information the Adamses include in their letters.

Reading Strategy

A writer's circumstances and point of view are often referred to as his or her "perspective." **Analyzing a writer's perspective** in a primary source document can help you step more fully into the time period in which he or she lived. For example, these letters describe the White House as it is being built. As you read, picture the structure exactly as the writers describe it. Analyze the perspectives using questions such as these:

- Does the writer have positive or negative feelings about the subject?
- Are broader *philosophical, religious, ethical, social, or historical events* influencing his or her perspective?
- Does the perspective seem appropriate, given the circumstances?

What is the **relationship** between literature and *place?*

Today, the White House is recognized as a symbol of power and democracy, but in 1800 it was just an unfinished structure. As you inspect these texts, notice details that express how the President and First Lady felt in such an environment as well as their hopes for the future.

Note-Taking Guide

Primary source documents are a rich source of information for researchers. As you read these documents, use a note-taking guide like the one shown to organize relevant and accurate information.

1 Type of Document (check one)
☐ Newspaper ☐ Advertisement ☐ Telegram ☐ Letter
☐ Floor Plan ☐ Diary or Journal ☐ E-mail ☐ Report

2 Date(s) of Document ______

3 Author of Document ______

4 Who is the intended audience for the work?
______

5 What is the main subject of this work? ______
______

6 List three observations or details in this document that you think are important:
a ______
b ______
c ______

7 Based on your answers to items 4–6, how would you describe the writer's perspective on the subject?
______
______

Reading Strategy
Analyzing a Writer's Perspective
A writer's perspective is often affected by his or her audience. As you study each document, ask yourself whether the relationship between writer and audience is intimate or formal, and how this relationship influences the work's content.

This guide was adapted from the **U.S. National Archives** document analysis worksheet.

Vocabulary

account (ə count′) *n.* a report or description (p. 181)

commissioners (kə mish′ ə nərz) *n.* government officials (p. 181)

inspection (in spek′ shən) *n.* examination (p. 181)

unabated (un ə bāt′ əd) *adj.* not lessened or reduced (p. 181)

interspersed (in′ tər spurst′) *v.* placed here and there (p. 182)

scale (skāl) *n.* the extent or size of something (p. 182)

establishment (ə stab′ lish mənt) *n.* a household or business (p. 182)

contract (kän′ trakt′) *n.* a written agreement (p. 183)

procure (prō kyoor′) *v.* bring about through some effort (p. 183)

recourse (rē′ kôrs′) *n.* access to a form of help or aid (p. 183)

THE STORY BEHIND THE DOCUMENTS

President John Adams

Abigail Adams

Benjamin Henry Latrobe

In 1790—two years after the ratification of the Constitution and one year after George Washington was elected the nation's first president—the U.S. Congress passed the Residence Act. This act established a permanent national capital in a 10-square-mile tract of land along the Potomac River. Washington himself selected the site for the President's House, later known as the White House, in a wooded area on the banks of the river. In 1792, a competition was held to choose an architect for the presidential residence. It was hoped that the design would reflect the nation's noble ideals. Irishman James Hoban (1762–1831) won the competition.

Hoban's design for the President's House was a basic rectangular structure. The classic simplicity of this design would allow later presidents to make alterations according to the needs of the day. Thomas Jefferson, for one, would ask architect **Benjamin Henry Latrobe (1764–1820)** to complete and extend Hoban's design. Latrobe transformed Hoban's boxy original into the grand house with columns and covered entrances that today is widely recognized as the home of the President of the United States.

Construction of the original President's House began on October 13, 1792. The house would not near completion until some eight years later, when the second President of the United States, **President John Adams (1735–1826)** and his wife **Abigail Smith Adams (1744–1818)** took up residence there in November, 1800. Although their stay in the house would be brief, the Adamses graciously made do with less-than-perfect living conditions. Many of the walls were still unplastered. A giant hole marked the place where the grand staircase would someday be, and the six out of thirty-six rooms that were habitable were poorly lit and drafty. To keep the house even mildly warm, President Adams paid for firewood out of his own pocket. Unwilling to have the president's laundry hung about the yard, Abigail had lines strung in the large, unfinished East Room.

These were trying times for the Adamses. John was on the brink of losing his reelection to Thomas Jefferson, and Abigail had been ill. The couple was no doubt bolstered by their close companionship, a relationship documented in their letters. Throughout their courtship and marriage, John and Abigail wrote more than one thousand letters to one another. Although their letters are often affectionate and even playful, they also reflect the couple's underlying awareness that they were key players in the unfolding of history.

Letter from the PRESIDENT'S HOUSE

John Adams

BACKGROUND As John Adams wrote this letter, the outcome of the election of 1801, in which Thomas Jefferson was his opponent, was still uncertain. Anxious for the company and consolation of his wife, Adams seems to sense that defeat is likely.

President's house,
Washington City,
Nov. 2. 1800

My Dearest Friend,

We arrived here last night, or rather yesterday, at one o Clock and here we dined and Slept. The Building is in a State to be habitable. And now we wish for your Company. The **Account** you give of the melancholly State of our dear Brother Mr. Cranch [1] and his family is really distressing and must severely afflict you. I most cordially Sympathize with you and them. I have seen only Mr. Marshall and Mr. Stoddert, General Wilkinson and the two **Commissioners** Mr. Scott and Mr. Thornton.[2] I shall say nothing of public affairs. I am very glad you consented to come on, for you would have been more anxious at Quincy[3] than here, and I, to all my other Solicitudines Mordaces as Horace[4] calls them i.e. "biting Cares" should have added a great deal on your Account. Besides it is fit and proper that you and I should retire together and not one before the other. Before I end my Letter I pray Heaven to bestow the best of Blessings on this House and all that shall hereafter inhabit it. May none but honest and wise Men ever rule under this roof. I shall not attempt a description of it. You will form the best Idea of it from **Inspection**. Mr. Brisler[5] is very anxious for the arrival of the Man and Women and I am much more so for that of the Ladies. I am with **unabated** Confidence and affection your

John Adams

Vocabulary

account (ə count´) *n.* a report or description

commissioners (kə mish´ ə nərz) *n.* government officials

inspection (in spek´ shən) *n.* examination

unabated (un ə bā´ təd) *adj.* not lessened or reduced

▲ sample of John Adams's handwriting

1. **Richard Cranch** President Adams's brother-in-law.
2. **Mr. Marshall. . . Mr. Thornton** Various officials and cabinet members.
3. **Quincy** the Adamses' hometown in Massachusetts.
4. **Horace** classical Roman poet.
5. **John Brisler** President Adams's servant.

Letter to Her Daughter from the NEW WHITE HOUSE

Abigail Adams

Washington,
21 November, 1800

My Dear Child:

I arrived here on Sunday last, and without meeting with any accident worth noticing, except losing ourselves when we left Baltimore and going eight or nine miles on the Frederick road, by which means we were obliged to go the other eight through woods, where we wandered two hours without finding a guide or the path. Fortunately, a straggling black came up with us, and we engaged him as a guide to extricate us out of our difficulty; but woods are all you see from Baltimore until you reach the *city*, which is only so in name. Here and there is a small cot, without a glass window, **interspersed** amongst the forests, through which you travel miles without seeing any human being. In the city there are buildings enough, if they were compact and finished, to accommodate Congress and those attached to it; but as they are, and scattered as they are, I see no great comfort for them. The river, which runs up to Alexandria,[1] is in full view of my window, and I see the vessels as they pass and repass. The house is upon a grand and superb **scale**, requiring about thirty servants to attend and keep the apartments in proper order, and perform the ordinary business of the house and stables; an **establishment** very well proportioned to the President's salary. The lighting of the apartments, from the kitchen to parlors and chambers, is a tax indeed; and the fires we are obliged to keep to secure us from daily agues is another very cheering comfort. To assist us in this great castle, and render less attendance necessary, bells are wholly wanting, not one single one being hung through the whole house, and promises are all you can obtain. This is so great an inconvenience, that I know not what to do, or how to do. The ladies from Georgetown[2] and in the city have many of them visited me. Yesterday I returned fifteen visits—but such a place as Georgetown appears—why, our Milton[3] is beautiful. But no comparisons—if they will put me up some bells and let me have wood enough to keep fires, I design to be pleased. I could content myself almost anywhere three

Vocabulary

interspersed (in′ tər spʉrst′) *v.* placed here and there

scale (skāl) *n.* the extent or size of something

establishment (ə stab′ lish mənt) *n.* a household or business

1. **Alexandria** city in northeastern Virginia.
2. **Georgetown** section of Washington, D.C.
3. **Milton** town in Massachusetts.

months; but, surrounded with forests, can you believe that wood is not to be had because people cannot be found to cut and cart it? Briesler entered into a **contract** with a man to supply him with wood. A small part, a few cords only, has he been able to get. Most of that was expended to dry the walls of the house before we came in, and yesterday the man told him it was impossible for him to **procure** it to be cut and carted. He has had **recourse** to coals; but we cannot get grates made and set. We have, indeed, come into a new country. You must keep all this to yourself, and, when asked how I like it, say that I write you the situation is beautiful, which is true. The house is made habitable, but there is not a single apartment finished, and all withinside, except the plastering, has been done since Briesler came. We have not the least fence, yard, or other convenience without and the great unfinished audience room I make a drying-room of, to hang up the clothes in. The principal stairs are not up, and will not be this winter. Six chambers are made comfortable; two are occupied by the President and Mr. Shaw; two lower rooms, one for a common parlor, and one for a levee room. Upstairs there is the oval room, which is designed for the drawing room, and has the crimson furniture in it. It is a very handsome room now; but, when completed, it will be beautiful. If the twelve years, in which this place has been considered as the future seat of government had been improved, as they would have been if in New England, very many of the present inconveniences would have been removed. It is a beautiful spot, capable of every improvement, and, the more I view it, the more I am delighted with it. Since I sat down to write, I have been called down to a servant from Mount Vernon,[4] with a billet[5] from Major Custis, and a haunch of venison, and a kind, congratulatory letter from Mrs. Lewis, upon my arrival in the city, with Mrs. Washington's love, inviting me to Mount Vernon, where, health permitting, I will go before I leave this place. Affectionally, your mother,

Abigail Adams

4. **Mount Vernon** home of George Washington, located in northern Virginia.
5. **billet** (bil′ it) *n.* brief letter.

Vocabulary

contract (kän′ trakt′) *n.* a written agreement

procure (prō kyoor′) *v.* to bring about through some effort

recourse (rē′ kôrs′) *n.* access to a form of help or aid

Primary Sources

Letters

In what ways does Mrs. Adams's statement about coming into a "new country" suggest a moment in time that is both historically and personally significant?

American stagecoach, mid-nineteenth century ▼

Floor Plan of the PRESIDENT'S HOUSE

Benjamin Henry Latrobe

Shown here is a floor plan of the President's House as it existed in 1803. Latrobe created this floor plan as a proposal for work that remained to be done on the house. Below is a detail showing all the rooms on the first floor; at right is the entire original drawing, including Latrobe's comments. Latrobe's original notations are blurred with age.

▼ Detail of Latrobe drawing

Latrobe's Notations

1. Public dining room
2. Porters Lodge
3. Private stairs
4. Hall
5. Staircase
6. This staircase is not yet put up
7. Library & Cabinet
8. President's antechamber
9. Drawing room
10. Common dining Room
11. Public audience chamber; entirely unfinished;
12. the ceiling has given way
13. Wooden platform

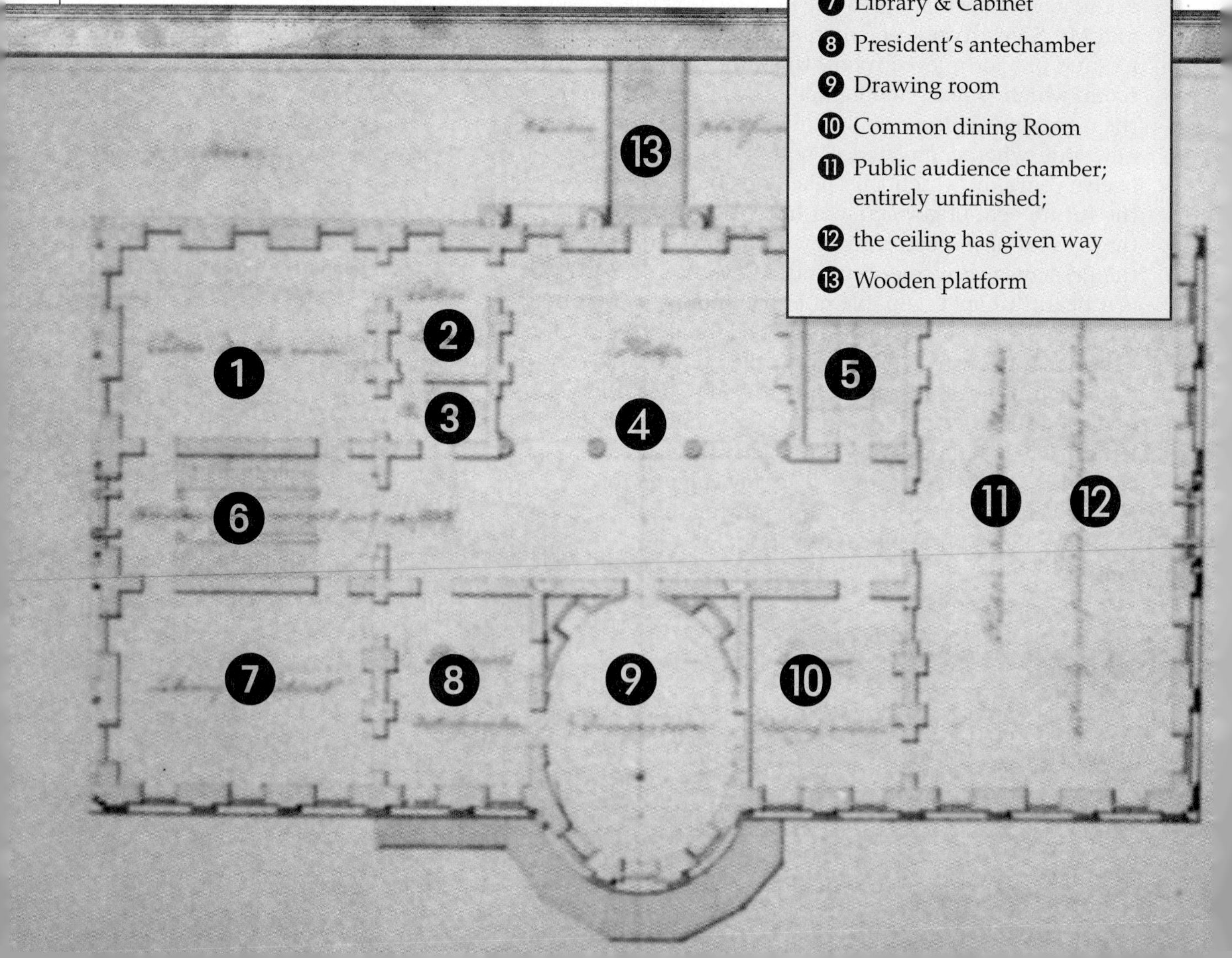

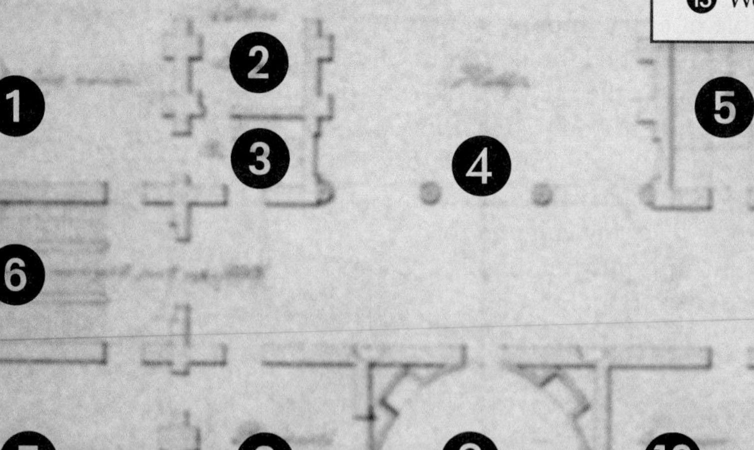

Latrobe's notes above and below the drawing contain observations about the President's House and its grounds. The drawing is signed and dated.

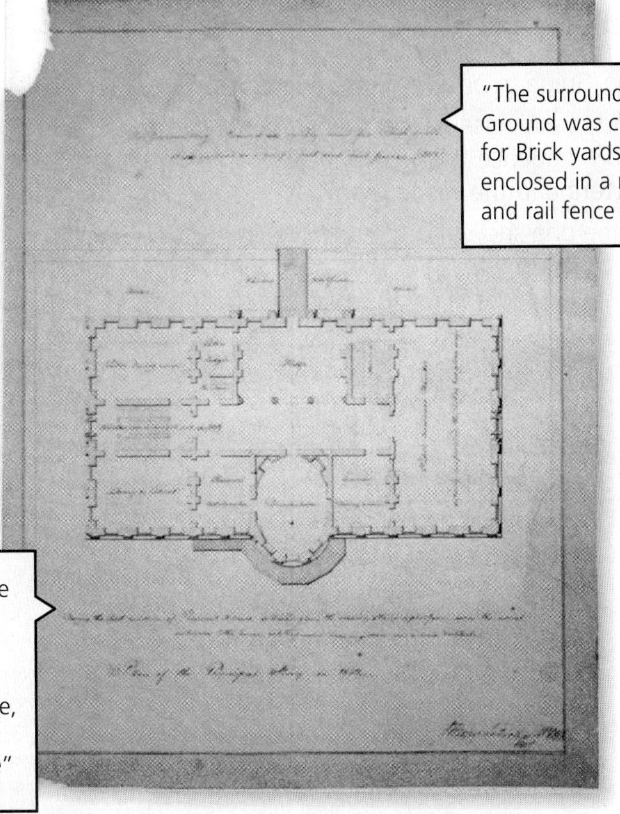

"The surrounding Ground was chiefly used for Brick yards, it was enclosed in a rough post and rail fence (1803)"

"During the short residence of President Adams at Washington, the wooden stairs & platform were the usual entrance to the house, and the present drawing room was a mere vestibule"

◀ Full image of Latrobe's original drawing of the White House floor plan

Critical Reading

Cite textual evidence to support your responses.

1. **Key Ideas and Details (a)** What is John Adams's stated wish for the house? **(b) Infer:** What does this wish tell you about the president's values and expectations?
2. **Key Ideas and Details (a)** What does Abigail Adams instruct her daughter to tell those who ask about the White House? **(b) Speculate:** Why might Mrs. Adams be greatly concerned about the opinions of others?
3. **Craft and Structure Analyze:** Which elements of the Latrobe floor plan show that the White House was designed to function as both a private residence and a public meeting place?
4. **Integration of Knowledge and Ideas (a)** Today, how are the White House and the city of Washington, D.C., different from the way they were when the Adamses lived there? **(b) Synthesize:** What do these differences tell you about changes in the United States since the eighteenth century?

Letters • Floor Plan

Comparing Primary Sources

Refer to your Note-Taking Guide to answer these questions.

1. **(a)** Who is the intended audience for each document? **(b)** How did the audience probably influence the type and style of information presented in the **letters** and the **floor plan**?
2. **(a)** Use a chart like the one shown to identify one important detail or observation from each document. **(b)** What **perspective** toward the President's House does each detail or observation reflect?

Source	Detail or Observation	Attitude It Reveals
John Adams		
Abigail Adams		
Benjamin Latrobe		

3. Which details do the Adamses present in their letters that you can verify or clarify by reviewing the floor plan and its notes? Explain.

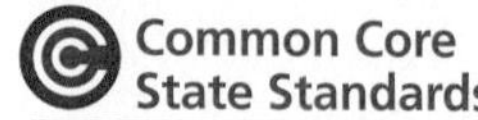

Common Core State Standards

Writing

7. Conduct short as well as more sustained research projects to answer a question or solve a problem; narrow or broaden the inquiry when appropriate; synthesize multiple sources on the subject, demonstrating understanding of the subject under investigation.

8. Gather relevant information from multiple authoritative print and digital sources, using advanced searches effectively; assess the strengths and limitations of each source in terms of the task, purpose, and audience; integrate information into the text selectively to maintain the flow of ideas, avoiding plagiarism and overreliance on any one source and following a standard format for citation.

Language

6. Acquire and use accurately general academic and domain-specific words and phrases, sufficient for reading, writing, speaking, and listening at the college and career readiness level; demonstrate independence in gathering vocabulary knowledge when considering a word or phrase important to comprehension or expression.

Vocabulary Acquisition and Use

Synonyms For each item, replace the italicized word with a synonym, or word of similar meaning, from the vocabulary list on page 179. Use each word once.

1. In a letter to her mother, Holly gave a(n) *description* of her train ride.
2. The scenery consisted of farmhouses with cows *scattered* in between.
3. The train station was a primitive *structure* with no indoor plumbing.
4. Holly felt *strong* pleasure at the idea of a week in the country.

Content-Area Vocabulary Answer each question. Explain your answers.

5. Do *commissioners* most likely work at a school or a state capitol?
6. How might restaurant owners prepare for an *inspection*?
7. Which group is more concerned with *scale*, city planners or dancers?
8. Would you use a *contract* to get a ride from a friend?
9. Should a successful campaign *procure* votes or voters?
10. Would you have *recourse* to the law if you had broken it?

Etymology Study The word *contract* comes from the Latin words *com*, which means "together," and *trahare*, which means "to draw." Explain how these meanings relate to both the noun and the verb form of *contract*. Then, use a dictionary to locate other words with the same Latin word parts.

Research Task

Topic: The Changing White House

Like America itself, the White House has come a long way since Abigail Adams hung her family's clothes to dry in "the great unfinished audience room." Starting with what you have learned from the Adams letters and the Latrobe floor plan, research the history of the building.

Assignment: Construct an annotated and illustrated timeline of the White House. Include each of these types of items:

- Architectural changes and additions
- Technological changes and additions
- Historical events that altered the building
- Influential presidents and first ladies
- Visual images—photos, drawings, diagrams

RESEARCH TIP

As you research, you may find it helpful to distinguish between interior and exterior changes to the White House.

Formulate a research plan. Locate authoritative print and electronic resources on the history of the White House. Identify key points to feature on your timeline and choose the most useful sources to cite.

Narrow the inquiry. Focus your research by listing questions, such as the following: When was electrical wiring installed? Who changed the house the most? What do specific changes to the White House say about our changing culture? Work to answer your specific questions.

Gather sources. Assemble the information in a systematic way, taking accurate notes, and separating factual data from opinions. Make sure to follow appropriate principles of citation (see pp. R21–R23 for details on how to cite varied sources.)

Synthesize multiple sources. When you synthesize information, you assemble data from varied sources and organize it into a unified presentation. As you work, critique your process. You may need to discard some details or continue researching to find additional information.

Model: Synthesizing Information with a Flexible Timeline

First Version

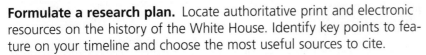

Construction 1792 — Changes 1817 — Changes 1952

Second Version

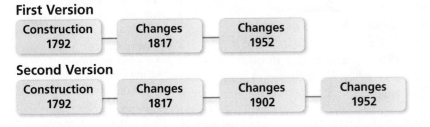

Construction 1792 — Changes 1817 — Changes 1902 — Changes 1952

Present your ideas. Make sure your timeline contains all of the essential information. Then, add annotations, quotations, and visuals.

Use a checklist like the one shown to evaluate your work.

Research Checklist

- ☐ Have I addressed all of my research questions?
- ☐ Have I clearly shown changes over time?
- ☐ Do my annotations support the basic facts?
- ☐ Do my visuals clearly illustrate historical changes?

Write a Narrative

Autobiographical Narrative Writers are often told to write about what they know. This advice has produced some of the best stories in literature. While some are pure works of imagination, others are true tales about the writer's own life. Such nonfiction stories are called autobiographical narratives. Autobiographical narratives often use the same types of narrative techniques you are used to seeing in works of fiction. Follow the steps outlined in this workshop to write your own autobiographical narrative.

Assignment Write an autobiographical narrative about a special or memorable experience.

What to Include Your autobiographical narrative should include the following elements:

- You, the writer, as the main character and other developed characters
- A clear depiction of a problem or situation
- An insight about the experience, an expression of its significance
- A logical organization that builds a smooth progression of events
- Narrative techniques that bring events, settings, and people to life
- Error-free conventions, including correct use of capitalization

To preview the criteria on which your autobiographical narrative may be assessed, see the rubric on page 195.

Writing

3. Write narratives to develop real or imagined experiences or events using effective techniques, well-chosen details, and well-structured event sequences.

3.a. Engage and orient the reader by setting out a problem, situation, or observation and its significance, establishing one or multiple point(s) of view, and introducing a narrator and/or characters; create a smooth progression of experiences or events.

5. Develop and strengthen writing as needed by planning, revising, editing, and rewriting, or trying a new approach, focusing on addressing what is most significant for a specific purpose and audience.

To get a feel for autobiographical narratives, read this mentor text. Notice how Olaudah Equiano explains what happened to him and how he felt about it. For the complete text, see pages 171–175.

from: The Interesting Narrative of the Life of Olaudah Equiano

During our passage, I first saw flying fishes, which surprised me very much; they used frequently to fly across the ship, and many of them fell on the deck. I also now first saw the use of the quadrant; I had often with astonishment seen the mariners make observations with it, and I could not think what it meant. They at last took notice of my surprise; and one of them, willing to increase it, as well as to gratify my curiosity, made me one day look through it. The clouds appeared to me to be land, which disappeared as they passed along. This heightened my wonder...

WRITE GUY
Jeff Anderson, M.Ed.

What Do You Notice?

Read the highlighted sentences several times. Then, with a partner, discuss the qualities that make them special. You might consider the following elements:

- Word choice
- Emotional appeal
- Structure
- Use of punctuation

Share your group's observations with the class.

Prewriting and Planning

Choosing Your Topic

Choose an event from your life that is meaningful to you, interesting to readers, and not awkward or painful to share. It may be an experience that showed you a different aspect of yourself, solved a problem, or gave you a new perspective. To find a topic, use one of these strategies:

- **Interview yourself.** List ten questions you might ask a stranger about his or her life. Add follow-up questions that would help you get deeper answers. Then, use your list to interview yourself.

Model: Interviewing Yourself

Main Question: What was the most surprising thing that ever happened to you?
Follow-Ups: How did you react? Would you react the same way today? Why or why not?

- **Make memory notes.** Go through a photo album or scrapbook and jot down notes about the events recorded there. Add details about what you did and how you felt at those times. Talk to a relative who might remember those moments from a different perspective.

Narrowing Your Topic

Find the turning point. Once you have chosen a basic topic, sharpen your focus. Narrow in on a moment—something that became a turning point in your life. Use an event chart like the one shown to locate such a key event. In the chart shown, the writer has highlighted the turning point in yellow.

We moved to CA when Dad got a promotion.
Lost my friends; felt afraid of new situations
Mom gave us surfboards and lessons.
I began to love the ocean.
I decided to study oceanography in college.

Gathering Details

Engage and orient the reader. Your purpose in writing is to explore your thoughts and feelings about an experience and to share your insights with readers. Once you have chosen a topic, gather details that will help your readers understand your meaning. To do so, answer questions like the following:

- What *background information* do my readers need to have in order to understand my experience?
- What *descriptive details* will bring my experience to life for my readers?
- What do readers need to know about what this experience means to me?

Drafting

Shaping Your Writing

Order events. Most autobiographical narratives relate events in *chronological order*, or the sequence in which they happened. They also center on a *conflict*, or problem, that is somehow resolved. As the conflict develops, the tension should increase until it reaches the *climax,* or point of greatest intensity. After that, the tension should decrease as you move toward the ending, or *resolution*. Within this overall structure, consider using narrative techniques. For example, you may jump back in time with a *flashback* or forward in time with a *flash-forward*. Use a plot diagram like the one shown here to order your events.

Begin with a strong lead. Write a simple but intriguing sentence that catches the reader's curiosity. Notice how these lead sentences *foreshadow*, or drop hints about the story to follow:

- ***My grandfather walked in and suddenly the room was silent.***
- ***My dog probably wouldn't want me to tell you this story.***

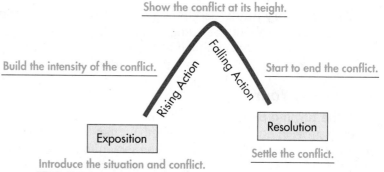

Climax
Show the conflict at its height.
Build the intensity of the conflict.
Rising Action
Falling Action
Start to end the conflict.
Exposition
Introduce the situation and conflict.
Resolution
Settle the conflict.

Provide a meaningful conclusion. End your narrative with a reflection, observation, or insight that confirms the importance of the experience.

Providing Elaboration

Use thought shots. As you write, follow these steps to expand your ideas:

- Scan your draft for uses of the word *I*. For each one, ask yourself how you reacted to what you described.
- For each reaction, draw a circle, or *thought shot*, in the margin. Inside the circle, jot details about what you saw, heard, felt, or thought.

Model: Using "Thought Shots"

And then I got my first surfboard.
I felt nervous but excited. Could I really do this?

Include dialogue. One of the best ways to make your writing more vivid is to include dialogue. People's words bring them alive as characters and help advance the story's conflict and climax.

Common Core State Standards

Writing

3.b. Use narrative techniques such as dialogue, pacing, description, reflection, and multiple plot lines, to develop experiences, events, and/or characters.

3.c. Use a variety of techniques to sequence events so that they build on one another to create a coherent whole and build toward a particular tone and outcome.

3.e. Provide a conclusion that follows from and reflects on what is experienced, observed, or resolved over the course of the narrative.

Writers on Writing

Susan Power On Choosing the Right Words

Susan Power is the author of "Museum Indians" (p. 34).

"Finding the precise word can be tricky."
—Susan Power

Beginnings are always difficult for me. I'll have an idea for a story, or, as in this excerpt from a nonfiction essay, a memory from childhood, but I won't know where to start. Here I wanted to write about the body of water where I'd spent many happy hours—Lake Michigan. Should I begin with hard facts, its depth and circumference? No. After many drafts, I began with my mother's stories.

from "Chicago Waters," from *Roofwalker*

My mother used to say that by the time I was an old woman, Lake Michigan would be the size of a silver dollar. She pinched her index finger with her thumb to show me the pitiful dimensions.

"People will gather around the tiny lake, what's left of it, and cluck over a spoonful of water," she told me.

I learned to squint at the 1967 shoreline until I had carved away the structures and roads built on landfill and could imagine the lake and its city as my mother found them in 1942 when she arrived in Chicago. I say *the lake and its city* rather than *the city and its lake*, because my mother taught me another secret: the city of Chicago belongs to Lake Michigan.

But which of my mother's pronouncements to believe? That Chicago would swallow the Midwestern sea, smother it in concrete, or that the lake wielded enough strength to outpolitick even Mayor Richard Daley?

Mayor Daley, Sr. is gone now, but the lake remains, alternately tranquil and riled, changing colors like a mood ring. I guess we know who won.

When my mother watches the water from her lakeside apartment building, she still sucks in her breath. "You have to respect the power of that lake," she tells me. And I do now. I do.

I mention that I'm looking at "the 1967 shoreline" so the reader will know the time frame, when I was a child.

I rely on the dictionary and thesaurus to help me find the precise, specific word. First I tried *sayings*, but that didn't exhibit my mother's strength as much as *pronouncements*.

Wrestling with word choice again, I used *beat* initially but later selected *outpolitick*—more appropriate when describing a politician.

Revising

Revising Your Overall Structure

Connect the past to the present. Your autobiographical narrative should show how the experience you are describing helped you become the person you are today. Make sure you have included details that help the reader understand what you learned or how you changed as a direct result of the experience you narrate. To strengthen those connections even more, follow these steps:

- Highlight passages in your draft that state or hint at how the experience affected you in a long-term way.
- ✔ Put a check mark beside those passages that could be clearer or explained better.
- Strengthen the checked passages by adding transitions to clarify connections, sensory details to make them more vivid, or a better explanation.

Common Core State Standards

Writing

3.d. Use precise words and phrases, telling details, and sensory language to convey a vivid picture of the experiences, events, setting, and/or characters.

Language

3.a. Vary syntax for effect.

Model: Revising to Connect the Past to the Present

I had never had a lot of friends, and now I had none.
✓Moving away from the place I had always lived was hard. ^
I was lonely and bored. My mom told me it would get better, but I thought I would never be happy again. ^
Eventually, my mom, a surfboard, and an open mind would change all that, but—for now—I was miserable.

These additions clarify the writer's conflict and hint at the importance of the experience.

Revising Your Sentences

Use subordination to give characters depth. Carefully reread the sentences that introduce the people in your story. If they seem bland and uninformative, use subordinate clauses to expand simple sentences and provide more information about who your characters are, what they are like, and how they affect the events of your narrative.

Simple Sentence: Alison taught me how to surf.

Complex Sentence: Alison, my mother's best friend, saw me fumbling in the waves, so she took pity on me and taught me how to surf.

Simple Sentence: She helped me a lot.

Complex Sentence: By showing that someone cared, she helped me a lot.

Peer Review: Have a partner review your draft, identifying sentences that introduce or describe characters. Answer questions your partner poses about the characters' personalities, their behavior or statements, and their roles in your narrative. Use your answers to expand the sentences your partner identified.

Developing Your Style

Improving Word Choice

If your writing is not as clear, sharp, or fresh as it should be, a careful look at your **word choice** might help. The use of strong verbs, precise nouns, and specific adjectives will make your writing come alive. It will also help you avoid clichés and say exactly what you mean.

Dull, Vague Words	Lively, Precise Words
The dog ran through the woods.	The terrier bounded through the underbrush.
I fell into the rough water.	I tumbled into the churning foam.
People yelled at the mayor.	Irate citizens harangued the mayor.

Find It in Your Reading

Read the excerpt from *The Interesting Narrative of the Life of Olaudah Equiano* on page 170.

1. Identify at least one specific noun, active verb, vivid adjective, and effective adverb.
2. Make a list of the words and identify their parts of speech.
3. Choose one word you think is a particularly good choice. Write a sentence or two in which you explain your reasons.

Apply It to Your Writing

Review the draft of your autobiographical narrative. Follow these steps for each paragraph:

1. Underline any nouns or verbs that seem vague or weak. Note each use of the verb *to be* (*am, is, are, was,* and *were*). In the margin, jot down a few interesting alternates for each bland word, and then choose the best replacement.
2. Highlight phrases that are wordy, and think about what you are really trying to say. Then, find one or two punchy words that mean the same thing but express your idea more forcefully.
3. Check to see if there are any sentences with no underlining or highlighting. Take a look at these sentences again. Challenge yourself to find places where you could add vivid words to create a clearer picture or convey a stronger attitude.

PH WRITING COACH

Further instruction and practice are available in *Prentice Hall Writing Coach*.

Student Model: Branden Boyer-White, Palm Springs, CA

Discovering Poetry

My mother was a night owl. She worked nights as a nurse at the hospital. She liked it; the schedule suited her. The nights she was off, she maintained her nocturnal routine—active at night and asleep in the early part of the day.

One early morning, I went into the living room to find my mother reading a thick book called *Best Loved Poems to Read Again and Again.* My interest was piqued solely by the fact that the word *Poems* appeared in big, hot pink letters.

Branden uses concrete details to set the scene.

"Is it good?" I asked her.

"Yeah, " she answered. "There's one you'll really like." She began to thumb through the grainy white pages. She finally stopped and asked, "Ready?" I certainly was! I leaned forward.

"'Patty Poem,'" she read the title. *Who is Patty?* my mind buzzed. The poem began:

She never puts her toys away,
Just leaves them scattered where they lay, . . .

The poem was just three short stanzas. The final one came quickly:

When she grows and gathers poise,
I'll miss her harum-scarum noise,
And look in vain for scattered toys,
And I'll be sad.

Excerpts from the poem help readers understand the writer's emotional reaction to what she heard.

A terrible sorrow washed over me. Whoever Patty was, she was a dreadful, mean girl. Then, the bombshell.

"It's you, honey," my mother sentimentalized.

To my mother, the poem captured a parent's nostalgic love when her child grows up and leaves. To me, the "she" in the poem was a horror. It was my mama who would be sad. It was so terrible I burst into tears.

"What's wrong?" my mother asked.

"Oh Mama," I babbled. "I don't want to grow up ever!"

Dialogue makes the narrative more realistic and poignant.

She smiled. "Honey, it's okay. You're not growing up anytime soon. And when you do, I'll still love you, okay?"

"Okay," I hiccuped. My panic had subsided. But I could not stop thinking about that silly poem. After what seemed like a safe amount of time, I read the poem again and was mystified. It all fit so well together, like a puzzle. The language was simple, so simple I could plainly understand its meaning, yet it was still beautiful. I was now transfixed by the idea of poetry, words that had the power to make or break a person's world. . . .

I have since fallen in love with other poems, but "Patty Poem" remains my poem. It was my first, and it will be mine to the end, because it brought me my love for poetry. This is a great testimony to the poignancy of the art. After all, "Patty Poem" gave me my love for poetry not because it was the verse that lifted my spirits, but because it was the one that hurt me the most.

Branden clearly demonstrates the significance of this experience.

Editing and Proofreading

Check your narrative for errors in grammar, usage, punctuation, and spelling.

Focus on capitalization. Double-check the capitalization of names and places. Common nouns name general categories and are lowercase. Proper nouns name specific people, places, or things and are capitalized.

Focus on spelling. The one-syllable word *full* has two *l's*. However, the suffix *-ful* has only one *l*. The orthographic, or spelling, rule is as follows: Words with two or more syllables, like *cheerful* and *successful*, end with the one-*l* suffix. Check your spelling of any words that end with this suffix.

Spiral Review: Conventions Earlier in this unit, you learned about coordinating conjunctions (p. 31), correlative conjunctions (p. 94), and subordinating conjunctions (p. 155). Check your narrative to be sure you have used those conventions correctly.

Common Core State Standards

Language
2.b. Spell correctly.

Speaking and Listening
6. Adapt speech to a variety of contexts and tasks.

Publishing, Presenting, and Reflecting

Consider one of the following ways to share your writing.

Deliver an oral presentation. Turn your narrative into an oral presentation and deliver it to the class. To do so, mark up a copy of your finished work, underlining words and phrases to emphasize. Also, identify places where you can add drama by changing your tone of voice or pausing. If you wish, choose photographs to display as a backdrop.

Create an illustrated class anthology. With classmates, combine several narratives in a binder. Include photographs or artwork that capture the mood or setting of each narrative.

Reflect on your writing. In a writer's journal, jot down your thoughts about the experience of writing an autobiographical narrative. Begin by answering these questions: *Which part of the process did you enjoy most and least? Did the work make you look at your life differently? If so, how?*

PH WRITING COACH
Further instruction and practice are available in *Prentice Hall Writing Coach*.

Rubric for Self-Assessment

Evaluate your reflective essay using the following criteria and rating scale.

Criteria	Rating Scale (not very – very)				
Focus: How clearly do you depict the conflict, its resolution, and your insight?	1	2	3	4	5
Organization: How clear and logical is the progression of events?	1	2	3	4	5
Support/Elaboration: How well do you build on your ideas with details and reactions?	1	2	3	4	5
Style: How effectively do you vary sentences and add details to bring characters alive?	1	2	3	4	5
Conventions: How correct are your grammar and mechanics, especially your use of capitalization?	1	2	3	4	5

SPEAKING AND LISTENING

Communications Workshop

Evaluate Persuasive Speech

Persuasive speech, also called *argument*, is the language people use when they want to convince us to think or act in a certain way. Advertisers use it to spread interest in their products; lawyers use it to establish the innocence of clients; and politicians use it to attract our support.

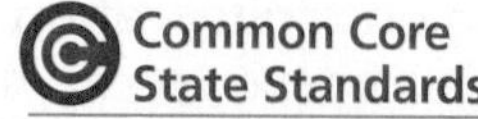

Speaking and Listening
3. Evaluate a speaker's point of view, reasoning, and use of evidence and rhetoric, assessing the stance, premises, links among ideas, word choice, points of emphasis, and tone used.

Types of Content and Positions

There are four main types of argumentation, or persuasive speech: propositions of fact, value, problem, and policy. All use language, reasoning, and proof differently in order to achieve specific ends.

Propositions	What They Establish	Examples
Fact	That something is so, or has happened	In fact, the defendant fled the scene.
Value	That something is good or bad, better or worse	Jazz is America's best music.
Problem	That something is a problem	The parking situation is a problem because...
Policy	That something should be done	Latin should be a required subject.

Types of Appeals and Evidence

Persuasive Appeals More than 2,000 years ago, Aristotle identified three types of appeals, or techniques, that can occur in any argument:

- **Ethos, or appeal to authority,** cites the speaker's credibility, or authority; for example, a noted scientist discussing issues in medical ethics.
- **Pathos, or appeal to sympathy,** engages the audience's emotions.
- **Logos, or appeal to logic,** applies reasoning and facts to build convincing arguments.

Some strategies may be more useful than others in certain situations. For example, a speaker asking for donations may use pathos more than logos.

Evidence Effective arguments employ strong evidence.

- **Facts:** data, statistical information, scientific observations
- **Anecdotes:** stories that illustrate a point
- **Expert Testimony:** statements by people who are widely viewed as authorities on a subject

When listening to persuasive speech, identify the speaker's position and evaluate the quality of the evidence he or she uses to support ideas.

Negative Persuasive Techniques

Logical fallacies are types of reasoning that may seem convincing but contain inherent flaws. Be alert to arguments built on such faulty reasoning.

- **Ad Hominem:** an attack on a person's character, not his or her ideas
- **False Causality:** an assumption that because A happened before B, A caused B
- **Red Herring:** something a speaker tosses into an argument to distract listeners from a more important issue or question
- **Overgeneralization:** a conclusion based on too little evidence
- **Bandwagon:** the assumption that something is right because it is popular

Propaganda, another negative technique, presents one-sided information and does not fairly represent an opposing view. It aims to win, but not to educate or invite discussion.

Activities: Evaluate Persuasive Speech

Comprehension and Collaboration For both activities, use an evaluation form like the one shown below.

A. Watch or listen to a persuasive speech. You may listen to a speech given by a classmate, find one in a movie, or locate one on the Internet.

B. With a partner, select two speeches that argue similar propositions but to different audiences. Critique their uses of appeals and evidence. Notice whether they use any negative persuasive techniques, and to what effect.

Evaluation Form for Persuasive Speech

Name of Speech ______________________________

Media Type ______________________________

Intended Audience ______________________________

Purpose ______________________________

Type of Proposition ______________________________

Types of Appeals:

Ethos: ☐ Example: ______________________________

Pathos: ☐ Example: ______________________________

Logos: ☐ Example: ______________________________

Specific Forms of Evidence: ______________________________

Special Uses of Language: ______________________________

Negative Persuasive Techniques: no ☐ yes ☐

Which Ones? ______________________________

Vocabulary Workshop

Using a Dictionary and Thesaurus

A **dictionary** is a reference work containing words and information about them. Dictionaries can help you find the exact meaning of a word or understand the different ways in which a word might be used. A print dictionary is arranged alphabetically. To use an **electronic dictionary,** you enter the word for which you are searching. **Specialized dictionaries** are those that define terms used in a particular field, such as law or business.

Common Core State Standards

Language

1.b. Resolve issues of complex or contested usage, consulting references as needed.

4.a. Use context as a clue to the meaning of a word or phrase.

4.c. Consult general and specialized reference materials, both print and digital, to find the pronunciation of a word or determine or clarify its precise meaning, its part of speech, its etymology, or its standard usage.

5.b. Analyze nuances in the meaning of words with similar denotations.

Sample Dictionary Entry

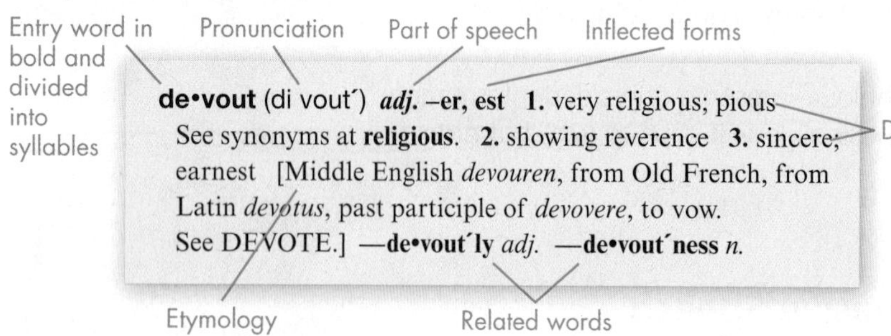
Entry word in bold and divided into syllables
Pronunciation
Part of speech
Inflected forms
de•vout (di vout′) *adj.* **–er, est** **1.** very religious; pious See synonyms at **religious**. **2.** showing reverence **3.** sincere; earnest [Middle English *devouren*, from Old French, from Latin *devotus*, past participle of *devovere*, to vow. See DEVOTE.] **—de•vout′ly** *adj.* **—de•vout′ness** *n.*
Definitions
Etymology
Related words

A **thesaurus** is a book of synonyms, or words with similar meanings. All of the synonyms listed for a word share denotation, or surface meaning, but their connotations, or shades of meaning, will probably vary. When writing, use a thesaurus to help vary your word choice. However, check your choices in a dictionary to make sure both their denotative and connotative meanings accurately represent your ideas.

Sample Thesaurus Entry

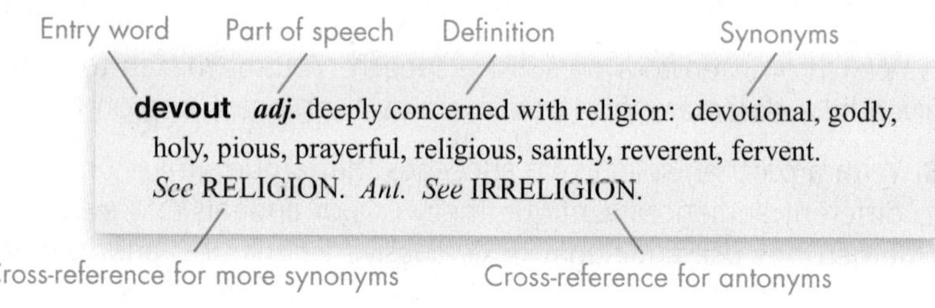
Entry word
Part of speech
Definition
Synonyms
devout *adj.* deeply concerned with religion: devotional, godly, holy, pious, prayerful, religious, saintly, reverent, fervent. *See* RELIGION. *Ant. See* IRRELIGION.
Cross-reference for more synonyms
Cross-reference for antonyms

Practice

Directions: Refer to the sample entries to answer questions 1 and 2. Use a print or electronic dictionary and thesaurus to answer question 3.

1. Trace the path by which the word *devout* entered the English language. Explain whether its meaning has changed or stayed the same.
2. **(a)** Analyze the context to determine which synonym for *devout* best completes this sentence: *Their hushed voices showed the pilgrims'___ attitude.* **(b)** Explain the nuances in word meanings that allowed you to make your choice.
3. Find two synonyms for *earnest* that have positive connotations and two that have negative connotations. For each synonym, write a sentence that reflects its connotative meaning.

Vocabulary Acquisition and Use: Context Clues

Context clues are words or phrases that help readers clarify the meanings of unfamiliar words in a text. Even fluent readers may not always know the dictionary definition of every word they read. By using context clues, readers make educated guesses, or inferences, about unfamiliar word meanings. This skill is often assessed on standardized tests.

Practice

This exercise is modeled after the Sentence Completion questions that appear in the Reading Comprehension section of the SAT.

Directions: Each of the following sentences is missing one or two words. Choose the word or set of words that best completes each sentence.

Test-Taking Tip
Immediately rule out any answer choices you *know* are wrong.

1. Many colonists felt that more ___?___ was necessary before war against Britain was declared.

A. disposition
B. provision
C. oblivion
D. deliberation
E. recompense

2. Revolutionaries such as Thomas Paine attempted to rouse the colonists' ___?___ desires for freedom and self-determination.

A. brittle
B. unconscious
C. tempered
D. omnipotent
E. vigilant

3. Paine and others argued that only a full split with Britain would create a peaceful world for ___?___.

A. posterity
B. tyranny
C. unanimity
D. diversity
E. urgency

4. With no sign of ___?___ for their complaints, colonial leaders declared independence from the crown.

A. privilege
B. vigilance
C. redress
D. peril
E. allegiance

5. Though the ___?___ of war would last for years, few would ___?___ the freedom it secured.

A. tempest . . . lament
B. assent . . . implore
C. tempest . . . relent
D. apparel . . . implore
E. privileges . . . redress

6. Nevertheless, the work of crafting a ___?___ for the new nation proved ___?___.

A. judgment . . . incorrigible
B. mediator . . . prudent
C. provision . . . copious
D. constitution . . . arduous
E. judgment. . . pensive

Test-Taking Practice

Reading Test: Social Science Passages

Social science reading passages are one type of reading selection found on standardized tests. The social sciences include disciplines such as anthropology, economics, geography, history, political science, and psychology. These passages tend to be tightly written and logically organized. They are informational, but they also express the author's point of view either directly or indirectly. Questions following these passages usually address elements such as structure, main idea, or author's purpose.

Common Core State Standards

RI.11-12.1, RI.11-12.4, RI.11-12.6; L.11-12.1, L.11-12.2, L.11-12.3, L.11-12.4.a

[For the full wording of the standards, see the standards chart in the front of your textbook.]

Practice

This exercise is modeled after the ACT Reading Test, Social Science section.

Directions: Read the following passage, taken from *The American Crisis* by Thomas Paine. Then, choose the best answer to each question.

I once felt all that kind of anger, which a man ought to feel, against the mean principles that are held by the Tories: a noted one, who kept a tavern at Amboy, was standing at this door, with as pretty a child in his hand, about eight or nine years old, as I ever saw, and after speaking his mind as freely as he thought was prudent, finished with this unfatherly expression, *"Well! give me peace in my day."* Not a man lives on the continent but fully believes that a separation must some time or other finally take place, and a generous parent should have said, *"If there must be trouble let it be in my day, that my child may have peace"*; and this single reflection, well applied, is sufficient to awaken every man to duty. . . .

I turn with the warm ardor of a friend to those who have nobly stood, and are yet determined to stand the matter out: I call not upon a few, but upon all; not on *this* state or *that* state, but on *every* state; up and help us; lay your shoulders to the wheel; better have too much force than too little, when so great an object is at stake. Let it be told to the future world, that in the depth of winter, when nothing but hope and virtue could survive, that the city and the country, alarmed at one common danger, came forth to meet and to repulse it. Say not that thousands are gone, turn out your tens of thousands; throw not the burden of the day upon Providence, but *"show your faith by your works,"* that God may bless you. It matters not where you live, or what rank of life you hold, the evil or the blessing will reach you all.

Strategy

Scan, then read.

- **First, scan the passage.** Take 20 seconds to skim the text. Look for a main topic and a few key terms.
- **Second, read the passage in full.** Ask yourself: *What is the author's purpose? What information is most important?*

1. The author includes the story about the father and child in order to:
   A. entertain his readers.
   B. shame his readers into action.
   C. stir up noble feelings in his readers.
   D. persuade his readers to do nothing.

2. The author uses the word *unfatherly* in reference to the tavern owner because he feels the man is:
   F. putting his child in danger.
   G. being selfish.
   H. behaving immaturely.
   J. ignoring his child.

3. What is the best summary of this passage?
   A. Let us band together to defend ourselves.
   B. We must labor to improve the lives of our children.
   C. The separation of one continent from another is inevitable.
   D. If we do good deeds, we will be blessed.

4. In the phrase "lay your shoulders to the wheel," what does the wheel symbolize?
   F. the Tories
   G. one's fellow soldiers
   H. Thomas Paine himself
   J. the task of war

5. When the author writes "I call not upon a few, but upon all; not on *this* state or *that* state, but on *every* state," which rhetorical device is he using?
   A. repetition
   B. restatement
   C. a rhetorical question
   D. an allusion

6. This passage LEAST resembles:
   F. a speech.
   G. an origin myth.
   H. a political document.
   J. a sermon.

7. According to the passage, what kind of anger does Paine believe is justified?
   A. anger at Tories
   B. anger at low-minded principles
   C. anger at bad parents
   D. anger at those who show little faith

8. Based on the passage, Paine's approach to his topic can best be characterized as:
   F. flexible and unbiased.
   G. contemplative and expansive.
   H. skeptical and tentative.
   J. passionate and uncompromising.

9. When the author urges his readers to "'*show your faith by your works,*' that God may bless you," he is using:
   A. a logical appeal.
   B. an emotional appeal.
   C. an ethical appeal.
   D. a political appeal.

10. Paine's overall purpose in this passage is to:
    F. urge Tories to defend themselves against abuse and ignorance.
    G. entertain soldiers who have recently returned from war.
    H. persuade colonists to fight in the cause of freedom.
    J. provide religious instruction to those who are troubled by anger.

Grammar and Writing: Editing in Context

In some tests you will encounter a passage with numbered sentences or parts of sentences, some of which contain errors in grammar, style, and usage. Your task is to choose the best version of the sentence from the choices offered. Some questions may also refer to the passage as a whole.

Practice

This exercise is modeled after the ACT English Test.

Directions: For each underlined sentence or portion of a sentence, choose the best alternative. If an item asks a question about the underlined portion, or about the passage as a whole, choose the best answer to the question.

[1]

Most people know that the mature Franklin was an important statesman but also [1] an innovative scientist. What they may *not* know is that even the young Franklin lived a noteworthy life.

[2]

As one of seventeen children and the son of a poor soap maker, the odds were against young Ben. [2] As a small boy, he taught himself to read; and though he had only two years of formal education, he stored the knowledge away for future use. When [3] he was apprenticed at age twelve to his brother, a printer, Franklin took his education into his own hands. He spent his spare moments copying essays out of a discarded literary magazine, translating them into poetry, translating them back into prose, and then memorizing them. He knew that good writing was rare, and could [4] lead him to both fame and fortune.

[3]

Finally, at age sixteen, Franklin saw himself in print. Adopting the persona of a widow named Silence Dogood, he penned a series of essays that poked fun at various aspects of colonial life that included [5] education, etiquette, and fashion. All fourteen essays were printed in his brother's newspaper, the *New-England Courant*. In fact, readers were so charmed by Silence Dogood that the nonexistent widow received several written proposals of marriage. [6]

Strategy

Try out each answer. Mentally test each answer before you choose one of them. The one that sounds the best is probably correct.

SAT® PREP ACT

1. **A.** NO CHANGE
   B. either an important statesman or
   C. both an important statesman and
   D. whether an important statesman nor

2. At this point, the writer is considering inserting the following: Nevertheless, he proved self-reliant from early on. Should the writer make this insertion?
   F. No, because the sentence directly expresses the essay's main idea.
   G. No, because the sentence distracts from the paragraph's main focus.
   H. Yes, because the sentence refers to Franklin's later writings.
   J. Yes, because the sentence provides a transition between two ideas.

3. What is the function of this word?
   A. It has no function and should be deleted.
   B. It is used as a subordinating conjunction.
   C. It is used as a correlative conjunction.
   D. It is used as a coordinating conjunction.

4. **F.** NO CHANGE
   G. is rare, but could
   H. was rare, as if it could
   J. though rare, could

5. **A.** NO CHANGE
   B. life and which included
   C. life, yet including
   D. life, including

6. Upon reviewing paragraph 3, the writer considers deleting the preceding sentence. If the writer were to delete the sentence, the paragraph would primarily lose:
   F. a humorous commentary that helps underscore Franklin's success.
   G. a colorful detail that shows how naive eighteenth-century readers were.
   H. a good-natured hint that Franklin's writing may have lacked clarity.
   J. nothing; it should be deleted.

7. This question asks about the passage as a whole.
   Review paragraphs 1 through 3. The text structure of this passage is:
   A. cause and effect.
   B. chronological order.
   C. problem and solution.
   D. comparison and contrast.

Timed Writing: Position Statement [25 minutes]

Consider these two commentaries on success:

I wished to live without committing any fault at any time; I would conquer all that either natural inclination, custom, or company might lead me into.

—Benjamin Franklin, *Autobiography*

I've managed to do a lot of things in my life I didn't think I was capable of and which many others didn't think me capable of either.

—Sandra Cisneros, "Straw Into Gold"

In your view, is success doing something perfectly, or doing something new and unexpected? Write an essay in which you develop your point of view on this issue. Support your position with reasoning and examples taken from your reading, studies, or experience.

Academic Vocabulary

An **issue** is a debatable idea. There is no right or wrong opinion. Choose the position for which you can offer the strongest support.

Performance Tasks

Follow the instructions to complete the tasks below as required by your teacher. As you work on each task, incorporate both general academic vocabulary and literary terms you learned in this unit.

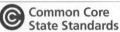

Common Core State Standards

RL.11-12.2, RL.11-12.9; RI.11-12.2, RI.11-12.4, RI.11-12.8, RI.11-12.9; W.11-12.9.a, W.11-12.9.b, W.11-12.10; SL.11-12.1.a, SL.11-12.1.b, SL.11-12.4, SL.11-12.5; L.11-12.2.b, L.11-12.3.a

[For the full wording of the standards, see the standards chart in the front of your textbook.]

Writing

Task 1: Literature [RL.11-12.2; W.11-12.9.a; L.11-12.3.a]

Analyze the Development of Theme

Write an ***essay*** *in which you determine two or more themes in a literary work from this unit.*

- Identify at least two themes in the work. Analyze how each theme is introduced and developed.
- Discuss similarities and differences among the insights each theme expresses.
- Note ways in which the themes interact and build on one another, and discuss how this interaction creates a complex account or deeper meaning.
- To ensure that readers understand your analysis, include an objective summary of each literary work.
- Vary your syntax by using coordinating or correlative conjunctions to combine short, choppy sentences.

Task 2: Informational Text [RI.11-12.2; W.11-12.9.b; L.11-12.3.a]

Analyze the Development of Central Ideas

Write an ***essay*** *in which you analyze the development of two or more central ideas in a work of literary nonfiction from this unit.*

- Clearly identify and explain at least two central ideas expressed in the work.
- Discuss how the author introduces and develops each idea.
- Identify specific details that shape and refine each central idea.
- Consider how the central ideas interact and build on one another to create a complex analysis of a topic.
- To ensure that readers understand your analysis, include an objective summary of the work.
- Vary your syntax by using subordinating conjunctions to combine sentences.

Task 3: Informational Text [RI.11-12.9; W.11-12.9.b; L.11-12.2.b]

Analyze Foundational U.S. Documents for Themes, Purposes, and Rhetorical Features

Write an ***essay*** *in which you analyze one of the foundational U.S. documents that appears in this unit, identifying its theme, purpose, and key rhetorical features.*

- Explain which document you chose and why you chose it.
- Identify the theme, or central idea, expressed in the document. If there are multiple themes or ideas, explain what they are and how they interact.
- Discuss the author's main purpose for writing as well as any secondary purposes.
- Analyze notable rhetorical features, considering how they help communicate the themes and advance the author's purpose for writing.
- Add to the strength of your writing and the clarity of your ideas by using strong verbs, precise nouns, and specific adjectives. Spell correctly.

Speaking and Listening

Task 4: Literature [RL.11-12.9; W.11-12.9.a; SL.11-12.5]

Demonstrate Knowledge of Foundational Works of American Literature

With a partner, deliver an ***oral presentation*** *in which you analyze how two or more literary works from this unit treat similar themes or topics.*

- Explain which works you will discuss and why you chose them.
- Identify the topics each work addresses and describe how each work presents characters, settings, and ideas.
- Explain the theme each work expresses and analyze the reasons for any similarities or differences.
- Incorporate digital media that enhances your presentation. For example, consider images, audio, graphics, or textual elements that help illustrate and clarify your ideas or those expressed in the works under discussion.

Task 5: Informational Texts [RI.11-12.8; SL.11-12.1.a, SL.11-12.1.b]

Evaluate the Reasoning in Seminal U.S. Texts

Conduct a ***panel discussion*** *in which you delineate and evaluate the reasoning in a seminal U.S. text from this unit.*

- Assign each member of the panel a specific role in the discussion.
- Each presenter should address at least one of the following elements: the text to be discussed and the reasons for the choice; the author's purpose for writing; the author's premises, reasoning, and arguments; the ways in which the author builds transitions and establishes meaningful connections among ideas; the types of evidence the author uses to support ideas and the quality of that evidence.
- As a group, ensure that the discussion is civil and democratic, or equally shared.
- As a group, ensure that each panel member has read the materials and completed any research needed to participate fully.

Task 6: Informational Text [RI.11-12.4; SL.11-12.4]

Determine the Meaning of Words and Phrases as They Are Used in a Text

With a partner, conduct a ***colloquy,*** *or formal discussion, about the meaning of a key term as it is used and refined in a text from this unit.*

- Explain which text you chose and why you chose it. Identify the key term you will discuss and explain why it is essential to the author's ideas.
- Discuss how the author introduces and defines the key term. Explain how the author then develops and refines that definition.
- Consider how the author incorporates connotations, or nuances, in the term's meaning as well as any figurative or technical meanings.
- As you speak, present information, findings, and evidence clearly so that listeners can follow your line of reasoning.
- Make sure your use of language, speaking style, and content are appropriate for a formal discussion.

What is the relationship between literature and place?

First Encounters When Europeans first arrived in North America, the native peoples had been living here for thousands of years. The first encounters between various groups not only affected the early settlements but continue to resonate in our society.

Assignment Choose at least two writers from this unit who describe an early encounter between two different groups. Write a **comparison-and-contrast essay** about the perspectives reflected in each text.

Featured Titles

In this unit, you have read a variety of precolonial and early American literature. Continue to read works related to this era on your own. Select books that you enjoy, but challenge yourself to explore new topics, new authors, and works offering varied perspectives or approaches. The titles suggested below will help you get started.

LITERATURE

Native American Literature
Pearson Prentice Hall

Anthology The literature of Native Americans is a rich collection of myths, legends, poems, histories, personal experiences, dreams, and songs. More than fifty such selections are collected in this anthology.

The Complete Writings
Phillis Wheatley EXEMPLAR TEXT 

Poetry Wheatley was the first enslaved African and the third woman in the United States to publish a book of poems. Wheatley's verse, including the poem "On Being Brought From Africa to America," explores religion, death, and the struggles of enslaved Africans.

[Wheatley's poem, "To His Excellency, General Washington," appears on p. 124 of this book. Build knowledge by reading Wheatley's complete works.]

INFORMATIONAL TEXTS

Historical Texts

Chronicle of the Narváez Expedition
Alvar Núñez Cabeza de Vaca;
translated by Fanny Bandelier

Narrative Account In the early sixteenth century, Spain sent the Narváez expedition to what is now the southern United States to claim vast territories for the Spanish empire. Cabeza de Vaca, who went on this journey, describes the fate of the nine-year expedition.

[An excerpt from de Vaca's account appears on p. 48 of this book. Build knowledge by reading the full text.]

Letters From an American Farmer
J. Hector St. John de Crevecoeur;
translated by Gerald Bevan

Epistolary Letters Early America's physical and cultural landscape is captured in these impassioned and engaging epistles, or essays fashioned as letters.

The Interesting Narrative of The Life of Olaudah Equiano
Olaudah Equiano

Autobiography Written in 1789, Equiano's autobiography is one of the most widely read "slave narratives." The author describes his childhood in eighteenth-century Guinea, Africa, where he was first enslaved. He also recounts his later experiences as a freedman and abolitionist in the United States.

[An excerpt from Equiano's autobiography appears on p. 170 of this book. Build knowledge by reading the full text.]

Democracy in America
Alexis de Tocqueville;
translated by Gerald Bevan EXEMPLAR TEXT 

Political Science In 1831, Alexis de Tocqueville, a twenty-five year old Frenchman, traveled throughout the United States for nine months. He had been sent by his government to observe American prisons, but he wound up taking notes about all aspects of American society. The resulting two-volume work, published in 1835 and 1840, is now a classic of political science.

Contemporary Scholarship

American Colonies: The Settling of North America
Alan Taylor

History The settling of the American colonies was not a simple story but an interweaving of many narratives. Pulitzer Prize–winning author Alan Taylor does justice to this multifaceted history by explaining the roles that different peoples played in this process.

1776
David McCullough EXEMPLAR TEXT 

History Esteemed historian McCullough describes the turbulence and promise of this most important year in American history.

Preparing to Read Complex Texts

Reading for College and Career In both college and the workplace, readers must analyze texts independently, draw connections among works that offer varied perspectives, and develop their own ideas and informed opinions. The questions shown below, and others that you generate on your own, will help you more effectively read and analyze complex college-level texts.

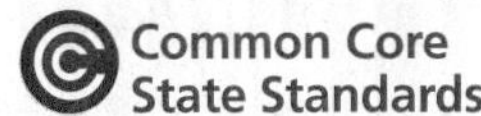

Reading Literature/Informational Text
10. By the end of grade 11, read and comprehend literature, including stories, dramas, and poems, and literary nonfiction, in the grades 11-CCR text complexity band proficiently, with scaffolding as needed at the high end of the range.

When reading analytically, ask yourself...

- What idea, experience, or story seems to have compelled the author to write? Has the author presented that idea, experience, or story in a way that I, too, find compelling?
- How might the author's era, social status, belief system, or personal experiences have affected the point of view he or she expresses in the text?
- How do my circumstances affect what I understand and feel about this text?
- What key idea does the author state explicitly? What key idea does he or she suggest or imply? Which details in the text help me to perceive implied ideas?
- Do I find multiple layers of meaning in the text? If so, what relationships do I see among these layers of meaning?
- Do I find the text believable and convincing? Why or why not?

- What patterns of organization or sequences do I find in the text? Do these patterns help me understand the ideas better? If so, how?
- What do I notice about the author's style, including his or her diction, uses of imagery and figurative language, and syntax?
- Do I like the author's style? Is the author's style memorable? Why or why not?
- What emotional attitude does the author express toward the topic, the story, or the characters? Does this attitude seem appropriate? Why or why not?
- What emotional attitude does the author express toward me, the reader? Does this attitude seem appropriate? Why, or why not?
- What do I notice about the author's voice—his or her personality on the page? Do I like this voice? Does it make me want to read on?

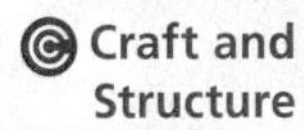

- Is the work fresh and original? How do I know?
- Do I agree with the author's ideas entirely or are there elements I find unconvincing?
- Do I disagree with the author's ideas entirely, or are there elements I can accept as true?
- How does this text relate to others I have read on the same or a similar topic?
- Based on my knowledge of American literature, history, and culture, does this work seem distinctly American? Why, or why not?

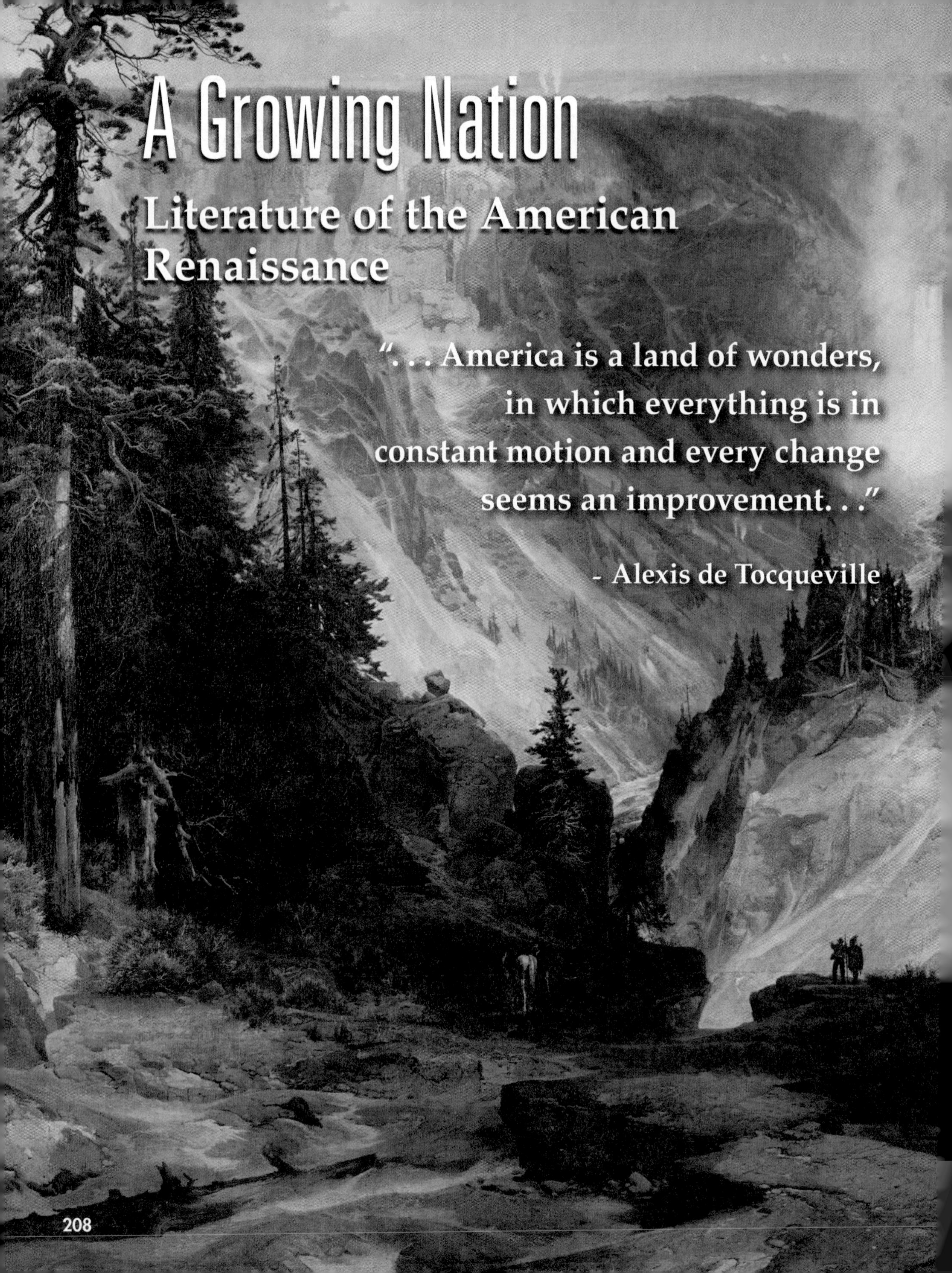

A Growing Nation

Literature of the American Renaissance

"... America is a land of wonders, in which everything is in constant motion and every change seems an improvement..."

- Alexis de Tocqueville

1800–1870

Unit 2

PHLit Online!

www.PHLitOnline.com

Hear It!

- Selection summary audio
- Selection audio

See It!

- Author video
- Essential Question video
- Get Connected videos
- Background videos
- More about the authors
- Illustrated vocabulary words
- Vocabulary flashcards

Do It!

- Interactive journals
- Interactive graphic organizers
- Grammar tutorials
- Interactive vocabulary games
- Test practice

Snapshot of the Period

In 1831, the French writer Alexis de Tocqueville (shown at right) traveled to America to write about its prisons. He was so enchanted by the bustling spirit of the young nation that he chose to write instead about American culture. While he celebrated the country's energy, Tocqueville also noted that America "has produced very few writers of distinction … [The literature of England] still darts its rays into the forests of the New World." By 1870, industrialism, population growth, economic changes, and the Civil War had all aged the nation's spirit. Along with that maturity came a new generation of writers who were the equal of any Europe had produced. Irving, Poe, Emerson, Thoreau, Dickinson, Whitman, and others shone their distinctly American light into and far beyond the "forests of the New World."

1804 Filter Coffee Pot

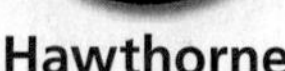

Hawthorne

Whitman

Poe

Emerson

Dickinson

Thoreau

As you read the selections in this unit, you will be asked to think about them in view of three key questions:

What is the **relationship** between literature and *place?*

How does **literature** shape or reflect *society?*

What makes **American** literature *American?*

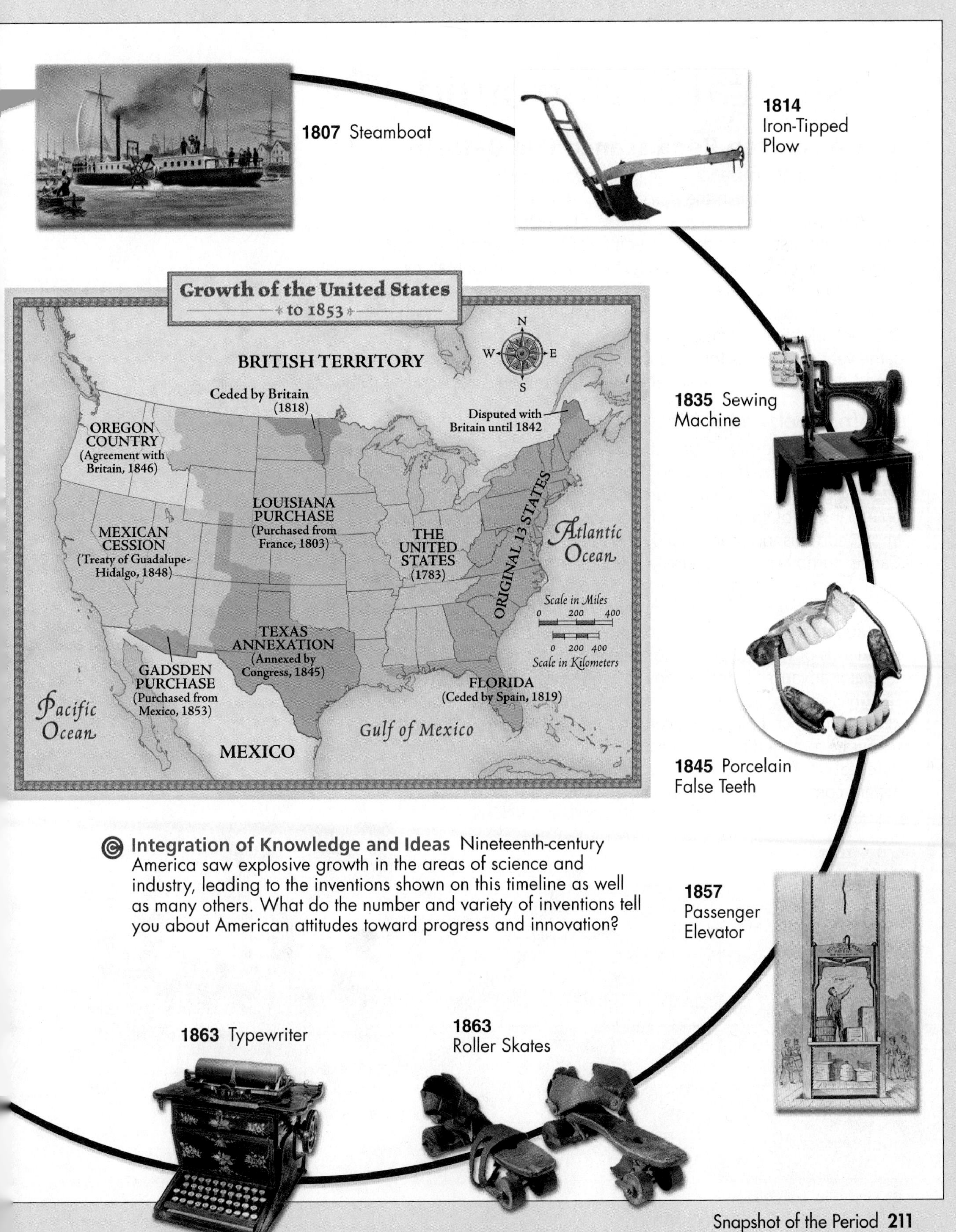

Integration of Knowledge and Ideas Nineteenth-century America saw explosive growth in the areas of science and industry, leading to the inventions shown on this timeline as well as many others. What do the number and variety of inventions tell you about American attitudes toward progress and innovation?

Historical Background

The American Renaissance (1800–1870)

The European Renaissance—the magnificent rebirth of classical art and learning—took place in the fourteenth, fifteenth, and sixteenth centuries. The American version—not a "rebirth" as much as a first flowering—took place in the first half of the nineteenth century. During these years, the nation came of age and entered its literary and cultural maturity.

Two turn-of-the-century events symbolized America's growing up. In 1800 the nation's capital was moved from Philadelphia to Washington, D.C., establishing a unique political center for a unique republic. In the same year, Americans founded the first cultural institution in the capital, the Library of Congress, a storehouse of law, scholarship, and creativity.

Steam, Steel, and Spirit

Underpinning the American cultural renaissance was sheer physical and technological growth. In 1803, Thomas Jefferson doubled the nation's size by signing the Louisiana Purchase. With the expansion of size came an expansion of spirit, an upsurge of national pride and self-awareness. Improved transportation helped bind the old and the new states together. Canals, turnpikes, and especially railroads—"the iron horse"—multiplied. Steamboats and sailing packets sped people and goods to their destinations. Everyone and everything was on the move. After California was added to the nation, the Gold Rush of 1849 drew hundreds of thousands of hopeful people to the western edge of the continent.

Major advances in technology spurred social and cultural change. Factories sprang up all over the Northeast, creating new industries, new kinds of jobs, and plenty of economic profit. The steel plow and the reaper encouraged more aggressive frontier settlement by making farming practical on the vast, sod-covered grasslands. The telegraph made almost instant communication possible across America's great distances.

TIMELINE

1800

1803: Louisiana Purchase extends the nation's territory to the Rocky Mountains.

"The object of our mission is to explore the Missouri River"
—Thomas Jefferson

▲ **1804:** Lewis and Clark begin expedition exploring and mapping vast regions of the West.

The Slow March of Democracy

The 1828 election of Andrew Jackson, "the People's President," ushered in the era of the common man, as property requirements for voting began to be eliminated. Only white males, however, benefited from these democratic advances. Little political attention was paid to women, and most African Americans remained enslaved. The tragic policy of "Indian removal" forced the westward migration of Native Americans as their tribal lands were confiscated. On the 1838 "Trail of Tears," for example, thousands of Cherokee perished on the trek from Georgia to Oklahoma.

On the World Stage

The first decades of the 1800s were hopeful ones. The War of 1812 convinced Europeans that the United States was on the world stage to stay. The Monroe Doctrine of 1823 warned Europe not to intervene in the new Latin American nations. In the 1830s, the U.S. became embroiled in a conflict over the secession of Texas from Mexico. When Texas was admitted to the Union in 1845, the resulting war with Mexico ended in a United States victory, adding more territory to the nation, including California.

Winds of Change

At mid-century the United States faced trouble as well as promise. The new prosperity unleashed fierce competition, leading to factories scarred by child labor and unsafe working conditions. Women's rights gained some ground, but the deepest social divide remained slavery. Advocates of states' rights argued that the federal government could not bend states to its will. Abolitionists, on the other hand, insisted that slavery was morally wrong. In 1861, the gathering storm finally burst into civil war.

Key Historical Theme: Coming of Age

- Physical expansion and technological progress lay the foundation for an American cultural flowering.
- Democracy advanced, although women, Native Americans, and African Americans did not fully share in it.
- The conflict over slavery eventually led to civil war.

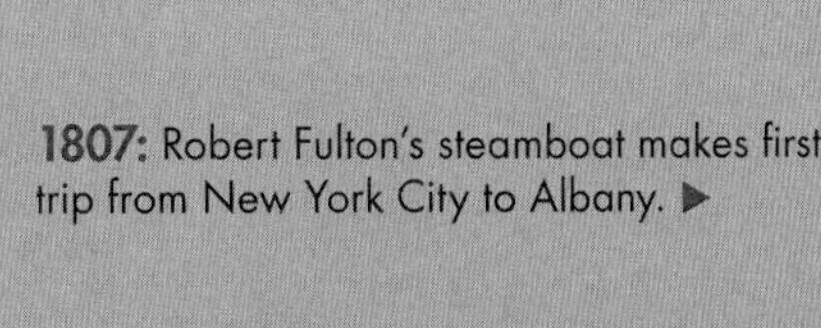

1807: Robert Fulton's steamboat makes first trip from New York City to Albany. ▶

1810

◀ **1804: France** Napoleon Bonaparte declares himself emperor.

Essential Questions Across Time

The American Renaissance (1800–1870)

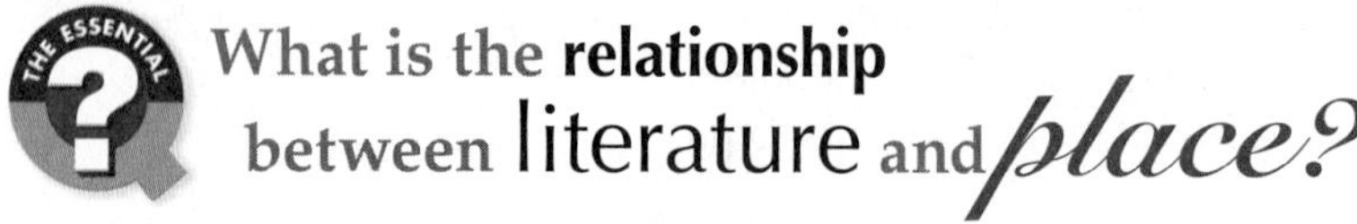

What did Americans discover as they explored the continent?

Starting as thirteen eastern seaboard colonies, hemmed in by mountain barriers blocking easy access to the interior, the United States gradually extended itself west. The Louisiana Purchase in 1803, the Mexican Cession of 1848, and the additions of Texas and the Oregon Territory filled out the nation and needed to be explored, surveyed, documented, and celebrated.

Size and Diversity Americans were inspired by the sheer size of the land. Vast open prairies in the Midwest, demanding deserts in the Southwest, unbroken forests in the Northwest, grand mountains and canyons in the West—the land ended only at an ocean. Explorers and settlers found countless natural resources. It seemed enough to last forever.

What attitudes developed toward the American land?

Commerce Americans covered the continent in a spirit of acquisition and pride of ownership. The land seemed to demand optimism and practical invention, calling continuously for one more step west. With exploration came exploitation. Commercial possibilities were as wide as the landscape.

Grandeur At the same time, many Americans developed an attitude that went beyond practical matters. The land struck them with awe. To them its spiritual possibilities, not its commercial ones, were as wide as the landscape. Its physical grandeur inspired them to reach for the sublime.

ESSENTIAL QUESTION VOCABULARY

These Essential Question words will help you think and write about literature and place:

barrier (bar′ē ər) *n.* something that prevents movement or separates

acquisition (ak′wə zish′ən) *n.* the act of obtaining something

exploration (eks′ plə rā′ shən) *n.* investigation of new lands

TIMELINE

1810

1812: U.S. declares war on Great Britain; early battles in War of 1812 are at sea.

1813: England Jane Austen publishes *Pride and Prejudice.* ▶

▲ **1814:** Bombardment of Fort McHenry inspires Francis Scott Key to write "The Star-Spangled Banner."

How did these attitudes show up in literature?

An American Mythology Explorers such as Meriwether Lewis and Captain William Clark recorded the facts of their expeditions in colorful words and drawings that made the farthest reaches of the continent accessible to every American, at least in imagination. Fiction writers Washington Irving and James Fenimore Cooper helped to create an American mythology by setting tales in the forests, towns, and outposts of the American landscape. In his exciting narrative poems, Henry Wadsworth Longfellow populated the wilderness with colonial Americans, Native Americans, and Revolutionary War heroes.

The American Masters The greatest of American writers—those whose work created the American Renaissance—were all profoundly involved in the American landscape. Edgar Allan Poe, Nathaniel Hawthorne, and Herman Melville saw the dark side of the wilderness, while Ralph Waldo Emerson and Henry David Thoreau emphasized its sublimity. Emily Dickinson explored the universal qualities of her local landscape, while Walt Whitman merged his all-encompassing self with the entire nation.

Nature and Culture The American place affected a wide variety of cultural figures. Thomas Cole and the other Hudson River painters based their work on the romantic and sublime features of the landscape. John James Audubon applied both science and art to American wildlife. Frederick Law Olmsted even found a way to bring nature into the city with his landscape design of New York City's Central Park.

The **American EXPERIENCE**

CLOSE-UP ON HISTORY

Sacajawea, Guide for Lewis and Clark

In 1804, a Shoshone woman named Sacajawea was staying with the Mandan Indians near present-day Bismarck, North Dakota. Meriwether Lewis and William Clark, who had been asked by President Thomas Jefferson to explore the new lands of the Louisiana Purchase, were spending the winter with the Mandans. Sacajawea offered to guide them in the spring across the Rocky Mountains, where the Shoshones lived. She knew the region well and she could translate for them in their encounters with different Indian tribes.

Sacajawea contributed greatly to the success of the expedition, gathering wild vegetables and advising the men where to fish and hunt. She also knew about the healing qualities of different herbs. When the party reached the mountains, Sacajawea recognized the lands of her people, and she persuaded her relatives to support the expedition with food and horses.

After crossing the Rockies, the explorers reached the west coast and returned to St. Louis in 1806. Thanks largely to Sacajawea, their relations with Indians had been almost entirely peaceful. Sadly, however, the westward movement inspired by the expedition would eventually lead to "Indian removal" and confiscation of Indian lands.

1817: William Cullen Bryant publishes early draft of "Thanatopsis" in a Boston magazine. ▶

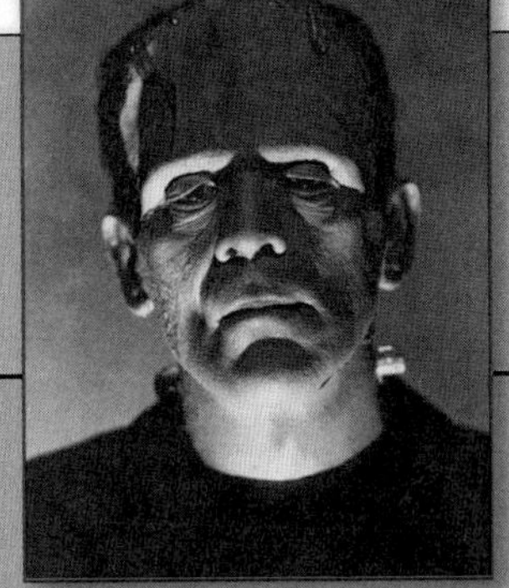

1818: England Mary Wollstonecraft Shelley creates a legend with *Frankenstein.* ▲

1820

How does **literature** shape or reflect *society?*

What social forces shaped America during this period?

Technology Bigger, better, stronger, faster—everything in America was rolling on the fast track, especially on the iron network of railroad tracks that crisscrossed the country. Railroads allowed farmers to get their crops to larger markets, and they made almost every corner of America a potential market. Factories made cities grow, and cities then built more factories. Shipbuilding, fishing, and whaling flourished. Inventions of all kinds made life easier: the telegraph and Morse code, the steamboat, the reaper, vulcanized rubber, powerful looms and lathes, the sewing machine, the elevator. Even the word *technology* was coined during this period.

Democracy As the nineteenth century moved forward in America, the right to vote was still largely restricted to white males who owned land. The election of Andrew Jackson as president and the rise of Jacksonian Democracy, however, signaled the rise of the common man to positions of unprecedented power. It was no longer necessary to be wealthy and highly educated to wield political authority in America. At the same time, the women's rights movement gained momentum, spurred on by the Seneca Falls Convention in 1848. Native Americans, on the other hand, felt the continuing hardship of forced removal from their traditional homelands.

Slavery The institution of slavery remained the most profound controversy in America. Eventually, slavery would be the social and political issue that would have the greatest effect on the lives—and deaths—of Americans.

What did nineteenth-century Americans read?

Americans had broken away from Britain politically, but they still devoured British literature, including the adventure tales of Walter Scott and the serial novels of Charles Dickens. However, no British author came close in popularity to two Americans. Harriet Beecher Stowe's anti-slavery novel *Uncle Tom's Cabin* became a national—and international—phenomenon, and Longfellow became the best-selling poet in the English language.

ESSENTIAL QUESTION VOCABULARY

These Essential Question words will help you think and write about literature and society:

market (mär′ kit) *n.* region in which goods can be bought and sold

invention (in ven′ shən) *n.* something originated by experiment; new device

technology (tek näl′ ə jē) *n.* scientific or industrial methods or products

TIMELINE

1820

1820: Missouri Compromise bans slavery in parts of new territories. ▼

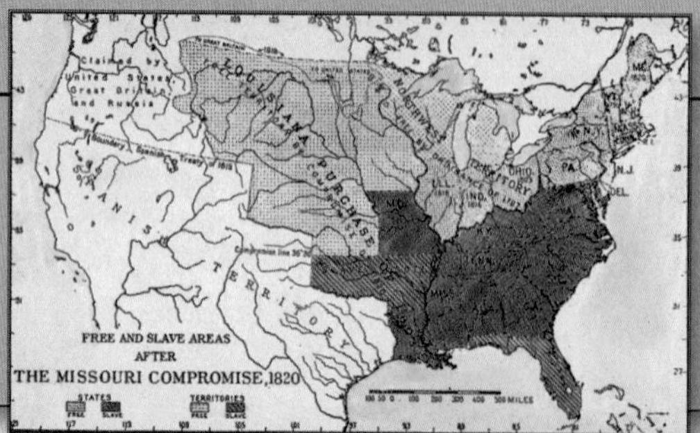

▲ **1825:** Completion and success of Erie Canal spurs canal building throughout the nation.

What did American writers want to achieve?

The Social Vision Thomas Jefferson's vision of America was grand, and the Louisiana Purchase helped make that vision a reality. The reports sent by Lewis and Clark and other explorers encouraged the country's physical, political, and commercial growth. At the same time, American journalism fed the idea that the New World could rival the Old World in every way. In lectures, essays, speeches, debates, pamphlets, editorials, and songs, Americans presented what they thought and felt about women's rights, slavery, treatment of Native Americans, land use, immigration, trade, and taxes. Public writing enabled America to define a public self.

The Romantic Vision Romanticism made clear that exploration of the private self was as important as exploration of the land. In prose and poetry, American writers described individual quests for self-definition. Romantic writers elevated imagination over reason, feeling over fact, and nature above all. The fantastical tales of Washington Irving and Edgar Allan Poe, and the agonized heroes of Nathaniel Hawthorne and Herman Melville made the Romantic vision an essential part of the American Renaissance.

The Transcendental Vision Literature, philosophy, and religion merged in New England Transcendentalism, producing a native blend that was Romantic, intuitive, and ethically engaged. For Transcendentalists, real truths lay outside sensory experience. Ralph Waldo Emerson explored those truths in brilliant, wide-ranging essays. Henry David Thoreau put his finger on those truths by merging nature writing and spiritual autobiography. Thoreau's *Walden* remains central to American literature.

The American EXPERIENCE

A LIVING TRADITION

Walden Pond and Tinker Creek

About 120 years after Thoreau embarked on the experiment of living "alone, in the woods ... on the shore of Walden Pond," Annie Dillard undertook a similar experiment with nature and solitude: "I live by a creek, Tinker Creek, in a valley in Virginia's Blue Ridge." Just as Thoreau wrote *Walden* to describe his experiences, she, too, wrote a book about what she saw and thought, the best-selling *Pilgrim at Tinker Creek*. Near the beginning of the book, she describes the home base for her observations:

"An anchorite's hermitage [hermit's secluded retreat] is called an anchor-hold; some anchor-holds were simple sheds clamped to the side of a church like a barnacle to a rock. I think of this house clamped to the side of Tinker Creek as an anchor-hold. It holds me at anchor to the rock bottom of the creek itself and it keeps me steadied in the current, as a sea anchor does, facing the stream of light pouring down. It's a good place to live; there's a lot to think about. The creeks—Tinker and Carvin's—are an active mystery, fresh every minute."

▲ **1827:** Edgar Allan Poe publishes *Tamerlane*, his first collection of poems.

1829: England George Stephenson perfects a steam locomotive for Liverpool-Manchester Railway.

1831: France Victor Hugo publishes *Notre Dame de Paris.* ▶

1830

"OUR FIELD IS THE WORLD."
LIGHT DRAFT, SUPERIOR DESIGN.
CLEAN AND RAPID CUTTER.
McCormick Harvesting Machine Co., Chicago.

◀ **1831:** Cyrus McCormick invents mechanical reaper.

The American EXPERIENCE

CONTEMPORARY CONNECTION

EMILY DICKINSON: POET, RECLUSE . . . GAMER?

In 2005, three prominent video-game designers set themselves a challenge to create games based on something surprising: the poetry of Emily Dickinson.

Clint Hocking, lead designer of *Splinter Cell*, created a game called *Muse*. Players would collect symbols based on Dickinson's Massachusetts. They would then assemble the symbols to make poems within a certain amount of time.

Peter Molyneux, designer of *Black & White*, created a game using a house modeled on Dickinson's. Players would wander around the house, trying to unlock Dickinson's experiences.

Will Wright, creator of *The Sims*, believes that Dickinson and hi-tech are a natural combination. "If she were alive today," he said, "she'd be an Internet addict, and she'd probably have a really amazing blog." The game Wright designed would be stored on a USB flash drive. The player and Emily would write to each other. Emily would appear randomly with IMs, e-mails, or desktop appearances. Ultimately, she could delete herself from the memory stick.

Wright's game won the challenge.

TIMELINE

1835

1837: Samuel F.B. Morse patents electromagnetic telegraph. ▶

1838: U.S. Army marches Cherokees of Georgia on long "Trail of Tears" to Oklahoma. ▶

1841: Antarctica is first explored by Englishman James Ross. ▶

1842: Asia Hong Kong becomes a British colony.

What makes American literature *American?*

What qualities made American literature sound American?

American English Most Americans, descended from English colonists, spoke English, but gradually the American way of speaking and writing took on many unique features. Dialects, the products of local communities, developed around the country, and local grammar and syntax often drove out standard British English. Spanish, French, Dutch, and Native American languages added to the mix, and Americans coined new words to describe their land, weather, plants, animals, and ways of daily life.

Triumph of the Colloquial American English, both spoken and written, became more colloquial, or informal, than British English. Contractions such as *can't, don't,* and *couldn't* were acceptable. Colorful idioms enlivened everyday speech. Americans might *set a spell, take a fork in a road,* or *bark up the wrong tree.* The British thought that Americans were ruining the language, but, like the nation itself, American English was intensely alive to change, variety, and new additions.

The "Barbaric Yawp" During the American Renaissance, American writers found their own voices. Emerson, Thoreau, Poe, Dickinson—each contributed to a recognizably American style, but no one sounded as utterly American as Walt Whitman. He was unafraid to sound his "barbaric yawp" across the continent. His style incorporated the plain and the elegant, the high and the low, the foreign and the native. It mixed grand opera, political oratory, journalistic punch, everyday conversation, and biblical cadences. Whitman's sound was the American sound.

What literary character types emerged during this period?

The Frontiersman As the frontier continued to open, the men and women who faced it head-on entered into the nation's literary imagination. Real-life backwoodsmen such as Daniel Boone and Davy Crockett were mythologized in almanacs and folktales, and Americans delighted in tall tales about

ESSENTIAL QUESTION VOCABULARY

These Essential Question words will help you think and write about American literature:

individualist (in′də vij′o͞o əl ist) *n.* one who lives life his or her own way, not influenced by others

colloquial (kə lō′kwē əl) *adj.* conversational; informal

self-reliant (self-ri lī′ənt) *adj.* depending upon one's own judgments and abilities

◀ **1845: Ireland** Famine results from failure of potato crop.

1845: Florida becomes the twenty-seventh state in the United States.

◀ **1848:** Women's Rights Convention held in Seneca Falls, New York.

1848: Mexican War ends; United States expands borders.

1848: Gold Rush begins in California. ▶

1848: Karl Marx and Friedrich Engels publish *The Communist Manifesto.*

1850

the superhuman lumberjack Paul Bunyan, the rowdy riverboat man Mike Fink, and the African American steel-driver John Henry. In fiction, the essential frontiersman was Natty Bumppo, the hero of James Fenimore Cooper's *Leatherstocking Tales.* At one with the wilderness, these hardy characters helped define the American identity as bold, self-reliant, and "uncorrupted" by civilization.

The Romantic Individualist Romanticism emphasized the individual over the institution and the person over the community. The American Romantic hero took many forms. In *The Scarlet Letter*, Nathaniel Hawthorne's Hester Prynne dared to put love and honor over the repressive rule of her town. In *Moby-Dick*, Herman Melville's Captain Ahab let nothing stand in the way of his obsession with the white whale. In *Leaves of Grass*, Walt Whitman's ecstatic self celebrated its own joyful existence at the center of the universe.

The Transcendental Seeker One type of Romantic individualist was the person who sought to reach the sublime, a feeling of oneness with all that is beautiful and good. This private soul craved unity with the Oversoul, a universal force that might be identified as the mind of God. As Emerson wrote, "the individual is the world," and an individual could reach the sublime through the world of nature. Emerson and Thoreau defined this character type, but other writers and artists contributed to the quest for the sublime. Margaret Fuller edited the Transcendentalist magazine *The Dial*, and the Hudson River school of visual artists painted landscapes that inspired a sense of the sublime in all who saw them.

What literary themes emerged during this era?

Westering The myth of America began as "a city upon a hill," but by the nineteenth century it had become "the garden of the world." The sheer bulk of the continent, with its treasury of natural resources, made continuous Western expansion a fundamental part of the national identity. Many Americans considered this movement west as a continental destiny. It became the right and duty of Americans to explore, expand, and exploit. However, if America was a garden, it was one being invaded by machines. This is a theme that continues to resonate in American literature.

TIMELINE

1850

1850: Nathaniel Hawthorne publishes *The Scarlet Letter.*

1850: England Elizabeth Barrett Browning publishes *Sonnets from the Portuguese.* ▶

◀ **1851:** Herman Melville publishes *Moby-Dick.*

1851: Nathaniel Hawthorne publishes *The House of Seven Gables.*

1851: Australia Gold discovered in New South Wales.

Bright and Dark Romanticism Romanticism had two faces, one bright and optimistic, the other dark and shadowed by evil. Emerson and Thoreau emphasized "the sun is but a morning star" aspect of Romanticism. They saw human beings as fundamentally good. Poe, Hawthorne, and Melville, on the other hand, were deeply disturbed by what they saw in the human heart. They believed that crime, cruelty, guilt, and self-destruction were the true earmarks of human nature. During the American Renaissance, writers explored both sides of the Romantic impulse.

Self-Reliance "Trust thyself," Emerson advised. Think for yourself, and act on what you think. "Live deliberately," Thoreau advised. Make your own choices, and do not let others choose for you. These principles had been built into American democracy, and they became fundamental themes of American culture. What applied to individuals also applied to the nation as a whole. The eighteenth century had seen the Declaration of Independence. The nineteenth century saw declarations of cultural independence. Self-reliance is key to why the American Renaissance happened at all. Literary culture had begun to grow; journalism and education prepared the ground. But it was extraordinary individuals who made it happen—self-reliant men and women who thought for themselves and refused to let social, political, religious, or cultural institutions overwhelm them.

The **American EXPERIENCE**

DEVELOPING AMERICAN ENGLISH

The Truth About O.K. by Richard Lederer

Americans seem to have a passion for stringing initial letters together. We use *A.M.* and *P.M.* to separate light from darkness and *B.C.* and *A.D.* to identify vast stretches of time. We may listen to a deejay or veejay on *ABC* or *MTV*, or a crusading *DA* quoting the *FBI* on *CNN*.

Perhaps the most widely understood American word in the world is *O.K.* The explanations for its origin have been imaginative and various. Some claim that *O.K.* is a version of the Choctaw affirmative *okeh*. Others assert that it is short for the Greek *olla kalla* ("all good") or *Orrin Kendall* crackers or chief *Old Keukuk*.

The truth is that in the 1830s there was a craze for initialisms, like our currently popular *T.G.I.F.* and *F.Y.I.* The fad went so far as to generate letter combinations of intentional misspellings: *K.Y.* for "know use," *O.W.* for "oll wright." *O.K.* for "oll korrect" followed.

Ultimately, *O.K.* survived because of a presidential nickname. President Martin Van Buren was born in Kinderhook, New York, and dubbed "Old Kinderhook." "O.K." became the rallying cry of the Old Kinderhook Club that supported him for re-election in 1840. Van Buren was defeated, but the word honoring his name remains what H. L. Mencken identified as "the most shining and successful Americanism ever invented."

135,000 SETS, 270,000 VOLUMES SOLD.
UNCLE TOM'S CABIN
FOR SALE HERE.
The Greatest Book of the Age.
1870
Leaves of Grass.
Walt Whitman

▲ **1852:** Harriet Beecher Stowe publishes *Uncle Tom's Cabin.*

1854: Henry David Thoreau publishes *Walden.* ▼

1855: England Robert Browning publishes *Men and Women.*

1855: Walt Whitman publishes *Leaves of Grass.* ▶

1858: Abraham Lincoln and Stephen Douglas run for Illinois Senate seat and conduct a series of famous debates.

Recent Scholarship

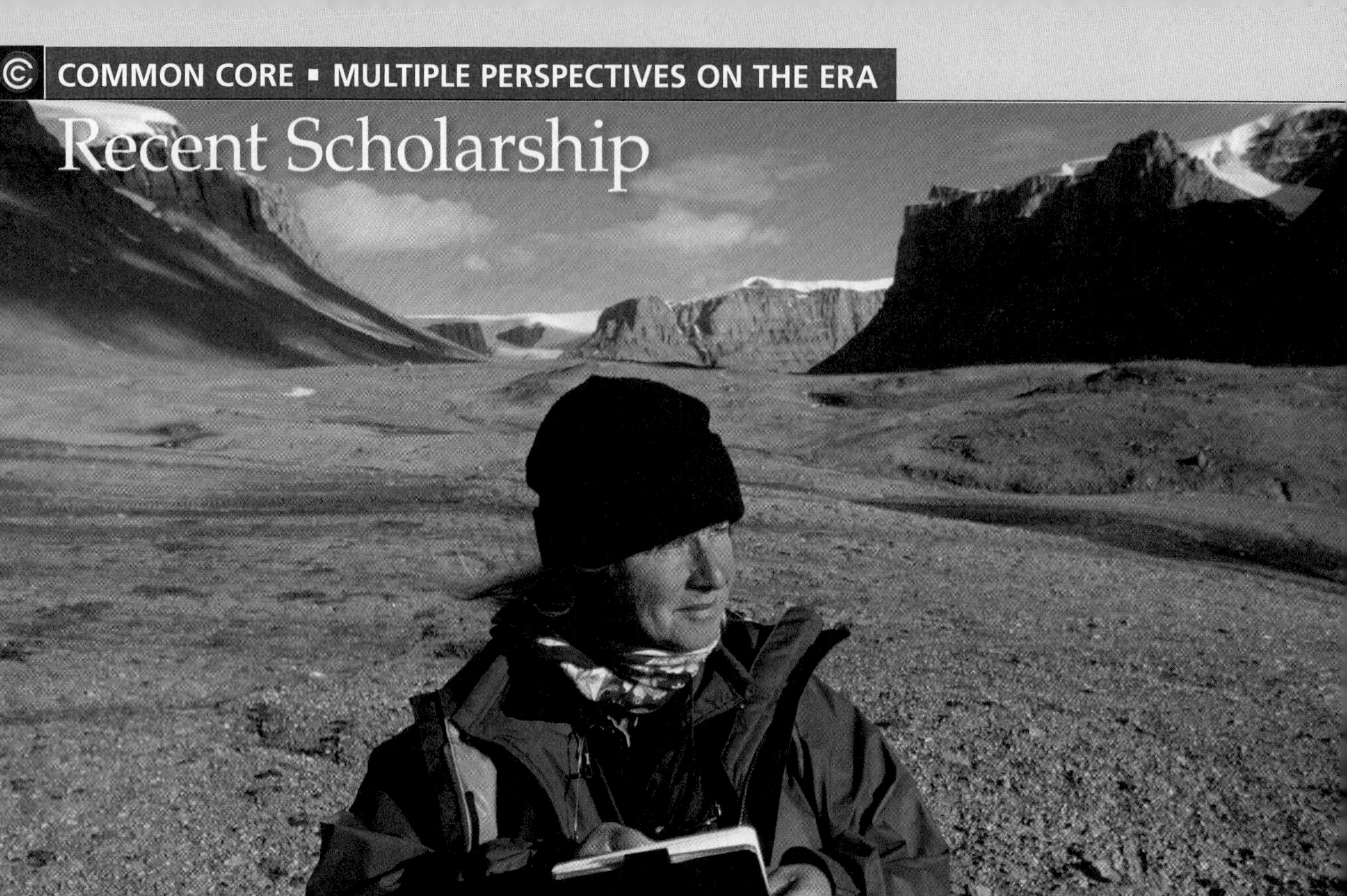

Inspired by Nature

Gretel Ehrlich

We are all born on a particular spot on the planet with its unique seasons, weather, and topography. Mountains, rivers, rocks, storms, glaciers, skies, trees, and grasses, as well as all living things, help shape who we are, how we see, how we move through our days, and how we know who we are. Those of us who have been called "nature writers" are simply people who observe and write about the living planet, who witness the birth and death of its residents, who understand that we all share the earth equally, and who tell the stories that come from the earth.

About the Author

Gretel Ehrlich was born in California. She has worked as a ranch hand, a sheepherder, and a documentary filmmaker. As a writer, she has been profoundly influenced by living in Wyoming, a place of intense extremes and breathtaking beauty. Ehrlich is the author of 13 books, including three collections of essays, a memoir, and three books of poetry. Her many honors include the 2010 PEN Thoreau Award. She is best known for her nature writing, which has focused most recently on the island of Greenland.

From Natural Fact Comes Human Meaning

The Inuit people of northern Greenland have a word, *sila*, that means "the power of nature, weather, and human and animal consciousness as one and the same": no separation between the "emotional weather" inside ourselves and the natural forces on the outside that affect us. Nature writers are always writing about two things at once: the ecosystem and continent that is our mind and body, and the greater one of the world surrounding us. They show us how human meaning can come from natural fact.

A One-Room Cabin on Walden Pond

Henry David Thoreau was one of the great natural history writers of all time. Broken-hearted over a lost love, he went to live on Walden Pond in Concord, Massachusetts, for two years and two months. His friend and mentor, Ralph Waldo Emerson, a brilliant essayist, bought an eleven-acre field on the north shore of the pond, and in March of 1845, Thoreau, with Emerson's encouragement, built a ten-by-fifteen-foot one-room cabin. Then, he borrowed a horse and plow and planted two acres in white beans, corn, and potatoes.

An Inventory of the Natural World

Thoreau was twenty-eight at the time, and he wanted to be free from the constraints of family and society. Reading widely, walking locally, writing obsessively—those were his priorities. He was not a great adventurer—others at the time were searching for the Northwest Passage in the Arctic, sailing the seas of the world, traveling by covered wagon across the country. Thoreau knew that his inventory of the natural world and his insights into human consciousness could be achieved right where he was: on Walden Pond. He wanted to live simply and quietly, to live deeply, to listen and observe, to become intimate with a place. In so doing, he allowed the outer landscape to shape the prose that came from within.

Where We Live Holds the Secrets of the Universe

"I went to the woods because I wished to live deliberately," he wrote, "to front only the essential facts of life, and see if I could not learn what it had to teach, and not, when I came to die, discover that I had not lived." What we learn from Thoreau's life and writings is that anywhere we happen to live is good enough. We don't have to go to some exotic place to find ourselves or understand the world. It's all right here, for each of us. Each place holds all the secrets of the universe, the history of the world in a raindrop.

© Collaboration: Speaking and Listening

One lesson of Thoreau's writing, according to Gretel Ehrlich, is that natural wonders exist in every corner of the natural world:

"What we learn from Thoreau's life and writings is that anywhere we happen to live is good enough… Each place holds all the secrets of the universe, the history of the world in a raindrop."

Hold a **small group discussion** about Ehrlich's ideas in the quoted passage. Decide whether you agree or disagree with her statement. Select a point person to share your ideas with the class.

Integrate and Evaluate Information

Common Core State Standards

Reading Informational Text
7. Integrate and evaluate multiple sources of information presented in different media or formats as well as in words in order to address a question or solve a problem.

Speaking and Listening
6. Adapt speech to a variety of contexts and tasks.

Language
6. Acquire and use accurately general academic and domain-specific words and phrases.

1. Use a chart like the one shown to determine the key ideas expressed in the Essential Question essays on pages 214–221. Fill in two ideas related to each Essential Question and note the authors most closely associated with each concept. One example has been done for you.

Essential Question	Key Concept	Key Author
Literature and Place	A kinship with nature	Thoreau
American Literature		
Literature and Society		

2. How do the visual sources in this section—artifacts, paintings, photographs, and illustrations—add to your understanding of the ideas expressed in words? Cite specific examples.

3. The vast, unexplored American West sparked the American imagination. Describe some of the different attitudes that developed toward the American land and its settlement, citing evidence from the multiple sources on pages 210–223. In your view, have these attitudes helped shape contemporary American culture? If so, how? If not, why not?

4. Address a Question In her discussion of Thoreau, Gretel Ehrlich writes: "We don't have to go to some exotic place to find ourselves or understand our world.... Each place holds all the secrets of the universe." How might this idea challenge certain values, such as the importance of progress, innovation, and expansion, that are often seen as essentially American? Integrate information from this textbook and other sources to support your ideas.

Speaking and Listening: Slide Presentation

During the nineteenth century, technology leaped forward. Using a variety of print and electronic resources, research one of the following nineteenth-century inventions. Then, write and deliver a **slide presentation** that explores the impact of the invention on American life:

- the mechanical reaper
- the cotton gin
- the steam locomotive
- the telegraph
- the bicycle

Your slide presentation should answer the following questions: What aspects of American life did the invention affect or change? What ripple effects did the invention cause? Whom did the invention most benefit? Whom, if anyone, did the invention harm?

Solve a Research Problem This assignment requires you to understand and integrate technical terms into your writing. To do so, find reliable print and online sources for definitions and explanations. Also, consult writings by scientists, inventors, and historians. As you present, make sure to explain technical terms that may be unfamiliar to your audience.

ESSENTIAL QUESTION VOCABULARY

Use these words in your responses:

Literature and Place
barrier
acquisition
exploration

American Literature
individualist
colloquial
self-reliant

Literature and Society
market
invention
technology

PART 1

Fireside and Campfire

Before You Read | *The Devil and Tom Walker*

Connecting to the Essential Question This dark yet comic story centers on greedy Tom Walker, who cares only for himself in his pursuit of riches. As you read, look for details that criticize selfishness and greed. This will help as you consider the Essential Question: **How does literature shape or reflect society?**

Reading Literature

3. Analyze the impact of the author's choices regarding how to develop and relate elements of a story or drama (e.g., where a story is set, how the characters are introduced and developed).

9. Demonstrate knowledge of nineteenth-century foundational works of American literature.

Literary Analysis

Characterization is the creation and development of a character. In **direct characterization,** a writer tells you what a character is like. In **indirect characterization,** the writer reveals a character's personality through the character's speech, thoughts, actions, appearance, and other characters' reactions. For example, Irving uses direct characterization when he tells the reader that Tom Walker was "not a man to be troubled with any fears." He uses indirect characterization in Tom's reply to the Devil, who has threateningly suggested that Tom is trespassing:

> *"Your grounds!" said Tom with a sneer, "no more your grounds than mine; they belong to Deacon Peabody."*

Indirect characterization provides valuable information and adds to a story's action, drama, or humor. As you read, notice Irving's use of characterization.

Reading Strategy

Preparing to Read Complex Texts Works of fiction are often shaped by the concerns of the historical period in which they are set. These may involve philosophical trends, religious beliefs, ethical issues, or social problems. As you read, **evaluate the influences of the historical period** on characters, plot, and settings. For example, the characters in this story hold attitudes common to New Englanders in the 1720s, when the story is set. Through his narrator, Irving criticizes some of those attitudes while accepting others. Use a chart like the one shown to track the effects of specific cultural attitudes on the characters, plot, and settings of this story.

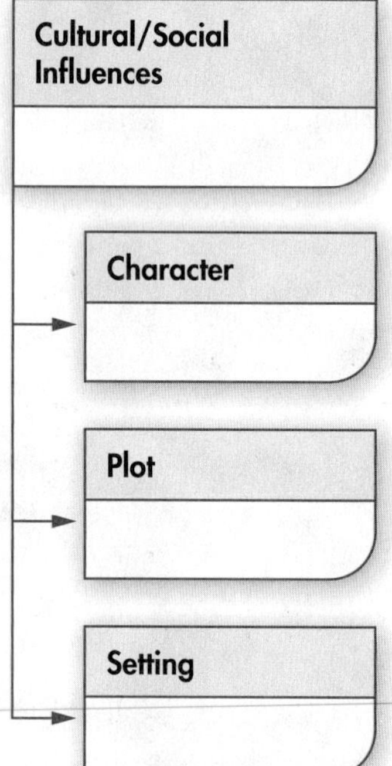

Vocabulary

prevalent (prev′ ə lənt) *adj.* widely existing or occurring (p. 229)

discord (dis′ kôrd′) *n.* lack of harmony; conflict (p. 230)

treacherous (trech′ ər əs) *adj.* dangerous (p. 230)

extort (eks tôrt′) *v.* obtain by threat or violence (p. 236)

ostentation (äs′ tən tā′ shən) *n.* boastful display (p. 237)

parsimony (pär′ sə mō′ nē) *n.* stinginess (p. 237)

Washington Irving *(1783–1859)*

Author of "The Devil and Tom Walker"

Named after President George Washington, Washington Irving became the first American fiction writer to achieve an international reputation. Irving was born into a wealthy New York family right at the close of the American Revolution. Although he planned to be a lawyer, he grew more interested in travel and writing and devoted his life to both pursuits.

A Career Blooms From 1807 to 1808, Irving wrote satirical essays under the pen name Jonathan Oldstyle. With his brother William, he anonymously published the magazine *Salmagundi*, named after a spicy appetizer. In 1809, he produced his first major work, *A History of New York From the Beginning of the World to the End of the Dutch Dynasty.* This humorous examination of New York in colonial times made Irving so famous that to this day native New Yorkers are known as "Knickerbockers" after Diedrich Knickerbocker, the character Irving created to narrate the work.

Americanizing Europe's Folklore Traveling in Europe from 1815 to 1832, Irving encountered European folklore that helped inspire his own writing. Two of his best-known works, "The Legend of Sleepy Hollow" and "Rip Van Winkle," turn German folk tales into distinctly American narratives set in New York's Hudson Valley. Their main characters—Ichabod Crane, the nervous Sleepy Hollow schoolteacher harassed by a headless horseman, and Rip Van Winkle, the lazy colonist who slept for decades—have become classic figures of American literature.

I am endeavoring to serve my country. Whatever I have written has been written with the feelings and published as the writing of an American. . . . If I can do any good in this world it is with my pen.

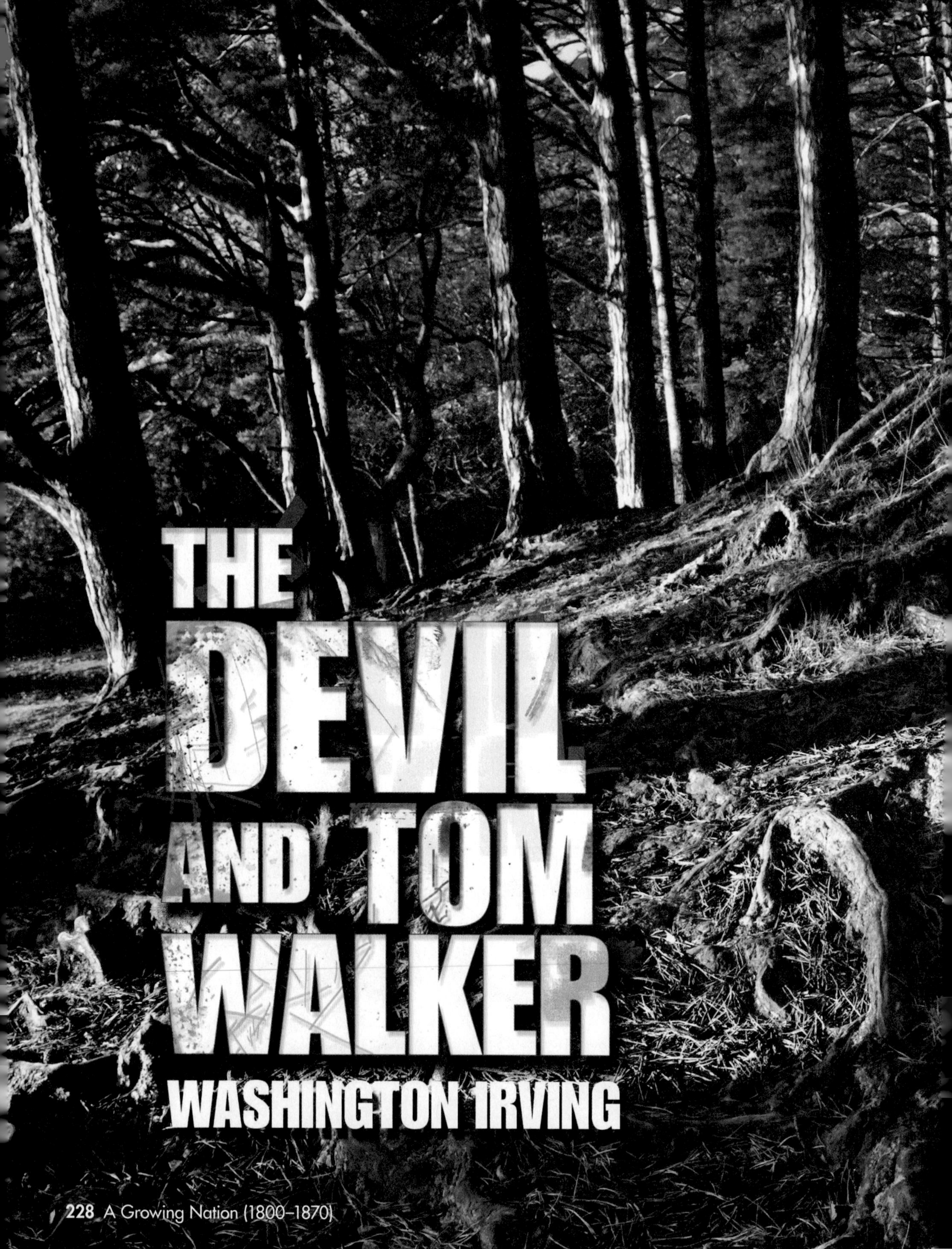
THE
DEVIL
AND TOM
WALKER
WASHINGTON IRVING

BACKGROUND This story appeared in 1824, when the American economy was booming. Advances in technology and transportation and the rapid growth of cities created large markets for goods. For the first time, manufactured items were widely available and people had money to buy them. Irving's story retells the European tale of Faust, a scholar who sold his soul for wisdom. Tom Walker, Washington Irving's American Faust, has no interest in wisdom; he is simply after riches. Irving may have set this story in an earlier America, but he revealed the materialism of his own era.

A few miles from Boston in Massachusetts, there is a deep inlet, winding several miles into the interior of the country from Charles Bay, and terminating in a thickly wooded swamp or morass. On one side of this inlet is a beautiful dark grove; on the opposite side the land rises abruptly from the water's edge into a high ridge, on which grow a few scattered oaks of great age and immense size. Under one of these gigantic trees, according to old stories, there was a great amount of treasure buried by Kidd the pirate.[1] The inlet allowed a facility to bring the money in a boat secretly and at night to the very foot of the hill; the elevation of the place permitted a good look-out to be kept that no one was at hand; while the remarkable trees formed good landmarks by which the place might easily be found again. The old stories add, moreover, that the Devil presided at the hiding of the money, and took it under his guardianship; but this it is well known he always does with buried treasure, particularly when it has been ill-gotten.

Be that as it may, Kidd never returned to recover his wealth; being shortly after seized at Boston, sent out to England, and there hanged for a pirate.

About the year 1727, just at the time that earthquakes were prevalent in New England, and shook many tall sinners down upon their knees, there lived near this place a meager, miserly fellow, of the name of Tom Walker. He had a wife as miserly as himself: they were so miserly that they even conspired to cheat each other. Whatever the woman could lay hands on, she hid away; a hen could not cackle but she was on the alert to secure the new-laid egg. Her husband was continually prying about to detect her secret hoards, and many and fierce were the conflicts that took place about what ought to have been common property.

Reading Strategy
Evaluate Influences of the Historical Period
What does this reference to the Devil and treasure suggest about period attitudes toward wealth?

Vocabulary
prevalent (prev′ ə lənt) *adj.* widely existing or occuring

What is buried under one of the gigantic trees?

1. **Kidd the pirate** Captain William Kidd (1645–1701).

▲ **Critical Viewing** How does this picture compare to Irving's description of the Walkers' home? **[Compare and Contrast]**

They lived in a forlorn-looking house that stood alone, and had an air of starvation. A few straggling savin trees, emblems of sterility, grew near it; no smoke ever curled from its chimney; no traveler stopped at its door. A miserable horse, whose ribs were as articulate as the bars of a gridiron, stalked about a field, where a thin carpet of moss, scarcely covering the ragged beds of puddingstone, tantalized and balked his hunger; and sometimes he would lean his head over the fence, look piteously at the passerby, and seem to petition deliverance from this land of famine.

The house and its inmates had altogether a bad name. Tom's wife was a tall termagant,[2] fierce of temper, loud of tongue, and strong of arm. Her voice was often heard in wordy warfare with her husband; and his face sometimes showed signs that their conflicts were not confined to words. No one ventured, however, to interfere between them. The lonely wayfarer shrunk within himself at the horrid clamor and clapperclawing;[3] eyed the den of **discord** askance; and hurried on his way, rejoicing, if a bachelor, in his celibacy.

Vocabulary

discord (dis′ kôrd′) *n.* lack of harmony; conflict

treacherous (trech′ ər əs) *adj.* dangerous

One day that Tom Walker had been to a distant part of the neighborhood, he took what he considered a shortcut homeward, through the swamp. Like most shortcuts, it was an ill chosen route. The swamp was thickly grown with great gloomy pines and hemlocks, some of them ninety feet high, which made it dark at noonday, and a retreat for all the owls of the neighborhood. It was full of pits and quagmires, partly covered with weeds and mosses, where the green surface often betrayed the traveler into a gulf of black, smothering mud; there were also dark and stagnant pools, the abodes of the tadpole, the bullfrog, and the watersnake; where the trunks of pines and hemlocks lay half-drowned, half-rotting, looking like alligators sleeping in the mire.

Tom had long been picking his way cautiously through this **treacherous** forest; stepping from tuft to tuft of rushes and roots, which afforded precarious footholds among deep sloughs; or pacing carefully, like a cat, along the prostrate trunks of trees; startled now and then by the sudden screaming of the bittern, or the quacking of a wild duck, rising on the wing from some solitary pool. At length he arrived at a piece of firm ground, which ran out like a peninsula into the deep bosom of the swamp. It had been one of the strongholds of the Indians during their wars with the first colonists. Here they had thrown up a kind of fort, which they had looked upon as almost impregnable, and had used as a place of refuge for their squaws and children. Nothing remained of the old Indian fort but a few embankments, gradually sinking to the level of the surrounding earth, and already overgrown in part by oaks and other forest trees, the foliage of which formed a contrast to the dark pines and hemlocks of the swamp.

2. **termagant** (tʉr′ mə gənt) *n.* quarrelsome woman.
3. **clapperclawing** (klap′ ər klô′ iŋ) *n.* clawing or scratching.

It was late in the dusk of evening when Tom Walker reached the old fort, and he paused there awhile to rest himself. Anyone but he would have felt unwilling to linger in this lonely, melancholy place, for the common people had a bad opinion of it, from the stories handed down from the time of the Indian wars; when it was asserted that the savages held incantations here, and made sacrifices to the evil spirit.

Tom Walker, however, was not a man to be troubled with any fears of the kind. He reposed himself for some time on the trunk of a fallen hemlock, listening to the boding cry of the tree toad, and delving with his walking staff into a mound of black mold at his feet. As he turned up the soil unconsciously, his staff struck against something hard. He raked it out of the vegetable mold, and lo! a cloven skull, with an Indian tomahawk buried deep in it, lay before him. The rust on the weapon showed the time that had elapsed since this deathblow had been given. It was a dreary memento of the fierce struggle that had taken place in this last foothold of the Indian warriors.

"Humph!" said Tom Walker, as he gave it a kick to shake the dirt from it.

"Let that skull alone!" said a gruff voice. Tom lifted up his eyes, and beheld a great black man seated directly opposite him, on the stump of a tree. He was exceedingly surprised, having neither heard nor seen anyone approach; and he was still more perplexed on observing, as well as the gathering gloom would permit, that the stranger was neither Negro nor Indian. It is true he was dressed in a rude half-Indian garb, and had a red belt or sash swathed round his body; but his face was neither black nor copper color, but swarthy and dingy, and begrimed with soot, as if he had been accustomed to toil among fires and forges. He had a shock of coarse black hair, that stood out from his head in all directions, and bore an ax on his shoulder.

He scowled for a moment at Tom with a pair of great red eyes.

"What are you doing on my grounds?" said the black man, with a hoarse growling voice.

"Your grounds!" said Tom with a sneer, "no more your grounds than mine; they belong to Deacon Peabody."

"Deacon Peabody be d—d," said the stranger, "as I flatter myself he will be, if he does not look more to his own sins and less to those of his neighbors. Look yonder, and see how Deacon Peabody is faring."

Tom looked in the direction that the stranger pointed, and beheld one of the great trees, fair and flourishing without, but rotten at the core, and saw that it had been nearly hewn through, so that the first high wind was likely to blow it down. On the bark of the tree was scored the name of Deacon Peabody, an eminent man, who had waxed wealthy by driving shrewd bargains with the Indians. He now looked round, and found most of the tall trees marked with the name of some great man of the colony, and all more or less scored by the ax. The one on which he had been seated, and which had evidently just been hewn down, bore the name of Crowninshield: and he recollected a mighty

Reading Strategy
Evaluate Influences of the Historical Period
What do details in the first two paragraphs on this page reveal about colonial attitudes toward Native Americans?

Where does Tom pause to rest?

rich man of that name, who made a vulgar display of wealth, which it was whispered he had acquired by buccaneering.

"He's just ready for burning!" said the black man, with a growl of triumph. "You see I am likely to have a good stock of firewood for winter."

"But what right have you," said Tom, "to cut down Deacon Peabody's timber?"

"The right of a prior claim," said the other. "This woodland belonged to me long before one of your white-faced race put foot upon the soil."

"And pray, who are you, if I may be so bold?" said Tom.

"Oh, I go by various names. I am the wild huntsman in some countries; the black miner in others. In this neighborhood I am known by the name of the black woodsman. I am he to whom the red men consecrated this spot, and in honor of whom they now and then roasted a white man, by way of sweet-smelling sacrifice. Since the red men have been exterminated by you white savages, I amuse myself by presiding at the persecutions of Quakers and Anabaptists;[4] I am the great patron and prompter of slave dealers, and the grandmaster of the Salem witches."

"And pray, who are you, if I may be so bold?" said Tom.

"The upshot of all which is, that, if I mistake not," said Tom, sturdily, "you are he commonly called Old Scratch."

"The same, at your service!" replied the black man, with a half-civil nod.

Such was the opening of this interview, according to the old story; though it has almost too familiar an air to be credited. One would think that to meet with such a singular personage, in this wild, lonely place, would have shaken any man's nerves; but Tom was a hard-minded fellow, not easily daunted, and he had lived so long with a termagant wife, that he did not even fear the Devil.

It is said that after this commencement they had a long and earnest conversation together, as Tom returned homeward. The black man told him of great sums of money buried by Kidd the pirate, under the oak trees on the high ridge, not far from the morass. All these were under his command, and protected by his power, so that none could find them but such as propitiated his favor. These he offered to place within Tom Walker's reach, having conceived an especial kindness for him; but they were to be had only on certain conditions. What these conditions were may easily be surmised, though Tom never disclosed them publicly. They must have been very hard, for he required time to think of them, and he was not a man to stick at trifles where money was in view. When they had reached the edge of the swamp, the stranger paused—"What proof have I that all you have been telling me is true?" said Tom. "There is my signature," said the black man, pressing his finger on Tom's forehead. So saying, he turned off among the thickets of the swamp, and seemed, as Tom

Literary Analysis
Characterization
Identify the direct characterization in the paragraph beginning "Such was the opening of this interview . . ."

4. Quakers and Anabaptists two religious groups that were persecuted for their beliefs.

said, to go down, down, down, into the earth, until nothing but his head and shoulders could be seen, and so on, until he totally disappeared.

When Tom reached home, he found the black print of a finger, burnt, as it were, into his forehead, which nothing could obliterate.

The first news his wife had to tell him was the sudden death of Absalom Crowninshield, the rich buccaneer. It was announced in the papers with the usual flourish, that "A great man had fallen in Israel."[5]

Tom recollected the tree which his black friend had just hewn down, and which was ready for burning, "Let the freebooter roast," said Tom, "who cares!" He now felt convinced that all he had heard and seen was no illusion.

He was not prone to let his wife into his confidence; but as this was an uneasy secret, he willingly shared it with her. All her avarice was awakened at the mention of hidden gold, and she urged her husband to comply with the black man's terms and secure what would make them wealthy for life. However Tom might have felt disposed to sell himself to the Devil, he was determined not to do so to oblige his wife; so he flatly refused, out of the mere spirit of contradiction. Many and bitter were the quarrels they had on the subject, but the more she talked, the more resolute was Tom not to be damned to please her.

Literary Analysis
Characterization
What does Mrs. Walker's reaction to Tom's news reveal about her character?

At length she determined to drive the bargain on her own account, and if she succeeded, to keep all the gain to herself. Being of the same fearless temper as her husband, she set off for the old Indian fort towards the close of a summer's day. She was many hours absent. When she came back, she was reserved and sullen in her replies. She spoke something of a black man, whom she had met about twilight, hewing at the root of a tall tree. He was sulky, however, and would not come to terms: she was to go again with a propitiatory offering, but what it was she forbore to say.

The next evening she set off again for the swamp, with her apron heavily laden. Tom waited and waited for her, but in vain; midnight came, but she did not make her appearance: morning, noon, night returned, but still she did not come. Tom now grew uneasy for her safety, especially as he found she had carried off in her apron the silver teapot and spoons, and every portable article of value. Another night elapsed, another morning came; but no wife. In a word, she was never heard of more.

What was her real fate nobody knows, in consequence of so many pretending to know. It is one of those facts which have become confounded by a variety of historians. Some asserted that she lost her way among the tangled mazes of the swamp, and sank into some pit or slough; others, more uncharitable, hinted that she had eloped with the household booty, and made off to some other province;

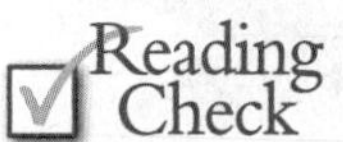

What does Tom's wife determine to do?

5. **A . . . Israel** a reference to II Samuel 3:38 in the Bible. The Puritans often called New England "Israel."

while others surmised that the tempter had decoyed her into a dismal quagmire, on the top of which her hat was found lying. In confirmation of this, it was said a great black man, with an ax on his shoulder, was seen late that very evening coming out of the swamp, carrying a bundle tied in a checked apron, with an air of surly triumph.

The most current and probable story, however, observes that Tom Walker grew so anxious about the fate of his wife and his property, that he set out at length to seek them both at the Indian fort. During a long summer's afternoon he searched about the gloomy place, but no wife was to be seen. He called her name repeatedly, but she was nowhere to be heard. The bittern alone responded to his voice, as he flew screaming by; or the bullfrog croaked dolefully from a neighboring pool. At length, it is said, just in the brown hour of twilight, when the owls began to hoot, and the bats to flit about, his attention was attracted by the clamor of carrion crows hovering about a cypress tree. He looked up, and beheld a bundle tied in a checked apron, and hanging in the branches of the tree, with a great vulture perched hard by, as if keeping watch upon it. He leaped with joy; for he recognized his wife's apron, and supposed it to contain the household valuables.

"Let us get hold of the property," said he, consolingly to himself, "and we will endeavor to do without the woman."

As he scrambled up the tree, the vulture spread its wide wings, and sailed off screaming into the deep shadows of the forest. Tom seized the checked apron, but woeful sight! found nothing but a heart and liver tied up in it!

Such, according to the most authentic old story, was all that was to be found of Tom's wife. She had probably attempted to deal with the black man as she had been accustomed to deal with her husband; but though a female scold is generally considered a match for the Devil, yet in this instance she appears to have had the worst of it. She must have died game, however; for it is said Tom noticed many prints of cloven feet deeply stamped about the tree, and found handfuls of hair, that looked as if they had been plucked from the coarse black shock of the woodsman.

▼ Critical Viewing
The narrator describes "a great vulture" and a checked apron hanging in a tree. What do you think happened to Tom Walker's wife? **[Infer]**

Tom knew his wife's prowess by experience. He shrugged his shoulders, as he looked at the signs of a fierce clapper-clawing. "Egad," said he to himself, "Old Scratch must have had a tough time of it!"

Tom consoled himself for the loss of his property, with the loss of his wife, for he was a man of fortitude. He even felt something like gratitude towards the black woodsman, who, he considered, had done him a kind-ness. He sought, therefore, to cultivate a further acquaintance with him, but for some time without success; the old blacklegs played shy, for whatever people may think, he is not always to be had for calling for: he knows how to play his cards when pretty sure of his game.

At length, it is said, when delay had whetted Tom's eagerness to the quick, and prepared him to agree to anything rather than not gain the promised treasure, he met the black man one evening in his usual woodsman's dress, with his ax on his shoulder, sauntering along the swamp, and humming a tune. He affected to receive Tom's advances with great indifference, made brief replies, and went on humming his tune.

By degrees, however, Tom brought him to business, and they began to haggle about the terms on which the former was to have the pirate's treasure. There was one condition which need not be mentioned, being generally understood in all cases where the Devil grants favors; but there were others about which, though of less importance, he was inflexibly obstinate. He insisted that the money found through his means should be employed in his service. He proposed, therefore, that Tom should employ it in the black traffic; that is to say, that he should fit out a slave ship. This, however, Tom resolutely refused: he was bad enough in all conscience, but the Devil himself could not tempt him to turn slave-trader.

Finding Tom so squeamish on this point, he did not insist upon it, but proposed, instead, that he should turn usurer; the Devil being extremely anxious for the increase of usurers, looking upon them as his peculiar[6] people.

To this no objections were made, for it was just to Tom's taste.

"You shall open a broker's shop in Boston next month," said the black man.

"I'll do it tomorrow, if you wish," said Tom Walker.

6. **peculiar** particular; special.

World LITERATURE IN CONTEXT

The Faust Legend

"The Devil and Tom Walker" is a variation of the Faust legend—a tale about a man who sells his soul to the Devil for earthly benefits. The legend was inspired by a real person, a wandering scholar and conjurer named Faust who lived in early sixteenth-century Germany. *Faustbach*, the first printed version of a Faust legend, was published in 1587. That story proposed that Faust had made a pact with the Devil for knowledge and power on Earth. Over the years, many variations of the Faust legend have appeared. Each retelling involves a person who trades his soul for experience, knowledge, or treasure. Adaptations do not share the same ending—in some, the protagonist is doomed; in others, he is redeemed.

Connect to the Literature

How do Irving's changes to the Faust story reveal the themes and issues of his era, in contrast to those of 16th century Europe?

What service does Tom refuse to provide for the Devil?

Vocabulary
extort (eks tôrt′)
v. to obtain by threat or violence

"You shall lend money at two per cent a month."

"Egad, I'll charge four!" replied Tom Walker.

"You shall extort bonds, foreclose mortgages, drive the merchant to bankruptcy—"

"I'll drive him to the D——l," cried Tom Walker.

"You are the usurer for my money!" said the blacklegs with delight. "When will you want the rhino?"[7]

"This very night."

"Done!" said the Devil.

"Done!" said Tom Walker. So they shook hands and struck a bargain.

A few days' time saw Tom Walker seated behind his desk in a countinghouse in Boston.

His reputation for a ready-moneyed man, who would lend money out for a good consideration, soon spread abroad. Everybody remembers the time of Governor Belcher,[8] when money was particularly scarce. It was a time of paper credit. The country had been deluged with government bills; the famous Land Bank[9] had been established; there had been a rage for speculating; the people had run mad with schemes for new settlements, for building cities in the wilderness; land jobbers[10] went about with maps of grants, and townships, and El Dorados,[11] lying nobody knew where, but which everybody was ready to purchase. In a word, the great speculating fever which breaks out every now and then in the country, had raged to an alarming degree, and everybody was dreaming of making sudden fortunes from nothing. As usual the fever had subsided; the dream had gone off, and the imaginary fortunes with it; the patients were left in doleful plight, and the whole country resounded with the consequent cry of "hard times."

At this propitious time of public distress did Tom Walker set up as usurer in Boston. His door was soon thronged by customers. The needy and adventurous, the gambling speculator, the dreaming land jobber, the thriftless tradesman, the merchant with cracked credit, in short, everyone driven to raise money by desperate means and desperate sacrifices, hurried to Tom Walker.

Thus Tom was the universal friend of the needy, and acted like a "friend in need"; that is to say, he always exacted good pay and good security. In proportion to the distress of the applicant was the hardness of his terms. He accumulated bonds and mortgages; gradually squeezed his customers closer and closer, and sent them

---

7. **rhino** (rī′ nō) slang term for money.
8. **Governor Belcher** Jonathan Belcher, the governor of Massachusetts Bay Colony from 1730 through 1741.
9. **Land Bank** a bank that financed transactions in real estate.
10. **land jobbers** people who bought and sold undeveloped land.
11. **El Dorados** (el′ də rä′ dōz) *n.* places that are rich in gold or opportunity. El Dorado was a legendary country in South America sought by early Spanish explorers for its gold and precious stones.

at length, dry as a sponge, from his door.

In this way he made money hand over hand, became a rich and mighty man, and exalted his cocked hat upon 'Change.[12] He built himself, as usual, a vast house, out of ostentation; but left the greater part of it unfinished and unfurnished, out of parsimony. He even set up a carriage in the fullness of his vainglory, though he nearly starved the horses which drew it; and as the ungreased wheels groaned and screeched on the axletrees, you would have thought you heard the souls of the poor debtors he was squeezing.

As Tom waxed old, however, he grew thoughtful. Having secured the good things of this world, he began to feel anxious about those of the next. He thought with regret on the bargain he had made with his black friend, and set his wits to work to cheat him out of the conditions. He became, therefore, all of a sudden, a violent churchgoer. He prayed loudly and strenuously, as if heaven were to be taken by force of lungs. Indeed, one might always tell when he had sinned most during the week, by the clamor of his Sunday devotion. The quiet Christians who had been modestly and steadfastly traveling Zionward,[13] were struck with self-reproach at seeing themselves so suddenly outstripped in their career by this new-made convert. Tom was as rigid in religious as in money matters; he was a stern supervisor and censurer of his neighbors, and seemed to think every sin entered up to their account became a credit on his own side of the page. He even talked of the expediency of reviving the persecution of Quakers and Anabaptists. In a word, Tom's zeal became as notorious as his riches.

Still, in spite of all this strenuous attention to forms, Tom had a lurking dread that the Devil, after all, would have his due. That he might not be taken unawares, therefore, it is said he always carried a small Bible in his coat pocket. He had also a great folio Bible on his countinghouse desk, and would frequently be found reading it when people called on business; on such occasions he would lay his green spectacles in the book, to mark the place, while he turned round to drive some usurious bargain.

Some say that Tom grew a little crackbrained in his old days, and that fancying his end approaching, he had his horse newly shod, saddled and bridled, and buried with his feet uppermost; because he supposed that at the last day the world would be turned upside down, in which case he should find his horse standing ready for mounting, and he was determined at the worst to give his old friend a run for it. This, however, is probably a mere old wives' fable. If he really did take such a precaution, it was totally superfluous; at least so says the authentic old legend, which closes his story in the following manner.

Vocabulary

ostentation (äs′ tən tā′ shən) *n.* boastful display

parsimony (pär′ sə mō′ nē) *n.* stinginess

Reading Strategy
Evaluate Influences of the Historical Period How do religious attitudes of the day inform Tom's feelings as he gets older?

Literary Analysis
Characterization What do you learn about Tom's character from the narrator's description of his religious zeal?

As he gets older, what does Tom always carry in his pocket?

12. 'Change exchange where bankers and merchants did business.

13. Zionward (zī′ ən wərd) toward heaven.

One hot summer afternoon in the dog days, just as a terrible black thunder-gust was coming up, Tom sat in his countinghouse in his white linen cap and India silk morning gown. He was on the point of foreclosing a mortgage, by which he would complete the ruin of an unlucky land speculator for whom he had professed the greatest friendship. The poor land jobber begged him to grant a few months' indulgence. Tom had grown testy and irritated, and refused another day.

"My family will be ruined and brought upon the parish," said the land jobber.

"Charity begins at home," replied Tom; "I must take care of myself in these hard times."

"You have made so much money out of me," said the speculator.

Tom lost his patience and his piety—"The Devil take me," said he, "if I have made a farthing!"

Just then there were three loud knocks at the street door. He stepped out to see who was there. A black man was holding a black horse, which neighed and stamped with impatience.

"Tom, you're come for," said the black fellow, gruffly. Tom shrunk back, but too late. He had left his little Bible at the bottom of his coat pocket, and his big Bible on the desk buried under the mortgage he was about to foreclose: never was sinner taken more unawares. The black man whisked him like a child into the saddle, gave the horse the lash, and away he galloped, with Tom on his back, in the midst of the thunderstorm. The clerks stuck their pens behind their ears, and stared after him from the windows. Away went Tom Walker, dashing down the streets, his white cap bobbing up and down, his morning gown fluttering in the wind, and his steed striking fire out of the pavement at every bound. When the clerks turned to look for the black man he had disappeared.

Tom Walker never returned to foreclose the mortgage. A countryman who lived on the border of the swamp, reported that in the height of the thunder-gust he had heard a great clattering of hoofs and a howling along the road, and running to the window caught sight of a figure, such as I have described, on a horse that galloped like mad across the fields, over the hills and down into the black hemlock swamp towards the old Indian fort; and that shortly after a thunderbolt falling in that direction seemed to set the whole forest in a blaze.

The good people of Boston shook their heads and shrugged their shoulders, but had been so much accustomed to witches and goblins and tricks of the Devil, in all kind of shapes from the first settlement of the colony, that they were not so much horror struck as might have been expected. Trustees were appointed to take charge of Tom's effects. There was nothing, however, to administer upon.

On searching his coffers all his bonds and mortgages were found reduced to cinders. In place of gold and silver his iron chest was filled with chips and shavings; two skeletons lay in his stable instead of his half-starved horses, and the very next day his great house took fire and was burned to the ground.

Such was the end of Tom Walker and his ill-gotten wealth. Let all griping money brokers lay this story to heart. The truth of it is not to be doubted. The very hole under the oak trees, whence he dug Kidd's money, is to be seen to this day; and the neighboring swamp and old Indian fort are often haunted in stormy nights by a figure on horseback, in morning gown and white cap, which is doubtless the troubled spirit of the usurer. In fact, the story has resolved itself into a proverb, and is the origin of that popular saying, so prevalent throughout New England, of "The Devil and Tom Walker."

Critical Reading

Cite textual evidence to support your responses.

1. **Key Ideas and Details (a)** What does the Devil offer Tom Walker? **(b) Analyze:** Why does Tom at first refuse?
2. **Key Ideas and Details (a)** What happens to Tom's wife? **(b) Interpret:** What do you learn about Tom, based on his reaction to the loss of his wife?
3. **Key Ideas and Details (a)** What agreement does Tom Walker ultimately make with the Devil? **(b) Draw Conclusions:** As the story progresses, why do you think Tom begins to go to church and carry a Bible with him at all times?
4. **Key Ideas and Details (a)** What does Tom do to cause the narrator to call him a "violent churchgoer"? **(b) Interpret:** In what way is Tom's approach to religion similar to his approach to financial dealings?
5. **Integration of Knowledge and Ideas (a) Take a Position:** Do you feel that Tom Walker deserved his fate? Explain. **(b) Defend:** Would you have felt more sympathy for Tom if he, like the original Faust, had sold his soul for knowledge instead of money? Explain.
6. **Integration of Ideas and Knowledge** Judging from the events of this story, what do you think Washington Irving might say about the effects of greed on society? In your response, use at least two of these Essential Question words: *avarice, failure, divide, charitable. [Connecting to the Essential Question: How does literature shape or reflect society?]*

After You Read *The Devil and Tom Walker*

Literary Analysis

1. **Key Ideas and Details** Identify three things you learn about Tom Walker through **direct characterization.**
2. **Key Ideas and Details (a)** Use a chart like the one shown to record dialogue, thoughts, actions, and other details that help reveal the key traits of Tom's personality. **(b)** What do these examples of **indirect characterization** show to be his chief personality traits?

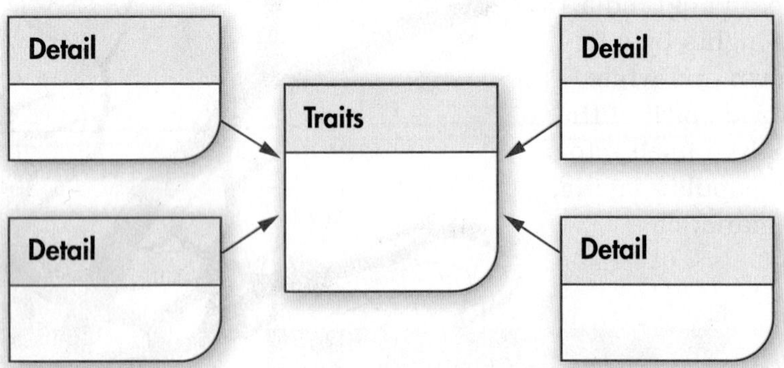

3. **Key Ideas and Details (a)** Describe Tom's wife based on the narrator's comments. **(b)** What do you learn about the relationship of Tom and his wife through indirect characterization? Explain.
4. **Key Ideas and Details (a)** What does the Walkers' home early in the story show about their personalities and values? **(b)** What does the home Tom builds later show about him?
5. **Craft and Structure** How would you describe the narrator's attitude toward Tom and his wife—for example, does he admire them? Is he amused by them? Cite details to support your answer.

Reading Strategy

6. **Evaluate the influences of the historical period on characters, plot, and settings** by identifying elements of the story that reflect an excessive concern for wealth in 1720s New England. **(a)** Note two characters who are driven by a desire for wealth. **(b)** Note at least one setting that demonstrates characters' concerns for the appearance of wealth. **(c)** Explain how the plot as a whole can be seen as an exploration of the dangers of excessive concern for wealth.
7. Does Irving effectively criticize this attitude? Cite details to support your evaluation.
8. **(a)** What does the story reveal about social attitudes toward Native Americans among New Englanders of European background in the 1720s? **(b)** Does Irving criticize these views? Cite story details to illustrate your thoughts.

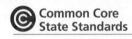

Common Core State Standards

Writing

3. Write narratives to develop real or imagined experiences or events using effective technique, well-chosen details, and well-structured event sequences. *(p. 241)*

3.d. Use precise words and phrases, telling details, and sensory language to convey a vivid picture of the experiences, events, setting, and/or characters. *(p. 241)*

Language

2.a. Observe hyphenation conventions. *(p. 241)*

PERFORMANCE TASKS

Integrated Language Skills

Vocabulary Acquisition and Use

Word Analysis: Latin Prefix *ex-*

When used without a hyphen, the Latin prefix *ex-* means "out; out of; away from." In the word *extort*, for example, it combines with the Latin root *-tort-*, meaning "twist," to form a verb meaning "to twist out of" or "to force." For each item below, form a word that combines the prefix *ex-* with the specified Latin root. You may need to make small changes to the spelling of the root. Explain the meaning of each word you form.

1. *-clam-*, "to cry; to shout"
2. *-hal-*, "to breathe"
3. *-tend-*, "to stretch"

When the prefix *ex-* is used with a hyphen, it means "former," as in ex-Governor. Write three words that correctly use the prefix *ex-* with a hyphen.

Vocabulary: Sentence Completions

Use a word from the vocabulary list on page 226 to complete each sentence, and explain your choice. Use each word only once.

1. Walking on that crumbling bridge is ______.
2. During those years of ______, politicians quarreled all the time.
3. Hurricanes in the Gulf of Mexico are ______ in summer but rare in winter.
4. The building's gold trim and ornate stone carvings were marks of ______.
5. The miser's ______ irritated his neighbors.
6. He would ______ money by threatening to harm those who would not pay.

Writing

Narrative Text Write a new version of Irving's **story,** updating it in a way that addresses a modern audience. Keep Irving's theme and the conflict of someone selling his or her soul to the devil for worldly gain.

Prewriting Use a two-column chart to plan your story. Reread Irving's tale, listing plot events, characters, and settings in the left column. Put a check next to details you want to update. Then, decide on the best way to update those details and write your ideas in the right-hand column. Finally, write down ideas for sensory details that will bring the new settings and characters to life for the reader.

Drafting Write your story using the updated details. Pay particular attention to the *concrete sensory details* you listed and take care to describe the specific actions, movements, gestures, and feelings of the characters. Consider using *interior monologue,* in which a character shares his or her thoughts with the reader but keeps them hidden from other characters.

Revising Confirm that your new version balances the original story elements with new details. Check to see that the conflict and message are the same, while the language and setting reflect today's world.

Model: Updating a Story

Tom was sitting at his computer, downloading promissory notes. Suddenly, he saw a pair of beady eyes glaring at him from the screen. Then, pixel by pixel, a strange-looking face took shape.

While maintaining the intent of the story, modern elements such as "pixel" and "computer" update the setting.

Primary Sources

Government Document
Commission of Meriwether Lewis

Field Report
Crossing the Great Divide

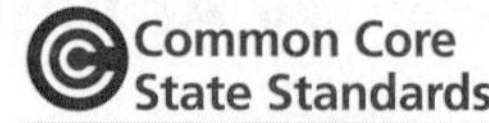

Reading Informational Text
9. Analyze nineteenth-century foundational U.S. documents of historical and literary significance for their themes, purposes, and rhetorical features.

About the Text Forms

The word *commission* has different meanings in different contexts. In a financial context, it refers to a payment based on percentages of a sale; in a legal context, it refers to the perpetration of a crime. When referring to a written work, a **commission** is a type of **government document** in which an official person or institution assigns a special task to someone. In this commission, Thomas Jefferson, then president of the United States, describes Meriwether Lewis's main goal and assigns him specific responsibilities. The language Jefferson uses reflects his position as leader of the young country, as well as an almost scientific curiosity about the vast territories acquired in the Louisiana Purchase.

A **field report** is a first hand record of observations and data written by researchers or explorers at the site of their work, or "in the field." Field reports present objective information and may also contain notes on personal thoughts. Depending on their subjects, writers of field reports may use *specialized scientific or technical language*, as well as graphs, charts, maps, or illustrations. Lewis's detailed report reflects his commitment to meeting Jefferson's expectations.

Reading Strategy

The *general purpose* of any written work may be *to inform, to entertain, to persuade, to describe*, or *to reflect*. The documents you are about to read were written to inform. However, their *specific purposes* and intended *audiences,* or readers, are different. Jefferson was sending Lewis on a mission. His commission describes the details of the task. Lewis was reporting his progress to his boss. As you read, **identify the writer's purpose** and the ways in which it shapes the text.

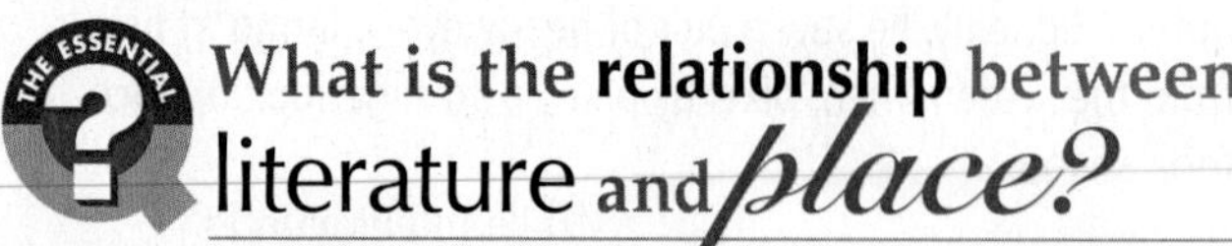

Reading these documents will help you understand how some nineteenth-century Americans felt about the vast continent they were beginning to explore. Notice details that show President Jefferson's interest in the resources provided by the new lands. Also, note details that tell you what Meriwether Lewis felt as he explored the wilderness.

Note-Taking Guide

Primary source documents are a rich source of information for researchers. As you read these documents, use a note-taking guide like the one shown to systematically organize relevant and accurate information.

1 Type of Document (check one)

☐ Newspaper ☐ Letter ☐ Map ☐ Memorandum ☐ Press release
☐ Report ☐ Government document ☐ E-mail ☐ Advertisement ☐ Other

2 Date(s) of Document ______

3 Author of Document ______

Author's Position or Title ______

4 Audience: For whom was the document written? ______

5 Purpose and Importance:

a **Why was this document written?** ______

Write down two details that support your answer: ______

______

b List two important ideas, statements, or observations from this document: ______

______

c What does this document show about life in the time and place in which it was written? ______

______

Reading Strategy
Purpose

A primary-source document may be written for more than one reason, or purpose. As you read, think about the different purposes each document may have served.

This guide was adapted from **U.S. National Archives** document-analysis worksheets.

Vocabulary

celestial (sə les′ tē əl) *adj.* of or in the sky, as planets or stars (p. 245)

practicable (prak′ ti kə bəl) *adj.* practical; possible (p. 245)

latitude (lat′ ə to͞od′) *n.* distance north or south from the equator (p. 245)

longitude (län′ jə to͞od) *n.* distance east or west on the earth's surface (p. 245)

membranes (mem′ branz′) *n.* thin, soft layers serving as coverings or linings (p. 247)

conciliatory (kən sil′ ē ə tôr′ ē) *adj.* intended to make peace or to reconcile; friendly (p. 249)

discretion (dis kre′ shən) *n.* judgment (p. 249)

dispatched (di spach′d′) *v.* sent off, usually on official business (p. 251)

prospect (pros′ spekt) *n.* something hoped for or expected (p. 251)

conspicuous (kən spik′ yo͞o əs) *adj.* obvious; easy to see or perceive (p. 252)

THE STORY BEHIND THE DOCUMENTS

President Thomas Jefferson

As the 19th century dawned, Ohio was the westward frontier of the United States, but that was not long to be. In 1803, **President Thomas Jefferson (1743–1826),** then the nation's third president, negotiated with France to buy a tract of land extending from the southern coast of Louisiana north into what is now Canada. This vast expanse included all of present-day Arkansas, Missouri, Iowa, Oklahoma, Kansas, and Nebraska. It also included parts of Minnesota, most of North and South Dakota, northeastern New Mexico, northern Texas, and portions of Colorado, Montana, and Wyoming. This enormous real-estate deal became known as **The Louisiana Purchase** and was one of the defining achievements of Thomas Jefferson's presidency. In a single treaty, Jefferson added more than 800,000 uncharted square miles to the holdings of the nation, effectively doubling the size of the country.

Jefferson had long wanted to pursue exploration of the Pacific Northwest. The completion of the Louisiana Purchase strengthened his resolve. He convinced Congress to allocate $2,500 to fund an expedition, writing:

The river Missouri, and Indians inhabiting it, are not as well known as rendered desirable by their connection with the Mississippi, and consequently with us. . . . An intelligent officer, with ten or twelve chosen men. . . might explore the whole line, even to the Western Ocean. . . .

Captain Meriwether Lewis

The "intelligent officer" he had in mind was his secretary, **Captain Meriwether Lewis (1774–1809).** On June 20, 1803, Jefferson wrote Lewis's commission to lead an expedition. He assigned Lewis the job of exploring the new territories with the particular objective of finding a water route from the Missouri River to the Pacific Ocean. Jefferson instructed Lewis to collect scientific data along the way, trace the boundaries of the Louisiana Territory, and claim the Oregon Territory for the United States. He also charged Lewis with the responsibility of recording almost every detail of his experiences.

Lewis had honed his leadership skills in the army. In preparation for the journey, he studied botany, biology, and cartography (map making). **Captain William Clark** became co-leader of the group, which numbered thirty-three people and one Newfoundland dog. Between 1804 and 1806, the team—which was known as **The Corps of Discovery**—completed an 8,000-mile trek from St. Louis to the source of the Missouri River, across the Rocky Mountains to the Pacific coast, and back to Missouri. Lewis started writing his report in May of 1804. Clark also maintained a journal in which he drew pictures of the people, plants, and animals the expedition encountered.

Commission of
MERIWETHER LEWIS

Thomas Jefferson

▲ Compass used by Lewis and Clark

To Meriwether Lewis,

Esquire, captain of the first regiment of infantry of the United States of America: Your situation as secretary of the president of the United States, has made you acquainted with the objects of my confidential message of January 18, 1803, to the legislature; you have seen the act they passed, which, though expressed in general terms, was meant to sanction those objects, and you are appointed to carry them into execution.

Instruments for ascertaining by celestial observations the geography of the country, through which you will pass, have been already provided. Light articles for barter, and presents among the Indians, arms for your attendants, say for from ten to twelve men, boats, tents, and other traveling apparatus, with ammunition, medicine, surgical instruments and provisions you will have prepared with such aids as the Secretary at War can yield in his department; and from him also you will receive authority to engage among our troops, by voluntary agreement, the number of attendants above-mentioned, over whom you, as their commanding officer, are invested with all the powers the laws give in such a case...

The object of your mission is to explore the Missouri river, and such principal streams of it, as, by its course and communication with the waters of the Pacific ocean, whether the Columbia, Oregan [*sic*], Colorado, or any other river, may offer the most direct and practicable water-communication across the continent, for the purposes of commerce.

Beginning at the mouth of the Missouri, you will take observations of latitude and longitude, at all remarkable points on the river, and especially at the mouths of rivers, at rapids, at islands, and other places and objects distinguished by such natural marks and characters, of a durable kind, as that they may with certainty be recognized hereafter. The courses of the river between these points of observation may

Vocabulary

celestial (sə les′ tē əl)
adj. of or in the sky, as planets or stars

practicable (prak′ ti kə bəl)
adj. practical; possible

latitude (lat′ə to͞od′)
n. distance north or south from the equator

longitude (län′ jə to͞od)
n. distance east or west on the earth's surface

What preparations for the journey does Jefferson instruct Lewis to make?

▲ Primary Source: Map How does this period map clarify your understanding of Jefferson's interest in the newly acquired lands? **[Connect]**

be supplied by the compass, the log-line, and by time, corrected by the observations themselves. The variations of the needle, too, in different places, should be noticed.

The interesting points of the portage between the heads of the Missouri, and of the water offering the best communication with the Pacific Ocean, should also be fixed by observation; and the course of that water to the ocean, in the same manner as that of the Missouri.

Your observations are to be taken with great pains and accuracy; to be entered distinctly and intelligibly for others as well as yourself; to comprehend all the elements necessary, with the aid of the usual tables, to fix the latitude and longitude of the places at which they were taken; and are to be rendered to the war-office, for the purpose of having the calculations made concurrently by proper persons within the United States. Several copies of these, as well as of your other notes, should be made at leisure times, and put into the care of the most trustworthy of your attendants to guard, by multiplying them against the accidental losses to which they will be exposed. A further guard would be, that one of these copies be on the cuticular membranes of the paper-birch, as less liable to injury from damp than common paper.

Vocabulary
membranes (mem′ branz′) *n.* thin, soft layers serving as coverings or linings

The commerce which may be carried on with the people inhabiting the line you will pursue, renders a knowledge of those people important. You will therefore endeavor to make your self acquainted, as far as a diligent pursuit of your journey shall admit, with the names of the nations and their numbers;

The extent and limits of their possessions;
Their relations with other tribes or nations;
Their language, traditions, monuments;
Their ordinary occupations in agriculture, fishing, hunting, war, arts, and the implements for these;
Their food, clothing, and domestic accommodations;
The diseases prevalent among them, and the remedies they use;
Moral and physical circumstances which distinguish them from the tribes we know;
Peculiarities in their laws, customs, and dispositions;
And articles of commerce they may need or furnish, and to what extent.

Captain Clark's magnet and compass ▼

And, considering the interest which every nation has in extending and strengthening the authority of reason and justice among the people around them, it will be useful to acquire what knowledge you can of the state of morality, religion, and information among them; as it may better enable those who may endeavor to civilize and instruct them, to adapt their measures to the existing notions and practices of those on whom they are to operate.

Other objects worthy of notice will be—The soil and face of the country, its growth and vegetable productions, especially those not of the United States;

The animals of the country generally, and especially those not known in the United States;
The remains and accounts of any which may be deemed rare or extinct;
The mineral productions of every kind, but more particularly metals, limestone, pitcoal, and saltpeter; salines and mineral waters, noting the temperature of the last, and such circumstances as may indicate their character;

What does Jefferson tell Lewis to look for between the heads of the Missouri River and the Pacific Ocean?

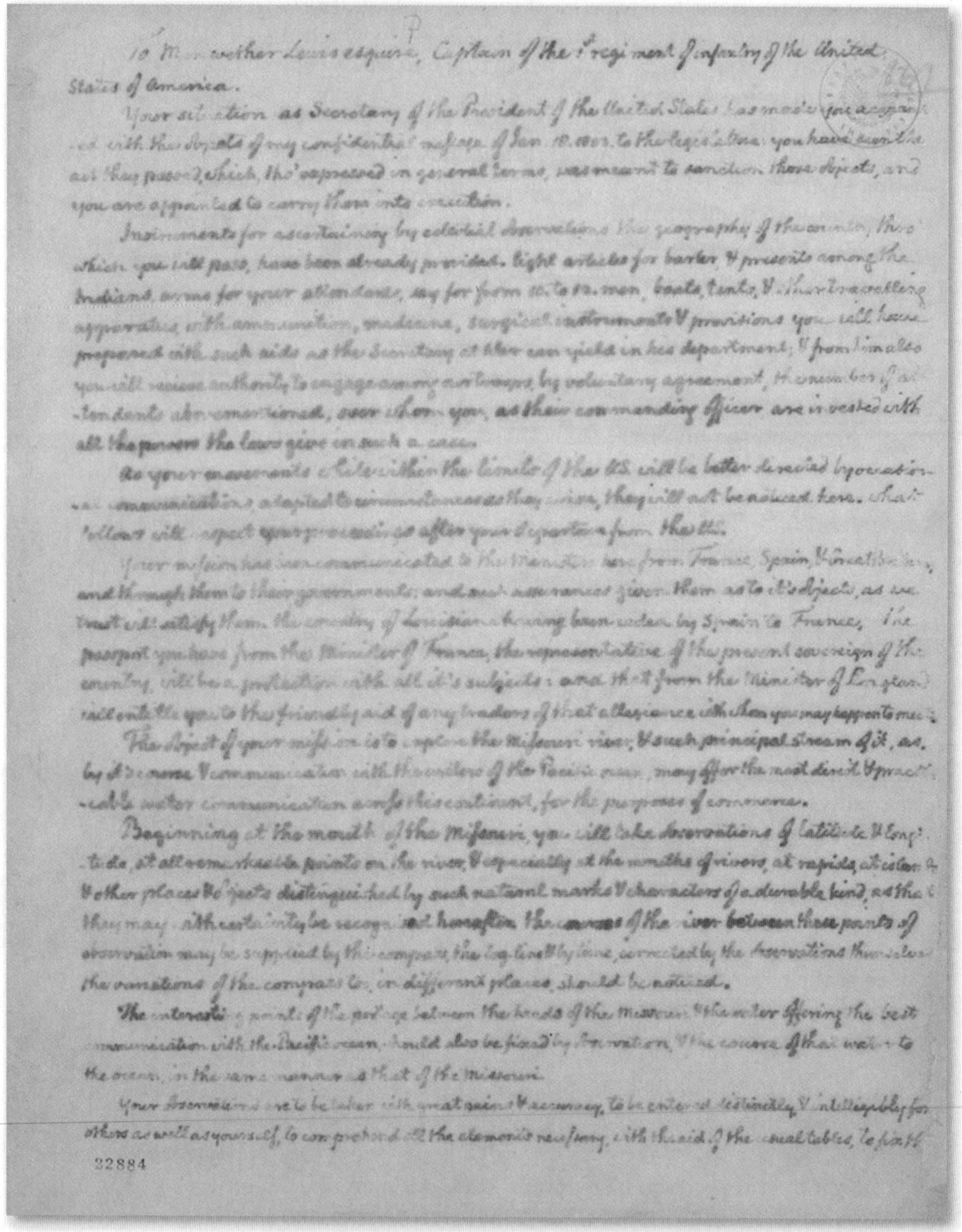

▲ Shown above is the original letter of commission President Jefferson wrote to Captain Lewis. The clarity of Jefferson's handwriting has been blurred by time.

Volcanic appearances;

Climate, as characterized by the thermo-meter, by the proportion of rainy, cloudy, and clear days; by lightning, hail, snow, ice; by the access and recess of frost; by the winds prevailing at different seasons; the dates at which particular plants put forth, or lose their flower or leaf; times of appearance of particular birds, reptiles or insects....

In all your [dealings] with the natives, treat them in the most friendly and conciliatory manner which their own conduct will admit; allay all jealousies as to the object of your journey; satisfy them of its innocence; make them acquainted with the position, extent, character, peaceable and commercial dispositions of the United States; of our wish to be neighborly, friendly, and useful to them, and of our dispositions to a commercial [relationship] with them; confer with them on the points most convenient as mutual emporiums, and the articles of most desirable interchange for them and us. If a few of their influential chiefs, within practicable distance, wish to visit us, arrange such a visit with them, and furnish them with authority to call on our officers on their entering the United States, to have them conveyed to this place at the public expense. If any of them should wish to have some of their young people brought up with us, and taught such arts as may be useful to them, we will receive, instruct, and take care of them. Such a mission, whether of influential chiefs, or of young people, would give some security to your own party. Carry with you some matter of the kine-pox; inform those of them with whom you may be of its efficacy as a preservative from the small-pox, and instruct and encourage them in the use of it. This may be especially done wherever you winter.

As it is impossible for us to foresee in what manner you will be received by those people, whether with hospitality or hostility, so is it impossible to prescribe the exact degree of perseverance with which you are to pursue your journey. We value too much the lives of citizens to offer them to probable destruction. Your numbers will be sufficient to secure you against the unauthorized opposition of individuals, or of small parties; but if a superior force, authorized, or not authorized, by a nation, should be arrayed against your further passage, and inflexibly determined to arrest it, you must decline its further pursuit and return. In the loss of yourselves we should lose also the information you will have acquired. By returning safely with that, you may enable us to renew the essay with better calculated means. To your own discretion, therefore, must be left the degree of danger you may risk, and the point at which you should decline, only saying, we wish you to err on the side of your safety, and to bring back your party safe, even if it be with less information. . . .

Vocabulary
conciliatory (kən sil′ ē ə tôr′ ē) *adj.* intended to make peace or to reconcile; friendly

Primary Sources
Commission In what ways do Jefferson's instructions to Lewis regarding the native peoples show his official interest in matters of public concern?

Vocabulary
discretion (dis kre′ shən) *n.* judgment

Crossing the GREAT DIVIDE

Meriwether Lewis

Lewis and Clark With Sacagawea at the Great Falls of the Missouri,
Olaf Seltzer, The Thomas Gilcrease Institute of Art, Tulsa, Oklahoma

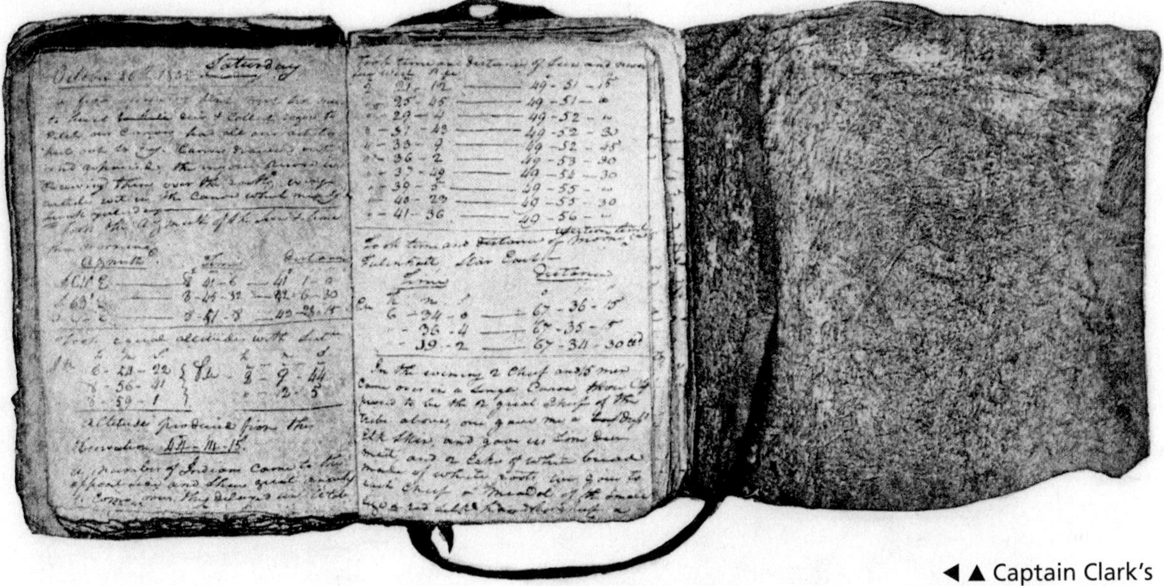

◀ ▲ Captain Clark's journal is shown here both closed (left) and open (right).

Saturday, August 17th, 1805

This morning I arose very early and **dispatched** Drewyer and the Indian down the river. Sent Shields to hunt. I made McNeal cook the remainder of our meat which afforded a slight breakfast for ourselves and the Chief. Drewyer had been gone about 2 hours when an Indian who had straggled some little distance down the river returned and reported that the white men were coming, that he had seen them just below. They all appeared transported with joy, and the chief repeated his fraternal hug. I felt quite as much gratified at this information as the Indians appeared to be. Shortly after Capt. Clark arrived with the Interpreter Charbono, and the Indian woman, who proved to be a sister of the Chief Cameahwait. The meeting of those was really affecting, particularly between Sah-ca-ga-we-ah and an Indian woman, who had been taken prisoner at the same time with her, and who had afterwards escaped from the Minnetares and rejoined her nation. At noon the canoes arrived, and we had the satisfaction once more to find ourselves all together, with a flattering **prospect** of being able to obtain as many horses shortly as would enable us to prosecute our voyage by land should that by water be deemed unadvisable.

Vocabulary
dispatched (di spach'd')
v. sent off, usually on official business

Vocabulary
prospect (pros' spekt)
n. something hoped for or expected

What information does the Indian bring to Lewis and his group?

◀ **Primary Source: Art** What does this painting of Lewis and Clark with Sacagawea suggest about the relationships among the people in it? Does Lewis's journal support the suggestion? **[Infer; Support]**

▲ **Primary Source: Art** What do the placement and size of these sketches in William Clark's journal reveal about his purpose in making them? **[Interpret]**

Reading Strategy
Identifying Writer's Purpose Which of Lewis's specific purposes for writing are evident in this paragraph?

We now formed our camp just below the junction of the forks on the Lard. side[1] in a level smooth bottom covered with a fine turf of greensward. Here we unloaded our canoes and arranged our baggage on shore; formed a canopy of one of our large sails and planted some willow brush in the ground to form a shade for the Indians to sit under while we spoke to them, which we thought it best to do this evening. Accordingly about 4 P.M. we called them together and through the medium of Labuish, Charbono and Sah-ca-ga-we-ah, we communicated to them fully the objects which had brought us into this distant part of the country, in which we took care to make them a conspicuous object of our own good wishes and the care of our government.

Vocabulary
conspicuous (kən spik′ yo͞o əs) *adj.* obvious; easy to see or perceive

1. **Lard. side** abbreviation for larboard, the port side of a ship. From their perspective, they camped on the left side of the river.

We made them sensible of their dependence on the will of our government for every species of merchandise as well for their defense and comfort; and apprised them of the strength of our government and its friendly dispositions towards them. We also gave them as a reason why we wished to penetrate the country as far as the ocean to the west of them was to examine and find out a more direct way to bring merchandise to them. That as no trade could be carried on with them before our return to our homes that it was mutually advantageous to them as well as to ourselves that they should render us such aids as they had it in their power to furnish in order to hasten our voyage and of course our return home.

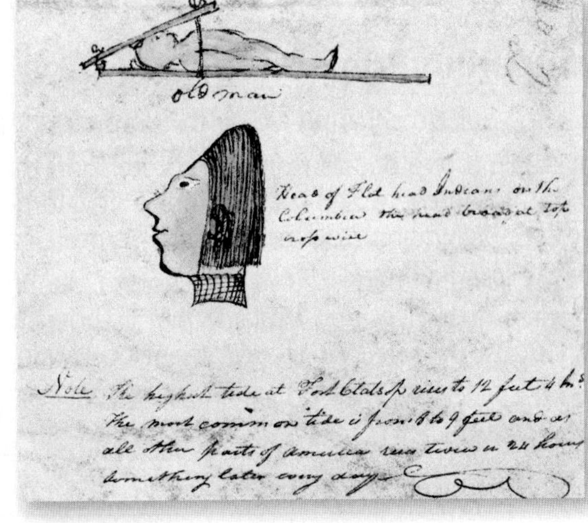
old man

▲ **Primary Source: Art**
Why do you think Clark used less detail in these sketches than in his drawings of plants and animals? **[Infer]**

Sextant used for celestial navigation by the expedition ▶

Critical Reading

Cite textual evidence to support your responses.

1. **Key Ideas and Details (a)** In the Commission, what information did Jefferson tell Lewis to write out in multiple copies? **(b)** To what office of the government was Lewis instructed to render these copies? **(c) Infer:** What do these instructions suggest about the importance of this information to Jefferson and the United States government? Explain.
2. **Key Ideas and Details (a)** In his report, how did Lewis feel about being reunited with his party? **(b) Analyze:** What are his reasons for feeling as he did?
3. **Key Ideas and Details (a)** Note two tasks that Jefferson instructed Lewis to perform. **(b) Evaluate:** Judging from this excerpt, how well do you think Lewis fulfilled his assignment?
4. **Integration of Knowledge and Ideas (a)** What did Lewis tell the Indians to expect from the United States government? **(b) Speculate:** In what ways does his dialogue with the Indians reflect specific instructions from Jefferson?

Government Document • Field Report

Comparing Primary Sources

Refer to your Note-Taking Guide to complete these questions.

1. **(a)** Find two details from the commission that show Jefferson is writing as a government official, not a private person. **(b)** In this excerpt, is Lewis writing from an official or a personal perspective? Explain.
2. **(a)** Using a chart like the one shown, identify one statement from each document and explain what it shows about life in the early 1800s. **(b)** From which document do you learn more? Explain.

Author	Statement	Life in early 1800s
Jefferson		
Lewis		

3. **(a)** Note one fact you learn from the commission about Jefferson's reasons for exploring the new lands. **(b)** Locate one statement in Lewis's report that *verifies or clarifies* that fact. Explain your choice.
4. **(a)** Identify two similarities and two differences in how these documents describe the Lewis and Clark expedition. **(b)** Explain the reasons for these similarities and differences.

Common Core State Standards

Writing

7. Conduct short as well as more sustained research projects to answer a question or solve a problem; narrow or broaden the inquiry when appropriate; synthesize multiple sources on the subject, demonstrating understanding of the subject under investigation. *(p. 255)*

8. Gather relevant information from multiple authoritative print and digital sources, using advanced searches effectively; assess the strengths and limitations of each source in terms of the task, purpose, and audience; integrate information into the text selectively to maintain the flow of ideas, avoiding plagiarism and overreliance on any one source and following a standard format for citation. *(p. 255)*

Vocabulary Acquisition and Use

Use New Words Correctly For each word pair, write a sentence in which you use both words correctly.

1. conspicuous/discretion
2. prospect/dispatched
3. conciliatory/practicable

Content-Area Vocabulary Answer each question. Then, explain your reasoning.

4. Would an astronomer or a biologist be more interested in ***celestial*** bodies?
5. Can a city change its ***latitude***?
6. Would a sailor be concerned about ***longitude***?
7. Would the outer bark of a tree be considered a ***membrane***?
8. Can a ***mineral*** be a living organism?

Etymology Study The word *celestial* comes from the Latin word *caelestis,* which means "heaven" or "sky." It often appears in opposition to the word *terrestrial.* Research the history of the word *terrestrial,* locate its root, and write a definition. Then, identify two other words that share the same root.

Research Task

Topic: The Life of Sacagawea

Sacagawea, the Shoshone woman who traveled with Lewis and Clark, was an invaluable source of help and information to the explorers. While some parts of Sacagawea's life are well documented, there is scarce and sometimes conflicting information about other periods of her life. She is, therefore, an intriguing topic for research.

Assignment: Write a biographical narrative designed as a **book for young readers** on the life of Sacagawea. As you research, differentiate between the theories about Sacagawea and the evidence that supports them. Determine the quality of the evidence you find for each theory in order to decide whether to include that information in your narrative.

Formulate a research plan. Working alone or in a group, formulate questions, such as the following, to answer through research:

- What are the basic facts of Sacagawea's life?
- What did she do on the Lewis and Clark expedition?
- What happened to her after the expedition?
- How does the popular cultural view of Sacagawea differ from the provable facts?

Gather sources. Use online and library sources to follow your research plan and find answers to your questions. Collect the information in a systematic way, grouping items about Sacagawea in categories such as "Family," "Accomplishments," and "Personal Qualities."

Synthesize information. When you synthesize information, you evaluate, assemble, and combine it in order to create a cogent argument—in this case, a reliable biography. Use a graphic organizer like the one shown to differentiate between theories about Sacagawea and the weak or strong evidence that supports them.

RESEARCH TIP

Pay careful attention to sources of online information. A Web site administered by a university or a recognized scholar is likely to be more reliable than one sponsored by a blogger, a club, a commercial company, or a popular media outlet.

Model: Differentiating Between Theories and Evidence

Theory	Evidence	Evaluation of Evidence
Sacagawea was calm and brave under pressure.	Personal diaries of members of the expedition agree.	Strong, reliable first-hand evidence from multiple sources.

Organize and present ideas. As you write, remember that you are addressing young readers. This means you may use shorter sentences and easier vocabulary and should plan to include useful visuals. However, a narrative for young readers should never be so simplified that it becomes incorrect or misleading. Make sure your facts are accurate according to the best sources. Include a Works Cited list in which you cite your sources, both print and electronic, correctly. (For more information on correct citations, see page R21 in this textbook.)

Use a checklist like the one shown to be sure your research results in a reliable biographical narrative.

Research Checklist

- ☐ Have I answered all my research questions?
- ☐ Have I differentiated between theories and evidence?
- ☐ Have I included strong evidence throughout?
- ☐ Do my visuals adequately illustrate the narrative?

Before You Read

from ***The Song of Hiawatha* • *The Tide Rises, The Tide Falls* • *Thanatopsis* • *Old Ironsides***

Connecting to the Essential Question The Fireside Poets' work helped to create a mythology of early American heroes. As you read, notice details that praise or celebrate American settings or characters. This will help as you consider the Essential Question: **What makes American literature American?**

Common Core State Standards

Reading Literature
5. Analyze how an author's choices concerning how to structure specific parts of a text contribute to its overall structure and meaning as well as its aesthetic impact.

Literary Analysis

In poetry, the systematic arrangement of stressed (´) and unstressed (˘) syllables is called **meter.** The basic unit of meter is the **foot,** which usually consists of one stressed and one or more unstressed syllables. The most frequently used foot in American verse is the *iamb*—one unstressed syllable followed by a stressed syllable. The type and number of feet in the lines of a poem determine its meter. For example, a pattern of five iambs per line is known as *iambic pentameter,* as in this line from Bryant's "Thanatopsis":

> The youth in life's green spring, and he who goes

In "The Song of Hiawatha," Longfellow uses the *trochee,* a stressed syllable followed by an unstressed syllable. This line has four trochees, a meter called *trochaic tetrameter*:

> Ye who love the haunts of Nature

Comparing Literary Works The meter of a poem can affect the **mood,** or emotional quality, it evokes in a reader. Meter can also contribute to a poem's meaning. For example, the drum-like rhythm of the trochees in "The Song of Hiawatha" reflects the Native American subject and adds to the poem's intensity. To better hear and understand these metered poems, read them aloud, listening for patterns. Identify the meter and compare the moods each helps to evoke. For each poem, consider how the meter contributes to the work's overall meaning.

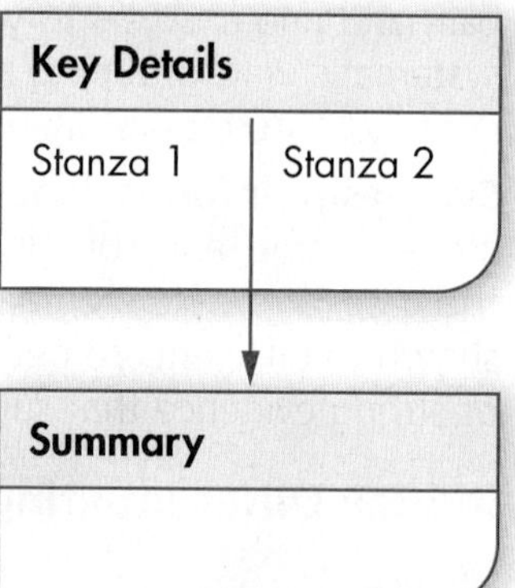

Reading Strategy

Preparing to Read Complex Texts To check your understanding of what you have read, **summarize** the work or parts of the work by briefly stating the main ideas and supporting details in your own words. As you read, use a graphic organizer like the one shown to summarize each poem.

Vocabulary

efface (ə fās′) *v.* erase, wipe out (p. 260)

eloquence (el′ ə kwəns) *n.* expressiveness (p. 262)

pensive (pen′ siv) *adj.* expressing deep thoughtfulness (p. 263)

venerable (ven′ ər ə bəl) *adj.* worthy of respect (p. 263)

Henry Wadsworth Longfellow (1807–1882)

Author of "The Song of Hiawatha"; "The Tide Rises, The Tide Falls"

Henry Wadsworth Longfellow enjoyed a long and successful career as a poet, publishing his first collection of poems, *Voices in the Night,* in 1839. By writing poetry that soothed and encouraged readers, Longfellow became the first American poet to reach a wide audience and create a national interest in poetry. His popular anthology *The Poets and Poetry of Europe,* published in 1845, accomplished his goal of bringing non-English poetry to the ordinary American reader.

Born and raised in Portland, Maine, Longfellow graduated from Bowdoin College and went on to teach modern languages at Harvard University for eighteen years, often writing and publishing his own textbooks for his classes. He also translated foreign literature into English, finding in foreign poetry inspirational models for his own work.

Longfellow experimented with adapting traditional European verse forms and themes to uniquely American subjects. Many of his narrative poems, such as "The Song of Hiawatha" (1855), "The Courtship of Miles Standish" (1858), and "Paul Revere's Ride" (1860), gave a romanticized view of America's early history and democratic ideals.

The Poet's Legacy Longfellow's poetry has been criticized for being overly optimistic and sentimental. Yet it was his optimism and sentimentality that made Longfellow the most popular poet of his day. In fact, Longfellow was so popular in his time that his seventy-fifth birthday was celebrated as if it were a national holiday.

"Talk not of wasted affection; affection never was wasted."

from *The Song of* HIAWATHA

Henry Wadsworth Longfellow

BACKGROUND "The Song of Hiawatha" is a long narrative poem based on a legend of the Ojibway, a Native American people of the Great Lakes region. Hiawatha was actually an Iroquois chief who joined with Dekanawidah (page 41) in efforts to unite the Iroquois people. In the Ojibway version, Hiawatha takes on godlike, heroic qualities. Published in 1855, Longfellow's famous poem contains over twenty sections recounting Hiawatha's adventures. The following lines are from the prologue, or introduction, to the poem.

Prologue

Should you ask me, whence these stories?
Whence these legends and traditions,
With the odours of the forest,
With the dew and damp of meadows,
With the curling smoke of wigwams,
With the rushing of great rivers,
With their frequent repetitions,
And their wild reverberations,
As of thunder in the mountains?

I should answer, I should tell you:
`From the forests and the prairies,
From the great lakes of the Northland,
From the land of the Ojibways,
From the land of the Dacotahs,[1]
From the mountains, moors, and fenlands,[2]
Where the heron, the Shuh-shuh-gah,[3]
Feeds among the reeds and rushes.
I repeat them as I heard them
From the lips of Nawadaha,
The musician, the sweet singer.'

Reading Strategy
Summarizing In two sentences, summarize the question and answer in lines 1–20.

1. **Dacotahs** *n.* a Native American people living near the Ojibway; usually spelled *Dakotas*. Minniehaha, Hiawatha's wife in Longfellow's poem, is Dacotah.
2. **moors . . . fenlands** swampy areas.
3. **Shuh-shuh-gah** Longfellow's attempt to spell the Ojibway word for the great blue heron, a large water bird.

Ye who love the haunts of Nature,
Love the sunshine of the meadow,
Love the shadow of the forest,
Love the wind among the branches,
And the rain-shower and the snowstorm,
And the rushing of great rivers
Through their palisades[4] of pine-trees,
And the thunder in the mountains,
Whose innumerable echoes
Flap like eagles in their eyries;[5]
Listen to these wild traditions,
To this Song of Hiawatha!

Ye who love a nation's legends,
Love the ballads of a people,
That like voices from afar off
Call to us to pause and listen,
Speak in tones so plain and childlike,
Scarcely can the ear distinguish
Whether they are sung or spoken;
Listen to this Indian Legend,
To this Song of Hiawatha!

---

4. **palisades** (pal′ ə sādz) *n.* stakes of a fence; used figuratively here.
5. **eyries** (ā′ ər ēz *or* ē′ rēz) *n.* high nests; often spelled *aeries*.

LITERATURE IN CONTEXT

Literary Connection

The Fireside Poets

The Fireside Poets—Henry Wadsworth Longfellow (1807–1882), Oliver Wendell Holmes (1809–1894), James Russell Lowell (1819–1891), and John Greenleaf Whittier (1807–1892)—got their nickname because their works were widely read as family entertainment at American firesides. The four poets—all New England born and bred—chose uniquely American settings and subjects but drew heavily on English tradition for their themes, meter, and imagery. Though this reliance on traditional styles prevented them from being truly innovative, the Fireside Poets were literary giants in their day and ranked for decades among America's best-loved poets.

Connect to the Literature

Fireside reading often meant oral recitation. Review the poems by the Fireside Poets (pages 258, 260, and 266) and list three qualities that make them well suited to oral recitation.

Critical Reading

1. **Key Ideas and Details (a)** According to this prologue, what are the sources of the Hiawatha legend? **(b) Analyze:** What details in lines 1–20 stress the authenticity of this retelling?
2. **Key Ideas and Details (a)** What attitude toward nature does the prologue say a reader who appreciates "The Song of Hiawatha" will have? **(b) Analyze:** What attitude toward nature does the prologue convey?
3. **Key Ideas and Details (a)** What attitude toward traditional legends and ballads is expressed in this prologue? **(b) Evaluate:** Based on this prologue, what values do you think the poem will express?

Cite textual evidence to support your responses.

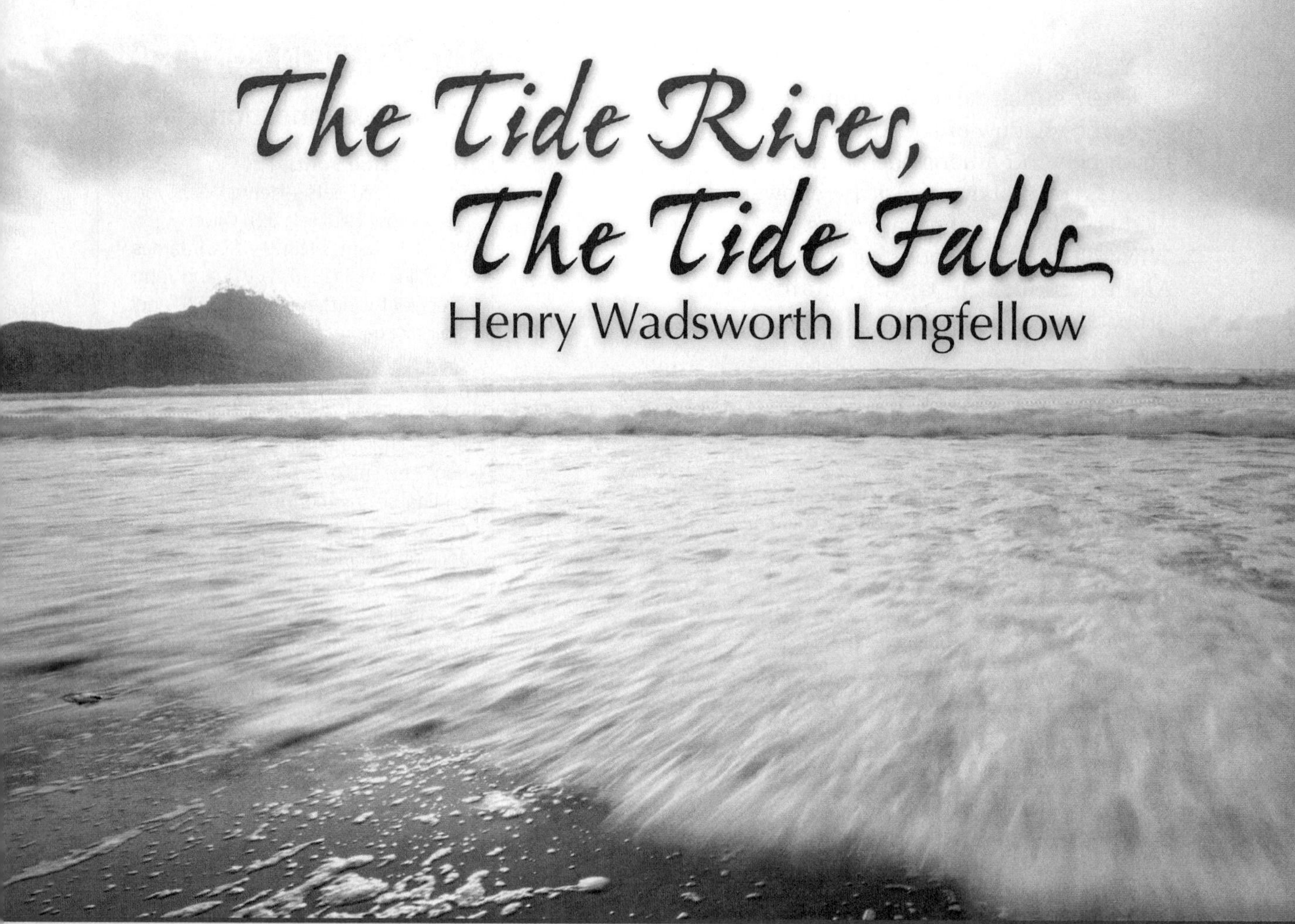

The Tide Rises, The Tide Falls

Henry Wadsworth Longfellow

Literary Analysis
Meter How does the broken meter in lines 1, 5, 10, and 15 reflect the content of those lines?

Vocabulary
efface (ə fās′) *v.* erase; wipe out

The tide rises, the tide falls.
The twilight darkens, the curlew[1] calls;
Along the sea sands damp and brown
The traveler hastens toward the town,
And the tide rises, the tide falls.

Darkness settles on roofs and walls,
But the sea, the sea in the darkness calls:
The little waves, with their soft, white hands,
Efface the footprints in the sands,
And the tide rises, the tide falls.

The morning breaks; the steeds in their stalls
Stamp and neigh, as the hostler[2] calls:
The day returns, but nevermore
Returns the traveler to the shore,
And the tide rises, the tide falls.

1. **curlew** (kʉr′ lo͞o) *n.* large wading bird associated with evening.
2. **hostler** (häs′ lər) *n.* person tending the horses at an inn or a stable.

William Cullen Bryant (1794–1878)

Author of "Thanatopsis"

As a journalist and political activist, William Cullen Bryant fought to ensure that industrialization did not obscure America's democratic values. Bryant began writing poetry at the age of nine and drafted the first version of "Thanatopsis," his most famous poem, when he was only nineteen. To support himself, Bryant practiced law for ten years while continuing to write poetry in his spare time. In 1825, he moved to New York City and became a journalist; by 1829, he had become editor-in-chief and part owner of the New York newspaper the *Evening Post.*

Voice for Justice Bryant used his position as an influential journalist to defend human rights and personal freedoms. He was an outspoken advocate of women's rights and a passionate foe of slavery. Bryant was the first American poet to win worldwide critical acclaim, and his work helped establish the Romantic Movement in America.

Romantic Influence Romanticism was an artistic and philosophical movement that stressed emotion over reason and celebrated individuality and the human imagination. Critical of science and the new industrial age, Romantic writers turned instead to nature as a source of spiritual comfort and guidance. Bryant was influenced by the work of the British Romantics William Wordsworth and Samuel Taylor Coleridge, whose 1798 publication of *Lyrical Ballads* revolutionized British poetry. After reading Wordsworth and Coleridge, Bryant incorporated aspects of romanticism into his poem "Thanatopsis."

> "To me it seems that one of the most important requisites for a great poet is a luminous style."

Thanatopsis

William Cullen Bryant

▲ Critical Viewing
What moods or emotions does this painting capture for you? Explain. **[Interpret]**

Vocabulary
eloquence (el´ ə kwəns) *n.* expressiveness

BACKGROUND The poem's title, which comes from Greek, means "a view or meditation on death." Bryant wrote his first draft of "Thanatopsis" while still a teenager, revised it often, and published his final longer version in 1821.

To him who in the love of Nature holds
Communion[1] with her visible forms, she speaks
A various language; for his gayer hours
She has a voice of gladness, and a smile
And eloquence of beauty, and she glides
Into his darker musings, with a mild
And healing sympathy, that steals away
Their sharpness, ere[2] he is aware. When thoughts
Of the last bitter hour come like a blight
Over thy spirit, and sad images
Of the stern agony, and shroud, and pall,
And breathless darkness, and the narrow house,[3]
Make thee to shudder, and grow sick at heart—
Go forth, under the open sky, and list
To Nature's teachings, while from all around—
Earth and her waters, and the depths of air—
Comes a still voice—Yet a few days, and thee

1. **Communion** (kə myo͞on´yən) *n.* the act of sharing one's thoughts; intimate conversation.
2. **ere** (er) *conj.* before.
3. **narrow house** coffin.

The all-beholding sun shall see no more
In all his course; nor yet in the cold ground,
Where thy pale form was laid, with many tears,
Nor in the embrace of ocean, shall exist
Thy image. Earth, that nourished thee, shall claim
Thy growth, to be resolved to earth again,
And, lost each human trace, surrendering up
Thine individual being, shalt thou go
To mix forever with the elements,
To be a brother to the insensible rock
And to the sluggish clod, which the rude swain
Turns with his share,[4] and treads upon. The oak
Shall send his roots abroad, and pierce thy mold.

Yet not to thine eternal resting place
Shalt thou retire alone, nor couldst thou wish
Couch[5] more magnificent. Thou shalt lie down
With patriarchs of the infant world—with kings,
The powerful of the earth—the wise, the good,
Fair forms, and hoary seers of ages past,
All in one mighty sepulcher.[6] The hills
Rock-ribbed and ancient as the sun—the vales
Stretching in **pensive** quietness between;
The **venerable** woods—rivers that move
In majesty, and the complaining brooks
That make the meadows green; and, poured round all,
Old Ocean's gray and melancholy waste—
Are but the solemn decorations all
Of the great tomb of man. The golden sun,
The planets, all the infinite host of heaven,
Are shining on the sad abodes of death,
Through the still lapse of ages. All that tread
The globe are but a handful to the tribes
That slumber in its bosom. Take the wings
Of morning,[7] pierce the Barcan[8] wilderness,
Or lose thyself in the continuous woods
Where rolls the Oregon,[9] and hears no sound,
Save his own dashings—yet the dead are there:
And millions in those solitudes, since first
The flight of years began, have laid them down
In their last sleep—the dead reign there alone.

Literary Analysis

Meter Identify two places in the first fifteen lines where the poem does not use perfect iambic pentameter.

Literary Analysis

Mood Describe the shift in mood that occurs in line 31.

Vocabulary

pensive (pen′ siv) *adj.* expressing deep thoughtfulness

venerable (ven′ ər ə bəl) *adj.* worthy of respect

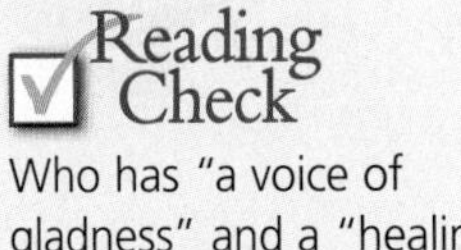

Who has "a voice of gladness" and a "healing sympathy"?

---

4. **clod, which . . . share** lump of earth, which the simple country youth turns with his plow-share.
5. **Couch** bed.
6. **sepulcher** (sep′ əl kər) *n.* tomb.
7. **Take . . . morning** a reference to Psalm 139:9.
8. **Barcan** (bär′ kən) *adj.* referring to Barca, a desert region in North Africa.
9. **Oregon** river flowing between Oregon and Washington State, now called the Columbia River.

So shalt thou rest, and what if thou withdraw
In silence from the living, and no friend
Take note of thy departure? All that breathe
Will share thy destiny. The gay will laugh
When thou art gone, the solemn brood of care
Plod on, and each one as before will chase
His favorite phantom; yet all these shall leave
Their mirth and their employments, and shall come
And make their bed with thee. As the long train
Of ages glide away, the sons of men,
The youth in life's green spring, and he who goes
In the full strength of years, matron and maid,
The speechless babe, and the gray-headed man—
Shall one by one be gathered to thy side,
By those, who in their turn shall follow them.

So live, that when thy summons comes to join
The innumerable caravan, which moves
To that mysterious realm, where each shall take
His chamber in the silent halls of death,
Thou go not, like the quarry-slave at night,
Scourged[10] to his dungeon, but, sustained and soothed
By an unfaltering trust, approach thy grave,
Like one who wraps the drapery of his couch
About him, and lies down to pleasant dreams.

Reading Strategy
Summarizing
Briefly state the poet's message in the final nine lines of the poem.

10. **Scourged** (skurjd) *v.* whipped.

Critical Reading

Cite textual evidence to support your responses.

1. **Key Ideas and Details (a) Analyze:** Which details in the second and third stanzas of "The Tide Rises…" suggest that the traveler has died? **(b) Interpret:** What does the contrast between the traveler and the waves suggest about human life?
2. **Craft and Structure (a)** What does the "still voice" in line 17 of "Thanatopsis" say will happen to the individual being? **(b) Analyze:** In what ways do the images in lines 27–30 reinforce this idea?
3. **Integrate Ideas and Knowledge (a) Connect:** Explain the connection between Bryant's poem and its title, which combines the Greek words *thanatos* ("death") and *opsis* ("view or vision"). **(b) Draw Conclusions:** What is the speaker's overall attitude toward death and the role nature plays in it?

Oliver Wendell Holmes *(1809–1894)*

Author of "Old Ironsides"

Another of the so-called Fireside Poets, Oliver Wendell Holmes penned humorous and celebratory verse with wide audience appeal. Famous for prose as well as poetry, he was also a significant figure in the world of medicine, serving as a professor of anatomy and physiology as well as dean of the Harvard Medical School and producing many important medical tracts.

A Cambridge Man A descendant of the poet Anne Bradstreet (page 75), Holmes grew up near Harvard in Cambridge, Massachusetts, where his father was a Congregationalist minister. After a brief flirtation with the law, he switched to medicine, studying at Harvard and also for two years in Paris. He obtained his medical degree in 1836, the same year he published his first collection of poetry.

A Keen Wit Whether lecturing at Harvard or rubbing elbows with Emerson, Longfellow, and other leading writers of the day, Holmes was known for his brilliant skills as a speaker. He found a way to exhibit those skills in written form in his best-known prose work, *The Autocrat of the Breakfast-Table,* a series of supposed dinner-table conversations at a fictional Boston boarding house that wittily examine a wide range of interesting topics. The popular work was serialized in *The Atlantic Monthly,* the influential magazine of art, literature, and politics that Holmes helped found with his friend and fellow Fireside Poet James Russell Lowell.

"One's mind, once stretched by a new idea, never regains its original dimensions."

Old Ironsides

Oliver Wendell Holmes

BACKGROUND The battleship *Constitution* earned its nickname of "Old Ironsides" for withstanding British attacks during the War of 1812. By 1830, having outworn its usefulness, the ship was slated for demolition. Holmes wrote this poem to protest this decision. The popular verse saved the ship and won Holmes early fame as a poet.

Ay, tear her tattered ensign[1] down!
Long has it waved on high,
And many an eye has danced to see
That banner in the sky;
Beneath it rung the battle shout,
And burst the cannons roar;—
The meteor of the ocean air
Shall sweep the clouds no more.

Her deck, once red with heroes' blood,
Where knelt the vanquished foe,
When winds were hurrying o'er the flood,
And waves were white below,
No more shall feel the victor's tread,
Or know the conquered knee;—
The harpies[2] of the shore shall pluck
The eagle of the sea!

Oh, better that her shattered hulk
Should sink beneath the wave;
Her thunders shook the mighty deep,
And there should be her grave;
Nail to the mast her holy flag.
Set every threadbare sail,
And give her to the god of storms,
The lightning and the gale!

1. **ensign** (en´ sin') *n.* the national flag displayed on a ship.
2. **harpies** (här´ pēz) *n.* a term for greedy, grasping people that comes from the name of the sharp-clawed half-bird, half-woman monsters in Greek mythology.

◀ Critical Viewing

To celebrate the 200th anniversary of her 1797 launch, the U.S.S. *Constitution* took a five-hour sail around Massachusetts Bay in 1997. The ship had not sailed in more than 116 years. Which lines from the poem still apply to "Old Ironsides" today? **[Apply]**

Literary Analysis

Meter Identify the three-syllable foot that breaks the iambic meter in line 7.

Critical Reading

1. **Key Ideas and Details (a) Infer:** Who or what are "the harpies of the shore" in line 15? **(b) Interpret:** What does the word *harpies* suggest about their motives in demolishing the ship?
2. **Key Ideas and Details (a) Draw Conclusions:** Why does the speaker think it would be better to let the ship sink? **(b) Evaluate:** Do you agree? Explain.
3. **Integration of Knowledge and Ideas** How is the subject matter of the poems in this grouping distinctly American? In your response, use at least two of these Essential Question words: *native, heroic, landscape. [Connecting to the Essential Question: What makes American literature American?]*

Cite textual evidence to support your responses.

After You Read

from *The Song of Hiawatha* • *The Tide Rises, The Tide Falls* • *Thanatopsis* • *Old Ironsides*

Literary Analysis

1. **Craft and Structure (a)** Copy the first two lines of "The Song of Hiawatha" and mark the syllables to show the **meter** (trochaic tetrameter). **(b)** What **mood** does line after line of trochaic tetrameter help establish? Explain.
2. **Craft and Structure (a)** In "Old Ironsides," which lines are in iambic tetrameter (four iambs)? **(b)** Which are in iambic trimeter (three iambs)? **(c)** The first two lines do not follow the exact metrical pattern. What effect does breaking the meter create?
3. **Craft and Structure (a)** Using a chart like the one shown, analyze the meter of two lines of poetry. **(b)** Which meter sounds the most like natural speech? Explain.

Line #	Stresses	# of feet
58 (Thanatopsis)		
9 (Old Ironsides)		

Meter

Common Core State Standards

Writing
2. Write informative texts to examine and convey complex ideas, concepts, and information clearly and accurately through the effective selection, organization, and analysis of content.

Language
5. Demonstrate understanding of word relationships.

Reading Strategy

4. **(a)** What is the main idea of the excerpt from "The Song of Hiawatha"? **(b)** What are three supporting details? **(c) Summarize** the excerpt.

PERFORMANCE TASKS
Integrated Language Skills

Vocabulary Acquisition and Use

Antonyms For each numbered word, choose the letter of its antonym, or word of opposite meaning. Then, explain your choice.

1. **venerable** **(a)** greedy **(b)** disregarded **(c)** quick **(d)** current
2. **efface** **(a)** clarify **(b)** insert **(c)** retire **(d)** loose
3. **eloquence** **(a)** slurring **(b)** persuasive **(c)** powerful **(d)** fearful
4. **pensive** **(a)** shallow **(b)** deep **(c)** curious **(d)** creative

Writing

Informative Text Choose two passages from the poems you have just read that evoke distinct moods in the reader. The passages should be between five and ten lines long. Write a **compare-and-contrast essay** in which you describe the mood evoked by each passage and discuss the *stylistic devices* the poet uses to create those moods. For example, in addition to meter, consider each poem's subject, striking images or word choices, and other aspects that you find noteworthy. Support your comparisons and contrasts with details from the passages.

Shadows of the Imagination

PART 2

Before You Read | *The Minister's Black Veil*

Connecting to the Essential Question Nathaniel Hawthorne wrote about America's Puritan past with puzzlement and shame but also with fascination. As you read this story, notice details that express specific attitudes toward Puritan New England. This will help as you consider the Essential Question: **What is the relationship between literature and place?**

Reading Literature
1. Cite strong and thorough textual evidence to support analysis of what the text says explicitly as well as inferences drawn from the text, including determining where the text leaves matters uncertain.

Literary Analysis

Hawthorne called "The Minister's Black Veil" a **parable,** or story that teaches a moral lesson. However, unlike religious parables such as those in the Bible, Hawthorne's parable teaches a lesson full of **ambiguity,** or uncertain meaning. Much of the ambiguity stems from the story's use of a symbol that is subject to different interpretations. A **symbol** is an object, setting, or even a character that has meaning as itself but also stands for something greater—often an abstract idea. The central symbol in this story is an article of clothing that the main character vows never to remove:

> ***Swathed about his forehead, and hanging down over his face ... Mr. Hooper had on a black veil.***

The veil's meaning is a mystery for both the characters in the story and the reader. As you read, look for details that will help you decide on your own interpretation of this ambiguous symbol.

Reading Strategy

Preparing to Read Complex Texts An inference is a logical guess you make about aspects of a text that are not explicitly, or directly, stated. You draw inferences by applying your own life experience to story details. To *interpret the essential meaning* of this story, **draw inferences** by noting descriptions, dialogue, and characters' actions and assessing them in view of your own understanding of human nature. As you read, use a chart like the one shown to draw inferences.

Description/Dialogue
"A sad smile gleamed faintly from beneath the black veil, . . ."

↓

Inference
The minister has suffered a loss.

Vocabulary

inanimate (in an′ ə mit) *adj.* not alive; lifeless (p. 274)

venerable (ven′ ər ə bəl) *adj.* commanding respect (p. 274)

pathos (pa′ thäs′ *or* thōs′) *n.* quality that arouses pity, sorrow, or sympathy in others (p. 275)

impertinent (im pʉr′ tə nənt) *adj.* not showing proper respect; saucy (p. 278)

obstinacy (äb′ stə nə sē) *n.* stubbornness (p. 279)

imperceptible (im′ pər sep′ tə bəl) *adj.* not easy to perceive; unnoticeable (p. 283)

Nathaniel Hawthorne

(1804–1864)

"Happiness is a butterfly, which when pursued, is always just beyond your grasp, but which, if you will sit down quietly, may alight upon you."

Author of **"The Minister's Black Veil"**

Sometimes called an "anti-Transcendentalist," Nathaniel Hawthorne admired Transcendentalists like Ralph Waldo Emerson but could not adopt their optimistic world view. Instead, as the descendant of New England Puritans who prosecuted witches and persecuted Quakers, Hawthorne was shaped by a sense of inherited guilt that gave him a darker vision. He believed that evil was a powerful force in the world, a sentiment that infuses most of his fiction.

A Shaky Start Hawthorne was born in Salem, Massachusetts, 112 years after the famous witchcraft trials in which one of his ancestors was a judge. After graduating from Bowdoin (bō′din) College in Maine, he secluded himself in his mother's home, determined to become a writer. In 1828 he published a novel, *Fanshawe,* but was so displeased with the effort that he tried to burn all the copies. Continuing to toil at his craft, he produced a story collection, *Twice-Told Tales* (1837), that won him critical regard but sold poorly.

Struggling to Earn a Living Hawthorne lived briefly at the Transcendentalist commune at Brook Farm and then at the Old Manse in Concord, Massachusetts, where he produced another story collection, *Mosses from an Old Manse* (1846). Still, to support his family, he was forced to accept a political post at the custom house back in Salem. A change of administrations lost him the job, but his stint there helped inspire his masterpiece, *The Scarlet Letter* (1850), a novel of sin and guilt among the early Puritans.

A Final Appointment When his college friend, Franklin Pierce, became president, Hawthorne was named American consul in Liverpool, England. He spent several years abroad, his travels in Italy inspiring his novel *The Marble Faun* (1860). Four years later, on a tour of New Hampshire with Franklin Pierce, Hawthorne died suddenly in his sleep.

The Minister's BLACK VEIL

A PARABLE ꩜ NATHANIEL HAWTHORNE

BACKGROUND Set in the 1600s, in a typical village of Puritan New England, this story reflects Nathaniel Hawthorne's deep awareness of his Puritan ancestry. The Puritans lived stern lives, emphasizing hard work and religious devotion. They believed that only certain people were predestined, or chosen, by God to go to heaven. This belief led them to search their souls continually for signs that God had selected them. At the same time, those who behaved unusually were often thought to be controlled by evil forces. This attitude contributed to the Salem witchcraft trials of 1692, during which at least twenty accused witches were executed. In this story, Hawthorne explores how such attitudes probably led to other, more commonplace acts of cruelty.

The sexton[1] stood in the porch of Milford meetinghouse, pulling busily at the bell rope. The old people of the village came stooping along the street. Children, with bright faces, tripped merrily beside their parents, or mimicked a graver gait, in the conscious dignity of their Sunday clothes. Spruce bachelors looked sidelong at the pretty maidens, and fancied that the Sabbath sunshine made them prettier than on weekdays. When the throng had mostly streamed into the porch, the sexton began to toll the bell, keeping his eye on the Reverend Mr. Hooper's door. The first glimpse of the clergyman's figure was the signal for the bell to cease its summons.

"But what has good Parson Hooper got upon his face?" cried the sexton in astonishment.

All within hearing immediately turned about, and beheld the semblance of Mr. Hooper, pacing slowly his meditative way towards the meetinghouse. With one accord they started, expressing more wonder than if some strange minister were coming to dust the cushions of Mr. Hooper's pulpit.

"Are you sure it is our parson?" inquired Goodman[2] Gray of the sexton.

"Of a certainty it is good Mr. Hooper," replied the sexton. "He was to have exchanged pulpits with Parson Shute, of Westbury; but Parson Shute sent to excuse himself yesterday, being to preach a funeral sermon."

1. sexton (seks′ tən) *n.* person in charge of the maintenance of a church.

2. Goodman title of respect similar to "Mister."

◀ **Critical Viewing**
How might a community react if a respected person were to wear a veil like the one shown in this illustration? **[Speculate]**

As the story begins, what weekly event is about to take place?

The cause of so much amazement may appear sufficiently slight. Mr. Hooper, a gentlemanly person, of about thirty, though still a bachelor, was dressed with due clerical neatness, as if a careful wife had starched his band, and brushed the weekly dust from his Sunday's garb. There was but one thing remarkable in his appearance. Swathed about his forehead, and hanging down over his face, so low as to be shaken by his breath, Mr. Hooper had on a black veil. On a nearer view it seemed to consist of two folds of crape,[3] which entirely concealed his features, except the mouth and chin, but probably did not intercept his sight, further than to give a darkened aspect to all living and inanimate things. With this gloomy shade before him, good Mr. Hooper walked onward, at a slow and quiet pace, stooping somewhat, and looking on the ground, as is customary with abstracted men, yet nodding kindly to those of his parishioners who still waited on the meetinghouse steps. But so wonderstruck were they that his greeting hardly met with a return.

Vocabulary
inanimate (in an′ ə mit) *adj.* not alive; lifeless

"I can't really feel as if good Mr. Hooper's face was behind that piece of crape," said the sexton.

"I don't like it," muttered an old woman, as she hobbled into the meetinghouse. "He has changed himself into something awful, only by hiding his face."

"Our parson has gone mad!" cried Goodman Gray, following him across the threshold.

"He has changed himself into something awful, only by hiding his face."

A rumor of some unaccountable phenomenon had preceded Mr. Hooper into the meetinghouse, and set all the congregation astir. Few could refrain from twisting their heads towards the door; many stood upright, and turned directly about; while several little boys clambered upon the seats, and came down again with a terrible racket. There was a general bustle, a rustling of the women's gowns and shuffling of the men's feet, greatly at variance with that hushed repose which should attend the entrance of the minister. But Mr. Hooper appeared not to notice the perturbation of his people. He entered with an almost noiseless step, bent his head mildly to the pews on each side, and bowed as he passed his oldest parishioner, a white-haired great-grandsire, who occupied an armchair in the center of the aisle. It was strange to observe how slowly this venerable man became conscious of something singular in the appearance of his pastor. He seemed not fully to partake of the prevailing wonder, till Mr. Hooper had ascended the stairs, and showed himself in the pulpit, face to face with his congregation, except for the black veil. That mysterious emblem was never once withdrawn. It shook with his measured breath, as he gave out the psalm; it threw its obscurity between him and the holy page, as he read the Scriptures; and while he prayed, the veil lay heavily on his uplifted countenance. Did he seek to hide it from the dread Being whom he was addressing?

Vocabulary
venerable (ven′ ər ə bəl) *adj.* commanding respect

Literary Analysis
Parable and Symbol
The passage beginning "That mysterious emblem" is the first suggestion that the veil is a symbol. What might the veil symbolize?

3. **crape** (krāp) *n.* piece of black cloth worn as a sign of mourning.

Such was the effect of this simple piece of crape, that more than one woman of delicate nerves was forced to leave the meetinghouse. Yet perhaps the palefaced congregation was almost as fearful a sight to the minister, as his black veil to them.

Mr. Hooper had the reputation of a good preacher, but not an energetic one: he strove to win his people heavenward by mild, persuasive influences, rather than to drive them thither by the thunders of the Word. The sermon which he now delivered was marked by the same characteristics of style and manner as the general series of his pulpit oratory. But there was something, either in the sentiment of the discourse itself, or in the imagination of the auditors, which made it greatly the most powerful effort that they had ever heard from their pastor's lips. It was tinged, rather more darkly than usual, with the gentle gloom of Mr. Hooper's temperament. The subject had reference to secret sin, and those sad mysteries which we hide from our nearest and dearest, and would fain conceal from our own consciousness, even forgetting that the Omniscient[4] can detect them. A subtle power was breathed into his words. Each member of the congregation, the most innocent girl, and the man of hardened breast, felt as if the preacher had crept upon them, behind his awful veil, and discovered their hoarded iniquity of deed or thought. Many spread their clasped hands on their bosoms. There was nothing terrible in what Mr. Hooper said, at least, no violence; and yet, with every tremor of his melancholy voice, the hearers quaked. An unsought **pathos** came hand in hand with awe. So sensible were the audience of some unwonted attribute in their minister, that they longed for a breath of wind to blow aside the veil, almost believing that a stranger's visage would be discovered, though the form, gesture, and voice were those of Mr. Hooper.

At the close of the services, the people hurried out with indecorous confusion, eager to communicate their pent-up amazement, and conscious of lighter spirits the moment they lost sight of the black veil. Some gathered in little circles, huddled closely together, with their mouths all whispering in the center; some went homeward alone, wrapt in silent meditation; some talked loudly, and profaned the Sabbath day with ostentatious laughter. A few shook their sagacious heads, intimating that they could penetrate the mystery; while one or two affirmed that there was no mystery at all, but only that Mr. Hooper's eyes were so weakened by the midnight lamp, as to require a shade. After a brief interval, forth came good Mr. Hooper also, in the rear of his flock. Turning his veiled face from one group to another, he paid due reverence to the hoary heads, saluted the middle-aged with kind dignity as their friend and spiritual guide, greeted the young with mingled authority and love, and laid his hands on the little children's heads to bless them. Such was always

Reading Strategy
Drawing Inferences
Has Mr. Hooper truly changed? What inferences can you draw based on this description of his sermon?

Vocabulary
pathos (pa´ thäs´ *or* thōs´)
n. quality that arouses pity, sorrow, or sympathy in others

What change has occurred in Mr. Hooper's appearance?

4. Omniscient (äm ni´ shənt) all-knowing God.

The
American
EXPERIENCE

Jonathan Edwards, Puritans, and Sermons of Fear

The congregation's fear of Mr. Hooper's veil recalls Jonathan Edwards, one of the greatest preachers of the colonial period. Edwards used his sermons to inspire fear of eternal damnation in the minds of his listeners. He insisted that the evidence they saw as proof of God's grace in their lives was false. According to Edwards, personal comfort, success, health, and a sense of being a good person were no proof that one was saved. Rather, these satisfactions in the earthly realm were mere distractions, providing comfort, but no substance, to the ignorant.

Though Hawthorne describes Mr. Hooper as a mild and benevolent preacher—certainly no spouter of fire-and-brimstone like Edwards—his veil inspires a similar fear and trembling among the villagers. You can read an excerpt of Jonathan Edwards's "Sinners in the Hands of an Angry God" on page 86.

Connect to the Literature

People in Hooper's congregation are taught to fear eternal damnation and to look for signs of evil in themselves and others. Why would they be inclined to fear anything that appears to be a mark of sin?

his custom on the Sabbath day. Strange and bewildered looks repaid him for his courtesy. None, as on former occasions, aspired to the honor of walking by their pastor's side. Old Squire Saunders, doubtless by an accidental lapse of memory, neglected to invite Mr. Hooper to his table, where the good clergyman had been wont to bless the food, almost every Sunday since his settlement. He returned, therefore, to the parsonage, and, at the moment of closing the door, was observed to look back upon the people, all of whom had their eyes fixed upon the minister. A sad smile gleamed faintly from beneath the black veil, and flickered about his mouth, glimmering as he disappeared.

"How strange," said a lady, "that a simple black veil, such as any woman might wear on her bonnet, should become such a terrible thing on Mr. Hooper's face!"

"Something must surely be amiss with Mr. Hooper's intellects," observed her husband, the physician of the village. "But the strangest part of the affair is the effect of this vagary, even on a sober-minded man like myself. The black veil, though it covers only our pastor's face, throws its influence over his whole person, and makes him ghostlike from head to foot. Do you not feel it so?"

"Truly do I," replied the lady; "and I would not be alone with him for the world. I wonder he is not afraid to be alone with himself!"

"Men sometimes are so," said her husband.

The afternoon service was attended with similar circumstances. At its conclusion, the bell tolled for the funeral of a young lady. The relatives and friends were assembled in the house, and the more distant acquaintances stood about the door, speaking of the good qualities of the deceased, when their talk was interrupted by the appearance of Mr. Hooper, still covered with his black veil. It was now an appropriate emblem. The clergyman stepped into the room where the corpse was laid, and bent over the coffin, to take a last farewell of his deceased parishioner. As he stooped, the veil hung straight down from his forehead, so that, if her eyelids had not been closed forever, the dead maiden might have seen his face. Could Mr. Hooper be fearful of her glance, that he so hastily caught back the black veil? A person who watched the interview between the dead and living, scrupled not to affirm, that, at the instant when the clergyman's features were disclosed,

the corpse had slightly shuddered, rustling the shroud and muslin cap, though the countenance retained the composure of death. A superstitious old woman was the only witness of this prodigy. From the coffin Mr. Hooper passed into the chamber of the mourners, and thence to the head of the staircase; to make the funeral prayer. It was a tender and heart-dissolving prayer, full of sorrow, yet so imbued with celestial hopes, that the music of a heavenly harp, swept by the fingers of the dead, seemed faintly to be heard among the saddest accents of the minister. The people trembled, though they but darkly understood him when he prayed that they, and himself, and all of mortal race, might be ready, as he trusted this young maiden had been, for the dreadful hour that should snatch the veil from their faces. The bearers went heavily forth, and the mourners followed, saddening all the street, with the dead before them, and Mr. Hooper in his black veil behind.

"Why do you look back?" said one in the procession to his partner.

"I had a fancy," replied she, "that the minister and the maiden's spirit were walking hand in hand."

"And so had I, at the same moment," said the other.

That night, the handsomest couple in Milford village were to be joined in wedlock. Though reckoned a melancholy man, Mr. Hooper had a placid cheerfulness for such occasions, which often excited a sympathetic smile where livelier merriment would have been thrown away. There was no quality of his disposition which made him more beloved than this. The company at the wedding awaited his arrival with impatience, trusting that the strange awe, which had gathered over him throughout the day, would now be dispelled. But such was not the result. When Mr. Hooper came, the first thing that their eyes rested on was the same horrible black veil, which had added deeper gloom to the funeral, and could portend nothing but evil to the wedding. Such was its immediate effect on the guests that a cloud seemed to have rolled duskily from beneath the black crape, and dimmed the light of the candles. The bridal pair stood up before the minister. But the bride's cold fingers quivered in the tremulous hand of the bridegroom, and her deathlike paleness caused a whisper that the maiden who had been buried a few hours before was come from her grave to be married. If ever another wedding were so dismal, it was that famous one where they tolled the wedding knell.[5] After performing the ceremony, Mr. Hooper raised a glass of wine to his lips, wishing happiness to the new-married couple in a strain of mild pleasantry that ought to have brightened the features of the guests, like a cheerful gleam from the hearth. At that instant, catching a glimpse of his figure in the looking glass, the black veil involved his own spirit in the horror with which it overwhelmed all others. His frame shuddered, his lips grew white, he spilt the untasted wine upon

rumors

Reading Strategy
Drawing Inferences What inferences can you draw from this dialogue about the veil's intensifying impact on the villagers?

Hooper using witchcraft?

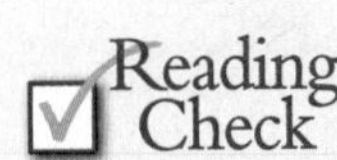

How does Mr. Hooper's veil affect the wedding party?

5. **If . . . knell** reference to Hawthorne's short story "The Wedding Knell." A knell is the slow ringing of a bell, as at a funeral.

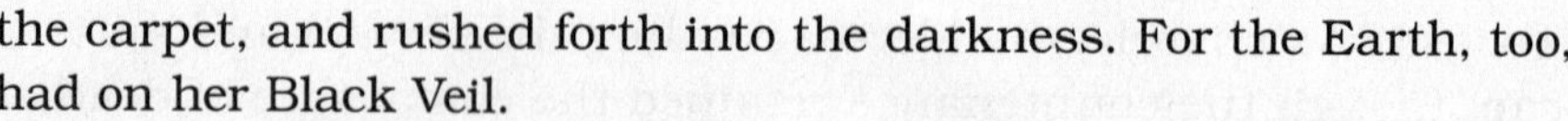

the carpet, and rushed forth into the darkness. For the Earth, too, had on her Black Veil.

The next day, the whole village of Milford talked of little else than Parson Hooper's black veil. That, and the mystery concealed behind it, supplied a topic for discussion between acquaintances meeting in the street, and good women gossiping at their open windows. It was the first item of news that the tavernkeeper told to his guests. The children babbled of it on their way to school. One imitative little imp covered his face with an old black handkerchief, thereby so affrighting his playmates that the panic seized himself, and he well nigh lost his wits by his own waggery.

Vocabulary
impertinent (im pur′ tə nənt) *adj.* not showing proper respect; saucy

It was remarkable that of all the busybodies and **impertinent** people in the parish, not one ventured to put the plain question to Mr. Hooper, wherefore he did this thing. Hitherto, whenever there appeared the slightest call for such interference, he had never lacked advisers, nor shown himself averse to be guided by their judgment. If he erred at all, it was by so painful a degree of self-distrust that even the mildest censure would lead him to consider an indifferent action as a crime. Yet, though so well acquainted with this amiable weakness, no individual among his parishioners chose to make the black veil a subject of friendly remonstrance. There was a feeling of dread, neither plainly confessed nor carefully concealed, which caused each to shift the responsibility upon another, till at length it was found expedient to send a deputation of the church, in order to deal with Mr. Hooper about the mystery, before it should grow into a scandal. Never did an embassy so ill discharge its duties. The minister received them with friendly courtesy, but became silent, after they were seated, leaving to his visitors the whole burden of introducing their important business. The topic, it might be supposed, was obvious enough. There was the black veil swathed round Mr. Hooper's forehead, and concealing every feature above his placid mouth, on which, at times, they could perceive the glimmering of a melancholy smile. But that piece of crape, to their imagination, seemed to hang down before his heart, the symbol of a fearful secret between him and them. Were the veil but cast aside, they might speak freely of it, but not till then. Thus they sat a considerable time, speechless, confused, and shrinking uneasily from Mr. Hooper's eye, which they felt to be fixed upon them with an invisible glance. Finally, the deputies returned abashed to their constituents, pronouncing the matter too weighty to be handled, except by a council of the churches, if, indeed, it might not require a general synod.[6]

But there was one person in the village unappalled by the awe with which the black veil had impressed all beside herself. When the deputies returned without an explanation, or even venturing to demand one, she, with the calm energy of her character, determined to chase away the strange cloud that appeared to be settling round Mr. Hooper,

6. **synod** (sin′ əd) *n.* high governing body in certain Christian churches.

every moment more darkly than before. As his plighted wife,[7] it should be her privilege to know what the black veil concealed. At the minister's first visit, therefore, she entered upon the subject with a direct simplicity, which made the task easier both for him and her. After he had seated himself, she fixed her eyes steadfastly upon the veil, but could discern nothing of the dreadful gloom that had so overawed the multitude: it was but a double fold of crape, hanging down from his forehead to his mouth, and slightly stirring with his breath.

"No," said she aloud, and smiling, "there is nothing terrible in this piece of crape, except that it hides a face which I am always glad to look upon. Come, good sir, let the sun shine from behind the cloud. First lay aside your black veil; then tell me why you put it on."

Mr. Hooper's smile glimmered faintly.

"There is an hour to come," said he, "when all of us shall cast aside our veils. Take it not amiss, beloved friend, if I wear this piece of crape till then."

"Your words are a mystery, too," returned the young lady. "Take away the veil from them, at least."

"Elizabeth, I will," said he, "so far as my vow may suffer me. Know, then, this veil is a type and a symbol, and I am bound to wear it ever, both in light and darkness, in solitude and before the gaze of multitudes, and as with strangers, so with my familiar friends. No mortal eye will see it withdrawn. This dismal shade must separate me from the world: even you, Elizabeth, can never come behind it!"

"What grievous affliction hath befallen you," she earnestly inquired, "that you should thus darken your eyes forever?"

"If it be a sign of mourning," replied Mr. Hooper, "I, perhaps, like most other mortals, have sorrows dark enough to be typified by a black veil."

"But what if the world will not believe that it is the type of an innocent sorrow?" urged Elizabeth. "Beloved and respected as you are, there may be whispers that you hide your face under the consciousness of secret sin. For the sake of your holy office, do away this scandal!"

The color rose into her cheeks as she intimated the nature of the rumors that were already abroad in the village. But Mr. Hooper's mildness did not forsake him. He even smiled again—that same sad smile, which always appeared like a faint glimmering of light, proceeding from the obscurity beneath the veil.

"If I hide my face for sorrow, there is cause enough," he merely replied; "and if I cover it for secret sin, what mortal might not do the same?"

And with this gentle, but unconquerable **obstinacy** did he resist all her entreaties. At length Elizabeth sat silent. For a few moments she appeared lost in thought, considering, probably, what new methods might be tried to withdraw her lover from so dark a fantasy,

7. **plighted wife** fiancée.

"There is an hour to come," said he, "when all of us shall cast aside our veils."

Reading Strategy
Drawing Inferences
In his reply to Elizabeth, what does Mr. Hooper suggest about the veil's meaning?

Vocabulary
obstinacy (äb′ stə nə sē) *n.* stubbornness

Are the villagers able to confront Mr. Hooper directly about the veil?

Winter Sunday in Norway, Maine, Unidentified artist, New York Historical Association, Cooperstown

▲ **Critical Viewing** In what ways does the atmosphere in this painting reflect the mood of the story? **[Connect]**

veil = fever until death

which, if it had no other meaning, was perhaps a symptom of mental disease. Though of a firmer character than his own, the tears rolled down her cheeks. But in an instant, as it were, a new feeling took the place of sorrow: her eyes were fixed insensibly on the black veil, when, like a sudden twilight in the air, its terrors fell around her. She arose, and stood trembling before him.

"And do you feel it then, at last?" said he mournfully.

She made no reply, but covered her eyes with her hand, and turned to leave the room. He rushed forward and caught her arm.

"Have patience with me, Elizabeth!" cried he, passionately. "Do not desert me, though this veil must be between us here on earth. Be mine, and hereafter there shall be no veil over my face, no darkness between our souls! It is but a mortal veil—it is not for eternity! O! you know not how lonely I am, and how frightened, to be alone behind my black veil. Do not leave me in this miserable obscurity forever!"

"Lift the veil but once, and look me in the face," said she.

"Never! It cannot be!" replied Mr. Hooper.

"Then farewell!" said Elizabeth.

She withdrew her arm from his grasp, and slowly departed, pausing at the door, to give one long shuddering gaze, that seemed almost to penetrate the mystery of the black veil. But, even amid his grief, Mr. Hooper smiled to think that only a material emblem had separated him from happiness, though the horrors, which it shadowed forth, must be drawn darkly between the fondest of lovers. From that time no attempts were made to remove Mr. Hooper's black veil, or, by a direct appeal, to discover the secret which it was supposed to hide. By persons who claimed a superiority to popular prejudice, it was reckoned merely an eccentric whim, such as often mingles with the sober actions of men otherwise rational, and tinges them all with its own semblance of insanity. But with the multitude, good Mr. Hooper was irreparably a bugbear.[8] He could not walk the street with any peace of mind, so conscious was he that the gentle and timid would turn aside to avoid him, and that others would make it a point of hardihood to throw themselves in his way. The impertinence of the latter class compelled him to give up his customary walk at sunset to the burial ground; for when he leaned pensively over the gate, there would always be faces behind the gravestones, peeping at his black veil. A fable went the rounds that the stare of the dead people drove him thence. It grieved him, to the very depth of his kind heart, to observe how the children fled from his approach, breaking up their merriest sports, while his melancholy figure was yet afar off. Their instinctive dread caused him to feel more strongly than aught else, that a preternatural[9] horror was interwoven with the threads of the black crape. In truth, his own antipathy to the veil was known to be so great that he never willingly passed before a mirror, nor stooped to drink at a still fountain, lest, in its peaceful bosom, he should be affrighted by himself. This was what gave plausibility to the whispers, that Mr. Hooper's conscience tortured him for some great crime too horrible to be entirely concealed, or otherwise than so obscurely intimated. Thus, from beneath the black veil, there rolled a cloud into the sunshine, an ambiguity of sin or sorrow, which enveloped the poor minister, so that love or sympathy could never reach him. It was said that ghost and fiend consorted with him there. With self-shudderings and outward terrors, he walked continually in its shadow, groping darkly within his own soul or gazing through a medium that saddened the whole world. Even the lawless wind, it was believed, respected his dreadful secret, and never blew aside the veil. But still good Mr. Hooper sadly smiled at the pale visages of the worldly throng as he passed by.

Among all its bad influences, the black veil had the one desirable effect, of making its wearer a very efficient clergyman. By the aid of his mysterious emblem—for there was no other apparent cause—he became a man of awful power over souls that were in agony for sin. His converts always regarded him with a dread peculiar to them-

8. **bugbear** *n.* something causing needless fear.
9. **preternatural** (prēt′ ər nāch′ ər əl) *adj.* supernatural.

Literary Analysis
Parable What message is conveyed by the passage beginning "But, even amid his grief,..."?

Reading Strategy
Drawing Inferences
Based on this description of the townspeople's reactions, what inferences can you draw about Mr. Hooper's happiness in life?

What one desirable effect does the veil have?

selves, affirming, though but figuratively, that, before he brought them to celestial light, they had been with him behind the black veil. Its gloom, indeed, enabled him to sympathize with all dark affections.

The Puritan, Frank E. Schoonover

▲ Critical Viewing
Does this image of a Puritan reflect Mr. Hooper's character? Explain. **[Connect]**

Dying sinners cried aloud for Mr. Hooper, and would not yield their breath till he appeared; though ever, as he stooped to whisper consolation, they shuddered at the veiled face so near their own. Such were the terrors of the black veil, even when Death had bared his visage! Strangers came long distances to attend service at his church, with the mere idle purpose of gazing at his figure, because it was forbidden them to behold his face. But many were made to quake ere they departed! Once, during Governor Belcher's[10] administration, Mr. Hooper was appointed to preach the election sermon. Covered with his black veil, he stood before the chief magistrate, the council, and the representatives, and wrought so deep an impression that the legislative measures of that year were characterized by all the gloom and piety of our earliest ancestral sway.

In this manner Mr. Hooper spent a long life, irreproachable in outward act, yet shrouded in dismal suspicions; kind and loving, though unloved, and dimly feared; a man apart from men, shunned in their health and joy, but ever summoned to their aid in mortal anguish. As years wore on, shedding their snows above his sable veil, he acquired a name throughout the New England churches, and they called him Father Hooper. Nearly all his parishioners, who were of mature age when he was settled, had been borne away by many a funeral: he had one congregation in the church, and a more crowded one in the churchyard; and having wrought so late into the evening, and done his work so well, it was now good Father Hooper's turn to rest.

Several persons were visible by the shaded candlelight, in the death chamber of the old clergyman. Natural connections[11] he had none. But there was the decorously grave, though unmoved physician, seeking only to mitigate the last pangs of the patient whom he could not save. There were the deacons, and other eminently pious members of his church. There, also, was the Reverend Mr. Clark, of Westbury, a young and zealous divine, who had ridden in haste to pray by the bedside of the expiring minister. There was the nurse, no hired handmaiden of death, but one whose calm affection had endured thus long in secrecy, in solitude, amid the chill of age, and would not perish, even at the dying hour. Who, but Elizabeth! And there lay the hoary head of good Father Hooper upon the death pillow, with the black veil still swathed

10. **Governor Belcher** Jonathan Belcher (1682–1757), the royal governor of the Massachusetts Bay Colony, from 1730 to 1741.
11. **Natural connections** relatives.

about his brow, and reaching down over his face, so that each more difficult gasp of his faint breath caused it to stir. All through life that piece of crape had hung between him and the world: it had separated him from cheerful brotherhood and woman's love, and kept him in that saddest of all prisons, his own heart; and still it lay upon his face, as if to deepen the gloom of his darksome chamber, and shade him from the sunshine of eternity.

For some time previous, his mind had been confused, wavering doubtfully between the past and the present, and hovering forward, as it were, at intervals, into the indistinctness of the world to come. There had been feverish turns, which tossed him from side to side, and wore away what little strength he had. But in his most convulsive struggles, and in the wildest vagaries of his intellect, when no other thought retained its sober influence, he still showed an awful solicitude lest the black veil should slip aside. Even if his bewildered soul could have forgotten, there was a faithful woman at his pillow, who, with averted eyes, would have covered that aged face, which she had last beheld in the comeliness of manhood. At length the death-stricken old man lay quietly in the torpor of mental and bodily exhaustion, with an **imperceptible** pulse, and breath that grew fainter and fainter, except when a long, deep, and irregular inspiration seemed to prelude the flight of his spirit.

The minister of Westbury approached the bedside.

"Venerable Father Hooper," said he, "the moment of your release is at hand. Are you ready for the lifting of the veil that shuts in time from eternity?"

Father Hooper at first replied merely by a feeble motion of his head; then, apprehensive, perhaps, that his meaning might be doubtful, he exerted himself to speak.

"Yea," said he, in faint accents, "my soul hath a patient weariness until that veil be lifted."

"And is it fitting," resumed the Reverend Mr. Clark, "that a man so given to prayer, of such a blameless example, holy in deed and thought, so far as mortal judgment may pronounce; is it fitting that a father in the church should leave a shadow on his memory, that may seem to blacken a life so pure? I pray you, my venerable brother, let not this thing be! Suffer us to be gladdened by your triumphant aspect as you go to your reward. Before the veil of eternity be lifted, let me cast aside this black veil from your face!"

And thus speaking, the Reverend Mr. Clark bent forward to reveal the mystery of so many years. But, exerting a sudden energy, that made all the beholders stand aghast, Father Hooper snatched both his hands from beneath the bedclothes, and pressed them strongly on the black veil, resolute to struggle, if the minister of Westbury would contend with a dying man.

"Never!" cried the veiled clergyman. "On earth, never!"

"Dark old man!" exclaimed the affrighted minister, "with what horrible crime upon your soul are you now passing to the judgment?"

Vocabulary
imperceptible (im′ pər sep′ tə bəl) *adj.* not easy to perceive; unnoticeable

Literary Analysis
Parable and Symbol
What does the minister of Westbury's question suggest about the veil's symbolic meaning?

On his deathbed, does Mr. Hooper wish the veil to be removed?

Father Hooper's breath heaved; it rattled in his throat; but, with a mighty effort, grasping forward with his hands, he caught hold of life, and held it back till he should speak. He even raised himself in bed; and there he sat, shivering with the arms of death around him, while the black veil hung down, awful, at that last moment, in the gathered terrors of a lifetime. And yet the faint, sad smile, so often there, now seemed to glimmer from its obscurity, and linger on Father Hooper's lips.

Spiral Review
Characterization What aspects of Mr. Hooper's character, especially his motivations, does this final speech reveal?

"Why do you tremble at me alone?" cried he, turning his veiled face round the circle of pale spectators. "Tremble also at each other! Have men avoided me, and women shown no pity, and children screamed and fled, only for my black veil? What, but the mystery which it obscurely typifies, has made this piece of crape so awful? When the friend shows his inmost heart to his friend; the lover to his best beloved; when man does not vainly shrink from the eye of his Creator, loathsomely treasuring up the secret of his sin; then deem me a monster, for the symbol beneath which I have lived, and die! I look around me, and, lo! on every visage a Black Veil!"

While his auditors shrank from one another, in mutual affright, Father Hooper fell back upon his pillow, a veiled corpse, with a faint smile lingering on the lips. Still veiled, they laid him in his coffin, and a veiled corpse they bore him to the grave. The grass of many years has sprung up and withered on that grave, the burial stone is moss-grown, and good Mr. Hooper's face is dust; but awful is still the thought that it moldered beneath the Black Veil!

Critical Reading

1. **Key Ideas and Details** **(a)** How did his congregation regard Mr. Hooper before he began wearing the veil? **(b) Analyze:** In what ways does the veil affect Mr. Hooper's relationship with his congregation?
2. **Key Ideas and Details** **(a)** What is the subject of Mr. Hooper's sermon on the day he first wears the veil? **(b) Compare and Contrast:** What emotions does Mr. Hooper evoke in his congregation that he never did before? **(c) Draw Conclusions:** To what do you attribute Mr. Hooper's newfound ability to affect his listeners?
3. **Craft and Structure** **(a)** According to the narrator, how does the "lawless wind" respond to the veil? **(b) Draw Conclusions:** Why is it significant that nature, as represented by the wind, has this reaction?
4. **Integration of Knowledge and Ideas** Does the portrait this story paints of Puritan New England seem too sympathetic, too harsh, or simply accurate? Explain. In your response, use at least two of these Essential Question words: *severe, powerful, community, struggle.* ***[Connecting to the Essential Question: What is the relationship between literature and place?]***

After You Read | *The Minister's Black Veil*

Literary Analysis

1. **Key Ideas and Details** A **parable** is a story that conveys a message. What message does this story convey? Support your answer with details from the text.
2. **Craft and Structure** **(a)** By calling this story a parable, what expectations does Hawthorne set up for the reader? **(b)** Does the story meet those expectations? Explain your response.
3. **Craft and Structure** What does Hawthorne's parable show about the way communities may treat those who are different or behave oddly? Explain your answer.
4. **Integration of Knowledge and Ideas** Hawthorne never makes clear why Mr. Hooper chooses to wear the veil. **(a)** By leaving the causes of Mr. Hooper's choice uncertain, what might he be saying about relationships among people? **(b)** Do you agree with this implicit message? Explain.
5. **Craft and Structure** Explain how the veil might be a **symbol** of each of these abstract ideas: **(a)** sin or guilt, **(b)** sorrow or mourning, **(c)** isolation, **(d)** the mystery of the self. Use a chart like the one shown to gather details from the story that support each interpretation.

Sin/Guilt	Sorrow/Mourning	Isolation	Mystery

6. **Craft and Structure** **(a)** In addition to the veil, identify at least one other possible symbol in the story. **(b)** Explain what this additional symbol might represent.
7. **Craft and Structure** Do you think Hawthorne's intentional use of **ambiguity,** or uncertain meaning, makes the story more or less effective? Explain your reasoning.

Reading Strategy

8. **(a)** From the description in the opening paragraph, **draw inferences** about the town of Milford's physical setting and its inhabitants. **(b)** How critical is the setting to the essential meaning of this story?
9. **(a)** Based on her actions in the story, what inferences can you draw about Elizabeth's personality and overall character? **(b)** Explain which of her actions lead you to draw your inferences.
10. On his deathbed, when Mr. Clark asks him to remove the black veil, Mr. Hooper replies, "On earth, never!" **(a)** What inference can you draw about when he *will* remove the veil? **(b)** What does this inference suggest about the essential meaning or significance of the veil?

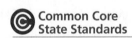

Common Core State Standards

Writing

2.b. Develop the topic thoroughly by selecting the most significant and relevant facts, concrete details, quotations, or other information and examples appropriate to the audience's knowledge of the topic. *(p. 286)*

2.c. Use appropriate and varied transitions and syntax to link the major sections of the text, create cohesion, and clarify the relationships among complex ideas and concepts. *(p. 286)*

Language

1. Demonstrate command of the conventions of standard English grammar and usage when writing or speaking. *(p. 287)*

3.a. Vary syntax for effect. *(p. 287)*

5. Demonstrate understanding of word relationships. *(p. 286)*

PERFORMANCE TASKS

Integrated Language Skills

Vocabulary Acquisition and Use

Word Analysis: Greek Root *-path-*

The word *pathos* contains the Greek root *-path-*, which means "suffering," "feeling," or "disease." Although the root appears in words related to the emotions, it is often found in *scientific and medical terminology*. Match each *-path-* word on the left with its definition on the right. Then, use each word in a sentence.

1. empathy	**(a)** caring about the feelings and suffering of others
2. pathetic	**(b)** a microorganism that causes disease
3. pathogen	**(c)** the branch of medicine that studies the nature of disease
4. pathology	**(d)** ability to experience the emotions of another person
5. sympathetic	**(e)** arousing feelings of pity in others; pitiful

Vocabulary: Word/Phrase Relationships

For each item, indicate the letter of the choice that best illustrates the phrase containing the italicized word. Explain your thinking.

1. an ***inanimate*** object: **(a)** a flower **(b)** a puppy **(c)** a rock **(d)** a dancer
2. a ***venerable*** figure: **(a)** a village elder **(b)** a criminal **(c)** an insect **(d)** a spoiled brat
3. a nearly ***imperceptible*** movement: **(a)** a twirl **(b)** a lurch **(c)** a blink **(d)** a stride
4. a play full of ***pathos:*** **(a)** a comedy **(b)** a tragedy **(c)** a fantasy **(d)** a farce
5. an ***impertinent*** act: **(a)** bowing **(b)** smiling **(c)** shaking hands **(d)** teasing
6. a creature of ***obstinacy:*** **(a)** a fickle friend **(b)** a puzzled student **(c)** a timid mouse **(d)** a stubborn mule

Writing

Explanatory Text Like Mr. Hooper's congregation, critics and general readers alike have puzzled over the uncertainties of the black veil in Hawthorne's story. Write an **interpretive essay** in which you explore the veil's significance. Explain the ambiguity that surrounds the veil, and give your own interpretation of its meaning.

Prewriting Reread the story, listing descriptions, dialogue, and character's actions relating to the veil. Review the details you listed, and look for relationships among them. Then, write a sentence in which you state your interpretation of the veil's meaning. Underline the details on your list that point to your interpretation.

Model: Using Exact Quotations

Hawthorne never tells us why Parson Hooper decides to wear the veil. We know only that the veil, which Hawthorne describes as a "gloomy shade," conceals his entire face except for his chin and mouth.

The most effective way to cite details from a literary work is to use word-for-word quotations.

Drafting Begin with a statement about the veil's ambiguity and the meaning that you give it. Then, defend your interpretation using the details you underlined as supporting evidence. *Use transitions* such as *first*, *next*, *in addition*, and *finally* to make the sequence of your examples clear.

Revising Reread your essay and make sure you have included enough passages or details from the story to support your ideas. Add additional direct quotations as needed to strengthen your work.

Conventions and Style: Adjective and Adverb Clauses

Sentence variety and flow are important elements of all good writing. Add to the fluidity of your writing by combining sentences with adjective or adverb clauses. An **adjective clause** is a subordinate clause that modifies a noun or pronoun by telling *what kind* or *which one*. An **adverb clause** is a subordinate clause that modifies a verb, adjective, adverb, or verbal by telling *where, when, in what way, to what extent, under what condition*, or *why*.

Starter Words for Types of Clauses

Adjective Clause: the relative pronouns *that, which, who, whom,* and *whose;* the relative adverbs *where, when*

Adverb Clause: the subordinating conjunctions *after, although, because, even though, so that, though, when*

Using Clauses to Combine Sentences

Choppy: The Puritans valued self-discipline. The Puritans devoted their lives to hard work.
Combined with adjective clause: The Puritans, *who valued self-discipline*, devoted their lives to hard work.

Choppy: People saw Mr. Hooper in his veil. People felt shocked.
Combined with adverb clause: People felt shocked *when they saw Mr. Hooper in his veil.*

Practice In items 1–5, identify each adjective clause or adverb clause. State what type of clause it is and tell what word or words it modifies. In items 6–10, use an adjective or adverb clause to combine the two sentences.

1. The sexton, who was the first to see Mr. Hooper, cried out in astonishment.
2. The sight that drew everyone's attention was a black veil.
3. The congregation stirred as the minister entered the church.
4. Although the villagers were curious, no one asked him about the veil.
5. As long as Mr. Hooper lived, he kept the veil on his face.
6. He would not remove the veil. His fiancée pleaded with him.
7. He would not answer Elizabeth's questions. Elizabeth left.
8. Through the veil, they could sometimes see a smile. The smile was melancholy.
9. The children were also there. The children seemed more frightened than the adults.
10. The mysterious preacher's sermon was powerful. The preacher's sermon upset his parishioners.

Writing and Speaking Conventions

A. Writing Use each subordinate clause in a sentence. Tell what word the clause modifies and what type of clause it is.

1. who had died young
2. which hid most of his face
3. after he delivered the sermon

Example: who loved him
Sentence: Elizabeth, who loved him, never understood Mr. Hooper's choice.
Word Modified: Elizabeth; **Type of Clause:** adjective

Further instruction and practice are available in *Prentice Hall Writing Coach.*

B. Speaking Write and present to the class a eulogy to be read at Father Hooper's funeral. Include at least one adjective clause and one adverb clause.

Edgar Allan Poe (1809–1849)

When Edgar Allan Poe died, Rufus Griswold, an editor and fellow writer who had an uneasy relationship with Poe, wrote a slanderous obituary that began, "Edgar Allan Poe is dead . . . . This announcement will startle many, but few will be grieved by it" (*New York Tribune*, October 9, 1849, p. 2). He went on to claim that Poe had been expelled from college, that he had neither good friends nor good qualities, and that he committed flagrant acts of plagiarism. Suspicious of this unconventional obituary, some speculated that Poe orchestrated the death notice himself to keep his name in the public eye. Yet, Poe's real life was almost as dark and dismal as the false obituary described it.

A TROUBLED CHILDHOOD Poe was born in Boston in 1809, the son of impoverished traveling actors. Shortly after Poe's birth, his father deserted the family; a year later, his mother died. Young Edgar was taken in—though never formally adopted—by the family of John Allan, a wealthy Virginia merchant. Poe lived with the Allans in England from 1815 to 1820, when they returned to the United States. It was from John Allan that Poe received his middle name. The Allans also provided for Poe's education; however, when his stepfather refused to pay Poe's large gambling debts at the University of Virginia, the young man was forced to leave the school.

BUILDING A LITERARY CAREER In 1827, after joining the army under an assumed name, Poe published his first volume of poetry, *Tamerlane and Other Poems*. Two years later, he published a second volume, *Al Aaraaf*. In 1830, John Allan helped Poe win an appointment to the United States Military Academy at West Point. Within a year, however, Poe was expelled for academic violations, and his dismissal resulted in an irreparable break with his stepfather.

STRUGGLING, WITH LITTLE REWARD During the second half of his short life, Poe pursued a literary career in New York, Richmond, Philadelphia, and Baltimore, barely supporting himself by writing and working as an editor for several magazines. After his third volume of poetry, *Poems* (1831), failed to bring him either money or acclaim, he turned from poetry to fiction and literary criticism. Five of his short stories were published in newspapers in 1832, and in 1838 he published his only novel, *The Narrative of Arthur Gordon Pym.*

AN UNHAPPY ENDING Although his short stories gained him some recognition, and his poem "The Raven" (1845) was greeted with enthusiasm, Poe could never escape from poverty. He suffered from bouts of depression and madness. His beloved wife, Virginia, seemed to be his one source of happiness. In 1846, he wrote these words to her: "[M]y little darling wife you are my greatest and only stimulus now, to battle with this uncongenial, unsatisfactory and ungrateful life...." Virginia died in 1847, at the age of 24. Some critics believe that Poe's despair over Virginia's lingering illness and death explains his fascination with doomed female characters, such as the lost Lenore of "The Raven" and the tormented Madeline Usher of "The Fall of the House of Usher." Two years after Virginia's death, Poe died in Baltimore, alone and unhappy.

A BOUNTIFUL LEGACY Since his death, Poe's work has been a magnet for attention and has influenced writers and artists of all types. His story "The Murders in the Rue Morgue" is widely accepted as the first detective story, making Poe the founder of an entire literary and theatrical genre. His psychological thrillers have been imitated by scores of modern writers, translated into nearly every language, and adapted for dozens of films. Since 1946, the Mystery Writers of America have honored their best and brightest by conferring upon them the Edgar Award for achievement in mystery writing. Today, Poe is regarded as a brilliant original whose tireless exploration of altered mental states and the dark side of human nature changed the landscape of literature, both in America and around the world.

In This Section

- Biography: Edgar Allan Poe *(p. 288)*
- Study: "The Fall of the House of Usher" by Edgar Allan Poe *(p. 292)*
- Critical Commentary: Edgar Allan Poe on writing "The Raven" *(p. 311)*
- Study: "The Raven" by Edgar Allan Poe *(p. 312)*
- Comparing Gothic Literature Past and Present *(p. 323)*
- Study: "Where Is Here?" by Joyce Carol Oates *(p. 325)*

ALL THAT WE SEE OR SEEM, IS BUT A DREAM WITHIN A DREAM.

Edgar A Poe

POE & POP CULTURE

Ever since his death in 1849, Poe's legend has grown. He has become a pop icon—a status usually reserved for movie stars or musicians. Consider this sampling of Poe's modern-day appearances:

- Poe is pictured on the Beatles' famous Sergeant Pepper album cover, and is referred to in the lyrics of "I Am the Walrus."
- Other musicians who have recorded Poe-related songs include Lou Reed, Joan Baez, Judy Collins, Iron Maiden, Good Charlotte, Public Enemy, Green Day, the Alan Parsons Project, and Japanese pop star Utada Hikaru.
- The 1990 Halloween edition of the TV show The Simpsons featured "The Raven." Poe is credited as a writer on the episode.
- Dozens of movies have been based on Poe's stories, including the famous films directed by Roger Corman.
- The Baltimore Ravens football team takes its name from Poe's famous poem.
- In the 1960s sitcom *The Munsters*, a raven often emerged from a cuckoo clock to squawk, "Nevermore, Nevermore."

Before You Read

The Fall of the House of Usher • The Raven

Connecting to the Essential Question Poe explored boundaries between reality and dreamlike states. The settings in his stories and poems are fantastic mental landscapes. As you read, find details that portray the setting as unreal or dreamlike. This will help as you think about the Essential Question: **What is the relationship between literature and place?**

Literary Analysis

This story and poem are examples of **Gothic literature,** a literary genre that began in England in the late 1700s. The word "Gothic" came from architecture, where it describes castles and cathedrals that served as the mysterious settings for early Gothic fiction. The Gothic style, which has the following elements, appealed to Edgar Allan Poe's dark view of the world:

- Bleak or remote settings
- Macabre or violent incidents
- Characters in psychological and/or physical torment
- Supernatural or otherworldly elements
- Strong language full of dangerous meanings

Poe's literary contributions extend beyond his stories. He was an important critic, who argued that a narrative should achieve a "certain unique or **single effect.**" He felt that every detail in a short story, play, or poem, should contribute to one impression. In Poe's work, the single effect is usually one of fear and a disturbing ambiguity about what is real. As you read, notice Gothic elements in both works that contribute to a single, unified effect.

Reading Strategy

Preparing to Read Complex Texts As you read, *monitor your comprehension* of Poe's complex sentences. If you are unsure of the meaning, **break down long sentences** into logical parts. First, look for a sentence's subject and verb. Then, look for clues in punctuation, conjunctions, and modifiers. Use a chart like the one shown to break Poe's intricate sentences into smaller parts.

Vocabulary

importunate (im pôr′ che nit) *adj.* insistent (p. 294)

munificent (myo͞o nif′ ə sənt) *adj.* generous (p. 296)

equivocal (i kwiv′ ə kəl) *adj.* having more than one possible interpretation (p. 296)

specious (spē′ shəs) *adj.* seeming to be but not actually sound (p. 297)

anomalous (ə näm′ ə ləs) *adj.* odd; out of the ordinary (p. 299)

sentience (sen′ shəns) *n.* capacity for feeling (p. 303)

Common Core State Standards

Reading Literature

1. Cite strong and thorough textual evidence to support analysis of what the text says explicitly as well as inferences drawn from the text, including determining where the text leaves matters uncertain.

3. Analyze the impact of the author's choices regarding how to develop and relate elements of a story.

9. Demonstrate knowledge of nineteenth-century foundational works of American literature, including how two or more texts from the same period treat similar themes or topics.

Sentence

As if . . . there had been found the potency of a spell, the huge antique panels to which the speaker pointed threw slowly back, upon the instant, their ponderous and ebony jaws.

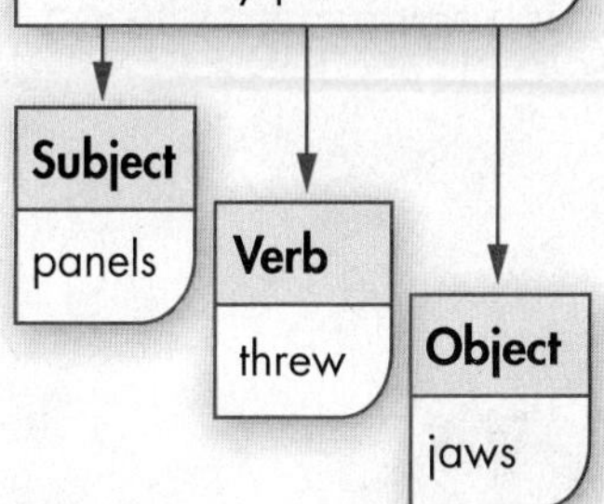

▲ **Critical Viewing**
What does this opening illustration suggest about the events that will take place in this story? **[Predict]**

THE FALL OF THE HOUSE OF USHER

EDGAR ALLAN POE

BACKGROUND In 1839, Edgar Allan Poe lived in Philadelphia and became coeditor of *Burton's Gentleman's Magazine*, a journal that published essays, fiction, reviews, and poems, as well as articles on sailing, hunting, and cricket. Poe's articles ran the gamut of topics. He explained the parallel bars, mused about the mysteries of Stonehenge, and reviewed more than eighty books on varied topics. It was in this magazine that he first published "The Fall of the House of Usher."

Son Coeur est un luth suspendu:
Sitôt qu'on le touche il résonne.[1]

During the whole of a dull, dark, and soundless day in the autumn of the year, when the clouds hung oppressively low in the heavens, I had been passing alone, on horseback, through a singularly dreary tract of country, and at length found myself, as the shades of evening drew on, within view of the melancholy House of Usher. I know not how it was—but, with the first glimpse of the building, a sense of insufferable gloom pervaded my spirit. I say insufferable; for the feeling was unrelieved by any of that half-pleasurable, because poetic, sentiment, with which the mind usually receives even the

Reading Check
What does the narrator feel at his first glimpse of the House of Usher?

1. ***Son . . . résonne*** "His heart is a lute strung tight: As soon as one touches it, it resounds." From "Le Refus" by Pierre Jean de Béranger (1780–1857).

sternest natural images of the desolate or terrible. I looked upon the scene before me—upon the mere house, and the simple landscape features of the domain—upon the bleak walls—upon the vacant eyelike windows—upon a few rank sedges[2]—and upon a few white trunks of decayed trees—with an utter depression of soul, which I can compare to no earthly sensation more properly than to the after-dream of the reveler upon opium—the bitter lapse into everyday life—the hideous dropping off of the veil. There was an iciness, a sinking, a sickening of the heart—an unredeemed dreariness of thought which no goading of the imagination could torture into aught[3] of the sublime. What was it—I paused to think—what was it that so unnerved me in the contemplation of the House of Usher? It was a mystery all insoluble; nor could I grapple with the shadowy fancies that crowded upon me as I pondered. I was forced to fall back upon the unsatisfactory conclusion, that while, beyond doubt, there are combinations of very simple natural objects which have the power of thus affecting us, still the analysis of this power lies among considerations beyond our depth. It was possible, I reflected, that a mere different arrangement of the particulars of the scene, of the details of the picture, would be sufficient to modify, or perhaps to annihilate its capacity for sorrowful impression; and, acting upon this idea, I reined my horse to the precipitous brink of a black and lurid tarn[4] that lay in unruffled luster by the dwelling, and gazed down—but with a shudder even more thrilling than before—upon the remodeled and inverted images of the gray sedge, and the ghastly tree stems, and the vacant and eyelike windows.

THERE WAS AN ICINESS, A SINKING, A SICKENING OF THE HEART.

Nevertheless, in this mansion of gloom I now proposed to myself a sojourn of some weeks. Its proprietor, Roderick Usher, had been one of my boon companions in boyhood; but many years had elapsed since our last meeting. A letter, however, had lately reached me in a distant part of the country—a letter from him—which, in its wildly **importunate** nature, had admitted of no other than a personal reply. The MS[5] gave evidence of nervous agitation. The writer spoke of acute bodily illness—of a mental disorder which oppressed him—and of an earnest desire to see me, as his best and indeed his only personal friend, with a view of attempting, by the cheerfulness of my society, some alleviation of his malady. It was the manner in which all this, and much more, was said—it was the apparent *heart* that went with his request—which allowed me no room for hesitation; and I accordingly obeyed forthwith what I still considered a very singular summons.

Although, as boys, we had been even intimate associates, yet I really knew little of my friend. His reserve had been always excessive and habitual. I was aware, however, that his very ancient family had

Vocabulary
importunate (im pôr′ che nit) *adj.* insistent

▶ **Critical Viewing**
Which details in this illustration reflect the description of the narrator's first impression of the house? **[Connect]**

2. **sedges** (sej′ iz) *n.* grasslike plants.
3. **aught** (ôt) anything.
4. **tarn** (tärn) *n.* small lake.
5. **MS.** *abbr.* manuscript.

Vocabulary
munificent
(myo͞o nif′ ə sənt)
adj. generous

Vocabulary
equivocal (i kwiv′ ə kəl)
adj. having more than one possible interpretation

Literary Analysis
Gothic Literature
How do the setting and mood of the story so far reflect Gothic literary style?

been noted, time out of mind, for a peculiar sensibility of temperament, displaying itself, through long ages, in many works of exalted art, and manifested, of late, in repeated deeds of **munificent** yet unobtrusive charity, as well as in a passionate devotion to the intricacies, perhaps even more than to the orthodox and easily recognizable beauties, of musical science. I had learned, too, the very remarkable fact, that the stem of the Usher race, all time-honored as it was, had put forth, at no period, any enduring branch: in other words, that the entire family lay in the direct line of descent, and had always, with very trifling and very temporary variations, so lain. It was this deficiency, I considered, while running over in thought the perfect keeping of the character of the premises with the accredited character of the people, and while speculating upon the possible influence which the one, in the long lapse of centuries, might have exercised upon the other—it was this deficiency, perhaps of collateral issue,[6] and the consequent undeviating transmission, from sire to son, of the patrimony[7] with the name, which had, at length, so identified the two as to merge the original title of the estate in the quaint and **equivocal** appellation of the "House of Usher"—an appellation which seemed to include, in the minds of the peasantry who used it, both the family and the family mansion.

I have said that the sole effect of my somewhat childish experiment—that of looking down within the tarn—had been to deepen the first singular impression. There can be no doubt that the consciousness of the rapid increase of my superstition—for why should I not so term it?—served mainly to accelerate the increase itself. Such, I have long known, is the paradoxical law of all sentiments having terror as a basis. And it might have been for this reason only, that, when I again uplifted my eyes to the house itself, from its image in the pool, there grew in my mind a strange fancy—a fancy so ridiculous, indeed, that I but mention it to show the vivid force of the sensations which oppressed me. I had so worked upon my imagination as really to believe that about the whole mansion and domain there hung an atmosphere peculiar to themselves and their immediate vicinity—an atmosphere which had no affinity with the air of heaven, but which had reeked up from the decayed trees, and the gray wall, and the silent tarn—a pestilent and mystic vapor, dull, sluggish, faintly discernible and leaden-hued.

Shaking off from my spirit what *must* have been a dream, I scanned more narrowly the real aspect of the building. Its principal feature seemed to be that of an excessive antiquity. The discoloration of ages had been great. Minute fungi overspread the whole exterior, hanging in a fine tangled web-work from the eaves. Yet all this was apart from any extraordinary dilapidation. No portion of the masonry had fallen; and there appeared to be a wild inconsistency between

6. **collateral** (kə lat′ ər əl) **issue** descended from the same ancestors but in a different line.
7. **patrimony** (pat′ rə mō′ nē) *n.* property inherited from one's father.

its still perfect adaptation of parts, and the crumbling condition of the individual stones. In this there was much that reminded me of the **specious** totality of old woodwork which has rotted for long years in some neglected vault, with no disturbance from the breath of the external air. Beyond this indication of extensive decay, however, the fabric gave little token of instability. Perhaps the eye of a scrutinizing observer might have discovered a barely perceptible fissure, which, extending from the roof of the building in front, made its way down the wall in a zigzag direction, until it became lost in the sullen waters of the tarn.

Noticing these things, I rode over a short causeway to the house. A servant in waiting took my horse, and I entered the Gothic[8] archway of the hall. A valet, of stealthy step, then conducted me, in silence, through many dark and intricate passages in my progress to the studio of his master. Much that I encountered on the way contributed, I know not how, to heighten the vague sentiments of which I have already spoken. While the objects around me—while the carvings of the ceilings, the somber tapestries of the walls, the ebon blackness of the floors, and the phantasmagoric[9] armorial trophies which rattled as I strode, were but matters to which, or to such as which, I had been accustomed from my infancy—while I hesitated not to acknowledge how familiar was all this—I still wondered to find how unfamiliar were the fancies which ordinary images were stirring up. On one of the staircases, I met the physician of the family. His countenance, I thought, wore a mingled expression of low cunning and perplexity. He accosted me with trepidation and passed on. The valet now threw open a door and ushered me into the presence of his master.

The room in which I found myself was very large and lofty. The windows were long, narrow, and pointed, and at so vast a distance from the black oaken floor as to be altogether inaccessible from within. Feeble gleams of encrimsoned light made their way through the trellised panes, and served to render sufficiently distinct the more prominent objects around; the eye, however, struggled in vain to reach the remoter angles of the chamber, or the recesses of the vaulted and fretted[10] ceiling. Dark draperies hung upon the walls. The general furniture was profuse, comfortless, antique, and tattered. Many books and musical instruments lay scattered about, but failed to give any vitality to the scene. I felt that I breathed an atmosphere of sorrow. An air of stern, deep, and irredeemable gloom hung over and pervaded all.

Upon my entrance, Usher arose from a sofa on which he had been lying at full length, and greeted me with a vivacious warmth which

Vocabulary

specious (spē′ shəs) *adj.* seeming to be but not actually sound

Reading Check

What flaw in the house might a careful observer find?

---

8. **Gothic** *adj.* high and ornate.
9. **phantasmagoric** (fan taz′ mə gôr′ ik) *adj.* fantastic or dreamlike.
10. **fretted** (fret′ id) *adj.* ornamented with a pattern of small, straight, intersecting bars.

had much in it, I at first thought, of an overdone cordiality—of the constrained effort of the *ennuyé*[11] man of the world. A glance, however, at his countenance convinced me of his perfect sincerity. We sat down; and for some moments, while he spoke not, I gazed upon him with a feeling half of pity, half of awe. Surely, man had never before so terribly altered, in so brief a period, as had Roderick Usher! It was with difficulty that I could bring myself to admit the identity of the wan being before me with the companion of my early boyhood. Yet the character of his face had been at all times remarkable. A cadaverousness of complexion; an eye large, liquid, and luminous beyond comparison; lips somewhat thin and very pallid, but of a surpassingly beautiful curve; a nose of a delicate Hebrew model, but with a breadth of nostril unusual in similar formations; a finely molded chin, speaking, in its want of prominence, of a want of moral energy; hair of a more than weblike softness and tenuity—these features, with an inordinate expansion above the regions of the temple, made up altogether a countenance not easily to be forgotten. And now in the mere exaggeration of the prevailing character of these features, and of the expression they were wont to convey, lay so much of change that I doubted to whom I spoke. The now ghastly pallor of the skin, and the now miraculous luster of the eye, above all things startled and even awed me. The silken hair, too, had been suffered to grow all unheeded, and as, in its wild gossamer texture, it floated rather than fell about the face, I could not, even with effort, connect its Arabesque[12] expression with any idea of simple humanity.

Reading Strategy
Breaking Down Long Sentences In your own words, restate the meaning of the sentence beginning "The silken hair. . ."

In the manner of my friend I was at once struck with an incoherence—an inconsistency; and I soon found this to arise from a series of feeble and futile struggles to overcome an habitual trepidancy—an excessive nervous agitation. For something of this nature I had indeed been prepared, no less by his letter than by reminiscences of certain boyish traits, and by conclusions deduced from his peculiar physical conformation and temperament. His action was alternately vivacious and sullen. His voice varied rapidly from a tremulous indecision (when the animal spirits seemed utterly in abeyance) to that species of energetic concision—that abrupt, weighty, unhurried, and hollow-sounding enunciation—that leaden, self-balanced, and perfectly modulated guttural utterance, which may be observed

11. ***ennuyé*** (än′ wē ā′) *adj.* bored (French).
12. **Arabesque** (ar′ ə besk′) *adj.* of complex and elaborate design.

in the lost drunkard, or the irreclaimable eater of opium, during the periods of his most intense excitement.

It was thus that he spoke of the object of my visit, of his earnest desire to see me, and of the solace he expected me to afford him. He entered, at some length, into what he conceived to be the nature of his malady. It was, he said, a constitutional and a family evil and one for which he despaired to find a remedy—a mere nervous affection,[13] he immediately added, which would undoubtedly soon pass off. It displayed itself in a host of unnatural sensations. Some of these, as he detailed them, interested and bewildered me; although, perhaps, the terms and the general manner of their narration had their weight. He suffered much from a morbid acuteness of the senses; the most insipid food was alone endurable; he could wear only garments of certain texture; the odors of all flowers were oppressive; his eyes were tortured by even a faint light; and there were but peculiar sounds, and these from stringed instruments, which did not inspire him with horror.

To an **anomalous** species of terror I found him a bounden slave. "I shall perish," said he, "I *must* perish in this deplorable folly. Thus, thus, and not otherwise, shall I be lost. I dread the events of the future, not in themselves, but in their results. I shudder at the thought of any, even the most trivial, incident, which may operate upon this intolerable agitation of soul. I have, indeed, no abhorrence of danger, except in its absolute effect—in terror. In this unnerved, in this pitiable, condition I feel that the period will sooner or later arrive when I must abandon life and reason together, in some struggle with the grim phantasm, FEAR."

I learned, moreover, at intervals, and through broken and equivocal hints, another singular feature of his mental condition. He was enchained by certain superstitious impressions in regard to the dwelling which he tenanted, and whence, for many years, he had never ventured forth—in regard to an influence whose supposititious[14] force was conveyed in terms too shadowy here to be restated—an influence which some peculiarities in the mere form and substance of his family mansion had, by dint of long sufferance, he said, obtained over his spirit—an effect which the physique of the gray walls and turrets, and of the dim tarn into which they all looked down, had at length, brought about upon the morale of his existence.

He admitted, however, although with hesitation, that much of the peculiar gloom which thus afflicted him could be traced to a more natural and far more palpable origin—to the severe and long-continued illness—indeed to the evidently approaching dissolution—of a tenderly beloved sister, his sole companion for long years, his last and only relative on earth. "Her decease," he said, with a bitterness

13. affection affliction.
14. supposititious (sə päz′ ə tish′ əs) *adj.* supposed.

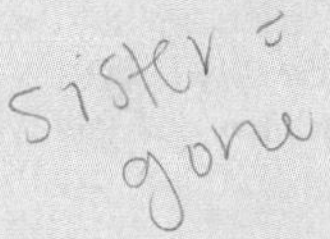

Literary Analysis
Gothic Literature
In what ways do Usher's mental state and the house itself typify a work of Gothic literature?

Vocabulary
anomalous (ə näm′ ə ləs) *adj.* odd; out of the ordinary

In what ways has Roderick Usher changed since the narrator last saw him?

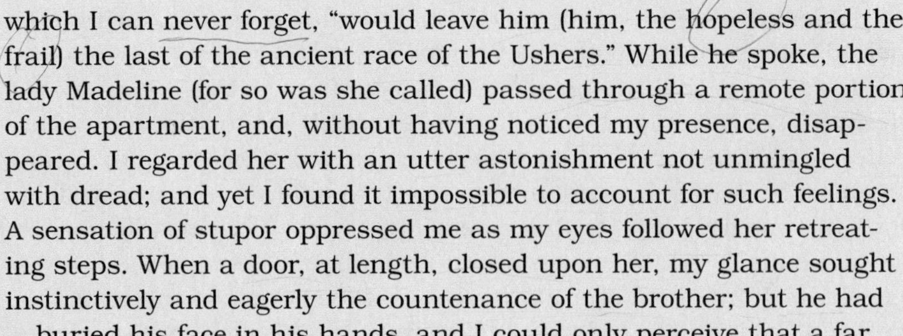

which I can never forget, "would leave him (him, the hopeless and the frail) the last of the ancient race of the Ushers." While he spoke, the lady Madeline (for so was she called) passed through a remote portion of the apartment, and, without having noticed my presence, disappeared. I regarded her with an utter astonishment not unmingled with dread; and yet I found it impossible to account for such feelings. A sensation of stupor oppressed me as my eyes followed her retreating steps. When a door, at length, closed upon her, my glance sought instinctively and eagerly the countenance of the brother; but he had buried his face in his hands, and I could only perceive that a far more than ordinary wanness had overspread the emaciated fingers through which trickled many passionate tears.

The disease of the lady Madeline had long baffled the skill of her physicians. A settled apathy, a gradual wasting away of the person, and frequent although transient affections of a partially cataleptical[15] character were the unusual diagnosis. Hitherto she had steadily borne up against the pressure of her malady, and had not betaken herself finally to bed; but on the closing in of the evening of my arrival at the house, she succumbed (as her brother told me at night with inexpressible agitation) to the prostrating power of the destroyer; and I learned that the glimpse I had obtained of her person would thus probably be the last I should obtain—that the lady, at least while living, would be seen by me no more.

For several days ensuing, her name was unmentioned by either Usher or myself; and during this period I was busied in earnest endeavors to alleviate the melancholy of my friend. We painted and read together, or I listened, as if in a dream, to the wild improvisations of his speaking guitar. And thus, as a closer and still closer intimacy admitted me more unreservedly into the recesses of his spirit, the more bitterly did I perceive the futility of all attempt at cheering a mind from which darkness, as if an inherent positive quality, poured forth upon all objects of the moral and physical universe in one unceasing radiation of gloom.

I shall ever bear about me a memory of the many solemn hours I thus spent alone with the master of the House of Usher. Yet I should fail in any attempt to convey an idea of the exact character of the studies, or of the occupations, in which he involved me, or led me the way. An excited and highly distempered ideality[16] threw a sulfureous[17] luster over all. His long improvised dirges will ring forever in my ears. Among other things, I hold painfully in mind a certain singular perversion and amplification

---

15. cataleptical (kat′ əl ep′ tik əl) *adj.* in a state in which consciousness and feeling are suddenly and temporarily lost and the muscles become rigid.
16. ideality (ī dē al′ i tē) *n.* something that is ideal and has no reality.
17. sulfureous (sul fyo͞or′ ē əs) *adj.* greenish-yellow.

of the wild air of the last waltz of von Weber.[18] From the paintings over which his elaborate fancy brooded, and which grew, touch by touch, into vaguenesses at which I shuddered the more thrillingly, because I shuddered knowing not why—from these paintings (vivid as their images now are before me) I would in vain endeavor to educe more than a small portion which should lie within the compass of merely written words. By the utter simplicity, by the nakedness of his designs, he arrested and overawed attention. If ever mortal painted an idea, that mortal was Roderick Usher. For me at least, in the circumstances then surrounding me, there arose out of the pure abstractions which the hypochondriac contrived to throw upon his canvas, an intensity of intolerable awe, no shadow of which felt I ever yet in the contemplation of the certainly glowing yet too concrete reveries of Fuseli.[19]

◀ Critical Viewing
Which of the qualities described by the narrator are captured in this illustration of Madeline Usher? **[Interpret]**

One of the phantasmagoric conceptions of my friend, partaking not so rigidly of the spirit of abstraction, may be shadowed forth, although feebly, in words. A small picture presented the interior of an immensely long and rectangular vault or tunnel, with low walls, smooth, white and without interruption or device. Certain accessory points of the design served well to convey the idea that this excavation lay at an exceeding depth below the surface of the earth. No outlet was observed in any portion of its vast extent, and no torch or other artificial source of light was discernible; yet a flood of intense rays rolled throughout, and bathed the whole in a ghastly and inappropriate splendor.

Literary Analysis
Gothic Literature and Single Effect What effect does this description of Usher's artwork help to create? Explain.

I have just spoken of that morbid condition of the auditory nerve which rendered all music intolerable to the sufferer, with the exception of certain effects of stringed instruments. It was, perhaps, the narrow limits to which he thus confined himself upon the guitar which gave birth, in great measure, to the fantastic character of his performances. But the fervid facility of his impromptus could not be so accounted for. They must have been, and were, in the notes, as well as in the words of his wild fantasias (for he not unfrequently accompanied himself with rhymed verbal improvisations), the result of that intense mental collectedness and concentration to which I have previously alluded as observable only in particular moments of the highest artificial excitement. The words of one of these rhapsodies I have easily remembered. I was, perhaps, the more forcibly impressed with it as he gave it because, in the under or mystic current of its meaning, I fancied that I perceived, and for the first time, a full consciousness on the part of Usher of the tottering of his lofty reason upon her throne. The verses, which were entitled "The Haunted Palace," ran very nearly, if not accurately, thus:

What conclusion does the narrator draw about Usher's mental state?

---

18. **von Weber** (fôn vā´ bər) Karl Maria von Weber (1786–1826), a German Romantic composer whose music was highly emotional and dramatic.
19. **Fuseli** (fo͞o ze´ lē) Johann Heinrich Fuseli (1741–1825), also known as Henry Fuseli, Swiss-born painter who lived in England and was noted for his depictions of dreamlike and sometimes nightmarish images.

I

In the greenest of our valleys,
By good angels tenanted,
Once a fair and stately palace—
Radiant palace—reared its head.
In the monarch Thought's dominion—
It stood there!
Never seraph[20] *spread a pinion*
Over fabric half so fair.

II

Banners yellow, glorious, golden,
On its roof did float and flow
(This—all this—was in the olden
Time long ago)
And every gentle air that dallied,
In that sweet day,
Along the ramparts plumed and pallid,
A winged odor went away.

III

Wanderers in that happy valley
Through two luminous windows saw
Spirits moving musically
To a lute's well-tunéd law;
Round about a throne, where sitting
(Porphyrogene!)[21]
In state his glory well befitting,
The ruler of the realm was seen.

Literary Analysis
Gothic Literature and Single Effect Which details of this poem mirror the narrator's sense of Usher's mental instability?

IV

And all with pearl and ruby glowing
Was the fair palace door,
Through which came flowing, flowing, flowing
And sparkling evermore,
A troop of Echoes whose sweet duty
Was but to sing,
In voices of surpassing beauty,
The wit and wisdom of their king.

---

20. seraph (ser′ əf) angel.
21. Porphyrogene (pôr fər ō jēn′) born to royalty or "the purple."

V

But evil things, in robes of sorrow,
Assailed the monarch's high estate;
(Ah, let us mourn, for never morrow
Shall dawn upon him, desolate!)
And, round about his home, the glory
That blushed and bloomed
Is but a dim-remembered story
Of the old time entombed.

VI

And travelers now within that valley,
Through the red-litten[22] windows see
Vast forms that move fantastically
To a discordant melody;
While, like a rapid ghastly river,
Through the pale door,
A hideous throng rush out forever,
And laugh—but smile no more.

I well remember that suggestions arising from this ballad led us into a train of thought wherein there became manifest an opinion of Usher's which I mention not so much on account of its novelty (for other men have thought thus), as on account of the pertinacity with which he maintained it. This opinion, in its general form, was that of the **sentience** of all vegetable things. But, in his disordered fancy the idea had assumed a more daring character, and trespassed, under certain conditions, upon the kingdom of inorganization.[23] I lack words to express the full extent, or the earnest abandon of his persuasion. The belief, however, was connected (as I have previously hinted) with the gray stones of the home of his forefathers. The conditions of the sentience had been here, he imagined, fulfilled in the method of collocation of these stones—in the order of their arrangement, as well as in that of the many fungi which overspread them, and of the decayed trees which stood around—above all, in the long undisturbed endurance of this arrangement, and in its reduplication in the still waters of the tarn. Its evidence—the evidence of the sentience—was to be seen, he said (and I here started as he spoke), in the gradual yet certain condensation of an atmosphere of their own about the waters and the walls. The result was discoverable, he added, in that silent yet importunate and terrible influence which for centuries had molded the destinies of his family, and which made him what I now saw him—what he was. Such opinions need no comment, and I will make none.

Vocabulary
sentience (sen′ shəns) *n.* capacity of feeling

Reading Check
What is "The Haunted Palace"?

22. litten lighted.
23. inorganization (in′ ôr gə ni zā′ shən) *n.* inanimate objects.

Our books—the books which, for years, had formed no small portion of the mental existence of the invalid—were, as might be supposed, in strict keeping with this character of phantasm. We pored together over such works as the *Ververt et Chartreuse*[24] of Gresset; the *Belphegor* of Machiavelli; the *Heaven and Hell* of Swedenborg; the *Subterranean Voyage of Nicholas Klimm* by Holberg; the *Chiromancy* of Robert Flud, of Jean D'Indaginé and of De la Chambre; the *Journey into the Blue Distance* of Tieck; and the *City of the Sun* of Campanella. One favorite volume was a small octavo edition of the *Directorium Inquisitorium,* by the Dominican Eymeric de Gironne; and there were passages in Pomponius Mela, about the old African Satyrs and Œgipans, over which Usher would sit dreaming for hours. His chief delight, however, was found in the perusal of an exceedingly rare and curious book in quarto Gothic—the manual of a forgotten church—the *Vigilae Mortuorum secundum Chorum Ecclesiae Maguntinae.*

HE STATED HIS INTENTION OF PRESERVING HER CORPSE FOR A FORTNIGHT.

I could not help thinking of the wild ritual of this work, and of its probable influence upon the hypochondriac, when, one evening, having informed me abruptly that the lady Madeline was no more, he stated his intention of preserving her corpse for a fortnight (previously to its final interment), in one of the numerous vaults within the main walls of the building. The worldly reason, however, assigned for this singular proceeding, was one which I did not feel at liberty to dispute. The brother had been led to his resolution (so he told me) by consideration of the unusual character of the malady of the deceased, of certain obtrusive and eager inquiries on the part of her medical men, and of the remote and exposed situation of the burial ground of the family. I will not deny that when I called to mind the sinister countenance of the person whom I met upon the staircase, on the day of my arrival at the house, I had no desire to oppose what I regarded as at best but a harmless, and by no means an unnatural precaution.

Reading Strategy
Breaking Down Long Sentences
Clarify the main idea of the sentence beginning "The vault in which we placed it. . ."

At the request of Usher, I personally aided him in the arrangements for the temporary entombment. The body having been encoffined, we two alone bore it to its rest. The vault in which we placed it (and which had been so long unopened that our torches, half smothered in its oppressive atmosphere, gave us little opportunity for investigation) was small, damp, and entirely without means of admission for light; lying, at great depth, immediately beneath that portion of the building in which was my own sleeping apartment. It had been used, apparently, in remote feudal times, for the worst purposes of a donjon-keep, and, in later days, as a place of deposit for powder, or some other highly combustible substance, as a portion of its floor, and the whole interior of a long archway through which we reached it, were carefully sheathed with copper. The door, of massive

24. ***Ververt et Chartreuse,* etc.** All the books listed deal with magic or mysticism.

iron, had been, also, similarly protected. Its immense weight caused an unusually sharp, grating sound, as it moved upon its hinges.

Having deposited our mournful burden upon trestles within this region of horror, we partially turned aside the yet unscrewed lid of the coffin, and looked upon the face of the tenant. A striking similitude between the brother and sister now first arrested my attention; and Usher, divining, perhaps, my thoughts, murmured out some few words from which I learned that the deceased and himself had been twins, and that sympathies of a scarcely intelligible nature had always existed between them. Our glances, however, rested not long upon the dead—for we could not regard her unawed. The disease which had thus entombed the lady in the maturity of youth, had left, as usual in all maladies of a strictly cataleptical character, the mockery of a faint blush upon the bosom and the face, and that suspiciously lingering smile upon the lip which is so terrible in death. We replaced and screwed down the lid, and, having secured the door of iron, made our way, with toil, into the scarcely less gloomy apartments of the upper portion of the house.

And now, some days of bitter grief having elapsed, an observable change came over the features of the mental disorder of my friend. His ordinary manner had vanished. His ordinary occupations were neglected or forgotten. He roamed from chamber to chamber with hurried, unequal, and object-less step. The pallor of his countenance had assumed, if possible, a more ghastly hue—but the luminousness of his eye had utterly gone out. The once occasional huskiness of his tone was heard no more; and a tremulous quaver, as if of extreme terror, habitually characterized his utterance. There were times, indeed, when I thought his unceasingly agitated mind was laboring with some oppressive secret, to divulge which he struggled for the necessary courage. At times, again, I was obliged to resolve all into the mere inexplicable vagaries[25] of madness, for I beheld him gazing upon vacancy for long hours, in an attitude of the profoundest attention, as if listening to some imaginary sound. It was no wonder that his condition terrified—that it infected me. I felt creeping upon me, by slow yet uncertain degrees, the wild influences of his own fantastic yet impressive superstitions.

It was, especially, upon retiring to bed late in the night of the seventh or eighth day after the placing of the lady Madeline within the donjon, that I experienced the full power of such feelings. Sleep came not near my couch—while the hours waned and waned away. I struggled to reason off the nervousness which had dominion over me. I endeavored to believe that much, if not all of what I felt, was due to the bewildering influence of the gloomy furniture of the room—of the dark and tattered draperies, which, tortured

Reading Check

What does the narrator notice about Madeline's appearance in her coffin?

---

25. vagaries (vā′ ger ēz) *n.* odd, unexpected actions or notions.

Literary Analysis
Gothic Literature
Which elements of Gothic literature are present in this description of the narrator's sleepless night?

into motion by the breath of a rising tempest, swayed fitfully to and fro upon the walls, and rustled uneasily about the decorations of the bed. But my efforts were fruitless. An irrepressible tremor gradually pervaded my frame; and, at length, there sat upon my very heart an incubus[26] of utterly causeless alarm. Shaking this off with a gasp and a struggle, I uplifted myself upon the pillows, and, peering earnestly within the intense darkness of the chamber, hearkened—I know not why, except that an instinctive spirit prompted me—to certain low and indefinite sounds which came, through the pauses of the storm, at long intervals, I knew not whence. Overpowered by an intense sentiment of horror, unaccountable yet unendurable, I threw on my clothes with haste (for I felt that I should sleep no more during the night), and endeavored to arouse myself from the pitiable condition into which I had fallen by pacing rapidly to and fro through the apartment.

I had taken but few turns in this manner, when a light step on an adjoining staircase arrested my attention. I presently recognized it as that of Usher. In an instant afterward he rapped, with a gentle touch, at my door, and entered, bearing a lamp. His countenance was, as usual, cadaverously wan—but, moreover, there was a species of mad hilarity in his eyes—an evidently restrained hysteria in his whole demeanor. His air appalled me—but anything was preferable to the solitude which I had so long endured, and I even welcomed his presence as a relief.

"And you have not seen it?" he said abruptly, after having stared about him for some moments in silence—"you have not then seen it?—but, stay! you shall." Thus speaking, and having carefully shaded his lamp, he hurried to one of the casements, and threw it freely open to the storm.

The impetuous fury of the entering gust nearly lifted us from our feet. It was, indeed, a tempestuous yet sternly beautiful night, and one wildly singular in its terror and its beauty. A whirlwind had apparently collected its force in our vicinity; for there were frequent and violent alterations in the direction of the wind; and the exceeding density of the clouds (which hung so low as to press upon the turrets of the house) did not prevent our perceiving the lifelike velocity with which they flew careering from all points against each other, without passing away into the distance. I say that even their exceeding density did not prevent our perceiving this—yet we had no glimpse of the moon or stars, nor was there any flashing forth of the lightning. But the under surfaces of the huge masses of agitated vapor, as well as all terrestrial objects immediately around us, were glowing in the unnatural light of a faintly luminous and distinctly visible gaseous exhalation which hung about and enshrouded the mansion.

"You must not—you shall not behold this!" said I, shuddering,

---

26. incubus (iŋ′ kyə bəs) *n.* something nightmarishly burdensome.

to Usher, as I led him, with a gentle violence, from the window to a seat. " These appearances, which bewilder you, are merely electrical phenomena not uncommon—or it may be that they have their ghastly origin in the rank miasma[27] of the tarn. Let us close this casement:—the air is chilling and dangerous to your frame. Here is one of your favorite romances. I will read, and you shall listen:—and so we will pass away this terrible night together."

The antique volume which I had taken up was the *Mad Trist* of Sir Launcelot Canning;[28] but I had called it a favorite of Usher's more in sad jest than in earnest; for, in truth, there is little in its uncouth and unimaginative prolixity which could have had interest for the lofty and spiritual ideality of my friend. It was, however, the only book immediately at hand; and I indulged a vague hope that the excitement which now agitated the hypochondriac, might find relief (for the history of mental disorder is full of similar anomalies) even in the extremeness of the folly which I should read. Could I have judged, indeed, by the wild overstrained air of vivacity with which he hearkened, or apparently hearkened, to the words of the tale, I might well have congratulated myself upon the success of my design.

"You must not—you shall not behold this!"

I had arrived at that well-known portion of the story where Ethelred, the hero of the Trist, having sought in vain for peaceable admission into the dwelling of the hermit, proceeds to make good an entrance by force. Here, it will be remembered, the words of the narrative run thus:

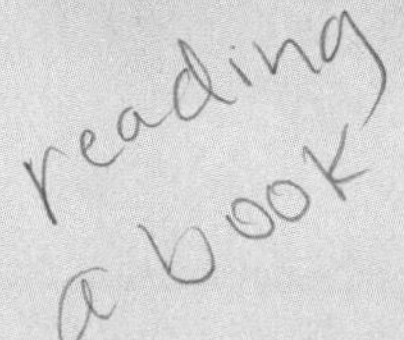

"And Ethelred, who was by nature of a doughty heart, and who was now mighty withal, on account of the powerfulness of the wine which he had drunken, waited no longer to hold parley with the hermit, who, in sooth, was of an obstinate and maliceful turn, but feeling the rain upon his shoulders, and fearing the rising of the tempest, uplifted his mace outright, and, with blows, made quickly room in the plankings of the door for his gauntleted hand; and now pulling therewith sturdily, he so cracked, and ripped, and tore all asunder, that the noise of the dry and hollow-sounding wood alarumed and reverberated throughout the forest."

At the termination of this sentence I started and, for a moment, paused; for it appeared to me (although I at once concluded that my excited fancy had deceived me)—it appeared to me that, from some very remote portion of the mansion, there came, indistinctly to my ears, which might have been, in its exact similarity of character, the echo (but a stifled and dull one certainly) of the very cracking and ripping sound which Sir Launcelot had so particularly described. It was, beyond doubt, the coincidence alone which had arrested my attention; for, amid the rattling of the sashes of the casements, and the ordinary commingled noises of the still increasing storm, the sound, itself, had nothing, surely, which should have interested or

What odd or unnatural sight does the narrator see when the curtains are opened?

27. miasma (mī az′ mə) *n.* unwholesome atmosphere.
28. ***Mad Trist* of Sir Launcelot Canning** fictional book and author.

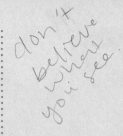

disturbed me. I continued the story:

"But the good champion Ethelred, now entering within the door, was sore enraged and amazed to perceive no signal of the maliceful hermit; but, in the stead thereof, a dragon of a scaly and prodigious demeanor, and of a fiery tongue, which sate in guard before a palace of gold, with a floor of silver; and upon the wall there hung a shield of shining brass with this legend enwritten—

Who entereth herein, a conqueror
hath bin;
Who slayeth the dragon, the shield
he shall win.

And Ethelred uplifted his mace, and struck upon the head of the dragon, which fell before him, and gave up his pasty breath, with a shriek so horrid and harsh, and withal so piercing, that Ethelred had fain to close his ears with his hands against the dreadful noise of it, the like whereof was never before heard."

Here again I paused abruptly, and now with a feeling of wild amazement—for there could be no doubt whatever that, in this instance, I did actually hear (although from what direction it proceeded I found it impossible to say) a low and apparently distant, but harsh, protracted, and most unusual screaming or grating sound—the exact counterpart of what my fancy had already conjured up for the dragon's unnatural shriek as described by the romancer.

Oppressed, as I certainly was, upon the extraordinary coincidence, by a thousand conflicting sensations, in which wonder and extreme terror were predominant, I still retained sufficient presence of mind to avoid exciting, by an observation, the sensitive nervousness of my companion. I was by no means certain that he had noticed the sounds in question; although, assuredly, a strange alteration had, during the last few minutes, taken place in his demeanor. From a position fronting my own, he had gradually brought round his chair; so as to sit with his face to the door of the chamber; and thus I could but partially perceive his features, although I saw that his lips trembled as if he were murmuring inaudibly. His head had dropped upon his breast—yet I knew that he was not asleep, from the wide and rigid opening of the eye as I caught a glance of it in profile. The motion of his body, too, was at variance with this idea—for he rocked from side to side with a gentle yet constant and uniform sway. Having rapidly taken notice of all this, I resumed the narrative of Sir Launcelot, which thus proceeded:

"And now, the champion, having escaped from the terrible fury of the dragon, bethinking himself of the brazen shield, and of the breaking up of the enchantment which was upon it, removed the carcass from out of the way before him, and approached valorously over the silver pavement of the castle to where the shield was upon the wall; which in sooth tarried not for his full coming, but fell down at his feet

Reading Strategy
Breaking Down Long Sentences
Summarize the action of the paragraph-long sentence beginning "And now, the champion. . ."

upon the silver floor, with a mighty great and terrible ringing sound."

No sooner had these syllables passed my lips, than—as if a shield of brass had indeed, at the moment, fallen heavily upon a floor of silver—I became aware of a distinct, hollow, metallic, and clangorous, yet apparently muffled, reverberation. Completely unnerved, I leaped to my feet; but the measured rocking movement of Usher was undisturbed. I rushed to the chair in which he sat. His eyes were bent fixedly before him, and throughout his whole countenance there reigned a stony rigidity. But, as I placed my hand upon his shoulder, there came a strong shudder over his whole person; a sickly smile quivered about his lips; and I saw that he spoke in a low, hurried, and gibbering murmur, as if unconscious of my presence. Bending closely over him I at length drank in the hideous import of his words.

"Not hear it?—yes, I hear it, and have heard it. Long—long—long—many minutes, many hours, many days, have I heard it—yet I dared not—oh, pity me, miserable wretch that I am!—I *dared* not—I dared not speak! *We have put her living in the tomb!* Said I not that my senses were acute? I *now* tell you that I heard her first feeble movement in the hollow coffin. I heard them—many, many days ago—yet I dared not—*I dared not speak!* and now—tonight—Ethelred—ha! ha!—the breaking of the hermit's door, and the death cry of the dragon, and the clangor of the shield—say, rather, the rending of her coffin, and the grating of the iron hinges of her prison, and her struggles within the coppered archway of the vault! Oh! wither shall I fly? Will she not be here anon? Is she not hurrying to upbraid me for my haste? Have I not heard her footstep on the stair? Do I not distinguish that heavy and horrible beating of her heart? Madman!"—here he sprang furiously to his feet, and shrieked out his syllables, as if in the effort he were giving up his soul—*"Madman! I tell you that she now stands without the door!"*

As if in the superhuman energy of his utterance there had been found the potency of a spell, the huge antique panels to which the speaker pointed threw slowly back, upon the instant, their ponderous and ebony jaws. It was the work of the rushing gust—but then without those doors there *did* stand the lofty and enshrouded figure of the lady Madeline of Usher. There was blood upon her white robes, and the evidence of some bitter struggle upon every portion of her emaciated frame. For a moment she remained trembling and reeling to and fro upon the threshold—then, with a low moaning cry, fell heavily inward upon the person of her brother, and in her violent and now final death agonies, bore him to the floor a corpse, and a victim to the terrors he had anticipated.

From that chamber, and from that mansion, I fled aghast. The storm was still abroad in all its wrath as I found myself crossing the old causeway. Suddenly there shot along the path a wild light, and I turned to see whence a gleam so unusual could have issued; for the vast house and its shadows were alone behind me. The radiance

Literary Analysis
Gothic Literature and Single Effect What effect does the description of Usher trembling and rocking help to create?

. . . A SICKLY SMILE QUIVERED ABOUT HIS LIPS . . .

Literary Analysis
Gothic Literature
Which aspects of Gothic literature are apparent in this description of Madeline Usher?

Reading Check
What unusual sounds does the narrator hear as he reads aloud?

was that of the full, setting, and bloodred moon, which now shone vividly through that once barely discernible fissure, of which I have before spoken as extending from the roof of the building, in a zigzag direction, to the base. While I gazed, this fissure rapidly widened—there came a fierce breath of the whirlwind—the entire orb of the satellite burst at once upon my sight—my brain reeled as I saw the mighty walls rushing asunder—there was a long tumultuous shouting sound like the voice of a thousand waters—and the deep and dank tarn at my feet closed sullenly and silently over the fragments of the *"House of Usher."*

Critical Reading 

1. **Key Ideas and Details (a)** Why has the narrator gone to visit Usher? **(b) Assess:** Does the narrator succeed in his purpose? Explain.
2. **Key Ideas and Details (a) Interpret:** What beliefs about the "sentience" of matter does Usher express to the narrator? **(b) Analyze:** How are Usher's beliefs and fears borne out by the final events of the story?
3. **Craft and Structure (a) Analyze:** In the description of the exterior of the house, which words suggest the presence of decay in the structure itself? **(b) Connect:** In what ways does this description foreshadow, or hint at, the ending of the story?
4. **Craft and Structure (a) Interpret:** Which descriptive details of the interior of the house suggest that the narrator has entered a realm that is very different from the ordinary world? **(b) Infer:** Which details in Usher's appearance suggest that he has been cut off from the outside world for many years? **(c) Connect:** In what ways is the appearance of the interior of the house related to Usher's appearance and to the condition of his mind?
5. **Integration of Knowledge and Ideas (a) Analyze:** What is the significance of the detail that the narrator finds himself becoming affected by Usher's condition? **(b) Evaluate:** Do you think the narrator is a reliable witness of the events he describes? Explain your opinion.

Critical Commentary

On Writing "The Raven"

Edgar Allan Poe

Poe's most famous poem, "The Raven," was an instant popular and critical hit. Just as people today are interested in "behind-the-scenes" information about their favorite movies or songs, Poe's fans wanted to know how their favorite poem was written. Poe obliged with an essay explaining that he wrote "The Raven" with almost mathematical precision. First, Poe explains that he wanted to write a poem that was short enough to be read in one sitting, but long enough to have an impact:

> *... there is a distinct limit, as regards length, to all works of literary art—the limit of a single sitting.... Holding in view these considerations, as well as that degree of excitement which I deemed not above the popular, while not below the critical, taste, I reached at once what I conceived the proper length for my intended poem—a length of about one hundred lines. It is, in fact, a hundred and eight.*

Poe goes on to tell how he chose both his subject matter and the mood of melancholy, or sadness, he wanted to convey:

> *Beauty of whatever kind, in its supreme development, invariably excites the sensitive soul to tears. Melancholy is thus the most legitimate of all the poetical tones.*

Poe then says that he wanted a **refrain,** or repeated set of phrases or lines, containing the *o* and *r* sounds, but he needed to find the right word:

> *... it became necessary to select a word embodying this sound, and at the same time in the fullest possible keeping with that melancholy which I had predetermined as the tone of the poem. In such a search it would have been absolutely impossible to overlook the word "Nevermore." In fact, it was the very first which presented itself.*

Now Poe had a problem: what kind of creature would speak the refrain?

> *Here, then, immediately arose the idea of a non-reasoning creature capable of speech; and, very naturally, a parrot, in the first instance, suggested itself, but was superseded forthwith by a Raven, as equally capable of speech, and infinitely more in keeping with the intended tone.*

Key Ideas and Details

- What tone did Poe want to achieve in "The Raven"?
- What subject did Poe believe is the most suitable for poetry?
- Why did Poe choose a Raven and not a parrot to deliver the refrain "Nevermore"?

The Raven

Edgar Allan Poe

Literary Analysis

Gothic Literature

In the very first line of the poem, which words contribute to a dark, mysterious Gothic mood?

Once upon a midnight dreary, while I pondered, weak and weary,
Over many a quaint and curious volume of forgotten lore—
While I nodded, nearly napping, suddenly there came a tapping,
As of some one gently rapping, rapping at my chamber door.
"'Tis some visitor," I muttered, "tapping at my chamber door—
Only this, and nothing more."

Ah, distinctly I remember it was in the bleak December;
And each separate dying ember wrought its ghost upon the floor.
Eagerly I wished the morrow;—vainly I had sought to borrow
From my books surcease[1] of sorrow—sorrow for the lost Lenore—
For the rare and radiant maiden whom the angels name Lenore—
Nameless *here* for evermore.

And the silken, sad, uncertain rustling of each purple curtain
Thrilled me—filled me with fantastic terrors never felt before;
So that now, to still the beating of my heart, I stood repeating
"'Tis some visitor entreating entrance at my chamber door—
Some late visitor entreating entrance at my chamber door;—
This it is and nothing more."

Presently my soul grew stronger; hesitating then no longer,
"Sir," said I, "or Madam, truly your forgiveness I implore;
But the fact is I was napping, and so gently you came rapping,
And so faintly you came tapping, tapping at my chamber door,
That I scarce was sure I heard you"—here I opened wide the door;—
Darkness there and nothing more.

1. **surcease** (sʉr sēs´) end.

Reading Strategy
Breaking Down Long Sentences
Summarize the action of the stanza-long sentence beginning "Presently my soul grew stronger. . ."

For whom is the speaker grieving?

Deep into that darkness peering, long I stood there wondering, fearing,
Doubting, dreaming dreams no mortal ever dared to dream before;
But the silence was unbroken, and the stillness gave no token,
And the only word there spoken was the whispered word, "Lenore?"
This I whispered, and an echo murmured back the word, "Lenore!"
Merely this and nothing more.

Back then into the chamber turning, all my soul within me burning,
Soon again I heard a tapping somewhat louder than before.
"Surely," said I, "surely that is something at my window lattice;
Let me see, then, what thereat is, and this mystery explore—
Let my heart be still a moment and this mystery explore;—
'Tis the wind and nothing more!"

Open here I flung the shutter, when, with many a flirt and flutter,
In there stepped a stately Raven of the saintly days of yore;
Not the least obeisance made he; not a minute stopped or stayed he;
But, with mien of lord or lady, perched above my chamber door—
Perched upon a bust of Pallas[2] just above my chamber door—
Perched, and sat, and nothing more.

Literary Analysis
Gothic Literature What element of Gothic literature does the Raven's speaking introduce into the poem? Explain.

Then this ebony bird beguiling[3] my sad fancy into smiling,
By the grave and stern decorum of the countenance[4] it wore,
"Though thy crest be shorn and shaven, thou," I said, "art sure no craven,
Ghastly grim and ancient Raven wandering from the Nightly shore—
Tell me what thy lordly name is on the Night's Plutonian[5] shore!"
Quoth the Raven, "Nevermore."

Much I marveled this ungainly fowl to hear discourse so plainly,
Though its answer little meaning—little relevancy bore;
For we cannot help agreeing that no living human being
Ever yet was blessed with seeing bird above his chamber door—
Bird or beast upon the sculptured bust above his chamber door,
With such name as "Nevermore."

But the Raven, sitting lonely on the placid bust, spoke only
That one word, as if his soul in that one word he did outpour.
Nothing farther than he uttered—not a feather then he fluttered—

2. **Pallas** (pal′ əs) Pallas Athena, the ancient Greek goddess of wisdom.
3. **beguiling** (bi gīl′ iŋ) *part.* charming.
4. **countenance** (koun′ tə nəns) *n.* facial expression.
5. **Plutonian** (plo͞o tō′ nē ən) *adj.* like the underworld or infernal regions; refers to Pluto, Greek and Roman god of the underworld.

Till I scarcely more than muttered, "Other friends have flown before—
On the morrow *he* will leave me, as my Hopes have flown before."
Then the bird said, "Nevermore."

Startled at the stillness broken by reply so aptly spoken,
"Doubtless," said I, "what it utters is its only stock and store
Caught from some unhappy master whom unmerciful Disaster
Followed fast and followed faster till his songs one burden bore—
Till the dirges of his Hope that melancholy burden bore
Of 'Never—nevermore.'"

But the Raven still beguiling my sad fancy into smiling,
Straight I wheeled a cushioned seat in front of bird, and bust and door;
Then, upon the velvet sinking, I betook myself to linking
Fancy unto fancy, thinking what this ominous[6] bird of yore—
What this grim, ungainly, ghastly, gaunt, and ominous bird of yore
Meant in croaking "Nevermore."

This I sat engaged in guessing, but no syllable expressing
To the fowl whose fiery eyes now burned into my bosom's core;
This and more I sat divining, with my head at ease reclining
On the cushion's velvet lining that the lamp-light gloated o'er,
But whose velvet-violet lining with the lamp-light gloating o'er,
She shall press, ah, nevermore!

Then, methought, the air grew denser, perfumed from an unseen censer
Swung by seraphim whose foot-falls tinkled on the tufted floor.
"Wretch," I cried, "thy God hath lent thee—by these angels he hath sent thee
Respite—respite and nepenthe[7] from thy memories of Lenore;
Quaff, oh quaff this kind nepenthe and forget this lost Lenore!"
Quoth the Raven, "Nevermore."

"Prophet!" said I, "thing of evil!—prophet still, if bird or devil!—
Whether Tempter sent, or whether tempest tossed thee here ashore,
Desolate yet all undaunted, on this desert land enchanted—
On this home by Horror haunted—tell me truly, I implore—
Is there—*is* there balm in Gilead?[8]—tell me—tell me, I implore!"

Literary Analysis
Gothic Literature
How is the speaker's psychological distress increasing?

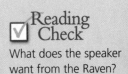

Reading Check
What does the speaker want from the Raven?

---

6. **ominous** (äm′ ə nəs) *adj.* threatening; sinister.
7. **nepenthe** (ni pen′ thē) *n.* drug that the ancient Greeks believed could relieve sorrow.
8. **balm in Gilead** (gil′ ē əd) in the Bible, a healing ointment made in Gilead, a region of ancient Palestine.

Quoth the Raven, "Nevermore."

"Prophet!" said I, "thing of evil!—prophet still, if bird or devil!
By that Heaven that bends above us—by that God we both adore—
Tell this soul with sorrow laden if, within the distant Aidenn,[9]
It shall clasp a sainted maiden whom the angels name Lenore—
Clasp a rare and radiant maiden whom the angels name Lenore."
Quoth the Raven, "Nevermore."

"Be that word our sign of parting, bird or fiend!" I shrieked, upstarting—
"Get thee back into the tempest and the Night's Plutonian shore!
Leave no black plume as a token of that lie thy soul hath spoken!
Leave my loneliness unbroken!—quit the bust above my door!
Take thy beak from out my heart, and take thy form from off my door!"
Quoth the Raven, "Nevermore."

And the Raven, never flitting, still is sitting, *still* is sitting
On the pallid bust of Pallas just above my chamber door;
And his eyes have all the seeming of a demon's that is dreaming;
And the lamp-light o'er him streaming throws his shadow on the floor;
And my soul from out that shadow that lies floating on the floor
Shall be lifted—nevermore!

◀ **Critical Viewing**
In this illustration of the poem's opening scene, how do the details in the setting and the angle of the image itself add to a sense of the speaker's fear and distress? **[Analyze]**

9. **Aidenn** (ā' den) Arabic for *Eden* or *heaven*.

Critical Reading

Cite textual evidence to support your responses.

1. **Key Ideas and Details** **(a)** With what emotion does the speaker first greet the Raven? **(b) Interpret:** As the poem progresses, how does the speaker's attitude toward the Raven change? **(c) Analyze Cause and Effect:** In what way is the word *nevermore* related to the emotional changes?
2. **Key Ideas and Details** **(a)** What does the speaker eventually order the Raven to do? **(b) Analyze:** At the end of the poem, what does the speaker mean when he says the Raven "still is sitting" above the door?
3. **Craft and Structure** **(a) Interpret:** What is the relationship between the Raven's shadow and the speaker's soul at the end of the poem? **(b) Analyze:** In your opinion, what does the Raven finally come to represent?
4. **Craft and Structure** Review your list of details that make Poe's settings seem dreamlike. Then, write a paragraph describing the power of Poe's landscapes. In your response, use at least two of these Essential Question words: *fantastic, personal, terrors, realistic.* ***[Connecting to the Essential Question: What is the relationship between literature and place?]***

After You Read

The Fall of the House of Usher • *The Raven*

Literary Analysis

1. **Craft and Structure** Use a chart like the one shown to identify the **Gothic** elements in "The Fall of the House of Usher" and "The Raven."

Gothic Element	House of Usher	Raven
Setting		
Violence		
Characterization		
The Supernatural		

2. **Craft and Structure** Describe the ways in which the following elements contribute to the **single effect** of a sense of terror in "The Fall of the House of Usher": **(a)** description of the house, **(b)** Madeline's entombment, **(c)** the storm.
3. **Craft and Structure** **(a)** In what ways is the ending of the story intentionally *ambiguous*? What does Poe leave uncertain? **(b)** What are some possible interpretations of the ending? **(c)** Which do you support, and why?
4. **Craft and Structure** In "The Raven," how do both the tapping and the Raven's fiery eyes add to the speaker's deteriorating emotional state?
5. **Integration of Knowledge and Ideas** **(a)** When Madeline appears at the end of the story, is she actually there, or is she a hallucination? Explain. **(b)** At the end of "The Raven," do you think the bird is actually in the room? Why or why not?
6. **Analyzing Visual Text** Explain the cartoon.

Reading Strategy

7. **Break down this long sentence** from the story and restate it in your own words:

   At times, again, I was obliged to resolve all into the mere inexplicable vagaries of madness, for I beheld him gazing upon vacancy for long hours, in an attitude of the profoundest attention, as if listening to some imaginary sound.

8. Choose another long sentence from the story or poem. Break the sentence down and restate it in your own words.

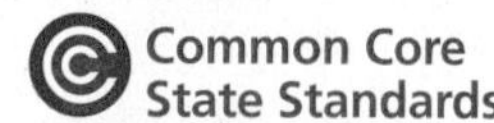

Common Core State Standards

Language
4.c. Consult general and specialized reference materials, both print and digital, to find the pronunciation of a word or determine or clarify its precise meaning or its standard usage. *(p. 319)*

PERFORMANCE TASKS

Integrated Language Skills

Vocabulary Acquisition and Use

Word Analysis: Latin Root *-voc-*

The word *equivocal* contains the Latin root *-voc-*, which derives from the Latin word *vox*, meaning "voice." Combined with the Latin prefix *equi-*, meaning "equal," *equivocal* can be defined as "having two equal voices" or "having more than one possible interpretation." Consider the meaning of these words containing *-voc-*. Then, answer the questions.

advocate *v.* speak or argue in favor of

equivocate *v.* avoid making a clear statement

vociferous *adj.* noisy or aggressive in making one's feelings known

1. The council *advocates* banning parking near the bridge. Is the council for or against it? Explain.
2. When the reporter asked the mayor about the new law, the mayor *equivocated.* Did the reporter like the mayor's answer? Explain.
3. Several citizens were *vociferous* in their response to the law. Do you think the mayor heard them? Why or why not?

Vocabulary: True or False?

Indicate which of the statements below are true and which are false. Explain your answers.

1. If historians decide that a document is *specious*, they will probably write a paper about its importance.
2. The quality of *sentience* is evident in rocks and other inanimate matter.
3. If a senator's position in a debate is *equivocal*, he probably believes strongly in his argument.
4. Misers are *munificent* and often give to the needy.
5. Someone who is in desperate need might be *importunate* about a request.
6. A professional's *anomalous* behavior will make others feel confident about using his or her services.

Using Resources to Build Vocabulary

Gothic Style: Words For a Character in Torment

In drawing a picture of his tormented friend, the narrator of "The Fall of the House of Usher" uses the following words:

agitation	leaden
feeble	tremulous
futile	trepidancy

Reread the last paragraph on page 298 to see these words in context. Then, *use a dictionary and a print or electronic thesaurus* to find synonyms for each word. On your own paper, rewrite the paragraph by replacing each of the words shown above with a duller, more ordinary word. Now, compare the original paragraph with your version. Write several sentences in which you describe the differences between the two versions.

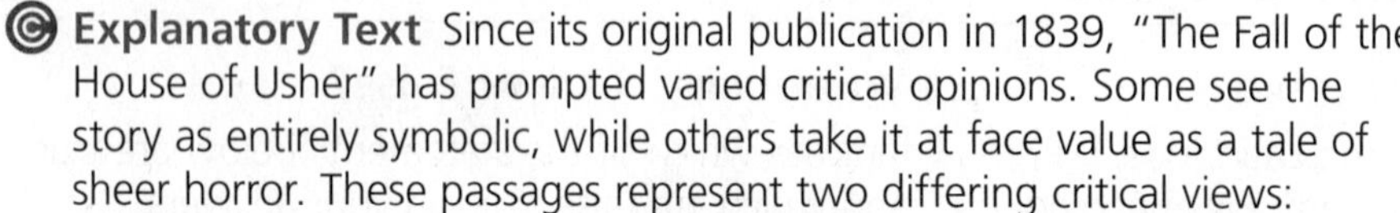
PERFORMANCE TASKS

Integrated Language Skills

Writing

Explanatory Text Since its original publication in 1839, "The Fall of the House of Usher" has prompted varied critical opinions. Some see the story as entirely symbolic, while others take it at face value as a tale of sheer horror. These passages represent two differing critical views:

> **Edward H. Davidson:** The three characters are unique people with distinct characters, but they are tied together by the same type of "mental disorder." All of them suffer from insanity....
>
> **H. P. Lovecraft:** "The Fall of the House of Usher"... displays an abnormally linked trinity of entities at the end of a long and isolated family history—a brother, his twin sister, and their incredibly ancient house all sharing a single soul ...

While both critics note strong connections among the characters, they see different meanings in these connections. Do you agree with Davidson that all the characters are separate, insane personalities, or do you prefer Lovecraft's analysis, that the brother, sister, and house represent different aspects of a single personality? Write an **essay** in which you evaluate these views and state your own judgment about Poe's story.

Common Core State Standards

Writing
2.c. Use appropriate and varied transitions and syntax to link the major sections of the text, create cohesion, and clarify the relationships among complex ideas and concepts.
9.a. Apply *grades 11-12 Reading standards* to literature.

Language
1. Demonstrate command of the conventions of standard English grammar and usage when writing or speaking. *(p. 321)*

Prewriting Review the story to develop your perspective. As you read, gather details that relate to the two critical views. Jot down details, looking for patterns among them. Then, determine which viewpoint—Davidson's or Lovecraft's—is more persuasive. Remember that *ambiguities, nuances, and complexities* are an integral part of Poe's writing. While you may not be able to fully explain them, assess the effect they have on the story's meaning.

Model: Using Transitions to Clarify Meaning

The idea that all the characters in the story are insane is intriguing. It would explain the story's strangeness. [insert: After all,] if the narrator is mad, he would not be able to relate events clearly.

This idea is intriguing. [insert: ; however,] ~~It~~ it is not convincing.

Use transitional words and phrases to make the flow of your ideas clear.

Punctuation Tip: The word "however" joins two complete sentences. When you combine sentences with a transitional word or phrase, use a semicolon.

Drafting Establish a logical organizational pattern for your essay. In your introduction, summarize the two critical viewpoints and state which one you support. Elaborate upon your reasoning in each body paragraph, citing details that are substantial, specific, and relevant to your position.

Revising Reread your essay, making sure you have established a logical flow of ideas. Improve the logic by adding transitional words and phrases at points where relationships among ideas are not perfectly clear.

Conventions and Style: Comparative and Superlative Adjectives and Adverbs

In academic writing, you will often be asked to explain how things are similar and different. To do so, use modifiers showing comparison and contrast correctly. Adjectives and adverbs can take three forms: **positive, comparative,** and **superlative.**

Positive	Comparative	Superlative
dark	darker	darkest
weary	wearier	weariest
nervous	more nervous	most nervous
painfully	more painfully	most painfully
bad	worse	worst
good	better	best

Using Comparative and Superlative Forms

Use the comparative degree to compare *two* persons, places, or things.

Comparative Adjective: Madeline is even *spookier* than her brother.
Comparative Adverb: The narrator describes Roderick *more fully* than he does Madeline.

Use the superlative degree to compare *three or more* persons, places, or things.

Superlative Adjective: The underground chamber is the *worst* place in the house.
Superlative Adverb: Usher's home is the *most elaborately* described mansion in all of literature.

Practice Complete each sentence below by supplying the correct form of the adjective or adverb shown in parentheses.

1. In your opinion, who is the ______ writer, Edgar Allan Poe or Stephen King? (*good*)
2. He got into trouble ______ than his friend did. (*frequently*)
3. Some scholars have criticized Poe's work ______ than others have. (*harshly*)
4. Of all the writers we have studied so far, I think Edgar Allan Poe had the ______ life. (*sad*)
5. Which deteriorated ______, the house or Usher's mental state? (*quick*)
6. He considers the narrator his ______ friend in the world. (*close*)
7. His last night at the mansion was by far the ______ one. (*bad*)
8. The second time he heard the tapping, it was ______ than before. (*loud*)
9. "The Raven" may be the ______ of Poe's poems. (*popular*)
10. Both selections are scary, but I think the poem is the ______ of the two. (*terrifying*)

Writing and Speaking Conventions

A. Writing For each item listed, write two sentences. In one, use the comparative form, and in the other, use the superlative form.

1. damp **2.** desperately **3.** sick **4.** gloomy **5.** hesitantly

Example: cold
Comparative: The bedroom is colder than the kitchen.
Superlative: The attic is the coldest place in the house.

B. Speaking Write and recite an alternate ending to the story in which you use at least one comparative form and one superlative form.

PH WRITING COACH

Further instruction and practice are available in *Prentice Hall Writing Coach*.

The Gothic Family Tree

British Author
Horace Walpole
(1717–1797)
The Castle of Otranto (1764)

BRITISH

Ann Radcliffe
(1764–1823)
Mysteries of Udolpho (1794)

Mary Shelley
(1797–1851)
Frankenstein, or the Modern Prometheus (1818)

Bram Stoker
(1847–1912)
Dracula (1897)

Daphne du Maurier
(1907–1989)
Rebecca (1938)

AMERICAN

Charles Brockden Brown
(1771–1810)
Wieland, or The Transformation (1798)

Edgar Allan Poe
(1809–1849)
Tales of the Grotesque and Arabesque (1839)

Detective/mystery stories

H. P. Lovecraft
(1890–1937)
The Colour Out of Space (1927)

MODERN GOTHIC

Joyce Carol Oates
(b. 1938)
Bellefleur (1980)

Anne Rice
(b. 1941)
Interview with the Vampire (1976)

Peter Straub
(b. 1943)
Ghost Story (1979)

Stephen King
(b. 1947)
The Dark Tower
(series: 1982–2004)

Comparing Literary Works

"The Fall of the House of Usher" by Edgar Allan Poe • "Where Is Here?" by Joyce Carol Oates

Comparing Gothic Literature Past and Present

Gothic Literature Edgar Allan Poe's work has roots deep in European Gothic literature. Horace Walpole's *The Castle of Otranto: A Gothic Tale* (1764) and Ann Radcliffe's *Mysteries of Udolpho* (1794) are just two of the books that probably influenced Poe (see the Gothic Family Tree on page 322). In a similar way, modern writers such as Joyce Carol Oates, author of "Where Is Here?," look back to Poe as the founding voice of an American Gothic tradition. The legacy of traditional Gothic literature cuts across genre classifications, and its elements can be found in poetry, drama, novels, and short stories. Regardless of the genre, traditional Gothic writing such as Poe's has these elements:

- A bleak or remote setting; often grand, such as a castle or mansion
- A gloomy atmosphere; a sense of impending doom
- Characters in physical or psychological torment
- Horrific or violent incidents
- Supernatural elements

Modern Gothic literature uses the same elements but does so with more subtlety or with details that reflect modern life. As you read "Where Is Here?," use a chart like the one shown to examine how Oates puts a new spin on traditional Gothic features.

	Traditional: Poe	Modern: Oates
Setting	a crumbling mansion	
Characters	Roderick Usher, who is ghostly and tormented	
Violence	Burying sister in vault	
The Supernatural	Link between house and Usher	

Common Core State Standards

Reading Literature
3. Analyze the impact of the author's choices regarding how to develop and relate elements of a story.

Language
4.c. Consult general and specialized reference materials, both print and digital, to find the precise meaning of a word and its etymology.

Gather Vocabulary Knowledge

Joyce Carol Oates uses related forms of the words *perplex*, *disturb*, and *resent*. Use a **dictionary** to define each word. Then, employ other references to further explore these words:

- **History of Language:** Use a book on the history of English to research each word's origins. Write a paragraph about the word's emergence in English.
- **Glossary of Affixes:** Consult a print or online list of affixes. For each word, explain how the addition of a specific affix modifies its meaning.

Comparing References Compare and contrast what you learn about the words from each reference.

Joyce Carol Oates

(b. 1938)

Author of "Where Is Here?"

Joyce Carol Oates was born in 1938 in Lockport, New York, a small, rural town. Though she grew up without many books, she always had a strong attraction to storytelling and began drawing picture stories even before she knew how to write.

Oates's elementary school years were spent in a one-room schoolhouse. At age 14, she received a typewriter as a gift and began writing in earnest. She was soon producing one book after another. In her college days, she would write one novel using one side of the paper, then write another novel on the reverse side. Then, she would throw the papers away.

Early Success Oates won the *Mademoiselle* short story contest, an important national fiction prize, while still in college, and published her first book at the age of twenty-five. Today, she is renowned not just for the quality of her work, but for her immense literary output. She has averaged two books a year during the course of her career. Her many honors include the National Book Award and three separate nominations for the Pulitzer Prize.

A Taste for the Gothic Oates's discovery of the Gothic novels of Ann Radcliff, an English writer, and of Edgar Allan Poe's remarkable short stories sparked her interest in Gothic fiction. Though she has written fiction and nonfiction in a wide variety of styles, she always returns to the Gothic. "Horror," she says, "Is a fact of life. As a writer I'm fascinated by all facets of life." Over her desk she keeps a quote from Henry James, another American master, which reads: "We work in the dark—we do what we can—we give what we have. Our doubt is our passion, and our passion is our task. The rest is the madness of art."

"Horror is a fact of life."

Where Is Here?

Joyce Carol Oates

For years they had lived without incident in their house in a quiet residential neighborhood when, one November evening at dusk, the doorbell rang, and the father went to answer it, and there on his doorstep stood a man he had never seen before. The stranger apologized for disturbing him at what was probably the dinner hour and explained that he'd once lived in the house— "I mean, I was a child in this house"—and since he was in the city on business he thought he would drop by. He had not seen the house since January 1949 when he'd been eleven years old and his widowed mother had sold it and moved away but, he said, he thought of it often, dreamt of it often, and never more powerfully than in recent months. The father said, "Would you like to come inside for a few minutes and look around?" The stranger hesitated, then said firmly, "I think I'll just poke around outside for a while, if you don't mind. That might be sufficient." He was in his late forties, the father's approximate age. He wore a dark suit, conservatively cut; he was hatless, with thin silver-tipped neatly combed hair; a plain, sober, intelligent face and frowning eyes. The father, reserved by nature, but genial and even *gregarious* when taken unaware, said amiably, "Of course we don't mind. But I'm afraid many things have changed since 1949."

So, in the chill, damp, deepening dusk, the stranger wandered around the property while the mother set the dining room table and the father peered covertly out the window. The children were upstairs in their rooms. "Where is he now?" the mother asked. "He just went into the garage," the father said. "The garage! What does he want in there!" the mother said uneasily. "Maybe you'd better go out there with him." "He wouldn't want anyone with him," the father said. He moved **stealthily** to another window, peering through the curtains. A moment passed in silence. The mother, paused in the act of setting down plates, neatly folded paper napkins, and stainless-steel cutlery, said impatiently, "And where is he now? I don't like this." The father said, "Now he's coming out of the garage," and stepped back hastily from the window. "Is he going now?" the mother asked. "I wish I'd answered the door." The father watched for a moment in silence then said, "He's headed into the backyard." "Doing what?" the mother asked. "Not doing anything, just walking," the father said. "He seems

Vocabulary
stealthily (stel´ thə lē) *adv.* slowly so as to avoid notice

Who invites the stranger in to the house?

to have a slight limp." "Is he an older man?" the mother asked. "I didn't notice," the father confessed. "Isn't that just like you!" the mother said.

She went on worriedly, "He could be anyone, after all. Any kind of thief, or mentally disturbed person, or even a murderer. Ringing our doorbell like that with no warning and you don't even know what he looks like!"

The father had moved to another window and stood quietly watching, his cheek pressed against the glass. "He's gone down to the old swings. I hope he won't sit in one of them, for memory's sake, and try to swing—the posts are rotted almost through." The mother drew breath to speak but sighed instead, as if a powerful current of feeling had surged through her. The father was saying, "Is it possible he remembers those swings from his childhood? I can't believe they're actually that old." The mother said vaguely, "They were old when we bought the house." The father said, "But we're talking about forty years or more, and that's a long time." The mother sighed again, involuntarily. "Poor man!" she murmured. She was standing before her table but no longer seeing it. In her hand were objects—forks, knives, spoons—she could not have named. She said, "We can't bar the door against him. That would be cruel." The father said, "What? No one has barred any door against anyone." "Put yourself in his place," the mother said. "He told me he didn't *want* to come inside," the father said. "Oh—isn't that just like you!" the mother said in **exasperation**.

Vocabulary
exasperation (eks äs pə rā′ shun) *n.* annoyance; frustration

Without a further word she went to the back door and called out for the stranger to come inside, if he wanted, when he had finished looking around outside.

They introduced themselves rather shyly, giving names, and forgetting names, in the confusion of the moment. The stranger's handshake was cool and damp and tentative. He was smiling hard, blinking moisture from his eyes; it was clear that entering his childhood home was enormously exciting yet intimidating to him. Repeatedly he said, "It's so nice of you to invite me in—I truly hate to disturb you—I'm really so grateful, and so—" But the perfect word eluded him. As he spoke his eyes darted about the kitchen almost like eyes out of control. He stood in an odd stiff posture, hands gripping the lapels of his suit as if he meant to crush them. The mother, meaning to break the awkward silence, spoke warmly of their satisfaction with the house and with the neighborhood, and the father concurred, but the stranger listened only politely, and continued to stare, and stare hard. Finally he said that the kitchen had been so changed—"so modernized"—he almost didn't recognize it. The floor tile, the size of the windows, something about the position of the cupboards—all

Comparing Gothic Literature
Which details in the description of the stranger create a sense of his agitation or distress?

were different. But the sink was in the same place, of course; and the refrigerator and stove; and the door leading down to the basement—"That is the door leading down to the basement, isn't it?" He spoke strangely, staring at the door. For a moment it appeared he might ask to be shown the basement but the moment passed, fortunately—this was not a part of their house the father and mother would have been comfortable showing to a stranger.

Finally, making an effort to smile, the stranger said, "Your kitchen is so—pleasant." He paused. For a moment it seemed he had nothing further to say. Then, "A—controlled sort of place. My mother—When we lived here—" His words trailed off into a dreamy silence and the mother and father glanced at each other with carefully neutral expressions.

On the windowsill above the sink were several lushly blooming African violet plants in ceramic pots and these the stranger made a show of admiring. **Impulsively** he leaned over to sniff the flowers—"Lovely!"—though African violets have no smell. As if embarrassed he said, "Mother too had plants on this windowsill but I don't recall them ever blooming."

The mother said tactfully, "Oh they were probably the kind that don't bloom—like ivy."

In the next room, the dining room, the stranger appeared to be even more deeply moved. For some time he stood staring, wordless. With **fastidious** slowness he turned on his heel, blinking, and frowning, and tugging at his lower lip in a rough gesture that must have hurt. Finally, as if remembering the presence of his hosts, and the necessity for some display of civility, the stranger expressed his admiration for the attractiveness of the room, and its coziness. He'd remembered it as **cavernous**, with a ceiling twice as high. "And dark most of the time," he said wonderingly. "Dark by day, dark by night." The mother turned the lights of the little brass chandelier to their fullest: shadows were dispersed like ragged ghosts and the cut-glass fruit bowl at the center of the table glowed like an exquisite multi-faceted jewel. The stranger exclaimed in surprise. He'd extracted a handkerchief from his pocket and was dabbing carefully at his face, where beads of perspiration shone. He said, as if thinking aloud, still wonderingly, "My father was a unique man. Everyone who knew him admired him. He sat *here*," he said, gingerly touching the chair that was in fact the father's chair, at one end of the table. "And Mother sat *there*," he said, merely pointing. "I don't recall my own place or my sister's but I suppose it doesn't matter. . . . I see you have four place settings, Mrs. . . .? Two children, I suppose?" "A boy eleven, and a girl thirteen," the mother said. The stranger stared not at her but at the table, smiling. "And so too we were—I mean, there were two of us: my sister and me."

Comparing Gothic Literature

How do the stranger's halted, or unfinished, statements affect your reading of his character?

Vocabulary

impulsively (im puhl′ siv lē) *adv.* spontaneously

fastidious (fa stid′ ē əs) *adj.* careful; meticulous

cavernous (cav′ ərn nəs) *adj.* cavelike; vast

What similarity does the stranger notice between his own family and that of the house's current occupants?

The mother said, as if not knowing what else to say, "Are you—close?"

The stranger shrugged, distractedly rather than rudely, and moved on to the living room.

This room, cozily lit as well, was the most carefully furnished room in the house. Deep-piled wall-to-wall carpeting in hunter green, cheerful chintz drapes, a sofa and matching chairs in nubby heather green, framed reproductions of classic works of art, a gleaming gilt-framed mirror over the fireplace: wasn't the living room impressive as a display in a furniture store? But the stranger said nothing at first. Indeed, his eyes narrowed sharply as if he were confronted with a disagreeable spectacle. He whispered, "Here too! Here too!"

...Who was this man, and how could they tactfully get rid of him?

He went to the fireplace, walking, now, with a decided limp; he drew his fingers with excruciating slowness along the mantel as if testing its materiality. For some time he merely stood, and stared, and listened. He tapped a section of wall with his knuckles—"There used to be a large water stain here, like a shadow.

"Was there!" murmured the father out of politeness, and "Was there!" murmured the mother. Of course, neither had ever seen a water stain there.

Then, noticing the window seat, the stranger uttered a soft surprised cry, and went to sit in it. He appeared delighted: hugging his knees like a child trying to make himself smaller. "This was one of my happy places! At least when Father wasn't home. I'd hide away here for hours, reading, daydreaming, staring out the window! Sometimes Mother would join me, if she was in the mood, and we'd plot together—oh, all sorts of fantastical things!" The stranger remained sitting in the window seat for so long, tears shining in his eyes, that the father and mother almost feared he'd forgotten them. He was stroking the velvet fabric of the cushioned seat, gropingly touching the leaded windowpanes. Wordlessly, the father and mother exchanged a glance: who was this man, and how could they tactfully get rid of him? The father made a face signaling impatience and the mother shook her head without seeming to move it. For they couldn't be rude to a guest in their house.

Comparing Gothic Literature
In this and the next two paragraphs, what is odd or unsettling in the stranger's responses? Explain.

The stranger was saying in a slow, dazed voice, "It all comes back to me now. How could I have forgotten! Mother used to read to me, and tell me stories, and ask me riddles I couldn't answer. 'What creature walks on four legs in the morning, two legs at midday, three legs in the evening?' 'What is round, and flat, measuring mere inches in one direction, and infinity in the other?' 'Out of what does our life arise? Out of what does our consciousness arise? Why are we here? Where *is* here?' "

The father and mother were perplexed by these strange words and hardly knew how to respond. The mother said uncertainly, "Our daughter used to like to sit here too, when she was younger. It *is* a lovely place." The father said with surprising passion, "I hate riddles—they're moronic some of the time and obscure the rest of the time." He spoke with such uncharacteristic rudeness, the mother looked at him in surprise.

Hurriedly she said, "Is your mother still living, Mr. . . .?" "Oh no. Not at all," the stranger said, rising abruptly from the window seat, and looking at the mother as if she had said something mildly preposterous. "I'm sorry," the mother said. "Please don't be," the stranger said. "We've all been dead—*they've* all been dead—a long time."

The stranger's cheeks were deeply flushed as if with anger and his breath was quickened and audible.

The visit might have ended at this point but so clearly did the stranger expect to continue on upstairs, so purposefully, indeed almost defiantly, did he limp his way to the stairs, neither the father nor the mother knew how to dissuade him. It was as if a force of nature, benign at the outset, now uncontrollable, had swept its way into their house! The mother followed after him saying nervously, "I'm not sure what condition the rooms are in, upstairs. The children's rooms especially—" The stranger muttered that he did not care in the slightest about the condition of the household and continued on up without a backward glance.

The father, his face burning with resentment and his heart accelerating as if in preparation for combat, had no choice but to follow the stranger and the mother up the stairs. He was flexing and unflexing his fingers as if to rid them of stiffness.

On the landing, the stranger halted abruptly to examine a stained-glass fanlight—"My God, I haven't thought of this in years!" He spoke excitedly of how, on tiptoe, he used to stand and peek out through the diamonds of colored glass, red, blue, green, golden yellow: seeing with amazement the world outside so *altered*. "After such a lesson it's hard to take the world on its own terms, isn't it?" he asked. The father asked, annoyed, "On what terms should it be taken, then?" The stranger replied, regarding him levelly, with a just perceptible degree of disdain, "Why, none at all."

It was the son's room—by coincidence, the stranger's old room—the stranger most wanted to see. Other rooms on the second floor, the "master" bedroom in particular, he decidedly did not want to see. As he spoke of it, his mouth twisted as if he had been offered something repulsive to eat.

Which room on the second floor does the stranger want to see and which does he "decidedly" not wish to see?

The mother hurried on ahead to warn the boy and to straighten up his room a bit. No one had expected a visitor this evening! "So you have two children," the stranger murmured, looking at the father with a small quizzical smile. "Why?" The father stared at him as if he hadn't heard correctly. "'Why'?" he asked. "Yes. *Why?*" the stranger repeated. They looked at each other for a long strained moment, then the stranger said quickly, "But you love them—of course." The father controlled his temper and said, biting off his words, "Of course."

"Of course, of course," the stranger murmured, tugging at his necktie and loosening his collar, "otherwise it would all come to an end." The two men were of approximately the same height but the father was heavier in the shoulders and torso; his hair had thinned more severely so that the scalp of the crown was exposed, flushed, damp with perspiration, sullenly alight.

No one had expected a visitor this evening!

With a stiff avuncular formality the stranger shook the son's hand. "So this is your room, now! So you live here, now!" he murmured, as if the fact were an astonishment. Not used to shaking hands, the boy was stricken with shyness and cast his eyes down. The stranger limped past him, staring. "The same!—the same!—walls, ceiling, floor—window—" He drew his fingers slowly along the windowsill; around the frame; rapped the glass, as if, again, testing materiality; stooped to look outside—but it was night, and nothing but his reflection bobbed in the glass, ghostly and insubstantial. He groped against the walls, he opened the closet door before the mother could protest, he sat heavily on the boy's bed, the springs creaking beneath him. He was panting, red-faced, dazed. "And the ceiling overhead," he whispered. He nodded slowly and repeatedly, smiling. "And the floor beneath. That is what *is*."

He took out his handkerchief again and fastidiously wiped his face. He made a visible effort to compose himself.

The father, in the doorway, cleared his throat and said, "I'm afraid it's getting late—it's almost six."

The mother said, "Oh yes I'm afraid— I'm afraid it *is* getting late. There's dinner, and the children have their homework—"

Comparing Gothic Literature
Which details suggest that the stranger's psychological torment has continued to intensify?

The stranger got to his feet. At his full height he stood for a precarious moment swaying, as if the blood had drained from his head and he was in danger of fainting. But he steadied himself with a hand against the slanted dormer ceiling. He said, "Oh yes!—I know!—I've disturbed you terribly! —you've been so kind." It seemed, surely, as if the stranger *must* leave now, but, as chance had it, he happened to spy, on the boy's desk, an opened mathematics textbook and several smudged sheets of paper, and impulsively offered to show the boy a mathematical riddle—"You can take it to school tomorrow and surprise your teacher!"

So, out of dutiful politeness, the son sat down at his desk and the stranger leaned familiarly over him, demonstrating adroitly with a ruler and a pencil how "what we call 'infinity' " can be contained within a small geometrical figure on a sheet of paper. "First you draw a square; then you draw a triangle to fit inside the square; then you draw a second triangle, and a third, and a fourth, each to fit inside the square, but without their points coinciding, and as you continue—here, son, I'll show you—give me your hand, and I'll show you—the border of the triangles' common outline gets more complex and measures larger, and larger, and larger—and soon you'll need a magnifying glass to see the details, and then you'll need a microscope, and so on and so forth, forever, laying triangles neatly down to fit inside the original square *without their points coinciding*—!" The stranger spoke with increasing fervor; spittle gleamed in the corners of his mouth. The son stared at the geometrical shapes rapidly materializing on the sheet of paper before him with no seeming comprehension but with a rapt staring fascination as if he dared not look away.

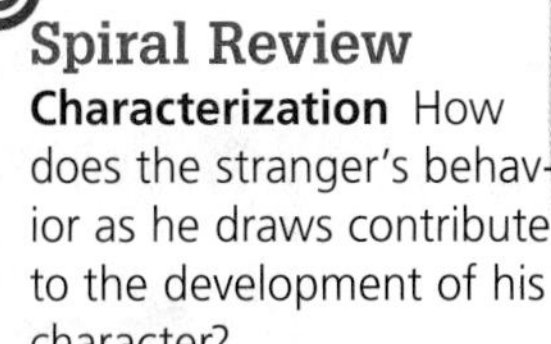

Spiral Review
Characterization How does the stranger's behavior as he draws contribute to the development of his character?

After several minutes of this the father came abruptly forward and dropped his hand on the stranger's shoulder. "The visit is over," he said calmly. It was the first time since they'd shaken hands that the two men had touched, and the touch had a galvanic effect upon the stranger: he dropped ruler and pencil at once, froze in his stooped posture, burst into frightened tears.

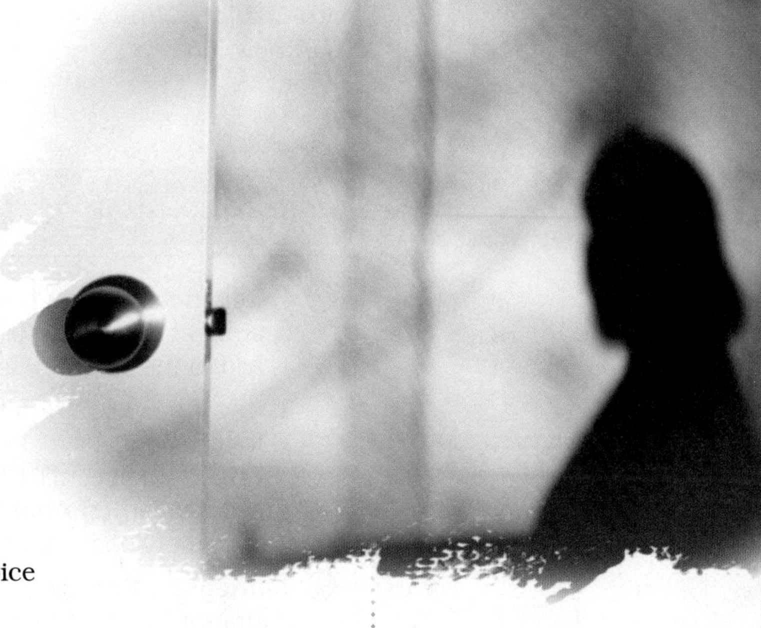

Now the visit truly was over; the stranger, at last, *was* leaving, having wiped away his tears and made a stoical effort to compose himself; but on the doorstep, to the father's astonishment, he made a final, preposterous appeal—he wanted to see the basement. "Just to sit on the stairs? In the dark? For a few quiet minutes? And you could close the door and forget me, you and your family could have your dinner and—"

The stranger was begging but the father was resolute. Without raising his voice he said, *"No. The visit is over."*

He shut the door, and locked it.

Locked it! His hands were shaking and his heart beat angrily.

He watched the stranger walk away—out to the sidewalk, out to the street, disappearing in the darkness. Had the streetlights gone out?

Behind the father the mother stood apologetic and defensive, wringing her hands in a classic stance. "Wasn't that *sad!* Wasn't that—*sad!* But we had no choice but to let him in, it was the only

Reading Check
Before he leaves, what request does the stranger make?

Everywhere the father looked, a pulse beat mute with rage.

decent thing to do." The father pushed past her without comment. In the living room he saw that the lights were flickering as if on the brink of going out; the patterned wallpaper seemed drained of color; a shadow lay upon it shaped like a bulbous cloud or growth. Even the robust green of the carpeting looked faded. Or was it an optical illusion? Everywhere the father looked, a pulse beat mute with rage. "*I* wasn't the one who opened the door to that man in the first place," the mother said, coming up behind the father and touching his arm. Without seeming to know what he did the father violently jerked his arm and thrust her away.

"Shut up. We'll forget it," he said.

"But—"

"We'll forget it."

The mother entered the kitchen walking slowly as if she'd been struck a blow. In fact, a bruise the size of a pear would materialize on her forearm by morning. When she reached out to steady herself she misjudged the distance of the door frame—or did the door frame recede an inch or two—and nearly lost her balance.

In the kitchen the lights were dim and an odor of sourish smoke, subtle but unmistakable, made her nostrils pinch.

She slammed open the oven door. Grabbed a pair of pot holders with insulated linings. "*I* wasn't the one, . . ." she cried, panting, "and you know it."

Critical Reading 

1. **Key Ideas and Details (a)** At what time of day does the stranger arrive at the house? **(b) Analyze:** In what ways does this choice add to the air of mystery surrounding the stranger?
2. **Key Ideas and Details (a) Describe:** How does the father react to the stranger's request to look around? **(b) Analyze Cause and Effect:** What conflict does this decision set up between the father and mother? **(c) Analyze Cause and Effect:** At the end of the story, how does the stranger's visit continue to affect the family?
3. **Integrate Knowledge and Ideas (a) Interpret:** How does the stranger react to the window seat? **(b) Interpret:** How does he react to the boy's bedroom? **(c) Speculate:** What do these details suggest about his relationship to his own father?
4. **Integrate Knowledge and Ideas (a) Deduce:** What apparent mistake does the stranger make when he responds to the mother's question about whether his family is still living?
(b) Make a Judgment: Is this a ghost story? Explain your answer.

After You Read *The Fall of the House of Usher • Where Is Here?*

Comparing Gothic Literature

1. **Craft and Structure (a)** Which character in Poe's story is most tormented? Explain. **(b)** Which character in Oates's story is tormented? **(c)** In what ways does the tormented character affect other characters in each story?
2. **Craft and Structure (a)** Where do readers first encounter a hint of the supernatural in Oates's story? **(b)** What are some supernatural elements in "The Fall of the House of Usher?" **(c)** Explain how these elements are both similar and different in the two stories.
3. **Craft and Structure (a)** What violent acts occur in "The Fall of the House of Usher?" **(b)** In what more subtle ways does Oates's story suggest the occurrence of mysterious but equally awful events?

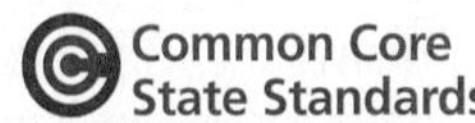

Common Core State Standards

Writing

9.a. Apply *grades 11-12 Reading standards* to literature.

10. Write routinely over shorter time frames for a range of tasks, purposes, and audiences.

Timed Writing

Explanatory Text: Analytical Essay

The castles and mansions that provide the settings for traditional Gothic tales are full of grandeur, darkness, and decay. These settings are one of the most recognizable elements of traditional Gothic fiction. Is setting equally important in a modern Gothic story?

Assignment: Write an **analytical essay** in which you explore the importance of setting in these two stories. Prewrite by answering the questions listed below to generate ideas and focus your analysis. **[40 minutes]**

- How are the settings in each story described? Note specific words each author uses to paint a picture of the setting.
- What *mood*, or atmosphere, does each setting have? Does this mood or atmosphere change as the story progresses? Explain.
- Which details in "Where Is Here?" show the setting as ordinary and which give it a frightening quality?
- Are the settings of "The Fall of the House of Usher" and "Where Is Here?" equally important to the events of each story? Explain.

As you write, support your ideas with detailed references to the stories.

5-Minute Planner

Complete these steps before you begin to write:

1. Read the prompt carefully. Underline key words and phrases.
2. Skim the stories and jot down notes about elements that address the focus questions in the prompt.
3. Write an outline to structure your ideas. **TIP** As part of your outline, note specific textual details you will use in each paragraph.
4. Reread the prompt, and draft your essay.

USE ACADEMIC VOCABULARY

As you write, use academic language, including the following words or their related forms:

quote
distinguish
illustrate
compare

For more on academic language, see the vocabulary charts in the introduction to this book.

Before You Read from *Moby-Dick*

Connecting to the Essential Question Americans tend to admire persistence. However, Captain Ahab, Herman Melville's most famous character, is persistent to the point of obsession. As you read, notice details that suggest the dark side of Ahab's determination. This will help as you consider the Essential Question: **What makes American literature American?**

Reading Literature
2. Determine two or more themes or central ideas of a text and analyze their development over the course of the text, including how they interact and build on one another to produce a complex account; provide an objective summary of the text.

Literary Analysis

A **symbol** is a person, place, or thing that has its own meaning and also represents something larger, usually an abstract idea. The main symbol in Melville's great novel—the whale that gives the book its title—is complex. To understand it as a symbol, reflect on all aspects of the whale's behavior and appearance, including the following qualities:

- Moby-Dick is enormous and powerful.
- Moby-Dick seems unpredictable but is controlled by natural laws.
- Moby-Dick seems immortal and indifferent to human suffering.

Analyzing the symbol of the whale will help you identify the novel's **theme,** its central message or comment on life. A writer develops theme through symbols, descriptions, characters, and imagery. A long and complex novel like *Moby-Dick* may have multiple themes. As you read, look for details related to concepts of good, evil, sacrifice, and revenge.

Reading Strategy

Preparing to Read Complex Texts Melville builds symbolic meaning and theme through details. As you read, **identify relevant details to determine the essential message.** Look for characters, settings, objects, and dialogue that suggest larger ideas. For example, Ahab's description of Moby-Dick provides a clue to the whale's essential meaning: "I see in him outrageous strength, with an inscrutable malice sinewing it." As you read, use a chart like the one shown to identify relevant details that will lead you to the novel's essential meanings.

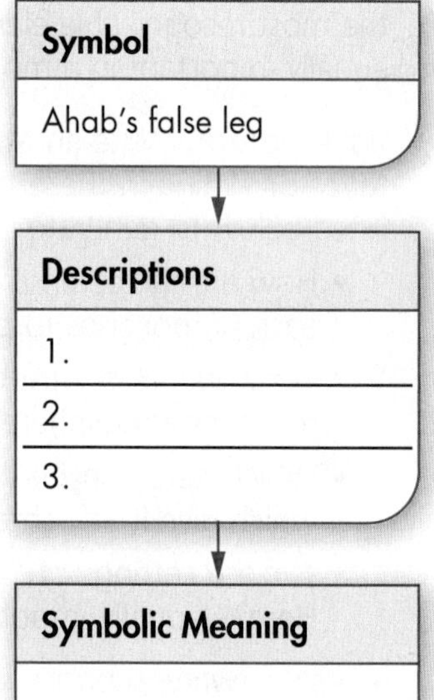

Symbol
Ahab's false leg
Descriptions
1.
2.
3.
Symbolic Meaning

Vocabulary

pedestrian (pi des′ trē ən) *adj.* going on foot; walking (p. 338)

impulsive (im pul′ siv) *adj.* done without thinking (p. 338)

inarticulate (in′ är tik′ yo͞o lət) *adj.* unclearly spoken or expressed (p. 339)

inscrutable (in skro͞ot′ ə bəl) *adj.* difficult to know or understand (p. 341)

maledictions (mal′ ə dik′ shənz) *n.* curses (p. 343)

prescient (presh′ ənt) *adj.* having foreknowledge (p. 348)

HERMAN MELVILLE *(1819–1891)*

Author of *Moby-Dick*

One of America's greatest novelists, Herman Melville was born in New York City, the son of a wealthy merchant. His family's comfortable situation changed drastically in 1830, however, when his father's business failed. Two years later, Melville's father died, leaving the family in debt. Melville spent the rest of his childhood working as a clerk, a farmhand, and a teacher to help support his family.

Whaling in the South Pacific Melville became a sailor at the age of nineteen and spent several years working on whaling ships in the South Pacific. He returned to the United States in 1844, after a brief period of service in the navy. Soon thereafter, Melville began his writing career, using his adventures in the South Seas as material for his fiction. He produced two popular novels, *Typee* (1846) and *Omoo* (1847), both set in the Pacific islands. His third novel, *Mardi* (1849), was more abstract and symbolic. When readers rejected the book, Melville grew melancholy. He continued writing, however, turning out two more novels over the next two years.

Writing in the Berkshires Using the profits from his popular novels, Melville bought Arrowhead, a farm near Pittsfield, Massachusetts. There, he befriended the author Nathaniel Hawthorne, who lived nearby. Encouraged by Hawthorne's interest, Melville redoubled his creative efforts. In 1851, he published his masterpiece, *Moby-Dick,* under the title *The Whale.*

A Moment of Pride *Moby-Dick* is a complex novel with several layers of meaning. On the surface, it is the story of the fateful voyage of a whaling ship. On another level, it is the story of a bitter man's quest for vengeance. On still another level, it is a philosophical examination of humanity's relationship to the natural world. When he finished the book, Melville sensed the magnitude of his achievement. Unfortunately, nineteenth-century readers rejected the book. They also spurned his next two novels and Melville fell into debt. The job he took as an inspector at the New York customs house became another experience that would inform his fiction, especially the story "Bartleby, the Scrivener."

Rediscovered In the latter part of his life, Melville privately published several volumes of poetry, a handful of short stories, and the novella *Billy Budd.* He died in 1891, unappreciated and unnoticed. In the 1920s, however, his work was rediscovered, and he finally received the recognition he deserved. Today, *Moby-Dick* is widely regarded as one of the finest novels in all of American literature.

FROM

MOBY-DICK

HERMAN MELVILLE

BACKGROUND *Moby-Dick* is the story of a man's obsession with the dangerous and mysterious white whale that years before had taken off one of his legs. The man, Captain Ahab, guides the *Pequod*, a whaling ship, and its crew in relentless pursuit of the whale, Moby-Dick. Among the more important members of the crew are Starbuck, the first mate; Stubb, the second mate; Flask, the third mate; Queequeg, Tashtego, and Daggoo, the harpooners; and Ishmael, the young sailor who narrates the story. When the crew signed aboard the *Pequod*, they believed the voyage to be a business venture. However, in the following excerpt, Ahab makes clear that his real purpose is to seek revenge against Moby-Dick.

◀ **Critical Viewing**
Which elements of this illustration emphasize human weakness in the face of nature? **[Analyze]**

FROM THE QUARTER-DECK

One morning shortly after breakfast, Ahab, as was his wont, ascended the cabin gangway to the deck. There most sea captains usually walk at that hour, as country gentlemen, after the same meal, take a few turns in the garden.

Soon his steady, ivory stride was heard, as to and fro he paced his old rounds, upon planks so familiar to his tread, that they were all over dented, like geological stones, with the peculiar mark of his walk. Did you fixedly gaze, too, upon that ribbed and dented brow; there also, you would see still stranger footprints—the footprints of his one unsleeping, ever-pacing thought.

But on the occasion in question, those dents looked deeper, even as his nervous step that morning left a deeper mark. And, so full of his thought was Ahab, that at every uniform turn that he made, now

Reading Check
Why are the *Pequod's* planks dented?

▲ **Critical Viewing**
How does this portrait of Ahab compare with your mental image of him? **[Compare and Contrast]**

at the mainmast and now at the binnacle,[1] you could almost see that thought turn in him as he turned, and pace in him as he paced; so completely possessing him, indeed, that it all but seemed the inward mold of every outer movement.

"D'ye mark him, Flask?" whispered Stubb; "the chick that's in him pecks the shell. 'Twill soon be out."

The hours wore on—Ahab now shut up within his cabin; anon, pacing the deck, with the same intense bigotry of purpose[2] in his aspect.

It drew near the close of day. Suddenly he came to a halt by the bulwarks, and inserting his bone leg into the auger hole there, and with one hand grasping a shroud, he ordered Starbuck to send everybody aft.

"Sir!" said the mate, astonished at an order seldom or never given on shipboard except in some extraordinary case.

"Send everybody aft," repeated Ahab. "Mastheads, there! come down!"

When the entire ship's company were assembled, and with curious and not wholly unapprehensive faces, were eyeing him, for he looked not unlike the weather horizon when a storm is coming up, Ahab, after rapidly glancing over the bulwarks, and then darting his eyes among the crew, started from his standpoint; and as though not a soul were nigh him resumed his heavy turns upon the deck. With bent head and half-slouched hat he continued to pace, unmindful of the wondering whispering among the men; till Stubb cautiously whispered to Flask, that Ahab must have summoned them there for the purpose of witnessing a pedestrian feat. But this did not last long. Vehemently pausing, he cried:

"What do ye do when ye see a whale, men?"

"Sing out for him!" was the impulsive rejoinder from a score of clubbed voices.

"Good!" cried Ahab, with a wild approval in his tones; observing the hearty animation into which his unexpected question had so magnetically thrown them.

"And what do ye next, men?"

"Lower away, and after him!"

"And what tune is it ye pull to, men?"

"A dead whale or a stove[3] boat!"

More and more strangely and fiercely glad and approving, grew the countenance of the old man at every shout; while the mariners began to gaze curiously at each other, as if marveling how it was that they themselves became so excited at such seemingly purposeless questions.

Vocabulary

pedestrian (pi des´ trē ən) *adj.* going on foot; walking

impulsive (im pul´ siv) *adj.* done without thinking

1. **binnacle** (bin´ ə kəl) *n.* case enclosing a ship's compass.
2. **bigotry of purpose** complete single-mindedness.
3. **stove** *v.* broken; smashed.

But, they were all eagerness again, as Ahab, now half-revolving in his pivot hole, with one hand reaching high up a shroud,[4] and tightly, almost convulsively grasping it, addressed them thus:

"All ye mastheaders have before now heard me give orders about a white whale. Look ye! d'ye see this Spanish ounce of gold?"—holding up a broad bright coin to the sun—"it is a sixteen-dollar piece, men. D'ye see it? Mr. Starbuck, hand me yon topmaul."

While the mate was getting the hammer, Ahab, without speaking, was slowly rubbing the gold piece against the skirts of his jacket, as if to heighten its luster, and without using any words was meanwhile lowly humming to himself, producing a sound so strangely muffled and inarticulate that it seemed the mechanical humming of the wheels of his vitality in him.

Vocabulary
inarticulate (in′ är tik′ yo͞o lit′) *adj.* unclearly spoken or expressed

Receiving the topmaul from Starbuck, he advanced towards the mainmast with the hammer uplifted in one hand, exhibiting the gold with the other, and with a high raised voice exclaiming: "Whosoever of ye raises me a white-headed whale with a wrinkled brow and a crooked jaw; whosoever of ye raises me that white-headed whale, with three holes punctured in his starboard fluke[5]—look ye, whosoever of ye raises me that same white whale, he shall have this gold ounce, my boys!"

"Huzza! huzza!" cried the seamen, as with swinging tarpaulins they hailed the act of nailing the gold to the mast.

"It's a white whale, I say," resumed Ahab, as he threw down the topmaul: "a white whale. Skin your eyes for him, men; look sharp for white water; if ye see but a bubble, sing out."

All this while Tashtego, Daggoo, and Queequeg had looked on with even more intense interest and surprise than the rest, and at the mention of the wrinkled brow and crooked jaw they had started as if each was separately touched by some specific recollection.

"Captain Ahab," said Tashtego, "that white whale must be the same that some call Moby-Dick."

"Moby-Dick?" shouted Ahab. "Do ye know the white whale then, Tash?"

"Does he fantail[6] a little curious, sir, before he goes down?" said the Gay-Header deliberately.

"And has he a curious spout, too," said Daggoo, "very bushy, even for a parmacetty,[7] and mighty quick, Captain Ahab?"

"And he have one, two, tree—oh! good many iron in him hide, too, Captain," cried Queequeg disjointedly, "all twiske-tee betwisk, like him—him—" faltering hard for a word, and screwing his hand round and round as though uncorking a bottle—"like him—him—"

"Corkscrew!" cried Ahab, "aye, Queequeg, the harpoons lie all twisted and wrenched in him; aye, Daggoo, his spout is a big one, like

What reward does Ahab offer to the man who spots the white whale?

4. **shroud** *n.* set of ropes from a ship's side to the masthead.
5. **starboard fluke** (flo͞ok) *n.* right half of a whale's tail.
6. **fantail** *v.* to spread the tail like a fan.
7. **parmacetty** (pär′ mə set′ ē) *n.* dialect for sperm whale, from which spermaceti was derived. Spermaceti is a high quality oil that was once used to make candles and other products.

▲ **Critical Viewing** What does this image suggest about the perils involved in whaling? **[Interpret]**

a whole shock of wheat, and white as a pile of our Nantucket wool after the great annual sheepshearing; aye, Tashtego, and he fantails like a split jib in a squall. Death and devils! men, it is Moby-Dick ye have seen—Moby-Dick—Moby-Dick!"

"Captain Ahab," said Starbuck, who, with Stubb and Flask, had thus far been eyeing his superior with increasing surprise, but at last seemed struck with a thought which somewhat explained all the wonder. "Captain Ahab, I have heard of Moby-Dick—but it was not Moby-Dick that took off thy leg?"

"Who told thee that?" cried Ahab; then pausing, "Aye, Starbuck; aye, my hearties all round; it was Moby-Dick that dismasted me; Moby-Dick that brought me to this dead stump I stand on now. Aye, aye," he shouted with a terrific, loud, animal sob, like that of a heartstricken moose; "Aye, aye! it was that accursed white whale that razeed me; made a poor pegging lubber[8] for me forever and a day!" Then tossing both arms, with measureless imprecations he shouted out: "Aye, aye! and I'll chase him round Good Hope, and round the Horn, and round the Norway Maelstrom, and round perdition's flames before I give him up. And this is what ye have shipped for, men! to chase that white whale on both sides of land, and over all sides of earth, till he spouts black blood and rolls fin out. What say ye, men, will ye splice hands on it, now? I think ye do look brave."

"Aye, aye!" shouted the harpooneers and seamen, running closer to the excited old man: "A sharp eye for the white whale; a sharp lance for Moby-Dick!"

"God bless ye," he seemed to half sob and half shout. "God bless

8. **lubber** (lub´ ər) *n.* slow, clumsy person.

ye, men. Steward! go draw the great measure of grog. But what's this long face about, Mr. Starbuck; wilt thou not chase the white whale? art not game for Moby-Dick?"

"I am game for his crooked jaw, and for the jaws of Death too, Captain Ahab, if it fairly comes in the way of the business we follow; but I came here to hunt whales, not my commander's vengeance. How many barrels will thy vengeance yield thee even if thou gettest it, Captain Ahab? it will not fetch thee much in our Nantucket market."

"Nantucket market! Hoot! But come closer, Starbuck; thou requirest a little lower layer. If money's to be the measurer, man, and the accountants have computed their great countinghouse the globe, by girdling it with guineas, one to every three parts of an inch; then, let me tell thee, that my vengeance will fetch a great premium *here!*"

Literary Analysis
Theme What do Ahab's comments suggest about the value of money compared with great desire?

"He smites his chest," whispered Stubb, "what's that for? methinks it rings most vast, but hollow."

"Vengeance on a dumb brute!" cried Starbuck, "that simply smote thee from blindest instinct! Madness! To be enraged with a dumb thing, Captain Ahab, seems blasphemous."

"Hark ye yet again—the little lower layer. All visible objects, man, are but as pasteboard masks. But in each event—in the living act, the undoubted deed—there, some unknown but still reasoning thing puts forth the moldings of its features from behind the unreasoning mask. If man will strike, strike through the mask! How can the prisoner reach outside except by thrusting through the wall? To me, the white whale is that wall, shoved near to me. Sometimes I think there's naught beyond. But 'tis enough. He tasks me; he heaps me; I see in him outrageous strength, with an **inscrutable** malice sinewing it. That inscrutable thing is chiefly what I hate; and be the white whale agent, or be the white whale principal, I will wreak that hate upon him. Talk not to me of blasphemy, man; I'd strike the sun if it insulted me. For could the sun do that, then could I do the other; since there is ever a sort of fair play herein, jealousy presiding over all creations. But not my master, man, is even that fair play. Who's over me? Truth hath no confines. Take off thine eye! more intolerable than fiends' glarings is a doltish stare! So, so; thou reddenest and palest; my heat has melted thee to anger-glow. But look ye, Starbuck, what is said in heat, that thing unsays itself. There are men from whom warm words are small indignity. I meant not to incense thee. Let it go. Look! see yonder Turkish cheeks of spotted tawn—living, breathing pictures painted by the sun. The pagan leopards—the unrecking and unworshiping things, that live, and seek, and give no reasons for the torrid life they feel! The crew, man, the crew! Are they not one and all with Ahab, in this matter of the whale? See Stubb! he laughs! See yonder Chilean! he snorts to think of it. Stand up amid the general hurricane, thy one tossed sapling cannot, Starbuck! And what is it? Reckon it. 'Tis but to help strike a fin; no wondrous feat for Starbuck. What is it more? From this one poor hunt, then, the

Vocabulary
inscrutable (in skroo̅t′ ə bəl) *adj.* difficult to know or understand

What is Starbuck's objection to Ahab's desire for vengeance on a "dumb brute"?

best lance out of all Nantucket, surely he will not hang back, when every foremasthand has clutched a whetstone. Ah! constrainings seize thee; I see! the billow lifts thee! Speak, but speak!—Aye, aye! thy silence, then, that voices thee. *(Aside)* Something shot from my dilated nostrils, he has inhaled it in his lungs. Starbuck now is mine; cannot oppose me now, without rebellion."

"God keep me!—keep us all!" murmured Starbuck, lowly.

Reading Strategy
Identifying Details to Determine Essential Message What important details in his environment does Ahab fail to notice?

But in his joy at the enchanted, tacit acquiescence of the mate, Ahab did not hear his foreboding invocation; nor yet the low laugh from the hold; nor yet the presaging vibrations of the winds in the cordage; nor yet the hollow flap of the sails against the masts, as for a moment their hearts sank in. For again Starbuck's downcast eyes lighted up with the stubbornness of life; the subterranean laugh died away; the winds blew on; the sails filled out; the ship heaved and rolled as before. Ah, ye admonitions and warnings! why stay ye not when ye come? But rather are ye predictions than warnings, ye shadows! Yet not so much predictions from without, as verifications of the fore-going things within. For with little external to constrain us, the innermost necessities in our being, these still drive us on.

"The measure! the measure!" cried Ahab.

Receiving the brimming pewter, and turning to the harpooneers, he ordered them to produce their weapons. Then ranging them before him near the capstan,[9] with their harpoons in their hands, while his three mates stood at his side with their lances, and the rest of the ship's company formed a circle round the group; he stood for an instant searchingly eyeing every man of his crew. But those wild eyes met his, as the bloodshot eyes of the prairie wolves meet the eye of their leader, ere he rushes on at their head in the trail of the bison; but, alas! only to fall into the hidden snare of the Indian.

"Drink and pass!" he cried, handing the heavy charged flagon to the nearest seamen. "The crew alone now drink. Round with it, round! Short drafts—long swallows, men; 'tis hot as Satan's hoof. So, so; it goes round excellently. It spiralizes in ye; forks out at the serpent-snapping eye. Well done; almost drained. That way it went, this way it comes. Hand it me—here's a hollow! Men, ye seem the years; so brimming life is gulped and gone. Steward, refill!

"Attend now, my braves. I have mustered ye all round this capstan; and ye mates, flank me with your lances; and ye harpooneers, stand there with your irons; and ye, stout mariners, ring me in, that I may in some sort revive a noble custom of my fishermen fathers before me. O men, you will yet see that—Ha! boy, come back? bad pennies come not sooner. Hand it me. Why, now, this pewter had run brimming again, wer't not thou St. Vitus' imp[10]—away, thou ague![11]

"Advance, ye mates! cross your lances full before me. Well done!

---

9. **capstan** (kap′ stən) *n.* large cylinder, turned by hand, around which cables are wound.
10. **St. Vitus' imp** offspring of St. Vitus, the patron saint of people stricken with the nervous disorder *chorea* which is characterized by irregular, jerking movements.
11. **ague** (ā′ gyo͞o) *n.* a chill or fit of shivering.

Let me touch the axis." So saying, with extended arm, he grasped the three level, radiating lances at their crossed center; while so doing, suddenly and nervously twitched them; meanwhile glancing intently from Starbuck to Stubb; from Stubb to Flask. It seemed as though, by some nameless, interior volition, he would fain have shocked into them the same fiery emotion accumulated within the Leyden jar[12] of his own magnetic life. The three mates quailed before his strong, sustained, and mystic aspect. Stubb and Flask looked sideways from him; the honest eye of Starbuck fell downright.

"In vain!" cried Ahab; "but, maybe, 'tis well. For did ye three but once take the full-forced shock, then mine own electric thing, *that* had perhaps expired from out me. Perchance, too, it would have dropped ye dead. Perchance ye need it not. Down lances! And now, ye mates, I do appoint ye three cupbearers to my three pagan kinsmen there—yon three most honorable gentlemen and noblemen, my valiant harpooneers. Disdain the task? What, when the great Pope washes the feet of beggars, using his tiara for ewer? Oh, my sweet cardinals! your own condescension, that shall bend ye to it. I do not order ye; ye will it. Cut your seizings and draw the poles, ye harpooneers!"

Silently obeying the order, the three harpooneers now stood with the detached iron part of their harpoons, some three feet long, held, barbs up, before him.

"Stab me not with that keen steel! Cant them; cant them over! know ye not the goblet end? Turn up the socket! So, so; now, ye cupbearers, advance. The irons! take them; hold them while I fill!" Forthwith, slowly going from one officer to the other, he brimmed the harpoon sockets with the fiery waters from the pewter.

"Now, three to three, ye stand. Commend the murderous chalices! Bestow them, ye who are now made parties to this indissoluble league. Ha! Starbuck! but the deed is done! Yon ratifying sun now waits to sit upon it. Drink, ye harpooneers! drink and swear, ye men that man the deathful whaleboat's bow—Death to Moby-Dick! God hunt us all, if we do not hunt Moby-Dick to his death!" The long, barbed steel goblets were lifted; and to cries and **maledictions** against the white whale, the spirits were simultaneously quaffed down with a hiss. Starbuck paled, and turned, and shivered. Once more, and finally, the replenished pewter went the rounds among the frantic crew; when, waving his free hand to them, they all dispersed; and Ahab retired within his cabin.

After Moby-Dick has been sighted in the Pacific Ocean, the Pequod's *boats pursue the whale for two days. One of the boats has been sunk, and Ahab's ivory leg has been broken off. However, as the next day dawns, the chase continues.*

Literary Analysis
Symbol What is Ahab's symbolic purpose in having his harpooners drink from their weapons?

Vocabulary
maledictions (mal′ ə dik′ shənz) *n.* curses

How do the three mates react to Ahab's gaze?

---

12. **Leyden** (līd′ ən) **jar** *n.* glass jar coated inside and out with tinfoil and having a metal rod connected to the inner lining; used to condense static electricity.

THE AMERICAN EXPERIENCE

The Golden Age of Yankee Whaling

▲ Model of a British whaling ship

During the nineteenth century, New England grew prosperous from whaling. Hundreds of ships set out from the ports of Nantucket, New Bedford, Boston, Sag Harbor, and New London and spread out across the world's seas in pursuit of whales. Whale oil and other by-products could make captains and ship owners rich, but whaling was a hard business. Voyages lasted as long as three years and many sailors died at sea. With the invention of the electric lamp (1879) and the development of spring steel (1906), whaling declined. However, during its heyday, whaling created fortunes.

CONNECT TO THE LITERATURE

How do these facts about the business of whaling enhance your understanding of *Moby-Dick*?

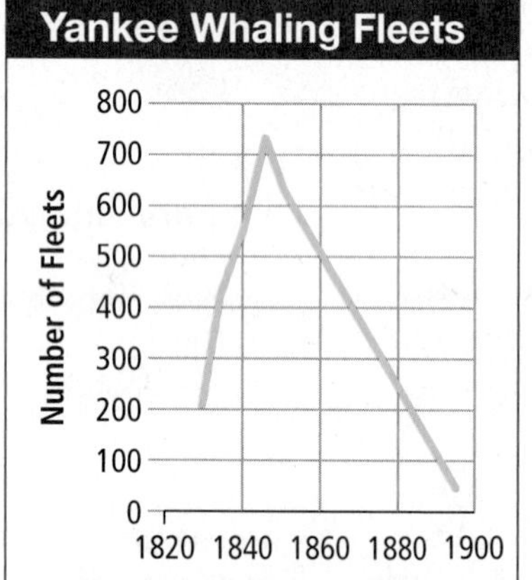

WHALE PRODUCTS

- Corsets (from whale bone)
- Lamp oil
- Candles
- Soaps
- Machine oil
- Vitamin supplement
- Perfume ambergris

▶ Bottle of whale liver oil

- Brushes
- Buggy whips
- Combs
- Hoop skirts
- Fishing rods

Baleen bristles shown with a floorbrush made from them. ▶

KENDALL MFG CO
Soapine
THE Dirt Killer
WILL NOT INJURE
HANDS or FABRIC

◀ Whale oil was used to make soap.

▼ An iron harpoon bent in the hunt

▲ Whale blubber pot
After a whale was caught, the crew stripped the blubber and heated it in giant pots like this one.

THE CHASE—THIRD DAY

The morning of the third day dawned fair and fresh, and once more the solitary night man at the foremasthead was relieved by crowds of the daylight lookouts, who dotted every mast and almost every spar.

"D'ye see him?" cried Ahab; but the whale was not yet in sight.

"In his infallible wake, though; but follow that wake, that's all. Helm there; steady, as thou goest, and hast been going. What a lovely day again! were it a new-made world, and made for a summerhouse to the angels, and this morning the first of its throwing open to them, a fairer day could not dawn upon that world. Here's food for thought, had Ahab time to think; but Ahab never thinks; he only feels, feels, feels; that's tingling enough for mortal man! to think's audacity. God only has that right and privilege. Thinking is, or ought to be, a coolness and a calmness; and our poor hearts throb, and our poor brains beat too much for that. And yet, I've sometimes thought my brain was very calm—frozen calm, this old skull cracks so, like a glass in which the contents turned to ice, and shiver it. And still this hair is growing now; this moment growing, and heat must breed it; but no, it's like that sort of common grass that will grow anywhere, between the earthy clefts of Greenland ice or in Vesuvius lava. How the wild winds blow it; they whip it about me as the torn shreds of split sails lash the tossed ship they cling to. A vile wind that has no doubt blown ere this through prison corridors and cells, and wards of hospitals, and ventilated them, and now comes blowing hither as innocent as fleeces.[13] Out upon it!—it's tainted. Were I the wind, I'd blow no more on such a wicked, miserable world. I'd crawl somewhere to a cave, and slink there. And yet, 'tis a noble and heroic thing, the wind! who ever conquered it? In every fight it has the last and bitterest blow. Run tilting at it, and you but run through it. Ha! a coward wind that strikes stark-naked men, but will not stand to receive a single blow. Even Ahab is a braver thing—a nobler thing than *that.* Would now the wind but had a body but all the things that most exasperate and outrage mortal man, all these things are bodiless, but only bodiless as objects, not as agents. There's a most special, a most cunning, oh, a most malicious difference! And yet, I say again, and swear it now, that there's something all glorious and gracious in the wind. These warm trade winds, at least, that in the clear heavens blow straight on, in strong and steadfast, vigorous mildness; and veer not from their mark, however the baser currents of the sea may turn and tack, and mightiest Mississippis of the land swift and swerve about, uncertain where to go at last. And by the eternal poles! these same trades that so directly blow my good ship on; these trades, or something like them—something so unchangeable, and

Literary Analysis
Symbol What does the wind symbolize to Ahab?

As the third day dawns, has the whale been sighted?

13. fleeces (flēs′ əz) *n.* sheep.

LITERATURE IN CONTEXT

Humanities Connection

The Whale as Archetype

An archetype is an image, a symbol, a character, or a plot that recurs so consistently across cultures and time that it is considered universal. The term comes from Swiss psychologist Carl Jung (1875–1961), who believed that certain human experiences have become a shared genetic memory. According to Jung, this "collective unconscious" explains why archetypes evoke strong feelings in people of all cultures.

The whale had made many appearances in myth, folklore, literature, and art well before Melville used it as a central symbol in *Moby-Dick*. Perhaps the most famous is the biblical tale in which Jonah is swallowed by a whale and then cast ashore. Because the whale is the largest of all animals, its image evokes fear and awe, as well as a sense of the power of nature. In *Moby-Dick*, Melville used these archetypal associations to create fiction of enduring power.

Connect to the Literature

Do you think modern readers react with fear and awe to the image of a whale? Explain.

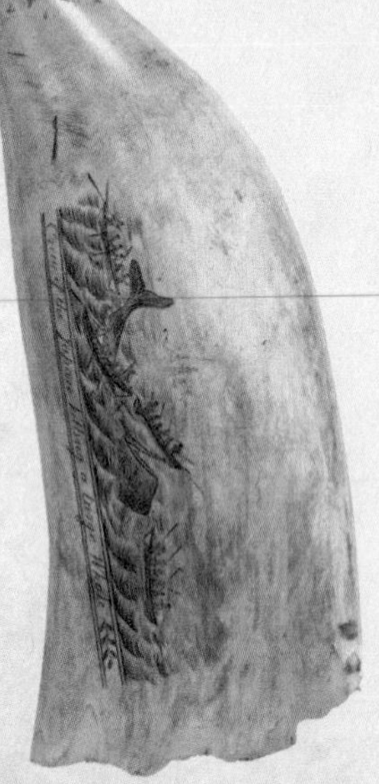

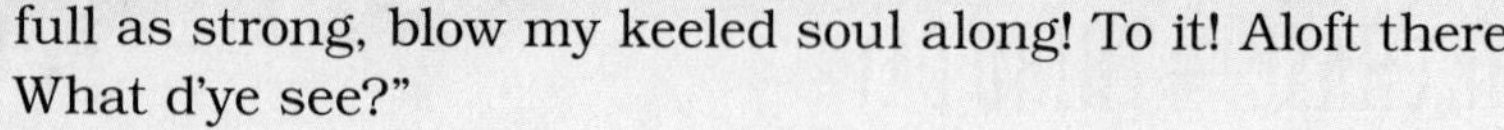

full as strong, blow my keeled soul along! To it! Aloft there! What d'ye see?"

"Nothing, sir."

"Nothing! and noon at hand! The doubloon[14] goes a-begging! See the sun! Aye, aye, it must be so. I've oversailed him. How, got the start? Aye, he's chasing me now; not I, him—that's bad; I might have known it, too. Fool! the lines—the harpoons he's towing.

Aye, aye, I have run him by last night. About! about! Come down, all of ye, but the regular lookouts! Man the braces!"

Steering as she had done, the wind had been somewhat on the Pequod's quarter, so that now being pointed in the reverse direction, the braced ship sailed hard upon the breeze as she rechurned the cream in her own white wake.

"Against the wind he now steers for the open jaw," murmured Starbuck to himself, as he coiled the new-hauled main brace upon the rail. "God keep us, but already my bones feel damp within me, and from the inside wet my flesh. I misdoubt me that I disobey my God in obeying him!"

"Stand by to sway me up!" cried Ahab, advancing to the hempen basket.[15] "We should meet him soon."

"Aye, aye, sir," and straightway Starbuck did Ahab's bidding, and once more Ahab swung on high.

A whole hour now passed; gold-beaten out to ages. Time itself now held long breaths with keen suspense. But at last, some three points off the weather bow, Ahab descried the spout again, and instantly from the three mastheads three shrieks went up as if the tongues of fire had voiced it.

"Forehead to forehead I meet thee, this third time, Moby-Dick! On deck there!—brace sharper up; crowd her into the wind's eye. He's too far off to lower yet, Mr. Starbuck. The sails shake! Stand over that helmsman with a topmaul! So, so; he travels fast, and I must down. But let me have one more good round look aloft here at the sea; there's time for that. An old, old sight, and yet somehow so young; aye, and not changed a wink since I first saw it, a boy, from the sand hills of Nantucket! The same!—the same!—the same to Noah as to me. There's a soft shower to leeward. Such lovely leewardings! They must lead somewhere—to something else than common land, more palmy than the palms. Leeward! the white whale goes that way; look to windward, then; the better if the bitterer quarter. But good-bye, good-bye, old masthead! What's this?—green? aye, tiny mosses in these warped cracks. No such green weather stains on Ahab's head! There's

14. **doubloon** (du blo͞on′) *n.* old Spanish gold coin. (Ahab offered it as a reward to the first man to spot the whale.)
15. **hempen basket** rope basket. (The basket was constructed earlier by Ahab, so that he could be raised, by means of a pulley device, to the top of the mainmast.)

the difference now between man's old age and matter's. But aye, old mast, we both grow old together; sound in our hulls, though, are we not, my ship? Aye, minus a leg, that's all. By heaven this dead wood has the better of my live flesh every way. I can't compare with it; and I've known some ships made of dead trees outlast the lives of men made of the most vital stuff of vital fathers. What's that he said? he should still go before me, my pilot; and yet to be seen again? But where? Will I have eyes at the bottom of the sea, supposing I descend those endless stairs? and all night I've been sailing from him, wherever he did sink to. Aye, aye, like many more thou told'st direful truth as touching thyself, O Parsee; but, Ahab, there thy shot fell short. Good-bye, masthead—keep a good eye upon the whale, the while I'm gone. We'll talk tomorrow, nay, tonight, when the white whale lies down there, tied by head and tail."

He gave the word; and still gazing round him, was steadily lowered through the cloven blue air to the deck.

In due time the boats were lowered; but as standing in his shallop's stern, Ahab just hovered upon the point of the descent, he waved to the mate—who held one of the tackle ropes on deck—and bade him pause.

"Starbuck!"

"Sir?"

"For the third time my soul's ship starts upon this voyage, Starbuck."

"Aye, sir, thou wilt have it so."

"Some ships sail from their ports, and ever afterwards are missing, Starbuck!"

"Truth, sir: saddest truth."

"Some men die at ebb tide; some at low water; some at the full of the flood—and I feel now like a billow that's all one crested comb, Starbuck. I am old—shake hands with me, man."

Their hands met; their eyes fastened; Starbuck's tears the glue.

"Oh, my captain, my captain!—noble heart—go not—go not!—see, it's a brave man that weeps; how great the agony of the persuasion then!"

"Lower away!"—cried Ahab, tossing the mate's arm from him. "Stand by the crew!"

In an instant the boat was pulling round close under the stern.

"The sharks! the sharks!" cried a voice from the low cabin window there; "O master, my master, come back!"

But Ahab heard nothing; for his own voice was high-lifted then; and the boat leaped on.

Yet the voice spake true; for scarce had he pushed from the ship, when numbers of sharks, seemingly rising from out the dark waters beneath the hull, maliciously snapped at the blades of the oars, every time they dipped in the water; and in this way accompanied the boat with their bites. It is a thing not uncommonly happen-

Literary Analysis
Symbol What symbolic meaning do you find in the comparison between Ahab and the mast?

What does Starbuck beg Ahab to do?

Vocabulary
prescient (presh′ ənt) *adj.* having foreknowledge

▼ Critical Viewing
Does this illustration seem like a realistic rendering of an actual situation? Explain. **[Evaluate]**

ing to the whaleboats in those swarming seas; the sharks at times apparently following them in the same prescient way that vultures hover over the banners of marching regiments in the east. But these were the first sharks that had been observed by the *Pequod* since the White Whale had been first descried; and whether it was that Ahab's crew were all such tiger-yellow barbarians, and therefore their flesh more musky to the senses of the sharks—a matter sometimes well known to affect them—however it was, they seemed to follow that one boat without molesting the others.

"Heart of wrought steel!" murmured Starbuck gazing over the side, and following with his eyes the receding boat—"canst thou yet ring boldly to that sight?—lowering thy keel among ravening sharks, and followed by them, open-mouthed to the chase; and this the critical third day?—For when three days flow together in one continuous intense pursuit; be sure the first is the morning, the second the noon, and the third the evening and the end of that thing—be that end what it may. Oh! my God! what is this that shoots through me, and leaves me so deadly calm, yet expectant—fixed at the top of a shudder! Future things swim before me, as in empty outlines and skeletons; all the past is somehow grown dim. Mary, girl; thou fadest in pale glories behind me; boy! I seem to see but thy eyes grown wondrous blue.[16] Strangest problems of life seem clearing; but clouds sweep between—Is my journey's end coming? My legs feel faint; like his who has footed it all day. Feel thy heart—beats it yet? Stir thyself, Starbuck!—stave it off—move, move! speak aloud!—Masthead there! See ye my boy's hand on the hill?—Crazed—aloft there!—keep thy keenest eye upon the boats—mark well the whale!—Ho! again!—drive off that hawk! see! he pecks—he tears the vane"—pointing to the red flag flying at the maintruck—"Ha, he soars away with it!—Where's the old man now? see'st thou that sight, oh Ahab!—shudder, shudder!"

The boats had not gone very far, when by a signal from the mastheads—a downward pointed arm, Ahab knew that the whale had sounded; but intending to be near him at the next rising, he held on his way a little sideways from the vessel; the becharmed crew maintaining the profoundest silence, as the head-beat waves

---

16. Mary . . . blue reference to Starbuck's wife and son.

hammered and hammered against the opposing bow.

"Drive, drive in your nails, oh ye waves! to their uttermost heads drive them in! ye but strike a thing without a lid; and no coffin and no hearse can be mine:—and hemp only can kill me! Ha! ha!"

Suddenly the waters around them slowly swelled in broad circles; then quickly upheaved, as if sideways sliding from a submerged berg of ice, swiftly rising to the surface. A low rumbling sound was heard; a subterraneous hum; and then all held their breaths; as bedraggled with trailing ropes, and harpoons, and lances, a vast form shot lengthwise, but obliquely from the sea. Shrouded in a thin drooping veil of mist, it hovered for a moment in the rainbowed air; and then fell swamping back into the deep. Crushed thirty feet upwards, the waters flashed for an instant like heaps of fountains, then brokenly sank in a shower of flakes, leaving the circling surface creamed like new milk round the marble trunk of the whale.

"Give way!" cried Ahab to the oarsmen, and the boats darted forward to the attack; but maddened by yesterday's fresh irons that corroded in him, Moby-Dick seemed combinedly possessed by all the angels that fell from heaven. The wide tiers of welded tendons overspreading his broad white forehead, beneath the transparent skin, looked knitted together; as head on, he came churning his tail among the boats; and once more flailed them apart; spilling out the irons and lances from the two mates' boats, and dashing in one side of the upper part of their bows, but leaving Ahab's almost without a scar.

While Daggoo and Queequeg were stopping the strained planks; and as the whale swimming out from them, turned, and showed one entire flank as he shot by them again; at that moment a quick cry went up. Lashed round and round to the fish's back; pinioned in the turns upon turns in which, during the past night, the whale had reeled the involutions of the lines around him, the half-torn body of the Parsee was seen; his sable raiment frayed to shreds; his distended eyes turned full upon old Ahab.

The harpoon dropped from his hand.

"Befooled, befooled!"—drawing in a long lean breath—"Aye, Parsee! I see thee again—Aye, and thou goest before; and this, this then is the hearse that thou didst promise. But I hold thee to the last letter of thy word. Where is the second hearse? Away, mates, to the ship! those boats are useless now; repair them if ye can in time, and return to me; if not, Ahab is enough to die—Down, men! the first thing that but offers to jump from this boat I stand in, that thing I harpoon. Ye are not other men, but my arms and my legs; and so obey me—Where's the whale? gone down again?"

But he looked too nigh the boat; for as if bent upon escaping with the corpse he bore, and as if the particular place of the last encounter had been but a stage in his leeward voyage, Moby-Dick was now again steadily swimming forward; and had almost passed the ship—which thus far had been sailing in the contrary direction to him,

Literary Analysis
Symbol What symbolic meaning is suggested by the description of the whale's behavior as he breaks the water's surface?

Reading Strategy
Identifying Details to Determine Essential Message What does Ahab realize when he sees Parsee's body lashed to Moby-Dick?

What happens to Parsee?

▼ **Critical Viewing** Which details from the story did the artist use to create this illustration? **[Analyze]**

though for the present her headway had been stopped. He seemed swimming with his utmost velocity, and now only intent upon pursuing his own straight path in the sea.

"Oh! Ahab," cried Starbuck, "not too late is it, even now, the third day, to desist. See! Moby-Dick seeks thee not. It is thou, thou, that madly seekest him!"

Setting sail to the rising wind, the lonely boat was swiftly impelled to leeward, by both oars and canvas. And at last when Ahab was sliding by the vessel, so near as plainly to distinguish Starbuck's face as he leaned over the rail, he hailed him to turn the vessel about, and follow him, not too swiftly, at a judicious interval. Glancing upwards he saw Tashtego, Queequeg, and Daggoo, eagerly mounting to the three mastheads; while the oarsmen were rocking in the two staved boats which had just been hoisted to the side, and were busily at work in repairing them, one after the other, through the portholes, as he sped, he also caught flying glimpses of Stubb and Flask, busying themselves on deck among bundles of new irons and lances. As he saw all this; as he heard the hammers in the broken boats; far other hammers seemed driving a nail into his heart. But he rallied. And now marking that the vane or flag was gone from the main masthead, he shouted to Tashtego, who had just gained that perch, to descend again for another flag, and a hammer and nails, and so nail it to the mast.

Whether fagged by the three days' running chase, and the resistance to his swimming in the knotted hamper he bore; or whether it was some latent deceitfulness and malice in him: whichever was true, the White Whale's way now began to abate, as it seemed, from the boat so rapidly nearing him once more; though indeed the whale's last start had not been so long a one as before. And still as Ahab glided over the waves the unpitying sharks accompanied him; and so pertinaciously stuck to the boat; and so continually bit at the plying oars, that the blades became jagged and crunched, and left small splinters in the sea, at almost every dip.

"Heed them not! those teeth but give new rowlocks to your oars. Pull on! 'tis the better rest, the sharks' jaw than the yielding water."

"But at every bite, sir, the thin blades grow smaller and smaller!"

"They will last long enough! pull on!—But who can tell"—he muttered—"whether these sharks swim to feast on the whale or on Ahab?—But pull on! Aye, all alive, now—we near him. The helm! take the helm! let me pass"—and so saying, two of the oarsmen helped him forward to the bows of the still flying boat.

At length as the craft was cast to one side, and ran ranging along with the White Whale's flank, he seemed strangely oblivious of its advance—as the whale sometimes will—and Ahab was fairly within the smoky mountain mist, which, thrown off from the whale's spout, curled round his great Monadnock[17] hump; he was even thus close to him; when, with body arched back, and both arms lengthwise high-lifted to the poise, he darted his fierce iron, and his far fiercer curse into the hated whale. As both steel and curse sank to the socket, as if sucked into a morass, Moby-Dick sidewise writhed; spasmodically rolled his nigh flank against the bow, and, without staving a hole in it, so suddenly canted the boat over, that had it not been for the elevated part of the gunwale to which he then clung, Ahab would once more have been tossed into the sea. As it was, three of the oarsmen—who foreknew not the precise instant of the dart, and were therefore unprepared for its effects—these were flung out; but so fell, that, in an instant two of them clutched the gunwale again, and rising to its level on a combing wave, hurled themselves bodily inboard again; the third man helplessly dropping astern, but still afloat and swimming.

Almost simultaneously, with a mighty volition of ungraduated, instantaneous swiftness, the White Whale darted through the weltering sea. But when Ahab cried out to the steersman to take new turns with the line, and hold it so; and commanded the crew to turn round on their seats, and tow the boat up to the mark; the moment the treacherous line felt that double strain and tug, it snapped in the empty air!

"What breaks in me? Some sinew cracks!—'tis whole again; oars! oars! Burst in upon him!"

Hearing the tremendous rush of the sea-crashing boat, the whale wheeled round to present his blank forehead at bay; but in that evolution, catching sight of the nearing black hull of the ship; seemingly seeing in it the source of all his persecutions; bethinking it—it may be—a larger and nobler foe; of a sudden, he bore down upon its advancing prow, smiting his jaws amid fiery showers of foam.

Ahab staggered; his hand smote his forehead. "I grow blind; hands! stretch out before me that I may yet grope my way. Is't night?"

"The whale! The ship!" cried the cringing oarsmen.

"Oars! oars! Slope downwards to thy depths. O sea that ere it be forever too late, Ahab may slide this last, last time upon his mark! I see: the ship! the ship! Dash on, my men! will ye not save my ship?"

But as the oarsmen violently forced their boat through the sledge-hammering seas, the before whale-smitten bow-ends of two planks burst through, and in an instant almost, the temporarily disabled

17. **Monadnock** (mə nad′ näk) mountain in New Hampshire.

Literary Analysis
Symbol What symbolic connection between his own body and the boat does Ahab seem to feel?

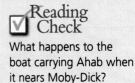

What happens to the boat carrying Ahab when it nears Moby-Dick?

boat lay nearly level with the waves; its half-wading, splashing crew, trying hard to stop the gap and bale out the pouring water.

Meantime, for that one beholding instant, Tashtego's masthead hammer remained suspended in his hand; and the red flag, half wrapping him as with a plaid, then streamed itself straight out from him, as his own forward-flowing heart; while Starbuck and Stubb, standing upon the bowsprit beneath, caught sight of the down-coming monster just as soon as he.

"The whale, the whale! Up helm, up helm! Oh, all ye sweet powers of air, now hug me close! Let not Starbuck die, if die he must, in a woman's fainting fit. Up helm I say—ye fools, the jaw! the jaw! Is this the end of all my bursting prayers? all my lifelong fidelities? Oh, Ahab, Ahab, lo, thy work. Steady! helmsman, steady. Nay, nay! Up helm again! He turns to meet us! Oh, his unappeasable brow drives on towards one, whose duty tells him he cannot depart. My God, stand by me now!"

"Stand not by me, but stand under me, whoever you are that will now help Stubb; for Stubb, too, sticks here. I grin at thee, thou grinning whale! Who ever helped Stubb, or kept Stubb awake, but Stubb's own unwinking eye? And now poor Stubb goes to bed upon a mattress that is all too soft; would it were stuffed with brushwood! I grin at thee, thou grinning whale! Look ye, sun, moon, and stars! I call ye assassins of as good a fellow as ever spouted up his ghost. For all that, I would yet ring glasses with thee, would ye but hand the cup! Oh, oh! oh, oh! thou grinning whale, but there'll be plenty of gulping soon! Why fly ye not, O Ahab! For me, off shoes and jacket to it; let Stubb die in his drawers! A most moldy and oversalted death, though—cherries! cherries! cherries! Oh, Flask, for one red cherry ere we die!"

"Cherries? I only wish that we were where they grow. Oh, Stubb, I hope my poor mother's drawn my part-pay ere this; if not, few coppers will now come to her, for the voyage is up."

From the ship's bows, nearly all the seamen now hung inactive; hammers, bits of plank, lances, and harpoons, mechanically retained in their hands, just as they had darted from their various employments; all their enchanted eyes intent upon the whale, which from side to side strangely vibrating his predestinating head, sent a broad band of overspreading semicircular foam before him as he rushed. Retribution, swift vengeance, eternal malice were in his whole aspect, and spite of all that mortal man could do, the solid white buttress of his forehead smote the ship's starboard bow, till men and timbers reeled. Some fell flat upon their faces. Like dislodged trucks, the heads of the harpooneers aloft shook on their bull-like necks. Through the breach, they heard the waters pour, as mountain torrents down a flume.

"The ship! The hearse!—the second hearse!" cried Ahab from the boat; "its wood could only be American!"

Literary Analysis

Symbol What is symbolized by the red flag streaming out from Tashtego?

◀ **Critical Viewing**

How does this illustration emphasize the symbolic aspects of this story? **[Evaluate]**

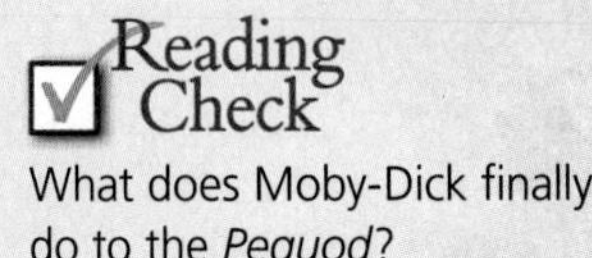

What does Moby-Dick finally do to the *Pequod*?

Literary Analysis
Symbol and Theme
What thematic elements come together in Ahab's climactic speech?

Diving beneath the settling ship, the whale ran quivering along its keel; but turning under water, swiftly shot to the surface again, far off the other bow, but within a few yards of Ahab's boat, where, for a time, he lay quiescent.

"I turn my body from the sun. What ho, Tashtego! let me hear thy hammer. Oh! ye three unsurrendered spires of mine; thou uncracked keel; and only god-bullied hull; thou firm deck, and haughty helm, and Polepointed prow—death-glorious ship! must ye then perish, and without me? Am I cut off from the last fond pride of meanest shipwrecked captains? Oh, lonely death on lonely life! Oh, now I feel my topmost greatness lies in my topmost grief. Ho, ho! from all your furthest bounds, pour ye now in, ye bold billows of my whole foregone life, and top this one piled comber of my death! Towards thee I roll, thou all-destroying but unconquering whale; to the last I grapple with thee; from hell's heart I stab at thee; for hate's sake I spit my last breath at thee. Sink all coffins and all hearses to one common pool! and since neither can be mine, let me then tow to pieces, while still chasing thee, though tied to thee, thou damned whale! *Thus,* I give up the spear!"

The harpoon was darted; the stricken whale flew forward; with igniting velocity the line ran through the groove;—ran foul. Ahab stooped to clear it; he did clear it; but the flying turn caught him round the neck, and voicelessly as Turkish mutes bowstring their victim, he was shot out of the boat, ere the crew knew he was gone. Next instant, the heavy eye splice in the rope's final end flew out of the stark-empty tub, knocked down an oarsman, and smiting the sea, disappeared in its depths.

For an instant, the tranced boat's crew stood still; then turned. "The ship? Great God, where is the ship?" Soon they through dim, bewildering mediums saw her sidelong fading phantom, as in the gaseous fata morgana,[18] only the uppermost masts out of water: while fixed by infatuation, or fidelity, or fate, to their once lofty perches, the pagan harpooneers still maintained their sinking lookouts on the sea. And now, concentric circles seized the lone boat itself, and all its crew, and each floating oar, and every lance pole, and spinning, animate and inanimate, all round and round in one vortex, carried the smallest chip of the *Pequod* out of sight.

But as the last whelmings intermixingly poured themselves over the sunken head of the Indian at the mainmast, leaving a few inches of the erect spar yet visible, together with long streaming yards of the flag, which calmly undulated, with ironical coincidings, over the destroying billows they almost touched—at that instant, a red arm and a hammer hovered backwardly uplifted in the open air, in the act of nailing the flag faster and yet faster to the subsiding spar. A sky hawk that tauntingly had followed the main-truck downwards

18. fata morgana (fät′ə môr gän ə) *n.* mirage seen at sea.

from its natural home among the stars, pecking at the flag, and incommoding Tashtego there: this bird now chanced to intercept its broad fluttering wing between the hammer and the wood: and simultaneously feeling that ethereal thrill, the submerged savage beneath, in his deathgasp, kept his hammer frozen there: and so the bird of heaven, with archangelic shrieks, and his imperial beak thrust upwards, and his whole captive form folded in the flag of Ahab, went down with his ship, which, like Satan, would not sink to hell till she had dragged a living part of heaven along with her, and helmeted herself with it.

Now small fowls flew screaming over the yet yawning gulf; a sullen white surf beat against its steep sides; then all collapsed, and the great shroud of the sea rolled on as it rolled five thousand years ago.

Critical Reading

Cite textual evidence to support your responses.

1. **Key Ideas and Details** **(a)** What happened to Ahab in his previous encounter with Moby-Dick? **(b) Interpret:** What does Ahab's obsession with Moby-Dick reveal about his character? **(c) Compare and Contrast:** In what ways is Starbuck different from Ahab?
2. **Key Ideas and Details** **(a)** How does Starbuck interpret Ahab's obsession with Moby-Dick? **(b) Analyze:** Why does Starbuck obey Ahab even though he disagrees with him?
3. **Key Ideas and Details** **(a)** What does Ahab believe exists "behind the unreasoning mask" of all visible things? **(b) Summarize:** Briefly, explain Ahab's beliefs about the nature of creation.
4. **Key Ideas and Details** **(a)** How does Moby-Dick react when the *Pequod* first approaches his flank? **(b) Compare and Contrast:** How does Moby-Dick's reaction illuminate the differences between the whale in reality and in Ahab's imagination?
5. **Integration of Knowledge and Ideas** **Take a Position:** This novel has been called a "voyage of the soul." Would you agree or disagree with that assessment? Explain.
6. **Integration of Knowledge and Ideas** **(a)** What happens to Ahab, Moby-Dick, and the *Pequod* at the story's end? **(b) Analyze:** What does the final paragraph indicate about the relationship between humanity and nature?
7. **Integration of Knowledge and Ideas** Does Ahab's persistence reflect aspects of a distinctly American character, or is it simply human? Explain. In your response, use at least two of these Essential Question words: *individualism, ambition, persistence, extreme.* ***[Connecting to the Essential Question: What makes American literature American?]***

After You Read from *Moby-Dick*

Literary Analysis

1. **Key Ideas and Details** What omens appear **(a)** as Ahab's whaleboat pulls away from the *Pequod* and **(b)** when Moby-Dick surfaces? **(c)** What is Ahab's reaction to these omens?
2. **Craft and Structure** The color white is often used as a **symbol** for innocence, as well as for absence and death. What contradictory symbolic meanings does the whale's whiteness convey?
3. **Craft and Structure** If the *Pequod* crew symbolizes humanity and Moby-Dick symbolizes nature, what might the ship's voyage symbolize?
4. **Key Ideas and Details** **(a)** Use a chart like the one shown to compare and contrast the characters of Starbuck and Ahab. **(b)** What message, or **theme,** is Melville expressing through these contrasting characters?

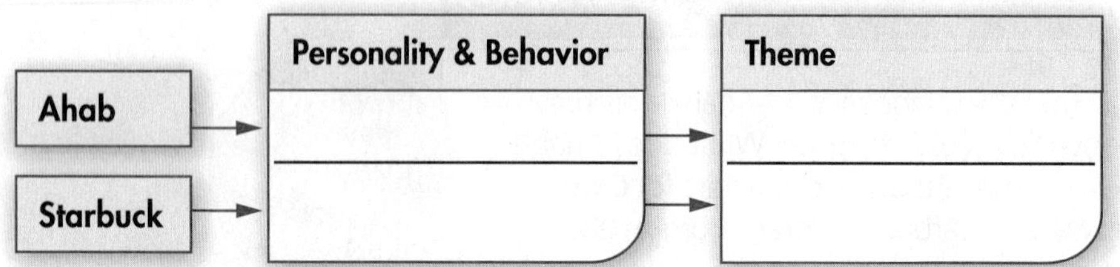

5. **Key Ideas and Details** Considering the journey's symbolic meaning and its terrible outcome, speculate about the novel's overall theme, or central idea.
6. **Analyze Visual Information** Explain the humor in this cartoon.

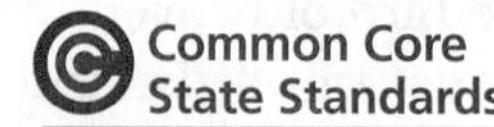

Common Core State Standards

Writing

1. Write arguments to support claims in an analysis of substantive topics or texts, using valid reasoning and relevant and sufficient evidence. *(p. 357)*

1.a. Introduce precise, knowledgeable claim(s), establish the significance of the claim(s), distinguish the claim(s) from alternate or opposing claims, and create an organization that logically sequences claim(s), counterclaims, reasons, and evidence. *(p. 357)*

Reading Strategy

7. **Identify relevant details to determine the essential message.** Which events, dialogue, or descriptions in the excerpt lead you to recognize Moby-Dick as a symbol of **(a)** nature's beauty; **(b)** nature's power; and **(c)** nature's immortality. For each meaning, explain your reasoning.
8. **(a)** What does Ahab mean when he says "Ahab never thinks; he only feels, feel, feels; that's tingling enough for mortal man! to think's audacity." **(b)** Considering the events that occur as a result of Ahab's feelings, what message do you derive from that statement?
9. How does this statement by Ishmael suggest a way to look at the essential meaning of the events he narrates?

"Ah, ye admonitions and warnings! why stay ye not when ye come? But rather are ye predictions than warnings, ye shadows! Yet not so much predictions from without, as verifications of the foregoing things within."

"Have ye seen a whale that matches this swatch?"

PERFORMANCE TASKS

Integrated Language Skills

Vocabulary Acquisition and Use

Word Analysis: Latin Prefix *mal-*

The word "maledictions" combines the Latin prefix *mal-*, which means "bad" or "badly," with the root *-dic-*, which means "to speak." Hence, the word "maledictions" means "bad speech," or curses. Write a definition for each numbered word below. Explain how the meaning of the prefix or root contributes to the meaning of the word.

1. malevolent
2. malice
3. malignant
4. dictate
5. predict
6. diction

Vocabulary: Synonyms

For each vocabulary word, select the best synonym from the column on the right. Then, explain your reasoning.

1. maledictions	**a.** thoughtless
2. prescient	**b.** curses
3. impulsive	**c.** walking
4. inscrutable	**d.** prophetic
5. pedestrian	**e.** inexpressive
6. inarticulate	**f.** mysterious

Writing

Argument A **character study** is a type of *literary criticism* in which a writer analyzes a character and argues for a certain interpretation of that figure. Often, a character study focuses on a subject, like Ahab, whose behavior can be interpreted in varied ways. For example, some readers feel Ahab's obsession borders on madness, while others feel it borders on greatness. Write an essay in which you analyze Ahab's character and present a convincing argument for your ideas.

Prewriting Review the excerpt and gather details about Ahab's appearance, statements, and behavior. Note what other characters say and feel about him. Use a format like the one shown to assemble the details and look for patterns among them. Write one sentence—your thesis—that expresses your analysis.

Model: Gathering Details and Forming an Opinion

Details:
- Ahab becomes more consumed by his thoughts as the story progresses.
- The crew members notice Ahab's excitement and his wild appearance when he gathers them on the quarter-deck.
- Ahab continues to take greater risks with life and lives of crew members in an effort to kill Moby-Dick.

Thesis: Ahab's obsession with Moby-Dick eventually leads to his madness.

Details taken from the selection as a whole show a character's development.

Drafting In your introduction, state your thesis and provide background information readers may need to understand your ideas. Then, devote one body paragraph to each of your supporting points. Make sure to address alternative explanations of Ahab's character but show why yours is better. Summarize your ideas in your conclusion.

Revising Reread your draft and make sure you have developed your thesis thoroughly. If there are stray details that do not support your thesis, either delete them or strengthen their connections to your main idea.

PERFORMANCE TASKS

Integrated Language Skills

Conventions and Style: Participles, Gerunds, and Infinitives (Verbals)

Your writing will be more interesting if you use varied sentences. Participles, gerunds, and infinitives, also called *verbals*, are good tools for creating sentence variety. A **participle** is a verb form, usually ending in *-ing* or *-ed*, that can be used as an adjective. A **gerund** is a verb form ending in *-ing* that acts as a noun. An **infinitive** is a verb form that appears with the word "to" and acts as a noun, an adjective, or an adverb. All of these verbals can be used with modifiers and complements to make a **phrase,** a group of words that lacks a subject or verb but adds detail to a sentence.

Varying Sentences with Verbals

Choppy: Ahab is filled with vengeance. Ahab chases Moby-Dick.
Combined Using Participial Phrase: *Filled with vengeance*, Ahab chases Moby-Dick.

Choppy: They are hunting whales. It is dangerous.
Combined Using Gerund Phrase: *Hunting whales* is dangerous.

Choppy: Their first task is clear. They must find the whale.
Combined Using Infinitive Phrase: Their first task is *to find the whale.*

Punctuation Tip: Always place a comma after an introductory participial phrase.

Practice In items 1–5, identify the italicized phrase as a participial, gerund, or infinitive phrase. In items 6–10, use the type of phrase indicated in parentheses to combine the two sentences into a single more detailed sentence.

1. Captain Ahab wants *to kill Moby-Dick.*
2. *Angering a huge whale* is not a good idea.
3. *To hunt whales for profit* was the men's original plan.
4. *Damaged by the sharks' bites,* the oars were useless.
5. Starbuck, *doubting the wisdom of his captain,* quietly mutters a prayer.
6. They use the basket. They lift Ahab to the top of the mainmast. (infinitive)
7. Most of the crew were eager. They wanted to obey the captain's orders. (infinitive)
8. Captain Ahab is obsessed with one thing. He is obsessed with getting revenge. (gerund)
9. The sailors follow Ahab's lead. They are motivated by their desire for the gold piece. (participial)
10. The whale initially swims away from the ship. The whale shows no aggression toward the men. (participial)

Writing and Speaking Conventions

A. Writing Use each phrase in a sentence and explain what type of phrase it is.

1. pacing the deck
2. to use their harpoons
3. obeying orders

Example: spying the whale
Sentence: Spying the whale, the men on watch shout out.
Type of Verbal: participial

B. Speaking Describe the final scene of the excerpt from Moby-Dick's point of view. As you speak, use at least one participial phrase, one gerund phrase, and one infinitive phrase.

Further instruction and practice are available in *Prentice Hall Writing Coach*.

The Human Spirit and the Natural World

PART 3

Literary History: Transcendentalism

▲ **Critical Viewing**
How might Thoreau feel about this statue and replica of his cabin that stand today at Walden Pond State Reservation? **[Speculate]**

According to Ralph Waldo Emerson, the preeminent Transcendentalist of his day, the human mind is so powerful it can unlock any mystery, from the intricacies of nature to the wonder of God.

Transcendentalism: The Seekers

For the Transcendentalists, the loose-knit group of writers, artists, and reformers who flourished in the 1830s and 1840s, the individual was at the center of the universe, more powerful than any institution, whether political or religious. So it is fitting that the most influential literary and philosophical movement in American history began with the struggles of one man.

A Crisis of Confidence In the early 1830s, a young Boston pastor found himself wrestling with his faith. His beloved wife had died, and he began questioning his beliefs. At the time, many institutions downplayed the importance of the individual. The Industrial Revolution had shown that machines could actually replace people, that individuals did not matter.

The pastor was troubled by this notion. He believed, on the contrary, that the human mind was the most important force in the universe. The pastor was so passionate about his search for a new way of thinking that he resigned his position and traveled to Europe to visit with some of the great philosophers of the day.

That pastor was Ralph Waldo Emerson, and his crisis of confidence became a revolution in American thought. When Emerson returned to the United States in 1833, he helped forge the Transcendentalist movement.

The Individual Is the World The Transcendentalist movement lasted a mere ten years and produced only two major books—Emerson's *Nature* (1836) and Thoreau's *Walden* (1854). Yet its influence on American life and letters continues to this day. According to Emerson, the human mind is so powerful it can unlock any mystery, from the intricacies of nature to the wonder of God. To Emerson, "the individual is the world." This was a radical thought in an age that gave all authority to the organized institutions of government, religion, and education.

Emerson first proposed his ideas in 1833 in a speech at Harvard University. Then, he took his ideas further, proposing that every soul and all of nature was part of an "Over-Soul," a universal spirit to which all beings return after death. In other words, every being is part of God's mind.

Meetings of Great Minds Many people denounced Emerson as a heretic, but his supporters flocked to his home in Concord, Massachusetts. During the height of Transcendentalist activities, Concord attracted so many great minds that it was dubbed the "Athens of America."

Among Emerson's admirers was **Amos Bronson Alcott**, whose beliefs about education revolutionized American schools. Alcott insisted that students should not be taught through routine memorization, but should instead be challenged to think, debate, and discuss. Feminist author and editor **Margaret Fuller** was another eminent Transcendentalist. Along with Emerson, Fuller was the driving force behind the Transcendentalist journal *The Dial.*

Emerson's most famous protégé was **Henry David Thoreau.** As a twenty-year-old student, Thoreau heard Emerson speak at Harvard and was thrilled by his ideas. Not content merely to discuss Transcendentalist philosophy, Thoreau wanted to put it into action. In 1845, he built a rough cottage in the woods at Walden Pond and went there to live alone, in harmony with nature, untied to material things. Thoreau lived at Walden Pond for two years and wrote about his experiences in his collection of essays, *Walden.*

A Lasting Legacy Like other Transcendentalists, Thoreau was a fierce abolitionist. To protest slavery and the Mexican War, he refused to pay taxes and was imprisoned. Although Thoreau spent only one night in jail, the experience gave him insights into the relationship of individuals to government. The theory of nonviolent civil disobedience that he developed has had a profound effect on society throughout the world. During India's struggle for independence in the 1940s, **Mahatma Gandhi** adopted Thoreau's ideas. In America, nonviolent protest served as the guiding principle for **Martin Luther King, Jr.,** during the civil rights movement.

The influence of the Transcendentalists is so woven into the fabric of American culture that we take it for granted. Yet whenever we celebrate the individual, look to the natural world as a mirror of human lives, or state a belief in the power of intuition to grasp fundamental truths, we owe a debt to the great, brief meeting of minds in Concord.

In This Section

- Literary History *(p. 360)*
- Themes Across Centuries: Charles Johnson on Ralph Waldo Emerson *(p. 362)*
- Biography: Ralph Waldo Emerson *(p. 365)*
- Study: "Nature," "Self-Reliance," and "Concord Hymn" by Ralph Waldo Emerson *(p. 366–371)*
- Themes Across Centuries: Gretel Ehrlich on *Walden* by Henry David Thoreau *(p. 374)*
- Biography: Henry David Thoreau *(p. 377)*
- Study: from *Walden* and "Civil Disobedience" by Henry David Thoreau *(p. 379–389)*

Speaking and Listening: Small Group Discussion

Comprehension and Collaboration The Transcendentalists believed that no institution should be as powerful as the individual. With a small group, discuss the role of the individual in our society today. Use these questions to guide your discussion:

- How much power do formal institutions have in our society? Support your position with examples.
- In what ways do individuals make a difference in our society?
- Should individuals have more power than they do? Why or why not?

Choose a point person to share your group's conclusions with the class.

Themes Across Centuries: Scholar's Insights

Charles Johnson on Ralph Waldo Emerson

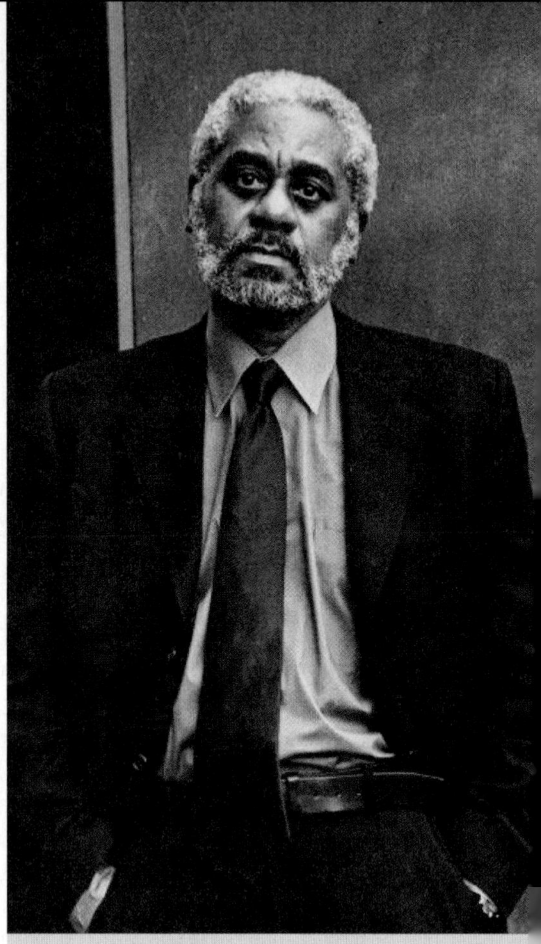

Emerson Gave Me Permission to Question Everything At age sixteen, when I was an Illinois boy trying to figure out where my place might be in the tempestuous, rapidly changing decade of the 1960s, and long before I became a black American novelist and philosopher, my teachers at Evanston Township High School placed the essays of Ralph Waldo Emerson in front of me. I'm thankful they did.

In grand fashion, "Self-Reliance" gave me permission to be a free thinker and to rigorously question *every*thing around me—from the status quo to social cliques in my school, from neighborhood gangs to eighty-year-old social "conventions" that enshrined racial segregation in the South and in the North. Emerson gave me the courage to resist the pressure to conform to things that were unreasonable, to always trust myself, to dream "impossible dreams," and to value my own individual voice and vision, even if doing so resulted in disapproval and being unpopular with the hip "in crowd."

Challenging Us to Go Beyond the Ordinary Just as he served me well in my teens, Emerson's belief in "the infinitude of the private man," and his identification with all forms of life, proved to be reliable guides during my adult years. First, that's because he defined so beautifully the values that eight generations of Americans regard as the basis for our national character and core beliefs, particularly his devotion to what he called "the republic of Man." He condemned the institution of slavery, championed the right of women to vote, and spoke out against the "wicked Indian policy."

In his journal, Emerson dreamed of an America that would one day be an "asylum of all nations, the energy of Irish, Germans, Swedes, Poles & Cossacks, & all the European tribes—of the Africans, & of the Polynesians [who] will construct a new race, a new religion, a new State, a new literature, which will be as vigorous as the new Europe which came out of the smelting pot of the Dark Ages. . . ." He truly believed, and made *me* see, how "It is our duty to be discontented, with the measure we have of knowledge & virtue, to forget the things behind & press toward those before."

Meet the Author

Charles Johnson has published in a wide variety of genres, including cartoons, philosophical and literary criticism, screenplays, and novels. His novel *Middle Passage* won the National Book Award in 1990.

▲ **Critical Viewing**
This print shows Emerson delivering a lecture. What details reveal what he might have been like as a speaker? **[Analyze]**

Secondly, Emerson has long inspired me—as he does anyone with an adventurous spirit—because he challenges us to be flexible and resourceful, like the "sturdy lad from New Hampshire or Vermont, who in turn tries all the professions, who *teams* it, *farms* it, *peddles*, keeps a school, preaches, edits a newspaper, goes to Congress, buys a township, and so forth, in successive years, and always, like a cat, falls on his feet" (from "Self-Reliance").

All those *are* our possibilities. There is nothing, Emerson says, that we cannot achieve if we believe in ourselves. As a Transcendentalist, he was a restless and superbly civilized man who went beyond (or transcended) the ordinary, the outdated, and the unoriginal, for, in his own words, he chose to "unsettle all things. No facts are to me sacred, none are profane; I simply experiment, an endless seeker, with no Past at my back" (from "Circles").

Critical Reading 

1. **Key Ideas and Details** **(a)** When Johnson was a teenager, what three important lessons did he learn from Emerson? **(b) Connect:** What important life lessons have you learned from a favorite author?
2. **Key Ideas and Details** **(a)** What two qualities does Emerson's "sturdy lad from New Hampshire or Vermont" display? **(b) Speculate:** Are these qualities still part of our "core beliefs" as Americans? Why or why not?

As You Read the Selections by Emerson . . .

3. **Integration of Knowledge and Ideas** Think about whether Emerson's work is still as relevant to today's high school students as it was to the young Charles Johnson.

Before You Read

from *Nature* • from *Self-Reliance* • *Concord Hymn*

Connecting to the Essential Question Emerson's ideas about individualism were radical to many people during his lifetime and remain challenging to many people today. As you read, look for passages in which Emerson alludes to the difficulty of being true to oneself. This will help as you consider the Essential Question: **How does literature shape or reflect society?**

Reading Informational Text
4. Determine the meaning of words and phrases as they are used in the text, including figurative, connotative, and technical meanings.

Language
5.a. Interpret figures of speech in context and analyze their role in the text.

Literary Analysis

Figurative language, which is also called **figures of speech,** is language that is used imaginatively instead of literally. Types of figurative language include the following:

- **Metaphor:** a stated similarity between two or more unlike things that does not use the words *"like"* or *"as"*
  Example: "Society is a joint-stock company."
- **Synecdoche:** the use of a part of something to stand for the whole
  Example: "the shot heard round the world" [The shot stands in for the whole of the Revolutionary War and the spread of American revolutionary ideals.]

In both his poetry and prose, Emerson uses metaphor and synecdoche to clarify ideas and stir readers' emotions. He also uses **imagery,** or word pictures, and is sensitive to the *sounds of words.* For example, the long *e* sounds in the phrase "the dark stream which seaward creeps" add to the beauty of the image. As you read, notice how figures of speech, images, and sound affect what you understand and feel about Emerson's ideas.

Reading Strategy

Preparing to Read Complex Texts As you read, check your understanding of Emerson's ideas by **challenging,** or **questioning,** the text. To do so, do not simply accept his arguments and evidence but evaluate them against your own experiences and other reading. As you read, use a chart like the one shown to record your challenges or questions and responses.

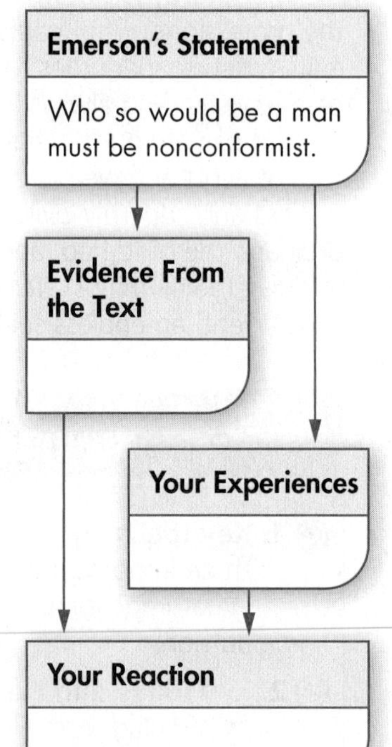

Vocabulary

perpetual (pər pech′ o͞o əl) *adj.* lasting forever (p. 367)

decorum (di kôr′ rəm) *n.* rightness; suitability (p. 367)

tranquil (traŋ′ kwəl) *adj.* calm, quiet, still (p. 368)

conviction (kən vik′ shən) *n.* strong belief (p. 369)

chaos (kā′ äs′) *n.* disorder of matter and space, supposed to have existed before the ordered universe (p. 369)

aversion (ə vʉr′ zhən) *n.* object arousing an intense dislike (p. 369)

absolve (ab zälv′) *v.* pardon; free from guilt (p. 370)

RALPH WALDO EMERSON *(1803–1882)*

Author of "Nature" • "Self-Reliance" • "Concord Hymn"

Individuality, independence, and an appreciation for the wonders of nature are just a few of the principles that Ralph Waldo Emerson helped to instill in our nation's identity. Although his ideas were sometimes considered controversial, they continue to inspire people to this day. Throughout his life, Emerson's mind was constantly in motion, generating new ideas and defining and redefining his view of the world. His natural eloquence in expressing these ideas—in essays, lectures, and poetry—makes him one of the most quoted writers in American literature.

A New England Childhood The son of a Unitarian minister, Emerson was born in Boston. When Emerson was seven, his father died. The boy turned to a brilliant aunt, Mary Moody Emerson, who encouraged his independent thinking. At fourteen, Emerson entered Harvard, where he began the journal he was to keep all his life. After postgraduate studies at Harvard Divinity School, he became pastor of the Second Church of Boston.

Finding His Niche Emerson's career as a minister was short-lived. Grief-stricken at the death of his young wife, and dissatisfied with Unitarianism, Emerson resigned after three years. He then went to Europe, where he met the English writers Thomas Carlyle, Samuel Taylor Coleridge, and William Wordsworth. On his return to the United States, Emerson settled in Concord, Massachusetts. He married Lydia Jackson of Plymouth and began to write seriously. Slowly, the Emerson household began to welcome a widening circle of friends and admirers that included many of the country's most important thinkers. In time, Emerson became widely sought as a lecturer.

Emerson first achieved national fame in 1841, when he published *Essays*, a collection based on material from his journals and lectures. He went on to publish several more volumes of nonfiction, including *Essays, Second Volume* (1844), *Representative Men* (1849), and *The Conduct of Life* (1860).

Though Emerson was known mostly for his essays and lectures, he considered himself a poet. "I am born a poet," he once wrote, "of a low class without doubt, yet a poet. That is my nature and my vocation." He published two successful volumes of poetry, *Poems* (1847) and *May-Day and Other Pieces* (1867). Like his essays, Emerson's poems express his beliefs in individuality and in humanity's spiritual connection to nature.

FROM NATURE

RALPH WALDO EMERSON

BACKGROUND *During the 1830s and 1840s, Emerson and a small group of like-minded friends gathered regularly in his study to discuss philosophy, religion, and literature. Among them were Emerson's protégé, Henry David Thoreau, as well as educator Bronson Alcott, feminist writer Margaret Fuller, and ex-clergyman and author George Ripley. The intimate group, known as the Transcendental Club, developed a philosophical system that stressed intuition, individuality, and self-reliance. In 1836, Emerson published Nature, the lengthy essay excerpted here that became the Transcendental Club's unofficial statement of belief.*

Nature is a setting that fits equally well a comic or a mourning piece. In good health, the air is a cordial of incredible virtue. Crossing a bare common,[1] in snow puddles, at twilight, under a clouded sky, without having in my thoughts any occurrence of special good fortune, I have enjoyed a perfect exhilaration. I am glad to the brink of fear. In the woods, too, a man casts off his years, as the snake his slough, and at what period soever of life is always a child. In the woods is perpetual youth. Within these plantations of God, a decorum and sanctity reign, a perennial festival is dressed, and the guest sees not how he should tire of them in a thousand years. In the woods, we return to reason and faith. There I feel that nothing can befall me in life—no disgrace, no calamity (leaving me my eyes), which nature cannot repair. Standing on the bare ground—my head bathed by the blithe air and uplifted into infinite space—all mean egotism vanishes. I become a transparent eyeball; I am nothing; I see all; the currents of the Universal Being circulate through me; I am part or parcel of God. The name of the nearest friend

Vocabulary

perpetual (pər pech´ o͞o əl) *adj.* lasting forever

decorum (di kôr´ əm) *n.* rightness; suitability

Reading Check

What effect does Emerson believe nature has on all people regardless of age?

1. **common** *n.* piece of open public land.

◀ **Critical Viewing** What different emotions might the natural setting shown in this photograph evoke in people? Explain. **[Interpret]**

Vocabulary
tranquil (traŋ′ kwəl) *adj.* calm, quiet, still

Reading Strategy
Questioning the Text
What question or challenge might you pose to Emerson's idea that one is not alone in nature?

sounds then foreign and accidental: to be brothers, to be acquaintances, master or servant, is then a trifle and a disturbance. I am the lover of uncontained and immortal beauty. In the wilderness, I find something more dear and connate than in the streets or villages. In the **tranquil** landscape, and especially in the distant line of the horizon, man beholds somewhat as beautiful as his own nature.

The greatest delight which the fields and woods minister is the suggestion of an occult relation between man and the vegetable. I am not alone and unacknowledged. They nod to me, and I to them. The waving of the boughs in the storm is new to me and old. It takes me by surprise, and yet is not unknown. Its effect is like that of a higher thought or a better emotion coming over me, when I deemed I was thinking justly or doing right.

Yet it is certain that the power to produce this delight does not reside in nature, but in man, or in a harmony of both. It is necessary to use these pleasures with great temperance. For nature is not always tricked[2] in holiday attire, but the same scene which yesterday breathed perfume and glittered as for the frolic of the nymphs is overspread with melancholy today. Nature always wears the colors of the spirit. To a man laboring under calamity, the heat of his own fire hath sadness in it. Then there is a kind of contempt of the landscape felt by him who has just lost by death a dear friend. The sky is less grand as it shuts down over less worth in the population.

2. **tricked** *v.* dressed.

Critical Reading

Cite textual evidence to support your responses.

1. **Key Ideas and Details** Under what circumstances, according to Emerson, does "mean egotism" vanish? **(b) Define:** How would you define Emerson's idea of "mean egotism"? **(c) Analyze Cause and Effect:** In nature, what emotion does Emerson believe replaces "mean egotism"?
2. **Key Ideas and Details (a)** When does Emerson become a "transparent eyeball"? **(b) Analyze:** What are the characteristics of this experience? **(c) Connect:** In what ways does this description reflect Transcendentalist belief in an Over-Soul?
3. **Integration of Knowledge and Ideas (a)** Where does the power to produce nature's delight come from? **(b) Define:** In describing a harmony between human beings and nature, do you think Emerson means the relationship is always serene? Explain.

FROM

SELF-RELIANCE

RALPH WALDO EMERSON

There is a time in every man's education when he arrives at the conviction that envy is ignorance; that imitation is suicide; that he must take himself for better, for worse, as his portion; that though the wide universe is full of good, no kernel of nourishing corn can come to him but through his toil bestowed on that plot of ground which is given to him to till. The power which resides in him is new in nature, and none but he knows what that is which he can do, nor does he know until he has tried. Not for nothing one face, one character, one fact makes much impression on him, and another none. This sculpture in the memory is not without preestablished harmony. The eye was placed where one ray should fall, that it might testify of that particular ray. We but half express ourselves, and are ashamed of that divine idea which each of us represents. It may be safely trusted as proportionate and of good issues, so it be faithfully imparted, but God will not have his work made manifest by cowards. A man is relieved and gay when he has put his heart into his work and done his best; but what he has said or done otherwise, shall give him no peace. It is a deliverance which does not deliver. In the attempt his genius deserts him; no muse befriends; no invention, no hope.

Trust thyself: every heart vibrates to that iron string. Accept the place the divine providence has found for you; the society of your contemporaries, the connection of events. Great men have always done so and confided themselves childlike to the genius of their age, betraying their perception that the absolutely trustworthy was stirring at their heart, working through their hands, predominating in all their being. And we are now men, and must accept in the highest mind the same transcendent destiny; and not minors and invalids in a protected corner, but guides, redeemers, and benefactors. Obeying the Almighty effort and advancing on chaos and the Dark. . . .

Society everywhere is in conspiracy against the manhood of every one of its members. Society is a joint-stock company in which the members agree for the better securing of his bread to each shareholder, to surrender the liberty and culture of the eater. The virtue in most request is conformity. Self-reliance is its aversion. It loves not realities and creators, but names and customs.

Vocabulary
conviction (kən vik′ shən) *n.* strong belief

Literary Analysis
Figurative Language
How does the metaphor of tilling soil help clarify Emerson's ideas in this opening paragraph?

Vocabulary
chaos (kā′ äs′) *n.* disorder of matter and space, supposed to have existed before the ordered universe

aversion (ə vʉr′ zhən) *n.* object arousing an intense dislike

According to Emerson, what have great men always done?

Vocabulary
absolve (ab zälv′) *v.* pardon; free from guilt

Whoso would be a man must be a nonconformist. He who would gather immortal palms must not be hindered by the name of goodness, but must explore if it be goodness. Nothing is at last sacred but the integrity of your own mind. **Absolve** you to yourself, and you shall have the suffrage of the world. . . .

A foolish consistency is the hobgoblin of little minds, adored by little statesmen and philosophers and divines. With consistency a great soul has simply nothing to do. He may as well concern himself with his shadow on the wall. Speak what you think now in hard words and tomorrow speak what tomorrow thinks in hard words again, though it contradict everything you said today. "Ah, so you shall be sure to be misunderstood?"—is it so bad, then, to be misunderstood? Pythagoras was misunderstood, and Socrates, and Jesus, and Luther, and Copernicus, and Galileo, and Newton,[1] and every pure and wise spirit that ever took flesh. To be great is to be misunderstood. . . .

1. **Pythagoras ... Newton** individuals who made major contributions to scientific, philosophical, or religious thinking.

Critical Reading

Cite textual evidence to support your responses.

1. **Key Ideas and Details (a)** What terms does Emerson use to describe society? **(b) Interpret:** According to Emerson, what is society's main purpose? **(c) Draw Conclusions:** In what ways does Emerson believe people should be affected by the way others perceive them?

2. **Key Ideas and Details (a) Interpret:** According to Emerson, what role does the "divine" have in determining each person's circumstances? **(b) Generalize:** What would Emerson say is each person's reason for living? Explain.

3. **Craft and Structure (a) Make a Judgment:** How important is Emerson's use of the adjective "foolish" in his discussion of consistency? **(b) Speculate:** Do you think there are any circumstances in which Emerson would advocate the benefits of consistency? Explain.

4. **Integration of Ideas and Knowledge** Which passage in these essays best expresses belief in the importance of the individual? Explain the reasons for your choice. In your response, use at least two of these Essential Question words: *conformity, integrity, society, agreement.* ***[Connecting to the Essential Question: What makes American literature American?]***

CONCORD HYMN

SUNG AT THE COMPLETION OF THE BATTLE MONUMENT, JULY 4, 1837

Ralph Waldo Emerson

By the rude[1] bridge that arched the flood,
Their flag to April's breeze unfurled,
Here once the embattled farmers stood,
And fired the shot heard round the world.

The foe long since in silence slept;
Alike the conqueror silent sleeps;
And Time the ruined bridge has swept
Down the dark stream which seaward creeps.

On this green bank, by this soft stream,
We set today a votive[2] stone;
That memory may their deed redeem,
When, like our sires, our sons are gone.

Spirit, that made those heroes dare
To die, and leave their children free,
Bid Time and Nature gently spare
The shaft we raise to them and thee.

---

1. **rude** (ro͞od) *adj.* crude or rough in form or workmanship.
2. **votive** (vōt′ iv) *adj.* dedicated in fulfillment of a vow or pledge.

▼ Critical Viewing
In 1875, the first verse of "Concord Hymn" was carved into the base of this statue commemorating the Minutemen who fought the British at Lexington and Concord on April 19, 1775. What aspects of the sculpture communicate the emotions of the poem? **[Connect]**

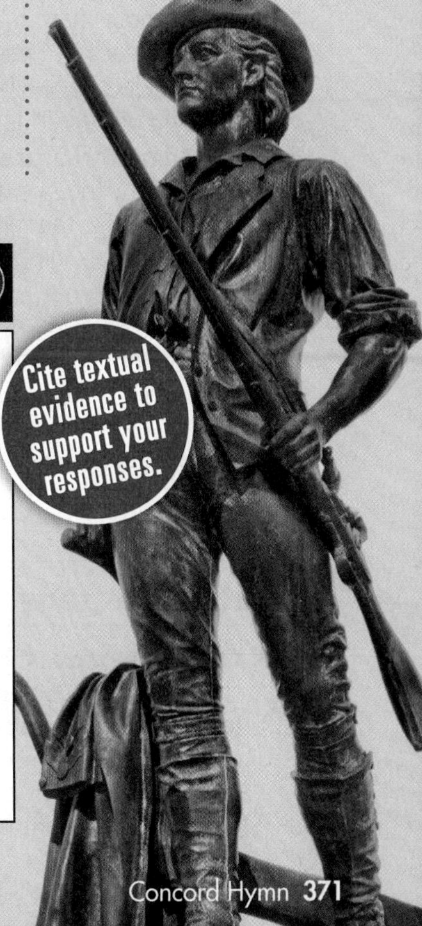

Critical Reading

Cite textual evidence to support your responses.

1. **Key Ideas and Details (a)** What event took place by the "rude bridge"? **(b) Interpret:** What does the poet mean by the image of "the shot heard round the world"?
2. **Craft and Structure (a)** What has happened to the bridge since the battle that took place there? **(b) Analyze:** How does the poem's organization reflect a sense of the passage of time?
3. **Craft and Structure (a)** In the last stanza, whom does the poet address directly? **(b) Infer:** In what way does this direct address reflect the Transcendentalist belief in an Over-Soul?
4. **Integration of Knowledge and Ideas Apply:** Which aspects of "Concord Hymn" would be appropriate for the dedication of other war monuments?

After You Read

from ***Nature*** • from ***Self-Reliance*** • ***Concord Hymn***

Literary Analysis

1. **Craft and Structure** **(a)** Identify one **metaphor** in each essay. **(b)** Explain the abstract idea each metaphor helps Emerson express in concrete terms. **(c)** What emotion do you think Emerson hopes to evoke with each example? Explain.
2. **Craft and Structure** **(a)** Explain Emerson's use of **synecdoche** in this passage: "Trust thyself: every heart vibrates to that iron string." **(b)** How does this use of synecdoche help to clarify Emerson's point about belief in oneself?
3. **Craft and Structure** Does the **image** of the "transparent eyeball" effectively convey the Transcendentalist idea of a universal Over-Soul? Explain.
4. **Craft and Structure** In "Nature," Emerson describes the woods as the "plantations of God." What type of figurative language is he using? Explain your thinking.
5. **Key Ideas and Details** In "Self-Reliance," Emerson describes "that divine idea which each of us represents." How do that phrase and the one noted in question 4 represent similar ideas about the relationship of God to nature and people?
6. **Craft and Structure** "Concord Hymn" commemorates events that happened more than sixty years before the poem was written. **(a)** Note one example each of imagery, metaphor, and synecdoche in the poem. **(b)** Explain how each example helps bring the events of the past and the passage of time to life in the reader's mind.
7. **Craft and Structure** **(a)** Restate the meaning of this sentence: "In the woods, too, a man casts off his years, as the snake his slough." **(b)** How does the repeated *s* sound in the phrase "snake his slough" add to the meaning?
8. **Craft and Structure** **(a)** Use a chart like the one shown to compare and contrast Emerson's descriptions of the bonds between people in society and those between people and nature. **(b)** Which bonds would Emerson say are more important? Explain.

People in Society	People and Nature

Reading Strategy

9. **Challenge or question the text** by answering the questions below about this statement from "Self-Reliance": "Nature always wears the colors of the spirit."
(a) What evidence does Emerson provide to support this statement?
(b) Is this evidence convincing? Explain.
(c) What argument can you make against this statement?
(d) What argument can you make in support of this statement?

Common Core State Standards

Writing

2. Write explanatory texts to examine and convey complex ideas, concepts, and information clearly and accurately through the effective selection, organization, and analysis of content. *(p. 373)*

2.b. Develop the topic thoroughly by selecting the most significant and relevant facts, extended definitions, concrete details, quotations, or other information and examples appropriate to the audience's knowledge of the topic. *(p. 373)*

Language

5. Demonstrate understanding of word relationships. *(p. 373)*

PERFORMANCE TASKS

Integrated Language Skills

Vocabulary Acquisition and Use

Word Analysis: Latin Prefix *ab-*

The word *absolve* includes the Latin prefix *ab-* meaning "away" or "from." This prefix contributes to the meaning of *absolve,* which means to take guilt away from someone. When Emerson exhorts his readers to "Absolve you to yourself," he urges them to release themselves from their own guilt or shame.

Explain how the prefix *ab-* relates to the meaning of each of the words below. If any of the words are unfamiliar, refer to a dictionary to clarify their meanings.

1. abnormal
2. absorb
3. abscond
4. abrupt
5. abduct
6. abhor

Vocabulary: Categorize Vocabulary

Review the vocabulary list on page 364. Then, study each item below to categorize each group of words as all synonyms or as a mixture of antonyms and synonyms. If necessary, consult a dictionary. Then, explain your reasoning.

1. chaos, order, clarity
2. conviction, principle, tenet
3. aversion, enticement, attraction
4. absolve, blame, castigate
5. decorum, propriety, politeness
6. perpetual, temporary, impermanent
7. tranquil, turbulent, moderate

Writing

Explanatory Text Ever since they were first published, Emerson's essays have stirred argument and inspired admiration. Now, it is your turn to add your voice. Write a **critical evaluation** of "Self-Reliance." Include a summary of Emerson's points, an assessment of his uses of *stylistic devices,* such as imagery and figurative language, and a statement of your opinion.

Prewriting Reread the excerpt from "Self-Reliance," noting key ideas, images, and uses of figurative language from the beginning, middle, and end. Then, write one sentence that summarizes Emerson's argument and another sentence that states your opinion about his presentation.

Drafting State the goals of your essay in your introduction. Then, write your summary of Emerson's essay. Follow the summary with a statement of your opinion of his ideas and how he presents them. Support your ideas with accurate and detailed citations from the text.

Model: Using Relevant Citations

Emerson pays tribute to the value of being true to oneself. While most of us would agree with him in theory, how many of us withstand the pressures to conform? Emerson notes, "The virtue in most request is conformity."

Citations specific to the argument keep the writing focused.

Revising As you revise, highlight any citations that do not effectively support your point. Replace weak citations with more relevant support.

Themes Across Centuries: Scholar's Insights

Gretel Ehrlich
Introduces *Walden* by Henry David Thoreau

When I was in high school, my parents took me to look at colleges on the East Coast, and on that trip, we visited Walden Pond. I'd bought a collection of Thoreau's essays at a bookstore in Boston, and standing at the edge of the pond, I read *Walden.* My parents had lived nearby before I was born, but I grew up on the central California coast. Thoreau's landscape was not familiar to me, and yet the ideas he expressed in his book-length essay *Walden* spoke to me as no others had.

Living From the Inside Out An essay is essentially a way of asking a question. It is an attempt to understand the nature of things: the human condition and the natural world. Thoreau's questions to me, the reader, asked me to think about where I lived and how I lived in that place. That "owning" land or a house is not as important as becoming friends with that place. That rich and poor are unimportant, but that how you meet your life and how you live from moment to moment, day to day, is most important of all.

Living comes from the inside out, not from an outsider's view of who you are. Life is change. The weather changes, our relationships with one another change, our bodies change. To be static is to be dead. To live in harmony with nature means to roll with those changes daily, yearly, moment by moment.

Contemplating One Ripple in the Pond These days we go about our lives with so much speed and so much extraneous information that it's difficult to contemplate just one thing, one sight, one evening or morning, one ripple in the pond. Thoreau would have us simplify, slow down, become quiet, and burrow into the heart of things with our minds. Not to "dumb down," but the opposite: to stop, listen, and see; to turn off the monologue in our minds; to erase our idea about how things are; to live in others' shoes.

Building a Fire in the Mind Thoreau would have us think like a river, a pond, a tree, another animal or human; to adopt their point of view instead of our own; to build a fire in the mind with real wood and a match that cannot be extinguished. Then, the fresh, dawnlike nature of things—what

Meet the Author

Gretel Ehrlich is the author of more than a dozen works of nonfiction, fiction, and poetry, including *The Solace of Open Spaces* and *A Match to the Heart.* For more information about Ehrlich, see page 222.

Thoreau calls "the auroral character"—will keep radiating, piercing the difficulties in our lives with new songs. A hut in the woods, a still pond, a fresh breeze: these morning winds carry poems, music, love, and loss into our days. Not a dreaminess, but the direct experience of life as it is.

Marching to a Different Drummer Thoreau encourages us to advance confidently in the direction of our dreams. He encourages each of us to be our own person—distinct, unique, thoughtful, precise, and passionate about what we love in the world. It is good to march to "a different drummer," if that's where our feet take us. To live fully, deeply, profoundly, unafraid to be ourselves—this is advice that travels forward for centuries, through all our lives.

▲ Critical Viewing
What details in this early hand-painted photograph of Walden Pond capture what Thoreau calls "the auroral character" of the setting? **[Connect]**

Critical Reading

1. **Key Ideas and Details (a)** What do Thoreau's questions ask Ehrlich—and all readers—to think about? **(b) Interpret:** In what way might Thoreau's questions help readers live "from the inside out"?
2. **Key Ideas and Details (a)** What would Thoreau have people do in a complex world? **(b) Speculate:** How might following Thoreau's advice change the way you live in the twenty-first century?

As You Read the excerpt from *Walden* . . .

3. **Integration of Knowledge and Ideas** Consider what relevance Thoreau's ideas have in today's world and in your own life.
4. **Integration of Knowledge and Ideas** Think about the ways in which Ehrlich's commentary enriches your understanding of specific passages in Thoreau's essays.

Cite textual evidence to support your responses.

Before You Read

from *Walden* • from *Civil Disobedience*

Connecting to the Essential Question In *Walden*, one of the most famous philosophical works in American literature, Thoreau explains his aim to live a simple life. As you read, look for details that demonstrate Thoreau's goals and values. This will help as you reflect on the Essential Question: **How does literature shape or reflect society?**

Common Core State Standards

Reading Informational Text

1. Cite strong and thorough textual evidence to support analysis of what the text says explicitly as well as inferences drawn from the text, including determining where the text leaves matters uncertain.

4. Determine the meaning of words and phrases as they are used in the text, including figurative meanings; analyze how an author uses and refines the meaning of a key term or terms over the course of a text.

Language

5.a. Interpret figures of speech in context and analyze their role in the text.

Literary Analysis

An **author's style** is the unique manner in which he or she puts thoughts into words. Elements of style include an author's *diction*, or word choice, and *syntax*, or arrangement of words in sentences. Thoreau's style has a conversational **tone,** or attitude, as though he is talking to a friend. This aspect of his style serves his purpose of enlightening the reader without seeming to lecture or scold. Thoreau also "thinks" in images, often using a series of **figurative expressions** to develop ideas. For example, in *Walden,* Thoreau explains that modern life is too complex. He illustrates the point with a series of concrete examples:

- First, he uses a **metaphor,** a figure of speech that shows a similarity between two or more unlike things without using the words "like" or "as": *In the midst of this chopping sea of civilized life, such are the clouds and storms and quicksands . . .*
- Next, he uses an **analogy,** an extended comparison of relationships: *"Our life is like a German Confederacy, made up of petty states . . ."*

As you read, notice how these elements help to enhance Thoreau's ideas.

Reading Strategy

Preparing to Read Complex Texts As a reader, you are not obligated to accept everything you see in print. When reading essays of opinion, **analyze the author's implicit and explicit philosophical assumptions**. Implicit ideas are only suggested, while explicit ideas are directly stated. First, ask yourself what fundamental beliefs the author holds about life. Then, identify the support the author provides. Decide if that support is convincing. As you read, use a chart like the one shown to analyze Thoreau's philosophical assumptions.

Thoreau's Idea:

People should simplify their lives: "Simplify, simplify."

↓

Supporting Details:

-
-
-

↓

Am I Convinced?

- Yes, because...
- No, because...

Vocabulary

dilapidated (də lap′ ə dāt′ id) *adj.* in disrepair (p. 381)

sublime (sə blīm′) *adj.* noble; majestic (p. 383)

superfluous (sə pʉr′ flo͞o əs) *adj.* excessive; not necessary (p. 383)

magnanimity (mag′ nə nim′ ə tē) *n.* generosity (p. 386)

expedient (ek spē′ dē ənt) *n.* resource (p. 388)

alacrity (ə lak′ rə tē) *n.* speed (p. 389)

Henry David Thoreau (1817–1862)

Author of *Walden* and "Civil Disobedience"

Henry David Thoreau was known by his Concord, Massachusetts, neighbors as an eccentric. As a child he rarely followed rules and was independent and strong-willed. He pursued a formal education at his mother's insistence. Thoreau attended Concord Academy, a college preparatory school, and later enrolled at Harvard University. Although Harvard's dress code required students to wear black coats, Thoreau wore a green one.

Questioning Authority When his objections to corporal punishment forced him to quit his first teaching job, Thoreau and his older brother John opened their own school in Concord. The school was successful, but they had to close it when John became ill.

In 1841, Thoreau moved into the house of another famous Concord resident, Ralph Waldo Emerson. He lived there for two years, performing odd jobs to pay for his room and board. Fascinated by Emerson's Transcendentalist ideas, Thoreau became Emerson's friend and disciple. Rather than return to teaching, he decided to devote his energies to exploring the spiritual relationship between humanity and nature and to living by his political and social beliefs.

On Walden Pond From 1845 to 1847, Thoreau lived alone in a one-room cabin he built at Walden Pond near Concord. This experience provided him with the material for his masterwork, *Walden* (1854). A blend of natural observation, social criticism, and philosophical insight, *Walden* is now generally regarded as the supreme work of Transcendentalist literature and one of the greatest examples of nature writing in American literature.

When he died of tuberculosis at the age of forty-four, Thoreau had received little public recognition. Only *A Week on the Concord and Merrimack Rivers* and some poems had been published—at his own expense—while he was alive. *The Maine Woods, Cape Cod,* and *A Yankee in Canada* were published posthumously. Nevertheless, Emerson knew that future generations would cherish Thoreau. Speaking at his funeral, Emerson said: "The country knows not yet, or in the least part, how great a son it has lost. . . . His soul was made for the noblest society; he had in a short life exhausted the capabilities of this world; wherever there is knowledge, wherever there is virtue, wherever there is beauty, he will find a home."

"Be true to your work, your word, and your friend."

from Walden

Henry David Thoreau

from Where I Lived, and What I Lived For

At a certain season of our life we are accustomed to consider every spot as the possible site of a house. I have thus surveyed the country on every side within a dozen miles of where I live. In imagination I have bought all the farms in succession, for all were to be bought, and I knew their price. I walked over each farmer's premises, tasted his wild apples, discoursed on husbandry[1] with him, took his farm at his price, at any price, mortgaging it to him in my mind; even put a higher price on it—took everything but a deed of it—took his word for his deed, for I dearly love to talk—cultivated it, and him too to some extent, I trust, and withdrew when I had enjoyed it long enough, leaving him to carry it on. This experience entitled me to be regarded as a sort of real-estate broker by my friends. Wherever I sat, there I might live, and the landscape radiated from me accordingly. What is a house but a *sedes*, a seat?—better if a country seat. I discovered many a site for a house not

Reading Check

Did Thoreau truly intend to purchase a farm?

1. **husbandry** (huz′ bən drē) *n.* farming.

◀ **Critical Viewing** Based on this picture of Walden Pond, what do you think it would be like to live in such a place? **[Speculate]**

Gretel Ehrlich
Scholar's Insight Thoreau is saying that every rock is our home, every vista is ours to drink in. And as a result, the landscape comes into us, and pours out again as an image, a poem, a bit of music.

likely to be soon improved, which some might have thought too far from the village, but to my eyes the village was too far from it. Well, there might I live, I said; and there I did live, for an hour, a summer and a winter life; saw how I could let the years run off, buffet the winter through, and see the spring come in. The future inhabitants of this region, wherever they may place their houses, may be sure that they have been anticipated. An afternoon sufficed to lay out the land into orchard woodlot and pasture, and to decide what fine oaks or pines should be left to stand before the door, and whence each blasted tree could be seen to the best advantage; and then I let it lie, fallow[2] perchance, for a man is rich in proportion to the number of things which he can afford to let alone.

My imagination carried me so far that I even had the refusal of several farms—the refusal was all I wanted—but I never got my fingers burned by actual possession. The nearest that I came to actual possession was when I bought the Hollowell Place, and had begun to sort my seeds, and collected materials with which to make a wheelbarrow to carry it on or off with; but before the owner gave me a deed of it, his wife—every man has such a wife—changed her mind and wished to keep it, and he offered me ten dollars to release him. Now, to speak the truth, I had but ten cents in the world, and it surpassed my arithmetic to tell, if I was that man who had ten cents, or who had a farm, or ten dollars, or all together. However, I let him keep the ten dollars and the farm too, for I had carried it far enough; or rather, to be generous, I sold him the farm for just what I gave for it, and, as he was not a rich man, made him a present of ten dollars, and still had my ten cents, and seeds, and materials for a wheelbarrow left. I found thus that I had been a rich man without any damage to my poverty. But I retained the landscape, and I have since annually carried off what it yielded without a wheelbarrow. With respect to landscapes:

> "I am monarch of all I *survey*,
> My right there is none to dispute."[3]

Literary Analysis
Author's Style and Metaphor Identify the metaphor Thoreau uses in this paragraph and the idea it helps him develop.

I have frequently seen a poet withdraw, having enjoyed the most valuable part of a farm, while the crusty farmer supposed that he had got a few wild apples only. Why, the owner does not know it for many years when a poet has put his farm in rhyme, the most admirable kind of invisible fence, has fairly impounded it, milked it, skimmed it, and got all the cream, and left the farmer only the skimmed milk.

The real attractions of the Hollowell farm, to me, were: its complete retirement, being about two miles from the village, half a mile from the nearest neighbor, and separated from the highway by a broad field; its bounding on the river, which the owner said protected

2. **fallow** (fal´ ō) *adj.* left uncultivated or unplanted.
3. **"I . . . dispute"** from William Cowper's *Verses Supposed to Be Written by Alexander Selkirk.*

it by its fogs from frosts in the spring, though that was nothing to me; the gray color and ruinous state of the house and barn, and the **dilapidated** fences, which put such an interval between me and the last occupant; the hollow and lichen-covered apple trees, gnawed by rabbits, showing what kind of neighbors I should have; but above all, the recollection I had of it from my earliest voyages up the river, when the house was concealed behind a dense grove of red maples, through which I heard the house-dog bark. I was in haste to buy it, before the proprietor finished getting out some rocks, cutting down the hollow apple trees, and grubbing up some young birches which had sprung up in the pasture, or, in short, had made any more of his improvements. To enjoy these advantages I was ready to carry it on; like Atlas,[4] to take the world on my shoulders—I never heard what compensation he received for that—and do all those things which had no other motive or excuse but that I might pay for it and be unmolested in my possession of it; for I knew all the while that it would yield the most abundant crop of the kind I wanted if I could only afford to let it alone. But it turned out as I have said.

All that I could say, then, with respect to farming on a large scale (I have always cultivated a garden) was that I had had my seeds ready. Many think that seeds improve with age. I have no doubt that time discriminates between the good and the bad; and when at last I shall plant, I shall be less likely to be disappointed. But I would say to my fellows, once for all, As long as possible live free and uncommitted. It makes but little difference whether you are committed to a farm or the county jail.

Old Cato,[5] whose "De Re Rustica" is my "Cultivator," says, and the only translation I have seen makes sheer nonsense of the passage, "When you think of getting a farm, turn it thus in your mind, not to buy greedily; nor spare your pains to look at it, and do not think it enough to go round it once. The oftener you go there the more it will please you, if it is good." I think I shall not buy greedily, but go round and round it as long as I live, and be buried in it first, that it may please me the more at last. . . .

I do not propose to write an ode to dejection, but to brag as lustily as chanticleer[6] in the morning, standing on his roost, if only to wake my neighbors up.

When first I took up my abode in the woods, that is, began to spend my nights as well as days there, which, by accident, was on Independence Day, or the fourth of July, 1845, my house was not finished for winter, but was merely a defense against the rain, without plastering or chimney, the walls being of rough weatherstained boards, with wide chinks, which made it cool at night. The upright white hewn studs and freshly planed door and window casings gave

Vocabulary

dilapidated (də lap′ ə dāt′ id) *adj.* in disrepair

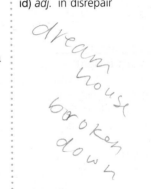

Reading Strategy

Analyzing the Author's Philosophical Assumptions

What do you think the idea of freedom means to Thoreau?

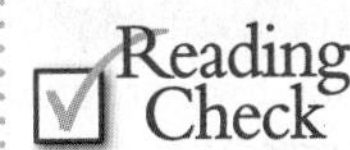

What were the "real attractions" of the Hollowell farm to Thoreau?

4. **Atlas** (at′ ləs) from Greek mythology, a Titan who supported the heavens on his shoulders.
5. **Old Cato** Roman statesman (234–149 B.C.). "De Re Rustica" is Latin for "Of Things Rustic."
6. **chanticleer** (chan′ tə klir′) *n.* rooster.

Where he's reminds him of a great cabin he visited once

Gretel Ehrlich
Scholar's Insight
Thoreau comes to Walden Pond with a "beginner's mind." He allows the earth to instruct him in its ways, leaving preconceptions behind. That is how writers must approach all things, as a student of the world.

it a clean and airy look, especially in the morning, when its timbers were saturated with dew, so that I fancied that by noon some sweet gum would exude from them. To my imagination it retained throughout the day more or less of this auroral[7] character, reminding me of a certain house on a mountain which I had visited the year before. This was an airy and unplastered cabin, fit to entertain a traveling god, and where a goddess might trail her garments. The winds which passed over my dwelling were such as sweep over the ridges of mountains, bearing the broken strains, or celestial parts only, of terrestrial

7. **auroral** (ô rōr′ əl) *adj.* resembling the dawn.

WORLD LITERATURE CONNECTION

Mount Olympus

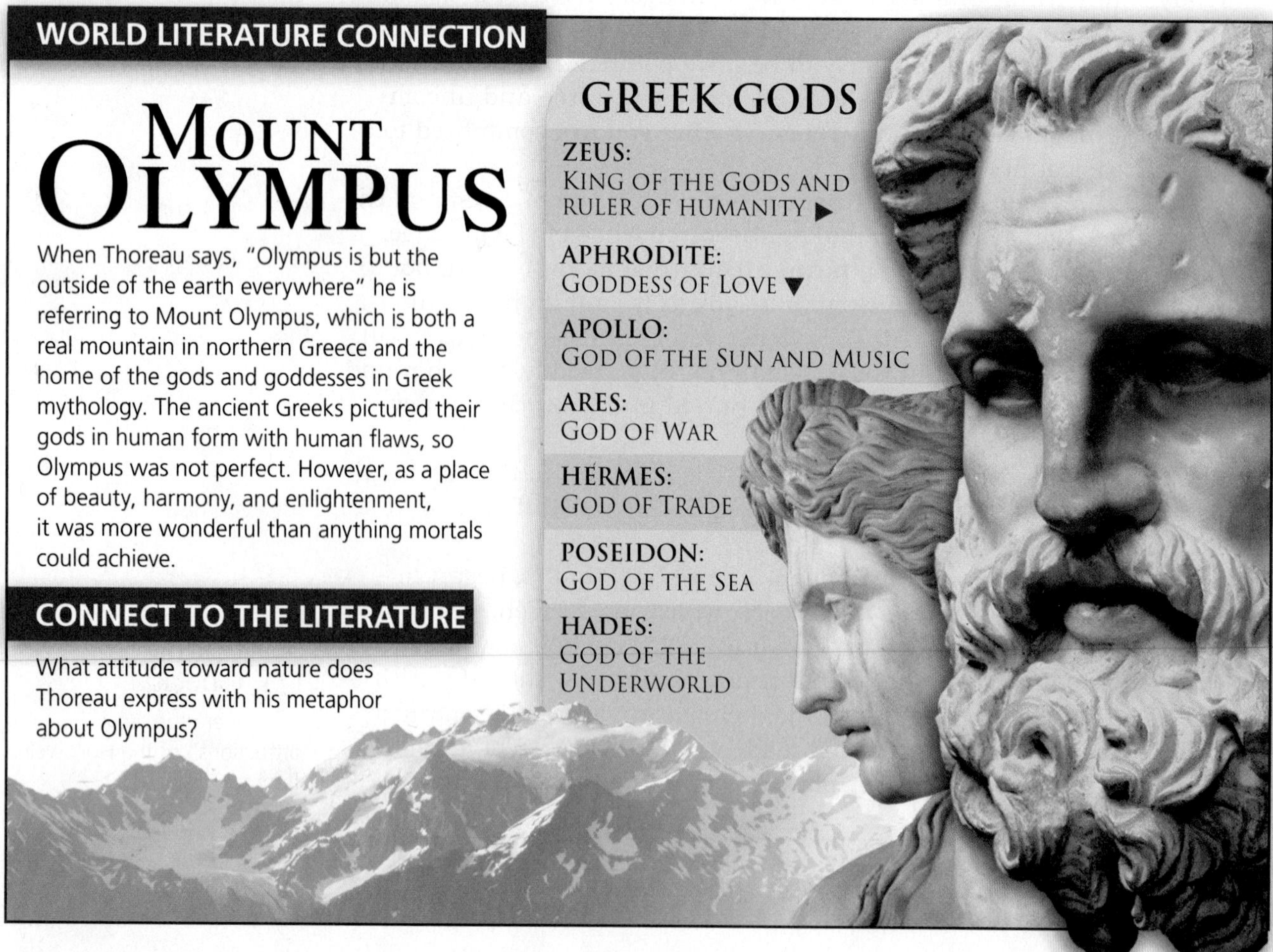

GREEK GODS
ZEUS:
KING OF THE GODS AND RULER OF HUMANITY ▶
APHRODITE:
GODDESS OF LOVE ▼
APOLLO:
GOD OF THE SUN AND MUSIC
ARES:
GOD OF WAR
HERMES:
GOD OF TRADE
POSEIDON:
GOD OF THE SEA
HADES:
GOD OF THE UNDERWORLD

When Thoreau says, "Olympus is but the outside of the earth everywhere" he is referring to Mount Olympus, which is both a real mountain in northern Greece and the home of the gods and goddesses in Greek mythology. The ancient Greeks pictured their gods in human form with human flaws, so Olympus was not perfect. However, as a place of beauty, harmony, and enlightenment, it was more wonderful than anything mortals could achieve.

CONNECT TO THE LITERATURE

What attitude toward nature does Thoreau express with his metaphor about Olympus?

music. The morning wind forever blows, the poem of creation is uninterrupted; but few are the ears that hear it. Olympus is but the outside of the earth everywhere. . . .

I went to the woods because I wished to live deliberately, to front only the essential facts of life, and see if I could not learn what it had to teach, and not, when I came to die, discover that I had not lived. I did not wish to live what was not life, living is so dear; nor did I wish to practice resignation, unless it was quite necessary. I wanted to live deep and suck out all the marrow of life, to live so sturdily and Spartanlike[8] as to put to rout all that was not life, to cut a broad swath and shave close, to drive life into a corner, and reduce it to its lowest terms, and, if it proved to be mean, why then to get the whole and genuine meanness of it, and publish its meanness to the world; or if it were **sublime**, to know it by experience, and be able to give a true account of it in my next excursion. For most men, it appears to me, are in a strange uncertainty about it, whether it is of the devil or of God, and have *somewhat hastily* concluded that it is the chief end of man here to "glorify God and enjoy him forever."[9]

Still we live meanly, like ants; though the fable tells us that we were long ago changed into men; like pygmies we fight with cranes:[10] it is error upon error, and clout upon clout, and our best virtue has for its occasion a **superfluous** and evitable wretchedness. Our life is frittered away by detail. An honest man has hardly need to count more than his ten fingers, or in extreme cases he may add his ten toes, and lump the rest. Simplicity, simplicity, simplicity! I say, let your affairs be as two or three, and not a hundred or a thousand; instead of a million count half a dozen, and keep your accounts on your thumbnail. In the midst of this chopping sea of civilized life, such are the clouds and storms and quicksands and thousand-and-one items to be allowed for, that a man has to live, if he would not founder and go to the bottom and not make his port at all, by dead reckoning,[11] and he must be a great calculator indeed who succeeds. Simplify, simplify. Instead of three meals a day, if it be necessary eat but one; instead of a hundred dishes, five; and reduce other things in proportion. Our life is like a German Confederacy,[12] made up of petty

8. **Spartanlike** like the people of Sparta, an ancient Greek state whose citizens were known to be hardy, stoical, simple, and highly disciplined.
9. **"glorify . . . forever"** the answer to the question "What is the chief end of man?" in the Westminster catechism.
10. **like . . . cranes** In the *Iliad*, the Trojans are compared to cranes fighting against pygmies.
11. **dead reckoning** navigating without the assistance of stars.
12. **German Confederacy** At the time, Germany was a loose union of thirty-nine independent states, with no common government.

Gretel Ehrlich
Scholar's Insight
Thoreau encourages us to face all that life brings to us, both its painful and beautiful sides. There cannot be one without the other.

Vocabulary

sublime (sə blīm′) *adj.* noble; majestic

superfluous (so͞o pur′ flo͞o əs) *adj.* excessive; not necessary

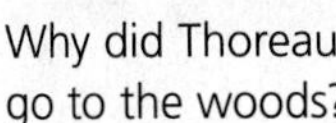

Reading Check

Why did Thoreau go to the woods?

states, with its boundary forever fluctuating, so that even a German cannot tell you how it is bounded at any moment. The nation itself, with all its so-called internal improvements, which, by the way, are all external and superficial, is just such an unwieldy and overgrown establishment, cluttered with furniture and tripped up by its own traps, ruined by luxury and heedless expense, by want of calculation and a worthy aim, as the million households in the land; and the only cure for it as for them is in a rigid economy, a stern and more than Spartan simplicity of life and elevation of purpose. It lives too fast. Men think that it is essential that the *Nation* have commerce, and export ice, and talk through a telegraph, and ride thirty miles an hour, without a doubt, whether *they* do or not; but whether we should live like baboons or like men, is a little uncertain. If we do not get out sleepers,[13] and forge rails, and devote days and nights to the work, but go to tinkering upon our *lives* to improve *them*, who will build railroads? And if railroads are not built, how shall we get to heaven in season? But if we stay at home and mind our business, who will want railroads? We do not ride on the railroad; it rides upon us. . . .

▼ Critical Viewing
This picture shows a replica of Thoreau's cabin. How does it help you understand his point that people should work on the quality of their lives rather than the things they own? **[Interpret]**

Time is but the stream I go a-fishing in. I drink at it; but while I drink I see the sandy bottom and detect how shallow it is. Its thin current slides away, but eternity remains. I would drink deeper; fish in the sky, whose bottom is pebbly with stars. I cannot count one. I know not the first letter of the alphabet. I have always been regretting that I was not as wise as the day I was born. The intellect is a cleaver; it discerns and rifts its way into the secret of things. I do not wish to be any more busy with my hands than is necessary. My head is hands and feet. I feel all my best faculties concentrated in it. My instinct tells me that my head is an organ for burrowing, as some creatures use their snout and forepaws, and with it I would mine and burrow my way through these hills. I think that the richest vein is somewhere here- abouts; so by the divining rod[14] and thin rising vapors I judge; and here I will begin to mine. . . .

13. **sleepers** (slē´ pərz) *n.* ties supporting railroad tracks.

14. **divining rod** a forked branch or stick alleged to reveal underground water or minerals.

from The Conclusion

I left the woods for as good a reason as I went there. Perhaps it seemed to me that I had several more lives to live, and could not spare any more time for that one. It is remarkable how easily and insensibly we fall into a particular route, and make a beaten track for ourselves. I had not lived there a week before my feet wore a path from my door to the pondside; and though it is five or six years since I trod it, it is still quite distinct. It is true, I fear that others may have fallen into it, and so helped to keep it open. The surface of the earth is soft and impressible by the feet of men; and so with the paths which the mind travels. How worn and dusty, then, must be the highways of the world, how deep the ruts of tradition and conformity! I did not wish to take a cabin passage, but rather to go before the mast and on the deck of the world, for there I could best see the moonlight amid the mountains. I do not wish to go below now.

I learned this, at least, by my experiment; that if one advances confidently in the direction of his dreams, and endeavors to live the life which he has imagined, he will meet with a success unexpected in common hours. He will put some things behind, will pass an invisible boundary; new, universal, and more liberal laws will begin to establish themselves around and within him; or the old laws be expanded, and interpreted in his favor in a more liberal sense, and he will live with the license of a higher order of beings. In proportion as he simplifies his life, the laws of the universe will appear less complex, and solitude will not be solitude, nor poverty poverty, nor weakness weakness. If you have built castles in the air, your work need not be lost; that is where they should be. Now put the foundations under them. . . .

Why should we be in such desperate haste to succeed, and in such desperate enterprises? If a man does not keep pace with his companions, perhaps it is because he hears a different drummer. Let him step to the music which he hears, however measured or far away. It is not important that he should mature as soon as an apple tree or an oak. Shall he turn his spring into summer? If the condition of things which we were made for is not yet, what were any reality which we can substitute? We will not be shipwrecked on a vain reality. Shall we with pains erect a heaven of blue glass over ourselves, though when it is done we shall be sure to gaze still at the true ethereal heaven far above, as if the former were not? . . .

However mean your life is, meet it and live it; do not shun it and call it hard names. It is not so bad as you are. It looks poorest when you are richest. The faultfinder will find faults even in paradise. Love your life, poor as it is. You may perhaps have some pleasant, thrilling, glorious hours, even in a poorhouse. The setting sun is reflected from the windows of the almshouse[15] as brightly as from the rich man's

Literary Analysis
Author's Style and Metaphor What metaphor does Thoreau use in the sentence beginning "If a man does not keep pace with his companions . . .?" What idea does it help him develop?

What does Thoreau claim to have learned from his experiment in living?

15. almshouse *n.* home for people too poor to support themselves.

Gretel Ehrlich
Scholar's Insight
To cultivate poverty is a radical thought and one that has been alive throughout history. Poverty in this sense means simplicity, like the "poverty" of an animal that wears only its own fur coat. The mind and the imagination are our true wealth.

Reading Strategy
Analyzing the Author's Philosophical Assumptions
Thoreau has strong opinions about how people should live, as shown in his advice to "cultivate poverty." Has he convinced you? Explain.

Vocabulary
magnanimity (mag′ nə nim′ ə tē) *n.* generosity

abode; the snow melts before its door as early in the spring. I do not see but a quiet mind may live as contentedly there, and have as cheering thoughts, as in a palace. The town's poor seem to me often to live the most independent lives of any. Maybe they are simply great enough to receive without misgiving. Most think that they are above being supported by the town; but it oftener happens that they are not above supporting themselves by dishonest means, which should be more disreputable. Cultivate poverty like a garden herb, like sage. Do not trouble yourself much to get new things, whether clothes or friends. Turn the old; return to them. Things do not change; we change. Sell your clothes and keep your thoughts. God will see that you do not want society. If I were confined to a corner of a garret[16] all my days, like a spider, the world would be just as large to me while I had my thoughts about me. The philosopher said: "From an army of three divisions one can take away its general, and put it in disorder; from the man the most abject and vulgar one cannot take away his thought." Do not seek so anxiously to be developed, to subject yourself to many influences to be played on; it is all dissipation. Humility like darkness reveals the heavenly lights. The shadows of poverty and meanness gather around us, "and lo! creation widens to our view."[17] We are often reminded that if there were bestowed on us the wealth of Croesus,[18] our aims must still be the same, and our means essentially the same. Moreover, if you are restricted in your range by poverty, if you cannot buy books and newspapers, for instance, you are but confined to the most significant and vital experiences; you are compelled to deal with the material which yields the most sugar and the most starch. It is life near the bone where it is sweetest. You are defended from being a trifler. No man loses ever on a lower level by magnanimity on a higher. Superfluous wealth can buy superfluities only. Money is not required to buy one necessary of the soul. . . .

The life in us is like the water in the river. It may rise this year higher than man has ever known it, and flood the parched uplands; even this may be the eventful year, which will drown out all our muskrats. It was not always dry land where we dwell. I see far inland the banks which the stream anciently washed, before science began to record its freshets. Everyone has heard the story which has gone the rounds of New England, of a strong and beautiful bug which came out of the dry leaf of an old table of apple-tree wood, which had stood in a farmer's kitchen for sixty years, first in Connecticut, and afterward in Massachusetts—from an egg deposited in the living tree many years earlier still, as appeared by counting the annual layers

---

16. garret (gar′ it) *n.* attic.
17. "and . . . view" from the sonnet "To Night" by British poet Joseph Blanco White (1775–1841).
18. Croesus (krē′ səs) King of Lydia (d. 546 B.C.), believed to be the wealthiest person of his time.

beyond it; which was heard gnawing out for several weeks, hatched perchance by the heat of an urn. Who does not feel his faith in a resurrection and immortality strengthened by hearing of this? Who knows what beautiful and winged life, whose egg has been buried for ages under many concentric layers of woodenness in the dead dry life of society, deposited at first in the alburnum[19] of the green and living tree, which has been gradually converted into the semblance of its well-seasoned tomb—heard perchance gnawing out now for years by the astonished family of man, as they sat round the festive board—may unexpectedly come forth from amidst society's most trivial and handselled furniture, to enjoy its perfect summer life at last!

I do not say that John or Jonathan[20] will realize all this; but such is the character of that morrow which mere lapse of time can never make to dawn. The light which puts out our eyes is darkness to us. Only that day dawns to which we are awake. There is more day to dawn. The sun is but a morning star.

---

19. **alburnum** (al bur´ nəm) *n.* soft wood between the bark and the heartwood, where water is conducted.
20. **John or Jonathan** average person.

Critical Reading 

Cite textual evidence to support your responses.

1. **Key Ideas and Details (a)** What advice does Thoreau offer to his "fellows" about ownership of land or property? **(b) Interpret:** What does Thoreau mean by his comment, "It makes but little difference whether you are committed to a farm or the county jail"?
2. **Key Ideas and Details (a)** What advice does Thoreau offer to those who live in poverty? **(b) Analyze:** What does this advice suggest about Thoreau's definition of true wealth?
3. **Key Ideas and Details (a)** According to Thoreau, by what is our life "frittered away"? **(b) Interpret:** What does Thoreau mean by his advice to "simplify, simplify"?
4. **Key Ideas and Details (a) Deduce:** What did Thoreau hope to achieve by living at Walden Pond? **(b) Make a Judgment:** Do you believe Thoreau felt his time at Walden was well spent? Explain.
5. **Integration of Knowledge and Ideas (a) Apply:** How would you define those things that are necessary to the soul? **(b) Take a Position:** Do you agree with Thoreau that "money is not required to buy one necessary of the soul"? Explain.

from

CIVIL DISOBEDIENCE

Henry David Thoreau

BACKGROUND The Mexican War was a conflict between Mexico and the United States that took place from 1846 to 1848. The war was caused by a dispute over the boundary between Texas and Mexico, as well as by Mexico's refusal to discuss selling California and New Mexico to the United States. Believing that President Polk had intentionally provoked the conflict before gaining congressional approval, Thoreau and many other Americans strongly objected to the war. In protest, Thoreau refused to pay his taxes and was forced to spend a night in jail. After that experience, Thoreau wrote "Civil Disobedience," urging people to resist governmental policies with which they disagree.

I heartily accept the motto, "That government is best which governs least";[1] and I should like to see it acted up to more rapidly and systematically. Carried out, it finally amounts to this, which also I believe: "That government is best which governs not at all"; and when men are prepared for it, that will be the kind of government which they will have. Government is at best but an **expedient**; but most governments are usually, and all governments are sometimes, inexpedient. The objections which have been brought against a standing army, and they are many and weighty, and deserve to prevail, may also at last be brought against a standing government. The standing army is only an arm of the standing government. The government itself, which is only the mode which the people have chosen to execute their will, is equally liable to be abused and perverted before the people can act through it. Witness the present Mexican war, the work of comparatively a few individuals using the standing government as their tool; for in the outset, the people would not have consented to this measure.

Vocabulary
expedient
(ek spē′ dē ənt)
n. resource

Spiral Review
Rhetorical Techniques What rhetorical technique does Thoreau use in the sentence beginning "This American government..."? Explain.

This American government—what is it but a tradition, though a recent one, endeavoring to transmit itself unimpaired to posterity, but each instant losing some of its integrity? It has not the vitality and force of a single living man; for a single man can bend it to his will. It is a sort of wooden gun to the people themselves; and, if ever

1. **"That . . . least"** the motto of the *United States Magazine and Democratic Review*, a literary-political journal.

they should use it in earnest as a real one against each other, it will surely split. But it is not the less necessary for this; for the people must have some complicated machinery or other, and hear its din, to satisfy that idea of government which they have. Governments show thus how successfully men can be imposed on, even impose on themselves, for their own advantage. It is excellent, we must all allow; yet this government never of itself furthered any enterprise, but by the alacrity with which it got out of its way. *It* does not keep the country free. *It* does not settle the West. *It* does not educate. The character inherent in the American people has done all that has been accomplished; and it would have done somewhat more, if the government had not sometimes got in its way. For government is an expedient by which men would fain succeed in letting one another alone; and, as has been said, when it is most expedient, the governed are most let alone by it. Trade and commerce, if they were not made of India rubber,[2] would never manage to bounce over the obstacles which legislators are continually putting in their way; and, if one were to judge these men wholly by the effects of their actions, and not partly by their intentions, they would deserve to be classed and punished with those mischievous persons who put obstructions on the railroads.

But, to speak practically and as a citizen, unlike those who call themselves no government men, I ask for, not at once no government, but *at once* a better government. Let every man make known what kind of government would command his respect, and that will be one step toward obtaining it. . . .

Vocabulary
alacrity (ə lak′ rə tē) *n.* speed

2. **India rubber** a form of crude rubber.

Critical Reading

Cite textual evidence to support your responses.

1. **Key Ideas and Details (a)** How does Thoreau define the best possible kind of government? **(b) Draw Conclusions:** According to Thoreau, when will Americans get the best possible kind of government?
2. **Key Ideas and Details (a) Summarize:** What is Thoreau asking his readers to do? **(b) Evaluate:** Does Thoreau present a convincing argument for acting on one's principles?
3. **Integration of Knowledge and Ideas (a) Criticize:** What arguments might you use to counter Thoreau's objections to the idea of a standing government? **(b) Support:** What examples might support an argument that government benefits individuals?
4. **Integration of Ideas and Knowledge** Do you find it surprising that the goals Thoreau tried to achieve have influenced generations of people around the world? Explain. In your response, use at least two of these Essential Question words: *self-reliance, vision, freedom, principle.* ***[Connecting to the Essential Question: How does literature shape or reflect society?]***

After You Read

from ***Walden*** •
from ***Civil Disobedience***

Literary Analysis

1. **Craft and Structure** Explain how the paragraph on simplicity in *Walden* demonstrates the following elements of Thoreau's **style:** **(a)** a conversational **tone**, or attitude; **(b)** a tendency to use a series of **figurative expressions**, including **metaphor** and **analogy**, to develop a key idea.
2. **Key Ideas and Details** **(a)** What is the central idea Thoreau develops in the paragraph on simplicity? Summarize it in one sentence. **(b)** Note another section in *Walden* where Thoreau repeats the idea for emphasis.
3. **Craft and Structure** Thoreau often starts a paragraph with specific examples. He then applies them to a larger truth. **(a)** Identify one such paragraph. **(b)** Do you think this approach is effective? Explain.
4. **Craft and Structure** Choose two metaphors and one analogy from these essays. Use a chart like the one shown to examine the meanings of each one.

Metaphor/Analogy	Things Compared	Meaning
I wanted to live deep and suck out all the marrow of life		

5. **Craft and Structure** In "Civil Disobedience," Thoreau describes government as a "wooden gun." In *Walden,* he describes civilized life as a "chopping sea." **(a)** Explain the meaning of each metaphor. **(b)** Then, explain how the metaphor helps Thoreau develop the logic of his ideas.
6. **Craft and Structure** **(a)** In which essay does Thoreau spend more time translating abstract ideas into concrete metaphors and analogies? **(b)** How does this choice reflect the purpose of the essay and the nature of his topic?
7. **Analyze Visual Information** Explain the humor in the cartoon at right.

Reading Strategy

8. Thoreau expresses his **explicit philosophical assumption** that people should simplify their lives. **(a)** What support for this belief does he provide? **(b)** How might someone argue against this idea?
9. **(a)** What evidence does Thoreau use to support his point that "It makes but little difference whether you are committed to a farm or the county jail"? **(b)** What **implicit philosophical assumption** does this statement suggest? **(c)** Do you agree? Explain.

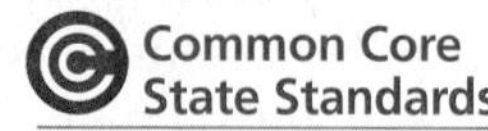

Common Core State Standards

Writing

1. Write arguments to support claims in an analysis of substantive topics or texts, using valid reasoning. *(p. 391)*

Language

4.b. Identify and correctly use patterns of word changes that indicate different meanings. *(p. 391)*

5. Demonstrate understanding of figurative language, word relationships, and nuances in word meanings. *(p. 391)*

▼ *Text in Bubble: "Dear Ralph, Talk about boring!! Nothing to do but take stupid walks in the dreary woods! You'd hate it!! Best regards, Henry" Caption: By Strategic Use of Postcards, Thoreau Manages to Keep Walden Pond Unspoiled.*

PERFORMANCE TASKS

Integrated Language Skills

Vocabulary Acquisition and Use

Word Analysis: Latin Root *-flu-*

The Latin root *-flu-*, found in words like *fluid,* means "flow." The word *superfluous* means "overflowing" or "exceeding what is sufficient." Consider the meanings of the *-flu-* words listed below. For each word, write an alternate explanation that contains the target word and the word *flow.* Follow the example shown here.

confluence *n.* a merging of two things
alternate definition: A confluence of two rivers occurs when they flow together.

1. affluence *n.* wealth; prosperity
2. fluent *adj.* effortlessly smooth
3. fluctuate *v.* change from high to low levels or change unpredictably
4. influx *n.* a sudden arrival of a large number of people or things
5. flue *n.* a shaft or tube used as an outlet for smoke or gas

Vocabulary: Synonyms

Synonyms are words that have the same or nearly the same meaning. Review the vocabulary list on page 376. Then, select the word below whose meaning is closest to that of the first word. For each answer, explain your reasoning.

1. **dilapidated: (a)** depressed **(b)** rundown **(c)** uneven
2. **sublime: (a)** lovely **(b)** enormous **(c)** awe-inspiring
3. **superfluous: (a)** toxic **(b)** extravagant **(c)** repetitive
4. **magnanimity: (a)** selflessness **(b)** tolerance **(c)** patience
5. **expedient: (a)** expense **(b)** instrument **(c)** barrier
6. **alacrity: (a)** awareness **(b)** preparedness **(c)** quickness

Writing

Argument In the century and a half since Thoreau wrote *Walden*, life for most Americans has become more complex rather than simpler. Write an **editorial**—a *persuasive article*—in which you argue for or against the relevance of Thoreau's ideas of simplicity in today's world. Refer to *Walden* and "Civil Disobedience" to support your ideas.

Prewriting Decide what you think of Thoreau's ideas, and brainstorm for examples that support your position. Plan to include specific *stylistic elements* to enhance meaning. Like Thoreau, develop *metaphors and analogies* that clarify your ideas.

Drafting Introduce Thoreau and his ideas. Write a statement either advocating or rejecting their relevance today. As you work, *use repetition* for emphasis; vary your wording, but drive home your key points. Conclude with a specific *call to action.*

Revising Reread your editorial, adding examples, anecdotes, or quotations as necessary to sharpen your argument. To complete your work, include photographs or illustrations that capture your ideas visually.

Model: Anticipating Reader's Concerns and Counterclaims
Today, Thoreau's ideas fall on deaf ears because everyone is glued to a cell phone. Instead of hearing his wisdom, people say, "But I can't live without my mobile GPS. It makes my life easier." Yet, people have less time with family, and less time for the simple pleasures of life than ever before.

Anticipating and answering opponents' arguments creates a more persuasive piece of writing.

Reading for Information

Analyzing Functional and Expository Texts

Consumer Guide • Report

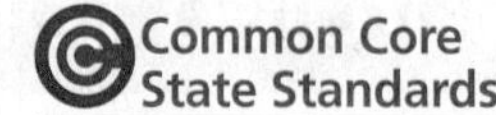

Reading Informational Text
7. Integrate and evaluate multiple sources of information presented in different media or formats as well as in words in order to address a question or solve a problem.

About the Texts

A **consumer guide** may be prepared by either a government agency or a private organization to educate the public about specific products or services. For a guide to be effective, it must be issued by a reliable source that does not stand to profit from the reporting. Most consumer guides contain basic facts about a product, service, or topic of interest; visual aids such as charts, graphs, or illustrations; and answers to frequently asked questions.

A **report** is a document written to inform officials and the public about issues such as environmental or health concerns. Reports are usually dated because they are often time sensitive. Most reports contain facts, statistics, and other data about an issue; dates and headings that organize the data; and a summary that omits all but the most essential information.

Reading Strategy

Many government and public documents use charts, graphs, and other visual aids to present complex data in an easy-to-read format. As you read, **evaluate the information from charts and graphs** and apply it to the information presented in the text. Notice the features listed in the chart below, and use a checklist like the one shown to identify, interpret, and evaluate the information each feature presents.

Content-Area Vocabulary

These words appear in the selections that follow. They may also appear in other content-area texts.

aquifer (ak´ wə fər) *n.* an underground rock formation in which water collects

contaminant (kən tam´ ə nənt) *n.* material that makes something impure or corrupt by contact or mixture

ecosystem (ē´ kō sis´ təm) *n.* a community of related organisms, together with their physical environment, considered as a unit

hydrologic (hī´ drə laj´ ik) *adj.* relating to the scientific study of water

Basic Elements		Purpose	Effectiveness
Titles and headings	Yes ❑ No ❑		
Charts or graphs	Yes ❑ No ❑		
Photos, maps, or illustrations	Yes ❑ No ❑		
Labels or captions	Yes ❑ No ❑		
Color-coding	Yes ❑ No ❑		
Issue dates	Yes ❑ No ❑		

WATER ON TAP
what you need to know

Where Does My Drinking Water Come From And How Is It Treated?

The headings anticipate questions readers may have.

Your drinking water comes from **surface water** or **ground water**. The water that systems pump and treat from sources open to the atmosphere, such as rivers, lakes, and reservoirs is known as surface water. Water pumped from wells drilled into underground **aquifers**, geologic formations containing water, is called ground water. The quantity of water produced by a well depends on the nature of the rock, sand, or soil in the aquifer from which the water is drawn. Drinking water wells may be shallow (50 feet or less) or deep (more than 1,000 feet). More water systems have ground water than surface water as a source (approx. 147,000 v. 14,500), but more people drink from a surface water system (195 million v. 101,400). Large-scale water supply systems tend to rely on surface water resources, while smaller water systems tend to use ground water. Your water utility or public works department can tell you the source of your public water supply.

How Does Water Get To My Faucet?

An underground network of pipes typically delivers drinking water to the homes and businesses served by the water system. Small systems serving just a handful of households may be relatively simple, while large metropolitan systems can be extremely complex—sometimes consisting of thousands of miles of pipes serving millions of people. Drinking water must meet required health standards when it leaves the treatment plant. After treated water leaves the plant, it is monitored within the distribution system to identify and remedy any problems such as water main breaks, pressure variations, or growth of microorganisms.

How Is My Water Treated To Make It Safe?

Water utilities treat nearly 34 billion gallons of water every day.[1] The amount and type of treatment applied varies with the source and quality of the water. Generally, surface water systems require more treatment than ground water systems because they are directly exposed to the atmosphere and runoff from rain and melting snow.Water suppliers use a variety of treatment processes to remove **contaminants** from drinking water. These individual processes can be arranged in a "treatment train" (a series of processes applied in a sequence). The most commonly used processes include coagulation (flocculation and sedimentation), filtration, and disinfection. Some water systems also use ion exchange and adsorption. Water utilities select the treatment combination most appropriate to treat the contaminants found in the source water of that particular system.

Coagulation (Flocculation & Sedimentation):

Flocculation: This step removes dirt and other particles suspended in the water. Alum and iron salts or synthetic organic polymers are added to the water to form tiny sticky particles called "floc," which attract the dirt particles.

All sources of drinking water contain some naturally occurring contaminants. At low levels, these contaminants generally are not harmful in our drinking water. Removing all contaminants would be extremely expensive, and in most cases, would not provide increased protection of public health. A few naturally occurring minerals may actually improve the taste of drinking water and may even have nutritional value at low levels.

Sedimentation: The flocculated particles then settle naturally out of the water.

Filtration:

Many water treatment facilities use filtration to remove all particles from the water. Those particles include clays and silts, natural organic matter, precipitates from other treatment processes in the facility, iron and manganese, and microorganisms. Filtration clarifies the water and enhances the effectiveness of disinfection.

Disinfection:

Disinfection of drinking water is considered to be one of the major public health advances of the 20th century. Water is often disinfected before it enters the distribution system to ensure that dangerous microbial contaminants are killed. Chlorine, chlorinates, or chlorine dioxides are most often used because they are very effective **disinfectants**, and residual concentrations can be maintained in the water system.

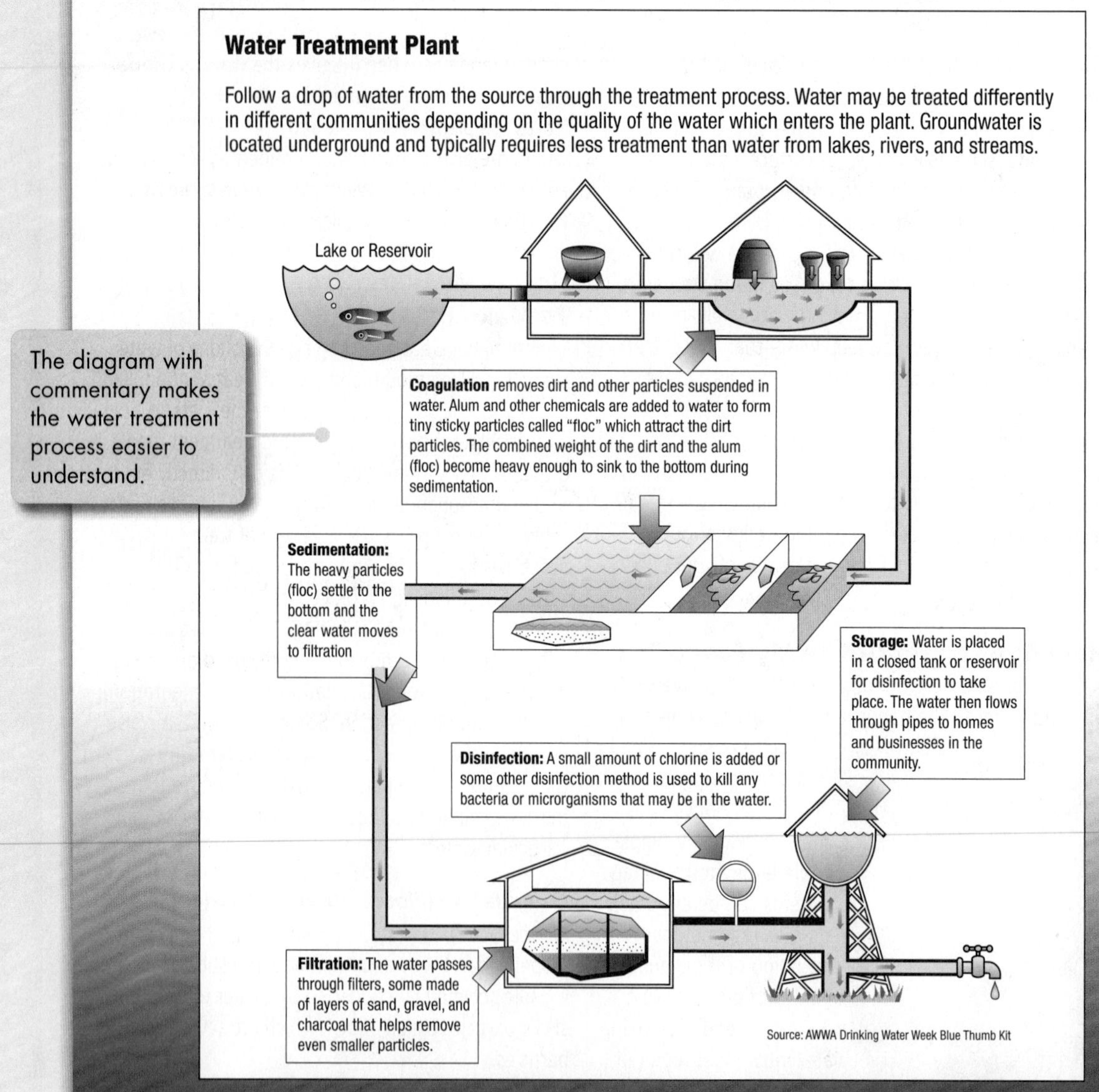

Water Treatment Plant
Follow a drop of water from the source through the treatment process. Water may be treated differently in different communities depending on the quality of the water which enters the plant. Groundwater is located underground and typically requires less treatment than water from lakes, rivers, and streams.
Lake or Reservoir
Coagulation removes dirt and other particles suspended in water. Alum and other chemicals are added to water to form tiny sticky particles called "floc" which attract the dirt particles. The combined weight of the dirt and the alum (floc) become heavy enough to sink to the bottom during sedimentation.
Sedimentation: The heavy particles (floc) settle to the bottom and the clear water moves to filtration
Storage: Water is placed in a closed tank or reservoir for disinfection to take place. The water then flows through pipes to homes and businesses in the community.
Disinfection: A small amount of chlorine is added or some other disinfection method is used to kill any bacteria or microrganisms that may be in the water.
Filtration: The water passes through filters, some made of layers of sand, gravel, and charcoal that helps remove even smaller particles.
Source: AWWA Drinking Water Week Blue Thumb Kit

The diagram with commentary makes the water treatment process easier to understand.

The heading indicates the topic covered in this section of the report.

2007
SOUTH FLORIDA
ENVIRONMENTAL
REPORT

The report is dated.

KISSIMMEE RIVER RESTORATION AND UPPER BASIN INITIATIVES

Covering approximately 3,000 square miles, the Kissimmee watershed forms the headwaters of the Kissimmee-Okeechobee-Everglades system. This watershed is comprised of a diverse group of wetland aquatic ecosystems within its Upper Basin—and Lower Basin, the Kissimmee River. The meandering Kissimmee River was channelized to prevent catastrophic flooding and much of the original floodplain was drained. However, there were pronounced impacts on the ecosystem—drastic declines in wintering waterfowl, wading bird, and fish populations and loss of ecosystem functions.

Another Year of Above-Average Rainfall In The Kissimmee Basin Poses Regional Water Management Challenges

During WY2006, hydrologic conditions in the Kissimmee watershed were quite variable, particularly due to extreme seasonal rainfall conditions. There were high levels of rainfall in June 2005, followed by a relatively dry spring and another surge of intense rainfall in October 2005 from Hurricane Wilma. The basin also experienced another year of above-average rainfall during WY2006, primarily due to Hurricane Wilma. The total rainfall during WY2006 in the Upper Basin (53 inches) and in the Lower Basin (49 inches) exceeded historical annual averages by about 3 to 4 inches, respectively. During this water year, discharges from the S-65 water control structure into the Kissimmee River peaked near 9,000 cubic feet per second and, were among the highest recorded in nearly 75 years.

The Next Phase of Kissimmee Basin Construction Was Launched In Water Year 2006

The District and the U.S. Army Corps of Engineers are collaborating in the Kissimmee River Restoration and the Kissimmee River Headwaters Revitalization projects.

Together, these large-scale restoration projects will **(1)** reestablish the river-floodplain system's ecological integrity by reconstructing the river's physical form, **(2)** provide the water storage and regulation

schedule modifications needed to approximate the historical flow characteristics of the Kissimmee River system, and **(3)** increase the quantity and quality of shoreline habitat in lakes Kissimmee, Hatchineha, Tiger, and Cypress for the benefit of fish and wildlife.

The first of four major phases of canal backfilling was completed in early 2001, reclaiming almost 6,000 acres of floodplain habitat. Initiated in June 2006, the second phase of construction will backfill 1.9 miles of C-38 canal, remove three weirs, and excavate some portions of river channel. It is projected that all restoration-related construction will be completed by 2012. In total, this project will restore ecological integrity to approximately 20 square miles of river/floodplain habitat and 44 continuous miles of meandering river channel.

Kissimmee River Restoration Produces Promising Results

A key element of the Kissimmee River Restoration is a comprehensive, multi-phased evaluation program for tracking ecological responses to restoration. To address the goal of ecological integrity, the evaluation program has a broad scope encompassing hydrology, water quality, and major biological communities such as plants, invertebrates, fish, and birds. Although restoration efforts only have been under way for a few years and will continue through 2012, many positive responses to the first phase are already being observed. These responses include increases in dissolved oxygen levels, reductions in accumulated sediments, and increased populations of bass and sunfishes in river channels, as well as increased use of the river and floodplain by various birds. Remarkably, the highest densities of both waterfowl and long-legged wading birds, such as white ibis (*Eudocimus albus*), on the restored floodplain were recorded in 2006, almost two times those observed in 2005 (see figure below). Since completion of Phase I construction in 2001, wading bird densities have exceeded the projected restoration expectation in this area.

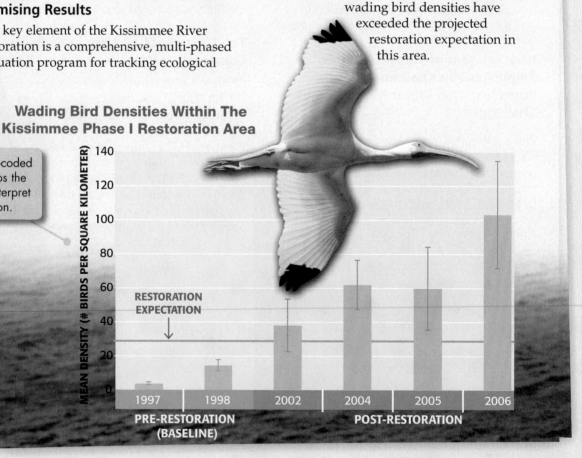

The color-coded chart helps the reader interpret information.

Critical Reading

1. **Key Ideas and Details (a)** What public issue or issues does the consumer guide address? **(b)** Cite one fact presented in the guide that a citizen might find reassuring and one that might raise concerns. Explain your choices.
2. **Key Ideas and Details (a)** What environmental concern does the project discussed in the report seek to correct? Explain. **(b)** At the time the report was issued, is the project showing clear success? Cite specific details to support your response.
3. **Integration of Knowledge and Ideas (a)** Identify two visual elements in each text that clarify or organize information presented verbally. **(b)** For each, explain how the visual element helps you interpret and integrate the information contained in the text.
4. **Content-Area Vocabulary (a)** Explain how the Greek prefix *hydro-* ("water") contributes to the meaning of the word *hydrologic.* **(b)** Determine the meaning of the following words that contain this Greek prefix: *hydraulic, hydrate, hydrant,* and *hydroplane.* Use a dictionary to verify the meanings.

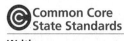

Common Core State Standards

Writing

1. Write arguments to support claims in an analysis of substantive topics or texts, using valid reasoning and relevant and sufficient evidence.

1.a. Introduce precise, knowledgeable claim(s) and establish the significance of the claim(s).

10. Write routinely over shorter time frames for a range of tasks and purposes.

Timed Writing

Argument: Persuasive Essay [40 minutes]

Format

In an argument, or **persuasive essay,** you present a well-reasoned position or opinion. In an essay, you must explain and support your argument.

Refer to both the Consumer Guide and the Government Report to write a position statement, a **persuasive essay** in which you state and support an opinion, about the management of **natural resources** both today and in the future. Cite facts, statistics, and quotations from the documents to support your case and persuade readers to agree with your position.

Academic Vocabulary

The prompt asks you to discuss the management of **natural resources.** Focus your response on land, water, and air and ways in which to improve the management of these resources.

5-Minute Planner

Complete these steps before you begin to write:

1. Read the prompt carefully. List key words.
2. Review the texts. Make notes about details pertaining to the management of natural resources. Cite specific details to include in your essay.
3. Draft a rough outline. Note ideas with which to introduce and conclude your essay. **TIP** In your outline, include notes about how to transition smoothly between ideas and evidence to convey meaning clearly and logically.
4. Reread the prompt, and then draft your essay.

CONTEMPORARY CONNECTION

Embracing WILDERNESS

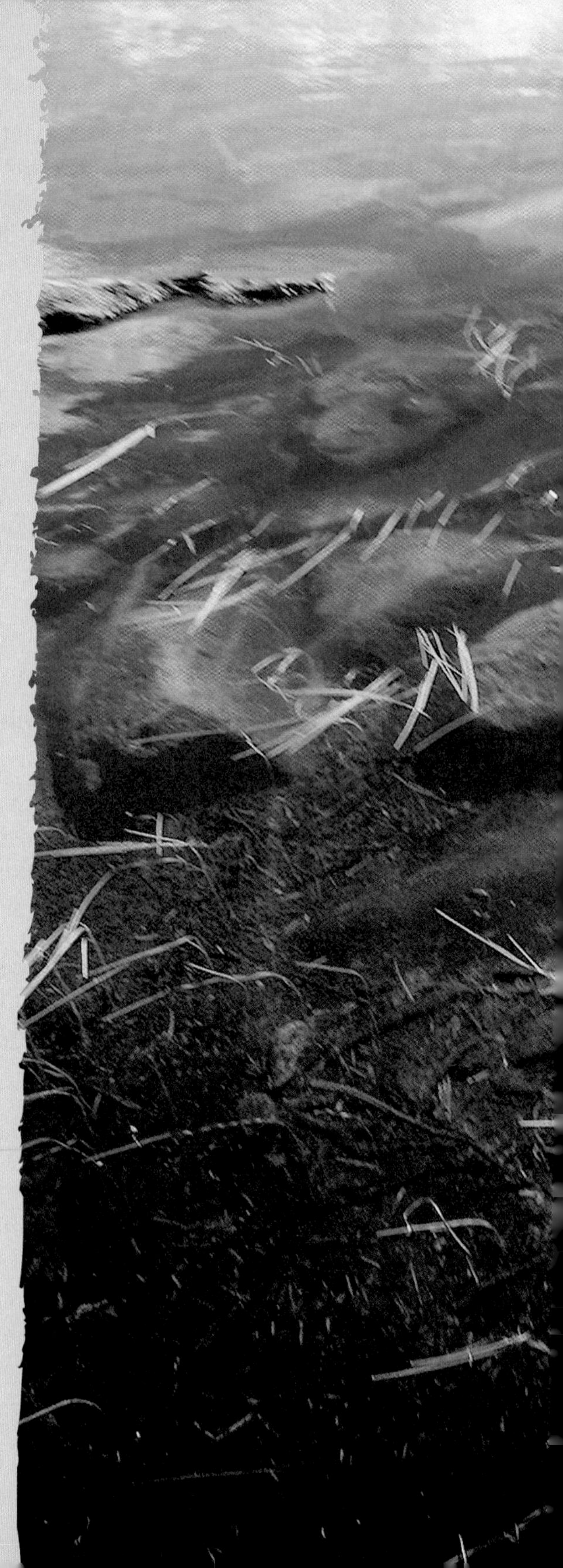

Past and Present

In 1846, 1853, and 1857, Henry David Thoreau traveled through vast stretches of Maine wilderness, following ancient canoe routes used by the Wabanaki Indians. In the Maine woods, Thoreau hiked and scaled mountains, writing, "I looked with awe at the ground I trod on...This was the Earth of which we have heard, made out of Chaos and Old Night." These Maine expeditions, far more grueling than Thoreau's walks around Massachusetts, "left such an impression of stern, yet gentle, wildness on [his] memory as will not soon be effaced."

Today, the Thoreau-Wabanaki Trail, as it is now called, is still in use. In the spring of 2005, photographer Bridget Besaw shot a series of photographs featuring people hiking, fishing, canoeing, camping, and climbing on the Thoreau-Wabanaki Trail. The photographs, captioned with quotes from Thoreau's writings, became an exhibit and a book. In her striking images, Besaw shows people rising to the challenges of the wilderness, celebrating its beauty, and standing in awe of its power. Her images suggest that the wilderness remains as important for us today as it was for Thoreau and the Wabanaki before him.

Bridget Besaw / Photographer

Bridget Besaw's award-winning photographs appear in a full spectrum of media: magazines, newspapers, advertisements, documentaries, books, and exhibits. Her current focus is on creating images for use as an advocacy tool for environmental protection.

Give me a WILDNESS whose glance no CIVILIZATION can endure . . .

Henry David Thoreau

Critical Reading

1. **Describe:** Select one of these images and describe the relationship between Besaw's images and Thoreau's words.
2. **(a) Compare and Contrast:** In what ways might a contemporary person's view of the wilderness be both similar to and different from Thoreau's perspective? **(b) Assess:** What circumstances might account for these similarities and differences?

Use this question to focus a class discussion:

3. Bridget Besaw's subject in this series is the north woods of Maine. If your assignment were to celebrate the beauty of nature in photographs, what locale would you select? Explain your choices.

American Masters

PART 4

IF I FEEL PHYSICALLY AS IF THE TOP OF MY HEAD WERE TAKEN OFF, I KNOW THAT IS POETRY.

— EMILY DICKINSON

In This Section

- Defining Poetry *(p. 402)*
- Model: "Man Listening to Disc" *(p. 403)*
- Study: Emily Dickinson's Poetry *(p. 406)*
- Study: Walt Whitman's Poetry *(p. 426)*

For more practice analyzing poetry, see numerous pages throughout this textbook, including 82, 125, 256, 312, 428, 636, 643, 708, 722, 874 , 902, 1064, 1072, and 1366.

Defining Poetry

Along with prose and drama, poetry is one of the three major genres, or forms, of literature. Poets usually employ highly charged language and arrange words in lines that form stanzas.

Types of Poetry Most poems fall into one of three categories:

- **Narrative poetry** tells a story and has the same literary elements as works of prose fiction. *Ballads* and *epics* are two types of narrative poem.
- **Dramatic poetry** uses the techniques of drama to present the speech of one or more characters in verse form.
- **Lyric poetry** expresses the thoughts and feelings of a single speaker.

Sound Devices Poets use the innate musical qualities of words to create patterns that emphasize meaning. **Meter,** the regular pattern of beats in a line, is one aspect of poetic sound. Other sound devices are

- **rhyme,** the repetition of sounds at the ends of words (*leaf* and *brief*);
- **consonance,** the repetition of final consonant sounds (*speak* and *break*);
- **assonance,** repetition of similar vowel sounds (*shade* and *ray*).

Alliteration, another sound device, is defined in the chart below.

Images and Figurative Language Images are words and phrases that appeal to the senses. Figurative language is language used imaginatively rather than literally. These, too, are hallmarks of poetry.

Close Read: Poetic Elements

These poetic elements appear in the Model text at right.

Alliteration: repetition of initial identical consonant sounds in accented syllables *Example: "What saint strained so much . . . ?" (Theodore Roethke)*	**Imagery:** language that appeals to the senses, creating word pictures that help to express meaning *Example: "a red wheelbarrow / glazed with rain water" (William Carlos Williams)*
Simile and Metaphor: figures of speech that compare two apparently unlike things. Similes use a connecting word (*like* or *as*); metaphors do not. *Simile: "The child's first step, / as awesome as an earthquake. (Anne Sexton)* *Metaphor: "...the fiery night that's in your eyes..." (Edward Arlington Robinson)*	**Precise Word Choice:** words that carry precise shades of meaning and express tone *Example: "Oh, but it is dirty!—this little filling station . . ." (Elizabeth Bishop)*

Model

About the Text Billy Collins (born 1941) has written many poems about other art forms. This poem celebrates the musical qualities and artistry of jazz.

"Man Listening to Disc" by Billy Collins

This is not bad—
ambling along 44th Street
with Sonny Rollins for company,
his music flowing through the soft calipers
of these earphones,

as if he were right beside me
on this clear day in March,
the pavement sparkling with sunlight,
pigeons fluttering off the curb,
nodding over a profusion of bread crumbs.

In fact, I would say
my delight at being suffused
with phrases from his saxophone—
some like honey, some like vinegar—
is surpassed only by my gratitude

to Tommy Potter for taking the time
to join us on this breezy afternoon
with his most unwieldy bass
and to the esteemed Arthur Taylor
who is somehow managing to navigate

this crowd with his cumbersome drums.
And I bow deeply to Thelonious Monk
for figuring out a way
to motorize—or whatever—his huge piano
so he could be with us today.

This music is loud yet so confidential
I cannot help feeling even more
like the center of the universe
than usual as I walk along to a rapid
little version of "The Way You Look Tonight,"

and all I can say to my fellow pedestrians,
to the woman in the white sweater,
the man in the tan raincoat and the heavy glasses,
who mistake themselves for the center of the universe—
all I can say is watch your step,

because the five of us, instruments and all,
are about to angle over
to the south side of the street
and then, in our own tightly knit way,
turn the corner at Sixth Avenue.

And if any of you are curious
about where this aggregation,
this whole battery-powered crew,
is headed, let us just say
that the real center of the universe,

the only true point of view,
is full of the hope that he,
the hub of the cosmos
with his hair blown sideways,
will eventually make it all the way downtown.

Alliteration Repetition of initial consonant *p* sounds mimics the popping rhythms of a jazz riff.

Simile The comparisons suggest the changing textures of the sound from sweet and flowing to sharp and jagged.

Imagery Word pictures appeal to the sense of sight. The speaker's head is filled with music, but he sees the world and its people clearly.

Precise Word Choice Precise word choices suggest the speaker's physical movement as he walks, the reality of his listening on a portable CD-player, and the virtuoso precision of the musicians.

Emily Dickinson
(1830–1886)

A unique voice of delicate intensity, Emily Dickinson is invariably named as one of our nation's greatest poets. Yet in her own lifetime, only a small circle of friends and relatives knew of Dickinson's poetic genius.

A Life Apart Born to a prominent family in Amherst, Massachusetts, Dickinson attended Amherst Academy and nearby Mount Holyoke Female Seminary. As a teenager she had an active social life, but over time she became increasingly reclusive, rarely venturing from her home after she was thirty. Devoting most of her time to writing poetry, she saw only the occasional visitor and communicated with friends and family mainly through letters.

Dickinson's Legacy Although she sometimes enclosed poetry in her letters, Dickinson published only a handful of her poems in her lifetime. When she died, her sister Lavinia found over a thousand poems in the drawers of her dresser, neatly tied in bundles known as **fascicles**. Dickinson left instructions that the poems be destroyed, but her family overrode that wish, recognizing that such a valuable legacy should be shared.

◀ This photograph shows the garden view of the Dickinson family homestead in Amherst, Massachusetts. The site is now a museum.

The Johnson Edition Unfortunately, Dickinson's early editors diminished the power of her verse by changing it to be more conventional in language and style. It was not until 1955 that Thomas H. Johnson published an edition of Dickinson's poetry that attempted to present the poems in their original form. With the appearance of the Johnson edition, Dickinson's poetic genius was more fully appreciated, and she is now acknowledged as a visionary who was far ahead of her time.

The Belle of Amherst In the years since the publication of her work, Dickinson has become the subject of plays, novels, and poems that have romanticized her life and celebrated her genius with varying levels of sentimentality and accuracy. In these works, she has been given a public personality that may or may not resemble the truth of who she was. However, in her work itself, the poets who have followed her find no peer.

In This Section

- Biography: Emily Dickinson *(p. 404)*
- Dickinson's Style *(p. 406)*
- Study: Emily Dickinson's Poetry *(pp. 408–417)*
- World Literature Connection: Tanka *(p. 413)*
- Critical Commentary: "Reckless Genius" by Galway Kinnell *(p. 418)*
- Biography: Walt Whitman *(p. 422)*
- Study: Walt Whitman's Poetry *(pp. 426–436)*
- Critical Commentary: America's Epic by James E. Miller, Jr. *(p. 437)*

FIND ECSTASY IN LIFE;
THE MERE SENSE OF
LIVING IS JOY ENOUGH.

— *Emily Dickinson*

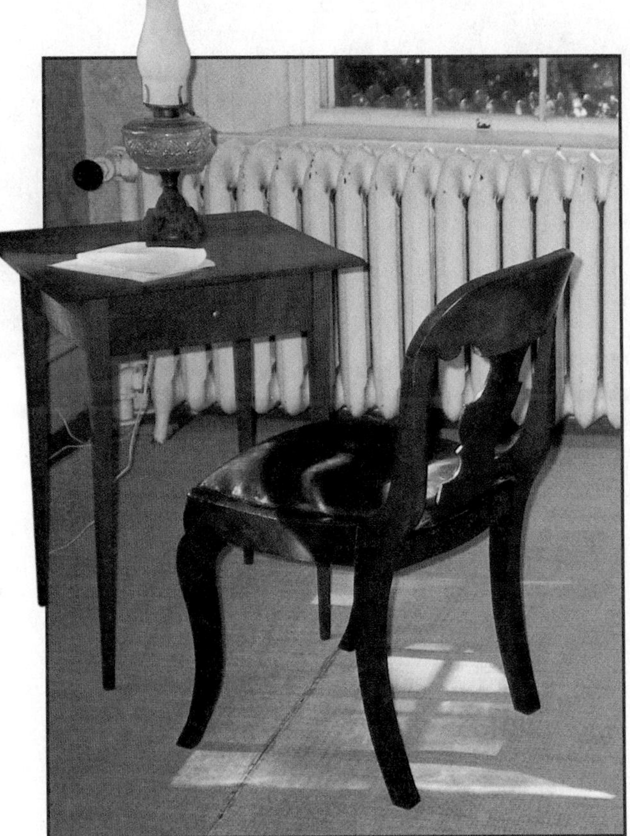

◀ Emily Dickinson's writing desk and chair still stand in her bedroom at the Homestead.

◀ This dress belonged to Emily Dickinson. It is now on display at the Emily Dickinson Homestead Museum.

Dickinson's Style

Uncertain about her abilities, in 1862 Dickinson sent four poems to the influential literary critic Thomas Wentworth Higginson. With the poems she enclosed a card on which she had written her name and the following unsigned letter:

MR. HIGGINSON, — Are you too deeply occupied to say if my verse is alive? The mind is so near itself it cannot see distinctly, and I have none to ask. Should you think it breathed, and had you the leisure to tell me, I should feel quick gratitude. If I make the mistake, that you dared to tell me would give me sincerer honor toward you. I inclose my name, asking you, if you please, sir, to tell me what is true? That you will not betray me it is needless to ask, since honor is it's own pawn.

In his response to Dickinson, Higginson recognized Dickinson's talent and encouraged her to keep writing, but he also sought to change her unconventional style. He was especially concerned by her unorthodox use of dashes and capitalization. After Dickinson died, Higginson was one of the early editors of her verse. Along with other early editors, he failed to recognize that Dickinson crafted her poems with great precision and that her eccentric capitalization and punctuation were important elements in her poetry. When Thomas H. Johnson came out with his edition of Dickinson's poetry in 1955, he restored original elements including the dashes and capital letters, so that today we can read the poems as Dickinson meant them to be read.

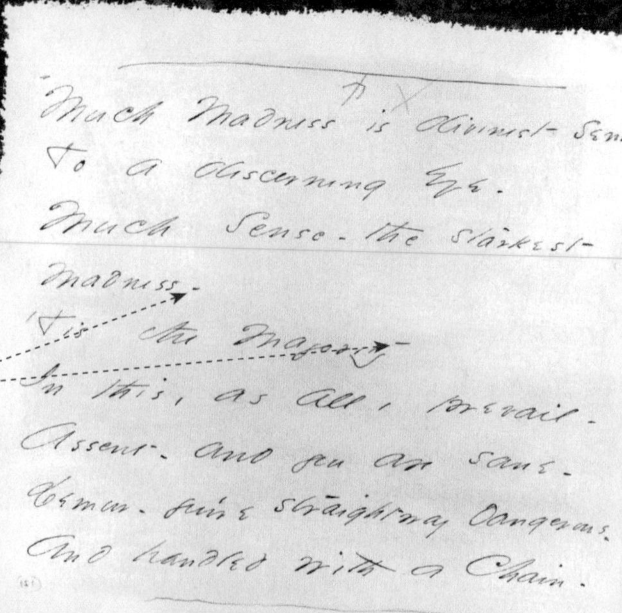
"Much Madness is divinest Sense
To a discerning Eye.
Much Sense - the starkest -
Madness -
'Tis the Majority
In this, as All, prevail -
Assent - and you are sane -
Demur - you're straightway dangerous -
And handled with a Chain -

This image shows Dickinson's original manuscript of her famous poem "Much Madness is Divinest Sense." Note her unconventional use of dashes throughout the poem.

Before You Read *Emily Dickinson's Poetry*

Connecting to the Essential Question Emily Dickinson's poems often express a preference for solitude, a value many people would not choose. As you read Dickinson's poems, notice references to the soul and society. This will help as you consider the Essential Question: **What makes American literature American?**

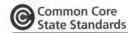

Common Core State Standards

Reading Literature

4. Determine the meaning of words and phrases as they are used in the text, including figurative and connotative meanings; analyze the impact of specific word choices on meaning and tone.

5. Analyze how an author's choices concerning how to structure specific parts of a text contribute to its overall structure and meaning as well as its aesthetic impact.

6. Analyze a case in which grasping a point of view requires distinguishing what is directly stated in a text from what is really meant.

Literary Analysis

Poets use rhyme to stress ideas, make poems musical, convey mood, and unify groups of lines. In **exact rhyme,** two or more words have identical sounds in their final stressed syllables, as in *one/begun*. In **slant rhyme** the final sounds are similar but not identical, as in *one/stone*. Dickinson's frequent use of slant rhyme at points where the reader expects an exact rhyme helps make her poetry surprising:

I've known her—from an ample nation—
Choose One—
Then—close the Valves of her attention—
Like Stone—

Another hallmark of Dickinson's style is her fondness for paradox. A **paradox** is a statement that seems contradictory but actually presents a truth. For example, the statement "The Brain—is wider than the Sky" is a paradox. It seems impossible but becomes true if you consider the brain's capacity to understand. As you read, analyze the effects of rhyme and notice examples of paradox in these poems.

Reading Strategy

Preparing to Read Complex Texts Dickinson writes with great precision, using carefully chosen words in statements that are dense with meaning. Sometimes, she omits words that are expected to be understood. This is called *elliptical phrasing*. To clarify this language, it may be helpful to **reread.** As you reread, mentally fill in words that seem to be missing, and be alert to different possible meanings. Use a chart like the one shown to help as you reread.

Original Line
Water, is taught by thirst

↓

Possible Meaning
Water is taught **something** by thirst.

↓

Probable Meaning
The concept of water is taught **to us** by thirst.

Vocabulary

surmised (sər mīzd′) *v.* guessed; concluded (p. 409)

eternity (ē turn′ ə tē) *n.* time without beginning or end (p. 409)

interposed (in′ tər pōzd′) *v.* came between (p. 411)

affliction (ə flik′ shən) *n.* anything causing pain or distress (p. 412)

ample (am′ pəl) *adj.* large in size; more than enough (p. 414)

finite (fī′ nīt) *adj.* having measurable or definable limits (p. 416)

infinity (in fin′ i tē) *n.* endless or unlimited space, time, or distance (p. 416)

Waiting Outside No. 12, Anonymous, Crane Kalman Gallery

BECAUSE I COULD NOT STOP FOR DEATH

Emily Dickinson

▲ Critical Viewing
In what ways do the details of this painting mirror Dickinson's poem? **[Analyze]**

BACKGROUND *The extent of Emily Dickinson's gift was not generally recognized until 1955, when a new edition of her poems was published under the guidance of Thomas H. Johnson. Previous editors had changed Dickinson's poems to reflect conventional ideas about poetry, but Johnson's edition restored the poet's original versions. For the first time, Dickinson's poetry was printed as she had meant it to be read, and the world experienced the power of her complex mind captured in concrete imagery and simple but forceful language. Dickinson's work is often compared with that of the modern poets, and she is now acknowledged as a visionary who was far ahead of her time.*

Because I could not stop for Death—
He kindly stopped for me—
The Carriage held but just Ourselves—
And Immortality.

We slowly drove—He knew no haste
And I had put away
My labor and my leisure too,
For his Civility—

We passed the School, where Children strove
At Recess—in the Ring—
We passed the Fields of Gazing Grain—
We passed the Setting Sun—

Or rather—He passed Us—
The Dews drew quivering and chill—
For only Gossamer,[1] my Gown—
My Tippet[2]—only Tulle[3]—

We paused before a House that seemed
A Swelling of the Ground—
The Roof was scarcely visible—
The Cornice—in the Ground—

Since then—'tis Centuries—and yet
Feels shorter than the Day
I first **surmised** the Horses' Heads
Were toward **Eternity**—

Reading Strategy
Reread Clarify the elliptical phrasing in lines 15–16 and restate the poet's meaning.

Vocabulary
surmised (sər mīzd′) *v.* guessed; concluded

eternity (ē tʉrn′ə tē) *n.* time without beginning or end

1. **Gossamer** *n.* very thin, soft, filmy cloth.
2. **Tippet** *n.* scarflike garment worn over the shoulders and hanging down in front.
3. **Tulle** (to͞ol) *n.* thin, fine netting used for scarves.

Critical Reading 

Cite textual evidence to support your responses.

1. **Craft and Structure (a)** In the first two lines, what adverb defines Death's actions? **(b) Analyze:** In what sense is this depiction surprising or ironic?
2. **Key Ideas and Details (a)** What three scenes does the carriage pass in stanza three? **(b) Interpret:** What meaning do you attribute to these scenes?
3. **Key Ideas and Details (a)** How much time passes for the speaker in this poem? **(b) Speculate:** Why do you think the speaker notes that the time "feels shorter than the Day"? **(c) Compare and Contrast:** What does the speaker seem to feel about the experience of death in contrast with life?
4. **Integration of Knowledge and Ideas Take a Position:** Do you think this poem has a single meaning or message? Explain your reasoning.

I HEARD A FLY BUZZ— WHEN I DIED

Emily Dickinson

I heard a Fly buzz—when I died—
The Stillness in the Room
Was like the Stillness in the Air—
Between the Heaves of Storm—

The Eyes around—had wrung them dry—
And Breaths were gathering firm
For that last Onset—when the King
Be witnessed—in the Room—

I willed my Keepsakes—Signed away
What portion of me be
Assignable—and then it was
There **interposed** a Fly—

With Blue—uncertain stumbling Buzz—
Between the light—and me—
And then the Windows failed—and then
I could not see to see—

Literary Analysis
Slant Rhyme What two words form a slant rhyme in the first stanza?

Vocabulary
interposed (in′tər pōzd′) *v.* came between

◀ **Critical Viewing**
Which details in this painting appropriately illustrate Dickinson's poem? **[Support]**

Critical Reading

Cite textual evidence to support your responses.

1. **Key Ideas and Details (a)** What do the speaker and those in attendance expect to experience when "the last Onset" occurs? **(b)** What happens instead? **(c) Analyze:** In what ways is this turn of events ironic?
2. **Key Ideas and Details (a)** What actions has the speaker taken in preparation for death? **(b) Interpret:** Which "portion" of the speaker is "assignable," or able to be willed to others, and which is not?
3. **Craft and Structure (a)** In the final stanza, what adjectives does the speaker use to describe the buzzing of the fly? **(b) Draw Conclusions:** What statement about dying is Dickinson making in this poem?
4. **Integration of Knowledge and Ideas Speculate:** If you were describing a deathbed scene from the perspective of the dying person, would you mention the buzzing of a fly? Why or why not?

THERE'S A CERTAIN SLANT OF LIGHT

EMILY DICKINSON

There's a certain Slant of light,
Winter Afternoons—
That oppresses, like the Heft
Of Cathedral Tunes—

Heavenly Hurt, it gives us—
We can find no scar,
But internal difference,
Where the Meanings, are—

None may teach it—Any—
'Tis the Seal Despair—
An imperial affliction
Sent us of the Air—

When it comes, the Landscape listens—
Shadows—hold their breath—
When it goes, 'tis like the Distance
On the look of Death—

Vocabulary
affliction (ə flik′ shən)
n. anything causing pain or distress

MY LIFE CLOSED TWICE BEFORE ITS CLOSE—

EMILY DICKINSON

My life closed twice before its close—
It yet remains to see
If Immortality unveil
A third event to me.

So huge, so hopeless to conceive
As these that twice befell.
Parting is all we know of heaven.
And all we need of hell.

WORLD LITERATURE CONNECTION

Capturing the Moment

In her poems, Emily Dickinson often seems to capture a moment and hold it still. The tanka is a Japanese form of poetry that also captures the moment. In the original Japanese, tanka is a 31-syllable poem that usually contains at least one distinct pause. This pause is often represented by a dash in English translations. When translated into English, tanka are usually written in five lines, and the syllable count often changes. In Japan, tanka-writing has been popular for more than 1300 years and is still practiced today.

Renowned tanka writers include **Ki Tsurayuki** (died c. 945), an important figure in the Japanese imperial court and a leading poet of his time; **Ono Komachi** (833 – 857), a great beauty whose poems were noted for their passion and energy; and **Priest Jakuren** (1139? – 1202), a Buddhist priest whose poems are filled with beautiful, melancholy imagery.

Tanka

Ki Tsurayuki
translated by Geoffrey Bownas

When I went to visit
The girl I love so much,
That winter night
The river blew so cold
That the plovers
were crying.

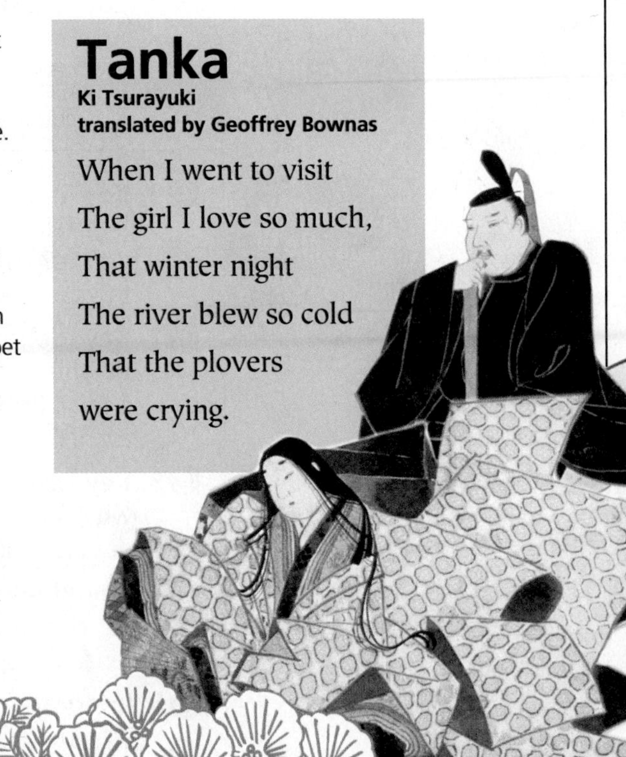

CONNECT TO THE LITERATURE

What similarities do you see in this tanka and the Emily Dickinson poems you have read? In what ways are they different?

The Soul Selects her own Society—

Emily Dickinson

The Soul selects her own Society—
Then—shuts the Door—
To her divine Majority—
Present no more—

Unmoved—she notes the Chariots—pausing—
At her low Gate—
Unmoved—an Emperor be kneeling
Upon her Mat—

I've known her—from an **ample** nation—
Choose One—
Then—close the Valves of her attention—
Like Stone—

Literary Analysis
Slant Rhyme What words create slant rhymes in the second stanza?

Vocabulary
ample (am′ pəl) *adj.* large in size; more than enough

Critical Reading

Cite textual evidence to support your responses.

1. **Key Ideas and Details (a)** According to the speaker of "There's a certain Slant of light," in what ways does the winter light affect people? **(b) Analyze:** What does this light seem to represent to the speaker?
2. **Key Ideas and Details (a) Interpret:** What is the third event to which the speaker of "My life closed twice before its close—" refers? **(b) Connect:** What is the relationship between the three events?
3. **Key Ideas and Details (a)** In "The Soul selects her own Society," what leaves the soul "unmoved"? **(b) Analyze:** How would you describe the soul's attitude toward the world's attractions?
4. **Key Ideas and Details (a)** What happens after the soul makes her choice? **(b) Assess:** What adjectives would you use to characterize the speaker based on this choice?
5. **Integration of Knowledge and Ideas Relate:** Our culture places a premium on popularity for its own sake. What do Dickinson's poems suggest about other ways to view human relationships?

The Brain— IS WIDER THAN THE SKY—

Emily Dickinson

The Brain—is wider than the Sky—
For—put them side by side—
The one the other will contain
With ease—and You—beside—

The Brain is deeper than the sea—
For—hold them—Blue to Blue—
The one the other will absorb—
As Sponges—Buckets—do—

The Brain is just the weight of God—
For—Heft them—Pound for Pound—
And they will differ—if they do—
As Syllable from Sound—

Literary Analysis

Paradox What paradoxes do you find in all three stanzas of this poem?

THERE IS A SOLITUDE OF SPACE

EMILY DICKINSON

Vocabulary

finite (fī´ nīt´) *adj.* having measurable or definable limits

infinity (in fin´ i tē) *n.* endless or unlimited space, time, or distance

There is a solitude of space
A solitude of sea
A solitude of death, but these
Society shall be
Compared with that profounder site
That polar privacy
A soul admitted to itself—
Finite Infinity.

Water, is taught by thirst

EMILY DICKINSON

Water, is taught by thirst.
Land—by the Oceans passed.
Transport[1]—by throe[2]—
Peace—by its battles told—
Love, by Memorial Mold[3]—
Birds, by the Snow.

1. **Transport** ecstasy; rapture.
2. **throe** spasm or pang of pain.
3. **Memorial Mold** memorial grounds or cemetery.

Cite textual evidence to support your responses.

Critical Reading

1. **Craft and Structure (a)** What comparisons does the speaker make in "The Brain—is wider than the Sky—"? **(b) Interpret:** What role does a surprising use of scale and size play in these comparisons?
2. **Key Ideas and Details (a)** In "There is a solitude of space," what three things does the speaker compare to "polar privacy"? **(b) Contrast:** How does the solitude of "a soul admitted to itself" differ from other types of solitude?
3. **Craft and Structure (a)** In "Water, is taught by thirst," what is the relationship between each line's first word and the words that follow? **(b) Interpret:** What is the theme or message of this poem?
4. **Integration of Ideas and Knowledge** Is the tension Dickinson sees between individuality and society true for most people, or is it simply the poet's view of her own life? In your response, use at least two of these Essential Question words: *unlimited, limited, social, private, public.* ***[Connecting to the Essential Question: What makes American literature American?]***

Critical Commentary

Reckless Genius

Galway Kinnell

A Pulitzer Prize-winning Poet Pays Tribute to the Belle of Amherst.

Emily Dickinson wrote about the kinds of experience few poets have the daring to explore or the genius to sing. She is one of the most intelligent of poets and also one of the most fearless. If the fearlessness ran out, she had her courage, and after that her heart-stopping recklessness.

More fully than most poets, Dickinson tells how it is to be a human being in a particular moment, in compressed, hard, blazingly vivid poems—which have duende![1] Her greatest seem not sung but forced into being by a craving for a kind of forbidden knowledge of the unknowable.

Being thoroughly conventional, the few literary men of the time who saw Dickinson's poems found nothing very special about them and attributed her experiments in rhyme and rhythm to the naiveté of an untaught lady poet with a tin ear.

Similar figures today think she cannot be considered a major poet because she writes tiny poems. Of course there is nothing inherently minor in smallish poems, and in any case, many of Dickinson's poems are little because she omits the warming-up, preface and situation—and begins where a more discursive poet might be preparing to end. Relative to their small surface, her poems have large inner bulk. And since her themes obsessively reappear, a group of the poems, when read together, sweeps one along inside another's consciousness much as a long poem does.

In my opinion, she could not have accomplished her great work without making two technical innovations.

Dickinson's chosen form requires rhymes, which are scarce in English, at frequent intervals. To avoid using an imprecise word for the sake of rhyme, she made a simple revolutionary innovation: expanding the kinds of echoes that qualify as rhyme. To exact rhyme *(room/broom)* and slant rhyme *(room/brim)* she added assonant rhyme *(room/bruise)*, thus multiplying the supply of rhyme words many times over. Sometimes, perhaps shocked by the rightness of an unrhymable word, she resorted to rhyme by vague resemblance *(freeze/privilege)* or skipped the rhyme entirely.

▲ Poet and translator Galway Kinnell is the recipient of the MacArthur Foundation "Genius" Grant and many other honors.

She is one of the most intelligent of poets and also one of the most fearless.

1. **duende** (dwen´ da) intensity; burning within.

Her other innovation protects the density and dissonance of her poems from the singsong latent in common meter's de dum, de dum, de dum, de dum / de dum, de dum, de dum / de dum, de dum, de dum, de dum / de dum, de dum, de dum. Using wee dashes, she divides lines into clusters of syllables (sometimes a single syllable) that are not unlike William Carlos Williams'[2] "variable feet"—rhythmic units of varying length that are all spoken in approximately the same amount of time.

Saying her poems aloud, we hear two rhythmic systems clashing and twining: the iambic beat, and superimposed upon it, Dickinson's own inner, speech-like, sliding, syncopated rhythm. The latter suggests an urge in her toward some kind of Creeley-like[3] free verse, and it is also what allows her to write in formal verse using all her passion and intelligence.

A poem by Dickinson that I particularly like is the widely admired "I heard a Fly buzz — when I died." Here, through what Keats[4] called "negative capability," Dickinson enters, imaginatively, a dying person and goes with her into death. To write this poem with authority, Dickinson had to "die" a moment in imagination, which may be to say that she had actually to die a little in reality. ... The brilliance of Emily Dickinson's greatest poems may have exacted a high price in emotional stamina and stability, and foreshortened by years that amazingly prolific period (in one year, she wrote 364 poems) when she was writing with her full powers...

To write this poem with authority, Dickinson had to "die" a moment in imagination...

2. **William Carlos Williams** (1883-1963) American poet and physician; one of the original Imagist poets, a group whose work stressed simplicity and the use of imagery.
3. **Creeley-like** The work of American poet Robert Creeley (1926-2005) was notable for its very short lines and simple language.
4. **Keats** John Keats (1795-1821), famous British poet whose work centered on the beauty found in ordinary things.

Check Your Comprehension

- According to Kinnell, what does Emily Dickinson do more fully than most other poets?
- What did Dickinson's contemporaries think of her work?
- With what two innovations does Kinnell credit Dickinson?

After You Read *Emily Dickinson's Poetry*

Literary Analysis

1. **Craft and Structure (a)** Use a chart like the one shown to examine the use of **slant rhyme** and **exact rhyme** in "I heard a Fly buzz—when I died." **(b)** What is the effect of the exact rhyme after so many slant rhymes?

Slant Rhyme	Lines	Exact Rhyme	Lines

2. **Craft and Structure (a)** How do the many slant rhymes in "Because I could not stop for Death" and "The Soul selects her own Society—" reflect the content of those poems? **(b)** How do the many exact rhymes in "The Brain—is wider than the Sky—" suit the content of that poem?
3. **Craft and Structure** Each line of "Water, is taught by thirst" expresses the same basic **paradox.** What is that paradox, and how can it be true?
4. **Craft and Structure (a)** Explain how the first line of "I heard a Fly buzz—when I died" is a paradox. **(b)** Which of the other poems presented here is built around a similar paradox? **(c)** For both poems, what explanation might make the situation possible, even though it seems impossible?
5. **Craft and Structure** A two-word paradox, such as *cruel kindness*, is called an *oxymoron*. Identify an oxymoron in "There is a solitude of space," and explain the apparent contradiction.
6. **Integration of Knowledge and Ideas** What is similar and different about the speaker's attitude toward the self and other people in "My life closed twice before its close—," "The Soul selects her own Society—," and "There is a solitude of space"?
7. **Integration of Knowledge and Ideas (a)** Which poems present human understanding as something boundless or unlimited? **(b)** Which present it as something small and limited? **(c)** How would you define Dickinson's view of the individual self?

Common Core State Standards

Writing

2. Write explanatory texts to examine and convey complex ideas, concepts, and information clearly and accurately through the effective selection, organization, and analysis of content.

2.b. Develop the topic thoroughly by selecting the most significant quotations or other information and examples appropriate to the audience's knowledge of the topic.

Language

5.a. Interpret figures of speech in context and analyze their role in the text.

Reading Strategy

8. **Reread** "I heard a Fly buzz—when I died." **(a)** In Dickinson's elliptical style, what words do you understand to be missing from lines 5 and 6? **(b)** Explain your interpretation of the poem's final line.
9. Reread "There's a certain Slant of light." What are two possible meanings of the last two lines?

PERFORMANCE TASKS

Integrated Language Skills

Vocabulary Acquisition and Use

Word Analysis: Latin Root *-fin-*

The Latin root *-fin-* means "end." In the word *finite* it combines with the suffix *-ite* to create an adjective meaning "having a definite end." In the word *infinite*, it combines with the suffix *-ite* and the prefix *in-*, meaning "not," to create an adjective meaning "without end." Use your knowledge of the root to explain the meaning of each italicized word below. Make clear how the word's meaning reflects the meaning of the root.

1. Perhaps you can count the stars, but to me they seem *infinite* in number.
2. The musical composition had an introduction, a long middle section, and a grand *finale*.
3. Stop being vague and give me a *definite* answer.
4. The contest began with fifty competitors, but I was one of only three *finalists*.
5. The coarse lad attended a special school, so his manners are now quite *refined*.

Vocabulary: Antonyms

For each numbered item, choose the letter of its antonym, or word that expresses an opposite meaning. Explain your choices.

1. **surmised:** **(a)** concluded **(b)** focused **(c)** asked **(d)** stated
2. **interposed:** **(a)** continuous **(b)** scattered **(c)** between **(d)** above
3. **affliction:** **(a)** poverty **(b)** passion **(c)** warfare **(d)** balm
4. **ample:** **(a)** smooth **(b)** huge **(c)** inhospitable **(d)** insufficient
5. **finite:** **(a)** countless **(b)** meaningless **(c)** worthwhile **(d)** thick
6. **infinity:** **(a)** trivia **(b)** limitation **(c)** confusion **(d)** endlessness

Writing

Explanatory Text A **blog** is a forum for writing that is part of a web site. Most blogs contain a series of postings on related topics and many have rules for content and posting.

Write a blog entry for a poetry site in which you analyze Dickinson's sense of infinity. Plan your work to meet the site's deadlines and other requirements.

Prewriting Reread Dickinson's poems, looking for references to infinity. List details and the poems in which they appear. Study the details, and write a statement in which you interpret patterns. This will serve as your controlling idea.

Drafting Develop your ideas in a logical sequence and support them with details from the poems. Follow correct requirements for citation.

Revising Make sure all the elements of your entry work to develop or support your controlling idea. Delete any stray ideas or unrelated details.

Model: Following Manuscript Requirements

In the "The Brain—is wider than the Sky—," Dickinson suggests that there is no limit to the amount of knowledge the human brain can take in. She compares the brain with the sky, writing, "For—put them side by side— / The one the other will contain."

A short quotation should be set off with quotation marks. If longer than four lines, a quotation should be set off and indented.

Walt Whitman (1819–1892)

In the preface to his first volume of poetry, the 1855 edition of *Leaves of Grass,* Walt Whitman wrote: "The proof of a poet is that his country absorbs him as affectionately as he absorbed it." Whitman's hopes for such proof of his own merit as a poet were deferred: He was harshly denounced for his first volume of poetry, but in the following decades, his poems gained popularity, and he became famous as "the Good Gray Poet" and "the Bard of Democracy." In his later years, Whitman was admired by writers and intellectuals on both sides of the Atlantic. Today, he is widely recognized as one of the greatest and most influential poets the United States has ever produced.

The Poet at Work Whitman was born on Long Island and raised in Brooklyn, New York. His education was not formal, but he read widely, including the works of Sir Walter Scott, Shakespeare, Homer, and Dante. Trained to be a printer, Whitman spent his early years alternating between printing jobs and newspaper writing. When he was twenty-seven, he became the editor of the *Brooklyn Eagle,* a respected newspaper, but the paper fired him in 1848 because of his opposition to slavery. After accepting a position on a paper in New Orleans, Whitman traveled across the country for the first time, observing the diversity of America's landscapes and people.

Whitman soon returned to New York City, however, and in 1850 quit journalism to devote his energy to writing poetry. Impressed by Ralph Waldo Emerson's prophetic description of a new kind of American poet, Whitman had been jotting down ideas and fragments of verse in a notebook for years. His work broke every poetic tradition of rhyme and meter as it celebrated America and the common man. When the first edition of *Leaves of Grass* was published in 1855, critics attacked Whitman's subject matter and abandonment of traditional poetic devices and forms. Noted poet John Greenleaf Whittier hated Whitman's poems so much that he hurled his copy of *Leaves of Grass* into the fireplace. Emerson, on the other hand, responded with great enthusiasm, remarking that the collection was "the most extraordinary piece of wit and wisdom that America has yet contributed."

The Bard of Democracy Though Whitman did publish other works in the course of his career, his life's work proved to be *Leaves of Grass,* which he continually revised, reshaped, and expanded until his death in 1892. The poems in later editions became less confusing, repetitious, and raucous, and more symbolic, expressive, and universal. He viewed the volume as a single long poem that expressed his evolving vision of the world. Using his poetry to convey his passionate belief in democracy, equality, and the spiritual unity of all forms of life, he celebrated the potential of the human spirit. Though Whitman's philosophy grew out of the ideas of the Transcendentalists, his poetry was mainly shaped by his ability to absorb and comprehend everything he observed. From its first appearance as twelve unsigned and untitled poems, *Leaves of Grass* grew to include 383 poems in its final, "death-bed" edition (1892). The collection captures the diversity of the American people and conveys the energy and intensity of all forms of life. In the century since Whitman's death, *Leaves of Grass* has become one of the most highly regarded collections of poetry ever written. There is little doubt that, according to his own definition, Whitman has proven himself as a poet.

"THE UNITED STATES THEMSELVES ARE ESSENTIALLY THE GREATEST POEM."

Before You Read *Walt Whitman's Poetry*

Connecting to the Essential Question The poetry of Walt Whitman is bold, adventurous, generous, and optimistic. As you read Whitman's poems, note word choices that signal a sense of boldness, adventure, and optimism. This will help as you consider the Essential Question: **What makes American literature American?**

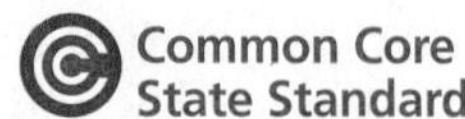

Reading Literature

4. Determine the meaning of words and phrases as they are used in the text, including figurative and connotative meanings; analyze the impact of specific word choices on meaning and tone, including words with multiple meanings or language that is particularly fresh, engaging, or beautiful. *(p. 425)*

5. Analyze how an author's choices concerning how to structure specific parts of a text contribute to its overall structure and meaning as well as its aesthetic impact.

9. Demonstrate knowledge of nineteenth-century foundational works of American literature, including how two or more texts from the same period treat similar themes or topics.

Language

5.a. Interpret figures of speech in context and analyze their role in the text.

Literary Analysis

Traditional **epic poetry** tells a long story about a hero whose adventures embody the values of a nation. Although many of his first readers were shocked by Whitman's *Leaves of Grass*, today the poem is considered a type of *American epic* that expresses national ideals. A true "poet of democracy," Whitman is broadly inclusive in his topics, which range from slavery and the Civil War to romantic love and immortality. Thrumming through these diverse subjects, though, is the constant echo of Whitman's **epic theme**—that all people of all times are connected by their shared experience of life. Whitman's **style** is marked by specific *structural and poetic elements* that contribute to a sense of epic sweep:

- **Free Verse:** Unlike formal verse, which has strict rules, free verse has irregular meter and line length and sounds like natural speech. Although free verse is as old as the Psalms in the Bible, Whitman was the first American poet to use it. It allows him to shape every line and stanza to suit his meaning, rather than fitting his message to a form:

  Do I contradict myself?
  Very well then I contradict myself. . . .

- **Long Lines:** Whitman uses long, sprawling lines for various effects. They may reflect the idea being expressed, capture a broad scene, develop a complex idea, or string together a list of objects:

  I lean and loaf at my ease observing a spear of summer grass.

- **Catalogues,** or **lists:** Whitman's use of catalogues, or lists, of people, objects, or situations, evokes the infinite range of elements that make up human experience. His catalogs create a colorful, inclusive parade of images while simultaneously suggesting that each element is of equal weight and worth. "I am enamor'd," he writes,

  Of men that live among cattle . . .
  Of the builders and steerers of ships and the wielders of axes and mauls, and the drivers of horses...

- **Anaphora,** or the repetition of phrases or sentences with similar structures or meanings: In the preface to *Leaves of Grass*, Whitman writes that America "perceives that the corpse" of old ideas is being moved out of the "house" of the national literature. His use of anaphora in this paragraph creates a tone and rhythm that is almost biblical, even as it delivers a message that is revolutionary:

  ... perceives that it waits a little while in the door ... that it was fittest for its days ... that its action has descended to the stalwart and well-shaped heir who approaches ... and that he shall be fittest for his days.

- **Diction,** or **word choice:** In the example used to illustrate anaphora above, the words *fittest* and *heir* enhance the passage's biblical quality. Whitman chooses other words for their clarity, precision, or sound quality.
- **Onomatopoeia,** or words whose sounds imitate their meanings: Whitman's use of words like *grunting*, *gab*, and *yawp* give his poetry an earthy quality, while also suggesting that his ideas transcend language itself.

Comparing Literary Works As you read, notice Whitman's use of these structural and poetic elements, and compare their effects in different poems. Think about the ideas or emotions individual elements help to emphasize.

Reading Strategy

Preparing to Read Complex Texts To increase your understanding of Whitman's ideas, **adjust your reading rate.** When a poem's lines are long and dense, read slowly, and when you feel pulled by the rhythm of the verse, read more rapidly. *Read aloud* to hear the flow of Whitman's language and to better appreciate his sprawling lines, evocative sounds, and rhythmic repetitions. As you read, use a chart like the one shown to record passages you read slowly and to note how this strategy enhances your understanding.

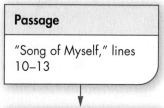

Passage
"Song of Myself," lines 10–13

Meaning
Whitman sets aside what he was taught through formal education, but these things cannot be completely forgotten. He will speak openly and freely in the lines to follow.

Vocabulary

stirring (stur′ iŋ) *adj.* busy; full of energy (p. 427)

abeyance (ə bā′ əns) *n.* temporary suspension (p. 428)

effuse (e fyo͞oz′) *v.* pour out (p. 431)

bequeath (bē kwēth′) *v.* hand down or pass on (p. 431)

stealthily (stelth′ ə lē) *adv.* slyly or secretively (p. 433)

robust (rō bust′) *adj.* strong and healthy; full of life (p. 435)

FROM PREFACE TO THE 1855 EDITION OF

LEAVES OF GRASS

WALT WHITMAN

BACKGROUND The 1855 edition of was the first edition of Whitman's opus. In the preface to his work, Whitman's prose sings much as his poetry does, full of poetic language, enthusiasm, and energy.

America does not repel the past or what it has produced under its forms or amid other politics or the idea of castes or the old religions. . . . accepts the lesson with calmness . . . is not so impatient as has been supposed that the slough still sticks to opinions and manners and literature while the life which served its requirements has passed into the new life of the new forms . . . perceives that the corpse is slowly borne from the eating and sleeping rooms of the house . . . perceives that it waits a little while in the door . . . that it was fittest for its days . . . that its action has descended to the stalwart and well-shaped heir who approaches . . . and that he shall be fittest for his days.

The Americans of all nations at any time upon the earth have probably the fullest poetical nature. The United States themselves are essentially the greatest poem. In the history of the earth hitherto the largest and most stirring appear tame and orderly to their ampler largeness and stir. Here at last is something in the doings of man that corresponds with the broadcast doings of the day and night. Here is not merely a nation but a teeming nation of nations. Here is action untied from strings necessarily blind to particulars and details magnificently moving in vast masses. Here is the hospitality which forever indicates heroes. . . . Here are the roughs and beards and space and ruggedness and nonchalance that the soul loves. Here the performance disdaining the trivial unapproached in the tremendous audacity of its crowds and groupings and the push of its perspective spreads with crampless and flowing breadth and showers its prolific and splendid extravagance. One sees it must indeed own the riches of the summer and winter, and need never be bankrupt while corn grows from the ground or the orchards drop apples or the bays contain fish or men beget children upon women. . . .

Vocabulary
stirring (stʉr´ iŋ) *adj.* busy; full of energy

Literary Analysis
Epic Theme What portrait of America does Whitman paint in his references to "roughs and beards and space and ruggedness"?

Critical Reading

Cite textual evidence to support your responses.

1. **Key Ideas and Details (a)** What subject does Whitman address in the first paragraph? **(b) Interpret:** What does Whitman mean when he says "the corpse is slowly borne from the eating and sleeping rooms of the house"?
2. **Key Ideas and Details (a)** According to Whitman, what makes America different from all other nations? **(b) Interpret:** What is the meaning of Whitman's notion that the United States is "a teeming nation of nations"?
3. **Key Ideas and Details (a)** According to Whitman, what is the greatest of all poems? **(b) Analyze:** Based on this statement, how is Whitman redefining the idea of a poem?

EXEMPLAR TEXT

from Song *of* Myself

WALT WHITMAN

1

I celebrate myself, and sing myself,
And what I assume you shall assume,
For every atom belonging to me as good belongs to you.

I loaf and invite my soul,
I lean and loaf at my ease observing a spear of summer grass.

My tongue, every atom of my blood, formed from this soil, this air,
Born here of parents born here from parents the same, and their parents the same,
I, now thirty-seven years old in perfect health begin,
Hoping to cease not till death.

Creeds and schools in **abeyance**,
Retiring back a while sufficed at what they are, but never forgotten,
I harbor for good or bad, I permit to speak at every hazard,
Nature without check with original energy.

Vocabulary
abeyance (ə bā´ əns) *n.* temporary suspension

6

A child said *What is the grass?* fetching it to me with full hands,
How could I answer the child? I do not know what it is any more than he.

I guess it must be the flag of my disposition, out of hopeful green stuff woven.

Or I guess it is the handkerchief of the Lord,
A scented gift and remembrancer[1] designedly dropped,
Bearing the owner's name someway in the corners, that we may see and remark, and say *Whose?*

. . .

What do you think has become of the young and old men?
And what do you think has become of the women and children?

They are alive and well somewhere,
The smallest sprout shows there is really no death,
And if ever there was it led forward life, and does not wait at the end to arrest it,
And ceas'd the moment life appear'd.
All goes onward and outward, nothing collapses,
And to die is different from what anyone supposed, and luckier.

9

The big doors of the country barn stand open and ready,
The dried grass of the harvest-time loads the slow-drawn wagon.
The clear light plays on the brown gray and green intertinged,
The armfuls are pack'd to the sagging mow.

I am there, I help, I came stretch'd atop of the load,
I felt its soft jolts, one leg reclined on the other,
I jump from the crossbeams and seize the clover and timothy,
And roll head over heels and tangle my hair full of wisps.

14

The wild gander leads his flock through the cool night,
Ya-honk he says, and sounds it down to me like an invitation,
The pert may suppose it meaningless, but I listening close,
Find its purpose and place up there toward the wintry sky.

The sharp-hoof'd moose of the north, the cat on the house-sill, the chickadee, the prairie dog,
The litter of the grunting sow as they tug at her teats,
The brood of the turkey hen and she with her half-spread wings,
I see in them and myself the same old law.

The press of my foot to the earth springs a hundred affections,
They scorn the best I can do to relate them.

1. **remembrancer** reminder.

◀ Critical Viewing

This drawing is based on a photograph of Whitman as a young man. What can you conclude about his attitudes and personality from this picture? How are they reflected in this poem? **[Infer; Support]**

Literary Analysis

Epic Theme and Diction

What attitude toward the cycle of life is suggested by Whitman's use of the words "onward," "outward," and "luckier"? Explain.

What aspects of life does the poet celebrate in this poem?

I am enamor'd of growing outdoors,
Of men that live among cattle or taste of the ocean or woods,
Of the builders and steerers of ships and the wielders of axes and mauls, and the drivers of horses,
I can eat and sleep with them week in and week out.

What is commonest, cheapest, nearest, easiest, is Me,
Me going in for my chances, spending for vast returns,
Adorning myself to bestow myself on the first that will take me,
Not asking the sky to come down to my good will,
Scattering it freely forever.

Literary Analysis
Epic Theme and Anaphora
How does Whitman's use of anaphora in Section 17 emphasize the ideas he is expressing?

17

These are really the thoughts of all men in all ages and lands, they are not original with me,
If they are not yours as much as mine they are nothing, or next to nothing,
If they are not the riddle and the untying of the riddle they are nothing,
If they are not just as close as they are distant they are nothing.
This is the grass that grows wherever the land is and the water is,
This is the common air that bathes the globe.

51

The past and present wilt—I have fill'd them, emptied them,
And proceed to fill my next fold of the future.

Listener up there! what have you to confide to me?
Look in my face while I snuff the sidle of evening,[2]
(Talk honestly, no one else hears you, and I stay only a minute longer.)

Do I contradict myself?
Very well then I contradict myself,
(I am large, I contain multitudes.)
I concentrate toward them that are nigh,[3] I wait on the door-slab.

Who has done his day's work? who will soonest be through with his supper?
Who wishes to walk with me?

Will you speak before I am gone? will you prove already too late?

---

2. **snuff . . . evening** put out the hesitant last light of day, which is moving sideways across the sky.
3. **nigh** near.

52

The spotted hawk swoops by and accuses me, he complains of my gab and my loitering.

I too am not a bit tamed, I too am untranslatable,
I sound my barbaric yawp over the roofs of the world.
The last scud[4] of day holds back for me,
It flings my likeness after the rest and true as any on the shadow'd wilds,
It coaxes me to the vapor and the dusk.

I depart as air, I shake my white locks at the runaway sun,
I effuse my flesh in eddies, and drift it in lacy jags.

I bequeath myself to the dirt to grow from the grass I love,

If you want me again look for me under your boot soles.

You will hardly know who I am or what I mean,
But I shall be good health to you nevertheless,
And filter and fiber your blood.

Failing to fetch me at first keep encouraged,
Missing me one place search another,
I stop somewhere waiting for you.

Vocabulary

effuse (e fyōōz´) *v.* to pour out

bequeath (bē kwēth´) *v.* to hand down or pass on

4. **scud** low, dark, wind-driven clouds.

Critical Reading

1. **Key Ideas and Details (a)** From what does Whitman say his tongue and blood are formed? **(b) Analyze:** How does he view his relationship with nature? **(c) Analyze:** How does he view his relationship with other people?
2. **Key Ideas and Details (a)** In Section 17, what natural images does Whitman use to communicate the idea that his thoughts belong to everyone? **(b) Generalize:** Which elements of these images convey a belief in the spiritual unity of all natural forms?
3. **Key Ideas and Details (a)** In Section 52, where does the speaker say readers can find him? **(b) Infer:** What does he suggest will happen to his spirit and message after he is gone?
4. **Integration of Knowledge and Ideas Evaluate:** In Section 52, Whitman proudly characterizes his poetry as "barbaric yawp." What terms would you use to evaluate his work?

Cite textual evidence to support your responses.

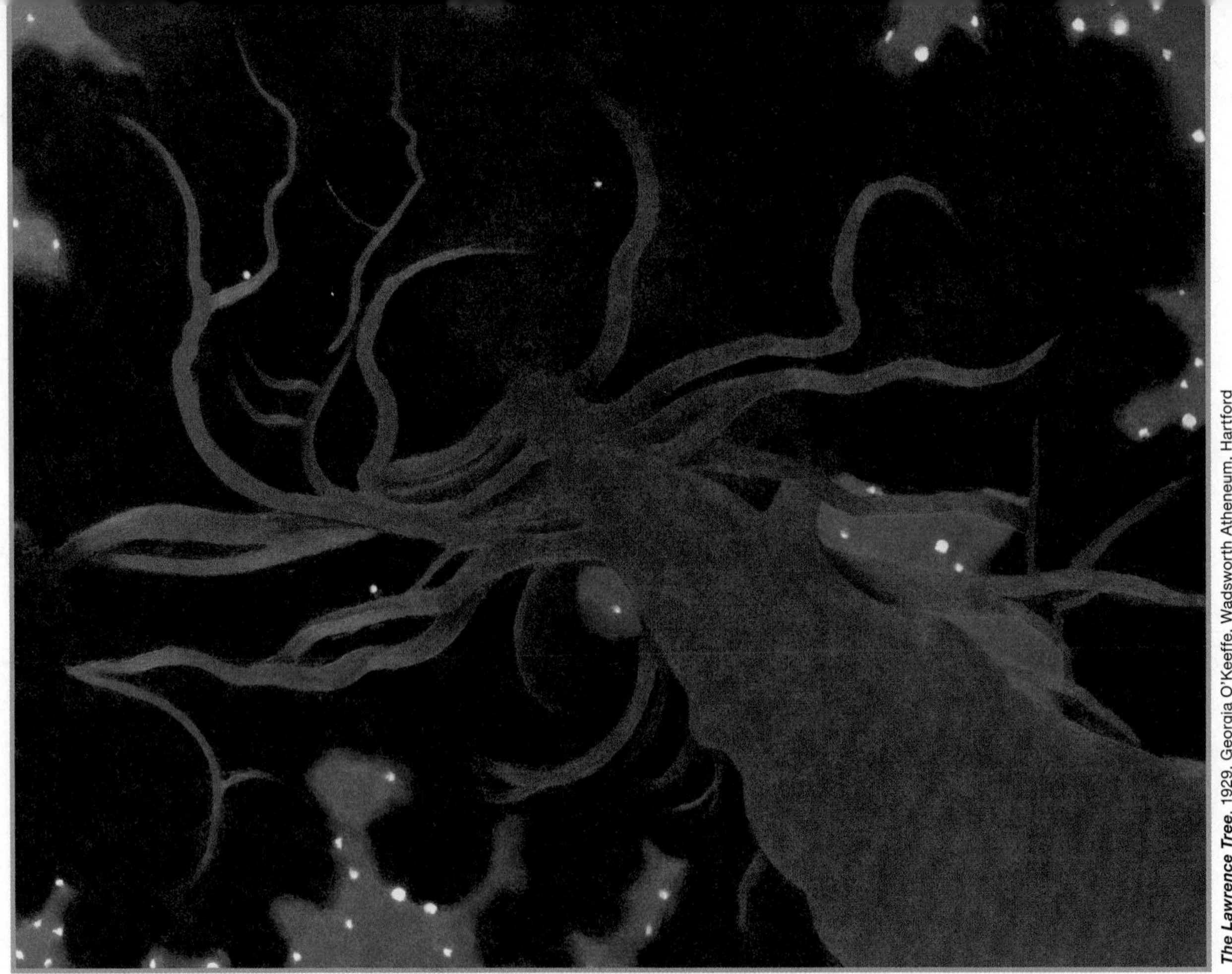

The Lawrence Tree, 1929, Georgia O'Keeffe, Wadsworth Atheneum, Hartford

When I Heard the Learn'd Astronomer

Walt Whitman

▲ Critical Viewing In what ways does the artist's viewpoint in this painting compare with Whitman's in this poem? **[Connect]**

When I heard the learn'd astronomer,
When the proofs, the figures, were ranged in columns before me,
When I was shown the charts and diagrams, to add, divide and measure them,
When I sitting heard the astronomer where he lectured with much applause in the lecture room,
How soon unaccountable I became tired and sick,
Till rising and gliding out I wander'd off by myself,
In the mystical moist night air, and from time to time,
Look'd up in perfect silence at the stars.

By the Bivouac's Fitful Flame

WALT WHITMAN

By the bivouac's[1] fitful flame,
A procession winding around me, solemn and sweet and slow—but first I note,
The tents of the sleeping army, the fields' and woods' dim outline,
The darkness lit by spots of kindled fire, the silence,
Like a phantom far or near an occasional figure moving,
The shrubs and trees, (as I lift my eyes they seem to be **stealthily** watching me,)
While wind in procession thoughts, O tender and wondrous thoughts,
Of life and death, of home and the past and loved, and of those that are far away;
A solemn and slow procession there as I sit on the ground,
By the bivouac's fitful flame.

Vocabulary
stealthily (stelth´ ə lē) *adv.* slyly or secretively

1. **bivouac** (biv´ wak´) *n.* night guard to prevent surprise attacks.

Critical Reading

Cite textual evidence to support your responses.

1. **Key Ideas and Details (a)** In "When I Heard the Learn'd Astronomer," what does the speaker do in reaction to the lecture? **(b) Connect:** What do his actions reveal about his character?
2. **Key Ideas and Details (a) Compare and Contrast:** In what ways does the "perfect silence" in the last line contrast with the lecture? **(b) Draw Conclusions:** What is the speaker saying about the value of science versus a personal experience with nature?
3. **Key Ideas and Details (a)** In lines 3–4 of "By the Bivouac's Fitful Flame," what sights does the speaker look upon? **(b) Infer:** What is the procession to which he refers in line 2?
4. **Key Ideas and Details (a)** Where does the speaker's mind go as he gazes upon the scene before him? **(b) Analyze:** Is the procession he refers to in line 9 the same one referred to earlier? Explain.
5. **Integration of Knowledge and Ideas Make a Judgment:** Whitman is known as a poet who celebrated life. Are these poems celebratory? If so, of what?

Haystack, 1938, Thomas Hart Benton, Museum of Fine Arts, Houston, Texas, USA, © DACS /Gift of Mr. Frank J. Hevrdejs / The Bridgeman Art Library International/©T.H. Benton and R.P. Benton Testamentary Trusts/Licensed by VAGA, New York, NY

I HEAR AMERICA SINGING

Walt Whitman

I hear America singing, the varied carols I hear,
Those of mechanics, each one singing his as it should be blithe and strong,
The carpenter singing his as he measures his plank or beam,
The mason singing his as he makes ready for work, or leaves off work,
The boatman singing what belongs to him in his boat, the deckhand singing on the steamboat deck,
The shoemaker singing as he sits on his bench, the hatter[1] singing as he stands,
The wood-cutter's song, the ploughboy's on his way in the morning, or at noon intermission or at sundown,
The delicious singing of the mother, or of the young wife at work, or of the girl sewing or washing,
Each singing what belongs to him or her and to none else,
The day what belongs to the day—at night the party of young fellows, robust, friendly,
Singing with open mouths their strong melodious songs.

1. **hatter** person who makes, sells, or cleans hats.

Vocabulary
robust (rō bust′) *adj.* strong and healthy; full of life

Who sings at night?

◀ **Critical Viewing** In this painting of farmwork, does the artist's style have qualities in common with Whitman's style? Explain. **[Compare and Contrast]**

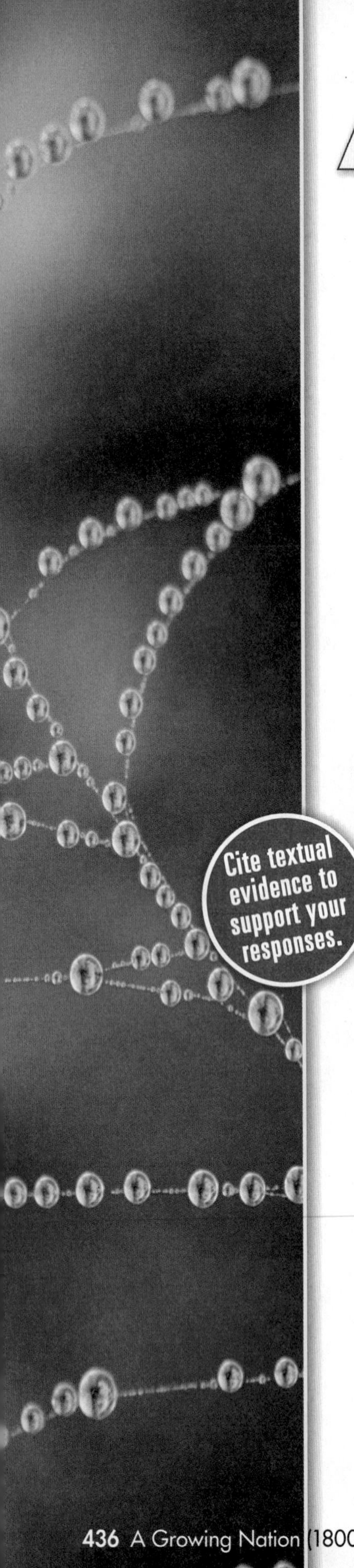
Cite textual evidence to support your responses.

A Noiseless Patient Spider

Walt Whitman

A noiseless patient spider,
I mark'd where on a little promontory it stood isolated,
Mark'd how to explore the vacant vast surrounding,
It launch'd forth filament, filament, filament, out of itself,
Ever unreeling them, ever tirelessly speeding them.

And you O my soul where you stand,
Surrounded, detached, in measureless oceans of space,
Ceaselessly musing, venturing, throwing, seeking the spheres
to connect them,
Till the bridge you will need be form'd, till the ductile anchor hold,
Till the gossamer thread you fling catch somewhere, O my soul.

Critical Reading

1. **Key Ideas and Details (a)** In "I Hear America Singing," what occupations does Whitman attribute to Americans? **(b) Draw Conclusions:** What does his catalog of occupations suggest about his vision of America?
2. **Key Ideas and Details (a)** What does Whitman describe the laborers doing at night? **(b) Analyze:** Why do you think the poem ends as it does?
3. **Key Ideas and Details (a)** In line three of "A Noiseless Patient Spider," what surrounds the spider? **(b) Interpret:** In line 7, what are the "measureless oceans of space" with which the speaker's soul is surrounded?
4. **Craft and Structure (a)** What verbs does Whitman use to describe the spider's actions? **(b)** What verbs does he use to describe the activities of his soul? **(c) Compare and Contrast:** How are the two explorations the same, and how are they different?
5. **Integration of Knowledge and ideas** What characteristics of America and the American spirit can you find in all the poems presented here? Use at least two of these Essential Question words in your response: *perseverance, bravery, spirit, unknown.* ***[Connecting to the Essential Question: What makes American literature American?]***

Critical Commentary

America's Epic

James E. Miller, Jr.

James E. Miller, Jr. is the Helen A. Regenstein Professor Emeritus of English at the University of Chicago. He is the author of two important critical studies of Walt Whitman and another focusing on T. S. Eliot.

Did Whitman write the epic for modern America? There have been many who contend that *Leaves of Grass* is merely a collection of lyric poetry, some good, some bad, all of it of a peculiarly personal nature that disqualifies its attitudes and philosophy generally. There have been others who have defended Whitman's book as the embodiment of the American reality and ideal, as superb fulfillment of all the genuine requirements of the national epic.

What did Whitman believe? The answer may be found in a number of prose works, beginning with the 1855 Preface. It is clear in this early work that Whitman desired *Leaves of Grass* to bear a unique relationship with America: "Here [in America] at last is something in the doings of man that corresponds with the broadcast doings of the day and night... It awaits the gigantic and generous treatment worthy of it." It is generally recognized that the entire Preface is a veiled account of Whitman's concept of his own role as a poet. Certainly he includes himself in the category when he asserts: "The poets of the kosmos advance through all interpositions and coverings and turmoils and stratagems to first principles." Although Whitman does not use the term, it is clear throughout the 1855 Preface that he believes his book to have the basic nature and general scope of the traditional national epic.

In *Democratic Vistas*, in the same indirect manner, Whitman again reveals his concept of the nature of his poetry: "Never was anything more wanted than, to-day, and here in the States, the poet of the modern is wanted, or the great literatus of the modern. At all times, perhaps, the central point in any nation, and that whence it is itself really sway'd the most and whence it sways others, is its national literature, especially its archetypal poems" (V, 54–55). Whitman was by this time (1871) acutely aware that America had not accepted his book as he had planned and hoped. There can be little doubt that he conceived *Leaves of Grass* as an "archetypal" poem produced and offered to America at its "central point"—a book "sway'd" by the nation and written to sway others. Such a work as Whitman calls for in *Democratic Vistas* is surely the epic of America. And, basically, it is his own work which he desires to be recognized as such.

Key Ideas and Details What question about Whitman's work does Miller pose? According to Miller, how does Whitman himself answer that question? What evidence does Miller provide to support this answer?

After You Read *Walt Whitman's Poetry*

Literary Analysis

1. **Craft and Structure** How does Whitman's use of **catalog,** or **list,** in the following line from the preface to *Leaves of Grass* help convey his **epic theme:**

   Here are the roughs and beards and space and ruggedness and nonchalance that the soul loves.

2. **Craft and Structure** **(a)** Note two ways in which his use of **free verse** in "Song of Myself" allows Whitman to express his ideas more effectively than would a formal structure. **(b)** Cite a passage that you think is a strong example of the relationship between free verse and meaning. Explain your choice.
3. **Craft and Structure** **(a)** In Section 51 of "Song of Myself," what does the speaker ask of the listener? **(b)** In line 5 of that section, do you think Whitman means exactly what he says? Why or why not? **(c)** In what ways does the **long line** enhance the poet's meaning?
4. **Craft and Structure** How does the use of **anaphora** in lines 1–4 of "When I Heard the Learn'd Astronomer" reinforce the speaker's idea of the astronomer?
5. **Craft and Structure** Note two examples of **word choice,** or **diction,** that add to the dreamlike quality of "By the Bivouac's Fitful Flame." Explain your choices.
6. **Comparing Literary Works** **(a)** Use a chart like the one shown to analyze and compare Whitman's epic theme of shared human experience in "Song of Myself" and at least two other poems in this grouping. **(b)** Based on your analysis, explain your understanding of Whitman's overall message or view of life.

Title	What Is Shared	Shared by Whom
"Song of Myself"	Atom	All, shared by everyone

Common Core State Standards

Writing

3.d. Use precise words and phrases, telling details, and sensory language to convey a vivid picture of the experiences, events, setting, and/or characters. *(p. 439)*

4. Produce clear and coherent writing in which the development, organization, and style are appropriate to task, purpose, and audience. *(p. 439)*

Language

4. Determine or clarify the meaning of unknown and multiple-meaning words and phrases based on *grades 11–12 reading and content,* choosing flexibly from a range of strategies. *(p. 439)*

4.d. Verify the preliminary determination of the meaning of a word or phrase. *(p. 439)*

Reading Strategy

7. Explain how you **adjusted your reading rate** as you read "Song of Myself." **(a)** Which stanzas or sections did you read more slowly? Why? **(b)** What new insight did slower reading help you gain?
8. **(a)** What reading rate did you use to read "I Hear America Singing"? Why? **(b)** Did your reading rate change over the course of the poem? Explain.
9. Which poems or sections of a poem did you *read aloud* slowly? How did doing so help you better understand the poet's meaning?

PERFORMANCE TASKS

Integrated Language Skills

Vocabulary Acquisition and Use

Multiple Meaning Words

Many words in English have more than one meaning. Usually, the meaning of a word changes according to its part of speech. For example, the word *bow* as a noun refers to a tied ribbon, to the implement that is drawn across a violin's strings, or to the front section of a boat. As a verb, it means "to bend one's head or body as a sign of respect." Explain the multiple meanings of each of the numbered words below. Use a dictionary to check your work.

1. stirring **3.** figures

2. note **4.** check

Then, choose two of the words, and use more than one meaning of both words in a brief paragraph describing the daily work of different kinds of Americans.

Vocabulary: Denotations

Denotations are the literal meanings of words, as opposed to their *connotative* meanings, which are the emotional associations the words bring forth. Answer each of the following questions. Then, explain your answers.

1. If a judge hands down a ruling in *abeyance* of a particular law, is she enforcing that law?

2. Does light that *effuses* from a lamp spread softly or shine in a sharply focused beam?

3. If you *bequeath* your bedroom to your little sister, could she use it?

4. If someone gave you a *robust* greeting, would you be likely to hear it?

5. Does a person typically move *stealthily* through a library?

6. If a town is *stirring*, is it peaceful and quiet?

Writing

Poem Write a poem to be read aloud as part of a group poetry reading honoring Walt Whitman. In addition to the use of free verse, choose several key elements of Whitman's unique style—his use of long lines, catalogs, anaphora, and onomatopoeia—and use them to enhance your own individual voice. Your poem should be your own while also demonstrating your understanding of Whitman's literary achievement.

Prewriting Decide on a "Whitmanesque" topic, and review the traits of free verse. Use a format like the one shown here to list or diagram sensory details and images related to your topic.

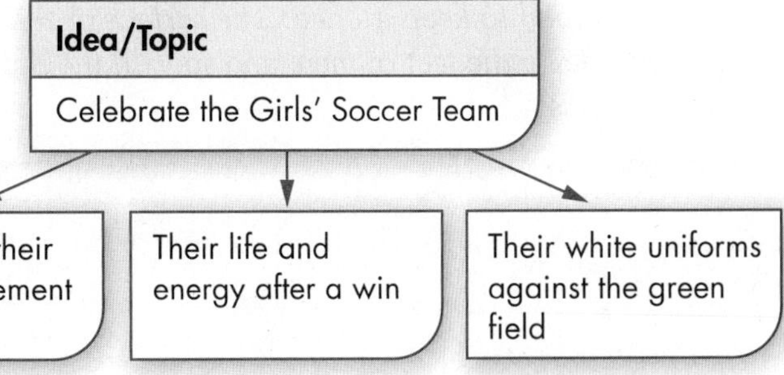
Idea/Topic
Celebrate the Girls' Soccer Team
The sound of their cleats on pavement
Their life and energy after a win
Their white uniforms against the green field

Drafting As you write, let your meaning determine the lengths of lines and stanzas. Be aware of your *tone*, or attitude toward your subject, and make sure your *diction*, or word choice, reflects that tone. Choose vivid words that contribute to the mood you want to evoke.

Revising Read your draft aloud. Listen for natural rhythms of speech rather than formal grammatical structures. Make any changes necessary to maintain natural rhythms and to enhance your meaning. If your word choices could be more precise, use a dictionary or thesaurus to select more effective language.

Write a Reflective Essay

Writing
2. Write informative texts to examine and convey complex ideas, concepts, and information clearly and accurately through the effective selection, organization, and analysis of content.
2.b. Develop the topic thoroughly by selecting the most significant and relevant facts, extended definitions, concrete details, quotations, or other information and examples appropriate to the audience's knowledge of the topic.

Reflective Essay Ralph Waldo Emerson and Henry David Thoreau wrote essays that do not just report on events but also interpret them and consider their deeper meanings. Their **reflective essays** make connections between each writer's personal life experiences and the larger world. Follow the steps outlined in this workshop to write your own reflective essay.

Assignment Write a reflective essay in which you explore a personal experience or an event and reflect on its deeper meaning.

What to Include Your reflective essay should have these elements:

- You, the writer, as the main speaker or character
- Your personal feelings and thoughts about a clearly defined topic
- Insights presented in a logical organization
- A balanced approach that presents incidents from your life and connects them to more general or abstract ideas
- Illlustration of your important beliefs
- An appropriate and consistent tone

To preview the criteria on which your reflective essay may be assessed, see the rubric on page 447.

To get a feel for reflective essays, read this mentor text. Note how Thoreau connects his personal experiences to a larger theme.

from: Walden by Henry David Thoreau

It is remarkable how easily and insensibly we fall into a particular route, and make a beaten track for ourselves. I had not lived there a week before my feet wore a path from my door to the pondside; and though it is five or six years since I trod it, it is still quite distinct. It is true, I fear that others may have fallen into it, and so helped to keep it open. The surface of the earth is soft and impressible by the feet of men; and so with the paths which the mind travels.

WRITE GUY
Jeff Anderson, M.Ed.

What Do You Notice?

Read the highlighted sentence several times. Then, with a partner, discuss the qualities that make it special. You might consider the following elements:

- Word choice
- Sentence length
- Vivid details
- Ideas or content

Share your group's observations with the class.

Prewriting and Planning

Choosing Your Topic

To choose an event for your essay, use one of these strategies:

- **Listing** List the activities that fill your week, paying attention to any incidents that made you pause or that seemed special. Choose one to explore in your essay.
- **Freewriting** Consider the important moments in your life, such as meeting your best friend, or making a tough choice. As you free-write, ask yourself how this moment changed your life. Choose one moment to explore further.

Narrowing Your Topic

Write a topic sentence. Narrow your focus by identifying a lesson you learned, or the instant you suddenly saw yourself or the world in a new light. Write one sentence about the event and the lesson it taught you.

Model: Expressing an Insight

When I saw how long it took me to walk home, (Event) I marveled at my ancestors who had cleared the land by themselves. (Insight)

Gathering Details

Make connections. Consider how your experience relates to themes in the world at large. Organize your thoughts in a diagram like the one shown below. You might also want to do some research to strengthen your knowledge about your subject. Talk with friends and family, or use the library or the Internet to gather details about past events or issues that relate to your personal experience.

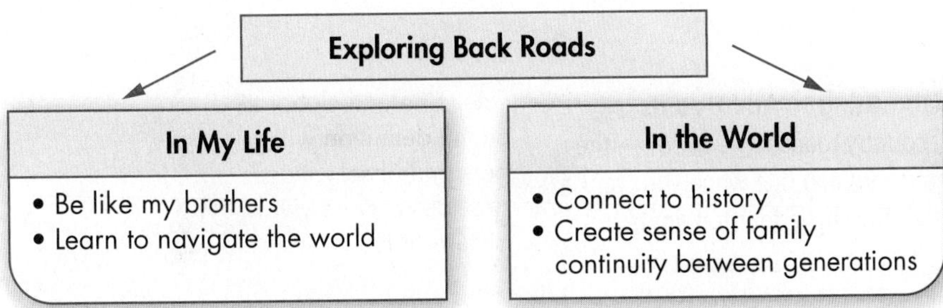

Exploring Back Roads
In My Life
• Be like my brothers
• Learn to navigate the world
In the World
• Connect to history
• Create sense of family continuity between generations

Drafting

Shaping Your Writing

Organize your ideas. Choose an organization that places the incident you are describing in a larger context. The format shown here is one effective way to build a reflective essay.

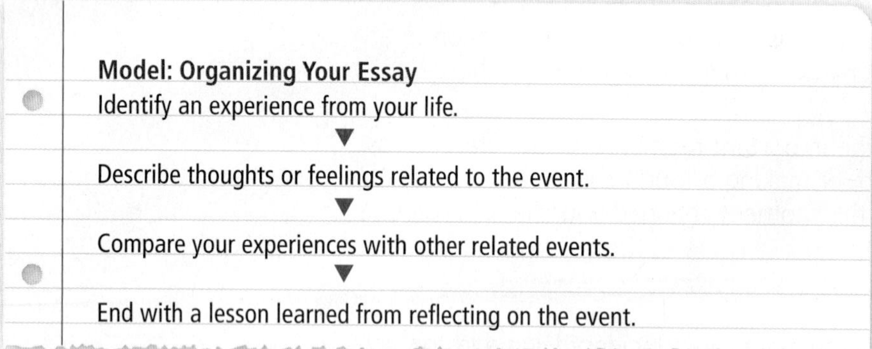

Model: Organizing Your Essay

Identify an experience from your life.

▼

Describe thoughts or feelings related to the event.

▼

Compare your experiences with other related events.

▼

End with a lesson learned from reflecting on the event.

Start with a strong lead. A simple, compelling lead, or opening sentence, provides enough information to activate readers' curiosity and make them want to read your essay. Notice how both of these leads raise questions in your mind:

- *Whenever I hear the song "Memory," I burst into laughter.*
- *My sister refuses to wear the color purple.*

Providing Elaboration

Use the SEE technique. The step-by-step approach of the SEE method can help you add details and develop your ideas. This is what the initials mean:

S **Statement:** Write a sentence to express a main idea.

E **Extension:** Restate or develop the main idea.

E **Elaboration:** Provide further information that amplifies or expands on the main idea.

Be generous as you extend and elaborate. Include sensory details, images, and personal thoughts that will make your writing vivid and interesting.

Model: Extending and Elaborating to Add Details

[*Statement*] They are small country roads [*Extension*] —the ones that change color [*Extension*] and ride when you cross a simple parish line. [*Extension*] They have four-ton limits…

Extending and elaborating on the definition with personal observations provides a more vivid picture of the topic.

Common Core State Standards

Writing

2.a. Organize complex ideas, concepts, and information so that each new element builds on that which precedes it to create a unified whole.

2.b. Develop the topic thoroughly by selecting the most significant and relevant facts, extended definitions, concrete details, quotations, or other information and examples appropriate to the audience's knowledge of the topic.

Writers on Writing

Gretel Ehrlich On Using Layers of Meaning

Gretel Ehrlich is the author of "Inspired by Nature" (p. 222).

These are the closing paragraphs of the title essay of my book *The Solace of Open Spaces*. Here, I stepped back from the details in the essay—those of anecdote and description—to contemplate the larger meaning of "space" and the way it shapes our minds and our experience of the world—the "internal weather" of our lives.

> *"Writing is an act of seeing through to the other side of our lives, then coming back and putting an expression of that otherness on the page."*
>
> —Gretel Ehrlich

from *The Solace of Open Spaces*

At night, by moonlight, the land is whittled to slivers—a ridge, a river, a strip of grassland stretching to the mountains, then the huge sky. One morning a full moon was setting in the west just as the sun was rising. I felt precariously balanced between the two as I loped across a meadow. For a moment, I could believe that the stars, which were still visible, work like cooper's bands, holding together everything above Wyoming.

Space has a spiritual equivalent and can heal what is divided and burdensome in us. My grandchildren will probably use space shuttles for a honeymoon trip or to recover from heart attacks, but closer to home we might also learn how to carry space inside ourselves in the effortless way we carry our skins. Space represents sanity, not a life purified or dull, or "spaced out," but one that might accommodate intelligently any idea or situation.

← In this paragraph, I turn the concept of "space" in four directions: as a spiritual guide, as a healer of physical maladies, as an actual component of our body's makeup, and as a state of mind.

From the clayey soil of northern Wyoming is mined bentonite, which is used as a filler in candy, gum, and lipstick. We Americans are great on fillers, as if what we have, what we are, is not enough. We have a cultural tendency toward denial, but, being affluent, we strangle ourselves with what we can buy. . . . We fill up space as if it were a pie shell, with things whose opacity further obstructs our ability to see what is already there.

← Here I take an actual geological substance—bentonite, which is a kind of clay—and use it metaphorically: to indicate the way we pack our heads, hearts, and homes with things we don't need.

← Here I am reminding the reader that "space" does not represent an "absence" but something positive.

Revising

Revising Your Overall Structure

Take a balanced approach. Your reflective essay will have more meaning for readers if you achieve a subtle balance between your personal experiences and broader themes or ideas about life. Use the following strategy to evaluate your draft:

★ Place a blue star next to sentences that describe your personal experiences.

✔ Place a red check next to sentences that refer to outside events or to reflections about the meaning of your experiences.

Check that your draft balances information about your personal experiences with reflections on larger, related themes. If you have too few red checks, revise to include statements that broaden your focus.

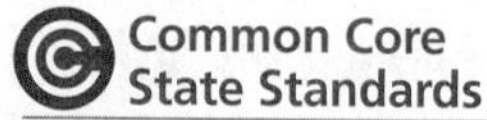
Common Core State Standards

Writing

2.d. Use precise language to manage the complexity of the topic.

2.e Establish and maintain a formal style and objective tone while attending to the norms and conventions of the discipline in which they are writing.

5. Develop and strengthen writing as needed by revising, rewriting, or trying a new approach.

Language

3.a. Vary syntax for effect.

Model: Revising for Balance

★ Now I am driving.★ Those old Bienville roads have acquired new meaning. ✓ I know that if I hang a right at the T, I can get to the cemetery that holds my relations from 150 years back, the same people that first helped settle North Louisiana. ★ None of my brothers ever knew about the cemetery, but I do. ★ I even know three ways to get to Minden that my brother Judd did not teach me. ✓ *On the roads that my family has traveled for over a century, I am just starting to find my way of traveling. . . .*

The writer added information that provides insight into the experiences he describes.

Revising Your Sentences

Vary your sentences. Even though your essay is about you, avoid beginning every sentence with *I*. Go through your draft and highlight the first word in every sentence. Make sure you are using a variety of sentence openers. If all or a majority of your sentences begin in the same way, combine or rewrite them to create more interest and variety.

Examples:

Monotonous: *I remember the door. I remember it was locked. I wanted to get inside. I was nervous about what I might find. I was very curious.*

Varied: *The door was locked, and I wanted to get in there. While I was nervous about what I might find, I was also curious.*

Peer Review: Exchange drafts with a partner. After you have read each other's essays, meet to discuss them. Focus on the clarity of the events and insights you present throughout your essay. Ask for specific suggestions, such as modifying sentences, omitting or adding transitions, or reordering paragraphs, to improve the logical flow of your ideas.

Developing Your Style

Voice: Controlling Your Tone and Diction

Voice is a writer's distinctive "sound" on the page. Voice is partly based on **tone,** the attitude you express toward your subject; and **diction,** your choice and arrangement of words. Your tone may be described as serious, lighthearted, humorous, insincere, soulful, and so on. Your diction may be casual, formal, technical, simple, or complex.

Serious Tone/Formal Diction

To my horror, I realized that I had absentmindedly mailed the urgent letter without a stamp.

Lighthearted Tone/Casual Diction

Oops, I must have goofed and forgotten to put a stamp on that!

Find It in Your Reading

Read the selection from *Walden* by Henry David Thoreau.

1. Describe Thoreau's tone. Note key passages that convey that tone.
2. For each passage you choose, list two words that help express Thoreau's attitude toward his subject or audience.
3. **Discuss:** Choose three of your key words, and replace them with words that have a different tone. With a partner, discuss how these changes in diction affect the overall tone of the writing and create a different sense of voice.

Apply It to Your Writing

For each paragraph in your draft reflective essay, follow these steps:

1. Read your essay aloud, paying attention to specific words that convey your attitude toward your reader or subject. Be sure that the overall tone of your essay is consistent throughout the essay. In addition, make sure your tone is appropriate to both personal reflection and the larger themes you discuss.
2. If your tone seems inappropriate, change it. Informal and friendly tones usually work best with personal observations, whereas formal or distant tones keep your far-reaching comments from sounding flippant or insincere.
3. Identify any words that do not support the tone you would like to have. Replace these words with ones that better express your attitudes. The voice of your essay will shift as a result.

PH WRITING COACH

Further instruction and practice are available in *Prentice Hall Writing Coach*.

Student Model: Graham Walker, Ruston, Louisiana

Back Roads to Tomorrow

They are small country roads—the ones that change color and ride when you cross a simple parish line. They have four-ton limits assigned to small bridges that hop over waters like Bear Creek and Black Lake Bayou. Their ragged shoulders are missing chunks of pavement and rise three inches above the packed red clay that supports the asphalt. Bright ribbons of tape hang from the lower limbs of pine trees to escort log trucks to jobs. Now and again a color will halt at a worn path entering a clean-bottomed plot of trees, but the others remain loyal to the country road.

These are the roads I grew up on.

It was usually just my oldest brother, Judd, and me. In a blue and gray Ford truck, we would branch out from our home in Taylor, Louisiana, with the windows down. Whether we went and looked at natural gas wells or whether we shot big turtles sunning themselves on logs in a bayou, it never took too much to keep us rolling along on those old Bienville back roads.

But it was not pure riding experience that I enjoyed so much. It was the infinite knowledge of the roads that I believed I gained from those trips. I was in Back Roads 101: Knowing the Road. I made sure that I asked my brother whether we would take a right here or keep straight at the intersections. I felt that I had to know three different ways to get to Minden, ten miles away, or which way the T below our house would take me in case I wanted to slip off for a spin in my pre–double digit years.

Looking back, I realize it was not my concern for my future driving years that led me to study those roads so intently and to map them in my memory. It was one of the lengths I went to so I could be like my three older brothers. All three of them knew the lay of the pavement throughout the Bienville Parish. They could tell me how to get wherever I wished by a backroad route—even to Shreveport, I am sure. And more than I wanted to get to Shreveport, I wanted to be like them.

So I soon knew most of the roads they knew. I could tell anyone three different ways to get to Minden, or which way the T would take me. But I was mapping more than Bienville Parish.

Now I am driving. Those old Bienville roads have acquired new meaning. I know that if I hang a right at the T, I can get to the cemetery that holds my relations from 150 years back, the same people who first helped settle North Louisiana. None of my brothers ever knew about the cemetery, but I do. I even know three ways to get to Minden that my brother Judd did not teach me. On the roads that my family has traveled for over a century, I am just starting to find my way of traveling. That journey, I now understand, is what all my rides with my brothers were really about.

This descriptive language creates a strong sense of place and establishes a personal tone.

Graham uses sensory details to convey a vivid picture of his experience.

Graham begins to draw connections between the specific experience and a deeper meaning.

Graham extends his personal experience into the abstract realm of family, identity, and history.

Editing and Proofreading

Check your essay to eliminate errors in grammar, spelling, or punctuation.

Focus on fragments. Look for sentence fragments and correct them.

Fragment: *Because I wanted to avoid traffic.*
Complete: *We took the back road because I wanted to avoid traffic.*

Fragment: *The orchestra uses many types of strings. Cellos, violins, and violas.*
Complete: *The orchestra uses many types of strings, including cellos, violins, and violas.*

Focus on spelling. In general, use *–tion* to spell the sound of ***shun,*** as in *exploration* and *portion*. Use *–sion* to spell the sound of ***zhun,*** as in *vision* and *incision*. Check your spelling of any words that end with these suffixes.

Spiral Review: Conventions Earlier in this unit, you learned about adjective and adverb clauses (p. 287) and comparative and superlative adjectives and adverbs (p. 321). Check your reflective essay to be sure you have used those conventions correctly.

Common Core State Standards

Writing

5. Develop and strengthen writing as needed by editing, focusing on addressing what is most significant for a specific purpose and audience.

Language

1. Demonstrate command of the conventions of standard English grammar and usage when writing.

2.b. Spell correctly.

Publishing, Presenting, and Reflecting

Consider one of the following ways to share your writing:

Deliver a reflective presentation. Use your reflective essay as the basis for an oral presentation. Select photographs, drawings, or other images to share with your audience, as well as music or sound effects.

Publish a literary magazine. Gather a variety of reflective essays to create a classroom magazine. Assign committees the tasks of designing the format, creating illustrations, proofreading, and distributing copies to other classes.

Reflect on your writing. Jot down your thoughts about the experience of writing a reflective essay. Begin by answering these questions: What new insights into your own life did you have? What did you learn about the effect of diction on your tone?

PH WRITING COACH

Further instruction and practice are available in *Prentice Hall Writing Coach*.

Rubric for Self-Assessment

Evaluate your reflective essay using the following criteria and rating scale.

Criteria	Rating Scale *not very* — *very*
Focus: How well do you establish yourself as the main character?	1 2 3 4 5
Organization: How well have you organized your feelings, thoughts, and views?	1 2 3 4 5
Support/Elaboration: How effectively do you use specific incidents to connect to broader themes?	1 2 3 4 5
Style: How well do you describe the insights you gained?	1 2 3 4 5
Conventions: How correct is your use of grammar, especially your use of complete sentences?	1 2 3 4 5

Write and Deliver a Persuasive Speech

Persuasive speech is language designed to influence the way other people think or act. You use persuasive speech often. Perhaps you want to convince a friend to see a certain movie, or a prospective employer to hire you. Both situations require you to speak persuasively. In daily life, persuasive speech is usually spontaneous. However, in formal speaking situations, you must develop persuasion with forethought and organization.

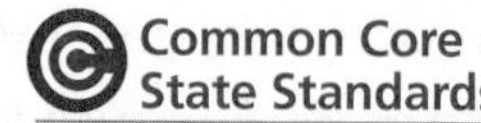

Writing

1. Write arguments to support claims in an analysis of substantive topics or texts, using valid reasoning and relevant and sufficient evidence.

Speaking and Listening

3. Evaluate a speaker's point of view, reasoning, and use of evidence and rhetoric, assessing the stance, premises, links among ideas, word choice, points of emphasis, and tone used.

6. Adapt speech to a variety of contexts and tasks, demonstrating a command of formal English when indicated or appropriate.

Topic, Focus, and Thesis

To write and deliver a formal persuasive speech, choose a topic that means something to you. Ask yourself, "What do people argue about when they discuss this topic?" The answer will help you narrow your focus. Then, determine your **thesis**—your specific position or claim. This should be a statement with which reasonable people could agree or disagree. *Example thesis:* "The Hillsboro Library is inadequate because it does not have enough computer workstations."

Appeals and Rhetorical Devices

Consider your audience. After defining your topic and thesis, think about your audience and what they may know or feel about your topic. This will help you choose effective *persuasive appeals* to reach them.

- To prove a position, use a **logical argument** that relies on *facts* and sound *reasoning.* Draw facts from credible sources, such as newspapers, journals, encyclopedias, and government Web sites.
- To gain your audience's trust, use an **ethical argument** that establishes your credibility as a speaker. Cite trusted sources and demonstrate knowledge of your topic.
- To move your audience, use an **emotional argument** that evokes sympathy or humor. Relate affecting stories and use vivid language that sets a specific *tone*, or attitude, toward the subject.

Structure your speech. Like an essay, a strong speech has a logical structure. In your **introduction,** engage your audience and show why your topic matters. In the **body** of your speech, develop your ideas point by point. In your **conclusion,** restate your thesis and issue a call to action, or urgent request that your audience do something or think in a new way.

Select language techniques. Make deliberate choices about the *diction*, or word choice, and *syntax*, or grammar and sentence structure, you use. To ensure your ideas are clear, use *formal English*, the version of English taught in school. Use *informal expressions,* such as slang, sparingly to connect to your audience. If your topic is scientific or technical, use *technical language*, such as the specific names of devices or processes.

There is also a rich variety of rhetorical devices and expressive language that can help you convince your audience in a clear and forceful way:

- **Rhetorical Questions:** questions asked for effect, not to get information. "Shouldn't the library be a valuable resource for students?"
- **Parallel Structure:** repeated grammatical patterns that create balance and emphasis. "The books are ancient, the computers are slow, and the lighting is terrible."
- **Concrete Images:** vividly described situations, places, or people
- **Figurative Language:** symbolic or non-literal language, such as similes and metaphors, used to make ideas memorable

Select appropriate persuasive techniques. To support your thesis and keep your audience interested, use a variety of supporting arguments:

- **Characterization:** using evaluative language, such as "essential" or "unfair" to classify a position or a situation
- **Irony:** pointing out incongruities. "The library has more computers for its staff than for the public."
- **Dialogue:** relating conversations or quoting directly from sources

Activities: Deliver and Evaluate Persuasive Speech

Comprehension and Collaboration For both activities, use an evaluation form like the one shown below.

A. Write and deliver a persuasive speech to the class. Have your audience assess your argument.

B. Using your class's responses, develop additional arguments and then present an *impromptu speech* to further defend your thesis.

Peer Evaluation Form for Persuasive Speech

Title of Speech ______________________

Thesis ______________________

Exhibits a Logical Structure: Yes ❑ No ❑

Explain ______________________

Diction and Syntax:

Standard English ❑ Rhetorical Questions ❑ Figurative Language ❑

Informal Language ❑ Parallel Structure ❑

Technical Language ❑ Concrete Images ❑

Examples ______________________

What would the speaker's opponents say in response to this argument?

____

What did the speaker do well? What could be improved? ______________________

____

Etymology: Political Science/History Terms

Many events have shaped the development of the English language. The timeline shown here identifies events that brought critical changes:

5th century
Angles and Saxons invade the British Isles. Anglo-Saxon becomes the dominant culture and language.
6th century
Christianity spreads into England, adding Latin and Greek words to Anglo-Saxon.
11th century
Normans invade from France, bringing thousands of French and Latin words.

The Romans and Greeks introduced numerous political ideas to the world, and English reflects those influences. The Normans became the ruling class of England, and many of their word contributions relate to politics, history, and law. Knowing key affixes and roots will help you define unfamiliar terms you encounter as you study political science and history.

	Word Part	Meaning	Example Words
Prefixes	*con-* (Latin)	with; together	constitution, congress
	auto- (Greek)	self	autocracy, autonomy
	dom- (Latin)	rule	dominion, dominant
Roots	*-belli-* (Latin)	war	bellicose, belligerent
	-dem- (Greek)	people	demographics, democracy
	-polis- (Greek)	city	politician, politics
Suffixes	*-cracy* (Greek)	government; rule	meritocracy, aristocracy
	-hood (Anglo-Saxon)	sharing a condition	statehood, knighthood
	-ism (Greek)	quality or practice of	nationalism, colonialism

Practice

1. Refer to the chart above to define **(a)** autocracy; **(b)** democracy.
2. Write definitions for each italicized word: **(a)** *Bellicose* acts caused greater conflict. **(b)** Members of the convention wrote a *constitution*.
3. Choose a word from the chart above and create a timeline *tracing its etymology*, or development as an English word. Include its language of origin, its movement from one language to another, changes in its meaning, and a discussion of any points at which its usage may have been contested. Consult reference materials, both print and digital, to aid your work.

Common Core State Standards

Language

1.a. Apply the understanding that usage is a matter of convention, can change over time, and is sometimes contested.

4.a. Use context as a clue to the meaning of a word or phrase.

4.c. Consult general and specialized reference materials, both print and digital, to find the pronunciation of a word or determine or clarify its precise meaning, its part of speech, its etymology, or its standard usage.

6. Acquire and use accurately general academic and domain-specific words and phrases.

Vocabulary Acquisition and Use: Context Clues

Sentence Completion questions appear in most standardized tests. One skill that Sentence Completions test is your ability to figure out what a word means by examining its context, or the surrounding words or sentences. In these types of questions, you are given sentences with one or more missing words. Your task is to choose the correct word or words to complete each sentence logically. Try using the following strategy: (1) Read the entire sentence and anticipate a word that would logically complete it. (2) Scan the answer choices for that word. (3) If the word you anticipated is not there, look for a synonym.

Practice

This exercise is modeled after the Sentence Completions exercises that appear in the Critical Reading section of the SAT.

Directions: Each of the following sentences is missing one or two words. Choose the word or set of words that best completes each sentence.

Test-Taking Tip
Before you mark an answer, carefully read the complete sentence to confirm that it makes sense.

1. Both his vengefulness and his __?__ prevent Captain Ahab from surrendering to the white whale.

A. parsimony
B. alacrity
C. obstinacy
D. magnanimity
E. flexibility

2. Those who celebrate the beauty of nature sometimes have an __?__ to industrialization.

A. eloquence
B. aversion
C. expedience
D. attraction
E. affinity

3. In the staid congregations of New England, __?__ was considered not only __?__, but sinful.

A. ostentation . . . indecorous
B. pathos . . . prevalent
C. discord . . . impulsive
D. avarice . . . superfluous
E. obstinacy . . . vengeful

4. Mr. Hooper's reasons for wearing the mysterious veil are __?__ to his parishioners.

A. impertinent
B. ample
C. inscrutable
D. stirring
E. sublime

5. In *Walden*, Thoreau voices his desire to lead a simple life and rid himself of __?__ concerns.

A. ominous
B. venerable
C. imperceptible
D. superfluous
E. essential

6. Though the human mind is limited and __?__, it is able to contemplate __?__.

A. tremulous . . . maledictions
B. finite . . . infinity
C. infinite . . . chaos
D. prescient . . . posterity
E. radiant . . . iniquity

Test-Taking Practice

Reading Test: Paired Passages

Paired reading passages are one type of critical reading passage used on standardized tests. Paired passages may be fiction or nonfiction, prose or poetry, and may vary in length. As you read, keep in mind that the passages will be **compared and contrasted.** Questions following paired passages will refer to each passage individually and to both passages as a unit. Note similarities and differences between the passages, especially the author's attitudes, word choices, and styles.

Common Core State Standards

RI.11-12.1, RI.11-12.2, RI.11-12.3, RI.11-12.4; L.11-12.4, L.11-12.5.a, L.11-12.6

[For the full wording of the standards, see the standards chart in the front of your textbook.]

Practice

The following exercise is modeled after the SAT Paired Passages Critical Reading section. This section usually includes 48 questions.

Directions: Read both passages. Then, answer the questions. Passage 1 is from *Walden* by Henry David Thoreau. Passage 2 is by Gretel Ehrlich.

Strategy

Break the task into parts.

- **Read Passage 1,** and answer the questions that refer only to the first passage.
- **Read Passage 2,** and answer the questions that refer only to the second passage.
- Finally, answer the compare-and-contrast questions.

PASSAGE 1

The life in us is like the water in the river. It may rise this year higher than man has ever known it, and flood the parched uplands. . . . It was not always dry land where we dwell. I see far inland the banks which the stream anciently washed, before science began to record its freshets. Everyone has heard the story which has gone the rounds of New England, of a strong and beautiful bug which came out of the dry leaf of an old table of apple-tree wood, which had stood in the farmer's kitchen for sixty years. . . . From an egg deposited in the living tree many years earlier still, as appeared by counting the annual layers beyond it; which was heard gnawing out for several weeks, hatched perchance by the heat of an urn. . . . Who knows what beautiful and winged life, whose egg has been buried for ages under many concentric layers of woodenness in the dead dry life of society . . . may unexpectedly come forth . . . to enjoy its perfect summer life at last.

PASSAGE 2

These days we go about our lives with so much speed and so much extraneous information that it's difficult to contemplate just one thing, one sight, one ripple in the pond. Thoreau would have us simplify, slow down, become quiet, and burrow into the heart of things without minds. Not to "dumb down," but the opposite: to stop, to listen, and see; to turn off the monologue in our minds; to erase our idea about how things are; to live in others' shoes. Thoreau would have us think like a river, a pond, a tree, another animal or human; to adopt their point of view instead of our own. Then, the fresh, dawnlike nature of things . . . will keep radiating, piercing the difficulties in our lives with new songs.

1. What is the best statement of the main idea of Passage 1?
   - **A.** It is unusual that a large bug should hatch from old wood.
   - **B.** One can determine the age of a tree by counting its rings.
   - **C.** Life ebbs and flows, sometimes surprisingly.
   - **D.** Science cannot measure life's force.
   - **E.** Summer is the best season.

2. In Passage 1, the hatched bug is used as a symbol for
   - **A.** life's irrepressibility.
   - **B.** unexpected beauty.
   - **C.** rebelliousness.
   - **D.** the act of writing.
   - **E.** a nightmare.

3. The main idea of Passage 2 is that
   - **A.** people should use less technology.
   - **B.** Americans should be less materialistic.
   - **C.** people are like bodies of water.
   - **D.** the truth can be found only in our minds.
   - **E.** serenity will bring us new understanding.

4. It would be most accurate to say that
   - **A.** Passage 2 is a commentary on Passage 1.
   - **B.** Passage 1 is a commentary on Passage 2.
   - **C.** Passage 1 is an excerpt of Passage 2.
   - **D.** Passage 2 is an unfavorable review of Passage 1.
   - **E.** Passage 1 was written after Passage 2.

5. In Passage 1, Thoreau uses a metaphor to compare
   - **A.** life to water in the river.
   - **B.** New England to a strong, beautiful bug.
   - **C.** the heat of an urn to the heat of the sun.
   - **D.** society to concentric layers of woodenness.
   - **E.** an egg to summer.

6. It can be inferred that the author of Passage 2
   - **A.** struggles to understand aspects of Thoreau's thinking.
   - **B.** embraces some of Thoreau's views, but rejects others.
   - **C.** thinks that Thoreau's philosophy is too simplistic.
   - **D.** has read all of Thoreau's writings.
   - **E.** respects Thoreau's philosophy.

7. In Passage 1, Thoreau's reference to the "parched uplands" (line 2) is
   - **A.** a description of the landscape he is viewing as he writes.
   - **B.** an image that evokes a sense of dryness and thirst.
   - **C.** a metaphor for the story that follows.
   - **D.** an example of synecdoche.
   - **E.** a symbol of summer.

8. Why does Thoreau mention the "dry leaf" (line 7) of the kitchen table?
   - **A.** to remind readers that the table was once a living tree
   - **B.** to create suspense
   - **C.** to create an atmosphere of dry lifelessness
   - **D.** to urge people not to abuse nature
   - **E.** as a metaphor for the page of a book

9. It can be inferred from the phrase "piercing the difficulties in our lives with new songs" that the author of Passage 2
   - **A.** uses straightforward language.
   - **B.** is not in tune with Thoreau's philosophy.
   - **C.** appreciates Thoreau, but does not echo his voice.
   - **D.** is attuned with Thoreau in both thought and writing style.
   - **E.** believes that problem solving is painful.

Grammar and Writing: Editing in Context

Editing in Context segments often appear in the writing sections of standardized tests. The passages or sample sentences used are usually drafts of student essays that may or may not contain errors in grammar, style, and usage. For each question, you must first decide if there is an error and then determine which of four possible answers will best correct a given sentence.

Practice

This exercise is modeled after the Identifying Sentence Errors portion of the SAT Writing test.

Directions: Each of the following sentences contains either a single error or no error at all. The error, if there is one, is underlined and lettered. If a sentence contains an error, select the letter of that underlined part. If the sentence is correct, select choice E.

Strategy

"Listen" for errors. Read the sentence straight through. If you mentally "trip" over one of the underlined portions, it is probably wrong.

1. Humankind (A) has been fascinated (B) with whales, the greater (C) of all sea mammals, for (D) the entire span of recorded history. No error (E)

   A.
   B.
   C.
   D.
   E.

2. Byzantine scholar and historian (A) Procopius wrote of a whale who (B) made its way into the inland Sea of Marmara (C), where it happily consumed the fisheries that (D) were maintained there. No error (E)

   A.
   B.
   C.
   D.
   E.

3. The whale is an (A) archetype that (B) appears repeatedly (C) throughout world religions, cultures, and literature (D). No error (E)

   A.
   B.
   C.
   D.
   E.

4. The King James Version of (A) the Bible makes (B) several mention (C) of whales (D). No error (E)

   A.
   B.
   C.
   D.
   E.

5. The more (A) famous one (B) is the story of Jonah, who is said (C) to have survived three days and nights in the belly of a great (D) whale. No error (E)
   A.
   B.
   C.
   D.
   E.

6. Because (A) whaling (B) was a lucrative and (C) dangerous industry in nineteenth-century America, it is no surprise so that (D) a whale would become the centerpiece of an American novel. No error (E)
   A.
   B.
   C.
   D.
   E.

7. Herman Melville's masterwork, *Moby-Dick*, widely regarded (A) as one of the finer (B) novels ever written, uses (C) the whale as a character (D), a symbol, and a force of nature. No error (E)
   A.
   B.
   C.
   D.
   E.

8. *Moby-Dick* is a rich (A), complex, and (B) entirely American rendition of (C) the archetypal (D) whale. No error (E)
   A.
   B.
   C.
   D.
   E.

Timed Writing: Position Statement [25 minutes]

Ralph Waldo Emerson wrote, "There is a time in every man's education when he arrives at the conviction that envy is ignorance; that imitation is suicide; that he must take himself for better, for worse, as his portion. . . ."

Write a position statement—an essay in which you express and support an opinion—in response to Emerson's statement. First, explain what the statement means. Then, explain your views: Do you believe the type of individualism he describes is an important value that people should try to develop? This assigment is similar to the essay portion of the SAT Writing Section.

Academic Vocabulary

The prompt asks you to *express,* or state, and *support,* or defend, your opinion.

Performance Tasks

Follow the instructions to complete the tasks below as required by your teacher. As you work on each task, incorporate both general academic vocabulary and literary terms you learned in this unit.

Common Core State Standards

RL.11-12.2, RL.11-12.3, RL.11-12.4, RL.11-12.5, RL.11-12.9; RI.11-12.4; W.11-12.2, W.11-12.9; SL.11-12.6; L.11-12.4, L.11-12.5

[For the full wording of the standards, see the standards chart in the front of your textbook.]

Writing

Task 1: Literature [RL.11-12.3; W.11-12.2]
Analyze the Development of a Story

*Write an **essay** in which you analyze and evaluate the development of a story from this unit.*

- Explain which story you chose and briefly summarize the plot.
- Identify key choices the author made in writing the story. For example, consider where the story is set, how the action is ordered, or how the characters are introduced and developed.
- Analyze the impact of the author's choices, discussing how these decisions affect both the story's meaning and the reader's experience.
- Organize your ideas so that each new idea builds on the one it follows to create a unified whole.
- Provide a concluding section that follows from the explanation presented.

Task 2: Literature [RL.11-12.4; W.11-12.9; L.11-12.4, L.11-12.5]
Analyze Word Choice

*Write an **essay** in which you analyze the word choice in a poem from this unit.*

- Explain which poem you chose and why you chose it.
- Identify specific examples of language in the poem that you find especially effective. Consider the following elements: figures of speech, such as similes or metaphors; specific words that are particularly interesting or beautiful; connotative meanings that are especially rich or striking. Explain your choices and the reasons for them.
- Identify any words in the poem that readers may not understand. Explain the meanings of these words. If any have multiple meanings, explain which ones are most important in this work.
- Consider how the combined word choices in the poem develop the author's tone.
- Cite specific examples from the poems to support your ideas. Quote precisely and accurately.

Task 3: Literature [RL.11-12.5; W.11-12.2]
Analyze Text Structure

*Write an **essay** in which you analyze the structure of a story in this unit.*

- Introduce your essay by discussing the overall structure of your chosen story. For example, does it follow simple chronological order or does it move about in time?
- Identify a specific section or aspect of the story you will analyze in depth. For example, you may discuss how the story begins, how events are ordered, or how it ends (happily, tragically, or inconclusively). Discuss how the specific section or aspect of the story contributes to the overall structure.
- Discuss the aesthetic, or artistic, impact of the author's structural choices. For example, consider how the structure affects the story's overall meaning.
- Choose varied transitional words and phrases to connect your ideas and clearly express the relationships you are analyzing.

Speaking and Listening

Task 4: Literature [RL.11-12.9; SL.11-12.6]
Demonstrate Knowledge of Foundational Works of American Literature

*Deliver a **speech** in which you analyze how two or more foundational literary works in this unit treat similar themes or topics.*

- Identify the works you will discuss and explain why you chose them. Discuss why these works are examples of foundational American literature.
- Identify the topic each work addresses and describe how each one presents characters, settings, or ideas.
- Explain the theme, or themes, the two works explore. Discuss similarities and differences—and the reasons for them—in these presentations or portrayals.
- Cite specific details to support your ideas.
- Include graphics or notes to support your analysis and clarify your ideas.
- Adapt your speech as you present. For example, you might slow your pace as you explain complex ideas.

Task 5: Informational Text [RI.11-12.4; SL.11-12.6]
Determine Author's Point of View

*Deliver an **oral presentation** in which you analyze the use of language in a nonfiction work from this unit.*

- Introduce the work you chose. Explain the historical context for the work and briefly summarize its central ideas.
- Identify specific word choices that are particularly critical to the writer's overall purpose and expression of ideas. State why you chose these words and phrases, and explain their figurative, technical, or connotative meanings.
- Speak clearly and precisely so that listeners can follow your line of reasoning, including your use of examples to illustrate your ideas.

Task 6: Literature [RL.11-12.2; SL.11-12.6]
Analyze Development of Theme

*Deliver an **oral presentation** in which you analyze the development of two or more themes in a work from this unit.*

- Explain which work you chose. Introduce your analysis by summarizing the work and identifying two distinct themes it conveys.
- Explain how the author develops the themes over the course of the work. For example, consider descriptions of the setting, characters' actions and reactions, and specific events. Also, consider symbols, imagery, or other literary elements that add to the development of two or more themes.
- Explain how the two themes interact and build on one another throughout the work.
- As you speak, use both general academic language and literary terms accurately. Employ formal English appropriate to an academic setting.

THE ESSENTIAL ?

How does literature shape or reflect society?

A Growing Nation Some writers in the 1800s celebrated the growing American nation and contributed to the sense of the country's unlimited potential. Others viewed the growing American culture less positively.

Assignment Choose two or more literary works from this unit that portray distinctly American settings and characters. Write a **comparison-and-contrast essay** in which you analyze these portrayals and characterize their perspective on American culture.

Featured Titles

In this unit, you have read a variety of literature from the American Renaissance. Continue to read works related to this era on your own. Select books that you enjoy, but challenge yourself to explore new topics, new authors, and works offering varied perspectives or approaches. The titles suggested below will help you get started.

LITERATURE

The Scarlet Letter

Nathaniel Hawthorne EXEMPLAR TEXT 

Novel Set in Puritan Boston in the early 1600s, *The Scarlet Letter* tells the story of Hester Prynne, a woman who is branded as an outcast for her sins and must struggle to create her own redemption.

["The Minister's Black Veil" by Hawthorne appears on page 272. Build knowledge by reading a longer work by this author.]

Leaves of Grass

Walt Whitman EXEMPLAR TEXT 

Poetry A landmark collection of free verse poetry that includes "Song of Myself," *Leaves of Grass* combines heroic and historical themes with deeply personal observations.

[Excerpts from Leaves of Grass *begin on page 426 in this book. Build knowledge by reading the full text.]*

Complete Stories and Poems of Edgar Allan Poe

Edgar Allan Poe
Doubleday, 1984 EXEMPLAR TEXT 

Short Story/Poetry This collection of Poe's short stories and poems reveals his talent for developing mysterious, macabre characters and plots. The collection includes his famous story "The Cask of Amontillado."

[Two of Edgar Allan Poe's works begin on pages 292 and 312 in this book. Build knowledge by reading Poe's complete works.]

The Complete Poems of Emily Dickinson

Emily Dickinson
Back Bay Books, 1976 EXEMPLAR TEXT 

Poetry Emily Dickinson's small, precise poems describe enormous topics, such as mortality and the nature of the imagination. She is one of the great poets of American literature. This volume, which includes "Because I Could Not Stop for Death," presents her collected works.

[Poems by Emily Dickinson appear on pages 408–417 of this book. Build knowledge by reading her complete works.]

INFORMATIONAL TEXTS

Historical Texts

Selected Writings of Ralph Waldo Emerson

Ralph Waldo Emerson
edited by William H. Gilman

Essay One of the great essayists in American letters, Ralph Waldo Emerson addressed subjects ranging from everyday experiences to the meaning of life.

[Excerpts from Emerson's essays begin on page 366 in this book. Build knowledge by reading the full texts.]

Walden and Civil Disobedience

Henry David Thoreau

Essay These essays by poet and philosopher Henry David Thoreau are among the most influential works of nonfiction in American literature.

[Excerpts from Thoreau's essays begin on page 378 of this book. Build knowledge by reading the full text.]

Eyewitness to America: 500 Years of American History in the Words of Those Who Saw It Happen

edited by David Colbert EXEMPLAR TEXT 

Primary Source Read first-hand accounts of 500 years of the American experience in this extraordinary book. Subjects range from Horace Porter's description of Robert E. Lee's surrender to Grant to Hunter S. Thompson's discussion of a Super Bowl game.

Contemporary Scholarship

An American Primer

edited by Daniel Boorstin EXEMPLAR TEXT 

Primary Source and Commentary This collection presents the most important documents in American history, accompanied by commentary from celebrated historians.

Preparing to Read Complex Texts

Reading for College and Career In both college and the workplace, readers must analyze texts independently, draw connections among works that offer varied perspectives, and develop their own ideas and informed opinions. The questions shown below, and others that you generate on your own, will help you more effectively read and analyze complex college-level texts.

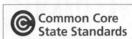

Reading Literature/Informational Text
10. By the end of grade 11, read and comprehend literature, including stories, dramas, and poems, and literary nonfiction, in the grades 11-CCR text complexity band proficiently, with scaffolding as needed at the high end of the range.

When reading complex texts, ask yourself...

- What idea, experience, or story seems to have compelled the author to write? Has the author presented that idea, experience, or story in a way that I, too, find compelling?
- How might the author's era, social status, belief system, or personal experiences have affected the point of view he or she expresses in the text?
- How do my circumstances affect what I understand and feel about this text?
- What key idea does the author state explicitly? What key idea does he or she suggest or imply? Which details in the text help me to perceive implied ideas?
- Do I find multiple layers of meaning in the text? If so, what relationships do I see among these layers of meaning?
- How do details in the text connect or relate to one another? Do I find any details unconvincing, unrelated, or out of place?
- Do I find the text believable and convincing?

Key Ideas and Details

- What patterns of organization or sequences do I find in the text? Do these patterns help me understand the ideas better?
- What do I notice about the author's style, including his or her diction, use of imagery and figurative language, and syntax?
- Do I like the author's style? Is the author's style memorable?
- What emotional attitude does the author express toward the topic, the story, or the characters? Does this attitude seem appropriate?
- What emotional attitude does the author express toward me, the reader? Does this attitude seem appropriate?
- What do I notice about the author's voice—his or her personality on the page? Do I like this voice? Does it make me want to read on?

Craft and Structure

- Is the work fresh and original?
- Do I agree with the author's ideas entirely, or are there elements I find unconvincing?
- Do I disagree with the author's ideas entirely, or are there elements I can accept as true?
- Based on my knowledge of American literature, history, and culture, does this work reflect the American tradition? Why or why not?

Integration of Ideas

Division, Reconciliation, and Expansion

Literature of the Civil War and the Frontier

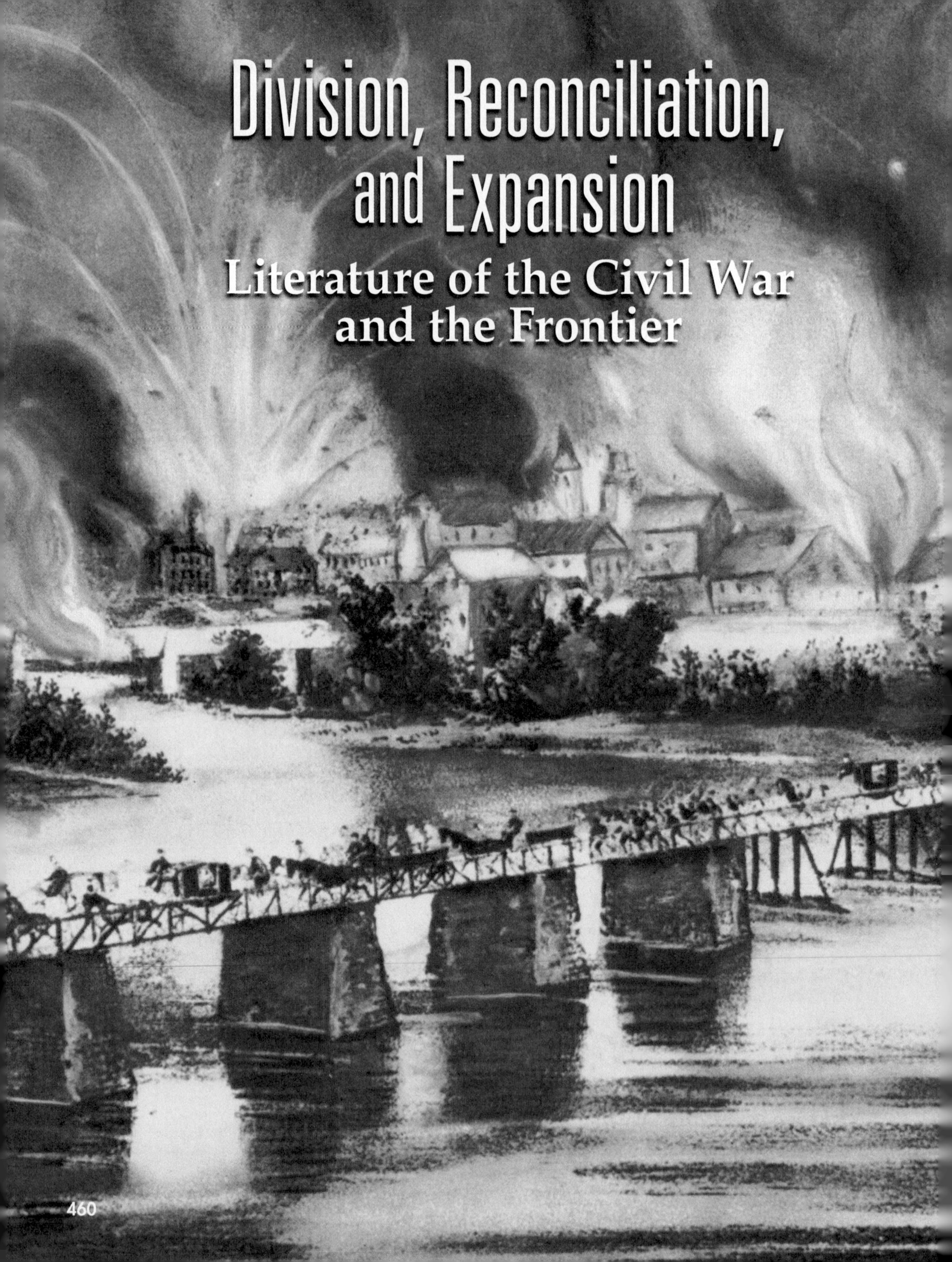

1850–1914

Unit 3

PHLit Online!
www.PHLitOnline.com

Hear It!

- Selection summary audio
- Selection audio

See It!

- Author videos
- Essential Question video
- Get Connected videos
- Background videos
- More about the authors
- Illustrated vocabulary words
- Vocabulary flashcards

Do It!

- Interactive journals
- Interactive graphic organizers
- Grammar tutorials
- Interactive vocabulary games
- Test practice

Fondly do we hope—fervently do we pray—that this mighty scourge of war may speedily pass away.

– Abraham Lincoln
Second Inaugural Address, 1865

Snapshot of the Period

The years between 1850 and 1914 witnessed a transformation of the United States. During those years, America came of age—the country changed from a decentralized, mostly agricultural nation to the modern industrial power that we know today. This transformation began in the period leading up to the Civil War. In that war, Americans took up arms against one another to determine which should prevail: The Union of the North or the Confederacy of the South? The federal Union or states' rights? Freedom or slavery? As the Civil War began, each side possessed significant strengths and notable weaknesses. The North had a tremendous advantage in population and was far more industrialized and thus better prepared to wage war than the agrarian South. However, the Confederacy had the psychological advantage of greater motivation: it was fighting for its very survival. The South also had a strong military tradition and notably fine leaders. When the struggle was over, the North won, the Union held, and slavery was abolished—but all at a devastating cost to the nation.

▲ Abraham Lincoln signed the Emancipation Proclamation in 1863, as the nation approached the third year of Civil War.

Twain

Douglass

Chopin

Crane

Cather

Chief Joseph

As you read the selections in this unit, you will be asked to think about them in view of three key questions:

What is the **relationship** between literature and *place?*

How does **literature** shape or reflect *society?*

What makes **American** literature *American?*

Integration of Knowledge and Ideas What does the information shown in the charts below help you understand about differences between the North and South in their economies, population densities, and overall lifestyles? How do you think these differences affected the outcome of the Civil War?

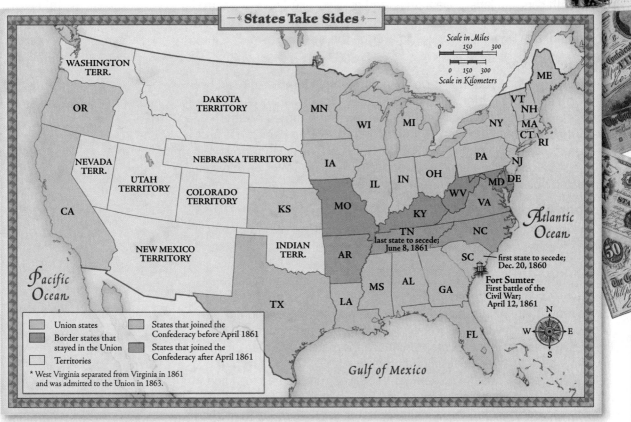

States Take Sides

Scale in Miles 0 150 300
Scale in Kilometers 0 150 300

- Union states
- Border states that stayed in the Union
- Territories
- States that joined the Confederacy before April 1861
- States that joined the Confederacy after April 1861

* West Virginia separated from Virginia in 1861 and was admitted to the Union in 1863.

SC first state to secede; Dec. 20, 1860

Fort Sumter First battle of the Civil War; April 12, 1861

TN last state to secede; June 8, 1861

WASHINGTON TERR. · OR · CA · NEVADA TERR. · UTAH TERRITORY · DAKOTA TERRITORY · NEBRASKA TERRITORY · COLORADO TERRITORY · NEW MEXICO TERRITORY · INDIAN TERR. · KS · TX · MN · IA · MO · AR · LA · WI · IL · MI · IN · OH · KY · TN · MS · AL · GA · FL · SC · NC · VA · WV · MD · DE · PA · NJ · NY · VT · NH · ME · MA · CT · RI

Pacific Ocean · Atlantic Ocean · Gulf of Mexico

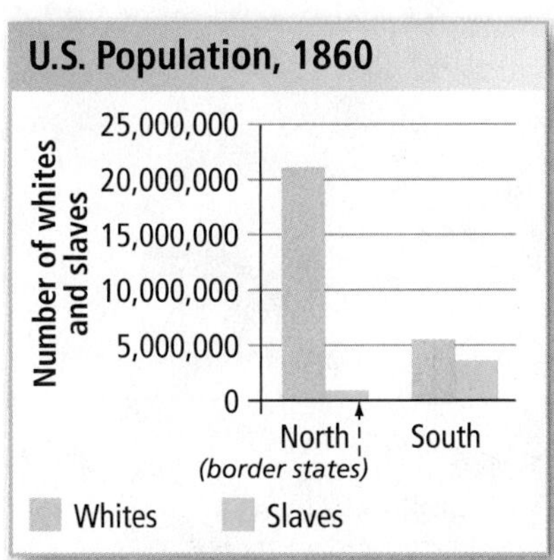

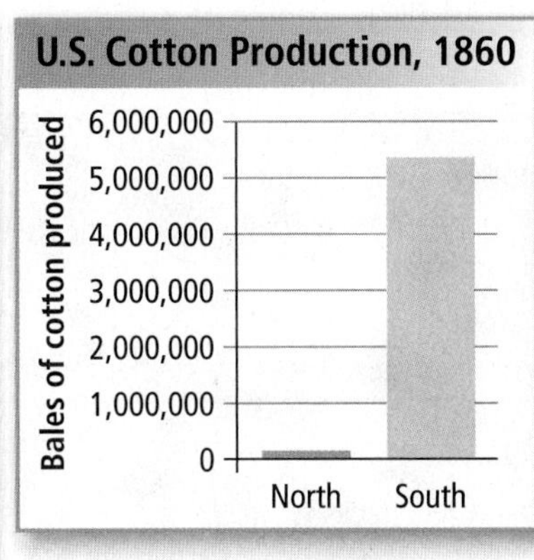

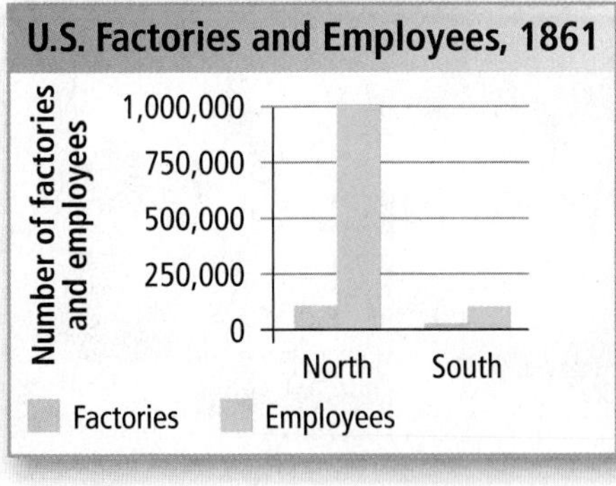

Historical Background

The Civil War Era (1850–1914)

Between the Civil War and World War I, America changed dramatically. The period began with cotton plantations and the Pony Express, and it ended with cars, airplanes, telephones, and movies. The Civil War scarred everyone—soldier, civilian, slave—and the shift from agriculture to industry accelerated. No American's life would ever be the same.

Prelude to War

The North and the South had developed differently. Commerce ruled the North and King Cotton ruled the South. The Industrial Revolution, advances in transportation, and a tide of immigration turned northern cities into centers of bustling activity. By contrast, cotton plantations and the system of slavery defined the South. Issues such as what to do about fugitive slaves and whether new states should be slave states or free states dominated politics. Rage and resentment grew. War was waiting.

Brother Against Brother

When Abraham Lincoln, dedicated to halting the spread of slavery, was elected president in 1860, South Carolina and five other states left the Union and established the Confederate States of America. Fighting began at Fort Sumter, in Charleston Harbor. Many on both sides anticipated a short war. No one could know what lay ahead: the carnage of Antietam, where more than 26,000 men fell in a single day; the deprivation of the siege of Vicksburg, where people survived only by eating dogs and rats; the destruction of Georgia, when Union troops marched to the coast. The devastating civil war lasted four long years.

By the time Confederate general Robert E. Lee surrendered to Union general Ulysses S. Grant in the spring of 1865, over 600,000 American soldiers had lost their lives. The South lay in ruins, its cities, farms, and plantations destroyed. The future looked grim. Just after the surrender, Abraham Lincoln was assassinated, and the exhausted, war-torn nation faced the huge task of reconstruction without him.

TIMELINE

1850

1850: China Taiping rebellion begins against the authority of the Qing government.

◀ **1856: France** Gustave Flaubert publishes *Madame Bovary,* a classic novel of realism.

1857: Dred Scott decision by the U.S. Supreme Court rules that people of African descent cannot become U.S. citizens.

▶ **1859:** John Brown, an abolitionist, leads a raid on the federal arsenal at Harpers Ferry, Virginia; he is hanged for treason.

1859: England Charles Darwin introduces theory of evolution in *The Origin of the Species.*

Americans Go West

After the Civil War, physical expansion and industrialization transformed the American landscape, economy, and society. The Homestead Act of 1862 promised 160 acres to anyone who would live on the land for a certain period and improve it. This shifted the westward movement into high gear. Half a million farmers, including tens of thousands of emancipated African Americans, staked their claims on the Great Plains. Miners went west, with dreams of gold sparkling in their eyes. In 1869, workers drove the last spike in the transcontinental railroad.

The Frontier Disappears

By 1890, the frontier had ceased to exist. Settlers, railroads, mines, ranches, and the slaughter of the buffalo had transformed the West. In place of open range were ploughed fields, grazing lands, and miles of fences. Gone, too, were the Indian nations; by 1890, almost all Native Americans in the West had been forced from their lands.

The "Electric" Society

When electricity entered the scene in the 1880s, the second Industrial Revolution began. Americans began to enjoy electric lights, telephones, automobiles, motion pictures, and skyscrapers, along with noise, traffic, and air pollution. Urban populations exploded; millions of immigrants provided cheap labor. Low wages, child labor, and disease were the norm for the working class, while a handful of industrial giants lived like kings. Mark Twain perfectly summarized the contradictions of this era when he called it "The Gilded Age."

Key Historical Theme: Painful Growth and Electric Change

- The Civil War left the nation physically, economically, and emotionally devastated as reconstruction began.
- Riding the railroad, Americans moved West and annihilated the frontier.
- The Age of Electricity transformed everyday life. Cities, with all their pleasures and problems, expanded rapidly.

1860: Abraham Lincoln is elected United States president. ▼

▲ **1861:** Civil War begins in April with firing on Fort Sumter.

1862: Emily Dickinson's poem "Safe in their Alabaster Chambers" is published in the Massachusetts newspaper *The Republican.*

▼ **1862: France** Louis Pasteur proposes modern germ theory of disease.

1865

1863: Lincoln issues the Emancipation Proclamation.

Essential Questions Across Time

The Civil War and the Frontier (1850–1914)

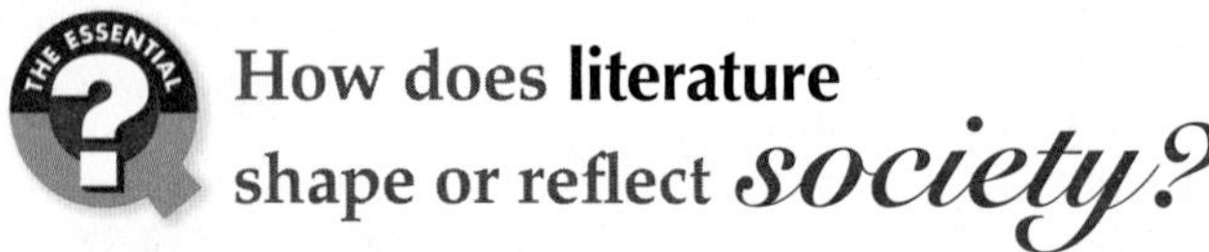

What literary forms did writers use to discuss social and political issues during this period?

Spirituals Although spirituals were sung, not written down, they were the form of literature that grew directly out of the major social and political issue of the time—slavery. Born in the rhythms of work and based on biblical imagery, spirituals were lyrical expressions of lamentation, comfort, and hope. Songs like "Go Down, Moses" and "Swing Low, Sweet Chariot" made it possible for slaves to at least imagine release into a better life.

Life Stories Nonfiction in which men and women related the dramatic events of their lives also gave literary form to the issues of the era. Sojourner Truth's first-person account of her life and Frederick Douglass's autobiography were true-life narratives of bondage and freedom. Richly detailed diaries, such as the one kept by Confederate wife Mary Chesnut, as well as the journals and letters of countless Civil War soldiers remain valuable and moving literary resources that turn abstract issues into the daily realities of actual human beings.

Fiction and Journalism With Harriet Beecher Stowe's *Uncle Tom's Cabin*, fiction stepped up to play a major role in the politics of the era. Newspapers, too, took stands on a wide variety of issues and provided forums for editorials, essays, and public letters. After the Civil War, investigative journalists called muckrakers wrote blistering exposés of corruption, scandal, and incompetence in American industries.

ESSENTIAL QUESTION VOCABULARY

These Essential Question words will help you think and write about literature and society:

lamentation (lam′ən tā′ shən) *n.* outward expression of grief; wail or cry

forum (fôr′əm) *n.* place for the discussion of public matters

unflinching (un flin′chiŋ) *adj.* steadfast; resolute

TIMELINE

1865

1865: The Thirteenth Amendment, outlawing slavery, is added to the U.S. Constitution.

1865: President Lincoln is assassinated by John Wilkes Booth.

▲ **1865: England** Lewis Carroll completes *Alice's Adventures in Wonderland.*

▲ **1867:** The United States buys the state of Alaska from Russia.

How did popular literature reflect the era's social and political issues?

Rags to Riches As America's cities grew, the struggle against crushing urban poverty became a fact of life for more and more people. Many readers turned to the young adult novels of Horatio Alger to find inspiration on the hard road to success. Alger's rags-to-riches stories of young men finding fame and fortune through right-thinking and moral actions were immensely popular, selling more than twenty million copies.

Twists and Turns William Sydney Porter started out as a journalist, worked in a bank, went to prison for embezzlement, and became a short story writer. Under the name "O. Henry," he published hundreds of tales of ordinary city dwellers and became one of the most popular writers in America. His stories are often humorous episodes that include twists of fate. Beneath the light-hearted surface, however, his ironic surprise endings suggest how much people felt their lives were subject to coincidence and chance.

The West and the Wizard Millions of Americans who never set foot on a prairie or an open range loved the Western novels of Zane Grey. The closing of the frontier encouraged a romantic view of the lost West, and Grey capitalized on that vision with exciting tales of self-reliant cowboys, many of which were later turned into movies. Industrial-age Americans found escapism of a different kind in L. Frank Baum's *The Wonderful Wizard of Oz* (1900), a fantasy so popular it led to thirteen sequels.

The American EXPERIENCE

ART IN THE HISTORICAL CONTEXT

Realism in Painting: The Ashcan School

At the turn of the twentieth century, a group of artists working in Philadelphia and New York realized that city life was fertile ground for a new kind of imagery. They shared the basic principles and attitudes of Realism, and they developed ways of conveying Realism visually. These painters were aware that America was becoming increasingly urban, and they wanted to depict this new steel-and-concrete reality. They painted the grubby and the drab as well as the hectic and the colorful. These frank and honest painters included Robert Henri, William Glackens, and George Luks. Some critics insultingly called them the Ashcan ("garbage can") School, a label that has endured but is no longer an insult.

One prominent Ashcan painter was John Sloan (1871–1951). Sloan said that he saw the city as a "vast stage set where all sorts of lively business was in progress." His painting *Six O'Clock, Winter* (c. 1912) shows the "lively business" of a New York City rush hour.

SIX O'CLOCK, WINTER, 1912, JOHN SLOAN, THE PHILLIPS COLLECTION

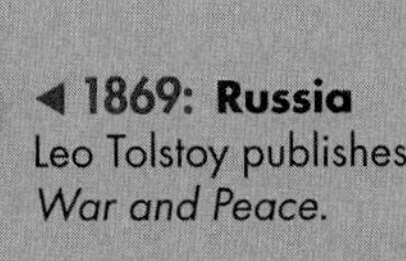

◀ **1869: Russia** Leo Tolstoy publishes *War and Peace.*

1874: France Claude Monet gathers Impressionist painters for first exhibition. ▶

1876: Baseball's National League is founded.

1877: Thomas Edison patents the phonograph.

1877: England First tennis championship held at Wimbledon.

1880

The American EXPERIENCE

CONTEMPORARY CONNECTION

Mark Twain, the Original Time Traveler

In his novel, *A Connecticut Yankee in King Arthur's Court*, Mark Twain places a present-day hero in the distant past. Twain said the idea was inspired by a dream in which he was "a knight errant in armor in the Middle Ages." When the book was published in 1889, *The Boston Herald* raved, "Of all the extraordinary conceits that have germinated in his fruitful imagination, nothing more delicious has ever occurred to Mark Twain than that of running riot among the legendary times of our ancestral race. . . .'"

While he must have enjoyed the book's success, Twain probably never imagined its long-term effect. Indeed, the time travel tale—now a familiar device in science fiction—is widely regarded to have begun with Twain's book. Perhaps because of this, many science fiction writers have a fondness for Twain. He often appears as a character in sci-fi books, films, television shows, and comics, including the following brief list of examples:

- *The Riverworld* series by Philip José Farmer
- *To Sail Beyond the Sunset* by Robert A. Heinlein
- *Star Trek: The Next Generation,* "Time's Arrow" episode
- *The Sandman* graphic novel series by Neil Gaiman
- *The Transformers: Evolutions* "Hearts of Steel" comic book series

TIMELINE

MARK TWAIN
KNOWN TO EVERYONE-LIKED BY ALL

1880

1883: Railroads adopt standard time zones.

1883: The Brooklyn Bridge is opened. ▶

◀ **1884:** Mark Twain publishes *The Adventures of Huckleberry Finn.*

1886: Statue of Liberty dedicated in New York Harbor. ▶

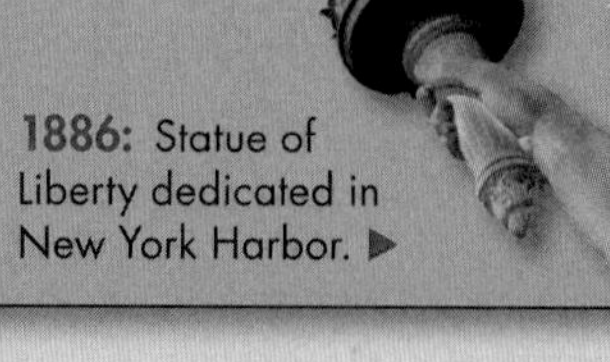

1888: Great mid-March blizzard in eastern United States piles 30-foot drifts in New York's Herald Square.

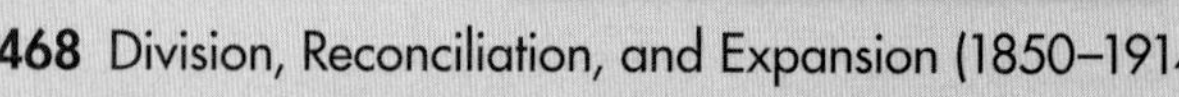

How did social and political issues lead to Realism and Naturalism?

The war was over. The unthinkable had happened: Americans had tried to slaughter each other. Although the outcome of the war had given the nation a hard-won sense of unity, the enormous cost in human life had shattered the nation's idealism. Like the hero of Stephen Crane's *Red Badge of Courage*, Americans had lost their innocence. The youthful sense of enthusiastic optimism that had built the country had faded away. Frustrated, unfulfilled, young writers turned away from the Romanticism that was popular before the war. They threw away their rose-colored glasses and saw the world for what it was. They became Realists.

The Common Life American writers began to focus on creating portrayals of "real life" as ordinary people lived it. They attempted to show characters and events in an honest, objective, almost factual way. In prose, Willa Cather wrote unflinchingly of the loneliness and cultural isolation of life on the prairie. In poetry, Edwin Arlington Robinson created unsparing psychological portraits of a variety of small-town characters. In *Spoon River Anthology*, Edgar Lee Masters presented a disturbingly candid portrait of small-town life in the form of epitaphs spoken by the dead themselves.

Naturalism Like Realists, Naturalists also depicted ordinary people in real-life situations, but they took it a step further. They believed that forces far more powerful than any individual shaped human destinies. Indifferent Nature, blind fate, heredity, pure chance—these determined the lives of men and women. Even fierce self-interest was not enough to guarantee success or survival. Jack London, for example, set much of his fiction in the Alaskan wilderness, where the frigid environment was unforgiving. The Naturalist theme of human endurance in the face of overwhelming natural forces pervades his fiction. The atmosphere of urban life fed Naturalism too, as people recognized that industrialization, mechanization, and anonymity were forces against which individuals were increasingly powerless.

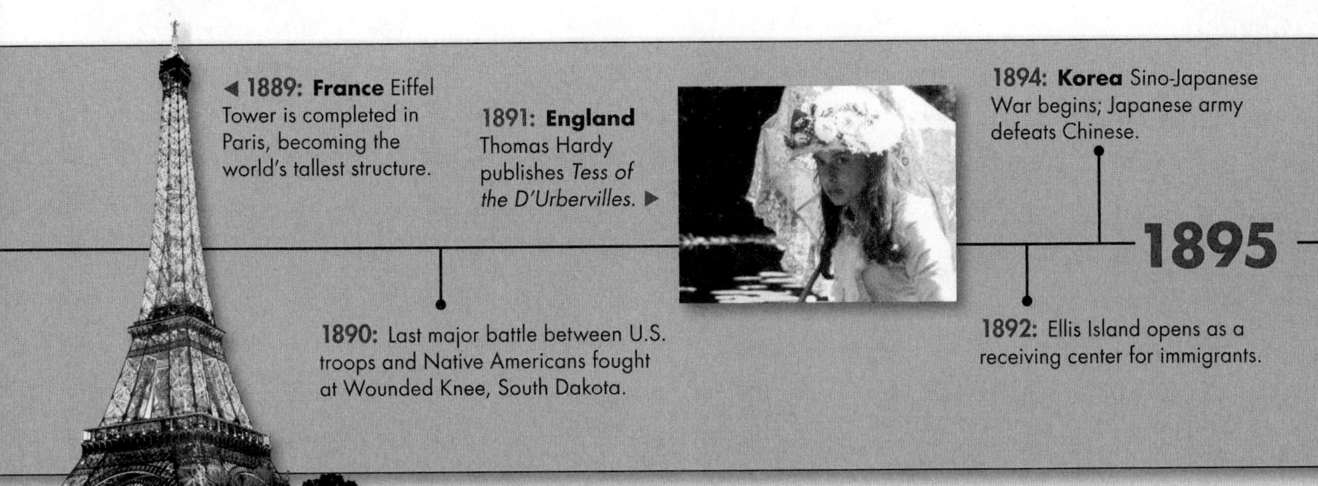

◀ **1889: France** Eiffel Tower is completed in Paris, becoming the world's tallest structure.
1891: England Thomas Hardy publishes *Tess of the D'Urbervilles.* ▶
1894: Korea Sino-Japanese War begins; Japanese army defeats Chinese.
1895
1890: Last major battle between U.S. troops and Native Americans fought at Wounded Knee, South Dakota.
1892: Ellis Island opens as a receiving center for immigrants.

What is the relationship between literature and *place?*

What elements of the physical environment affected Northern writers' attitudes?

Industry The growth of industry in the North radically changed the landscape, and the landscape profoundly affected the thoughts, attitudes, and values of the people. In fact, change itself became a significant value. Technological advances in manufacturing, transportation, and the conveniences of daily life encouraged Northerners to believe that anything bigger, stronger, faster, and newer was necessarily better.

Urban Life On the other hand, the increased sizes and populations of Northern cities led to a host of urban problems and discontents. Conflicts arose over the treatment of immigrants, the role of organized labor, and the causes and effects of poverty. Writers were particularly sensitive to what was happening to the spirits—the emotions and values—of people crowded into cities and working at mind-numbing jobs in factories.

What elements of the physical environment affected Southern writers' attitudes?

Regionalism The South of course had cities too, but overall it remained a predominantly rural environment. Agriculture had always been at the heart of the economy, but the war had devastated the plantation system and abolished slavery, radically altering the Southern way of life. Nevertheless, Southern writers focused on the distinctive qualities of their geographical setting. Like writers in other parts of the country, Southern regionalists used the features and color of their local landscapes to tell stories that seemed to grow out of the land itself.

How did expressions of place show up in literature?

Local Color Almost as a conscious national reaction to the Civil War, writers all over the country seemed to realize how precious each separate part of the country could be. In the Northeast, South, Midwest, and West,

ESSENTIAL QUESTION VOCABULARY

These Essential Question words will help you think and write about literature and place:

industry (in′dəs trē) *n.* the production of goods; manufacturing enterprises collectively

transportation (trans′pər tā′shən) *n.* system for carrying passengers or goods from one place to another

rural (ro͝or′əl) *adj.* characteristic of the country or farm rather than the city

TIMELINE

1895

1895: **Germany** Wilhelm Roentgen discovers X-rays.

1895: First professional football game played in Latrobe, Pennsylvania. ▶

1896: *The Country of the Pointed Firs,* Sarah Orne Jewett's masterpiece, is published.

1898: **France** Pierre and Marie Curie discover radium and polonium. ▲

1901: **Italy** First transatlantic radio telegraphic message is sent by Marconi.

writers began to feature characters and details that were unique to a particular geographic area. Characters spoke in dialect, linking themselves to a specific locale. Landscapes were so fully integrated into stories that they virtually became characters. Descriptions of customs, clothing, manners, and attitudes all contributed to a literature of local color.

The mining-camp sketches and stories of Bret Harte made the West, especially California, a lively locale in the American literary imagination. Hamlin Garland and Willa Cather found hardship and tragedy, sometimes touched with romance, on the farms of the Midwest. Mark Twain told stories, like *The Adventures of Huckleberry Finn*, that are so deeply entwined with the landscape of the Mississippi River we cannot imagine them happening in any other place. In Maine, Sarah Orne Jewett created delicate and unforgettable New England idylls, and in Louisiana Kate Chopin told wrenchingly realistic stories of life in the bayous.

Urban Sophistication Not all realism, however, was set on farms, in small towns, and on riverboats. Some American writers were also comfortable in elegant drawing rooms. Edith Wharton wrote novels and stories about repressive customs in the Eastern high society into which she had been born. William Dean Howells applied his brand of realism to New England novels of manners and class. Urban subtlety and sophistication found its greatest American analyst in Henry James. Often placing his Americans back in Europe, James probed deeply into characters motivated by complex mixes of desire, honor, ambition, and guilt.

The **American EXPERIENCE**

DEVELOPING AMERICAN ENGLISH

Mark Twain and the American Language by Richard Lederer

On February 18, 1885, thirty thousand copies of *The Adventures of Huckleberry Finn* were released, and the novel changed the direction of American letters. Twain used everyday speech instead of formal, standard English. He used seven distinct dialects to reflect the speech patterns of his characters, and he showed the vitality of the American idiom in narrative as well as in dialogue. *Huckleberry Finn* is the first novel of world rank written entirely in American.

Readin', Writin', and Twain

Twain held strong opinions about a passel of subjects. Here are a few things he had to say about the American language that he helped to shape.

- *On dialects*: I have traveled more than anyone else, and I have noticed that even the angels speak English with an accent.
- *On choosing words*: The difference between the almost right word and the right word is really a large matter—'tis the difference between the lightning-bug and the lightning.
- *On style* (in a letter to a twelve-year-old): I notice that you use plain, simple language, short words, and brief sentences. That is the way to write English—it is the modern way and the best way. Stick to it; and don't let fluff and flowers and verbosity creep in.

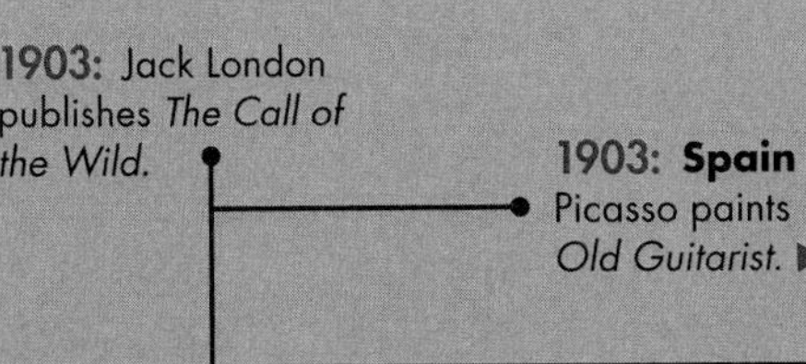

1903: Jack London publishes *The Call of the Wild.*

1903: Spain Pablo Picasso paints *The Old Guitarist.* ▶

1903: Wright Brothers fly 852 feet in their airplane at Kitty Hawk, North Carolina. ▼

1903: W.E.B. DuBois publishes *The Souls of Black Folk,* a collection of essays.

The Old Guitarist, 1903, Pablo Picasso, The Art Institute of Chicago, ©2004 Estate of Pablo Picasso/Artists Rights Society (ARS), New York

1904: Russo-Japanese War begins.

1905

What makes American literature *American?*

What literary elements contributed to an American style?

Settings and Plots Unique local settings were essential in creating the "Americanness" of literature during this period. A Civil War battlefield, a Mississippi riverboat, a Western mining town, a Yukon wilderness—these and other sites grounded American literature in truly American places.

Dialogue and Style Common speech and dialects contributed to an American style. The way characters talked linked them to specific parts of the country and gave them distinct identities. Straightforward, deliberately "unliterary" speech defined a plain and powerful American style.

Humor Mark Twain said, "The humorous story is American." He felt that a good comic story depended on *how* it was told. Twain and other American writers often used humor to expose corruption and dissect human foibles.

What roles did writers play in shaping American identity?

Writer as Realist During the first half of the nineteenth century, Romantic subjectivity dominated American writing. The adventure tales of Irving and Cooper, the romances and fantasies of Hawthorne and Poe, and the otherworldly quests of Emerson and Melville defined American literature. However, after the horrors of the Civil War, the second half of the century saw the rise of a more objective attitude toward the world and human affairs. Hard fact took on more value than the search for the Transcendentalist Oversoul.

Local color writers such as Bret Harte, Sarah Orne Jewett, and Kate Chopin took great pains to depict details of the places they loved. As a result, their readers came to love those places as well. Local colorists were storytellers—Mark Twain the finest of them all—but they were also documentarians, recording life as it was lived.

TIMELINE

1905: **Germany** Albert Einstein proposes his relativity theory. ▼

▲ 1906: The San Francisco earthquake results in the deaths of at least 3,000 people.

1908: Henry Ford builds the first Model T. ▲

1905

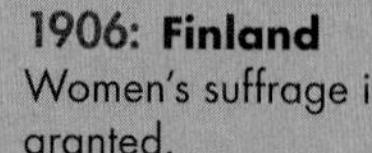

1906: **Finland** Women's suffrage is granted.

1907: Frank Lloyd Wright hosts his first solo exhibition at the Art Institute of Chicago.

1908: The electric washing machine is invented.

These were also the years when a new invention, photography, began to flourish, further feeding the demand for realistic images of life.

Writer as Naturalist The writers associated with Naturalism, including Stephen Crane, Frank Norris, and Jack London, were even more detached. They were deeply influenced by the writings of British naturalist Charles Darwin, German political economist Karl Marx, and French novelist Emile Zola, who believed that heredity, environment, and social conditions determined people's actions. To the American Naturalists, Emerson's self-reliance was an illusion, and the role of the writer was to make that clear.

At the dawn of the twentieth century, what did literature reveal about American attitudes?

Pragmatism The American Romantic impulse had faded. The dream-life expressed by Hawthorne and Poe had given way to a hard-edged pragmatism. Melville's Captain Ahab, an obsessive, tragic figure on a doomed whaling ship, was succeeded by Twain's Huck Finn, a clear-eyed and clear-headed boy on a raft.

Loss of Idealism The Civil War tarnished many of the ideals that had characterized the pre-war nation. In the face of Civil War deaths, postwar poverty, urban crowding, and mass production, Emersonian self-reliance lost its relevance. Henry David Thoreau, living alone at Walden and becoming one with nature, was succeeded by Jack London's doomed Yukon camper in "To Build a Fire."

Democracy Americans continued to put their faith in democracy. Realism emphasized the common person. It praised the everyday and the ordinary, even at the risk of glorifying mediocrity. Hawthorne's Hester Prynne, an exceptional woman reviled by her community, was succeeded by Edgar Lee Masters' Lucinda Matlock, an ordinary woman in small-town America.

Science As the nation entered the twentieth century, science and technology took on ever greater importance. Americans believed in progress and measured it in concrete ways. Over 27 million people visited the 1893 World's Columbian Exposition in Chicago, a massive world's fair that celebrated culture, craft, and commerce. The fair symbolized America's future as a leader in the practical industries that would continue to transform the world and create the Modern Age.

ESSENTIAL QUESTION VOCABULARY

These Essential Question words will help you think and write about American literature:

objective (əb jek´tiv) *adj.* real; actual

realistic (rē ə lis´tik) *adj.* practical or concrete rather than visionary

pragmatism (prag´mə tiz´əm) *n.* quality of being practical, sensible

1909: A multi-racial group of activists founds the National Association for the Advancement of Colored People.

TITANIC
WHITE STAR LINE
The World's Largest Liner
SOUTHAMPTON ~ NEW YORK
VIA CHERBOURG & QUEENSTOWN

1912: Over 1,500 people die in the sinking of the *Titanic.* ▶

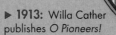

▶ **1913:** Willa Cather publishes *O Pioneers!*

1914

1914: The world's first scheduled airline service begins taking flight from St. Petersburg to Tampa.

Recent Scholarship

Defining an Era

Nell Irvin Painter

One of my most-read books, *Standing at Armageddon: The United States, 1877–1919,* showed me how politics changes as the times change. (The word *Armageddon* in the title refers to the end of the world, and the phrase *Standing at Armageddon* comes from a statement Theodore Roosevelt made in 1912.)

Historians, of course, know that timing is everything. We call one of our specialties "periodization," meaning the breaking up of the past into meaningful chunks of time. Historians decided that certain dates—in this textbook, for example, 1750, 1800, 1850, 1870, 1914, and 1946—carried special meaning, that what came before was different from what came afterward. The periodization in this unit (1850–1914) generally corresponds to the periodization of my book (1877–1919), although this unit includes the Civil War and Reconstruction and my book does not.

I made my own discoveries as I was just starting to work on *Standing at Armageddon.* I had to decide where to start and end a book on the period that covered roughly 1885 to 1915. The years 1885 and 1915 had no particular resonance: Nothing earthshaking occurred in either of those years to change the course of United States history. So I set about finding meaningful years by reading newspapers and news magazines, where I could follow the news of the day as it unfolded, day by day and week by week.

Meet the Author

Introducing Nell Irvin Painter (b. 1942)
Nell Irvin Painter served as the director of Princeton University's Program in African American Studies from 1997 to 2000. She is the author of numerous books, including *Standing at Armageddon: The United States, 1877–1919; Southern History Across the Color Line;* and *Sojourner Truth: A Life, A Symbol.*

A Shift from Land to Labor Issues

At the beginning of the 1870s, the news still bristled with violence related to the politics of the Civil War, as Democrats attacked Republicans and killed off the people associated with Reconstruction. Reconstruction—the reorganization of Southern states from 1867 to 1877—was dying a bloody death in the South, as Democrats took back by force the power they had held before the war. In 1877, however, new conflicts eclipsed the focus on Southern political terrorism. The news also revealed a great deal of labor conflict outside the South. A nationwide strike of railroad workers occurred in 1877 that began a whole new era in which politics revolved around working people and strikes. Before the Civil War, politics had been about land and access to land. After Reconstruction, postwar politics focused on industries and workers; 1877—the year national attention shifted from land to labor—became the starting point for *Standing at Armageddon*.

What about the end? Where should my period and my book end? Still reading the newspapers and news magazines, I found an echo of 1877's strikes and riots in 1919, the year contemporaries called the "Great Upheaval." There was the end of my period, a time in which working people and their issues once again dominated American politics.

Organized Labor Becomes a Force

Before 1877, American politics revolved around questions of land. But after 1877, politics revolved around industry and the people who worked in it. Organized labor became a force in U.S. politics between 1877 and 1919 and, building on this foundation, labor unions would surge to the fore in the 1930s. My periodization of 1877–1919 reflects my belief that working people and their concerns lie at the heart of the politics of the era. I begin and end *Standing at Armageddon* at moments in which workers attract the attention of Americans as a whole.

© Speaking and Listening: Collaboration

Nell Irvin Painter discusses "periodization," the breaking up of the past into meaningful time periods. Some periods begin or end with major dramatic events, such as a war or an economic change. The beginning or ending of other periods, such as a "renaissance," are more difficult to pinpoint.

Hold a **small group discussion** about your own time period. What event or events define it? When would you say it started? What name or label would you give it? As a group, arrive at a consensus and then share your ideas with the class.

◄ **Critical Viewing**
Explain how this photograph of a railroad strike reflects Painter's discussion of American workers. **[Connect]**

Integrate and Evaluate Information

1. Use a chart like the one shown to determine the key ideas expressed in the Essential Question essays on pages 466–473. Fill in two ideas related to each Essential Question and note the authors most closely associated with each concept. One example has been done for you.

Essential Question	Key Concept	Key Author
Literature and Place		
American Literature	Influence of heredity and environment	Crane
Literature and Society		

2. How do the visual sources in this section—map, charts, paintings, and photographs—add to your understanding of the ideas expressed in words? Cite specific examples.
3. After the Civil War, Americans were more conscious than ever of their regional identities. How did writers of this era express and preserve the distinct perspectives of Americans across the land? Cite evidence from the various sources presented on pages 462–473 in your answer.
4. **Address a Question:** In her essay "Defining an Era," Nell Irvin Painter states her contention that politics before the Civil War dealt with issues related to land, while politics after the Civil War dealt with issues related to labor. In what ways does her point echo other societal changes occurring during this era? Consider information presented in this textbook about urbanization and industrialization. In addition, integrate information from other sources to support your ideas.

Common Core State Standards

Reading Informational Text
7. Integrate and evaluate multiple sources of information presented in different media or formats as well as in words in order to address a question or solve a problem.

Speaking and Listening
5. Make strategic use of digital media in presentations to enhance understanding of findings, reasoning, and evidence and to add interest.

Speaking and Listening: Oral Presentation

During the Civil War era, speeches and debates played an important role in American life. Research and develop an **oral presentation** about the public-speaking style of one of these famous American orators:

- Abraham Lincoln
- Sojourner Truth
- Henry Ward Beecher
- Mark Twain

Solve a Research Problem: To complete this assignment, you will need to locate examples of and commentaries about the public speaking of a person who lived before the age of sophisticated recording devices. Formulate a plan to meet this research challenge. Consider primary and secondary sources such as:

- Journal and newspaper articles written during the speaker's life
- Writings of later scholars familiar with the speaker's works
- Recordings of other people reenacting the speaker's speeches

As part of your presentation, explain the process you used to identify and evaluate information and solve the research problem. To add interest and evidence to your presentation, use a digital recording of a reenactment of the speaker's words or of an expert discussing the speaker's abilities and ideas.

ESSENTIAL QUESTION VOCABULARY

Use these words in your responses:

Literature and Place
industry
transportation
rural

American Literature
objective
realistic
pragmatism

Literature and Society
lamentation
forum
unflinching

PART 1

A Nation Divided

Before You Read

An Occurrence at Owl Creek Bridge

Connecting to the Essential Question Everyday locations become charged with strategic importance and danger during times of war. As you read this story, which takes place during the Civil War, notice ominous details about the setting. This will help as you reflect on the Essential Question: **What is the relationship between literature and place?**

Literary Analysis

Point of view is the perspective, or vantage point, from which a story is told. An author's choice of point of view affects every aspect of a story. For example, different points of view convey different types of information to the reader.

- In stories told from an **omniscient point of view,** the narrator is an observer who can relate everything that happens, as well as the private thoughts and feelings of all the characters. The opening scene of this story is related from an omniscient, "bird's eye" perspective: "A man stood on a railroad bridge in northern Alabama . . ."
- In stories told from a **limited third-person point of view,** readers' information is limited to what a single character feels, thinks, and observes: "A piece of dancing driftwood caught his attention . . ."

The point of view in this story shifts from omniscient to limited third-person. As the point of view shifts, so do the emotional tone and sense of time. To emphasize this change, Bierce introduces yet another narrative approach. He uses **stream of consciousness,** a technique in which a character's thoughts are presented as the mind experiences them—in short bursts without obvious logic. As you read, consider which events spark the thoughts and feelings the main character experiences.

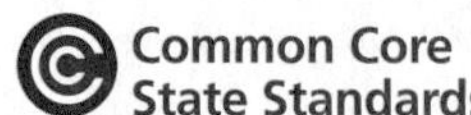

Reading Literature

3. Analyze the impact of the author's choices regarding how to develop and relate elements of a story.

5. Analyze how an author's choices concerning how to structure specific parts of a text contribute to its overall structure and meaning as well as its aesthetic impact.

Reading Strategy

Preparing to Read Complex Texts Bierce chooses to structure this story in three sections, each representing a shift in time and in chronological order. Clarify meaning by **analyzing the story's pattern of organization,** or *text structure*. Use a chart like the one shown to identify the time frame and events for each section. Then, analyze how this pattern of organization contributes to the story's meaning and impact.

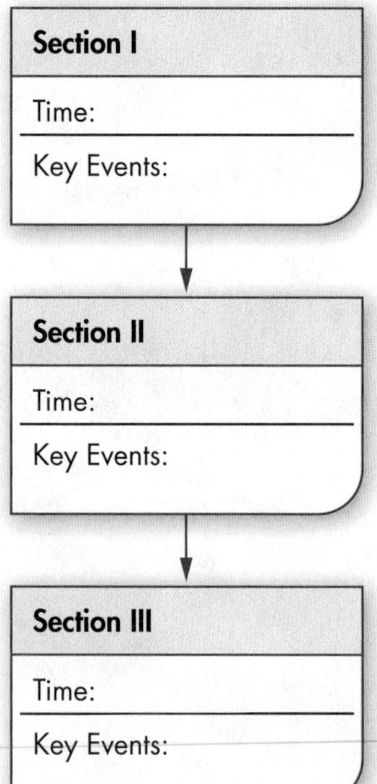

Vocabulary

etiquette (et′ i kit) *n.* appropriate behavior and ceremonies (p. 482)

deference (def′ ər əns) *n.* respect; courtesy; regard (p. 482)

dictum (dik′ təm) *n.* formal statement of fact or opinion (p. 483)

summarily (sə mer′ ə lē) *adv.* without formality; hastily (p. 484)

apprised (ə prīzd′) *v.* informed; notified (p. 485)

ineffable (in ef′ ə bəl) *adj.* too overwhelming to be spoken (p. 489)

AMBROSE BIERCE *(1842–1914?)*

Author of **"An Occurrence at Owl Creek Bridge"**

Ambrose Bierce's writing and worldview were shaped by his career as a Union officer in the Civil War. The poverty in which he was raised helped to foster Bierce's unsentimental outlook; the brutality he saw during the war cemented his cynicism. Bierce explored themes of cruelty and death in his writing, earning himself the nickname "Bitter Bierce."

A Civil War Soldier Bierce was born in Ohio and raised on a farm in Indiana. Having educated himself by reading his father's books, he left the farm while in his teens to attend a military academy in Kentucky. When the Civil War broke out, he enlisted in the Union army. Bierce fought in several important battles, rose from private to lieutenant, and won many awards for bravery. Toward the end of the war he was seriously wounded, but he returned to battle a few months later.

Poisoned Pen After the war, Bierce settled in San Francisco as a journalist. His "Prattler" column, which appeared in *The Argonaut* (1877–1879), the *Wasp* (1881–1886), and the *San Francisco Sunday Examiner* (1887–1896), mixed political and social satire, literary reviews, and gossip. The broodingly handsome writer was dubbed "the wickedest man in San Francisco" for his cynical and often malicious commentary. Yet Bierce's dark reputation only added to his personal popularity. He was a magnetic figure who charmed those around him despite the malice of his words.

Establishing His Legacy Although Bierce published many of his finest short stories in his column, he decided in the early 1890s to publish his collected short stories in two volumes entitled *Tales of Soldiers and Civilians* (1891) and *Can Such Things Be?* (1893). The concise, carefully plotted stories in these collections, set for the most part during the Civil War, capture the cruelty and futility of war and the indifference of death.

The Perfect Cynic Writer George Sterling wrote of Bierce, his longtime friend, that he "never troubled to conceal his justifiable contempt of humanity. . . . Bierce was a 'perfectionist,' a quality that in his case led to an intolerance involving merciless cruelty."

While he was successful professionally, Bierce found little happiness in a world where so few people met his expectations. His marriage ended in divorce, and both of his sons died at an early age. In 1913, at age 71, Bierce traveled to Mexico, a country in the midst of a bloody civil war. To this day, his fate is unknown, although a reasonable speculation is that he was killed during the siege of Ojinaga in 1914.

An Occurrence at Owl Creek Bridge

Ambrose Bierce

BACKGROUND *The senseless violence, death, and destruction Ambrose Bierce witnessed during the American Civil War (1861–1865) convinced him that war was terrible and futile. He set much of his best fiction, including this story, against the backdrop of this divisive war in which the agricultural South, whose economy was based on slavery, battled the more industrialized North. Fought mostly in the South, the war caused hundreds of thousands of casualties on both sides.*

I

A man stood upon a railroad bridge in northern Alabama, looking down into the swift water twenty feet below. The man's hands were behind his back, the wrists bound with a cord. A rope closely encircled his neck. It was attached to a stout cross timber above his head and the slack fell to the level of his knees. Some loose boards laid upon the sleepers supporting the metals of the railway supplied a footing for him and his executioners—two private soldiers of the Federal army, directed by a sergeant who in civil life may have been a deputy sheriff. At a short remove upon the same temporary platform was an officer in the uniform of his rank, armed. He was a captain. A sentinel at each end of the bridge stood with his rifle in the position known as "support," that is to say, vertical in front of the left shoulder, the hammer resting on the forearm thrown straight across the chest—a formal and unnatural position, enforcing an erect carriage of the body. It did not appear to be the duty of these two men to know what was occurring at the center of the bridge; they merely blockaded the two ends of the foot planking that traversed it.

Literary Analysis
Point of View Which details in the first paragraph show the use of the omniscient point of view? Explain.

Beyond one of the sentinels nobody was in sight; the railroad ran straight away into a forest for a hundred yards, then, curving, was lost to view. Doubtless there was an out-post farther along. The other bank of the stream was open ground—a gentle acclivity[1] topped with a stockade of vertical tree trunks, loopholed for rifles, with a single embrasure through which protruded the muzzle of a brass cannon commanding the bridge. Midway of the slope between bridge and fort were the spectators—a single company of infantry in line, at "parade rest," the butts of the rifles on the ground, the barrels inclining slightly backward against the right shoulder, the hands crossed upon the stock. A lieutenant stood at the right of the line, the point of his sword upon the ground, his left hand resting upon his right. Excepting the group of four at the center of the bridge, not a man moved. The company faced the bridge, staring stonily, motionless. The sentinels, facing the banks of the stream, might have been statues to adorn the

What event is about to take place on the bridge?

1. **acclivity** (ə kliv′ ə tē) *n.* upward slope.

Vocabulary

etiquette (et′ i kit) *n.* appropriate behavior and ceremonies

deference (def′ ər əns) *n.* respect; courtesy; regard

bridge. The captain stood with folded arms, silent, observing the work of his subordinates, but making no sign. Death is a dignitary who when he comes announced is to be received with formal manifestations of respect, even by those most familiar with him. In the code of military **etiquette** silence and fixity are forms of **deference**.

The man who was engaged in being hanged was apparently about thirty-five years of age. He was a civilian, if one might judge from his habit, which was that of a planter. His features were good—a straight nose, firm mouth, broad forehead, from which his long, dark hair was combed straight back, falling behind his ears to the collar of his well-fitting frock coat. He wore a mustache and pointed beard, but no whiskers; his eyes were large and dark gray, and had a kindly expression which one would hardly have expected in one whose neck was in the hemp. Evidently this was no vulgar assassin. The liberal military code makes provision for hanging many kinds of persons, and gentlemen are not excluded.

The preparations being complete, the two private soldiers stepped aside and each drew away the plank upon which he had been standing. The sergeant turned to the captain, saluted and placed himself immediately behind that officer, who in turn moved apart one pace. These movements left the condemned man and the sergeant standing on the two ends of the same plank, which spanned three of the crossties of the bridge. The end upon which the civilian stood almost, but not quite, reached a fourth. This plank had been held in place by the weight of the captain; it was now held by that of the sergeant. At a signal from the former the latter would step aside, the plank would tilt and the condemned man go down between two ties. The arrangement commended itself to his judgment as simple and effective. His face had not been covered nor his eyes bandaged. He looked a moment at his "unsteadfast footing," then let his gaze wander to the swirling water of the stream racing madly beneath his feet. A piece of dancing driftwood caught his attention and his eyes followed it down the current. How slowly it appeared to move! What a sluggish stream!

He closed his eyes in order to fix his last thoughts upon his wife and children. The water, touched to gold by the early sun, the brooding mists under the banks at some distance down the stream, the fort, the soldiers, the piece of drift—all had distracted him. And now he became conscious of a new disturbance. Striking through the thought of his dear ones was a sound which he could neither ignore nor understand, a sharp, distinct, metallic percussion like the stroke of a blacksmith's hammer upon the anvil; it had the same ringing quality. He wondered what it was, and whether immeasurably distant or near by—it seemed both. Its recurrence was regular, but as slow as the tolling of a death knell. He awaited each stroke with impatience and—he knew not why—apprehension. The intervals of silence grew progressively longer; the delays became maddening. With their greater infrequency the sounds increased in strength and sharpness. They hurt his ear like the thrust of a knife; he feared he would shriek. What he heard was the ticking of his watch.

He unclosed his eyes and saw again the water below him. "If I could free my hands," he thought, "I might throw off the noose and spring into the stream. By diving I could evade the bullets and, swimming vigorously, reach the bank, take to the woods and get away home. My home, thank God, is as yet outside their lines; my wife and little ones are still beyond the invader's farthest advance."

As these thoughts, which have here to be set down in words, were flashed into the doomed man's brain rather than evolved from it the captain nodded to the sergeant. The sergeant stepped aside.

II

Peyton Farquhar was a well-to-do planter, of an old and highly respected Alabama family. Being a slave owner and like other slave owners a politician he was naturally an original secessionist and ardently devoted to the Southern cause. Circumstances of an imperious nature, which it is unnecessary to relate here, had prevented him from taking service with the gallant army that had fought the disastrous campaigns ending with the fall of Corinth,[2] and he chafed under the inglorious restraint, longing for the release of his energies, the larger life of the soldier, the opportunity for distinction. That opportunity, he felt, would come, as it comes to all in war time. Meanwhile he did what he could. No service was too humble for him to perform in aid of the South, no adventure too perilous for him to undertake if consistent with the character of a civilian who was at heart a soldier, and who in good faith and without too much qualification assented to at least a part of the frankly villainous **dictum** that all is fair in love and war.

One evening while Farquhar and his wife were sitting on a rustic bench near the entrance to his grounds, a gray-clad soldier rode up to the gate and asked for a drink of water. Mrs. Farquhar was only too happy to serve him with her own white hands. While she was fetching the water her husband approached the dusty horseman and inquired eagerly for news from the front.

"The Yanks are repairing the railroads," said the man, "and are getting ready for another advance. They have reached the Owl Creek bridge, put it in order and built a stockade on the north

Spiral Review
Characterization
Identify one example of direct and one example of indirect characterization in this paragraph. Explain what you learn about Farquhar from each example.

Vocabulary
dictum (dik´ təm) *n.* formal statement of fact or opinion

In the war that divides his nation, which side does Farquhar support?

2. Corinth Mississippi town that was the site of an 1862 Civil War battle.

Vocabulary
summarily (sə mer′ ə lē) *adv.* without formality; hastily

bank. The commandant has issued an order, which is posted everywhere, declaring that any civilian caught interfering with the railroad, its bridges, tunnels or trains will be **summarily** hanged. I saw the order."

"How far is it to the Owl Creek bridge?" Farquhar asked.

"About thirty miles."

"Is there no force on this side the creek?"

"Only a picket post[3] half a mile out, on the railroad, and a single sentinel at this end of the bridge."

"Suppose a man—a civilian and student of hanging—should elude the picket post and perhaps get the better of the sentinel," said Farquhar, smiling, "what could he accomplish?"

The soldier reflected. "I was there a month ago," he replied. "I observed that the flood of last winter had lodged a great quantity of driftwood against the wooden pier at this end of the bridge. It is now dry and would burn like tow."[4]

The lady had now brought the water, which the soldier drank. He thanked her ceremoniously, bowed to her husband and rode away. An hour later, after nightfall, he repassed the plantation, going northward in the direction from which he had come. He was a Federal scout.

Reading Strategy
Analyzing Patterns of Organization
Describe the shift in time that occurs between sections II and III.

As Peyton Farquhar fell straight downward through the bridge he lost consciousness and was as one already dead. From this state he was awakened—ages later, it seemed to him—by the pain of a sharp pressure upon his throat, followed by a sense of suffocation. Keen, poignant agonies seemed to shoot from his neck downward through every fiber of his body and limbs. These pains appeared to flash along well-defined lines of ramification[5] and to beat with an inconceivably rapid periodicity. They seemed like streams of pulsating fire heating him to an intolerable temperature. As to his head, he was conscious of nothing but a feeling of fullness—of congestion. These sensations were unaccompanied by thought. The intellectual part of his nature was already effaced: he had power only to feel, and feeling was torment. He was conscious of motion. Encompassed in a luminous cloud, of which he was now merely the fiery heart, without material substance, he swung through unthinkable arcs of oscillation, like a vast pendulum. Then all at once, with terrible suddenness, the light about him shot upward with the noise of a loud plash; a frightful roaring was in his ears, and all was cold and dark. The power of thought was restored; he knew that the rope had broken and he had fallen into the stream. There was no additional strangulation; the

3. **picket post** troops sent ahead with news of a surprise attack.
4. **tow** (tō) *n.* coarse, broken fibers of hemp or flax before spinning.
5. **flash along well-defined lines of ramification** spread out quickly along branches from a central point.

noose about his neck was already suffocating him and kept the water from his lungs. To die of hanging at the bottom of a river!—the idea seemed to him ludicrous. He opened his eyes in the darkness and saw above him a gleam of light, but how distant, how inaccessible! He was still sinking, for the light became fainter and fainter until it was a mere glimmer. Then it began to grow and brighten, and he knew that he was rising toward the surface—knew it with reluctance, for he was now very comfortable. "To be hanged and drowned," he thought, "that is not so bad; but I do not wish to be shot. No; I will not be shot; that is not fair."

He was not conscious of an effort, but a sharp pain in his wrist **apprised** him that he was trying to free his hands. He gave the struggle his attention, as an idler might observe the feat of a juggler, without interest in the outcome. What splendid effort!—what magnificent, what superhuman strength! Ah, that was a fine endeavor! Bravo! The cord fell away; his arms parted and floated upward, the hands dimly seen on each side in the growing light. He watched them with a new interest as first one and then the other pounced upon the noose at his neck. They tore it away and thrust it fiercely aside, its undulations resembling those of a water-snake. "Put it back, put it back!" He thought he shouted these words to his hands, for the undoing of the noose had been succeeded by the direst pang that he had yet experienced. His neck ached horribly; his brain was on fire; his heart, which had been fluttering faintly, gave a great leap, trying to force itself out at his mouth. His whole body was racked and wrenched with an insupportable anguish! But his disobedient hands gave no heed to the command. They beat the water vigorously with quick, downward strokes, forcing him to the surface. He felt his head emerge; his eyes were blinded by the sunlight; his chest expanded convulsively, and with a supreme and crowning agony his lungs engulfed a great draft of air, which instantly he expelled in a shriek!

He was now in full possession of his physical senses. They were, indeed, preternaturally[6] keen and alert. Something in the awful disturbance of his organic system had so exalted and refined them that they made record of things never before perceived. He felt the ripples upon his face and heard their separate sounds as they struck. He looked at the forest on the bank of the stream, saw the individual trees, the leaves and the veining of each leaf—saw the very insects upon them: the locusts, the brilliant-bodied flies, the gray spiders

6. **preternaturally** (prēt′ ər nach′ ər əl ē) *adv.* abnormally; extraordinarily.

LITERATURE IN CONTEXT

History Connection

The Battle of Shiloh

Owl Creek is the stream that runs through Tennessee at the site of one of the bloodiest battles of the Civil War—the Battle of Shiloh—where more than 20,000 soldiers died. Railroad bridges like Owl Creek Bridge were important because they gave the armies access over bodies of water.

Connect to the Literature

Why does Farquhar ask so many questions about the bridge?

Vocabulary

apprised (ə prīzd′) *v.* informed; notified

What surprising event happens after Farquhar first loses consciousness?

▲ Critical Viewing
Explain the connection between the illustrations on this and the facing page and their relationship to the story. **[Connect]**

stretching their webs from twig to twig. He noted the prismatic colors in all the dewdrops upon a million blades of grass. The humming of the gnats that danced above the eddies of the stream, the beating of the dragonflies' wings, the strokes of the water spiders' legs, like oars which had lifted their boat—all these made audible music. A fish slid along beneath his eyes and he heard the rush of its body parting the water.

He had come to the surface facing down the stream; in a moment the visible world seemed to wheel slowly round, himself the pivotal point, and he saw the bridge, the fort, the soldiers upon the bridge, the captain, the sergeant, the two privates, his executioners. They were in silhouette against the blue sky. They shouted and gesticulated, pointing at him. The captain had drawn his pistol, but did not fire; the others were unarmed. Their movements were grotesque and horrible, their forms gigantic.

Suddenly he heard a sharp report and something struck the water smartly within a few inches of his head, spattering his face with spray. He heard a second report, and saw one of the sentinels with his rifle at his shoulder, a light cloud of blue smoke rising from the muzzle. The man in the water saw the eye of the man on the bridge gazing into his own through the sights of the rifle. He observed that it was a gray eye and remembered having read that gray eyes were keenest, and that all famous marksmen had them. Nevertheless, this one had missed.

A counterswirl had caught Farquhar and turned him half round; he was again looking into the forest on the bank opposite the fort. The sound of a clear, high voice in a monotonous singsong now rang out behind him and came across the water with a distinctness that pierced and subdued all other sounds, even the beating of the ripples in his ears. Although no soldier, he had frequented camps enough to know the dread significance of that deliberate, drawling, aspirated chant; the lieutenant on shore was taking a part in the morning's work. How coldly and pitilessly—with what an even, calm intonation, presaging,[7] and enforcing tranquillity in the men—with what accurately measured intervals fell those cruel words:

"Attention, company! . . . Shoulder arms! . . . Ready! . . . Aim! . . . Fire!"

Farquhar dived—dived as deeply as he could. The water roared in his ears like the voice of Niagara, yet he heard the dulled thunder of the volley and, rising again toward the surface, met shining bits of metal, singularly flattened, oscillating slowly downward. Some of them touched him on the face and hands, then fell away, continuing their descent. One lodged between his collar and neck; it was uncomfortably warm and he snatched it out.

As he rose to the surface, gasping for breath, he saw that he had been a long time under water; he was perceptibly farther down stream—nearer to safety. The soldiers had almost finished reloading; the metal ramrods flashed all at once in the sunshine as they were drawn from the barrels, turned in the air, and thrust into their sockets. The two sentinels fired again, independently and ineffectually.

The hunted man saw all this over his shoulder; he was now swimming vigorously with the current. His brain was as energetic as his arms and legs; he thought with the rapidity of lightning.

"The officer," he reasoned, "will not make that martinet's[8] error a second time. It is as easy to dodge a volley as a single shot. He has probably already given the command to fire at will. God help me, I cannot dodge them all!"

How do the soldiers try to stop Farquhar after he dives?

An appalling plash within two yards of him was followed by a loud, rushing sound, *diminuendo,*[9] which seemed to travel back through the air to the fort and died in an explosion which stirred the very river to its deeps! A rising sheet of water curved over him, fell down upon him, blinded him, strangled him! The cannon had taken a hand in the game. As he shook his head free from the commotion of the smitten water he heard the deflected shot humming through the air ahead, and in an instant it was cracking and smashing the branches in the forest beyond.

"They will not do that again," he thought; "the next time they

---

7. **presaging** (prē sāj′ iŋ) *v.* predicting; warning.
8. **martinet** (märt′ 'n et′) *n.* strict military disciplinarian.
9. **diminuendo** (də min′ yo͞o en′ dō) *adj.* musical term used to describe a gradual reduction in volume.

will use a charge of grape.[10] I must keep my eye upon the gun; the smoke will apprise me—the report arrives too late; it lags behind the missile. That is a good gun."

Literary Analysis
Point of View and Stream of Consciousness
What clues suggest Farquhar may not be totally reliable as a witness?

Suddenly he felt himself whirled round and round—spinning like a top. The water, the banks, the forests, the now distant bridge, fort and men—all were commingled and blurred. Objects were represented by their colors only; circular horizontal streaks of color—that was all he saw. He had been caught in a vortex and was being whirled on with a velocity of advance and gyration that made him giddy and sick. In a few moments he was flung upon the gravel at the foot of the left bank of the stream—the southern bank—and behind a projecting point which concealed him from his enemies. The sudden arrest of his motion, the abrasion of one of his hands on the gravel, restored him, and he wept with delight. He dug his fingers into the sand, threw it over himself in handfuls and audibly blessed it. It looked like diamonds, rubies, emeralds; he could think of nothing beautiful which it did not resemble. The trees upon the bank were giant garden plants; he noted a definite order in their arrangement, inhaled the fragrance of their blooms. A strange, roseate[11] light shone through the spaces among their trunks and the wind made in their branches the music of aeolian harps.[12] He had no wish to perfect his escape—was content to remain in that enchanting spot until retaken.

Suddenly he felt himself whirled round and round—spinning like a top.

A whiz and rattle of grapeshot among the branches high above his head roused him from his dream. The baffled cannoneer had fired him a random farewell. He sprang to his feet, rushed up the sloping bank, and plunged into the forest.

All that day he traveled, laying his course by the rounding sun. The forest seemed interminable; nowhere did he discover a break in it, not even a woodman's road. He had not known that he lived in so wild a region. There was something uncanny in the revelation.

By night fall he was fatigued, footsore, famishing. The thought of his wife and children urged him on. At last he found a road which led him in what he knew to be the right direction. It was as wide and straight as a city street, yet it seemed untraveled. No fields bordered it, no dwelling anywhere. Not so much as the barking of a dog suggested human habitation. The black bodies of the trees formed a straight wall on both sides, terminating on the horizon in a point, like a diagram in a lesson in perspective. Overhead, as he looked up through this rift in the wood, shone great golden stars looking unfamiliar and grouped in strange constellations. He was sure they were arranged in some order which had a secret and malign significance. The wood on either side was full of singular noises, among which—once, twice, and again, he distinctly heard whispers in an unknown tongue.

---

10. **charge of grape** cluster of small iron balls—"grape shot"—that disperse once fired from a cannon.

11. **roseate** (rō′ zē it) *adj.* rose-colored.

12. **aeolian** (ē ō′ lē ən) **harps** stringed instruments that produce music when played by the wind. In Greek mythology, Aeolus is the god of the winds.

His neck was in pain and lifting his hand to it he found it horribly swollen. He knew that it had a circle of black where the rope had bruised it. His eyes felt congested: he could no longer close them. His tongue was swollen with thirst; he relieved its fever by thrusting it forward from between his teeth into the cold air. How softly the turf had carpeted the untraveled avenue—he could no longer feel the roadway beneath his feet!

Doubtless, despite his suffering, he had fallen asleep while walking, for now he sees another scene—perhaps he has merely recovered from a delirium. He stands at the gate of his own home. All is as he left it, and all bright and beautiful in the morning sunshine. He must have traveled the entire night. As he pushes open the gate and passes up the wide white walk, he sees a flutter of female garments: his wife, looking fresh and cool and sweet, steps down from the veranda to meet him. At the bottom of the steps she stands waiting, with a smile of **ineffable** joy, an attitude of matchless grace and dignity. Ah, how beautiful she is! He springs forward with extended arms. As he is about to clasp her he feels a stunning blow upon the back of the neck; a blinding white light blazes all about him with a sound like the shock of a cannon—then all is darkness and silence!

Vocabulary
ineffable (in ef′ ə bəl) *adj.* too overwhelming to be spoken

Peyton Farquhar was dead; his body, with a broken neck, swung gently from side to side beneath the timbers of the Owl Creek bridge.

Critical Reading

Cite textual evidence to support your responses.

1. **Key Ideas and Details** **(a)** Identify one example of Farquhar's distorted perceptions. **(b) Interpret:** What causes this distortion?
2. **Key Ideas and Details** **(a)** What does Farquhar visualize moments before he is hanged? **(b) Connect:** How is his journey connected with this earlier vision?
3. **Craft and Structure** **(a)** What sensation does Farquhar experience "with terrible suddenness"? **(b) Distinguish:** Which details suggest that Farquhar's escape occurs in his mind?
4. **Key Ideas and Details** **(a)** What does this story suggest about the psychology of a person facing a life or death situation? **(b) Speculate:** Are such insights applicable in daily life, or merely in extreme circumstances, like those of war? Explain.
5. **Integration of Knowledge and Ideas** How does the contrast between the ordinary settings and the awful events of this story add to its power? Explain. In your response, use at least two of these Essential Question words: *heighten, conflict, tension, perspective.* ***[Connecting to the Essential Question: What is the relationship between literature and place?]***

After You Read | An Occurrence at Owl Creek Bridge

Literary Analysis

1. **Craft and Structure** Reread the story to find examples of the two different **points of view** Bierce uses. Then, using a chart like the one shown, analyze the effects of these choices.

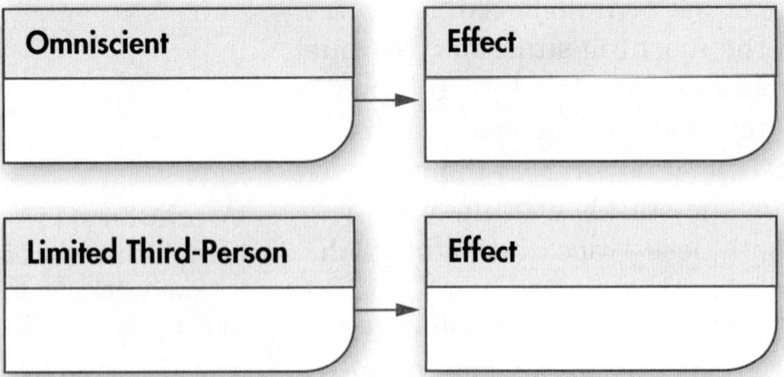

2. **Craft and Structure (a)** What point of view does Bierce use in Section III? **(b)** Explain why this choice of point of view is essential to the story's overall impact.
3. **Craft and Structure** What is the effect of the shift in point of view in the last paragraph of the story? Explain.
4. **Craft and Structure (a)** Which details in the second paragraph of Section III are revealed through the use of **stream of consciousness? (b)** What is the "sharp pain" that sparks Farquhar's thoughts? **(c)** In what ways does this passage mimic the natural, jumbled flow of thought?
5. **Craft and Structure** Why is the stream-of-consciousness technique particularly appropriate for this story?

Reading Strategy

6. Clarify meaning by **analyzing the story's pattern of organization. (a)** Explain how the time frame of the story shifts from Section I to Section II and from Section II to Section III. **(b)** How does the style of writing shift from section to section?
7. **(a)** What do you learn in Section II about the main character's home life, political loyalties, and motivations? **(b)** How does this detailed information shed light on the scene described in Section I? Explain.
8. At the end of the story, what do you suddenly understand about both the scene described in Section I and the incident described in Section II?
9. How important do you think the structure of this story is to its overall power and effect on the reader? Explain, citing specific story details in your response.

Common Core State Standards

Writing

2. Write explanatory texts to examine and convey complex ideas, concepts, and information clearly and accurately through the effective selection, organization, and analysis of content. *(p. 491)*

2.b. Develop the topic thoroughly by selecting the most significant quotations or other information and examples appropriate to the audience's knowledge of the topic. *(p. 491)*

9.a. Apply *grades 11–12 Reading* standards to literature. *(p. 491)*

Language

3. Apply knowledge of language to make effective choices for meaning. *(p. 491)*

PERFORMANCE TASKS

Integrated Language Skills

Vocabulary Acquisition and Use

Word Analysis: Latin Root *-dict-*

The noun *dictum* derives from the Latin root *-dict-*, meaning "saying; expression; word." Words that share this root include *verdict* and *dictionary.* Decide whether each of the following statements is true or false and explain each answer. In your explanation, demonstrate your understanding of the meaning of the root *-dict-* in words with different meanings and parts of speech.

1. If two arguments are nearly identical, there is a *contradiction* of terms.
2. An *unpredictable* disaster is one that cannot be avoided.
3. A governmental *edict* is usually written in a formal style.
4. A school board often has *jurisdiction* to establish regulations relating to school safety.
5. Writers who prefer not to type might *dictate* their stories for someone to transcribe.
6. Radio announcers do not need clear *diction* in order to do their jobs well.

Vocabulary: Revising Sentences for Logic

Revise each sentence below so that the underlined vocabulary word is used logically and effectively. Do not change the word.

Example: His preparation for the exam gave him a feeling of apprehension.
Corrected Sentence: His lack of preparation for the exam gave him a feeling of apprehension.

1. He followed proper etiquette and offended nearly everyone in attendance.
2. The judge acted so summarily that we were certain her decision was just.
3. A dictum is likely to use slang or dialect in order to keep an informal tone.
4. In deference to the elders' frailty, we asked them to walk to the reunion.
5. The moment had an ineffable quality that was perfectly described by the soldier.
6. The reporter had not been apprised of the breaking news, so she scooped the story.

Writing

Explanatory Text Bierce was among the first writers to use stream of consciousness, a *stylistic device* that imitates the natural flow of thoughts and feelings. In an **essay,** explain how Bierce's use of this technique adds to the story's drama.

Prewriting Reread the story and generate a list of selected passages in which the use of stream of consciousness helps you understand Farquhar's thoughts and feelings. Then, select the two or three most significant passages to discuss.

Drafting Focus on one passage at a time. Explain why the use of stream-of-consciousness narration reveals the character's thoughts with heightened realism and drama.

Model: Incorporating Quotations From the Story
Through stream of consciousness, Bierce enables readers to empathize with Farquhar as he desperately imagines a struggle to save his life. The moment of full peace when he reunites with his wife is especially powerful. In his own words, Farquhar thinks he "must have traveled the entire night."

Appropriate quotations from the story create strong connections between the writer's opinions and the text.

Revising As you review your draft, note points where quotations from the story will help support your opinions and analysis. To assure effective organization, make strong connections between your opinions and each passage you are quoting.

Primary Sources

Civil War Diaries and Journals

Mary Chesnut's Civil War

A Confederate Account of the Battle of Gettysburg

Recollections of a Private

Common Core State Standards

Reading Informational Text

1. Cite strong and thorough textual evidence to support analysis of what the text says explicitly as well as inferences drawn from the text, including determining where the text leaves matters uncertain.

6. Determine an author's point of view or purpose in a text.

9. Analyze nineteenth-century foundational U.S. documents of historical and literary significance for their themes, purposes, and rhetorical features.

About the Text Forms

Diaries and **journals** are personal records of events, thoughts, feelings, and observations. These texts are written informally in a series of dated entries, express the writer's immediate responses to events, and use the first-person pronouns *I* and *we*.

Diaries and journals tell us a great deal about each writer's beliefs, political leanings, values, and experience of life. While most remain unpublished, some that are especially powerful or shed light on historical events, such as these Civil War writings, may be published after the writer's death.

Reading Strategy

Generating questions, or asking questions about a text as you read, can help you focus your reading and better understand the *authors' purposes and perspectives* in historical documents. As you read these diaries and journals, pose questions such as the following:

- *What main purpose prompts the writer to record these experiences?*
- *What does the writer's use of language suggest about his or her position in life?*
- *What does the writer feel or believe about the Civil War? Why? Does the writer express a thematic insight about war in general? If so, how does it relate to those expressed in similar texts?*
- *Does the writer state opinions, feelings, and beliefs directly or implicitly through observation and descriptions?*
- *What clues suggest an opinion or belief is being stated?*

As you read, generate questions to help you better understand each author's position on the Civil War and other aspects of life during that era.

What is the **relationship** between literature and *place?*

The Civil War was fought on American soil and in American waters. Reading these diary and journal entries will help you see how the war caused people to view their own towns, hillsides, and harbors differently. As you read, note details that describe various locations as being unfamiliar, comforting, strange, or frightening.

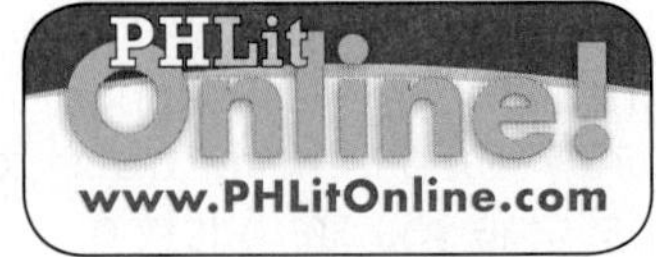

Note-Taking Guide

Primary-source documents are a rich source of information for researchers. As you read these documents, use a note-taking guide like the one shown to organize relevant and accurate information.

1 Type of Document (check one)
☐ Newspaper ☐ Advertisement ☐ Telegram ☐ Letter
☐ Press Release ☐ Diary or Journal ☐ E-mail ☐ Report

2 Date(s) of Document ______________________________

3 Author of Document ______________________________

Author's Position, Title, or Circumstances ______________________________

4 Purpose and Audience: Why and for whom was the document written? ______________________________

____

5 Document Information

a List two observations or pieces of information given near the beginning of the document that strike you as important. ______________________________

____

b Ask a question about each piece of information. ______________________________

____

c Identify answers. ______________________________

____

d If answers are not clear, explain how you might find them. ______________________________

____

____

Reading Strategy
Generating Questions
A primary source document may raise questions in your mind about a historical event. Pay attention to these questions and use them to focus your reading.

This guide was adapted from the **U.S. National Archives** Document Analysis Worksheets.

Vocabulary

adjourned (ə jʉrnd´) *v.* closed for a time (p. 495)

convention (kən ven´ shən) *n.* a meeting attended by members or delegates (p. 495)

intercepted (in´ tər sept´ əd) *v.* seized or stopped something on its way from one place to another (p. 496)

obstinate (äb´ stə nət) *adj.* stubborn (p. 497)

recruits (ri kro͞ots) *n.* newly drafted soldiers (p. 500)

fluctuation (fluk´ cho͞o ā´ shən) *n.* a change in level or intensity (p. 500)

spectator (spek´ tāt´ ər) *n.* a person who watches something without taking part in it (p. 501)

offensive (ô´ fen´ siv) *n.* an attitude or position of attack (p. 502)

brigade (bri gād´) *n.* a unit of soldiers (p. 502)

entrenchments (en trench´ mənts) *n.* long, deep holes with steep sides, used as defense against enemy fire (p. 503)

THE STORY BEHIND THE DOCUMENTS

Mary Chesnut

Randolph McKim

In the early days of April 1861, the nation held its collective breath. South Carolina and six other Southern states had recently seceded, or split away; formed their own government; and elected Jefferson Davis as the president of their new Confederacy. Meanwhile, Abraham Lincoln had been inaugurated as president of the United States. When he refused to acknowledge the Confederacy as a separate entity, an armed conflict between the two regions seemed inevitable.

The drama was centered on a massive fort that stood in the harbor of Charleston, South Carolina. Since December 26, 1860, Fort Sumter had housed 85 unwelcome Union soldiers and their commander. In spite of stern warnings from the Confederate army, the Union troops refused to budge. Meanwhile, their food supplies began to dwindle.

It was an uneasy stalemate: neither the North nor the South wanted to fire the first shot. On April 6, President Lincoln ordered supplies sent to Fort Sumter. The gesture was seen as a threat. Southern leaders decided to attack the fort before the shipment arrived.

As the attack began at 4:30 A.M. on April 12, 1861, citizens of Charleston clambered to their rooftops to watch the action. **Mary Boykin Chesnut** (1823–1886) was one of these spectators. Raised in a wealthy aristocratic family, Boykin married James Chesnut, Jr., a senator and a Confederate officer. While her diary provides a detailed account of the events at Fort Sumter, it also conveys the mixture of optimism and dread felt by most Southern aristocrats during the opening days of the war.

Once the war was underway, men hurried to enlist in what most believed would be a swift and glorious conflict. Some saw the military as an opportunity for adventure and advancement, as we learn from the journal of Union soldier **Warren Lee Goss.** Like Goss, most soldiers were young—21 on average—and had no military experience. These naive young men quickly learned that war meant misery, not glory.

Perhaps no other Civil War battle was as painful as the Battle of Gettysburg, in which 51,000 men were either wounded or killed. From July 1 to July 3, 1863, Union and Confederate troops fought near the small town of Gettysburg, Pennsylvania. After Union troops gained control of the nearby hills, the Confederate troops launched a risky attack on the strongest Union position. The attack—described as both "gallant" and "terrible" in the diary of Confederate soldier **Randolph McKim**—was a bitter failure.

Although Chesnut, Goss, and McKim experienced the Civil War in different ways, their diaries and journals reveal profound similarities. They all try to make sense of a fearful unknown, and to contribute, in some way, to the safety and well-being of their loved ones, their companions, and the country and ideals they cherish.

from Mary Chesnut's CIVIL WAR

Mary Chesnut

BACKGROUND As Mary Chesnut notes in the first diary entry below, plans for an attack on Fort Sumter have been made, and the citizens of Charleston wait with both excitement and anxiety for something—or nothing—to happen.

APRIL 7, 1861. Today things seem to have settled down a little.

One can but hope still. Lincoln or Seward[1] have made such silly advances and then far sillier drawings back. There may be a chance for peace, after all.

Things are happening so fast.

My husband has been made an aide-de-camp[2] of General Beauregard.

Three hours ago we were quietly packing to go home. The convention has adjourned.

Now he tells me the attack upon Fort Sumter[3] may begin tonight. Depends upon Anderson and the fleet outside. The *Herald* says that this show of war outside of the bar is intended for Texas.

John Manning came in with his sword and red sash. Pleased as a boy to be on Beauregard's staff while the row goes on. He has gone with Wigfall to Captain Hartstene with instructions.

Mr. Chesnut is finishing a report he had to make to the convention.

Mrs. Hayne called. She had, she said, "but one feeling, pity for those who are not here."

Jack Preston, Willie Alston—"the take-life-easys," as they are called—with John Green, "the big brave," have gone down to the island—volunteered as privates.

Seven hundred men were sent over. Ammunition wagons rumbling along the streets all night. Anderson burning blue lights—signs and signals for the fleet outside, I suppose.

Primary Sources

Diaries and Journals What details of style and form tell you that you are reading a diary or journal entry?

Vocabulary

adjourned (ə jurnd′) *v.* closed for a time

convention (kən ven′ shən) *n.* a meeting attended by members or delegates

What event might happen on the night of April 7, 1861?

1. **Seward** William Henry Seward (1801–1872), U.S. Secretary of State from 1861 through 1869.
2. **aide-de-camp** (ād′ də kamp′) *n.* officer serving as assistant and confidential secretary to a superior.
3. **Fort Sumter** fort in Charleston Harbor, South Carolina. At the time, the fort was occupied by Union troops commanded by Major Robert Anderson.

Bombardment of Sumter, Harper's Weekly, 1861

▶ **Primary Source: Art**
Describe the spectators' differing reactions to the attack on Fort Sumter as shown in this illustration. **[Distinguish]**

Primary Sources
Diaries and Journals
Judging from her list of dinner guests, what do you understand about Mary Chesnut's social circumstances?

Today at dinner there was no allusion to things as they stand in Charleston Harbor. There was an undercurrent of intense excitement. There could not have been a more brilliant circle. In addition to our usual quartet (Judge Withers, Langdon Cheves, and Trescot) our two governors dined with us, Means and Manning.

These men all talked so delightfully. For once in my life I listened.

That over, business began. In earnest, Governor Means rummaged a sword and red sash from somewhere and brought it for Colonel Chesnut, who has gone to demand the surrender of Fort Sumter.

And now, patience—we must wait.

Why did that green goose Anderson go into Fort Sumter? Then everything began to go wrong.

Now they have intercepted a letter from him, urging them to let him surrender. He paints the horrors likely to ensue if they will not.

He ought to have thought of all that before he put his head in the hole.

Vocabulary
intercepted (in′ tər sept′ əd) *v.* seized or stopped something on its way from one place to another

APRIL 12, 1861. Anderson will not capitulate.

Yesterday was the merriest, maddest dinner we have had yet. Men were more audaciously wise and witty. We had an unspoken foreboding it was to be our last pleasant meeting. Mr. Miles dined with us today. Mrs. Henry King rushed in: "The news, I come for the latest news—all of the men of the King family are on the island"—of which fact she seemed proud.

While she was here, our peace negotiator—or envoy—came in. That is, Mr. Chesnut returned—his interview with Colonel Anderson had been deeply interesting—but was not inclined to be communicative, wanted his dinner. Felt for Anderson. Had telegraphed to President Davis[4] for instructions.

What answer to give Anderson, etc., etc. He has gone back to Fort Sumter with additional instructions.

When they were about to leave the wharf, A. H. Boykin sprang into the boat, in great excitement; thought himself ill-used. A likelihood of fighting—and he to be left behind!

I do not pretend to go to sleep. How can I? If Anderson does not accept terms—at four—the orders are—he shall be fired upon.

I count four—St. Michael chimes. I begin to hope. At half-past four, the heavy booming of a cannon.

I sprang out of bed. And on my knees—prostrate—I prayed as I never prayed before.

There was a sound of stir all over the house—pattering of feet in the corridor—all seemed hurrying one way. I put on my double gown and a shawl and went, too. It was to the housetop.

The shells were bursting. In the dark I heard a man say "waste of ammunition."

I knew my husband was rowing about in a boat somewhere in that dark bay. And that the shells were roofing it over—bursting toward the fort. If Anderson was obstinate—he was to order the forts on our side to open fire. Certainly fire had begun. The regular roar of the cannon—there it was. And who could tell what each volley accomplished of death and destruction.

The women were wild, there on the housetop. Prayers from the women and imprecations from the men, and then a shell would light up the scene. Tonight, they say, the forces are to attempt to land.

The *Harriet Lane*[5] had her wheelhouse[6] smashed and put back to sea.

Reading Strategy
Generating Questions What questions might you ask about Chesnut's daily life?

Vocabulary
obstinate (äb´ stə nət) *adj.* stubborn

What happens at half past four on April 12, 1861?

---

4. **President Davis** Jefferson Davis (1808–1889), president of the Confederacy (1861–1865).
5. **The *Harriet Lane*** federal steamer that had brought provisions to Fort Sumter.
6. **wheelhouse** *n.* enclosed place on the upper deck of a ship, in which the helmsman stands while steering.

We watched up there—everybody wondered. Fort Sumter did not fire a shot.

Today Miles and Manning, colonels now—aides to Beauregard—dined with us. The latter hoped I would keep the peace. I give him only good words, for he was to be under fire all day and night, in the bay carrying orders, etc.

Last night—or this morning truly—up on the housetop I was so weak and weary I sat down on something that looked like a black stool.

"Get up, you foolish woman—your dress is on fire," cried a man. And he put me out.

It was a chimney, and the sparks caught my clothes. Susan Preston and Mr. Venable then came up. But my fire had been extinguished before it broke out into a regular blaze.

Do you know, after all that noise and our tears and prayers, nobody has been hurt. Sound and fury, signifying nothing.[7] A delusion and a snare. . . .

Somebody came in just now and reported Colonel Chesnut asleep on the sofa in General Beauregard's room. After two such nights he must be so tired as to be able to sleep anywhere. . . .

Primary Sources
Diaries and Journals
What do you learn from the entry of April 13, 1861, that you would probably not learn from a textbook?

APRIL 13, 1861. Nobody hurt, after all. How gay we were last night.

Reaction after the dread of all the slaughter we thought those dreadful cannons were making such a noise in doing.

Not even a battery[8] the worse for wear.

Fort Sumter has been on fire. He has not yet silenced any of our guns. So the aides—still with swords and red sashes by way of uniform—tell us.

But the sound of those guns makes regular meals impossible. None of us go to table. But tea trays pervade the corridors, going everywhere.

Some of the anxious hearts lie on their beds and moan in solitary misery. Mrs. Wigfall and I solace ourselves with tea in my room.

These women have all a satisfying faith.

APRIL 15, 1861. I did not know that one could live such days of excitement.

---

7. Sound . . . nothing from Shakespeare's *Macbeth*, Act V, Scene v, lines 27–28. Macbeth is contemplating the significance of life and death after learning of his wife's death.
8. battery *n.* artillery unit.

They called, “Come out—there is a crowd coming.”

A mob indeed, but it was headed by Colonels Chesnut and Manning.

The crowd was shouting and showing these two as messengers of good news. They were escorted to Beauregard’s headquarters. Fort Sumter had surrendered.

Those up on the housetop shouted to us, “The fort is on fire.” That had been the story once or twice before.

When we had calmed down, Colonel Chesnut, who had taken it all quietly enough—if anything, more unruffled than usual in his serenity—told us how the surrender came about.

Wigfall was with them on Morris Island when he saw the fire in the fort, jumped in a little boat and, with his handkerchief as a white flag, rowed over to Fort Sumter. Wigfall went in through a porthole.

When Colonel Chesnut arrived shortly after and was received by the regular entrance, Colonel Anderson told him he had need to pick his way warily, for it was all mined.

As far as I can make out, the fort surrendered to Wigfall.

But it is all confusion. Our flag is flying there. Fire engines have been sent to put out the fire.

Everybody tells you half of something and then rushes off to tell something else or to hear the last news. . . .

Critical Reading

1. **Key Ideas and Details (a)** What significant events does Chesnut describe in her diary? **(b) Interpret:** What does her diary reveal about daily life during these historical events? **(c) Evaluate:** Do you find anything surprising about Chesnut’s depiction of the events themselves or of people’s reactions to them? Explain.
2. **Key Ideas and Details (a)** What role does Chesnut’s husband play in the events at Fort Sumter? **(b) Infer:** What does his response to the events and the people involved tell you about him? **(c) Hypothesize:** Do you think the Chesnuts’ feelings about the events mirror those of most other Southerners? Explain.
3. **Key Ideas and Details (a)** Does Chesnut seem worried about the fate of her hometown, or does she seem to feel safe even in the face of battle? Cite details to support your answer. **(b)** What do you think explains Chesnut’s attitude?

▲ **Primary Source: Art** What attitude toward war does this 1861 painting of a young Civil War soldier convey? Explain. **[Analyze]**

Recollections of A PRIVATE

Warren Lee Goss

In the weeks that followed the attack on Fort Sumter, thousands of men on both sides volunteered to fight. Among the early enlistees was young Warren Lee Goss of Massachusetts.

"Cold chills" ran up and down my back as I got out of bed after the sleepless night, and shaved preparatory to other desperate deeds of valor. I was twenty years of age, and when anything unusual was to be done, like fighting or courting, I shaved.

With a nervous tremor convulsing my system, and my heart thumping like muffled drumbeats, I stood before the door of the recruiting office, and before turning the knob to enter read and reread the advertisement for recruits posted thereon, until I knew all its peculiarities. The promised chances for "travel and promotion" seemed good, and I thought I might have made a mistake in considering war so serious after all. "Chances for travel!" I must confess now, after four years of soldiering, that the "chances for travel" were no myth; but "promotion" was a little uncertain and slow.

I was in no hurry to open the door. Though determined to enlist, I was half inclined to put it off awhile; I had a fluctuation of desires; I was fainthearted and brave; I wanted to enlist, and yet— Here I turned the knob, and was relieved. . . .

My first uniform was a bad fit: My trousers were too long by three or four inches; the flannel shirt was coarse and unpleasant, too large at the neck and too short elsewhere. The forage cap[1] was an ungainly bag with pasteboard top and leather visor; the blouse was the only part which seemed decent; while the overcoat made me feel like a little nubbin of corn in a large preponderance of husk. Nothing except "Virginia mud" ever took down my ideas of military pomp quite so low.

Vocabulary

recruits (ri kro͞ots) *n.* newly drafted soldiers

fluctuation (fluk′ cho͞o ā′ shən) *n.* a change in level or intensity

1. **forage cap** cap worn by infantry soldiers.

After enlisting I did not seem of so much consequence as I had expected. There was not so much excitement on account of my military appearance as I deemed justly my due. I was taught my facings, and at the time I thought the drillmaster needlessly fussy about shouldering, ordering, and presenting arms. At this time men were often drilled in company and regimental evolutions long before they learned the manual of arms, because of the difficulty of obtaining muskets. These we obtained at an early day, but we would willingly have resigned them after carrying them a few hours. The musket, after an hour's drill, seemed heavier and less ornamental than it had looked to be.

The first day I went out to drill, getting tired of doing the same things over and over, I said to the drill sergeant: "Let's stop this fooling and go over to the grocery." His only reply was addressed to a corporal: "Corporal, take this man out and drill him"; and the corporal did! I found that suggestions were not so well appreciated in the army as in private life, and that no wisdom was equal to a drillmaster's "Right face," "Left wheel," and "Right, oblique, march." It takes a raw recruit some time to learn that he is not to think or suggest, but obey. Some never do learn. I acquired it at last, in humility and mud, but it was tough. Yet I doubt if my patriotism, during my first three weeks' drill, was quite knee high. Drilling looks easy to a spectator, but it isn't. After a time I had cut down my uniform so that I could see out of it, and had conquered the drill sufficiently to see through it. Then the word came: on to Washington! . . .

Reading Strategy
Generating Questions
What question might you ask about Goss's future as a soldier?

Vocabulary
spectator (spek´ tāt´ ər) *n.* a person who watches something without taking part in it

Critical Reading

1. **Key Ideas and Details (a) Summarize:** Describe Warren Lee Goss's feelings on the day he was to enlist in the army. **(b) Analyze:** How did Private Goss's attitudes and expectations change after he enlisted?
2. **Key Ideas and Details (a)** According to Goss, what takes a long time for a recruit to learn? **(b) Infer:** What do you think happened to cause him to say, "I acquired it at last, in humility and in mud, but it was tough"?
3. **Integration of Knowledge and Ideas (a) Make a Judgment:** In your view, how well suited is Goss for military life? **(b) Generalize:** How similar or different do you think Goss might be to other young men in his situation? Explain.

A Confederate Account of the BATTLE OF GETTYSBURG

Randolph McKim

The Battle of Gettysburg is often referred to as the "turning point" in the Civil War—the point at which the North gained the upper hand. In his diary, Confederate soldier Randolph McKim recounts the bravery of his companions, many of whom were killed or wounded during the advance on Culp's Hill. The advance was led by McKim himself.

Vocabulary
offensive (ô´ fen´ siv) *n.* an attitude or position of attack
brigade (bri gād´) *n.* a unit of soldiers

Then came General Ewell's order to assume the offensive and assail the crest of Culp's Hill, on our right. . . . The works to be stormed ran almost at right angles to those we occupied. Moreover, there was a double line of entrenchments, one above the other, and each filled with troops. In moving to the attack we were exposed to enfilading fire[1] from the woods on our left flank, besides the double line of fire which we had to face in front, and a battery of artillery posted on a hill to our left rear opened upon us at short range. . . .

On swept the gallant little brigade, the Third North Carolina on the right of the line, next the Second Maryland, then the three Virginia regiments (10th, 23d, and 37th), with the First North Carolina on the extreme left. Its ranks had been sadly thinned, and its energies greatly depleted by those six fearful hours of battle that morning; but its nerve and spirit were undiminished. Soon, however, the left and center were checked and then repulsed, probably by the severe flank fire from the woods; and the small remnant of the Third North Carolina, with the stronger Second Maryland (I do not recall the banners of any other regiment), were far in advance of the rest of the line. On they pressed to within about twenty or thirty paces of the works—a small but gallant band of heroes daring to attempt what could not be done by flesh and blood.

Primary Sources
Diaries and Journals
Which words in this description of the battle show McKim's political leanings?

The end soon came. We were beaten back to the line from which we had advanced with terrible loss, and in much confusion, but the enemy did not make a countercharge. By the strenuous efforts of the officers of the line and of the staff, order was restored, and we re-formed in the breastworks[2] from which we had emerged, there to be again exposed to an artillery fire exceeding in violence that of the

1. **enfilading** (en´ fə lād´ iŋ) **fire** gunfire directed along the length of a column or line of troops.
2. **breastworks** low walls put up quickly as a defense in battle.

◀ **Primary Source: Art** Does this painting of the Battle of Gettysburg help you understand McKim's pride in his brigade? Explain. **[Connect]**

early morning. It remains only to say that, like Pickett's men[3] later in the day, this single brigade was hurled unsupported against the enemy's works. Daniel's brigade remained in the breastworks during and after the charge, and neither from that command nor from any other had we any support. Of course it is to be presumed that General Daniel acted in obedience to orders. We remained in this breastwork after the charge about an hour before we finally abandoned the Federal entrenchments and retired to the foot of the hill.

Vocabulary
entrenchments (en trench′ mənts) *n.* long, deep holes with steep sides, used as defense against enemy fire

3. **Pickett's men** General George Pickett was a Confederate officer who led the unsuccessful attack on the Union position.

Critical Reading

1. **Integration of Knowledge and Ideas (a) Summarize:** Describe in your own words the attack on Culp's Hill. **(b) Speculate:** In your view, who or what was responsible for the Confederates' defeat?
2. **Key Ideas and Details (a)** According to McKim, how was the attack like Pickett's charge later in the day? **(b) Infer:** How do you think McKim felt about his superiors' decisions and orders during the battle? Support your inference with a quotation from the text.
3. **Integration of Knowledge and Ideas Make a Judgment:** Is McKim's account trustworthy? Explain.

Diaries and Journals

Comparing Primary Sources

Refer to your Note-Taking Guide to answer these questions.

1. **(a)** Why do you think each of these writers felt compelled to write a diary or journal? **(b)** What connection do you see between each writer's purpose and the details he or she includes in a diary entry?
2. **(a)** Using a chart like the one shown below, identify one detail or observation from each diary or journal that reveals something important about the writer's beliefs. **(b)** Which writers state their beliefs explicitly? **(c)** Which express their beliefs implicitly? Explain.

Writer	Detail or Observation	What It Reveals
Chesnut		
Goss		
McKim		

3. Write several paragraphs in which you compare and contrast these writers' stations in life and the perspectives they bring to their descriptions of the war. Consider each writer's objectivity, political feelings, and philosophical beliefs.

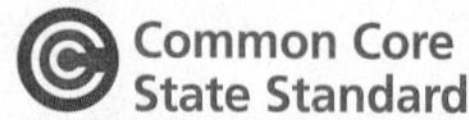

Common Core State Standards

Writing

7. Conduct short as well as more sustained research projects to answer a question or solve a problem; narrow or broaden the inquiry when appropriate; synthesize multiple sources on the subject, demonstrating understanding of the subject under investigation.

8. Gather relevant information from multiple authoritative print and digital sources, using advanced searches effectively; assess the strengths and limitations of each source in terms of the task, purpose, and audience; integrate information into the text selectively to maintain the flow of ideas, avoiding plagiarism and overreliance on any one source.

Language

4.c. Consult general and specialized reference materials to find the etymology of a word.

Vocabulary Acquisition and Use

True or False Indicate whether each sentence below is true or false. Explain your answer.

1. The police would foil a crime if they *intercepted* stolen goods.
2. An *obstinate* person makes a good negotiator.
3. A sudden summer rainstorm can cause a *fluctuation* in temperature.
4. At a sports event, a *spectator* is often responsible for a team's win.

Content-Area Vocabulary Link each word on the left with a set of words on the right. Explain why the word belongs to that set.

5. adjourned
6. recruits
7. brigade
8. offensive
9. convention
10. entrenchments

a. delegates, capitol, elect, legislature
b. combat, campaign, tactic, siege
c. soldiers, enlist, drill, military

Etymology Study The word *adjourned* comes from the Latin word *diurnus*, which means "day" or "daily." Use a dictionary to determine how the words ***journal*** and ***diary*** are also related to this Latin root. Then, locate other words that share the same root.

Research Task

Topic: Women and the Civil War

Waiting wives and mourning mothers, fighters and farmers, abolitionists and slaves, nurses and spies—American women during the Civil War played many roles. Before, during, and after the war, women's lives told a vital and often heartrending part of the tragic American story.

▲ Clara Barton traveled behind enemy lines to bring medical care to wounded Union soldiers.

Assignment: Write a **research report** on women and the Civil War. Do not rely strictly on texts written for students; instead, include evidence from texts written by experts for informed, scholarly audiences.

Formulate your research plan. "Women and the Civil War" is a huge topic that cannot be covered adequately in a brief research report. Therefore, narrow the topic to make it manageable and interesting. Alone or in a group, brainstorm for a list of focused topics such as the following:

- women who participated in military action
- the domestic lives of women during the war
- women who worked as spies during the war
- wartime for Northern women vs. Southern women
- one particular woman, such as Mary Chesnut

Choose a focused topic that grabs your interest. Then, formulate a brief list of major questions to answer through research.

Gather sources. Answer your questions using online and library materials. To avoid overreliance on one source, create a chart of the different kinds of information you acquire from a variety of sources.

RESEARCH TIP

Read author information, often on a jacket flap or back page, to evaluate a writer's authority. On a Web site, read the "About Me" section to evaluate credentials.

Model: Researching Using Multiple Sources

Source	Type of Source	Type of Information
"Belle Boyd"	encyclopedia	biographical facts
"Belle Boyd"	history Web site	other women spies
Belle Boyd	2007 biography	details of spy missions

Use a checklist like the one shown to ensure the reliability of your research report.

Synthesize information. As you synthesize details from different sources, flexibility is key. You may need to further refine the topic, shift the focus of your research, or add or discard sources. Be prepared to pursue new thoughts and new directions.

Organize and present your ideas. Organize your report into sections identified by subheads. This will clarify the flow of your ideas and information and make the job of writing easier. Add summary statements at the end of each section to make the final report clearer.

Research Checklist

- ☐ Have I answered all my research questions?
- ☐ Does my evidence come from experts and texts written for informed audiences in the field?
- ☐ Have I avoided relying too much on one source?
- ☐ Is my report clearly organized, with sections, subheads, and summary statements?

Before You Read *An Episode of War*

Connecting to the Essential Question Stephen Crane presents the stark realities of war, omitting lofty reflections on honor or courage. As you read, notice details that downplay the drama of war. This will help as you consider the Essential Question: **How does literature shape or reflect society?**

Common Core State Standards

Reading Literature

3. Analyze the impact of the author's choices regarding how to develop and relate elements of a story (e.g., how the characters are introduced and developed).

9. Demonstrate knowledge of nineteenth-century foundational works of American literature, including how two or more texts from the same period treat similar themes or topics.

Literary Analysis

Naturalism is a literary movement that developed in reaction to *Romanticism.* The horrors of the Civil War caused many American writers to question Romantic ideas about human goodness and nature's beauty. In stark contrast to the Romantic view, Naturalists felt that people's lives are controlled by forces beyond their understanding or control. These forces include heredity, people's surroundings, and sheer chance. In Naturalistic works, characters are often victims of their own instincts or of a violent world, and they endure their suffering with a quiet dignity. For example, the wounded main character in "An Episode of War" wanders aimlessly through a Civil War encampment:

> *He wore the look of one who knows he is the victim of a terrible disease and understands his helplessness.*

Like other Naturalistic writers, Crane presents a bleak reality without explaining it. Instead, he allows the reader to draw his or her own conclusions. As you read, look for these Naturalistic elements in Crane's story.

Reading Strategy

Preparing to Read Complex Texts Knowledge of the Civil War era can clarify your understanding of the characters and action in this story. The diaries and journals that appear on pages 494–503, as well as the unit introduction, background note, and other features in this textbook offer valuable insights into the realities of the Civil War experience. As you read, **apply background knowledge** you gain from these texts to clarify details. Doing so will also help you *predict* the story's events. Use a chart like the one shown to record your observations.

Background Knowledge	Story Details

Vocabulary

precipitate (prē sip′ ə tāt′) *v.* cause to happen before expected or desired (p. 510)

aggregation (ag′ rə gā′ shən) *n.* group of distinct objects or individuals (p. 511)

commotion (kə mō′ shən) *n.* noisy confusion (p. 512)

disdainfully (dis dān′ fəl ē) *adv.* showing scorn or contempt (p. 513)

sinister (si′ nəs tər) *adj.* threatening harm, evil, or misfortune (p. 513)

Stephen Crane (1871–1900)

Author of "An Episode of War"

Stephen Crane had not been born when the last battle of the American Civil War was fought, yet he is best remembered for his compelling depiction of the conflict. During his brief life, Crane established himself as both a leader of the Naturalist movement and one of the greatest writers of his time.

Early in his career, Crane worked as a journalist in New York City. His experiences there inspired his first novel, *Maggie: A Girl of the Streets* (1893). Its grimly realistic portrayal of life in the city's slums was so frank and shocking that Crane was unable to find a publisher, and he printed the book at his own expense.

The Red Badge of Courage Crane's second novel, published in 1895, was *The Red Badge of Courage: An Episode of the American Civil War.* A psychological exploration of a young soldier's mental and emotional reactions under enemy fire, the wildly successful novel earned international acclaim for the twenty-four-year-old writer. Crane had never experienced military combat, but he interviewed Civil War veterans and studied photographs, battle plans, and biographical accounts before writing the realistic battle scenes.

Crane later viewed war firsthand when he served as a newspaper correspondent during the Greco-Turkish War in 1897 and the Spanish-American War in 1898. His war experiences provided material for a collection of poetry, *War Is Kind* (1899), but they took their toll on his health. He died of tuberculosis at the age of twenty-eight.

A Short, Passionate Life Like other Naturalists, Crane depicts characters who are manipulated by forces that are beyond their understanding or control. His most common themes include the harsh reality of war, the degradation of humanity, social rebellion, betrayal, and guilt. Knowing he would not live long, Crane worked intensely in the last years of his life. His novels, short stories, poems, and other writings fill twelve volumes. He is considered a literary prodigy who wrote as quickly and passionately as he lived.

An Episode of War

Stephen Crane

BACKGROUND Until World War II, the American Civil War was the bloodiest conflict in American history. It claimed the lives of 600,000 soldiers. Hundreds of thousands more were left maimed by battle wounds and crude medical care. In fact, the conditions in field hospitals were so primitive that twice as many soldiers died from infections as from combat wounds. As you read this story, keep in mind that amputation was the routine treatment for injured limbs. A wounded soldier knew that he faced the high probability of losing his arm or leg to a surgeon's saw.

The lieutenant's rubber blanket lay on the ground, and upon it he had poured the company's supply of coffee. Corporals and other representatives of the grimy and hot-throated men who lined the breast-work[1] had come for each squad's portion.

The lieutenant was frowning and serious at this task of division. His lips pursed as he drew with his sword various crevices in the heap, until brown squares of coffee, astoundingly equal in size, appeared on the blanket. He was on the verge of a great triumph in mathematics, and the corporals were thronging forward, each to reap a little square, when suddenly the lieutenant cried out and looked quickly at a man near him as if he suspected it was a case of personal assault. The others cried out also when they saw blood upon the lieutenant's sleeve.

He had winced like a man stung, swayed dangerously, and then straightened. The sound of his hoarse breathing was plainly audible. He looked sadly, mystically, over the breast-work at the green face of a wood, where now were many little puffs of white smoke. During this moment the men about him gazed statuelike and silent, astonished and awed by this catastrophe which happened when catastrophes were not expected—when they had leisure to observe it.

As the lieutenant stared at the wood, they too swung their heads, so that for another instant all hands, still silent, contemplated the distant forest as if their minds were fixed upon the mystery of a bullet's journey.

The officer had, of course, been compelled to take his sword into his left hand. He did not hold it by the hilt. He gripped it at the middle of the blade, awkwardly. Turning his eyes from the hostile wood, he looked at the sword as he held it there, and seemed puzzled as to what to do with it, where to put it. In short, this weapon had of a sudden become a strange thing to him. He looked at it in a kind of stupefaction, as if he had been endowed with a trident, a sceptre,[2] or a spade.

Finally he tried to sheathe it. To sheathe a sword held by the left hand, at the middle of the blade, in a scabbard hung at the left hip, is a feat worthy of a sawdust ring.[3] This

The **American EXPERIENCE**

Humanities Connection

Photographer Mathew Brady

Thanks to photography pioneer Mathew Brady (1823?–1896), the Civil War was the first war to be captured on film. As a young man, Brady met Samuel Morse, the inventor of the telegraph. Morse taught Brady how to make daguerreotypes, the forerunners of photographs. By the 1850s, Brady owned a thriving studio in New York City and was known for his portraits of distinguished Americans. When the Civil War broke out, Brady hired twenty photographers and sent them out to document the conflict. Due to the limitations of their technology, the photographers rarely captured battlefield action. Instead, they took pictures of events behind the scenes and of the carnage after battles. **The photographs that illustrate this story were taken by Brady and his team.** Their images, often horrific, forced viewers to face the realities of war more directly than ever before.

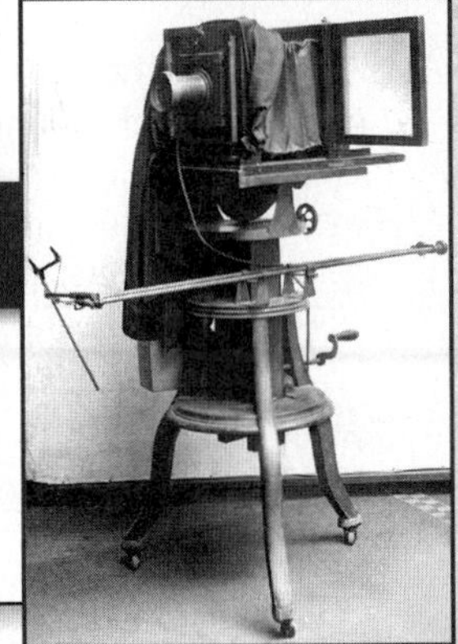

Connect to the Literature

How is documentary photography, like the images on these pages, similar to Naturalism?

1. **breast-work** low wall put up quickly as a defense in battle.
2. **a trident, a sceptre** (trīd′ ənt; sep′ tər) three-pronged spear; decorated ornamental rod or staff symbolizing royal authority.
3. **sawdust ring** ring in which circus acts are performed.

◀ **Critical Viewing** What similarities do you see between this photograph and Crane's description of the wounded lieutenant being helped by his men? **[Connect]**

Literary Analysis
Naturalism What Naturalist ideas are evident in this passage about the orderly-sergeant's reaction to the lieutenant's wound?

Vocabulary
precipitate (prē sip′ ə tāt′) *v.* cause to happen before expected or desired

Reading Strategy
Applying Background Knowledge How does your knowledge of the Civil War clarify your understanding of these battlefield details?

wounded officer engaged in a desperate struggle with the sword and the wobbling scabbard, and during the time of it breathed like a wrestler.

But at this instant the men, the spectators, awoke from their stone-like poses and crowded forward sympathetically. The orderly-sergeant took the sword and tenderly placed it in the scabbard. At the time, he leaned nervously backward, and did not allow even his finger to brush the body of the lieutenant. A wound gives strange dignity to him who bears it. Well men shy from his new and terrible majesty. It is as if the wounded man's hand is upon the curtain which hangs before the revelations of all existence—the meaning of ants, potentates,[4] wars, cities, sunshine, snow, a feather dropped from a bird's wing; and the power of it sheds radiance upon a bloody form, and makes the other men understand sometimes that they are little. His comrades look at him with large eyes thoughtfully. Moreover, they fear vaguely that the weight of a finger upon him might send him headlong, precipitate the tragedy, hurl him at once into the dim, grey unknown. And so the orderly-sergeant, while sheathing the sword, leaned nervously backward.

There were others who proffered assistance. One timidly presented his shoulder and asked the lieutenant if he cared to lean upon it, but the latter waved him away mournfully. He wore the look of one who knows he is the victim of a terrible disease and understands his helplessness. He again stared over the breast-work at the forest, and then, turning, went slowly rearward. He held his right wrist tenderly in his left hand as if the wounded arm was made of very brittle glass.

And the men in silence stared at the wood, then at the departing lieutenant; then at the wood, then at the lieutenant.

As the wounded officer passed from the line of battle, he was enabled to see many things which as a participant in the fight were unknown to him. He saw a general on a black horse gazing over the lines of blue infantry at the green woods which veiled his problems. An aide galloped furiously, dragged his horse suddenly to a halt, saluted, and presented a paper. It was, for a wonder, precisely like a historical painting.

To the rear of the general and his staff a group, composed of a bugler, two or three orderlies, and the bearer of the corps standard,[5] all upon maniacal horses, were working like slaves to hold their ground, preserve their respectful interval, while the shells boomed in the air about them, and caused their chargers to make furious quivering leaps.

A battery, a tumultuous and shining mass, was swirling toward the right. The wild thud of hoofs, the cries of the riders shouting

4. **potentates** (pōt′ ən tāts) *n.* rulers; powerful people.
5. **corps standard** (kôr) flag or banner representing a military unit.

blame and praise, menace and encouragement, and, last, the roar of the wheels, the slant of the glistening guns, brought the lieutenant to an intent pause. The battery swept in curves that stirred the heart; it made halts as dramatic as the crash of a wave on the rocks, and when it fled onward this **aggregation** of wheels, levers, motors had a beautiful unity, as if it were a missile. The sound of it was a war-chorus that reached into the depths of man's emotion.

The lieutenant, still holding his arm as if it were of glass, stood watching this battery until all detail of it was lost, save the figures of the riders, which rose and fell and waved lashes over the black mass.

Later, he turned his eyes toward the battle, where the shooting sometimes crackled like bush-fires, sometimes sputtered with exasperating irregularity, and sometimes reverberated like the thunder. He saw the smoke rolling upward and saw crowds of men who ran and cheered, or stood and blazed away at the inscrutable distance.

He came upon some stragglers, and they told him how to find the field hospital. They described its exact location. In fact, these men, no longer having part in the battle, knew more of it than others. They told the performance of every corps, every division, the opinion of every general. The lieutenant, carrying his wounded arm rearward, looked upon them with wonder.

At the roadside a brigade was making coffee and buzzing with talk like a girls' boarding school. Several officers came out to him

▲ Critical Viewing
What mood do the expressions and body language of these Civil War officers convey? Explain. **[Analyze]**

Vocabulary
aggregation (ag′ rə gā′ shən) *n.* group of distinct objects or individuals

What does the lieutenant stop to watch on his way to the field hospital?

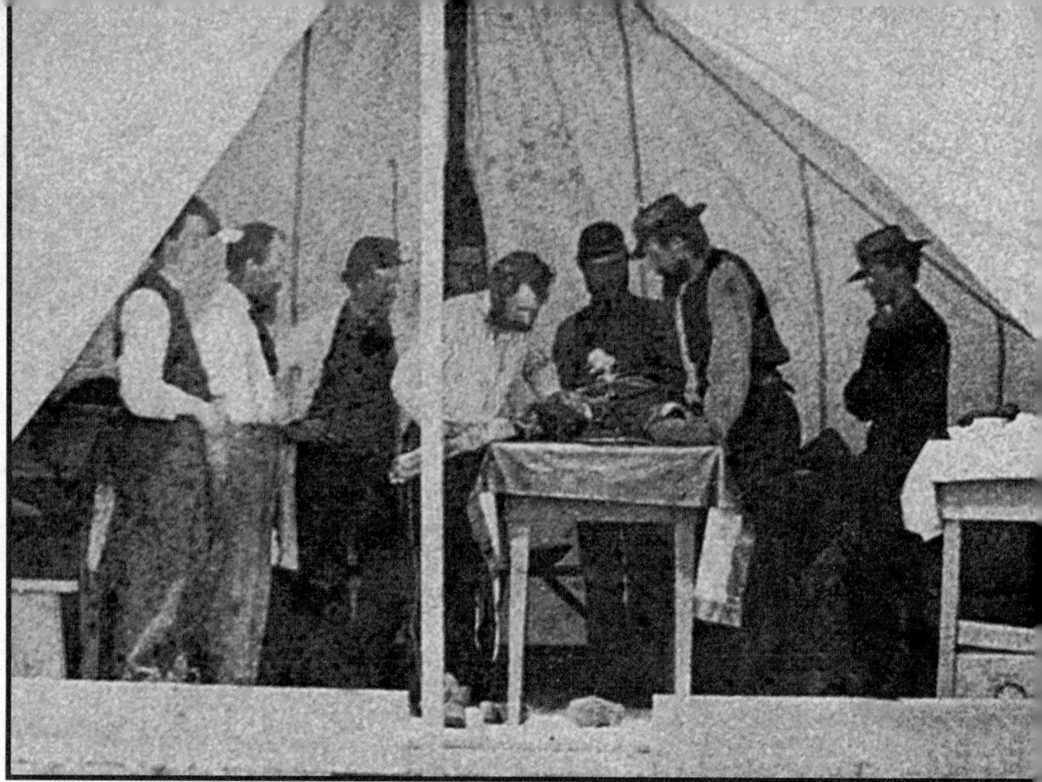

▶ **Critical Viewing** This is a photograph of a Civil War field hospital. Do you think that soldiers received quality treatment in this setting? Explain. **[Deduce]**

and inquired concerning things of which he knew nothing. One, seeing his arm, began to scold. "Why, man, that's no way to do. You want to fix that thing." He appropriated the lieutenant and the lieutenant's wound. He cut the sleeve and laid bare the arm, every nerve of which softly fluttered under his touch. He bound his handkerchief over the wound, scolding away in the meantime. His tone allowed one to think that he was in the habit of being wounded every day. The lieutenant hung his head, feeling, in this presence, that he did not know how to be correctly wounded.

The low white tents of the hospital were grouped around an old schoolhouse. There was here a singular commotion. In the foreground two ambulances interlocked wheels in the deep mud. The drivers were tossing the blame of it back and forth, gesticulating and berating, while from the ambulances, both crammed with wounded, there came an occasional groan. An interminable crowd of bandaged men were coming and going. Great numbers sat under the trees nursing heads or arms or legs. There was a dispute of some kind raging on the steps of the schoolhouse. Sitting with his back against a tree a man with a face as grey as a new army blanket was serenely smoking a corncob pipe. The lieutenant wished to rush forward and inform him that he was dying.

A busy surgeon was passing near the lieutenant. "Good-morning," he said, with a friendly smile. Then he caught sight of the

Vocabulary
commotion (kə mō′ shən) *n.* noisy confusion

▶ **Critical Viewing** What do the Civil War era surgical instruments shown on the next page suggest about the care the lieutenant will receive? **[Infer]**

lieutenant's arm, and his face at once changed. "Well, let's have a look at it." He seemed possessed suddenly of a great contempt for the lieutenant. This wound evidently placed the latter on a very low social plane. The doctor cried out impatiently, "What mutton-head had tied it up that way anyhow?" The lieutenant answered, "Oh, a man."

When the wound was disclosed the doctor fingered it **disdainfully**. "Humph," he said. "You come along with me and I'll 'tend to you." His voice contained the same scorn as if he were saying: "You will have to go to jail."

The lieutenant had been very meek, but now his face flushed, and he looked into the doctor's eyes. "I guess I won't have it amputated," he said.

"Nonsense, man! Nonsense! Nonsense!" cried the doctor. "Come along, now. I won't amputate it. Come along. Don't be a baby."

"Let go of me," said the lieutenant, holding back wrathfully, his glance fixed upon the door of the old schoolhouse, as **sinister** to him as the portals of death.

And this is the story of how the lieutenant lost his arm. When he reached home, his sisters, his mother, his wife, sobbed for a long time at the sight of the flat sleeve. "Oh, well," he said, standing shamefaced amid these tears, "I don't suppose it matters so much as all that."

Vocabulary

disdainfully (dis dān′ fəl ē) *adv.* showing scorn or contempt

sinister (si′ nəs tər) *adj.* threatening harm, evil, or misfortune

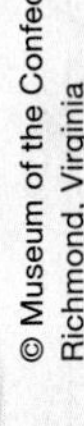
© Museum of the Confederacy, Richmond, Virginia

Critical Reading

1. **Key Ideas and Details (a)** What happens to cause the lieutenant's injury? **(b) Analyze:** How do the details of his injury make him a sympathetic character?
2. **Key Ideas and Details (a)** What is the lieutenant's reaction when a soldier offers a helpful shoulder? **(b) Infer:** Why does he react this way?
3. **Integration of Knowledge and Ideas (a)** Note three examples of the lieutenant's distance from the uninjured people around him. **(b) Interpret:** What do these examples suggest about the way others see him and the way he sees himself?
4. **Integration of Knowledge and Ideas** In your view, does society benefit from frank portrayals of suffering? In your response, use at least two of these Essential Question words: *awareness, assumption, reality, despair. **[Connecting to the Essential Question: How does literature shape or reflect society?]***

Cite textual evidence to support your responses.

After You Read **An Episode of War**

Literary Analysis

1. **Key Ideas and Details (a)** What is the lieutenant doing when he is injured? **(b)** How does this detail reflect the **Naturalist** idea that people are victims of chance?
2. **Key Ideas and Details (a)** Why do you think Crane chooses to have the lieutenant remain nameless? **(b)** Does the lieutenant's namelessness heighten or lessen the emotional impact of the story? Explain.
3. **Key Ideas and Details** Note two details that show how the lieutenant exhibits a quiet endurance typical of characters in Naturalist works. Explain your choices.
4. **Key Ideas and Details (a)** Identify three descriptions of human actions in the story that could also describe the actions of animals. **(b)** How do these descriptions reflect Naturalist ideas about people's helplessness in the face of nature and circumstance?
5. **Key Ideas and Details (a)** At various points in the story, people make gestures of kindness toward the lieutenant. Use a chart like the one shown to record these details and explain why they fail. **(b)** What Naturalist ideas about the possibility of kindness does this series of details imply?

Event or Detail	Why It Fails	Naturalist Idea

6. **Integration of Knowledge and Ideas** What differences might exist in the mood, events, or outcome of this story if it had been written by a *Romantic* writer who believed in the harmony of humanity and nature? Explain.

Reading Strategy

7. **(a) Apply your background knowledge** of Civil War medical practices to explain why the doctor promises the lieutenant he will not amputate. **(b)** How did your background knowledge help you anticipate, or *predict,* the type of medical treatment the lieutenant would receive?
8. Apply the background knowledge you gain from reading the Civil War documents on pages 494–503. **(a)** List at least three details from the primary sources that relate to the setting, characters, and events in *An Episode of War.* **(b)** For each detail you cite, explain how it adds to your understanding of the story.

Common Core State Standards

Writing

2. Write informative/explanatory texts to examine and convey complex ideas, concepts, and information clearly and accurately through the effective selection, organization, and analysis of content. *(p. 515)*

2.a. Introduce a topic; organize complex ideas, concepts, and information so that each new element builds on that which precedes it to create a unified whole. *(p. 515)*

Language

4.b. Identify and correctly use patterns of word changes that indicate different meanings or parts of speech. *(p. 515)*

PERFORMANCE TASKS

Integrated Language Skills

Vocabulary Acquisition and Use

Word Analysis: Latin Root *-greg-*

The word *aggregation* contains the Latin root *-greg-*, meaning "herd" or "flock." An *aggregation* is a group of people or things taken as a whole. A *congregation* is a group, and a *gregarious* person is someone who enjoys being part of a crowd. Copy the paragraph below, filling in each blank with the appropriate *-greg-* word from the list. Be sure to fill in each blank with a word that is appropriate in meaning and part of speech.

aggregate gregarious congregated

The wounded soldiers _______ on the steps, waiting to see the doctor. They were silent, except for one _______ private who described his injury in great detail to the rest of the group. In the _______, an orderly reflected, wounded men are a quiet bunch.

Vocabulary: Analogies

Analogies show the relationships between pairs of words. Complete each analogy using a word from the vocabulary list on page 506. In each, your choice should create a word pair that matches the relationship between the first two words given. Then, explain your answer.

1. *Quickly* is to *rapidly* as _______ is to *scornfully.*
2. *Hidden* is to *revealed* as _______ is to *harmless.*
3. *Storm* is to *peace* as _______ is to *serenity.*
4. *Laugh* is to *cry* as _______ is to *delay.*
5. *Sum* is to *parts* as _______ is to *individual.*

Writing

Explanatory Text Many critics have observed that Crane's fiction asks questions but does not provide answers, challenging readers to evaluate their ideas about people's behavior, feelings, and thoughts. Write an **essay** in which you respond to this assessment of Crane's work. Determine whether "An Episode of War" provides strong support for this critical view.

Prewriting Use a format like the one shown to list assumptions about war that people commonly hold. Then, reread the story. Note details that relate to your list of assumptions. Decide if you think this story poses challenges to those assumptions and whether it provides support for the critical view. Write a statement that summarizes your observations.

Model: Questioning Assumptions

Assumption: Soldiers have what they need to do their job well.
Challenge question: Do soldiers always have what they need?
Related detail: The soldiers are each being rationed a small bit of coffee.

To challenge an assumption, ask, "Is this always true?"

Drafting Clearly state the critical assessment of Crane's work. Then, state your position. Using your prewriting notes, devote one paragraph to each assumption and its expression in the story.

Revising Reread your essay to make sure that your ideas are fully developed, that your ideas flow in a logical order, and that each idea builds on the one that comes before. If necessary, reorder your paragraphs to improve the flow of ideas.

> There are events which are so great that if a writer has participated in them his obligation is to write truly rather than assume the presumption of altering them with invention.
>
> ~ Ernest Hemingway

Defining Narrative Nonfiction

Narrative nonfiction is prose writing that tells the stories of real people, places, objects, or events. It features many of the same elements as fiction—including characters, setting, and a sequence of events—but these are based on actual, lived experiences, rather than imagination.

Types of Narrative Nonfiction These are the most common forms of narrative nonfiction:

- **Biography and Autobiography:** works that tell life stories. A biography is a life story written by another person, while an autobiography is an account of the writer's own life.
- **Historical Narrative:** a work that relates historical events that the writer may or may not have experienced firsthand
- **Memoir:** an autobiographical work that focuses on a particular time period or aspect of the writer's life
- **Diary and Journal:** an informal account of the writer's daily experiences
- **Narrative Essay:** a short work that explores ideas while relating a story

Style and Tone Style is a writer's particular way of using language, and tone is his or her attitude toward the audience and subject. Both are key ingredients in narrative nonfiction.

In This Section

- Defining Narrative Nonfiction *(p. 516)*
- Model: from *Black Boy* by Richard Wright *(p. 517)*
- Study: from *My Bondage and My Freedom* by Frederick Douglass *(p. 519)*

For more practice analyzing narrative nonfiction, see pages 34, 48, 58, 69, 140, 171, 251, 495, 554, 570, 589, 617, 930, and 1426.

Close Read: Style and Tone

Many literary elements contribute to a writer's style and tone. The following elements appear in the Model Text.

Diction: the types of words a writer favors. Diction may be ornate, plain, familiar, formal, technical, or any combination thereof. *Example: "Why did that green goose Anderson go into Fort Sumter?" (Mary Chesnut)*	**Rhetorical Devices:** meaningful patterns of words and ideas. *Parallelism* is the repetition of the same grammatical structure. *Rhetorical questions* are asked for effect. *Example (parallelism): "She had bread for the hungry, clothes for the naked, and comfort for every mourner. . . ." (Frederick Douglass)*
Syntax: sentence length and complexity. Syntax may involve any combination of long, short, complex, or simple sentences. *Example: "When I was a boy, there was but one permanent ambition among my comrades in our village on the west bank of the Mississippi River. That was, to be a steamboatman." (Mark Twain)*	**Telling Details:** precise details that reveal important information about the characters, setting, or situation. *Example: ". . . she had two shopping bags full of canned peaches, real peaches, beans wrapped in taro leaves, cookies, Thermos bottles, enough food for everybody . . ." (Maxine Hong Kingston)*

Model

About the Text Richard Wright (1908–1960) was one of the first African American writers to achieve international fame. His autobiography, *Black Boy,* was published in 1945, five years after the appearance of his acclaimed first novel, *Native Son.* In this excerpt, he refers to *A Book of Prefaces* by journalist and social critic H. L. Mencken.

from *Black Boy*
by Richard Wright

That night in my rented room, while letting the hot water run over my can of pork and beans in the sink, I opened *A Book of Prefaces* and began to read. I was jarred and shocked by the style, the clear, clean, sweeping sentences. Why did he write like that? And how did one write like that? I pictured the man as a raging demon, slashing with his pen, consumed with hate, denouncing everything American, extolling everything European or German, laughing at the weakness of people, mocking God, authority. What was this? I stood up, trying to realize what reality lay behind the meaning of the words. Yes, this man was fighting, fighting with words. He was using words as a weapon, using them as one would use a club. Could words be weapons? Well, yes, for here they were. Then maybe, perhaps, I could use them as a weapon? No. It frightened me. I read on and what amazed me was not what he said, but how on earth anybody had the courage to say it.

Occasionally I glanced up to reassure myself that I was alone in the room. Who were these men about whom Mencken was talking so passionately? Who was Anatole France? Joseph Conrad? Sinclair Lewis, Sherwood Anderson, Dostoevski, George Moore, Gustave Flaubert, Maupassant, Tolstoy, Frank Harris, Mark Twain, Thomas Hardy, Arnold Bennett, Stephen Crane, Zola, Norris, Gorky, Bergson, Ibsen, Balzac, Bernard Shaw, Dumas, Poe, Thomas Mann, O. Henry, Dreiser, H. G. Wells, Gogol, T. S. Eliot, Gide, Baudelaire, Edgar Lee Masters, Stendhal, Turgenev, Huneker, Nietzsche,[1] and scores of others? Were these men real? Did they exist or had they existed? And how did one pronounce their names?

Telling Details Specific details, such as "rented room," and "can of pork and beans" clearly establish both the setting and Wright's less than affluent circumstances.

Rhetorical Devices Note the use of parallel structure in Wright's description of Mencken's prose: "slashing," "denouncing," "extolling," and "mocking."

Syntax Wright's syntax—featuring short, staccato sentences—reflects the intensity and speed of his thoughts. It is as though the reader is allowed to experience Wright's internal, highly charged conversation.

Diction Wright uses an idiomatic expression: "how on earth." This strengthens the sense of authenticity in his impassioned, emotional reaction to Mencken's words.

[1]**Anatole France...Nietzche** This list identifies some of the most celebrated European and American philosophers, poets, playwrights, and fiction writers of the 19th and 20th centuries.

Before You Read from *My Bondage and My Freedom*

Connecting to the Essential Question In both his writing and, implicitly, in the example he provided through his own life, Frederick Douglass argued for freedom and equality. As you read, notice details that reveal Douglass's character. Doing so will help as you consider the Essential Question: **How does literature shape or reflect society?**

Common Core State Standards

Reading Informational Text

6. Determine an author's point of view or purpose in a text in which the rhetoric is particularly effective, analyzing how style and content contribute to the power, persuasiveness, or beauty of the text.

9. Analyze nineteenth-century foundational U.S. documents for their themes, purposes, and rhetorical features.

Literary Analysis

An **autobiography** is a person's account of his or her own life. Most autobiographers feel their lives are noteworthy and can somehow help others. This belief is part of the **author's purpose,** or reason for writing. Douglass's purpose was to show through his own life that African Americans are as intelligent, capable, and feeling as whites:

> *I could talk and sing; I could laugh and weep;*
> *I could reason and remember . . .*

Douglass's formal and dignified writing style, or specific way of using language, contributes to his purpose. It also helps to expresses his *tone*, or attitude, which is both passionate and compassionate. As you read, think about Douglass's purpose for relating the events in this excerpt and analyze how his style contributes to that purpose.

Reading Strategy

Preparing to Read Complex Texts **Setting a purpose** for reading gives you a concept on which to focus. When reading literature from other eras, one useful purpose is to note how *influences of the historical period shape characters, events, and settings*. Historical influences may include the following broad areas:

- *philosophical ideas* or *religious beliefs* that motivate specific actions
- *political events* or *social problems* that affect individuals or groups
- *ethical issues,* such as the moral conflicts caused by slavery

As you read, identify the historical influences in Douglass's narrative. Record your observations in a chart like the one shown.

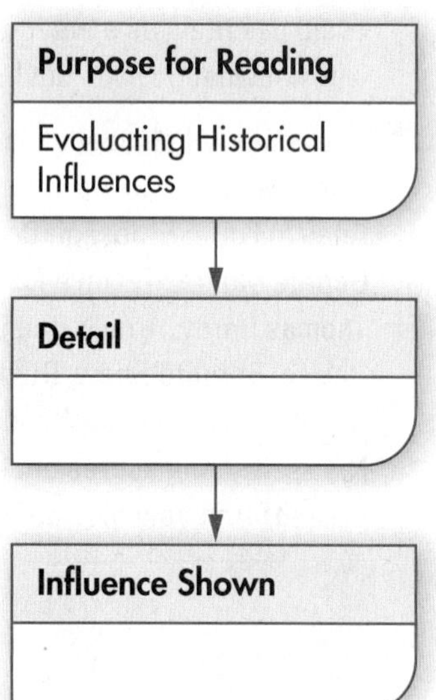

Vocabulary

benevolent (bə nev′ ə lənt) *adj.* kindly; charitable (p. 521)

deficient (di fi′ shənt) *adj.* incomplete; defective (p. 522)

fervent (fər′ vənt) *adj.* intensely devoted or earnest (p. 523)

opposition (ä pə zi′ shən) *n.* resistance; hostility (p. 523)

consternation (kän′ stər nā′ shən) *n.* fear or shock that makes one feel helpless or bewildered (p. 523)

intolerable (in täl′ ər ə bəl) *adj.* unbearable; too severe (p. 525)

Frederick Douglass (1817–1895)

Author of *My Bondage and My Freedom*

Frederick Douglass rose out of slavery to become one of the most gifted writers and orators of his time. He used his talents to fight for the abolition of slavery and for civil rights. His life served as an inspiration and example for all Americans, both black and white throughout the country.

Early Years Douglass was born on a Maryland plantation. Historians believe that his name at birth was Frederick Augustus Bailey. At the age of eight, he was sent as a slave to the Baltimore home of the Auld family, where he learned to read and write. Learning became an unquenchable thirst for Douglass. As his knowledge grew, so did his desire for freedom. At age twenty, he escaped to Massachusetts, a free state, and took the surname Douglass to avoid arrest as a fugitive.

A Public Life In 1841, despite the fear of being arrested, Douglass began lecturing against slavery and for civil rights for all people. Rumors spread that a man of such eloquence could not possibly have been a slave. In response, Douglass published his first autobiography, *Narrative of the Life of Frederick Douglass, an American Slave, Written By Himself* (1845). Fearing re-enslavement, Douglass then fled to England, where he worked to gain British support for the abolitionist movement in the United States.

Freedom at Last After English friends raised money to buy his freedom, Douglass returned to the United States, founded a newspaper for African Americans, and resumed lecturing. In 1855, he published *My Bondage and My Freedom*, an updated version of his autobiography.

After slavery was abolished, Douglass fought vigorously for civil rights for African Americans. He became a consultant to President Lincoln and held several government positions, including United States minister to Haiti.

A Vision for the Future In 1883, Douglass said "I expect to see the colored people of this country enjoying the same freedom, voting at the same ballot-box, . . . going to the same schools, attending the same churches, . . . proud of the same country, fighting the same foe, and enjoying the same peace and all its advantages. . . ."

from

My Bondage and My Freedom

FREDERICK DOUGLASS

BACKGROUND *Frederick Douglass was perhaps the most prominent African American leader of the nineteenth century, and his influence is still felt. As a crusader for human rights, Douglass served as a role model for African American leaders such as Booker T. Washington and W.E.B. DuBois. In our own era, the civil rights movement has drawn inspiration from Douglass, who opposed segregation decades before other voices were raised. As a young man, Douglass protested segregated seating on trains by sitting in cars reserved for whites until the authorities forcibly removed him. Later, he fought job discrimination against African Americans, protested segregation in school, and fought for civil rights for all Americans.*

I lived in the family of Master Hugh, at Baltimore, seven years, during which time—as the almanac makers say of the weather—my condition was variable. The most interesting feature of my history here, was my learning to read and write, under somewhat marked disadvantages. In attaining this knowledge I was compelled to resort to indirections by no means congenial to my nature, and which were really humiliating to me. My mistress—who had begun to teach me—was suddenly checked in her benevolent design, by the strong advice of her husband. In faithful compliance with this advice, the good lady had not only ceased to instruct me, herself, but had set her face as a flint against my learning to read by any means. It is due, however, to my mistress to say, that she did not adopt this course in all its stringency at the first. She either thought it unnecessary, or she lacked the depravity indispensable to shutting me up in mental darkness.

Vocabulary
benevolent (bə nev′ ə lənt) *adj.* kindly; charitable

Why did Douglass's mistress stop teaching him to read?

◀ **Critical Viewing** What might the light shining on the reader in this painting symbolize? **[Interpret]**

The Chimney Corner, 1863, Eastman Johnson, Munson-Williams-Proctor Institute Museum of Art, Utica, New York

It was, at least, necessary for her to have some training, and some hardening, in the exercise of the slaveholder's prerogative, to make her equal to forgetting my human nature and character, and to treating me as a thing destitute of a moral or an intellectual nature. Mrs. Auld—my mistress—was, as I have said, a most kind and tender-hearted woman; and, in the humanity of her heart, and the simplicity of her mind, she set out, when I first went to live with her, to treat me as she supposed one human being ought to treat another.

It is easy to see, that, in entering upon the duties of a slaveholder, some little experience is needed. Nature has done almost nothing to prepare men and women to be either slaves or slaveholders. Nothing but rigid training, long persisted in, can perfect the character of the one or the other. One cannot easily forget to love freedom; and it is as hard to cease to respect that natural love in our fellow creatures. On entering upon the career of a slaveholding mistress, Mrs. Auld was singularly deficient; nature, which fits

Vocabulary
deficient (di fi′ shənt)
adj. incomplete; defective

▲ Critical Viewing
Is the situation and relationship shown in this image similar to Douglass's? Explain. **[Distinguish]**

nobody for such an office, had done less for her than any lady I had known. It was no easy matter to induce her to think and to feel that the curly-headed boy, who stood by her side, and even leaned on her lap; who was loved by little Tommy, and who loved little Tommy in turn; sustained to her only the relation of a chattel.[1] I was *more* than that, and she felt me to be more than that. I could talk and sing; I could laugh and weep; I could reason and remember; I could love and hate. I was human, and she, dear lady, knew and felt me to be so. How could she, then, treat me as a brute, without a mighty struggle with all the noble powers of her own soul. That struggle came, and the will and power of the husband was victorious. Her noble soul was overthrown; but, he that overthrew it did not, himself, escape the consequences. He, not less than the other parties, was injured in his domestic peace by the fall.

When I went into their family, it was the abode of happiness and contentment. The mistress of the house was a model of affection and tenderness. Her **fervent** piety and watchful uprightness made it impossible to see her without thinking and feeling—"that woman is a Christian." There was no sorrow nor suffering for which she had not a tear, and there was no innocent joy for which she did not [have] a smile. She had bread for the hungry, clothes for the naked, and comfort for every mourner that came within her reach. Slavery soon proved its ability to divest her of these excellent qualities, and her home of its early happiness. Conscience cannot stand much violence. Once thoroughly broken down, *who* is he that can repair the damage? It may be broken toward the slave, on Sunday, and toward the master on Monday. It cannot endure such shocks. It must stand entire, or it does not stand at all. If my condition waxed bad, that of the family waxed not better. The first step, in the wrong direction, was the violence done to nature and to conscience, in arresting the benevolence that would have enlightened my young mind. In ceasing to instruct me, she must begin to justify herself *to* herself; and, once consenting to take sides in such a debate, she was riveted to her position. One needs very little knowledge of moral philosophy, to see *where* my mistress now landed. She finally became even more violent in her **opposition** to my learning to read, than was her husband himself. She was not satisfied with simply doing as *well* as her husband had commanded her, but seemed resolved to better his instruction. Nothing appeared to make my poor mistress—after her turning toward the downward path—more angry, than seeing me, seated in some nook or corner, quietly reading a book or a newspaper. I have had her rush at me, with the utmost fury, and snatch from my hand such newspaper or book, with something of the wrath and **consternation** which a traitor might be supposed to feel on being discovered in a plot by some dangerous spy.

1. **chattel** (chat′ 'l) *n.* a movable item of personal property, as a piece of furniture or a head of livestock.

Reading Strategy
Purpose for Reading: Historical Influences How do the ethical conflicts of slavery affect everyone in the Auld household?

Vocabulary
fervent (fər′ vənt) *adj.* intensely devoted or earnest

Vocabulary
opposition (ä pə zi′ shən) *n.* resistance; hostility

consternation (kän′ stər nā′ shən) *n.* fear or shock that makes one feel helpless or bewildered

What extreme measure does Mrs. Auld take?

Reading Strategy
Purpose for Reading: Historical Influences What multiple influences of the period are evident in this paragraph? Explain.

Mrs. Auld was an apt woman, and the advice of her husband, and her own experience, soon demonstrated, to her entire satisfaction, that education and slavery are incompatible with each other. When this conviction was thoroughly established, I was most narrowly watched in all my movements. If I remained in a separate room from the family for any considerable length of time, I was sure to be suspected of having a book, and was at once called upon to give an account of myself. All this, however, was entirely *too late*. The first, and never to be retraced, step had been taken. In teaching me the alphabet, in the days of her simplicity and kindness, my mistress had given me the "inch," and now, no ordinary precaution could prevent me from taking the "ell."[2]

Seized with a determination to learn to read, at any cost, I hit upon many expedients to accomplish the desired end. The plea which I mainly adopted, and the one by which I was most successful, was that of using my young white playmates, with whom I met in the street, as teachers. I used to carry, almost constantly, a copy of Webster's spelling book in my pocket; and, when sent on errands, or when play time was allowed me, I would step, with my young friends, aside, and take a lesson in spelling. I generally paid my *tuition fee* to the boys, with bread, which I also carried in my pocket. For a single biscuit, any of my hungry little comrades would give me a lesson more valuable to me than bread. Not everyone, however, demanded this consideration, for there were those who took pleasure in teaching me, whenever I had a chance to be taught by them. I am strongly tempted to give the names of two or three of those little boys, as a slight testimonial of the gratitude and affection I bear them, but prudence forbids; not that it would injure me, but it might, possibly, embarrass them; for it is almost an unpardonable offense to do anything, directly or indirectly, to promote a slave's freedom, in a slave state. It is enough to say, of my warm-hearted little play fellows, that they lived on Philpot Street, very near Durgin & Bailey's shipyard.

For a single biscuit, any of my hungry little comrades would give me a lesson more valuable to me than bread.

Although slavery was a delicate subject, and very cautiously talked about among grownup people in Maryland, I frequently talked about it—and that very freely—with the white boys. I would, sometimes, say to them, while seated on a curbstone or a cellar door, "I wish I could be free, as you will be when you get to be men." "You will be free, you know, as soon as you are twenty-one, and can go where you like, but I am a slave for life. Have I not as good a right to be free as you have?" Words like these, I observed, always troubled them; and I had no small satisfaction in wringing from the boys, occasionally, that fresh and bitter condemnation of slavery, that springs from nature, unseared and unperverted.[3] Of all consciences let me have those to deal with which have not been bewildered by the cares of

2. **ell** *n.* former English measure of length, equal to forty-five inches.
3. **unperverted** (un´ pər vʉrt´ id) *adj.* uncorrupted; pure.

A Home on the Mississippi, Currier & Ives, The Museum of the City of New York

life. I do not remember ever to have met with a *boy*, while I was in slavery, who defended the slave system; but I have often had boys to console me, with the hope that something would yet occur, by which I might be made free. Over and over again, they have told me, that "they believed *I* had as good a right to be free as *they* had"; and that "they did not believe God ever made anyone to be a slave." The reader will easily see, that such little conversations with my play fellows, had no tendency to weaken my love of liberty, nor to render me contented with my condition as a slave.

When I was about thirteen years old, and had succeeded in learning to read, every increase of knowledge, especially respecting the free states, added something to the almost **intolerable** burden of the thought—"I am a slave for life." To my bondage I saw no end. It was a terrible reality, and I shall never be able to tell how sadly that thought chafed my young spirit. Fortunately, or unfortunately, about this time in my life, I had made enough money to buy what was then a very popular schoolbook, the *Columbian Orator.* I bought this addition to my library, of Mr. Knight, on Thames street, Fell's Point, Baltimore, and paid him fifty cents for it. I was first led to buy this book, by hearing some little boys say they were going to learn some little pieces out of it for the exhibition. This volume was, indeed, a rich treasure, and every opportunity afforded me, for a time, was spent in diligently perusing it. . . . The dialogue and the

▲ Critical Viewing
How does this idealized picture of plantation life contrast with Douglass's experiences as an enslaved African American? **[Contrast]**

Vocabulary
intolerable (in ´täl ər ə bəl) *adj.* unbearable; too severe

What beliefs do Douglass's playmates express about slavery?

The American EXPERIENCE

Slave Narratives

Between 1760 and the end of the Civil War, when slavery was officially abolished, testimonies of hundreds of fugitives and former slaves appeared in the form of slave narratives. These narratives exposed the inhumanities of the slave system as former slaves recorded the harsh conditions they suffered at the hands of their owners. Their writings did more than document their personal experiences for the enlightenment of others. They also served to create permanent reminders that could not be easily ignored by the reunified nation. In the 1920s and 1930s, The Federal Writers Project created an archive of these narratives, preserving the memory of the painful realities of American slavery.

Connect to the Literature

Douglass intended his narrative to be read by both black and white audiences. What do you think his purpose was in describing his white playmates' attitudes toward slavery?

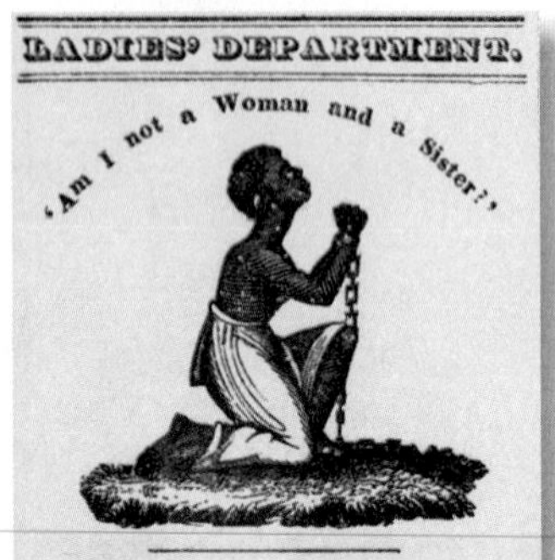
LADIES' DEPARTMENT.
'Am I not a Woman and a Sister?'
White Lady, happy, proud and free,
Lend awhile thine ear to me ;
Let the Negro Mother's wail
Turn thy pale cheek still more pale.
Can the Negro Mother joy
Over this her captive boy,
Which in bondage and in tears,
For a life of wo she rears?
Though she bears a Mother's name,
A Mother's rights she may not claim ;
For the white man's will can part,
Her darling from her bursting heart.

speeches were all redolent of the principles of liberty, and poured floods of light on the nature and character of slavery. As I read, behold! the very discontent so graphically predicted by Master Hugh, had already come upon me. I was no longer the light-hearted, gleesome boy, full of mirth and play, as when I landed first at Baltimore. Knowledge had come. . . . This knowledge opened my eyes to the horrible pit, and revealed the teeth of the frightful dragon that was ready to pounce upon me, but it opened no way for my escape. I have often wished myself a beast, or a bird—anything, rather than a slave. I was wretched and gloomy, beyond my ability to describe. I was too thoughtful to be happy. It was this everlasting thinking which distressed and tormented me; and yet there was no getting rid of the subject of my thoughts. All nature was redolent of it. Once awakened by the silver trump[4] of knowledge, my spirit was roused to eternal wakefulness. Liberty! the inestimable birthright of every man, had, for me, converted every object into an asserter of this great right. It was heard in every sound, and beheld in every object. It was ever present, to torment me with a sense of my wretched condition. The more beautiful and charming were the smiles of nature, the more horrible and desolate was my condition. I saw nothing without seeing it, and I heard nothing without hearing it. I do not exaggerate, when I say, that it looked from every star, smiled in every calm, breathed in every wind, and moved in every storm.

I have no doubt that my state of mind had something to do with the change in the treatment adopted, by my once kind mistress toward me. I can easily believe, that my leaden, downcast, and discontented look, was very offensive to her. Poor lady! She did not know my trouble, and I dared not tell her. Could I have freely made her acquainted with the real state of my mind, and given her the reasons therefor, it might have been well for both of us. Her abuse of me fell upon me like the blows of the false prophet upon his ass; she did not know that an *angel* stood in the way;[5] and—such is the relation of master and slave—I could not tell her. Nature had made us *friends*; slavery made us *enemies.* My interests were in a direction opposite to hers, and we both had our private thoughts and plans. She aimed to keep me ignorant; and I resolved to know, although knowledge only increased my discontent. My feelings were

---

4. **trump** trumpet.
5. **blows . . . the way** allusion to a biblical tale (Numbers 22:21–35) about an ass that cannot move, though she is beaten by her master, because her path is blocked by an angel.

not the result of any marked cruelty in the treatment I received; they sprung from the consideration of my being a slave at all. It was *slavery*—not its mere *incidents*—that I hated. I had been cheated. I saw through the attempt to keep me in ignorance. . . . The feeding and clothing me well, could not atone for taking my liberty from me. The smiles of my mistress could not remove the deep sorrow that dwelt in my young bosom. Indeed, these, in time, came only to deepen my sorrow. She had changed; and the reader will see that I had changed, too. We were both victims to the same overshadowing evil—*she,* as mistress, *I,* as slave. I will not censure her harshly; she cannot censure me, for she knows I speak but the truth, and have acted in my opposition to slavery, just as she herself would have acted, in a reverse of circumstances.

I have often wished myself a beast, or a bird—anything, rather than a slave.

Critical Reading

1. **Key Ideas and Details (a)** What does Mrs. Auld initially think about Douglass's reading? **(b) Draw Conclusions:** Why do you think she is later "violent in her opposition" to Douglass's reading?
2. **Key Ideas and Details (a)** What book does Douglass buy when he is about thirteen years old? **(b) Analyze Causes and Effects:** How does reading this transform Douglass from "light-hearted" to "wretched and gloomy"?
3. **Key Ideas and Details (a)** What consumed Douglass once he obtained knowledge? **(b) Support:** How does his experience prove his mistress's belief that education and slavery are incompatible?
4. **Integration of Knowledge and Ideas** What personal qualities do you think helped Douglass become an effective champion of human rights? Use at least two of these Essential Question words in your response: *conviction, determination, goal, justice, humanity. **[Connecting to the Essential Question: How does literature shape or reflect society?]***

Cite textual evidence to support your responses.

After You Read from *My Bondage and My Freedom*

Literary Analysis

1. **Key Ideas and Details (a)** Describe the treatment Douglass receives as a slave in the Auld household. **(b)** In what ways does his **autobiography** make a powerful case against slavery?
2. **Craft and Structure (a)** Using a chart like the one shown, select three events from this excerpt, and explain the **purpose,** or reason, Douglass includes each one in his narrative. **(b)** How does each event advance his overall purpose for writing?

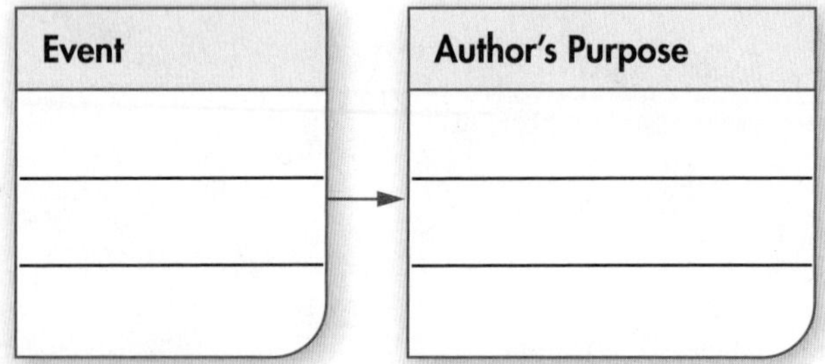

Event	Author's Purpose

3. **Craft and Structure (a)** Note at least three positive words or phrases Douglass uses to describe Mrs. Auld. **(b)** How does he seem to feel about her? Explain.
4. **Craft and Structure (a)** Considering their relationship as owner and slave, what is remarkable about Douglass's *tone* in his discussion of Mrs. Auld? **(b)** What does this suggest about Douglass's purpose in writing his life story?
5. **Integration of Knowledge and Ideas** In what ways would this account be different if it had been written by another member of the Auld household, such as Mrs. Auld? Explain.

Reading Strategy

6. In approaching this selection, you **set a purpose for reading**—to *evaluate the historical influences that shape the narrative.* Note two specific observations you made as a result of setting this focus. Explain.
7. Note three specific ways in which Douglass's narrative—indeed, his life itself—is shaped by historical influences of the period.
8. What *ethical, political, and social* conflicts are evident in Mrs. Auld's changing behavior toward Douglass? Explain.
9. **(a)** How does his reading of the *Columbian Orator* affect Douglass? **(b)** To what *philosophical* ideas does it awaken him?
10. As an adult, Douglass was a staunch advocate of human rights. How do you think the philosophical influences he encountered as a child affected his adult decisions? Explain.
11. Based on this account, how did some people of Douglass's era justify owning slaves?

Common Core State Standards

Writing

2. Write informative/explanatory texts to examine and convey complex ideas, concepts, and information clearly and accurately through the effective selection, organization, and analysis of content. *(p. 529)*

2.a. Introduce a topic; organize complex ideas, concepts, and information so that each new element builds on that which precedes it to create a unified whole. *(p. 529)*

2.b. Develop the topic thoroughly by selecting the most significant and relevant facts, concrete details, quotations, or other information and examples. *(p. 529)*

2.c. Use appropriate and varied transitions and syntax to link the major sections of the text, create cohesion, and clarify the relationships among complex ideas and concepts. *(p. 529)*

Language

4.b. Identify and correctly use patterns of word changes that indicate different meanings or parts of speech. *(p. 529)*

4.d. Verify the preliminary determination of the meaning of a word or phrase. *(p. 529)*

PERFORMANCE TASKS

Integrated Language Skills

Vocabulary Acquisition and Use

Word Analysis: Latin Root *-bene-*

The Latin root *-bene-* means "well" or "good." In the word *benevolent*, it combines with a form of the Latin word *velle*, which means "to want," or "to wish." Thus, *benevolent* literally means "a disposition to do good," or "with good wishes." Define each of the numbered words, incorporating the meaning of the root *–bene-* into your definition. If necessary, consult a dictionary to check your work.

1. benefit
2. benefactor
3. benediction
4. beneficence
5. benign

Vocabulary: Sentence Completions

Fill in the blanks in each sentence below with the appropriate vocabulary word from the list on page 518. Then, explain your reasoning.

1. Douglass holds a _______ belief that slavery is morally wrong.
2. His eloquent prose proves that slaves are not _______ in intellect.
3. Douglass argues that slavery is an _______ institution that must be eliminated.
4. His _______ to slavery could not be more firm.
5. Douglass's _______ attitude toward Mrs. Auld suggests his greatness of spirit.
6. The conflicts and _______ of violating her own good nature changes Mrs. Auld's personality.

Writing

Informative Text College applications often require a **reflective essay** about an experience that helped shape you as a person. Just as Douglass described how knowledge freed him, identify a key event in your life, and write an essay communicating its significance. Follow the model Douglass set of combining *narration*, or storytelling, with other rhetorical strategies, such as *description, exposition,* or *explanation,* and—if appropriate—*persuasion.*

Prewriting Outline the details of the event and its effect on you. List details in chronological order to establish organization. Identify points at which your essay will benefit from description, explanation, or persuasion.

Drafting Introduce the experience and explain why it is important. Then, write the body paragraphs to follow your outline. Conclude with a paragraph that insightfully sums up the meaning of the experience in your life.

Revising Review your essay and make sure you have balanced the narrative, or storytelling aspect, with a discussion of its meaning. If necessary, add transitional words, concrete sensory details, or more in-depth explanation to clarify that balance.

Model: Planning a Clear and Logical Organization

A. Experience: I worked in a local campaign office.
B. What happened:
1. met the candidate; was inspired to join her campaign
2. distributed flyers; polled voters
3. phoned residents to encourage voting

C. Outcome: I learned teamwork and the power of democracy.

Chronological order makes it easy for readers to follow events.

Before You Read

Go Down, Moses • Swing Low, Sweet Chariot

Connecting to the Essential Question The sense of place in spirituals is often a longed-for promised land that offers delivery from pain. As you read, noticing how settings are described will help as you consider the Essential Question: **What is the relationship between literature and place?**

Reading Literature

4. Determine the meaning of words and phrases as they are used in the text, including figurative meanings; analyze the impact of specific word choices on meaning and tone, including language that is particularly fresh, engaging, or beautiful.

5. Analyze how an author's choices concerning how to structure specific parts of a text contribute to its overall structure and meaning as well as its aesthetic impact.

Literary Analysis

Spirituals are folk songs that were often sung by enslaved African Americans. The following structures are shared by virtually all spirituals:

- A **refrain** is a word, phrase, line, or group of lines repeated at regular intervals. A refrain emphasizes key ideas, sets a rhythm, and makes a song easier to remember. Refrains also allowed spirituals to have a call-and-response format in which a leader sang the verses and the rest of the group acted like a chorus and sang the refrain.
- **Biblical allusions** and **allegory:** Spirituals are full of allusions, or references, to people, places, and events from the Bible. These allusions often have allegorical meaning. An allegory is a story in which all the literal elements are also symbols. For example, in the Old Testament story, Moses led the ancient Israelites out of slavery. References to Moses in the spirituals are allegorical; the slaves are referring to both the Biblical story and to their own yearning for a guide who will lead them to freedom. As you read, analyze the meaning of Biblical allusions in specific passages as well as in each spiritual as a whole.

Comparing Literary Works Compare and contrast the messages of freedom expressed in the refrains to these songs. In particular, consider similarities and differences in the emotional quality of those messages.

Reading Strategy

Preparing to Read Complex Texts Songs are created to be heard; **listening,** therefore, is an especially important skill for appreciating lyrics. Read each spiritual aloud, listening to its *rhythm, rhymes,* and *repeated sounds.* Think about the *moods,* or emotions, these sound devices help to express. Record your observations in a chart like the one shown.

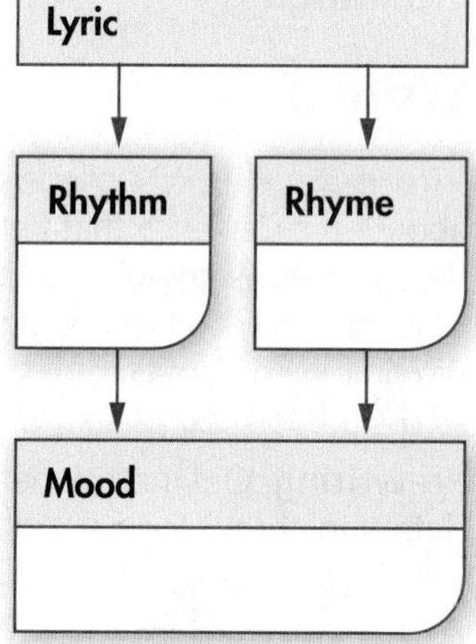

Vocabulary

oppressed (ə prest′) *v.* kept down by cruel or unjust power (p. 533)

smite (smīt) *v.* kill by a powerful blow (p. 533)

SPIRITUALS

Spirituals are folk songs that originated among enslaved and oppressed African Americans. Spirituals took the forms of anthems, ballads, shouts, and jubilees to reflect different moods and circumstances. Containing both social and religious content, spirituals helped to shape the conscious identity of an enslaved people. They also helped slaves persevere under the physical and psychological pressures of their daily lives. These songs conveyed the singers' pain, their yearning for freedom, and their rage against slavery. In doing so, they brought to life the emotional impact of slavery, which divided our nation for decades and played a key role in causing the Civil War. Frederick Douglass, a slave who became one of the most important writers of his time, wrote of the spirituals, "Every tone was a testimony against slavery and a prayer to God for deliverance from chains."

Song of the Fields Plantation owners encouraged field hands to sing, reasoning that people who were busy singing could not plot escape or rebellion. They generally accepted spirituals because of their religious content. The slaves, however, found ways to benefit from singing. These songs provided an outlet for the grief and frustration they often kept bottled up inside. Spirituals also communicated messages of hope and encouragement. Likewise, their traditional African sounds and rhythms helped slaves maintain a connection to their homelands and heritages. In addition, the language in some spirituals provided a means to communicate forbidden thoughts and feelings. For example, songs that referred to the escape of Biblical slaves expressed the slaves' own hope that they would someday escape to a "promised land." Other songs did more than express feelings; they actually provided specific directions for escape. In "Follow the Drinking Gourd," fugitive slaves were advised to follow the Big Dipper north to freedom.

"Every tone was a testimony against slavery and a prayer to God for deliverance from chains."

—Frederick Douglass

Path to Popularity Spirituals were almost unknown outside the South until after the Civil War. In 1867, a collection of African American music called *Slave Songs of the United States* was published. In 1871, a black choral group, The Jubilee Singers from Fisk University, traveled throughout the United States and to England and Germany singing spirituals to raise money for their school. The Jubilee Singers were extremely gifted and became highly successful, even singing for Queen Victoria in England. Students from other schools followed their example and helped popularize the spiritual. Today, spirituals are performed by singers of all types, and their influence is apparent in contemporary music forms such as blues and jazz.

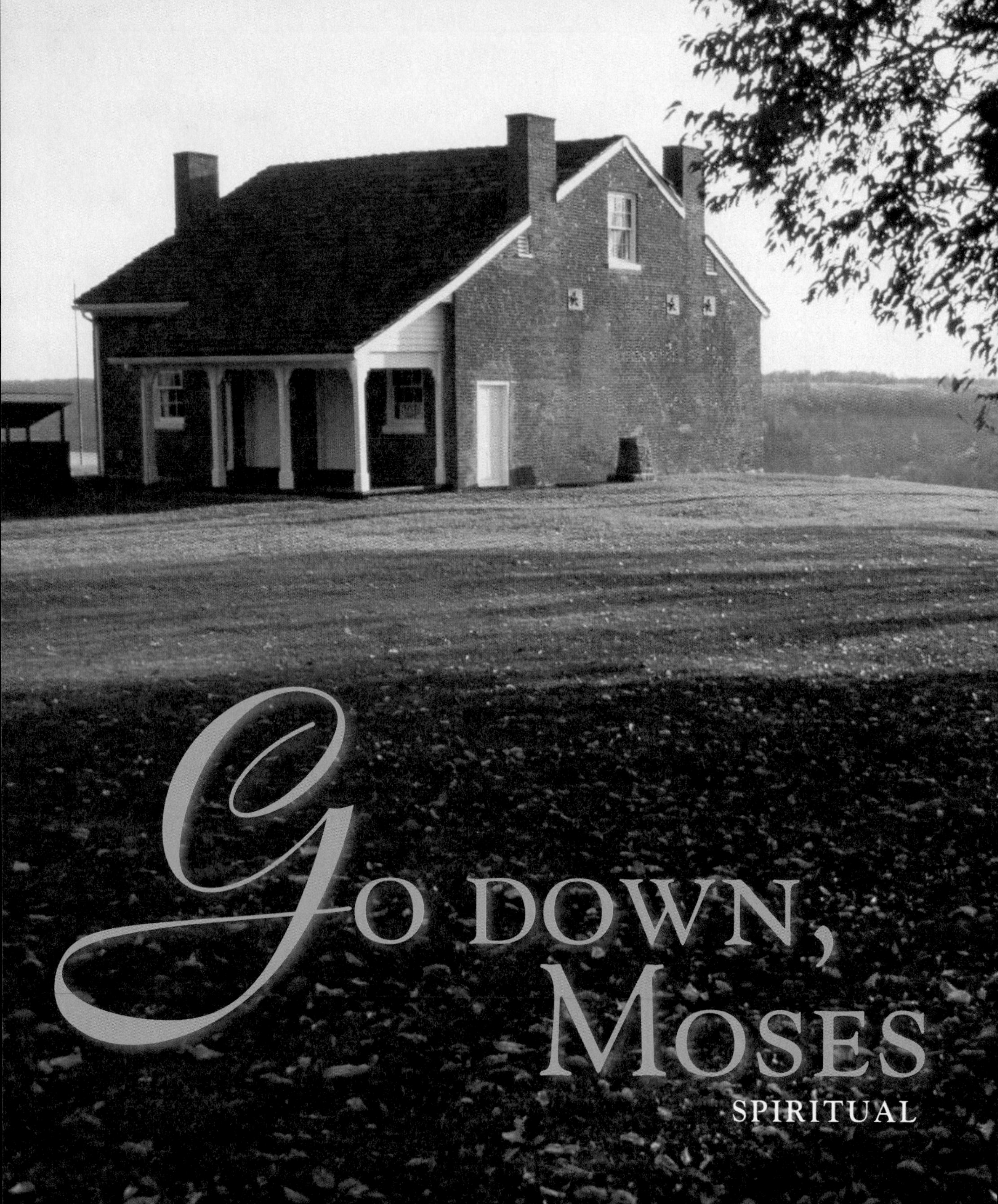

Go Down, Moses

Spiritual

BACKGROUND Africans were first brought to this country as slaves in 1619. Although the slave trade was banned in 1808, slavery itself remained legal. In the years before the Civil War, many enslaved Africans fled captivity. They were hidden and transported by the Underground Railroad, a secret network of activists dedicated to helping fugitives reach freedom in the North and in Canada. One of these activists was Harriet Tubman, who was born a slave around 1820. Tubman's remarkable efforts earned her the name "Moses." In the Bible, Moses led the Israelites out of captivity in Egypt. Tubman escaped slavery via the Underground Railroad and then risked her life to return for her family. She returned to the South repeatedly to rescue other enslaved Africans, eventually leading more than 300 people to freedom.

▲ Portrait of Harriet Tubman, also known as "Moses"

Go down, Moses,
Way down in Egypt land
Tell old Pharaoh
To let my people go.

When Israel was in Egypt land
Let my people go
Oppressed so hard they could not stand
Let my people go.

Go down, Moses,
Way down in Egypt land
Tell old Pharaoh
"Let my people go."

"Thus saith the Lord," bold Moses said,
"Let my people go;
If not I'll smite your first-born dead
Let my people go."

Go down, Moses,
Way down in Egypt land,
Tell old Pharaoh,
"Let my people go!"

Vocabulary

oppressed (ə prest′) *v.* kept down by cruel or unjust power

smite (smīt) *v.* kill by a powerful blow

◀ **Critical Viewing** The Rankin House, shown here, was a stop on the Underground Railroad. How does the mood of this picture reflect the role the home played? **[Connect]**

Swing Low, Sweet Chariot

SPIRITUAL

Swing low, sweet chariot,
Coming for to carry me home,
Swing low, sweet chariot,
Coming for to carry me home.

I looked over Jordan[1] and what did I see
Coming for to carry me home,
A band of angels coming after me,
Coming for to carry me home.

If you get there before I do,
Coming for to carry me home,
Tell all my friends I'm coming too,
Coming for to carry me home.

Swing low, sweet chariot,
Coming for to carry me home,
Swing low, sweet chariot,
Coming for to carry me home.

Reading Strategy
Listening Read the song aloud. What is the effect of the repetition of the word *home*?

1. **Jordan** river of the Middle East that flows from the Lebanon Mountains through the Sea of Galilee to the Dead Sea. Many spirituals use the phrase "crossing over Jordan" as a metaphor for crossing the Ohio River to freedom or going to heaven.

Critical Reading

Cite textual evidence to support your responses.

1. **Key Ideas and Details (a)** In "Go Down, Moses," who is oppressed? **(b) Connect:** What connection might these oppressed people have with the slaves?
2. **Key Ideas and Details (a)** Whom does Moses tell to "let my people go"? **(b) Interpret:** If this song is related to the slaves, whom might this figure represent?
3. **Key Ideas and Details (a)** In "Swing Low, Sweet Chariot," who is coming to carry the speaker home? **(b) Interpret:** What might these figures represent?
4. **Key Ideas and Details Interpret:** Knowing that spirituals were often "code" songs for escape, do you see any hidden messages in these songs? Explain.
5. **Integration of Knowledge and Ideas** What qualities do the places described in these songs have? How do they compare to the actual places inhabited by the slaves? In your response, use at least two of these Essential Question words: *escape, desire, respite, expression. **[Connecting to the Essential Question: What is the relationship between literature and place?]***

After You Read

Go Down, Moses • Swing Low, Sweet Chariot

Literary Analysis

1. **Craft and Structure** What **refrains,** both lines and entire stanzas, appear in each **spiritual?**
2. **Key Ideas and Details** **(a)** Using a chart like the one shown, identify one **Biblical allusion** in each spiritual. **(b)** Explain how each allusion functions as an **allegory.**

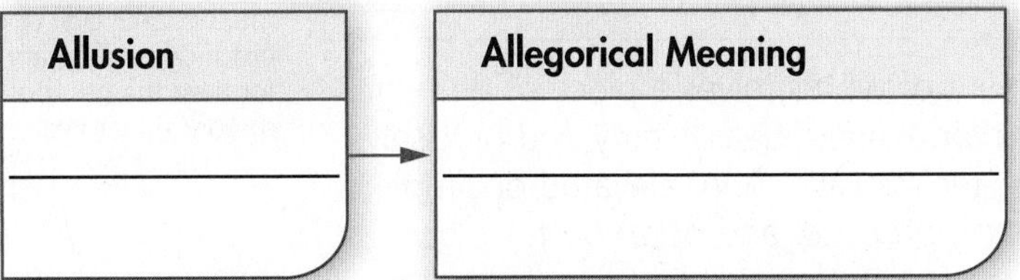

3. **Comparing Literary Works** **(a)** In what ways are the messages about freedom in each song similar and different? **(b)** How are the moods or emotional qualities of each song similar and different? Explain.

Reading Strategy

4. Read the spirituals aloud, **listening** to their sound elements. **(a)** Identify the uses of *rhythm, rhyme, and repetition* in both songs. **(b)** Explain how these musical elements help reinforce each song's meaning.

Common Core State Standards

Writing
6. Use technology, including the Internet, to produce, publish, and update individual or shared writing products in response to ongoing feedback, including new arguments or information.

Language
5. Demonstrate understanding of word relationships.

PERFORMANCE TASKS

Integrated Language Skills

Vocabulary Acquisition and Use

Antonyms For each numbered word, select the letter of the answer that is the best antonym, or word of opposite meaning. Explain your choices.

1. oppressed	**(a)** crushed	**(b)** assisted	**(c)** punished
2. smite	**(a)** hit	**(b)** question	**(c)** caress

Writing

Informative Text Using the Internet and library resources, find recordings of several spirituals and related art or illustrations from the historical period discussed in this unit. Incorporate the recordings and images into a **slide presentation** about spirituals in their historical context. Write a brief introduction for each song and a general introduction to the presentation as a whole. Consider including quotations from the following types of writers or speakers:

- scholars who have written about this genre of music
- important African American figures, such as Harriet Tubman or Frederick Douglass

If possible, post your presentation to an approved Internet site, such as a class or school Web site. Invite constructive comments and incorporate feedback into a revised presentation.

Before You Read

The Gettysburg Address • Letter to His Son

Connecting to the Essential Question These selections were written by two patriotic men on opposite sides of a conflict. As you read, look for ideas that express each writer's patriotism. This will help as you consider the Essential Question: **How does literature shape or reflect society?**

Reading Informational Text
9. Analyze nineteenth-century foundational U.S. documents of historical and literary significance for their themes, purposes, and rhetorical features.

Literary Analysis

Diction, the choice and arrangement of words, gives a piece of writing its unique quality and helps the writer express ideas clearly and precisely. Diction may be formal or informal, technical or plain, elevated or simple. Diction is influenced by the *audience, purpose,* and *occasion* for a given text. For example, in this public speech, Lincoln's diction has a formality that suits the occasion and purpose of the event:

> Four score and seven years ago, our fathers brought forth on this continent a new nation . . .

In this private letter to his son, Lee's informal diction suits his audience:

> As far as I can judge by the papers, we are between a state of anarchy and civil war . . .

As you read, note how each writer's diction reflects the audience, purpose, and occasion of his writing.

Comparing Literary Works Each selection communicates a writer's views about the Civil War, but from very different vantage points. Lee, a Southerner, wrote on the eve of conflict, whereas Lincoln, the Union leader, wrote from a battlefield two years into the war. Compare and contrast the insights each writer brings to this painful conflict.

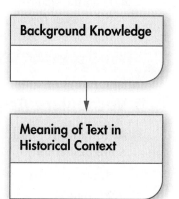

Background Knowledge
↓
Meaning of Text in Historical Context

Reading Strategy

Preparing to Read Complex Texts When reading historical documents, it is helpful to understand the situations that inspired them. **Use your background knowledge** of the Civil War to analyze the ideas these writers express in their historical context. Complete a chart like the one shown to organize your ideas.

Vocabulary

consecrate (kän′ si krāt′) *v.* cause to be revered or honored (p. 539)

hallow (hal′ ō) *v.* honor as sacred (p. 539)

virtuous (vʉr′ cho͞o əs) *adj.* characterized by moral virtue (p. 541)

anarchy (an′ ər kē) *n.* absence of government (p. 541)

Abraham Lincoln

(1809–1865)

Author of the Gettysburg Address

Serving as president during one of the most tragic periods in American history, Abraham Lincoln fought to reunite a nation torn apart by war. His courage, strength, and dedication in the face of an overwhelming national crisis have made him one of the most admired and respected American presidents.

Lincoln was born into a family of humble means. As a child, his duties on his parents' farm limited his opportunities to receive a formal education. Still, he was an avid reader and developed an early interest in politics. He served in the Illinois state legislature and the United States Congress, where he earned a reputation as a champion of emancipation. In 1858, he ran for the United States Senate against Stephen Douglas. Lincoln lost the election, but his heated debates with Douglas brought him national recognition and helped him win the presidency in 1860.

Troubled Times Shortly after his election, the Civil War erupted. Throughout the war, Lincoln showed great strength and courage. He also demonstrated his gift for oratory. He was invited to make "a few appropriate remarks" in November 1863 for a dedication of the Gettysburg battlefield as a national cemetery. The world has long remembered what he said there.

Lincoln's great care as a writer shows in the Gettysburg Address, as it does in many of his other speeches. He worked diligently and thoughtfully to prepare messages that would have the effect he desired. Two important aspects of the Gettysburg speech are its brevity—just 272 words—and its reaffirmation of the democratic principles at the heart of American government. Lincoln was killed by an assassin's bullet in 1865 while attending the theater with his wife.

"As I would not be a slave, so I would not be a master. This expresses my idea of democracy. Whatever differs from this, to the extent of the difference, is no democracy."

THE GETTYSBURG ADDRESS

Abraham Lincoln

November 19, 1863

BACKGROUND The battle of Gettysburg, Pennsylvania, fought in July 1863, was an important Union victory and marked a turning point in the war. More than 51,000 soldiers were injured in the battle. On November 19, 1863, while the war still raged, a military cemetery on the battlefield was dedicated. Unsure of President Lincoln's availability, the dedication organizers slated him as a secondary speaker, asking him to make only "a few appropriate remarks." In drafting that brief address, Lincoln wanted to lead the 15,000 American citizens attending the dedication through an emotional, final rite of passage. He also needed to gain continuing support for a bloody conflict that was far from over.

Four score and seven years ago our fathers brought forth on this continent a new nation, conceived in Liberty, and dedicated to the proposition that all men are created equal.

Now we are engaged in a great civil war, testing whether that nation, or any nation so conceived and so dedicated, can long endure. We are met on a great battle-field of that war. We have come to dedicate a portion of that field, as a final resting place for those who here gave their lives that that nation might live. It is altogether fitting and proper that we should do this.

But, in a larger sense, we can not dedicate—we can not consecrate—we can not hallow—this ground. The brave men, living and dead, who struggled here, have consecrated it, far above our poor power to add or detract. The world will little note, nor long remember what we say here, but it can never forget what they did here. It is for us the living, rather, to be dedicated here to the unfinished work which they who fought here have thus far so nobly advanced. It is rather for us to be here dedicated to the great task remaining before us—that from these honored dead we take increased devotion to that cause for which they gave the last full measure of devotion—that we here highly resolve that these dead shall not have died in vain—that this nation, under God, shall have a new birth of freedom—and that government of the people, by the people, for the people, shall not perish from the earth.

Literary Analysis

Diction What impression do you get of the speaker from the level of diction in "four score and seven years ago"?

Vocabulary

consecrate (kän′ si krāt′) *v.* cause to be revered or honored

hallow (hal′ ō) *v.* honor as sacred

◀ **Critical Viewing** What do the details in this painting of Lincoln suggest about the esteem in which he was held by people of his time? **[Infer]**

Robert E. Lee (1807–1870)

Author of "Letter to His Son"

Robert E. Lee was born into a respected Virginia family with a strong military tradition and graduated with high honors from the United States Military Academy at West Point. During the Mexican War, he established a reputation as one of the finest leaders in the United States Army.

Divided Loyalties Despite his military training and talent, the job of commanding the Confederate army during the Civil War was not one that Robert E. Lee wanted. As the dispute over slavery grew, Lee was torn. A descendant of a number of distinguished patriots and statesmen, he believed in the Union and opposed both slavery and secession. Still, when President Lincoln offered him command of the Union forces, Lee refused to lead an army against his native state and resigned from the army, vowing to fight only in defense of Virginia.

A Difficult Task Unlike many Confederate leaders, Lee had no illusions about the South's power. Serving initially as commander of the army of northern Virginia and later of all the Confederate armies, he expected the widespread bloodshed and destruction caused by the war. He was an extraordinary military leader whose accomplishments and personal integrity in the face of overwhelming odds inspired great loyalty in both soldiers and civilians.

An avid letter writer, Lee wrote frequently to family members explaining his actions and expressing his feelings. On the eve of resigning his U.S. Army commission, Lee explored his divided loyalties in "Letter to His Son." After the war, Lee served as president of Washington College (now Washington and Lee) until his death.

"Do your duty in all things. You cannot do more, you should never wish to do less."

Letter to His Son

Robert E. Lee
January 23,1861

I received Everett's[1] *Life of Washington* which you sent me, and enjoyed its perusal. How his spirit would be grieved could he see the wreck of his mighty labors! I will not, however, permit myself to believe, until all ground of hope is gone, that the fruit of his noble deeds will be destroyed, and that his precious advice and virtuous example will so soon be forgotten by his countrymen. As far as I can judge by the papers, we are between a state of anarchy and civil war. May God avert both of these evils from us! I fear that mankind will not for years be sufficiently Christianized to bear the absence of restraint and force. I see that four states[2] have declared themselves out of the Union; four more will apparently follow their example. Then, if the border states are brought into the gulf of revolution, one half of the country will be arrayed against the other. I must try and be patient and await the end, for I can do nothing to hasten or rètard it.

The South, in my opinion, has been aggrieved by the acts of the North, as you say. I feel the aggression and am willing to take every proper step for redress. It is the principle I contend for, not individual or private benefit. As an American citizen, I take great pride in my country, her prosperity and institutions, and would defend any state if her rights were invaded. But I can anticipate

1. **Everett's** referring to Edward Everett (1794–1865), an American scholar and orator who made a long speech at Gettysburg before Lincoln delivered his famous address.
2. **four states** South Carolina, Mississippi, Florida, and Alabama.

▲ Critical Viewing
What sense of Lee as a leader does this painting convey? **[Interpret]**

Vocabulary
virtuous (ˈvʉrˊ choo əs) *adj.* characterized by moral virtue

anarchy (anˊ ər kē) *n.* absence of government

According to Lee, what is the political state of the country?

Reading Strategy
Using Background Knowledge Given what you know about Lee, why was he so committed to both the Union and to Virginia?

> *I* shall mourn for my country and for the welfare and progress of mankind.

no greater calamity for the country than a dissolution of the Union. It would be an accumulation of all the evils we complain of, and I am willing to sacrifice everything but honor for its preservation. I hope, therefore, that all constitutional means will be exhausted before there is a resort to force. Secession is nothing but revolution. The framers of our Constitution never exhausted so much labor, wisdom, and forbearance in its formation, and surrounded it with so many guards and securities, if it was intended to be broken by every member of the Confederacy at will. It was intended for "perpetual union," so expressed in the preamble, and for the establishment of a government, not a compact, which can only be dissolved by revolution or the consent of all the people in convention assembled. It is idle to talk of secession. Anarchy would have been established, and not a government, by Washington, Hamilton, Jefferson, Madison, and the other patriots of the Revolution. . . . Still, a Union that can only be maintained by swords and bayonets, and in which strife and civil war are to take the place of brotherly love and kindness, has no charm for me. I shall mourn for my country and for the welfare and progress of mankind. If the Union is dissolved, and the government disrupted, I shall return to my native state and share the miseries of my people; and, save in defense, will draw my sword on none.

Critical Reading

1. **Key Ideas and Details (a)** What vision of the nation does Lincoln describe at the close of his speech? **(b) Connect:** In what way does an expression of this vision further his purpose for speaking?
2. **Key Ideas and Details (a)** What gift has Lee's son given him? **(b) Connect:** How is Lee's recognition of this gift linked to his feelings about secession? Explain.
3. **Key Ideas and Details (a)** How would you explain Lee's use of the word *Union*? **(b)** In what ways does he clarify or refine the meaning of the word *Union*? **(c) Summarize:** In your own words, explain Lee's argument against secession.
4. **Integration of Knowledge and Ideas** Based on these selections, how do you think both Lincoln and Lee define American patriotism? In your response, use at least two of these Essential Question words: *devotion, unity, conviction, aspiration.* ***[Connecting to the Essential Question: How does literature shape or reflect society?]***

Cite textual evidence to support your responses.

After You Read

The Gettysburg Address • Letter to His Son

Literary Analysis

1. **Craft and Structure** Using a chart like the one shown, analyze how the **diction** used by each writer is appropriate to the audience, occasion, and purpose of the text.

	Examples of Diction	Audience	Occasion	Purpose
Lincoln				
Lee				

2. **Craft and Structure** Choose one passage from each selection in which the diction seems especially effective in expressing and clarifying the writer's meaning. Explain your choices.

3. **Comparing Literary Works** **(a)** What words does Lincoln use to describe the war? **(b)** What words does Lee use to describe it? **(c)** What personal views about the war do you think the two men share?

4. **Craft and Structure** Which voice do you find more engaging, Lincoln's or Lee's? Why?

Reading Strategy

5. **Using background knowledge,** explain why President Lincoln wrote such a short speech for his address at Gettysburg.

6. Why did Lincoln connect the honoring of those who died at Gettysburg with the goal of continuing the war toward a Union victory?

7. Why was Lee so opposed to secession?

Common Core State Standards

Writing

2. Write informative/explanatory texts to examine and convey complex ideas, concepts, and information clearly and accurately through the effective selection, organization, and analysis of content.

2.c. Use appropriate and varied transitions and syntax to link the major sections of the text, create cohesion, and clarify the relationships among complex ideas and concepts.

PERFORMANCE TASKS

Integrated Language Skills

Vocabulary Acquisition and Use

Use New Words in Sentences For each word pair, write one sentence using both words correctly.

1. consecrate/hallow
2. anarchy/virtuous

Writing

Explanatory Text Abraham Lincoln and Robert E. Lee wrote from different sides of the Civil War conflict, yet both take a historical view about the founding principles of the United States. Write a **compare-and-contrast essay** in which you describe each writer's understanding of the relationship between the Civil War strife of their own generation and the ideas on which the United States was founded. To clarify the flow of your ideas, *use transitional words and phrases* that show contrast or similarity, such as "alternatively," "on the other hand," and "in a similar way."

CONTEMPORARY CONNECTION

Civil War Writings Past and Present

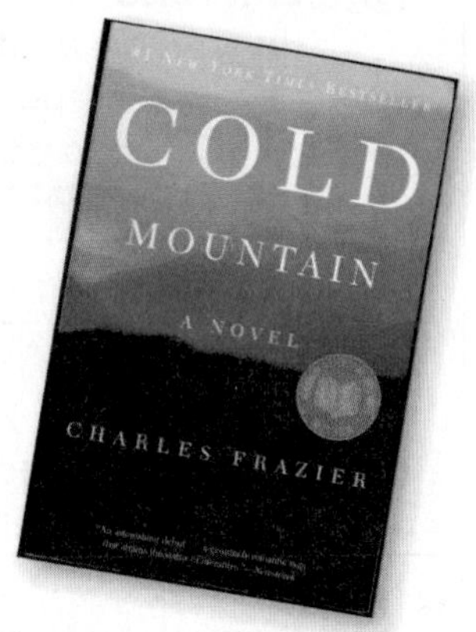

A turbulent and tragic stage in America's story, the Civil War has captured the imaginations of generations of American writers. Ambrose Bierce wrote about the war from firsthand experience as a Union soldier. Stephen Crane steeped himself in knowledge about the war in order to write his vivid stories. Margaret Mitchell set her sweeping 1936 bestseller *Gone With the Wind* during the Civil War. Ken Burns's documentary series, *Civil War*, debuted on public television stations in 1990. With 40 million viewers, it was the most-watched PBS series ever aired.

Charles Frazier's novel *Cold Mountain* continues this tradition. The story of a man's quest to return from the battlefield to his home in the Carolina mountains, the book stormed onto bestseller lists when it was published in 1997. In 2003, Nicole Kidman, Jude Law, and Renée Zellwegger starred in the feature film based on the book.

ANTHONY MINGHELLA Screenwriter/Director

British director and screenwriter Anthony Minghella's film career took off in 1990 with the release of *Truly, Madly, Deeply*, a drama he wrote and directed for Britain's BBC. He later wrote the screenplay adaptation of Patricia Highsmith's novel *The Talented Mr. Ripley* and directed the 1999 film starring Matt Damon. In 1996, Minghella won the Academy Award for Best Director for his work on *The English Patient,* a film he adaptated from his friend Michael Ondaatje's novel. Minghella once described a screenplay as "not beautiful in the way a book is beautiful . . . It's much more sort of a plan. So I tried not to even think of the screenplay as a defining document, as a piece of work in itself, but only as a route." Minghella was in Toronto, Canada, when Ondaatje gave him a copy of *Cold Mountain.* Upon his return home to London, he discovered two other people had sent him copies of the novel. He said, "I felt there must be some augury," or prophecy, in the coincidence. The film he wrote and directed was a critical and box office success and received seven Academy Award nominations. Sadly, Minghella's thriving career was cut short by his death in 2008.

JUDE LAW NICOLE KIDMAN RENÉE ZELLWEGER

FIND YOUR WAY HOME

from COLD MOUNTAIN

▲ Nicole Kidman plays Ada Monroe, a cultured young woman struggling to survive during the Civil War in the film version of *Cold Mountain*.

from COLD MOUNTAIN

a screenplay by

Anthony Minghella

based on the novel by

Charles Frazier

BACKGROUND The following scenes are set at Black Cove Farm, the home of Ada Monroe. Ada is a privileged young woman who has never had to work the land before. With the Civil War in full force, she has fallen on desperate times. The arrival of capable and tough Ruby Thewes saves both Ada's farm and her life.

79.[1] INT.[2] ADA'S BEDROOM, BLACK COVE FARM. PREDAWN. SUMMER 1864.

Ada wakes up to persistent knocking.

RUBY. (O.S.[3]) Ada? Ada? You up?

1. Numbers indicate scene numbers.
2. **INT.** abbreviation for "interior" or a scene shot indoors.
3. **O.S.** off screen, a voice heard without the actor appearing on screen.

ADA. Yes. *(opening her eyes)* It's still dark.

RUBY. (O.S.) Tell the cows that. It's late.

80. INT. KITCHEN, BLACK COVE FARM. PREDAWN. SUMMER 1864.

Ada enters blearily, clutching her novel. Ruby is already busy.

ADA. I have to eat something.

RUBY. Then you have to get up earlier. *(at Ada's book)* What's that?

ADA. A novel.

RUBY. *(heading outside)* You want to carry a book, carry one you can write in—

81. EXT.[4] BLACK COVE FARM. DAWN. SUMMER 1864.

Ruby emerges, followed by Ada, chewing on a carrot.

RUBY. —we got our own story. Called Black Cove Farm : a catastrophe.

She looks back at Ada for a reaction.

RUBY. (CONT.[5]) I can spell it, too. Learned the same place you did, in the schoolhouse. That's one of the first words they taught me. Ruby Thewes, you are a c-a-t-a-s-t-r-o-p-h-e.

They're heading for the stable.

82. INT. STABLE, BLACK COVE FARM. DAY. SUMMER 1864.

Ruby's already pitching hay. Turns to Ada, hands her a rake. Ada, half asleep, accepts obediently, stunned by this energy.

RUBY. Three years I was in school before my daddy—saying God rest his soul is like wishing him what he had in life, 'cause he lived to rest, he was born tired—before my daddy decided there was better use for me than have me sat all day in front of a chalkboard.

83. EXT. A FIELD OF WEEDS, BLACK COVE FARM. DAY.

▲ Renée Zellweger plays the feisty and practical Ruby Thewes.

4. **EXT.** exterior, a scene shot outdoors.
5. **CONT.** continued, here dialogue that is interrupted for a moment, but begins again.

SUMMER 1864.

Ruby dictates a list to Ada as they bustle along.

RUBY. Number one—lay out a winter garden for cool-season crops: turnips, onions, cabbage, greens.

Ada scribbles, walks, scribbles.

84. EXT. BARN, BLACK COVE FARM. DAY. SUMMER 1864.

Ruby up a ladder, inspecting the roof.

RUBY. Number two: patch the shingles on the barn roof. Do we have a maul and froe?

ADA. *(writing, holding the ladder)* Maul?

RUBY. Maul. M-a-u-l.

ADA. I have no idea.

85. INT. SPRINGHOUSE, BLACK COVE FARM. DAY. SUMMER 1864.

Ruby cleans out leaves and detritus from the stone channel, allowing the stream to flow free and cool.

RUBY. Number three: clay crocks for preserves. Peppers. Beans. Jams.

86. EXT. BOTTOM FIELD, BLACK COVE FARM. DUSK. SUMMER 1864.

Ruby doing her version of soil analysis, scrunching the earth, tasting it, spitting it out. Ada makes a face.

RUBY. Clear and turn this field. No harm done letting it go fallow, now we'll do well.

87. EXT. OUTBUILDINGS, BLACK COVE FARM. AFTERNOON. SUMMER 1864.

Ruby looks up. Ada catches up with her.

RUBY. Number fifteen—

ADA. Sixteen.

RUBY. Number sixteen: let's hang some gourds for a martin colony. Keep away crows. You got one thing in abundance on this farm, and that's crows. Shut the gate.

88. EXT. APPLE ORCHARD, BLACK COVE FARM. DUSK. SUMMER 1864.

Ruby, delighted, contemplates the bounty of apples.

RUBY. There's survival. On them trees. *(turns to an exhausted Ada)* You got a cider press or would that be wishing on a blessing?

ADA. Actually, yes, I think we do.

Ruby whoops, jogs away. Ada, exhausted, takes a bite of an apple, watching her.

Critical Reading

1. **(a)** When Ruby wakes Ada, what does each woman say about breakfast? **(b) Compare and Contrast:** Explain the similarities and differences in the two women's perceptions of morning. **(c)** What does this suggest about other differences in their characters?
2. **(a)** As Ada and Ruby walk, what does Ruby say about the farm? **(b) Describe:** How does Ada respond? **(c) Infer:** What does each woman know about farming?

Use these questions to focus a class discussion of *Cold Mountain:*

3. Why do you think writers and filmmakers are interested in characters who do not see battle but nevertheless struggle during a war?
4. In what ways are depictions of events in a screenplay different from their presentation in short stories or novels?

Nell Irvin Painter Introduces

An Account of an Experience with Discrimination

by Sojourner Truth

A Public Figure Encounters Discrimination Sojourner Truth, an African American abolitionist born in upstate New York in 1797, belonged to a group of antislavery women volunteering with the ex-slave refugees in Washington, D.C., during the Civil War. Poor people from the battlefields of Virginia and from slaveholding Maryland sought protection and jobs in the nation's capital. Volunteers like Truth and her comrades, Josephine Griffing and Laura Haviland, helped them cope with their situation. Although Truth did not read or write, she dictated this account for publication in the anti-slavery press. In this way, people who cared about human rights would know that one Washington, D.C., streetcar conductor had not stopped for her and another had tried to push her from the platform of the car, even though she was a well-known public figure.

Two American Histories Truth's experience of discrimination in public transportation belongs to two American histories, both beginning in the early nineteenth century and both ending with the passage and enforcement of federal legislation against discrimination in public services in the 1950s and 1960s. The first history is that of Washington, D.C., a Southern city. The second history is that of discrimination against African Americans throughout the United States.

In 1791, President George Washington chose land on the border of Maryland and Virginia near his own home to serve as the nation's capital. In the 1790s, slavery existed in virtually the whole country. But during the early nineteenth century the Northern states abolished slavery, while the institution grew stronger in the South, of which Washington, D.C., was a part. The Washington slave market sat near the capitol building, and slavery flourished in the District until abolition in 1862. The discrimination Sojourner Truth experi-

Meet the Author

Nell Irvin Painter is an award-winning historian and professor. Her book *Sojourner Truth: A Life, A Symbol* was a choice of both the Book of the Month Club and the History Book Club.

enced belonged partly to Washington, D.C.'s Southern traditions. However, even after the abolition of slavery, racial discrimination in transportation remained a national problem. The war between black people and American railroads was national in scope, because racial discrimination was national in scope.

Truth's Experience Was Not Unique Sojourner Truth's painful experience caused her psychic and physical pain—she was in her sixties at the time. However, the insult she suffered was one she shared with many other black people trying to get from one place to another before the middle of the twentieth century.

Before the Civil War, the black abolitionists Frederick Douglass and David Ruggles had traded blows with conductors pushing them out of their seats. During the war, Harriet Tubman, who had guided Union troops during the Civil War, suffered shoulder injuries in New Jersey, when a conductor and three other men dragged her out of her seat and threw her into the baggage car. After the war, Frances Ellen Watkins Harper, the most prominent black woman writer of the era, experienced humiliating and bruising conflicts on railroads and streetcars. George T. Downing, an African American businessman, encountered difficulties in railroad transportation during Reconstruction. The Civil War and Reconstruction ended slavery but not discrimination and exclusion.

Critical Reading

1. **Key Ideas and Details** **(a)** Who was Sojourner Truth? **(b)** What was she doing in Washington, D.C., during and after the Civil War? **(c) Connect:** Was the act of making public her own experience with discrimination related to her purpose for being in Washington? Explain.
2. **Key Ideas and Details** **(a)** According to Nell Irvin Painter, to what two American histories does Truth's experience of discrimination belong? **(b) Speculate:** Why do you think discrimination persisted in both the North and South even after slavery ended?

As You Read "An Account of an Experience With Discrimination" . . .

3. **Integration of Knowledge and Ideas** Identify two ways in which Painter's commentary helps you better understand Sojourner Truth's experiences and reactions.
4. **Integration of Knowledge and Ideas** Decide what an individual who experiences or witnesses discrimination should do.

Before You Read

An Account of an Experience With Discrimination

Connecting to the Essential Question Sojourner Truth showed courage in the face of injustice—one aspect of the American ideal. As you read, notice details that show Truth's reactions to harsh treatment and injustice. Doing so will help as you consider the Essential Question: **What makes American literature American?**

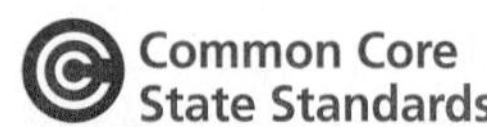

Reading Informational Text
6. Determine an author's point of view or purpose in a text in which the rhetoric is particularly effective, analyzing how style and content contribute to the power, persuasiveness, or beauty of the text.

Literary Analysis

Every author has both a general and a specific purpose for writing. An **author's general purpose for writing** may be *to inform, to persuade, to entertain,* or *to describe*. Authors also have at least one **specific purpose for writing** any given literary work. For example, in this account Truth seeks to inform readers about a distressing experience. She also has an implicit, or unstated, persuasive purpose: by describing her experiences, she may move readers to put an end to prejudice and injustice.

An author's purpose affects all elements of a literary work, including the **tone,** or attitude, the writer assumes toward the subject and audience. Tone, a key aspect of a writer's style, may be formal or informal, personal or distant, modest or pretentious. For an account of a distressing experience, Truth chooses a surprisingly factual, unemotional tone:

> *A few weeks ago I was in company with my friend Josephine S. Griffing, when the conductor of a streetcar refused to stop his car for me . . . They dragged me a number of yards before she succeeded in stopping them.*

As you read this account, think about why Truth adopted this even tone and how it helps her achieve her purpose for writing.

Reading Strategy

Preparing to Read Complex Texts In this account, Truth presents a series of factual events. Taken together, these facts build toward a powerful main idea or **essential message**. As you read, **identify relevant facts and details** to determine the essential message of Truth's account. Use a chart like the one shown to collect important details and identify the essential message of Truth's narrative.

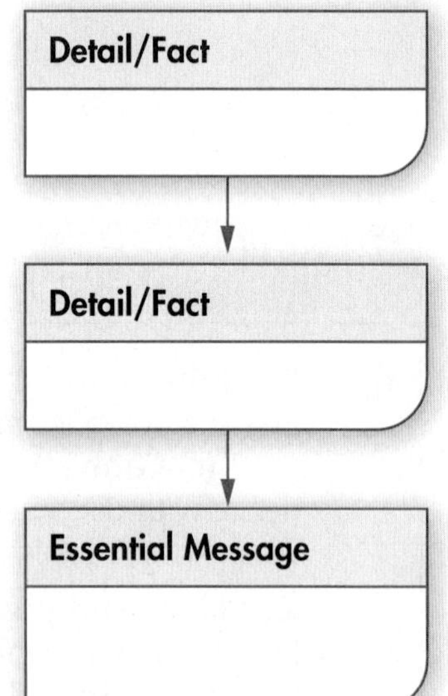

Vocabulary

ascended (ə send′ əd) *v.* climbed up (p. 556)

assault (ə sôlt′) *n.* violent attack (p. 556)

Sojourner Truth *(1797–1883)*

Author of "An Account of an Experience With Discrimination"

Sojourner Truth was born into slavery in Ulster County, New York. At the age of nine, she was separated from her family and sold several times, facing abuse at the hands of harsh masters. She was finally bought by John and Sally Dumont. As a slave in the Dumont household, she was forced into marriage with a fellow slave, Thomas, with whom she had at least four children. In 1826, one year before New York state emancipated slaves, Truth escaped from her master's household with her youngest son. She was later able to recover custody of another son, who was illegally sold as a slave in the South. In 1829, Truth and her two youngest children moved to New York City, where she found work as a domestic employee.

A Passion for Preaching Throughout her life, Truth felt a strong commitment to religion. In New York City, she became a missionary, preaching on the streets. Truth was a powerful speaker whose passion and charisma often drew large crowds. In 1843, she assumed the name Sojourner Truth and began preaching along the east coast. She began to travel through the Midwest in 1850, spreading her opinions and beliefs. She dictated her autobiography, *The Narrative of Sojourner Truth,* to Olive Gilbert and sold copies to support her tours.

A Voice for Justice Truth became a noted abolitionist, eloquently arguing against the horrifying injustices of slavery. After the Civil War ended in 1865, she continued to battle the lasting effects of slavery, including discrimination and racism. Working as a counselor, she helped former slaves find employment and build new lives. During her lifetime, Truth also earned fame as an advocate for women's rights and for workplace and prison reform.

"*That man over there says that women need to be helped into carriages, and lifted over ditches, and to have the best place everywhere. Nobody ever helps me into carriages, or over mud-puddles, or gives me any best place! And ain't I a woman?*"

An Account of an Experience with Discrimination

Sojourner Truth

Background *Although the Civil War brought an end to slavery, the struggle against racial discrimination was far from over. Before the war, Sojourner Truth worked to free slaves. After the war, she fought for a number of causes, including the woman's suffrage movement and the desegregation of public transportation. Once, when a driver of a streetcar refused her passage, she brought a local street to a standstill. With the support of a crowd behind her, the driver was forced to allow her on board. In the following account, dictated by Truth on October 1, 1865, Sojourner Truth describes other encounters with racism.*

A few weeks ago I was in company with my friend Josephine S. Griffing, when the conductor of a streetcar refused to stop his car for me, although [I was] closely following Josephine and holding on to the iron rail. They dragged me a number of yards before she succeeded in stopping them. She reported the conductor to the president of the City Railway, who dismissed him at once, and told me to take the number of the car whenever I was mistreated by a conductor or driver. On the 13th I had occasion to go for

What does Josephine S. Griffing do to help her friend?

◀ **Critical Viewing** In what ways does this image of Sojourner Truth compare with the impression you gain from this account? Explain. **[Compare and Contrast]**

necessities for the patients in the Freedmen's Hospital where I have been doing and advising for a number of months. I thought now I would get a ride without trouble as I was in company with another friend, Laura S. Haviland of Michigan. As I ascended the platform of the car, the conductor pushed me, saying "Go back—get off here." I told him I was not going off, then "I'll put you off" said he furiously, clenching my right arm with both hands, using such violence that he seemed about to succeed, when Mrs. Haviland told him he was not going to put me off. "Does she belong to you?" said he in a hurried angry tone. She replied, "She does not belong to me, but she belongs to humanity." The number of the car was noted, and conductor dismissed at once upon the report to the president, who advised his arrest for assault and battery as my shoulder was sprained by his effort to put me off. Accordingly I had him arrested and the case tried before Justice Thompson. My shoulder was very lame and swollen, but is better. It is hard for the old slaveholding spirit to die. But die it must. . . .

Vocabulary

ascended (ə send′ əd) *v.* climbed up

assault (ə sôlt′) *n.* violent attack

Nell Irvin Painter

Scholar's Insight The African American journalist Ida B. Wells went to court in 1884 after being denied first-class passage despite having purchased a first-class ticket. (She won her case, then lost on appeal.)

Critical Reading

Cite textual evidence to support your responses.

1. **Key Ideas and Details (a)** What does the streetcar conductor say to Laura Haviland about Sojourner Truth? **(b) Infer:** What does his question reveal about the "old slaveholding spirit"?
2. **Key Ideas and Details (a)** What action does Truth take following each incident of discrimination described in her account? **(b) Evaluate:** Do you think this is the best course of action in each situation? Explain.
3. **Key Ideas and Details (a)** What happens to the conductor who refuses service to Truth? **(b) Synthesize:** What do details of these events of 1865 have in common with the civil rights movement of the 1950s?
4. **Integration of Knowledge and Ideas Take a Position:** Do you think the conductors received appropriate punishments for their acts? Explain.
5. **Integration of Knowledge and Ideas** What does Truth's account suggest about the individual's responsibility to act with courage to promote positive social change? In your response, use at least two of these Essential Question words: *integrity, self-determination, freedom, challenge.* ***[Connecting to the Essential Question: What makes American literature American?]***

After You Read

An Account of an Experience With Discrimination

Literary Analysis

1. **Craft and Structure (a)** Truth's **general purposes** for writing this account were to inform and persuade. How would you describe her **specific purpose for writing? (b)** Do you think she achieved that purpose? Explain.
2. **Craft and Structure (a)** How would you describe Truth's **tone** in this account? **(b)** Using a chart like the one shown, note three examples that reflect this tone. Then, explain how Truth's tone suits her purpose for writing.

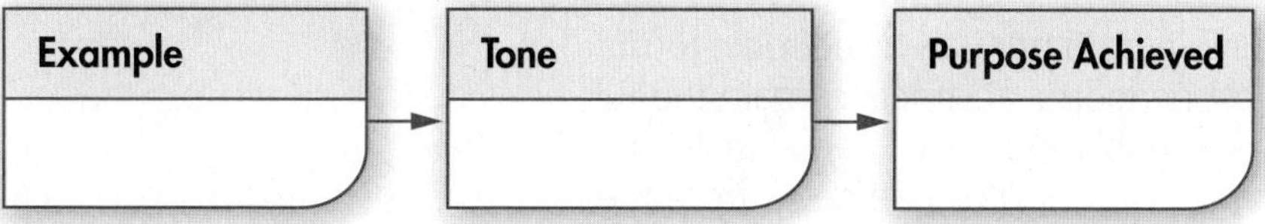

Reading Strategy

3. **(a)** What is the **essential message** of this account? **(b)** Cite three **relevant details** from Truth's account that support that message.
4. Well-chosen details often shed light on a situation in more than one way. Identify two details Truth includes that do so. Write a paragraph in which you *defend and clarify* your choices.

Common Core State Standards

Writing

2. Write informative/explanatory texts to examine and convey complex ideas, concepts, and information clearly and accurately through the effective selection, organization, and analysis of content.

2.a. Introduce a topic; organize complex ideas, concepts, and information; include formatting when useful to aiding comprehension.

2.b. Develop the topic thoroughly by selecting the most significant and relevant facts, concrete details, quotations, or other information and examples appropriate to the audience's knowledge of the topic.

2.e. Establish and maintain a formal style and objective tone while attending to the norms and conventions of the discipline in which they are writing.

PERFORMANCE TASKS

Integrated Language Skills

Vocabulary Acquistion and Use

True or False Determine whether each statement below is true or false. Explain your answers.

1. Someone who experiences an *assault* will have positive feelings.
2. Someone who is trying to get to a rooftop restaurant would take an elevator that *ascended.*

Writing

Informative Text Rewrite Truth's account as a **newspaper article.** First, determine how the change of form will affect your approach. For example, a newspaper article, written by a reporter rather than a participant, should maintain a formal style and objective, or neutral, tone. As you write your article, incorporate the changes you have outlined. Your article should include

- a *headline* that summarizes the event and engages readers' interest.
- a gripping first sentence, or *lead.*
- relevant facts that identify *who, what, where, when,* and *why.*
- *quotes* from participants and eyewitnesses that shed additional light on the events described.

Reading for Information

Analyzing Functional and Expository Texts

Periodical Abstract • Government Form

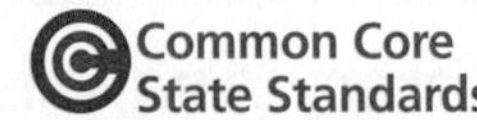

Writing

8. Assess the strengths and limitations of each source in terms of the task, purpose, and audience.

About the Texts

A **periodical abstract** is a summary of a long article from a magazine or scholarly journal. An abstract allows you to quickly evaluate the relevance of a source or gain a general overview of the subject. Abstracts can be found in both print and electronic form. In addition to a summary, most periodical abstracts contain the full article's title, author's name, and publication information; a list of the full article's key points; and photos or other elements from the original article.

A **government form** is a document that allows organizations to compile information efficiently. Forms use quick-response features and a minimal amount of extended text. Basic features include the label or logo of the relevant organization; headings for different categories of information; and checklists, short answer lists, write-on lines, and other text features that capture and organize information.

Reading Strategy

Researchers use abstracts and forms to locate information and evaluate its usefulness. They apply various strategies to assess the quality of information, connect facts and concepts, and outline key points. As you read, **apply systematic strategies to organize and record information.** The chart below highlights strategies you may use at different stages of your own research.

Content-Area Vocabulary

These words appear in the selections that follow. They may also appear in other content-area texts.

archaeology (är′ kē′ äl′ ə jē′) *n.* the study of material evidence from human life in the past

dig (dig) *n.* an archaeological excavation to explore human life from the past

site (sīt) *n.* the place or setting of an event

Note-Taking Strategy	When to Use
Anecdotal Scripting (highlighting texts and making marginal notes)	When first surveying a source (only on a personal copy or photocopy)
Outlining	When you want to extract key points or trace a line of reasoning
Making an Annotated Bibliography	When you want to keep track of information in a wide variety of sources
Concept Mapping (a diagram that uses key words and branching lines to show relationships among related ideas)	When many concepts are linked

ARCHAEOLOGY

A Publication of the Archaeological Institute of America

abstracts

Volume 59 Number 6, November/December 2006

The title, date, volume, and number of the source magazine for this abstract are clearly identified.

A Community's Roots

by Samir S. Patel

(National Portrait Gallery, Smithsonian Institution/Art Resource)

With Frederick Douglass's help, the past and present come together on a Maryland plantation.

The first section of the abstract includes an element from the article.

In Talbot County, Eastern Shore, State of Maryland, near Easton, the county town, there is a small district of country, thinly populated, and remarkable for nothing that I know of more than for the worn-out, sandy, desert-like appearance of its soil, the general dilapidation of its farms and fences, the indigent and spiritless character of its inhabitants, and the prevalence of ague and fever. It was in this dull, flat, and unthrifty district or neighborhood, bordered by the Choptank river, among the laziest and muddiest of streams surrounded by a white population of the lowest order, indolent and drunken to a proverb, and among slaves who, in point of ignorance and indolence, were fully in accord with their surroundings, that I, without any fault of my own, was born, and spent the first years of my childhood.

—Frederick Douglass,
Life and Times of Frederick Douglass (1881)

The summary of the full article begins here.

Under the boughs of a huge tulip poplar, buried among clumps of roots and piles of oyster shells, is the brick foundation of a building, a remnant of a once-thriving slave community. For 18 months in the early nineteenth century, it was home to a young Frederick Douglass, the future African-American statesman, diplomat, orator, and author. Here, at the age of seven or eight, a shoeless, pantless, precocious Douglass first saw whippings and petty cruelties. Here, he first realized he was a slave. "A lot of the horror that comes through his autobiographies is grounded in those months that he was there," says James Oakes, a historian at the City University of New York who is working on a book about Douglass's relationship with Abraham Lincoln. The modest excavation at Wye House Farm,

Archaeologist Mark Leone and site supervisor Jenn Babiarz show the site to Derek Lloyd, an engineer at Howard University who may be descended from slaves who lived on the farm. (Samir S. Patel)

a 350-year-old estate on Maryland's Eastern Shore, has yielded sherds, buttons, pipe stems, beads, and precious knowledge about everyday slave life, and is allowing the descendants of that slave community, many of whom live in the nearby rural African-American town of Unionville, to reclaim a lost cultural heritage.

A team of archaeologists and students started digging here in 2005 after archaeologist Lisa Kraus proposed the dig, on the basis of Douglass's descriptions of the site, to Mark Leone, director of the urban archaeology field school at the University of Maryland. Before beginning the excavation, Leone approached St. Stephen's African Methodist Episcopal Church, the social and religious center of Unionville, to ask what the people of the community wanted to learn from the archaeology. "You should ask the people who think it's their heritage what they want to know about it," Leone says. "The answers automatically dissolve the difference between then and now." This, he adds, is the heart of social archaeology, working with descendant communities and understanding that the past and present inform one another. The people of Unionville wanted to know about slave spirituality, what remained of African life, how the owner of the slaves did or did not support freedom, and how slaves found the strength to survive. They are questions a single dig is unlikely to answer, but they have opened an avenue of dialogue between the archaeologists and the people to whom their work matters most.

Photographs and captions from the actual article make this a particularly useful abstract.

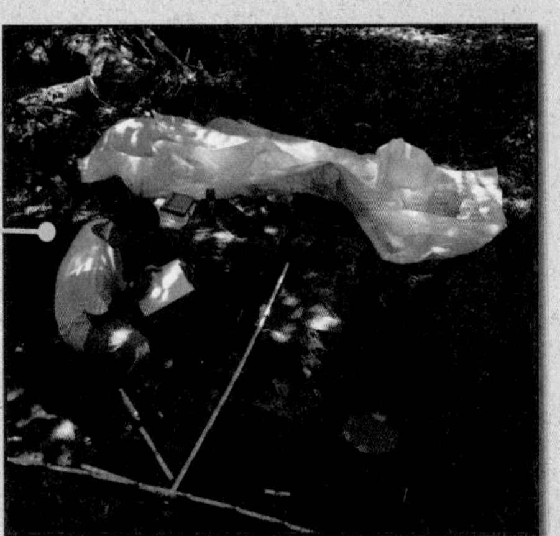

Pete Quantock, a University of Maryland student, profiles the site of a workshop, where slaves probably both slept and worked. (Samir S. Patel)

Samir S. Patel is an associate editor at ARCHAEOLOGY.

Virginia Department of Historic Resources

GENERAL PROPERTY INFORMATION

City/County:

Site Class: ______ Terrestrial, Open Air ______ Terrestrial, Cave/ Rockshelter ______ Submerged

Temporary Designation:

Specialized Contexts:

Resource Name:

Open to public: Y N

Ownership Status: ______ Private
______ Public/Local
______ Public/State
______ Public/Federal

Gov. Modifier:

Checklists provide an efficient way to gather important information.

Cultural Affiliation: ______ African-American ______ Native American
______ Euro-American ______ Other
______ Indeterminate

LOCATION INFORMATION

Physiographic Province:

Elevation: ______ ft

Aspect:

Site Soils:

Drainage:

Adjacent Soils:

Direction:

Distance: ______ ft

Landform:

Nearest Water Source:

Site Dimensions: ________ × ________ ft

Acreage:

Slope: ________ percent

Survey Description:

SPECIMENS AND FIELD NOTES INFORMATION

Specimens Obtained: ____ Yes ____ No Depository:

Assemblage Description:

Specimens Reported: ____ Yes ____ No

Owner Name:

Owner Address:

Assemblage Description:

Field Notes: ____ Yes ____ No

Depository:

Headings define the information being collected in each section.

INDIVIDUAL/ORG AGENCY MAILING INFORMATION

Category: Informant Occupant Owner Owner of Specimens Property Mgr. Tenant

Honorific: ________ First Name: ________ Last Name: ________ Suffix: ________

Title: ________ Company: ________ Mailing Address: ________ City: ________

Zip Code: ________ Country: ________ Phone 1/Ext.: ________ Phone 2/Ext.: ________ Surveyor's Notes:

After You Read

Periodical Abstract • Government Form

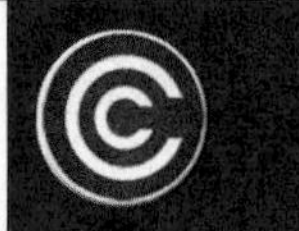

Literary Analysis

1. **Key Ideas and Details (a)** If you were to use anecdotal scripting to identify the key points in the abstract, which passages would you highlight? **(b)** Which passages would you note because they contain other important details? Explain.
2. **Key Ideas and Details (a)** What information does the government form capture quickly and efficiently? **(b)** What types of workers or professionals would use this form and for what purposes?
3. **Key Ideas and Details** Why do you think the government form attempts to capture specific data about elevation, soils, and water sources?
4. **Key Ideas and Details** If you were to draw a concept map for both the abstract and the government form, what key concepts would you identify and how would you connect them?
5. **Key Ideas and Details** Do you think a government form like the one on page 561 would be useful to the researchers described in the abstract? Why or why not?

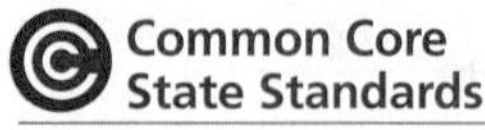

Common Core State Standards

Writing

1.a. Introduce precise, knowledgeable claim(s), establish the significance of the claim(s), distinguish the claim(s) from alternate or opposing claims, and create an organization that logically sequences claim(s), counterclaims, reasons, and evidence.

Timed Writing

Argument [40 minutes]

Format

In a **persuasive essay**, you build a well-reasoned and compelling case for a position or claim. Strengthen your argument by introducing counterclaims, or opposing opinions, and demonstrating that your position is more convincing.

Write a **persuasive essay** about the importance of archaeology and whether society has a responsibility to preserve historical sites and objects. Take and **defend** a position about the types of documents, sites, or objects that are most important and explain your reasons. Support your opinions with details from the Periodical Abstract and the Government Form.

Academic Vocabulary

When you **defend** a position, you supply varied, convincing evidence that supports your point of view. Evidence can include facts, quotations from reliable sources, and personal observation.

5-Minute Planner

Complete these steps before you begin to write.

1. Read the prompt carefully. List key words.
2. Scan the texts for details that relate to the prompt.
3. Briefly sketch an outline for your essay. **TIP** In a Timed Writing situation, an outline can be a simple numbered list of key words.
4. Reread the prompt, and draft your essay.

PART 2

Forging New Frontiers

Literary History: Twain's World

At a time when most American writers were copying European novelists, Twain wrote about American themes.

Mark Twain: The American Bard

In the late 1800s, readers might have known him as Thomas Jefferson Snodgrass, W. Epaminandos Adrastus Blab, or simply Josh. Today, we know Samuel Langhorne Clemens as Mark Twain, his most famous literary pseudonym. Whichever name he used, Twain pulled off a rare literary feat—he created stories, novels, and essays that were both wildly popular in his own day and models of wit and skill more than a century later. Twain was so influential that fifty years after his death, Ernest Hemingway said that "all modern American literature begins" with Twain's novel *The Adventures of Huckleberry Finn.*

Life on the Mississippi Born in 1835, Samuel Clemens grew up in the small river town of Hannibal, Missouri. Steamboat men, religious revivalists, circus performers, minstrel companies, showboat actors, and every other kind of traveler imaginable made appearances in Hannibal. As a boy, Clemens met many of the characters that he would later write about.

After his father's death in 1847, Clemens was forced to leave school and became a printer's apprentice. During the 1850s, he published a few stories and traveled the country. A boat trip down the Mississippi brought back childhood memories, and he decided to become a riverboat pilot. He served as a pilot until 1861, when the Civil War closed the Mississippi to boat traffic.

Mark Twain Is Born In 1862, Clemens took a job as a reporter on a Virginia City newspaper, where he found his calling as a humorist under the byline Mark Twain. The new name, which is actually a signal yelled out by riverboat pilots, freed him to develop a new style. Before becoming "Twain," his work was typical of the low humor of the time, filled with bad puns and intentional misspellings. But in 1865, Twain published a short story entitled "The Notorious Jumping Frog of Calaveras County" (p. 576). The story won

▶ Critical Viewing What do you think it would have been like to captain a Mississippi riverboat like the one shown in this photograph? **[Speculate]**

the author fame and financial success, and it marked the first appearance of his distinctive comic style.

Ordinary American Speech The targets of Twain's jokes were not new. He distrusted technology and railed against political figures, calling them swindlers and con men. What was new was Twain's feel for ordinary American people and their language. He wrote using the American English that people actually spoke. In that source, he found rich and comic poetry.

Twain's novels, such as *The Adventures of Tom Sawyer* and *The Adventures of Huckleberry Finn*, were unlike any books the world had ever seen. At a time when most American writers were copying European novelists, Twain wrote about American themes. His heroes were dirt-poor and plain-spoken, but in Twain's hands, their moral choices had as much drama as those of any tormented aristocrat in a European novel.

Not everyone appreciated Twain's humor. The author fled Virginia City when a rival journalist, offended by a story, challenged him to a pistol duel. He was chased out of San Francisco by policemen angered by critical articles. Even as his fame grew, some critics dismissed him as little more than a jokester. Yet the American public loved Twain. He made a fortune from his writings, settling with his family into a Hartford, Connecticut, mansion that was decorated to look like the inside of a steamboat.

The Old Man in a White Suit In the late 1800s, the deaths of Twain's wife and daughters left the writer bitter and cynical. Twain became so reclusive that a newspaper reported he was dead. Twain immediately wired the editors: "Reports of my death have been greatly exaggerated." History has not exaggerated Twain's legacy. He was the first, and possibly the greatest, authentically American writer.

In This Section

- Literary History *(p. 564)*
- Biography: Mark Twain *(p. 566)*
- Study: from *Life on the Mississippi (p. 570)*
- Critical Commentary: from "How to Tell a Story" *(p. 575)*
- Study: "The Notorious Jumping Frog of Calaveras County" *(p. 576)*
- Comparing American Humor *(p. 587)*
- Study: from *The Life and Times of the Thunderbolt Kid (p. 589)*

Speaking and Listening: Oral Presentation

Comprehension and Collaboration Like Twain, contemporary humor writers and comedians find ordinary American life a rich source of material. With a small group, research current humor on television, in movies, in periodicals, and in books. Then, using the research, write and deliver a **formal oral presentation:**

- As a group, prepare a set of focus questions, such as: What roles does comedy play today? What values does current humor transmit? Does contemporary humor challenge or perpetuate stereotypes?
- Use *systematic strategies, such as anecdotal scripting* (underlining, highlighting, and writing notes in the margins of a text) to identify key information.

Select examples to maintain a tone that is appropriate for the classroom. Work together to set goals and deadlines, organize your observations, write the text, and divide up responsibilities for the presentation.

Common Core State Standards

SL.11-12.1.a, SL.11-12.1.b, SL.11-12.1.c, SL.11-12.1.d.

[For the full wording of the standards, see the standards chart in the front of your textbook.]

MARK TWAIN 1835–1910

Be good + you will be lonesome.
Clemens
Mark Twain
3-15-

Although Mark Twain is widely regarded as one of the greatest American writers, the world-renowned author once indicated that he would have preferred to spend his life as a Mississippi riverboat pilot. The comment was probably not entirely serious, but Twain so loved life on the river that, as a young man, he did in fact work as a riverboat pilot for several years. His childhood on the banks of the Mississippi fostered more than a love of riverboats—it also became the basis for many of his most famous works, including *The Adventures of Tom Sawyer* (1876) and *The Adventures of Huckleberry Finn* (1884).

Life on the River

Twain, whose given name was Samuel Langhorne Clemens, felt so closely tied to the Mississippi River that he even took his pen name, Mark Twain, from a river man's call meaning "two fathoms deep," indicating that the river is deep enough for a boat to pass safely. He grew up in the Mississippi River town of Hannibal, Missouri. His father died when he was eleven, and he left school to become a printer's apprentice. He worked as a printer in a number of different cities before deciding at age twenty-one to pursue a career as a riverboat pilot.

IT IS WISER TO FIND OUT THAN SUPPOSE.

A Traveling Man

When the Civil War closed traffic on the Mississippi, Twain went west to Nevada. There, he supported himself as a journalist and lecturer, developing the entertaining writing style that made him famous. In 1865, Twain published "The Notorious Jumping Frog of Calaveras County," his version of a tall tale he had heard in a mining camp in California while he was working as a gold prospector. The story made him an international celebrity.

Following the publication of *The Innocents Abroad* (1869), a successful book of humorous travel letters, Twain moved to Hartford, Connecticut, where he was to make his home for the rest of his life. There, Twain began using his past experiences as raw material for his books. He drew on his travels in the western mining region for *Roughing It* (1872). He turned to his childhood experiences on the Mississippi for *The Adventures of Tom Sawyer, Life on the Mississippi,* and his masterpiece, *The Adventures of Huckleberry Finn.*

A Restless Soul

Twain traveled widely throughout his life, including residential stints in such major American cities as St. Louis, New York, Philadelphia, Cincinnati, and San Francisco. He made extended visits to England, Germany, Switzerland, Italy, and Palestine. His adventures, both at home and abroad, were fuel for a number of books. After living in Europe for several years, he returned home with his family. Following the death of his wife and three of their four children, Twain was unable to reproduce the balance between pessimism and humor that he had captured so brilliantly in *The Adventures of Huckleberry Finn.* In his later works, such as *A Connecticut Yankee in King Arthur's Court* (1889), *Pudd'nhead Wilson* (1894), and *The Man That Corrupted Hadleyburg* (1900), Twain's writing depicted an increasingly pessimistic view of society and human nature. However, he continued to display the same masterful command of language that had already established him as one of America's finest fiction writers.

The Quotable Twain

"CLOTHES MAKE THE MAN," Mark Twain once wrote. In his case, it was words that made the man. From novels to travel correspondence to social commentary, Twain's words were passionately celebrated and hotly criticized. As the great writer and humorist himself declared, "An author values a compliment even when it comes from a source of doubtful competency." What follows are ten more quotable quotes from Twain.

1. "When in doubt, tell the truth."
2. "Let us be thankful for the fools. But for them the rest of us could not succeed."
3. "Don't part with your illusions. When they are gone you may still exist, but you have ceased to live."
4. "It is curious—curious that physical courage should be so common in the world, and moral courage so rare."
5. "It could probably be shown by facts and figures that there is no distinctly native American criminal class except Congress."
6. "We find not much in ourselves to admire, we are always privately wanting to be like somebody else. If everybody was satisfied with himself there would be no heroes."
7. "It is better to keep your mouth shut and appear stupid than to open it and remove all doubt."
8. "All generalizations are false, including this one."
9. "Always do right. That will gratify some of the people, and astonish the rest."
10. "The only way to keep your health is to eat what you don't want, drink what you don't like, and do what you'd rather not."

Before You Read

from *Life on the Mississippi* • *The Notorious Jumping Frog of Calaveras County*

Connecting to the Essential Question Mark Twain portrayed America in a way that continues to define our national character. As you read, look for images, expressions, characters, and ways of thinking that strike you as distinctly American. This will help as you consider the Essential Question: **What makes American literature American?**

Literary Analysis

Humor, which may appear in all literary genres, is writing intended to amuse. Humorists use a variety of devices and techniques to achieve that goal:

- **Incongruity,** or differences in logic or degree. For example, a speaker may use a serious tone to describe ridiculous events.
- **Hyperbole,** or the exaggeration of details or embellishment of events beyond what is logical
- **Comic uses of language,** including funny names

Twain's humor is not just funny. Even his most comic works carry an undercurrent of **social commentary,** or critique of society. His social commentary is infused with Twain's keen observations *of human foibles,* or weaknesses, which he usually describes with affection. Twain is also a master of **dialect**—ways of speaking that are specific to a particular area or group of people. This, too, adds to the humor of his writing. As you read, look for these hallmarks of Twain's comic style.

Reading Strategy

Preparing to Read Complex Texts Twain uses *technical language* to describe steamboats and *dialect* to convey a sense of authentic speech. Both types of language may be unfamiliar to you. To **clarify** technical language, consult footnotes. To **interpret** regional dialect, read unfamiliar words aloud to find that they are simply different pronunciations of words you know. Use a chart like the one shown to translate dialect into modern Standard English.

Vocabulary

transient (tran′ zē ənt) *adj.* not permanent (p. 571)

prodigious (prə dij′ əs) *adj.* of great power or size (p. 572)

eminence (em′ ə nəns) *n.* greatness; celebrity (p. 573)

garrulous (gar′ ə ləs) *adj.* talking too much (p. 576)

conjectured (kən jek′ chərd) *v.* guessed (p. 576)

monotonous (mə nät′ ən əs) *adj.* tiresome because unvarying (p. 576)

interminable (in tʉr′ mi nə bəl) *adj.* seeming to last forever (p. 576)

Common Core State Standards

Reading Literature

6. Analyze a case in which grasping a point of view requires distinguishing what is directly stated in a text from what is really meant.

9. Demonstrate knowledge of nineteenth-century foundational works of American literature, including how two or more texts from the same period treat similar themes or topics.

Reading Informational Text

4. Determine the meaning of words and phrases as they are used in a text, including technical meanings.

Language

5.a. Interpret figures of speech in context and analyze their role in the text.

Regional Dialect

. . . there couldn't be no solit'ry thing mentioned but that feller'd offer to bet on it, and take ary side you please. . . .

Standard English

Not one thing could be mentioned without him offering to bet on it, taking any side.

FROM

LIFE ON THE MISSISSIPPI

MARK TWAIN

BACKGROUND Mark Twain was an eyewitness to the nineteenth-century expansion of the western frontier. He was a young man when wagon trains left his home state of Missouri to cross the prairies, and he later saw the transcontinental railroad built. He traveled throughout the nation, working first on the Mississippi and then in the West, before settling in Connecticut. However, as this excerpt shows, the Mississippi River held a special place in his memory.

THE BOYS' AMBITION

When I was a boy, there was but one permanent ambition among my comrades in our village[1] on the west bank of the Mississippi River. That was, to be a steamboatman. We had transient ambitions of other sorts, but they were only transient.

Vocabulary
transient (tran′ zē ənt) *adj.* not permanent

When a circus came and went, it left us all burning to become clowns; the first Negro minstrel show that came to our section left us all suffering to try that kind of life; now and then we had a hope that if we lived and were good, God would permit us to be pirates. These ambitions faded out, each in its turn; but the ambition to be a steamboatman always remained.

◀ **Critical Viewing** How does this painting convey a sense of the glamour steamboats brought to the Mississippi River? **[Analyze]**

Once a day a cheap, gaudy packet[2] arrived upward from St. Louis, and another downward from Keokuk.[3] Before these events, the day was glorious with expectancy; after them, the day was a dead and empty thing. Not only the boys, but the whole village, felt this. After all these years I can picture that old time to myself now, just as it was then: the white town drowsing in the sunshine of a summer's morning; the streets empty, or pretty nearly so; one or two clerks sitting in front of the Water Street stores, with their splint-bottomed chairs tilted back against the wall, chins on breasts, hats slouched over their faces, asleep—with shingle shavings enough around to show what broke them down; a sow and a litter of pigs loafing along the sidewalk, doing a good business in watermelon rinds and seeds; two or three lonely little freight piles scattered about the levee;[4] a pile of skids[5] on the slope of the stone-paved wharf, and the fragrant town drunkard asleep in the shadow of them; two or three wood flats[6] at the head of the wharf, but nobody to listen to the peaceful lapping of the wavelets against them; the great Mississippi, the majestic, the magnificent Mississippi, rolling its mile-wide tide along, shining in the sun; the dense forest away on the other side; the point above the town, and the point below, bounding the river-glimpse and turning it into a sort of sea, and withal a very still and brilliant and lonely one. Presently a film of dark smoke appears above one of those remote

How did the boys' ambitions change with each new visitor to their town?

1. **our village** Hannibal, Missouri.
2. **packet** *n.* boat that travels a regular route, carrying passengers, freight, and mail.
3. **Keokuk** (kē′ ə kuk′) town in southeastern Iowa.
4. **levee** (lev′ ē) *n.* landing place along the bank of a river.
5. **skids** *n.* low, movable wooden platforms.
6. **flats** *n.* small, flat-bottomed boats.

▶ Critical Viewing What does this painting suggest about some of the challenges steamboat captains faced in navigating the river? **[Infer]**

Vocabulary
prodigious (prə dij′ əs) *adj.* of great power or size

Reading Strategy
Clarifying and Interpreting Language How do footnotes clarify your understanding of the technical terms in this paragraph?

points; instantly a Negro drayman,[7] famous for his quick eye and prodigious voice, lifts up the cry, "S-t-e-a-m-boat a-comin'!" and the scene changes! The town drunkard stirs, the clerks wake up, a furious clatter of drays follows, every house and store pours out a human contribution, and all in a twinkling the dead town is alive and moving. Drays, carts, men, boys, all go hurrying from many quarters to a common center, the wharf. Assembled there, the people fasten their eyes upon the coming boat as upon a wonder they are seeing for the first time. And the boat is rather a handsome sight, too. She is long and sharp and trim and pretty; she has two tall, fancy-topped chimneys, with a gilded device of some kind swung between them; a fanciful pilothouse, all glass and gingerbread, perched on top of the texas deck[8] behind them; the paddleboxes are gorgeous with a picture or with gilded rays above the boat's name; the boiler deck, the hurricane deck, and the texas deck are fenced and ornamented with clean white railings; there is a flag gallantly flying from the jackstaff;[9] the furnace doors are open and the fires glaring bravely; the upper decks are black with passengers; the captain stands by the big bell, calm, imposing, the envy of all; great volumes of the blackest smoke are rolling and tumbling out of the chimneys—a husbanded grandeur created with a bit of pitch pine just before arriving at a town; the crew are grouped on the forecastle;[10] the broad stage is run far out over the port bow, and an envied deckhand stands picturesquely on the end of it with a coil of rope in his hand; the pent steam is screaming through the gauge cocks; the captain lifts his hand, a bell rings, the wheels stop; then they turn back, churning the water to foam, and the steamer is at rest. Then such a scramble as there is to get aboard, and to get ashore, and to take in freight and to discharge

7. **drayman** (drā′ mən) *n.* driver of a dray, a low cart with detachable sides.
8. **texas deck** deck adjoining the officers' cabins, the largest cabins on the ship.
9. **jackstaff** (jak′ staf) *n.* small staff at the bow of a ship for flying flags.
10. **forecastle** (fōk′ səl) *n.* front part of the upper deck.

freight, all at one and the same time; and such a yelling and cursing as the mates facilitate it all with! Ten minutes later the steamer is under way again, with no flag on the jackstaff and no black smoke issuing from the chimneys. After ten more minutes the town is dead again, and the town drunkard asleep by the skids once more.

My father was a justice of the peace, and I supposed he possessed the power of life and death over all men and could hang anybody that offended him. This was distinction enough for me as a general thing; but the desire to be a steamboatman kept intruding, nevertheless. I first wanted to be a cabin boy, so that I could come out with a white apron on and shake a tablecloth over the side, where all my old comrades could see me; later I thought I would rather be the deckhand who stood on the end of the stage plank with the coil of rope in his hand, because he was particularly conspicuous. But these were only daydreams—they were too heavenly to be contemplated as real possibilities. By and by one of our boys went away. He was not heard of for a long time. At last he turned up as apprentice engineer or striker on a steamboat. This thing shook the bottom out of all my Sunday school teachings. That boy had been notoriously worldly, and I just the reverse; yet he was exalted to this **eminence**, and I left in obscurity and misery. There was nothing generous about this fellow in his greatness. He would always manage to have a rusty bolt to scrub while his boat tarried at our town, and he would sit on the inside guard and scrub it, where we could all see him and envy him and loathe him. And whenever his boat was laid up he would come home and swell around the town in his blackest and greasiest clothes, so that nobody could help remembering that he was a steamboatman; and he used all sorts of steamboat technicalities in his talk, as if he were so used to them that he forgot common people could not understand them. He would speak of the labboard[11] side of a horse in an easy, natural way that would make one wish he was dead. And he was always talking about "St. Looey" like an old citizen; he would refer casually to occasions when he "was coming down Fourth Street," or when he was "passing by the Planter's House," or when there was a fire and he took a turn on the brakes of "the old Big Missouri"; and then he would go on and lie about how many towns the size of ours were burned down there that day. Two or three of the boys had long been persons of consideration among us because they had been to St. Louis once and had a vague general knowledge of its wonders, but the day of their glory was over now. They lapsed into a humble silence, and learned to disappear when the ruthless cub engineer approached. This fellow had money, too, and hair oil. Also an ignorant silver watch and a showy brass watch chain. He wore a leather belt and used no suspenders. If ever a youth was cordially

Spiral Review
Tone How would you describe the author's tone in this paragraph? Explain.

Vocabulary
eminence (em′ i nəns) *n.* greatness; celebrity

Reading Strategy
Clarifying Regional Dialect What does the apprentice engineer's use of riverboat jargon reveal about him?

What activities and actions of the boy who worked on a steamship inspired envy?

11. **labboard** (lab′ ərd) larboard, the left-hand side of a ship.

Literary Analysis

Humor How does the use of the word *reptile* add to the humor of this passage?

admired and hated by his comrades, this one was. No girl could withstand his charms. He cut out every boy in the village. When his boat blew up at last, it diffused a tranquil contentment among us such as we had not known for months. But when he came home the next week, alive, renowned, and appeared in church all battered up and bandaged, a shining hero, stared at and wondered over by everybody, it seemed to us that the partiality of Providence for an undeserving reptile had reached a point where it was open to criticism.

This creature's career could produce but one result, and it speedily followed. Boy after boy managed to get on the river. The minister's son became an engineer. The doctor's and the postmaster's sons became mud clerks; the wholesale liquor dealer's son became a barkeeper on a boat; four sons of the chief merchant, and two sons of the county judge, became pilots. Pilot was the grandest position of all. The pilot, even in those days of trivial wages, had a princely salary—from a hundred and fifty to two hundred and fifty dollars a month, and no board to pay. Two months of his wages would pay a preacher's salary for a year. Now some of us were left disconsolate. We could not get on the river—at least our parents would not let us.

So by and by I ran away. I said I never would come home again till I was a pilot and could come in glory. But somehow I could not manage it. I went meekly aboard a few of the boats that lay packed together like sardines at the long St. Louis wharf, and very humbly inquired for the pilots, but got only a cold shoulder and short words from mates and clerks. I had to make the best of this sort of treatment for the time being, but I had comforting daydreams of a future when I should be a great and honored pilot, with plenty of money, and could kill some of these mates and clerks and pay for them.

Critical Reading

Cite textual evidence to support your responses.

1. **Key Ideas and Details (a)** What is the one permanent ambition of the narrator and his boyhood friends? **(b) Connect:** How does this childhood ambition reflect the American spirit that gave rise to the settlement of new frontiers?
2. **Key Ideas and Details (a)** How do the people of Hannibal respond to the arrival of the steamboat? **(b) Interpret:** What impression of the town does Twain convey by this response?
3. **Craft and Structure (a) Hypothesize:** Do you think Twain could have written so well about riverboat life had he not become a pilot himself? Explain. **(b) Apply:** In what ways do you think Twain's love for the Mississippi River contributed to his success as a writer?
4. **Integration of Knowledge and Ideas Evaluate:** The last paragraph suggests that the young Twain was driven by a desire for glory. Is a desire for glory a reasonable motivation in life? Explain.

Critical Commentary

from "How to Tell a Story"

An Essay by Mark Twain

I do not claim that I can tell a story as it ought to be told. I only claim to know how a story ought to be told, for I have been almost daily in the company of the most expert story-tellers for many years.

There are several kinds of stories, but only one difficult kind—the humorous. I will talk mainly about that one. The humorous story is American, the comic story is English, the witty story is French. The humorous story depends for its effect upon the *manner* of the telling; the comic story and the witty story upon the *matter.*

The humorous story may be spun out to great length, and may wander around as much as it pleases, and arrive nowhere in particular; but the comic and witty stories must be brief and end with a point. The humorous story bubbles gently along, the others burst.

The humorous story is strictly a work of art—high and delicate art—and only an artist can tell it; but no art is necessary in telling the comic and the witty story; anybody can do it. The art of telling a humorous story—understand, I mean by word of mouth, not print—was created in America, and has remained at home.

The humorous story is told gravely; the teller does his best to conceal the fact that he even dimly suspects that there is anything funny about it; but the teller of the comic story tells you beforehand that it is one of the funniest things he has ever heard, then tells it with eager delight, and is the first person to laugh when he gets through. And sometimes, if he has had good success, he is so glad and happy that he will repeat the "nub" of it and glance around from face to face, collecting applause, and then repeat it again. It is a pathetic thing to see.

Very often, of course, the rambling and disjointed humorous story finishes with a nub, point, snapper, or whatever you like to call it. Then the listener must be alert, for in many cases the teller will divert attention from that nub by dropping it in a carefully casual and indifferent way, with the pretense that he does not know it is a nub. . . .

But the teller of the comic story does not slur the nub; he shouts it at you—every time. And when he prints it, in England, France, Germany, and Italy, he italicizes it, puts some whooping exclamation-points after it, and sometimes explains it in a parenthesis. All of which is very depressing, and makes one want to renounce joking and lead a better life.

Key Ideas and Details Why does Twain think Americans are skilled at telling humorous stories? What is the difference between a humorous story and a comic story?

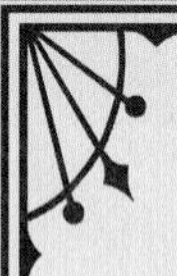

THE NOTORIOUS JUMPING FROG OF CALAVERAS COUNTY

MARK TWAIN

Vocabulary

garrulous (gar′ ə ləs) *adj.* talking too much

conjectured (kən jek′ chərd) *v.* guessed

monotonous (mə nät′ ən əs) *adj.* tiresome because unvarying

interminable (in tʉr′ mi nə bəl) *adj.* seeming to last forever

In compliance with the request of a friend of mine, who wrote me from the East, I called on good-natured, garrulous old Simon Wheeler, and inquired after my friend's friend, Leonidas W. Smiley, as requested to do, and I hereunto append the result. I have a lurking suspicion that *Leonidas W.* Smiley is a myth; that my friend never knew such a personage: and that he only conjectured that if I asked old Wheeler about him, it would remind him of his infamous *Jim* Smiley, and he would go to work and bore me to death with some exasperating reminiscence of him as long and as tedious as it should be useless to me. If that was the design, it succeeded.

I found Simon Wheeler dozing comfortably by the barroom stove of the dilapidated tavern in the decayed mining camp of Angel's, and I noticed that he was fat and baldheaded, and had an expression of winning gentleness and simplicity upon his tranquil countenance. He roused up, and gave me good day. I told him a friend of mine had commissioned me to make some inquiries about a cherished companion of his boyhood named *Leonidas W.* Smiley—*Rev. Leonidas W.* Smiley, a young minister of the Gospel, who he had heard was at one time a resident of Angel's Camp. I added that if Mr. Wheeler could tell me anything about this Rev. Leonidas W. Smiley, I would feel under many obligations to him.

Simon Wheeler backed me into a corner and blockaded me there with his chair, and then sat down and reeled off the monotonous narrative which follows this paragraph. He never smiled, he never frowned, he never changed his voice from the gentle-flowing key to which he tuned his initial sentence, he never betrayed the slightest suspicion of enthusiasm; but all through the interminable narrative there ran a vein of impressive earnestness and sincerity, which showed me plainly that, so far from his imagining that there was anything ridiculous or funny about his story, he regarded it as a really important matter, and admired its two heroes as men of transcendent genius in *finesse*. I let him go on in his own way, and never interrupted him once.

"Rev. Leonidas W. H'm, Reverend Le—well, there was a feller here once by the name of *Jim* Smiley, in the winter of '49—or maybe it was the spring of '50—I don't recollect exactly, somehow, though what makes me think it was one or the other is because I remember the big flume[1] warn't finished when he first come to the camp; but anyway, he was the curiousest man about always betting on anything that turned up you ever see, if he could get anybody to bet on the other side; and if he couldn't he'd change sides. Any way that suited the other man would suit *him*—any way just so's he got a bet, *he* was satisfied. But still he was lucky, uncommon lucky; he most always come out winner. He was always ready and laying for a chance; there couldn't be no solit'ry thing mentioned but that feller'd offer to bet on it, and take ary side you please, as I was just telling you. If there was a horse race, you'd find him flush or you'd find him busted at the end of it; if there was a dogfight, he'd bet on it; if there was a cat fight, he'd bet on it; if there was a chicken fight, he'd bet on it; why, if there was two birds setting on a fence, he would bet you which one would fly first; or if there was a camp meeting,[2] he would be there reg'lar to bet on Parson Walker, which he judged to be the best exhorter about here and so he was too, and a good man. If he even see a straddle bug[3] start to go anywheres, he would bet you how long it would take him to get to—to wherever he was going to, and if you took him up, he would foller that straddle bug to Mexico but what he would find out where he was bound for and how long he was on the road. Lots of the boys here has seen that Smiley, and can tell you about him. Why, it never made no difference to *him*—he'd bet on *any* thing—the dangdest feller. Parson Walker's wife laid very sick once, for a good while, and it seemed as if they warn't going to save her; but one morning he come in, and Smiley up and asked him how she was, and he said she was considable better—thank the Lord for his inf'nite

▼ **Critical Viewing** Would Twain have been amused or offended by this caricature of himself? Explain. **[Speculate]**

What does the narrator suspect about Leonidas W. Smiley?

1. **flume** (flo͞om) *n.* artificial channel for carrying water to provide power and transport objects.
2. **camp meeting** religious gathering at the mining camp.
3. **straddle bug** insect with long legs.

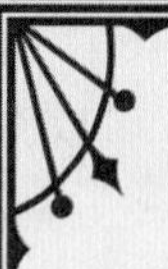

mercy—and coming on so smart that with the blessing of Prov'dence she'd get well yet; and Smiley, before he thought, says, 'Well, I'll resk two-and-a-half she don't anyway.'

Literary Analysis
Humor What is funny about this description of the mare?

Thish-yer Smiley had a mare—the boys called her the fifteen-minute nag, but that was only in fun, you know, because of course she was faster than that—and he used to win money on that horse, for all she was so slow and always had the asthma, or the distemper, or the consumption, or something of that kind. They used to give her two or three hundred yards start, and then pass her under way; but always at the fag end[4] of the race she'd get excited and desperate like, and come cavorting and straddling up, and scattering her legs around limber, sometimes in the air, and sometimes out to one side among the fences, and kicking up m-o-r-e dust and raising m-o-r-e racket with her coughing and sneezing and blowing her nose—and *always* fetch up at the stand just about a neck ahead, as near as you could cipher it down.

Literary Analysis
Humor Why is the dog's name—Andrew Jackson—funny?

And he had a little small bull-pup, that to look at him you'd think he warn't worth a cent but to set around and look ornery and lay for a chance to steal something. But as soon as money was up on him he was a different dog; his under-jaw'd begin to stick out like the fo'castle[5] of a steamboat, and his teeth would uncover and shine like the furnaces. And a dog might tackle him and bullyrag him, and bite him, and throw him over his shoulder two or three times, and Andrew Jackson—which was the name of the pup—Andrew Jackson would never let on but what *he* was satisfied, and hadn't expected nothing else—and the bets being doubled and doubled on the other side all the time, till the money was all up; and then all of a sudden he would grab that other dog jest by the j'int of his hind leg and freeze to it—not chaw, you understand, but only just grip and hang on till they throwed up the sponge, if it was a year. Smiley always come out winner on that pup, till he harnessed a dog once that didn't have no hind legs, because they'd been sawed off in a circular saw, and when the thing had gone along far enough, and the money was all up, and he come to make a snatch for his pet holt,[6] he see in a minute how he'd been imposed on, and how the other dog had him in the door, so to speak, and he 'peared surprised, and then he looked sorter discouraged-like, and didn't try no more to win the fight, and so he got shucked out bad. He give Smiley a look, as much as to say his heart was broke, and it was his fault, for putting up a dog that hadn't no hind legs for him to take holt of, which was his main dependence in a fight, and then he limped off a piece and laid down and died. It was a good pup, was that Andrew Jackson, and would have made a name for hisself if he'd lived, for the stuff was in him and he had genius—I know it, because he hadn't no opportunities to

---

4. **fag end** last part.
5. **fo'castle** (fōk´ səl) *n.* the forward part of the upper deck.
6. **holt** hold.

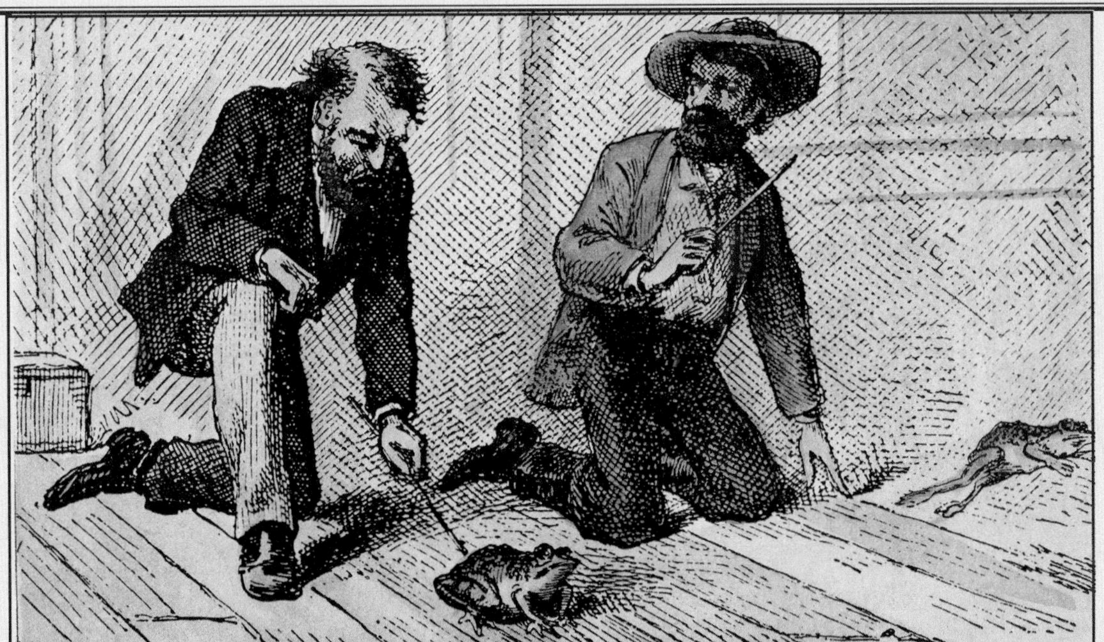

speak of, and it don't stand to reason that a dog could make such a fight as he could under them circumstances if he hadn't no talent. It always makes me feel sorry when I think of that last fight of his'n, and the way it turned out.

▲ **Critical Viewing** Which moment of the story is depicted in this illustration? **[Connect]**

Well, thish-yer Smiley had rat terriers,[7] and chicken cocks,[8] and tomcats and all them kind of things, till you couldn't rest, and you couldn't fetch nothing for him to bet on but he'd match you. He ketched a frog one day, and took him home, and said he cal'lated to educate him; and so he never done nothing for three months but set in his back yard and learn that frog to jump. And you bet you he *did* learn him, too. He'd give him a little punch behind, and the next minute you'd see that frog whirling in the air like a doughnut—see him turn one summerset, or maybe a couple, if he got a good start, and come down flatfooted and all right, like a cat. He got him up so in the matter of ketching flies, and kep' him in practice so constant, that he'd nail a fly every time as fur as he could see him. Smiley said all a frog wanted was education, and he could do 'most anything—and I believe him. Why, I've seen him set Dan'l Webster down here on this floor—Dan'l Webster was the name of the frog—and sing out, "Flies, Dan'l, flies!" and quicker'n you could wink he'd spring straight up and snake a fly off 'n the counter there, and flop down on the floor ag'in as solid as a gob of mud, and fall to scratching the side of his head with his hind foot as indifferent as if he hadn't no idea he'd been doin' any more'n any frog might do. You never see a frog so modest and straightfor'ard as he was, for all he was so gifted. And when it come to fair and square jumping on a dead level, he could get over more ground at one straddle than any animal of his breed you ever

Literary Analysis
Humor What exaggerations in this passage make the description funnier?

Reading Check
What was most unusual about Smiley and his betting habits?

7. **rat terriers** dogs skilled in catching rats.
8. **chicken cocks** roosters trained to fight.

see. Jumping on a dead level was his strong suit, you understand; and when it come to that, Smiley would ante up money on him as long as he had a red.[9] Smiley was monstrous proud of his frog, and well he might be, for fellers that had traveled and been everywheres all said he laid over any frog that ever *they* see.

'IT MIGHT BE A PARROT, OR IT MIGHT BE A CANARY, MAYBE, BUT IT AIN'T—IT'S ONLY JUST A FROG.'

Well, Smiley kep' the beast in a little lattice box, and he used to fetch him downtown sometimes and lay for a bet. One day a feller—a stranger in the camp, he was—come acrost him with his box, and says:

'What might it be that you've got in the box?'

And Smiley says, sorter indifferent-like, 'It might be a parrot, or it might be a canary, maybe, but it ain't—it's only just a frog.'

And the feller took it, and looked at it careful, and turned it round this way and that, and says, 'H'm—so 'tis. Well, what's *he* good for?'

'Well,' Smiley says, easy and careless, 'he's good enough for *one* thing, I should judge—he can outjump any frog in Calaveras county.'

The feller took the box again, and took another long, particular look, and give it back to Smiley, and says, very deliberate, 'Well,' he says, 'I don't see no p'ints about that frog that's any better'n any other frog.'

'Maybe you don't,' Smiley says. 'Maybe you understand frogs and maybe you don't understand 'em; maybe you've had experience, and maybe you ain't only a amature, as it were. Anyways, I've got *my* opinion, and I'll resk forty dollars that he can outjump any frog in Calaveras county.'

And the feller studied a minute, and then says, kinder sad like, 'Well, I'm only a stranger here, and I ain't got no frog; but if I had a frog, I'd bet you.'

And then Smiley says, 'That's all right—that's all right—if you'll hold my box a minute, I'll go and get you a frog.' And so the feller took the box, and put up his forty dollars along with Smiley's, and set down to wait.

So he set there a good while thinking and thinking to hisself, and then he got the frog out and prized his mouth open and took a teaspoon and filled him full of quailshot[10]—filled him pretty near up to his chin—and set him on the floor. Smiley he went to the swamp and slopped around in the mud for a long time, and finally he ketched a frog, and fetched him in, and give him to this feller, and says:

'Now, if you're ready, set him alongside of Dan'l, with his forepaws just even with Dan'l's, and I'll give the word.' Then he says, 'One—two—three—*git*!' and him and the feller touched up the frogs from behind, and the new frog hopped off lively, but Dan'l give a heave, and hysted up his shoulders—so—like a Frenchman, but it warn't no use—he couldn't budge; he was planted as solid as a church, and he couldn't no more stir than if he was anchored out. Smiley was a good

9. a red red cent; colloquial expression for "any money at all."
10. quailshot small lead pellets used for shooting quail.

deal surprised, and he was disgusted too, but he didn't have no idea what the matter was, of course.

The feller took the money and started away; and when he was going out at the door, he sorter jerked his thumb over his shoulder—so—at Dan'l, and says again, very deliberate, 'Well,' he says, 'I don't see no p'ints about that frog that's any better'n any other frog.'

Smiley he stood scratching his head and looking down at Dan'l a long time, and at last he says, 'I do wonder what in the nation that frog throw'd off for—I wonder if there ain't something the matter with him—he 'pears to look mighty baggy, somehow.' And he ketched Dan'l by the nap of the neck, and hefted him, and says, 'Why blame my cats if he don't weigh five pound!' and turned him upside down and he belched out a double handful of shot. And then he see how it was, and he was the maddest man—he set the frog down and took out after that feller, but he never ketched him. And—"

Reading Strategy
Clarifying and Interpreting Language How would you rephrase the sentence beginning "And he ketched Dan'l . . ." in Standard English?

Here Simon Wheeler heard his name called from the front yard, and got up to see what was wanted. And turning to me as he moved away, he said: "Just set where you are, stranger, and rest easy—I ain't going to be gone a second."

But, by your leave, I did not think that a continuation of the history of the enterprising vagabond *Jim* Smiley would be likely to afford me much information concerning the Rev. *Leonidas W.* Smiley, and so I started away.

At the door I met the sociable Wheeler returning, and he buttonholed me and recommenced:

"Well, thish-yer Smiley had a yaller one-eyed cow that didn't have no tail, only just a short stump like a bannanner, and—"

However, lacking both time and inclination, I did not wait to hear about the afflicted cow, but took my leave.

Critical Reading

1. **Key Ideas and Details (a)** What prompts Simon Wheeler to tell the story of Jim Smiley? **(b) Infer:** Why had the narrator's friend suggested that he ask Wheeler about Leonidas Smiley?
2. **Key Ideas and Details (a)** What was Jim Smiley's response to any event? **(b) Infer:** Based on this behavior, what can you infer about his character?
3. **Integration of Knowledge and Ideas** What image of America do both the excerpt from Twain's memoir and this comic story paint? Consider the sense of place, character, and event. In your response, use at least two of these Essential Question words: *adventure, individualism, sincerity, ambition.* ***[Connecting to the Essential Question: What makes American literature American?]***

Cite textual evidence to support your responses.

After You Read

from *Life on the Mississippi* • *The Notorious Jumping Frog of Calaveras County*

Literary Analysis

1. **Craft and Structure** In the excerpt from *Life on the Mississippi*, how does Twain's use of the word *heavenly* to describe ordinary activities (shaking out a tablecloth or holding a rope) add to the **humor** of his narrative?
2. **Craft and Structure** **(a)** What place and way of life does Twain describe in the excerpt? **(b)** How does humor help Twain avoid sentimentality in dealing with this subject?
3. **Craft and Structure** **(a)** In "The Notorious Jumping Frog of Calaveras County," what basic **incongruity** exists between the narrator and Simon Wheeler? **(b)** How does this contrast add to the story's humor?
4. **Craft and Structure** Use a chart like the one shown to analyze two examples of **hyperbole** in "The Notorious Jumping Frog of Calaveras County."

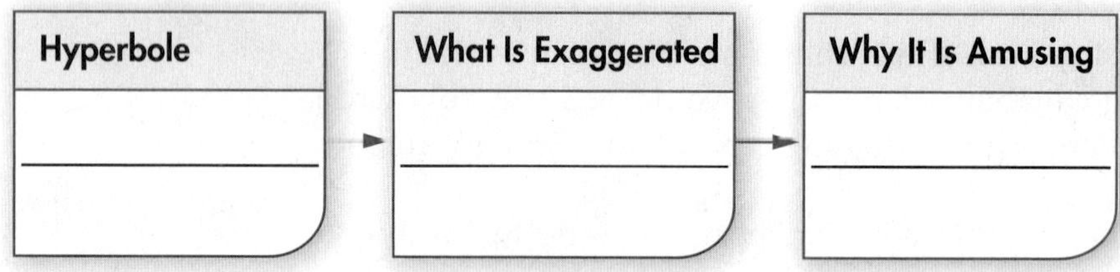

5. **Craft and Structure** **(a)** How does the use of **dialect** in "The Notorious Jumping Frog of Calaveras County" add to the story's humor? **(b)** Why would the story be less effective if Wheeler spoke in Standard English?
6. **Key Ideas and Details** **(a)** What is Wheeler's main activity in "The Notorious Jumping Frog..."? **(b)** What **social commentary** about this activity might Twain be making through humor?
7. **Integration of Knowledge and Ideas** In which selection does Twain view the characters' foibles, or weaknesses, with more sympathy? Explain.
8. **Analyze Visual Information** What does this drawing, made after Twain's death, show about his place in American culture?

Reading Strategy

9. In the excerpt from *Life on the Mississippi,* the narrator—the older Twain—peppers his account with steamboat terminology. **(a)** Identify two examples of this use of *technical language.* **(b)** Explain what each example means and how you **clarify** that information.
10. **Interpret** the regional dialect in this passage by "translating" it into modern Standard English: *...he 'peared surprised, and then he looked sorter discouraged-like, and didn't try no more to win the fight, and so he got shucked out bad.*

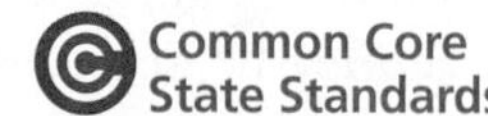

Common Core State Standards

Language

4. Determine or clarify the meaning of unknown and multiple-meaning words and phrases based on *grades 11–12 reading and content,* choosing flexibly from a range of strategies. *(p. 583)*

4.b. Identify and correctly use patterns of word changes that indicate different meanings or parts of speech. *(p. 583)*

4.c. Consult general and specialized reference materials, both print and digital, to determine or clarify the precise meaning of a word. *(p. 583)*

5. Demonstrate understanding of word relationships and nuances in word meanings. *(p. 583)*

5.b. Analyze nuances in the meanings of words with similar denotations. *(p. 583)*

THERE IS A TIME TO LAUGH AND THERE IS A TIME TO WEEP

PERFORMANCE TASKS

Integrated Language Skills

Vocabulary Acquisition and Use

Word Analysis: Greek Prefix *mono-*

The Greek prefix *mono-* means "alone," "one," or "single." A *monotonous* storyteller, therefore, uses a single tone, without varying volume or pace. Likewise, a *monosyllabic* word is made up of one syllable, and a *monocle* is a form of eyeglass with only one lens. Add the prefix *mono-* to each word root listed below. Using your understanding of the prefix and the definition of each root, tell the meaning of each newly created word.

1. *theism* = belief in a god or gods
2. *logue* = speech; speaking
3. *lith* = stone
4. *syllable* = unit of sound

Which of the new words best describes Simon Wheeler's tale? Explain.

Vocabulary: Antonyms

Antonyms are words with opposite or nearly opposite meanings. Review the words in the vocabulary list on page 569. Then, select the letter of the word in the right column that is the best antonym for each vocabulary word in the left column. Explain your answers.

1. transient	**a.** varied
2. prodigious	**b.** meager
3. eminence	**c.** quiet
4. garrulous	**d.** permanent
5. conjectured	**e.** verified
6. monotonous	**f.** obscurity
7. interminable	**g.** brief

Using Resources to Build Vocabulary

Funny Business: Words for Overstating the Case

Twain infuses his prose with humor by using overblown words to describe common feelings, experiences, and situations. Here are a few of them:

glorious	heavenly
fragrant	tranquil
grandeur	transcendent

Return to Twain's stories to review these words in context. Then, *use a print or an electronic thesaurus* to find a less inflated synonym for each one. (For example, a milder synonym for *glorious* might be *bright.*) On your own paper, rewrite the sentence in which the word appears by replacing the word with the deflated synonym. Read over your new lines, and, in a sentence or two, explain why they are less amusing than Twain's originals.

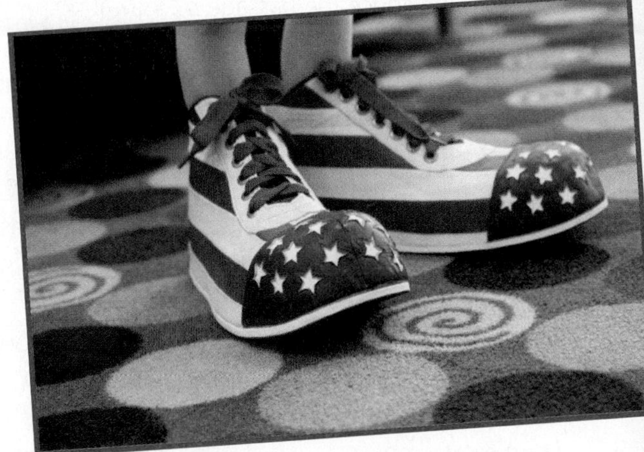

PERFORMANCE TASKS

Integrated Language Skills

Writing

Expository Text In the essay excerpted on page 575, Twain defines some of the elements that contribute to a humorous story:

> ***The humorous story may be spun out to great length, and may wander around as much as it pleases, and arrive nowhere in particular. . . . [It] is told gravely; the teller does his best to conceal the fact that he even dimly suspects there is anything funny about it.***

Write an **essay** in which you analyze Twain's application of these techniques in his own story "The Notorious Jumping Frog of Calaveras County." Include in your analysis an evaluation of Twain's definition. Determine whether his definition is universal—true in most times and places—or true only in Twain's day and age.

Prewriting Select several humorous passages from the story to analyze according to the main ideas in Twain's definition. Use a chart like the one shown to organize your thoughts.

Model: Organizing to Show Comparison

spins out at length	arrives nowhere	is told gravely	conceals humor

Drafting Organize your essay point by point, connecting Twain's definition to passages from the story. For each passage, do the following:

- Introduce the passage by indicating which aspect of the definition it will illustrate.
- Provide the passage in the form of a quotation. Introduce shorter passages with a colon, and enclose them in quotation marks. Set longer passages off from the text. Include a parenthetical page reference after each quotation.
- Explain the connection between the passage and Twain's definition. Strengthen your analysis by adding your own insights about how and why a certain technique creates humor.

Conclude your draft with an assessment of Twain's definition. To end the essay on a lively note, consider imitating Twain's style or otherwise injecting your own variety of respectful humor.

Revising Review your essay to find ideas that you can support more effectively with additional examples, details, or quotations. Return to your notes or to the story to find additional supporting evidence.

Common Core State Standards

Writing

2. Write explanatory texts to examine and convey complex ideas, concepts, and information clearly and accurately through the effective selection, organization, and analysis of content.

2.a. Introduce a topic; organize complex ideas, concepts, and information so that each new element builds on that which precedes it to create a unified whole.

2.b. Develop the topic thoroughly by selecting the most significant and relevant facts, extended definitions, concrete details, quotations, or other information and examples appropriate to the audience's knowledge of the topic.

2.f. Provide a concluding statement or section that follows from and supports the information or explanation presented.

Language

1. Demonstrate command of the conventions of standard English grammar and usage when writing or speaking. *(p. 585)*

Conventions and Style: Fixing Misplaced and Dangling Modifiers

A **misplaced modifier** seems to modify the wrong word in a sentence because it is too far away from the word it really modifies. A **dangling modifier** seems to modify the wrong word or no word at all because the word it *should* modify is not in the sentence. Misplaced and dangling modifiers can be single words, phrases, or clauses. Your writing will be clearer if you avoid misplaced and dangling modifiers.

Misplaced: *Disappointed*, the riverboat captain ignored the boy.
Fixed: The riverboat captain ignored the disappointed boy.

Misplaced: Twain's adventures inspired a number of books *in foreign countries.*
Fixed: Twain's adventures in foreign countries inspired a number of books.

Dangling: *Full of quailshot*, jumping was impossible.
Fixed: Full of quailshot, the frog could not jump.

Dangling: *While working as a journalist*, an entertaining writing style developed.
Fixed: While working as a journalist, Twain developed an entertaining writing style.

TIP Dangling modifiers most often appear as introductory phrases or clauses.

Practice Rewrite each sentence to fix the misplaced or dangling modifier and make the sentence clear. You may have to change the wording slightly. In items 1–5, the misplaced or dangling modifier is in italics.

1. The frog *only* lost one race.
2. The pup would grab the other dog *to win the fight* by the hind leg.
3. *Determined*, Twain's plan was to work on a steamboat.
4. *Eager to make a bet*, Smiley's frog is left with the stranger.
5. *After his wife's death*, pessimism overcame Mark Twain.
6. The young men were talking about their future jobs on steamboats yesterday.
7. Having found a second frog, the jumping contest was started.
8. Clemens met many characters that he would write about later as a boy.
9. Assembled at the wharf, their eyes were fixed on the handsome steamboat.
10. The boy would become a writer who dreamed of piloting a riverboat.

Writing and Speaking Conventions

A. Writing For each numbered item, write a sentence using the phrase or clause as a modifier. Then, tell what word or words the phrase or clause modifies.

1. near the Mississippi River
2. who envied him
3. gone for a long time
4. placing his bet

Example: near the Mississippi River
Sentence: As a boy, Clemens lived near the Mississippi River.
Word Modified: lived

B. Speaking Describe an occupation you dream of having. Correctly use at least three different types of modifiers.

PH WRITING COACH
Further instruction and practice are available in *Prentice Hall Writing Coach*.

"School" of American Humor

"Semper Ridere"

Mark Twain, President & Founder
Robert Benchley, Punster & Wordsmith
Dorothy Parker, Resident Wit
James Thurber, Fabulist
S. J. Perelman, Wry *Feuilletonist*
Russell Baker, Memoirist & Humorist
Art Buchwald, Political Satirist
Garrison Keillor, Storyteller
Bill Cosby, Comedian of Stage, Screen, and Print
Erma Bombeck, Humorous Housewife
Dave Barry, Humor Columnist
Bill Bryson, Backpacking Comic

COURSE CATALOGUE

Humor Writing 101
Dry Wit, Dialect, and Local Color
Prof. **Mark Twain**
Meets: M-W-F, 11:00–12:00 *4 credits*

Knowing your audience is the key to effective humor, and Prof. Twain shares his time-tested techniques in this required humor course. Learn to be an observer and develop a keen ear for speech to make your writing richer and funnier.

Humor Writing 102
Bon Mots, Biting Wit, and Blistering Sarcasm
Prof. **Dorothy Parker**
Meets: F 5:00–11:00 *4 credits*

If Oscar Wilde had an American sister, it would have been Prof. Parker. She'll teach you to write satirical fiction, brutal barbs and viciously funny poems. Wield wit as a weapon. Torpedo the double standard. Subvert the status quo. Students will emerge as seasoned professionals. "The most beautiful words in English," says Parker, "are 'check enclosed.'"

Humor Writing 103
Satire, Punch Lines, Cartoons, and Deadpan Delivery
Prof. **James Thurber**
Meets T-TH, 9:00 – 10:00 *4 credits*

Unlock the absurdity in your secret life. Prof. Thurber will show how writing about small, timid protagonists can earn you a whale of a reputation. Humor, as Prof. Thurber will demonstrate, is emotional chaos remembered in tranquility. This is his class and welcome to it.

Humor Writing 104
Humorous Sketches and Absurdist Screenplays
Prof. **S. J. Perelman**
Meets: W 2:00–5:00 *4 credits*

Feuilletons is a French literary term meaning "little leaves." Prof. Perelman shows how he produces his *feuilletons*—brief, amusing sketches for *The New Yorker*. On the syllabus: making wry observations, tossing up non- sequiturs, infusing everyday events with irony, and writing absurdist screenplays a la *Horsefeathers* and *Monkey Business.*

Humor Writing 105
Hyperbole and Screwball Characters
Prof. **Erma Bombeck**
Meets: M-W-F 10:00–11:00 *4 credits*

Learn how to turn mundane household chores into comic opera for a newspaper column. Master screwball characters, down-home hyperbole, and the self-deprecating voice. Prof. Bombeck will show you how to make outrageous claims—such as, "Motherhood is the second oldest profession," —without bursting your own balloon.

Humor Writing 106
Anthropology, Incongruity, and Human Foibles
Prof. **Bill Bryson**
Meets: T-TH 9:00–11:00 *4 credits*

If you look at your own backyard and see an exhibit on alien culture, you may have what it takes to become a best-selling author. After Prof. Bryson leads you on a tour of Main Street USA, it will never seem quite the same again. His tools of the trade include regional detail, hyperbole, embellishment, and comic characters. Wear your walking shoes.

Comparing Literary Works

Mark Twain's Writings* • from *The Life and Times of the Thunderbolt Kid

Comparing American Humor Past and Present

Writing Humor American humor writing falls roughly into two categories: the refined, moral wit of figures such as Benjamin Franklin and Washington Irving; and the folk humor, or "humor of the people," of writers such as Mark Twain and contemporary writer **Bill Bryson.** While the first type of humor is characterized by a subtle, high-minded cleverness, the second makes use of more obvious humorous devices, including the following:

- **hyperbole:** the exaggeration of details or embellishment of events
- **incongruity:** elements that seem not to fit their context
- **regionalism:** language or behaviors specific to a certain part of the country
- **foibles:** a focus on human flaws

When used in conjunction with everyday subject matter, such as making a bet or cooking dinner, these elements produce snapshots of real life that are familiar, funny, and revealing of larger ideas about human nature.

Like Mark Twain, Bill Bryson began his career as a journalist; also like Twain, Bryson used his observational skills in humorous works on a wide range of subjects, including travel. Both authors deal in the humor of the everyday—the amusing aspects of regular folks trying to live in a world that is anything but "regular." Use the following chart to compare and contrast Twain's and Bryson's humor.

Humorous Device	Twain	Bryson
hyperbole	describes an apprentice engineer as an "exalted . . . eminence"	
regional elements	Simon Wheeler's dialect	
comic characters	the "trapped" narrator of "The Notorious Jumping Frog..."	

Common Core State Standards

Reading Informational Text
4. Determine the meaning of words and phrases as they are used in a text, including figurative and connotative meanings.

Language
4.c. Consult general and specialized reference materials, both print and digital, to find the pronunciation of a word or determine or clarify its precise meaning, its part of speech, its etymology, or its standard usage.
5.a. Interpret figures of speech in context and analyze their role in the text.

Gather Vocabulary Knowledge

Bryson uses related forms of the words *explode, perish,* and *recoil* to relate his early experiences with food. Use print or online glossaries and other references to explore these words.

- **Related References**: Using an etymology guide or vocabulary builder, learn more about each word's origin and meaning. Select one word and build a word map for it that includes synonyms, antonyms, and examples of use in sentences.
- **Glossaries:** Refer to the glossary of a cookbook and find three verbs that normally apply to cooking processes. Use the words in a paragraph.

Bill Bryson *(b. 1951)*

Author of *The Life and Times of the Thunderbolt Kid: A Memoir*

Bill Bryson was born and raised in Des Moines, Iowa, where his father was a sports writer and his mother a home furnishings editor for the daily newspaper the *Des Moines Register.* Bryson's two older siblings had left home by the time he was a teenager, and his busy parents granted Bryson a great deal of freedom: On any given evening he might be given five dollars and told to eat out and catch a movie. This lifestyle suited Bryson, who has led what he describes as a "rootless" life ever since.

Back and Forth In 1972, Bryson abandoned his studies at Drake University in order to spend four months backpacking through Europe. The following year, he returned to England for a longer stay. While working in a psychiatric hospital near London, Bryson met his wife, a nurse. The couple returned to the United States in order for Bryson to complete his college degree. They crossed the Atlantic yet again, settled in northern England, and stayed put for almost twenty years before moving back to the United States in 1995. After eight years in New Hampshire, the couple returned to England, where they remain.

Word Wanderings During his early years in Britain, Bryson worked as a journalist. The work left him restless, though, and he retired from journalism in 1987. Bryson's first book, *The Lost Continent*, appeared two years later. True to its author's ambling spirit, the book describes a visit to the United States—38 of them, to be exact—in search of the perfect American small town. Subsequent books have ranged across the globe and across a wide spectrum of subjects, including travels in Europe, hiking the Appalachian Trail, British culture, the history of the English language, the history of science, and the life of William Shakespeare.

Looking Back Bryson's memoir, *The Life and Times of the Thunderbolt Kid*, is a portrait of his childhood that also provides insight into the stuff of Bryson's humor, which he finds in our chaotic daily lives, in our oddball habits, in those forgotten containers at the backs of our refrigerators. Bryson admits that the memoir is also a kind of lament for the loss of our collective innocence. If you were a kid in the 1950s, he reflects, "You really did expect, any day, that we'd all have jet-packs or be going on vacation to Mars. . . . And now that's completely gone."

from The Life and Times of the Thunderbolt Kid

Bill Bryson

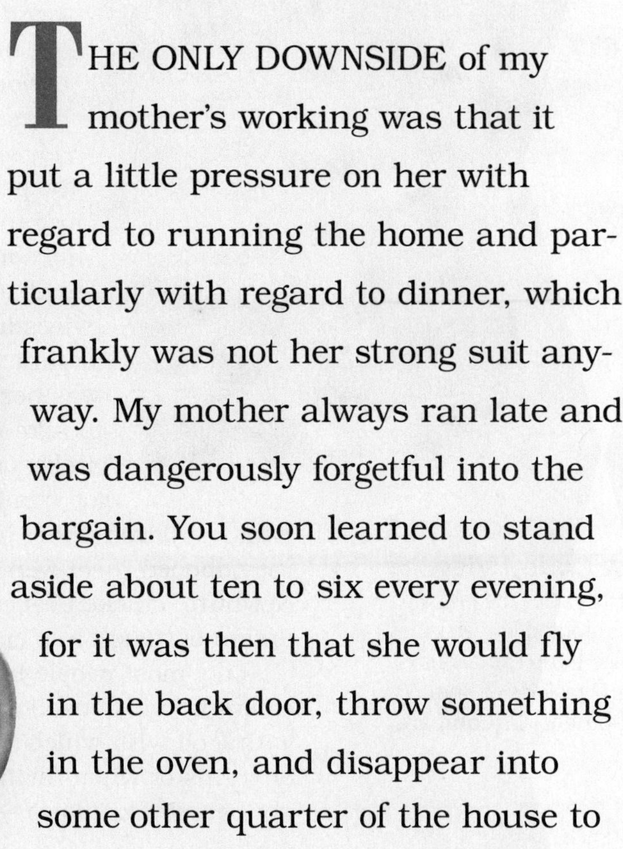

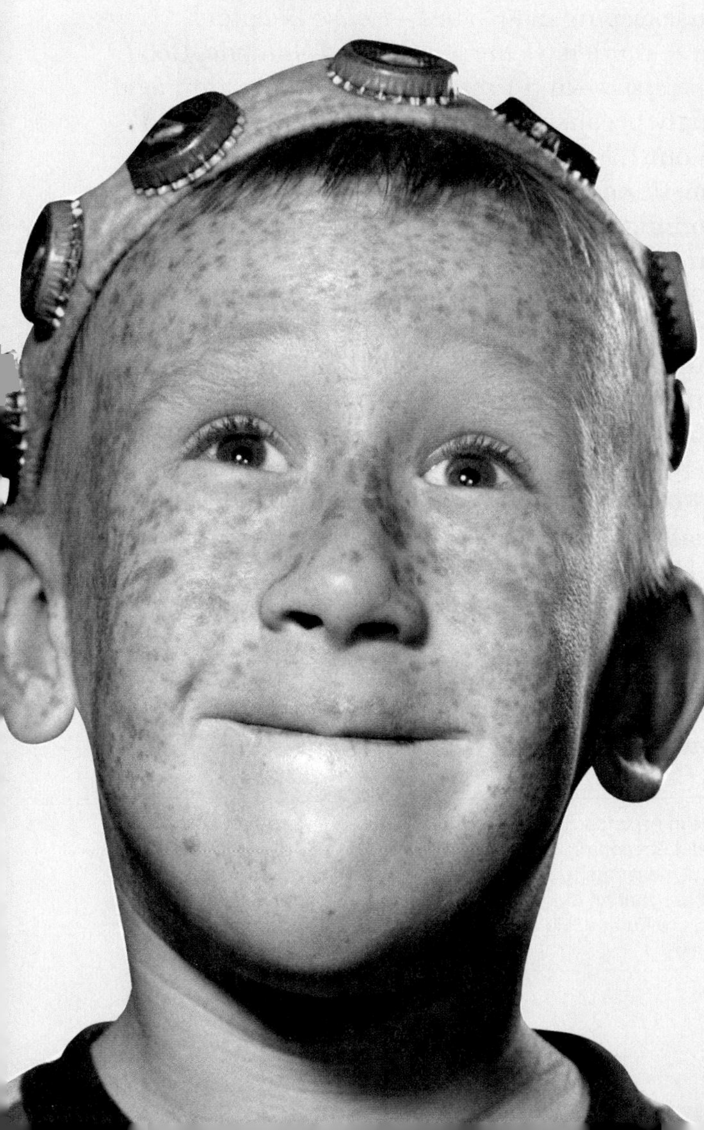

THE ONLY DOWNSIDE of my mother's working was that it put a little pressure on her with regard to running the home and particularly with regard to dinner, which frankly was not her strong suit anyway. My mother always ran late and was dangerously forgetful into the bargain. You soon learned to stand aside about ten to six every evening, for it was then that she would fly in the back door, throw something in the oven, and disappear into some other quarter of the house to

Vocabulary
embark (em bärk′) *v.* to begin a venture, project, or activity

embark on the thousand other household tasks that greeted her each evening. In consequence she nearly always forgot about dinner until a point slightly beyond way too late. As a rule you knew it was time to eat when you could hear potatoes exploding in the oven.

We didn't call it the kitchen in our house. We called it the Burns Unit.

"It's a bit burned," my mother would say apologetically at every meal, presenting you with a piece of meat that looked like something—a much-loved pet perhaps—salvaged from a tragic house fire. "But I think I scraped off most of the burned part," she would add, overlooking that this included every bit of it that had once been flesh.

Happily, all this suited my father. His palate only responded to two tastes—burned and ice cream—so everything suited him so long as it was sufficiently dark and not too startlingly flavorful. Theirs truly was a marriage made in heaven, for no one could burn food like my mother or eat it like my dad.

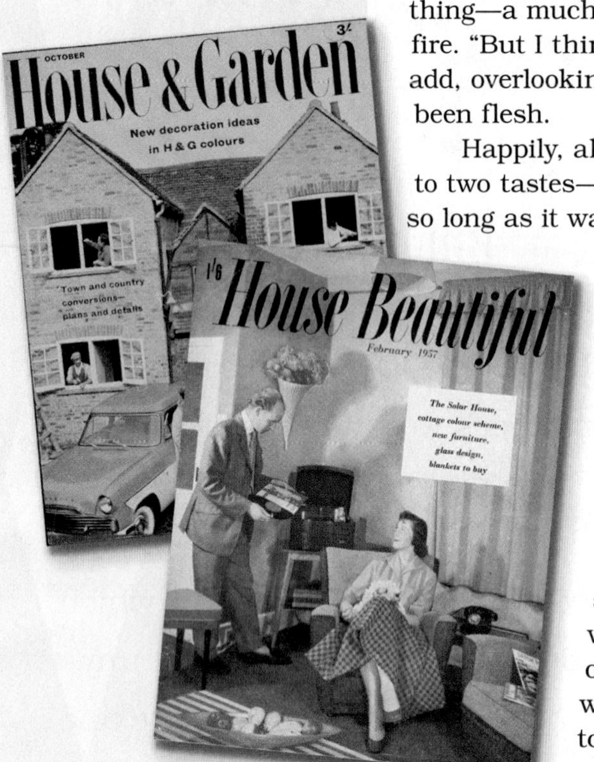

As part of her job, my mother bought stacks of housekeeping magazines—*House Beautiful, House & Garden, Better Homes and Gardens, Good Housekeeping*—and I read these with a certain avidity, partly because they were always lying around and in our house all idle moments were spent reading something, and partly because they depicted lives so absorbingly at variance with our own. The housewives in my mother's magazines were so collected, so organized, so calmly on top of things, and their food was perfect—their *lives* were perfect. They dressed up to take their food out of the oven! There were no black circles on the ceiling above their stoves, no mutating goo climbing over the sides of their forgotten saucepans. Children didn't have to be ordered to stand back every time they opened *their* oven doors. And their foods—baked Alaska, lobster Newburg, chicken cacciatore—why, these were dishes we didn't even dream of, much less encounter, in Iowa.

▲ Critical Viewing
How does the lifestyle presented in magazines like these compare to the realities of Bryson's household? **[Compare]**

Like most people in Iowa in the 1950s, we were more cautious eaters in our house.* On the rare occasions when we were presented with food with which we were not comfortable or familiar—on planes or trains or when invited to a meal cooked by someone who was not herself from Iowa—we tended to tilt it up carefully with a knife

---

* In fact, like most other people in America. The leading food writer of the age, Duncan Hines, author of the hugely successful *Adventures in Good Eating*, was himself a cautious eater and declared with pride that he never ate food with French names if he could possibly help it. Hines's other proud boast was that he did not venture out of America until he was seventy years old, when he made a trip to Europe. He disliked much of what he found there, especially the food.

and examine it from every angle as if determining whether it might need to be defused. Once on a trip to San Francisco my father was taken by friends to a Chinese restaurant and he described it to us afterward in the somber tones of someone recounting a near-death experience.

"And they eat it with sticks, you know," he added knowledgeably.

"Goodness!" said my mother.

"I would rather have gas gangrene than go through that again," my father added grimly.

All of our meals consisted of leftovers.

In our house we didn't eat

- pasta, rice, cream cheese, sour cream, garlic, mayonnaise, onions, corned beef, pastrami, salami, or foreign food of any type, except French toast
- bread that wasn't white and at least 65 percent air
- spices other than salt, pepper, and maple syrup
- fish that was any shape other than rectangular and not coated in bright orange bread crumbs, and then only on Fridays and only when my mother remembered it was Friday, which in fact was not often
- soups not blessed by Campbell's and only a very few of those
- anything with **dubious** regional names like "pone" or "gumbo," or foods that had at any time been an esteemed staple of slaves or peasants

Vocabulary
dubious (do͞o′ bē əs) *adj.* questionable; suspicious

All other foods of all types—curries, enchiladas, tofu, bagels, sushi, couscous, yogurt, kale, arugula, Parma ham, any cheese that was not a vivid bright yellow and shiny enough to see your reflection in—had either not yet been invented or was yet unknown to us. We really were radiantly unsophisticated. I remember being surprised to learn at quite an advanced age that a shrimp cocktail was not, as I had always imagined, a predinner alcoholic drink with a shrimp in it.

All our meals consisted of leftovers. My mother had a seemingly inexhaustible supply of foods that had already been to the table, sometimes repeatedly. Apart from a few perishable dairy products, everything in the fridge was older than I was, sometimes by many years. (Her oldest food possession of all, it more or less goes without saying, was a fruitcake that was kept in a metal tin and dated from the colonial period.) I can only assume that my mother did all of her cooking in the 1940s so that she could spend the rest of her life surprising herself with what she could find under cover at the back of the fridge. I never knew her to reject a food. The rule of thumb seemed to be that if you opened the lid and the stuff inside didn't make you actually recoil and take at least one staggered step backward, it was deemed okay to eat.

Why was Bryson's parents' marriage "made in heaven"?

My mother routinely washed and dried paper plates...

Both of my parents had grown up during the Great Depression and neither of them ever threw anything away if they could possibly avoid it. My mother routinely washed and dried paper plates, and smoothed out for reuse spare aluminum foil. If you left a pea on your plate, it became part of a future meal. All our sugar came in little packets spirited out of restaurants in deep coat pockets, as did our jams, jellies, crackers (oyster *and* saltine), tartar sauces, some of our ketchup and butter, all of our napkins, and a very occasional ashtray; anything that came with a restaurant table really. One of the happiest moments in my parents' life was when maple syrup started to be served in small disposable packets and they could add those to the household hoard.

Critical Reading

Cite textual evidence to support your responses.

1. **Key Ideas and Details (a)** What was the kitchen called in the Bryson house? **(b) Infer:** What does this name suggest about the family?
2. **Key Ideas and Details (a)** How does Bryson describe the eaters in his house—and in Iowa in the 1950s? **(b) Infer:** What does this attitude toward food tell you about other aspects of life in Iowa in the 1950s?
3. **Craft and Structure Evaluate:** Which word choices or descriptions do you think add most to the humor of this excerpt? Explain.
4. **Craft and Structure (a) Distinguish:** What tone, or attitude toward his subject, does Bryson take in this excerpt? **(b) Apply:** Keeping his attitude in mind, write a one-sentence rule for responding to exasperating situations.

After You Read

Mark Twain's Writings* • from *The Life and Times of the Thunderbolt Kid

Comparing Humor

1. **Key Ideas and Details (a)** What specific **regional** elements of place and time does Twain bring to light in *Life on the Mississippi*? **(b)** What specific place and time does Bryson bring to life? **(c)** What do the boys in these two different settings have in common?
2. **Key Ideas and Details (a)** Identify a **human foible,** or flaw, that is emphasized in Bryson's memoir. **(b)** Identify a foible Twain spotlights in one of his works. **(c)** For which foible do you have greater sympathy? Why?
3. **Craft and Structure (a)** Note one example each of **hyperbole** and **incongruity** in Bryson's memoir. **(b)** Identify one example of each of these devices in Twain's story "The Notorious Jumping Frog of Calaveras County." **(c)** Which examples do you find funnier? Explain.

Common Core State Standards

Writing

2. Write informative/explanatory texts to examine and convey complex ideas, concepts, and information clearly and accurately through the effective selection, organization, and analysis of content.

2.b. Develop the topic thoroughly by selecting the most significant and relevant facts, extended definitions, concrete details, quotations, or other information and examples appropriate to the audience's knowledge of the topic.

9.a. Apply *grades 11–12 Reading standards* to literature.

Timed Writing

Explanatory Text: Essay

Stock characters, or character "types," are personalities that have become conventional in literature over time. The "overworked career woman" and the conniving trickster are both stock characters. Humor writers use character types to evoke laughter and sympathy and, sometimes, to critique society.

Assignment: Write a **compare-and-contrast** essay in which you examine two character "types" presented by Twain and Bryson. Prewrite by answering the questions listed below to generate ideas and focus your analysis.

- What aspects of each character suggest they are "types"?
- Why is each character funny? What makes each character sympathetic?

As you write, follow the conventions of a strong analytical essay:

- Analyze humorous nuances in the texts.
- Analyze the effects of each author's use of figurative language, such as hyperbole.

5-Minute Planner

Complete these steps before you begin to write.

1. Read the assignment carefully, noting key words and phrases.
2. Scan the selections, looking for details about your chosen characters. **TIP** Jot down details that support your interpretation in two columns, devoting one column to each character.
3. Create a rough outline for your essay.
4. Reread the prompt, and draft your essay.

USE ACADEMIC VOCABULARY

As you write, use academic language, including the following words or their related forms:

compare
contrast
analyze
characterize

For more information about academic language, see the vocabulary charts in the introduction to this book.

Before You Read *To Build a Fire*

Connecting to the Essential Question For "armchair adventurers" at the turn of the twentieth century, this and other stories by Jack London brought to life a distant world of danger and extreme conditions. As you read, note details of extreme peril specific to the setting. This will help as you consider the Essential Question: **What is the relationship between literature and place?**

Reading Literature

3. Analyze the impact of the author's choices regarding how to develop and relate elements of a story or drama.

6. Analyze a case in which grasping a point of view requires distinguishing what is directly stated in a text from what is really meant.

Literary Analysis

Conflict, the struggle between opposing forces, can take two forms:

- **Internal,** occurring within the mind of a character
- **External,** occurring between a character and society, nature, another person, God, or fate

A character's efforts to resolve a conflict form the basis for the plot of a narrative. In "To Build a Fire," a man is in the throes of a deadly external conflict, struggling to survive in the bitter cold of the Alaskan wilderness. In this case, the story's **setting**—the time and place of the action—serves as the opposing force against which the protagonist struggles.

Irony involves a discrepancy between what is stated and what is meant, or between what is expected and what actually happens. In the case of **dramatic irony,** there is a contradiction between what a character thinks and what the reader knows to be true. For example, in this story the reader knows that the frigid temperature poses a much greater danger than the man realizes. The result is an ironic quality that permeates the entire story, affecting the reader's understanding of the characters, plot, and setting. As you read, notice passages where it is clear that you understand more than the man does about the conflict he faces.

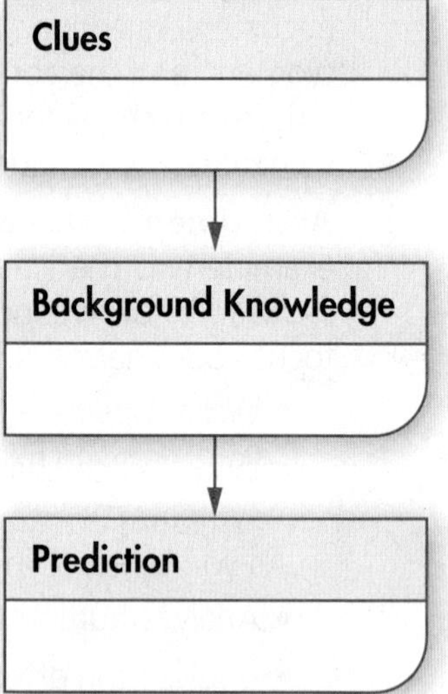

Reading Strategy

Preparing to Read Complex Texts As you read this story, **predict,** or anticipate, what will happen by noting clues that hint at later events. You can apply your *background knowledge* about the Yukon and survival at extreme temperatures to identify clues. Then, determine what the clues suggest about the main character's plight. Use a chart like the one shown to record your predictions.

Vocabulary

conjectural (kən jek′ chər əl) *adj.* based on guesswork (p. 597)

unwonted (un wän′ tid) *adj.* unusual; unfamiliar (p. 598)

appendage (ə pen′ dij) *n.* an external part of a plant or animal, such as a tail or a limb (p. 599)

conflagration (kän′ flə grā′ shən) *n.* big, destructive fire (p. 605)

peremptorily (pər emp′ tə rə lē) *adv.* decisively; commandingly (p. 608)

JACK LONDON (1876–1916)

Author of "To Build a Fire"

Jack London had endured more hardships by the age of twenty-one than most people experience in a lifetime. His struggles gave him a sympathy for the working class and a lasting distaste for drudgery. They also provided inspiration for novels and short stories, and became the foundation of his success as a writer.

Difficult Beginnings London grew up in San Francisco in extreme poverty. At the age of eleven, he left school and supported himself through a succession of unskilled jobs. Despite the long hours spent toiling at these jobs, London was able to read constantly, borrowing travel and adventure books from the library.

The books he read inspired London to travel, and he did so as a "tramp," using the name "Frisco Kid." After being arrested for vagrancy near Buffalo, New York, London decided to educate himself and reshape his life. He completed high school in eighteen months and enrolled at the University of California.

After only one semester, however, the lure of adventure proved irresistible. In 1897, London abandoned his studies and traveled to the Alaskan Yukon in an unsuccessful search for gold. His experiences in Alaska taught him about people's desire for wealth and power, and about our inability to control the forces of nature.

A Writing Life Once back in California, London became determined to earn a living as a writer. He rented a typewriter and worked up to fifteen hours a day, spinning his Alaskan adventures into short stories and novels. According to legend, London's stack of rejection slips from publishers grew to five feet in height. Even so, he wrote diligently every morning, setting himself a 1,000-word minimum.

In 1903, London earned national fame when he published *The Call of the Wild*. He soon became the highest-paid and most industrious writer in the country. During his career, London produced more than fifty fiction and nonfiction books, including *The Sea-Wolf* (1904) and *White Fang* (1906), which, along with *The Call of the Wild*, have become American classics.

Recognition by His Peers The well-known writer Upton Sinclair wrote that Jack London "was the true king of our storytellers." London's friend Oliver Madox Hueffer recalled that London "was the ideal yarnster . . . and one reason why I think him likely to be numbered as among the writers of real mark was that he was perfectly unconscious of it. Like Peter Pan, he never grew up, and he lived in his own stories with such intensity that he ended by believing them himself."

TO BUILD A FIRE

JACK LONDON

BACKGROUND The United States purchased Alaska from Russia for two cents an acre in 1867. Three decades later, thousands of prospectors, including Jack London, headed north after gold was discovered in the Yukon wilderness. London may have been searching for more than gold. He once commented: "True, the new territory was mostly barren; but its several hundred thousand square miles of frigidity at least gave breathing space to those who else would have suffocated at home."

Day had broken cold and gray, exceedingly cold and gray, when the man turned aside from the main Yukon[1] trail and climbed the high earth-bank, where a dim and little-traveled trail led eastward through the fat spruce timberland. It was a steep bank, and he paused for breath at the top, excusing the act to himself by looking at his watch. It was nine o'clock. There was no sun nor hint of sun, though there was not a cloud in the sky. It was a clear day, and yet there seemed an intangible pall over the face of things, a subtle gloom that made the day dark, and that was due to the absence of sun. This fact did not worry the man. He was used to the lack of sun. It had been days since he had seen the sun, and he knew that a few more days must pass before that cheerful orb, due south, would just peep above the skyline and dip immediately from view.

The man flung a look back along the way he had come. The Yukon lay a mile wide and hidden under three feet of ice. On top of this ice were as many feet of snow. It was all pure white, rolling in gentle undulations where the ice jams of the freeze-up had formed. North and south, as far as his eye could see, it was unbroken white, save for a dark hairline that curved and twisted from around the spruce-covered island to the south, and that curved and twisted away into the north, where it disappeared behind another spruce-covered island. This dark hairline was the trail—the main trail—that led south five hundred miles to the Chilcoot Pass, Dyea,[2] and salt water; and that led north seventy miles to Dawson, and still on to the north a thousand miles to Nulato,[3] and finally to St. Michael on Bering Sea, a thousand miles and half a thousand more.

But all this—the mysterious, far-reaching hairline trail, the absence of sun from the sky, the tremendous cold, and the strangeness and weirdness of it all—made no impression on the man. It was not because he was long used to it. He was a newcomer in the land, a *chechaquo*,[4] and this was his first winter. The trouble with him was that he was without imagination. He was quick and alert in the things of life, but only in the things, and not in the significances. Fifty degrees below zero meant eighty-odd degrees of frost. Such fact impressed him as being cold and uncomfortable, and that was all. It did not lead him to meditate upon his frailty as a creature of temperature, and upon man's frailty in general, able only to live within certain narrow limits of heat and cold; and from there on it did not lead him to the conjectural field of immortality and man's place in the universe. Fifty degrees below zero stood for a bite of frost that hurt and that must be guarded against by the use of mittens, earflaps, warm

Reading Strategy
Predicting What do you predict will happen to the "newcomer" who is "without imagination"?

Vocabulary
conjectural (kən jek′ chər əl) *adj.* based on guesswork

Where is the man, and what weather conditions is he experiencing?

1. **Yukon** (yo͞o′ kän) territory in northwestern Canada, east of Alaska; also, a river.
2. **Dyea** (dī′ ā) former town in Alaska at the start of the Yukon trail.
3. **Dawson . . . Nulato** former gold-mining villages in the Yukon.
4. ***chechaquo*** (chē chä′ kwō) slang for newcomer.

moccasins, and thick socks. Fifty degrees below zero was to him just precisely fifty degrees below zero. That there should be anything more to it than that was a thought that never entered his head.

As he turned to go on, he spat speculatively. There was a sharp, explosive crackle that startled him. He spat again. And again, in the air, before it could fall to the snow, the spittle crackled. He knew that at fifty below spittle crackled on the snow, but this spittle had crackled in the air. Undoubtedly it was colder than fifty below—how much colder he did not know. But the temperature did not matter. He was bound for the old claim on the left fork of Henderson Creek, where the boys were already. They had come over across the divide from the Indian Creek country, while he had come the roundabout way to take a look at the possibilities of getting out logs in the spring from the islands in the Yukon. He would be in to camp by six o'clock; a bit after dark, it was true, but the boys would be there, a fire would be going, and a hot supper would be ready. As for lunch, he pressed his hand against the protruding bundle under his jacket. It was also under his shirt, wrapped up in a handkerchief and lying against the naked skin. It was the only way to keep the biscuits from freezing. He smiled agreeably to himself as he thought of those biscuits, each cut open and sopped in bacon grease, and each enclosing a generous slice of fried bacon.

Literary Analysis
Conflict With what or whom is the man in conflict?

He plunged in among the big spruce trees. The trail was faint. A foot of snow had fallen since the last sled had passed over, and he was glad he was without a sled, traveling light. In fact, he carried nothing but the lunch wrapped in the handkerchief. He was surprised, however, at the cold. It certainly was cold, he concluded, as he rubbed his numb nose and cheekbones with his mittened hand. He was a warm-whiskered man, but the hair on his face did not protect the high cheekbones and the eager nose that thrust itself aggressively into the frosty air.

At the man's heels trotted a dog, a big native husky, the proper wolf dog, gray-coated and without any visible or temperamental difference from its brother, the wild wolf. The animal was depressed by the tremendous cold. It knew that it was no time for traveling. Its instinct told it a truer tale than was told to the man by the man's judgment. In reality, it was not merely colder than fifty below zero; it was colder than sixty below, than seventy below. It was seventy-five below zero. Since the freezing point is thirty-two above zero, it meant that one hundred and seven degrees of frost obtained. The dog did not know anything about thermometers. Possibly in its brain there was no sharp consciousness of a condition of very cold such as was in the man's brain. But the brute had its instinct. It experienced a vague but menacing apprehension that subdued it and made it slink along at the man's heels, and that made it question eagerly every unwonted movement of the man as if expecting him to go into camp or to seek shelter somewhere and build a fire. The dog had learned fire, and it wanted fire, or else to burrow under the snow and cuddle its warmth away from the air.

Reading Strategy
Predicting What prediction can you make based on the description of the dog's instincts?

Vocabulary
unwonted (un wän′ tid) *adj.* unusual; unfamiliar

The frozen moisture of its breathing had settled on its fur in a fine powder of frost, and especially were its jowls, muzzle, and eyelashes whitened by its crystalled breath. The man's red beard and mustache were likewise frosted, but more solidly, the deposit taking the form of ice and increasing with every warm, moist breath he exhaled. Also, the man was chewing tobacco, and the muzzle of ice held his lips so rigidly that he was unable to clear his chin when he expelled the juice. The result was that a crystal beard of the color and solidity of amber was increasing its length on his chin. If he fell down it would shatter itself, like glass, into brittle fragments. But he did not mind the appendage. It was the penalty all tobacco-chewers paid in that country, and he had been out before in two cold snaps. They had not been so cold as this, he knew, but by the spirit thermometer[5] at Sixty Mile he knew they had been registered at fifty below and at fifty-five.

Vocabulary
appendage (ə pen′ dij) *n.* an external part of a plant or animal, such as a tail or a limb

He held on through the level stretch of woods for several miles, crossed a wide flat, and dropped down a bank to the frozen bed of a small stream. This was Henderson Creek, and he knew he was ten miles from the forks. He looked at his watch. It was ten o'clock. He was making four miles an hour, and he calculated that he would arrive at the forks at half past twelve. He decided to celebrate that event by eating his lunch there.

Spiral Review
Point of View From what point of view is this story related? How do you know?

The dog dropped in again at his heels, with a tail drooping discouragement, as the man swung along the creek bed. The furrow of the old sled trail was plainly visible, but a dozen inches of snow covered the marks of the last runners. In a month no man had come up or down that silent creek. The man held steadily on. He was not much given to thinking, and just then particularly he had nothing to think about save that he would eat lunch at the forks and that at six o'clock he would be in camp with the boys. There was nobody to talk to; and, had there been, speech would have been impossible because of the ice-muzzle on his mouth. So he continued monotonously to chew tobacco and to increase the length of his amber beard.

Once in a while the thought reiterated itself that it was very cold and that he had never experienced such cold. As he walked along he rubbed his cheekbones and nose with the back of his mittened hand. He did this automatically, now and again changing hands. But rub as he would, the instant he stopped his cheekbones went numb, and the following instant the end of his nose went numb. He was sure to frost his cheeks; he knew that, and experienced a pang of regret that he had not devised a nose strap of the sort Bud wore in cold snaps. Such a strap passed across the cheeks, as well, and saved them. But it didn't matter much, after all. What were frosted cheeks? A bit painful, that was all: they were never serious.

What physical effects of the cold does the man experience?

Empty as the man's mind was of thoughts, he was keenly observant, and he noticed the changes in the creek, the curves and

5. **spirit thermometer** thermometer containing alcohol; used in extreme cold.

▲ Critical Viewing
Which words or passages from the story could be used to describe this scene? **[Analyze]**

bends and timber jams, and always he sharply noted where he placed his feet. Once, coming around a bend, he shied abruptly, like a startled horse, curved away from the place where he had been walking, and retreated several paces back along the trail. The creek he knew was frozen clear to the bottom—no creek could contain water in that arctic winter—but he knew also that there were springs that bubbled out from the hillsides and ran along under the snow and on top the ice of the creek. He knew that the coldest snaps never froze these springs, and he knew likewise their danger. They were traps. They hid pools of water under the snow that might be three inches deep, or three feet. Sometimes a skin of ice half an inch thick covered them, and in turn was covered by the snow. Sometimes there were alternate layers of water and ice skin, so that when one broke through he kept on breaking through for a while, sometimes wetting himself to the waist.

Reading Strategy
Predicting Based on the description of the creek and hidden pools, what do you predict might happen?

That was why he had shied in such panic. He had felt the give under his feet and heard the crackle of a snow-hidden ice skin. And to get his feet wet in such a temperature meant trouble and danger. At the very least it meant delay, for he would be forced to stop and build a fire, and under its protection to bare his feet while he dried his socks and moccasins. He stood and studied the creek bed and its banks, and decided that the flow of water came from the right. He reflected awhile, rubbing his nose and cheeks, then skirted to the left, stepping gingerly and testing the footing for each step. Once clear of the danger, he took a fresh chew of tobacco and swung along at his four-mile gait.

In the course of the next two hours he came upon several similar traps. Usually the snow above the hidden pools had a sunken, candied appearance that advertised the danger. Once again, however, he had a close call; and once, suspecting danger, he compelled the dog to go on in front. The dog did not want to go. It hung back until the man shoved it forward, and then it went quickly across the white, unbroken surface. Suddenly it broke through, floundered to one side, and got away to firmer footing. It had wet its forefeet and legs, and almost immediately the water that clung to it turned to ice. It made quick efforts to lick the ice off its legs, then dropped down in the snow and began to bite out the ice that had formed between the toes. This was a matter of instinct. To permit the ice to remain would mean sore feet. It did not know this. It merely obeyed the mysterious prompting that arose from the deep crypts of its being. But the man knew, having achieved a judgment on the subject, and he removed the mitten from his right hand and helped tear out the ice particles. He did not expose his fingers more than a minute, and was astonished at the swift numbness that smote them. It certainly was cold. He pulled on the mitten hastily, and beat the hand savagely across his chest.

At twelve o'clock the day was at its brightest. Yet the sun was too far south on its winter journey to clear the horizon. The bulge of the earth intervened between it and Henderson Creek, where the man walked under a clear sky at noon and cast no shadow. At half-past twelve, to the minute, he arrived at the forks of the creek. He was pleased at the speed he had made. If he kept it up, he would certainly be with the boys by six. He unbuttoned his jacket and shirt and drew forth his lunch. The action consumed no more than a quarter of a minute, yet in that brief moment the numbness laid hold of the exposed fingers. He did not put the mitten on, but, instead, struck the fingers a dozen sharp smashes against his leg. Then he sat down on a snow-covered log to eat. The sting that followed upon the striking of his fingers against his leg ceased so quickly that he was startled. He had had no chance to take a bite of biscuit. He struck the fingers repeatedly and returned them to the mitten, baring the other hand for the purpose of eating. He tried to take a mouthful, but

...SUSPECTING **DANGER,** HE COMPELLED THE DOG TO GO ON IN FRONT.

Why does the man want to avoid getting his feet wet?

LITERATURE IN CONTEXT

History Connection

Dogs and the Yukon

Dogs like the one in "To Build a Fire" have long played a key role in the Yukon. For centuries, native people in Alaska have bred dogs for a variety of purposes, including transportation. When the Klondike gold rush brought thousands of miners to the Yukon, the problem of transportation became acute. In 1910, the federal government constructed a trail more than 1,000 miles long for use by dog sled teams. That trail became known as the Iditarod.

Sled dogs are among the most powerful draft animals on earth. A team of twenty dogs can pull a ton or more. Though the man in London's story does not treat his dog with affection, for many dog sled drivers these valiant dogs provided warmth and companionship on the long, cold trail.

Connect to the Literature

Why do you think London chooses to portray the dog's thoughts and feelings?

the ice muzzle prevented. He had forgotten to build a fire and thaw out. He chuckled at his foolishness, and as he chuckled he noted the numbness creeping into the exposed fingers. Also, he noted that the stinging which had first come to his toes when he sat down was already passing away. He wondered whether the toes were warm or numb. He moved them inside the moccasins and decided that they were numb.

He pulled the mitten on hurriedly and stood up. He was a bit frightened. He stamped up and down until the stinging returned into the feet. It certainly was cold, was his thought. That man from Sulphur Creek had spoken the truth when telling how cold it sometimes got in the country. And he had laughed at him at the time! That showed one must not be too sure of things. There was no mistake about it, it was cold. He strode up and down, stamping his feet and threshing his arms, until reassured by the returning warmth. Then he got out matches and proceeded to make a fire. From the undergrowth, where high water of the previous spring had lodged a supply of seasoned twigs, he got his firewood. Working carefully from a small beginning, he soon had a roaring fire, over which he thawed the ice from his face and in the protection of which he ate his biscuits. For the moment the cold of space was outwitted. The dog took satisfaction in the fire, stretching out close enough for warmth and far enough away to escape being singed.

When the man had finished, he filled his pipe and took his comfortable time over a smoke. Then he pulled on his mittens, settled the earflaps of his cap firmly about his ears, and took the creek trail up the left fork. The dog was disappointed and yearned back toward the fire. This man did not know cold. Possibly all the generations of his ancestry had been ignorant of cold, of real cold, of cold one hundred and seven degrees below freezing point. But the dog knew; all its ancestry knew, and it had inherited the knowledge. And it knew that it was not good to walk abroad in such fearful cold. It was the time to lie snug in a hole in the snow and wait for a curtain of cloud to be drawn across the face of outer space whence this cold came. On the other hand, there was no keen intimacy between the dog and the man. The one was the toil slave of the other, and the only caresses it had ever received were the caresses of the whiplash and of harsh and menacing throat sounds that threatened the whiplash. So the dog made no effort to communicate its apprehension to the man. It was not concerned in the welfare of the man; it was for its own sake that it yearned back toward the fire. But the man whistled, and spoke to it with the sound of whiplashes, and the dog swung in at the man's heels and followed after.

The man took a chew of tobacco and proceeded to start a new amber beard. Also, his moist breath quickly powdered with white his mustache, eyebrows, and lashes. There did not seem to be so many springs on the left fork of the Henderson, and for half an hour the man saw no signs of any. And then it happened. At a place where there were no signs, where the soft, unbroken snow seemed to advertise solidity beneath, the man broke through. It was not deep. He wet himself halfway to the knees before he floundered out to the firm crust.

He was angry, and cursed his luck aloud. He had hoped to get into camp with the boys at six o'clock, and this would delay him an hour, for he would have to build a fire and dry out his footgear. This was imperative at that low temperature—he knew that much; and he turned aside to the bank, which he climbed. On top, tangled in the underbrush about the trunks of several small spruce trees, was a high-water deposit of dry firewood—sticks and twigs, principally, but also larger portions of seasoned branches and fine, dry, last year's grasses. He threw down several large pieces on top of the snow. This served for a foundation and prevented the young flame from drowning itself in the snow it otherwise would melt. The flame he got by touching a match to a small shred of birch bark that he took from his pocket. This burned even more readily than paper. Placing it on the foundation, he fed the young flame with wisps of dry grass and with the tiniest dry twigs.

He worked slowly and carefully, keenly aware of his danger. Gradually, as the flame grew stronger, he increased the size of the twigs with which he fed it. He squatted in the snow, pulling the twigs out from their entanglement in the brush and feeding directly to the flame. He knew there must be no failure. When it is seventy-five below zero, a man must not fail in his first attempt to build a fire—that is, if his feet are wet. If his feet are dry, and he fails, he can run along the trail for half a mile and restore his circulation. But the circulation of wet and freezing feet cannot be restored by running when it is seventy-five below. No matter how fast he runs, the wet feet will freeze the harder.

All this the man knew. The old-timer on Sulphur Creek had told him about it the previous fall, and now he was appreciating the advice. Already all sensation had gone out of his feet. To build the fire he had been forced to remove his mittens, and the fingers had quickly gone numb. His pace of four miles an hour had kept his heart pumping blood to the surface of his body and to all the extremities. But the instant he stopped, the action of the pump eased down. The cold of space smote the unprotected tip of the planet, and he, being on that unprotected tip, received the full force of the blow. The blood of his body recoiled before it. The blood was alive, like the dog, and like the dog it wanted to hide away and cover itself up from the fearful cold. So long as he walked four

WHEN IT IS SEVENTY-FIVE BELOW ZERO, A MAN MUST NOT FAIL IN HIS FIRST ATTEMPT TO BUILD A FIRE—

What does the man do after he falls into the creek?

miles an hour, he pumped that blood, willy-nilly, to the surface; but now it ebbed away and sank down into the recesses of his body. The extremities were the first to feel its absence. His wet feet froze the faster, and his exposed fingers numbed the faster, though they had not yet begun to freeze. Nose and cheeks were already freezing, while the skin of all his body chilled as it lost its blood.

But he was safe. Toes and nose and cheeks would be only touched by the frost, for the fire was beginning to burn with strength. He was feeding it with twigs the size of his finger. In another minute he would be able to feed it with branches the size of his wrist, and then he could remove his wet foot-gear, and, while it dried, he could keep his naked feet warm by the fire, rubbing them at first, of course, with snow. The fire was a success. He was safe. He remembered the advice of the old-timer on Sulphur Creek, and smiled. The old-timer had been very serious in laying down the law that no man must travel alone in the Klondike after fifty below. Well, here he was; he had had the accident; he was alone; and he had saved himself. Those old-timers were rather womanish, some of them, he thought. All a man had to do was to keep his head, and he was all right. Any man who was a man could travel alone. But it was surprising, the rapidity with which his cheeks and nose were freezing. And he had not thought his fingers could go lifeless in so short a time. Lifeless they were, for he could scarcely make them move together to grip a twig, and they seemed remote from his body and from him. When he touched a twig, he had to look and see whether or not he had hold of it. The wires were pretty well down between him and his finger ends.

All of which counted for little. There was the fire, snapping and

Literary Analysis

Conflict and Irony What does the reader understand about the old-timer's advice that the man does not?

▼ Critical Viewing

What aspects of the Alaskan landscape pictured here clarify the challenge the man faces in building a fire? **[Connect]**

crackling and promising life with every dancing flame. He started to untie his moccasins. They were coated with ice; the thick German socks were like sheaths of iron halfway to the knees; and the moccasin strings were like rods of steel all twisted and knotted as by some **conflagration**. For a moment he tugged with his numb fingers, then, realizing the folly of it, he drew his sheath-knife.

But before he could cut the strings, it happened. It was his own fault or, rather, his mistake. He should not have built the fire under the spruce tree. He should have built it in the open. But it had been easier to pull the twigs from the brush and drop them directly on the fire. Now the tree under which he had done this carried a weight of snow on its boughs. No wind had blown for weeks, and each bough was fully freighted. Each time he had pulled a twig he had communicated a slight agitation to the tree—an imperceptible agitation, so far as he was concerned, but an agitation sufficient to bring about the disaster. High up in the tree one bough capsized its load of snow. This fell on the boughs beneath, capsizing them. This process continued, spreading out and involving the whole tree. It grew like an avalanche, and it descended without warning upon the man and the fire, and the fire was blotted out! Where it had burned was a mantle of fresh and disordered snow.

The man was shocked. It was as though he had just heard his own sentence of death. For a moment he sat and stared at the spot where the fire had been. Then he grew very calm. Perhaps the old-timer on Sulphur Creek was right. If he had only had a trail mate he would have been in no danger now. The trail mate could have built the fire. Well, it was up to him to build the fire over again, and this second time there must be no failure. Even if he succeeded, he would most likely lose some toes. His feet must be badly frozen by now, and there would be some time before the second fire was ready.

Such were his thoughts, but he did not sit and think them. He was busy all the time they were passing through his mind. He made a new foundation for a fire, this time in the open, where no treacherous tree could blot it out. Next, he gathered dry grasses and tiny twigs from the high-water flotsam. He could not bring his fingers together to pull them out, but he was able to gather them by the handful. In this way he got many rotten twigs and bits of green moss that were undesirable, but it was the best he could do. He worked methodically, even collecting an armful of the larger branches to be used later when the fire gathered strength. And all the while the dog sat and watched him, a certain yearning wistfulness in its eyes, for it looked upon him as the fire provider, and the fire was slow in coming.

When all was ready, the man reached in his pocket for a second piece of birch bark. He knew the bark was there, and, though he could not feel it with his fingers, he could hear its crisp rustling as he fumbled for it. Try as he would, he could not clutch hold of it. And all the time, in his consciousness, was the knowledge that each instant his feet were freezing. This thought tended to put him in a panic, but

Vocabulary

conflagration (kän′ flə grā′ shən) *n.* big, destructive fire

What happens to ruin the man's fire?

he fought against it and kept calm. He pulled on his mittens with his teeth, and threshed his arms back and forth, beating his hands with all his might against his sides. He did this sitting down, and he stood up to do it; and all the while the dog sat in the snow, its wolf brush of a tail curled around warmly over its forefeet, its sharp wolf ears pricked forward intently as it watched the man. And the man, as he beat and threshed with his arms and hands, felt a great surge of envy as he regarded the creature that was warm and secure in its natural covering.

After a time he was aware of the first faraway signals of sensation in his beaten fingers. The faint tingling grew stronger till it evolved into a stinging ache that was excruciating, but which the man hailed with satisfaction. He stripped the mitten from his right hand and fetched forth the birch bark. The exposed fingers were quickly going numb again. Next he brought out his bunch of sulphur matches. But the tremendous cold had already driven the life out of his fingers. In his effort to separate one match from the others, the whole bunch fell in the snow. He tried to pick it out of the snow, but failed. The dead fingers could neither touch nor clutch. He was very careful. He drove the thought of his freezing feet, and nose, and cheeks, out of his mind, devoting his whole soul to the matches. He watched, using the sense of vision in place of that of touch, and when he saw his fingers on each side of the bunch, he closed them—that is, he willed to close them, for the wires were down, and the fingers did not obey. He pulled the mitten on the right hand, and beat it fiercely against his knee. Then, with both mittened hands, he scooped the bunch of matches, along with much snow, into his lap. Yet he was no better off.

Reading Strategy
Predicting As the man struggles to light the matches, what do you predict about his success? Why?

After some manipulation he managed to get the bunch between the heels of his mittened hands. In this fashion he carried it to his mouth. The ice crackled and snapped when by a violent effort he opened his mouth. He drew the lower jaw in, curled the upper lip out of the way, and scraped the bunch with his upper teeth in order to separate a match. He succeeded in getting one, which he dropped on his lap. He was no better off. He could not pick it up. Then he devised a way. He picked it up in his teeth and scratched it on his leg. Twenty times he scratched before he succeeded in lighting it. As it flamed he held it with his teeth to the birch bark. But the burning brimstone went up his nostrils and into his lungs, causing him to cough spasmodically. The match fell into the snow and went out.

Literary Analysis
Conflict What is the conflict with which the man now struggles desperately?

The old-timer on Sulphur Creek was right, he thought in the moment of controlled despair that ensued: after fifty below, a man should travel with a partner. He beat his hands, but failed in exciting any sensation. Suddenly he bared both hands, removing the mittens with his teeth. He caught the whole bunch between the heels of his hands. His arm muscles not being frozen enabled him to press the hand heels tightly against the matches. Then he scratched the bunch along his leg. It flared into flame, seventy sulphur matches at once!

There was no wind to blow them out. He kept his head to one side to escape the strangling fumes, and held the blazing bunch to the birch bark. As he so held it, he became aware of sensation in his hand. His flesh was burning. He could smell it. Deep down below the surface he could feel it. The sensation developed into pain that grew acute. And still he endured it, holding the flame of the matches clumsily to the bark that would not light readily because his own burning hands were in the way, absorbing most of the flame.

At last, when he could endure no more, he jerked his hands apart. The blazing matches fell sizzling into the snow, but the birch bark was alight. He began laying dry grasses and the tiniest twigs on the flame. He could not pick and choose, for he had to lift the fuel between the heels of his hands. Small pieces of rotten wood and green moss clung to the twigs, and he bit them off as well as he could with his teeth. He cherished the flame carefully and awkwardly. It meant life, and it must not perish. The withdrawal of blood from the surface of his body now made him begin to shiver, and he grew more awkward. A large piece of green moss fell squarely on the little fire. He tried to poke it out with his fingers, but his shivering frame made him poke too far, and he disrupted the nucleus of the little fire, the burning grasses and tiny twigs separating and scattering. He tried to poke them together again, but in spite of the tenseness of the effort, his shivering got away with him, and the twigs were hopelessly scattered. Each twig gushed a puff of smoke and went out. The fire provider had failed. As he looked apathetically about him, his eyes chanced on the dog, sitting across the ruins of the fire from him, in the snow, making restless, hunching movements, slightly lifting one forefoot and then the other, shifting its weight back and forth on them with wistful eagerness.

The sight of the dog put a wild idea into his head. He remembered the tale of the man, caught in a blizzard, who killed a steer and crawled inside the carcass, and so was saved. He would kill the dog and bury his hands in the warm body until the numbness went out of them. Then he could build another fire. He spoke to the dog, calling it to him; but in his voice was a strange note of fear that frightened the animal, who had never known the man to speak in such way before. Something was the matter, and its suspicious nature sensed danger—it knew not what danger, but somewhere, somehow, in its brain arose an apprehension of the man. It flattened its ears down at the sound of the man's voice, and its restless, hunching movements and the liftings and shiftings of its forefeet became more pronounced; but it would not come to the man. He got on his hands and knees and crawled toward the dog. This unusual posture again excited suspicion, and the animal sidled mincingly away.

The man sat up in the snow for a moment and struggled for calmness. Then he pulled on his mittens, by means of his teeth, and got upon his feet. He glanced down at first in order to assure himself that

HIS FLESH WAS BURNING. HE COULD SMELL IT.

Literary Analysis

Conflict What conflict is intensified in the passage beginning "The sight of the dog . . ."?

What happens to the man's second attempt to build a fire?

Vocabulary
peremptorily (pər emp′ tə rə lē) *adv.* decisively; commandingly

A CERTAIN FEAR OF DEATH, DULL AND OPPRESSIVE, CAME TO HIM.

he was really standing up, for the absence of sensation in his feet left him unrelated to the earth. His erect position in itself started to drive the webs of suspicion from the dog's mind; and when he spoke peremptorily, with the sound of whiplashes in his voice, the dog rendered its customary allegiance and came to him. As it came within reaching distance, the man lost his control. His arms flashed out to the dog, and he experienced genuine surprise when he discovered that his hands could not clutch, that there was neither bend nor feeling in the fingers. He had forgotten for the moment that they were frozen and that they were freezing more and more. All this happened quickly, and before the animal could get away, he encircled its body with his arms. He sat down in the snow, and in this fashion held the dog, while it snarled and whined and struggled.

But it was all he could do, hold its body encircled in his arms and sit there. He realized that he could not kill the dog. There was no way to do it. With his helpless hands he could neither draw nor hold his sheath-knife nor throttle the animal. He released it, and it plunged wildly away, with tail between its legs, and still snarling. It halted forty feet away and surveyed him curiously, with ears sharply pricked forward. The man looked down at his hands in order to locate them, and found them hanging on the ends of his arms. It struck him as curious that one should have to use his eyes in order to find out where his hands were. He began threshing his arms back and forth, beating the mittened hands against his sides. He did this for five minutes, violently, and his heart pumped enough blood up to the surface to put a stop to his shivering. But no sensation was aroused in the hands. He had an impression that they hung like weights on the ends of his arms, but when he tried to run the impression down, he could not find it.

A certain fear of death, dull and oppressive, came to him. This fear quickly became poignant as he realized that it was no longer a mere matter of freezing his fingers and toes, or of losing his hands and feet, but that it was a matter of life and death with the chances against him. This threw him into a panic, and he turned and ran up the creek-bed along the old, dim trail. The dog joined in behind and kept up with him. He ran blindly, without intention, in fear such as he had never known in his life. Slowly, as he plowed and floundered through the snow, he began to see things again—the banks of the creek, the old timber jams, the leafless aspens, and the sky. The running made him feel better. He did not shiver. Maybe, if he ran on, his feet would thaw out; and, anyway, if he ran far enough, he would reach camp and the boys. Without doubt he would lose some fingers and toes and some of his face; but the boys would take care of him, and save the rest of him when he got there. And at the same time there was another thought in his mind that said he would never get to the camp and the boys; that it was too many miles away, that the freezing had too great a start on him, and that he would soon be stiff and dead. This thought he kept in the background and refused to consider. Sometimes it pushed itself forward and demanded to be heard, but he thrust it back and strove to think of other things.

It struck him as curious that he could run at all on feet so frozen that he could not feel them when they struck the earth and took the weight of his body. He seemed to himself to skim along above the surface, and to have no connection with the earth. Somewhere he had once seen a winged Mercury,[6] and he wondered if Mercury felt as he felt when skimming over the earth.

His theory of running until he reached camp and the boys had one flaw in it: he lacked the endurance. Several times he stumbled, and finally he tottered, crumpled up, and fell. When he tried to rise, he failed. He must sit and rest, he decided, and next time he would merely walk and keep on going. As he sat and regained his breath, he noted that he was feeling quite warm and comfortable. He was not shivering, and it even seemed that a warm glow had come to his chest and trunk. And yet, when he touched his nose or cheeks, there was no sensation. Running would not thaw them out. Nor would it thaw out his hands and feet. Then the thought came to him that the frozen portions of his body must be extending. He tried to keep this thought down, to forget it, to think of something else; he was aware of the panicky feeling that it caused, and he was afraid of the panic. But the thought asserted itself, and persisted, until it produced a vision of his body totally frozen. This was too much, and he made another wild run along the trail. Once he slowed down to a walk, but the thought of the freezing extending itself made him run again.

Literary Analysis
Conflict and Irony As the man begins to feel warm, what does the reader know that the man does not?

And all the time the dog ran with him, at his heels. When he fell down a second time, it curled its tail over its forefeet and sat in front of him, facing him, curiously eager and intent. The warmth and security of the animal angered him, and he cursed it till it flattened down its ears appeasingly. This time the shivering came more quickly upon the man. He was losing in his battle with the frost. It was creeping into his body from all sides. The thought of it drove him on, but he ran no more than a hundred feet, when he staggered and pitched headlong. It was his last panic. When he had recovered his breath and control, he sat up and entertained in his mind the conception of meeting death with dignity. However, the conception did not come to him in such terms. His idea of it was that he had been making a fool of himself, running around like a chicken with its head cut off—such was the simile that occurred to him. Well, he was bound to freeze anyway, and he might as well take it decently. With this new-found peace of mind came the first glimmerings of drowsiness. A good idea, he thought, to sleep off to death. It was like taking an anaesthetic. Freezing was not so bad as people thought. There were lots worse ways to die.

What thought does the man refuse to consider?

6. **Mercury** from Roman mythology, the wing-footed messenger of the gods.

He pictured the boys finding his body next day. Suddenly he found himself with them, coming along the trail and looking for himself. And, still with them, he came around a turn in the trail and found himself lying in the snow. He did not belong with himself any more, for even then he was out of himself; standing with the boys and looking at himself in the snow. It certainly was cold, was his thought. When he got back to the States he could tell the folks what real cold was. He drifted on from this to a vision of the old-timer on Sulphur Creek. He could see him quite clearly, warm and comfortable, and smoking a pipe.

"You were right, old hoss; you were right," the man mumbled to the old-timer of Sulphur Creek.

Then the man drowsed off into what seemed to him the most comfortable and satisfying sleep he had ever known. The dog sat facing him and waiting. The brief day drew to a close in a long, slow twilight. There were no signs of a fire to be made, and, besides, never in the dog's experience had it known a man to sit like that in the snow and make no fire. As the twilight drew on, its eager yearning for the fire mastered it, and with a great lifting and shifting of forefeet, it whined softly, then flattened its ears down in anticipation of being chidden[7] by the man. But the man remained silent. Later, the dog whined loudly. And still later it crept close to the man and caught the scent of death. This made the animal bristle and back away. A little longer it delayed, howling under the stars that leaped and danced and shone brightly in the cold sky. Then it turned and trotted up the trail in the direction of the camp it knew, where were the other food providers and fire providers.

7. **chidden** scolded.

Critical Reading

Cite textual evidence to support your responses.

1. **Key Ideas and Details (a)** What do the dog's instincts tell it about the cold? **(b) Compare and Contrast:** Why does the extreme cold "make no impression" on the man? **(c) Make a Judgment:** Who is better equipped to survive in the cold, the dog or the man? Explain.
2. **Key Ideas and Details (a)** What trap does the man unsuccessfully try to avoid? **(b) Analyze Cause and Effect:** What deadly chain of events does this begin?
3. **Integration of Knowledge and Ideas** What does London suggest about human strength in the face of nature's power? In your response, use at least two of these Essential Question words: *vulnerable, resolve, frailty, wilderness.* ***[Connecting to the Essential Question: What is the relationship between literature and place?]***

After You Read *To Build a Fire*

Literary Analysis

1. **Key Ideas and Details** Use a chart like the one shown to analyze the **conflict** in "To Build a Fire." **(a)** What **external conflict** drives the plot? **(b)** Identify at least three details in the **setting** that contribute to the central conflict.

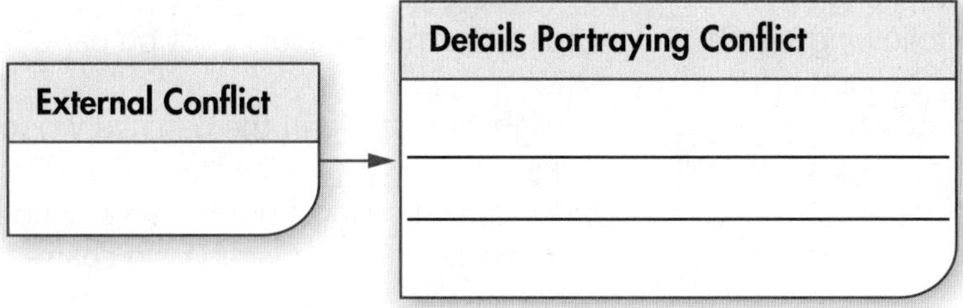

2. **Key Ideas and Details** In what ways does the main character's awareness of the conflict intensify as the story unfolds? Explain.
3. **Key Ideas and Details** What **internal conflict** develops as the plot progresses? Explain, using details from the story.
4. **Key Ideas and Details** What events finally resolve, or settle, the conflict?
5. **Craft and Structure** The man breaks through the snow and steps in the hidden spring. In what ways is this event an example of **irony?**
6. **Craft and Structure** What is ironic about the location in which the man builds his fire?
7. **Craft and Structure** In what way do London's descriptions of the dog's feelings and its instincts about survival increase the story's **dramatic irony?**

Reading Strategy

8. Early in the story, the narrator reveals that the man does not really know the temperature outside. What can you **predict** from this clue?
9. **(a)** What *background knowledge* about the Yukon did you bring to your reading of the story? **(b)** What predictions were you able to make based on this knowledge? **(c)** Were your predictions correct? Explain.
10. **(a)** What information do the man's recollections of his conversation with the old-timer provide? **(b)** What clues about the man can you draw based on his responses to the old-timer? **(c)** How do these clues help you predict what will happen at the end of the story?
11. **(a)** At what point did you first predict that the man would not survive his journey? **(b)** On what clues did you base your prediction?

Common Core State Standards

Writing

1. Write arguments to support claims in an analysis of substantive topics or texts, using valid reasoning and relevant and sufficient evidence. *(p. 612)*

Language

1. Demonstrate command of the conventions of standard English grammar and usage when writing or speaking. *(p. 613)*

4.b. Identify and correctly use patterns of word changes that indicate different meanings or parts of speech. *(p. 612)*

4.d. Verify the preliminary definition of the meaning of a word or phrase. *(p. 612)*

5. Demonstrate understanding of word relationships. *(p. 612)*

PERFORMANCE TASKS

Integrated Language Skills

Vocabulary Acquisition and Use

Word Analysis: Latin Root *-pend-*

The Latin root *-pend-* means "to hang." Your *appendages*—your arms and legs, toes and feet—hang or extend from your torso. Likewise, if you *depend* on someone, you may be "hanging on" to him or her for help. Each of the following words contains the root *-pend-*. Write a definition for each word and explain how the idea of hanging or extending relates to the term. If a word is unfamiliar, use a dictionary to clarify its meaning.

1. impending
2. pendulum
3. suspend
4. perpendicular
5. pendant

Vocabulary: Word/Phrase Relationships

Scan the paragraph below. For each blank, write a sentence explaining what type of word—noun, adjective, or adverb—you would expect to find there. Then, fill in the blanks with appropriate words from the vocabulary list on page 594.

A lightning storm in the parched woodland sparked a(n) _______. The tree's dry limbs and branches fell flaming from the trees, and soon the forest floor was covered with charred _______ of the tree. This was a(n) _______ scene for the young and inexperienced fire chief. Yet, he acted _______ ordering all firefighters to work around the clock. His estimates of how long it would take to overcome the fire, however, were _______ at best.

Writing

Argument Critical writing often presents and defends an interpretation of a literary work. The writer examines how elements, such as plot, setting, character, and point of view, work together to convey an insight about life. Write a work of **literary criticism** in which you present and defend your interpretation of the message expressed in"To Build a Fire."

Prewriting Review the story to identify London's message about the relationship between humanity and nature. Gather details that support your interpretation.

Drafting In your introduction, state your thesis and outline your main points. Focus each body paragraph on one main point. Cite supporting details from the story.

Model: Elaborating to Support an Argument

The dog, equipped by centuries of evolution for life in the bitter cold, serves as a symbolic foil to the man. Unlike the man, who disregards plain evidence,". . . the dog knew; all its ancestry knew, and it had inherited the knowledge. And it knew that it was not good to walk abroad in such fearful cold."

Providing details from the work helps to elaborate on the main point, underlined here.

Revising Review your draft, making sure your thesis is clear and your support is convincing. Look for opportunities to *elaborate ideas through supporting details*.

Conventions and Style: Introductory Phrases and Clauses

To keep your reader's interest, try *varying sentence structures* in your writing. For example, instead of starting every sentence with the subject, begin some sentences with phrases or clauses. A **phrase** is a group of words that acts as a single part of speech and lacks a complete subject and verb. A **clause** is a group of words that has both a subject and verb.

Using Introductory Phrases and Clauses to Vary Sentence Structure

Subject First: He stopped at the top of a steep bank to catch his breath.
Phrase First: *At the top of a steep bank*, he stopped to catch his breath. (prepositional phrase)

Subject First: The dog seemed hesitant as he slinked along behind the man.
Phrase First: *Slinking along behind the man*, the dog seemed hesitant. (participial phrase)

Subject First: He sends the dog ahead to check the thickness of the ice.
Phrase First: *To check the thickness of the ice*, he sends the dog ahead. (infinitive phrase)

Subject First: The spittle crackled and froze when he spit into the air.
Clause First: *When he spit into the air*, the spittle crackled and froze. (adverb clause)

Punctuation Tip: Place a comma after most introductory phrases and clauses.

Practice Revise each sentence by using the italicized part as an introductory phrase or clause. In some sentences, you will have to make slight changes to the original wording.

1. Huskies burrow beneath the snow *to stay warm.*
2. Thousands of prospectors *lured by visions of gold and wealth* headed to the Yukon.
3. His nose and cheekbones turned numb *even though he kept rubbing them.*
4. He could not build a third fire *in spite of all his efforts.*
5. The dog *grew suspicious* and moved away from the man.
6. He heard the crackle of ice *as he came around a bend in the creek.*
7. The dog *curled his tail around his forefeet* and sat there watching the man.
8. The man beat his hands against his sides *to restore feeling to his fingers.*
9. Jack London produced more than fifty books *during his career.*
10. London was *determined to earn a living as a writer,* so he often worked fifteen hours a day.

Writing and Speaking Conventions

A. Writing Use each phrase or clause to begin a sentence.

1. in his pocket **3.** numbed by the extreme cold
2. to build a fire **4.** after his legs are wet

Example: If he kept the pace
Sentence: If he kept the pace, he would be at the camp by six.

B. Speaking Suppose the dog in the story could speak. Tell the story as he would relate it to the men at the camp. In your story, begin at least four sentences with an introductory phrase or clause.

Further instruction and practice are available in *Prentice Hall Writing Coach*.

Primary Sources

Personal History
Heading West

Speech
I Will Fight No More Forever

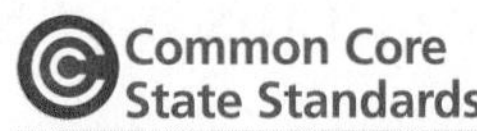
Common Core State Standards

Reading Informational Text

1. Cite strong and thorough textual evidence to support analysis of what a text says explicitly as well as inferences drawn from the text, including determining where the text leaves matters uncertain.

9. Analyze nineteenth-century foundational U.S. documents of historical and literary significance for their themes, purposes, and rhetorical features.

About the Text Forms

A **personal history** is a type of autobiographical nonfiction in which a writer relates his or her experiences during a particular event or era. Personal histories can take many forms, from straightforward narratives to the dated entries of a journal or diary.

A **speech** is a nonfiction work that is delivered orally to an audience. There are many types of speeches, each suited to a different kind of public gathering and setting. Speakers use a variety of strategies to express their ideas and move listeners. They may appeal to listeners' values or emotions, or to their sense of reason and logic.

Reading Strategy

In addition to facts, primary-source documents written by individuals often include subjective statements, such as opinions, beliefs, prejudices, and assumptions. For later readers and researchers, these subjective statements are important for a number of reasons:

- They provide a window into history as it was truly experienced.
- They provide a sense of the principles and values that drove a society.

While authors may state these ideas explicitly, more often they will merely imply, or suggest, them. Teasing out these unstated claims, or **making inferences about an author's implicit and explicit philosophical assumptions and beliefs,** is an important part of reading primary-source documents. As you read these documents, notice references, details, opinions, and other clues to the underlying assumptions that motivate these writers.

THE ESSENTIAL ?

What is the **relationship** between literature and *place?*

Most settlers of the American West were farmers who sought a better life for themselves and their children. This meant settling on fertile land that they could own, cultivate, and pass on to later generations. For Native Americans, however, the land was the source of all life and belonged to no one person. As you read these texts, watch for words and phrases that reflect these competing worldviews.

Note-Taking Guide

Primary-source documents are a rich source of information for researchers. As you read these documents, use a note-taking guide like the one shown to organize relevant and accurate information.

1 Type of Document (check one)

☐ Telegram ☐ Press Release ☐ Personal History ☐ Letter
☐ Speech ☐ Newspaper ☐ Report ☐ E-Mail

2 Date(s) of Document ______

3 Author of Document ______

Author's Position, Title, or Circumstances ______

4 Audience: For whom was the document written? ______

5 Document Information

a What is the main subject of the document? ______

b Find in the document a stated opinion, or belief, about the subject you listed above. Write it here. ______

c List one additional thing the author says that you think is important. ______

d Find in the document an implied—not directly stated—opinion. Write it here. ______

Reading Strategy Inferring an Author's Philosophical Assumptions and Beliefs Remember that an opinion is a person's belief or judgment about something. Unlike a fact, an opinion cannot be proved. As you read, look for statements that express feelings, attitudes, or desires.

This guide was adapted from the **U.S. National Archives** document analysis worksheets.

Vocabulary

shares (sherz) *n.* portions of ownership of a company or a piece of property (p. 617)

pervading (per vād′ iŋ) *v.* spreading throughout (p. 618)

levee (lev′ ē) *n.* an embankment built along the side of a river to prevent flooding (p. 618)

emigrants (em′ i grənts) *n.* people who leave one place to settle in another (p. 618)

profusion (prō fyo͞o′ zhən) *n.* abundance; rich supply (p. 619)

foothold (fo͝ot′ hōld′) *n.* a secure position from which further actions can be taken (p. 619)

prairie (prer′ ē) *n.* a treeless, grass-covered plain (p. 620)

forded (fôrd′ əd) *v.* crossed a river at a low point (p. 620)

ravine (rə vēn′) *n.* a long, deep hollow in the ground; a gully (p. 621)

THE STORY BEHIND THE DOCUMENTS

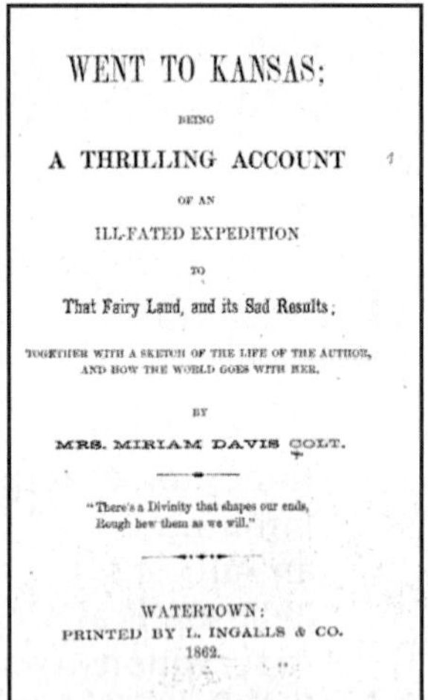

WENT TO KANSAS;

BEING

A THRILLING ACCOUNT

OF AN

ILL-FATED EXPEDITION

TO

That Fairy Land, and its Sad Results;

TOGETHER WITH A SKETCH OF THE LIFE OF THE AUTHOR, AND HOW THE WORLD GOES WITH HER.

BY

MRS. MIRIAM DAVIS COLT.

"There's a Divinity that shapes our ends, Rough hew them as we will."

WATERTOWN:
PRINTED BY L. INGALLS & CO.
1862.

▲ The title page of Colt's published book

The history of America from its beginnings to 1900 might be summarized in two words: *westward expansion*. For more than 300 years, European explorers, colonial settlers, and American pioneers pushed west from the Atlantic Ocean toward the distant Pacific. Urged onward by curiosity, these travelers—and the ever-strengthening national government behind them—also believed that it was their right and duty to settle the continent. The consequences of this policy came to a dramatic climax during the 1800s, as unprecedented numbers of pioneers flocked westward. **Miriam Davis Colt** (1815–1900) and her family were among them. In 1856, the Colts set out on a month-long journey from upstate New York to Kansas. At the time, Kansas was in turmoil. In 1854, Congress had passed an act giving the people of the territory the freedom to decide for themselves whether to allow slavery. Both anti-slavery Northerners and pro-slavery Southerners streamed there from the East. The resulting conflicts were frequent and bloody.

Aware that their journey was history in the making, many Kansas pioneers kept a written record of their experiences. Some, like Colt, described their journeys in personal histories meant for a public audience, including relatives and future generations. Occasionally, as in Colt's case, the histories were later published as books.

▲ Chief Joseph

Though the settlers often lived harrowing lives, the most endangered people on the western frontier were the American Indians. As the frontier advanced past the Mississippi River, tribe after tribe was driven from its ancient homeland. The cycle was always the same: As white settlers encroached upon new lands, the tribes in that region would resist. United States soldiers would be sent to secure the area, and war would ensue. Eventually, the Indians would be defeated. They would either be forced onto a reservation, or made to sign a treaty in which they were promised food or money in exchange for their lands. More often than not, these promises went unfulfilled.

One such ill-fated tribe was the Nez Percé of the Pacific northwest. When an 1863 treaty reduced the size of the tribe's lands to a small reservation in Idaho, a group of the Nez Percé continued living outside the reservation boundaries in Oregon's Wallowa Valley. They were allowed to do so until 1877, when General Oliver O. Howard issued an ultimatum. Unwilling to concede, Nez Percé leader **Chief Joseph** (1840–1904) and six hundred of his people fled northeast through the mountains of Montana, toward the Canada border. Hotly pursued by legions of soldiers and finally weakened by the onset of winter, the Nez Percé were compelled to admit defeat. The speech in which Chief Joseph surrenders contains some of the most achingly beautiful words ever spoken.

HEADING WEST

Miriam Davis Colt

BACKGROUND Miriam Davis Colt and her family were among a group of families forming a vegetarian commune in the Kansas territory. The personal history from which this excerpt is taken was published in 1862 under the title "Went to Kansas; Being a Thrilling Account of an Ill-Fated Expedition to that Fairy Land, and its Sad Results."

JANUARY 5TH, 1856. We are going to Kansas. The Vegetarian Company that has been forming for many months, has finally organized, formed its constitution, elected its directors, and is making all necessary preparations for the spring settlement. . . . We can have, I think, good faith to believe, that our directors will fulfill on their part; and we, as settlers of a new country, by going in a company will escape the hardships attendant on families going in singly, and at once find ourselves surrounded by improving society in a young and flourishing city. It will be better for ourselves pecuniarily,[1] and better in the future for our children.

My husband has long been a practical vegetarian, and we expect much from living in such a genial clime, where fruit is so quickly grown, and with people whose tastes and habits will coincide with our own.

JANUARY 15TH. We are making every necessary preparation for our journey, and our home in Kansas. My husband has sold his farm, purchased shares in the company, sent his money as directed by H. S. Clubb. . . . I am very busy in repairing all of our clothing, looking over bags of pieces, tearing off and reducing down, bringing everything into as small a compass as possible, so that we shall have no unnecessary baggage.

APRIL 15TH. Have been here in West Stockholm, at my brother's, since Friday last. Have visited Mother very hard, for, in all probability, it is the last visit we shall have until we meet where parting never comes—believe we have said everything we can think of to say.

▲ Primary Source: Photograph
What does this photograph suggest about the quality of life people led while on the journey west? **[Analyze]**

Vocabulary
shares (sherz) *n.* portions into which a company or a piece of property is divided

Reading Check
Why do the Colts decide to travel to Kansas?

1. **pecuniarily** (pi kyo͞o′ nē er′ i lē) *adv.* financially.

APRIL 16TH. Antwerp, N.Y. Bade our friends good bye, in Potsdam, this morning, at the early hour of two o'clock.

APRIL 22ND. Have been on the cars[2] again since yesterday morning. Last night was a lovely moonlit night, a night of thought, as we sped almost with lightning speed, along in the moonlight, past the rail fences.

Found ourselves in this miserable hotel before we knew it. Miserable fare—herring boiled with cabbage—miserable, dirty beds, and an odor pervading the house that is not at all agreeable. Mistress gone.

Vocabulary
pervading (per vād′ iŋ) *v.* spreading throughout
levee (lev′ ē) *n.* an embankment built along the side of a river to prevent flooding
emigrants (em′i grənts) *n.* people who leave one place to settle in another

APRIL 23RD. On board steamer "Cataract," bound for Kansas City.

APRIL 24TH. A hot summer day. The men in our company are out in the city, purchasing wagons and farming implements, to take along on the steamer up to Kansas City.

APRIL 28TH. The steamer struck a "snag" last night; gave us a terrible jar; tore off a part of the kitchen; ladies much frightened. Willie is not very well; the water is bad; it affects all strangers.

APRIL 30TH. Here we are, at Kansas City, all safely again on terra firma. Hasten to the hotel—find it very much crowded. Go up, up, up, and upstairs to our lodging rooms.

Primary Sources
Personal History What two contrasting aspects of the pioneers' journey does Colt describe in the May 1st entry?

MAY 1ST. Take a walk out onto the levee—view the city, and see that it takes but a few buildings in this western world to make a city. The houses and shops stand along on the levee, extending back into the hillsides. The narrow street is literally filled with huge merchandise wagons bound for Santa Fe. The power attached to these wagons is seven or eight and sometimes nine pair of long-eared mules, or as many pair of oxen, with a Mexican driver who wields a whip long enough to reach the foremost pair, and who does not hesitate to use it with severity, and a noise, too.

Large droves of cattle are driven into town to be sold to emigrants, who like us, are going into the Territory. Our husbands are all out today buying oxen, provisions and cooking utensils for our ox-wagon journey into the Territory.

This is the anniversary of my wedding-day, and as I review the past pleasant years as they have passed, one after another, until they now number eleven, a shadow comes over me, as I try to look away into the future and ask, "What is my destiny?"

Ah! away with all these shadowings. We shall be very busy this year in making our home comfortable, so that no time can be spared for that dreaded disease, "home-sickness," to take hold of us, and we mean to obey physical laws,[3] thereby securing to ourselves strength of body and vigor of mind.

2. **cars** train cars.
3. **physical laws** community's by-laws that dictated members abstain from alcohol and meat.

MAY 2ND. A lovely day. Our husbands are loading the ox-wagons. . . . Women and children walk along up the hill out of this "Great City," wait under a tree—what a beautiful country is spread out before us! Will our Kansas scenery equal this . . .?

One mile from the city, and Dr. Thorn has broke his wagon tongue;[4] it must be sent back to Kansas City to be mended. Fires kindled—women cooking—supper eaten sitting round on logs, stones and wagon tongues. This I am sure is a "pic-nic." We expect "pic-nic" now all the time. We are shaded by the horse-chestnut, sweet walnut, and spreading oak; flowers blooming at our feet, and grasshoppers in profusion hopping in every direction. This is summer time.

MAY 3RD. The women and children, who slept in their wagons last night, got a good drenching from the heavy shower. It was fortunate for mother, sister, myself and children, that lodgings were found for us in a house. My husband said not a rain drop found him; he had the whole wagon to himself, besides all of our Indian blankets. Father, it seems, fell back a little and found a place to camp in a tavern (not a hotel), where he fell in with the scores of Georgians who loaded a steamer and came up the river the same time that we did. He said he had to be very shrewd indeed not to have them find out that he was a "Free States"[5] man. These Bandits have been sent in here, and will commit all sorts of depredations on the Free State settlers, and no doubt commit many a bloody murder.

Have passed Westport, the foothold for Border-Ruffianism. The town looks new, but the hue is dingy. Our drivers used their goads to hurry up the oxen's heavy tread, for we felt somewhat afraid, for we learned the Georgians had centered here. Here, too, came in the Santa Fe and Indian trade—so here may be seen the huge Mexican wagon, stubborn mule, swarthy driver with his goad-like whip, and the red man of the prairie on his fleet Indian pony, laden with dried meat, furs, and buffalo robes.

"What! fast in the mud, and with our wagon tongue broke?" "Why yes, to be sure." So a long time is spent before my husband and Dr. House can put our vehicle in moving order again. Meanwhile, we women folks and children must sit quietly in the wagon to keep out of the rain—lunch on soda biscuit, look at the deep, black mud in which our wagon is set, and inhale the sweet odor that comes from the blossoms of the crab-apple trees that are blooming in sheets of whiteness along the roadside. . . .

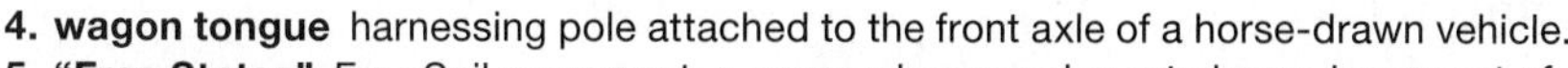

4. **wagon tongue** harnessing pole attached to the front axle of a horse-drawn vehicle.
5. **"Free States"** Free Soil movement; a group whose goal was to keep slavery out of the western territories.

Vocabulary

profusion (prō fyo͞o′ zhən) *n.* abundance; rich supply

foothold (fo͝ot′ hōld′) *n.* a secure position from which further actions can be taken

Reading Strategy

Inferring Philosophical Assumptions and Beliefs
What assumptions does Colt hold about the opponents of "Free States" settlers?

▼ Wagon used by Dr. Marcus and Narcissa Whitman, 19th century pioneers in the Oregon Territory

Vocabulary
prairie (prer´ ē) *n.* a treeless, grass-covered plain
forded (fôrd´ əd) *v.* crossed a river at a low point

MAY 6TH. Dined on the prairie, and gathered flowers, while our tired beasts filled themselves with the fresh, green grass. . . . Have driven 18 miles to-day . . . so here we are, all huddled into this little house 12 by 16—cook supper over the fire . . . fill the one bed lengthwise and crosswise; the family of the house take to the trundle-bed,[6] while the floor is covered . . . with men, women and children, rolled in Indian blankets like silk worms in cocoons.

MAY 11TH. "Made" but a few miles yesterday. Forded the Little Osage; the last river, they say, we have to ford . . . our "noble lords" complained of the great weight of the wagons. . . . That our wagon is heavily loaded, have only to make a minute of what we have stowed away in it—eight trunks, one valise, three carpet bags, a box of soda crackers, 200 lbs. flour, 100 lbs. corn meal, a few lbs. of sugar, rice, dried apple, one washtub of little trees, utensils for cooking, and two provision boxes—say nothing of mother, a good fat sister, self, and two children, who ride through the rivers. . . .

Reading Strategy
Inferring Philosophical Assumptions and Beliefs What beliefs underlie Colt's ironic reference to the owner of the log cabin as the "Lord of the Castle"?

At nightfall came to a log-cabin at the edge of the wood, and inquired of the "Lord of the Castle" if some of the women and children could take shelter under his roof for the night; the masculine number and whichever of the women that chose, couching in the wagons and under them. He said we could. His lady, who was away, presently came, with bare feet, and a white sack twisted up and thrown over her shoulder, with a few quarts of corn meal in the end that hung down her back. I said to myself—"Is that what I have got to come to?" She seemed pleased to have company—allowed us the first chance of the broad, Dutch-backed fireplace with its earthy hearth, and without pot hooks or trammels,[7] to make ready our simple evening repast. . . .

Are now [May 11th] crossing the 20 mile prairie, no roads—Think Mrs. Voorhees will get walking enough crossing this prairie. She is quite a pedestrian, surely, for she has walked every bit of the way in, so far, from Kansas City, almost 100 miles.

Arrive at Elm Creek—no house to lodge in tonight—campfire kindled—supper cooked, and partaken of with a keen relish, sitting in family groups around the "great big" fire. Some will sleep in wagons, others under the canopy of the blue vault of Heaven. The young men have built some shady little bowers of the green boughs; they are looking very cosily under them, wrapped in their white Indian blankets.

We ladies, or rather, "emigrant women," are having a chat around the camp-fire—the bright stars are looking down upon us—we wonder if we shall be neighbors to each other in the great "Octagon City. . . ."

6. **trundle-bed** low, portable bed that can be stored beneath a larger bed.
7. **trammels** (tram´ əlz) *n.* devices for hanging several pothooks in a fireplace.

MAY 12TH. Full of hope, as we leave the smoking embers of our camp-fire this morning. Expect tonight to arrive at our new home.

It begins to rain, rain, rain, like a shower; we move slowly on, from high prairie, around the deep ravine—are in sight of the timber that skirts the Neosho river. Have sent three men in advance to announce our coming; are looking for our Secretary, (Henry S. Clubb) with an escort to welcome us into the embryo city. If the booming of cannon is not heard at our approach, shall expect a salute from the firing of Sharp's rifles, certainly.

No escort is seen! no salute is heard! We move slowly and drippingly into town just at nightfall—feeling not a little nonplused on learning that our worthy, or unworthy Secretary was out walking in the rain with his *dear* wife. We leave our wagons and make our way to the large camp-fire. It is surrounded by men and women cooking their suppers—while others are busy close by, grinding their hominy[8] in hand mills.

Look around, and see the grounds all around the camp-fire are covered with tents, in which the families are staying. Not a house is to be seen. In the large tent here is a cook stove—they have supper prepared for us; it consists of hominy, soft Johnny cake (or corn bread, as it is called here), stewed apple, and tea. We eat what is set before us, "asking no questions for conscience' sake."

The ladies tell us they are sorry to see us come to this place; which shows us that all is not right. Are too weary to question, but with hope depressed go to our lodgings, which we find around in the tents, and in our wagons.

Vocabulary
ravine (rə vēn′) *n.* a long, deep hollow in the ground; a gully

8. **hominy** (häm′ ə nē) *n.* dry corn, usually ground and boiled for food.

Critical Reading

1. **Key Ideas and Details (a)** What financial arrangements did the Colts make as part of their preparations for heading west? **(b) Evaluate:** Do you think they were too naive and trusting? Explain.
2. **Key Ideas and Details (a)** Describe the settler woman Colt mentions in her entry of May 11. **(b) Analyze:** What does this settler woman suggest to Colt about her own future?
3. **Key Ideas and Details Compare and Contrast:** How do Colt's expectations about life at "Octagon City" compare with the reality she finds there?
4. **Integration of Knowledge and Ideas Synthesize:** Based on Colt's experiences, explain which character traits you feel were necessary to being a successful pioneer.

I WILL FIGHT NO MORE FOREVER

Chief Joseph

BACKGROUND *In company with fellow chiefs, Chief Joseph gave this speech on October 4, 1877, to an aide of General Oliver Howard. The aide recorded and delivered the speech to his commander.*

Primary Sources
Speech Chief Joseph appeals to values and beliefs that he hopes his listeners share. What are they?

Tell General Howard I know his heart. What he told me before, I have in my heart. I am tired of fighting. Our chiefs are killed. Looking Glass is dead. Toohoolhoolzote is dead. The old men are all dead. It is the young men who say yes and no. He who led on the young men is dead. It is cold and we have no blankets. The little children are freezing to death. My people, some of them, have run away to the hills and have no blankets, no food; no one knows where they are—perhaps freezing to death. I want to have time to look for my children and see how many I can find. Maybe I shall find them among the dead. Hear me, my chiefs. I am tired; my heart is sick and sad. From where the sun now stands I will fight no more forever.

Critical Reading

1. **Key Ideas and Details (a)** What has happened to many of the Nez Percé chiefs? **(b) Infer:** Who has been left to carry on the fight? **(c) Speculate:** Why do you think Chief Joseph directs part of his speech to his chiefs?
2. **Key Ideas and Details (a)** What reasons does Chief Joseph give for his surrender? **(b) Evaluate:** Would the speech have been more or less effective had it contained more detailed explanations?
3. **Integration of Knowledge and Ideas Synthesize:** Although Chief Joseph delivered this speech to confirm his tribe's surrender, his eloquent words serve another purpose for people today. What is that purpose?

Personal History • Speech

Comparing Primary Sources

Refer to your Note-Taking Guide to answer these questions.

1. **(a)** Note three details you learn about pioneer families from Colt's **personal history. (b)** Note two details you understand about the Native American experience based on Chief Joseph's brief **speech.**
2. **(a)** Use a chart like the one shown to identify one statement from each document about the subject on the left. **(b)** What **philosophical assumption,** or unstated belief, underlies each statement?

	Colt		Joseph	
	Statement	Assumption	Statement	Assumption
leaving home →				
children →				

3. Write three paragraphs in which you compare and contrast each author's understanding of nineteenth-century westward expansion. Explain the reasons for any similarities and differences.

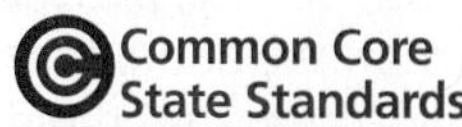

Common Core State Standards

Writing

7. Conduct short as well as more sustained research projects to answer a question or solve a problem; narrow or broaden the inquiry when appropriate, synthesize multiple sources on the subject, demonstrating understanding of the subject under investigation. *(p. 624)*

8. Gather relevant information from multiple authoritative print and digital sources, using advanced searches effectively; assess the strengths and weaknesses of each source in terms of the task, purpose, and audience; integrate information into the text selectively to maintain the flow of ideas, avoiding plagiarism and overreliance on any one source and following a standard format for citation. *(p. 624)*

Language

4.b. Identify and correctly use patterns of word changes that indicate different meanings or parts of speech.

Vocabulary Acquisition and Use

Evaluating Logic Decide whether each sentence below is logical. If not, revise the sentence so that the italicized word is used in a logical way.

1. The smell of wet paint is *pervading* the art room.
2. The *levee* will cause the town to flood when the river rises.
3. A *profusion* of weeds is every gardener's dream.
4. The army established a *foothold* near the border.
5. The hikers *forded* the river by piling large rocks along its bank.

Content-Area Vocabulary Answer each question. Then, explain your answer.

6. Who is more likely to sell *shares*: a stockbroker or a musician?
7. Would *emigrants* be more likely to ask or give directions?
8. Who would have less success on a *prairie*: a lumberjack or a farmer?
9. What might a *ravine* become during heavy rains?

Etymology Study The word *mile* comes from the Latin word *mille*, for "thousand." Use a dictionary to discover how each of the following words are related to "thousand": *millennium, milligram, millimeter, million, millisecond.*

Research Task

Topic: Westward Expansion

Ambition, politics, principles, greed, restlessness, curiosity—all of these motives, and others, drove people West during the nineteenth century. Perhaps even more powerful than practical reasons was the image of the West created by those who wrote about it in government documents, newspaper reports, and personal histories.

Assignment: Make a **display**—a poster, a trifold poster, or a museum-style exhibit—about the Westward Expansion. In your research, investigate the reliability of early media sources that informed people about opportunities in the West. Avoid over-reliance on any one source.

Formulate your research plan. To plan your display, make a list of relevant questions, such as the following:

- How did the government announce opportunities?
- What did people learn from pamphlets and posters?
- What did people learn from newspapers?
- How reliable was word-of-mouth news about the West?
- How reliable were the visual images of the West?

Then, choose a question or questions that will enable you to focus on a limited, manageable topic.

Gather sources. Use online and library searches to find answers to your research questions. Just like a smart American planning to go West, avoid relying too much on one source of information. Consult multiple sources, including texts written by experts in the field for scholarly audiences, as well as primary-source documents. Collect all details needed to prepare accurate citations.

Synthesize information. In deciding which information to use and which to discard, distinguish carefully between reliable and unreliable sources. A text that is awkwardly written may nevertheless be a trustworthy primary source. A source that seems dull may be accurate. A source that is entertaining may be oversimplified.

Organize and present your ideas. When you present information, use parallel structures to communicate parallel, or related, ideas. This will help viewers sift through a variety of data and clearly see your point. For example, you might organize a trifold poster with three parallel headings so that viewers can easily compare and contrast different information.

Model: Using Parallelism to Present Information

What People Learned from the Government	What People Learned from Newspapers	What People Learned from Word of Mouth

▲ Advertisements such as this one from 1876 captured the imagination of adventurous Americans.

RESEARCH TIP

Set the preferences on your printer so that the full address of each Web site is included on each page you choose to print. In this way, you will have an automatic record of your Web-related sources.

Use a checklist like the one shown to create a display that is reliable, informative, and easy to understand.

Research Checklist

- ☐ Have I answered my research questions?
- ☐ Does my evidence come from experts on the topic and texts written for informed audiences in the field?
- ☐ Have I avoided relying too much on one source?
- ☐ Have I cited all sources according to a standard format?

Living in a Changing World

PART 3

Before You Read *The Story of an Hour*

Connecting to the Essential Question Chopin's heroine appears to be mild and dependent, but she secretly hungers for independence. As you read, notice details that emphasize Mrs. Mallard's independence. Doing so will help as you consider the Essential Question: **How does literature shape or reflect society?**

Common Core State Standards

Reading Literature
6. Analyze a case in which grasping point of view requires distinguishing what is directly stated in a text from what is really meant.

Literary Analysis

Irony is a contradiction between appearance and reality, between expectation and outcome, or between meaning and intention. In literature, readers frequently encounter three types of irony:

- **Verbal irony** occurs when someone says something that deliberately contradicts what that person actually means.
- **Situational irony** occurs when something happens that contradicts readers' expectations.
- **Dramatic irony** occurs when the reader or audience is aware of something that a character does not know.

Authors may use irony to create humor or to add an element of surprise to a story. The use of irony may also develop a story's **theme**—its central message. When irony is used in this way, the theme of the work may concern a discrepancy between surface appearances and inner truths. As you read this story, decide which type of irony Chopin primarily uses and whether it functions to create an effect or to develop the theme.

Reading Strategy

Preparing to Read Complex Texts Kate Chopin was among the first American authors to write with intention about women who suffer from the restrictions imposed on them by society. Her fiction is driven by a philosophy—the belief that men and women are equals but that society denies women their full humanity. As you read this story, **analyze the philosophical argument** that drives the plot. Determine how Chopin's philosophy *contributes to the credibility* of Mrs. Mallard's character. Note your ideas in a chart like the one shown.

Detail
Louise would "have no one follow her" up to her room.

↓

Related Issue
Women seek independence.

Vocabulary

forestall (fôr stôl′) *v.* prevent by acting ahead of time (p. 630)

repression (ri presh′ ən) *n.* restraint (p. 630)

elusive (ē lo͞o′ siv) *adj.* hard to grasp (p. 630)

tumultuously (to͞o mul′ cho͞o əs lē) *adv.* in an agitated way (p. 630)

Kate Chopin (1850–1904)

Author of **"The Story of an Hour"**

Despite her conservative, aristocratic upbringing, Kate O'Flaherty Chopin (shō´ pan) became one of the most powerful and controversial writers of her time. In her writing, she captured the local color of Louisiana and boldly explored the role of women in society.

Family Life Kate O'Flaherty was born in St. Louis, Missouri, the daughter of a wealthy businessman who died five years later in a railroad accident. When she was twenty, Kate married Oscar Chopin, a Louisiana cotton trader. The couple settled in New Orleans, where they lived for ten years before moving to a plantation in rural Louisiana.

In 1882, Chopin's husband died, leaving her to raise their six children. Chopin carried on the work of the plantation alone until 1884, when she returned with her children to St. Louis. Then, in 1885, Chopin's mother died, leaving her in deep sorrow. Her family doctor, concerned about her emotional health, suggested that she begin to write fiction. Chopin spent the rest of her life in St. Louis, devoting much of her energy to writing.

Chopin the Writer and Rebel Chopin focused on capturing the essence of life in Louisiana in her writing. Her first novel, *At Fault* (1890), was set in a small Louisiana town inhabited by Creoles, descendants of the original French and Spanish settlers, and Cajuns, descendants of French Canadian settlers. Her charming portraits of Louisiana life often obscured the fact that she explored themes considered radical at the time: the nature of marriage, racial prejudice, and women's desire for equality.

The Awakening Chopin's finest novel, *The Awakening* (1899), is a psychological account of a woman's search for independence and fulfillment. Because the novel explored the issue of infidelity, it aroused a storm of protest. The book was eventually banned and Chopin's reputation was badly damaged. Then, in the 1950s, *The Awakening* was resurrected. Today, the book is among the five most-read American novels in colleges and universities. Chopin is now considered an early practitioner of American Realism—a literary style that seeks to avoid sentimental depictions of life. She is widely respected for her portrayal of the psychology of women and her ability to capture local color.

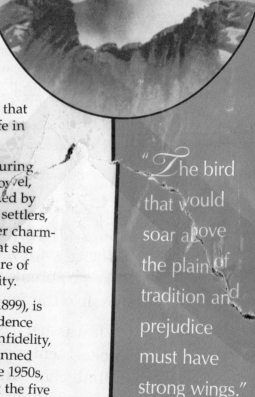

"The bird
that would
soar above
the plain of
tradition and
prejudice
must have
strong wings."

THE STORY OF AN *Hour*

Kate Chopin

BACKGROUND "The Story of an Hour" was considered daring in the nineteenth century. The editors of at least two magazines refused the story because they thought it was immoral. They wanted Chopin to soften her female character, to make her less independent and unhappy in her marriage. Undaunted, Chopin continued to deal with issues of women's growth and emancipation in her writing, advancing ideas that are widely accepted today.

Knowing that Mrs. Mallard was afflicted with a heart trouble, great care was taken to break to her as gently as possible the news of her husband's death.

It was her sister Josephine who told her, in broken sentences; veiled hints that revealed in half concealing. Her husband's friend Richards was there, too, near her. It was he who had been in the newspaper office when

▶ **Critical Viewing** This story presents a "subtle and elusive" revelation. What connection do you see between the light shining through the window and such a discovery? **[Connect]**

Vocabulary
forestall (fôr stôl′) *v.* prevent by acting ahead of time

intelligence of the railroad disaster was received, with Brently Mallard's name leading the list of "killed." He had only taken the time to assure himself of its truth by a second telegram, and had hastened to forestall any less careful, less tender friend in bearing the sad message.

She did not hear the story as many women have heard the same, with a paralyzed inability to accept its significance. She wept at once, with sudden, wild abandonment, in her sister's arms. When the storm of grief had spent itself she went away to her room alone. She would have no one follow her.

There stood, facing the open window, a comfortable, roomy armchair. Into this she sank, pressed down by a physical exhaustion that haunted her body and seemed to reach into her soul.

She could see in the open square before her house the tops of trees that were all aquiver with the new spring life. The delicious breath of rain was in the air. In the street below a peddler was crying his wares. The notes of a distant song which someone was singing reached her faintly, and countless sparrows were twittering in the eaves.

Literary Analysis
Irony Considering the news she has just received, what is ironic about the details Mrs. Mallard notices through her window?

There were patches of blue sky showing here and there through the clouds that had met and piled one above the other in the west facing her window.

She sat with her head thrown back upon the cushion of the chair, quite motionless, except when a sob came up into her throat and shook her, as a child who has cried itself to sleep continues to sob in its dreams.

She was young, with a fair, calm face, whose lines bespoke repression and even a certain strength. But now there was a dull stare in her eyes, whose gaze was fixed away off yonder on one of those patches of blue sky. It was not a glance of reflection, but rather indicated a suspension of intelligent thought.

Vocabulary
repression (ri presh′ ən) *n.* restraint
elusive (ē lo͞o′ siv) *adj.* hard to grasp
tumultuously (to͞o mul′ cho͞o əs lē) *adv.* in an agitated way

There was something coming to her and she was waiting for it, fearfully. What was it? She did not know; it was too subtle and elusive to name. But she felt it, creeping out of the sky, reaching toward her through the sounds, the scents, the color that filled the air.

Now her bosom rose and fell tumultuously. She was beginning to recognize this thing that was approaching to possess her, and she was striving to beat it back with her will—as powerless as her two white slender hands would have been.

When she abandoned herself, a little whispered word escaped her slightly parted lips. She said it over and over under her breath: "free, free, free!" The vacant stare and the look of terror that had followed it went from her eyes. They stayed keen and bright. Her pulses beat fast, and the coursing blood warmed and relaxed every inch of her body.

She did not stop to ask if it were or were not a monstrous joy that held her. A clear and exalted perception enabled her to dismiss the suggestion as trivial.

She knew that she would weep again when she saw the kind, tender hands folded in death; the face that had never looked save with love upon her, fixed and gray and dead. But she saw beyond that bitter moment a long procession of years to come that would belong to her absolutely. And she opened and spread her arms out to them in welcome.

There would be no one to live for her during those coming years; she would live for herself. There would be no powerful will bending hers in that blind persistence with which men and women believe they have a right to impose a private will upon a fellow creature. A kind intention or a cruel intention made the act seem no less a crime as she looked upon it in that brief moment of illumination.

And yet she had loved him—sometimes. Often she had not. What did it matter! What could love, the unsolved mystery, count for in face of this possession of self-assertion which she suddenly recognized as the strongest impulse of her being!

"Free! Body and soul free!" she kept whispering.

Josephine was kneeling before the closed door with her lips to the keyhole, imploring for admission. "Louise, open the door! I beg; open the door—you will make yourself ill. What are you doing, Louise? For heaven's sake open the door."

"Go away. I am not making myself ill." No; she was drinking in a very elixir of life[1] through that open window.

Her fancy was running riot along those days ahead of her. Spring days, and summer days, and all sorts of days that would be her own. She breathed a quick prayer that life might be long. It was only yesterday she had thought with a shudder that life might be long.

She arose at length and opened the door to her sister's importunities.[2] There was a feverish triumph in her eyes, and she carried herself unwittingly like a goddess of Victory. She clasped her sister's waist, and together they descended the stairs. Richards stood waiting for them at the bottom.

---

1. **elixir of life** (i liks′ ər) imaginary substance believed in medieval times to prolong life indefinitely.
2. **importunities** (im′ pôr to͞on′ i tēz) *n.* persistent requests or demands.

World LITERATURE CONNECTION

Challenging Women's Roles

Chopin was one of a growing number of writers in the late nineteenth and early twentieth centuries who challenged women's traditional social roles. A generation earlier in Britain, novelist Mary Ann Evans adopted the pen name **George Eliot** (1819–1880) to explore the theme of women's independence. In France, Amadine Dupin (1804–1876) did the same, publishing as **George Sand.** In 1929, novelist and critic **Virginia Woolf** (1882–1941), pictured below, published the essay "A Room of One's Own" in which she argued that women need community in order to realize their potential as writers. She wrote: "Masterpieces are not solitary births."

Connect to the Literature

Do you think Kate Chopin would have trouble publishing "The Story of An Hour" today? Why or why not?

What does Mrs. Mallard think about while alone in her room?

Someone was opening the front door with a latchkey. It was Brently Mallard who entered, a little travel-stained, composedly carrying his gripsack[3] and umbrella. He had been far from the scene of accident, and did not know there had been one. He stood amazed at Josephine's piercing cry; at Richards's quick motion to screen him from the view of his wife.

But Richards was too late.

When the doctors came they said she had died of heart disease—of joy that kills.

3. **gripsack** (grip′ sak) *n.* small bag for holding clothes.

"Free! Body and soul free!"

Critical Reading 

Cite textual evidence to support your responses.

1. **Key Ideas and Details (a)** At the beginning of the story, what does the narrator call the ailment that afflicts Mrs. Mallard? **(b) Interpret:** In addition to a medical condition, what might the narrator mean by this phrase?
2. **Key Ideas and Details (a)** What does Mrs. Mallard see as she gazes out her window? **(b) Connect:** How does the scene outside the window foreshadow the feelings that sweep over her as she sits in her chair?
3. **Key Ideas and Details (a)** According to the doctors, what causes Mrs. Mallard's death? **(b) Draw Conclusions:** What do you believe is the actual cause of her death? **(c) Speculate:** Why do you think Chopin does not elaborate more about Mrs. Mallard's death?
4. **Integration of Knowledge and Ideas** How does Chopin emphasize differences between Mrs. Mallard's true self and the ways in which she is perceived? In your response, use at least two of these Essential Question words: *perception, subservient, illusion, fragile.* ***[Connecting to the Essential Question: How does literature shape or reflect society?]***

After You Read | *The Story of an Hour*

Literary Analysis

1. **Craft and Structure** In what ways is Mrs. Mallard's reaction to her husband's death an example of **situational irony?**
2. **Craft and Structure** How might the diagnosis of Mrs. Mallard's cause of death be an example of **dramatic irony?**
3. **Craft and Structure** Use a chart like the one shown to examine elements of irony in the story's descriptive passages.

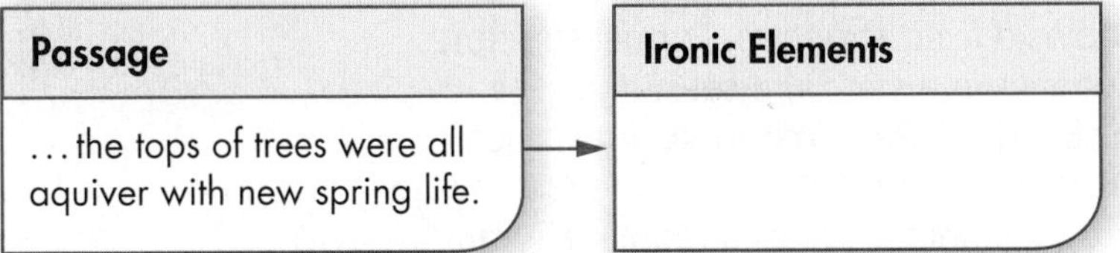

Passage
. . . the tops of trees were all aquiver with new spring life.
Ironic Elements

4. **Integration of Knowledge and Ideas** How does the story's central **theme** relate to a discrepancy between perception and reality?

Reading Strategy

5. Reread the paragraph beginning, "There would be no one to live for during those coming years. . . ." **(a) Analyze the philosophical argument** about human interactions Chopin describes in that paragraph. **(b)** How does this argument illuminate Mrs. Mallard's conflict?
6. Is Mrs. Mallard a *credible* character? Explain, relating story details to Chopin's philosophy regarding women at that time period.

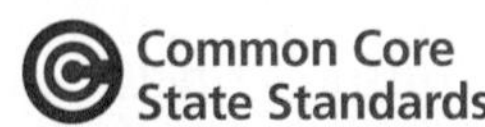

Writing

3. Write narratives to develop real or imagined experiences or events using effective technique, well-chosen details, and well-structured event sequences.

3.c. Use a variety of techniques to sequence events so that they build on one another to create a coherent whole and build toward a particular tone and outcome.

PERFORMANCE TASKS

Integrated Language Skills

Vocabulary Acquisition and Use

Synonyms For each item, choose the letter of the synonym, or word that most closely expresses the same meaning. Explain your reasoning.

1. forestall	**a.** intercept	**b.** facilitate	**c.** arrange
2. repression	**a.** indulgence	**b.** constraint	**c.** tolerance
3. elusive	**a.** tangible	**b.** vivid	**c.** evanescent
4. tumultuously	**a.** severely	**b.** thoughtlessly	**c.** briskly

Writing

Narrative Text In a **reflective essay,** a writer describes personal experiences and conveys his or her feelings about them. Draw upon your memory and observations to write your own "story of an hour" about a moment when your life dramatically changed. Organize precise details either chronologically or in order of importance. *Create a fresh, authentic tone* by using words and phrases that come naturally to you.

Before You Read

Douglass • We Wear the Mask

Connecting to the Essential Question Paul Laurence Dunbar depicts the struggles of African Americans in "Douglass" and "We Wear the Mask." As you read, take note of the issues that Dunbar raises. Doing so will help as you reflect on the Essential Question: **How does literature shape or reflect society?**

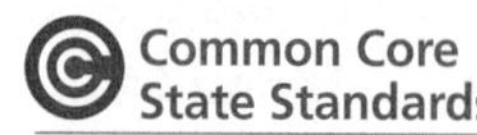

Reading Literature
5. Analyze how an author's choices concerning how to structure specific parts of a text contribute to its overall structure and meaning as well as its aesthetic impact.

Literary Analysis

Formal verse is poetry that follows a fixed structure. Formal structures may require a specific number of lines in a stanza, a set number of stanzas, or the use of repeated sounds. A **Petrarchan sonnet,** such as Dunbar's poem "Douglass," has fourteen lines separated into one stanza of eight lines and one of six lines. A sonnet also has a regular **rhyme scheme,** or pattern of rhyming words at the ends of lines. When notating rhyme scheme, the same sounds are indicated with lower case letters:

> Ah, Douglass, we have fall'n on evil days, (a)
> Such days as thou, not even thou didst know, (b)
> When thee, the eyes of that harsh long ago (b)
> Saw, salient, at the cross of devious ways . . . (a)

Poets also use formal structures in poems that do not use a specific fixed form. For example, "We Wear the Mask" is not written in a fixed form, but it has formal elements, including rhyme scheme. Formal elements enhance a poem's meaning and *mood*, or emotion. They also contribute to a poem's *aesthetic qualities*—the sense of art and beauty it conveys. As you read, notice how Dunbar's use of formal elements adds to the meaning, power, and beauty of these poems.

Reading Strategy

Preparing to Read Complex Texts Dunbar wrote in the decades following the Civil War. To fully appreciate his poems, consider how the period in which he wrote affected his point of view. As you read, **analyze the effect of the historical period** on the ideas, values, and themes that Dunbar expressed. A complete interpretation of the poem will account for both its *universal themes* and the ideas that reflect the poet's historical period. Use a chart like the one shown to record your interpretations.

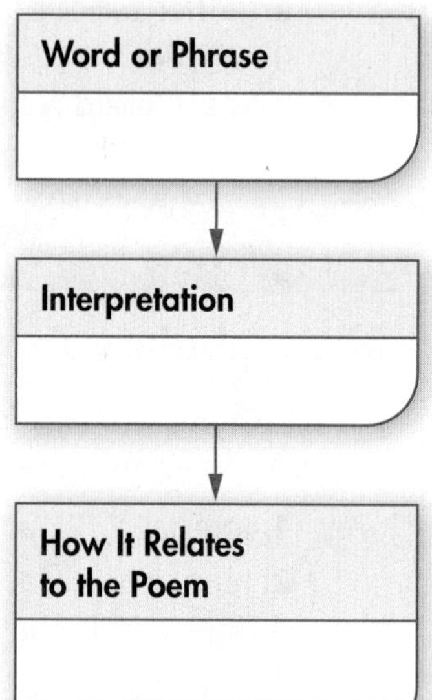

Vocabulary

salient (sāl′ yənt) *adj.* standing out from the rest (p. 637)

dissension (di sen′ shən) *n.* disagreement; discord (p. 637)

stark (stärk) *adj.* stiff; rigid (p. 637)

guile (gīl) *n.* craftiness (p. 638)

myriad (mir′ ē əd) *adj.* countless (p. 638)

Paul Laurence Dunbar *(1872–1906)*

Author of "Douglass" and "We Wear the Mask"

Paul Laurence Dunbar was the first African American author to attain national recognition and support himself entirely with his writing. Throughout his short career, he wrote many books of poetry, as well as four novels and four volumes of short stories.

A Literary Child Dunbar was born in Dayton, Ohio, the son of former slaves. Encouraged by his mother, he began writing poetry at an early age. The only African American student in his high school class, Dunbar served as president of the literary society, class poet, and editor of the school newspaper.

Gaining Recognition After graduation, Dunbar sought work in a newspaper or legal office, but he found it difficult because of his race. He finally took a job as an elevator operator, supporting himself while continuing to write. He first earned recognition among writers and critics in 1892, when he read his poetry during a meeting of the Western Association of Writers. A year later, he took out a loan and published his first collection of poetry, *Oak and Ivy*. In 1895, he published a second collection, *Majors and Minors*. William Dean Howells, the leading critic of the day, was so impressed with the book that he wrote an introduction for Dunbar's next collection, *Lyrics of a Lowly Life* (1896).

Characters, Themes, and Forms Dunbar's fiction often focuses on daily life in the vanished world of the southern plantation. Sometimes, however, his writing revolves around social problems facing African Americans in Midwestern towns and urban ghettoes at the turn of the century. His characters include farmers, politicians, preachers, traders, entertainers, and professionals.

Popularity at a Price Dunbar composed poems in two styles—one formal and elegant, the other informal, using a rural dialect. His gift for re-creating dialect and using it to create believable characters was profound. However, it also drew criticism from those who believed Dunbar was pandering to white readers' desire for stereotypes of prewar African Americans. In poems such as "Douglass" and "We Wear the Mask," however, Dunbar demonstrates a command of the English language that was often overlooked, capturing the struggles of African Americans in a dignified, graceful manner.

An Untimely Death By his late twenties, Dunbar was a nationally recognized poet. Sadly, his life was cut short by tuberculosis in 1906. By the end of his life, his poetry was so popular that he was able to write from Florida, "Down here one finds my poems recited everywhere."

DOUGLASS

Paul Laurence Dunbar

Background *Paul Laurence Dunbar was among the last generation to have an ongoing contact with former African American slaves. As a child, Dunbar heard stories from his father, who had escaped captivity and fought during the Civil War. In his poems, Dunbar expresses the pain of racial injustice and the struggles of African Americans to achieve equality. In "Douglass," he calls upon the memory of Frederick Douglass (1817–1895), the great African-American abolitionist.*

Ah, Douglass, we have fall'n on evil days,
  Such days as thou, not even thou didst know,
  When thee, the eyes of that harsh long ago
Saw, salient, at the cross of devious ways,
And all the country heard thee with amaze.
  Not ended then, the passionate ebb and flow.
  The awful tide that battled to and fro;
We ride amid a tempest of dispraise.

Now, when the waves of swift dissension swarm,
  And Honor, the strong pilot, lieth[1] stark,
Oh, for thy voice high-sounding o'er the storm,
  For thy strong arm to guide the shivering bark,[2]
The blast-defying power of thy form,
  To give us comfort through the lonely dark.

---

1. **lieth** (lī′ eth) *v.* lies.
2. **bark** boat.

Vocabulary

salient (sāl′ yənt) *adj.* standing out from the rest

dissension (di sen′ shən) *n.* disagreement; discord

stark (stärk) *adj.* stiff; rigid

What does the speaker say is the difference between the current time and the time in which Douglass lived?

◀ **Critical Viewing** Do you think this portrait and Dunbar's poem convey similar understandings of Frederick Douglass's character? Explain. **[Interpret]**

We Wear the Mask

Paul Laurence Dunbar

Vocabulary
guile (gīl) *n.* craftiness
myriad (mir′ ē əd) *adj.* countless

We wear the mask that grins and lies,
It hides our cheeks and shades our eyes—
This debt we pay to human guile;
With torn and bleeding hearts we smile,
And mouth with myriad subtleties.

Why should the world be overwise,
In counting all our tears and sighs?
Nay, let them only see us, while
We wear the mask.

Literary Analysis
Rhyme Scheme Where does the poet use exact rhyme? Which lines do not rhyme?

We smile, but, O great Christ, our cries
To thee from tortured souls arise.
We sing, but oh the clay is vile
Beneath our feet, and long the mile;
But let the world dream otherwise,
We wear the mask!

Critical Reading

Cite textual evidence to support your responses.

1. **Key Ideas and Details (a)** In "Douglass," when was Douglass's voice heard by the nation? **(b) Compare:** How does Douglass's message relate to what the speaker of "Douglass" describes?
2. **Key Ideas and Details (a) Infer:** Who is the "we" in "We Wear the Mask"? **(b) Analyze:** What struggles do they face? **(c) Draw Conclusions:** Why do you think they wear the mask?
3. **Integration of Knowledge and Ideas** If Dunbar were alive today, do you think he would still have the views he expresses in these poems? Why or why not?
4. **Integration of Knowledge and Ideas** Based on your reading of these poems, how do you think the expression of personal emotion might lead to social change? In your response, use at least two of these Essential Question words: *bigotry, disclose, endurance, justice.* ***[Connecting to the Essential Question: How does literature shape or reflect society?]***

After You Read Douglass • We Wear the Mask

Literary Analysis

1. **Craft and Structure** Which words in "We Wear the Mask" rhyme with "lies"? With "guile"?
2. **Craft and Structure** Using a chart, notate the **rhyme scheme** of each poem. Use a lower-case letter to identify each rhyming sound.

Rhyme Scheme →

"Douglass"	"We Wear..."
1	1
2	2
	3

3. **Craft and Structure** **(a)** What elements of **formal verse** does Dunbar use in "We Wear the Mask"? **(b)** How do these elements add to the poem's *mood* and *aesthetic qualities?* Explain.
4. **Key Ideas and Details** **(a)** What ideas does Dunbar introduce in the first stanza of the **sonnet** "Douglass"? **(b)** How does the second stanza build on these ideas? **(c)** What plea does he make in the final lines?

Reading Strategy

5. **Analyze the effect of the historical period** in "Douglass" by noting details that reveal the speaker's understanding of his times.
6. **(a)** What is the *theme*, or message, of "We Wear the Mask"? **(b)** How does that theme reflect problems African Americans faced during Dunbar's lifetime? Explain.

Common Core State Standards

Writing
1. Write arguments to support claims in an analysis of substantive topics or texts, using valid reasoning and relevant and sufficient evidence.

Language
5. Demonstrate understanding of word relationships and nuances in word meanings.

PERFORMANCE TASKS
Integrated Language Skills

Vocabulary Acquisition and Use

Antonyms For each word below, select the antonym, or word of opposite meaning, from the vocabulary list on page 634. Explain your answers.

1. inconspicuous
2. agreement
3. few
4. honesty
5. flexible

Writing

Argument When it was first published, Dunbar's work received mixed reviews. Conduct research to find examples of both positive and negative responses to Dunbar's work. In a report, summarize your findings and take a position about Dunbar's legacy. Examine how ideas held during Dunbar's era—including prejudice—may have influenced critics.

Before You Read

Luke Havergal • Richard Cory • Lucinda Matlock • Richard Bone

Connecting to the Essential Question The vision of small-town America in these poems is full of contradictions. As you read, notice details that portray the light and dark sides of small-town life. This activity will help as you consider the Essential Question: **What is the relationship between literature and place?**

Common Core State Standards

Reading Literature

3. Analyze the impact of the author's choices regarding how to develop and relate elements of a story or drama.

9. Demonstrate knowledge of early-twentieth-century foundational works of American literature, including how two or more texts from the same period treat similar themes or topics.

Literary Analysis

Narrative poetry is poetry that tells a story and includes the same literary elements as narrative prose such as short stories and novels:

- **Plot:** a related sequence of events, driven by a *conflict* or problem
- **Setting:** the time and place in which a story takes place
- **Characters:** people who participate in the action

In some narrative poems, one character acts as the **speaker,** or voice that tells the story. For example, the speakers in the poems from Masters's *Spoon River Anthology* are characters buried in the cemetery of the fictional town of Spoon River: "At ninety-six I had lived enough, that is all. . . ." Instead of using a neutral speaker, Masters lets characters tell their own stories. As you read, notice how the poet's choice of speaker affects the drama and emotional power of each poem.

Reading Strategy

Preparing to Read Complex Texts **Comparing and contrasting** poems in a group can give you a deeper understanding of each individual poem. It also allows you to see shared elements of works representing a certain region, time period, or literary style. As you read, use a chart like the one shown to compare and contrast the following elements:

- **Poetic Elements:** Which poems use rhyme and meter? To what effect?
- **Point of View:** How are the speakers similar and different?
- **Theme:** How are the central messages or insights about life in each poem similar and different?

Point of View	Theme

Vocabulary

repose (ri pōz′) *n.* state of being at rest (p. 646)

degenerate (dē jen′ ər it) *adj.* morally corrupt (p. 646)

epitaph (ep′ ə taf′) *n.* inscription on a tombstone (p. 647)

chronicles (krän′ i kəlz) *n.* stories; histories (p. 647)

Edwin Arlington Robinson *(1869–1935)*

Author of **"Luke Havergal"** and **"Richard Cory"**

In his mid-thirties, Edwin Arlington Robinson earned twenty cents per hour as a New York City subway inspector. Yet, friends helped him arrange the private printing of three books of his poetry during these lean times, allowing Robinson to become the most successful American poet of the 1920s.

Robinson grew up in Gardiner, Maine, a small town that was the model for Tilbury Town, the fictional setting of many of his poems. He attended Harvard University for two years, but he was forced to return to Gardiner after his father's death. Upon his return, Robinson began writing poetry, depending on friends and patrons for financial support. In a letter to a friend, Robinson wrote: "Writing has been my dream ever since I was old enough to lay a plan for an air castle. Now for the first time I seem to have something like a favorable opportunity and this winter I shall make a beginning."

Four years later, Robinson returned to New York City, hoping to improve his financial situation. When President Theodore Roosevelt, an admirer of Robinson's poems, appointed him to a post at the New York Customhouse, Robinson was set free from his financial worries.

The Inner Struggle Robinson's years of poverty and struggle shaped his world view. He filled his poems with the voices and stories of the lost and the sorrowful, exploring the themes of personal defeat and unfulfilled longing. His best poems paint portraits of desperate characters who view their lives as trivial and meaningless or who long to live in another place or time. Despite his characters' pessimistic outlook, Robinson's poems possess a certain dignity that results from his traditional style, command of language, imagination, and wit.

Robinson found success when his fourth volume of verse, *The Town Down the River* (1910), sold well and received much critical praise. He went on to publish many acclaimed books and receive three Pulitzer Prizes.

Luke Havergal

Edwin Arlington Robinson

Go to the western gate, Luke Havergal,
There where the vines cling crimson on the wall,
And in the twilight wait for what will come.
The leaves will whisper there of her, and some,
Like flying words, will strike you as they fall;
But go, and if you listen she will call.
Go to the western gate, Luke Havergal—
Luke Havergal.

No, there is not a dawn in eastern skies
To rift the fiery night that's in your eyes;
But there, where western glooms are gathering,
The dark will end the dark, if anything:
God slays Himself with every leaf that flies,
And hell is more than half of paradise.
No, there is not a dawn in eastern skies—
In eastern skies.

Out of a grave I come to tell you this,
Out of a grave I come to quench the kiss
That flames upon your forehead with a glow
That blinds you to the way that you must go.
Yes, there is yet one way to where she is,
Bitter, but one that faith may never miss.
Out of a grave I come to tell you this—
To tell you this.

There is the western gate, Luke Havergal,
There are the crimson leaves upon the wall.
Go, for the winds are tearing them away,—
Nor think to riddle the dead words they say,
Nor any more to feel them as they fall;
But go, and if you trust her she will call.
There is the western gate, Luke Havergal—
Luke Havergal.

Literary Analysis
Speaker Who is the "I" who speaks in this poem? Is there more than one possible interpretation?

What will happen at the western gate if Luke Havergal goes there?

The Thinker (Portrait of Louis N. Kenton, 1900), Thomas Eakins, The Metropolitan Museum of Art

RICHARD CORY

EDWIN ARLINGTON ROBINSON

Whenever Richard Cory went down town,
We people on the pavement looked at him:
He was a gentleman from sole to crown,
Clean favored, and imperially slim.

And he was always quietly arrayed,
And he was always human when he talked;
But still he fluttered pulses when he said,
"Good-morning," and he glittered when he walked.

And he was rich—yes, richer than a king—
And admirably schooled in every grace:
In fine, we thought that he was everything
To make us wish that we were in his place.

So on we worked, and waited for the light,
And went without the meat, and cursed the bread;
And Richard Cory, one calm summer night,
Went home and put a bullet through his head.

▲ Critical Viewing
Do you think this painting suggests Richard Cory or the poem's speaker? Explain. **[Evaluate]**

Critical Reading

Cite textual evidence to support your responses.

1. **Key Ideas and Details (a)** Why should Luke Havergal go to the gate? **(b) Speculate:** What might the gate symbolize?
2. **Key Ideas and Details (a)** In "Luke Havergal," from where has the speaker come? **(b) Interpret:** What is the speaker's message?
3. **Key Ideas and Details (a)** Why was Richard Cory the envy of the town? **(b) Contrast:** In what ways does Richard Cory differ from the other townspeople?
4. **Key Ideas and Details (a)** What does Cory do one night? **(b) Infer:** Do you think the town was surprised by his action? Explain.
5. **Integration of Knowledge and Ideas (a) Apply:** Why might Richard Cory have been miserable? **(b) Relate:** What does this poem suggest about differences between people's inner realities and their outward appearances? **(c) Extend:** In what ways is the message of this poem applicable to contemporary American culture today? Explain.

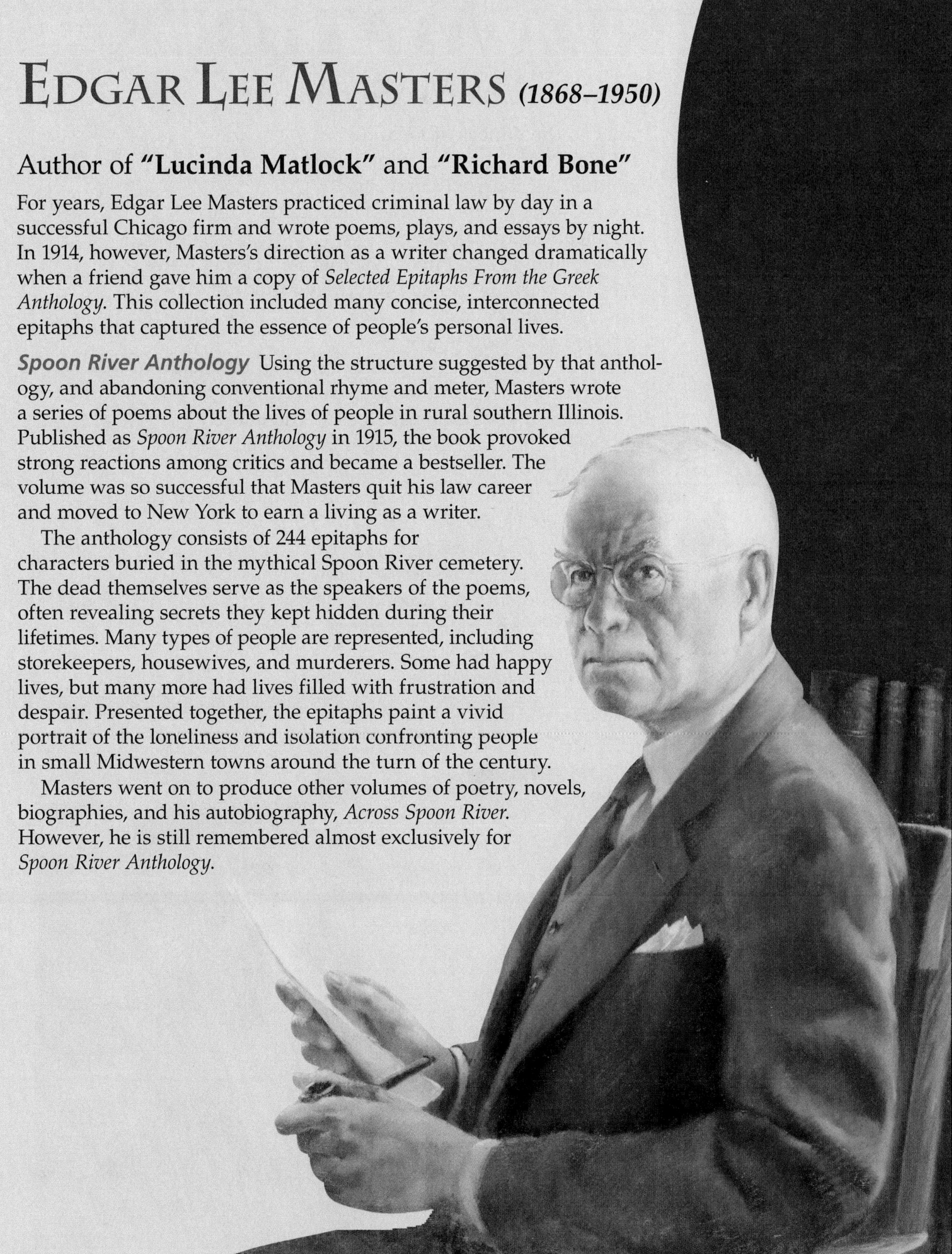

Edgar Lee Masters *(1868–1950)*

Author of "Lucinda Matlock" and "Richard Bone"

For years, Edgar Lee Masters practiced criminal law by day in a successful Chicago firm and wrote poems, plays, and essays by night. In 1914, however, Masters's direction as a writer changed dramatically when a friend gave him a copy of *Selected Epitaphs From the Greek Anthology*. This collection included many concise, interconnected epitaphs that captured the essence of people's personal lives.

Spoon River Anthology Using the structure suggested by that anthology, and abandoning conventional rhyme and meter, Masters wrote a series of poems about the lives of people in rural southern Illinois. Published as *Spoon River Anthology* in 1915, the book provoked strong reactions among critics and became a bestseller. The volume was so successful that Masters quit his law career and moved to New York to earn a living as a writer.

The anthology consists of 244 epitaphs for characters buried in the mythical Spoon River cemetery. The dead themselves serve as the speakers of the poems, often revealing secrets they kept hidden during their lifetimes. Many types of people are represented, including storekeepers, housewives, and murderers. Some had happy lives, but many more had lives filled with frustration and despair. Presented together, the epitaphs paint a vivid portrait of the loneliness and isolation confronting people in small Midwestern towns around the turn of the century.

Masters went on to produce other volumes of poetry, novels, biographies, and his autobiography, *Across Spoon River.* However, he is still remembered almost exclusively for *Spoon River Anthology.*

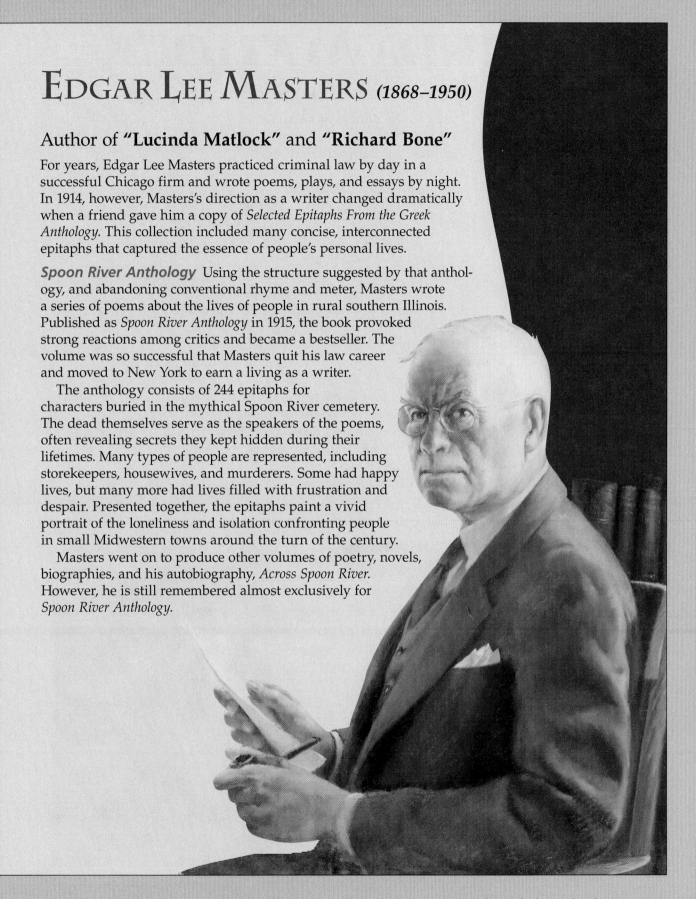

LUCINDA MATLOCK

EDGAR LEE MASTERS

I went to the dances at Chandlerville,
And played snap-out[1] at Winchester.
One time we changed partners,
Driving home in the moonlight of middle June,
And then I found Davis.
We were married and lived together for seventy years,
Enjoying, working, raising the twelve children,
Eight of whom we lost
Ere I had reached the age of sixty.
I spun, I wove, I kept the house, I nursed the sick,
I made the garden, and for holiday
Rambled over the fields where sang the larks,
And by Spoon River gathering many a shell,
And many a flower and medicinal weed—
Shouting to the wooded hills, singing to the green valleys.
At ninety-six I had lived enough, that is all,
And passed to a sweet **repose**.
What is this I hear of sorrow and weariness,
Anger, discontent and drooping hopes?
Degenerate sons and daughters,
Life is too strong for you—
It takes life to love Life.

Vocabulary
repose (ri pōz′) *n.* state of being at rest
degenerate (dē jen′ ər it) *adj.* morally corrupt

1. **snap-out** game in which a long line of players who are holding hands spin around in a circle, causing the players on the ends to be flung off by centrifugal force.

WORLD LITERATURE CONNECTION

Dramatic Monologue

The poems from *Spoon River Anthology* are dramatic monologues, a form developed by British poets during the Victorian period. In a dramatic monologue, the speaker of the poem is a character who addresses the reader, just as a character in a play might speak directly to the audience.

The most famous writer of dramatic monologues is Robert Browning, born near London in 1812. Browning first gained celebrity with *The Ring and the Book*, a series of poems spoken by characters that describe a murder case. Today, Browning's best-known poem is "My Last Duchess," a dramatic monologue spoken by a rich Italian duke who unwittingly admits to having killed his wife: "That's my last Duchess painted on the wall, /Looking as if she were alive."

CONNECT TO THE LITERATURE

Do you think the dramatic monologues from *Spoon River Anthology* could provide the basis for an interesting television series? Why or why not?

***Proserpine*, 1984** Dante Gabriel Rosetti. Tate Gallery

RICHARD BONE

EDGAR LEE MASTERS

When I first came to Spoon River
I did not know whether what they told me
Was true or false.
They would bring me the epitaph
And stand around the shop while I worked
And say "He was so kind," "He was wonderful,"
"She was the sweetest woman," "He was a consistent Christian."
And I chiseled for them whatever they wished,
All in ignorance of its truth.
But later, as I lived among the people here,
I knew how near to the life
Were the epitaphs that were ordered for them as they died.

But still I chiseled whatever they paid me to chisel
and made myself party to the false chronicles
Of the stones,
Even as the historian does who writes
Without knowing the truth,
Or because he is influenced to hide it.

Vocabulary
epitaph (ep′ ə taf′) *n.* inscription on a tombstone
chronicles (krän′ i kəlz) *n.* stories; histories

Critical Reading

Cite textual evidence to support your responses.

1. **Key Ideas and Details (a)** How old was Lucinda Matlock when she died? **(b) Infer:** Why might she have thought she "lived enough"?
2. **Key Ideas and Details (a)** Whom does she address at the end of the poem? **(b) Interpret:** What is the meaning of Matlock's message to those she addresses?
3. **Key Ideas and Details (a)** What is Richard Bone's occupation? **(b) Infer:** What does he learn after years in Spoon River?
4. **Key Ideas and Details (a) Interpret:** Why does Bone think the epitaphs are "false chronicles"? **(b) Speculate:** Is it likely Bone is correct in his assessment? Explain.
5. **Integration of Knowledge and Ideas** What image of life in small-town America do these poems project? In your response, use at least two of these Essential Question words: *conflict, appearance, secretive, familiar. **[Connecting to the Essential Question: What is the relationship between literature and place?]***

After You Read

Luke Havergal • Richard Cory • Lucinda Matlock • Richard Bone

Literary Analysis

1. **Craft and Structure (a)** Use a chart like the one shown to identify the **plot, setting,** and **characters** in the **narrative poem** "Richard Cory." **(b)** Do the same for "Lucinda Matlock."

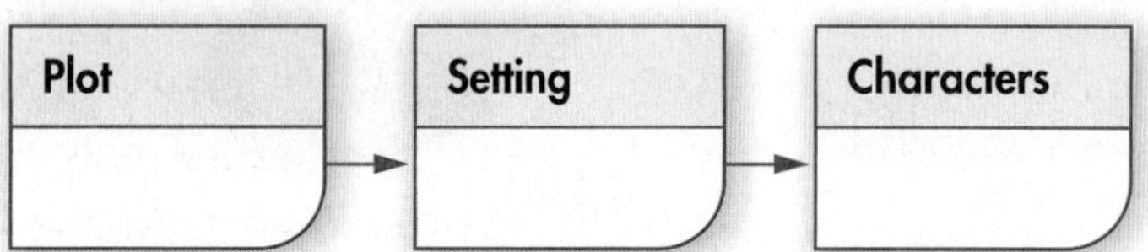

2. **Key Ideas and Details (a)** For each poem in this grouping, identify the *conflict*—the obstacles or problems—the characters face. **(b)** Do all the characters resolve, or solve, their conflicts? Explain.
3. **Craft and Structure** Identify the **speaker** of each poem in this grouping.
4. **Key Ideas and Details** Which details suggest that the speaker of "Richard Cory" is the voice of an entire town? Explain.
5. **Craft and Structure** In what ways does the speaker's admiration for Richard Cory add to the drama and surprise of the poem?
6. **Craft and Structure (a)** In what ways might "Lucinda Matlock" be different if Masters had used a different speaker? **(b)** If "Richard Cory" spoke for himself, how might the poem be different?
7. **Integration of Knowledge and Ideas** The speakers in Masters's *Spoon River Anthology* are dead. Why might this allow them to discuss their lives more openly?

Common Core State Standards

Writing
3. Write narratives to develop real or imagined experiences or events using effective technique, well-chosen details, and well-structured event sequences. *(p. 649)*

Language
4.b. Identify and correctly use patterns of word changes that indicate different meanings or parts of speech. *(p. 649)*

Reading Strategy

8. **(a)** Write several sentences in which you **compare and contrast** the uses of *rhyme* and *meter* in Robinson's poems and Masters's poems. **(b)** In your opinion, which type of poetic form is better suited to the topic of life in small-town America? Explain.
9. **(a)** If Richard Bone were to inscribe a true epitaph for each of the four speakers of these poems, including himself, what might each one say? **(b)** Compare and contrast those messages.
10. Taken together, is there a single *theme* all these poems express? If not, why not? If so, what is that theme?

PERFORMANCE TASKS

Integrated Language Skills

Vocabulary Acquisition and Use

Word Analysis: Latin Root *-genus-*

The word *degenerate* combines the Latin root *-genus-*, meaning "birth, race, species, or kind," with the prefix *de-*, meaning "away from" or "unlike." If a person is *degenerate*, he or she has fallen away from the ancestral qualities of his or her species. Use each of the following *-genus-* words below to complete the sentences. If the meaning of a word is unclear, consult a dictionary.

genetic	genealogy	homogenous
ingenious	generate	general

1. Is the human race truly ____: are we really all alike?
2. We all have a nearly identical ____ makeup.
3. Most of us can ____ good solutions to everyday problems.
4. However, each of us inherits a unique ____.
5. Some of us think in ____ terms, while others dwell on the tiniest of details.
6. And while many of us can be described as "bright," only a few can be considered ____!

Vocabulary: Evaluating Logic

Indicate whether the underlined word in each sentence below is used logically. If it is, explain your answer. If it is not, explain why not and correct the sentence to restore the logic.

1. Just as I drifted off for my afternoon nap, I heard a loud yapping outside the window and was instantly wrenched into a state of annoyed repose.
2. Throwing up the blind, I could see that the source of the yapping was the degenerate beast my neighbor refers to as his pet.
3. I began to fantasize about a small gravestone bearing an epitaph that read *Rover, detested dog of Denton Drive.*
4. Sadly, I thought, the chronicle of my own life will feature a tired grump with an overactive imagination.

Writing

Narrative Text Choose the poem in this grouping that you think would make the most poignant short story. Then, create an outline that would aid you in translating the verse into a prose narrative.

Prewriting First, use a chart like the one shown to identify the beginning, middle, and end of the story. Refer back to the poem for key story events.

Beginning	Middle	End

Drafting Decide how each part of the story will unfold. Decide what new elements or events would make the beginning more engaging, the middle more suspenseful, and the end more satisfying. As you think of ways to enrich the plot, make notes in the relevant columns of your chart.

Revising Convert the contents of your chart into an outline, using Roman numerals *I, II,* and *III* for the story's beginning, middle, and end. Use the letters *A, B, C,* etc., for details within each section. Organize the story events in chronological order.

Before You Read | *A Wagner Matinée*

Connecting to the Essential Question In this story, a woman's move to a distant state changes her life and character. As you read, notice how setting affects both Aunt Georgiana and Clark. Doing so will help as you reflect on the Essential Question: **What is the relationship between literature and place?**

Common Core State Standards

Reading Literature
3. Analyze the impact of the author's choices regarding how to develop and relate elements of a story or drama.

Literary Analysis

Characterization is the art of revealing characters' personalities. In **direct characterization,** a writer simply states what a character is like, as in this sentence: "She was a pious woman." In **indirect characterization,** the writer uses the following methods to provide clues about the character:

- descriptions of the character's appearance, manner, and behavior
- the character's own words, inner thoughts, and actions
- comments about the character made by other characters
- the ways in which other characters react to the character

The point of view in which a story is told also affects how readers learn about characters. For example, this story uses **first-person point of view**—the narrator is part of the action and uses the pronouns *I, me,* and *we.* As a result, readers' impressions filter through the narrator's eyes. As you read, notice what characters are like and identify the clues that help you understand them.

Reading Strategy

Preparing to Read Complex Texts To fully understand a story, **ask questions to clarify meaning.** You might ask the following types of questions: What problems or obstacles do characters face? What motivates characters to think, feel, or act as they do? How do characters respond to cultural or historical influences? Then, to find answers, *reread* or *refer to footnotes and sidebars.* Use a chart like the one shown to ask questions and clarify details as you read this story.

Question

Why did Georgiana go to Nebraska?

Clarifying Strategy

Reread.

Vocabulary

reverential (rev′ ə ren′ shəl) *adj.* showing deep respect and love (p. 655)

tremulously (trem′ yo͞o ləs lē) *adv.* fearfully; timidly (p. 655)

inert (in ʉrt′) *adj.* motionless (p. 656)

prelude (prel′ yo͞od′) *n.* introductory section or movement of a musical work (p. 659)

jocularity (jäk′ yo͞o lar′ ə tē) *n.* joking good humor (p. 660)

Willa Cather (1873–1947)

Author of "A Wagner Matinée"

Although Willa Cather lived more than half her life in New York City, she turned again and again to the Nebraska prairie of her youth—at the time, a recently settled area of the American frontier—for inspiration and material for her writing. Cather captured with unflinching honesty the difficulties of life on the expanding frontier.

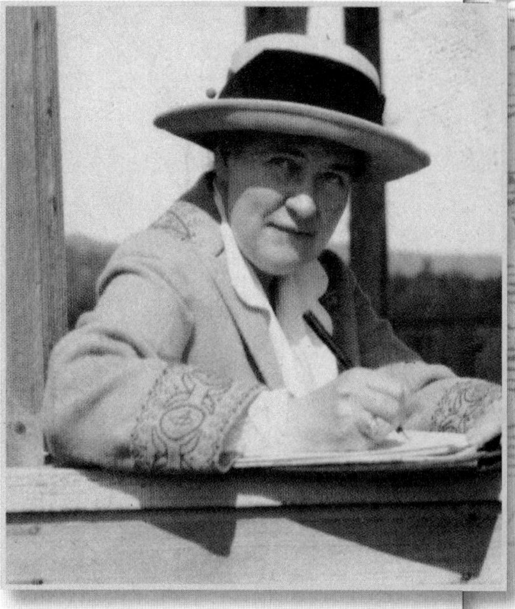

A Prairie Childhood Born in a small town in western Virginia, Cather moved to the Nebraska frontier when she was nine. Many of her new neighbors were immigrants struggling to build new lives while preserving their native cultures. Commenting on the diversity that surrounded her during her childhood, Cather once wrote, "On Sundays we could drive to a Norwegian church and listen to a sermon in that language, or to a Danish or Swedish church. We could go to a French Catholic settlement or into a Bohemian township and hear one in Czech, or we could go to the church with the German Lutherans."

Cather received a rich formal education, studying foreign languages, history, classical music, and opera. In 1891, she left home to study at the University of Nebraska, becoming one of the first women to receive a college education.

"Most of the basic material a writer works with is acquired before the age of fifteen."

The Making of a Literary Giant After her graduation in 1895, Cather worked as an editor at a Pittsburgh newspaper while writing poems and short stories in her spare time. Her first collection of stories, *The Troll Garden,* was published in 1905. In 1906, she moved to New York and joined the editorial staff of *McClure's Magazine.* After her first novel, *Alexander's Bridge,* was published in 1912, Cather devoted herself to writing full-time. She remained in New York for the rest of her life, but her memories of the prairie inspired her greatest work.

Over the next 35 years, Cather produced ten novels, two short-story collections, and two collections of essays. Among her outstanding works are *O Pioneers!* (1913), *My Ántonia* (1918), and *One of Ours* (1922), all of which capture the flavor of life on the Midwestern prairie. *One of Ours* won the Pulitzer Prize in 1923. Cather then shifted her attention from the Midwest to New Mexico in *Death Comes for the Archbishop* (1927) and to seventeenth-century Canada in *Shadows on the Rock* (1931).

A Wagner Matinée

Willa Cather

BACKGROUND When "A Wagner Matinée" first appeared in 1904, Cather's readers would have been as familiar with Richard Wagner (väg nər) as people are today with the Beatles. Wagner, who was German, was one of the nineteenth century's great composers. His operas are characterized by adventurous harmonic language and an innovative intermarriage of music and drama. To many, Wagner represents the idea of high culture. In this story, Cather contrasts the stark realities of frontier life with life in a more cultured world.

I received one morning a letter written in pale ink, on glassy, blue-lined notepaper, and bearing the postmark of a little Nebraska village. This communication, worn and rubbed, looking as though it had been carried for some days in a coat pocket that was none too clean, was from my Uncle Howard. It informed me that his wife had been left a small legacy by a bachelor relative who had recently died, and that it had become necessary for her to come to Boston to attend to the settling of the estate. He requested me to meet her at the station, and render her whatever services might prove necessary. On examining the date indicated as that of her arrival, I found it no later than tomorrow. He had characteristically delayed writing until, had I been away from home for a day, I must have missed the good woman altogether.

The name of my Aunt Georgiana called up not alone her own figure, at once pathetic and grotesque, but opened before my feet a gulf

◀ **Critical Viewing**
What sort of life do you think the woman depicted in this painting has lived? Explain **[Interpret]**

Why is Aunt Georgiana going to Boston?

◀ ***From Arkansas,*** 1939, George Schreiber, Sheldon Swope Art Museum, Terre Haute, Indiana of recollections so wide and deep that, as the letter dropped from my hand, I felt suddenly a stranger to all the present conditions of my existence, wholly ill at ease and out of place amid the surroundings of my study. I became, in short, the gangling farmer boy my aunt had known, scourged with chilblains and bashfulness, my hands cracked and raw from the corn husking. I felt the knuckles of my thumb tentatively, as though they were raw again. I sat again before her parlor organ, thumbing the scales with my stiff, red hands, while she beside me made canvas mittens for the huskers.

The next morning, after preparing my landlady somewhat, I set out for the station. When the train arrived I had some difficulty in finding my aunt. She was the last of the passengers to alight, and when I got her into the carriage she looked not unlike one of those charred, smoked bodies that firemen lift from the *débris* of a burned building. She had come all the way in a day coach; her linen duster[1] had become black with soot and her black bonnet gray with dust during the journey. When we arrived at my boardinghouse the landlady put her to bed at once, and I did not see her again until the next morning.

Whatever shock Mrs. Springer experienced at my aunt's appearance she considerately concealed. Myself, I saw my aunt's misshapen figure with that feeling of awe and respect with which we behold explorers who have left their ears and fingers north of Franz Josef Land,[2] or their health somewhere along the upper Congo.[3] My Aunt Georgiana had been a music teacher at the Boston Conservatory, somewhere back in the latter sixties. One summer, which she had spent in the little village in the Green Mountains[4] where her ancestors had dwelt for generations, she had kindled the callow[5] fancy of the most idle and shiftless of all the village lads, and had conceived for this Howard Carpenter one of those absurd and extravagant passions which a handsome country boy of twenty-one sometimes inspires in a plain, angular, spectacled woman of thirty. When she returned to her duties in Boston, Howard followed her; and the upshot of this inexplicable infatuation was that she eloped with him, eluding the reproaches of her family and the criticism of her friends by going with him to the Nebraska frontier. Carpenter, who of course had no money, took a homestead in Red Willow County,[6] fifty miles from the railroad. There they measured off their eighty acres by driving across the prairie in a wagon, to the wheel of which they had tied a red cotton handkerchief, and counting its revolutions. They built a dugout in the red hillside, one of those cave dwellings whose

Literary Analysis

Characterization What do the contrasting details of Aunt Georgiana's life in Boston and Nebraska reveal about her character?

1. **duster** *n.* short, loose smock worn while traveling to protect clothing from dust.
2. **Franz Josef Land** group of islands in the Arctic Ocean.
3. **Congo** river in central Africa.
4. **Green Mountains** mountains in Vermont.
5. **callow** (kal′ ō) *adj.* immature; inexperienced.
6. **Red Willow County** county in southwestern Nebraska that borders on Kansas.

inmates usually reverted to the conditions of primitive savagery. Their water they got from the lagoons where the buffalo drank, and their slender stock of provisions was always at the mercy of bands of roving Indians. For thirty years my aunt had not been farther than fifty miles from the homestead.

But Mrs. Springer knew nothing of all this, and must have been considerably shocked at what was left of my kinswoman. Beneath the soiled linen duster, which on her arrival was the most conspicuous feature of her costume, she wore a black stuff dress whose ornamentation showed that she had surrendered herself unquestioningly into the hands of a country dressmaker. My poor aunt's figure, however, would have presented astonishing difficulties to any dressmaker. Her skin was yellow from constant exposure to a pitiless wind, and to the alkaline water which transforms the most transparent cuticle into a sort of flexible leather. She wore ill-fitting false teeth. The most striking thing about her physiognomy, however, was an incessant twitching of the mouth and eyebrows, a form of nervous disorder resulting from isolation and monotony, and from frequent physical suffering.

Literary Analysis
Characterization In this paragraph, which details are examples of indirect characterization?

In my boyhood this affliction had possessed a sort of horrible fascination for me, of which I was secretly very much ashamed, for in those days I owed to this woman most of the good that ever came my way, and had a **reverential** affection for her. During the three winters when I was riding herd for my uncle, my aunt, after cooking three meals for half a dozen farmhands, and putting the six children to bed, would often stand until midnight at her ironing board, hearing me at the kitchen table beside her recite Latin declensions and conjugations, and gently shaking me when my drowsy head sank down over a page of irregular verbs. It was to her, at her ironing or mending, that I read my first Shakespeare; and her old textbook of mythology was the first that ever came into my empty hands. She taught me my scales and exercises, too, on the little parlor organ which her husband had bought her after fifteen years, during which she had not so much as seen any instrument except an accordion, that belonged to one of the Norwegian farmhands. She would sit beside me by the hour, darning and counting, while I struggled with the "Harmonious Blacksmith"; but she seldom talked to me about music, and I understood why. She was a pious woman; she had the consolation of religion; and to her at least her martyrdom was not wholly sordid. Once when I had been doggedly beating out some passages from an old score of "Euryanthe" I had found among her music books, she came up to me and, putting her hands over my eyes, gently drew my head back upon her shoulder, saying **tremulously**, "Don't love it so well, Clark, or it may be taken from you. Oh! dear boy, pray that whatever your sacrifice be it is not that."

Vocabulary
reverential (rev′ ə ren′ shəl) *adj.* showing deep respect and love

Vocabulary
tremulously (trem′ yo͞o ləs lē) *adv.* fearfully; timidly

When Clark was a boy, what subjects did he learn from his aunt?

LITERATURE IN CONTEXT

Music Connection

Wagnerian Opera

Aunt Georgiana has a strong reaction to the music of Richard Wagner, the composer of *The Flying Dutchman* (1843). Wagner rejected some of the traditions of opera. He usually avoided lengthy musical speeches and instead originated the *leitmotif*, a recurring musical theme used to symbolize an emotion or event. Wagner also wrote what he called "music dramas." An entire series of these works, called *The Ring of the Nibelung*, consumed twenty-six years of his life. In "A Wagner Matinée," the audience hears excerpts from *The Ring* and *Siegfried*, an opera based on the adventures of a legendary German hero.

Connect to the Literature

Does the reader need to be familiar with Wagner's operas to understand Aunt Georgiana's response? Explain.

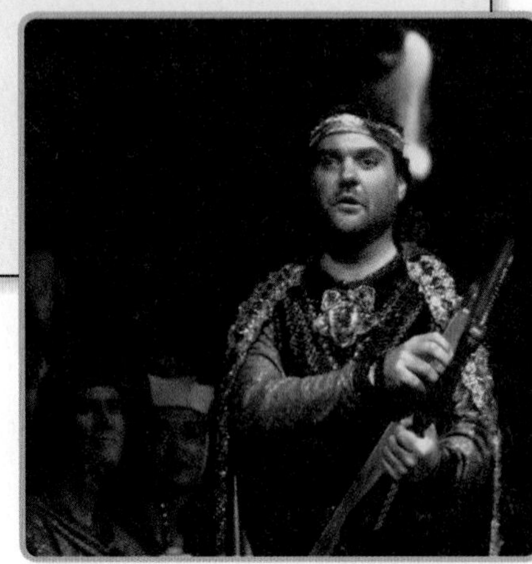

When my aunt appeared on the morning after her arrival, she was still in a semi-somnambulant[7] state. She seemed not to realize that she was in the city where she had spent her youth, the place longed for hungrily for half a lifetime. She had been so wretchedly trainsick throughout the journey that she had no recollection of anything but her discomfort, and, to all intents and purposes, there were but a few hours of nightmare between the farm in Red Willow County and my study on Newbury Street. I had planned a little pleasure for her that afternoon, to repay her for some of the glorious moments she had given me when we used to milk together in the straw-thatched cowshed, and she, because I was more than usually tired, or because her husband had spoken sharply to me, would tell me of the splendid performance of Meyerbeer's *Les Huguenots*[8] she had seen in Paris in her youth. At two o'clock the Boston Symphony Orchestra was to give a Wagner program, and I intended to take my aunt, though as I conversed with her I grew doubtful about her enjoyment of it. Indeed, for her own sake, I could only wish her taste for such things quite dead, and the long struggle mercifully ended at last. I suggested our visiting the Conservatory and the Common[9] before lunch, but she seemed altogether too timid to wish to venture out. She questioned me absently about various changes in the city, but she was chiefly concerned that she had forgotten to leave instructions about feeding half-skimmed milk to a certain weakling calf, "Old Maggie's calf, you know, Clark," she explained, evidently having forgotten how long I had been away. She was further troubled because she had neglected to tell her daughter about the freshly opened kit of mackerel in the cellar, that would spoil if it were not used directly.

I asked her whether she had ever heard any of the Wagnerian operas, and found that she had not, though she was perfectly familiar with their respective situations and had once possessed the piano score of *The Flying Dutchman*. I began to think it would have been best to get her back to Red Willow County without waking her, and regretted having suggested the concert.

From the time we entered the concert hall, however, she was a trifle less passive and inert, and seemed to begin to perceive her

Vocabulary
inert (in urt′) *adj.* motionless

7. **semi-somnambulant** (se mī säm′ nam byə lənt) *adj.* resembling a sleepwalker.
8. ***Les Huguenots*** (lāz hyōō′ gə nät′) opera written in 1836 by Giacomo Meyerbeer (1791–1864).
9. **Common** Boston Common, a small park in Boston.

surroundings. I had felt some trepidation[10] lest one might become aware of the absurdities of her attire, or might experience some painful embarrassment at stepping suddenly into the world to which she had been dead for a quarter of a century. But again I found how superficially I had judged her. She sat looking about her with eyes as impersonal, almost as stony, as those with which the granite Ramses[11] in a museum watches the froth and fret that ebbs and flows about his pedestal, separated from it by the lonely stretch of centuries. I have seen this same aloofness in old miners who drift into the Brown Hotel at Denver, their pockets full of bullion, their linen soiled, their haggard faces unshorn, and who stand in the thronged corridors as solitary as though they were still in a frozen camp on the Yukon, or in the yellow blaze of the Arizona desert, conscious that certain experiences have isolated them from their fellows by a gulf no haberdasher could conceal.

The audience was made up chiefly of women. One lost the contour of faces and figures, indeed any effect of line whatever, and there was only the color contrast of bodices past counting, the shimmer and shading of fabrics soft and firm, silky and sheer, resisting and yielding: red, mauve, pink, blue, lilac, purple, ecru, rose, yellow, cream, and white, all the colors that an impressionist finds in a sunlit landscape, with here and there the dead black shadow of a frock coat. My Aunt Georgiana regarded them as though they had been so many daubs of tube paint on a palette.

When the musicians came out and took their places, she gave a little stir of anticipation, and looked with quickening interest down over the rail at that invariable grouping; perhaps the first wholly familiar thing that had greeted her eye since she had left old Maggie and her weakling calf. I could feel how all those details sank into her soul, for I had not forgotten how they had sunk into mine when I came fresh from plowing forever and forever between green aisles of corn, where, as in a treadmill, one might walk from daybreak to dusk without perceiving a shadow of change in one's environment. I reminded myself of the impression made on me by the clean profiles of the musicians, the gloss of their linen; the dull black of their coats, the beloved shapes of the instruments, the patches of yellow light thrown by the green-shaded stand-lamps on the smooth, varnished bellies of the cellos and the bass viols in the rear, the restless, wind-tossed forest of fiddle necks and bows; I recalled how, in the first orchestra I had ever heard, those long bow strokes seemed to draw the soul out of me, as a conjuror's stick reels out paper ribbon from a hat.

The first number was the Tannhäuser overture. When the violins

Literary Analysis
Characterization What do Clark's descriptions of his own first reactions to a concert reveal about his character?

Reading Check
What is Clark's initial feeling about being in public with Aunt Georgiana? How does that attitude change?

---

10. **trepidation** (trep´ ə dā´ shən) *n.* fearful anxiety; apprehension.
11. **Ramses** (ram´ sēz) one of the eleven Egyptian kings by that name who ruled from c. 1292 to c. 1075 B.C.

drew out the first strain of the Pilgrims' chorus, my Aunt Georgiana clutched my coat sleeve. Then it was that I first realized that for her this singing of basses and stinging frenzy of lighter strings broke a silence of thirty years, the inconceivable silence of the plains. With the battle between the two motifs, with the bitter frenzy of the Venusberg[12] theme and its ripping of strings, came to me an overwhelming sense of the waste and wear we are so powerless to combat. I saw again the tall, naked house on the prairie, black and grim as a wooden fortress; the black pond where I had learned to swim, the rain-gullied clay about the naked house; the four dwarf ash seedlings on which the dishcloths were always hung to dry before the kitchen door. The world there is the flat world of the ancients; to the east, a cornfield that stretched to daybreak; to the west, a corral that stretched to sunset; between, the sordid conquests of peace, more merciless than those of war.

The overture closed. My aunt released my coat sleeve, but she said nothing. She sat staring at the orchestra through a dullness of thirty years, through the films made, little by little, by each of the three hundred and sixty-five days in every one of them. What, I wondered, did she get from it? She had been a good pianist in her day, I knew, and her musical education had been broader than that of most music teachers of a quarter of a century ago. She had often told me of Mozart's operas and Meyerbeer's, and I could remember hearing her sing, years ago, certain melodies of Verdi. When I had fallen ill with a fever she used to sit by my cot in the evening, while the cool night wind blew in through the faded mosquito netting tacked over the window, and I lay watching a bright star that burned red above the cornfield, and sing "Home to our mountains, oh, let us return!" in a way fit to break the heart of a Vermont boy near dead of homesickness already.

I watched her closely through the prelude to *Tristan and Isolde*, trying vainly to conjecture what that warfare of motifs, that seething turmoil of strings and winds, might mean to her. Had this music any message for her? Did or did not a new planet swim into her ken? Wagner had been a sealed book to Americans before the sixties. Had she anything left with which to comprehend this glory that had flashed around the world since she had gone from it? I was in a fever of curiosity, but Aunt Georgiana sat silent upon her peak in Darien.[13] She preserved this utter immobility throughout the numbers from the *Flying Dutchman*, though her fingers worked mechanically upon her black dress, as though of themselves they were recalling the piano score they had once played. Poor old hands! They

Reading Strategy
Asking Questions to Clarify Meaning What questions might you ask about Clark's description of the plains?

◄ Critical Viewing
In what ways does this painting mirror Clark's description of the audience at the opera house? **[Connect; Compare]**

Vocabulary
prelude (prel′ yo͞od) *n.* introductory section or movement of a musical work

Reading Check

Describe Aunt Georgiana's musical education.

12. **Venusberg** (vē′ nəs bʉrg′) legendary mountain in Germany where Venus, the Roman goddess of love, held court.
13. **peak in Darien** (der′ ē ən′) mountain on the Isthmus of Panama; from "On First Looking into Chapman's Homer" by English poet John Keats (1795–1821).

were stretched and pulled and twisted into mere tentacles to hold, and lift, and knead with; the palms unduly swollen, the fingers bent and knotted, on one of them a thin worn band that had once been a wedding ring. As I pressed and gently quieted one of those groping hands, I remembered, with quivering eyelids, their services for me in other days.

Soon after the tenor began the "Prize Song," I heard a quick-drawn breath, and turned to my aunt. Her eyes were closed, but the tears were glistening on her cheeks, and I think in a moment more they were in my eyes as well. It never really dies, then, the soul? It withers to the outward eye only, like that strange moss which can lie on a dusty shelf half a century and yet, if placed in water, grows green again. My aunt wept gently throughout the development and elaboration of the melody.

Reading Strategy
Asking Questions to Clarify Meaning What questions might you ask about the episode of the farm hand to clarify your understanding of its meaning to Georgiana?

During the intermission before the second half of the concert, I questioned my aunt and found that the "Prize Song" was not new to her. Some years before there had drifted to the farm in Red Willow County a young German, a tramp cow puncher who had sung in the chorus at Bayreuth,[14] when he was a boy, along with the other peasant boys and girls. On a Sunday morning he used to sit on his blue gingham-sheeted bed in the hands' bedroom, which opened off the kitchen, cleaning the leather of his boots and saddle, and singing the "Prize Song," while my aunt went about her work in the kitchen. She had hovered about him until she had prevailed upon him to join the country church, though his sole fitness for this step, so far as I could gather, lay in his boyish face and his possession of this divine melody. Shortly afterward he had gone to town on the Fourth of July, lost his money at a faro[15] table, ridden a saddled Texas steer on a bet, and disappeared with a fractured collarbone.

Vocabulary
jocularity (jäk′ yo͞o lar′ ə tē) *n.* joking good humor

"Well, we have come to better things than the old *Trovatore* at any rate, Aunt Georgie?" I queried, with well-meant **jocularity**.

Her lip quivered and she hastily put her handkerchief up to her mouth. From behind it she murmured, "And you've been hearing this ever since you left me, Clark?" Her question was the gentlest and saddest of reproaches.

"But do you get it, Aunt Georgiana, the astonishing structure of it all?" I persisted.

"Who could?" she said, absently; "why should one?"

The second half of the program consisted of four numbers from the *Ring*. This was followed by the forest music from *Siegfried*[16] and the program closed with Siegfried's funeral march. My aunt wept quietly, but almost continuously. I was perplexed as to what

14. Bayreuth (bī roit′) city in Germany known for its annual Wagnerian music festivals.
15. faro (fer′ ō) gambling game in which players bet on the cards to be turned up from the top of the dealer's deck.
16. Siegfried (sēg′ frēd) opera based on the adventures of Siegfried, a legendary hero in medieval German literature.

measure of musical comprehension was left to her, to her who had heard nothing for so many years but the singing of gospel hymns in Methodist services at the square frame schoolhouse on Section Thirteen. I was unable to gauge how much of it had been dissolved in soapsuds, or worked into bread, or milked into the bottom of a pail.

The deluge of sound poured on and on; I never knew what she found in the shining current of it; I never knew how far it bore her, or past what happy islands, or under what skies. From the trembling of her face I could well believe that the *Siegfried* march, at least, carried her out where the myriad graves are, out into the gray, burying grounds of the sea; or into some world of death vaster yet, where, from the beginning of the world, hope has lain down with hope, and dream with dream and, renouncing, slept.

The concert was over; the people filed out of the hall chattering and laughing, glad to relax and find the living level again, but my kinswoman made no effort to rise. I spoke gently to her. She burst into tears and sobbed pleadingly, "I don't want to go, Clark, I don't want to go!"

"I don't want to go, Clark, I don't want to go!"

I understood. For her, just outside the door of the concert hall, lay the black pond with the cattle-tracked bluffs, the tall, unpainted house, naked as a tower, with weather-curled boards; the crook-backed ash seedlings where the dishcloths hung to dry, the gaunt, moulting turkeys picking up refuse about the kitchen door.

Critical Reading

Cite textual evidence to support your responses.

1. **Key Ideas and Details (a)** What part did Boston play in Aunt Georgiana's earlier life? **(b) Compare and Contrast:** In what ways would you compare and contrast life in Boston and life in Red Willow County?
2. **Key Ideas and Details (a)** As a boy, what did the narrator practice on the "parlor organ" in the Nebraska farmhouse? **(b) Interpret:** What does Aunt Georgiana mean when she says, "Don't love it so well, Clark, or it may be taken from you"? **(c) Connect:** Do the events of the story reinforce her statement? Explain.
3. **Integration of Knowledge and Ideas Take a Position:** Would it have been better for Aunt Georgiana if she had not come to Boston? Explain.
4. **Integration of Knowledge and Ideas** What do you think Cather would say about the importance of artistic and cultural outlets to the health of a community? Do you agree or disagree? Explain. In your response, use at least two of these Essential Question words: *expression, freedom, individualism, self-reliance.* ***[Connecting to the Essential Question: What is the relationship between literature and place?]***

After You Read A Wagner Matinée

Literary Analysis

1. **Craft and Structure** Note two examples of **direct characterization** in this story.
2. **Craft and Structure** What do you learn about Aunt Georgiana's personality through **indirect characterization?** Use a chart like the one shown to record your observations.

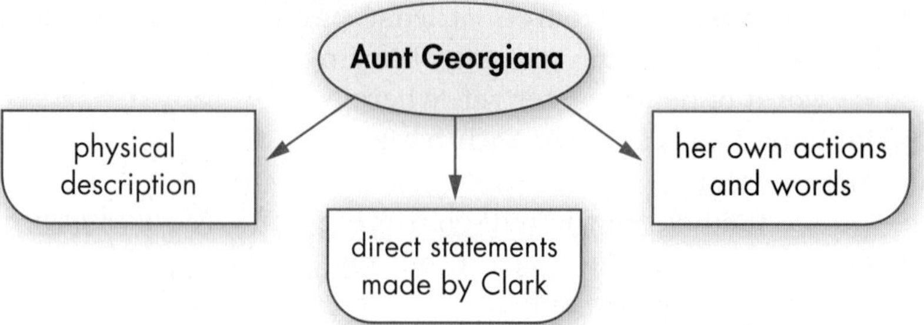

3. **Craft and Structure** What do Clark's thoughts and feelings about his aunt indirectly reveal about his personality? Explain.
4. **Craft and Structure** What effect does Clark's **first-person point of view** have on your perception of Aunt Georgiana?
5. **Key Ideas and Details** **(a)** Find two examples of events Clark recalls from living with Aunt Georgiana. **(b)** How do these events shape your impressions of her?
6. **Key Ideas and Details** **(a)** How do Clark's feelings toward his aunt change during the story? **(b)** How do his feelings affect your response to her? **(c)** How do Clark's feelings about his aunt affect your attitude toward him as a character?
7. **Craft and Structure** Aunt Georgiana's husband bought her a "little parlor organ." Explain what this small detail suggests about his character.

Reading Strategy

8. **(a)** What **questions** might you ask about the difficulties of Aunt Georgiana's life in Nebraska? **(b)** *Reread* to find two details in the story that help you understand Nebraska life at that time in history. **(c)** In what ways do these details **clarify the meaning** of the story for you?
9. **(a)** What questions might you ask about Boston life at the time of the story? **(b)** Which story details provide answers to your questions?
10. How do the questions you asked and answered in items 8 and 9 above help clarify your understanding of Aunt Georgiana's experiences in Boston?
11. **(a)** As you read this story, what questions might you ask about the composer Richard Wagner? **(b)** How do *footnotes or sidebars* help to answer these questions? **(c)** In what ways did learning about Wagner deepen your understanding of the story?

Common Core State Standards

Writing

1. Write arguments to support claims in an analysis of substantive topics or texts, using valid reasoning and relevant and sufficient evidence. *(p. 663)*

5. Develop and strengthen writing as needed by revising, focusing on addressing what is most significant for a specific purpose and audience. *(p. 663)*

Language

4. Determine or clarify the meaning of unknown and multiple-meaning words and phrases based on *grades 11–12 reading and content,* choosing flexibly from a range of strategies. *(p. 663)*

6. Acquire and use accurately general academic and domain-specific words and phrases, sufficient for reading, writing, and speaking at the college and career readiness level. *(p. 663)*

PERFORMANCE TASKS

Integrated Language Skills

Vocabulary Acquisition and Use

Multiple-Meaning Words from Music

Musical vocabulary often has multiple meanings. For example, a *prelude* can be the introduction to a musical work or preparation for any important matter. For each numbered item below, select the correct definition of the italicized word.

chord: (a) two or more notes played or sung simultaneously, **(b)** an emotional response

concert: (a) a performance of several short compositions, **(b)** working together

harmony: (a) a pleasing combination of musical sounds, **(b)** a peaceful situation

overture: (a) an introductory movement to an extended musical work, **(b)** any first movement

1. We put a *concerted* effort into the game.
2. The chorus sang in glorious *harmony*.
3. He made an *overture* to pay for lunch.
4. The speech struck a *chord* in the audience.

Vocabulary: Word Meanings

Answer the following questions in complete sentences. Be sure to use the underlined words in your responses.

1. If students are <u>reverential</u> toward a teacher, do they ignore or respect her?
2. Who is most likely to speak <u>tremulously</u>—a musician, a truck driver, or a child?
3. What is an example of a substance that is usually—but not always—<u>inert?</u>
4. As a <u>prelude</u> to bad news, would you expect sarcasm or seriousness?
5. Is <u>jocularity</u> more likely to be the trademark of a talk-show host or a funeral director?

Writing

Argument "A Wagner Matinée" provoked an outcry among Nebraskans who felt Cather had portrayed the state unfairly. Cather responded that the story was a tribute to pioneer strength and endurance. As the editor of a Nebraska newspaper, take a position and write an **editorial** defending your view. Structure your argument in a persuasive way, supported by precise and relevant examples.

Prewriting Review the story. Analyze the details Cather uses to portray Nebraska and Boston. Decide whether you agree with her views. Jot down ideas, observations, and facts that support your opinion.

Drafting Arrange your ideas in order of importance. Include factual evidence and emotional appeals to support your statements.

Revising Reread your work to make sure your language is specific and persuasive and that you present a sustained, unified argument. Replace irrelevant statements, and add support as needed.

Model: Using Specific Language

Cather implies that Boston offers more than Nebraska. While it may be true that Boston is a center for art, Nebraska offers many ~~things~~ *cultural resources* without the ~~trouble~~ *pollution and congestion* of a major city.

Specific references such as *cultural resources* and *pollution and congestion* make the editorial clear and persuasive.

Write a Research Report

Writing

2. Write informative/ explanatory texts to examine and convey complex ideas, concepts, and information clearly and accurately through the effective selection, organization, and analysis of content.

7. Conduct short as well as more sustained research projects to answer a question or solve a problem; narrow or broaden the inquiry when appropriate; synthesize multiple sources on the subject, demonstrating understanding of the subject under investigation.

Historical Investigation Report You can learn a great deal about a literary work by investigating the historical context in which it was written. To focus such an investigation, write a report in which you present information you have gathered, along with your own insights. An effective historical investigation report synthesizes information from multiple sources and connects ideas to form a coherent analysis. Follow the steps outlined in this workshop to write a historical investigation report.

Assignment Write a research report about the historical context in which a literary work or group of related works was written.

What to Include Your research report should have these elements:

- a clear thesis statement or main proposition
- factual support from varied sources, including primary and secondary sources found in both electronic and print texts
- direct quotations and proper citations of sources
- logical organization, including an introduction, body, and conclusion
- a formal bibliography or works-cited list

To preview the criteria on which your research report may be assessed, see the rubric on page 675.

To get a feel for historical research, read this mentor text. Notice how Painter uses clear language and logical organization to present information. For the complete text, see pages 550–551.

from: Nell Irvin Painter's Introduction to "An Account of an Experience With Discrimination"

In 1791, President George Washington chose land on the border of Maryland and Virginia near his own home to serve as the nation's capital. In the 1790s, slavery existed in virtually the whole country. But during the early nineteenth century the Northern states abolished slavery, while the institution grew stronger in the South, of which Washington, D.C., was a part. The Washington slave market sat near the capitol building, and slavery flourished in the District until abolition in 1862.

WRITE GUY
Jeff Anderson, M.Ed.

What Do You Notice?

Read the highlighted sentence several times. Then, with a partner, discuss the qualities that make it special. You might consider the following elements:

- word choice
- use of facts
- structure
- tone

Share your group's observations with the class.

Prewriting and Planning

Choosing Your Topic

To find a suitable topic, use the following strategies:

- **Notebook and Textbook Review** Flip through your notebooks, literature textbooks, and writing journals, and list selections or authors you find interesting. Write down specific questions you have about the historical context in which your favorite works were written.
- **Research Preview** Once you have several possible topic choices and questions, spend 10–15 minutes researching each one on the Internet or at the library. Seek out both primary and secondary sources. A quick research preview will confirm the availability of information on each topic.

Narrowing Your Topic

Find your focus. Make sure your topic is substantial but not too ambitious for a short research paper. Narrow an overly broad topic by finding a more focused subject that fits within the larger area of interest. Use a flowchart like the one shown to do so.

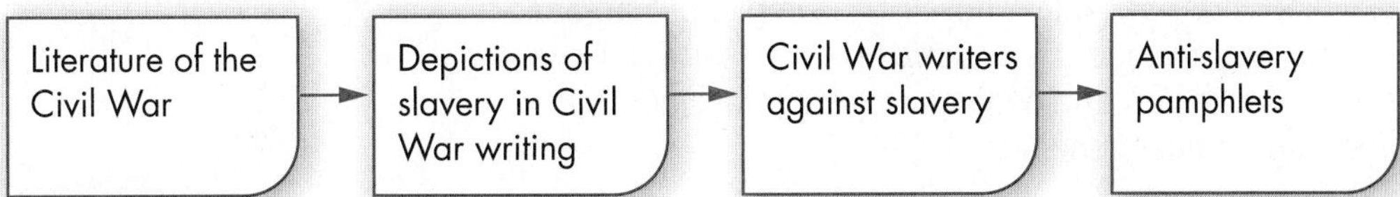

Gathering Details

Organize your notes. As you gather information, use index cards to keep track of important ideas, facts, and scholarly opinions. Write down the general subject, fact or quotation, page numbers, and an identifying letter or number you will assign to the source.

Prepare to credit sources. Use another set of index cards to keep track of your sources. Use one card for each source you consult. Record the author's name, title, publisher, city, and date of publication. Label each source card with a letter or number so you can refer to sources quickly.

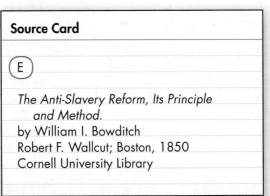

Fact Card

basic principles p. 17

"What is the principle which underlies the anti-slavery movement? It is that slaveholding is always wrong; not in this case or that case only, but in all cases..."

Source Card: E

Source Card

E

The Anti-Slavery Reform, Its Principle and Method.
by William I. Bowditch
Robert F. Wallcut; Boston, 1850
Cornell University Library

Drafting

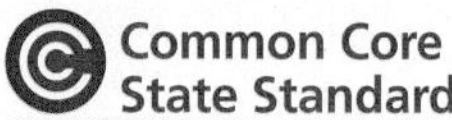

Writing

2.a. Introduce a topic; organize complex ideas, concepts, and information so that each new element builds on that which precedes it to create a unified whole.

2.b. Develop the topic thoroughly by selecting the most significant and relevant facts, extended definitions, concrete details, quotations, or other information and examples appropriate to the audience's knowledge of the topic.

8. Gather relevant information from multiple authoritative print and digital sources, using advanced searches effectively; assess the strengths and limitations of each source in terms of the task, purpose, and audience.

Shaping Your Writing

Propose a thesis statement. Your research report should develop a coherent thesis statement or controlling idea. Review your notes and write a statement that is supported by the evidence you discovered in primary and secondary resources. Your thesis should make a claim that your report will support; it should not state a simple fact.

Weak Argument	Strong Argument
• Anti-slavery pamphlets first appeared in 1704. • Pamphlets were very influential in ending slavery.	Beginning in 1704, anti-slavery pamphlets increasingly used the tools of advertising to persuade readers that slavery was immoral.

Write a formal outline. After you have selected a controlling idea, prepare an outline. Consider points at which you might include rhetorical strategies other than exposition, or explanation. For example, use an anecdote, a form of ***narration***, or include the ***description*** of a setting. Note ideas for a conclusion in which you attain closure by summarizing your main points and presenting a final generalization.

Providing Elaboration

Include a variety of sources. As you draft, use direct quotations, paraphrases, and visuals from sources that are reliable, valid, and varied. Do not rely on the ideas or information you find in a single source. Referencing multiple resources gives your writing more validity because it takes into account a variety of perspectives.

Analyze relationships among sources. In your research, you may have encountered differences of opinion in secondary sources or conflicting accounts of the same events in primary sources. Provide analysis and explanation about the reasons for such differences. To present a complete analysis, include answers to the questions listed in the following chart.

When Sources Agree	When Sources Disagree
• Do the writers of primary sources share similar biases that influenced their writing? • Do secondary resources confirm this perspective?	• Which primary sources do I think are more reliable and valid? Why? • Do I have a secondary resource that takes a side on this issue? Do I agree with it?

Developing Your Style

Choosing an Effective Organization

To choose the best pattern of organization for your report, consider your thesis and your findings. Then, structure your report with one of the methods listed in the chart below. You may choose an overall organizational strategy and use other methods to support it. For example, your essay might follow a chronological organization, but an individual paragraph might evaluate the causes and effects of a single important event.

Method	Description
Chronological	Discuss events in the order in which they occurred.
Cause/Effect	Analyze the causes and/or effects of an event.
Problem/Solution	Identify a specific problem and present a solution.
Parts to Whole	Relate elements of a single event or topic to a whole.
Order of Importance	Present your support from most to least important or from least to most important.
Compare and Contrast	Discuss similarities and differences between two topics.

Find It in Your Reading

Review Nell Irvin Painter's introduction to "An Account of an Experience With Discrimination" on page 664.

1. Identify the overall organizational method Painter uses.
2. Note her organization within individual paragraphs. Find examples of chronological and cause-and-effect organizations.

PH WRITING COACH

Further instruction and practice are available in *Prentice Hall Writing Coach*.

Apply It to Your Writing

To select an appropriate organizational method, follow these steps:

1. Review the strategies listed in the chart and consider their pros and cons. For example, chronological order can present a sequence of events clearly, but it may not establish the importance of a person or event.
2. Choose the overall organizational method that best supports your thesis statement. Draft an outline that reflects that strategy.
3. Think about the organization of information within paragraphs. Consider using cause-and-effect or problem-and-solution organization if relevant to the ideas you are presenting in that paragraph.
4. Use transitions to make your organization clear to readers.

Revising

Revising Your Paragraphs

Integrate source material smoothly. A strong research report is not a choppy collection of facts and quotations. It presents a smooth flow of ideas that are supported by valid, researched information. Review your paper, looking for points at which your source material can be integrated better. When you paraphrase another writer's ideas, include a citation that identifies the source of the idea. When you include exact quotations, follow this strategy:

- First, introduce the quotation by naming the writer or by connecting the quotation to the subject being discussed.
- Then, present the quoted material.
- Finally, explain the quotation by showing how it supports the point you are making.

Revising Your Word Choice

Define specialized vocabulary. General readers may not be familiar with specialized terms you have encountered in your research. Some words may be familiar only to experts in the field and will present obstacles to your readers' appreciation of your ideas. To aid readers' understanding, define jargon that is specific to a topic.

- Review your work and identify specialized words, such as *broadsheet* in the example shown. Add necessary definitions.
- Consider whether definitions are sufficient. If necessary, add descriptions or comparisons to more familiar concepts or objects.
- If the terms are still too challenging for your readers, consider replacing the specialized vocabulary with simpler language.

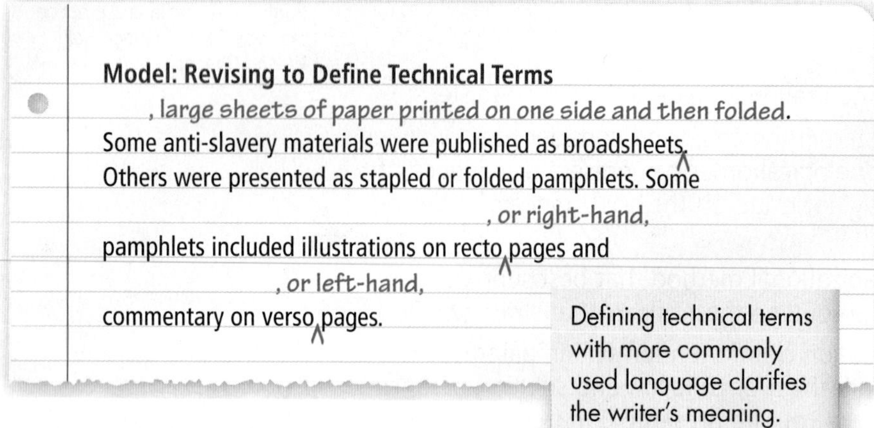

Model: Revising to Define Technical Terms
, large sheets of paper printed on one side and then folded.
Some anti-slavery materials were published as broadsheets.
Others were presented as stapled or folded pamphlets. Some
, or right-hand,
pamphlets included illustrations on recto pages and
, or left-hand,
commentary on verso pages.

Defining technical terms with more commonly used language clarifies the writer's meaning.

Peer Review: Ask a partner to review your draft and identify specialized terms. Discuss whether each term should be defined, deleted, or simplified.

Common Core State Standards

Writing

2.d. Use precise language, domain-specific vocabulary, and techniques such as metaphor, simile, and analogy to manage the complexity of the topic.

4. Produce clear and coherent writing in which the development, organization, and style are appropriate to task, purpose, and audience.

5. Develop and strengthen writing as needed by rewriting, focusing on addressing what is most significant for a specific purpose and audience.

8. Integrate information into the text selectively to maintain the flow of ideas, avoiding plagiarism and overreliance on any one source and following a standard format for citation.

Writers on Writing

Nell Irvin Painter On Using Research

Nell Irvin Painter is the author of "Defining an Era" (p. 474).

The broader your research, the more appealing your writing.

—Nell Irvin Painter

These words come from the introduction to my history of the United States between 1877 and 1919. I wanted to break down gross generalizations about Americans based on race (black/white) and ethnicity (Irish, German, Jewish) by talking about socio-economic class. Men and women experience class in different ways. In order to speak broadly, I had to research the incomes and lifestyles of many kinds of Americans, not just middle-class white people.

from *Standing at Armageddon, 1877–1919*

In both 1877 and 1919 native-born white Protestant Americans were presumed to belong to the middle (or upper) classes, even though in the South, West, and Midwest large numbers of such people belonged to the agricultural and industrial working classes. The standing of descendants of immigrants changed over time because the arrival of new groups of immigrants altered assumptions about relative class status. The Irish, who had seemed in 1877 to constitute a permanent class of casual laborers and domestic servants, had by 1919 become skilled workers and foremen, while many Irishwomen had become the teachers of eastern and southern European immigrants who early in the twentieth century formed a new industrial working class. Similarly, German Jews, many of whom in the mid-nineteenth century had been itinerant peddlers, were largely middle- and upper-class by the time of heavy Russian Jewish immigration after 1905. And the process continued. By 1920 the children of Europeans who had immigrated in the late nineteenth century had become the teachers and foremen of southern black migrants in the North and Midwest.

I purposefully included the words *white* and *Protestant* to break up an equation that many readers take for granted: that middle-class is the same as white and Protestant. I also did research in sources that discussed the lives of many kinds of people.

I specifically mentioned Irish immigrants, because many readers forget the history of Irish Americans as immigrants. I wanted this section to convey the sense of change over time in the status of Irish Americans in relation to later immigrants.

I used these two particular vocations because one, teachers, is associated with women, and the other, foremen, is associated with men.

Providing Appropriate Citations

Writing

8. Integrate information into the text selectively to maintain the flow of ideas, avoiding plagiarism and overreliance on any one source and following a standard format for citation.

You must cite the sources for the information and ideas you use in your report. In the body of your paper, include a footnote, an endnote, or a parenthetical citation, identifying the sources of facts, opinions, and quotations. At the end of your paper, provide a bibliography or a works-cited list, a list of all the sources you cite. Follow the format your teacher recommends, such as Modern Language Association (MLA) Style or American Psychological Association (APA) Style. See pages R20–R23 for more information about how to prepare citations for different kinds of sources.

If you do not credit sources accurately, you commit the serious offense of **plagiarism,** presenting someone else's work as your own. Plagiarism is stealing someone else's ideas, so it is both illegal and dishonest. Avoid this problem by fairly and thoroughly citing every source you use.

Deciding What to Cite

You do not need to cite every fact that you report. For example, facts that are considered common knowledge do not require citation. A fact that can be found in three or more sources is probably common knowledge. However, you should cite any facts and statistics that are not common knowledge. The examples in this chart reflect the difference between common knowledge and facts that should be cited.

Common Knowledge
• Slavery was abolished in the United States in 1863. • William Lloyd Garrison was a leader of the abolitionist movement. • *Uncle Tom's Cabin* was published in 1852.
Facts to Be Cited
• From the 17th to 19th centuries, about 12 million Africans were captured and sent as slaves to the Americas. Source: Ronald Segal, *The Black Diaspora: Five Centuries of the Black Experience Outside Africa* (New York: Farrar, Straus and Giroux, 1995, page 4). • Harriet Beecher Stowe's anti-slavery novel *Uncle Tom's Cabin* (1852) increased tensions between the North and the South. Source: Will Kaufman, *The Civil War in American Culture* (Edinburgh: Edinburgh University Press, 2006, page 18).

In your report, give credit for the following:

- ideas, opinions, or theories presented by other writers
- facts or statistics that are not common knowledge
- direct quotations of spoken or written words
- paraphrases of spoken or written words

Notice that you must still provide a citation even if you paraphrase someone else's ideas. It is appropriate to give credit to someone else's thoughts, whether or not you use his or her exact words. In general, it is a good idea to provide more citations rather than risk not providing enough.

Works-Cited List (MLA Style)

A works-cited list must contain the following information:

- name of the author, editor, translator, or group responsible for the work
- title
- place and date of publication
- publisher

For print materials, the information required for a citation generally appears on the copyright and title pages of a work.

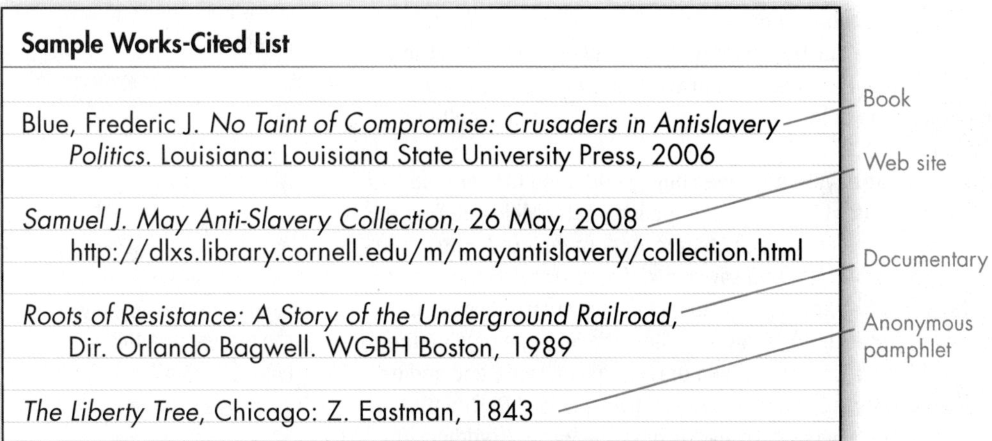

Sample Works-Cited List

Blue, Frederic J. *No Taint of Compromise: Crusaders in Antislavery Politics.* Louisiana: Louisiana State University Press, 2006

Samuel J. May Anti-Slavery Collection, 26 May, 2008 http://dlxs.library.cornell.edu/m/mayantislavery/collection.html

Roots of Resistance: A Story of the Underground Railroad, Dir. Orlando Bagwell. WGBH Boston, 1989

The Liberty Tree, Chicago: Z. Eastman, 1843

Parenthetical Citations (MLA Style)

A parenthetical citation appears in the body of your text and identifies the source at point of use. It refers the reader to an entry on your works-cited list. A parenthetical citation appears in parentheses. It identifies the source by the last name of the author, editor, or translator. It also gives a page reference, identifying the page of the source on which the information can be found.

Model: Parenthetical Citations

Although most of the anti-slavery pamphlets were expected to exist for only a short time, some rare examples have survived in carefully preserved collections. The founders of one large collection acknowledged the "great importance that the literature of the Anti-Slavery movement…be preserved and handed down…" (Samuel J. May Anti-Slavery Collection, "Collection Description") The variety of opinions reflected in this collection show that there were many divisions among the beliefs of abolitionists. (Blue, p. 1)

Manuscript Preparation

The final copy of your research report should be prepared according to your teacher's recommended style. Here are some common preferences:

- double-spaced lines
- 12-point type (Times New Roman or Courier is often requested.)
- italics to replace underscoring (for example, in titles of novels)
- one-inch margins on each side of the text

Student Model: Lauren Shepherd, Tupelo, MS

The Writing Style of Phillis Wheatley

In an era when African Americans were struggling to carve an identity for themselves, Phillis Wheatley emerged as the first truly significant black poet in American literature. Although many do not consider her to be an important writer, judged by today's values of originality, she persevered through the challenges of her social status to become not only a celebrated poet, but the starting point for the study of African American literature. In this paper, I will discuss her work as a whole and present a detailed analysis of one of her most famous poems, "To His Excellency General Washington."

Lauren clearly states her thesis in the opening paragraph.

Religious Message Wheatley was highly educated for her time and had read the classics as well as the best English poets (Miller, de Dwyer, Wood 48). She was deeply influenced by the work of the great English poet John Milton (1608–1674), who saw himself as a writer in the service of God. Like Milton, Wheatley expressed a constant awareness of "God, His Son, His beneficence and His Power." Almost every one of Wheatley's poems develops around a central theme of religious morality and sometimes has an "air of message from the pulpit" (Mason 15–17). One theme, Christian salvation, underlies nearly everything she wrote (Redding 10).

Lauren provides thorough support for the opinions she expresses in this passage.

Wheatley's religious messages are often conveyed through embellished Bible stories. In fact, a tradition within African American literature of augmenting biblical accounts with creative license and poetic flair can be traced directly to Wheatley. Both her poems "Goliath and Gath" and "Isaiah LXIII" add creative information to a foundation of biblical narrative.

Subheads add to the clarity and order of the essay.

African Influences In addition to the key role of Christian religious messages in Wheatley's work, many of her writings also exhibit a subtle presence of African traditions. For example, Wheatley uses solar imagery throughout her body of poems. Her frequent use of sun imagery in such poems as "A Hymn to the Morning" and "A Hymn to the Evening" suggest that her early religious training in Africa may have consisted of some kind of hierophantic—or sun—worship (Smith, Baechler, Litz 474). Wheatley usually uses such sun imagery as a metaphor for Christian revelation, thus connecting the two essential elements of her religious life.

Lauren provides factual support for an interesting literary analysis.

Also reminiscent of Wheatley's childhood in Africa is her constant interest in panegyric—or praise—poetry. In many of the cultures of Africa, poets were instructed that political praise constituted the very core of their responsibility as writers (Smith Baechler, Litz 476). In keeping with that tradition, the majority of Wheatley's works are directed towards politically and socially prominent individuals, such as George Whitehead, a famous English clergyman, and George Washington (Johnson 29).

Racial Consciousness Although many have ventured to say that Wheatley's "unquestioning embrace of New England and white cultures" prompted her to neglect the issue of slavery (Smith, Baechler, Litz 476), a closer examination of her poetry reveals that she was quite "race conscious" (Davis 192). She refers to herself on several occasions as "Africa's muse," and even uses her skin color and presumed low social status as a reference point for her religious message of salvation (Davis 192–193).

The essay presents a variety of interpretations of the material.

Neoclassical Style The majority of Wheatley's poems adhere to the established patterns of the neoclassical style. Neoclassicism was a widespread movement in the visual and literary arts that began in the 1700s and lasted until the 1840s and 1850s. Classical history and mythology provided much of the subject matter of Neoclassical works. The poetry of Homer, Virgil, and Ovid, and the plays of Aeschylus, Sophocles, and Euripides provided the bulk of classical sources. Neoclassical writers, such as Alexander Pope (1688–1744), stressed order, harmony, and restraint.

Necessary background information is essential to the readers' understanding.

Like the Neoclassicists she admired, Wheatley's work was noted for an unfaltering preoccupation with regular rhyme and rhythm (Mason 14). Breaking out of her usual form on only six occasions, Wheatley most frequently wrote using the heroic couplet—two-line stanzas written in iambic pentameter—that Alexander Pope made so effective (Mason 20). Considering that she is labeled as a spontaneous poet who would write during bouts of inspiration, the general regularity of her meter is remarkable. The influence of the Neoclassical writers also shows in Wheatley's use of elevated language (Mason 16) and in her numerous classical and mythological allusions.

Lauren refers to other points of view regarding Wheatley's work.

"To His Excellency General Washington" The poem "To His Excellency General Washington" serves as a good example of Wheatley's style. Troubled by poor health since her arrival in America in 1761, when she was only eight years old (Perkins et al. 272), Wheatley traveled from Boston to London in 1773 in hope that the sea air would improve her well-being. Upon her return to the rebellious colonies in 1774, she found the fighting in the Boston vicinity had escalated. Wheatley composed her poem to George Washington and crossed the battle lines to deliver it in person. Two years later, Wheatley received a letter from the general himself thanking her for her adulation but insisting that she had placed him on too high a pedestal. In April 1776, Thomas Paine published her poem, its accompanying note, and Washington's reply in Pennsylvania Magazine or American Monthly Museum (Sheeler 8–10).

The essay makes use of a variety of historical documents, including a primary source.

Although Washington's response to Wheatley's poem was modest, Wheatley gives the reader clear insight as to her opinions of the man. The entire poem is devoted to the veneration of the Continental Army and the leadership of General Washington. Wheatley adheres to her favorite poetic form of heroic couplets. She does not merely revere Washington, she portrays him as a royal figure, referring to him as "Your Excellency," and ascribing to him "a crown, a mansion and a throne that shine."

Wheatley resorts to a striking use of personification in the poem. In the opening lines, she mentions the sorrow of "mother earth" at the bloodshed ravaging the land. In line 15, she personifies heaven as a maiden with a "fair face." Her use of alliteration in that image adds to its effect. Wheatley also gives life to the "nations" in line 33 and describes Brittania as a defeated being who "droops the pensive head" (line 35).

Perhaps Wheatley's most notable use of personification lies in her image of the American colonies as the Goddess Columbia (line 9), who is a "native of the skies" (line 11). Wheatley created this new goddess in honor of Christopher Columbus. Later popularized by Revolutionary War poets such as Philip Freneau, the image of Columbia has its first appearance in Wheatley's poem (Jensen).

Wheatley also weaves various allusions into her poem. For example, the European countries in conflict with America are said to be "Gallic powers" (line 30). This allusion refers to the Gallic Wars at the time of Julius Caesar when France was called Gaul. Further evidence of her classical knowledge appears in the reference to "Aeolus," the God of the wind (line 15). Aeolus appeared in Homer's Odyssey (Tripp 24), which Wheatley read in Alexander Pope's famous translation. Wheatley scholars generally agree that Pope's translation of Homer greatly affected her poetry (Mason 16).

Although Phillis Wheatley never achieved a truly original poetic style, she is undoubtedly an important figure in American literature. She transcended racial and language barriers to occupy a significant position in the social and intellectual scene of both Boston and London. If one judges her work based on the impact of her poetry on her contemporaries, she is an important pioneer in the development of American literature.

Lauren concludes by restating her thesis.

Works Cited

Davis, Arthur P. "Personal Elements in the Poetry of Phillis Wheatley." *Phylon: The Atlanta University Review of Race and Culture*. 13 vols. June 1953, pp. 191–198.

Johnson, James Weldon., ed. *The Book of American Negro Poetry.* New York: Harcourt Brace Jovanovich Inc., 1922.

Mason, Julian D., Jr., ed. *The Poems of Phillis Wheatley.* North Carolina: The University of North Carolina Press, 1989.

Miller, James E., Jr., Carlota Cárdenas de Dwyer, and Kerry M. Wood. *The United States in Literature*. Illinois: Scott Foresman and Company, 1985.

Perkins, George, et al., eds. *The American Tradition in Literature.* 1 vol. New York: McGraw-Hill Publishing Company, 1990.

Redding, J. Saunders. *To Make a Poet Black*. New York: Cornell University Press, 1988.

Sheeler, Karissa L. Phillis Wheatley. 11 February 2000. <http://www.kutztown.edu/faculty/reagan/wheat1.html>

Smith, Valerie, Lea Baechler, and A. Walton Litz, eds. *African American Writers.* New York: Charles Scribner's Sons, 1991.

Tripp, Edward. *Cromwell's Handbook of Classical Mythology.* New York: Thomas Y. Cromwell Company, 1970.

A complete works-cited list provides information on the sources Lauren references in the report.

Editing and Proofreading

Review your historical investigation report to eliminate errors in grammar, usage, punctuation, and spelling.

Focus on accuracy. Consult your note cards to be sure you have quoted material exactly. Check all dates and statistics. You may need to return to the original source to check a specific fact.

Focus on capitalization and spelling. Make sure you have capitalized proper nouns correctly. Then, check your spelling. Follow this ***spelling rule:*** If an adjective ends in *-ent*, such as the word *expedient*, its parallel forms end in *-ence (expedience)* or *-ency (expediency).*

Spiral Review: Conventions Earlier you learned that misplaced and dangling modifiers can be confusing (p. 585). Check your report to make sure you have not used any misplaced or dangling modifiers.

Common Core State Standards

Writing
5. Develop and strengthen writing as needed by editing, focusing on addressing what is most significant for a specific purpose and audience.

Language
2. Demonstrate command of the conventions of standard English capitalization, punctuation, and spelling when writing.
2.b. Spell correctly.

Publishing, Presenting, and Reflecting

Consider the following ways to share and think further about your writing.

Present an oral historical investigation report. Deliver your paper as an oral report. Incorporate visual aids and images to illustrate specific information. Provide classmates with a handout listing your sources.

Submit your paper for publication. Submit your paper to a magazine or Web site that publishes student writing or that covers your research topic.

Reflect on your writing. Jot down your thoughts on the experience of writing a historical investigation report. Begin by answering these questions: What strategies would you use again? How was conducting in-depth research on a topic different from other types of research you have done?

PH WRITING COACH
Further instruction and practice are available in *Prentice Hall Writing Coach*.

Rubric for Self-Assessment

Evaluate your research report using the following criteria and rating scale.

Criteria	Rating Scale (*not very* – *very*)				
Focus: How clearly does your thesis statement guide your report?	1	2	3	4	5
Organization: How logical and effective is the organization?	1	2	3	4	5
Support/Elaboration: How well do you use a variety of primary and secondary sources to support your thesis?	1	2	3	4	5
Style: How well do you explain differences among your sources?	1	2	3	4	5
Conventions: According to an accepted format, how complete and accurate are your citations?	1	2	3	4	5

Oral Interpretation of a Literary Work

An *oral interpretation* is a performance of a literary work that highlights its most important qualities as the performer sees, or interprets, them. Generally, oral interpretations do not use scenery or other theatrical effects. Instead, they call upon a performer's ability to analyze a literary work and present it meaningfully, using *tone, vocal inflection, pacing,* and *body language.*

Prepare an Analysis of a Literary Work

Analyze the literature. To prepare a compelling oral interpretation, start by reading, analyzing, and researching a work of literature. As you read, consider the *stylistic devices* and elements shown in the chart.

Literary Element	Description	How to Identify
Tone	the author's attitude	Determine if the author is serious, playful, or critical.
Language and Style	the manner in which ideas are expressed	Study the lengths and rhythm of sentences, details, repetition, and changes to pronunciation, spelling, or grammar.
Imagery	word pictures that appeal to the senses	Analyze descriptions of places, objects, settings, or experiences.
Theme	a work's central idea, message, or insight about life	Identify the author's purpose and note images or ideas that repeat.
Nuance and Ambiguity	literary elements that can be interpreted in multiple ways	Look for significant words, figurative language, symbols, changes in characters, and the variety of meanings they may have.

Read, analyze, and research. Read your selection closely and analyze how specific literary elements help develop significant ideas and meaning. Consider both denotative, or literal, meanings, and connotative meanings, or the associations or feelings that words suggest. Make sure to address any elements that are open to interpretation. Research the selection by reviewing other texts, such as critical essays, to support your ideas. Then, write a brief analytical essay detailing your findings. Incorporate *rhetorical strategies* into your writing, such as describing your first impressions of the text or recalling conversations you had with others about your selection. You will use this essay to introduce your oral interpretation.

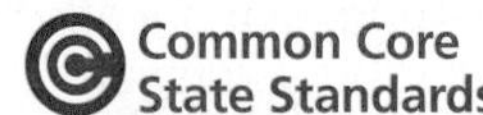

Reading Literature
7. Analyze multiple interpretations of a story, drama, or poem, evaluating how each version interprets the source text.

Writing
2. Write explanatory texts to examine and convey complex ideas, concepts, and information clearly and accurately through the effective selection, organization, and analysis of content.

Speaking and Listening
3. Evaluate a speaker's point of view, reasoning, and use of evidence and rhetoric, assessing the stance, premises, links among ideas, word choice, points of emphasis, and tone used.

4. Present information, findings, and supporting evidence, conveying a clear and distinct perspective, such that listeners can follow the line of reasoning, alternative or opposing perspectives are addressed, and the organization, development, substance, and style are appropriate to purpose, audience, and a range of formal and informal tasks.

Language
2. Demonstrate command of the conventions of standard English capitalization, punctuation, and spelling when writing.

5.a. Interpret figures of speech in context and analyze their role in the text.

5.b. Analyze nuances in the meaning of words with similar denotations.

Plan Your Interpretation

Focus on delivery techniques. Your oral interpretation should help listeners understand characters, follow shifts in plot, and hear changes in emotion. Consider how you will use the techniques shown in the graphic to add depth and drama to your interpretation.

Research other ways to enhance your performance by observing the body language and vocalization of an actor, poet, or other polished reader as he or she presents a literary work.

Vocalization

Reflect characters' speech patterns and *dialects*, and enunciate and project your voice.

Appropriate Eye Contact

Look at your listeners and make eye contact with people in the back as well as the front of the room.

Voice Register

Make characters distinct by using the high, low, and middle tones in your voice.

Gesture/Movement

Use hand gestures and move around your stage to show actions in the work.

Mark up the selection. Make notes on your copy of the selection indicating how you will use your voice and movement to communicate your understanding of the work. Also, consider using music, images, or sound effects to enhance the artistry of your interpretation.

Practice. Plan *staging and performance details* as you rehearse in front of a mirror or record yourself. For example, consider when to move, use gestures, or include simple props. Then, practice for family or friends and apply their feedback to improve your presentation.

Activities: Deliver and Analyze Oral Interpretations

Comprehension and Collaboration For both activities, use an evaluation form like the one shown below.

A. Deliver your oral interpretation to your class. First, read your analytical essay—or a shorter, less formal version—to introduce the literary work. Then, deliver your interpretation. After your performance, apply feedback from listeners to improve your delivery.

B. With a small group, analyze a variety of interpretations of the same literary work. You may use audio or video recordings, your own interpretations, or a combination of the two. Analyze how each version interprets the source text.

Evaluation Form for Oral Interpretation
Title and Author of Literary Work: ______
How well does the speaker convey the main idea of the selection? ______
How well does the speaker use gestures? Give examples. ______
Comment on one effective use of voice. ______
How well does the speaker maintain eye contact with the audience? ______
What can the speaker improve? ______

Vocabulary Workshop

Words from Mythology and Religious Traditions

Common Core State Standards

Language

4.a. Use context as a clue to the meaning of a word or phrase.

5. Demonstrate understanding of word relationships in word meanings.

6. Acquire and use accurately general academic and domain-specific words and phrases, sufficient for reading, writing, speaking, and listening at the college and career readiness level.

Many of the words in the English language have their origins in Greek or Roman mythology or the Bible. They entered the language during the Renaissance, a time when translations of classical and Biblical works became more readily available. Knowing the story behind the figure or event from which an English word developed will help you to infer its meaning and remember it more clearly.

For example, Hercules was an ancient Greek hero noted for his strength and his undertaking of enormous physical tasks. The word *herculean* derives from the qualities of this mythological hero, as seen in the sentence "*I was unable to face the herculean chore of cleaning my room.*" Based on the story of Hercules, you can figure out that the job of cleaning the room is huge and challenging. The chart below provides information on the mythological or Biblical origins of some common words.

Word	Origin	Myth
jovial	Roman	**Jove,** the chief Roman god, was believed to be the source of happiness.
mentor	Greek	In Homer's *Odyssey,* the goddess Athena disguises herself as **Mentor,** a human male, and guides Telemachus while his father is away.
nemesis	Greek	**Nemesis** was the goddess who punished mortals for their crimes against the gods.
panic	Greek	**Pan** was the god of untamed nature. His sudden appearance and the sound of his music inspired fear.
scapegoat	Biblical	An **escape goat** was sent into the wilderness to carry away the sins of the people.
tantalize	Greek	**Tantalus,** punished for murdering his son, was surrounded by food and water that moved out of reach whenever he wanted them.

Practice

Directions: Refer to the chart above to complete the **analogies.** Then, write an explanation of the word relationships for each pairing.

1. jovial : happiness :: _______ : panic

a. dark **b.** run **c.** afraid **d.** wild

2. mentor : _______ :: nemesis : enemy

a. lead **b.** teacher **c.** friend **d.** student

Directions: Make a four-column chart tracing the origins of each word below. The column heads should read: "Word," "Meaning Today," "Origin," "Sample Sentence." Use a dictionary as necessary.

1. dire **2.** spartan **3.** nectar

Vocabulary Acquisition and Use: Context Clues

Sentence Completion questions appear in most standardized tests. They are designed to test your ability to understand what a word means from its *context*, or the way it is used in a text. In these types of questions, you are given sentences with one or more missing words. Your task is to choose the correct word or words to complete each sentence logically. Try using the following strategy: (1) Define each word in the answer options. (2) Identify clues to the meanings of words that are unfamiliar. For example, identify root words, prefixes, suffixes, or related words. (3) Test possible meanings by plugging them into the original sentence.

Practice

This exercise is modeled after the Sentence Completion exercises that appear in the Critical Reading section of the SAT.

Test-Taking Tip
Later questions in this section of the test are more difficult than earlier ones.

Directions: Each of the following sentences is missing one or two words. Choose the word or set of words that best completes each sentence.

1. The untrained soldiers, a loose _______ of men, heard a _______ and surged forward.

A. monopoly . . . tempest
B. aggregation . . . commotion
C. congregation . . . spy
D. regiment . . . bark
E. amalgamation . . . whisper

2. The officers in the tent rose in _______ when their commander entered.

A. insubordination
B. alarm
C. deference
D. condemnation
E. disgust

3. Many in the audience yawned as the _______ speaker droned on.

A. intrepid
B. prodigious
C. compelling
D. garrulous
E. fervent

4. The frowning judge _______ banged the gavel to _______ the lawyer's statement.

A. peremptorily . . . forestall
B. aggressively . . . permit
C. repeatedly . . . encourage
D. happily . . . punctuate
E. playfully . . . contradict

5. The philosopher cautioned that fame is a(n) _______ goal.

A. transporting
B. transparent
C. transient
D. transcendental
E. transitional

6. Before dying, the miserly loner made sure to write his own _______ .

A. epigram
B. epitaph
C. epigraph
D. epitome
E. epistle

Test-Taking Practice

Reading Test: Humanities Passage

Humanities passages are one type of reading selection found on standardized tests. These passages may be excerpts from essays, biographies, or memoirs and address diverse topics including the arts, philosophy, and literary criticism. Questions may focus on main ideas and supporting details, the author's tone and style, or on the meanings of particular words or sentences. Some questions may require you to make generalizations or think about causes and effects.

Common Core State Standards

RL.11-12.3, RL.11-12.5, RL.11-12.6; RI.11-12.1, RI.11-12.4, RI.11-12.6; L.11-12.1, L.11-12.2, L.11-12.3, L.11-12.4.a.

[For the full wording of the standards, see the standards chart in the front of your textbook.]

Practice

The following exercise is modeled after the ACT Reading Test, Humanities section. The full test has 40 questions.

Directions: Read the following passage from Frederick Douglass's *My Bondage and My Freedom*. Then, choose the *best* answer to each question.

Strategy

- Look for words and phrases that convey the author's attitude toward the subject. Such words may be clues to nuances in the author's intended meaning or point of view.

Passage 1

It is easy to see, that, in entering upon the duties of a slaveholder, some little experience is needed. Nature has done almost nothing to prepare men and women to be either slaves or slaveholders. Nothing but rigid training, long persisted in, can perfect the character of the one or the other. One cannot easily forget to love freedom; and it is as hard to cease to respect that natural love in our fellow creatures. On entering upon the career of slaveholding mistress, Mrs. Auld was singularly deficient; nature, which fits nobody for such an office, had done less for her than any lady I had known. It was no easy matter to induce her to think and to feel that the curly-headed boy, who stood by her side, and even leaned on her lap; who was loved by little Tommy, and who loved little Tommy in turn; sustained to her only the relation of a chattel. I was *more* than that, and she felt me to be more than that. I could talk and sing; I could laugh and weep; I could reason and remember; I could love and hate. I was human, and she, dear lady, knew and felt me to be so. How could she, then, treat me as a brute, without a mighty struggle with all the noble powers of her own soul. That struggle came, and the will and power of the husband was victorious. Her noble soul was overthrown; but, he that overthrew it did not, himself, escape the consequences. He, not less than the other parties, was injured in his domestic peace by the fall.

1. Which of the following statements best summarizes lines 1–6?
   - **A.** Human history has a long record of slavery.
   - **B.** Slavery is an unnatural condition for both owner and slave.
   - **C.** Slaveholders who treat slaves kindly have been taught to do so.
   - **D.** Slaveholders are uncaring, cruel people.

2. In the context of lines 1–9, it can reasonably be inferred that *singularly* means:
   - **F.** alone.
   - **G.** on one occasion.
   - **H.** notably.
   - **J.** lonely.

3. Which best explains what Douglass means by calling Mrs. Auld "deficient" (line 8)?
   - **A.** She suffered from a disability.
   - **B.** She lacked financial resources.
   - **C.** She wasted few resources when running the home.
   - **D.** She lacked a certain characteristic.

4. In the context of the passage, it can reasonably be inferred that "little Tommy" (lines 11 and 12) is:
   - **F.** Mrs. Auld's favorite pet.
   - **G.** Mrs. Auld's child.
   - **H.** a slave like Douglass.
   - **J.** a neighbor.

5. Which best describes Douglass's overall opinion of Mrs. Auld?
   - **A.** She was a kindly woman with a generous nature.
   - **B.** She was a stiff and uncompromising person.
   - **C.** She stood up to her husband, defying him.
   - **D.** She was difficult to live with due to wild mood swings.

6. In the context of the first part of the passage, it can reasonably be inferred that *chattel* (line 12) means:
   - **F.** a lowly creature.
   - **G.** a kind of house.
   - **H.** constant talking.
   - **J.** a piece of property.

7. The ideas expressed in lines 9 through 15 can best be described as:
   - **A.** Douglass's view of his own situation at the time.
   - **B.** what Douglas came to believe as an adult.
   - **C.** Mrs. Auld's rationale for treating Douglass well.
   - **D.** the general attitude of Southerners toward slaves.

8. In the context of lines 9–21, it can reasonably be inferred that:
   - **F.** Mrs. Auld's treatment of Douglass changed.
   - **G.** Mr. Auld was convinced to be kind to Douglass as well.
   - **H.** Douglass ran away from the home.
   - **J.** Mrs. Auld suffered a nervous breakdown.

9. In the context of lines 18–21, which best describes Mr. Auld's "injury"?
   - **A.** He was struck in the head by a falling object.
   - **B.** The tranquility of his home was shattered.
   - **C.** His wife turned against him.
   - **D.** All his slaves revolted against him.

10. Which of the following statements best describes the structure of the passage?
    - **F.** It begins with an arresting anecdote and then draws general principles from that incident.
    - **G.** It contains several general arguments and supporting details to substantiate each one.
    - **H.** It opens with a generalization that helps explain the events that follow.
    - **J.** It follows a chronological structure and ends with a surprising twist.

Grammar and Writing: Editing in Context

Editing-in-context segments test your understanding of grammar and sentence structure. You may be presented with a reading passage that has numbered sentences, some of which contain errors in grammar, style, or usage. Your task is to choose the best way to correct each sentence.

Practice

The exercise is modeled after the ACT English Test, which usually has 75 questions.

Directions: For each underlined sentence or portion of a sentence, choose the best alternative. If an item asks a question about the underlined portion, choose the best answer to the question.

[1]

Lincoln begins the Second Inaugural Address formally but he (1) ends with an eloquent plea for reconciliation. In the opening paragraph (2), his use of the passive voice and refusal even to identify himself as an actor in the inaugural drama give the passage a stiff formality. This (3) matches his understated message, which is that he has nothing to say about the previous four years that he hasn't (4) said already.

[2]

When he begins (5) discussing slavery, though, Lincoln injects a moral seriousness into the address that is reinforced by his growing eloquence. Speculated (6) that the war might be divine retribution for decades of suffering endured by enslaved African Americans his speech (7) uses language and rhythms that deepen the impact of his message. Then the opening words of his final paragraph suggest a vision of reconciliation made memorable by his cadences—"With malice toward none; with charity for all" (8)—and the contrasting absolutes of "none" and "all." Lincoln concludes by expressing his sense of mission for the remainder of the war—"to bind up the nation's wounds" and to "achieve a just and lasting peace, among ourselves, and with all nations."

Strategy

Narrow the answer options.

Make your task simpler by eliminating any answers you know to be incorrect.

SAT® PREP ACT

1. A. NO CHANGE
   B. formally, but
   C. formally; but,
   D. formally. But

2. What is the function of this phrase?
   F. independent clause
   G. adverbial prepositional phrase
   H. adverbial dependent clause
   J. adjectival phrase

3. A. NO CHANGE
   B. This strategy
   C. This passive construction
   D. This formality

4. F. NO CHANGE
   G. has not
   H. have not
   J. hadn't

5. While reviewing Paragraph 2, the author considers deleting these two words. If the writer were to do so, the sentence would lose:
   A. the idea that the eloquence starts with the discussion of slavery.
   B. the idea that Lincoln views slavery as a moral evil.
   C. the idea that Lincoln delayed discussing slavery for much of the speech.
   D. nothing; they should be deleted.

6. F. NO CHANGE
   G. Speculating
   H. Lincoln speculated
   J. Asserted

7. A. NO CHANGE
   B. his speeches
   C. he speaks
   D. Lincoln

8. In reviewing the draft, the author considers moving this phrase to follow "his final paragraph" in the preceding line. If the writer were to do so, the effect would be:
   F. to misquote Lincoln and distort his meaning.
   G. to gain clarity about which phrases the author has in mind.
   H. to lose the author's emphasis on the rhythm of the phrases.
   J. to underscore Lincoln's moral message.

 Timed Writing: Position Statement [30 minutes]

The Civil War was the first war that people were able to witness through photographs. Some might say that images of war are important because they convey much more than words alone. Others might hold that showing pain and destruction is coldhearted and disrespectful to the victims.

Write an essay in which you express and support an opinion on this question. Whichever side you take, cite specific reasons and examples to support your position. This exercise is similar to the optional ACT Writing Test.

Academic Vocabulary

To "express and support an opinion" you must first decide **what** you think, and then tell **why** you think it.

Performance Tasks

Follow the instructions to complete the tasks below as required by your teacher. As you work on each task, incorporate both general academic vocabulary and literary terms you learned in this unit.

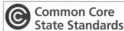

Common Core State Standards

RL.11-12.3, RL.11-12.6, RL.11-12.9; RI.11-12.1, RI.11-12.4, RI.11-12.6, RI.11-12.9; W.11-12.2, W.11-12.9.a, W.11-12.9.b; SL.11-12.1, SL.11-12.4, SL.11-12.6

[For the full wording of the standards, see the standards chart in the front of your textbook.]

Writing

Task 1: Literature [RL.11-12.3; W.11-12.2]

Analyze Characterization in a Story

*Write an **essay** in which you analyze the character development in a story from this unit.*

- Choose a story from this unit with memorable characters.
- Describe one of the main characters. Then, provide at least two examples of indirect and at least two examples of direct characterization from the story to support your description.
- Identify the setting and point of view of the story. Analyze the role each of these choices plays in influencing the development of the main character you chose.
- Describe how the story's plot events influence the main character's development.
- Conclude by briefly restating the impression that the main character creates for the reader and evaluating which story element (setting, point of view, or plot) has the greatest influence in creating that impression.

Task 2: Literature/Informational Text [RL.11-12.4; RI.11-12.4; W.11-12.2]

Analyze Word Choice

*Write an **essay** in which you analyze the meaning and impact of the word choices in a work of fiction or nonfiction from this unit.*

- Choose a work from this unit in which the writer uses a variety of interesting word choices.
- Choose particular passages in the work in order to highlight ones that you find especially effective.
- Analyze word choice by interpreting the meaning of key language in each passage and explaining why it is effective.
- Distinguish between literal meanings and figurative and connotative meanings in each passage you choose. Explain how figurative and connotative meanings add to the power of the passage and the overall work.
- Conclude by explaining how the word choice creates a tone and meaning that is appropriate to the author's audience and purpose.

Task 3: Informational Text [RI.11-12.5; W.11-12.2]

Analyze and Evaluate Text Structure

*Write an **essay** in which you analyze and evaluate the effectiveness of the structure of a work of literary nonfiction from this unit.*

- Choose a work of literary nonfiction from this unit that has a clear organizational structure.
- Identify and analyze the structure of the author's argument. For example, does the author use cause and effect, comparison and contrast, or main idea and details?
- Evaluate the effectiveness of the structure for conveying the author's main argument. Assess whether the structure makes individual points clear and helps make the overall argument convincing.
- Support your analysis with examples from the work.
- Organize your ideas logically, using transitional words, phrases, and clauses to clearly show the link between ideas.

Speaking and Listening

Task 4: Literature/Informational Text [RL.11-12.6; RI.11-12.6; SL.11-12.1]

Analyze Irony

Hold a ***panel discussion*** *in which you analyze various authors' use of irony in works from this unit.*

- Identify all works from this unit in which irony features prominently.
- As a group, discuss why each selection you choose is ironic and identify the type of irony it represents.
- Evaluate what the author's use of irony adds to the theme or meaning of each selection.
- Finally, compare a single author's use of irony in one selection with another author's use of irony in a work from the same unit or in something else you have read or seen.
- Make sure that each person on the panel gets an opportunity to speak. Allow time for follow-up questions and debate, and try to build on each other's ideas to reach a final consensus.

Task 5: Informational Text [RI.11-12.9; SL.11-12.4]

Evaluate a Work of Nonfiction and Two Foundational Documents

Deliver an ***oral presentation*** *in which you assess whether the social injustices described by Frederick Douglass in the excerpt from* My Bondage and My Freedom *were addressed by the Emancipation Proclamation and the Fourteenth Amendment.*

- Review the excerpt from *My Bondage and My Freedom.* Identify the individual injustices that Douglass describes in the excerpt.
- Find the texts of the Emancipation Proclamation and the Fourteenth Amendment online or in print.
- Analyze and compare the purposes, themes, and language of the autobiographical account and the two historical documents.
- Assess the two documents to determine whether they address Douglass's grievances completely, partially, or not at all.
- Organize and present your findings logically, so your audience can easily follow your reasoning.

Task 6: Literature [RL.11-12.3, RL.11-12.6; SL.11-12.4]

Identify and Analyze Point of View

Deliver an ***oral presentation*** *in which you identify and analyze the point of view in a work of fiction from this unit.*

- Choose a story that effectively uses point of view.
- Identify point of view by describing whether a story is written from a first- or third-person and limited or omniscient perspective. Explain to your audience how you made this determination.
- Analyze the impact of the author's choice of point of view on the story. Do this by relating point of view to other elements in the story, such as character development or plot, and to the use of devices such as irony or understatement.
- Present your ideas in a way that makes them easy for listeners to follow.

What makes American literature American?

Primary Sources and Fiction Primary sources, such as journals and speeches, speak to readers with great immediacy, even centuries after they were written. They help us understand how people experienced life in the past. Short stories and poems also shed light on people's sense of identity and aspects of their culture at a particular time in history, but their effect is often different from that of a primary source.

Assignment Choose one primary source and one work of fiction from this unit. Write a **compare-and-contrast essay** about how the two works add to your understanding of American identity during the Civil War era.

Featured Titles

In this unit, you have read a variety of literature of the Civil War and Frontier eras. Continue to read works related to these eras on your own. Select books that you enjoy, but challenge yourself to explore new topics, new authors, and works offering varied perspectives or approaches. The titles suggested below will help you get started.

LITERATURE

The Adventures of Huckleberry Finn
Mark Twain

Novel Set in pre-Civil War Missouri, this influential novel describes the adventures of two runaways on a raft on the Mississippi River—Huck Finn, who is escaping his abusive father, and Jim, a slave hoping to gain his freedom.

[Works by Twain begin on page 570 of this book. Build knowledge by reading a novel by this author.]

My Ántonia
Willa Cather

Novel The story of Ántonia, a self-reliant, spirited young woman growing up on the Nebraska frontier, is told by her friend and confidant, Jim Burden. *My Ántonia* chronicles their friendship and reveals both the beauty and hardship of frontier life.

[Cather's "A Wagner Matinée" appears on page 652 of this book. Build knowledge by reading a novel by this author.]

Spoon River Anthology
Edgar Lee Masters

Poetry The former residents of an Illinois town, now long dead, tell the stories of their lives from the graveyard in which they lie.

[On pages 646 and 647, you'll find "Lucinda Matlock" and "Richard Bone," two of the poems from Spoon River Anthology*. Build knowledge by reading the complete anthology.]*

INFORMATIONAL TEXTS

Historical Texts

The Classic Slave Narratives
edited by Henry Louis Gates, Jr.

Autobiographical Narrative This book presents the accounts of two men and two women who had been enslaved and describes their extraordinary experiences, ranging from surviving the dangerous Atlantic Crossing to enduring the brutal, and often short, life of a slave in the Caribbean colonies and in America.

Narrative of the Life of Frederick Douglass
Frederick Douglass

Autobiographical Narrative Born into slavery, Frederick Douglass escaped to become an abolitionist leader as well as a gifted writer and orator. This narrative describes the cruelty of slavery and gives a powerful voice to a disenfranchised people.

[An excerpt from My Bondage and My Freedom *appears on page 520 of this book. Build knowledge by reading Douglass's autobiographical narrative.]*

The American Reader: Words That Moved a Nation
edited by Diane Ravitch
HarperCollins, 1990

Prose and Poetry This collection of prose and poetry by famous and ordinary Americans from different socioeconomic and racial backgrounds provides the reader with a rich view of American culture and history.

Contemporary Scholarship

Empire Express: Building the First Transcontinental Railroad
David Haward Bain

History On May 10, 1868, the last spike was driven to complete the transcontinental railroad. *Empire Express* describes the race to complete the railroad and presents a fresh view of the history and impact of this engineering triumph.

What They Fought For 1861–1865
James McPherson
Anchor Books, 1995

EXEMPLAR TEXT 

History Scholar James McPherson investigates what motivated Civil War soldiers to fight, based on their letters and journals. Through the voices of these long-dead soldiers, McPherson gives readers a strong sense of the intense passions and ideological conflicts of the time.

Preparing to Read Complex Texts

Reading for College and Career In both college and the workplace, readers must analyze texts independently, draw connections among works that offer varied perspectives, and develop their own ideas and informed opinions. The questions shown below, and others that you generate on your own, will help you more effectively read and analyze complex college-level texts.

Reading Literature/Informational Text
10. By the end of grade 11, read and comprehend literature, including stories, dramas, and poems, and literary nonfiction, in the grades 11-CCR text complexity band proficiently, with scaffolding as needed at the high end of the range.

When reading analytically, ask yourself...

- What idea, experience, or story seems to have compelled the author to write? Has the author presented that idea, experience, or story in a way that I, too, find compelling?
- How might the author's era, social status, belief system, or personal experiences have affected the point of view he or she expresses in the text?
- How do my circumstances affect what I understand and feel about this text?
- What key idea does the author state explicitly? What key idea does he or she suggest or imply? Which details in the text help me to perceive implied ideas?
- Do I find multiple layers of meaning in the text? If so, what relationships do I see among these layers of meaning?
- How do details in the text connect or relate to one another? Do I find any details unconvincing, unrelated, or out of place?
- Do I find the text believable and convincing?

Key Ideas and Details

- What patterns of organization or sequences do I find in the text? Do these patterns help me understand the ideas better?
- What do I notice about the author's style, including his or her diction, use of imagery and figurative language, and syntax?
- Do I like the author's style? Is the author's style memorable?
- What emotional attitude does the author express toward the topic, the story, or the characters? Does this attitude seem appropriate?
- What emotional attitude does the author express toward me, the reader? Does this attitude seem appropriate?
- What do I notice about the author's voice—his or her personality on the page? Do I like this voice? Does it make me want to read on?

Craft and Structure

- Is the work fresh and original?
- Do I agree with the author's ideas entirely, or are there elements I find unconvincing?
- Do I disagree with the author's ideas entirely, or are there elements I can accept as true?
- Based on my knowledge of American literature, history, and culture, does this work reflect the American tradition? Why or why not?

Integration of Ideas

Resources

Reading and Vocabulary Handbook **R1**
English Glossary R1
Spanish Glossary R7
Life of the English Language R14
Tips for Improving Fluency R16

Literary Handbook **R18**
Approaches to Criticism R18
Citing Sources and Preparing Manuscript R21
Literary Terms R24

Writing Handbook **R34**
College Application Essay R34
Workplace Writing R35
Job Search Documents: Cover Letter, Résumé Job Application
Business Communications: Business Letter, Memo, E-mail, Meeting Minutes, Technical Writing
Guide to Rubrics R43

21st Century Skills **R47**
Blogs, Web Safety, Social Networking, Podcasts, Wikis R47
Research and Technology Guide R51

Communications Handbook **R53**
Tips for Discussing Literature R53
Oral and Visual Communication R54

Grammar, Usage, and Mechanics Handbook (with Spelling Tips) **R56**

Indexes **R64**

Acknowledgments **R80**

Credits **R81**

English Glossary

Essential Question vocabulary appears in **blue type**. High-Utility Academic Vocabulary is **underlined**.

A

abeyance (uh BAY uhns) *n.* temporary suspension

absolve (ab ZOLV) *v.* pardon; free from guilt

absurdity (ab SUR duh tee) *n.* nonsense; ridiculousness

accosted (uh KAWST uhd) *v.* approached and spoke to in an eager way

account (uh KOWNT) *n.* a report or description

acknowledges (ak NOL ihj) *v.* to admit the existence, reality, or truth of

acquiesce (AK wee EHS) *v.* agree without protest

adamant (AD uh mant) *adj.* firm; unyielding

adjourned (uh JURND) *v.* closed for a time

advantageous (ad vuhn TAY juhs) *adj.* favorable; beneficial

adversary (AD vuhr sehr ee) *n.* opponent; enemy

adversity (ad VUR suh tee) *n.* hardship; difficulty

affections (uh FEHK shuhnz) *n.* emotions

affliction (uh FLIHK shuhn) *n.* anything causing pain or distress

agape (uh GAYP) *adj.* in surprise; wonder

aggregation (ag ruh GAY shuhn) *n.* group of distinct objects or individuals

agricultural (ag ruh KUHL chuhr uhl) *adj.* with farming as the main way of life

alacrity (uh LAK ruh tee) *n.* speed

alienation (AY lee uh NAY shuhn) *n.* a withdrawing or separation of feeling or affection

alliance (uh LY uhns) *n.* union of nations for a specific purpose

ambiguity (AM buh GYOO uh tee) *n.* state of having two or more possible meanings

ambition (am BIHSH uhn) *n.* strong desire to gain a particular objective; drive to succeed

ameliorate (uh MEEL yuh rayt) *v.* make better

ample (AM puhl) *adj.* large in size; more than enough

<u>analyze</u> (AN uh lyz) *v.* break down a topic into parts and explain them

anarchy (AN uhr kee) *n.* absence of government

ancestor (AN sehs tuhr) *n.* person from whom other people descend

anonymity (an uh NIHM uh tee) *n.* the condition of being unknown

<u>anticipate</u> (an TIHS uh payt) *v.* prepare for or signal something

anxiety (ang ZY uh tee) *n.* state of being uneasy, apprehensive, or worried about what may happen.

apparel (uh PAR uhl) *n.* clothing

apparition (ap uh RIHSH uhn) *n.* act of appearing or becoming visible

appease (uh PEEZ) *v.* satisfy

appendage (uh PEHN dihj) *n.* external part of a plant or animal, such as a tail or a limb

<u>appraise</u> (uh PRAYZ) *v.* evaluate something's worth, significance, or status

apprehension (ap rih HEHN shuhn) *n.* an anxious feeling of foreboding; dread

appropriate (uh PROH pree ayt) *v.* to take or use something without permission

arduous (AHR joo uhs) *adj.* difficult

<u>argue</u> (AHR gyoo) *v.* give reasons for or against; prove by giving reasons

<u>arrange</u> (uh RAYNJ) *v.* put into order or sequence

ascended (uh SEHND uhd) *v.* climbed up

aspirations (as puh RAY shuhnz) *n.* strong desires or ambitions

assault (uh SAWLT) *n.* violent attack

assent (uh SEHNT) *n.* agreement

<u>assess</u> (uh SEHS) *v.* determine importance, size, or value

austerity (aw STEHR uh tee) *n.* sternness in manner or appearance; harshness; severity

auxiliary (awg ZIHL yuhr ee) *adj.* giving help or support

avarice (AV uhr ihs) *n.* greed

aversion (uh VUR zhuhn) *n.* object arousing an intense dislike

avidly (AV ihd lee) *adv.* eagerly

awe (aw) *n.* mixed feelings of fear and wonder

B

base (bays) *adj.* low; mean

beguile (bih GYL) *v.* charm or delight

benediction (behn uh DIHK shuhn) *n.* prayer asking for God's blessing

benevolent (buh NEHV uh luhnt) *adj.* kindly; charitable

benign (bih NYN) *adj.* not injurious or malignant; not cancerous

bequeath (bih KWEETH) *v.* hand down; pass on

blaspheming (BLAS feem ihng) *v.* cursing

brazenness (BRAY zuhn nehs) n. shamelessness; boldness; impudence

brigade (brih GAYD) n. a unit of soldiers

brutal (BROO tuhl) adj. cruel and without feeling; savage; violent

C

cadence (KAY duhns) *n.* a series of notes or chords near the end of a musical work

calamity (kuh LAM uh tee) *n.* disaster; catastrophe

calumny (KAL uhm nee) *n.* false accusation; slander

candid (KAN dihd) *adj.* straightforward

canvass (KAN vuhs) *v.* go through an area asking people for votes, orders, or participation

capable (KAY puh buhl) *adj.* having the skills needed to do something

caper (KAY puhr) *n.* prank

casualties (KAZH oo uhl teez) *n.* members of the armed forces who die in combat

<u>categorize</u> (KAT uh guh ryz) *v.* place in related groups

cavernous (KAV uhr nuhs) *adj.* cavelike; vast

celestial (suh LEHS chuhl) *adj.* of or in the sky, as planets or stars

chaos (KAY os) *n.* disorder of matter and space, supposed to have existed before the ordered universe

chronicles (KRON uh kuhlz) *n.* stories; histories

circumvent (sur kuhm VEHNT) *v.* prevent; get around

civilian (suh VIHL yuhn) *n.* any person who is not a member of the armed forces

<u>classify</u> (KLAS uh fy) *v.* assign to a category

cleave (kleev) *v.* adhere; cling

coinage (KOY nihj) *n.* an invented word or expression

coincide (koh ihn SYD) *v.* to occur at the same time

collective (kuh LEHK tihv) *n.* gathered into a whole

collusion (kuh LOO zhuhn) *n.* secret agreement; conspiracy

commercial (kuh MUR shuhl) *adj.* connected with trade or business

commissioners (kuh MIHSH uh nuhrz) *n.* government officials

commonplace (KOM uhn PLAYS) *adj.* everyday; ordinary

commotion (kuh MOH shuhn) *n.* noisy confusion

community (kuh MYOO nuh tee) *n.* all the people living a particular district, city, or area

<u>compare</u> (kuhm PAIR) *v.* point out similarities or differences

conciliatory (kuhn SIHL ee uh tawr ee) *adj.* intended to make peace or to reconcile; friendly

conclude (kuhn KLOOD) *v.* reach as a logically necessary end by reasoning

condolences (kuhn DOH luhns ez) *n.* expressions of sympathy

conduct (KON duhkt) *n.* behavior

conflagration (kon fluh GRAY shuhn) *n.* big, destructive fire

conformity (kuhn FAWR muh tee) *n.* action in agreement with generally accepted standards

confounded (kon FOWN dihd) *adj.* confused; dismayed

conjectural (kuhn JEHK chuhr uhl) *adj.* based on guesswork

conjectured (kuhn JEHK chuhrd) *v.* guessed

conjuring (KON juhr ihng) *v.* causing to be; appearing as by magic

consecrate (KON suh krayt) *v.* cause to be revered or honored

conspicuous (kuhn SPIHK yoo uhs) *adj.* obvious; easy to see or perceive

consternation (kon stuhr NAY shuhn) *n.* great fear or shock that makes one feel helpless or bewildered

constitute (KON stuh toot) *v.* serve as the parts or basis of; form; comprise

constitution (kon stuh TOO shuhn) *n.* physical makeup of a person

contentious (kuhn TEHN shuhs) *adj.* argumentative

contiguous (kuhn TIHG yoo uhs) *adj.* bordering; adjacent

contract (KON trakt) *n.* written agreement

contrast (KON trast) *v.* examine to discover differences

convention (kuhn VEHN shuhn) *n.* a meeting attended by members or delegates

conviction (kuhn VIHK shuhn) *n.* strong belief

convivial (kuhn VIHV ee uhl) *adj.* fond of good company; sociable

copious (KOH pee uhs) *adj.* plentiful; abundant

correspond (KAWR uh SPOND) *v.* be in agreement; relate to

countenance (KOWN tuh nuhns) *v.* approve; tolerate

cowering (KOW uhr ihng) *v.* trembling or cringing, as with fear

create (kree AYT) *v.* produce through imaginative skill

crevices (KREHV ihs iz) *n.* narrow openings caused by cracks or splits

critic (KRIHT ihk) *n.* person who disapproves or finds fault

critique (krih TEEK) *v.* examine critically; review

cunning (KUHN ihng) *adj.* skillful in deception; crafty; sly

cyberspace (SY buhr SPAYS) *n.* online world of computer networks

D

daunting (DAWNT ihng) *adj.* intimidating

decorum (dih KAWR uhm) *n.* rightness; suitability

deduce (dih DOOS) *v.* infer from a general principle

defend (dih FEHND) *v.* maintain or support in the face of argument

deference (DEHF uhr uhns) *n.* courteous regard or respect

deficient (dih FIHSH uhnt) *adj.* lacking; not having something needed

define (dih FYN) *v.* tell the qualities that make something what it is

degenerate (dih JEHN uh ruht) *adj.* morally corrupt

dejected (dih JEHK tihd) *v.* in low spirits; downcast; depressed

deliberation (dih lihb uh RAY shuhn) *n.* careful consideration

deposition (dehp uh ZIHSH uhn) *n.* testimony of a witness made under oath but not in open court

depths (dehpths) *n.* deepest areas

derivative (dih RIHV uh tihv) *adj.* not original; based on something else

derive (dih RYV) *v.* trace to or from a source; get by reasoning

describe (dih SKRYB) *v.* represent in words

design (dih ZYN) *v.* create, fashion, execute, or construct according to plan

desolate (DEHS uh liht) *adj.* deserted; isolated

despondent (dih SPON duhnt) *adj.* without courage or hope

despotism (DEHS puh tihz uhm) *n.* absolute rule; tyranny

destitute (DEHS tuh toot) *adj.* living in complete poverty

destruction (dih STRUHK shuhn) *n.* act of demolishing or defeating

detached (dih TACHT) *adj.* not emotionally involved

devise (dih VYZ) *v.* form in the mind by new combinations of ideas; invent

dictum (DIHK tuhm) *n.* formal statement of fact or opinion

differentiate (DIHF uh REHN shee ayt) *v.* recognize a dissimilarity

digress (duh GREHS) *v.* depart temporarily from the main subject

dilapidated (duh LAP uh day tuhd) *adj.* in disrepair

diligence (DIHL uh juhns) *n.* constant, careful effort; perseverance

discern (duh SURN) *v.* perceive or recognize; make out clearly

discord (DIHS kawrd) *n.* difference of opinion; disputing

discretion (dihs KREHSH uhn) *n.* judgment

discriminate (dihs KRIHM uh nayt) *v.* recognize differences between or among things

disdainfully (dihs DAYN fuhl ee) *adv.* showing scorn or contempt

disgrace (dihs GRAYS) *n.* something that brings shame or dishonor

disillusion (DIHS ih LOO zhuhn) *n.* freedom from a false idea; disenchantment

dispatched (dihs PACHT) *v.* sent off, usually on official business

dispersal (dihs PUR suhl) *n.* distribution

disposition (dihs puh ZIHSH uhn) *n.* inclination; tendency

disregard (dihs rih GAHRD) *v.* to pay no attention to; leave out of consideration; ignore

dissembling (dih SEHM buhl ihng) *v.* disguising one's real nature or motives

dissention (dih SEHN shuhn) *n.* disagreement; discord as expressed in intense quarreling

dissuade (dih SWAYD) *v.* convince someone not to do something

distinguish (dihs TIHNG gwihsh) *v.* mark as separate or different

diversity (duh VUR suh tee) *n.* variety; point of unlikeness

divine (duh VYN) *v.* find out by intuition

docile (DOS uhl) adj. easy to direct or manage: obedient

doctrine (DOK truhn) *n.* what is taught

dogma (DAWG muh) *n.* authoritative doctrines or beliefs

dubious (DOO bee uhs) *adj.* questionable; suspicious

duplicate (DOO pluh kayht) *v.* make a copy

duration (du RAY shuhn) *n.* the time during which something continues or exists

dusky (DUHS kee) *adj.* dark; dim; shadowy

dyspepsia (dihs PEHP see uh) *n.* indigestion

E

ecstasy (EHKS tuh see) *n.* a feeling of overpowering joy; great delight

efface (uh FAYS) *v.* erase; wipe out

effigies (eh FIHJ eez) *n.* images or likenesses, especially of people

effrontery (uh FRUHN tuhr ee) *n.* shameless boldness

effuse (ih FYOOZ) *v.* pour out; gush

eloquence (EHL uh kwuhns) *n.* talent for vivid, forceful speech

elusive (ih LOO sihv) *adj.* hard to grasp

embankment (ehm BANGK muhnt) *n.* mound of earth or stone built to hold back water or support or a roadway

embark (ehm BAHRK) *v.* to begin a venture, project, or activity

emigrants (EHM uh gruhnts) *n.* people who leave one place to settle in another

eminence (EHM uh nuhns) *n.* greatness; celebrity

emit (ih MIHT) *v.* utter words or sounds

enamored (ehn AM uhrd) *adj.* charmed; captivated

encroached (ehn KROHCHT) *v.* intruded

endured (ehn DURD) *v.* held up under

engrossed (ehn GROHST) *v.* occupied wholly; absorbed

entreated (ehn TREET uhd) *v.* begged; pleaded

entrenchments (ehn TREHNCH muhnts) *n.* long deep holes with steep sides, used as defense against enemy fire

environment (ehn VY ruhn muhnt) *n.* the surrounding objects or conditions

epitaph (EHP uh taf) *n.* inscription on a tombstone or grave marker

equivocal (ih KWIHV uh kuhl) *adj.*having more than one possible interpretation

eradicate (ih RAD uh kayt) *v.* wipe out; destroy

establishment (ehs TAB lihsh muhnt) *n.* household or business

estimates (EHS tuh mihts) *n.* general, careful calculations

etiquette (EHT uh keht) *n.* appropriate behavior and ceremonies

evacuated (ih VAK yu ayt uhd) *v.* emptied; withdrawn

evade (ih VAYD) *v.* avoid or escape from by deceit or cleverness

evaluate (ih VAL yu ayt) *v.* determine something's significance, worth, or condition through careful study

exalted (ehg ZAWL tihd) *adj.* filled with joy or pride; elated

examine (ehg ZAM uhn) *v.* carefully inquire into a topic

exasperation (ehg zas puh RAY shuhn) *n.* annoyance; frustration

exhaust (ehg ZAWST) *n.* discharge of used steam or gas from an engine

exile (EHG zyl) *n.* the state or period of being banished

expansion (ehk SPAN shuhn) *n.* act or process of increasing in extent, size, or volume

expedient (ehk SPEE dee uhnt) *n.* method used to achieve a goal quickly

expenditures (ehk SPEHN duh churz) *n.* expenses; uses of money or resources

exposures (ehk SPOH zhuhrz) *n.* sections of film on which light falls when a photograph is taken

extort (ehk STAWRT) *v.* obtain by threat or violence

extraneous (ehk STRAY nee uhs) *adj.* unrelated; unconnected

F

fallowness (FAL oh nuhs) *n.* inactivity

fantastic (fan TAS tihk) *adj.* excellent; unbelievable

fastidious (fas TIHD ee uhs) *adj.* careful; meticulous

fatigues (fuh TEEGZ) *n.* sturdy clothing worn by soldiers doing hard work

feigned (faynd) *v.* pretended

fervent (FUR vuhnt) *adj.* extremely passionate; very enthusiastic

finite (FY nyt) *adj.* having measurable or definable limits

fitfully (FIHT fuhl ee) *adv.* characterized by irregular or intermittent activity

flagrant (FLAY gruhnt) *adj.* glaring; outrageous

flourished (FLUR ihsht) *v.* grew strong, healthy, and happy; prospered

fluctuation (fluhk chu AY shuhn) *n.* a change in level or intensity

foothold (FUT hohld) *n.* secure position from which further actions can be taken

forded (FAWRD uhd) *v.* crossed a river at a low point

forestall (fawr STAWL) *v.* prevent by acting ahead of time

formulate (FAWR myuh layt) *v.* express fully and clearly

fortuitous (fawr TOO uh tuhs) *adj.* fortunate

fortune (FAWR chuhn) *n.* wealth; luck

fragmentation (frag muhn TAY shuhn) *n.* act or process of breaking up into parts

frantic (FRAN tihk) *adj.* marked by frenzy

frayed (frayd) *adj.* tattered

freedom (FREE duhm) *n.* not being under another's control

frontier (fruhn TIHR) *n.* border between inhabited regions; a developing region of field of thought

furtive (FUR tihv) *adj.* sneaky

G

garrulous (GAR uh luhs) *adj.* talking too much

gaudy (GAW dee) *adj.* showy in a tasteless way

generalize (JEHN uhr uh lyz) *v.* draw a larger principle from details

genial (JEEN yuhl) *adj.* cheerful; friendly

genre (zhahn ruh) *n.* catagory, or style

global (GLOH buhl) *adj.* spread throughout the world

govern (GUHV uhrn) *v.* to rule; control; manage

grandeur (GRAN juhr) *n.* greatness

grave (grayv) *adj.* serious; solemn

gravity (GRAV uh tee) *n.* seriousness

guile (gyl) *n.* craftiness

H

habitation (hab uh TAY shuhn) *n.* place to live; group of homes or dwellings

hallow (HAL oh) *v.* honor as sacred

handiwork (HAN dee wurk) *n.* work done by the hands; work done personally

harass (HUH ras) *v.* attack; bother

heady (HEHD ee) *adj.* intoxicating

heightened (HY tuhnd) *v.* raised the level of

heritage (HEHR uh tihj) *n.* traits, beliefs, or customs passed on from one's ancestors

homages (HOM ihj uhz) *n.* acts showing honor and reverence

homely (HOHM lee) *adj.* not elegant or polished; crude

huddled (HUHD uhld) *v.* gathered closely; nestled

humor (HYOO muhr) *n.* funny or amusing quality

hypothesize (hy POTH uh syz) *v.* develop a theory about

I

idealism (y DEE uh lihz uhm) *n.* thought based on following standards of perfection or beauty

identify (y DEHN tuh fy) *v.* establish the identity of something

identity (y DEHN tuh tee) *n.* who a person is

illiterate (ih LIHT uhr iht) *adj.* unable to read or write

illustrate (IHL uh strayt) *v.* give examples that support an idea

immigration (ihm uh GRAY shuhn) *n.* act of coming into a foreign country or region to live

imperceptible (ihm puhr SEHP tuh buhl) *adj.* not easy to perceive; unnoticeable

impertinent (ihm PUR tuh nuhnt) *adj.* not showing proper respect; saucy

implore (ihm PLAWR) *v.* ask or beg earnestly; plead

imply (ihm PLY) *v.* hint or suggest

impulsive (ihm PUHL sihv) *adj.* done without thinking

impulsively (ihm PUHL sihv lee) *adv.* spontaneously; suddenly

inanimate (ihn AN uh miht) *adj.* not alive; lifeless

inarticulate (ihn ahr TIHK yuh liht) *adj.* unclearly spoken or expressed

inaudibly (ihn AW duh blee) *adv.* in a manner that cannot be heard

incessant (ihn SEHS uhnt) *adj.* constant; seemingly endless

incorporated (ihn KAWR puh rayt uhd) *v.* organized as a legal corporation

incorrigible (ihn KAWR uh juh buhl) *adj.* impossible to correct; incurable

incredulously (ihn KREHD juh luhs lee) *adv.* skeptically

increment (IHN kruh muhnt) *n.* increase, as in a series

indelible (ihn DEHL uh buhl) *adj.* permanent; that cannot be erased

independence (IHN dih PEHN duhns) *n.* freedom from the control of others

individualism (IHN duh VIHJ u uh LIHZ uhm) *n.* belief that personal freedom is most important

induce (ihn DOOS) *v.* cause; bring about

industry (IHN duh stree) *n.* any branch of business, trade, or manufacturing

ineffable (ihn EHF uh buhl) *adj.* too overwhelming to be spoken

inert (ihn URT) *adj.* motionless

inextricable (ihn EHK struh kuh buhl) *adj.* unable to be separated or freed from

infer (ihn FUR) *v.* derive a conclusion from facts or premises

infinity (ihn FIHN uh tee) *n.* endless or unlimited space, time, or distance

ingratiating (ihn GRAY shee ay tihng) *adj.* charming or flattering

innovation (ihn uh VAY shuhn) *n.* a new idea, method, or device

innumerable (ih NOO muhr uh buhl) *adj.* too many to count

insatiable (ihn SAY shuh buhl) *adj.* constantly wanting more

inscrutable (ihn SKROO tuh buhl) *adj.* not able to be easily understood

inseparable (ihn SEHP uhr uh buhl) *adj.* not able to be divided; linked

insidious (ihn SIHD ee uhs) *adj.* deceitful; treacherous

inspection (ihn SPEHK shuhn) *n.* examination

intent (ihn TEHNT) *n.* purpose or aim

intently (ihn TEHNT lee) *adv.* in a focused, purposeful manner

intercepted (ihn tuhr SEHPT uhd) *v.* seized or stopped something on its way from one place to another

interminable (ihn TUR muh nuh buhl) *adj.* seeming to last forever

interposed (ihn tuhr POHZD) *v.* came between

interspersed (ihn tuhr SPURSD) *v.* placed here and there

intervene (ihn tuhr VEEN) *v.* take action in order to prevent something

intolerable (ihn TOL uhr uh buhl) *adj.* difficult or painful that it cannot be endured; unbearable

intonation (ihn toh NAY shuhn) *n.* the quality of playing musical notes in or out of tune

intricate (IHN truh kiht) *adj.* complex; having many small, interrelated parts

intuitively (ihn TOO uh tihv lee) *adv.* without having to be taught; instinctively

invective (ihn VEHK tihv) *n.* verbal attack; strong criticism

invent (ihn VEHNT) *v.* devise by thinking

investigate (ihn VEHS tuh gayt) *v.* make a systematic examination

J

jocularity (jok yuh LAR uh tee) *n.* joking good humor

jubilant (JOO buh luhnt) *adj.* joyful and triumphant

judge (juhj) *v.* form an estimate or evaluation of something

judgment (JUHJ muhnt) *n.* power to form an opinion well; good sense

justify (JUHS tuh fy) v. prove or show to be just, right, or reasonable

L

label (LAY buhl) *v.* describe or designate

lament (luh MEHNT) *v.* to express sorrow for; mourn aloud for

landscape (LAND skayp) *n.* an area that can be seen at one time from one place

latent (LAY tuhnt) *adj.* present but invisible or inactive

latitude (LAT uh tood) *n.* distance north or south from the equator

levee (LEHV ee) *n.* embankment built along the side of a river to prevent flooding

liberty (LIHB uhr tee) *n.* freedom

license (LY suhns) *n.* freedom from appropriate behavior or speech

licentious (ly SEHN shuhs) *adj.* lacking moral restraint

limber (LIHM buhr) *adj.* flexible

list (lihst) *v.* make a list; enumerate

listed (LIHST uhd) *v.* tilted; inclined

locate (LOH kayt) *v.* find the place of something

longitude (LON juh tood) *n.* distance east or west on the earth's surface

lulled (luhld) *v.* calmed or soothed by a gentle sound or motion

luminary (LOO muh nehr ee) *adj.* giving off light

M

machetes (muh SHEHT eez) *n.* large heavy knives with broad blades

magnanimity (mag nuh NIHM uh tee) *n.* generosity

magnitude (MAG nuh tood) *n.* greatness of size

maledictions (mal uh DIHK shuhnz) *n.* curses

malign (muh LYN) *adj.* malicious; very harmful

malingers (muh LIHNG guhrz) *v.* pretends to be ill

maneuver (muh NOO vuhr) *v.* to move something by some plan or scheme

manifold (MAN uh fohld) *adj.* in many ways

martial (MAHR shuhl) *adj.* relating to war

marvel (MAHR vuhl) *n.* wonderful or astonishing thing

master (MAS tuhr) *v.* become an expert in

media (MEE dee uh) *n.* systems of communication designed to reach the masses

mediator (MEE dee ay tuhr) *n.* one who reconciles opposing groups

melancholy (MEHL uhn kol ee) *adj.* sad and depressed; gloomy

membrane (MEHM brayn) *n.* thin, soft layer serving as a covering or lining

memorials (muh MAWR ee uhlz) *n.* objects displayed in memory of a person or event

meticulous (muh TIHK yuh luhs) *adj.* extremely careful about details

metropolis (muh TROP uh lihs) *n.* large city

migrant (MY gruhnt) *adj.* moving from place to place

monotonous (muh NOT uh nuhs) *adj.* tiresome because unvarying

morose (muh ROHS) *adj.* gloomy; sullen

mundane (muhn DAYN) *adj.* commonplace, everyday, ordinary

munificent (myoo NIHF uh suhnt) *adj.* generous

myriad (MIHR ee uhd) *adj.* countless

N

native (NAY tihv) *adj.* belonging to a place by birth

natural (NACH uhr uhl) *adj.* not man-made or artificial

nostalgia (nos TAL juh) *n.* a longing for something

nuance (NOO ahns) *n.* a slight or delicate variation in tone, color, meaning

O

oblivion (uh BLIHV ee uhn) *n.* condition of being completely forgotten

oblivious (uh BLIHV ee uhs) *adj.* lacking all awareness

obstinacy (OB stuh nuh see) *n.* stubbornness

obstinate (OB stuh niht) *adj.* stubborn

obtuse (uhb TOOS) *adj.* slow to understand or perceive

offensive (uh FEHN sihv) *n.* an attitude or position of attack

ominous (OM uh nuhs) *adj.* threatening; sinister

omnipotent (om NIHP uh tuhnt) *adj.* all-powerful

opposition (op uh ZIHSH uhn) *n.* hostile or resistant attitude toward something

oppressed (uh PREHST) *v.* kept down by cruel or unjust power

optimism (OP tuh mihz uhm) *n.* tendency to be positive

order (AWR duhr) *v.* arrange

ordinances (AWR duh nuhns uhz) *n.* sacraments or religious rites

ostentation (os tehn TAY shuhn) *n.* boastful display

P

pacify (PAS uh fy) *v.* to calm or soothe

pallor (PAL uhr) *n.* paleness

palpable (PAL puh buhl) *adj.* able to be touched, felt, or handled

parsimony (PAHR suh moh nee) *n.* stinginess

pastoral (PAS tuhr uhl) *adj.* characteristic of rural life; idealized as peaceful, simple, and natural

pathos (PAY thohs) *n.* quality that arouses pity, sorrow, or sympathy in others

pedestrian (puh DEHS tree uhn) *adj.* going on foot; walking

pensive (PEHN sihv) *adj.* thinking earnestly; plead

perdition (puhr DIHSH uhn) *n.* complete and irreparable loss; ruin

peremptorily (puh REHMP tuhr uh lee) *adv.* decisively; commandingly

peril (PEHR uhl) *n.* danger

permeated (PUR mee ayt uhd) *v.* soaked through with

perpetual (puhr PEHCH oo uhl) *adj.* lasting forever

persevere (pur suh VIHR) *v.* continue despite hardship; persist

persistent (puhr SIHS tuhnt) *adj.* repeated; continual

personal (PUR suh nuhl) *adj.* belonging to an individual; private

pessimism (PEHS uh mihz uhm) *n.* tendency to be negative

piety (PY uh tee) *n.* devotion to religion

platitudes (PLAT uh toodz) *n.* empty statements; tired expressions

plodding (PLOD ihng) *v.* walking or moving heavily and laboriously; trudging

poignant (POY nuhnt) *adj.* sharply painful to the feelings

poise (poyz) *n.* balance; stability

posterity (pos TEHR uh tee) *n.* all future generations

practicable (PRAK tuh kuh buhl) *adj.* practical, possible

prairie (PRAIR ee) *n.* a treeless, grass-covered plain

precipitate (prih SIHP uh tayt) *v.* cause to happen before expected or desired

preconceptions (prih kuhn SEHP shuhnz) *n.* ideas formed beforehand

predict (prih DIHKT) *v.* foretell on the basis of observation, experience, or reason

predilection (pree duh LEHK shuhn) *n.* preexisting preference

prelude (PREHL yood) *n.* introductory section or movement of a work of music

prescient (PREE shee uhnt) *adj.* having foreknowledge

pervading (puhr VAYD ihng) *v.* spreading throughout

prevalent (PREHV uh lehnt) *adj.* widely existing or occurring

privileges (PRIHV uh lihj uhz) *n.* special rights; advantages

proclaiming (pruh KLAYM ihng) *v.* announcing

procure (pruh KYUR) *v.* bring about through some effort

prodigious (pruh DIHJ uhs) *adj.* of great power or size

profundity (pruh FUHN duh tee) *n.* intellectual depth

profusion (pruh FYOO zhuhn) *n.* abundance; rich supply

propitiation (pruh pihsh ee AY shuhn) *n.* action designed to soothe or satisfy a person, a cause, etc.

propitious (pruh PIHSH uhs) *adj.* favorably inclined or disposed

prospect (PROS pehkt) *n.* something hoped for or expected

prosperity (pros PEHR uh tee) *n.* condition of being successful; wealth

protruded (proh TROOD uhd) *v.* stuck out

prudence (PROO duhns) *n.* carefulness; caution

prudent (PROO duhnt) *adj.* sensible; careful

psychology (sy KOL uh jee) *n.* science dealing with the mind and with mental and emotional processes

punitive (PYOO nuh tihv) *adj.* concerned with punishment

purged (purjd) *v.* cleansed

Q

quail (kwayl) *v.* draw back in fear; lose heart

quench (kwehnch) *v.* satisfy a thirst

quote (kwoht) *v.* speak or write a passage by someone else

R

range (raynj) *n.* distance between certain limits; extent

ravenous (RAV uh nuhs) *adj.* extremely hungry for something

ravine (ruh VEEN) *n.* long, deep hollow in the ground; a gully

realist (REE uh lihst) *n.* person or artist concerned with things as they are, rather than as they could or should be

realistic (REE uh LIHS tihk) *adj.* based on facts; practical

reaped (reept) *v.* gathered; brought in

receipts (rih SEETS) *n.* amounts of money received

recognize (REHK uhg nyz) *v.* perceive clearly

recompense (REHK uhm pehns) *n.* something given or done in return for something else; repayment

recourse (REE kawrs) *n.* access to a form of help or aid

recruits (rih KROOTS) *n.* newly drafted soldiers

rectitude (REHK tuh tood) *n.* correctness; righteousness

redress (rih DREHS) *n.* compensation for a wrong done

refuge (REHF yooj) *n.* shelter or protection from danger

regiment (REHJ uh muhnt) *n.* military unit

regional (REE juh nuhl) *adj.* of or in a particular localized area

regionalism (REE juh nuh LIHZ uhm) *n.* strong or loyal attachment to a certain region or area

relent (rih LEHNT) *v.* become less harsh; be more merciful

reluctant (rih LUHK tuhnt) *adj.* unwilling; disinclined

rendezvous (RAHN duh voo) *n.* meeting place

repeat (rih PEET) *v.* say or state again

repent (rih PEHNT) *v.* feel sorry for what one has done and vow to change one's behavior

repose (rih POHZ) *n.* state of being at rest

repression (rih PREHSH uhn) *n.* restraint

reproduce (REE pruh DOOS) *v.* imitate closely

repugnant (rih PUHG nuhnt) *adj.* offensive; disagreeable

resign (rih ZYN) *v.* accept something as unavoidable; submit oneself to a something negative

resources (rih SAWR sihz) *n.* supplies

retaliation (rih tal ee AY shuhn) *n.* act of returning an injury or wrong

revelations (rehv uh LAY shuhnz) *n.* newly revealed information; disclosures

reverential (rehv uh REHN shuhl) *adj.* showing deep respect and love

revise (rih VYZ) *v.* make a new, improved version

rights (ryts) *n.* that which a person has claim to

rituals (RIHCH oo uhlz) *n.* established forms of ceremonies; ceremonial acts

robust (roh BUHST) *adj.* strong and healthy; full of life

rueful (ROO fuhl) *adj.* feeling or showing someone sorrow or pity

rural (RUR uhl) *adj.* of or relating to the country or agriculture

S

salient (SAY lee uhnt) *adj.* standing out from the rest

salutary (SAL yuh tehr ee) *adj.* beneficial; promoting a good purpose

salvage (SAL vihj) *v.* the saving of goods or materials from waste

satire (SAT yr) *n.* literary work mocking human vices or mistakes

saunter (SAWN tuhr) *n.* a slow, leisurely gait

savagery (SAV ihj ree) *n.* barbarity

scale (skayl) *n.* the extent or size of something

scenario (sih NAIR ee oh) *n.* situation

sediment (SEHD uh muhnt) *n.* material that settles to the bottom of a liquid

seeping (SEEP ihng) *v.* flowing slowly

self-conscious (SEHLF KON shuhs) *adj.* uncomfortable, especially by the presence or the thought of other people

self-reliance (SEHLF rih LY uhns) *n.* dependence on one's own acts

self-reliant (SEHLF rih LY uhnt) *adj.* dependent on one's own acts

sensible (SEHN suh buhl) *adj.* emotionally or intellectually aware

sentience (SEHN shuhns) *n.* capacity for feeling

separate (SEHP uh rayt) *v.* make a distinction between

shard (shahrd) *n.* a fragment or broken piece

shares (shairz) *n.* portions of ownership of a company or a piece of property

sinister (SIHN uh stuhr) *adj.* threatening harm, evil or misfortune

sinuous (SIHN yoo uhs) *adj.* moving in and out; wavy

skyscraper (SKY SKRAY puhr) *n.* very tall building

smite (smyt) *v.* kill by a powerful blow

solemn (SOL uhm) *adj.* serious or grave

somnolent (SOM nuh luhnt) *adj.* sleepy; drowsy

sort (sawrt) *v.* put in place according to kind, class, or nature

sowed (sohd) *v.* scattered; planted

specious (SPEE shuhs) *adj.* seeming to be good or sound without actually being so

spectator (SPEHK tay tuhr) *n.* a person who watches something without taking part in it

speculate (SPEHK yuh layt) *v.* use evidence to guess what might happen

splendor (SPLEHN duhr) *n.* great display of riches; great brightness

squander (SKWON duhr) *v.* spend or use wastefully

stark (stahrk) *adj.* stiff; rigid

state (stayt) *v.* express in words

statute (STACH oot) *n.* the document in which such an enactment is expressed

steal (steel) *v.* creep

stealthily (STEHLTH uh lee) *adv.* slyly or secretively

stirring (STUR ihng) *adj.* busy; full of energy

storytelling (STAWR ee TEHL ihng) *n.* act or art of telling tales or anecdotes

striking (STRYK ihng) *adj.* very noticeable or impressive

structure (STRUHK chuhr) *v.* create a general plot or outline

subject to (SUHB jihkt too) *adj.* likely to be affected by something

sublime (suh BLYM) *adj.* noble; majestic

subsisted (suhb SIHST uhd) *v.* remained alive; were sustained

suburbia (suh BUR bee uh) *n.* region outside of a major city

successive (suhk SEHS ihv) *adj.* following one after another

suffice (suh FYS) *v.* be adequate; meet the needs of

summarily (SUHM uhr uh lee) *adv.* promptly and without formality

summarize (SUHM uh ryz) *v.* briefly state the most important ideas and details

summation (suh MAY shuhn) *n.* summing up; giving all the key details of in a brief form

superficial (SOO puhr FIHSH uhl) *adj.* on the surface; shallow

superfluous (su PUR floo uhs) *adj.* strong belief

supple (SUHP uhl) adj. able to bend and move easily and nimbly

surmised (suhr MYZD) *v.* guessed; concluded

surveyed (suhr VAYD) *v.* measured and marked to show boundaries

swerve (swurv) *v.* to turn aside sharply or suddenly from a straight course

synonymous (sih NON uh muhs) *adj.* equivalent or similar in meaning

systemic (sihs TEHM ihk) *adj.* affecting the entire organism or bodily system

T

taboo (tuh BOO) *n.* something forbidden within a particular society or culture

tactful (TAKT fuhl) *adj.* concerned about upsetting or offending others

tantalized (TAN tuh lyzd) *v.* tormented; frustrated

taut (tawt) adj. tightly stretched

technology (tehk NOL uh jee) *n.* science of the mechanical and industrial arts

tedious (TEE dee uhs) *adj.* long or verbose and wearisome

tempered (TEHM puhrd) *v.* treated to achieve just the right strength or balance

tempest (TEHM pihst) *n.* violent storm with high winds

terrain (teh RAYN) *n.* ground or track of ground, especially with regard to its natural features

terrors (TEHR uhrz) *n.* great fears

theology (thee OL uh jee) *n.* the study of religion

tranquil (TRANG kwuhl) *adj.* calm; quiet; still

transcribed (tran SKRYBD) *v.* wrote or typed a copy

transformed (trans FAWRMD) *adj.* altered; changed

transfusion (trans FYOO zhuhn) *n.* the act of transference or transmission

transient (TRAN shuhnt) *adj.* not permanent

transition (tran ZIHSH uhn) *n.* change or passing from one condition to another

traversed (trav UHRST) *v.* moved over, across, or through

treacherous (TREHCH uhr uhs) *adj.* giving a false appearance of security; dangerous

tremulously (TREHM yuh luhs lee) *adv.* fearfully; timidly

tumultuously (too MUHL choo uhs lee) *adv.* in an agitated way

tyranny (TIHR uh nee) *n.* oppressive power

U

unabated (uhn uh BAY tihd) *adj.* not lessened or reduced

unanimity (yoo nuh NIHM uh tee) *n.* complete agreement

unconscious (uhn KON shuhs) *adj.* having temporarily lost awareness; in a faint

undertaking (UHN duhr tay kihng) *n.* task or challenge

unscrupulous (uhn SKROO pyuh luhs) *adj.* unethical; dishonest

unwonted (uhn WOHN tihd) *adj.* unusual; unfamiliar

urban (UR buhn) *adj.* characteristic of a city

V

validate (VAL uh dayt) *v.* prove to be factual or effective

vanquished (VAN kwihsht) *v.* thoroughly defeated

venerable (VEHN uhr uh buhl) *adj.* commanding respect

verify (VEHR uh fy) *v.* prove to be true by evidence

vernacular (vuhr NAK yuh luhr) *n.* native language

vigilance (VIHJ uh luhns) *n.* watchfulness

vigilant (VIHJ uh luhnt) *adj.* alert to danger

vigorously (VIHG uhr uhs lee) *adv.* forcefully or powerfully

vindicated (VIHN duh kayt ihd) *v.* cleared from blame

virtuous (VUR choo uhs) *adj.* characterized by moral virtue; righteous

virulent (VIHR yuh luhnt) *adj.* extremely hurtful or infectious

vision (VIHZH uhn) *n.* sense of sight; something seen in a dream or the imagination

volition (voh LIHSH uhn) *n.* act of using the will; decision

voluminous (vuh LOO muh nuhs) *adj.* of enough material to fill volumes

votive (VOH tihv) *adj.* designed to accomplish or fulfill a special intention

vulnerability (vuhl nuhr uh BIHL uh tee) *n.* open to moral attack, criticism, temptation, etc

W

wanton (WON tuhn) *adj.* senseless; unjustified

wasteland (WAYST LAND) *n.* land that is uncultivated or barren

wilderness (WIHL duhr nihs) *n.* region with no people living in it

wily (WY lee) *adj.* sly; cunning

wretched (REHCH uhd) *adj.* deeply distressed; miserable

Spanish Glossary

El vocabulario de Pregunta Esencial aparece en **azul**. El vocabulario acadēmico de alta utilidad está **subrayado**.

A

abeyance / suspensión *s.* cesación temporal

absolve / absolver *v.* perdonar; liberar de culpa

absurdity / absurdo *s.* disparate; irracionalidad

accosted / abordó *v.* se dirigió a o habló con alguien de manera vehemente

account / cuenta *s.* informe o detalle

acknowledges / reconoce *v.* acepta la existencia, realidad o verdad de algo

acquiesce / asentir *v.* aceptar sin protesta

adamant / obstinado *adj.* firme; inflexible

adjourned / suspendió *v.* clausuró temporalmente

advantageous / ventajoso *adj.* provechoso; beneficioso

adversary / adversario *s.* opositor; enemigo

adversity / adversidad *s.* desgracia, calamidad

affections / afectos *s.* emociones

affliction / aflicción *s.* algo que causa dolor o angustia

agape / boquiabierto *adj.* con sorpresa; con asombro

aggregation / conjunto *s.* agrupación de objetos o individuos distintos

agricultural / agrícola *adj.* donde la agricultura es el principal medio de vida

alacrity / alacridad *s.* velocidad

alienation / enajenación *s.* distanciamiento o separación de sentimiento o afecto

alliance / alianza *s.* unión de naciones para un fin específico

ambiguity / ambigüedad *s.* estado de tener dos o más significados posibles

ambition / ambición *s.* deseo vehemente de lograr un objetivo específico; ímpetu por triunfar

ameliorate / mejorar *v.* hacer mejor

ample / amplio *adj.* de gran tamaño; más que suficiente

analyze / analizar *v.* descomponer un tema en partes y explicarlas

anarchy / anarquía *s.* ausencia de gobierno

ancestor / antepasado *s.* persona de la que descienden otras personas

anonymity / anonimato *s.* la condición de ser desconocido

anticipate / prever *v.* prepararse para algo o indicar algo

anxiety / ansiedad *s.* estado de sentirse intranquilo, aprehensivo o preocupado por lo que pudiera ocurrir

apparel / vestido *s.* ropa

apparition / aparición *s.* acto de aparecer o hacerse visible

appease / saciar *v.* satisfacer

appendage / apéndice *s.* parte externa de una planta o animal, como una rama o cola

appraise / evaluar *v.* calcular el valor, la importancia o el estatus de algo

apprehension / aprensión *s.* inquietante sensación de premonición; pavor

appropriate / apropiar *v.* tomar o usar algo sin permiso

arduous / arduo *adj.* difícil

argue / argumentar *v.* expresar razones a favor o en contra; comprobar expresando razones

arrange / acomodar *v.* poner en orden o en secuencia

ascended / ascendió *v.* subió

aspirations / aspiraciones *s.* fuertes deseos o ambiciones

assault / asalto *s.* ataque violento

assent / asentir *v.* acordar

assess / evaluar *v.* determinar la importancia, el tamaño o el valor de algo

austerity / austeridad *s.* adustez en la conducta o la apariencia; dureza; severidad

auxiliary / auxiliar *adj.* que brinda ayuda o apoyo

avarice / avaricia *s.* codicia

aversion / aversión *s.* objeto que provoca una fuerte antipatía

avidly / ávidamente *adv.* ansiosamente

awe / asombro *s.* sentimientos encontrados de temor y admiración

B

base / bajo *adj.* ruin; vil

beguile / cautivar *v.* encantar o deleitar

benediction / bendición *s.* plegaria que invoca la gracia de Dios

benevolent / benévolo *adj.* bondadoso; caritativo

benign / benigno *adj.* no injurioso ni maligno; no canceroso

bequeath / legar *v.* transmitir; pasar a otro

brazenness / descaro *s.* desfachatez; atrevimiento; insolencia

brigade / brigada *s.* unidad de soldados

brutal / brutal *adj.* cruel y sin sentimientos; salvaje; violento

C

cadence / cadencia *s.* serie de notas o acordes hacia el final de una obra musical

calamity / calamidad *s.* desastre; catástrofe

calumny / calumnia *s.* falsa acusación; difamación

candid / franco *adj.* sincero

canvass / solicitar *v.* recorrer cierta área solicitando los votos, mandatos o participación de la gente

capable / capaz *adj.* poseer las destrezas necesarias para realizar algo

caper / travesura *s.* picardía

casualties / bajas *s.* miembros de las fuerzas armadas que mueren en combate

categorize / categorizar *v.* colocar en grupos relacionados

cavernous / cavernoso *adj.* que se asemeja a una caverna; vasto

celestial / celestial *adj.* que pertenece o está en el cielo, como los planetas o las estrellas

chaos / caos *s.* desorden de la materia y el espacio, que presuntamente existió antes del universo ordenado

chronicles / crónicas *s.* cuentos; historias

circumvent / circundar *v.* evitar; rodear

civilian / civil *s.* cualquier persona que no es miembro de las fuerzas armadas

classify / clasificar *v.* asignar a una categoría

cleave / asir *v.* adherirse; pegarse

coinage / invención *s.* palabra o expresión inventada

coincide / coincidir *v.* que sucede al mismo tiempo

collective / colectividad *s.* acto de agrupar en un todo

collusion / confabulación *s.* acuerdo secreto; conspiración

commercial / comercial *adj.* relacionado con el comercio o los negocios

commissioners / comisionados *s.* funcionarios de gobierno

commonplace / común *adj.* habitual; ordinario

commotion / conmoción *s.* confusión ruidosa

community / comunidad *s.* todas las personas que viven en un distrito, ciudad o área específica

compare / comparar *v.* señalar las similitudes o las diferencias

conciliatory / conciliatorio *adj.* que busca la paz o la conciliación; amistoso

conclude / concluir *v.* llegar a un fin lógicamente necesario por medio de razonamiento

condolences / condolencias *s.* expresiones de pesar

conduct / conducta *v.* comportamiento

conflagration / conflagración *s.* incendio extenso y destructivo

conformity / conformidad *s.* acción que concuerda con las normas generalmente aceptadas

confounded / confundido *adj.* confuso; consternado

conjectural / conjetural *adj.* basado en la suposición

conjectured / conjeturó *v.* supuso

conjuring / conjurando *v.* invocando; apareciendo como por arte de magia

consecrate / consagrar *v.* motivo para ser venerado u honrado

conspicuous / conspicuo *adj.* obvio; fácilmente visible o perceptible

consternation / consternación *s.* gran temor o conmoción que provoca sentimientos de impotencia e incertidumbre

constitute / constituir *v.* servir de base o parte de algo; formar; abarcar

constitution / constitución *s.* composición física de una persona

contentious / contencioso *adj.* disputable

contiguous / contiguo *adj.* lindante; adyacente

contract / contrato *s.* acuerdo escrito

contrast / contrastar *v.* inspeccionar para descubrir las diferencias

convention / convención *s.* reunión a la que asisten miembros o delegados

conviction / convicción *s.* creencia profunda

convivial / jovial *adj.* que goza de la buena compañía; sociable

copious / copioso *adj.* cuantioso; abundante

correspond / corresponder *v.* concordar; relacionarse con

countenance / aprobar *v.* sancionar; tolerar

cowering / encogiendo *v.* temblando o agachándose, como con miedo

create / crear *v.* producir por medio de habilidad imaginativa

crevices / grietas *s.* estrechas aberturas causadas por resquebraduras o fisuras

critic / crítico *s.* persona que desaprueba o detecta fallas

critique / criticar *v.* examinar críticamente; reseñar

cunning / astuto *adj.* hábil para el engaño; artificioso; taimado

cyberspace / ciberespacio *s.* mundo en línea de redes informáticas

D

daunting / atemorizante *adj.* intimidante

decorum / decoro *s.* rectitud; idoneidad

deduce / deducir *v.* inferir a partir de un principio general

defend / defender *v.* mantener o apoyar en vista de un argumento

deference / deferencia *s.* estimación o respeto cortés

deficient / deficiente *adj.* con falta de; que carece de algo necesario

define / definir *v.* expresar las cualidades que hacen de algo lo que es

degenerate / degenerado *adj.* moralmente corrupto

dejected / abatido *v.* desanimado; cabizbajo; deprimido

deliberation / deliberación *s.* consideración meticulosa

deposition / deposición *s.* declaración de un testigo bajo juramento, aunque no en un tribunal en pleno

depths / profundidades *s.* áreas más profundas

derivative / derivado *adj.* que no es original; que se basa en otra cosa

derive / derivar *v.* rastrear hasta o desde una fuente; obtener por medio de razonamiento

describe / describir *v.* representar en palabras

design / diseñar *v.* crear, elaborar, ejecutar o construir según un plan

desolate / desolado *adj.* abandonado; aislado

despondent / desalentado *adj.* sin valor ni esperanza

despotism / despotismo *s.* dominio absoluto; tiranía

destitute / indigente *adj.* que vive en abyecta pobreza

destruction / destrucción *s.* acto de demoler o abatir

detached / indiferente *adj.* no involucrado emocionalmente

devise / idear *v.* formar en la mente por medio de nuevas combinaciones de ideas; inventar

dictum / dictamen *s.* declaración formal de hecho u opinión

differentiate / diferenciar *v.* reconocer una disparidad

digress / divagar *v.* alejarse temporalmente del tema principal

dilapidated / dilapidado *adj.* ruinoso

diligence / diligencia *s.* esfuerzo constante y minucioso; perseverancia

discern / discernir *v.* percibir o reconocer; distinguir claramente

discord / desacuerdo *s.* diferencia de opinión; disputa

discretion / discreción *s.* Prudencia

discriminate / discriminar *v.* reconocer diferencias entre elementos

disdainfully / desdeñosamente *adv.* que muestra desdén o desprecio

disgrace / ignominia *s.* algo que genera vergüenza o deshonra

disillusion / desengaño *s.* libertad de una idea falsa; desencanto

dispatched / despachó *v.* envió, generalmente en asuntos oficiales

dispersal / dispersión *s.* distribución

disposition / disposición *s.* inclinación; tendencia

disregard / desatender *v.* no prestar atención a; hacer caso omiso de; ignorar

dissembling / disimulando *v.* encubriendo la verdadera naturaleza o los motivos propios

dissention / disensión *s.* desacuerdo; discordia expresada mediante fuertes discusiones

dissuade / disuadir *v.* convencer a alguien de no hacer algo

distinguish / distinguir *v.* marcar como independiente o diferente

diversity / diversidad *s.* variedad; punto de disimilitud

divine / adivinar *v.* averiguar mediante la intuición

docile / dócil *adj.* fácil de dirigir o manejar; obediente

doctrine / doctrina *s.* lo que se enseña

dogma / dogma *s.* doctrinas o credos autorizados

dubious / dudoso *adj.* cuestionable; sospechoso

duplicate / duplicar *v.* hacer una copia

duration / duración *s.* tiempo durante el cual algo continúa o existe

dusky / obscuro *adj.* poco claro; sombrío; tenebroso

dyspepsia / dispepsia *s.* indigestión

E

ecstasy / éxtasis *s.* sentimiento de alegría abrumadora; enorme deleite

efface / tachar *v.* borrar; eliminar

effigies / efigies *s.* imágenes o retratos, especialmente de personas

effrontery / desvergüenza *s.* audacia descarada

effuse / derramar *v.* verter; brotar

eloquence / elocuencia *s.* talento para la oratoria vívida y enérgica

elusive / evasivo *adj.* difícil de comprender

embankment / dique *s.* montículo de tierra o piedra construido para retener agua, o como soporte para una carretera

embark / embarcar *v.* iniciar una empresa, proyecto o actividad

emigrants / emigrantes *s.* personas que abandonan un sitio para establecerse en otro

eminence / eminencia *s.* grandeza; celebridad

emit / emitir *v.* articular palabras o sonidos

enamored / enamorado *adj.* encantado; cautivado

encroached / usurpó *v.* invadió

endured / soportó *v.* aguantó

engrossed / absorto *adj.* completamente ocupado; enfrascado

entreated / suplicó *v.* rogó; imploró

entrenchments / trincheras *s.* zanjas profundas y extensas con paredes empinadas, utilizadas para defenderse del fuego enemigo

environment / entorno *s.* objetos o condiciones circundantes

epitaph / epitafio *s.* inscripción en una lápida o piedra sepulcral

equivocal / ambiguo *adj.* que se puede interpretar de más de una manera

eradicate / erradicar *v.* eliminar; destruir

establishment / establecimiento *s.* casa o negocio

estimates / estimaciones *s.* cálculos generales minuciosos

etiquette / etiqueta *s.* comportamiento correcto y formal

evacuated / evacuó *v.* desalojó; retiró

evade / evadir *v.* eludir o escapar mediante el engaño o ingenio

evaluate / evaluar *v.* determinar la importancia, el valor o la condición de algo estudiándolo detalladamente

exalted / exaltado *adj.* lleno de júbilo u orgullo; regocijado

examine / examinar *v.* indagar detalladamente sobre un tema

exasperation / exasperación *s.* enojo; frustración

exhaust / escape *s.* descarga de vapor o gas ya usado de un motor

exile / exilio *s.* estado o período de destierro

expansion / expansión *s.* acto o proceso de aumentar la amplitud, el tamaño o el volumen

expedient / recurso *s.* método utilizado para alcanzar un objetivo rápidamente

expenditures / desembolsos *s.* gastos; usos del dinero o recursos

exposures / exposiciones *s.* secciones de una película donde se refleja la luz al tomar una fotografía

extort / extorsionar *v.* obtener mediante amenaza o violencia

extraneous / extraño *adj.* no relacionado; desvinculado

F

fallowness / ociosidad *s.* inactividad

fantastic / fantástico *adj.* excelente; increíble

fastidious / exigente *adj.* cuidadoso; meticuloso

fatigues / trajes de fatiga *s.* ropa resistente que usan los soldados para trabajos pesados

feigned / fingió *v.* simuló

fervent / ferviente *adj.* extremadamente apasionado; muy entusiasta

finite / finito *adj.* que tiene límites mensurables o definibles

fitfully / irregularmente *adv.* se distingue por actividad interrumpida o intermitente

flagrant / flagrante *adj.* deslumbrante; escandaloso

flourished / floreció *v.* creció fuerte, saludable y feliz; prosperó

fluctuation / fluctuación *s.* cambio de nivel o intensidad

foothold / asidero *s.* posición estable para emprender acciones subsiguientes

forded / vadeó *v.* cruzó el río en el punto menos profundo

forestall / impedir *v.* prevenir mediante una acción anticipada

formulate / formular *v.* expresar plena y claramente

fortuitous / fortuito *adj.* que ocurre por suerte

fortune / fortuna *s.* riqueza; suerte

fragmentation / fragmentación *s.* acto o proceso de descomponer en partes

frantic / frenético *adj.* marcado por el frenesí

frayed / raído *adj.* andrajoso

freedom / libertad *s.* no estar bajo el control de otros

frontier / frontera *s.* frontera entre regiones deshabitadas; región en desarrollo de un campo de conocimiento

furtive / furtivo *adj.* sigiloso

G

garrulous / gárrulo *adj.* que habla demasiado

gaudy / llamativo *adj.* que llama la atención con mal gusto

generalize / generalizar *v.* llegar a un principio más amplio a partir de detalles

genial / afable *adj.* jovial; cordial

genre / género *s.* categoría o estilo

global / global *adj.* extendido por todo el mundo

govern / gobernar *v.* regir; controlar; manejar

grandeur / grandiosidad *s.* grandeza

grave / grave *adj.* serio; solemne

gravity / gravedad *s.* seriedad

guile / maña *s.* astucia

H

habitation / morada *s.* lugar para vivir; conjunto de casas o viviendas

hallow / venerar *v.* honrar como sagrado

handiwork / manualidad *s.* trabajo hecho a mano; obra hecha con las propias manos

harass / hostigar *v.* acosar; molestar

heady / embriagante *adj.* intoxicante

heightened / enalteció *v.* elevó el nivel de

heritage / patrimonio *s.* rasgos, creencias o costumbres transmitidos de una generación a otra

homages / homenaje *s.* actos que expresan honor y reverencia

homely / sencillo *adj.* que no es elegante ni refinado; tosco

huddled / amontonó *v.* apiñó; acurrucó

humor / humor *s.* cualidad de ser gracioso o divertido

hypothesize / hipotetizar *v.* desarrollar una teoría acerca de algo

I

idealism / idealismo *s.* pensamiento basado en seguir las normas de perfección o belleza

identify / identificar *v.* establecer la identidad de algo

identity / identidad *s.* lo que caracteriza a una persona

illiterate / analfabeto *adj.* incapaz de leer o escribir

illustrate / ilustrar *v.* dar ejemplos para apoyar una idea

immigration / inmigración *s.* acto de llegar a otro país o región para vivir ahí

imperceptible / imperceptible *adj.* difícil de distinguir; desapercibido

impertinent / impertinente *adj.* que no muestra el respeto apropiado; insolente

implore / implorar *v.* pedir o suplicar con devoción; rogar

imply / insinuar *v.* dar a entender o sugerir

impulsive / impulsivo *adj.* que se realiza sin pensar

impulsively / impulsivamente *adv.* espontáneamente; repentinamente

inanimate / inanimado *adj.* sin vida; muerto

inarticulate / inarticulado *adj.* pronunciado o expresado sin claridad

inaudibly / imperceptiblemente *adv.* que no puede ser escuchado

incessant / incesante *adj.* constante; aparentemente interminable

incorporated / constituido *adj.* establecido legalmente como corporación

incorrigible / incorregible *adj.* imposible de corregir; irremediable

incredulously / incrédulamente *adv.* escépticamente

increment / incrementar *v.* aumentar, como en serie

indelible / indeleble *adj.* permanente; que no se puede borrar

independence / independencia *s.* libertad del control de otros

individualism / individualismo *s.* creencia de que la libertad personal es lo más importante

induce / inducir *v.* causar; provocar

industry / industria *s.* cualquier ramo de negocios, comercio o manufactura

ineffable / inefable *adj.* demasiado abrumador para ser expresado

inert / inerte *adj.* sin movimiento

inextricable / inextricable *adj.* que no puede separarse o liberarse de

infer / inferir *v.* derivar una conclusión a partir de hechos o premisas

infinity / infinito *s.* espacio, tiempo o distancia interminable o ilimitado

ingratiating / congraciador *adj.* encantador o halagador

innovation / innovación *s.* una nueva idea, método o dispositivo

innumerable / innumerable *adj.* son tantos que no se pueden contar

insatiable / insaciable *adj.* que constantemente desea más

inscrutable / inescrutable *adj.* que no puede comprenderse fácilmente

inseparable / inseparable *adj.* que no puede dividirse; enlazados

insidious / insidioso *adj.* engañoso; traicionero

inspection / inspección *s.* examen

intent / intención *s.* propósito u objetivo

intently / asiduamente *adv.* de manera concentrada y con un propósito determinado

intercepted / interceptó *v.* capturó o detuvo a algo o a alguien en su trayecto de un lugar a otro

interminable / interminable *adj.* que parece perdurar para siempre

interposed / interpuso *v.* intermedió

interspersed / esparció *v.* colocó por doquier

intervene / intervenir *v.* tomar medidas con el fin de prevenir algo

intolerable / intolerable *adj.* tan difícil o doloroso que resulta insoportable; inaguantable

intonation / entonación *s.* la capacidad de tocar notas musicales de manera afinada o desafinada

intricate / intrincado *adj.* complicado; que tiene muchas partes pequeñas correlacionadas

intuitively / intuitivamente *adv.* que no hace falta aprenderlo; instintivamente

invective / invectiva *s.* ataque verbal; crítica violenta

invent / inventar *v.* crear pensando

investigate / investigar *v.* realizar una inspección sistemática

J

jocularity / jocosidad *s.* buen humor chistoso

jubilant / jubiloso *adj.* alegre y triunfante

judge / juzgar *v.* formar una estimación o evaluación de algo

judgment / juicio *s.* capacidad de formar una opinión apropiadamente; buen razonamiento

justify / justificar *v.* comprobar o demostrar que algo es justo, correcto o razonable

L

label / etiquetar *v.* describir o designar

lament / lamentar *v.* expresar pesar por algo; sufrir en voz alta

landscape / paisaje *s.* área que puede verse a la vez desde un lugar

latent / latente *adj.* presente pero invisible o inactivo

latitude / latitud *s.* distancia al norte o al sur del ecuador

levee / dique *s.* muro construido en las márgenes de un río para detener las inundaciones

liberty / libertad *s.* autonomía

license / libertad de acción *s.* exención de una conducta o lenguaje correcto

licentious / licencioso *adj.* sin refrenamiento moral

limber / flexible *adj.* elástico

list / enumerar *v.* hacer una lista; incluir

listed / inclinado *adj.* ladeado; en declive

locate / ubicar *v.* hallar el lugar de algo

longitude / longitud *s.* distancia este u oeste en la superficie de la Tierra

lulled / arrulló *v.* calmó o sosegó mediante un sonido o movimiento suave

luminary / luminaria *adj.* que irradia luz

M

machetes / machetes *s.* cuchillos grandes y pesados de hoja ancha

magnanimity / magnanimidad *s.* generosidad

magnitude / magnitud *s.* grandeza de tamaño

maledictions / maldiciones *s.* maleficios

malign / maligno *adj.* maléfico; muy dañino

malingers / fingirse enfermo *v.* simular una enfermedad

maneuver / maniobrar *v.* mover algo utilizando un plan o conspiración

manifold / múltiple *adj.* de muchas maneras

martial / marcial *adj.* relativo a la guerra

marvel / maravilla *s.* cosa maravillosa o sorprendente

master / dominar *v.* volverse experto en

media / medios *s.* sistemas de comunicación diseñados para llegar a las masas

mediator / mediador *s.* aquél que reconcilia grupos opositores

melancholy / melancólico *adj.* triste y deprimido; lúgubre

membrane / membrana *s.* capa delgada y suave que sirve de cubierta o forro

memorials / monumentos *s.* objetos que se exhiben en memoria de una persona o suceso

meticulous / meticuloso *adj.* extremadamente cuidadoso de los detalles

metropolis / metrópolis *s.* ciudad grande

migrant / migrante *adj.* que se traslada de un lugar a otro

monotonous / monótono *adj.* tedioso porque no varía

morose / esquivo *adj.* melancólico; retraído

mundane / mundano *adj.* común, cotidiano, ordinario

munificent / munificente *adj.* generoso

myriad / innumerable *adj.* incontable

N

native / nativo *adj.* que pertenece a un lugar por nacimiento

natural / natural *adj.* que no ha sido elaborado por el hombre ni es artificial

nostalgia / nostalgia *s.* sentimiento de añoranza por algo

nuance / matiz *s.* una pequeña o sutil variación en tono, color o significado

O

oblivion / olvido *s.* condición de ser totalmente olvidado

oblivious / abstraído *adj.* falto de todo conocimiento

obstinacy / obstinación *s.* terquedad

obstinate / obstinado *adj.* terco

obtuse / obtuso *adj.* lento para comprender o percibir

offensive / ofensiva *s.* actitud o posición de ataque

ominous / ominoso *adj.* amenazador; siniestro

omnipotent / omnipotente *adj.* todopoderoso

opposition / oposición *s.* actitud hostil o resistente hacia algo

oppressed / oprimió *v.* reprimió mediante un poder injusto o cruel

optimism / optimismo *s.* tendencia a ser positivo

order / ordenar *v.* acomodar

ordinances / ordenanzas *s.* sacramentos o ritos religiosos

ostentation / ostentación *s.* exhibición jactanciosa

P

pacify / pacificar *v.* calmar o apaciguar

pallor / palor *s.* palidez

palpable / palpable *adj.* que puede ser tocado, sentido o manipulado

parsimony / parsimonia *s.* tacañería

pastoral / pastoril *adj.* característico de la vida rural; idealizado como pacífico, sencillo y natural

pathos / pathos *s.* cualidad que inspira lástima, pena o compasión en otros

pedestrian / peatonal *adj.* a pie; caminando

pensive / pensativo *adj.* que piensa intensamente; que suplica

perdition / perdición *s.* pérdida total e irreparable; ruina

peremptorily / perentoriamente *adv.* terminantemente; autoritariamente

peril / peligro *s.* riesgo

permeated / permeó *v.* impregnó

perpetual / perpetuo *adj.* que dura para siempre

persevere / perseverar *v.* continuar a pesar de las penurias; persistir

persistent / persistente *adj.* recurrente; constante

personal / personal *adj.* que pertenece a una persona; privado

pessimism / pesimismo *s.* tendencia a ser negativo

piety / piedad *s.* devoción a la religión

platitudes / trivialidades *s.* declaraciones sin sentido; expresiones desgastadas

plodding / caminar pausadamente *v.* avanzar o moverse pesadamente y con dificultad; recorrer penosamente

poignant / conmovedor *adj.* que hiere profundamente los sentimientos

poise / equilibrio *s.* balance; estabilidad

posterity / posteridad *s.* todas las futuras generaciones

practicable / practicable *adj.* factible, posible

prairie / llanura *s.* planicie cubierta de pasto sin árboles

precipitate / precipitar *v.* provocar que ocurra antes de lo esperado o deseado

preconceptions / preconcepciones *s.* ideas preconcebidas

predict / predecir *v.* vaticinar basándose en observación, experiencia o raciocinio

predilection / predilección *s.* preferencia preexistente

prelude / preludio *s.* parte o movimiento preliminar de una obra musical

prescient / presciente *adj.* que se conoce de antemano

pervading / difundirse *v.* que se esparce a través de

prevalent / extendido *adj.* que existe u ocurre abundantemente

privileges / privilegios *s.* derechos especiales; ventajas

proclaiming / proclamar *v.* anunciar

procure / procurar *v.* llevar a cabo con cierto esfuerzo

prodigious / prodigioso *adj.* de enorme poder o tamaño

profundity / profundidad *s.* profundidad intelectual

profusion / profusión *s.* abundancia; provisión cuantiosa

propitiation / apaciguamiento *s.* acción que busca aquietar o satisfacer a una persona, causa, etc.

propitious / propicio *adj.* favorablemente inclinado hacia o dispuesto a

prospect / prospecto *s.* algo deseado o esperado

prosperity / prosperidad *s.* condición de tener éxito; riqueza

protruded / sobresalió *v.* destacó

prudence / prudencia *s.* cuidado; cautela

prudent / prudente *adj.* perceptible; cauteloso

psychology / psicología *s.* la ciencia que estudia la mente y los procesos mentales y emocionales

punitive / punitivo *adj.* relativo al castigo

purged / purgó *v.* limpió

Q

quail / acobardar *v.* amedrentarse; descorazonarse

quench / aplacar *v.* calmar la sed

quote / citar *v.* decir o escribir un pasaje de la autoría de otra persona

R

range / rango *s.* distancia entre ciertos límites; alcance

ravenous / voraz *adj.* extremadamente hambriento

ravine / cañada *s.* zanja larga y profunda en la tierra; hondonada

realist / realista *s.* persona o artista que se interesa en las cosas como son y no como podrían o deberían ser

realistic / realista *adj.* basado en hechos; práctico

reaped / recolectó *v.* recogió; cosechó

receipts / ingresos *s.* cantidades de dinero recibidas

recognize / reconocer *v.* percibir claramente

recompense / recompensa *s.* algo que se da o se hace como retribución por otra cosa; compensación

recourse / recurso *s.* acceso a cierta forma de ayuda o asistencia

recruits / reclutas *s.* soldados recién alistados

rectitude / rectitud *s.* corrección; probidad

redress / resarcimiento *s.* compensación por un mal cometido

refuge / refugio *s.* amparo o protección del peligro

regiment / regimiento *s.* unidad militar

regional / regional *adj.* de o en un área específica

regionalism / regionalismo *s.* apego intenso o leal a cierta región o área

relent / aplacar *v.* hacerse menos tosco; ser más compasivo

reluctant / reacio *adj.* renuente; maldispuesto

rendezvous / punto de reunión *s.* sitio de encuentro

repeat / repetir *v.* decir o expresar de nuevo

repent / arrepentir *v.* sentir remordimiento por una mala acción y prometer cambiar su comportamiento

repose / reposo *s.* estado de descanso

repression / represión *s.* restricción

reproduce / reproducir *v.* imitar con detalle

repugnant / repugnante *adj.* ofensivo; desagradable

resign / resignar *v.* aceptar que algo es inevitable; someterse a algo negativo

resources / recursos *s.* suministros

retaliation / represalia *s.* acto de desquitarse por un perjuicio o mal

revelations / revelaciones *s.* información recientemente revelada; divulgaciones

reverential / reverencial *adj.* que muestra gran respeto y devoción

revise / revisar *v.* hacer una versión nueva y mejorada

rights / derechos *s.* aquello que una persona puede exigir

rituals / rituales *s.* formas establecidas de ceremonias; actos ceremoniales

robust / robusto *adj.* fuerte y saludable; vigoroso

rueful / desconsolado *adj.* sentir o mostrarle pena o lástima a alguien

rural / rural *adj.* relacionado con el campo o la agricultura

S

salient / sobresaliente *adj.* que se destaca entre los demás

salutary / saludable *adj.* benéfico; que promueve una buena causa

salvage / recuperar *v.* rescatar bienes o materiales de los desechos

satire / sátira *s.* obra literaria que se burla de los vicios o errores humanos

saunter / deambular *s.* paso lento y sin prisa

savagery / salvajismo *s.* barbarie

scale / escala *s.* el alcance o tamaño de algo

scenario / circunstancias *s.* situación

sediment / sedimento *s.* material que se deposita en el fondo de un líquido

seeping / filtrando *v.* fluyendo lentamente

self-conscious / cohibido *adj.* incómodo, especialmente por la presencia de otras personas o lo que ellas piensan

self-reliance / autosuficiencia *s.* dependencia únicamente en los actos propios

self-reliant / autosuficiente *adj.* dependiente únicamente de los actos propios

sensible / sensato *adj.* emocional o intelectualmente razonable

sentience / sensible *s.* que responde a o es conciente de las sensaciones

separate / separar *v.* hacer distinción entre

shard / fragmento *s.* pequeña parte o pedazo roto

shares / acciones *s.* porciones de participación en una compañía o propiedad

sinister / siniestro *adj.* que amenaza con perjuicio, maldad o infortunio

sinuous / sinuoso *adj.* con movimiento serpenteante; ondulante

skyscraper / rascacielos *s.* edificio de gran altura

smite / aniquilar *v.* matar de un fuerte golpe

solemn / solemne *adj.* serio o grave

somnolent / soñoliento *adj.* adormecido; amodorrado

sort / clasificar *v.* ordenar por tipo, clase o calidad

sowed / sembrado *adj.* esparcido; plantado

specious / especioso *adj.* que aparenta estar bueno o sano sin estarlo realmente

spectator / espectador *s.* persona que observa algo sin tomar parte

speculate / especular *v.* usar evidencia para predecir lo que puede ocurrir

speculation / especulación *s.* idea; conjetura

splendor / esplendor *s.* gran exhibición de riqueza; gran brillo

squander / despilfarrar *v.* gastar o derrochar

stark / rígido *adj.* tieso; inflexible

state / establecer *v.* expresar en palabras

statute / estatuto *s.* documento en el cual se expresa la promulgación, aprobación y sanción del mismo

steal / arrastrar *s.* reptar

stealthily / furtivamente *adv.* astuta o disimuladamente

stirring / incitante *adj.* activo; lleno de energía

storytelling / contar cuentos *s.* acto o arte de narrar cuentos o anécdotas

striking / impresionante *adj.* excesivamente llamativo o impactante

structure / estructurar *v.* crear una trama o un esquema general

subject / propenso *adj.* que puede ser afectado por algo

sublime / sublime *adj.* noble; majestuoso

subsisted / subsistieron *v.* permanecieron con vida; soportaron

suburbia / suburbio *s.* región fuera de una ciudad principal

successive / sucesivo *adj.* uno tras otro

suffice / bastar *v.* ser idóneo; satisfacer las necesidades de

summarily / sumariamente *adv.* brevemente y sin formalidades

summarize / resumir *v.* expresar brevemente las ideas y detalles más importantes

summation / recapitulación *s.* compendio; acto de dar todos los detalles principales en forma sucinta

superficial / superficial *adj.* en la superficie; poco profundo

superfluous / superfluo *adj.* innecesario

supple / flexible *adj.* capaz de doblarse y moverse fácil y ágilmente

surmised / conjeturó *v.* adivinó; dedujo

surveyed / deslindó *v.* midió y marcó para mostrar los linderos

swerve / desviar *v.* virar hacia un lado brusca o repentinamente y salirse del rumbo fijo

synonymous / sinónimo *adj.* con significado igual o similar

systemic / sistémico *adj.* que afecta el organismo o sistema físico completo

T

taboo / tabú *adj.* algo prohibido dentro de una sociedad o cultura en particular

tactful / discreto *adj.* que se preocupa por no enfadar u ofender a otros

tantalized / exasperó *v.* atormentó; frustró

taut / tirante *adj.* muy estirado

technology / tecnología *s.* ciencia de las artes mecánicas e industriales

tedious / tedioso *adj.* extenso o verboso y fastidioso

tempered / temperado *adj.* tratado para alcanzar exactamente la fuerza o equilibrio correcto

tempest / tempestad *s.* poderosa tormenta con fuertes vientos

terrain / terreno *s.* tierra o trocha de tierra, principalmente en lo relativo a sus características naturales

terrors / terrores *s.* grandes temores

theology / teología *s.* el estudio de la religión

tranquil / tranquilo *adj.* calmado; quieto; sosegado

transcribed / transcribió *v.* escribió o mecanografió una copia

transform / transformar *v.* cambiar en forma o apariencia

transformed / transformó *v.* cambió la condición o naturaleza de

transfusion / transfusión *s.* acto de transferencia o transmisión

transient / transitorio *adj.* no permanente

transition / transición *s.* cambiar o pasar de una condición a otra

traversed / atravesó *v.* cruzó sobre, a través de, o de un extremo a otro

treacherous / traicionero *adj.* que da una falsa apariencia de seguridad; peligroso

tremulously / trémulamente *adv.* con temor; tímidamente

tumultuously / tumultuosamente *adv.* de forma agitada

tyranny / tiranía *s.* poder opresor

U

unabated / cabal *adj.* no disminuido ni reducido

unanimity / unanimidad *s.* acuerdo total

unconscious / inconsciente *adj.* temporalmente sin conocimiento; desmayado

undertaking / empresa *s.* tarea o desafío

unscrupulous / inescrupuloso *adj.* poco ético; deshonesto

unwonted / inusitado *adj.* inusual; poco familiar

urban / urbano *adj.* característico de una ciudad

V

validate / validar *v.* demostrar que algo se basa en hechos o es efectivo

vanquished / venció *v.* derrotó completamente

venerable / venerable *adj.* que inspira respeto imponente

verify / verificar *v.* demostrar que algo es cierto con evidencia

vernacular / lengua vernácula *s.* idioma nativo

vigilance / vigilancia *s.* cuidado

vigilant / vigilante *adj.* alerta al peligro

vigorously / vigorosamente *adv.* enérgicamente o poderosamente

vindicated / vindicado *adj.* liberado de culpa

virtuous / virtuoso *adj.* que se distingue por sus virtudes morales; con rectitud

virulent / virulento *adj.* extremadamente doloroso o infeccioso

vision / visión *s.* sentido de la vista; algo que se ve en un sueño o en la imaginación

volition / volición *s.* acto de usar la voluntad; determinación

voluminous / voluminoso *adj.* con suficiente material como para llenar volúmenes

votive / votivo *adj.* diseñado para lograr o cumplir una intención especial

vulnerability / vulnerabilidad *s.* exposición a ataques morales, críticas, tentaciones, etc.

W

wanton / displicente *adj.* insensible; injustificable

wasteland / tierra baldía *s.* tierra en su estado natural, sin cultivar

wilderness / tierra salvaje *s.* región en la que no habitan personas

wily / artero *adj.* solapado; astuto

wretched / miserable *adj.* profundamente atormentado; desdichado

Life of the English Language

The life of every language depends on the people who use it. Whenever you use English by asking a question, talking on the phone, going to a movie, reading a magazine, or writing an e-mail, you keep it healthy and valuable.

Using a Dictionary

Use a **dictionary** to find the meaning, the pronunciation, and the part of speech of a word. Consult a dictionary also to trace the word's *etymology*, or its origin. Etymology explains how words change, how they are borrowed from other languages, and how new words are invented, or "coined."

Here is an entry from a dictionary. Notice what it tells about the word *anthology*.

> **anthology** (an thäl′ ə jè) *n., pl.* –gies [Gr. anthologia, a garland, collection of short poems < *anthologos*, gathering flowers < *anthos*, flower + *legein*, to gather] a collection of poems, stories, songs, excerpts, etc., chosen by the compiler.

Dictionaries provide the *denotation* of each word, or its objective meaning. The symbol < means "comes from" or "is derived from." In this case, the Greek words for "flower" and "gather" combined to form a Greek word that meant a garland, and then that word became an English word that means a collection of literary flowers—a collection of literature like the one you are reading now.

Using a Thesaurus

Use a **thesaurus** to increase your vocabulary. In a thesaurus, you will find synonyms, or words that have similar meanings, for most words. Follow these guidelines to use a thesaurus:

- Do not choose a word just because it sounds interesting or educated. Choose the word that expresses exactly the meaning you intend.
- To avoid errors, look up the word in a dictionary to check its precise meaning and to make sure you are using it properly.

Here is an entry from a thesaurus. Notice what it tells about the word *book*.

> **book** *noun* A printed and bound work: tome, volume. See WORDS.
> **book** *verb* **1.** To register in or as if in a book: catalog, enroll, inscribe, list, set down, write down. *See* REMEMBER. **2.** To cause to be set aside, as for one's use, in advance: bespeak, engage, reserve. *See* GET.

If the word can be used as different parts of speech, as book can, the thesaurus entry provides synonyms for the word as each part of speech. Many words also have connotations, or emotional associations that the word calls to mind. A thesaurus entry also gives specific synonyms for each connotation of the word.

Activity Look up the words *knight* and *chivalry* in a dictionary. **(a)** What are their etymologies?
(b) Explain what their etymologies reveal about the development of English. Then, check the word *chivalry* in a thesaurus.
(c) What are two synonyms for this word?
(d) In what way do the connotations of the synonyms differ?

The Origin and Development of English

Old English English began about the year 500 when Germanic tribes settled in Britain. The language of these peoples—the Angles, Saxons, and Jutes—combined with Danish and Norse when Vikings attacked Britain and added some Latin elements when Christian missionaries arrived. The result was Old English, which looked like this:

Hwaet! We Gar-Dena in gear-dagum,
peod-cyninga, prym gefrunon,
hu da aepelingas ellen fremedon!

These words are the opening lines of the Old English epic poem *Beowulf*, probably composed in the eighth century. In modern English, they mean: "Listen! We know the ancient glory of the Spear-Danes, and the heroic deeds of those noble kings!"

Middle English The biggest change in English took place after the Norman Conquest of Britain in 1066. The Normans spoke a dialect of Old French, and Old English changed dramatically when the Normans became the new aristocracy. From about 1100 to 1500, the people of Britain spoke what we now call Middle English.

A Knyght ther was, and that a worthy man,
That fro the tyme that he first bigan
To riden out, he loved chivalrie,
Trouthe and honour, fredom and curtesie.

These lines from the opening section of Chaucer's *Canterbury Tales* (c. 1400) are much easier for us to understand than the lines from *Beowulf*. They mean: "There was a knight, a worthy man who, from the time he began to ride, loved chivalry, truth, honor, freedom, and courtesy."

Modern English During the Renaissance, with its emphasis on reviving classical culture, Greek and Latin languages exerted a strong influence on the English language. In addition, Shakespeare added about two thousand words to the language. Grammar, spelling, and pronunciation continued to change. Modern English was born.

> *But soft! What light through yonder window breaks?*
> *It is the East, and Juliet is the sun!*

These lines from Shakespeare's *Romeo and Juliet* (c. 1600) need no translation, although it is helpful to know that "soft" means "speak softly." Since Shakespeare's day, conventions of usage and grammar have continued to change. For example, the *th* at the ends of many verbs has become s. In Shakespeare's time, it was correct to say "Romeo *hath* fallen in love." In our time, it is right to say "he *has* fallen in love." However, the changes of the past five hundred years are not nearly as drastic as the changes from Old English to Middle English, or from Middle English to Modern English. We still speak Modern English.

Old Words, New Words

Modern English has a larger vocabulary than any other language in the world. The *Oxford English Dictionary* contains about a half million words, and it is estimated that another half million scientific and technical terms do not appear in the dictionary. Here are the main ways that new words enter the language:

- **War**—Conquerors introduce new terms and ideas—and new vocabulary, such as anger, from Old Norse.
- **Immigration**—When large groups of people move from one country to another, they bring their languages with them, such as *boycott*, from Ireland.
- **Travel and Trade**—Those who travel to foreign lands and those who do business in faraway places bring new words back with them, such as *shampoo*, from Hindi.
- **Science and Technology**—In our time, the amazing growth of science and technology adds multitudes of new words to English, such as *Internet.*

English is also filled with **borrowings,** words taken directly from other languages. Sometimes borrowed words keep basically the same meanings they have in their original languages: *pajamas* (Hindi), *sauna* (Finnish), *camouflage* (French), *plaza* (Spanish). Sometimes borrowed words take on new meanings. *Sleuth,* for example, an Old Norse word for trail, has come to mean the person who follows a *trail*—a detective.

Mythology contributed to our language too. Some of the days of the week are named after Norse gods—Wednesday was Woden's Day, Thursday was Thor's Day. Greek and Roman myths have given us many words, such as jovial (from Jove), *martial* (from Mars), *mercurial* (from Mercury), and *herculean* (from Hercules).

Americanisms are words, phrases, usages, or idioms that originated in American English or that are unique to the way Americans speak. They are expressions of our national character in all its variety: *easy as pie, prairie dog, bamboozle, panhandle, halftime, fringe benefit, bookmobile, jackhammer, southpaw, lickety split.*

Activity Look up the following words in a dictionary. Describe the ways in which you think these words entered American English.

sabotage *burrito* *moccasin* *mecca* *megabyte*

The Influence of English

English continues to have an effect on world cultures and literature. There are about three hundred million native English speakers, and about the same number who speak English as a second language. Although more people speak Mandarin Chinese, English is the dominant language of trade, tourism, international diplomacy, science, and technology.

Language is a vehicle of both communication and culture, and the cultural influence of English in the twenty-first century is unprecedented in the history of the world's languages. Beyond business and science, English spreads through sports, pop music, Hollywood movies, television, and journalism. A book that is translated into English reaches many more people than it would in its native language alone. Perhaps most significantly, English dominates the Internet. The next time you log on, notice how many Web sites from around the world also have an English version. The global use of English is the closest the world has ever come to speaking an international language.

Activity Choose one area of culture—such as sports, fashion, the arts, or technology—and identify three new words that English has recently added to the *world's* vocabulary.
(a) How do you think non-English speakers feel about the spread of English? **(b)** Do you think English helps to bring people together? Why or why not?

Tips for Improving Fluency

When you were younger, you learned to read. Then, you read to expand your experiences or for pure enjoyment. Now, you are expected to read to learn. As you progress in school, you are given more and more material to read. The tips on these pages will help you improve your reading fluency, or your ability to read easily, smoothly, and expressively. Use these tips as you read daily.

Keeping Your Concentration

One common problem that readers face is the loss of concentration. When you are reading an assignment, you might find yourself rereading the same sentence several times without really understanding it. The first step in changing this behavior is to notice that you do it. Becoming an active, aware reader will help you get the most from your assignments. Practice using these strategies:

- Cover what you have already read with a note card as you go along. Then, you will not be able to reread without noticing that you are doing it.
- Set a purpose for reading beyond just completing the assignment. Then, read actively by pausing to ask yourself questions about the material as you read. Check the accuracy of your answers as you continue to read.
- Use the Reading Strategy instruction and notes that appear with each selection in this textbook.
- Look at any art or illustrations that accompany the reading and use picture clues to help your comprehension.
- Stop reading after a specified period of time (for example, 5 minutes) and summarize what you have read. To help you with this strategy, use the Reading Check questions that appear with each selection in this textbook. Reread to find any answers you do not know.

Reading Phrases

Fluent readers read phrases rather than individual words. Reading this way will speed up your reading and improve your comprehension. Here are some useful ideas:

- Experts recommend rereading as a strategy to increase fluency. Choose a passage of text that is neither too hard nor too easy. Read the same passage aloud several times until you can read it smoothly. When you can read the passage fluently, pick another passage and keep practicing.
- Read aloud into a tape recorder. Then, listen to the recording, noting your accuracy, pacing, and expression. You can also read aloud and share feedback with a partner.
- Use the *Prentice Hall Audio Program Literature Hear It!* to hear the selections read aloud. Read along silently in your textbook, noticing how the reader uses his or her voice and emphasizes certain words and phrases.
- Set a target reading rate. Time yourself as you read and work to increase your speed without sacrificing the level of your comprehension.

Understanding Key Vocabulary

If you do not understand some of the words in an assignment, you may miss out on important concepts. Therefore, it is helpful to keep a dictionary nearby when you are reading. Follow these steps:

- Before you begin reading, scan the text for unfamiliar words or terms. Find out what those words mean before you begin reading.
- Use context—the surrounding words, phrases, and sentences—to help you determine the meanings of unfamiliar words.
- If you are unable to understand the meaning through context, refer to the dictionary.

Paying Attention to Punctuation

When you read, pay attention to punctuation. Commas, periods, exclamation points, semicolons, and colons tell you when to pause or stop. They also indicate relationships between groups of words. When you recognize these relationships you will read with greater understanding and expression. Look at the chart below.

Punctuation Mark	Meaning
comma	brief pause
period	pause at the end of a thought
exclamation point	pause that indicates emphasis
semicolon	pause between related but distinct thoughts
colon	pause before giving explanation or examples

Using the Reading Fluency Checklist

Use the checklist below each time you read a selection in this textbook. In your Language Arts journal or notebook, note which skills you need to work on and chart your progress each week.

Reading Fluency Checklist

- ❑ Preview the text to check for difficult or unfamiliar words.
- ❑ Practice reading aloud.
- ❑ Read according to punctuation.
- ❑ Break down long sentences into the subject and its meaning.
- ❑ Read groups of words for meaning rather than reading single words.
- ❑ Read with expression (change your tone of voice to add meaning to the word).

Reading is a skill that can be improved with practice. The key to improving your fluency is to read. The more you read, the better your reading will become.

Approaches to Criticism

By writing **criticism**—writing that analyzes literature—readers share their responses to a written work. Criticism is also a way for a reader to deepen his or her own understanding and appreciation of the work, and to help others to deepen theirs.

The information in this handbook will guide you through the process of writing criticism. In addition, it will help you to refine your critical perceptions to ensure that you are ready to produce work at the college level.

Understanding Criticism

There are a few different types of criticism. Each can enhance understanding and deepen appreciation of literature in a distinctive way. All types share similar functions.

The Types of Criticism

Analysis Students are frequently asked to analyze, or break into parts and examine, a passage or a work. When you write an analysis, you must support your ideas with references to the text.

Archetypal Criticism Archetypal criticism evaluates works of literature by identifying and analyzing the archetypes contained within them. An archetype, sometimes called a "universal symbol," is a plot, character, symbol, image, setting, or idea that recurs in the literature of many different cultures. Archetypes and patterns of archetypes can be seen as representing common patterns of human life and experience.

Biographical Criticism Biographical criticism uses information about a writer's life to shed light on his or her work.

Historical Criticism Historical criticism traces connections between an author's work and the events, circumstances, or ideas that shaped the writer's historical era.

Political Criticism Political criticism involves viewing an author's work with a focus on political assumptions and content—whether explicit or implicit—and, possibly, assessing the political impact of the work. Similar to historical criticism, political criticism draws connections between an author's work and the political issues and assumptions of the times.

Philosophical Criticism In philosophical criticism, the elements of a literary work such as plot, characters, conflict, and motivations are examined through the lens of the author's philosophical arguments and stances. The critic taking a philosophical approach will analyze philosophical arguments presented in a literary work and determine how those arguments have molded the work.

The Functions of Criticism

Critical writing serves a variety of important functions:

Making Connections All criticism makes connections between two or more things. For instance, an analysis of a poem may show similarities among different images.

Making Distinctions Criticism must make distinctions as well as connections. In an analysis of a poem, a critic may distinguish between two possible purposes for poetry: first, to create an enduring image and, second, to present a deeper meaning.

Achieving Insight By making connections and distinctions, criticism achieves insight. An analysis of a poem may reach the insight that the poem stands on its own as a work of beauty apart from any deeper meaning.

Making a Judgment Assessing the value of a work is an important function of criticism. A critic may assess a work by comparing it with other works and by using a standard such as enjoyment, insight, or beauty.

"Placing" the Work Critics guide readers not by telling them *what* to think but by giving them *terms in which to think.* Critical writing may help readers apply varied perspectives to illuminate different aspects of a work.

Writing Criticism

Like all solid writing, a work of criticism presents a thesis (a central idea) and supports it with arguments and evidence. Follow the strategies below to develop a critical thesis and gather support for it.

Formulate a Working Thesis

Once you have chosen a work or works on which to write, formulate a working thesis. First, ask yourself questions like these:

- What strikes you most about the work or the writer that your paper will address? What puzzles you most?
- In what ways is the work unlike others you have read?
- What makes the techniques used by the writer so well-suited to (or so poorly chosen for) conveying the theme of the work?

Jot down notes answering your questions. Then, reread passages that illustrate your answers, jotting down notes about what each passage contributes to the work. Review your notes, and write a sentence that draws a conclusion about the work.

If your thesis concerns . . .	look for support in the form of . . .
Character	• dialogue • character's actions • writer's descriptions of the character • other characters' reactions to the character
Theme	• fate of characters • patterns and contrasts of imagery, character, or events • mood • writer's attitude toward the action
Style	• memorable descriptions, observations • passages that "sound like" the writer • examples of rhetorical devices, such as exaggeration and irony
Historical Context	• references to historical events and personalities • evidence of social or political pressures on characters • socially significant contrasts between characters (for example, between the rich and the poor)
Literary Influences	• writer's chosen form or genre • passages that "sound like" another writer • events or situations that resemble those in other works • evidence of an outlook similar to that of another writer

Gather Support

Taking Notes From the Work
Once you have a working thesis, take notes on passages in the work that confirm it. To aid your search for support, consider the type of support suited to your thesis, as in the chart.

Conducting Additional Research If you are writing biographical or historical criticism, you will need to consult sources on the writer's life and era. Even if you are writing a close analysis of a poem, you should consider consulting the works of critics to benefit from their insights and understanding.

Take Notes

Consider recording notes from the works you are analyzing, as well as from any critical works you consult, on a set of note cards. A good set of note cards enables you to recall details accurately, to organize your ideas effectively, and to see connections between ideas.

One Card, One Idea If you use note cards while researching, record each key passage, theme, critical opinion, or fact on a separate note card. A good note card includes a brief quotation or summary of an idea and a record of the source, including the page number, in which you found the information. When copying a sentence from a work, use quotation marks and check to make sure you have copied it correctly.

Coding Sources Keep a working bibliography, a list of all works you consult, as you conduct research. Assign a code, such as a letter, to each work on the list. For each note you take, include the code for the source.

Coding Cards Organize your note cards by labeling each with the subtopic it concerns.

Present Support Appropriately

As you draft, consider how much support you need for each point and the form that support should take. You can provide support in the following forms:

- **Summaries** are short accounts in your own words of important elements of the work, such as events, a character's traits, or the writer's ideas. They are appropriate for background information.
- **Paraphrases** are restatements of passages from a work in your own words. They are appropriate for background and for information incidental to your main point.
- **Quotations of key passages** are direct transcriptions of the writer's words, enclosed in quotation marks or, if longer than three lines, set as indented text. If a passage is crucial to your thesis, you should quote it directly and at whatever length is necessary.

Quotations of multiple examples are required to support claims about general features of a work, such as a claim about the writer's ironic style or use of cartoonlike characters.

DOs and DON'Ts of Academic Writing

Avoid gender and cultural bias. Certain terms and usages reflect the bias of past generations. To eliminate bias in any academic work you do, edit with the following rules in mind:

- **Pronoun usage** When referring to an unspecified individual in a case in which his or her gender is irrelevant, use forms of the pronoun phrase he or she. Example: "A lawyer is trained to use his or her mind."
- **"Culture-centric" terms** Replace terms that reflect a bias toward one culture with more generally accepted synonyms. For instance, replace terms such as primitive (used of hunting-gathering peoples), the Orient (used to refer to Asia), and Indians (used of Native Americans), all of which suggest a view of the world centered in Western European culture.

Avoid plagiarism. Presenting someone else's ideas, research, or exact words as your own is plagiarism, the equivalent of stealing or fraud. Laws protect the rights of writers and researchers in cases of commercial plagiarism. Academic standards protect their rights in cases of academic plagiarism.

To avoid plagiarism, follow these practices:

- Read from several sources.
- Synthesize what you learn.
- Let the ideas of experts help you draw your own conclusions.
- Always credit your sources properly when using someone else's ideas to support your view.

By following these guidelines, you will also push yourself to think independently.

Forming Your Critical Vocabulary

To enhance your critical perceptions—the connections you find and the distinctions you make—improve your critical vocabulary. The High-Utility Academic Words that appear in this textbook and are underlined in the Glossary (pp. R1–R13) are useful in critical writing.

Citing Sources and Preparing Manuscript

In research writing, cite your sources. In the body of your paper, provide a footnote, an endnote, or an internal citation, identifying the sources of facts, opinions, or quotations. At the end of your paper, provide a bibliography or a Works Cited list, a list of all the sources you cite. Follow an established format, such as Modern Language Association (MLA) Style or American Psychological Association (APA) Style.

Works Cited List (MLA Style)

A Works Cited list must contain accurate information sufficient to enable a reader to locate each source you cite. The basic components of an entry are as follows:

- Name of the author, editor, translator, or group responsible for the work
- Title
- Place and date of publication
- Publisher

For print materials, the information required for a citation generally appears on the copyright and title pages of a work. For the format of Works Cited list entries, consult the examples at right and in the chart on page R22.

Parenthetical Citations (MLA Style)

A parenthetical citation briefly identifies the source from which you have taken a specific quotation, factual claim, or opinion. It refers the reader to one of the entries on your Works Cited list. A parenthetical citation has the following features:

- It appears in parentheses.
- It identifies the source by the last name of the author, editor, or translator.
- It gives a page reference, identifying the page of the source on which the information cited can be found.

Punctuation A parenthetical citation generally falls outside a closing quotation mark but within the final punctuation of a clause or sentence. For a long quotation set off from the rest of your text, place the citation at the end of the excerpt without any punctuation following.

Special Cases

- If the author is an organization, use the organization's name, in a shortened version if necessary.
- If you cite more than one work by the same author, add the title or a shortened version of the title.

Sample Works-Cited Lists (MLA 7th Edition)

Carwardine, Mark, Erich Hoyt, R. Ewan Fordyce, and Peter Gill. *The Nature Company Guides: Whales, Dolphins, and Porpoises.* New York: Time-Life, 1998. Print.

"Discovering Whales." *Whales on the Net.* 1998. Whales in Danger Information Service. Web. 18 Oct. 1999.

Neruda, Pablo. "Ode to Spring." *Odes to Opposites.* Trans. Ken Krabbenhoft. Ed. and illus. Ferris Cook. Boston: Little, 1995. Print.

The Saga of the Volsungs. Trans. Jesse L. Byock. London: Penguin, 1990. Print.

List an anonymous work by title.

List both the title of the work and the collection in which it is found.

Sample Parenthetical Citations

It makes sense that baleen whales such as the blue whale, the bowhead whale, the humpback whale, and the sei whale (to name just a few) grow to immense sizes (Carwardine, Hoyt, and Fordyce 19–21). The blue whale has grooves running from under its chin to partway along the length of its underbelly. As in some other whales, these grooves expand and allow even more food and water to be taken in (Ellis 18–21).

Author's last name

Page numbers where information can be found

MLA Style for Listing Sources

Book with one author	Pyles, Thomas. *The Origins and Development of the English Language.* 2nd ed. New York: Harcourt, 1971. Print.
Book with two or three authors	McCrum, Robert, William Cran, and Robert MacNeil. *The Story of English*. New York: Penguin, 1987. Print.
Book with an editor	Truth, Sojourner. *Narrative of Sojourner Truth.* Ed. Margaret Washington. New York: Vintage, 1993. Print.
Book with more than three authors or editors	Donald, Robert B., et al. *Writing Clear Essays*. Upper Saddle River: Prentice, 1996. Print.
Single work in an anthology	Hawthorne, Nathaniel. "Young Goodman Brown." *Literature: An Introduction to Reading and Writing*. Ed. Edgar V. Roberts and H. E. Jacobs. Upper Saddle River: Prentice, 1998. 376–385. Print. [Indicate pages for the entire selection.]
Introduction to a work in a published edition	Washington, Margaret. Introduction. *Narrative of Sojourner Truth.* By Sojourner Truth. Ed. Washington. New York: Vintage, 1993. v–xi. Print.
Signed article from an encyclopedia	Askeland, Donald R. "Welding." *World Book Encyclopedia.* 1991 ed. Print.
Signed article in a weekly magazine	Wallace, Charles. "A Vodacious Deal." *Time* 14 Feb. 2000: 63. Print.
Signed article in a monthly magazine	Gustaitis, Joseph. "The Sticky History of Chewing Gum." *American History* Oct. 1998: 30–38. Print.
Newspaper	Thurow, Roger. "South Africans Who Fought for Sanctions Now Scrap for Investors." *Wall Street Journal* 11 Feb. 2000: A1+. Print. [For a multipage article that does not appear on consecutive pages, write only the first page number on which it appears, followed by the plus sign.]
Unsigned editorial or story	"Selective Silence." Editorial. *Wall Street Journal* 11 Feb. 2000: A14. Print. [If the editorial or story is signed, begin with the author's name.]
Signed pamphlet or brochure	[Treat the pamphlet as though it were a book.]
Work from a library subscription service	Ertman, Earl L. "Nefertiti's Eyes." *Archaeology* Mar.–Apr. 2008: 28–32. *Kids Search*. EBSCO. New York Public Library. Web. 18 June 2008 [Indicate the date you accessed the information.]
Filmstrips, slide programs, videocassettes, DVDs, and other audiovisual media	*The Diary of Anne Frank*. Dir. George Stevens. Perf. Millie Perkins, Shelley Winters, Joseph Schildkraut, Lou Jacobi, and Richard Beymer. 1959. Twentieth Century Fox, 2004. DVD.
CD-ROM (with multiple publishers)	Simms, James, ed. *Romeo and Juliet.* By William Shakespeare. Oxford: Attica Cybernetics; London: BBC Education; London: Harper, 1995. CD-ROM.
Radio or television program transcript	"Washington's Crossing of the Delaware." *Weekend Edition Sunday.* Natl. Public Radio. WNYC, New York. 23 Dec. 2003. Television transcript.
Internet Web page	"Fun Facts About Gum." NACGM site. 1999. National Association of Chewing Gum Manufacturers. Web. 19 Dec. 1999 [Indicate the date you accessed the information.]
Personal interview	Smith, Jane. Personal interview. 10 Feb. 2000.

All examples follow the style given in the *MLA Handbook for Writers of Research Papers,* seventh edition, by Joseph Gibaldi.

APA Style for Listing Sources

Book with one author	Pyles, T. (1971). *The origins and development of the English language* (2nd ed.). New York: Harcourt Brace Jovanovich.
Book with two or three authors	McCrum, R., Cran, W., & MacNeil, R. (1987). *The story of English.* New York: Penguin Books.
Book with an editor	Truth, S. (1993). *Narrative of Sojourner Truth* (M. Washington, Ed.). New York: Vintage Books.
Book with more than three authors or editors	Donald, R. B., Morrow, B. R., Wargetz, L. G., & Werner, K. (1996). *Writing clear essays.* Upper Saddle River, NJ: Prentice Hall. [With eight or more authors, abbreviate all authors after the sixth as "et al."]
Single work from an anthology	Hawthorne, N. (1998). Young Goodman Brown. In E. V. Roberts, & H. E. Jacobs (Eds.), *Literature: An introduction to reading and writing* (pp. 376–385). Upper Saddle River, NJ: Prentice Hall.
Introduction in a published edition	Washington, M. (1993). Introduction. In M. Washington (Ed.), S. Truth, *Narrative of Sojourner Truth* (pp. v–xi). New York: Vintage Books.
Signed article from an encyclopedia	Askeland, D. R. (1991). Welding. In *World Book Encyclopedia.* (Vol. 21. pp. 190–191). Chicago: World Book.
Signed article in a weekly magazine	Wallace, C. (2000, February 14). A vodacious deal. *Time, 155,* 63. [The volume number appears in italics before the page number.]
Signed article in a monthly magazine	Gustaitis, J. (1998, October). The sticky history of chewing gum. *American History*, 33, 30–38.
Newspaper	Thurow, R. (2000, February 11). South Africans who fought for sanctions now scrap for investors. *Wall Street Journal*, pp. A1, A4. [If an article appears on discontinuous pages, give all page numbers and separate the numbers with a comma.]
Unsigned editorial or story	Selective silence [Editorial]. (2000, February 11). *Wall Street Journal*, p. A14.
Signed pamphlet	Pearson Education. (2000). *LifeCare* (2nd ed.) [Pamphlet]. New York: Smith, John: Author.
Filmstrips, slide programs, videocassettes, DVDs, and other audiovisual media	Wallis, H. B. (Producer), & Curtiz, M. (Director). (1942). *Casablanca* [Motion Picture]. United States: Warner.
Radio or television program transcript	Hackett Fischer, D. (Guest), & Hansen, L. (Host). (2003, December 23). Washington's crossing of the Delaware. [Radio series installment]. *Weekend Edition Sunday.* New York: National Public Radio. Retrieved March 6, 2008 from http://www.npr.org/templates/story/story.php?storyId=1573202
Internet	National Association of Chewing Gum Manufacturers. (1999). Retrieved December 19, 1999, from http://www.nacgm.org/consumer/funfacts.html [References to Websites should begin with the author's last name, if available. Indicate the site name and the available path or URL address.]
Work from a library subscription service	Ertman, E. L. (2008 March–April). Nefertiti's eyes. *Archaeology, 61,* 28–32. Retrieved June 18, 2008, from EBSCO Science Reference Center database.
CD	Shakespeare, W. (1995). *Romeo and Juliet.* (J. Simms, Ed.) [CD-ROM]. Oxford: Attica Cybernetics.
Personal interview	[APA states that, since interviews (and other personal communications) do not provide "recoverable data," they should only be cited in text.]

Literary Terms

ALLEGORY An ***allegory*** is a story or tale with two or more levels of meaning—a literal level and one or more symbolic levels. The events, setting, and characters in an allegory are symbols for ideas or qualities. Arthur Miller's play *The Crucible* (p. 1124) is an allegory.

ALLITERATION ***Alliteration*** is the repetition of consonant sounds at the beginning of words or accented syllables. Sara Teasdale uses alliteration in these lines from her poem "Understanding":

> Your spirit's secret hides like gold
>
> Sunk in a Spanish galleon

ALLUSION An ***allusion*** is a reference to a well-known person, place, event, literary work, or work of art. Writers often make allusions to stories from the Bible, to Greek and Roman myths, to plays by Shakespeare, to political and historical events, and to other materials with which they can expect their readers to be familiar. In "The Love Song of J. Alfred Prufrock" (p. 708), T. S. Eliot alludes to, among other things, Dante's *Inferno*, Italian artist Michelangelo, Shakespeare's *Hamlet*, and the Bible. By using allusions, writers can suggest complex ideas simply and easily.

AMBIGUITY ***Ambiguity*** is the effect created when words suggest and support two or more divergent interpretations. Ambiguity may be used in literature to express experiences or truths that are complex or contradictory. Ambiguity often derives from the fact that words have multiple meanings.

See also ***Irony.***

ANALOGY An ***analogy*** is an extended comparison of relationships. It is based on the idea that the relationship between one pair of things is like the relationship between another pair. Unlike a metaphor, an analogy involves an explicit comparison, often using the words *like* or *as.*

See also ***Metaphor*** and ***Simile.***

ANECDOTE An ***anecdote*** is a brief story about an interesting, amusing, or strange event. An anecdote is told to entertain or to make a point. In the excerpt from *Life on the Mississippi* (p. 570), Mark Twain tells several anecdotes about his experiences on the Mississippi River.

ANTAGONIST An ***antagonist*** is a character or force in conflict with a main character, or protagonist. In Jack London's "To Build a Fire" (p. 596), the antagonist is neither a person nor an animal but rather the extreme cold. In many stories, the conflict between the antagonist and the protagonist is the basis for the plot.

See also ***Conflict, Plot,*** and ***Protagonist.***

APHORISM An ***aphorism*** is a general truth or observation about life, usually stated concisely. Often witty and wise, aphorisms appear in many kinds of works. An essay writer may have an aphoristic style, making many such statements. Ralph Waldo Emerson was famous for his aphoristic style. His essay entitled "Fate" contains the following aphorisms:

> Nature is what you may do.
>
> So far as a man thinks, he is free.
>
> A man's fortunes are the fruit of his character.

Used in an essay, an aphorism can be a memorable way to sum up or to reinforce a point or an argument.

APOSTROPHE An ***apostrophe*** is a figure of speech in which a speaker directly addresses an absent person or a personified quality, object, or idea. Phillis Wheatley uses apostrophe in this line from "To the University of Cambridge, in New England":

> Students, to you 'tis given to scan the heights

See also ***Figurative Language.***

ARCHETYPAL LITERARY ELEMENTS ***Archetypal literary elements*** are patterns in literature found around the world. For instance, the occurrence of events in threes is an archetypal element of fairy tales. Certain character types, such as mysterious guides, are also archetypal elements of such traditional stories. Archetypal elements make stories easier to remember and retell. In Moby-Dick (p. 336), Melville uses the archetype of a whale—like the biblical mammal in conflict with Jonah—to address man's conflict with nature.

ARGUMENT See ***Persuasion.***

ASSONANCE ***Assonance*** is the repetition of vowel sounds in conjunction with dissimilar consonant sounds. Emily Dickinson uses assonance in the line "The mountain at a given distance." The *i* sound is repeated in *given* and *distance*, in the context of the dissimilar consonant sounds *g–v* and *d–s.*

ATMOSPHERE See ***Mood.***

AUTOBIOGRAPHY An ***autobiography*** is a form of nonfiction in which a person tells his or her own life story. Notable examples of autobiographies include those by Benjamin Franklin and Frederick Douglass. *Memoirs,* first-person accounts of personally or historically significant events in which the writer was a participant or an eyewitness, are a form of autobiographical writing.

See also ***Biography*** and ***Journal.***

BALLAD A ***ballad*** is a songlike poem that tells a story, often one dealing with adventure and romance. Most ballads include simple language, four- or six-line stanzas, rhyme, and regular meter.

BIOGRAPHY A ***biography*** is a form of nonfiction in which a writer tells the life story of another person. Carl Sandburg's *Abe Lincoln Grows Up* is a biography of President Lincoln.

See also ***Autobiography.***

BLANK VERSE ***Blank verse*** is poetry written in unrhymed iambic pentameter. An iamb is a poetic foot consisting of one weak stress followed by one strong stress. A pentameter line has five poetic feet. Robert Frost's "Birches" (p. 874) is written in blank verse.

CHARACTER A ***character*** is a person or an animal that takes part in the action of a literary work. The following are some terms used to describe various types of characters:

The ***main character*** in a literary work is the one on whom the work focuses. ***Major characters*** in a literary work include the main character and any other characters who play significant roles. A ***minor character*** is one who does not play a significant role. A ***round character*** is one who is complex and multifaceted, like a real person. A ***flat character*** is one who is one-dimensional. A ***dynamic character*** is one who changes in the course of a work. A ***static character*** is one who does not change in the course of a work.

See also ***Characterization*** and ***Motivation.***

CHARACTERIZATION ***Characterization*** is the act of creating and developing a character. In ***direct characterization,*** a writer simply states a character's traits, as when F. Scott Fitzgerald writes of the main character in his story "Winter Dreams" (p. 730), "He wanted not association with glittering things and glittering people—he wanted the glittering things themselves." In ***indirect characterization,*** character is revealed through one of the following means:

1. words, thoughts, or actions of the character
2. descriptions of the character's appearance or background
3. what other characters say about the character
4. the ways in which other characters react to the character

See also ***Character.***

CINQUAIN See ***Stanza.***

CLASSICISM ***Classicism*** is an approach to literature and the other arts that stresses reason, balance, clarity, ideal beauty, and orderly form in imitation of the arts of ancient Greece and Rome. Classicism is often contrasted with ***Romanticism,*** which stresses imagination, emotion, and individualism. ***Classicism*** also differs from ***Realism,*** which stresses the actual rather than the ideal.

See also ***Realism*** and ***Romanticism.***

CLIMAX The ***climax*** is the high point of interest or suspense in a literary work. For example, Jack London's "To Build a Fire" (p. 596) reaches its climax when the man realizes that he is going to freeze to death. The climax generally appears near the end of a story, play, or narrative poem.

See also ***Plot.***

COMEDY A ***comedy*** is a literary work, especially a play, that has a happy ending.

CONFLICT A ***conflict*** is a struggle between opposing forces. Sometimes this struggle is internal, or within a character, as in Bernard Malamud's "The First Seven Years" (p. 1028). At other times, this struggle is external, or between a character and an outside force, as in Jack London's "To Build a Fire" (p. 596). Conflict is one of the primary elements of narrative literature because most plots develop from conflicts.

See also ***Antagonist, Plot,*** and ***Protagonist.***

CONNOTATION A ***connotation*** is an association that a word calls to mind in addition to the dictionary meaning of the word. Many words that are similar in their dictionary meanings, or denotations, are quite different in their connotations. Consider, for example, José García Villa's line, "Be beautiful, noble, like the antique ant." This line would have a very different effect if it were "Be pretty, classy, like the old ant." Poets and other writers choose their words carefully so that the connotations of those words will be appropriate.

See also ***Denotation.***

CONSONANCE ***Consonance*** is the repetition of similar final consonant sounds at the ends of words or accented syllables. Emily Dickinson uses consonance in these lines:

> But if he ask where you are hid
> Until to-morrow,—happy letter!
> Gesture, coquette, and shake your head!

COUPLET See ***Stanza.***

CRISIS In the plot of a narrative, the ***crisis*** is the turning point for the protagonist—the point at which the protagonist's situation or understanding changes dramatically. In Bernard Malamud's "The First Seven Years" (p. 1028), the crisis occurs when Feld recognizes that Sobel loves Miriam.

DENOTATION The ***denotation*** of a word is its objective meaning, independent of other associations that the word brings to mind.

See also ***Connotation.***

DENOUEMENT See ***Plot.***

DESCRIPTION A ***description*** is a portrayal, in words, of something that can be perceived by the senses. Writers create descriptions by using images, as John Wesley Powell does in this passage from "The Most Sublime Spectacle on Earth," his description of the Grand Canyon:

> Clouds creep out of canyons and wind into other canyons. The heavens seem to be alive, not moving as move the heavens over a plain, in one direction with the wind, but following the multiplied courses of these gorges.

See also ***Image.***

DEVELOPMENT See ***Plot.***

DIALECT A ***dialect*** is the form of a language spoken by people in a particular region or group. Writers often use dialect to make their characters seem realistic and to create local color. See, for example, Mark Twain's "The Notorious Jumping Frog of Calaveras County" (p. 576).

See also ***Local Color.***

DIALOGUE A ***dialogue*** is a conversation between characters. Writers use dialogue to reveal character, to present events, to add variety to narratives, and to arouse their readers' interest.

See also ***Drama.***

DICTION ***Diction*** is a writer's or speaker's word choice. Diction is part of a writer's style and may be described as formal or informal, plain or ornate, common or technical, abstract or concrete.

See also ***Style.***

DRAMA A ***drama*** is a story written to be performed by actors. The playwright supplies dialogue for the characters to speak, as well as stage directions that give information about costumes, lighting, scenery, properties, the setting, and the characters' movements and ways of speaking. Dramatic conventions include soliloquies, asides, or the passage of time between acts or scenes.

See also ***Genre.***

DRAMATIC MONOLOGUE A ***dramatic monologue*** is a poem or speech in which an imaginary character speaks to a silent listener. T. S. Eliot's "The Love Song of J. Alfred Prufrock" (p. 708) is a dramatic monologue.

See also ***Dramatic Poem*** and ***Monologue.***

DRAMATIC POEM A ***dramatic poem*** is one that makes use of the conventions of drama. Such poems may be monologues or dialogues or may present the speech of many characters. Robert Frost's "The Death of the Hired Man" is a famous example of a dramatic poem.

See also ***Dramatic Monologue.***

DYNAMIC CHARACTER See ***Character.***

EPIGRAM An ***epigram*** is a brief, pointed statement, in prose or in verse. Benjamin Franklin was famous for his epigrams, which include "Fools make feasts, and wise men eat them," and "A plowman on his legs is higher than a gentleman on his knees."

EPIPHANY An ***epiphany*** is a sudden revelation or flash of insight. The shoemaker in Bernard Malamud's "The First Seven Years" (p. 1028) experiences an epiphany when he suddenly and thoroughly comprehends that the actions of his apprentice, Sobel, are motivated by his secret love for Miriam.

ESSAY An ***essay*** is a short nonfiction work about a particular subject. Essays can be classified as ***formal*** or ***informal***, ***personal*** or ***impersonal***. They can also be classified according to purpose, such as ***cause-and-effect*** (see the excerpt from "One Day, Now Broken in Two" on p. 1404), ***satirical*** (see "Coyote v. Acme" on p. 1384), or ***reflective*** (see Amy Tan's "Mother Tongue" on p. 1410). Modes of discourse, such as ***expository***, ***descriptive***, ***persuasive***, or ***narrative***, are other means of classifying essays.

See also ***Satire, Exposition, Description, Persuasion,*** and ***Narration.***

EXPOSITION ***Exposition*** is writing or speech that explains, informs, or presents information. The main techniques of expository writing include analysis, classification, comparison and contrast, definition, and exemplification, or illustration. An essay may be primarily expository, as is William Safire's "Onomatopoeia" (p. 1378), or it may use exposition to support another purpose, such as persuasion or argumentation, as in Ian Frazier's satirical essay "Coyote v. Acme" (p. 1384).

In a story or play, the exposition is that part of the plot that introduces the characters, the setting, and the basic situation.

See also ***Plot.***

FALLING ACTION See ***Plot.***

FICTION ***Fiction*** is prose writing that tells about imaginary characters and events. Short stories and novels are works of fiction.

See also ***Genre, Narrative, Nonfiction,*** and ***Prose.***

FIGURATIVE LANGUAGE ***Figurative language*** is writing or speech not meant to be taken literally. Writers use figurative language to express ideas in vivid and imaginative ways. For example, Emily Dickinson begins one poem with the following description of snow:

> It sifts from leaden sieves, / It powders all the wood
>
> By describing the snow as if it were flour, Dickinson renders a precise and compelling picture of it.

See also ***Figure of Speech.***

FIGURE OF SPEECH A ***figure of speech*** is an expression or a word used imaginatively rather than literally.

See also ***Figurative Language.***

FLASHBACK A ***flashback*** is a section of a literary work that interrupts the chronological presentation of events to relate an event from an earlier time. A writer may present a flashback as a character's memory or recollection, as part of an account or story told by a character, as a dream or a daydream, or simply by having the narrator switch to a time in the past.

FLAT CHARACTER See ***Character.***

FOIL A ***foil*** is a character who provides a contrast to another character. In F. Scott Fitzgerald's "Winter Dreams" (p. 730), Irene Scheerer is a foil for the tantalizing Judy Jones.

FOLK LITERATURE ***Folk literature*** is the body of stories, legends, myths, ballads, songs, riddles, sayings, and other works arising out of the oral traditions of peoples around the globe. The folk literature traditions of the United States, including those of Native Americans and of the American pioneers, are especially rich.

FOOT See ***Meter.***

FORESHADOWING ***Foreshadowing*** in a literary work is the use of clues to suggest events that have yet to occur.

FREE VERSE ***Free verse*** is poetry that lacks a regular rhythmical pattern, or meter. A writer of free verse is at liberty to use any rhythms that are appropriate to what he or she is saying. Free verse has been widely used by twentieth-century poets such as Leslie Marmon Silko, who begins "Where Mountain Lion Lay Down With Deer" with these lines:

> I climb the black rock mountain
>
> stepping from day to day
>
> silently.

See also ***Meter.***

GENRE A ***genre*** is a division, or type, of literature. Literature is commonly divided into three major genres: poetry, prose, and drama. Each major genre can in turn be divided into smaller genres. Poetry can be divided into lyric, concrete, dramatic, narrative, and epic poetry. Prose can be divided into fiction and nonfiction. Drama can be divided into serious drama, tragedy, comic drama, melodrama, and farce.

See also ***Drama, Poetry,*** and ***Prose.***

GOTHIC ***Gothic*** refers to the use of primitive, medieval, wild, or mysterious elements in literature. Gothic novels feature places like mysterious and gloomy castles, where horrifying, supernatural events take place. Their influence on Edgar Allan Poe is evident in "The Fall of the House of Usher" (p. 292).

GROTESQUE ***Grotesque*** refers to the use of bizarre, absurd, or fantastic elements in literature. The grotesque is generally characterized by distortions or striking incongruities. ***Grotesque characters***, like those in Flannery O'Connor's "The Life You Save May Be Your Own" (p. 1012), are characters who have become bizarre through their obsession with an idea or a value or as a result of an emotional problem.

HARLEM RENAISSANCE The ***Harlem Renaissance,*** which occurred during the 1920s, was a time of African American artistic creativity centered in Harlem, in New York City. Writers of the Harlem Renaissance include Countee Cullen, Claude McKay, Jean Toomer, and Langston Hughes.

HYPERBOLE ***Hyperbole*** is a deliberate exaggeration or overstatement, often used for comic effect. In Mark Twain's "The Notorious Jumping Frog of Calaveras County" (p. 576), the claim that Jim Smiley would follow a bug as far as Mexico to win a bet is hyperbole.

IAMBIC PENTAMETER ***Iambic pentameter*** is a line of poetry with five iambic feet, each containing one unstressed syllable followed by one stressed syllable (˘ ´). Iambic pentameter may be rhymed or unrhymed. Unrhymed iambic pentameter is called blank verse. These lines from Anne Bradstreet's "The Author to Her Book" are in iambic pentameter:

> Ănd fór thy̆, Móthĕr, shĕ ălás ĭs póor,
>
> Whĭch caúsed hĕr thús tŏ sénd thĕe oút ŏf dóor.

See also ***Blank Verse*** and ***Meter.***

IDYLL An ***idyll*** is a poem or part of a poem that describes and idealizes country life. John Greenleaf Whittier's "Snowbound" is an idyll.

IMAGE An ***image*** is a word or phrase that appeals to one or more of the five senses—sight, hearing, touch, taste, or smell.

See also ***Imagery.***

IMAGERY ***Imagery*** is the descriptive or figurative language used in literature to create word pictures for the reader. These pictures, or images, are created by details of sight, sound, taste, touch, smell, or movement.

IMAGISM ***Imagism*** was a literary movement that flourished between 1912 and 1927. Led by Ezra Pound and Amy Lowell, the Imagist poets rejected nineteenth-century poetic forms and language. Instead, they wrote short poems that used ordinary language and free verse to create sharp, exact, concentrated pictures. Pound's poetry (p. 722) provides examples of Imagism.

IRONY ***Irony*** is a contrast between what is stated and what is meant, or between what is expected to happen and what actually happens. In ***verbal irony***, a word or a phrase is used to suggest the opposite of its usual meaning. In ***dramatic irony***, there is a contradiction between what a character thinks and what the reader or audience knows. In ***irony of situation***, an event occurs that contradicts the expectations of the characters, of the reader, or of the audience.

JOURNAL A ***journal*** is a daily autobiographical account of events and personal reactions. For example, Mary Chesnut's journal (p. 495) records events during the Civil War.

LEGEND A ***legend*** is a traditional story. Usually a legend deals with a particular person—a hero, a saint, or a national leader. Often legends reflect a people's cultural values. American legends include those of the early Native Americans and those about folk heroes such as Davy Crockett.

See also ***Myth.***

LETTER A ***letter*** is a written message or communication addressed to a reader or readers and is generally sent by mail. Letters may be ***private*** or ***public***, depending on their intended audience. A public letter, also called a ***literary letter*** or ***epistle***, is a work of literature written in the form of a personal letter but created for publication. Michel-Guillaume Jean de Crèvecoeur's "Letters From an American Farmer" are public letters.

LOCAL COLOR ***Local color*** is the use in a literary work of characters and details unique to a particular geographic area. It can be created by the use of dialect and by descriptions of customs, clothing, manners, attitudes, and landscape. Local-color stories were especially popular after the Civil War, bringing readers the West of Bret Harte and the Mississippi River of Mark Twain.

See also ***Realism*** and ***Regionalism.***

LYRIC POEM A ***lyric poem*** is a melodic poem that expresses the observations and feelings of a single speaker. Unlike a narrative poem, a lyric poem focuses on producing a single, unified effect. Types of lyric poems include the ***elegy***, the ***ode***, and the ***sonnet***. Among contemporary American poets, the lyric is the most common poetic form.

MAIN CHARACTER See ***Character.***

MEMOIR A ***memoir*** is a type of nonfiction autobiographical writing that tells about a person's own life, usually focusing on the writer's involvement in historically or culturally significant events—either as a participant or an eyewitness.

METAPHOR A ***metaphor*** is a figure of speech in which one thing is spoken of as though it were something else. The identification suggests a comparison between the two things that are identified, as in "death is a long sleep."

A ***mixed metaphor*** occurs when two metaphors are jumbled together. For example, thorns and rain are illogically mixed in "the thorns of life rained down on him." A ***dead metaphor*** is one that has been overused and has become a common expression, such as "the arm of the chair" or "nightfall."

METER The ***meter*** of a poem is its rhythmical pattern. This pattern is determined by the number and types of stresses, or beats, in each line. To describe the meter of a poem, you must scan its lines. ***Scanning*** involves marking the stressed and unstressed syllables, as follows:

> Sóon ăs | thĕ sún | fŏrsóok | thĕ éas|tĕrn máin
>
> Thĕ péal | ĭng thún | dĕr shóok | thĕ héav'n | lў pláin;
>
> —"An Hymn to the Evening," Phillis Wheatley

As the example shows, each strong stress is marked with a slanted line (´) and each weak stress with a horseshoe symbol (˘). The weak and strong stresses are then divided by vertical lines (|) into groups called feet. The following types of feet are common in poetry written in English:

1. ***Iamb:*** a foot with one unstressed syllable followed by one stressed syllable, as in the word "around"
2. ***Trochee:*** a foot with one stressed syllable followed by one unstressed syllable, as in the word "broken"
3. ***Anapest:*** a foot with two unstressed syllables followed by one stressed syllable, as in the phrase "in a flash"
4. ***Dactyl:*** a foot with one stressed syllable followed by two unstressed syllables, as in the word "argument"
5. ***Spondee:*** a foot with two stressed syllables, as in the word "airship"
6. ***Pyrrhic:*** a foot with two unstressed syllables, as in the last foot of the word "imag|ining"

Lines of poetry are often described as iambic, trochaic, anapestic, or dactylic. Lines are also described in terms of the number of feet that occur in them, as follows:

1. ***Monometer:*** verse written in one-foot lines

   Évĭl
   Bĕgéts
   Évĭl

   —Anonymous

2. ***Dimeter:*** verse written in two-foot lines

   Thĭs ís | thĕ tíme
   ŏf thĕ trág|ĭc mán

   —"Visits to St. Elizabeth's," Elizabeth Bishop

3. ***Trimeter:*** verse written in three-foot lines:

   Over | the win|ter glaciers
   I see | the sum|mer glow,
   And through | the wild-|piled snowdrift
   The warm | rosebuds | below.

   —"Beyond Winter," Ralph Waldo Emerson

4. ***Tetrameter:*** verse written in four-foot lines:

   The sun | that brief | Decem|ber day
   Rose cheer|less ov|er hills | of gray

   —"Snowbound," John Greenleaf Whittier

5. ***Pentameter:*** verse written in five-foot lines:

> I doubt | not God | is good, | well-mean|ing, kind,
>
> And did | He stoop | to quib|ble could | tell why
>
> The lit|tle bur|ied mole | contin|ues blind
>
> —"Yet Do I Marvel," Countee Cullen

A complete description of the meter of a line tells both how many feet there are in the line and what kind of foot is most common. Thus, the lines from Countee Cullen's poem would be described as ***iambic pentameter. Blank verse*** is poetry written in unrhymed iambic pentameter. Poetry that does not have a regular meter is called ***free verse***.

MONOLOGUE A ***monologue*** is a speech delivered entirely by one person or character.

See also ***Dramatic Monologue.***

MOOD ***Mood***, or atmosphere, is the feeling created in the reader by a literary work or passage. Elements that can influence the mood of a work include its setting, tone, and events.

See also ***Setting*** and ***Tone.***

MOTIVATION A ***motivation*** is a reason that explains a character's thoughts, feelings, actions, or speech. Characters are motivated by their values and by their wants, desires, dreams, wishes, and needs. Sometimes the reasons for a character's actions are stated directly, as in Willa Cather's "A Wagner Matinée" (p. 652), when Clark explains his reception of his aunt by saying, "I owed to this woman most of the good that ever came my way in my boyhood." At other times, the writer will just suggest a character's motivation.

MYTH A ***myth*** is a fictional tale that explains the actions of gods or heroes or the causes of natural phenomena. Myths that explain the origins of earthly life, as do the Onondaga, Navajo, and Modoc myths in this text, are known as origin myths. Other myths express the central values of the people who created them.

NARRATION ***Narration*** is writing that tells a story. The act of telling a story is also called ***narration***. The ***narrative***, or story, is told by a storyteller called the ***narrator***. A story is usually told chronologically, in the order in which events take place in time, though it may include flashbacks and foreshadowing. Narratives may be true, like the events recorded in Mary Chesnut's journal (p. 495), or fictional, like the events in Flannery O'Connor's "The Life You Save May Be Your Own" (p. 1012). Narration is one of the forms of discourse and is used in novels, short stories, plays, narrative poems, anecdotes, autobiographies, biographies, and reports.

See also ***Narrative Poem*** and ***Narrator.***

NARRATIVE A ***narrative*** is a story told in fiction, nonfiction, poetry, or drama. Narratives are often classified by their content or purpose. An ***exploration narrative*** is a firsthand account of an explorer's travels in a new land. Alvar Núñez Cabeza de Vaca's account of his exploration of the wilderness that is now Texas, "A Journey Through Texas," appears on page 48. "The Interesting Narrative of the Life of Olaudah Equiano" (excerpt on p. 170) is a ***slave narrative***, an account of the experiences of an enslaved person. A ***historical narrative*** is a narrative account of significant historical events, such as William Bradford's *Of Plymouth Plantation.* (p. 58).

See also ***Narration.***

NARRATIVE POEM A ***narrative*** poem tells a story in verse. Three traditional types of narrative verse are ***ballads***, songlike poems that tell stories; ***epics***, long poems about the deeds of gods or heroes; and ***metrical romances***, poems that tell tales of love and chivalry.

See also ***Ballad.***

NARRATOR A ***narrator*** is a speaker or character who tells a story. A story or novel may be narrated by a main character, by a minor character, or by someone uninvolved in the story. The narrator may speak in the first person or in the third person. An ***omniscient narrator*** is all-knowing, while a ***limited narrator*** knows only what one character does.

See also ***Point of View.***

NATURALISM ***Naturalism*** was a literary movement among novelists at the end of the nineteenth century and during the early decades of the twentieth century. The Naturalists tended to view people as hapless victims of immutable natural laws. Early exponents of Naturalism included Stephen Crane, Jack London, and Theodore Dreiser.

See also ***Realism.***

NONFICTION ***Nonfiction*** is prose writing that presents and explains ideas or that tells about real people, places, objects, or events. Essays, biographies, autobiographies, journals, and reports are all examples of nonfiction.

See also ***Fiction*** and ***Genre.***

NOVEL A ***novel*** is a long work of fiction. A novel often has a complicated plot, many major and minor characters, a significant theme, and several varied settings. Novels can be classified in many ways, based on the historical periods in which they are written, the subjects and themes that they treat, the techniques that are used in them, and the literary movements that inspired them. Classic nineteenth-century novels include Herman Melville's *Moby-Dick* (p. 336) and Nathaniel Hawthorne's *The Scarlet Letter* (an extended reading suggestion). Well-known twentieth-century novels include F. Scott Fitzgerald's *The Great Gatsby* and Edith Wharton's *Ethan Frome* (recommended selections for extended reading). A ***novella*** is not as long as a novel but is longer than a short story. Ernest Hemingway's *The Old Man and the Sea* is a novella.

ODE An ***ode*** is a long, formal lyric poem with a serious theme that may have a traditional stanza structure. Odes often honor people, commemorate events, respond to natural scenes, or consider serious human problems.

See also ***Lyric Poem***.

OMNISCIENT NARRATOR See ***Narrator*** and ***Point of View***.

ONOMATOPOEIA ***Onomatopoeia*** is the use of words that imitate sounds. Examples of such words are *buzz, hiss, murmur,* and *rustle*.

ORAL TRADITION ***Oral tradition*** is the passing of songs, stories, and poems from generation to generation by word of mouth. The oral tradition in America has preserved Native American myths and legends, spirituals, folk ballads, and other works originally heard and memorized rather than written down.

See also ***Ballad, Folk Literature, Legend, Myth,*** and ***Spiritual***.

ORATORY ***Oratory*** is public speaking that is formal, persuasive, and emotionally appealing. Patrick Henry's "Speech in the Virginia Convention" (p. 100) is an example of oratory.

OXYMORON An ***oxymoron*** is a figure of speech that combines two opposing or contradictory ideas. An oxymoron, such as "freezing fire," suggests a paradox in just a few words.

See also ***Figurative Language*** and ***Paradox***.

PARADOX A ***paradox*** is a statement that seems to be contradictory but that actually presents a truth. Marianne Moore uses paradox in "Nevertheless" when she says, "Victory won't come / to me unless I go / to it." Because a paradox is surprising, it draws the reader's attention to what is being said.

See also ***Figurative Language*** and ***Oxymoron***.

PARALLELISM ***Parallelism*** is the repetition of a grammatical structure. Robert Hayden concludes his poem "Astronauts" with these questions in parallel form:

> What do we want of these men?
>
> What do we want of ourselves?

Parallelism is used in poetry and in other writing to emphasize and to link related ideas.

PARODY A ***parody*** is a humorous imitation of a literary work, one that exaggerates or distorts the characteristic features of the original.

PASTORAL ***Pastoral*** poems deal with rural settings, including shepherds and rustic life. Traditionally, pastoral poems have presented idealized views of rural life. In twentieth-century pastorals, however, poets like Robert Frost introduced ethical complexity into an otherwise simple landscape.

PERSONIFICATION ***Personification*** is a figure of speech in which a nonhuman subject is given human characteristics. In "April Rain Song," Langston Hughes personifies the rain:

> Let the rain sing you a lullaby.

Effective personification of things or ideas makes them seem vital and alive, as if they were human.

See also ***Figurative Language***.

PERSUASION ***Persuasion*** is writing or speech that attempts to convince a reader to think or act in a particular way. During the Revolutionary War period, leaders such as Patrick Henry, Thomas Paine, and Thomas Jefferson used persuasion in their political arguments. Persuasion is also used in advertising, in editorials, in sermons, and in political speeches. An ***argument*** is a logical way of presenting a belief, conclusion, or stance. A good argument is supported with reasoning and evidence.

PLAIN STYLE ***Plain style*** is a type of writing in which uncomplicated sentences and ordinary words are used to make simple, direct statements. This style was favored by those Puritans who wanted to express themselves clearly, in accordance with their religious beliefs. In the twentieth century, Ernest Hemingway was a master of plain style.

See also ***Style***.

PLOT ***Plot*** is the sequence of events in a literary work. In most fiction, the plot involves both characters and a central conflict. The plot usually begins with an ***exposition*** that introduces the setting, the characters, and the basic situation. This is followed by the ***inciting incident***, which introduces the central conflict. The conflict then increases during the ***development*** until it reaches a high point of interest or suspense, the ***climax***. The climax is followed by the end, or resolution, of the central conflict. Any events that occur after the ***resolution*** make up the ***denouement***. The events that lead up to the climax make up the ***rising action***. The events that follow the climax make up the ***falling action***.

See also ***Conflict***.

POETRY ***Poetry*** is one of the three major types of literature. In poetry, form and content are closely connected, like the two faces of a single coin. Poems are often divided into lines and stanzas and often employ regular rhythmical patterns, or meters. Most poems use highly concise, musical, and emotionally charged language. Many also make use of imagery, figurative language, and special devices such as rhyme.

See also ***Genre***.

POINT OF VIEW ***Point of view*** is the perspective, or vantage point, from which a story is told. Three commonly used points of view are first person, omniscient third person, and limited third person.

In the ***first-person point of view***, the narrator is a character in the story and refers to himself or herself with the first-person pronoun "I." "The Fall of the House of Usher" (p. 292) is told by a first-person narrator.

The two kinds of third-person point of view, limited and omniscient, are called "third person" because the narrator uses third-person pronouns such as "he" and "she" to refer to the characters. There is no "I" telling the story.

In stories told from the ***omniscient third-person point of view***, the narrator knows and tells about what each character feels and thinks. "The Devil and Tom Walker" (p. 228) is written from the omniscient third-person point of view.

In stories told from the ***limited third-person point of view***, the narrator relates the inner thoughts and feelings of only one character, and everything is viewed from this character's perspective. "An Occurrence at Owl Creek Bridge" (p. 480) is written from the limited third-person point of view.

See also ***Narrator.***

PROSE ***Prose*** is the ordinary form of written language. Most writing that is not poetry, drama, or song is considered prose. Prose is one of the major genres of literature. It occurs in two forms: fiction and nonfiction.

See also ***Fiction, Genre,*** and ***Nonfiction.***

PROTAGONIST The ***protagonist*** is the main character in a literary work. In "The Jilting of Granny Weatherall" (p. 834), the protagonist is the dying grandmother.

See also ***Antagonist.***

QUATRAIN See ***Stanza.***

REALISM ***Realism*** is the presentation in art of the details of actual life. Realism was also a literary movement that began during the nineteenth century and stressed the actual as opposed to the imagined or the fanciful. The Realists tried to write objectively about ordinary characters in ordinary situations. They reacted against Romanticism, rejecting heroic, adventurous, or unfamiliar subjects. Naturalists, who followed the Realists, traced the effects of heredity and environment on people helpless to change their situations.

See also ***Local Color, Naturalism,*** and ***Romanticism.***

REFRAIN A ***refrain*** is a repeated line or group of lines in a poem or song. Most refrains end stanzas, as does "And the tide rises, the tide falls," the refrain in Henry Wadsworth Longfellow's poem (p. 260), or "Coming for to carry me home," the refrain in "Swing Low, Sweet Chariot" (p. 534). Although some refrains are nonsense lines, many increase suspense or emphasize character and theme.

REGIONALISM ***Regionalism*** in literature is the tendency among certain authors to write about specific geographical areas. Regional writers, like Willa Cather and William Faulkner, present the distinct culture of an area, including its speech, customs, beliefs, and history. Local-color writing may be considered a type of Regionalism, but Regionalists, like the Southern writers of the 1920s, usually go beyond mere presentation of cultural idiosyncrasies and attempt, instead, a sophisticated sociological or anthropological treatment of the culture of a region.

See also ***Local Color*** and ***Setting.***

RESOLUTION See ***Plot.***

RHYME ***Rhyme*** is the repetition of sounds at the ends of words. Rhyming words have identical vowel sounds in their final accented syllables. The consonants before the vowels may be different, but any consonants occurring after these vowels are the same, as in *frog* and *bog* or *willow* and *pillow.* End rhyme occurs when rhyming words are repeated at the ends of lines. Internal rhyme occurs when rhyming words fall within a line. ***Approximate,*** or ***slant, rhyme*** occurs when the rhyming sounds are similar, but not exact, as in *prove* and *glove.*

See also ***Rhyme Scheme.***

RHYME SCHEME A ***rhyme scheme*** is a regular pattern of rhyming words in a poem. To describe a rhyme scheme, one uses a letter of the alphabet to represent each rhyming sound in a poem or stanza. Consider how letters are used to represent the *abab* rhyme scheme rhymes in the following example:

With innocent wide penguin eyes, three **a**
large fledgling mocking-birds below **b**
the pussywillow tree, **a**
stand in a row **b**

—"Bird-Witted," Marianne Moore

See also ***Rhyme.***

RHYTHM ***Rhythm*** is the pattern of beats, or stresses, in spoken or written language. Prose and free verse are written in the irregular rhythmical patterns of everyday speech. Consider, for example, the rhythmical pattern in the following free-verse lines by Gwendolyn Brooks:

Life for my child is simple, and is good.

He knows his wish. Yes, but that is not all.

Because I know mine too.

Traditional poetry often follows a regular rhythmical pattern, as in the following lines by America's first great female poet, Anne Bradstreet:

In critic's hands beware thou dost not come,

And take thy way where yet thou art not known

—"The Author to Her Book"

See also ***Meter.***

RISING ACTION See ***Plot.***

ROMANTICISM ***Romanticism*** was a literary and artistic movement of the nineteenth century that arose in reaction against eighteenth-century Neoclassicism and placed a premium on imagination, emotion, nature, individuality, and exotica. Romantic elements can be found in the works of American writers as diverse as Cooper, Poe, Thoreau, Emerson, Dickinson, Hawthorne, and Melville. Romanticism is particularly evident in the works of the Transcendentalists.

See also ***Classicism*** and ***Transcendentalism.***

ROUND CHARACTER See ***Character.***

SATIRE ***Satire*** is writing that ridicules or criticizes individuals, ideas, institutions, social conventions, or other works of art or literature. The writer of a satire, the satirist, may use a tolerant, sympathetic tone or an angry, bitter tone. Some satire is written in prose and some, in poetry. Examples of satire in this text include W. H. Auden's "The Unknown Citizen" (p. 774) and Ian Frazier's "Coyote v. Acme" (p. 1384).

SCANSION ***Scansion*** is the process of analyzing a poem's metrical pattern. When a poem is scanned, its stressed and unstressed syllables are marked to show what poetic feet are used and how many feet appear in each line. The last two lines of Edna St. Vincent Millay's "I Shall Go Back Again to the Bleak Shore" may be scanned as follows:

> But I | shall find | the sul|len rocks | and skies
>
> Unchanged | from what | they were | when I | was young.

See also ***Meter.***

SENSORY LANGUAGE ***Sensory language*** is writing or speech that appeals to one or more of the five senses.

See also ***Image.***

SETTING The ***setting*** of a literary work is the time and place of the action. A setting may serve any of a number of functions. It may provide a background for the action. It may be a crucial element in the plot or central conflict. It may also create a certain emotional atmosphere, or mood.

SHORT STORY A ***short story*** is a brief work of fiction. The short story resembles the novel but generally has a simpler plot and setting. In addition, the short story tends to reveal character at a crucial moment rather than developing it through many incidents. For example, Thomas Wolfe's "The Far and the Near" concentrates on what happens to a train engineer when he visits people who had waved to him every day.

See also ***Fiction*** and ***Genre.***

SIMILE A ***simile*** is a figure of speech that makes a direct comparison between two subjects, using either *like* or *as*. Here are two examples of similes:

> The trees looked like pitch forks against the sullen sky.
>
> Her hair was as red as a robin's breast.

See also ***Figurative Language.***

SLANT RHYME See ***Rhyme.***

SONNET A ***sonnet*** is a fourteen-line lyric poem focused on a single theme. Sonnets have many variations but are usually written in iambic pentameter, following one of two traditional patterns: the ***Petrarchan***, or ***Italian***, ***sonnet***, which is divided into two parts, the eight-line octave and the six-line sestet; and the ***Shakespearean***, or ***English***, ***sonnet***, which consists of three quatrains and a concluding couplet.

See also ***Lyric Poem.***

SPEAKER The ***speaker*** is the voice of a poem. Although the speaker is often the poet, the speaker may also be a fictional character or even an inanimate object or another type of nonhuman entity. Interpreting a poem often depends upon recognizing who the speaker is, whom the speaker is addressing, and what the speaker's attitude, or tone, is.

See also ***Point of View.***

SPIRITUAL A ***spiritual*** is a type of African American folk song dating from the period of slavery and Reconstruction. A typical spiritual deals both with religious freedom and, on an allegorical level, with political and economic freedom. In some spirituals the biblical river Jordan was used as a symbol for the Ohio River, which separated slave states from free states; and the biblical promised land, Canaan, was used as a symbol for the free northern United States. Most spirituals made use of repetition, parallelism, and rhyme. See "Go Down Moses" (p. 532) and "Swing Low, Sweet Chariot" (p. 534).

STAGE DIRECTIONS See ***Drama.***

STANZA A ***stanza*** is a group of lines in a poem that are considered to be a unit. Many poems are divided into stanzas that are separated by spaces. Stanzas often function just like paragraphs in prose. Each stanza states and develops a single main idea.

Stanzas are commonly named according to the number of lines found in them, as follows:

1. Couplet: a two-line stanza
2. Tercet: a three-line stanza
3. Quatrain: a four-line stanza
4. Cinquain: a five-line stanza
5. Sestet: a six-line stanza
6. Heptastich: a seven-line stanza
7. Octave: an eight-line stanza

STATIC CHARACTER See ***Character.***

STREAM OF CONSCIOUSNESS ***Stream of consciousness*** is a narrative technique that presents thoughts as if they were coming directly from a character's mind. Instead of being arranged in chronological order, the events are presented from the character's point of view, mixed in with the character's thoughts just as they might spontaneously occur. Katherine Anne Porter uses this technique in "The Jilting of Granny Weatherall" (p. 834) to capture Granny's dying thoughts and feelings. Ambrose Bierce also uses the stream of consciousness technique in "An Occurrence at Owl Creek Bridge" (p. 480).

See also ***Point of View.***

STYLE A writer's ***style*** includes word choice, tone, degree of formality, figurative language, rhythm, grammatical structure, sentence length, organization—in short, every feature of a writer's use of language. Ernest Hemingway, for example, is noted for a simple prose style that contrasts with Thomas Paine's aphoristic style and with N. Scott Momaday's reflective style.

See also ***Diction*** and ***Plain Style.***

SUSPENSE ***Suspense*** is a feeling of growing uncertainty about the outcome of events. Writers create suspense by raising questions in the minds of their readers. Suspense builds until the climax of the plot, at which point the suspense reaches its peak.

See also ***Climax*** and ***Plot.***

SYMBOL A ***symbol*** is anything that stands for or represents something else. A ***conventional symbol*** is one that is widely known and accepted, such as a voyage symbolizing life or a skull symbolizing death. A ***personal symbol*** is one developed for a particular work by a particular author. Examples in this textbook include Hawthorne's black veil and Melville's white whale.

SYMBOLISM ***Symbolism*** was a literary movement during the nineteenth century that influenced poets, including the Imagists and T. S. Eliot. Symbolists turned away from everyday, realistic details to express emotions by using a pattern of symbols.

See also ***Imagism*** and ***Realism.***

THEME A ***theme*** is a central message or insight into life revealed by a literary work. An essay's theme is often directly stated in its thesis statement. In most works of fiction, the theme is only indirectly stated: A story, poem, or play most often has an ***implied theme***. For example, in "A Worn Path" (p. 848), Eudora Welty does not directly say that Phoenix Jackson's difficult journey shows the power of love, but readers learn this indirectly by the end of the story.

TONE The ***tone*** of a literary work is the writer's attitude toward his or her subject, characters, or audience. A writer's tone may be formal or informal, friendly or distant, personal or pompous. For example, William Faulkner's tone in his "Nobel Prize Acceptance Speech" (p. 828) is earnest and serious, whereas James Thurber's tone in "The Night the Ghost Got In" (p. 860) is humorous and ironic.

See also ***Mood.***

TRAGEDY A ***tragedy*** is a work of literature, especially a play, that shows the downfall or death of the main character, or ***tragic hero***.

TRANSCENDENTALISM ***Transcendentalism*** was an American literary and philosophical movement of the nineteenth century. The Transcendentalists, who were based in New England, believed that intuition and the individual conscience "transcend" experience and thus are better guides to truth than are the senses and logical reason. Influenced by Romanticism, the Transcendentalists respected the individual spirit and the natural world, believing that divinity was present everywhere, in nature and in each person. The Transcendentalists included Ralph Waldo Emerson, Henry David Thoreau, Bronson Alcott, W. H. Channing, Margaret Fuller, and Elizabeth Peabody.

See also ***Romanticism.***

College Application Essay

If you are applying for admission to a college, you will probably need to submit an essay as part of your application. This essay will help admissions committee members get a sense of you as a person and as a student. Review the chart at right for general strategies, and follow the guidelines below to produce an effective college application essay.

Strategies for Writing an Effective College Application Essay

- **Choose the right topic**. If you have a choice of essay topics, choose one that truly interests you.
- **Organize.** Use a strong organization that carries the reader from introduction to conclusion.
- **Begin Strongly.** Open with an introduction that has a good chance of sparking the reader's interest.
- **Elaborate.** Be sure to explain why the experiences you discuss are important to you or what you learned from them.
- **Show style.** Bring life to your essay through vivid descriptions, precise word choice, and sophisticated sentence structure, such as parallelism. Consider including dialogue where appropriate.
- **Close with a clincher.** Write a conclusion that effectively sums up your ideas.
- **Do a clean job**. Proofread your essay carefully. It should be error-free.

Selecting a Topic

Read the essay question on the application form with care. Mark key criteria and direction words such as *describe* and *explain*. After you have written a first draft, check to make sure you have met all of the requirements of the question. Your essay has a better chance of succeeding if it meets the requirements exactly.

General Questions About You

The essay question on a college application may be as general as "Describe a significant experience or event in your life and explain its consequences for you." To choose the right topic for such a question, think of an event or experience that truly is meaningful to you—a camping trip, a volunteer event, a family reunion. Test the subject by drafting a letter about it to a good friend or relative. If you find that your enthusiasm for the subject grows as you write, and if your discussion reveals something about your growth or your outlook on life, the topic may be the right one for your essay.

Directed Questions

The essay question on an application may be a directed question, rather than a general question. For instance, you may be asked to select three figures from history you would like to meet and to explain your choices.

In such cases, do not give an answer just because you think it will please reviewers. Rely on your own interests and instincts. Your most convincing writing will come from genuine interest in the subject.

Style

Remember that an essay is a formal document addressed to strangers. Use a formal to semiformal style. Avoid incomplete sentences and slang unless you are using them for clear stylistic effect. Use words with precision, selecting one or two accurate words to express your meaning. Do not use a word if you are unsure of its meaning.

Format

Most applications limit the length of essays. Do not exceed the allowed space or word count. Your college application essay should be neatly typed or printed, using adequate margins. Proofread your final draft carefully. If you submit a separate copy of the essay (rather than writing on the application form), number the pages and include your name and contact information on each page.

Reusing Your Essay

Most students apply to a number of different colleges. Once you have written a strong essay for one application, you may adapt it for others. However, do not submit a single essay to several schools blindly. Always read the application essay question carefully to insure that the essay you submit fulfills all of its requirements.

Workplace Writing

Job Search Document: Cover Letter

A cover letter is a formal letter in which the writer asks to be considered for a job. It usually accompanies, or "covers," a completed job application, a résumé, or both. A good cover letter relates specifically to the job for which the writer is applying.

Write a Cover Letter

Consider a part-time job or a summer job you would like to have. Then, write a cover letter to accompany a job application. Include a header, an inside address, an introductory paragraph, one or two body paragraphs, a closing paragraph, and a signature. Mention your main qualifications, and explain how they make you a good fit for the job.

000 Park Avenue
San Marcos, Texas 00000
512-000-0000
emailaddress@theinternet.com

January 15, 20—

The heading should include the writer's name, address, phone number, e-mail address, and the date of the letter.

Barbara Jones, Director
River Place Day Camp
500 S. Camp Street
Austin, TX 00000

The inside address includes the name, title, and address of the recipient.

Dear Ms. Jones:

I am writing to apply for the position of Activities Coordinator for your summer camp. The job description posted on the Texas Summer Camps job board perfectly parallels my own interests and experience.

As noted on the enclosed résumé, I have four years' experience as a camp counselor, including one as Lead Counselor and one as Assistant Activities Director. In these roles, I learned not only to work as a team leader, but also to help tailor a camp's programs to the needs of its campers. As an education student at Texas State University, I have completed basic education courses as well as electives in counseling, recreational learning, and youth leadership. These courses, along with my volunteer work as an after-school mentor, have sparked my interest in non-classroom education. In fact, I plan to base my entire career on the idea that learning can be fun—and can happen anywhere.

The body paragraph describes how the writer's experiences relate specifically to the job responsibilities.

I hope to help make River Place Day Camp a fun, educational, and well-organized experience for both its campers and its staff. I look forward to meeting with you and discussing my qualifications in more detail.

Sincerely,
Cesar Moreno

Job Search Document: Résumé

A **résumé** is a written summary or outline of a person's job qualifications. It plays a key part in most career or job searches. An effective résumé has the following elements:

- candidate's name, current address, phone number, and e-mail address;
- educational background, work experience, and other relevant life experiences;
- logical organization;
- clearly labeled sections.

Compile a Résumé

Write a résumé to use in a job search. Consider a specific job you would like to pursue. Then, brainstorm for relevant information in your schooling or work experience. Include important details and maintain a professional tone.

As you develop your document, experiment with different fonts to create a professional-looking, readable document.

CESAR MORENO
000 Park Avenue
San Marcos, Texas 00000
512-000-0000 • emailaddress@theinternet.com

Place contact information at the top of the résumé.

EDUCATION
- **Texas State University**, San Marcos, TX
  Bachelor of Science in Education
  Expected: May, 20—
- **Austin High School**, Austin, TX
  Graduated with honors, May, 20—

WORK EXPERIENCE
- **Summer 2008–Summer 2010**
  Camp Lazy J, Fredericksburg, TX
  Camp Counselor: Supervised groups of campers aged 8–12. Served as Lead Counselor in 20– and as Assistant Activities Director in 20–.
- **2009–2010**
  YMCA, Austin, Texas
  Life Guard and Swim Instructor: Guarded weekend free-swim sessions and taught beginning and intermediate youth swim classes.

The headings *Education, Work Experience,* and so on indicate that this résumé is organized by topic.

The items under each topic are bulleted and arranged from most to least recent.

VOLUNTEER EXPERIENCE
- **2009–present**
  San Marcos Community Center, San Marcos, TX
  After-School Mentor: Help elementary and middle school students organize and complete schoolwork, develop skills and interests, and resolve personal issues.
- **2008–2009**
  Stepping Up Preschool, Austin, TX
  Teacher's Aide: Assisted in the 3- and 4-year-old classroom; helped plan and execute special summer programs.

ADDITIONAL SKILLS AND CERTIFICATIONS
- CPR certified, 2007 to the present
- Fluent in Spanish
- Proficient in water sports, including rowing, kayaking, and rafting
- Proficient in Microsoft Word, Excel, and PowerPoint
- Completed childcare training course, YMCA, 2007

REFERENCES
Furnished on request.

A résumé should be no longer than a single page.

Job Search Document: Job Application

Many employers require job applicants to complete a **job application.** A job application is a standard form that asks for particular kinds of information, including the candidate's contact information, education, and work experience.

Complete a Job Application

Consider a part-time job you would like to have. Then, copy and complete the job application shown here using your own information.

Employment Application

PERSONAL INFORMATION

Full Name: Cesar Moreno
Address: 000 Park Ave., San Marcos, TX, 00000
Phone Number: (512) 000-0000
E-mail Address: emailaddress@theinternet.com

POSITION AND AVAILABILITY

Position Applied For: Activities Coordinator

EDUCATION

School	Degree/Diploma	Graduation Date
Texas State University Austin High School	B.S./Education diploma	expected 5/20— May, 20—
Additional Skills, Qualifications, Licenses, Training, Awards		
CPR and childcare certified, 2007–present Fluent in Spanish		

EMPLOYMENT HISTORY

Present/Last Position and Dates: Camp Counselor, Summer 2006–Summer 2009
Employer: Camp Lazy J
Responsibilities: supervised campers aged 8–12
Supervisor: Mr. Smith
May we contact Supervisor? If so, phone number: yes; (512) 000-0000

Previous Position: Lifeguard and Swim Instructor, 2007–2008
Employer: Austin YMCA
Responsibilities: Guarded free-swim sessions; taught youth swim classes
Supervisor: Mrs. Smith
May we contact Supervisor? If so, phone number: yes; (512) 000-0000

Please list additional employment information on a separate sheet of paper.

I certify that the information contained in this application is true and complete. I authorize the verification of any or all information listed above.

Signature: Cesar Moreno
Date: January 15, 20—

Include only relevant information, and condense it to fit the space available.

Get your former supervisor's permission before responding "yes" to this item.

The applicant's signature gives the employer permission to check the information provided.

Business Communications: Business Letter

Business letters are formal letters in which the content is other than personal. Whatever the subject, an effective business letter has the following elements:

- a heading, inside address, salutation or greeting, body, closing, and signature
- one of several acceptable formats, including *block format,* in which each part of the letter begins at the left margin, and *modified block format,* in which the heading, closing, and signature are indented to the center of the page
- formal and courteous language

Write a Business Letter

Choose one of the following purposes and write a business letter to accomplish it. Include heading, inside address, salutation, body, closing, and signature. Use polite and formal language.

- complain about poor service in a restaurant
- accompany a short story you hope to have published
- praise the work of an artist or musician
- gain support for a beautification plan in your community

Bright Orange Lodge
000 Orange Dr.
Orchard, FL 00000

May 1, 20—

The heading shows the writer's address, organization, and date.

Tom Manager, Business Manager
Universal Bank, Inc.
00000 Adams Park Drive
Miami, FL 00000

The inside address includes the name, title, company, and address of the recipient.

Dear Mr. Manager:

I am writing to confirm the reservation you have made for your organization's annual corporate retreat.

Per our phone conversation of April 28, you requested that the Bright Orange Lodge facilities be reserved for Universal Bank, Inc. from Friday, June 10, at 6:00 p.m. to Sunday, June 12, at 3:00 p.m. Facilities are to include the large meeting room, the kitchen, and a block of between 20 and 30 double-occupancy rooms. As we discussed, I anticipate a firm room count from you by the end of this month.

This letter is organized in block format.

Per the same conversation, I understand that Universal Bank is planning to use its own caterers for all meals. Should this change, Bright Orange can provide food services in its main dining hall, but we will need advance notice.

A bill for the above-specified services will be sent to your attention under separate cover.

Thank you for choosing Bright Orange for your corporate retreat. If I can be of any further assistance, or if you have any questions, please contact me directly at (352) 000-0000.

Sincerely,
Pat Brown

Pat Brown
Event Coordinator

Business letters end with formal closings, such as *Sincerely* or *Respectfully yours,* followed by the writer's signature and typed name.

Business Communications: Memo

A **memo**—short for *memorandum*—is a brief printed message between co-workers. It usually focuses on information necessary for the completion of a particular task or project. An effective memo has the following elements:

- block organization, with each new element beginning at the left margin
- sender's name, intended audience, date, and topic
- clear and brief description, including statement of actions required

MEMO

TO: Members of the Corporate Retreat Staff
FROM: Ann Smith, Vice President
DATE: May 11, 20—
RE: PLANNING SESSION

Most memos follow this format: To, From, Date, and Re (Regarding). The word *re* is Latin for "about." It introduces the subject of the memo.

Our annual corporate retreat is fast approaching. To ensure that all aspects of the retreat are coordinated, let's meet this Friday, May 14, at 9:00 a.m. in the second-floor conference room.

We will discuss the following topics, so please be prepared to report the status of your assigned area of responsibility.

- finalized dates, times, and location of the retreat (Tom)
- schedule of sessions and events (Bruno)
- presenters and topics (Yolanda)
- caterers and pricing (Barry)
- employee communications — invitations, RSVPs, etc. (DeShon)

The body of a memo is brief and informative, and should clearly state a course of action.

I appreciate the many hours you have already invested in the planning process, and hope that our meeting on Friday will be brief and productive.

AS

Memos are often initialed (either at the conclusion or next to the "FROM" line) in order to indicate that the contents have been approved by the sender.

Business Communications: E-Mail

An **e-mail** is a message sent through an electronic communication system such as a computer network or the Internet. Like a memo, an e-mail may be sent to many recipients at once; however, an e-mail has the added benefit of traveling instantaneously. It can also be used to send an attachment—a file that travels with the e-mail but that must be opened using a separate application. While e-mail messages are often more casual than memos, a workplace e-mail (unlike a personal e-mail) should maintain an appropriately formal tone.

Write a Memo and an E-mail

Choose one of the topics below and write a memo that states the message quickly and efficiently. Then, recast the memo as an e-mail.

- announcement of an upcoming event to members of a club or organization
- reminder to fellow workers in a gift shop about store procedures
- information about a surprise party for a teacher
- details about about transportation to a sports competition

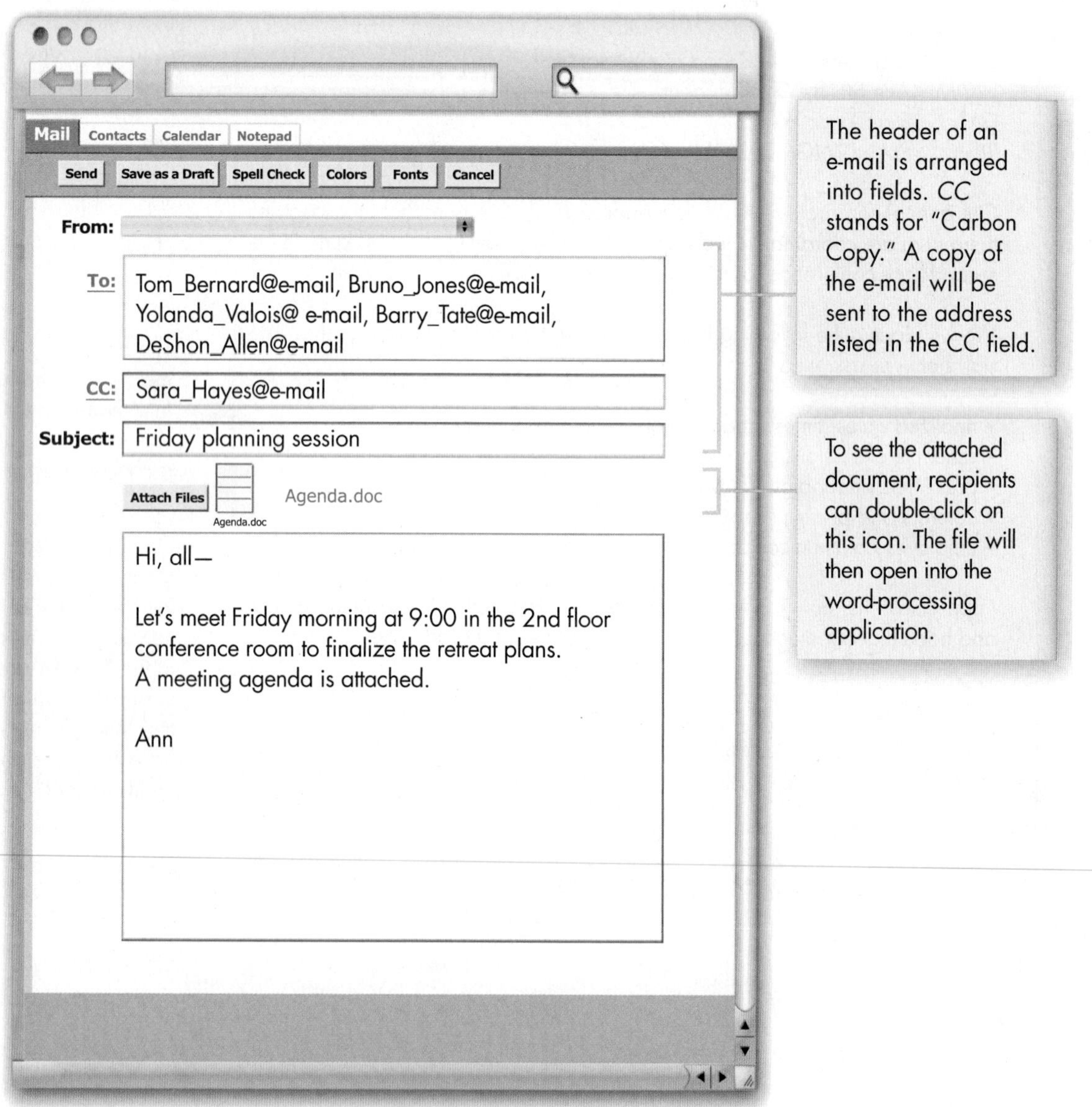

Business Communications: Meeting Minutes

Meeting minutes are notes that tell what transpired at a meeting: what was said, what was decided, and what was left unresolved. Often, the person taking the minutes will jot down abbreviated notes during the meeting, and then rewrite the minutes afterward to distribute to meeting participants.

Write Meeting Minutes

In a small group, conduct a business meeting. Take notes during the meeting. Afterward, write a set of minutes to distribute to your fellow group members.

WRITING HANDBOOK

Meeting to Finalize Corporate Retreat Plans
Friday, May 14, 20–
Main Office, 2nd Floor Conference Room, 9:00 a.m.

The header should include the name of the meeting and its date, location, and time.

Committee Members Present: Ann Smith, Tom Bernard, Yolanda Valois, DeShon Allen
Committee Members Absent: Bruno Jones
Others Present: Sara Hayes, assistant to Ann Smith

Proceedings:
Meeting called to order at 9:00 a.m. by Ann Smith.
Agenda was distributed by Sara Hayes.

First Agenda Item: Retreat dates, times, and location, presented by Tom Bernard.
Tom reported that he has received a letter from Bright Orange Lodge that confirms reservation of their retreat facilities for Universal Bank, Inc. from Friday, June 10, at 6:00 p.m. through Sunday, June 12, at 3:00 p.m. A copy of this letter is attached to the minutes.

These minutes are formatted to show that the meeting followed an agenda.

Second Agenda Item: Schedule of sessions and events, presented by Ann Smith for Bruno Jones.
Bruno is out of the office today, but e-mailed Ann the finalized retreat schedule. Ann distributed copies of the schedule to all members. MOTION to approve schedule; passed unanimously.

A *motion* is a proposal to vote on something. All motions and their results should be carefully noted in meeting minutes.

Assessment of the meeting: Members agreed that the retreat promises to be very successful. Jeff congratulated committee members on a job well done.

Meeting adjourned at 10:05 a.m.
Meeting minutes compiled by Sarah Hayes.

Business Communications: Technical Writing

Technical writing refers to any kind of writing that presents specialized information to help someone perform a task. Scientific reports, troubleshooting guides, assembly instructions, and school handbooks are all examples of technical writing. Although the format varies with the purpose, all technical writing must be clear and easy to use—in other words, "user friendly." It must also be absolutely precise.

Write a Section of a Technical Document

Think of something you know how to do well and write a set of procedures for completing the task. Remember to use specific language that accurately describes the details of the task.

Porterdale Community Library rev. 7/09
Policies and Procedures
Section IV: Collection Maintenance

A page header identifies the publication title, the section, and the revision date.

IV.D. PROCESSING NEW MATERIALS

When new items are delivered to the library, they must be processed, or prepared for use by patrons. The steps for processing a new shipment of items are as follows.

A brief introduction tells the reader what is included in this section.

1. Before unpacking the items:

- **a.** Remove the packing slip from the box.
- **b.** Find the matching order form in the main filing cabinet. Order forms are filed alphabetically by vendor.

2. Unpacking the items:

- **a.** Check each item against both the order form and the packing slip.
- **b.** Place a checkmark on each document next to the title of the item.
- **c.** If all items in the shipment correspond with those on the order form, send the order form and invoice to the business office for payment. The invoice is usually inside the shipment or affixed to the outside in an envelope.
- **d.** If an item is missing or damaged, make a note and/or set the item aside. (See section IV.B. for Ordering and Returning procedures.)

(To process books, see item 3, below. To process other media items, proceed to item 4 on the following page.)

Cross-references and navigational guides are included to help the reader find additional needed information with ease.

3. Processing books:

- **a.** Attach a bar code label to the upper left-hand corner of the front cover.
- **b.** Stamp books with the library name on the front inside cover and back inside cover.
- **c.** Prepare a spine label for books. (See section II.A. for call number designation.) Affix the label to the spine with a label protector.
- **d.** Enter information for the new item into the library catalog database. (See section III.B. for cataloging procedures.)

Guide to Rubrics

What is a rubric?

A rubric is a tool, often in the form of a chart or a grid, that helps you assess your work. Rubrics are particularly helpful for writing and speaking assignments.

To help you or others assess, or evaluate, your work, a rubric offers several specific criteria to be applied to your work. Then the rubric helps you or an evaluator indicate your range of success or failure according to those specific criteria. Rubrics are often used to evaluate writing for standardized tests.

Using a rubric will save you time, focus your learning, and improve the work you do. When you know what the rubric will be before you begin writing a persuasive essay, for example, you will be aware as you write of specific criteria that are important in that kind of an essay. As you evaluate the essay before giving it to your teacher, you will focus on the specific areas that your teacher wants you to master—or on areas that you know present challenges for you. Instead of searching through your work randomly for any way to improve it or correct its errors, you will have a clear and helpful focus on specific criteria.

How are rubrics constructed?

Rubrics can be constructed in several ways.

- Your teacher may assign a rubric for a specific assignment.
- Your teacher may direct you to a rubric in your textbook.
- Your teacher and your class may construct a rubric for a particular assignment together.
- You and your classmates may construct a rubric together.
- You may create your own rubric with criteria you want to evaluate in your work.

How will a rubric help me?

A rubric will help you assess your work on a scale. Scales vary from rubric to rubric but usually range from 6 to 1, 5 to 1, or 4 to 1, with 6, 5, or 4 being the highest score and 1 being the lowest. If someone else is using the rubric to assess your work, the rubric will give your evaluator a clear range within which to place your work. If you are using the rubric yourself, it will help you make improvements to your work.

What are the types of rubrics?

- A holistic rubric has general criteria that can apply to a variety of assignments. See p. R45 for an example of a holistic rubric.
- An analytic rubric is specific to a particular assignment. The criteria for evaluation address the specific issues important in that assignment. See p. R44 for examples of analytic rubrics.

Sample Analytic Rubrics

Rubric With a 4-point Scale

The following analytic rubric is an example of a rubric to assess a persuasive essay. It will help you evaluate focus, organization, support/elaboration, and style/convention.

	Focus	Organization	Support/Elaboration	Style/Convention
4	Demonstrates highly effective word choice; clearly focused on task.	Uses clear, consistent organizational strategy.	Provides convincing, well-elaborated reasons to support the position.	Incorporates transitions; includes very few mechanical errors.
3	Demonstrates good word choice; stays focused on persuasive task.	Uses clear organizational strategy with occasional inconsistencies.	Provides two or more moderately elaborated reasons to support the position.	Incorporates some transitions; includes few mechanical errors.
2	Shows some good word choices; minimally stays focused on persuasive task.	Uses inconsistent organizational strategy; presentation is not logical.	Provides several reasons, but few are elaborated; only one elaborated reason.	Incorporates few transitions; includes many mechanical errors.
1	Shows lack of attention to persuasive task.	Demonstrates lack of organizational strategy.	Provides no specific reasons or does not elaborate.	Does not connect ideas; includes many mechanical errors.

Rubric With a 6-point Scale

The following analytic rubric is an example of a rubric to assess a persuasive essay. It will help you evaluate presentation, position, evidence, and arguments.

	Presentation	Position	Evidence	Arguments
6	Essay clearly and effectively addresses an issue with more than one side.	Essay clearly states a supportable position on the issue.	All evidence is logically organized, well presented, and supports the position.	All reader concerns and counterarguments are effectively addressed.
5	Most of essay addresses an issue that has more than one side.	Essay clearly states a position on the issue.	Most evidence is logically organized, well presented, and supports the position.	Most reader concerns and counterarguments are effectively addressed.
4	Essay adequately addresses issue that has more than one side.	Essay adequately states a position on the issue.	Many parts of evidence support the position; some evidence is out of order.	Many reader concerns and counterarguments are adequately addressed.
3	Essay addresses issue with two sides but does not present second side clearly.	Essay states a position on the issue, but the position is difficult to support.	Some evidence supports the position, but some evidence is out of order.	Some reader concerns and counterarguments are addressed.
2	Essay addresses issue with two sides but does not present second side.	Essay states a position on the issue, but the position is not supportable.	Not much evidence supports the position, and what is included is out of order.	A few reader concerns and counterarguments are addressed.
1	Essay does not address issue with more than one side.	Essay does not state a position on the issue.	No evidence supports the position.	No reader concerns or counterarguments are addressed.

Sample Holistic Rubric

Holistic rubrics are sometimes used to assess writing assignments on standardized tests. Notice that the criteria for evaluation are focus, organization, support, and use of conventions.

Points	Criteria
6 Points	• The writing is strongly focused and shows fresh insight into the writing task. • The writing is organized with a logical progression of ideas. • A main idea is fully developed, and support is specific and substantial. • A mature command of the language is evident. • Sentence structure is varied, and writing is free of all but purposefully used fragments. • Virtually no errors in writing conventions appear.
5 Points	• The writing is clearly focused on the task. • The writing is well organized and generally shows a logical progression of ideas. • A main idea is well developed and supported with relevant detail. • Sentence structure is varied, and the writing is free of unintended fragments. • Writing conventions are followed correctly.
4 Points	• The writing is clearly focused on the task, but extraneous material may intrude at times. • Clear organizational pattern is present, though lapses may occur. • A main idea is adequately supported, but development may be uneven. • Sentence structure is generally fragment free but shows little variation. • Writing conventions are generally followed correctly.
3 Points	• Writing is generally focused on the task, but extraneous material may intrude at times. • An organizational pattern is evident, but writing may lack a logical progression of ideas. • Support for the main idea is generally present but is sometimes illogical. • Sentence structure is generally free of fragments, but there is almost no variation. • The work generally demonstrates a knowledge of writing conventions, with occasional misspellings.
2 Points	• The writing is related to the task but generally lacks focus. • There is little evidence of organizational pattern, and there is little sense of cohesion. • Support for the main idea is generally inadequate, illogical, or absent. • Sentence structure is unvaried, and serious errors may occur. • Errors in writing conventions and spellings are frequent.
1 Point	• The writing may have little connection to the task and is generally unfocused. • There has been little attempt at organization or development. • The paper seems fragmented, with no clear main idea. • Sentence structure is unvaried, and serious errors appear. • Poor word choice and poor command of the language obscure meaning. • Errors in writing conventions and spelling are frequent.
Unscorable	The paper is considered unscorable if: • The response is unrelated to the task or is simply a rewording of the prompt. • The response has been copied from a published work. • The student did not write a response. • The response is illegible. • The words in the response are arranged with no meaning. • There is an insufficient amount of writing to score.

Student Model

Persuasive Writing

This persuasive letter, which would receive a top score according to a persuasive rubric, is a response to the following writing prompt, or assignment:

Write a letter to a government official strongly supporting an environmental issue that is important to you and urging the official to take a specific action that supports your cause.

Dear Secretary of the Interior:

It's a normal carefree day in the forest. The birds are singing and all of the animals are relaxing under the refreshing glow of the sun. But suddenly the thunderous sound of a chainsaw echoes throughout the woodlands, and trees fall violently. The creatures of the forest run in terror. Many of these beautiful creatures will starve to death slowly and painfully as their homes are destroyed, and this precious ecosystem will not be able to regrow to its previous greatness for many years to come.

A descriptive and interesting introduction grabs the reader's attention and shows a persuasive focus.

This sad story is a true one in many places around the globe. We must slow deforestation and replant trees immediately to save our breathable air, fertile soil, and fragile ecosystems.

If entire forests continue to be obliterated, less oxygen will be produced and more CO_2 emitted. In fact, deforestation accounts for a quarter of the CO_2 released into the atmosphere each year: about 1–2 billion tons. Forests provide the majority of the oxygen on earth, and if these forests disappear our air will soon be unbreathable.

Second, deforestation results in a loss of topsoil. Many of the companies who are involved in deforestation claim that the land is needed for farms, but deforestation makes the land much less fertile because it accelerates the process of erosion. According to the UN Food and Agriculture Organization, deforestation has damaged almost 6 million square kilometers of soil.

Finally, if cutting doesn't slow, many species will die off and many ecosystems will be destroyed. The 2000 UN Global Environment Outlook says that forests and rain forests have the most diverse plant and animal life in the world. The GEO also notes that there are more than 1,000 threatened species living in the world's forests. Imagine someone destroying all the houses in your neighborhood and leaving all of the residents homeless. This is how it is for the organisms that live in the forests.

The writer supports the argument with facts and evidence, and also uses the persuasive appeal to the reader's emotions.

In conclusion, deforestation must slow down and trees must be replanted immediately, or we will lose clean air, topsoil, and many precious organisms. Furthermore, a loss in forests will result in a generation that knows very little about nature. So, to prevent the chaotic disturbance of peace in the forests, please do whatever you can to prevent deforestation. Vote YES on any UN bills that would help the condition of our world's forests.

The conclusion restates the argument and presents a call to action.

Sincerely Yours,
Jamil Khouri

21st Century Skills

Changing technology creates new ways to communicate. This handbook provides an overview of some ways you can use today's technology to create, share, and find information. You will find brief descriptions of the following topics in this section:

- ✔ Blogs
- ✔ Social Networking
- ✔ Widgets and Feeds
- ✔ Podcasts
- ✔ Wikis
- ✔ Internet Research Guide

BLOGS

A **blog** is a common form of online writing. The word *blog* is a contraction of *Web log.* Most blogs include a series of entries known as posts. The posts appear in a single column and are displayed in reverse chronological order. That means that the most recent post is at the top of the page. As you scroll down, you will find earlier posts.

Blogs have become increasingly popular. Researchers estimate that 75,000 new blogs are launched every day. Blog authors are often called bloggers. They can use their personal sites to share ideas, experiences, and impressions. Because blogs are designed so that they are easy to update, bloggers can post new messages as often as they like, often daily.

Another key component of blogs is interactivity with their audience. Many blogs allow readers to post their responses by using a comments feature found in each new post. Popular blog entries often inspire extended conversations and debates.

Kinds of Blogs

Not all blogs are the same. Many blogs have a single author, but others are group projects.

Blogs also serve a variety of purposes. Here are some common types of blogs:

- Personal blogs often have a general focus. Bloggers post about any topic they find interesting in their daily lives.
- Topical blogs focus on a specific theme, such as movie reviews, political news, class assignments, or health care opportunities.
- Open Forum blogs are open to any Internet user.
- Closed Forum blogs are allowed only to members of a site. Bloggers can further limit readership by giving only invited users full access to their site.

Web Safety

Always be aware of the information you post on the Internet. Remember that whatever information you post can be read by everyone with access to that page. Once you post a picture or text, it can be saved on someone else's computer, even if you later remove it.

Using the Internet safely means keeping personal information personal. Do not post sensitive information. Never include your address (e-mail or real), last name, telephone numbers, or mention places you can be frequently found. Do not give out this information for other people. Never give out passwords you use to access other Web sites and do not respond to e-mails from strangers.

Anatomy of a Blog

Here are some of the features you can include in a blog.

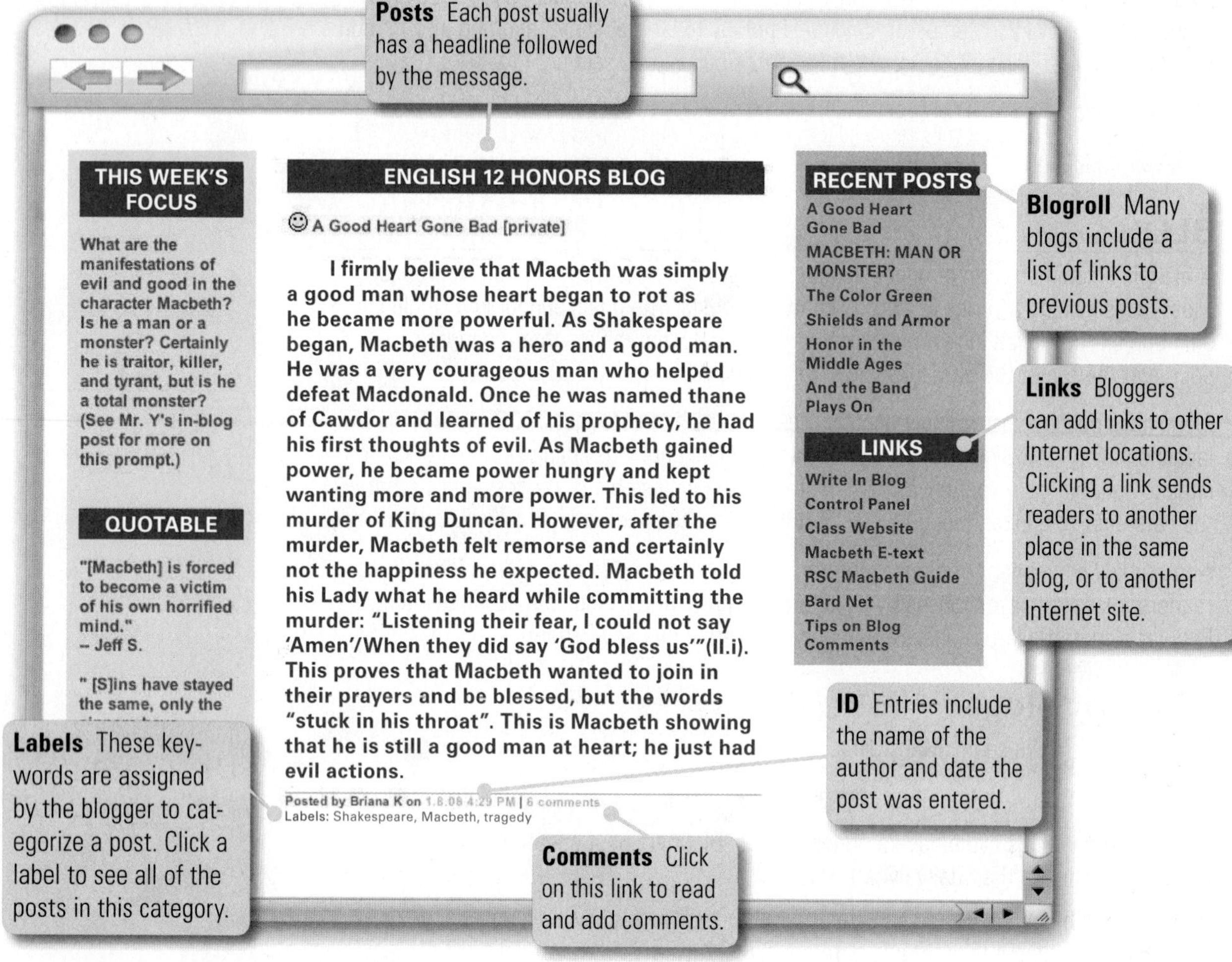

Posts Each post usually has a headline followed by the message.
THIS WEEK'S FOCUS
What are the manifestations of evil and good in the character Macbeth? Is he a man or a monster? Certainly he is traitor, killer, and tyrant, but is he a total monster? (See Mr. Y's in-blog post for more on this prompt.)
QUOTABLE
"[Macbeth] is forced to become a victim of his own horrified mind." – Jeff S.
" [S]ins have stayed the same, only the
ENGLISH 12 HONORS BLOG
A Good Heart Gone Bad [private]
I firmly believe that Macbeth was simply a good man whose heart began to rot as he became more powerful. As Shakespeare began, Macbeth was a hero and a good man. He was a very courageous man who helped defeat Macdonald. Once he was named thane of Cawdor and learned of his prophecy, he had his first thoughts of evil. As Macbeth gained power, he became power hungry and kept wanting more and more power. This led to his murder of King Duncan. However, after the murder, Macbeth felt remorse and certainly not the happiness he expected. Macbeth told his Lady what he heard while committing the murder: "Listening their fear, I could not say 'Amen'/When they did say 'God bless us'"(II.i). This proves that Macbeth wanted to join in their prayers and be blessed, but the words "stuck in his throat". This is Macbeth showing that he is still a good man at heart; he just had evil actions.
Posted by Briana K on 1.8.08 4:29 PM | 6 comments
Labels: Shakespeare, Macbeth, tragedy
RECENT POSTS
A Good Heart Gone Bad
MACBETH: MAN OR MONSTER?
The Color Green
Shields and Armor
Honor in the Middle Ages
And the Band Plays On
LINKS
Write In Blog
Control Panel
Class Website
Macbeth E-text
RSC Macbeth Guide
Bard Net
Tips on Blog Comments
Blogroll Many blogs include a list of links to previous posts.
Links Bloggers can add links to other Internet locations. Clicking a link sends readers to another place in the same blog, or to another Internet site.
ID Entries include the name of the author and date the post was entered.
Labels These key-words are assigned by the blogger to cat-egorize a post. Click a label to see all of the posts in this category.
Comments Click on this link to read and add comments.

Creating a Blog

Like any form of writing, blogging is a form of communication. Keep these hints and strategies in mind to help you create an interesting and fair blog:

- Focus each blog entry on a single topic. If you have two ideas you want to write about, create two separate blog entries. This can help readers find topics that interest them.
- Vary the length of your posts. Sometimes, all you need is a line or two to share a quick thought. Other posts will be much longer.
- Make your main ideas pop out by using clear or clever headlines and boldfacing key terms.
- Use labels to categorize entries, allowing readers to find material that interests them.
- Give credit to other people's work and ideas. Mention the names of people whose ideas you are quoting. You can also add a link that will take readers directly to that person's blog or site.
- If you post comments, try to make them brief and polite. Even if you disagree, state the reasons for your disagreement clearly and without exaggeration.

SOCIAL NETWORKING

Social networking refers to any interaction between members of an online community. People can exchange many different kinds of information, from text and voice messages to video images.

Many social network communities, such as MySpace and Facebook, allow users to create permanent pages that describe themselves. Users create home pages to share ideas about their lives and post messages to other members in the network. Each user is responsible for adding and updating the content on his or her profile page. You can create a social network page for an individual or a group, such as a school or special interest club. Many hosting sites do not charge to register, so you can also have fun by creating a page for a pet or a fictional character.

Here are some features you are likely to find on a social network profile:

- A biographical description, including photographs and artwork.
- Lists of favorite things, such as books, movies, music, and fashions.
- Playable media elements, such as videos and sound recordings.
- Message boards, or "walls," in which members of the community can exchange messages.

Privacy in Social Networks

Social networks allow users to decide how open their profiles will be. Be sure to read introductory information carefully before you register at a new site. Once you have a personal profile page, monitor your privacy settings regularly. Remember that any information you post will be available to anyone in your network.

Users often post messages anonymously or using false names, or pseudonyms. People can also post using someone else's name. Judge all information on the net critically. Do not assume that you know who posted information simply because you recognize the name of the post author. The rapid speed of communication on the Internet can make it easy to jump to conclusions. Be careful to avoid this trap.

Think twice before posting anything on a social networking page or blog. Once you have posted a photo or text, it can be saved on someone else's computer. Even if you remove the material later, the Web user still has a copy. Once another user has your photo, he or she might post it to other sites, or alter it using photo editing software. This practice may not be legal, but many users are not familiar with privacy laws, or choose to ignore them.

In fact, the user might not even be a person. A Web crawler is a computer program that browses the Internet and collects and saves data posted on Web sites. Also known as Web spiders or Web robots, these automated programs might gather information for marketing research or targeted sales.

PODCASTS

A **podcast** is a digital audio or video recording of a program that is made available on the Internet. Users can replay the podcast on a computer, or download and replay it on a personal audio player. You might think of podcasts as radio or television programs that you create yourself. They can be embedded on a Web site or fed to a Web page through a podcast widget.

Creating an Effective Podcast

To make a podcast, you will need a recording device, such as a microphone or digital video camera, as well as editing software. Open source editing software is widely available and free of charge. Most audio podcasts are converted into the MP3 format. Bulleted list of hints and strategies for creating a podcast that is clear and entertaining (such as rehearsing before recording, preparing a time outline, limiting length, and so on).

- Listen to several podcasts by different authors to get a feeling for the medium. Make a list of features and styles you like, as well as those you want to avoid.
- Test your microphone to find the best recording distance. You will stand close to the microphone so that your voice sounds full, but not so close that you create an echo.
- Create an outline that gives your estimated timing for each element.
- Be prepared before you record. Rehearse, but do not create a script. Podcasts are best when they have a natural, easy flow.
- Talk directly to your listeners. Slow down enough so they can understand you.
- Use software to edit your podcast before publishing it.

WIKIS

A **wiki** is a collaborative Web site that lets visitors create, add, remove, and edit content. The term comes from the Hawaiian phrase *wiki wiki,* which means "quick." Web users at a wiki are both the readers and the writers of the site. Some wikis are open to contributions from anyone. Others require visitors to register before they can edit the content.

Wikipedia is a well-known wiki encyclopedia. All of the text was created by people who use the site. Articles are constantly changing, as visitors find and correct errors and improve texts.

Wikis have both advantages and disadvantages as sources of information. They are valuable open forums for the exchange of ideas. The unique collaborative writing process allows entries to change over time. However, entries can also be modified incorrectly. Careless or malicious users can delete good content and add inappropriate or inaccurate information.

You can change the information on a wiki, but be sure your information is correct and clear before you add it. Wikis keep track of all changes, so your work will be recorded and can be evaluated by other users.

Wiki users must agree to use the sites responsibly so they can offer accurate information. As with blogs and social networking pages, the informal nature of wikis can lead to trouble. Remember that all information you post to a wiki—including text or images you erase—can not only be seen but also tracked, since all versions of the wiki are saved for security purposes.

USING THE INTERNET FOR RESEARCH

Key Word Search

Before you begin a search, you should identify your specific topic. To make searching easier, narrow your subject to a key word or a group of key words. These are your search terms, and they should be as specific as possible. For example, if you are looking for the latest concert dates for your favorite musical group, you might use the band's name as a key word. However, if you were to enter the name of the group in the query box of the search engine, you might be presented with thousands of links to information about the group that is unrelated to what you want to know. You might locate such information as band member biographies, the group's history, fan reviews of concerts, and hundreds of sites with related names containing information that is irrelevant to your search. Because you used such a broad key word, you might need to navigate through all that information before you could find a link or subheading for concert dates. In contrast, if you were to type in "Duplex Arena and [band name]," you would have a better chance of locating pages that contain this information.

How to Narrow Your Search

If you have a large group of key words and still do not know which ones to use, write out a list of all the words you are considering. Once you have completed the list, scrutinize it. Then, delete the words that are least important to your search, and highlight those that are most important.

These **key search connectors** can help you fine-tune your search:

AND: Narrows a search by retrieving documents that include both terms. For example: ***baseball*** AND ***playoffs***

OR: Broadens a search by retrieving documents including any of the terms. For example: ***playoffs*** OR ***championships***

NOT: Narrows a search by excluding documents containing certain words. For example: ***baseball*** NOT ***history of***

Tips for an Effective Search

1. Remember that search engines can be case-sensitive. If your first attempt at searching fails, check your search terms for misspellings and try again.
2. If you are entering a group of key words, present them in order from the most important to the least important key word.
3. Avoid opening the link to every single page in your results list. Search engines present pages in descending order of relevancy. The most useful pages will be located at the top of the list. However, read the description of each link before you open the page.
4. Some search engines provide helpful tips for specializing your search. Take the opportunity to learn more about effective searching.

Other Ways to Search

Using Online Reference Sites How you search should be tailored to what you are hoping to find. If you are looking for data and facts, use reference sites before you jump onto a simple search engine. For example, you can find reference sites to provide definitions of words, statistics about almost any subject, biographies, maps, and concise information on many topics. Here are some useful online reference sites:

Online libraries
Online periodicals
Almanacs
Encyclopedias

You can find these sources using subject searches.

Conducting Subject Searches As you prepare to go online, consider your subject and the best way to find information to suit your needs. If you are looking for general information on a topic and you want your search results to be extensive, consider the subject search indexes on most search engines. These indexes, in the form of category and subject lists, often appear on the first page of a search engine. When you click on a specific highlighted word, you will be presented with a new screen containing subcategories of the topic you chose.

Evaluating the Reliability of Internet Resources

Just as you would evaluate the quality, bias, and validity of any other research material you locate, check the source of information you find online. Compare these two sites containing information about the poet and writer Langston Hughes:

Site A is a personal Web site constructed by a college student. It contains no bibliographic information or links to sites that he used. Included on the site are several poems by Langston Hughes and a student essay about the poet's use of symbolism. It has not been updated in more than six months.

Site B is a Web site constructed and maintained by the English Department of a major university. Information on Hughes is presented in a scholarly format, with a bibliography and credits for the writer. The site includes links to other sites and indicates new features that are added weekly.

For your own research, consider the information you find on Site B to be more reliable and accurate than that on Site A. Because it is maintained by experts in their field who are held accountable for their work, the university site will be a better research tool than the student-generated one.

Tips for Evaluating Internet Sources

1. Consider who constructed and who now maintains the Web page. Determine whether this author is a reputable source. Often, the URL endings indicate a source.
   - Sites ending in ***.edu*** are maintained by educational institutions.
   - Sites ending in ***.gov*** are maintained by government agencies (federal, state, or local).
   - Sites ending in ***.org*** are normally maintained by nonprofit organizations and agencies.
   - Sites ending in ***.com*** are commercially or personally maintained.
2. Skim the official and trademarked Web pages first. It is safe to assume that the information you draw from Web pages of reputable institutions, online encyclopedias, online versions of major daily newspapers, or government-owned sites produce information as reliable as the material you would find in print. In contrast, unbranded sites or those generated by individuals tend to borrow information from other sources without providing documentation. As information travels from one source to another, it could have been muddled, misinterpreted, edited, or revised.
3. You can still find valuable information in the less "official" sites. Check for the writer's credentials, and then consider these factors:
   - Do not be misled by official-looking graphics or presentations.
   - Make sure that the information is updated enough to suit your needs. Many Web pages will indicate how recently they have been updated.
   - If the information is borrowed, notice whether you can trace it back to its original source.

Respecting Copyrighted Material

Because the Internet is a relatively new and quickly growing medium, issues of copyright and ownership arise almost daily. As laws begin to govern the use and reuse of material posted online, they may change the way that people can access or reprint material.

Text, photographs, music, and fine art printed online may not be reproduced without acknowledged permission of the copyright owner.

Tips for Discussing Literature

As you read and study literature, discussions with other readers can help you understand, enjoy, and develop interpretations of what you read. Use the following tips to practice good speaking and listening skills in group discussions of literature.

- **Understand the purpose of your discussion.**

  Your purpose when you discuss literature is to broaden your understanding and appreciation of a work by testing your own ideas and hearing the ideas of others. Be sure to stay focused on the literature you are discussing and to keep your comments relevant to that literature. Starting with one focus question will help to keep your discussion on track.

- **Communicate effectively.**

  Effective communication requires thinking before speaking. Plan the points that you want to make and decide how you will express them. Organize these points in logical order and cite details from the work to support your ideas. Jot down informal notes to help keep your ideas focused.

  Remember to speak clearly, pronouncing words slowly and carefully so that your listeners will understand your ideas. Also, keep in mind that some literature touches readers deeply—be aware of the possibility of counterproductive emotional responses and work to control them.

- **Make relevant contributions.**

  Especially when responding to a short story or a novel, avoid simply summarizing the plot. Instead, consider *what* you think might happen next, *why* events take place as they do, or *how* a writer provokes a response in you. Let your ideas inspire deeper thought or discussion about the literature.

- **Consider other ideas and interpretations.**

  A work of literature can generate a wide variety of responses in different readers—and that can make your discussions really exciting. Be open to the idea that many interpretations can be valid. To support your own ideas, point to the events, descriptions, characters, or other literary elements in the work that led to your interpretation. To consider someone else's ideas, decide whether details in the work support the interpretation he or she presents. Be sure to convey your criticism of the ideas of others in a respectful and supportive manner.

- **Ask questions and extend the contributions of others.**

  Get in the habit of asking questions to help you clarify your understanding of another reader's ideas. You can also use questions to call attention to possible areas of confusion, to points that are open to debate, or to errors in the speaker's points.

  In addition, offer elaboration of the points that others make by providing examples and illustrations from the literature. To move a discussion forward, summarize and evaluate tentative conclusions reached by the group members.

Oral and Visual Communication

You use speaking and listening skills every day. When you talk with your friends, teachers, or parents, or when you interact with store clerks, you are communicating orally. In addition to everyday conversation, oral communication includes class discussions, speeches, interviews, presentations, debates, and performances. The following terms will give you a better understanding of the many elements that are part of communication and help you eliminate barriers to listening by managing any distractions:

Body language refers to the use of facial expressions, eye contact, gestures, posture, and movement to communicate a feeling or an idea.

Connotation is the set of associations a word calls to mind. The connotations of the words you choose influence the message you send. For example, most people respond more favorably to being described as "slim" rather than as "skinny." The connotation of *slim* is more appealing than that of *skinny.*

Eye contact is direct visual contact with another person's eyes.

Feedback is the set of verbal and nonverbal reactions that indicate to a speaker that a message has been received and understood.

Gestures are the movements made with arms, hands, face and fingers to communicate.

Listening is understanding and interpreting sound in a meaningful way. You listen differently for different purposes.

> ***Listening for key information:*** For example, when a teacher gives an assignment, or when someone gives you directions to a place, you listen for key information.
>
> ***Listening for main points:*** In a classroom exchange of ideas or information, or while watching a television documentary, you listen for main points.
>
> ***Listening critically:*** When you evaluate a performance, song, or a persuasive or political speech, you listen critically, questioning and judging the speaker's message.

Medium is the material or technique used to present a visual image. Common media include paint, clay, and film.

Nonverbal communication is communication without the use of words. People communicate nonverbally through gestures, facial expressions, posture, and body movements. Sign language is an entire language based on nonverbal communication. Be aware of your nonverbal communication and make sure that your gestures and facial expressions do not conflict with your words.

Projection is speaking in such a way that the voice carries clearly to an audience. It's important to project your voice when speaking in a large space like a classroom or an auditorium.

Viewing is observing, understanding, analyzing, and evaluating information presented through visual means. You might use the following questions to help you interpret what you view:

- What subject is presented?
- What is communicated about the subject?
- Which parts are factual? Which are opinion?
- What mood, attitude, or opinion is conveyed?
- What is your emotional response?

Vocal delivery is the way in which you present a message. Your vocal delivery involves all of the following elements:

> ***Volume:*** the loudness or quietness of your voice
>
> ***Pitch:*** the high or low quality of your voice
>
> ***Rate:*** the speed at which you speak; also called pace
>
> ***Stress:*** the amount of emphasis placed on different syllables in a word or on different words in a sentence

All of these elements individually, and the way in which they are combined, contribute to the meaning of a spoken message.

Speaking, Listening, and Viewing Situations

Here are some of the many types of situations in which you apply speaking, listening, and viewing skills:

Audience Your audience in any situation refers to the person or people to whom you direct your message. An audience can be a group of people observing a performance or just one person. When preparing for any speaking situation, it's useful to analyze your audience, so that you can tailor your message to them.

Charts and graphs are visual representations of statistical information. For example, a pie chart might indicate how the average dollar is spent by government, and a bar graph might compare populations in cities over time.

Debate A debate is a formal public-speaking situation in which participants prepare and present arguments on opposing sides of a question, stated as a **proposition.**

The two sides in a debate are the *affirmative* (pro) and the *negative* (con). The affirmative side argues in favor of the proposition, while the negative side argues against it. Each side has an opportunity for *rebuttal,* in which they may challenge or question the other side's argument.

Documentaries are nonfiction films that analyze news events or other focused subjects. You can watch a documentary for the information on its subject.

Graphic organizers summarize and present information in ways that can help you understand the information. Graphic organizers include charts, outlines, webs, maps, lists, and diagrams. For example, a graphic organizer for a history chapter might be an outline. A Venn diagram is intersecting circles that display information showing how concepts are alike and different.

Group discussion results when three or more people meet to solve a common problem, arrive at a decision, or answer a question of mutual interest. Group discussion is one of the most widely used forms or interpersonal communication in modern society.

Interview An interview is a form of interaction in which one person, the interviewer, asks questions of another person, the interviewee. Interviews may take place for many purposes: to obtain information, to discover a person's suitability for a job or a college, or to inform the public of a notable person's opinions.

Maps are visual representations of Earth's surface. Maps may show political boundaries and physical features and provide information on a variety of other topics. A map's titles and its key identify the content of the map.

Oral interpretation is the reading or speaking of a work of literature aloud for an audience. Oral interpretation involves giving expression to the ideas, meaning, or even the structure of a work of literature. The speaker interprets the work through his or her vocal delivery. **Storytelling,** in which a speaker reads or tells a story expressively, is a form of oral interpretation.

Panel discussion is a group discussion on a topic of interest common to all members of a panel and to a listening audience. A panel is usually composed of four to six experts on a particular topic who are brought together to share information and opinions.

Pantomime is a form of nonverbal communication in which an idea or a story is communicated completely through the use of gesture, body language, and facial expressions, without any words at all.

Political cartoons are drawings that comment on important political or social issues. Often, these cartoons use humor to convey a message about their subject. Viewers use their own knowledge of events to evaluate the cartoonist's opinion.

Readers theatre is a dramatic reading of a work of literature in which participants take parts from a story or play and read them aloud in expressive voices. Unlike a play, however, sets and costumes are not part of the performance, and the participants remain seated as they deliver their lines.

Role play To role-play is to take the role of a person or character and act out a given situation, speaking, acting, and responding in the manner of the character.

Speech A speech is a talk or address given to an audience. A speech may be **impromptu** or **extemporaneous**—delivered on the spur of the moment with no preparation—or formally prepared and delivered for a specific purpose or occasion.

- ***Purposes:*** the most common purposes of speeches are to persuade, to entertain, to explain, and to inform.
- ***Occasions:*** Different occasions call for different types of speeches. Speeches given on these occasions could be persuasive, entertaining, or informative, as appropriate.

Visual representation refers to informative texts, such as newspapers and advertisements, and entertaining texts, such as magazines. Visual representations use elements of design—such as texture and color, shapes, drawings, and photographs—to convey the meaning, message, or theme.

Grammar, Usage, and Mechanics Handbook

Parts of Speech

Every English word, depending on its meaning and its use in a sentence, can be identified as one of the eight parts of speech. These are nouns, pronouns, verbs, adjectives, adverbs, prepositions, conjunctions, and interjections. Understanding the parts of speech will help you learn the rules of English grammar and usage.

Part of Speech	Definition	Examples
Noun	**Names a person, place, or thing**	
Common	• Names any one of a class of persons, places, or things	writer, country, novel
Proper	• Names a specific person, place or thing	Charles Dickens, Great Britain, *Hard Times*
Pronoun	**Stands for a noun or for a word that takes the place of a noun**	
Personal	• Refers to the person speaking (first person); the person spoken to (second person); or the person, place, or thing spoken about (third person)	I, me, my, mine, we, us, our, ours, you, our, yours, he, him, his, she, her, hers, it, its, they, them, their, theirs, myself, ourselves, yourself, yourselves, himself, herself, itself, themselves
Reflexive	• Names the person or thing receiving an action when that person or thing is the same as the one performing the action	"They click upon *themselves/* As the breeze rises,…" –Robert Frost
Intensive	• Adds emphasis to a noun or pronoun	"The United States *themselves* are essentially the greatest poem…" –Walt Whitman
Demonstrative	• Singles out specific person(s), place(s), or thing(s)	this, that, these, those
Relative	• Begins a subordinate clause and connects it to another idea in the sentence	that, which, who, whom, whose
Interrogative	• Begins a question	what, which, who, whom, whose
Indefinite	• Refers to a person, place, or thing that may or may not be specifically named	another, everyone, nobody, one, both, few, all, most, none

(Parts of Speech continues)

(continued)

Part of Speech	Definition	Examples
Verb	**Expresses time while showing an action, condition, or the fact that something exists**	
Action	• Tells what action someone or something is performing	gather, read, work, jump, imagine, analyze, conclude
Linking	• Connects the subject with another word that identifies or describes the subject	appear, be, become, feel, look,remain, sound, stay, taste
Helping	• Added to another verb to make a verb phrase	be, do, have, should, can, could, may
Adjective	**Used to describe a noun or pronoun or give it a more specific meaning**	*purple* hat, *happy* face, *this* bowl, *three* cars, *enough* food, *a loud* sound
Adverb	**Modifies a verb, an adjective, or another adverb by telling *where, when, how* or *to what extent***	will answer *soon, extremely* sad, calls *more* often
Preposition	**Relates a noun or pronoun that appears with it to another word in the sentence**	Dad made a meal *for* us. We talked *till* dusk. Bo missed school *because of* his illness.
Conjunction	**Connects words or groups of words**	
Coordinating	• Connects equal words or word groups	bread *and* cheese, brief *but* powerful
Correlative	• Used in pairs to connect equal words or word groups	*both* Luis *and* Rosa, neither you *nor I*
Subordinating	• Indicates the connection between two ideas by placing one below the other in rank or importance	We will miss her *if* she leaves. Hank shrieked *when* he slipped on the ice.
Interjection	**Expresses feeling or emotion**	ah, hey, ouch, well, yippee

Phrases and Clauses

Phrases A **phrase** is a group of words that does not have a subject and verb and that functions as one part of speech.

Prepositional Phrases A **prepositional phrase** is a group of words that includes a preposition and a noun or pronoun.

beyond the horizon   **according to** the manager

An **adjective phrase** is a prepositional phrase that modifies a noun or pronoun.

The works **of Benjamin Franklin** appeal to me.

An **adverb phrase** is a prepositional phrase that modifies a verb, an adjective, or an adverb.

I often read **about early American writers.**

Appositive Phrases An **appositive phrase** is a noun or pronoun with modifiers, placed next to a noun or pronoun to add information.

Tamika, **one of my best friends,** is moving away.

Verbal Phrases A **participial phrase** is a participle that is modified by an adverb or an adverb phrase or that has a complement. The entire phase acts as an adjective.

Be alert for snakes **sunning themselves on the rocks.**

A **gerund** is a noun formed from the present participle of a verb (ending in *–ing*). A **gerund phrase** is a gerund with modifiers or a complement, all acting together as a noun.

Her favorite pastime is **hiking in the mountains.**

An **infinitive phrase** is an infinitive with modifiers, complements, or a subject, all acting together as a single part of speech.

I would like **to learn about wilderness survival.**

Clauses A **clause** is a group of words with its own subject and verb.

Independent Clauses An independent clause can stand by itself as a complete sentence.

Henry David Thoreau was considered an eccentric.

Subordinate Clauses A subordinate clause cannot stand by itself as a complete sentence.

Henry David Thoreau, **who did not follow society's rules,** was considered an eccentric.

An **adjective clause** is a subordinate clause that modifies a noun or pronoun by telling what kind or which one.

The journey **that Lewis undertook** was dangerous.

An **adverb clause** is a subordinate clause that modifies a verb, an adjective, an adverb, or a verbal by telling *where, when, in what way, to what extent, under what condition,* or *why.*

As I read the poem, I pictured the Grand Canyon.

A **noun clause** is a subordinate clause that acts as a noun.

Whoever visits the Grand Canyon should remember John Wesley Powell's contributions.

Sentence Structure

Subject and Predicate A **sentence** is a group of words with two main parts: a *subject* and a *predicate*. Together, these parts express a complete thought.

The **complete subject** tells *whom* or *what* the sentence is about. The **complete predicate** tells what the complete subject of the sentence does or is.

Complete Subject **Complete Predicate**

One of those poems | was written by Claude McKay.

The **simple subject** is the essential noun, pronoun, or group of words acting as a noun that cannot be left out of the complete subject. The **simple predicate** is the essential verb or verb phrase that cannot be left out of the complete predicate.

Simple Subject **Simple Predicate**

One of those poems | **was written** by Claude McKay.

Complements A **complement** is a word or word group that completes the meaning of the predicate. There are five kinds of complements: *direct objects, indirect objects, objective complements, predicate nominatives,* and *predicate adjectives.*

A **direct object** is a noun, a pronoun, or a group of words acting as a noun that receives the action of a transitive verb.

Washington Irving used several **pseudonyms.**

An **indirect object** is a noun or pronoun that appears with a direct object and names the person or thing that something is given to or done for.

Folk tales gave **Irving** inspiration for his stories. [The direct object is *inspiration.*]

An **objective complement** is an adjective or noun that appears with a direct object and describes or renames it.

Ms. Gates considers Phillis Wheatley a brilliant **poet.** [The direct object is *Phillis Wheatley.*]

A **predicate nominative** is a noun or pronoun that appears with a linking verb and tells something about the subject.

John Smith became a famous **explorer.**

A **predicate adjective** is an adjective that appears with a linking verb and describes the subject of the sentence.

Smith was **adventurous** and **daring**.

Classifying Sentences by Structure

Sentences are often classified according to the kind and number of clauses they contain. The four basic sentence structures are *simple, compound, complex,* and *compound-complex.*

A **simple sentence** consists of one independent clause.

Alisa enjoys contemporary American poetry.

A **compound sentence** consists or two or more independent clauses.

Alisa enjoys contemporary American poetry, but Joyce prefers earlier works.

A **complex sentence** consists of one independent clause and one or more subordinate clauses.

Alisa, who likes all things modern, enjoys contemporary American poetry.

A **compound-complex sentence** consists of two or more independent clauses and one or more subordinate clauses.

Alisa, who likes all things modern, enjoys contemporary American poetry, but Joyce prefers earlier works.

Paragraph Structure

An effective paragraph is organized around one **main idea,** which is often stated in a topic sentence. The other sentences support the main idea. To give the paragraph unity, make sure the connection between each sentence and the main idea is clear.

Usage

Lessons throughout your literature book will help you with many usage problems. See Unit 1 for help with **using coordinating conjunctions** (p. 31), **using correlative conjunctions** (p. 94), and **using subordinating conjunctions** (p. 155). See Unit 2 for help with **using adjective and adverb clauses** (p. 287), **comparative and superlative adjectives and adverbs** (p. 321), and **using participles, gerunds, and infinitives** (p. 358). In Unit 3 you will find lessons on **misplaced and dangling modifiers** (p. 585) and **introductory phrases and clauses** (p. 613). See Unit 4 for help with **subject-verb agreement problems** (p. 755) and **pronoun-antecedent agreement problems** (p. 911). In Unit 5 you will find lessons on **avoiding shifts in verb tense** (p. 1093), **using active, not passive, voice** (p. 1115), and **sentence fragments and run-ons** (p. 1237). Go to Unit 6 for lessons on **transitional expressions** (p. 1323), using **parallel structure** (p. 1423), and **creating sentence variety** (p. 1441).

Unintended Shift in Person

Do not change needlessly from one person to another. Keep the person consistent in your sentences.

Tara is a good babysitter, but **you** have to pay her well. [shift from third person to second person]

Tara is a good babysitter, but **she** charges high rates. [consistent]

Modifier Placement

To avoid confusion, a modifying word, phrase, or clause should be placed as close as possible to the word or words it is supposed to modify.

We saw a large swan **rowing the boat near the shore.** [misplaced modifier]

Rowing the boat near the shore, we saw a large swan. [correct placement]

Agreement

Subject and Verb Agreement

A singular subject must have a singular verb. A plural subject must have a plural verb.

Daniel cooks chicken tortilla soup to perfection.

The **boys cook** several different casseroles.

A phrase or clause that comes between a subject and verb does not affect subject-verb agreement.

My **sister**, along with her friends, **plays** softball.

Two subjects joined by *and* usually take a plural verb.

The **players** and the **coach take** the game seriously.

Two singular subject joined by *or* or *nor* must have a singular verb.

Neither the **coach** nor the **player is** ready.

Two plural subjects joined by *or* or *nor* must have a plural verb.

The **players** or the **coaches suggest** special plays.

Pronoun and Antecedent Agreement

Pronouns must agree with their antecedents in number and gender. Use singular pronouns with singular antecedents and plural pronouns with plural antecedents.

Kate Chopin became a bold and controversial writer in spite of **her** conservative upbringing.

Writers must be courageous in facing **their** critics.

Use a singular pronoun when the antecedent is a singular indefinite pronoun such as *anybody, each, either, everybody, neither, no one, one,* or *someone.*

Anybody can offer **his or her** help with the report.

Use a plural pronoun when the antecedent is a plural indefinite pronoun (*both, few, many,* or *several.*)

Few of the students offered **their** help.

The indefinite pronouns *all, any, more, most, none,* and *some* can be singular or plural depending on the number of the word to which they refer.

All of the *books* are missing **their** covers.

All of the *book* is ready for **its** final edit.

Using Verbs

Principal Parts of Regular and Irregular Verbs

A verb has four principal parts:

Present	Present Participle	Past	Past Participle
learn	learning	learned	learned
discuss	discussing	discussed	discussed
stand	standing	stood	stood
begin	beginning	began	begun

Regular verbs such as *talk* and *maintain* form the past and past participle by adding *–ed* to the present form. **Irregular verbs** such as *keep* and *give* form the past and past participle in other ways. If you are in doubt about the principal parts of an irregular verb, check a dictionary.

The Tenses of Verbs

The different tenses of verbs indicate the time an action or condition occurred.

The **present tense** is most often used to show one of the following:

Present action or condition:	Jamal **hikes** to the lake. The sky **is** clear.
Regularly occurring action or condition:	Tourists **flock** to the site yearly. **I am** usually tired by 9:00.
Constant action or condition:	The earth **orbits** the sun. Pets **are** good for our health.

The **past tense** is used to express a completed action or condition.

The dog **grabbed** the bone and **ran** away.

The **present perfect tense** is used to express (1) an action or condition that happened at an indefinite time in the past or (2) an action or condition from the past that is continuing into the present.

The mayor **has made** changes in the city code.

My clothes **have been** in the dryer all day.

The **past perfect tense** shows an action or condition completed before another past action or condition.

Micah **had hidden** the gift before he left the house.

The **future tense** is used to show a future action or condition.

The Garcias **will travel** to Rome this summer.

The future perfect tense is used to show a future action or condition that is completed before another future action or condition.

Jess **will have washed** the dishes by the time we return.

Using Modifiers

Degrees of Comparison

Adjectives and adverbs take different forms to show the three degrees of comparison: the *positive*, the *comparative*, and the *superlative*.

Positive	Comparative	Superlative
fast	faster	fastest
crafty	craftier	craftiest
abruptly	more abruptly	most abruptly
bad	worse	worst
much	more	most

Using Comparative and Superlative Adjectives and Adverbs

Use comparative adjectives and adverbs to compare two things. Use superlative adjectives and adverbs to compare three or more things.

The bread is fresher than the rolls.

Of all the foods here, this bread is the freshest.

Using Pronouns

Pronoun Case

The **case** of a pronoun is the form it takes to show its use in a sentence. There are three pronoun cases: *nominative, objective,* and *possessive.*

Nominative	Objective	Possessive
I, you, he, she, it, we, you, they	me, you, him, her, it, us, you, them	my, your, his, her, its, our, their, mine, yours, his, hers, its, ours, theirs

Use the **nominative case** for the *subject* or for a *predicate nominative.*

They worked together to write the play. [subject]

The biggest theater fan is **he.** [predicate nominative]

Use the **objective case** for a *direct object,* an *indirect object,* or the *object of a preposition.*

Jamal drove **me** to the game. [direct object]

Aunt Lil bought **us** the tickets. [indirect object]

The fans cheered for **her.** [object of preposition]

The **possessive case** is used to show ownership.

I think the blue jacket is **his.**

Commonly Confused Words

Diction refers to word choice. The words you choose contribute to the overall effectiveness of your writing. One aspect of diction has to do with choosing between commonly confused words, such as the pairs listed below.

affect, effect

Affect is almost always a verb meaning "to influence." *Effect* is usually a noun meaning "result." Effect can also be a verb meaning "to bring about" or "to cause."

An understanding of T.S. Eliot's multiple allusions can *affect* one's appreciation of his poetry.

In Cather's story, the concert has a profound *effect* on Aunt Georgina.

The aim of persuasive writing is often to *effect* a change in the attitudes of the audience.

farther, further

Use *farther* when you refer to distance. Use *further* when you mean "to a greater degree."

In "A Worn Path," the *farther* Phoenix Jackson travels, the more her determination grows.

In his speech, Patrick Henry urges his countrymen to trust the British no *further.*

good, well

Use the predicate adjective *good* after linking verbs such as *feel, look, smell, taste,* and *seem.* Use *well* whenever you need an adverb.

At the end of "Winter Dreams," Devon implies that Judy does not look as *good* as she used to.

Anne Tyler writes especially *well* about ordinary people and family relationships.

its, it's

Do not confuse the possessive pronoun its with the contraction it's, which stands for "it is" or "it has."

One memorable line in Emerson's poem "The Rhodera" is "Beauty is *its* own excuse for being."

Wallace Stevens's "Anecdote of the Jar" suggests that *it's* impossible to mediate completely between the wilderness and the world of civilization.

set, sit

Set is a transitive verb meaning "to put (something) in a certain place." Its principal parts are *set, setting, set, set. Sit* is an intransitive verb meaning "to be seated." Its principal parts are *sit, sitting, sat, sat.*

Phillis Wheatley's poem is so complimentary to Washington that it seems to *set* him on a pedestal.

As Mrs. Mallard *sits* upstairs alone, she contemplates the death of her husband.

Editing For English Language Conventions

Capitalization

First Words

Capitalize the first word of a sentence.

Compare and contrast the works of Poe and Emerson.

Capitalize the first word of a direct quotation.

Bill asked, "**W**hat are the similarities?"

Proper Nouns and Proper Adjectives

Capitalize all proper nouns.

Carl **S**andburg   **N**ovember   **H**arvard **U**niversity

Capitalize all proper adjectives.

Turkish heritage   **P**uerto **R**ican writers

Academic Course Names

Capitalize course names only if they are language courses, are followed by a number, or are preceded by a proper noun or adjective.

German   **S**ocial **S**cience 101   **H**onors **E**nglish

geometry   **p**hysics   **l**anguage **a**rts

Titles

Capitalize titles showing family relationships when they refer to a specific person unless they are preceded by a possessive noun or pronoun.

Granny Weatherall my **g**randfather Mammedaty

Capitalize the first word and all other key words in the titles of books, stories, songs, and other works of art.

*The **C**rucible*   "**M**ending **W**all"

Punctuation

End Marks

Use a **period** to end a declarative sentence or an imperative sentence.

War literature can be quite powerful**.**

Discuss the historical context of Hemingway's story**.**

Use periods with abbreviations.

T.S. Eliot   Mr. Shiftlet

Use a **question mark** to end an interrogative sentence.

Why did Mr. Hooper wear the black veil**?**

Use an **exclamation mark** after an exclamatory sentence or a forceful imperative sentence.

Our team won in overtime**!**Come here now**!**

Commas

Use a **comma** before the conjunction to separate two independent clauses in a compound sentence.

I read a story by Eudora Welty**,** and I liked it.

Use commas to separate three or more words, phrases, or clauses in a series.

Benjamin Franklin was a statesman**,** a scientist**,** and a journalist.

Use a comma after an introductory word, phrase, or clause.

When the crew heard Ahab's plan**,** they were stunned.

Use commas to set of nonessential expressions.

Captain Ahab**,** as you know**,** was seeking revenge.

Use commas with places and dates.

Boston**,** Massachusetts   November 17**,** 1915

Semicolons

Use a **semicolon** to join closely related independent clauses that are not already joined by a conjunction.

Byron is a point guard**;** Mick usually plays center.

Use semicolons to avoid confusion when items in a series contain commas.

Kevin, the team captain**;** Mr. Reece, the coach**;** and Mr. Jenkins, the assistant coach, had a long talk.

Colons

Use a **colon** before a list of items following an independent clause.

Great literature provides us with many things**:** entertainment, enrichment, and inspiration.

Use a colon to introduce an independent clause that summarizes or explains the sentence before it.

Joleen left for a walk**:** She wanted to clear her mind.

Quotation Marks

Use **quotation marks** to enclose a direct quotation.

"A good poet,**"** Mr. Charles said, **"**uses words skillfully and carefully.**"**

An **indirect quotation** does not require quotation marks.

Mr. Charles said that good poets use words skillfully and carefully.

Use quotation marks around the titles of short written works, episodes in a series, songs, and titles of works mentioned as parts of collections.

"Winter Dreams**"** **"**Go Down, Moses**"**

Italics

Italicize the titles of long written works, movies, television and radio shows, lengthy works of music, paintings, and sculptures.

Mary Poppins *House by the Railroad*

For handwritten material, you can use underlining instead of italics.

<u>The Great Gatsby</u> <u>Aida</u>

Dashes

Use **dashes** to indicate an abrupt change of thought, a dramatic interrupting idea, or a summary statement.

I told my teacher—and I was being entirely sincere—that I loved studying American drama.

Parentheses

Use **parentheses** to set off asides and explanations when the material is not essential or when it consists of one or more sentences.

The chair of the city council **(**she also happens to be our neighbor**)** explained the new ordinance to us.

In the example above, the sentence in parentheses interrupts the larger sentence, so it does not have a capital letter and a period. When a sentence in parentheses falls between two other complete sentences, it should start with a capital letter and end with a period.

My family often travels to El Paso. **(**It is the nearest large city.**)** We like to shop there.

Apostrophes

Add an **apostrophe** and an *s* to show the possessive case of most singular nouns and of plural nouns that do not end in –s or *–es*.

Taylor**'**s poetry women**'**s hats

Names ending in *s* form their possessives in the same way, except for classical and biblical names, which add only an apostrophe to form the possessive.

Adams**'**s letter Achilles**'** death

Add an apostrophe to show the possessive case of plural nouns ending in *–s* and *–es.*

the boys**'** ambition the Cruzes**'** house

Use an apostrophe in a contraction to indicate the position of the missing letter or letters.

We**'**ve been studying the works of Edgar Allan Poe.

Brackets

Use **brackets** to enclose a word or words you insert in a quotation when you are quoting someone else.

Columbus's journal entry from October 21, 1492, begins as follows: "At 10 o'clock, we arrived at a cape of the island **[**San Salvador**]**, and anchored, the other vessels in company."

Ellipses

Use three **ellipses** to indicate where you have omitted words from quoted material.

It was Thoreau who wrote, " **. . .** if one advances confidently in the direction of his dreams, **. . .** he will meet with a success unexpected **. . . .**"

In the example above, the four dots at the end of the sentence are the three ellipses plus the period from the original sentence.

Spelling

Spelling Rules

Learning the rules of English spelling will help you make **generalizations** about how to spell words.

Rules for Spelling with Word Parts

The three word parts that can combine to form a word are roots, prefixes, and suffixes. Many of these word parts come from the Greek, Latin, and Anglo-Saxon languages.

The **root word** carries a word's basic meaning.

Root and Origin	Meaning	Examples
-ject- [L.]	to throw	re*ject*
-leg- (-log-) [Gr.]	to say, speak	*leg*al, *log*ic

A **prefix** is one or more syllables at the beginning of a word. A prefix adds to the meaning of the root.

Prefix and Origin	Meaning	Examples
in- (il-, im-, ir-) [L.]	not	*in*human, *il*legal
mono- [Gr.]	alone, one	*mono*poly
over- [A.S.]	above, in excess	*over*flow

A **suffix** is added to the end of a root word and can change the word's meaning or part of speech.

Suffix and Origin	Meaning	Part of Speech
-fy [L.]	to cause to become: clari*fy*	verb
-ish [A.S.]	of, tending to: fool*ish*	adjective
-ism [Gr.]	act, practice, or result of: tru*ism*	noun
-ly [A.S.]	in a manner: quick*ly*	adverb

Rules for Adding Suffixes to Root Words

When adding a suffix to a root word ending in *y* preceded by a consonant, change *y* to *i* unless the suffix begins with *i*.

funny + -est = funniest silly + -ness = silliness
modify + -ing = modifying cry + -ing = crying

For a root word ending in *e*, drop the *e* when adding a suffix beginning with a vowel.

nature + -al = natural seize + -ure = seizure
SOME EXCEPTIONS: courageous, mileage, dyeing

For root words ending with a consonant + vowel + consonant in a stressed syllable, double the final consonant when adding a suffix that begins with a vowel.

slim + -er = slimmer permit + -ed = permitted
SOME EXCEPTIONS: rowing, conference

Rules for Adding Prefixes to Root Words

When a prefix is added to a root word, the spelling of the root remains the same.

in- + sincere = insincere over- + eat = overeat

With some prefixes, the spelling of the prefix changes when joined to the root to make the pronunciation easier.

in- + pact = impact com- + found = confound

Orthographic Patterns

Certain letter combinations in English make certain sounds. For instance, *ph* sounds like *f*, *eigh* usually makes a long *a* sound, and the *k* before an *n* is often silent.

phase w**eigh**t **kn**eeling

Understanding orthographic patterns such as these can help you improve your spelling.

Forming Plurals

The plural form of most nouns is formed by adding *–s* or *–es* to the singular.

merit**s** sparrow**s** American**s**

For words ending in *s, ss, x, z, sh, ch,* add *–es.*

dress**es** waltz**es** pouch**es**

For words ending in *y* or *o* preceded by a vowel, add *–s.*

way**s** rodeo**s** bouy**s**

For words ending in *y* preceded by a consonant, change the *y* to an *i* and add *–es.*

quer**ies** cemeter**ies** luxur**ies**

For most words ending in *o* preceded by consonant, add *–es.*

potato**es** echo**es**

Some words form the plural in irregular ways.

mice alumni women crises

Foreign Words Used in English

Some words used in English are actually foreign words we have adopted. Learning to spell these words requires memorization. When in doubt, check a dictionary.

origami desperado protégé
laissez faire croissant

GRAMMAR, USAGE, AND MECHANICS HANDBOOK

Index of Authors and Titles

Note: Page numbers in *italics* refer to biographical information for authors, or commentary for titles; nonfiction and informational text appears in red.

A

Account of An Experience With Discrimination, An, *550*, *555*
Acquainted With the Night, 882
Adams, Abigail, *180*, 182
Adams, John, *180*, 181
Albee, Edward, *1184*
Alvarez, Julia, *1290*, *1294*, *1297*, 1298, *1451*
Ambush, *808*, 810
American Crisis (No. 1), from *The*, 117
American Forests, from *The*, lxv
American Slang, from *The American Language*, 1375
Andrews, William L., *147*, *166*
Another Country, In, 800
Antojos, 1298
Antojos, from, 1451
anyone lived in a pretty how town, 781
Ars Poetica, 789
Atkinson, Brooks, 1251
Atlanta Braves, 941
Auden, Wystan Hugh, *773*, 774
Autobiography, from *The*, 141

B

Backing the Attack, 1005
Baldwin, James, *1081*, 1082
Battle of the Easy Chair, The, 1004
Because I could not stop for Death, 408
Ben Franklin: America's Everyman, 147
Bierce, Ambrose, *479*, 480
Birches, 874
Bishop, Elizabeth, *1071*, 1072, 1075
Black Boy, from, 517
Black Man Talks of Reaping, A, 924
Bontemps, Arna, *920*, 924
Boulders Taller Than the Great Tower of Seville, 52
Boys' Ambition, The, 570
Bradford, William, *57*, 58
Bradstreet, Anne, *75*, 76
Brave New Words, 1287
Brecht, Bertolt, *1171*
Brooks, Gwendolyn, *1063*, 1064
Bryant, William Cullen, *261*, 262
Bryson, Bill, *588*, 589
By the Bivouac's Fitful Flame, 433

C

Cabeza de Vaca, Alvar Núñez, *47*, 48
Camouflaging the Chimera, 1350
Carver, Raymond, *1325*, 1326
Cather, Willa, *651*, 652
Chesnut, Mary, *494*, 495
Chicago, 868
Chief Joseph, *616*, 622
Chopin, Kate, *627*, 628
Cisneros, Sandra, *158*, 159
Civil Disobedience, from, 388
Clifton, Lucille, *914*, 915
Clooney, George, *1240*, 1241
Cofer, Judith Ortiz, *1365*, 1366
Cold Mountain (screenplay), from, 546
Collins, Billy, 403
Colt, Miriam Davis, *616*, 617
Commission of Meriwether Lewis, 245
Community's Roots, A, 559
Conant, James Bryant, lxiii
Concord Hymn, 371
Confederate Account of the Battle of Gettysburg, A, 502
Constantly Risking Absurdity, 1042
Courage, 1053
Coyote v. Acme, 1384
Crane, Stephen, *507*, 508
Crossing the Great Divide, 250
Crucible, The
  Act I, 1126
  Act II, 1161
  Act III, 1187
  Act IV, 1217
  critical reviews, 1251, 1252, 1253
Cullen, Countee, *921*, 926
Cummings, E.E., *779*, 780, 781
Cuttings, 1058
Cuttings (later), 1060

D

Death of the Ball Turret Gunner, The, 997
Declaration of Independence, The, 112
Devil and Tom Walker, The, 228
Dickinson, Emily, *404*, *406*, 408, 410–417, *418*
Doolittle, Hilda. See H.D.
Douglass, Frederick, 97, *519*, 520
Douglass, 636
Dove, Rita, *1417*, 1418
Dr. Seuss, *1002*, 1004
Dream Variations, 906
Dunbar, Paul Laurence, *635*, 636, 638
Dust Bowl Blues, 768
Dust Tracks On a Road, from, 930

E

Earth on Turtle's Back, The, 20
Edwards, Jonathan, *85*, 86
Ehrlich, Gretel, *222*, *374*, 443
Eliot, T.S., *707*, 708
Emerson, Ralph Waldo, *362*, *365*, 366, 369, 371
Emily Dickinson, Reckless Genius, 418
Episode of War, An, 508
Equiano, Olaudah, *169*, 170
Espada, Martín, *1347*, 1348
Everyday Use, 1312
Everything Stuck to Him, 1326
Explorer, The, 1064

F

Fall of the House of Usher, The, 292
Faulkner, William, *815*, 817, 828
Feiffer, Jules, *888*, 889
Ferlinghetti, Lawrence, *1041*, 1042
Few Don'ts, A, 719
Filling Station, 1074
First Seven Years, The, 1028
Fitzgerald, F. Scott, *729*, 730
Floor Plan of the President's House, 185
For My Children, 916
For the Love of Books, 1418
Franklin, Benjamin, *104*, 105, *136*, 140, 148
Frazier, Charles, 546
Frazier, Ian, *1383*, 1384
Frederick Douglass, 1066
From the Dark Tower, 926
Frost, Robert, *873*, 874, 877, 878, 880, 882, 884

G

Geisel, Theodor Seuss. See Dr. Seuss
Gettysburg Address, The, 538
Gift, The, 1342
Gift Outright, The, 884
Go Down, Moses, 532
Good Night, and Good Luck, from, 1241
Gorky, Maxim, *1137*
Goss, Warren Lee, *494*, 500
Grapes of Wrath, from *The*, 758
Grass, 870
Great Figure, The, 724
Guthrie, Woody, *766*, 768

H

Halley's Comet, 1358
Hansberry, Lorraine, 1117, *1184*
Harvey, William, *1400*, 1403
Hawthorne, Nathaniel, *271*, 272
Hayden, Robert, *1065*, 1066
H.D., *717*, 725
Help North Texas Vote/*Heading West*, 132
Hemingway, Ernest, *799*, 800
Henry, Patrick, *99*, 100
Hersey, John, *983*, 984
Heslov, Grant, *1240*, 1241
Hiroshima, from, 984
Holmes, Oliver Wendell, *265*, 266
How to Tell a Story, from 575
Hughes, Langston, *898*, *900*, 902, 904, 906, 907
Hurston, Zora Neale, *929*, 930
Huswifery, 82

I

I, Too, 904
I Hear America Singing, 434
I heard a Fly buzz—when I died—, 410
I Will Fight No More Forever, 622
Improv Everywhere, *1047*
In a Station of the Metro, 722
Inaugural Address, 1104
Interesting Narrative of the Life of Olaudah Equiano, from *The*, *166*, 170
Iroquois, The *41*
Iroquois Constitution, from *The*, 42
Irving, Washington, *227*, 228

J

Jefferson, Thomas, *111*, 112, *244*, 245
Jewett, Sarah Orne, 797
Jilting of Granny Weatherall, The, 834
Johnson, Charles, *362*
Journey Through Texas, A, 48
Junk Rally (poster), 1003

K

Keller, Helen, lxvii
Kennedy, John Fitzgerald, *1103*, 1104
King, Martin Luther, Jr., *1108*, 1109
Kingston, Maxine Hong, *1425*, 1426
Kinnell, Galway, 418
Komunyakaa, Yusef, *1349*, 1350
Kunitz, Stanley, *1357*, 1358

L

Lange, Dorothea, *766*, 767
Latin Deli: An Ars Poetica, The, 1366
Latrobe, Benjamin Henry, *180*, 184
Leaves of Grass: America's Epic, 437
Leaves of Grass, from Preface to 1855 Edition of, 426
Lederer, Richard, 9, 221, 471, 701, 1287
Lee, Li-Young, *1341*, 1342
Lee, Robert E., *540*, 541
Letter From Birmingham City Jail, from, 1109
Letter From the President's House, 181
Letter to Her Daughter From the New White House, 182
Letter to His Son, 541
Levertov, Denise, *1338*, 1339
Lewis, Meriwether, *244*, 250
Life and Times of the Thunderbolt Kid, from, 589
Life in His Language, 1096
Life on the Mississippi, from, 570
Life You Save May Be Your Own, The, 1012
Lincoln, Abraham, *537*, 539
Literature as a Magic Carpet, 702
London, Jack, *595*, 596
Longfellow, Henry Wadsworth, *257*, 258, 260
López de Cárdenas, García, *47*, 52
Lorca, Federico García, *1199*
Love Song of J. Alfred Prufrock, The, 708
Lucinda Matlock, 646
Luke Havergal, 642

M

MacLeish, Archibald, *788*, 789
Malamud, Bernard, *1027*, 1028
Man Listening to Disc, 403
Mark Twain and the American Language, 471
Mars Rover Mission Update, from, 69
Mary Chesnut's Civil War, from, 495
Masters, Edgar Lee, *645*, 646, 647
McCullough, David, lxiii
McElroy, Colleen, *914*, 916
McKay, Claude, *920*, 923
McKim, Randolph, *494*, 502
Melville, Herman, *335*, 337
Mencken, H. L., 1375
Mending Wall, 878
Migrant Mother, 767
Miller, Arthur, *978*, *1118*, *1120*, *1122*, 1124, *1184*, *1253*, *1259*
Miller, James E. Jr., 437
Minghella, Anthony, *544*, 546
Minister's Black Veil, The, 272
Miranda v. Arizona, from, lxix
Mirror, 1052
Moby-Dick, from, 336
Modern Poetry, Of, 786
Modoc (tellers), *19*, 24
Momaday, N. Scott, *1433*, 1434
Moore, Marianne, *788*, 791
Morrison, Toni, *1095*, 1096
Mother Tongue, 1410
Muir, John, lxv
Museum Indians, 34
My Bondage and My Freedom, from, 520
My life closed twice before its close, 413

N

Names, from *The*, 1434
Nature, from, 366
Navajo (tellers), *19*, 27
Navajo Origin Legend, The, 27
Negro Speaks of Rivers, The, 902
New York Times, from *The*, 1005, 1251, 1253
Night the Ghost Got In, The, 860
Nobel Prize Acceptance Speech, 828
Noiseless Patient Spider, A, 436
Notorious Jumping Frog of Calaveras County, The, 576
Nye, Naomi Shihab, *1352*, 1353

O

Oates, Joyce Carol, *324*, 325
O'Brien, Tim, *702*, *811*, 810, 947
Occurrence at Owl Creek Bridge, An, 480
O'Connor, Flannery, *1011*, 1013
Of Plymouth Plantation, from, 58
old age sticks, 780
Old Ironsides, 266
One Art, 1072
One Day, Now Broken in Two, 1394
Onomatopoeia, 1378
Onondaga (tellers), *19*, 20
Our Native American Heritage, 9
"Out, Out–," 880

P

Paine, Thomas, *116*, 117
Painter, Nell Irvin, *474*, *550*, 669
Pear Tree, 725
Perils of Indifference, from *The*, lxi
Plath, Sylvia, *1051*, 1052
Playing for the Fighting Sixty-Ninth, 1403
Poe, Edgar Allan, *288*, 293, 311, 312
Poetry, 791
Poor Richard's Almanack from, 148
Porter, Katherine Anne, *833*, 834
Pound, Ezra, *716*, 719, 722
Power, Susan, *32*, 34, 191

Q

Quindlen, Anna, *1393*, 1394

R

Raisin in the Sun, A, from, 1117
Ramsay, Sean, *1400*, 1401
Randall, Jarrell, *996*, 997
Raven, The, 312
Recollections of a Private, 500
Red Wheelbarrow, The, 723
Refugee in America, 907
Richard Bone, 647
Richard Cory, 644
Robinson, Edwin Arlington, *641*, 642, 644
Rockpile, The, 1082
Roethke, Theodore, *1057*, 1058, 1060
Roofwalker, from, 191
Rose for Emily, A, 816

S

Safire, William, *1377*, 1378
Sandburg, Carl, *867*, 868, 870
Secret, The, 1339
Self-Reliance, from, 369
1776, from, lxiii
Sexton, Anne, *1051*, 1053
Shakespeare, William, lix
Sinners in the Hands of an Angry God, from, 86
Sliding With Slang, 701
Solace of Open Spaces, The, 443
Song of Hiawatha, from *The*, 258
Song of Myself, from, 428
Sonnet 27, lix
Soyinka, Wole, *1223*
Speech in the Convention, 105
Speech in the Virginia Convention, 100
Spiritual, *531*, 532, 534
Squyres, Steve, *68*, 69
Stafford, William, *1335*, 1336
Standing at Armageddon, 1877–1919, from, 669
Steinbeck, John, *757*, 758
Stevens, Wallace, *785*, 786
Stopping by Woods on a Snowy Evening, 877
Story of an Hour, The, 628
Straw into Gold: The Metamorphosis of the Everyday, 159
Streets, 1353
Strickland, Stephanie, *1288*
Strike Against War, from, lxvii
Study the Masters, 915
Subway Birthday, 1047
Swing Low, Sweet Chariot, 534

T

Tan, Amy, *1409*, 1410
Taylor, Edward, *81*, 82
Thanatopsis, 262
The Brain—is wider than the Sky, 415
The Soul selects her own Society—, 414
There is a solitude of space, 416
There's a certain Slant of light, 412
Things They Carried, from *The*, 947
This Is Just to Say, 723
Thoreau, Henry David, *377*, 378, 388
Thurber, James, *859*, 860
Tide Rises, the Tide Falls, The, 260
To Build a Fire, 596
To His Excellency, General Washington, 124
To My Dear and Loving Husband, 76
Todd, Charlie, *1046*, 1047
Trapped in a Comic Book, 889
Traveling Through the Dark, 1336
Tropics in New York, The, 923
Truth, Sojourner, *550*, *553*, 555
Truth About O.K., The, 221
Turtle, The, 758
Twain, Mark, *566*, *568*, 570, 575, 576

U

Unknown Citizen, The, 774
Urban Renewal, 1401
U.S. National Archives document analysis worksheets, from, 179, 243, 493, 615, 765, 1001, 1399

W

Wagner Matinée, A, 652
Walden, from, 378
Walker, Alice, *1311*, 1312
Water, is taught by thirst, 417
We Wear the Mask, 638
Weisel, Elie, lxi
Welty, Eudora, *847*, 848
What Are We Arming to Defend?, from, lxiii
What to the Slave is the Fourth of July, from, 97
Wheatley, Phillis, *123*, 124
When Grizzlies Walked Upright, 24
When I Heard the Learn'd Astronomer, 432
Where Is Here? 325
White Heron, A, from, 797
Whitman, Walt, *422*, 426, 428, 432, 433, 434, 436, *437*
Who Burns for the Perfection of Paper, 1348
Wilder, Thornton, *1184*
Williams, William Carlos, *717*, 723, 724
Winter Dreams, 730
Woman Warrior, from *The*, 1426
Worn Path, A, 848
Wright, Richard, 517

Index of Skills

Boldface numbers indicate pages where terms are defined.

Literary Analysis

Action, rising/falling, **796**, **1026**, **1123**, 1158, **1449**
Actors, **1116**
Acts (drama), **1116**
Ad hominem, **197**, **953**
Address (speech), **96**
Advertisements, **952**
Allegory, **530**, 541, **756**, 762, **1216**, 1219, 1230, 1234, **R24**
Alliteration, **402**, 403, **1056**, 1061, **R24**
Allusion, **98**, 101, 108, 541, **706**, 709, 714, **R24**
Ambiguity, **270**, **676**, **R24.** *See also* Irony
Analogy, **196**, **376**, 390, **R24**
Analysis, **R18**
Analytic rubrics, **R44**
Anapest, **R28**
Anaphora, **96**, **425**, 430, 438
Antithesis, **96**, **97**, **1102**, 1105, 1113
APA (American Psychological Association) Style, **R23**
Aphorisms, **139**, 152
Apostrophe, **866**, 871
Appeals. *See* Persuasive techniques
Archetypal criticism, **R18**
Archetypal literary elements, **R24**
Archetype, **18**, **84**, 92
Archetype of the quest, **846**, 850, 853, 854, 857
Argument, lxiv–lxvii, lxx–lxxi, **196**, **448**, **1260**
Argument/support structure, **1102**, 1113
Assonance, **402**, **1056**, 1061, **R24**
Atmosphere. *See* Mood
Audience, **1456**
Authority, appeal to, **110**, **196**
Author's insights
  drama (Miller), **1120**, 1126, 1135, 1165, 1196
  oral tradition (Power), **32**, 35, 36, 38
  short story (O'Brien), **808**, 811, 812, 813
  See also Scholar's insights
Author's opinion, **1116**, 1117
Author's perspective, **982**, 989, 993, **1456**
Author's purpose
  essays, **1374**, 1375
  general/specific, **56**, 62, 64, 66, **552**, 557
  information texts, **242**
  information/public/private, **516**, **517**, **518**, 528
print media, **1456**
Author's style
  analysis, **676**
  Carver's, **1324**, 1328, 1330, 1331, 1332
  Cummings's, **778**, 782, 783
  Dickinson's, **406**, **407**
  Hemingway's, **798**, 805, 807
  narrative nonfiction, **516**
  Thoreau's, **376**, 380, 385, 390
  Whitman's, **424**
Autobiographical essay, 165
Autobiographical narrative, **188**
Autobiographical writing, **157**
Autobiography, **139**, 141, 143, 145, 152, 165, **517**, 528, **928**, 937
Ballad, **764**, **R24**
Bandwagon, **197**, **1260**
Bias, **R20**
Biased accounts, **516**, 517
Biblical allusion, **530**, 541, **1160**, 1163, 1175, 1179, 1182
Biographical criticism, **R18**
Biography, **516**
Blank verse, **872**, 877, 880, 883, 886, **R25**
Blog, **421**, **R47**
Blogroll, **R48**
Business letter, **R38**
Camera angles, **1265**
Cartoon, **1000**
Catalogue, use of, in poetry, **424**, 438
Causality, false, **197**
Cause and effect, **667**
Central idea, **1374**
Challenging the text, 364
Character study, **357**
Characterization, direct/indirect, **R25**, **728**, 732, 734, 741, 743, 744, 748, 749, 753
  comic story, **226**, 232, 233, 237, 240
  contemporary fiction, **1310**, 1313, 1321
  drama, **1186**, 1188, 1189, 1191, 1200, 1201, 1206, 1214
  short story, **650**, 654, 655, 657, 662, **796**, **1010**, 1014, 1016, 1018, 1019, 1024
Characters, **728**, 753, **796**, **1116**, **R25**. *See also* Comic characters; Grotesque characters
Chronological order, **46**, 55, **190**, **667**
Cinquain, **R25**
Citation organizer, online, **938**
Climax, **190**, **796**, **1026**, 1038, **1123**, 1158, **1449**, **R25**
College application essay, **R34**
Comedy, **R25**.
Comic characters, 587
Comic uses of language, **569**
Comments, blog, **R47**, **R48**
Commission, **242**
Comparison-and-contrast essay, **1392**, 1397
Conceit, **80**, 83
Concrete images, **449**
Conflict, internal/external, **R25**
  autobiographical narrative, **190**
  drama, **1160**, 1162, 1164, 1167, 1173, 1182
  short story, **594**, 598, 604, 606, 607, 609, 611, **814**, 819, 822, 826, 830
Connotation, **909**, **1050**, **R25**, **R54**
Consonance, **403**, **1056**, 1061, **R25**
Consumer guide, **392**
Controversial Issues, **1116**, 1117
Copyright, **R55**
Couplet, **402**, **R25**, **R32**
Cover letter, **R35**
Critical perspectives (types), **901**
Critical review, **1250**
Cultural identity, **913**
Culture, 1264
Culture-centric terms, **R20**
Dactyl, **R28**
Debate, **R55**
Deductive reasoning, **196**, **1258**
Denotation, **909**, **R25**
Description, **796**, **R26**
Descriptive essay, **1374**
Details, **516**, **764**
Development, **1026**
Dialect, **569**, 582, **858**, **928**, 937, **1310**, 1316, 1319, 1321, **R26**
Dialogue, **449**, **928**, 937, **1116**, **1450**, **R26**
Diary, **492**, **516**
Diction, **516**, **796**, **1374**, **R26**
  patriotic writing, **536**, 539, 543
  persuasive speech, **448**
  poetry, **1070**, 1077
  Safire's style, **1376**, 1381
  Whitman's style, **425**, 429, 430, 438
  Writer's Toolbox, **445**
Dimeter, **R28**
Discussion (defined), small group, **R55**
Document, **764**
Documentary, **R55**
Drama, **1116**, **R26**
Dramatic exposition, **1123**, 1127, 1129, 1138, 1146, 1147, 1151, 1158
Dramatic irony. *See* Irony

Dramatic monologue, **706**, 709, 710, 714, **R26**
Dramatic poem, **402**, **R26**
Editorial, **1000**
Editorial cartoon, **1000**
Elegy, **R28**
Elizabethan sonnet, **634**
Elliptical phrasing, **407**
E-mail, **1398**, **R40**
Emoticons, **R50**
Emotional appeal, **97**, **110**, **196**, **448**, **1258**
Emotional attitude, **798**
Encyclopedia, online, **938**
End-stopped line, **1356**, 1360
Enjambed line, **1356**, 1360
Epic, **R29**
Epic poetry, **424**
Epic theme, **424**, 427, 429, 430, 438
Epigram, **R26**
Epiphany, **1026**, 1037, 1038, **1334**, 1340, 1344, **R26**
Essay, **1374**, **R26**
Ethical appeal/argument, **97**, **110**, **196**, **448**, **1258**
Ethos. *See* Ethical appeal
Eulogy, **1094**, 1097, 1101
Evidence, **1374**
Exclamation, **96**, **97**, **1070**, 1077
Exploration narratives, **46**, 50, 51, 55
Exposition, 190, **1026**, 1038, **1449**
Expository essay, **1374**, **1376**, 1381
Fact, **953**, **1250**, **1257**, 1264
Fact propositions, **196**
Feature article, **1250**
Feed (widget), **R51**
Fiction, **R26**
Field report, **242**
Figurative expressions, **376**, 390
Figurative language, **364**, 369, **402**, 403, **449**, **1050**, **R26**
Figures of speech, **364**
Firsthand accounts, **516**
Flashback, **190**, **832**, 838, 844, **1296**, 1308, **1449**
Flash-forward, **190**
Floor plan, **178**
Foibles, **587**, 593
Folk Literature, **R27**
Folksy/familiar diction, **1376**
Foot, **256**, **402**, **R27**. *See also* Meter
Foreshadowing, **1026**, 1034, 1038, **1296**, 1308, **1449**
Formal essay, **1374**
Formal verse, **634**, 639
Frame story, **1324**
Free verse, **424**, 438, **1356**, 1360, **R27**
Generalizations, **953**
Gothic literature, **291**, 296, 299, 301, 302, 306, 309, **312**, 314, 315, 318, 322, **323**, 326, 327, 328, 330, **R27**
Government form, **558**
Government report, **392**
Grotesque characters, **1010**, 1014, 1016, 1018, 1019, 1024
Heptastich, **R32**
Heroic couplets, **122**, 127
Hero's quest, **846**, 857
Historical investigation, **664**
Historical narrative, **516**
History/roots, **913**
Holistic rubric, **R45**
Humor, **569**, 574, 578, 579, 582, **587**
Humorous devices, **587**
Humorous essay, **858**, 860, 865
Hyperbole, **569**, 582, **587**, 593, **858**, **R27**
Iamb, **256**, **872**, **R28**
Iambic pentameter, **256**, **872**, **R27**, **R29**
Idioms, **858**, **1376**
Image (word/phrase), **449**, **718**, 723, 726, **R27**
Imagery, **364**, 372, **402**, 403, **676**, **784**, 792, 793, **1364**, 1367, 1369, **R27**
Imagism, **718**
Imagist poetry, **718**, 720, 726
Imperative, **1070**, 1077
Inciting incident, **1026**, 1038
Incongruity, **569**, 582, **587**, 593
Inductive reasoning, **196**, **1258**
Informal essay, **1374**
Informal expressions, **448**
Internet, writing for, **R50**
Internet search connectors, key, **R53**
Internet sources, **R52**
Interview, **R55**
Inversion, **74**, 79
Irony, **R27**
  dramatic, **594**, 604, 609, 611, **626**, 633, **1186**, 1200, 1207, 1212, 1214
  persuasive, **449**
  verbal/situational, **626**, 630, 633, **1186**, 1193, 1194, 1195, 1214
Job application, **R37**
Job search writing, **R35**
Journal, **492**, **516**, **R28**
Knowledge (your), **764**
Label, Internet post, **R48**
Language, **676**, **913**
Legend, **R28**. *See also* Myth
Letter, **178**, **R28**
Link, Internet, **R48**
List, use of, in poetry, **424**, 438
List structure, **1102**, 1113
Literary criticism, **R18**
Loaded words, **97**, **1260**
Logical appeal/argument, **97**, **110**, **196**, **448**, **1258**, **1260**
Logical fallacies, **197**, **953**
Logos. *See* Logical appeal
Long lines in poetry, **424**, 438
Lyric poem, **402**, **1334**, 1340, 1344, **R28**
Magazine, **1456**
Manual, **128**
Manuscript preparation, **671**
In medias res, **1296**, 1308
Media techniques, **1265**
Medium, **R56**
Meeting minutes, **R41**
Memo, **R39**
Memoir, **516**, **1424**, 1427, 1428, 1429, 1436, 1439
Metaphor, **80**, 83, **364**, 372, **376**, 380, 385, 390, **402**, **1040**, 1045, **1050**, 1055, **R28**
Meter, **256**, 260, 263, 267, 268, **402**, **872**, **R28**
MLA (Modern Language Association) Style, **R22**
Modern realistic drama, **1116**
Monologue, interior, **1450**, **R30**. *See also* Dramatic monologue; Soliloquy
Monometer, **R28**
Mood, **256**, 263, 268, **1094**, 1101, **R29**
Mud slinging, **953**
Multimedia presentation, **944**
Music, **1265**
Myth, **18**, 22, 25, **R29**
Mythology, classical, **122**, 127
Narration, **R29**
Narrative essay, **516**
Narrative nonfiction, **516**
Narrative poem, **402**, **640**, 648, **R29**
Narrator, **797**, **1450**, **R29**
Naturalism, **506**, 510, 514, **R29**
Newspaper, **1456**
Nonfiction, **R29**
Nonverbal communication, **R54**
Novel, **R29**
Nuance, **676**
Objective summary, lvi, lvii
Octave, **R32**
Ode, **R30**
Online citation organizer, **938**
Online encyclopedia, **938**, **R50**
Onomatopoeia, **425**, **1376**, **R30**
Opinion, **1250**, **1257**
Oral history, **1398**
Oral interpretation, **R55**

Oral tradition, 15, **18**, 32, **R30**
Oratory, **84**, 92
Order of importance, **667**
Ordinary language, **1116**, 1117
Organizational structure, **1102**
Overgeneralization, **197**
Oxymoron, **R30**
Panel discussion, **R57**
Pantomime, **R57**
Parable, **270**, 281, 283, 285
Paradox, **407**, 415, 420, **R30**
Parallel structure, **449**
Parallelism, **96**, **97**, 108, **1062**, 1068, **1102**, 1113, **1261**
Paraphrase, **R20**
Parenthetical (MLA style), **671**
Parody, 1265, **1382**, 1386, 1390, **R30**
Parts to whole, **667**
Pastoral, **872**, 878, 881, 886, **R30**
Pathos. *See* Emotional appeal
Pentameter, **R29**
Periodical abstract, **558**
Personal essay, **1374**
Personal history, **614**
Personification, **784**, 793, **866**, 869, 871, **R30**
Perspective, objective/subjective, **982**. *See also* Author's perspective; Critical perspectives (types); Point of view
Persuasion, **97**, **110**, 113, 120, 1264
Persuasive essay, **1256**, **1374**
Persuasive speech, **196**, **448**
Persuasive techniques, **97**, **110**, **196**, **448**, **1260**
Philosophical criticism, **R18**
Photograph, **764**
Plagiarism, **670**, **R20**
Play (drama), **1116**
Plot, **640**, 648, **796**, **1026**, 1032, 1034, 1037, 1038, 1116, **1123**, 1129, 1130, 1133, 1139, 1144, 1150, 1156, 1158, **R30**
Plot device, **1296**, 1299, 1300, 1303, 1308
Podcast, **R50**
Poetry, **402**, 403, **424**, **R14**, **R30**
Point of view, **478**, 481, 488, 490, **650**, 662, **796**, **1424**, 1439, **1450**, **R30**
Policy, **196**
Political advertisement (nonprint), **952**
Political cartoons, **R55**
Political criticism, **R18**
Political document, **40**, 44, 45
Political drama, **1116**
Political speech, **96**
Poster, **1000**
Posts, blog, **R48**
Print media, **1456**
Privacy, networking, **R49**
Problem/solution, **196**, **667**
Profile, social networking, **R49**
Projection, **R54**
Propaganda, **197**, **953**
Prose, **R31**
Public service advertisement (PSA), **128**
Puns, **1040**, 1045
Puritan Plain Style, 56, **74**, 79
Purpose. *See* Author's purpose
Purpose for writing. *See* Author's purpose
Pyrrhic, **R28**
Quatrain, **R32**
Questioning the text, 368
Questions. *See* Rhetorical questions
Quotations, **R20**
Reaction shots, **1265**
Readers theatre, **R55**
Realism, **R31**
Realistic characters, **1116**, 1117
Reasoning, circular, **1260**
Recent scholarship, 14, 222, 474, 702, 978, 1290
Red herring, **197**
Reflective essay, **440**, **1408**, 1413, 1414, 1418, 1421
Refrain, **311**, **530**, 541, **R31**
Regionalism, **587**, 593, **R31**
Religious parable, **270**
Repetition, **96**, **97**, 108, **425**, **1062**, 1068
Resolution and conflict, **190**, **814**, 826, 830, **1026**, **1123**, **1449**
Restatement, **97**, **98**, 108
Résumé, **R36**
Review, **1250**
Rhetorical devices, **97**, **98**, 108, **516**, **1070**, **1102**, 1106
Rhetorical question, **97**, **98**, 102, 108, **449**, **1070**, 1077
Rhyme, **402**, **407**, **R31**
Rhyme scheme, **634**, 638, 639, **R31**
Rhythm (meter), **R31**
Role play, **R55**
Romanticism, **506**, **R32**
Rubric, **R43**
Satire, **772**, 776, **1382**, 1390, **R32**
Scansion, **R32**
Scenes (drama), **1116**
Scholarly diction, **1376**
Scholar's insights
discrimination experience (Painter), **550**, 556
philosophical works (Ehrlich), **374**, 380, 382, 383, 386
slave narrative (Andrews), **166**, 172, 173, 175
See also Author's insights
Sequence of events, **46**, 55, **1265**
Sermon, **84**, 92, **96**
Sestet, **R32**
Setting, **594**, 611, **640**, 648, **796**, **1080**, 1083, 1084, 1086, 1091, **R32**
Short story, **796**, **1448**, **R24**, **R32**
Simile, **402**, **784**, 793, **1050**, 1055, **R32**
Single effect (short story), **291**, 301, 302, 309, 318
Slant rhyme, **407**, 411, 414, 420
Slave narrative, **168**, 176, 517
Social commentary, **569**, 582, **1346**, 1354
Social context, **928**, 932, 934, 937
Social networking, **R49**
Sonnet, 639, **R32**
Sound devices, **403**, **1056**, 1061
Sounds, word, 364, 372, **425**
Sources. *See* Citations
Speaker, **640**, 643, 648, **901**, 906, 908, **R32**
Special effects, **1265**
Speeches, **96**, **98**, 101, 102, 108, **614**, **R57**
Spiritual, **530**, **531**, 541
Spondee, **R28**
Stage directions, **1116**
Stanza, **80**, 83, **402**, **922**, 927, **R32**
Stanza structure, **922**, 923, 927
Stream of consciousness, **478**, 488, 490, **832**, 835, 837, 838, 840, 842, 844
Style, **516**, **796**, **1374**, 1375
See also Author's style; Puritan Plain Style
Style formats for manuscript, **R21**
Summary, **R20**
Syllogism, **196**
Symbol, **40**, 44, 45, **270**, 283, 285, **334**, 343, 345, 347, 349, 351, 353, 354, 356, **796**, 797, **1080**, 1083, 1084, 1091, **R33**
Symposium, 201
Synecdoche, **364**, 372
Syntax, **74**, 79, **448**, **516**, **778**, **796**, **1374**
Tales, 32
Technical report, **1442**
Technical writing, **R42**
Tercet, **R32**
Tetrameter, **256**, **R28**

Theme, **R33**
allegory, **756**, 760, 762
analysis, **676**
Gothic literature, **334**, 341, 354
Hemingway's, **798**, 807
implied, **982**, 987, 990, 998
irony and, **626**, 633
more than one, **901**, 908
poetry, **403**, **424**, **1334**
reflective essay, **1408**, 1411, 1421
short story, **797**
Themes Across Centuries
Author's insights, 166, 808, 1120
Scholar's insights, 362
Thesis, **448**, **1374**, 1375 **R19**
Time, passage of, **1117**
Tone, **376**, 390, **517**, **552**, 557, **676**, **772**, 776, **796**, 797, **1374**, 1375, **R33**
Tragedy, **1216**, 1221, 1223, 1227, 1231, 1232, 1234, **R33**
Tragic flaw, **1216**
Tragic hero, **1216**, 1234
Trimeter, **402**, **R28**
Trochaic tetrameter, **256**
Trochee, **256**, **402**, **R28**
Understatement, **858**
Values, **196**, **913**, 1264
Visual representation, **R55**
Voice, **445**, **1346**, 1355
Web crawler/spider/robot, **R49**
Web safety, **R47**
Widget, **R51**
Wiki, **R50**
Word choice, **425**, 438, **448**, **796**, 797
Workplace writing, **R35**, **R36**, **R37**, **R38**, **R39**, **R40**, **R41**, **R42**
Works cited list (MLA style), **671**
Writer's style. *See* Author's style

Reading

READING FOR INFORMATION

Analyzing Functional and Expository Text

Assessment, 133, 397, 562, 943, 1255, 1447
Consumer guide, 393
Government form, 561
Government report, 395
Manual, 129
Mission statement, 1446
Newspaper feature article, 1253
Online citation organizer, 939
Online encyclopedia, 941
Periodical abstract, 559
Public service advertisement (PSA), 132
Technical report, 1443
Theater/film review, 1251, 1252

Primary Sources

Art, 246, 250, 252, 253, 496, 500, 503
Assessment, 187, 255, 505, 624, 764, 1008, 1398
Ballad, 768
Cartoon, editorial, 1004
Commission, 245
Comparing, 186, 254, 504, 623, 770, 1007, 1406
Diaries (personal history), 495, 502, 617
Editorial, 1005
E-mail, 1403
Field report, 250
Floor plan, 185
Journals, 500
Letters, 181
Note-taking guides, 179, 243, 493, 615, 765, 1001, 1399
Oral history transcript, 1401
Photographs, 617, 767
Poster, 1003
Speeches, 622

READING STRATEGIES

Action, visualize/picture, **1040**, 1045
Ambiguity, clarify, **814**, 824, 830
Anecdotal scripting, **558**
Annotated bibliography, make, **558**
Aphorisms, compare, 139, 152
Appeal to audience, critique, **98**, 105, 108
Archetypal perspective, apply, **901**, 908
Archetypes, compare and contrast, 18, 29
Arguments, evaluate, **1186**, 1190, 1192, 1194, 1198, 1201, 1203, 1207, 1214
Audience, shape message for, 110, 120
Author's perspective. *See* Writer's perspective
Author's purpose. *See* Writer's purpose
Autobiographies, compare, **157**, 160, 162, 165
Background knowledge, use, **506**, 510, 514, 536, 542, 543, **1056**, 1061, **1160**, **1398**, 1399, 1407
Bias, check for, **517**
Biographical perspective, apply, **901**, 908
Cause and effect, analyze/identify, **139**, 152, **858**, 861, 865, **1080**, 1085, 1086, 1088, 1091, **1382**, 1388, 1390
Challenge the text, **364**, 372
Characters
compare and contrast, **1310**, 1314, 1319, 1321
draw inferences about, **728**, 737, 739, 745, 747, 750, 753
identify with, **798**, 802, 807
Sample Test Item, 958
Compare and contrast Sample Test Item, 454
Comprehension, monitor, 46, 80
Concentration, keep, **R16**
Concept mapping, **558**
Conclusions, draw, **1010**, 1015, 1020, 1024, **1398**, 1393, 1407
Conflict, identify/analyze, **797**, **1117**
Connotations, interpret, **1050**, 1055
Context clues, use, **84**, 90, 92, **1442**
Contrast, relate, 46
Critical perspectives, apply, **901**, 905, 908
Cultural identity, compare, 917, 918, 919
Details
analyze sensory, **1364**, 1369
identify key, **1356**, 1360
identify relevant, **334**, 342, 349, 356, **552**, 557
identify supporting, **1102**, 1110, 1113
Details chart, use, 18
Dictionary, use, 74
Drama, reading, **1117**
Essays, reading, **1375**
Essential message
determine, **334**, 342, 349, 356, **552**, 557
paraphrase to understand, **74**
summarize to identify, **168**
Fact and opinion, distinguish between, **1250**
Fluency, improve, **R16**
Fluency checklist, use, **R17**
Footnotes, integrate, 83
Gothic literature, comparing, 323, 326, 327, 328, 330, 333
Historical period, evaluate influences of, **226**, 229, 231, 237, 240, **634**, 639, **1216**, 1218, 1234
Historical perspective, apply, **901**, 908
Humor, comparing past/present, **587**, 593
Imagery, compare, **922**, 927, 1462
Images, compare, **718**, 726
Inference, draw
about poet's beliefs, **1346**, 1355
informational texts, **764**, 765, 769
to interpret meaning, **270**, 275, 277, 279, 285
Test Practice, 771
Information, organize/record, **558**
Integrate and evaluate information, 16, 224, 476, 704, 980, 1292
Interpret, **1334**, 1342, 1344
Listening to lyrics, **530**, 534, 541
Literary criticism, apply political approach to, 922
Main idea, **1102**
identify support of, 1110, 1113
summarize to identify, **168**
Meaning, clarify, 56, **650**, 659, 660, 662
Moods, compare, **256**, 268
Multiple themes, compare, **901**, 908
Narrative accounts, reading, **517**
Note-taking, **558**
Online source, evaluate, **938**
Organizational patterns, analyze, **128**, **478**, 484, 490, **1094**, 1098, 1101
Outline, **558**, **1408**, 1421
Parallelism, find, 1062, 1068

Paraphrase to determine meaning, **74**, 76, 79, **778**, 781, 783, **1376**, 1381
Performance, visualize action in, **1117**
Personification, compare use of, **866**, 871
Perspectives, compare, **982**, 998
Persuasive techniques, identify, **97**
Philosophical argument, analyze, **626**, 633, **784**, 793
Philosophical assumptions, analyze, **40**, 43, 45, **376**, 381, 386, 390, **614**, 615, 619, 620, 624
Plot turning points, Sample Test to identify, 1270
Poems, compare and contrast, **403**, **640**, 648
Poetry, reading/responding to, **403**
Poetry of cultural identity, compare, **913**
Points of view, compare, **1424**, 1439
Political approach, apply, 922, 925
Political assumptions, analyze, **98**, 108, **982**, 998
Political drama, compare past/present, **1239**, 1244, 1249
Predictions, make
- applying background knowledge, **594**, 597, 598, 600, 606, 611
- drama, **1160**, 1163, 1168, 1176, 1177, 1180, 1182
- generate questions, then, **846**, 857
- short story, **1296**, 1304, 1307, 1308

Primary sources, relate literary work to, 1392, 1397
Problems, compare and contrast, 46, 55
Purpose for reading, set/establish, **18**, 22, 26, 29, **518**, 523, 524, 528
Questioning the text, **364**, 372
Questions, ask
- to clarify connections, **1324**, 1332
- to clarify meaning, **650**, 659, 660, 662
- to distinguish between fact/opinion, **1250**
- Questions, generate, **492**, 493, 497, 501, 505, **846**, 850, 853, 854

Read
- according to punctuation, **R17**
- phrases not words, **R16**

Read aloud, **425**, 438, **797**, **1062**, 1068
Read poetry
- according to punctuation, **1070**, 1077
- in sentences, **872**, 876, 879, 885, 886

Reading rate, adjust
- dramatic monologue, **706**, 711, 714
- epic poetry, **425**, 438
- political document, **80**, 83

Reason, relate, 46
Refrains of songs, compare and contrast, 530, 535
Regional dialect, interpret, **569**, 573, 581, 582
Relate to own experience, **1424**, 1428, 1439
Repetition
- evaluate effects of, **866**, 870, 871
- find and compare, **1062**, 1068

Reread
- to clarify elliptical phrasing, **407**, 409, 420
- to clarify understanding, **122**, 127
- to clarify unfamiliar material, **1442**

Restate
- in own words, 74
- in simplified form, 66

Rewrite, to understand, 74
Rhetorical devices, analyze/compare, **97**, **1102**, 1113
Scan, 66
Senses, engage, **718**, 721, 723, 726
Sentences, break down long, **56**, 64, 66, **291**, 298, 304, 308, 313, 318
Sequence of events, clarify, 46, **832**, 844
Short stories, reading, **797**
Signal words, recognize, **46**, 49, 54, 55
Social commentary, compare, 1346, 1355
Social perspective, apply, **901**, 908
Speaker's attitude, compare and contrast, 406, 420
Speeches, reading, **97**
Structure/meaning, evaluate, **772**, 776
Subjectivity, check for, **517**
Summarize
- to identify main idea, **168**, 176
- main and supporting ideas, **256**, 258, 264, 268
- short story, **1026**, 1030, 1038

Symbolism, analyze patterns of, **756**, 761, 762
Symbols, evaluate persuasive use of, **1000**, 1001, 1008
Technical language, clarify, **569**, 572, 582
Text structures/features
- analyze informational, **392**
- analyze/evaluate information from, **128**
- identify, **1123**, 1126, 1130, 1137, 1139, 1141, 1143, 1149, 1155, 1156, 1158

Themes, interpret/compare, **797**, **1408**, 1421
Thesis, identify author's, **1375**
Time of events, clarify, 46
Tone, identify author's, **1375**
Understanding, monitor, 56
Vocabulary, understand key, **R17**
Word choice, analyze, **110**, 114, 120
Writer's perspective, analyze, **178**, 179, 181, 184, 186, 187, 682
Writer's purpose, identify/analyze, 202, **242**, 243, 252, 253, **517**, **928**, 933, 934, 937, **1375**
Writer's views/insights, compare, **536**, 543

CRITICAL READING

Achieve insight, **R18**
Analyze, 28, 33, 39, 44, 72, 77, 82, 91, 103, 107, 115, 119, 150, 164, 175, 185, 239, 253, 259, 264, 284, 310, 317, 332, 355, 368, 371, 387, 409, 411, 414, 427, 431, 433, 436, 501, 513, 610, 621, 638, 721, 722, 724, 752, 761, 769, 787, 790, 792, 806, 843, 856, 876, 879, 881, 907, 918, 926, 995, 997, 1006, 1023, 1054, 1100, 1181, 1213, 1233, 1307, 1337, 1343, 1354, 1372, 1380, 1396, 1405, 1420, 1438
Analyze cause and effect, 28, 91, 317, 332, 368, 527, 1060
Apply, 23, 164, 185, 371, 387, 574, 592, 644, 806, 1064, 1157, 1213, 1432
Assess, 310, 400, 414, 725, 856, 1049, 1076, 1181, 1213, 1340, 1359
Classify, 864, 995
Compare, 638, 1354, 1368
Compare and contrast, 28, 33, 54, 150, 284, 355, 409, 433, 436, 549, 610, 621, 661, 761, 782, 806, 813, 1037, 1320, 1380, 1396, 1416
Connect, 33, 164, 264, 310, 363, 368, 414, 433, 489, 534, 542, 551, 556, 574, 632, 661, 712, 724, 752, 769, 787, 843, 881, 885, 1006, 1307, 1337, 1420, 1432, **R18**
Contrast, 39, 417, 644
Criticize, 389
Deduce, 82, 103, 126, 332, 387, 769, 813, 827, 829, 843, 869, 894, 905, 1090, 1337
Defend, 239
Define, 368, 721, 790, 829
Describe, 72, 332, 400, 549, 712, 827, 894, 1049
Distinguish, 77, 164, 489, 592, 721, 761, 864, 1060, 1112, 1359, **R18**
Draw conclusions, 54, 65, 72, 77, 103, 119, 164, 175, 239, 264, 267, 284, 370, 389, 411, 433, 436, 527, 549, 632, 638, 827, 870, 925, 995, 997, 1054, 1181, 1233, 1248, 1331, 1359, 1405, 1432, 1438

Essential Questions
- **How does literature shape or reflect society? 11**, 91, 107, 175, **216**, 239, 370, 389, **466**, 513, 527, 542, 632, 638, **696**, 712, 752, 761, 775, 782, 792, 827, 843, 936, **970**, 997, 1043, 1054, 1067, 1090, 1100, 1112, 1233, **1282**, 1320, 1343, 1354, 1389, 1396
- **What is the relationship between literature and place? 6**, 28, 44, 54, **214**, 284, 317, **470**, 489, 542, 610, 647, 661, **694**, 725, 856, 885, 926, **976**, 1060, 1076, **1285**, 1307, 1359, 1368, 1438
- **What makes American literature American? 9**, 65, 77, 82, 119, 126, 150, **219**, 267, 355, 417, 436, **472**, 556, 581, **699**, 806, 864, 870, 907, **974**, 1023, 1037, **1287**, 1331, 1380, 1420

Evaluate, 65, 91, 107, 115, 150, 253, 259, 267, 310, 389, 431, 499, 556, 574, 592, 621, 622, 721, 722, 724, 752, 769, 782, 864, 907, 1006, 1049, 1107, 1157, 1181, 1213, 1320, 1331, 1380, 1405, 1416
Extend, 103, 489, 638, 644, 790, 829, 1233
Generalize, 23, 39, 107, 150, 370, 400, 431, 501, 1023, 1076
Hypothesize, 65, 499, 574, 829
Identify, 769, 1076, 1372, 1399
Identify cause and effect, 54

Infer, 23, 44, 54, 103, 126, 150, 167, 175, 185, 253, 267, 284, 310, 371, 431, 433, 499, 501, 503, 513, 549, 556, 581, 592, 622, 638, 644, 647, 722, 725, 787, 806, 809, 827, 843, 864, 879, 885, 905, 925, 936, 995, 1006, 1023, 1060, 1067, 1112, 1121, 1157, 1213, 1233, 1307, 1331, 1337, 1340, 1343, 1359, 1372, 1416, 1432, 1438
Interpret, 23, 33, 39, 54, 65, 72, 82, 91, 119, 126, 150, 164, 239, 264, 267, 310, 317, 332, 355, 370, 371, 375, 387, 400, 409, 411, 414, 417, 427, 436, 489, 499, 513, 534, 574, 632, 644, 647, 661, 712, 722, 724, 725, 752, 769, 775, 782, 787, 790, 792, 806, 813, 829, 843, 856, 869, 870, 876, 881, 885, 894, 905, 907, 918, 925, 926, 995, 997, 1023, 1037, 1043, 1054, 1060, 1064, 1076, 1107, 1157, 1181, 1213, 1233, 1248, 1295, 1307, 1320, 1337, 1340, 1343, 1354, 1359, 1368, 1396, 1416, 1420, 1432
List, 1372
Make a decision, 721
Make a judgement, 332, 370, 387, 433, 501, 503, 610, 712, 761, 775, 813, 1023, 1380, 1389, **R18**
Make inferences, 1076
Place the work, **R18**
Relate, 414, 644
Respond, 23, 28, 44, 54, 65, 77, 82, 91, 103, 107, 115, 119, 126, 150, 164, 175, 185, 239, 253, 259, 264, 267, 284, 310, 317, 355, 368, 370, 371, 387, 389, 409, 411, 414, 427, 431, 433, 436, 489, 499, 501, 503, 513, 527, 534, 542, 556, 574, 581, 592, 610, 621, 622, 632, 638, 644, 647, 661, 712, 721, 722, 725, 752, 761, 769, 775, 782, 790, 792, 806, 813, 827, 829, 843, 856, 864, 869, 870, 876, 879, 881, 885, 905, 907, 918, 925, 926, 936, 995, 997, 1006, 1023, 1037, 1043, 1054, 1060, 1064, 1067, 1076, 1090, 1100, 1107, 1112, 1157, 1181, 1213, 1233, 1248, 1307, 1320, 1331, 1340, 1343, 1354, 1359, 1368, 1380, 1389, 1396, 1399, 1416, 1420, 1432, 1438
Speculate, 28, 39, 103, 150, 167, 185, 253, 332, 363, 370, 375, 400, 409, 411, 489, 503, 551, 622, 632, 644, 647, 721, 782, 787, 790, 813, 827, 843, 876, 879, 1037, 1049, 1067, 1121, 1295, 1331, 1354, 1359, 1372, 1420
Summarize, 28, 44, 355, 389, 501, 503, 542, 787, 827, 869, 894, 1006, 1049, 1157, 1416
Support, 389, 527, 864, 936, 1090, 1157, 1181, 1354, 1389, 1438
Synthesize, 44, 115, 126, 185, 284, 556, 621, 622, 792, 856, 905, 1340
Take a position, 44, 239, 355, 387, 409, 556, 661, 809, 918, 995, 997

Vocabulary

ESSENTIAL QUESTION VOCABULARY,
8, 10, 13, 214, 216, 219, 466, 470, 473, 694, 696, 699, 970, 974, 976, 1284, 1286, 1289

GRAMMAR, USAGE, AND MECHANICS
Academic course names (capitalization), **R61**
ACT English Test: Editing in Context, 206, 686, 1274
Adjective, **321**, **R57**
Adjective clause, **287**, **R58**
Adjective phrase, **R57**
Adverb, **321**, **R57**
Adverb clause, **287**, **R58**
Adverb phrase, **R57**
Apostrophe, **R62**
Appositive phrase, **R57**
Brackets, **R62**
Capitalization, **R61**
Clause, **613**, **R58**
Colons, **R62**
Commas, 31, 1263, **R61**
Commonly confused words, **R60**
Complement, **R58**
Complex sentence, **R58**
Compound sentence, **R58**
Compound-complex sentence, **R58**
Conjunction, 31, **94**, **155**, **R57**
Connotation, **909**
Conventions, **R61**
Dashes, **R62**
Denotation, **909**
Diction, **R60**
Dictionary, using, **198**, **R14**
Electronic dictionary, using, **198**
Ellipses, **R62**
End marks, **R61**
English language, **R14**
Exclamation mark, **R61**
Gerund phrase, **R58**
Gerunds, **358**
Idioms/idiomatic expressions, **1266**
Independent clause, **R58**
Infinitive, **358**
Infinitive phrase, **R58**
Interjection, **R57**
Italics, **R62**
Modifier placement, 585, **R59**
Modifiers (degrees of comparison), **R60**
Nominative case, **R60**
Noun, **755**, **R56**
Noun clause, **R58**
Object, direct/indirect, **R58**
Objective case, **R60**
Objective complement, **R58**
Paragraph structure, **R58**
Parallel structure, **1423**
Parentheses, **R62**
Participial phrase, **R57**
Participle, **358**
Parts of speech, **R56**
Period (end mark), **R61**
Person, unintended shift in, **R59**
Phrase, 358, **613**, **R59**
Plurals, forming, **R63**
Possessive case, **R60**
Predicate adjective, **R58**
Predicate nominative, **R58**
Preposition, **R57**
Prepositional phrase, **R57**
Pronoun, **755**, **R56**
Pronoun case, **R60**
Pronoun-antecedent agreement, **911**, **R59**
Punctuation, 31, 1263, **R61**
Question mark, **R61**
Quotation marks, **R62**
Semicolons, **R62**
Sentences
  classifying, **R58**
  combining, 31, 94, **1237**
  first words of (capitalization), **R61**
  SAT Writing Test: Identifying Errors, 962, 1466
  SAT Writing Test: Improving, 458
  structure, **R58**
  varying, 613, **1441**
Simple sentence, **R58**
Specialized dictionaries, using, **198**
Spelling rules, **R63**
Subject and predicate, **R58**
Subject-verb agreement, **755**, **R59**
Subordinate clause, **R58**
Subordination, **155**
Thesaurus, using, **198**, **R14**
Titles (capitalization), **R61**
Transitional expressions, **1323**
Verb, **1115**, **R57, R59**
Verb phrase, **R57**
Verb tense, 1093, **R60**
Voice, active/passive, **1115**
Word choice, **R60**

Sentences
choose correct, 755, 911, 1115
combine, 31, 94, 1237, 1323
complete, 45, 94, 127, 155, 205, 241, 321, 457, 529, 612, 685, 794, 871, 919, 961, 999, 1007, 1055, 1093, 1101, 1159, 1273, 1369, 1381, 1422, 1440, 1465
revise, 254, 358, 491, 543, 585, 593, 613, 623, 649, 770, 777, 937, 1045, 1061, 1069, 1332, 1345, 1397, 1423, 1441
Synonyms/Antonyms 67, 165, 177, 186, 319, 333, 357, 373, 391, 583, 633, 715, 1078, 1092, 1114, 1215, 1235, 1309, 1355, 1361, 1406, 1458

True or false statements Explain choice, 83, 121, 319, 504, 557, 727, 857, 1183
Word mapping, 1361
Word meanings, 954, 1391
Word/phrase relationships, 79, 286, 763

WORD ANALYSIS

Etymology
- *appear*, 727
- *civis*, 1007
- cognates, **1458**
- *com*, 186
- *diurnus*, 504
- English language, **R14**
- *fatigare*, 1406
- legal terms, 1215
- *migrare*, 770
- military words from other languages, 999
- *mille*, 623
- mythological/Biblical, 678
- *peril*, 67
- political science/history terms, 450
- scientific/medical/mathematical terms, 954
- *terrestrial*, 254
- words from myths, 1235
- words from other languages, **R63**

words from Spanish, 1309, 1458
Multiple-meaning words, 439, 663, 1069, 1345
Orthographic patterns, **R63**
Prefixes
- *ab-*, 373
- adding, to root words, **R63**
- *di-*, 715
- *ex-*, 241
- *extra-*, 1078
- *in-*, 831
- *mal-*, 357
- *mono-*, 583
- *omni-*, 93
- political science/history terms, 450
- *pro-*, 763, 1361
- scientific/medical/mathematical terms, 954
- spelling rules, **R63**
- *super-*, 1092
- *uni-*, 109

Roots
- *-anima-*, 109
- *-aud-*, 1440
- *-bene-*, 529
- *-corpus-*, 1391
- *-dict-*, 491
- *-doc-*, 1322
- *-doct-*, 1322
- *-est-*, 254
- *-fin-*, 421
- *-flu-*, 391
- *-genus-*, 649
- *-grat-*, 1159
- *-greg-*, 515
- *-ject-*, 177
- legal terms, 1215
- *-liber-*, 909
- *-litera-*, 1039
- *-lum-*, 887
- *-path-*, 286
- *-pend-*, 612
- political science/history terms, 450
- *-psych-*, 777
- *-rect-*, 121
- *-satis-*, 794
- scientific/medical/mathematical terms, 954
- *-scrib-*, 1422
- *-script-*, 1422
- *-sed-*, 754
- *-sol-*, 1025
- spelling using, **R65**
- *-trud-*, 30
- *-trus-*, 30
- *-vers-*, 1114
- *-vert-*, 1114
- *-voc-*, 319

Suffixes
- adding, to root words, **R65**
- *-ance*, 153
- *-ence*, 153
- *-logy*, 1183
- political science/history terms, 450
- scientific/medical/mathematical terms, 954
- spelling using, **R65**
- *-tude*, 121

VOCABULARY WORKSHOPS

Cognates, 1458
Dictionary and Thesaurus, 198
Etymology: Scientific/Medical/Mathematical Terms, 954
Idioms/Idiomatic Expressions, 1266
Mythology and Religious Traditions, Words from, 678
Political Science/History Terms, 450

Writing

WRITING APPLICATIONS

Analytical essay
- humor, 584, 865
- poetry, 871, 1055
- response to literature, 910
- story's ending, 1332
- theme, 1355

Argument, lxx, lxxi
Assessment essay (timed), 943
Autobiographical narrative
- Student Model, 194
- Workshop, 188
- Writers on Writing (Power), 191

Blog entry about poetry, 421
Business letter, **R38**
Character analysis, 715
Character study, 357
College application essay, 529, **R34**
Comparison-and-contrast essay
- authors' political viewpoints, 1249
- character types, 593
- cultural heritage poems, 919
- How does literature shape or reflect society? 452, 956
- poetry, 268, 794, 927, 1345
- speeches, 109
- theme, 999
- Timed Writing, 133
- What is the relationship between literature and place? 200, 1268
- What makes American literature American? 680, 1460
- writer's understanding, 543

Cover letter, **R35**
Critical essay, 491, 807, 887
Critical review, 831, 1322
Criticism. *See* Literary criticism
Editorial, 391, 663
Editor's review of manuscript, 727
E-mail, **R40**
Essay
- comparing science to poetry, 1061
- of interpretation, 1025
- in response to criticism, 515
- of tribute, 1101

Essential Questions
- **How does literature shape or reflect society?** 1080, 1094
  - American Renaissance, 226, 364, 376, 452
  - Civil War Era, 506, 518, 536, 626, 634
  - Contemporary Period, 1290, 1310, 1334, 1346, 1382, 1392
  - Early America, 84, 98, 168
  - Modern Age, 706, 728, 756, 772, 778, 784, 814, 832, 928, 956
  - Post-War Era, 982, 1040, 1050, 1062, 1123
- **What is the relationship between literature and place?**
  - American Renaissance, 270, 286
  - Civil War Era, 478, 530, 594, 640, 650
  - Contemporary Period, 1290, 1296, 1356, 1364, 1424
  - Early America, 18, 46, 200
  - Modern Age, 718, 846, 872, 922, 956
  - Post-War Era, 1010, 1056, 1070
- **What makes American literature American?** 1324
  - American Renaissance, 256, 334, 406, 424
  - Civil War Era, 552, 569, 680
  - Contemporary Period, 1290, 1376, 1408, 1460
  - Early America, 56, 74, 80, 110, 122, 139
  - Modern Age, 798, 858, 866, 901, 956
  - Post-War Era, 1026, 1102, 1268

Evaluation
- of persuasion, 93
- of philosophical essay, 373

Evaluation essay of differing views, 320
Expository essay (timed), 1447
Free verse poem in honor of Whitman, 439
Historical context essay, 763
Historical investigation report
- Student Model, 672
- Workshop, 664
- Writers on Writing (Painter), 669

Interpretive essay, 79, 286, 1369
Job application, **R37**
Journal entry, explorer's, 55
Letter to author, 1397, 1422
Letter to editor, 1114
Literary criticism
  approaches to, 777, 1069, **R18**
  how elements convey message, 612
  how main concept supported, 754
  supporting, **R19**
  on universal theme, 1236
  writing, **R19**
Meeting minutes, **R41**
Memo, **R39**
Memoir, 1440
Multimedia presentation
  Student Model, 950
  Workshop, 944
  Writers on Writing (O'Brien), 947
  Writer's Toolbox, 949
Museum placard, 177
Newspaper article, 557, 1159
Objective summary, lvi, lvii
Outline for short story, 649
Parody of opening statement, 1391
Personality profile, 1039
Persuasive essay
  Student Model, 1262, R46
  Timed Writing, 562
  Workshop, 1256
  Writers on Writing (Miller), 1259
Persuasive letter, 1183
Persuasive memorandum, 127
Persuasive speech, 448
Philosophical essay, evaluation of, 373
Play, 30
Poem
  found, 45
  using extended metaphor, 1045
Poet's introduction, 783
Position statement (timed)
  ACT Prep, 207, 687, 1275
  Informational texts, 397, 1255
  SAT Prep, 459, 963, 1467
Radio play, 1092
Reflective essay
  Student Model, 446
  Workshop, 440
  Writers on Writing (Ehrlich), 443
  writing lessons, 83, 633, 937, 1361
Report on literary history, 639
Research paper on word origins, 1381
Response to literature
  analysis, 154, 333
  compare and contrast, 165
  multi-genre, 910, 1078
Résumé, **R36**
Sequel, 857
Short story (retell same)
  from different point of view, 1309
  update, 241
Short story
  Student Model, 1454
  Workshop, 1448
  Writers on Writing (Alvarez), 1451
Slide presentation, introductions for, 535
Speaker introduction, 67
Technical writing, **R42**
Workplace document: legal brief, 1215

WRITING STRATEGIES

Prewriting

About, in writing process, **R19**
Analogies, 391
Argument summary, 373
Artwork, consider including, 535
Assumptions, challenge, 515
Audience, consider, 189
Blueprint, use, 1449
Brainstorm, 391, 1440
Characters, analyze/interview, 357, 1092, 1449
Chart, using, 67, 109, 154, 241, 1025
Citations, decide, 670
Coding cards, use, **R20**
Conflict, 1449
Details, 109, 241, 286, 439, 529, 754, 999, 1039, 1309, 1361
Details, gather, 55, 79, 189, 441, 612, 663, 665, 1257, 1449
Dialogue, 30, 1092
Electronic sources, use, 67
Emotional appeals, 93
Evidence, 1183, 1257
Examples, 945
Facts, verify/clarify, 177
Focus, find, 665, 937
Freewrite, 441, 1361
Graphics, consider including, 541
Ideas, 121, 794, 1025, 1114, 1159
Imagery, 93
Images, visual, 1078
Internet research, 639
Interview yourself, 189
Introduction/body/conclusion, 649
Issue, analyze both sides of, 1257
Key similarities/differences, jot down, 999
Library research, 177, 639
List, using, 30, 121, 441, 491, 1045, 1322, 1422
Location, choose specific, 55
Logical reasoning, 93
Looping, focus by, 1257
Main ideas chart, 584
Media checklist, 945
Memory notes, 189
Metaphors, 391
Narrator/dialogue, 30, 1092
News notebook, use, 1257
Notes, organize/use, 665, 831, 887, 1025, **R20**
Opinion, form/summarize/support, 357, 373, 663, 1322
Organization, logical, 794
Outline support, 1215
Perspectives, different, 910
Position, support/outline, 391, 1215
Preferences, list, 945
Print sources, use, 67
Purpose, consider, 189
Questions, address, 67, 680, 777, 1249, 1355, 1369
Quotations, consider, 541
Reread
  to identify relationships, 286
  to interpret patterns, 421
  for natural dialogue, 30
  for questions, 67
Research, quick preview, 665
Review literature for details, 79
Sources, research, 67, 121, 665, 763
Story chart, use, 1449
Strengths/weaknesses, note, 727
Support, **R19**
Textbook review, 665
Thesis statement, 910, 945
Thoughts, cluster diagram, 1391
Titles, compare/contrast, 1345
Topic, choose/narrow, 189, 441, 665, 945, 1114, 1257, 1449, **R34**
Turning point, find, 189
Universal themes, chart, 1236
Viewpoint, determine/support, 320, 715
Vocabulary, identify specialized, 177
Word choice, 1381

Drafting

About, in writing process, **R19**
Action, 30
Analysis, support of, 754
Appeals, effective, 1258
Archetypal perspective, from, 1069
Arguing techniques, 1258
Arguments, 391, 612, 666, 1215, 1391
Audience, consider, 177, 1450
Balance, strike a, 946
Business letter, 1114
Cause/effect relationships, 1391
Characters' dialog/directions, 30
Citations, 373, 421, 670, 671
Concerns/counterclaims, 391
Conclusions, draw, 200, 865
Conversational style, appropriate, 783
Counterargument, 1215
Cultural bias, avoid, **R20**
Delivery diagram/chart, 946
Description, 55, 83
Details, 83, 241, 442, 910, 1039, 1309, 1322, 1332
Dialogue, 30, 190, 1092, 1309, 1450
Documentation, internal, 763
Elaboration, 190, 666, 1258, **R34**
Emotional appeal, 663
Emotional depth, 1440
Events, order of, 190
Evidence, factual, 200, 663
Examples, 121
Facts, relevant, 557
Findings summary, 639
Gender bias, avoid, **R20**
Headline, 557
Ideas, 79, 109, 121, 442, 663, 794, 831, 910, 1045, 1322
Illustrations, connections to, 1078
Insights, thoughtful, 83, 584
Interpretation, statement of, 286
Interpretations support, 452, 777

Introduction/body/conclusion, 93, 154, 373, 391, 442, 529, 557, 754, 910, 999, 1025, 1101, 1258, 1422, **R34**
Journalistic distance, with, 1159
Language, use appropriate, 121
Main points summary/support, 93, 109
Manuscript preparation, 671
Monologue, interior, 241, 1450
Name calling, avoid, 121
Opinion, state/support, 715, 887
Organization method, 320, 584, 633, 667, 1236, 1258, 1345, 1361, **R34**
Outline, 666, 946
Paraphrases, **R20**
Plagiarism, avoid, 670, **R20**
Plot, decide/enrich, 649
Point of view, 1450
Position statement, 515, 639, 1061, 1332
Purpose, consider, 177
Questions, ask/answer, 1159
Quotations, 109, 421, 557, 584, 715, 754, 777, 927, 1159, **R20**
Read aloud after, 67
Reader's questions, anticipate, 177
References, elaborate with, 831
Repetition for emphasis, 391
Respect, demonstrate, 121
Rhetorical devices, 1183
Scenes, organize action into, 30
Sequence, logical, 421
Settings, decide action for, 30
Social perspective, from, 1069
Sources, 79, 666, 763, **R21**
Speech, natural-sounding, 67
Stage directions, 30, 946, 1092
Stream of consciousness, 491
Style, show, **R34**
Summaries, **R20**
Support, **R19**
Tense, 1450
Theme, 1236
Thesis, 154, 357, 452, 612, 666, 680, **R19**
Thought shots, 190
Tone, authentic/appropriate, 67, 439, 633
Topic, state, 109
Transitions, 286
Understanding, demonstrate, 807
Viewpoint, determine/support, 727, 1114
Word choice, 191, 200, 391, 439, 452, 680, 927, 946
Works cited list (MLA style), 671

Student Models
Autobiographical narrative, 194
Historical investigation report, 672
Multimedia presentation, 950
Persuasive essay, 1262
Reflective essay, 446
Short story, 1454

Revising
About, in writing process, **R19**
Adjectives/adverbs, use precise, 1322
Argument, 391, 1260
Audience, knowledge level for, 999
Avoid too much, 1045
Balance, 444, 529, 1025
Cause/effect relationships, 1391
Characters depth, 192
Citations, 373, 668, 763
Clarity, 727
Cluster diagram, 1039
Connect past to present, 192
Connections, strengthen, 154, 357
Details, 67, 421, 529, 1309, 1361
Dialogue, 30
Effects, variety of, 948
Explanations, depth of, 177, 529
Facts/data, 177
Feedback, use, 1440
Historical context, 763
Ideas, 109, 154, 286, 421, 515, 543, 584, 612, 777, 794, 831, 1025, 1078
Illustrations/photographs, 391
Language, 121, 663, 1452
Logic, clarify, 320, 1260, 1345
Main idea focus, 93, 754
Media selection, 391, 948, 949
Modifiers, replace weak, 1322
New version of original story, 241
Parallelism form, 1114
Peer review, use, 55, 192, 444, 668, 948, 1260, 1452
Point of view, 1452
Proper names, 1159
Punctuation, 320
Quotations, 109, 286, 320, 491, 794, 999, 1069, 1159
Read aloud
to catch awkward sections, 154
for natural rhythms, 439
to practice, 67
for smooth flow, 1092
Reread for accuracy/effectiveness, 67, 1183
Rhythms, 439
Sentences, vary, 192, 444, 1114
Sequence, improve, 948
Show instead of tell, 1452
Source material, integrate, 668
Structure, overall, 192, 444
Subordination, use, 192
Support, review and evaluate, 121
Themes, connections between, 1236
Thesaurus, use, 727, 1322
Transitional words/phrases, 154, 320, 529, 543, 887, 948, 1025, 1078, 1114, 1236, 1260, 1345, 1391
Word choice, 55, 67, 193, 439, 668, 715, 727, 910, 1114, 1183, 1215, 1422, 1452

Six Traits
Sentence Fluency, 1453
Ideas, 949
Organization, 667
Conventions, 1261
Voice, 445
Word choice, 193

Editing/Proofreading
Accuracy, 675
Capitalization, 195
Commas, 1263
Culture-centric terms, **R20**
Dialogue punctuation, 1455
Pronoun usage, **R20**
Punctuation, 951
Sentence fragments, 447, 951
Spelling, 195, 447, 675, 1263, 1455

Publishing/Presenting
Anthology, class, 195
Illustrated story, 1455
Literary magazine, 447
Multimedia portfolio, 951
Newspaper article, 1263
Oral historical investigation report, 675
Oral presentation, 195
Recitation of story, 1455
Reflective presentation, 447
Speech, 1263
Stage showing, 951

Reflect on Writing (Writer's journal)
Autobiographical narrative, 195
Historical investigation report, 675
Multimedia presentation, 951
Persuasive essay, 1263
Reflective essay, 447
Short story, 1455

Rubric for Self-Assessment
Autobiographical narrative, 195
Historical investigation report, 675
Multimedia presentation, 951
Persuasive essay, 1263
Reflective essay, 447
Short story, 1455

Writers on Writing
Flashback and Exposition (Alvarez), 1451
Layers of Meaning (Ehrlich), 443
Revision (O'Brien), 947
Using Historical Facts (Miller), 1259
Using Research (Painter), 669
Word Choice (Power), 191

Writing for Assessment *See* Test Practice; Test-Taking Practice

Research and Technology

Advertising campaign, 1363
Blog, creating, R48
Culture fair, 1461
Documentary, 1269
Evaluation: magazine designs, 957
Internet research, R51
Internet resources evaluation, R52
Multimedia presentation, 702
Panel discussion, 453
Podcast, R50
Proposal for mini-series, 681
Research Task, 187, 255, 505, 624, 771, 1008, 1407
Slide presentation, 222
Social networking, R49
Solve a Research Project, 16, 224, 476, 704, 980, 1292
Survey, 201
Symposium, 201
Travel Directions, 1290

Speaking, Listening, and Viewing

Critical Viewing

Analyze, 77, 86, 101, 107, 117, 134, 167, 317, 337, 350, 363, 408, 500, 511, 571, 600, 617, 737, 825, 860, 878, 915, 916, 931, 1013, 1030, 1067, 1202, 1229, 1378, 1394

Analyze visual information, 59, 390, 1234, 1360

Apply, 20, 267

Assess, 862, 991, 994, 1087, 1131, 1188, 1211, 1339

Compare, 590, 659, 1299, 1302

Compare and contrast, 34, 37, 172, 230, 338, 435, 555, 733, 738, 805, 818, 877, 924, 1198, 1327, 1430

Connect, 53, 161, 280, 282, 294, 371, 375, 432, 476, 486, 509, 533, 579, 604, 628, 659, 704, 724, 791, 823, 835, 849, 868, 875, 902, 906, 1017, 1052, 1083, 1172, 1351, 1418

Contrast, 525

Deduce, 731, 758, 811, 1388

Describe, 1387

Distinguish, 496, 522, 1412

Draw conclusions, 141, 780

Evaluate, 348, 353, 644, 725, 774, 801, 852, 863, 1022, 1205

Generalize, 1142

Hypothesize, 1435

Infer, 149, 234, 429, 512, 539, 572, 1104, 1128, 1154, 1224, 1411, 1426

Interpret, 49, 50, 125, 135, 262, 301, 340, 367, 384, 512, 521, 541, 637, 653, 708, 839, 896, 1073, 1136, 1138, 1152, 1178, 1184

Judge, 63

Make a decision, 905

Make a judgement, 1075, 1170, 1385

Predict, 292

Relate, 597, 988

Speculate, 273, 360, 379, 564, 577, 809, 980, 1134, 1220, 1295

Support, 63, 411, 429

Synthesize, 720

Take a position, 985

Verify, 171

Listening and Speaking

Discussion, small group
- Essential Questions, 14, 474, 978, 1290
- Collaboration: Speaking and Listening, 224, 361, 476, 897, 1185, 1292
- Handbook tips for, R50

Entertainment media analysis, 1264

Impromptu speech, 222

Interview, 16, 453, 980

Media review, 135

Multimedia presentation, 704

Oral interpretation, 676, 957

Oral presentation, 16, 476,
- Essential Questions, 702, 1269
- Extend Your Learning, 14, 474, 565

Oral report: historical investigation, 681

Performance of essay, 910

Persuasive speech, 197, 448

Political advertisement (nonprint) analysis, 953

Press conference, 201

Print coverage comparison, 1457

Read written statement, 980

Situations applying communication skills, R54

Small group discussion, 1292

Talk show script, 1461

Slide presentation, 224

Testimonial, 704

Test-Taking Practice

Grammar
- ACT English Test: Editing in Context, 202, 682, 1270
- SAT Writing Test: Identifying Sentence Errors, 453
- SAT Writing Test: Improving Sentences, Paragraphs, 958, 1462

Reading
- ACT: Humanities Passage, 680
- ACT: Prose Fiction, 1268
- ACT: Social Science Passage, 200
- SAT: Long Reading Passage, 956
- SAT: Paired Passages, 452
- SAT: Short Reading Passage, 1460

Timed Writing
- ACT: Position statements, 203, 683, 1271
- SAT: Position statements, 455, 959, 1463

Vocabulary in Context
- SAT Sentence Completions, 199, 451, 679, 955, 1267, 1459

Index of Features

American Experience, The

Arthur Miller and the Blacklist, 1166
Benjamin Franklin in Our World, 146
Jazz Age, 746
Jonathan Edwards, Puritans, and Sermons of Fear, 276
Modernism, 713
Slave Narratives, 526
Southern Regionalism, 1021
Two Influential Writers, 820
World War II, 992
Zora Neale Hurston Rediscovered, 935

Close-Up on History
African Americans and Women in the Revolution, 11
Rachel Carson and Environmental Writing, 977

Contemporary Connection
Emily Dickinson: Poet, Recluse. . .Gamer?, 218
Jack Kerouac: King of the Road Trip, 972
Mark Twain: Original Time-Traveler, 468
Stephanie Strickland: Hypertext Poetry Pioneer, 1288
Thomas Paine: Essayist, Hero of the Revolution. . .Father of the Internet?, 12
Walden Pond and Tinker Creek, 217
William Faulkner: Hollywood Script Doctor, 698

Developing American English
Brave New Words (Lederer), 1287
Mark Twain and the American Language (Lederer), 471
Our Native American Heritage (Lederer), 9
Sliding With Slang (Lederer), 701
Truth About O.K. (Lederer), 221

Economic Connection
Slave Trade, The, 174
Golden Age of Yankee Whaling, The, 344

History Connection
The Beats, 1044
Biblical Imagery, 88
The Mayflower, 60

Humanities Connection
Photographer Mathew Brady, 509

Illustrated Literary History
A Gallery of Autobiography, 156
Gothic Family Tree, The, 322
Poetry of Identity, 912
Political Drama Around the World, 1238
"School" of American Humor, 586

Literature Connection
Biblical Imagery, 88

Living Tradition
A.R. Ammons: Emersonian Postmodernist, 1285

Philosophy Connection
John Locke and the Social Contract, 114

Assessment Workshops

Performance Tasks, 204, 455, 684, 960, 1272, 1464

Communications Workshop

Entertainment Media Analysis/Evaluation, 1264
Oral Interpretation of Literary Work, 676
Persuasive Speech, 196, 448
Political Advertisement (nonprint) Analysis, 952
Print Media News Coverage, 1456

Comparing Literary Works

Aphorisms, 139, 152
Audiences, 110, 120
Autobiography Past and Present, 157, 165
Conflicts/Problems, 46, 55
Gothic Literature Past and Present, 323, 333
Humor Past and Present, 587, 593
Imagery, 922, 927
Images, 718, 726
Moods, 256, 268
Multiple Themes, 901, 908
Mythic Archetypes, 18, 29
Personification, 866, 871
Perspective, 982, 998
Poetry of Cultural Identity, 913, 919
Points of view, 1424, 1439
Political Assumptions, 98, 108
Political Drama Past and Present, 1239, 1249
Refrains of Songs, 530, 541
Repetition/Parallelism, 1062, 1068
Rhetorical devices, 1102, 1113
Social Commentary, 1346, 1355
Speaker's Attitude, 406, 420
Themes, 1408, 1421
Writer's Views/Insights, 536, 543

Contemporary Connection (Past/present)

Artistic Upstarts (Todd), 1046
Cartooning as Literature (Feiffer), 888
Civil War Writings (Minghella), 544
Embracing the Wilderness (Besaw), 398
Exploration (Squyres), 68
Poetry and Numbers: The Fibonacci Sequence, 1371

Essential Questions Across Time

How does literature shape or reflect society?
American Renaissance, 216, 222, 226, 239, 364, 370, 376, 389, 452
Civil War Era, 466, 474, 506, 513, 518, 527, 536, 542, 626, 632, 634, 638, 680
Contemporary Period, 1282, 1290, 1310, 1320, 1334, 1343, 1346, 1354, 1382, 1389, 1392, 1396, 1398, 1460
Early America, 11, 14, 84, 91, 98, 107, 168, 175, 200
Modern Age, 696, 702, 706, 712, 728, 752, 756, 761, 764, 772, 775, 778, 782, 784, 792, 814, 827, 832, 843, 928, 936, 956
Post-War Era, 970, 978, 982, 997, 1000, 1040, 1043, 1050, 1054, 1062, 1067, 1080, 1090, 1094, 1100, 1112, 1123, 1233, 1268

What is the relationship between literature and place?
American Renaissance, 214, 222, 242, 270, 284, 291, 317, 452
Civil War Era, 470, 474, 478, 489, 492, 530, 534, 594, 610, 614, 640, 647, 650, 661, 680
Contemporary Period, 1285, 1290, 1296, 1307, 1356, 1359, 1364, 1368, 1424, 1438, 1460
Early America, 6, 14, 18, 28, 40, 44, 46, 54, 178, 200
Modern Age, 694, 702, 718, 725, 846, 856, 872, 885, 922, 926, 956
Post-War Era, 976, 978, 1010, 1056, 1060, 1070, 1076, 1268

What makes American literature American?
American Renaissance, 219, 222, 256, 267, 334, 355, 406, 417, 424, 436, 452

Civil War Era, 472, 474, 552, 556, 569, 581, 680
Contemporary Period, 1287, 1290, 1324, 1331, 1376, 1380, 1408, 1420, 1460
Early America, 9, 14, 56, 65, 74, 77, 80, 82, 110, 119, 122, 126, 139, 150, 200
Modern Age, 699, 702, 798, 806, 858, 864, 866, 870, 901, 907
Post-War Era, 974, 978, 1023, 1026, 1037, 1102

Extended Study

Authors
Franklin, Benjamin, 136
Hughes, Langston 898
Miller, Arthur, 1118
Poe, Edgar Allan, 288
Twain, Mark, 566

Literary Forms
Drama, 1116
Essay, 1374
Narrative Nonfiction, 516
Poetry, 402
Short Stories, 796
Speeches, 96

Literary History
Colonial Newspapers, 134
Harlem Renaissance, 896
Mark Twain: American Bard, 564
Transcendentalists, 360
Twentieth-Century Drama, 1184

Independent Reading

American Renaissance, 458
Civil War Era, 686
Contemporary Period, 1466
Early America, 206
Modern Age, 961
Post-War Era, 1273

Literary Criticism/ Commentary

Approaches to, R18

Alvarez, Julia
All-American Writer, 1290
Flashback and Exposition, 1451
Introduces *Antojos*, 1294

Andrews, William L.
America Begins With a Promise and a Paradox, 14
Ben Franklin: America's Everyman, 147
Olaudah Equiano, 166

Ehrlich, Gretel
Introduces Henry David Thoreau, 374
Inspired by Nature, 222
Using Layers of Meaning, 443

Johnson, Charles
Ralph Waldo Emerson, 362

Kinnell, Galway
Emily Dickinson: Reckless Genius, 418

Miller, Arthur
The Crucible, 1120
Purpose of Theater, The 978
Using Historical Facts, 1259

Miller, James E., Jr.
Leaves of Grass: America's Epic, 437

O'Brien, Tim
Introduces *Ambush*, 808
Literature as a Magic Carpet, 702
Revision, 947

Painter, Nell Irvin
Defining an Era, 474
Introduces Sojourner Truth, 550
Using Research, 669

Poe, Edgar Allan
Writing "The Raven," 311

Power, Susan
Choosing the Right Word, 191
Introduces *Museum Indians*, 32

Twain, Mark
from "How to Tell a Story," 575

Literature in Context

Cultural Connection
Benjamin Franklin in Our World, 146
Fitzgerald's Elusive Women, 742
James Baldwin and the Church, 1088
Poe and Pop Culture, 290

History Connection
B-29 Bombers, 986
Battle of Shiloh, The, 485
Dogs and the Yukon, 602
History Repeats Itself, 1132
House Calls, 836
Inquisition, The, 1145
Puritans and Nathaniel Hawthorne, 1208

Humanities Connection
Whale as Archetype, The 346

Literature Connection
Fireside Poets, 259
Villanelle, The, 1073
Parodies in American Culture, 1386

Media Connection
Being Abigail Williams, 1226

Music Connection
Wagnerian Opera, 656

Mythology Connection
Centaur, The, 1437

World Literature Connection
Ars Poetica, 1368
Bertolt Brecht, 1171
Capturing the Moment, 413
Challenging Women's Roles, 631
Dramatic Monologue: Robert Browning, 646
Faust Legend, The, 235
Federico Garcia Lorca
Hero's Quest, The, 851
Maxim Gorky, 1137
Mount Olympus, 382
Proverbs, The Wisdom of Many, 151
Tenth Muse, The, 79
Terza Rima, 883
Wole Soyinka, 1223

Reading for Information

Analyzing Functional and Expository Text
Consumer Documents, 128, 392
Digital Reference Tools, 938
Newspaper Articles, 1250
Public/Government Documents, 392, 558
Workplace Documents, 1442

Primary Sources
Commission/Field Report, 242
Diaries/Journals (Civil War), 492
Letters/Floor Plan, 178
Oral History Transcript/E-mail, 1398
Personal History/Speech, 614
Photographs/Ballad, 764
Poster/Editorial Cartoon/Editorial, 1000

Recent Scholarship

Alvarez, Julia, 1290
Andrews, WIlliam L., 14
Ehrlich, Gretel, 222
Miller, Arthur, 978
O'Brien, Tim, 702
Painter, Nell Irvin, 474

Test-Taking Practice

Grammar
ACT English Test: Editing in Context, 202, 682, 1270
SAT Writing Test: Identifying Sentence Errors, 454
SAT Writing Test: Improving Sentences, 958, 1462

Reading
ACT: Humanities, 680
ACT: Prose Fiction, 1268
ACT: Social Science, 200
SAT: Long Reading Passage, 956
SAT: Paired Passages, 452
SAT: Short Reading Passage, 1460

Timed Writing
ACT: Position statements, 203, 683, 1271
SAT: Position statements, 455, 959, 1463

Vocabulary in Context
SAT Critical Reading, 679, 956, 1267, 1459
SAT Reading Comprehension, 199, 451

Themes Across Centuries

Author's Insights, 166, 808, 1120
Scholar's Insights, 362

Unit Introduction

American Renaissance, Literature of the, 208
Historical Background, 212
Snapshot of the Period, 210
Timeline, 212–221

Civil War and the Frontier, Literature of the, 460
Historical Background, 464
Snapshot of the Period, 462
Timeline, 464–473

Contemporary Period, Literature of the, 1276
Historical Background, 1280
Snapshot of the Period, 1278
Timeline, 1280–1289

Literature of Early America, 1
Historical Background, 4
Snapshot of the Period, 2
Timeline, 4–13

Modern Age, Literature of the, 688
Historical Background, 692
Snapshot of the Period, 690
Timeline, 692–701

Post-War Era, Literature of the, 964
Historical Background, 968
Snapshot of the Period, 966
Timeline, 968–977

Vocabulary Workshop

Cognates, 1458
Dictionary and Thesaurus, 198
Idioms/Idiomatic Expressions, 1266
Mythology and Religious Traditions, Words from, 678
Political Science/History Terms, 450
Etymology: Scientific/Medical/Mathematical Terms, 954

Writing Workshop

Autobiographical Narrative, 188
Historical Investigation Report, 664
Multimedia Presentation, 944
Persuasive Essay, 1256
Reflective Essay, 440
Short Story, 1448

Acknowledgments

Acknowledgments continued from copyright page.

William Harvey "Playing for the Fighting Sixty-Ninth" by William Harvey from *Playing for the Fighting Sixty-Ninth.* Copyright © 2001 by William Harvey. Used by permission.

Historical Museum of Southern Florida "Museum Mission/History" from *http://www.hmsf.org.* Copyright © Historical Museum of Southern Florida. Used by permission.

The Barbara Hogenson Agency, Inc. "The Night the Ghost Got In" by James Thurber. Copyright © 1933, 1961 by James Thurber, © Rosemary Thurber. Used by permission.

Henry Holt and Company, Inc. "Acquainted with the Night" by Robert Frost from *The Poetry of Robert Frost* edited by Edward Connery Latham. Copyright © 1956 by Robert Frost. Copyright 1928, © 1969 by Henry Holt and Co. "The Gift Outright" by Robert Frost from *The Poetry of Robert Frost.* Copyright 1942 by Robert Frost, © 1970 by Lesley Frost Ballantine, © 1969 by Henry Holt & Company. "Stopping By Woods on a Snowy Evening" by Robert Frost from *The Poetry of Robert Frost,* edited by Edward Connery Lathem. Copyright 1951 by Robert Frost, © 1923, 1969 by Henry Holt and Company. Used by permission of Henry Holt and Company, LLC.

Houghton Mifflin Company, Inc. "Ambush" from *The Things They Carried by Tim O'Brien.* Copyright © 1990 by Tim O'Brien. "Ars Poetica" from Collected Poems, 1917–1982 by Archibald MacLeish. Copyright © 1985 by The Estate of Archibald MacLeish. "Courage" by Anne Sexton from *The Awful Rowing Toward God* by Anne Sexton. Copyright © 1975 by Loring Conant, Jr., Executor of the Estate of Anne Sexton. Used by permission of Houghton Mifflin Company. All rights reserved.

Hyperion From *Cold Mountain: The Screenplay* by Anthony Minghella, based on a novel by Charles Frazier. Copyright © 2003 by Anthony Minghellla. Used by permission of Hyperion. All rights reserved.

International Creative Management, Inc. "One Day, Now Broken in Two" by Anna Quindlen from *Newsweek.* Copyright © 2002 by Anna Quindlen. First appeared in *Newsweek.* "Life in His Language" by Toni Morrison from *James Baldwin.* Copyright © 1989 by Toni Morrison. Published in James Baldwin: The Legacy (Quincy Troupe, ed.), Simon & Schuster, 1989. Copyright © 1989 by Simon & Schuster. Used by permission of International Creative Management, Inc.

Athena Kildegaard "untitled" poem by Athena Kildegaard used from *Rare Momentum,* Red Dragonfly Press, 2006, by permission of the author.

The Estate of Dr. Martin Luther King, Jr. c/o Writer's House LLC From "Letter from Birmingham Jail" by Dr. Martin Luther King, Jr. from *A Testament of Hope:The Essential Writings of Martin Luther King, Jr.* Used by arrangement with the Heirs to the Estate of Martin Luther King, Jr. c/o Writers House as agent for the proprietor. Copyright 1963 Martin Luther King, Jr.; renewed 1991 Coretta Scott King.

Galway Kinnell "Reckless Genius" by Galway Kinnell from *http://www.salon.com.* Used by permission.

Alfred A. Knopf, Inc. "Dream Variations" by Langston Hughes from *The Selected Poems of Langston Hughes.* Copyright © 1926 by Alfred A. Knopf, Inc. and renewed 1954 by Langston Hughes. "I, Too" by Langston Hughes from *The Selected Poems of Langston Hughes.* Copyright © 1994 by the Estate of Langston Hughes. "Refugee in America" by Langston Hughes from *The Selected Poems of Langston Hughes.* Copyright © 1943 by The Curtis Publishing Company. "The Negro Speaks of Rivers" by Langston Hughes from *Selected Poems of Langston Hughes.* Copyright © 1926 by Alfred A. Knopf, Inc. and renewed 1954 by Langston Hughes. From "The Woman Warrior" by Maxine Hong Kingston from *The Woman Warrior.* Copyright © 1975, 1976 by Maxine Hong Kingston. "Of Modern Poetry" by Wallace Stevens from *The Collected Poems of Wallace Stevens.* Copyright 1942 by Wallace Stevens and renewed 1970 by Holly Stevens from by Wallace Stevens. "Of Plymouth Plantation" by William Bradford from Of Plymouth Plantation 1620–1647 by William Bradford, edited by Samuel Eliot Morison, copyright 1952 by Samuel Eliot Morison and renewed 1980 by Emily M. Beck. From "Hiroshima" by John Hersey. Copyright 1946 and renewed 1974 by John Hersey. Used by permission of Alfred A. Knopf, a division of Random House, Inc. Excerpt from *The American Language,* 4th Edition by H.L. Mencken. Copyright © 1919, 1921, 1923, 1936 by Alfred A. Knopf, Inc. All rights reserved.

The Landmark Project "Son of Citation Machine and Landmarks Son of Citation Machine Masthead" from *http://citationmachine.net.* Copyright © 2006 by David Warlick & The Landmark Project. Used by permission of The Landmark Project.

League of Women Voters "How to Watch a Debate" from *www.lwv.org.* The material in this publication on "How to Watch a Debate" was excerpted from a League of Women Voters of the United States (LWVUS) online document of the same title, located at www.lwv.org, with express permission of the LWVUS for this one-time use in Pearson Prentice Hall Literature 8e Program. Secondary users must request permission directly from the LWVUS, the copyright owner. Copyright © 2007 League of Women Voters. All rights reserved. Used by permission.

Patricia Lee Lewis "(0)" by Patricia Lee Lewis.

Liveright Publishing Corporation "anyone lived in a pretty how town" by E. E. Cummings from *Complete Poems, 1904–1962.* Copyright 1940, © 1968, 1991 by the Trustees for the E.E. Cummings Trust. "old age sticks" by E. E. Cummings. Copyright 1958 © 1986, 1991 by the Trustees for the E. E. Cummings Trust, from *Complete Poems: 1904–1962* by E. E. Cummings, edited by George J. Firmage. "Frederick Douglass" by Robert Hayden. Copyright © 1966 by Robert Hayden, from *Collected Poems of Rober Hayden* by Robert Hayden, edited by Frederick Glaysher. "Runagate Runagate" by Robert Hayden from *The Collected Poems of Robert Hayden* by Robert Hayden, edited by Frederick Glaysher. Copyright © 1966 by Robert Hayden. "Storm Ending" by Jean Toomer from Cane. Copyright 1923 by Boni & Liveright, renewed 1951 by Jean Toomer. Used by permission of Liveright Publishing Corporation.

Los Angeles Times Syndicate "Hysteria Resides at Heart of the Frantic Crucible" by Kenneth Turan from Los Angeles Times, 12/13/96. Copyright © 1996 The Times Mirror Company, Los Angeles Times. Used by permission.

Ludlow Music c/o The Richmond Organization (TRO) "Dust Bowl Blues" Words and Music by Woody Guthrie TRO-© Copyright 1964 (Renewed) 1977 Ludlow Music, Inc., New York, NY Used by permission.

The Estate of Edgar Lee Masters "Lucinda Matlock" by Edgar Lee Masters from *The Spoon River Anthology.* Permission by Hilary Masters.

The Miami Herald "Crucible Casts a Newly Contempo rary Spell/Free from Chains of McCarthyism, Arthur Miller's Classic Soars" by Rene Rodriguez from *The Miami Herald,* 12/20/96. Copyright © 1996 The Miami Herald. Used by permission.

Milkweed Editions "Museum Indians" by Susan Power from *Roofwalker* (Minneapolis: Milkweed Editions, 2002). Copyright © 2002 by Susan Power. Used with permission from Milkweek Editions.

Navarre Scott Momaday From "The Names" by N. Scott Momaday. Copyright © by N. Scott Momaday. Used by permission.

New Directions Publishing Corporation From "A Retrospect: Few Don'ts By an Imagiste" by Ezra Pound, from *The Literary Essays of Ezra Pound,* copyright © 1935 by Ezra Pound. "Constantly Risking Absurdity" by Lawrence Ferlinghetti from *These Are My Rivers: New and Selected Poems 1955–1993.* Copyright © 1955, 1958, 1959, 1960, 1961, 1964, 1966, 1967, 1968, 1969, 1971, 1972, 1975, 1976, 1977, 1978, 1979, 1981, 1984, 1988, 1993 by Lawrence Ferlinghetti. All rights reserved. "The Great Figure" by William Carlos Williams from *Collected Poems: 1909–1939, Volume I,* copyright © 1938 by New Directions Publishing Corp. "Heat" by H. D. from *Collected Poems, 1912–1944,* copyright © 1982 by The Estate of Hilda Doolittle. "In a Station of the Metro" by Ezra Pound from *Personae,* copyright © 1926 by Ezra Pound. "Pear Tree" by H. D. from *Collected Poems, 1912–1944,* copyright © 1982 by The Estate of Hilda Doolittle. "The Red Wheelbarrow" by William Carlos Williams from *Collected Poems: 1909–1939, Volume 1,* copyright © 1938 by New Directions Publishing Corp. "The Secret" by Denise Levertov from *Poems 1960–1967.* Copyright © 1964 by Denise Levertov Goodman. "This is Just to Say" by William Carlos Williams from *Collected Poems 1909–1939, Volume I,* copyright © 1938 by New Directions Publishing Corp. Used by permission of New Directions Publishing Corp.

New York Times Agency "At the Theater/The Crucible" by Brooks Atkinson from *The New York Times,* January 23, 1953. Copyright © 1953 by the New York Times Co. "Onomatopoeia" originally titled "Zapmanship" by William Safire from *You Could Look It Up.* Copyright 1984, The New York Times. "The Nation: Backing the Attack" from *The New York Times,* September 12, 1943. Copyright © The New York Times. "Rock of the Modern Age, Arthur Miller is Everywhere" by Mel Gussow from *diversityjobmarket.com.* Used by permission and protected by the copyright Laws of the United States. The printing, copying, redistribution, or retransmission of the material without express written permission is prohibited.

Newmarket Press From "Good Night, and Good Luck: The Screenplay and History behind the Landmark Movie". Screenplay by George Clooney and Grant Heslov. Copyright © 2005 by Section Eight Production. Used by permission of Newmarket Press, 18 East 48th Street, New York, New York 10017. www.newmarketpress.com.

Naomi Shihab Nye "Streets" by Naomi Shihab Nye from *Words Under the Words: Selected Poems.* Copyright © Naomi Shihab Nye. Used by permission.

Harold Ober Associates, Inc. "A Black Man Talks of Reaping" by Arna Bontemps from *American Negro Poetry.* Copyright © 1963 by Arna Bontemps. Used by permission of Harold Ober Associates Incorporated.

Gregory K. Pincus "Fib" by Gregory K. Pincus, originally posted online at *http://gottabook.blogspot.com/2006/04/fib.html.* Used by permission of the author.

Popular Photography Magazine From "The Assignment I'll Never Forget" by Dorothea Lange from *Popular Photography,* February 1960, Vol. 46, No. 2. Copyright © Popular Photography, 1960.

Princeton University Press From "Walden" by Henry David Thoreau. Copyright © 1971 by Princeton University Press, 1999 renewed PUP, 1989 paperback edition. Used by permission of Princeton University Press.

Sean Ramsay "Urban Renewal" by Sean Ramsay. Copyright © 2001 by Sean Ramsay. Used by permission.

Random House, Inc. "A Rose for Emily" by William Faulkner from *Collected Stories of William Faulkner* copyright © 1930 and renewed © 1958 by William Faulkner. "The Unknown Citizen", copyright 1940 & copyright renewed 1968 by W.H. Auden from Collected Poems by W.H. Auden. Used by permission of Random House, Inc. "A Raisin in the Sun" by Lorraine Hansberry. Copyright © 1958 by Robert Nemiroff, as an unpublished work. Copyright © 1959, 1966, 1984, by Robert Nemiroff.

Random House, Inc. & Sterling Lord Literistic, Inc. "Man Listening to Disc" by Billy Collins from Random House Trade Paperbacks. Copyright © 2001 by Billy Collins. Used by permission.

Schomburg Center for Research in Black Culture "The Tropics in New York" by Claude McKay from *The Poems of Claude McKay.* Courtesy of the Literary Representative for the Works of Claude McKay, Schomburg Center for Research in Black Culture, The New York Public Library, Astor, Lenox and Tilden Foundations. Used by permission.

Scribner, an imprint of Simon & Schuster "In Another Country" by Ernest Hemingway from *Men Without Woman.* Copyright 1927 by Charles Scribner's Sons. Copyright renewed 1955 by Ernest Hemingway. Used by permission of Scribner, an imprint of Simon & Schuster Adult Publishing Group. "Poetry" by Marianne Moore from *The Collected Poems of Marianne Moore.* Copyright © 1935 by Marianne Moore, copyright renewed © 1963 by Marianne Moore and T.S. Eliot. Used with the permission of Scribner, an imprint of Simon & Schuster Adult Publishing Group.

Simon & Schuster, Inc. "1776" by David McCullough from Chapter 3, "Dorchester Heights." New York: Simon & Schuster, 2005. All rights reserved.

South Florida Water Management District "Kissimmee River Restoration and Upper Basin Initiatives" by Staff from *2007 South Florida Environmental Report.* Copyright © 2007 South Florida Water Management District. Courtesy of South Florida Water Management District. Used by permission.

Donald D. Stanford "Huswifery" from *The Poems of Edward Taylor* ed. by Donald E. Stanford, University of North Carolina Press, 1989. Copyright © 1960, renewed 1988 by Donald E. Stanford.

State of California—Dept. of Parks and Recreation "Archaeological Site Record" from *http://ohp.parks.ca.gov.* Used by permission.

The Statue of Liberty-Ellis Island Foundation, Inc. "Statue of Liberty-Ellis Island Foundation Mission and Background" from *www.statueofliberty.org.* Copyright © The Statue of Liberty-Ellis Island Foundation, Inc. *www.ellisisland.org.* Used by permission.

Sterling Lord Literistic, Inc. "Mission Update blog" by Steve Squyres from *http://athena.cornell.edu/news/mubss/.* Used by permission of SLL/Sterling Lord Literistic, Inc. Copyright by Steven Squyres.

Syracuse University Press "The Iroquois Constitution" from *Arthur C. Parker on the Iroquois: Iroquois Uses of Maize and Other Food Plants, The Code of Handsome Lake; The Seneca Prophet; The Constitution of the Five Nations* by Arthur C. Parker, edited by William N. Fenton (Syracuse University Press, Syracuse, NY, 1981). Copyright © 1968 by Syracuse University Press.

Thompson and Thompson From "The Dark Tower" by Countee Cullen. Published in *Copper Sun* © 1927 Harper & Bros, NY. Renewed 1954 by Ida M. Cullen. Copyrights held by Amistad Research Center, Tulane University. Administered by Thompson and Thompson, New York, NY. Used by permission.

Anthony Thwaite "When I went to visit" by Ki no Tsurayuki translated by Geoffrey Bownas and Anthony Thwaite from *The Penguin Book of Japanese Verse*. Penguin Books copyright © 1964, revised edition 1998. Translation copyright © Geoffrey Bownas and Anthony Thwaite, 1964, 1998. Used by permission.

Charlie Todd "Surprise! Subway Birthday" by Charlie Todd and improve everywhere.com Copyright © 2002. Used by permission of Charlie Todd.

The University of Chicago Press "America's Epic" by James Miller, Jr. from Whitman: A Collection of Critical Essays. Copyright © 1957 by The University of Chicago. © 1962 by Prentice Hall, Inc.

University of Nebraska Press "Crossing the Great Divide" by Meriweather Lewis from *The Journals of the Lewis and Clark Expedition, volume 5*. Edited by Gary E. Moulton, used by permission of the University of Nebraska Press. Copyright © 1988 by the University of Nebraska Press.

University of North Carolina Press "To His Excellency, General Washington" by Phillis Wheatley from *The Poems of Phillis Wheatley*. Edited and with an introduction by Julian D. Mason Jr. Copyright © 1966 by the University of North Carolina Press, renewed 1989. Used by permission of the publisher. www.uncpress.unc.edu.

University of North Texas "Help North Texas Vote" from *http://www.eac.gov*.

Viking Penguin, Inc. "The Turtle (Chapter 3)" by John Steinbeck from The Grapes of Wrath. Copyright © 1939, renewed copyright © 1967 by John Steinbeck. "The Crucible" by Arthur Miller from *The Crucible*. Copyright 1952, 1953, 1954, renewed © 1980, 1981, 1982 by Arthur Miller. Used by permission of Viking Penguin, a division of Penguin Books USA Inc. CAUTION: Professionals and amateurs are hereby warned that "The Crucible" being fully protected under the copyright laws of the United States of America, the British Commonwealth countries, including the Dominion of Canada, and the other countries of the Universal Copyright and Berne Conventions, are subject to royalty. All rights, including professional, amateur, motion picture, recitation, lecturing, public reading, radio, television and cable broadcasting, and the rights of translation into foreign languages, are strictly reserved. Particular emphasis is laid on the question of readings, permission for which must be secured in writing. Any inquiries for The Crucible should be addressed to Viking Penguin, 375 Hudson Street, NY, NY 10014.

Virginia Department of Historic Resources "Virginia Department of Historic Resources Archaeological Site Inventory Form" from Virginia Department of Historic Resources. Used by permission.

Patricia Vogel "untitled" (Fibonacci poem) by Patricia Vogel. Used by permission of the author.

W. W. Norton & Company, Inc. "Halley's Comet" by Stanley Kunitz from *Passing Through: The Later Poems*, New and Selected. Copyright © 1995 by Stanley Kunitz. Used by permission of W.W. Norton & Company, Inc. Copyright © 1985 by Stanley Kunitz. "Who Burns for the Perfection of Paper" by Martin Espada from *City of Coughing and Dead Radiators*. Copyright © 1993 by Martin Espada. Used by permission of W. W. Norton & Company, Inc.

Wesleyan University Press "Camouflaging the Chimera" by Yusef Komunyakaa from *Neon Vernacular*. From Dien Cai Dau (Wesleyan University Press, 1988). Used by permission of Wesleyan University Press.

Wikipedia.org "Kennedy Space Center" from *http://en.wikipedia.org/wiki/Kennedy_Space_Center*; retrieved from http://en.wikpedia.org accessed on 07/06/07. "Atlanta Braves" from *http://en.wikipedia.org/wiki/Atlanta_Braves*; retrieved from http://en.wikpedia.org accessed on 07/06/07. "Mojave Desert" from *http://en.wikipedia.org/wiki/Mojave_desert*; retrieved from http://en.wikpedia.org accessed on 07/06/07.

The Wylie Agency, Inc. "Everything Stuck to Him" by Raymond Carver from *What We Talk About When We Talk About Love*. Copyright © 1981 by Tess Gallagher, used with the permission of the Wylie Agency. "Journey to the Crucible" by Arthur Miller, first published in *The New York Times*, February 8,1953 © 1953 by Arthur Miller. Copyright renewed 2008 by The Arthur Miller Estate, used with the permission of The Wylie Agency Inc.

Yale University Press From "Sinners in the Hands of an Angry God" by Jonathan Edwards from *The Sermons of Jonathan Edwards: A Reader* published by Yale University Press. Copyright © 1999 by Yale University Press. From "Mary Chesnut's Civil War" by Mary Chesnut edited by C. Vann Woodward. Copyright © 1981 by C. Vann Woodward, Sally Bland Metts, Barbara G. Carpenter, Sally Bland Johnson, and Katherine W. Herbert. All rights reserved. Used by permission of the publisher, Yale University Press.

Note: Every effort has been made to locate the copyright owner of material reproduced on this component. Omissions brought to our attention will be corrected in subsequent editions.

Credits

Photo Credits

xlvi: gallimaufry/Shutterstock; **lxxx:** © Classic Image / Alamy; **1:** ©Imtek Imagineering/ Masterfie; **5:** © Sandra Templeton/Stock; **1:** The Art Archive / Gift of Mrs. Karl Frank / Buffalo Bill Historical Center, Cody, Wyoming / 14.86; **2:** b. Courtesy of the Library of Congress; **2:** Library of Congress; 4: l. Bettmann/ CORBIS; **4:** r. Bettmann/CORBIS; **5:** l. The Gallery Collection/CORBIS; **5:** r. Blue Lantern Studio/CORBIS; **6:** r. The Granger Collection, New York; **6:** l. Lee Snider/ Photo Images/CORBIS; **7:** t. topora/Shutterstock; **7:** bl. Bettmann/CORBIS; **7:** br. Scala/Art Resource; **8:** l. Burstein Collection/CORBIS; **8:** r. istockphoto.com; **9** br. Chris Hillier/CORBIS; **9:** t. istockphoto.com; **9:** bl. The Granger Collection, New York; **10:** l. Bettmann/CORBIS; **10:** r. Blue Lantern Studio/CORBIS; **10:** m. Bettmann/CORBIS; **11:** r. The Granger Collection, New York; **11:** l. istockphoto.com; **12:** m. The Gallery Collection/CORBIS; **12:** r. Cynthia Hart Designer/ CORBIS; **12:** l. The Granger Collection, New York; **13:** r. Francis G. Mayer/ CORBIS; **13:** l. Gerrit Greve/CORBIS; **15:** r. Photo by Rebecca Dallinger; Courtesy of Susan Power; **15:** t. Michael Storrings; **16:** Smithsonian American Art Museum, Washington, DC / Art Resource, NY; **17:** Smithsonian American Art Museum, Washington, DC / Art Resource, NY; **21:** Mary Ann McDonald?CORBIS; **23:** istockphoto.com; **24:** © /Masterfile (Royalty-Free Div.); **26:** l. Yva Momatiuk/CORBIS; **26:** r. istockphoto.com; **27:** CORBIS; **30:** Julie Downing and Grahame Corbett/© Dorling Kindersley; **32:** The Granger Collection, New York; **32:** t. Photo by Rebecca Dallinger; Courtesy of Susan Power; **32:** rm. The Grass Dancer, Susan Power. Penguin Putnam, Inc. Copyright © 1994 by Susan Power; **32:** bl. The Roofwalker, Susan Power. Milkweed Editions. †Â 2002, Text by Susan Power. Cover and Interior design by Dale Cooney. Cover painting, *Migrations*, oil, 1996 by Ojibwe artist Jim Denomie; **34:** ©Brooklyn Museum/CORBIS; **35:** istockphoto.com; **37:** The Old Guitarist, 1903, Pablo Picasso, Spanish, 1881–1973, oil on panel 122.9 x 82.6 cm, Helen Birch Bartlett Memorial Collection, 1926.253. Reproduction, The Art Institute of Chicago, ©2004 Estate of Pablo Picasso/Artists Rights Society (ARS), New York; **38:** Buffalo Bill Historical Center; Cody, Wyoming; Gift of Hon. and Mrs. William Henry Harrison; NA. 202.70; **39:** DLILLC/CORBIS; **41:** John Kahionhes Fadden; **42:** CORBIS; **42:** bkgrnd. istockphoto.com; **43:** W. Perry Conway/CORBIS; **46: 50:** Courtesy Catholic Archives of Texas, Austin; **52:** © Daryl Benson/Masterfile; **53:** Jay Krishnan/Shutterstock; **55:** Geoffrey Clements/ CORBIS; **56:** The Granger Collection, New York; **57:** Bettmann/CORBIS; **60:** Bettmann/CORBIS; **61:** istockphoto.com; **68:** Ric Francis/epa/CORBIS; **69:** FILATOV ALEXEY/Shutterstock; **70**: NASA/Handout/Getty Images; **70–71:** b. Getty Images; **71:** inset AP/Wide World Photos; **73:** Pilgrims Going to Church, George Henry Boughton, Collection of The New-York Historical Society; **75:** The Granger Collection, New York; **76:** istockphoto.com; **77:** Anne Bradstreet , The Tenth Muse Lately Sprung Up in America, Ladonna Gulley Warrick, Courtesy of the artist; **78:** m. Mimmo Jodice/CORBIS; **78:** t. The Granger Collection, New York; **78:** bl. Demetrio Carrasco © CONACULTA-INAH-MEX. Authorized by the Instituto Nacional de Antropologia e Historia; **78:** br. Dance of Apollo with the Nine Muses (tempera on panel), Peruzzi, Baldassarre (1481–1536) / Palazzo Pitti, Florence, Italy, Alinari / The Bridgeman Art Library; **85:** CORBIS; **86: 0087:** b. istockphoto.com; **87:** t. istockphoto.com; **89:** ©North Wind/North WInd Picture Archives; **90–91:** istockphoto.com; **95:** George Washington (1732–1799) (colour litho) by John Trumbull (1756–1843) (after); Private Collection/ Peter Newark American Pictures/ The Bridgeman Art Library; Nationality / copyright status: American / out of copyright;**96:** The Granger Collection, New York; **99:** National Portrait Gallery, Smithsonian Institution / Art Resource, NY; **99:** inset istockphoto.com; **100:** ©Superstock; **104:** Bettmann/CORBIS; **106:** Swim Ink 2, LLC/CORBIS; **111:** John Elk III/Getty Images; **112:** National Archives and Records Adminisitration; **112:** inset istockphoto.com; **116:** The Granger Collection, New York; **117:** The Granger Collection, New York; **118:** The Granger Collection, New York; **123:** Bettmann/CORBIS; **124:** Liberty and Washington, New York State Historical Association, Cooperstown; **129:** © ZUMA Press, Inc. / Alamy; **131:** © Bob Daemmrich / Alamy; **132:** AP/Wide World Photos; **132:** b. istockphoto.com; **132:** b. istockphoto.com; **132:** t. istockphoto.com; **132:** t. istockphoto.com; **134:** The Granger Collection, New York; **135:** l. The Granger Collection, New York; **135:** m. The Granger Collection, New York; **135:** r. The Granger Collection, New York; **136:** l. Photo by Michael J. Deas/Time Magazine/Time & Life Pictures/Getty Images; **136:** r. The Granger Collection, New York; **137:** m. The Granger Collection, New York; **137:** r. The Granger Collection, New York; **137:** l. The Granger Collection, New York; **138:** tm. The Granger Collection, New York; **138:** br. Courtesy of the Bakken Library, Minneapolis; **138:** tr. The Granger Collection, New York; **138:** tl. The Granger Collection, New York; **140:** Christieís Images/SuperStock; **146:** t. Richard Cummings/CORBIS; **146:** br. Liberty Kids is a registered trademark of DIC Entertainment Corp. Used under license. All rights reserved; **146:** bl. Accoutrements LLC; **146:** bm. istockphoto.com; **148:** The Granger Collection, New York; **149:** The Granger Collection, New York; **151:** tl. The Granger Collection, New York; **151:** bl. Seattle Art Museum, Gift of Katherine White and the Boeing Company. Photo by Paul Macapia; **151:** br. Seattle Art Museum, Gift of Katherine White and the Boeing Company. Photo by Paul Macapia; **152:** © The New Yorker Collection 1965 William Hamiliton from cartoonbank.com. All Rights Reserved.; **153:** Hulton-Deutsch Collection/ CORBIS; **156: #6:** Getty Images; **156: #8:** Bassouls Sophie/CORBIS; **156: #10:** AP/ Wide World Photos; **156: #4:** The Granger Collection, New York; **156: #2:** Bettmann/CORBIS; **156: #3:** Bettmann/CORBIS; **156: #7:** Rune Hellestad/CORBIS; **156: #1:** Bettmann/ CORBIS; **156: #5:** Getty Images; **156: #9:** AP/Wide World Photos; **158:** AP/Wide World Photos; **159:** DK Limited/CORBIS; **160–161:** border Michael Storrings; **161:** Rivera, Diego (1866–1957). The grinder (La molendera). 1926. Oil on canvas, 35 7/16 x 46 1/16 in. Museo Nacional de Arte Moderno, Instituto Nacional de Bellas Artes, Mexico City, D.F., Mexico. © Banco de Mexico Diego Rivera & Frida Kahlo Museums Trust. Av. Cinco de Mayo No. 2, Col. Centro, Del. Cuauhtemoc 06059, Mexico, D.F. Reproduction authorized by the Instituto Nacional de Bellas Artes y Literatura. Courtesy of Art Resource, NY; **162:** © JUPITERIMAGES/ PHOTOS.COM / Alamy; **162–163:** border Michael Storrings; **164:** b. © Imagebroker / Alamy; **164:** t. Michael Storrings; **166:** t.

Prentice Hall; **166:** b. From To Tell a Free Story: The First Century of Afro-American Autobiography, 1760–1865. © 1986 by the Board of Trustees of the University of Illinois. Used with permission of the author and the University of Illinois Press; **167:** Courtesy of the Library of Congress; **169:** Royal Albert Memorial Museum, Exeter, Devon, UK/The Bridgeman Art Library, London/New York; **170:** The Art Archive/Maritime Museum Kronborg Castle Denmark/Dagli Orti; **171:** b. © Dorling Kindersley, Courtesy of the Wilberforce House Museum; **171:** bkgd. THE WAY WE LIVED IN NORTH CAROLINA edited by Joe A. Mobley. Maps by Mark Anderson Moore. Copyright © 2003 by the University of North Carolina Press. Published in association with the North Carolina Department of Cultural Resources, Office of Archives and History. Used by permission of the publisher; **172:** The Granger Collection, New York; **175:** istockphoto.com; **180:** m. The Granger Collection, New York; **180:** t. Bettmann/CORBIS; **180:** b. The Granger Collection, New York; **181:** b. Profiles in History/CORBIS; **181:** t. Judith Miller / Dorling Kindersley / Dreweatt Neate; **183:** The Granger Collection, New York; **184:** Library of Congress; **185:** Library of Congress; **188:** Deeble & Stone/OSF/Animals Animals-Earth Scenes; **191:** Photo by Rebecca Dallinger; Courtesy of Susan Power; **199:** no credit; **199:** no credit; **199:** no credit; **199:** no credit; **199:** no credit; **199:** no credit; **206:** (BR) © Associated Press; **208–209:** Geoffrey Clements/CORBIS; **210:** tr. The Granger Collection, New York; **210:** t. Krause, Johansen/Archivo Iconografico, SA/Corbis; **210:** m. Cover of Democracy in America by Alexis De Tocqueville, © 1965 by Harper & Row, Publishers, Inc. Reprinted by permission of HarperCollins Publishers; **211:** br. Bettmann/CORBIS; **211:** bmr. Science Museum; **211:** mr. Science Museum; **211:** tr. Old Sturbridge Village; **211:** tl. Bettmann/CORBIS; **211:** bl. National Museum of American History, Smithsonian Institution; **211:** rt. National Museum of American History, Smithsonian Institution; **212:** bl. The Granger Collection, New York; **213:** br. The Granger Collection, New York; **213:** bl. The Art Archive / MusÈe du Ch,teau de Versailles / Gianni Dagli Orti; **214:** br. Bettmann/CORBIS; **214:** bm. **215:** bl. The Granger Collection, New York; **215:** br. The National Academy of Science of Philadelphia/CORBIS; **216:** bm. Bettmann/CORBIS; **216:** bl. The Granger Collection, New York; **217:** br. Image Source/CORBIS; **217:** bm. The Granger Collection, New York; **217:** bl. Stefano Bianchetti/CORBIS; **218:** bl. The Granger Collection, New York; **218:** bm. The Granger Collection, New York; **218:** br. Frank Lukasseck/CORBIS; **219:** bl. The Granger Collection, New York; **219:** bm. The Granger Collection, New York; **219:** br. The Granger Collection, New York; **220:** bm. Bettmann/CORBIS; **220:** bm. The Granger Collection, New York; **221:** bl. Bettmann/CORBIS; **221:** ml. Bettmann/CORBIS; **221:** bm. Joseph Sohm/Visions of America/CORBIS; **221:** br. North Wind Picture Archives; **223:** t. Aurora/Getty Images; **224:** t. Aurora/Getty Images; **225:** © Private Collection/ Photo © Christie's Images/ The Bridgeman Art Library; **227:** Bettmann/CORBIS; **228:** b. © Dorling Kindersley; **228–233:** Richard Bowden/Shutterstock; **230:** t. CORBIS; **233:** © johannesspreter/Fotolia; **233:** unknown; **233:** t. Hardy/zefa/CORBIS; **234:** b. Phil Schermeister/CORBIS; **235:** b. Bettmann/CORBIS; **236:** t. Phil Schermeister/CORBIS; **238:** l. Lothar Lenz/zefa/CORBIS; **239:** Peter Johnson/CORBIS; **239:** Geoffrey Clements/CORBIS; **239:** Geoffrey Clements/CORBIS; **239:** Peter Johnson/CORBIS; **242–243:** Courtesy of the Library of Congress; **243:** **244:** tl. The Granger Collection, New York; **244:** b. National Portrait Gallery, Smithsonian Institution/Art Resource, NY; **245:** t. Smithsonian Institution, 95-3550; **246:** t. North Wind Picture Archives; **248:** Library of Congress; **250:** b. Lewis and Clark with Sacajawea at the Great Falls on the Missouri, O.C. Seltzer, 0137.871, From the Collection of Gilcrease Museum, Tulsa; **250:** t. Missouri Historical Society, St. Louis, David Schultz; **251:** t. North Wind Picture Archives; **252:** l. Missouri Historical Society; **253:** t. North Wind Picture Archives; **253:** m. Library of Congress; **256:** CORBIS; **257:** r. CORBIS; **258:** tl. **260:** t. Craig Tuttle/CORBIS; **261:** The Granger Collection, New York; **262:** t. Image copyright © The Metropolitan Museum of Art/Art Resource, NY; **265:** r. The Granger Collection, New York; **266:** CORBIS Sygma; **269:** MARY EVANS/ARTHUR RACKHAM; **271:** Smithsonian Institution/CORBIS; **276:** b. Louis R. Linscott and S.B. Goddard & Son Co.; **280:** t. New York State Historical Association, Cooperstown, New York; **282:** t. The Puritan, c. 1898, Frank E. Schoonover, Oil on canvas, Collection of The Brandywine River Museum, Gift of Mr. and Mrs. Jacob J. Foster, 1981. © 2002 Brandywine Conservancy; **283:** **288:** b. CORBIS; **289:** b. © Classic Image / Alamy; **290:** t. Shutterstock, Inc.; **290:** ml. AIP/THE KOBAL COLLECTION; **290:** mr. Accoutrements LLC; **290:** ml. Steven Bourelle/Shutterstock, Inc.; **290:** b. National Football League; **290:** bkgd. Istockphoto.com; **292:** Royal Photographic Society/Science & Society Picture Library; **299:** **312–313:** Patrick Cocklin/Getty Images; **316:** University of Delaware Library, Newark, Delaware; **318:** © The New Yorker Collection 1990 Ed Frascino from cartoonbank.com. All Rights Reserved.; **318:** Bettmann/CORBIS; **322:** ©age/fotostock/SuperStock; **322:** CORBIS; **324:** CORBIS; **324:** Peter Freed/CORBIS; **325:** rt. Paul Knight, Trevillion Images; **326:** t. Yolande de Kort, Trevillion Images; **327:** SuperStock; **329:** r. Geoff Eley, Trevillion Images; **331:** Karl J. Kuerner III/SuperStock; **331:** r. Gaetan Charbonneau/Getty Images; **335:** r. Bettmann/CORBIS; **335:** b. Bettmann/CORBIS; **336:** © 1998 Kinuko Y. Craft. All rights reserved; **338:** t. Bettmann/CORBIS; **340:** t. Private Collection/The Bridgeman Art Library; insert: **344:** t. Frank Greenaway © Dorling Kindersley, Courtesy of the Town Docks Museum, Hull: mt. Frank Greenaway © Dorling Kindersley, Courtesy of the Town Docks Museum, Hull; mbm. Courtesy of the New Bedford Whaling Museum; mbr. Frank Greenaway © Dorling Kindersley, Courtesy of the Town Docks Museum, Hull; bl. Frank Greenaway © Dorling Kindersley, Courtesy of the Town Docks Museum, Hull; br. Christian Darkin/Photo Researchers. **344:** mbr. Courtesy of the New Bedford Whaling Museum; **346:** b. James Stevenson and Tina Chambers © Dorling Kindersley, Courtesy of the National Maritime Museum, London; **350:** l. Bettmann/CORBIS; **352:** The Granger Collection, New York; **359:** Mark Karrass/CORBIS; **362:** tr. ©Elisheba Johnson; **Z362:** m. **363:** t. Bettmann/CORBIS; **365:** r. Bettmann/CORBIS; **366–367:** Momatiuk - Eastcott/CORBIS; **371:** b. © Christian Delbert; **374:** rt. Pearson Education/PH School Division; **375:** t. Courtesy Concord Free Public Library, Concord Massachusetts; **377:** br. The Granger Collection, New York; **378:** Curtis Hamilton © Rough Guides; **382:** b. Pat OiHara/CORBIS; **382:** r. Bildarchiv Preussischer Kulturbesitz / Art Resource, NY; **384:** MyLoupeRF\UIG/AGE Fotostock America; **388:** r. istockphoto.com; **388:** br. istockphoto.com; **389:** bkgrnd. Mitchell, S. Augustus 1792-1868/Library of Congress; **389:** b. Bettmann/CORBIS; **392:** Lee Snider/CORBIS; **393:** t. Hulton-Deutsch Collection/CORBIS; **393:** b. istockphoto.com; **395:** t. istockphoto.com; **395:** tr. Theo Allofs/zefa/CORBIS; **395:** b. istock-photo.com; **396:** b. istockphoto.com; **398:** b. Rune Hellestad/CORBIS; **399:** r. moodboard/CORBIS; **401:** Christieís Images/CORBIS; **404:** b. ames Marshall/CORBIS; **404:** t. The Granger Collection, New York; **405:** b. Courtesy of the Emily Dickinson Museum, Amherst, Massachusetts; **405:** t. **406:** inset Bettmann/CORBIS; **406:** Amherst College Archives and Special Collections, by permission of the Trustees of Amherst College; **408:** t. Waiting Outside No. 12, Anonymous, Crane Kalman Gallery; **410:** Bildarchiv Preussischer Kulturbesitz/Art Resource, NY.; **412:** © British Museum; **412:** t. istockphoto.com; **413:** b. Heibonsha/Pacific Press Service; **413:** m. Heibonsha/Pacific Press Service; **415:** istockphoto.com; **416:** istockphoto.com; **426–427:** © Janina Dierks/Fotolia; **434–435:** Haystack, 1938 (tempera with oil glaze on linen on panel), Benton, Thomas Hart (1889–1975) / Museum of Fine Arts, Houston, Texas, USA, © DACS /Gift of Mr. Frank J. Hevrdejs / The Bridgeman Art Library International/©T.H. Benton and R.P. Benton Testamentary Trusts/Licensed by VAGA, New York, NY; **440:** b. Royalty-Free/CORBIS; **443:** rt. Pearson Education/PH School Division; **462:** Library of Congress; **462:** mr. The Granger Collection, New York; **462:** tr. Getty Images; **463:** tr. detail from the original painting,The Museum of the Confederacy, Richmond, Virginia, Photography by Katharine Wetzel; **463:** l. The British Museum/HIP/The Image Works; **463:** mr. The Granger Collection, New York; **463:** r. Chas Howson© Dorling Kindersley; **463:** rt. Dave King© Dorling Kindersley; **464:** bl. The Art Archive / Bibliothèque des Arts Dècoratifs Paris / Gianni Dagli Orti; **464:** br. CORBIS; **465:** bl. Getty Images; **465:** bm. **465:** br. The Gallery Collection/CORBIS; **465:** The Granger Collection, New York; **466:** Courtesy of the Library of Congress; **466:** br. pinky/Shutterstock; **466:** bl. The Granger Collection, New York; **467:** Courtest of the Henry B. Plant Museum; Tampa, FL; **467:** br. The Gallery Collection/CORBIS; **467:** bl. The Art Archive; **468:** bl. Museum of the City of New York/CORBIS; **468:** ml. The Granger Collection, New York; **468:** br. istockphoto.com; **468:** Dunstanburgh Castle in a Thunderstorm, Thomas Girtin, Ashmolean Museum, Oxford, UK/Bridgeman Art Library, London/New York; **469:** bl. Jose Fuste Raga/CORBIS; **469:** br. Columbia Pictures/Photofest; **470:** The Lawrence Tree,1929, Georgia O'Keeffe, Wadsworth Atheneum, Hartford, CT. The Ella Gallup Sumner and Mary Catlin Sumner Collection, ©1998 The Georgia O'Keeffe Foundation/Artists Rights Society (ARS), New York; **470:** bl. H. Armstrong Roberts/CORBIS; **470:** br. Underwood & Underwood/CORBIS; **471:** bl. Bettmann/CORBIS; **471:** istockphoto.com; **471:** br. The Old Guitarist, 1903, Pablo Picasso, Spanish, 1881–1973, oil on panel 122.9 x 82.6 cm, Helen Birch Bartlett Memorial Collection, 1926.253. Reproduction, The Art Institute of Chicago, ©2004 Estate of Pablo Picasso/Artists Rights Society (ARS), New York; **472:** bm. Ted Streshinsky/CORBIS; **472:** br. Science Museum/Science & Society Picture Library; **472:** bl. Deborah Betz Collection/CORBIS; **473:** bl. The Granger Collection, New York; **473:** br. Bettmann/CORBIS; **474:** istockphoto.com; **476:** Bettmann/ CORBIS; **477:** **479:** r. Bettmann/CORBIS; **494:** Mulberry Plantation, Camden, S.C.; **499:** Bettmann/CORBIS; **500:** l. Young Soldier: Separate Study of a Soldier Giving Water to a Wounded Companion, (detail) 1861, Winslow Homer, Oil, gouache, black crayon on canvas, 36 x 17.5 cm., United States, 1836–1910, Cooper-Hewitt, National Museum of Design, Smithsonian Institution, Gift of Charles Savage Homer, Jr., 1912-12-110, Photo by Ken Pelka, Courtesy of Art Resource, New York; **503:** t. The Granger Collection, New York; **507:** r. Bettmann/CORBIS; **508:** **509:** r. Bettmann/ CORBIS; **511:** t. CORBIS; **513:** r. Museum of the Confederacy, Richmond, Virginia; **515:** tr. ANCIENT ART & ARCHITECTURE / DanitaDelimont.com; **519:** Frederick Douglass (detail), c.1844, Attributed to Elisha Hammond, The National Portrait Gallery, Smithsonian Institution, Washington, D.C./Art Resource, New York; **520:** Smithsonian American Art Museum, Washington, DC / Art Resource, NY; **522:** The Granger Collection, New York; **525:** A Home on the Mississippi, 1871, Currier & Ives, The Museum of the City of New York, Harry T. Peters Collection; **526:** Bettmann/CORBIS; **532:** Layne Kennedy/CORBIS; **537:** Bettmann/CORBIS; **538:** Bettmann/CORBIS; **540:** CORBIS; **541:** The Granger Collection, New York; **544:** b. AFP/Getty Images; **544:** b. Cover design by John Gall. Cover photograph courtesy of National Geographic. Grove Press and imprint of Grove Atlantic, Inc. Distributed by Publishers Group West; **545:** Miramax/Photofest; **546:** Miramax/Photofest; **546–547:** Purestock; **547:** Miramax/Photofest; **548–549:** Purestock; **550:** t. Prentice Hall; **550:** Courtesy of the National Museum of the U.S. Army, Army Art Collection.; **550:** b. Cover design by Francine Kass. Cover photograph courtesy of the National Portrait Gallery, Smithsonian Institution. W.W. Norton; **553:** **554:** Bettmann/ CORBIS; **555:** istockphoto.com; **559:** National Portrait Gallery, Smithsonian Institution / Art Resource, NY; **560:** t. Samir S. Patel; **560:** b. Samir S. Patel; **563:** North Wind Picture Archives; **564:** b. Corel Professional Photos CD-ROM; **564:** t. Courtesy National Archives; **566:** Bettmann/CORBIS; **566–567:** Joseph Sohm/Visions of America/CORBIS; **567:** CORBIS; **567:** The Granger Collection, New York; **568:** Bettmann/CORBIS; **568:** bkgrnd. istockphoto.com; **570:** Minnesota Historical Society/CORBIS; **572:** Historical Picture Archive/CORBIS; **577:** The Granger Collection, New York; **579:** The Granger Collection, New York; **588:** Rick Friedman/CORBIS; **589:** t. Tom Kelley/Getty Images; **589:** b. ClassicStock; **590:** t. **590:** b. **592:** WALTER SANDERS /Getty Images; **593:** U.S. Department of the Interior, Geological Survey; **595:** CORBIS; **596:** Peter Lilja/Getty Images; **600:** Shutterstock, Inc.; **602:** Paul A. Souders/CORBIS; **604:** Jeff Curtes/CORBIS; **610:** Will Datene/Alamy; **616:** © National Anthropological Archives, Smithsonian Institute, NAA INV 00942000; **617:**

619: Connie Ricca/CORBIS; 620: Courtesy of the Lane County Historical Museum; 622: Chief Joseph (detail), 1878, Cyrenius Hall, National Portrait Gallery, Smithsonian Institution, Washington, D.C./Art Resource, New York; 625: Channel to the Mills, 1913, Edwin M. Dawes, oil on canvas, 51 x 39 1/2 in. Minneapolis Institute of Arts, anonymous gift.; 627: Missouri Historical Society; 628: Afternoon in Piedmont, (Elsie at the Window), c.1911, Xavier Martìnez, Collection of The Oakland Museum of California, Gift of Dr. William S. Porter; 631: Hulton-Deutsch Collection/CORBIS; 632: Corel Professional Photos CD-ROMô; 635: The Granger Collection, New York; 636: Bettmann/CORBIS; 638: Wayne Lynch/DRK Photo; 638: istockphoto.com; 641: 642: 643: istockphoto.com; 644: THE THINKER (Portrait of Louis N. Kenton, 1900), Thomas Eakins, The Metropolitan Museum of Art, John Stewart Kennedy Fund, 1917. (17.172) Photograph © 2001 The Metropolitan Museum of Art; 645: Edgar Lee Masters (detail), 1946, Francis J. Quirk, National Portrait Gallery, Smithsonian Institution, Washington, D.C./Art Resource, New York; 646: Christie's Images/CORBIS; 647: Joel Greenstein/Omni-Photo Communications, Inc.; 651: New York Times Co./Getty Images, Inc.; 652: George Schreiber (1904–1977), From Arkansas, 1939, oil on canvas, Sheldon Swope Art Museum, Terre Haute, Indiana; 653: The Granger Collection, New York; 654–655: border The Granger Collection, New York; 656: Time & Life Pictures/Getty Images; 656–657: border The Granger Collection, New York; 658: Erich Lessing / Art Resource, NY; 659: border The Granger Collection, New York; 660–661: border The Granger Collection, New York; 688–689: Drought Stricken Area, 1934 (oil on canvas), Hogue, Alexandre (1898–1994) / Dallas Museum of Art, Texas, USA, / The Bridgeman Art Library; 690: l. Bettmann/CORBIS; 690: r. Underwood & Underwood/CORBIS; 691: #4: MGM/Photofest; 691: #3: United Artists/Photofest; 691: #8: Warner Bros. Pictures/Photofest; 691: #1: Chaplin/Photofest; 691: #5: Getty Images; 691: #2: 20th Century Fox/Photofest; 692: b. © Bettmann/CORBIS; 692: t. 2007 Getty Images/ Hulton Archive/Stringer; 693: bl. © CORBIS; 693: br. © Bettmann/CORBIS; 693: t. Photo by Mansell/Mansell/Time & Life Pictures/Getty Images; 694: l. 2007 Getty Images/Hulton Archive/Stringer; 694: r. 2004 AFP/FRAN CAFFREY/Stringer; 695: b. © 2008 The Associated Press. All rights reserved.; 695: m. © JazzSign/Lebrecht Music & Arts/Corbis; 696: l. © Bettmann/CORBIS; 696: r. Photo by Lipnitzki/Roger Viollet/Getty Images; 697: bl. Photo by FPG/Getty Images; 697: tl. © Bettmann/CORBIS; 697: br. © Bettmann/CORBIS; 697: tr. © Bettmann/CORBIS; 698: l. 2007 Getty Images/Hulton Archive/Stringer; 698: RB © Bettmann/CORBIS; 698: rt. © 2008 The Associated Press. All rights reserved.; 699: l. © Bettmann/CORBIS; 699: r. The Granger Collection, New York; 700: t. The Granger Collection, New York; 700: b. The Granger Collection, New York; 701: b. 2007 Getty Images/ Richard Peter Snr/Stringer; 701: t. © Radius Images/Alamy; 703: t. Prentice Hall; 703: m. image copyright © The Metropolitan Museum of Art / Art Resource, NY; 703: b. Random House Inc.; 704: Getty Images; 705: CORBIS; 707: Hulton-Deutsch Collection/CORBIS; 708: Erich Lessing / Art Resource, NY; 713: t. CNAC/MNAM/Dist. RÈunion des MusÈes Nationaux / Art Resource, NY; 713: b. erry Cooke/Pix Inc./Time Life Pictures/Getty Images; 714: © The New Yorker Collection 1994 Bruce Eric Kaplan from cartoonbank.com. All Rights Reserved.; 716: © CORBIS; 717: b. © Bettmann/ CORBIS; 717: t. © Bettmann/CORBIS; 719: istockphoto.com/stephen mulcahey; 720: The Granger Collection, New York; 722: © Paul Seheult/Eye Ubiquitous/Corbis; 723: t. istockphoto.com/Branko Miokovic; 723: b. istockphoto.com/ James Pauls; 724: Art Resource/ The Metropolitan Museum of Art; 725: © age fotostock / SuperStock; 1566-148636-N-X006; 729: Bettmann/CORBIS; 730: 731: tr. istockphoto.com/GARY GODBY; 732: l. Getty Images/C Squared Studios; 732: r. istockphoto.com/ VINCENT GIORDANO; 733: 734: tl. istockphoto.com/GARY GODBY; 735: 736: 738: 738: tl. istockphoto.com/GARY GODBY; 740: l. 741: tr. istockphoto.com/GARY GODBY; 742: Bettmann/CORBIS; 743: tr. istockphoto.com/GARY GODBY; 745: tr. istockphoto.com/GARY GODBY; 747: 748: tl. istockphoto.com/GARY GODBY; 749: tr. istockphoto.com/GARY GODBY; 750: tl. istockphoto.com/GARY GODBY; 751: istockphoto.com/GARY GODBY; 752: 752: m. istockphoto.com/GARY GODBY; 757: b. Bettmann/CORBIS; 758–759: David Lee/Shutterstock; 760: SuperStock, Inc; 766: b. CORBIS; 766: t. Library of Congress; 766: m. John Springer Collection/CORBIS; 767: l. Library of Congress; 767: rt. Library of Congress; 767: RB Library of Congress; 768: Library of Congress, Washington D.C., USA/The Bridgeman Art Library; 773: Bettmann/CORBIS; 774: The Turret Lathe Operator (J.G. Cherry series), 1925, Grant Wood, oil on canvas 18" x 24" Cedar Rapids Museum of Art, Cedar Rapids, Iowa, Gift of the Cherry Burrell Charitable Foundation Collection. 75.5.8, ©Estate of Grant Wood/Figge Art Museum, successors to the Estate of Nan Wood Graham/Licensed by VAGA, New York, NY; 779: Bettmann/CORBIS; 780: Hood Museum of Art, Dartmouth College, Hanover, New Hampshire; gift of Frank L. Harrington, Class of 1924; 785: Corbis/Bettmann; 786: istockphoto.com/Dmytro Konstantynov; 788: t. Bettmann/CORBIS; 788: b. © Bettmann/CORBIS; 789: istockphoto.com; 791: Untitled, 1964, Alexander Calder, (one of seven lithographs in series), 19 1/2" x 25 1/2" Solomon R. Guggenheim Museum, New York, Gift of the artist, 1965, Photo by David Heald, © The Solomon R. Guggenheim Foundation, New York, ©1998 Estate of Alexander Calder/Artists Rights Society (ARS), New York; 795: © Columbus Museum of Art, Ohio: Gift of Ferdinand Howald 1931.146; 799: © Bettmann/CORBIS; 800: Military Ambulance, First World War (bodycolour on paper), Simpson, Charles Walter (1885–1971) / Private Collection, © Chris Beetles, London, U.K. / The Bridgeman Art Library; 803: © CORBIS; 804: © CORBIS; 805: © CORBIS; 808: Prentice Hall; 808: b. Random House Inc.; 809: AP/Wide World Photos; 810: MARY EVANS/JACK NOVAK; 812: Philip Jones Griffiths/Magnum Photos; 815: CORBIS; 816: Woman by a Window, Gustav Vermehren Snark/Art Resource, NY; 818: Collection of the Prentice and Paul Sack Photographic Trust of the San Francisco Museum of Modern Art; 819: istockphoto.com; 821: istockphoto.com; 823: Rèunion des Musèes Nationaux / Art Resource, NY; 823: istockphoto.com; 824: Markus Amon/Getty Images; 825: CORBIS SYGMA; 826: age fotostock / SuperStock; 827: istockphoto.com; 828: ANSA/Corbis; 833: inset Getty Images; 833: t. istockphoto.com; 833: istockphoto.com; 834: l. Verlog Suddeutscher-Bilderdienst; 834: Garden of Memories, 1917, Charles Burchfield, The Museum of Modern Art, New York. Gift of Abby Aldrich Rockefeller (by exchange). Digital Image © The Museum of Modern Art/Licensed by SCALA/Art Resource, NY; 839: The Bride, 1886 (w/c on paper), Zorn, Anders Leonard (1860–1920) / © Nationalmuseum, Stockholm, Sweden, / The Bridgeman Art Library International; 840: ©1993 J. Fishkin. All Rights Reserved.; 847: Philip Gould/CORBIS; 848: Miz Emily, Joseph Holston, 24" x 16", Courtesy of Joseph Holston (www.holstonart.com); 852: Georgia Red Clay, 1946, Nell Choate Jones, oil on canvas, 25 x 30 inches, 1989.01.094, Morris Museum of Art, Augusta, Georgia; 859: Bettmann/CORBIS; 860: My Life and Hard Times Copyright ©1933 by James Thurber. Copyright © renewed 1961 by James Thurber. Reprinted by arrangement with Rosemary A. Thurber and The Barbara Hogenson Agency.; 862: My Life and Hard Times Copyright ©1933 by James Thurber. Copyright © renewed 1961 by James Thurber. Reprinted by arrangement with Rosemary A. Thurber and The Barbara Hogenson Agency.; 863: My Life and Hard Times Copyright ©1933 by James Thurber. Copyright © renewed 1961 by James Thurber. Reprinted by arrangement with Rosemary A. Thurber and The Barbara Hogenson Agency.; 867: © Bettmann/CORBIS; 868: Stock Montage, Inc.; 870: istockphoto.com; 873: CORBIS; 874: © Photodisc / SuperStock; 877: istockphoto.com; 878–879: The Irish Image Collection/CORBIS; 880: Corel Professional Photos CD-ROMô; 882: Fine Art Photographic Library/CORBIS; 883: ©Duomo, Florence, Italy/ The Bridgeman Art Library; 884: Bettmann/CORBIS; 886: ©The New Yorker Collection 1993 Mick Stevens from cartoonbank.com. All Rights Reserved.; 888: Walter Weissman/Corbis; 889: 890: 891: 892: 893: 894: 895: Evans-Tibbs Collection, Washington, D.C.; 896: Zora and Langston, Phoebe Beasley, Bettmann/CORBIS; 898: CORBIS; 899: Atlantide Phototravel/CORBIS; 900: t. istockphoto.com; 900: b. Winold Reiss (1886–1953), Portrait of Langston Hughes (1902–1967 Poet), pastel on artist board, 76.3 x 54.9 cm. National Portrait Gallery, Washington, DC, USA. Art Resource, N.Y.; 903: Aaron Douglas, Into Bondage, 1936, 60 3/8 x 60 1/2, oil on canvas. In the collection of the Corcoran Gallery of Art, Washington, DC. Museum Purchase and Partial Gift of Thurlow Tibbs Jr., The Evans-Tibbs Collection. 1996.9; 904: Nobody Around Here Calls Me Citizen, 1943, Robert Gwathmey, oil on canvas, H. 14-1/4" x W. 17" Collection Frederick R. Weisman Art Museum at the University of Minnesota, Minneapolis, Bequest of Hudson Walker from the Ione and Hudson Walker Collection. ©Estate of Robert Gwathmey/Licensed by VAGA, New York, NY; 906: Girls Skipping, 1949, Hale Woodruff, oil on canvas, 24" x 32" , Private Collection. Courtesy of Michael Rosenfeld Gallery, New York; 914: b. Miriam Berkley/Authorpix; 914: t. Christopher Felver/CORBIS; 915: Smithsonian American Art Museum, Washington, DC / Art Resource, NY; 916: The Madonna And Child, 1990, Momodou Ceesay, Dialogue Systems, Inc.; 920: CORBIS; 920: b. National Portrait Gallery, Smithsonian Institution / Art Resource, NY; Image Reference : ART155673; 921: Bettmann/CORBIS; 923: t. Dave G. Houser/CORBIS; 924: b. Hoeing, 1934, Robert Gwathmey, Oil on canvas, 40 by 60 1/4 (101.6 by 153), Carnegie Institute Museum of Art, Pittsburgh, Pennsylvania, Patrons Art Fund, 44.3. Photograph by Richard Stoner, ©Estate of Robert Gwathmey/Licensed by VAGA, New York, NY; 924: t. istockphoto.com; 926: istockphoto.com; 929: Library of Congress; 930: b. The Granger Collection, New York; 930: t. Lake County Museum/CORBIS; 931: ©Hulton Getty/Archive Photos; 931: border Lake County Museum/CORBIS; 932: border Lake County Museum/CORBIS; 933: border Lake County Museum/CORBIS; 934: border Lake County Museum/CORBIS; 935: border Lake County Museum/CORBIS; 936: Lake County Museum/CORBIS; 941: t. MLB Photos via Getty Images; 941: b. Getty Images; 941: MAPS.com/CORBIS; 941: David Muench/CORBIS; 942: AFP/Getty Images; 947: Prentice Hall; 963: 964–965: Digital Image © The Museum of Modern Art/Licensed by SCALA / Art Resource, NY; 966: tl. NASA/Photo Researchers. Inc.; 966: tr. © Everett Collection Inc / Alamy; 967: #3: 967: T1: Herbert Orth/Time Life Pictures/Getty Imagess, Inc.; 967: 5.#4: Herbert Orth/Time Life Pictures/Getty Imagess, Inc.; 967: #2: David J. and Janice L. Frent/Corbis; 967: #5: David J. and Janice L. Frent/Corbis; 967: #6: Hulton Archives/Getty Images Inc.; 968: r. John Springer Collection/CORBIS; 968: l. © Bettmann/CORBIS; 969: b. Bettmann/CORBIS; 969: t. Image Source Pink; 970: t. Bettmann/ CORBIS; 970: b. Time & Life Pictures/Getty Images; 971: r. Robert W. Kelley/Time Life Pictures/Getty Images: 971: b. Alfred Pasieka/ Photo Researchers, Inc.; 972: Bettmann/CORBIS; 973: l. Credit: Novosti / Photo Researchers, Inc.; 973: r. Bettmann/CORBIS; 974: bl. ©Judith Miller / Dorling Kindersley / Bauman Rare Books; 974: t. Bettmann/CORBIS; 974: br. Getty Images; 975: bl. Bettmann/CORBIS; 975: br. Charles E. Rotkin/CORBIS; 975: t. Bettmann/CORBIS; 976: b. Bettmann/CORBIS; 976: t. Bettmann/CORBIS; 977: m. ©Judith Miller / Dorling Kindersley / Bauman Rare Books; 977: l. Bettmann/CORBIS; 977: r. Bettmann/CORBIS; 979: b. PlaybillÇ is a registered trademark of Playbill, Inc. All rights reserved. Used by permission.; 979: t. Deborah Feingold/Corbis; 981: Photo by MPI/Getty Images; 983: © Bettmann/CORBIS; 984: ASSOCIATED PRESS/STANLEY TROUTMAN; 986: ©CORBIS; 988: The Granger Collection, New York; 990–991: The Granger Collection, New York; 994: The Granger Collection, New York; 996: Rosalie Thorne McKenna Foundation. Courtesy Center for Creative Photography, University of Arizona Foundation.; 997: © Nik Keevil / Alamy; 1002: t. Bettmann/CORBIS; 1002: b. Bettmann/CORBIS; 1003: Courtesy Harry S. Truman Library; 1004: The Granger Collection, New York; 1009: Choke, 1964, Robert Rauschenberg, Oil and screenprint on canvas, 60" x 48", Washington University Gallery of Art, St. Louis, Gift of Mr. and Mrs. Richard K. Weil, 1972, ©Robert Rauschenberg/Licensed by VAGA, New York, NY; 1011: 1012: Deep Fork Overlook, Joan Marron-LaRue, Courtesy of the artist; 1017: Black Walnuts, Joseph Pollet, Collection of Whitney Museum of American Art. Purchase and gift of Gertrude Vanderbilt Whitney, by exchange (52.30). Photograph Copyright © 2000: Whitney Museum of American Art; 1022T Vlaminck,

Maurice de (1876–1958) © ARS, NY Banque d'Images, ADAGP / Art Resource, NY; **1027:** © David Lees/CORBIS; **1028:** Reading by the Oven, 1961 (oil on canvas), Sokolovskaya, Oksana Dmitrievna (fl.1961) / Springville Museum of Art, Utah, USA, / The Bridgeman Art Library; **1028:** Copyright: Pertusinas; **1030:** istockphoto.com/Robyn Mackenzie; **1031:** Culver Pictures, Inc.; **1031:** Copyright: Pertusinas; **1032:** b. istockphoto.com; **1032–1033:** b. istockphoto.com; **1033:** Copyright: Pertusinas; **1034:** istockphoto.com/Roel Smart; **1035:** Copyright: Pertusinas; **1036:** Judson Abts; **1037:** Copyright: Pertusinas; **1041: 1042:** Todd Davidson; **1044: #3:** Allen Ginsberg/CORBIS; **1044: #1:** Bettmann/CORBIS; **1044: #4:** Bettmann/CORBIS; **1044: #2:** AFP/Getty Images; **1046:** www.improveverywhere.com; **1047:** www.improveverywhere.com; **1048:** br. www.improveverywhere.com; **1048:** t. www.improveverywhere.com; **1048:** bl. www.improveverywhere.com; **1053–1054:** Sunny Forest; **1057:** © Bettmann/CORBIS; **1058:** © 2008 Masterfile Corporation; **1059:** istockphoto.com/Dar Yang Yan; **1060:** istockphoto.com/Dar Yang Yan; **1063:** © Bettmann/CORBIS; **1064:** istockphoto.com/ Valerie Loiseleux; **1065:** Bettmann/CORBIS; **1066:** Photo: The Jacob and Gwendolyn Lawrence Foundation / Art Resource, NY; Image Reference : ART188169; **1071:** © Everett Collection Inc / Alamy; **1072: 1074–1075:** Smithsonian American Art Museum, Washington, DC / Art Resource, NY; **1079:** Bettmann/CORBIS; **1079: 1081:** tl. © Bettmann/CORBIS; **1081:** br. Photo by Ian Cook//Time Life Pictures/Getty Images; **1081:** Peter Turnley/CORBIS; **1082:** t. Mirror II, George Tooker, (1920–1938), Egg tempera on gesso panel, 20 x 20 in., 1968.4, Gift of R. H. Donnelley Erdman (PA 1956), ©Addison Gallery of American Art, Phillips Academy, Andover, Massachusetts. All Rights Reserved.; **1082:** Push to Walk, collage 48" x 48" Phoebe Beasley; **1083:** t. Lester Lefkowitz/CORBIS; **1084:** t. Lester Lefkowitz/CORBIS; **1087: 1095:** © Katy Winn/Corbis; **1096:** © Bettmann/CORBIS; **1099:** Getty Images/Walter Daran/Contributor; **1103:** © CORBIS; **1104:** Retroactive I, Robert Rauschenberg, 1964, Wadsworth Atheneum, Hartford, CT, Gift of Susan Morse Hilles, ©Robert Rauschenberg/Licensed by VAGA, New York, NY; **1107:** Time & Life Pictures/Getty Images; **1108:** © Flip Schulke/CORBIS; **1109:** Bettmann/CORBIS; **1110:** r. Express Newspapers/Staff/Hulton Archive/Getty Images; **1110:** l. © Bettmann/CORBIS; **1110:** m. **1111:** © Hulton-Deutsch Collection/CORBIS; **1116:** Boden/Ledingham/Masterfile; **1118: #2:** The Granger Collection, New York; **1118: #4:** Photofest; **1118: #4:** Courtesy Everett Collection; **1118: #1:** PlaybillÇ is a registered trademark of Playbill, Inc. All rights reserved. Used by permission.; **1119:** Deborah Feingold/Corbis; **1120:** b. **1120:** t. Deborah Feingold/Corbis; **1121:** t. 20TH CENTURY FOX / THE KOBAL COLLECTION; **1121:** b. 20TH CENTURY FOX / THE KOBAL COLLECTION; **1122:** br.: **1122:** ml. Time & Life Pictures/Getty Images; **1122:** mr. TimeWireImage & Life PictuWire res/Getty Images; **1122:** bl. FilmMagic; **1122:** bm. Popperfoto/Getty Images; **1122:** t. PUNCH/ROXBURY/BIOSKOP FILM / THE KOBAL COLLECTION; **1124: 1131:** Twentieth Century Fox Film Corporation/Photofest; **1132:** AP/Wide World Photos; **1134:** 20TH CENTURY FOX / THE KOBAL COLLECTION / WETCHER, BARRY; **1136:** Twentieth Century Fox Film Corporation/Photofest; **1137:** l. Bettmann/ CORBIS; **1137:** r. **1138:** Getty Images; **1142:** Twentieth Century Fox Film Corporation/Photofest; **1145:** Musee Conde, Chantilly, France/ Bridgeman Art Library, London/New York; **1146:** Steve Cole/Getty Images; **1153:** Twentieth Century Fox Film Corporation/Photofest; **1154:** 20th Century-Fox / Photofest; **1170:** Twentieth Century Fox Film Corporation/Photofest; **1171:** l. The Art Archive/CORBIS; **1171:** r. Robbie Jack/CORBIS; **1172:** Twentieth Century Fox Film Corporation/Photofest; **1174:** Pocumtuck Valley Memorial Association, Memorial Hall Museum, Deerfield, Massachusetts; **1178:** Twentieth Century Fox Film Corporation/Photofest; **1184:** ©Bettmann/CORBIS; **1188:** Twentieth Century Fox Film Corporation/Photofest; **1198:** Twentieth Century Fox Film Corporation/ Photofest; **1199:** r. Robbie Jack/CORBIS; **1199:** l. Archivo Iconografico, S.A./ CORBIS; **1202:** Twentieth Century Fox Film Corporation/Photofest; **1204:** Twentieth Century Fox Film Corporation/Photofest; **1208:** Penguin USA; **1209:** The Trial of Two "Witches" at Salem, Massachusetts, in 1662, Howard Pyle, The Granger Collection, New York; **1211:** Twentieth Century Fox Film Corporation/Photofest; **1221:** 20th Century-Fox/Photofest; **1223:** PELLETIER MICHELINE/CORBIS SYGMA; **1224:** Twentieth Century Fox Film Corporation/ Photofest; **1226:** ©Reuters/Brad Rickerby/Archive Photos; **1229:** 20TH CENTURY FOX / THE KOBAL COLLECTION; **1234:** "It's Okay—We're Hunting Communists". From "Herblock Special Report (W.W. Norton, 1974). Reprinted by permission of the Herb Block Foundation.; **1240:** © Fred Prouser/Reuters/Corbis; **1241:** WARNER INDEPENDENT/2929 PROD / THE KOBAL COLLECTION; **1242:** WARNER INDEPENDENT/2929 PROD / THE KOBAL COLLECTION / GORDON, MELINDA SUE; **1243:** WARNER INDEPENDENT/2929 PROD / THE KOBAL COLLECTION / GORDON, MELINDA SUE; **1244:** WARNER INDEPENDENT/2929 PROD / THE KOBAL COLLECTION / GORDON, MELINDA SUE; **1245:** WARNER INDEPENDENT/2929 PROD / THE KOBAL COLLECTION / GORDON, MELINDA SUE; **1246:** WARNER INDEPENDENT/2929 PROD / THE KOBAL COLLECTION / GORDON, MELINDA SUE; **1247:** WARNER INDEPENDENT/2929 PROD / THE KOBAL COLLECTION / GORDON, MELINDA SUE; **1248:** WARNER INDEPENDENT/2929 PROD / THE KOBAL COLLECTION / GORDON, MELINDA SUE; **1256:** © CORBIS; **1259:** Deborah Feingold/Corbis; **1274:** (TCR) Getty Images; **1276–1277:** © Louis K. Meisel Gallery, Inc./CORBIS; **1278:** b.: **1278:** t. Ricky Flores/ The Journal News/Corbis; **1279:** t. istockphoto.com; **1279:** b. Bob Rowan; Progressive Image/CORBIS; **1280:** l. © Bettmann/CORBIS; **1280:** l.: **1281:** t. © Bettmann/CORBIS; **1281:** b. © rudi1976/Fotolia; **1282:** © Tim Graham/Corbis; **1283:** br. PhotoEdit Inc.; **1283:** t. Courtesy of International Business Machines Corporation, © International Business Machines Corporation; **1283:** r. Getty Images; **1283:** bl. © Bettmann/CORBIS; **1284:** t. Corbis/Bettmann; **1284:** b. Wally McNamee/CORBIS; **1285:** t. **1285:** b. © Peter Turnley/CORBIS; **1286:** bl.: **1286:** t. © Reuters/CORBIS; **1286:** br. © Reuters/CORBIS; **1287:** © Reuters/Corbis; **1288:** l. © Roger Ressmeyer/CORBIS; **1288:** r. © AP Photo/The Express-Times, Joe Gill; **1289:** tr. istockphoto.com/Marie-france Bèlanger; **1289:** b. © Car Culture/Corbis; **1289:** tr. © Denis Scott/Corbis; **1289:** tl. © MOLLY RILEY/Reuters/Corbis; **1291:** Prentice Hall; **1293:** Do It Yourself Landscape (detail), 1962, Andy Warhol. photo: The Andy Warhol Foundation, Inc./Art Resource, NY. ©2010 Andy Warhol Foundation for the Visual Arts/ARS, New York; **1294:** Photo: Daniel Cima ©; **1295:** © Leslie Hinrichs / SuperStock; 1083-20005-I-P2A; **1297:** Prentice Hall; **1298:** Will & Deni McIntyre/Getty Images, Inc.; **1298–1299:** istockphoto.com/ Teresa Hurst; **1298–1299:** t. istockphoto.com/Teresa Hurst; **1300–1301:** istockphoto.com/Teresa Hurst; **1302:** © Catherine Karnow/CORBIS; **1302–1303:** istockphoto.com/Teresa Hurst; **1304–1305:** istockphoto.com/Teresa Hurst; **1306–1307:** istockphoto.com/Teresa Hurst; **1311:** © Keith Bedford/Reuters/Corbis; **1312:** b. istockphoto.com/Maksim Sokolov; **1312:** t. istockphoto.com; **1312–1313:** istockphoto.com/Emilia Kun; **1314–1315:** istockphoto.com/Emilia Kun; **1316–1317:** istockphoto.com/Emilia Kun; **1318:** Erich Lessing / Art Resource, NY; **1318–1319:** istockphoto.com/Emilia Kun; **1318–1319:** istockphoto.com/Emilia Kun; **1320:** b. istockphoto.com/Maksim Sokolov; **1320:** m. istockphoto.com; **1320:** t. istockphoto.com/Emilia Kun; **1325:** Sophie Bassouls/Sygma/CORBIS; **1326:** © David Lees/CORBIS; **1333:** Louis K. Meisel Gallery, Inc./CORBIS; **1335:** Kit Stafford; **1336–1337: 1338:** © Christopher Felver/CORBIS; **1339:** Art Resource, NY; **1341:** Donna Lee, courtesy of BOA Editions, Ltd. http://www.boaeditions.org; **1342:** © Daniel Aeschlimann/zefa/Corbis; **1347:** Shelley Rotner/Omni-Photo Communications, Inc.; **1349:** Miriam Berkley/Authorpix; **1350–1351: 1351:** istockphoto.com; **1352:** James McGoon Photography; **1353–1354:** © Christie's Images/CORBIS; **1353–1354:** border istockphoto.com; **1357: 1358–1359:** Mark R; **1360:** ©2008 Bob Eckstein from cartoonbank.com. All Rights Reserved.; **1362:** b. istockphoto.com/ Lee Pettet; **1362: #3:** Christopher Felver/CORBIS; **1362: #6:** Christopher Felver/CORBIS; **1362: #5:** Bettmann/CORBIS; **1362: #2:** Bettmann/CORBIS; **1362: #1:** Library of Congress; **1362: #4:** AP Images; **1365:** Miriam Berkley/Authorpix; **1366:** © Jack Gunter/CORBIS; **1368:** The Granger Collection, New York; **1370:** t. istockphoto.com/James Thew; **1370:** b. **1371:** istockphoto.com/ Manik Ratan; **1372:** l. istockphoto.com/aleksandar velasevic; **1372:** r. istockphoto.com/Oleksandr Bondarenko; **1373: 1374:** Images.com/CORBIS; **1377:** © Alex Gotfryd/CORBIS; **1378:** Yale University Art Gallery / Art Resource, NY; **1383:** Time & Life Pictures/Getty Images; **1384:** Warner Bros./Photofest; **1385:** Warner Bros./Photofest; **1387:** Warner Bros./Photofest; **1388:** Warner Bros./Photofest; **1394:** t. Delta Hunter; **1394:** b. William Harvey; **1395:** © US Navy Photo / Alamy; **1396:** © Peter Turnley/Corbis; **1397:** istockphoto.com/Tomaz Levstek; **1398:** © Peter Turnley/Corbis; **1403:** AP/Wide World Photos; **1404:** David Butow/CORBIS SABA; **1405:** m. Reuters/CORBIS; **1405:** r. Richard Levine / Alamy; **1405:** l. vario images GmbH & Co.KG / Alamy; **1406:** istockphoto.com; **1409:** © Todd France/ Corbis **1410** b. Jim McHugh; **1410:** t. istockphoto.com; **1411:** istockphoto.com; **1412:** © Andrew Gunners/ Digital vision/ gettyimages; **1415:** © Rudy Sulgan/ Corbis; **1417:** © Tim Wright/CORBIS; **1418:** Clarke, Daniel (Contemporary Artist); **1425:** © Doug Menuez/CORBIS; **1426:** Redchopsticks.com; **1430–1431:** Getty Images Inc.—Stone Allstock; **1433:** © BASSOULS SOPHIE/CORBIS SYGMA; **1434:** istockphoto.com; **1435:** istockphoto.com; **1437:** Museo de Santa Cruz/ Bridgeman Art Library, London/New York; **1437:** istockphoto.com; **1448:** Erich Lessing / Art Resource, NY; **1451:** Photo: Daniel Cima ©.

Staff Credits

The people who made up the Pearson Prentice Hall Literature team—representing design, editorial, editorial services, education technology, manufacturing and inventory planning, market research, marketing services, planning and budgeting, product planning, production services, project office, publishing processes, and rights and permissions—are listed below. Boldface type denotes the core team members.

Tobey Antao, Margaret Antonini, Rosalyn Arcilla, Penny Baker, James Ryan Bannon, Stephan Barth, **Tricia Battipede,** Krista Baudo, Rachel Beckman, Julie Berger, Lawrence Berkowitz, Melissa Biezin, **Suzanne Biron,** Rick Blount, **Marcela Boos, Betsy Bostwick,** Kay Bosworth, Jeff Bradley, Andrea Brescia, Susan Brorein, Lois Brown, **Pam Carey,** Lisa Carrillo, **Geoffrey Cassar,** Patty Cavuoto, Doria Ceraso, Jennifer Ciccone, Jaime Cohen, Rebecca Cottingham, Joe Cucchiara, Jason Cuoco, **Alan Dalgleish, Karen Edmonds, Irene Ehrmann,** Stephen Eldridge, Amy Fleming, Dorothea Fox, Steve Frankel, Cindy Frederick, Philip Fried, Diane Fristachi, Phillip Gagler, **Pamela Gallo,** Husain Gatlin, **Elaine Goldman,** Elizabeth Good, John Guild, Phil Hadad, Patricia Hade, Monduane Harris, Brian Hawkes, Jennifer B. Heart, Martha Heller, John Hill, Beth Hyslip, Mary Jean Jones, Grace Kang, Nathan Kinney, Roxanne Knoll, **Kate Krimsky,** Monisha Kumar, Jill Kushner, Sue Langan, Melisa Leong, Susan Levine, Dave Liston, **Mary Luthi, George Lychock, Gregory Lynch, Joan Mazzeo, Sandra McGloster,** Eve Melnechuk, Kathleen Mercandetti, Salita Metha, Artur Mkrtchyan, Karyn Mueller, Alison Muff, Christine Mulcahy, Kenneth Myett, Elizabeth Nemeth, Stefano Nese, Carrie O'Connor, April Okano, Kim Ortell, Sonia Pap, Raymond Parenteau, Dominique Pickens, Linda Punskovsky, **Sheila Ramsay,** Maureen Raymond, Mairead Reddin, **Erin Rehill-Seker, Renee Roberts, Laura Ross,** Bryan Salacki, Sharon Schultz, Jennifer Serra, Melissa Shustyk, Rose Sievers, Christy Singer, Yvonne Stecky, **Cynthia Summers,** Steve Thomas, Merle Uuesoo, Roberta Warshaw, Patricia Williams, Daniela Velez

Additional Credits

Lydie Bemba, Victoria Blades, Denise Data, Rachel Drice, Eleanor Kostyk, Jill Little, Loraine Machlin, Evan Marx, Marilyn McCarthy, Patrick O'Keefe, Shelia M. Smith, Lucia Tirondola, Laura Vivenzio, Linda Waldman, Angel Weyant